SUPPLEMENTS

Teaching and Learning Supplements are a special part of this book. Each supplement is customer driven, user friendly, and fully integrated. No other financial statement analysis book offers instructors a greater wealth of instructional and learning resources.

- *Instructor's Solutions Manual*—on Instructor Resource CD-ROM,ISBN: 0-07-253655-1
- *Test Bank*—on Instructor Resource CD-ROM, ISBN: 0-07-253655-1
- *Chapter Lecture Slides*—PowerPoint version; on Instructor Resource CD-ROM, ISBN: 0-07-253655-1; and on book's website
- *Book Website:* http://www.mhhe.com/Wild 8e
- *Understanding Annual Reports (Project),* ISBN: 0-07-286821-X
- *Case Materials—Primis custom case selection:* www.mhhe.com/primis
- Power Web—includes current articles curriculum-based materials, weekly updates with assessment, refereed Web links, research tools, student study tools, and interactive exercises: http://www.dushkin.com/powerweb
- Financial Accounting Video Library, Volumes 1 through 4: ISBN: 0-07-237616-3
- *Prerequisite Skills Development:* *MBA Survival Kit CD,* ISBN: 0-07-251199-0 *Essentials of Finance with Accounting CD,* ISBN: 0-07-256472-5
- *Financial Shenanigans (casebook),* ISBN: 0-07-138626-2
- *Online Resources*— http://www.mhhe.com/oscar
- *IEM: Iowa Electronic Markets*— ISBN 0-256-23307-1
- *Customer Service*— 1-800-338-3987

ORGANIZATION AND FOCUS

Financial statement analysis is part of the broader task of business analysis. Chapters 1 and 2 provide an overview and describe this broader task, including industry and strategy analysis. Chapters 3,4,5 and 6 focus on accounting analysis and the necessary adjustments to financial statements. Chapters 7, 8, 9, 10, 11, and 12 focus on financial analysis, including prospective analysis. The following diagram reflects this organization and focus:

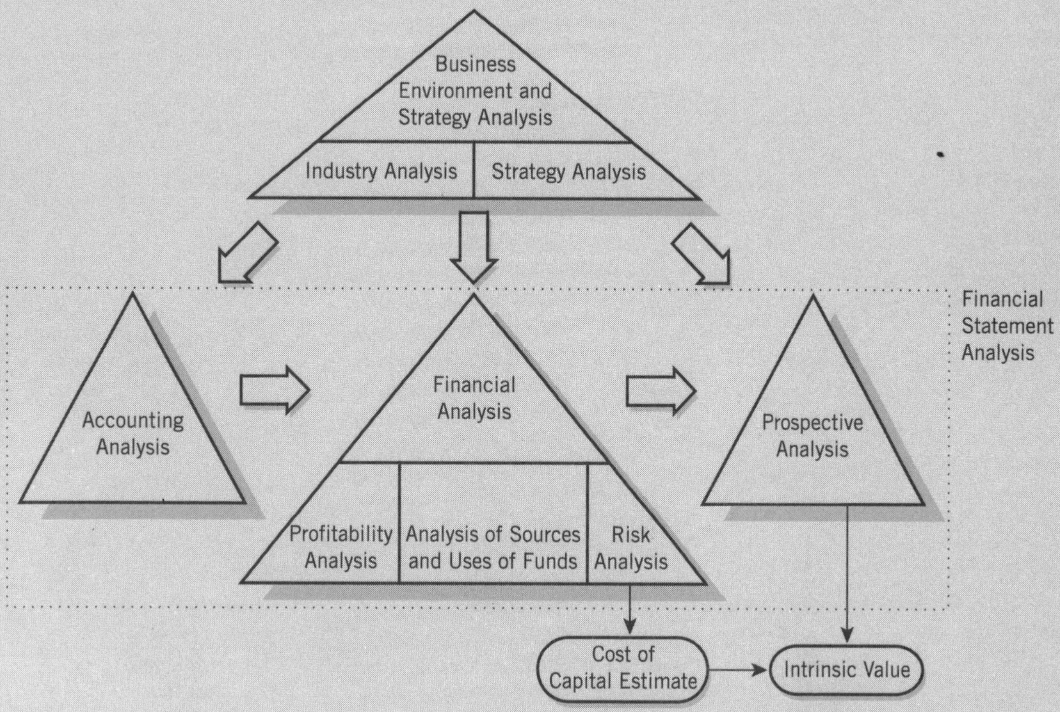

FINANCIAL STATEMENT ANALYSIS

EIGHTH EDITION

JOHN J. WILD
University of Wisconsin at Madison

K. R. SUBRAMANYAM
University of Southern California

ROBERT F. HALSEY
Babson College

Boston Burr Ridge, IL Dubuque, IA Madison, WI New York
San Francisco St. Louis Bangkok Bogotá Caracas Kuala Lumpur
Lisbon London Madrid Mexico City Milan Montreal New Delhi
Santiago Seoul Singapore Sydney Taipei Toronto

To my wife Gail and children Kimberly, Jonathan, Stephanie, and Trevor

—J. J. W.

To my wife Jayasree, son Sujay, and our parents

—K. R. S.

To my wife Ellie and children Christian and Grace

—R. F. H.

FINANCIAL STATEMENT ANALYSIS

Published by McGraw-Hill/Irwin, an imprint of The McGraw-Hill Companies, Inc., 1221 Avenue of the Americas, New York, NY 10020.

This book is printed on acid-free paper.

1 2 3 4 5 6 7 8 9 0 CCW/CCW 0 9 8 7 6 5 4 3

ISBN 0-07-253651-9

Publisher: *Brent Gordon*
Sponsoring editor: *Steve DeLancey*
Managing developmental editor: *Gail Korosa*
Marketing manager: *Richard Kolasa*
Senior producer, Media technology: *David Barrick*
Senior project manager: *Kimberly D. Hooker*
Senior production supervisor: *Michael R. McCormick*
Designer: *Matthew Baldwin*
Supplement producer: *Matthew Perry*
Senior digital content specialist: *Brian Nacik*
Design: *Matthew Baldwin*
Cover design: *Jenny El-Shamy*
Typeface: *10/12 Caslon Book BE*
Cover images: © GettyOne
Compositor: *GAC Indianapolis*
Printer: *Courier Westford*

Library of Congress Cataloging-in-Publication Data

Wild, John J.
Financial statement analysis / John J. Wild, K. R. Subramanyam, Robert F. Halsey.
8th ed.
p. cm
Includes bibliographical references and index.
ISBN 0-07-253651-9 (alk. paper)
1. Financial statements. I. Subramanyam, K. R. II. Halsey, Robert F. III. Title.
HF5681.B2 B46 2004
657'.3–dc21 2002043190

www.mhhe.com

Welcome to the eighth edition of *Financial Statement Analysis*. This book is the product of extensive market surveys, chapter reviews, and correspondence with instructors and students. We are delighted that an overwhelming number of instructors, students, practitioners, and organizations agree with our approach to analysis of financial statements. This book forges a unique path in financial statement analysis, one that responds to the requests and demands of modern-day analysts. From the outset, a main goal in writing this book has been to respond to these needs by providing the most progressive, accessible, current, and user-driven textbook in the field. We are pleased that the book's reception in the United States and across the world has exceeded expectations.

Analysis of financial statements is exciting and dynamic, with enormous implications for business decisions, resource allocation, and individual wealth. This book reveals the keys to effective analysis to give readers a competitive advantage in an increasingly competitive marketplace. We know financial statements are relevant to the decisions of many individuals including investors, creditors, consultants, managers, auditors, directors, analysts, regulators, and employees. This book equips these individuals with the analytical skills necessary to succeed in business. Yet, experience in teaching this material tells us that we can only engage readers by demonstrating the relevance of analysis. This book continually demonstrates that relevance with applications to real world companies. The book aims to benefit a broad readership, ranging from those with a simple curiosity in financial markets to those with years of experience in accounting and finance.

ORGANIZATION AND CONTENT

This book's organization accommodates different teaching styles. While the book is comprehensive, its layout allows instructors to choose topics and depth of coverage as desired. Readers are told in Chapter 1 how the book's topics are related to each other and how they fit within the broad discipline of financial statement analysis. The book is organized into three parts:

1. Analysis Overview
2. Accounting Analysis
3. Financial Analysis

ANALYSIS OVERVIEW

Part One gives an overview of financial statement analysis. We introduce financial statement analysis as an integral part of the broader framework of business analysis. We examine the role of financial statement analysis in different types of business analysis such as equity analysis and credit analysis. We emphasize the understanding of business activities–planning, financing, investing, and operating. We describe the strategies underlying business activities and their effects on financial statements. We also emphasize the importance of accrual accounting for analysis and the relevance of conducting accounting analysis to make appropriate adjustments to financial statements before embarking on financial analysis. We apply several popular tools and techniques in analyzing and interpreting financial statements. An important and unique feature is our use of Eastman Kodak's annual report as a means to immediately engage readers and to instill relevance. Part One comprises two chapters:

- *Chapter 1.* We begin the analysis of financial statements by considering their relevance to business decisions. This leads to a focus on users, including what they need and how analysis serves them. We describe business activities and how they are reflected in financial statements. We also discuss both debt and equity valuation.
- *Chapter 2.* This chapter explains the nature and purpose of financial accounting and reporting, including the broader environment under which financial statements are prepared and used. We highlight the importance of accrual accounting in comparison to cash accounting. We identify and discuss myths and truths of these two measurement systems. The importance and limitations of accounting data for analysis purposes are described along with the significance of conducting accounting analysis for financial analysis.

ACCOUNTING ANALYSIS

To aid in accounting analysis, Part Two explains and analyzes the accounting measurement and reporting practices underlying financial statements. We organize this analysis around financing (liabilities and equity), investing (assets), and operating (income) activities. We show how operating activities are outcomes of changes in investing and financing activities. We provide insights into income determination and asset and liability measurement. Most important, we discuss procedures and clues for the analysis and adjustment of financial statements to enhance their economic content for meaningful financial analysis. Part Two comprises four chapters:

- *Chapter 3.* Chapter 3 begins the detailed analysis of the numbers reflecting financing activities. It explains how those numbers are the raw material for financial analysis. Our focus is on explaining, analyzing, interpreting, and adjusting those reported numbers to better reflect financing activities. Crucial topics include leases, pensions, off-balance-sheet financing, and shareholders' equity.
- *Chapter 4.* This chapter extends the analysis to investing activities. We show how to analyze and adjust (as necessary) numbers that reflect assets such as securities, receivables, derivatives, inventories, property, equipment, and intangibles. We explain what those numbers reveal about financial position and performance, including future performance.
- *Chapter 5.* Chapter 5 extends the analysis to special investing activities–intercompany and international. We analyze intercorporate investments and business combinations from the perspective of a parent company. We examine international investments and their reporting implications for financial statements. We show how interpreting and adjusting the disclosures on intercompany and international activities are an important part of analysis.
- *Chapter 6.* This chapter focuses on analysis of operating activities and income. We discuss the concept and measurement of income as distinct from cash flows. We analyze accrual measures in yielding net income. Understanding recognition methods of both revenues and expenses is stressed. We analyze and adjust the income statement and its components, including nonrecurring items such as restructuring charges, asset impairments, and employee stock options.

FINANCIAL ANALYSIS

Part Three examines the processes and methods of financial analysis (including prospective analysis). We stress the objectives of different users and describe analytical tools and techniques to meet those objectives. The means of analysis range from computation of ratio and cash flow measures to earnings prediction and equity valuation. We apply analysis tools that enable one to reconstruct the economic reality embedded in financial statements. We demonstrate how analysis tools and techniques enhance users' decisions–including company valuation and lending decisions. We show how financial statement analysis reduces uncertainty and increases confidence in business decisions. Part Three consists of six chapters and a Comprehensive Case:

- *Chapter 7.* This chapter begins our study of the application and interpretation of financial analysis tools. We analyze cash flow measures for insights into all business activities, with special emphasis on operating activities. Attention is directed at company and industry conditions when analyzing cash flows.
- *Chapter 8.* Chapter 8 emphasizes return on invested capital and explains variations in its measurement. Attention is directed at return on assets and return on equity. We disaggregate both return measures and describe their relevance. Financial leverage also is explained.
- *Chapter 9.* This chapter expands the returns analysis to profitability. We emphasize the components of income and the adjustments necessary for their proper evaluation. Attention is directed at sales, cost of sales, taxes, selling, and financing expenses. Profitability-based analysis tools are demonstrated, including their interpretation and application.
- *Chapter 10.* We describe forecasting and pro forma analysis of financial statements. We present forecasting of the balance sheet, income statement, and statement of cash flows with a detailed example. We then provide an example to link prospective analysis to equity valuation.
- *Chapter 11.* This chapter focuses on credit analysis, both liquidity and solvency. We first present analysis tools to assess liquidity–including accounting-based ratios, turnover, and operating activity measures. Then, we focus on capital structure and its implications for solvency. We analyze the importance of financial leverage and its effects on risk and return. Analytical adjustments are explained for tests of liquidity and solvency. We describe earnings-coverage measures and their interpretation.
- *Chapter 12.* The final chapter emphasizes earnings-based analysis and equity valuation. The earnings-based analysis focuses on earnings quality, earnings persistence, and earning power. Attention is directed at techniques for measuring and applying these concepts. Discussion of equity valuation focuses on forecasting accounting numbers and estimating company value.
- *Comprehensive Case.* This case is a comprehensive analysis of financial statements and related notes. We describe steps in analyzing the statements and the essential attributes of an analysis report. Our analysis is organized around key components of financial statement analysis: cash analysis, return on invested capital, asset utilization, operating performance, profitability, forecasting, liquidity, capital structure, and solvency.

KEY CHANGES IN THIS EDITION

Many readers provided useful suggestions through chapter reviews, surveys, and correspondence. We made the following changes in response to these suggestions:

- Extensively revised the text to streamline the discussion. We have reduced the total text pages by 20% with no loss of content.

- Expanded the discussion of off-balance-sheet financing in Chapter 3, focusing particularly on special purpose entities.
- Rewrote Chapter 10 on Prospective Analysis from a valuation perspective. Detailed examples of balance sheet, income statement, and statement of cash flows forecasting procedures are now provided. Prospective analysis is linked directly with equity valuation through a detailed example.
- Revised the Comprehensive Case to incorporate prospective analysis and valuation concepts and illustrations.
- Rewrote the equity method accounting and business combinations sections of Chapter 5 to reflect the new accounting standards.
- Placed greater emphasis on accounting analysis. This includes further explanations of the necessary adjustments to financial statements.
- Increased excerpts of actual company disclosures on each topic–typically, we select a company, probe its detailed note disclosures, and then demonstrate the adjustments needed for effective financial analysis.
- Added numerous new examples throughout the book to illustrate concepts and applications from current practice.
- Increased the emphasis on making the material accessible and engaging. Several features are apparent, others are more subtle. For example, we describe theoretical concepts and specialized analyses in simple terms. We present data and illustrations in readable and understandable frameworks. We introduce industry and economic data throughout the book, often in graphical form.
- Enhanced visual appeal. Extensive use of graphs, charts, and schedules engage the reader.

INNOVATIVE PEDAGOGY

We believe people learn best when provided with motivation and structure. The pedagogical features of this book facilitate those learning goals. Features include:

- **Analysis Feature.** An article featuring an actual company launches each chapter to highlight the relevance of that chapter's materials. In-chapter analysis is performed on that company. Experience shows readers are motivated to learn when their interests are piqued.
- **Analysis Objectives.** Chapters open with key analysis objectives that highlight important chapter goals.
- **Analysis Linkages.** Linkages launch each chapter to establish bridges between topics and concepts in prior, current, and upcoming chapters. This roadmap–titled *A Look Back, A Look at This Chapter,* and *A Look Ahead*–provides structure for learning.
- **Analysis Preview.** A preview kicks off each chapter by describing its content and importance.
- **Analysis Viewpoint.** Multiple role-playing scenarios in each chapter are a unique feature that show the relevance of financial statement analysis to a wide assortment of decision makers.
- **Analysis Excerpt.** Numerous excerpts from practice–including annual report disclosures, newspaper clippings, and press releases–illustrate key points and topics. Excerpts reinforce the relevance of the analysis and engage the reader.
- **Analysis Research.** Multiple, short boxes in each chapter discuss current research relevant to the analysis and interpretation of financial statements.
- **Analysis Annotations.** Each chapter includes marginal annotations. These are aimed at relevant, interesting, and topical happenings from business that bear on financial statement analysis.

- **Analysis Feedback.** End-of-chapter assignments include numerous traditional and innovative assignments augmented by several cases that draw on actual financial statements such as those from Wal-Mart, Kmart, Nike, Reebok, Allied Signal, Lucent Technologies, IBM, Dell, Rite Aid, Motorola, Yahoo!, Baxter International, Columbia Pictures, Abbott, Philip Morris, Merck, and Coca-Cola. Assignments are of five types: *Questions, Exercises, Problems, Cases,* and *Web Activities.* Each assignment is titled to reflect its purpose–many require critical thinking, communication skills, interpretation, and decision making. This book stands out in both its diversity and number of end-of-chapter assignments. Key check figures are selectively printed in the margins.
- **Analysis Focus Companies.** Entire financial statements of three companies–Eastman Kodak, Campbell Soup, and Quaker Oats–are reproduced in the book and used in numerous assignments. Experience shows that frequent use of annual reports heightens interest and learning. These reports include notes and other financial information.

TARGET AUDIENCE

This best-selling book is targeted to readers of all business-related fields. Students and professionals alike find the book beneficial in their careers as they are rewarded with an understanding of both the techniques of analysis and the expertise to apply them. Rewards also include the skills to successfully recognize business opportunities and the knowledge to capitalize on them.

The book accommodates courses extending over one quarter, one semester, or two quarters. It is suitable for a wide range of courses focusing on analysis of financial statements, including upper-level "capstone" courses. The book is used at both the undergraduate and graduate levels, as well as in professional programs. It is the book of choice in modern financial statement analysis education.

SUPPLEMENT PACKAGE

This book is supported by a wide array of supplements aimed at the needs of both students and instructors of financial statement analysis. They include:

- **Instructor Resource CD-ROM.** The CD-ROM contains the Instructor's Solutions Manual, Test Bank, and Lecture Slides in one easily accessible version. IBSN 0-07-253655-1.
- **Instructor's Solutions Manual.** An Instructor's Solutions Manual contains complete solutions for assignments. It is carefully prepared, reviewed, and checked for accuracy. The Manual contains chapter summaries, analysis objectives, and other helpful materials. It has transition notes to instructors for ease in moving from the seventh to the eighth edition, including cross-referencing of assignment material between both editions. It is available on the text website and on the Instructor CD-ROM.
- **Test Bank.** The Test Bank contains a variety of test materials with varying levels of difficulty. All materials are carefully reviewed for consistency with the book and thoroughly examined for accuracy. It is available on the Instructor CD-ROM.
- **Chapter Lecture Slides.** A set of PowerPoint slides is available for each chapter. They can be used to augment the instructor's lecture materials or as an aid to students in supplementing in-class lectures. It is available on the text website and on the Instructor CD-ROM.
- **Book Website.** [http://www.mhhe.com/wild8e] The Web is increasingly important for financial statement analysis. This book has its own dedicated website, which is an excellent starting point for analysis resources. The site includes links

to key websites as well as additional support materials for both instructors and students. There is online delivery of PowerPoint slides and other instructional materials.

- **PowerWeb.** [http://www.dushkin.com/powerweb] This website is a reservoir of news articles, cases, questions, and exercises on accounting and analysis.
- **Analysis Project.** A computerized analysis project aids students in the basics of financial statement analysis (*Understanding Annual Reports*–ISBN: 0-07-286821-X).
- **Casebook Support.** Some instructors augment the book with additional case materials. While practical illustrations and case materials are abundant in the text, more are available. These include (1) *Primis* custom case selection [www.mhhe.com/primis] and (2) *Financial Shenanigans*–ISBN: 0-07-138626-2.
- **Financial Accounting Video Library.** The Financial Accounting Video Library includes short, action-oriented videos for lively classroom discussion of topics, including disclosure practices, accounting quality, the role of International Accounting Standards, and the impact of regulators. (ISBN 0-07-237616-3)
- **Prerequisite Skills Development.** There are materials to aid readers in understanding basic accounting and finance concepts: (1) *MBA Survival Kit–Accounting Interactive CD*–ISBN: 0-07-251199-0, and (2) *Essentials of Finance with Accounting CD*–ISBN: 0-07-256472-5.
- **Online Resources.** [http://www.mhhe.com/oscar] McGraw-Hill offers additional Internet resources on a number of accounting and analysis-related topics.
- **IEM: Iowa Electronic Markets.** ISBN 0-256-23307-1 IEM is an interactive, real-money electronics futures market designed as a teaching supplement. Students learn about markets and follow company, industry, and economic news. [http://www.biz.uiowa.edu/iem]
- **Customer Service.** 1-800-338-3987 or access http://www.mhhe.com/business.

ACKNOWLEDGMENTS

We are thankful for the encouragement, suggestions, and counsel provided by many instructors, professionals, and students in writing this book. It has been a team effort and we recognize the contributions of all these individuals. They include the following professionals who read portions of this book in various forms:

Kenneth Alterman
(Standard & Poor's)

Michael Ashton
(Ashton Analytics)

Clyde Bartter
(Portfolio Advisory Co.)

Laurie Dodge
(Interbrand Corp.)

Vincent C. Fung
(PricewaterhouseCoopers)

Hyman C. Grossman
(Standard & Poor's)

Richard Huff
(Standard & Poor's)

Michael A. Hyland
(First Boston Corp.)

Robert J. Mebus
(Standard & Poor's)

Robert Mednick
(Arthur Andersen)

William C. Norby
(Financial Analyst)

David Norr
(First Manhattan Corp.)

Thornton L. O'Glove
(Quality of Earnings Report)

Paul Rosenfield
(AICPA)

George B. Sharp
(CITIBANK)

Fred Spindel
(PricewaterhouseCoopers)

Frances Stone
(Merrill Lynch & Co.)

Jon A. Stroble
(Jon A. Stroble & Associates)

Jack L. Treynor
(Treynor-Arbit Associates)

Neil Weiss
(Jon A. Stroble & Associates)

Gerald White
(Grace & White, Inc.)

We also want to recognize the following instructors and colleagues who provided valuable comments and suggestions for this edition:

Florence Atiase
(University of Texas at Austin)

Steven Balsam
(Temple University)

William Belski
(Virginia Tech)

Don Giacomino
(Marquette University)

James William Harden
(University of North Carolina at Greensboro)

Janet Kimbrell
(Oklahoma State University)

Ralph Lim
(Sacred Heart University)

Krishnagopal Menon
(Boston University)

Eric Press
(Temple University)

Chris Prestigiacomo
(University of Missouri at Columbia)

Larry Prober
(Riber University)

Phil Shane
(University of Colorado at Boulder)

Pamela Stuerke
(Case Western Reserve University)

Karen Taranto
(George Washington University)

Gary Taylor
(University of Alabama)

John M. Trussel
(Penn State University at Harrisburg)

Joseph Weintrop
(CUNY–Baruch)

We once again thank those individuals whose contributions to past editions have helped the book evolve to its present form:

Rashad Abdel-Khalik
(University of Illinois)

M. J. Abdolmohammadi
(Bentley College)

Robert N. Anthony
(Harvard University)

Hector R. Anton
(New York University)

Terry Arndt
(Central Michigan University)

Dick Baker
(Northern Illinois University)

Mark Bauman
(University of Wisconsin–Milwaukee)

William T. Baxter
(CUNY–Baruch)

Martin Benis
(CUNY–Baruch)

Shyam Bhandari
(Bradley University)

Fred Bien
(Louisiana State University)

John S. Bildersee
(New York University)

Vince Brenner
(Louisiana State University)

Abraham J. Briloff
(CUNY–Baruch)

Gary Bulmash
(American University)

Joseph Bylinski
(University of North Carolina)

Douglas Carmichael
(CUNY–Baruch)

Philip Chuey
(Youngstown State University)

Benny R. Copeland
(University of North Texas)

Maurice P. Corrigan
(Teikyo Post University)

Wallace N. Davidson III
(University of North Texas)

Harry Davis
(CUNY–Baruch)

Peter Lloyd Davis
(CUNY–Baruch)

Peter Easton
(Ohio State University)

James M. Emig
(Villanova University)

Eric S. Emory
(Sacred Heart University)

William P. Enderlein
(Golden Gate University)

Calvin Engler
(Iona College)

Thomas J. Frecka
(University of Notre Dame)

John Gentis
(Ball State University)

Philip Gerdin
(University of New Haven)

Edwin Grossnickle
(Western Michigan University)

Peter M. Gutman
(CUNY–Baruch)

J. Larry Hagler
(East Carolina University)

Jerry Han
(SUNY–Buffalo)

Frank Heflin
(Purdue University)

Steven L. Henning
(Southern Methodist University)

Yong-Ha Hyon
(Temple University)

Henry Jaenicke
(Drexel University)

Keith Jakob
(University of Montana)

Kenneth H. Johnson
(Georgia Southern University)

Jo Koehn
(Central Missouri State)

Homer Kripke
(New York University)

Russ Langer
(San Francisco State University)

Burton T. Lefkowitz
(C. W. Post College)

Barbara Leonard
(Loyola University, Chicago)

Steven Lillien
(CUNY–Baruch)

Thomas Lopez
(Pace University)

Mostafa Maksy
(Northeastern Illinois University)

Brenda Mallouk
(University of Toronto)

Ann Martin
(University of Colorado–Denver)

Martin Mellman
(Hofstra University)

William G. Mister
(Colorado State University)

Stephen Moehrle
(University of Missouri–St. Louis)

Belinda Mucklow
(University of Wisconsin)

Hugo Nurnberg
(CUNY-Baruch)

Per Olsson
(Duke University)

Stephen Penman
(Columbia University)

Tom Porter
(Boston College)

William Ruland
(CUNY–Baruch)

Stanley C. W. Salvary
(Canisius College)

Emanuel Saxe
(CUNY–Baruch)

Don Shannon
(DePaul University)

Ken Shaw
(University of Missouri)

Lenny Soffer
(Northwestern University)

Reed Storey
(Financial Accounting Standards Board)

Rebecca Todd
(Boston University)

Bob Trezevant
(University of Southern California)

Jerrold Weiss
(Lehman College)

J. Scott Whisenant
(University of Houston)

Kenneth L. Wild
(University of London)

Richard F. Williams
(Wright State University)

Philip Wolitzer
(Marymount Manhattan College)

Christine V. Zavgren
(Clarkson University)

Stephen Zeff
(Rice University)

We acknowledge permission to use materials adapted from examinations of the Association for Investment Management and Research (AIMR) and the American Institute of Certified Public Accountants (AICPA). Special thanks to Eric Press of Temple University and Joel Stiebel for preparing the Test Bank. Also, we are fortunate to work with an outstanding team of McGraw-Hill/lrwin professionals, extending from editorial to marketing to sales.

Special thanks go to our families for their patience, understanding, and inspiration in completing this book, and we dedicate the book to them.

John J. Wild
K. R. Subramanyam
Robert F. Halsey

As a team, John Wild, K. R. Subramanyam, and Robert Halsey provide a blend of skills uniquely suited to writing a financial statement analysis and valuation textbook. They combine award-winning teaching and research with a broad view of accounting and analysis gained through years of professional and teaching experiences.

John J. Wild is professor of accounting and the Robert and Monica Beyer Distinguished Professor at the University of Wisconsin at Madison. He previously held appointments at Michigan State University and the University of Manchester in England. He received his BBA, MS, and PhD from the University of Wisconsin.

Professor Wild teaches courses in accounting and analysis at both the undergraduate and graduate levels. He has received the Chipman Excellence-in-Teaching Award and the Departmental Excellence-in-Teaching Award from the University of Wisconsin. He also received the Beta Alpha Psi and Salmonson Excellence-in-Teaching Award from Michigan State University. Professor Wild is a past KPMG Peat Marwick National Fellow and is a prior recipient of fellowships from the American Accounting Association and the Ernst & Young Foundation.

Professor Wild is an active member of the American Accounting Association and its sections. He has served on several committees of these organizations, including the Outstanding Accounting Educator Award, Wildman Award, National Program Advisory, Publications, and Research Committees. Professor Wild is author of the best-selling book, *Financial Accounting,* published by McGraw-Hill/Irwin. His many research articles on financial accounting and analysis appear in *The Accounting Review, Journal of Accounting Research, Journal of Accounting and Economics, Contemporary Accounting Research, Journal of Accounting, Auditing & Finance, Journal of Accounting and Public Policy, Journal of Business Finance and Accounting, Auditing: A Journal of Theory and Practice,* and other accounting and business periodicals. He is past associate editor of *Contemporary Accounting Research* and has served on editorial boards of several respected journals, including *The Accounting Review* and the *Journal of Accounting and Public Policy.*

K. R. Subramanyam is associate professor of accounting at the Marshall School of Business, University of Southern California. He received his MBA from the Indian Institute of Management and his PhD from the University of Wisconsin. Prior to obtaining his PhD he worked as an international management consultant and as a financial planner for General Foods.

Professor Subramanyam has taught courses in financial statement analysis, financial accounting, and managerial accounting at both the graduate and undergraduate levels. He is a highly regarded teacher, recognized for his commitment and creativity in business education. His course in financial statement analysis is one of the most popular courses in the Marshall School of Business. Professor Subramanyam is a National Talent Scholar, a member of Beta Alpha Psi, and a Deloitte and Touche National Fellow. He is also the recipient of the Robert Beyer and Arthur Andersen Scholarships. Professor Subramanyam is actively involved in several national and international organizations, including the American Accounting Association. He has served these organizations in several capacities, including as a member of the Committee to Identify Seminal Contributions to Accounting.

Professor Subramanyam's research interests span a wide range, including the economic effects of financial statements, implications of earnings management, and financial statement analysis and valuation. He has won both national and international awards for his research contributions. His articles appear in leading academic journals such as *The Accounting Review, Contemporary Accounting Research, Journal of Accounting Research, Journal of Accounting and Economics,* and the *Journal of Business Finance and Accounting.*

Robert F. Halsey is an assistant professor at Babson College. He received his MBA and PhD from the University of Wisconsin. Prior to obtaining his PhD he worked as the CFO of a privately held retailing and manufacturing company and as the vice president and senior loan officer of a large bank.

Professor Halsey teaches courses in financial and managerial accounting at both the graduate and undergraduate levels, including a popular course in financial statement analysis for second year MBA students. He has also taught in numerous executive education courses for large multinational companies through Babson's School of Executive Education as well as for a number of stock brokerage firms in the Boston area. He is regarded as an innovative teacher and has been recognized for outstanding teaching at both the University of Wisconsin and Babson College. He is the recipient of an Ernst & Young Fellowship and is a member of the Beta Gamma Sigma and Phi Eta Sigma honor societies.

Professor Halsey's research interests are in the area of financial reporting, including firm valuation, financial statement analysis, and disclosure issues. He has published in *Advances in Quantitative Analysis of Finance and Accounting, The Journal of the American Taxation Association, Issues in Accounting Education, The Portable MBA in Finance and Accounting,* 3rd ed., the *CPA Journal, AICPA Professor/Practitioner Case Development Program,* and in other accounting and analysis periodicals. He has also developed exam preparation materials for the CFA examination and administers numerous CFA review courses in the Northeast, including the Boston and New York areas.

PART ONE
INTRODUCTION AND OVERVIEW

PART TWO
ACCOUNTING ANALYSIS

PART THREE
FINANCIAL ANALYSIS

FINANCIAL STATEMENT ANALYSIS

1

OVERVIEW OF FINANCIAL STATEMENT ANALYSIS

A LOOK AT THIS CHAPTER

We begin our analysis of financial statements by considering its relevance in the broader task of business analysis. We use Eastman Kodak Company as an example to help us illustrate the importance of assessing financial performance in light of industry and economic conditions. This leads us to focus on financial statement users, their information needs, and how financial statement analysis addresses those needs. We describe major types of business activities and how they are reflected in financial statements. A preliminary financial analysis illustrates these important concepts.

A LOOK AHEAD

Chapter 2 describes the financial reporting environment and the information included in financial statements. Chapters 3 through 6 deal with accounting analysis, which is the task of analyzing, adjusting, and interpreting accounting numbers that make up financial statements. Chapters 7 through 12 focus on mastering the tools of financial statement analysis and valuation. A comprehensive financial statement analysis of Campbell Soup Company follows Chapter 12.

ANALYSIS OBJECTIVES

- Explain business analysis and its relation to financial statement analysis.
- Identify and discuss different types of business analysis.
- Describe the component analyses that constitute business analysis.
- Explain business activities and their relation to financial statements.
- Describe the purpose of each financial statement and linkages between them.
- Identify the relevant analysis information beyond financial statements.
- Analyze and interpret financial statements as a preview to more detailed analyses.
- Apply several basic financial statement analysis techniques.
- Define and formulate some fundamental valuation models.
- Explain the purpose of financial statement analysis in an efficient market.
- Describe some basic investment theories and their implications for analysis (Appendix 1A).

Kodak's Hazy Picture

Financial statement analysis includes the study of a company's strategic goals and its business environment. For example, take the case of Eastman Kodak [**www.Kodak.com**] whose sales are languishing in an increasingly competitive market in which unit sales increase only as a result of price discounting. Profitability can be achieved only through reduction of operating costs. Over the past six years, Kodak has slashed 20% of its workforce and, until the recession of 2001, had steadily increased its operating profit margin. This major restructuring effort has cost the company over $2.25 billion and has resulted in the severance of more than 20,000 employees.

The increasing competitiveness of its markets, coupled with the lack of positive investment opportunities and the growth of digital imaging, has decimated Kodak's stock price and placed increasing pressure on management to find long-term solutions. To date, Kodak has repurchased over one-quarter of its outstanding common shares at a cost of $5.8 billion in a futile attempt to bolster its sagging stock price. Despite the fact that Kodak generates over $2 billion of operating cash flow per year, management has found little to do with its cash other than to repurchase its stock and pay dividends to shareholders.

. . . management has found little to do with its cash . . .

Kodak has misread the market, plowing hundreds of millions of dollars into the advanced photo system (APS) film-based camera that never took off. Instead, digital cameras have captured consumers' attention and Kodak has found itself mired in a brutal price war with Fuji Photo on the film side and struggling to catch up in the digital world. Although sales of its new EasyShare digital camera have been promising, the company desperately needs a home-run product line. Until its strategies produce significant sales growth, it is a hazy Kodak moment.

Sources: Solomon Lehman Brothers and Smith Barney investment analysis, June/July 2002; Kodak website, January 2003; Business Week, May 13, 2002, and January 14, 2002.

PREVIEW OF CHAPTER 1

Financial statement analysis is an integral and important part of the broader field of business analysis. **Business analysis** is the process of evaluating a company's economic prospects and risks. This includes analyzing a company's business environment, its strategies, and its financial position and performance. Business analysis is useful in a wide range of business decisions such as whether to invest in equity or in debt securities, whether to extend credit through

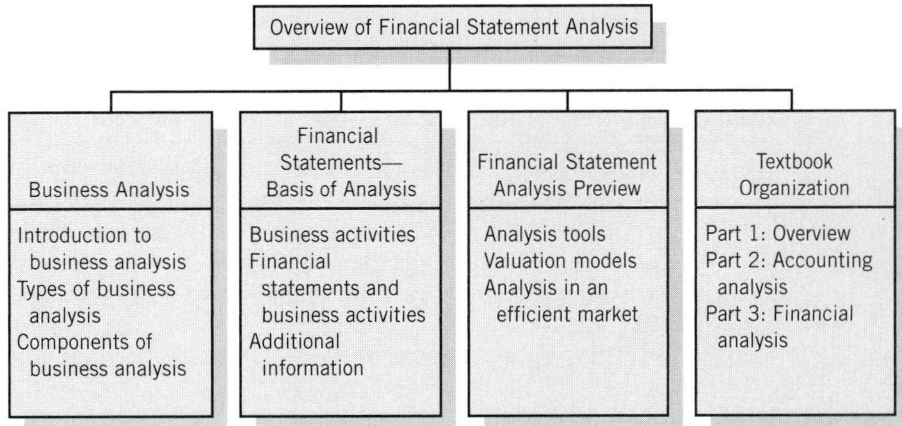

short- or long-term loans, how to value a business in an initial public offering (IPO), and how to evaluate restructurings including mergers, acquisitions, and divestitures. **Financial statement analysis** is the application of analytical tools and techniques to general-purpose financial statements and related data to derive estimates and inferences useful in business analysis. Financial statement analysis reduces reliance on hunches, guesses, and intuition for business decisions. It decreases the uncertainty of business analysis. It does not lessen the need for expert judgment but, instead, provides a systematic and effective basis for business analysis. This chapter describes business analysis and the role of financial statement analysis. The chapter also introduces financial statements and explains how they reflect underlying business activities. We introduce several tools and techniques of financial statement analysis and apply them in a preliminary analysis of Kodak. We also show how business analysis helps us understand Kodak's prospects and the role of business environment and strategy for financial statement analysis.

BUSINESS ANALYSIS

This section explains business analysis, describes its practical applications, identifies separate analyses that make up business analysis, and shows how it all fits in with financial statement analysis.

Introduction to Business Analysis

Financial statement analysis is part of business analysis. Business analysis is the evaluation of a company's prospects and risks for the purpose of making business decisions. These business decisions extend to equity and debt valuation, credit risk assessment, earnings predictions, audit testing, compensation negotiations, and countless other decisions. Business analysis aids in making informed decisions by helping structure the decision task through an evaluation of a company's business environment, its strategies, and its financial position and performance.

An initial step in business analysis is to evaluate a company's business environment and strategies. To illustrate this initial step we turn to Kodak. Much financial information about Kodak–including its financial statements, explanatory notes, and selected news about its past performance, future plans, and strategies–is communicated in its *annual report* reproduced in Appendix A near the end of this book. We begin by studying Kodak's business activities and learn that it is a global leader in photographic and imaging products. This investigation reveals that Kodak is a major provider of photo processing equipment, chemicals and services, medical imaging, motion picture films, copiers, printers, scanners, and microfilm equipment and media. Exhibit 1.1 identifies

Exhibit 1.1 ***Kodak's Operating Divisions****

	Photography	Health Imaging	Commercial Imaging/Other
	Photographic film, paper, chemicals, photo processing equipment, and cameras (traditional and digital)	Medical film and processing equipment, laser and radiography imaging equipment for health care sector	Microfilm equipment and media, and graphics film products; Other includes organic light emitting diode displays and optical products
Sales	$9,403	$2,262	$1,569
Operating assets	6,288	1,426	866
Operating earnings	787	323	105

*In millions.

three major divisions of Kodak as taken from Note 21 of its financial statements. These data show that photography is its largest division, both in asset size and in its sales and earnings levels.

Despite Kodak's well-accepted and diversified product lines and its perceived commitment to research and product development, the last decade has been difficult. This is reflected in its weak stock price performance for this period relative to the overall market trend (see Exhibit 1.2).

Exhibit 1.2

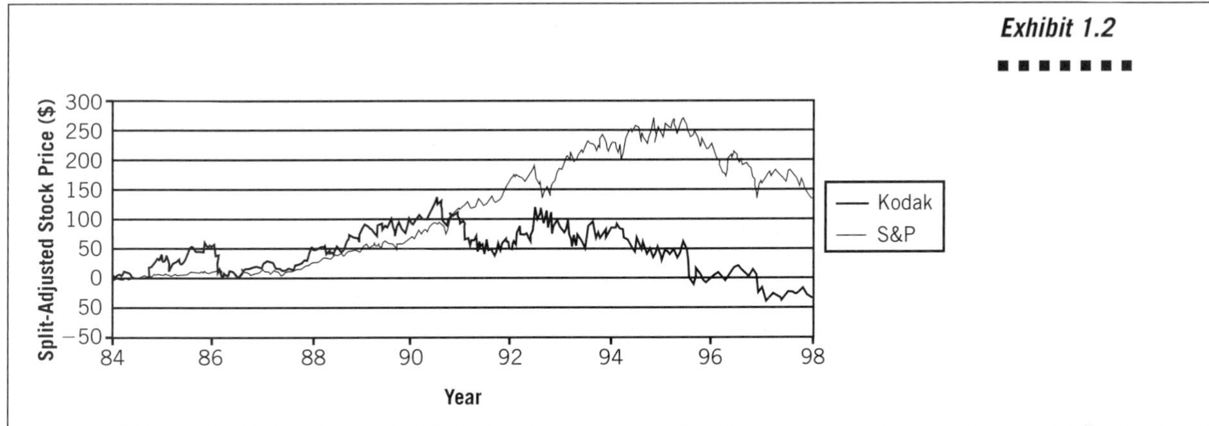

Further analysis shows that one of Kodak's weaknesses is its high cost structure. This makes it difficult for Kodak to compete with low cost producers, especially in the mature consumer photography market. In response, Kodak is in the midst of major restructuring that began in 1996–97. It has already reduced its workforce by 20 percent, divested poorly performing and nonstrategic segments, and launched a cost reduction program–at a total cost of $2.25 billion. Kodak is also launching several strategic initiatives to ensure long-term growth, including entering new and emerging markets such as digital photography and pursuing strategic investments, joint ventures, and alliances. By 1998, Kodak's cost reduction program trimmed $730 million from expenses, helping Kodak enjoy one of its most profitable years, and it continued to report strong earnings until the recession of 2001. It introduced new products, notably its EasyShare digital camera, and it strengthened its entry into digital photography by acquisitions and partnerships with Intel and America Online. Kodak also made sizable investments in China, potentially the largest consumer market in the world.

These actions suggest that Kodak might be positioned for a positive reversal in fortunes. Yet, the market does not appear convinced of such a turnaround. For example, Kodak's stock price has declined steadily since its restructuring began six years ago. Accordingly, we might ask whether or not we should buy Kodak stock, and if so, what price we should be willing to pay.

The mostly qualitative information we've examined to this point, while useful, is inadequate for answering such questions. Instead, we need "hard" information about Kodak such as its net earnings, its sales and growth rates, its profit margins, its return on investment, and a host of other financial details. This realization highlights one of the most important roles for financial statements, namely, that as a source of reliable financial information. They reveal how a company obtains its resources (financing), where and how those resources are deployed (investing), and how effectively those resources are deployed (operating profitability).

Many individuals and organizations use financial statements to improve business decisions. Investors and creditors use them to assess company prospects for investing and lending decisions. Boards of directors, as investor representatives, use them to monitor managers' decisions and actions. Employees and unions use financial statements in labor negotiations. Suppliers use financial statements in setting credit terms. Investment advisors and information intermediaries use financial statements in making buy-sell recommendations and in credit rating. Investment bankers use financial statements in determining company value in an IPO, merger, or acquisition.

To show how financial statement information helps in business analysis, let's turn to the data in Exhibit 1.3. These data reveal that Kodak's net earnings in 2000, prior to the recession of 2001, were at their highest level of the past four years. This is despite stagnating sales during that period. Kodak appears profitable–earnings in 2000 are 10% of sales, and 41% of shareholders' equity. Kodak's increased profitability has come from cost reduction rather than from increased sales, a result of its restructuring activities during the period. The lack of sales growth, however, does not bode well for the future and cost control will become increasingly more important. This is particularly troublesome for a company so dependent on research and development.

Exhibit 1.3 ***Kodak's Summary Financial Data****

	2001	2000	1999	1998	1997
Sales	13,234	13,994	14,089	13,406	14,538
Total assets	13,362	14,212	14,370	14,733	13,145
Shareholders' equity	2,894	3,428	3,912	3,988	3,161
Net earnings	76	1,407	1,392	1,390	5
Basic earnings per share	0.26	4.62	4.38	4.30	0.01
Book value per share	9.95	11.80	12.60	12.35	9.78
Dividend per share	2.21	1.76	1.76	1.76	1.76
Average stock price	34.40	52.81	69.13	66.28	70.41

*In millions, except per share data.

The financial statement information in Exhibit 1.3 enhances our ability to assess Kodak's prospects and risks. Indeed, many investors use the ratio of a company's stock price to either its earnings or book value as a preliminary screening tool for investment analysis. However, is this summary financial information sufficient to use as a basis for deciding whether or not to invest in Kodak's stock or in making other business decisions? The answer is no. To make informed business decisions, it is important to evaluate Kodak's business activities in a more systematic and complete manner. For example, equity investors desire answers to the following types of questions before deciding to buy, hold, or sell Kodak stock:

- What are Kodak's future business prospects? Are Kodak's markets expected to grow? What are Kodak's competitive strengths and weaknesses? What strategic initiatives has Kodak taken, or does it plan to take, in response to business opportunities and threats?
- What is Kodak's earnings potential? What is its recent earnings performance? How sustainable are current earnings? What are the "drivers" of Kodak's profitability? What estimates can be made about earnings growth?
- What is Kodak's current financial condition? What risks and rewards does Kodak's financing structure portray? Are Kodak's earnings vulnerable to variability? Does Kodak possess the financial strength to overcome a period of poor profitability?
- How does Kodak compare with its competitors, both domestically and globally?
- What is a reasonable price for Kodak's stock?

FALLING STAR
Regulators slapped a $5 million fine on Smith Barney, charging that its star analyst privately questioned a telecom stock while he publicly boosted it.

Creditors and lenders also desire answers to important questions before entering into lending agreements with Kodak. Their questions include the following:

- What are Kodak's business plans and prospects? Why does Kodak need additional financing? What are Kodak's needs for future financing?
- What are Kodak's likely sources for payment of interest and principal? How much cushion does Kodak have in its earnings and cash flows to pay interest and principal?
- What is the likelihood Kodak will be unable to meet its financial obligations? How volatile are Kodak's earnings and cash flows? Does Kodak have the financial strength to pay its commitments in a period of poor profitability?

Answers to these and other questions about company prospects and risks require analysis of both qualitative information about a company's business plans and quantitative information about its financial position and performance. Proper analysis and interpretation of information is crucial to good business analysis. This is the role of financial statement analysis. Through it, an analyst will better understand and interpret both qualitative and quantitative financial information so that reliable inferences are drawn about company prospects and risks.

Types of Business Analysis

Financial statement analysis is an important and integral part of business analysis. The goal of business analysis is to improve business decisions by evaluating available information about a company's financial situation, its management, its plans and strategies, and its business environment. Business analysis is applied in many forms and is an important part of the decisions of security analysts, investment advisors, fund managers, investment bankers, credit raters, corporate bankers, and individual investors. This section considers major types of business analysis.

Credit Analysis

Creditors lend funds to a company in return for a promise of repayment with interest. This type of financing is temporary since creditors expect repayment of their funds with interest. Creditors lend funds in many forms and for a variety of purposes. **Trade** (or operating) **creditors** deliver goods or services to a company and expect payment within a reasonable period, often determined by industry norms. Most trade credit is short term, ranging from 30 to 60 days, with cash discounts often granted for early payment. Trade creditors do not usually receive (explicit) interest for an extension of credit. Instead, trade creditors earn a return from the profit margins on the business transacted. **Nontrade creditors** (or debtholders) provide financing to a company in return for a promise, usually in writing, of repayment with interest (explicit or implicit) on specific future dates. This type of financing can be either short or long term and arises in a variety of transactions.

In pure credit financing, an important element is the fixed nature of benefits to creditors. That is, should a company prosper, creditors' benefits are limited to the debt contract's rate of interest or to the profit margins on goods or services delivered. However, creditors bear the *risk of default.* This means a creditor's interest and principal are jeopardized when a borrower encounters financial difficulties. This asymmetric relation of a creditor's risk and return has a major impact on the creditor's perspective, including the manner and objectives of credit analysis.

Credit analysis is the evaluation of the creditworthiness of a company. *Creditworthiness* is the ability of a company to honor its credit obligations. Stated differently, it is the ability of a company to pay its bills. Accordingly, the main focus of credit analysis is on

RATINGS INFO
One can find company debt ratings at **standardandpoors.com**, **moodys.com**, and **fitchratings.com**.

BOND FINANCING
The value of the U.S. bond market exceeds $13 trillion.

risk, not profitability. Variability in profits, especially the sensitivity of profits to downturns in business, is more important than profit levels. Profit levels are important only to the extent they reflect the margin of safety for a company in meeting its obligations.

Credit analysis focuses on downside risk instead of upside potential. This includes analysis of both liquidity and solvency. **Liquidity** is a company's ability to raise cash in the short term to meet its obligations. Liquidity depends on a company's cash flows and the makeup of its current assets and current liabilities. **Solvency** is a company's long-run viability and ability to pay long-term obligations. It depends on both a company's long-term profitability and its capital (financing) structure.

The tools of credit analysis and their criteria for evaluation vary with the term (maturity), type, and purpose of the debt contract. With short-term credit, creditors are concerned with current financial conditions, cash flows, and the liquidity of current assets. With long-term credit, including bond valuation, creditors require more detailed and forward-looking analysis. Long-term credit analysis includes projections of cash flows and evaluation of extended profitability (also called *sustainable earning power*). Extended profitability is a main source of assurance of a company's ability to meet long-term interest and principal payments.

Credit analysis is performed in a variety of decision contexts. For example, a commercial bank must do credit analysis when extending a new line of credit to a company. In this case, credit analysis helps determine whether the loan is granted and, if it is, how it is structured and priced. Banks also need to periodically analyze the creditworthiness of their borrowers, both to ensure the safety of loans granted and to process requests for additional loans. Other decision makers who perform credit analysis are a pension fund manager, bond analyst, or investor who must do credit analysis when deciding to invest in bonds and other types of debt securities. Rating agencies periodically do credit analysis to set credit ratings, and suppliers do it to evaluate the probability a customer will pay its bills. Auditors who evaluate a client's going-concern status also do credit analysis, as does the treasury department of a company to assess its ability to raise debt when the need arises.

Equity Analysis

Equity investors provide funds to a company in return for the risks and rewards of ownership. Equity investors are major providers of company financing. Equity financing, also called *equity* or *share capital,* offers a cushion or safeguard for all other forms of financing that are senior to it. This means equity investors are entitled to the distributions of a company's assets only after the claims of all other senior claimants are met, including interest and preferred dividends. As a result, equity investors are said to hold a *residual interest.* This implies equity investors are the first to absorb losses when a company liquidates, although their losses are usually limited to the amount invested. However, when a company prospers, equity investors share in the gains with unlimited upside potential. Thus, unlike credit analysis, equity analysis is symmetric in that it must assess both downside risks and upside potential. Because equity investors are affected by all aspects of a company's financial condition and performance, their analysis needs are among the most demanding and comprehensive of all users.

Individuals who apply active investment strategies primarily use technical analysis, fundamental analysis, or a combination. **Technical analysis**, or charting, searches for patterns in the price or volume history of a stock to predict future price movements. **Fundamental analysis,** which is more widely accepted and applied, is the process of determining the value of a company by analyzing and interpreting key factors for the economy, the industry, and the company. A main part of fundamental analysis is evaluation of a company's financial position and performance.

GREATEST INVESTORS

The "top 10" greatest equity investors of the 20th century, as compiled in a recent survey:

1. Warren Buffett, Berkshire Hathaway
2. Peter Lynch, Fidelity Funds
3. John Templeton, Templeton Group
4. Benjamin Graham & David Dodd, professors
5. George Soros, Soros Fund
6. John Neff, Vanguard Group
7. John Bogle, Vanguard Group
8. Michael Price, Franklin Mutual
9. Julian Robertson, Tiger Management
10. Mark Mobius, Templeton Group

A major goal of fundamental analysis is to determine intrinsic value, also called *fundamental value.* **Intrinsic value** is the value of a company (or its stock) determined through fundamental analysis without reference to its market value (or stock price). While a company's market value can equal or approximate its intrinsic value, this is not necessary. An investor's strategy with fundamental analysis is straightforward: buy when a stock's intrinsic value exceeds its market value, sell when a stock's market value exceeds its intrinsic value, and hold when a stock's intrinsic value approximates its market value.

To determine intrinsic value, an analyst must forecast a company's earnings or cash flows and determine its risk. This is achieved through a comprehensive, in-depth analysis of a company's business prospects and its financial statements. Once a company's future profitability and risk are estimated, the analyst uses a valuation model to convert these estimates into a measure of intrinsic value. Intrinsic value is used in many contexts, including equity investment and stock selection, initial public offerings, private placements of equity, mergers and acquisitions, and the purchase/sale of companies without traded securities.

Other Uses of Business Analysis

Business analysis and financial statement analysis are important in a number of other contexts.

- **Managers.** To ensure their own well-being and future earnings potential, managers need to be concerned with the financial condition, profitability, and prospects of their company. Both business analysis and financial statement analysis take an outsider's perspective on the company, much as creditors and equity investors must view it. Analysis of financial statements can provide managers with clues to strategic changes in operating, investing, and financing activities. Managers also analyze the businesses and financial statements of competing companies to evaluate a competitor's profitability and risk. Such analysis allows for *interfirm comparisons,* both to evaluate relative strengths and weaknesses and to *benchmark* performance.
- **Mergers, acquisitions, and divestitures.** Business analysis is performed whenever a company restructures its operations, through mergers, acquisitions, divestitures, and spin-offs. Investment bankers need to identify potential targets and determine their values, and security analysts need to determine whether and how much additional value is created by the merger for both the acquiring and the target companies. Mergers and acquisitions are nearly always based on estimated intrinsic values, even when stock prices are available for both the target and acquiring companies. The goals of mergers and acquisitions analysis are similar to equity analysis.
- **Financial management.** Managers must evaluate the impact of financing decisions and dividend policy on company value. Business analysis helps assess the impact of financing decisions on both future profitability and risk. Managers also must determine intrinsic value before pursuing a share repurchase program. It is commonly believed that companies repurchase shares when managers view their shares as underpriced. To determine this, managers must estimate the company's intrinsic value.
- **External auditors.** The product of an audit is an expression of opinion on the fairness of the client's financial statements. At the completion of an audit, financial analysis can serve as a final check on the reasonableness of the financial statements as a whole. Auditors also use credit analysis in evaluating the ability of their client to remain a going concern.

MERGER BOOM
Nearly $4 trillion worth of mergers occurred from 1998 through 2000—more than in the entire preceding 30 years.

NEW DEALS
Experts say the *defining deals* for the next decade will be the alliance, the joint venture, and the partnership. Such deals will be more common in industries with rapid change.

- **Directors.** As elected representatives of the shareholders, directors are responsible for protecting the shareholders' interests by vigilantly overseeing the company's activities. This demands an understanding and appreciation of financing, investing, and operating activities. Both business analysis and financial statement analysis aid directors in fulfilling their oversight responsibilities.
- **Regulators.** The Internal Revenue Service applies tools of financial statement analysis to audit tax returns and check the reasonableness of reported amounts. Other regulatory agencies use analysis techniques in their supervisory and rate-determination roles. Politicians often use financial statements to support the perceived need, or lack thereof, for legislation affecting companies. For example, excessive profitability in an industry can invite additional taxation, while poor profitability can result in tax breaks and subsidies.
- **Labor unions.** Techniques of financial statement analysis are useful to labor unions in collective bargaining negotiations.
- **Customers.** Analysis techniques to determine profitability (or staying power) of their suppliers along with estimating the suppliers' profits from their mutual transactions.

PROFIT TAKERS
Microsoft's profitability levels encouraged recent antitrust actions against it.

Components of Business Analysis

Business analysis encompasses several interrelated processes. Exhibit 1.4 identifies these processes in the context of estimating company value–one of the many important applications of financial statement analysis. Company value, or intrinsic value, is estimated using a valuation model. Inputs to the valuation model include estimates of future payoffs (prospective cash flows or earnings) and the cost of capital. The process of forecasting future payoffs is called *prospective analysis.* To accurately forecast future payoffs, it is important to evaluate both the company's business prospects and its financial

Exhibit 1.4 **Component Processes of Business Analysis**

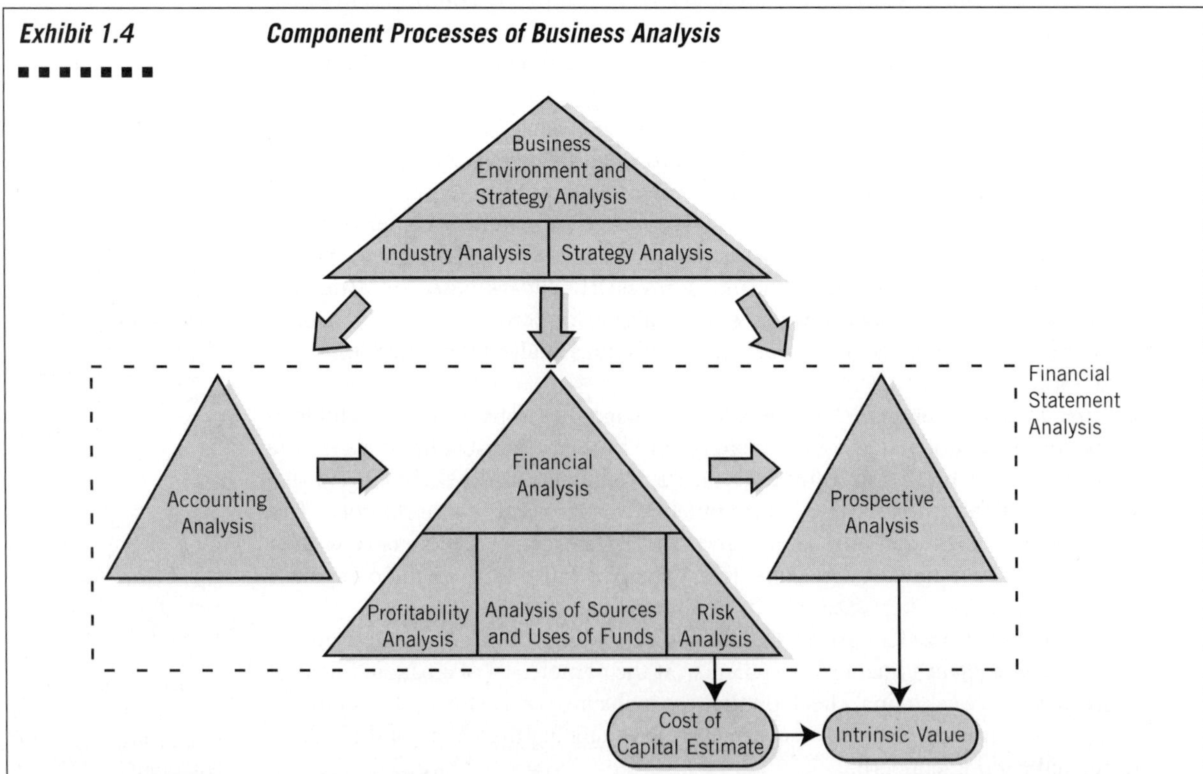

statements. Evaluation of business prospects is a major goal of *business environment and strategy analysis*. A company's financial status is assessed from its financial statements using *financial analysis*. In turn, the quality of financial analysis depends on the reliability and economic content of the financial statements. This requires *accounting analysis* of financial statements. Financial statement analysis involves all of these component processes–accounting, financial, and prospective analyses. This section discusses each of these component processes in the context of business analysis.

Business Environment and Strategy Analysis

Analysis of a company's future prospects is one of the most important aims of business analysis. It also is a subjective and complex task. To effectively accomplish this task we must adopt an interdisciplinary perspective. This includes attention to analysis of the business environment and strategy. Analysis of the business environment seeks to identify and assess a company's economic and industry circumstances. This includes analysis of its product, labor, and capital markets within its economic and regulatory setting. Analysis of business strategy seeks to identify and assess a company's competitive strengths and weaknesses along with its opportunities and threats.

Business environment and strategy analysis consists of two parts–industry analysis and strategy analysis. **Industry analysis** is the usual first step since the prospects and structure of its industry largely drive a company's profitability. Industry analysis is often done using the framework proposed by Porter (1980, 1985) or value chain analysis. Under this framework, an industry is viewed as a collection of competitors that jockey for bargaining power with consumers and suppliers and that actively compete among themselves and face threats from new entrants and substitute products. Industry analysis must assess both the industry prospects and the degree of actual and potential competition facing a company. **Strategy analysis** is the evaluation of both a company's business decisions and its success at establishing a competitive advantage. This includes assessing a company's expected strategic responses to its business environment and the impact of these responses on its future success and growth. Strategy analysis requires scrutiny of a company's competitive strategy for its product mix and cost structure.

Where do we obtain the information necessary for conducting business environment and strategy analysis? Part of the information is available from a company's annual report. This includes the Chairperson's Letter, Management's Discussion and Analysis (MD&A), and any other Vision, Mission, or Business sections. These items convey information about a company's environment and strategies from management's perspective. We also obtain information from industry and trade reports and journals, government publications, the financial press, and in some cases directly from the company's website or its promotional materials. Voluntary disclosures and press releases provide still other sources of information about company plans and progress to date.

Business environment and strategy analysis requires knowledge of both economic and industry forces. It also requires knowledge of strategic management, business policy, production, logistics management, marketing, and managerial economics. Because of its broad, multidisciplinary nature, it is beyond the scope of this book to cover all of these areas in the context of business environment and strategy analysis and how they relate to financial statements. Still, this analysis is necessary for meaningful business decisions and is implicit, if not explicit, in all analyses in this book.

BENCHMARKING
The Web offers benchmarking info to help with analysis of business environment and strategy:
www.asq.org
www.apqc.org
www.trainingforum.com/MRT
www.benchnet.com
www.bmpcoe.org

BOARDROOM ETHICS
Recent NYSE rules require that independent directors with "no material relationship" to the company be appointed to certain board committees. This is a major problem for many companies as a recent study estimates that up to 75% of S&P 500 companies are not in concert with these rules.

Accounting Analysis

Accounting analysis is a process of evaluating the extent to which a company's accounting reflects economic reality. This is done by studying a company's transactions and events, assessing the effects of its accounting policies on financial statements, and adjusting the statements to both better reflect the underlying economics and make them more amenable to analysis. Financial statements are the primary source of information for financial analysis. This means the quality of financial analysis depends on the reliability of financial statements that in turn depends on the quality of accounting analysis. Accounting analysis is especially important for comparative analysis.

We must remember that accounting is a process involving judgment guided by fundamental principles. While accounting principles are governed by standards, the complexity of business transactions and events makes it impossible to adopt a uniform set of accounting rules for all companies and all time periods. Moreover, most accounting standards evolve as part of a political process to satisfy the needs of diverse individuals and their sometimes conflicting interests. These individuals include *users* such as investors, creditors, and analysts; *preparers* such as corporations, partnerships, and proprietorships; *regulators* such as the Securities and Exchange Commission and the Financial Accounting Standards Board; and still others such as auditors, lawyers, and educators. Accordingly, accounting standards sometimes fail to meet the needs of specific individuals. Another factor potentially impeding the reliability of financial statements is error from accounting estimates that can yield incomplete or imprecise information.

NUMBERS CRUNCH
In a recent survey, nearly 20% of CFO respondents admitted that CEOs pressured them to misrepresent results.

These accounting limitations affect the usefulness of financial statements and can yield at least two problems in analysis. First, lack of uniformity in accounting leads to comparability problems. **Comparability problems** arise when different companies adopt different accounting for similar transactions or events. Comparability problems also arise when a company changes its accounting across time, leading to difficulties with temporal comparability.

Second, discretion and imprecision in accounting can distort financial statement information. **Accounting distortions** are deviations of accounting information from the underlying economics. These distortions occur in at least three forms. (1) Managerial estimates can be subject to honest errors or omissions. This *estimation error* is a major cause of accounting distortions. (2) Managers might use their discretion in accounting to manipulate or window-dress financial statements. This *earnings management* can cause accounting distortions. (3) Accounting standards can give rise to accounting distortions from a failure to capture economic reality. These three types of accounting distortions create accounting risk in financial statement analysis. **Accounting risk** is the uncertainty in financial statement analysis due to accounting distortions. A major goal of accounting analysis is to evaluate and reduce accounting risk and to improve the economic content of financial statements, including their comparability. Meeting this goal usually requires restatement and reclassification of financial statements to improve their economic content and comparability. The type and extent of adjustments depend on the analysis. For example, adjustments for equity analysis can differ from those for credit analysis.

ANALYSIS SNITCH
Filing a complaint with the SEC is easy online http://www.sec.gov. E-mail the SEC with details of the suspected scam. Include website, newsgroup, and E-mail addresses; names of companies or people mentioned; and any information that can help the SEC track those involved. Your name, address, and phone number are optional.

Accounting analysis includes evaluation of a company's *earnings quality* or, more broadly, its accounting quality. Evaluation of earnings quality requires analysis of factors such as a company's business, its accounting policies, the quantity and quality of information disclosed, the performance and reputation of management, and the opportunities and incentives for earnings management. Accounting analysis also includes evaluation of earnings persistence, sometimes called *sustainable earning power*. We explain analysis of both earnings quality and persistence in Chapters 2 and 12.

Accounting analysis is often the least understood, appreciated, and effectively applied process in business analysis. Part of the reason might be that accounting analysis requires accounting knowledge. Analysts that lack this knowledge have a tendency to brush accounting analysis under the rug and take financial statements as reported. This is a dangerous practice because accounting analysis is crucial to any successful business or financial analysis. Chapters 3–6 of this book are devoted to accounting analysis.

Financial Analysis

Financial analysis is the use of financial statements to analyze a company's financial position and performance, and to assess future financial performance. Several questions can help focus financial analysis. One set of questions is future oriented. For example, does a company have the resources to succeed and grow? Does it have resources to invest in new projects? What are its sources of profitability? What is the company's future earning power? A second set involves questions that assess a company's track record and its ability to deliver on expected financial performance. For example, how strong is the company's financial position? How profitable is the company? Did earnings meet analyst forecasts? This includes an analysis of why a company might have fallen short of (or exceeded) expectations.

Financial analysis consists of three broad areas–profitability analysis, risk analysis, and analysis of sources and uses of funds. **Profitability analysis** is the evaluation of a company's return on investment. It focuses on a company's sources and levels of profits and involves identifying and measuring the impact of various profitability drivers. It also includes evaluation of the two major sources of profitability–margins (the portion of sales not offset by costs) and turnover (capital utilization). Profitability analysis also focuses on reasons for changes in profitability and the sustainability of earnings. The topic is discussed in detail in Chapters 8 and 9. **Risk analysis** is the evaluation of a company's ability to meet its commitments. Risk analysis involves assessing the solvency and liquidity of a company along with its earnings variability. Since risk is of foremost concern to creditors, risk analysis is often discussed in the context of credit analysis. Still, risk analysis is important to equity analysis, both to evaluate the reliability and sustainability of company performance and to estimate a company's cost of capital. We explain risk analysis along with credit analysis in Chapter 11. **Analysis of sources and uses of funds** is the evaluation of how a company is obtaining and deploying its funds. This analysis provides insights into a company's future financing implications. For example, a company that funds new projects from internally generated cash (profits) is likely to achieve better future performance than a company that either borrows heavily to finance its projects or, worse, borrows to meet current losses. We explain analysis of sources and uses of funds along with cash flow analysis in Chapter 7.

ANALYSTS' CONFLICTS
Regulators wrung a $100 million penalty from Merrill Lynch after revealing internal E-mails in which analysts privately disparaged as "junk" and "crap" stocks they were pushing to the public.

Prospective Analysis

Prospective analysis is the forecasting of future payoffs–typically earnings, cash flows, or both. This analysis draws on accounting analysis, financial analysis, and business environment and strategy analysis. The output of prospective analysis is a set of expected future payoffs used to estimate company value.

While quantitative tools help improve forecast accuracy, prospective analysis remains a relatively subjective process. This is why prospective analysis is sometimes referred to as an art, not a science. Still, there are many tools we can draw on to help enhance this analysis. We explain prospective analysis in detail in Chapter 10.

KEEN PREDICTOR
Accounting professor and Morgan Stanley Dean Witter analyst Trevor Harris sounded an early alarm about Qwest Communications' accounting woes in June 2001, one year before the SEC began investigating the issues he raised.

Valuation

Valuation is a main objective of many types of business analysis. Valuation refers to the process of converting forecasts of future payoffs into an estimate of company value. To determine company value, an analyst must select a valuation model and must also estimate the company's cost of capital. While most valuation models require forecasts of future payoffs, there are certain ad hoc approaches that use current financial information. We examine valuation in a preliminary manner later in this chapter and again in Chapter 12.

Financial Statement Analysis and Business Analysis

Exhibit 1.4 and its discussion emphasizes that financial statement analysis is a collection of analytical processes that are part of business analysis. These separate processes share a common bond in that they all use financial statement information, to varying degrees, for analysis purposes. While financial statements do contain information on a company's business plans, analysis of a company's business environment and strategy is sometimes viewed outside of conventional financial statement analysis. Also, prospective analysis pushes the frontier of conventional financial statement analysis. Yet most agree that an important part of financial statement analysis is analyzing a company's business environment and strategy. Most also agree that valuation, which requires forecasts, is part of financial statement analysis. Therefore, financial statement analysis should be, and is, viewed as an important and integral part of business analysis and all of its component analyses. At the same time, it is important to understand the scope of financial statement analysis. Specifically, this book focuses on financial statement analysis and not on aspects of business analysis apart from those involving analysis of financial statements.

KNOW-NOTHING CEOs

The know-nothing defense of CEOs such as Global Crossing's Gary Winnick and Enron's Jeffrey Skilling and Kenneth Lay was shattered by novel legal moves. They created problems for CEOs when investigators proved that CEOs knew the internal picture was materially different than the external picture presented to shareholders.

FINANCIAL STATEMENTS—BASIS OF ANALYSIS

Business Activities

A company pursues a number of activities in a desire to provide a salable product or service and to yield a satisfactory return on investment. Its financial statements and related disclosures inform us about the four major activities of the company: planning, financing, investing, and operating. It is important to understand each of these major business activities before we can effectively analyze a company's financial statements.

Planning Activities

A company exists to implement specific goals and objectives. For example, Kodak aspires to remain the world leader in imaging products and services. A company's goals and objectives are captured in a **business plan** that describes the company's purpose, strategy, and tactics for its activities. A business plan assists managers in focusing their efforts and identifying expected opportunities and obstacles. Insight into the business plan considerably aids our analysis of a company's current and future prospects and is part of the analysis of business environment and strategy. We look for information on company objectives and tactics, market demands, competitive analysis, sales strategies (pricing, promotion, distribution), management performance, and financial projections. Information of this type, in varying forms, is often revealed in financial statements. It is also available through less formal means such as press releases, industry publications, analysts' newsletters, and the financial press.

Two important sources of information on a company's business plan are the Letter to Shareholders (or Chairperson's Letter) and Management's Discussion and Analysis (MD&A). Kodak, in its Chairperson's Letter found in its annual report, discusses various business opportunities and plans as reproduced here:

ANALYSIS EXCERPT

We will continue to invest in R&D as a critical path to our financial success—delivering innovative, customer-focused imaging products, systems, and services. . . . We will work to maintain or increase share positions in all of our businesses and we will continue to pay close attention to costs, managing the business for maximum cash. . . . We will leverage our unparalleled reputation for quality to ALL infoimaging processes and products, a category with $225 billion total market potential.

Additional discussion appears in the Management's Discussion and Analysis section of Kodak's annual report. These two sources are excellent starting points in constructing a company's business plan and in performing a business environment and strategy analysis.

It is important to stress that business planning is not cast in stone and is fraught with uncertainty. Can Kodak be certain of the future of consumer and professional photography? Can Kodak be certain its raw material costs will not increase? Can Kodak be sure how competitors will react? These and other questions add risk to our analysis. While all actions involve risk, some actions involve more risk than others. Financial statement analysis helps us estimate the degree of risk, or uncertainty, and yields more informed and better decisions. While information taken from financial statements does not provide irrefutable answers, it does help us to gauge the soundness of a company's business opportunities and strategies and to better understand its financing, investing, and operating activities.

SERIAL ACQUIRERS
CEOs who built up their companies with a blitz of deals include GE's Jack Welch who did 534 deals, Tyco International Ltd.'s Dennis Kozlowski with 169 deals, and AutoNation's H. Wayne Huizenga with 114 deals.

Financing Activities

A company requires financing to carry out its business plan. Kodak needs financing for purchasing raw materials for production, paying its employees, acquiring complementary companies and technologies, and for research and development. **Financing activities** refer to methods that companies use to raise the money to pay for these needs. Because of their magnitude and their potential for determining the success or failure of a venture, companies take care in acquiring and managing financial resources.

There are two main sources of external financing–equity investors (also called owners or shareholders) and creditors (lenders). Decisions concerning the composition of financing activities depend on conditions existing in financial markets. Financial markets are potential sources of financing. In looking to financial markets, a company considers several issues, including the amount of financing necessary, sources of financing (owners or creditors), timing of repayment, and structure of financing agreements. Decisions on these issues determine a company's organizational structure, affect its growth, influence its exposure to risk, and determine the power of outsiders in business decisions.

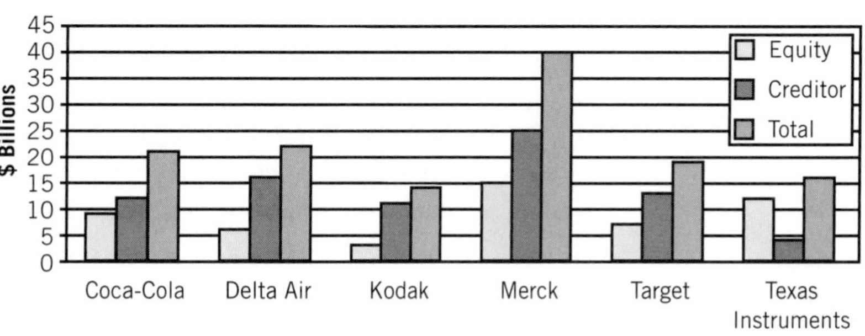

Equity investors are a major source of financing. Kodak's balance sheet shows it raised $1.827 billion by issuing stock to equity investors. Investors provide financing in a desire for a return on their investment, after considering both expected return and risk.

Return is the equity investor's share of company earnings in the form of either earnings distribution or earnings reinvestment. **Earnings distribution** is the payment of dividends to shareholders. Dividends can be paid directly in the form of cash or stock dividend, or indirectly through stock repurchase. **Dividend payout** refers to the proportion of earnings distributed. It is often expressed as a ratio or a percentage. Kodak has paid a stable dividend of between $1.76 and $2.21 per share in the past five years, a dividend payout ratio (dividends/net earnings) in the range of 40%. **Earnings reinvestment** (or earnings retention) refers to retaining earnings within the company for use in its business; this is also called *internal financing*. Earnings reinvestment is often measured by a retention ratio. The **earnings retention ratio**, reflecting the proportion of earnings retained, is defined as one less the dividend payout ratio. Earnings reinvestment also is measured by equity growth. Kodak's earnings retention ratio is approximately 60 percent. Total 2001 equity financing for Kodak is nearly $2.89 billion, which is 22% of its total financing of $13.36 billion. The chart in the margin on the previous page shows the makeup of total financing for selected companies.

Equity financing can be in cash or any asset or service contributed to a company in exchange for equity shares. Private offerings of shares usually involve selling shares to one or more individuals or organizations. Public offerings involve selling shares to the public. There are significant costs with public offerings of shares, including government regulatory filings, stock exchange listing requirements, and brokerage fees to selling agents. The main benefit of public offerings of shares is the potential to raise substantial funds for business activities. Many corporations offer their shares for trading on organized exchanges like the New York, Tokyo, Singapore, and London stock markets. Kodak's common stock trades on the New York Stock Exchange under the symbol EK. The chart in the margin shows the makeup of equity financing for selected companies. Note the negative amounts of contributed capital for Coca-Cola, Kodak, and Merck. This represents significant repurchases of common stock (called treasury stock).

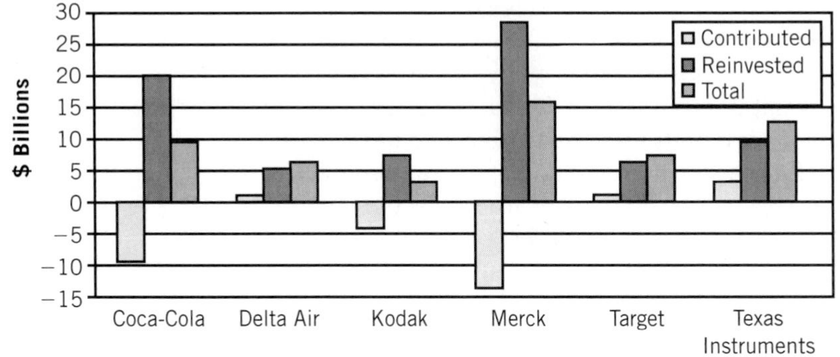

Companies also obtain financing from creditors. Creditors are of two types: (1) debt creditors, who directly lend money to the company, and (2) operating creditors, to whom the company owes money as part of its operations. Debt financing often occurs through loans or through issuance of securities such as bonds. Debt financers include organizations like banks, savings and loans, and other financial or nonfinancial institutions. Operating creditors include suppliers, employees, the government, and any other entity to whom the company owes money. Even employees who are paid periodically, say weekly or monthly, are implicitly providing a form of credit financing until they are paid for their efforts. Kodak's balance sheet shows total creditor financing of over $10 billion, which is about 78% of its total financing. Of this amount, around $3.2 billion, or 31% of total financing, is debt financing, while the remaining $7.3 billion, or 69%, is operations financing.

SCAM SOURCING

According to regulators, the five most common ways investors get duped are (1) unlicensed securities dealers, (2) unscrupulous stockbrokers, (3) research analyst conflicts, (4) fraudulent promissory notes, and (5) prime bank schemes.

Creditor financing is different from equity financing in that an agreement, or contract, is usually established that requires repayment of the loan with interest at specific dates. While interest is not always expressly stated in these contracts, it is always implicit. Loan periods are variable and depend on the desires of both creditors and companies. Loans can be as long as 50 years or more, or as short as a week or less.

Like equity investors, creditors are concerned with return and risk. Unlike equity investors, creditors' returns are usually specified in loan contracts. For example, a 20-year, 10 percent, fixed-rate loan means that creditors receive a 10 percent annual return on their investment for 20 years. Kodak's long-term loans are due from 2002 to 2021 and carry different interest rates. The returns of equity investors are not guaranteed and depend on the level of future earnings. Risk for creditors is the possibility a business will default in repaying its loans and interest. In this situation, creditors might not receive their money due, and bankruptcy or other legal remedies could ensue. Such remedies impose costs on creditors.

Creditor Financing

30
25
20
15
10
5
0
$ Billions
Operating debt
Debt
Total
Coca-Cola
Delta Air
Kodak
Merck
Target
Texas Instruments

> ***ANALYSIS VIEWPOINT . . . YOU ARE THE CREDITOR***
>
> Kodak requests a $500 million loan from your bank. How does the composition of Kodak's financing sources (creditor and equity) affect your loan decision? Do you have any reluctance making the loan to Kodak given its current financing composition? *[Note: Solutions to Viewpoints are at the end of each chapter.]*

Answer–p. 45

Investing Activities

Investing activities refer to a company's acquisition and maintenance of investments for purposes of selling products and providing services, and for the purpose of investing excess cash. Investments in land, buildings, equipment, legal rights (patents, licenses, copyrights), inventories, human capital (managers and employees), information systems, and similar assets are for the purpose of conducting the company's business operations. Such assets are called **operating assets.** Also, companies often temporarily or permanently invest excess cash in securities such as other companies' equity stock, corporate and government bonds, and money market funds. Such assets are called **financial assets.** Kodak's balance sheet shows its 2001 investment, or asset, base is $13.4 billion, of which $448 million is in financial assets and the rest is in operating assets. The chart in the margin shows the operating and financial assets of selected companies.

Information on both financing and investing activities assists us in evaluating business performance. Note the value of investments always equals the value of financing obtained. Any excess financing not invested is simply reported as cash (or some other noncash asset). Companies differ in the amount and composition of their investments. Many companies demand huge investments in acquiring,

Operating and Financing Assets

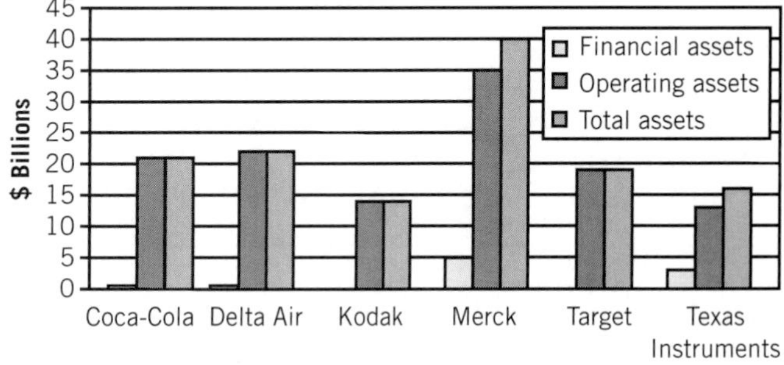

developing, and selling their products, while others require little investment. Size of investment does not necessarily determine company success. It is the efficiency and effectiveness with which a company carries out its operations that determine earnings and returns to owners.

Investing decisions involve several factors such as type of investment necessary (including technological and labor intensity), amount required, acquisition timing, asset location, and contractual agreement (purchase, rent, and lease). Like financing activities, decisions on investing activities determine a company's organizational structure (centralized or decentralized), affect growth, and influence riskiness of operations. Investments in short-term assets are called **current assets.** These assets are expected to be converted to cash in the short term. Investments in long-term assets are called **noncurrent assets.** Kodak invests \$4.7 billion in current assets (35% of total assets) and \$5.66 billion in plant and machinery (42% of total assets). Its remaining assets include intangibles such as goodwill (\$948 million) and other long-term assets (\$2.07 billion), including investments in other companies, deferred tax assets, and prepaid pension costs.

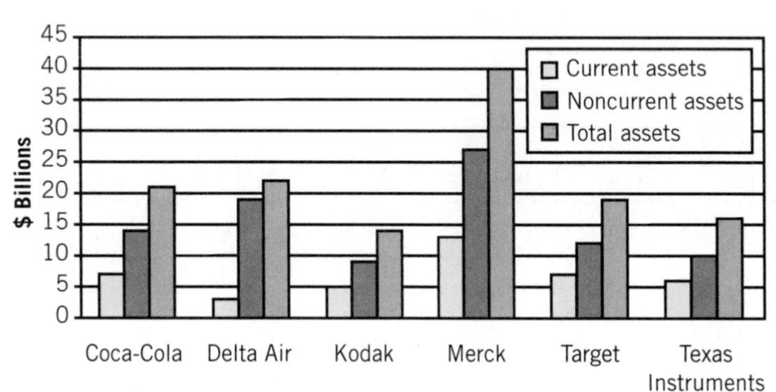

Operating Activities

One of the more important pieces in analyzing a company is operating activities. **Operating activities** represent the "carrying out" of the business plan given its financing and investing activities. Operating activities involve at least five possible components: research and development, procurement, production, marketing, and administration. A proper mix of the components of operating activities depends on the type of business, its plans, and its input and output markets. Management decides on the most efficient and effective mix for the company's competitive advantage.

Operating activities are a company's primary source of earnings. Earnings reflect a company's success in buying from input markets and selling in output markets. How well a company does in devising business plans and strategies, and deciding the mix of operating activities, determines its success or failure. Analysis of earnings figures, and their component parts, reflects a company's success in efficiently and effectively managing business activities.

Kodak earned \$76 million in the recession year of 2001. This number by itself is not very meaningful. Instead, it must be compared with the level of investment used to generate these earnings. Kodak's return on beginning-of-year investment of \$14,212 million is 0.5% (\$76 million/\$14,212 million)–an inadequate return by any standard. The same \$14,212 million invested in a savings account earning 5% interest would yield earnings of over \$700 million.

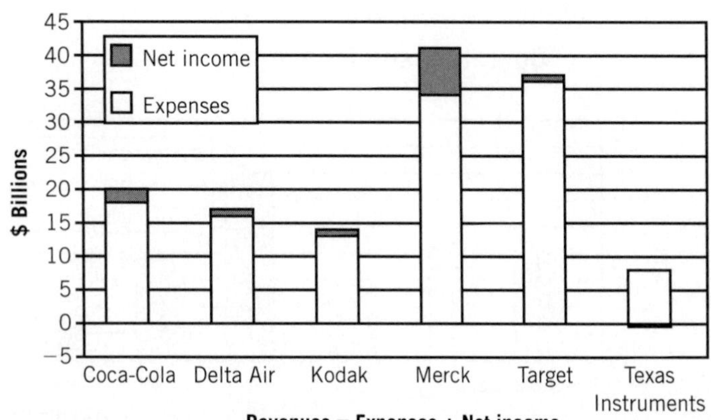

For 2000, a more representative year, Kodak earned $1,407 million on an initial investment of $14,370 million, a respectable return of 9.8%. Such analysis, while revealing, is incomplete. We need to consider costs of financing. For example, even though a 10% return looks appealing, we might think otherwise if financing costs are 15%. Moreover, we must compare a company's earnings with its sales. Kodak's sales in 2000 were $13.9 billion, showing that its earnings of $1.41 billion are 10.1% of sales, seemingly adequate for this industry.

Financial Statements Reflect Business Activities

At the end of a period–typically a quarter or a year–financial statements are prepared to report on financing and investing activities at that point in time, and to summarize operating activities for the preceding period. This is the role of financial statements and the object of analysis. It is important to recognize that financial statements report on financing and investing activities at a point in time, whereas they report on operating activities for a period of time.

Balance Sheet

The **accounting equation** (also called the balance sheet identity) is the basis of the accounting system: Assets = Liabilities + Equity. The left-hand side of this equation relates to the resources controlled by a company, or **assets.** These resources are investments that are expected to generate future earnings through operating activities. To engage in operating activities, a company needs financing to fund them. The right-hand side of this equation identifies funding sources. **Liabilities** are funding from creditors and represent obligations of a company or, alternatively, claims of creditors on assets. **Equity** (or shareholders' equity) is the total of (1) funding invested or contributed by owners (contributed capital) and (2) accumulated earnings in excess of distributions to owners (retained earnings) since inception of the company. From the owners', or shareholders', point of view, equity represents their claim on company assets. A slightly different way to describe the accounting equation is in terms of sources and uses of funds. That is, the right-hand side represents sources of funds (either from creditors or shareholders, or internally generated) and the left-hand side represents uses of funds.

Assets and liabilities are separated into current and noncurrent amounts. **Current assets** are expected to be converted to cash or used in operations within one year or the operating cycle, whichever is longer. **Current liabilities** are obligations the company is expected to settle within one year or the operating cycle, whichever is longer. The difference between current assets and current liabilities is called **working capital**.

It is revealing to rewrite the accounting equation in terms of business activities–namely, investing and financing activities: Total investing = Total financing; or alternatively: Total investing = Creditor financing + Owner financing.

Remember the accounting equation is a balance sheet identity reflecting a *point* in time. Operating activities arise over a *period* of time and are not reflected in this identity. However, operating activities can affect both sides of this equation.

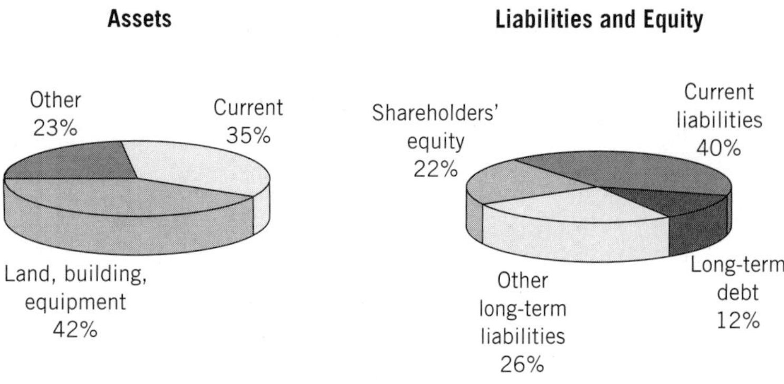

That is, if a company is profitable, both investing (assets) and financing (equity) levels increase. Similarly, when a company is unprofitable, both investing and financing decline.

The balance sheet of Kodak is reproduced in Appendix A at the end of the text. Kodak's total investments (assets) on December 31, 2001, are $13.362 billion (see Appendix A). Of this amount, creditor financing totals $10.468 billion, while the remaining $2.894 billion represents claims of shareholders.

Income Statement

An income statement measures a company's financial performance between balance sheet dates. It is a representation of the operating activities of a company. The income statement provides details of revenues, expenses, gains, and losses of a company for a time period. The bottom line, **earnings** (also called *net income*), indicates the profitability of the company. Earnings reflects the return to equity holders for the period under consideration, while the line items of the statement detail how earnings are determined. Earnings approximate the increase (or decrease) in equity before considering distributions to and contributions from equity holders. For income to exactly measure change in equity, we need a slightly different definition of income, called *comprehensive income,* which we discuss in the section on links between financial statements later in this chapter.

The income statement includes several other indicators of profitability. **Gross profit** (also called *gross margin*) is the difference between sales and cost of sales (also called *cost of goods sold*). It indicates the extent to which a company is able to cover costs of its products. This indicator is not especially relevant for service and technology companies where production costs are a small part of total costs. **Earnings from operations** refers to the difference between sales and all operating costs and expenses. It usually excludes financing costs (interest) and taxes. **Earnings before taxes,** as the name implies, represents earnings from continuing operations before the provision for income tax. **Earnings from continuing operations** is the income from a company's continuing business after interest and taxes. It is also called *earnings before extraordinary items and discontinued operations.* We discuss these alternative earnings definitions in Chapters 6 and 9.

EBITDA MESS

Some companies have convinced investors that they should measure performance not by earnings but by earnings before interest, taxes, depreciation, and amortization (EBITDA). EBITDA shelters companies from the harsh judgment of a net income calculation. For example, results (in millions) for cable-TV companies follow after adding back the cost of capital expenditures:

	EBITDA	EBITDA adding cap. expend.
Cox Comm.	$1,569	$ (636)
Charter Comm.	1,811	(1,239)
Cablevision Sys.	708	(663)

Earnings are determined using the **accrual basis** of accounting. Under accrual accounting, revenues are recognized when a company sells goods or renders services, regardless of when it receives cash. Similarly, expenses are matched to these recognized revenues, regardless of when it pays cash. The income statement of Kodak, titled consolidated statement of earnings, for the preceding three years is shown in Appendix A. Kodak's 2001 sales total $13.234 billion. Of this amount, $13.158 billion are expenses and costs of operations, yielding net earnings of $76 million. The reduction of Kodak's profitability from previous years reflects the extraordinary events of September 11, 2001, and the recession of that year, coupled with the effects of Kodak's ongoing restructuring activities.

Statement of Shareholders' Equity

The statement of shareholders' equity reports changes in the accounts that make up equity. This statement is useful in identifying reasons for changes in equity holders' claims on the assets of a company. Kodak's statement of shareholders' equity for its most recent year is shown in Appendix A. During this period, shareholders' equity changes due to the issuing and repurchasing of (treasury) stock, and reinvesting earnings. Kodak details these changes under five columns: Common Stock, Additional Paid-In Capital, Retained Earnings, Accumulated Other Comprehensive Income (Loss), and Treasury Stock. Common Stock and Additional Paid-In Capital together represent Contributed Capital and are often collectively called *share capital.*

Although many companies such as Kodak show Accumulated Other Comprehensive Income (Loss) separate from retained earnings, in reality it is an integral component of retained earnings. Accordingly, our analysis will always refer to them collectively as retained earnings. The change in Kodak's retained earnings is especially important because this account links consecutive balance sheets through the income statement. For example, consider Kodak's collective retained earnings decrease from \$7.387 billion in 2000 to \$6.834 billion in 2001. This decrease of \$0.553 billion is explained by net earnings of \$0.076 billion less other comprehensive loss of \$0.115 billion–collectively called *comprehensive income*–and less a decrease of \$0.514 billion from dividends. Since dividends almost always are distributed from retained earnings, the retained earnings balance often represents an upper limit on the amount of potential dividend distributions. The fifth column in the statement of shareholders' equity shows details of treasury stock. Treasury stock is discussed in Chapter 3. For now, it is sufficient to view the treasury stock amount as the difference between cash paid for share repurchases and the proceeds from selling stock to employees. The treasury stock amount reduces equity.

Statement of Cash Flows

Earnings do not typically equal net cash flows, except over the life of a company. Since accrual accounting yields numbers different from cash flow accounting, and we know that cash flows are important in business decisions, there is a need for reporting on cash inflows and outflows. For example, analyses involving reconstruction and interpretation of business transactions often require the statement of cash flows. Also, certain valuation models use cash flows. The statement of cash flows reports cash inflows and outflows separately for a company's operating, investing, and financing activities over a period of time.

Kodak's statement of cash flows is reproduced in Appendix A. Kodak's 2000 cash balance increases by \$202 million, from \$246 million to \$448 million. Of this net cash increase, Kodak's operating activities provided \$2.065 billion, its investing activities used \$1.047 billion, its financing activities used \$0.808 billion, and exchange rate changes used \$.008 billion.

Links between Financial Statements

Financial statements are linked at points in time and across time. These links are portrayed in Exhibit 1.5 using Kodak's financial statements. Kodak began 2001 with the investing and financing amounts reported in the balance sheet on the left side of Exhibit 1.5. Its investments in assets, comprising both cash (\$246 million) and noncash assets (\$13,966 million), total \$14,212 million. These investments are financed by both creditors (\$10,784 million) and equity investors, the latter comprising share capital (\$1,849 million), retained earnings (\$7,387 million), and treasury stock (\$5,808 million). Kodak's operating activities are shown in the middle column of Exhibit 1.5. The statement of cash flows explains how operating, investing, and financing activities increase Kodak's cash balance from \$246 million at the beginning of the year to \$448 million at year-end. This end-of-year cash amount is reported in the year-end balance sheet on the right side of Exhibit 1.5. Kodak's net earnings of \$76 million, computed from revenues less expenses, is reported in the income statement. Adding net earnings to other comprehensive loss of \$115 million gives comprehensive loss of \$39 million. This comprehensive loss amount less the dividends paid (\$514 million) helps explain the change in retained earnings reported in the statement of shareholders' equity. This

Exhibit 1.5 ***Financial Statement Links—Kodak***

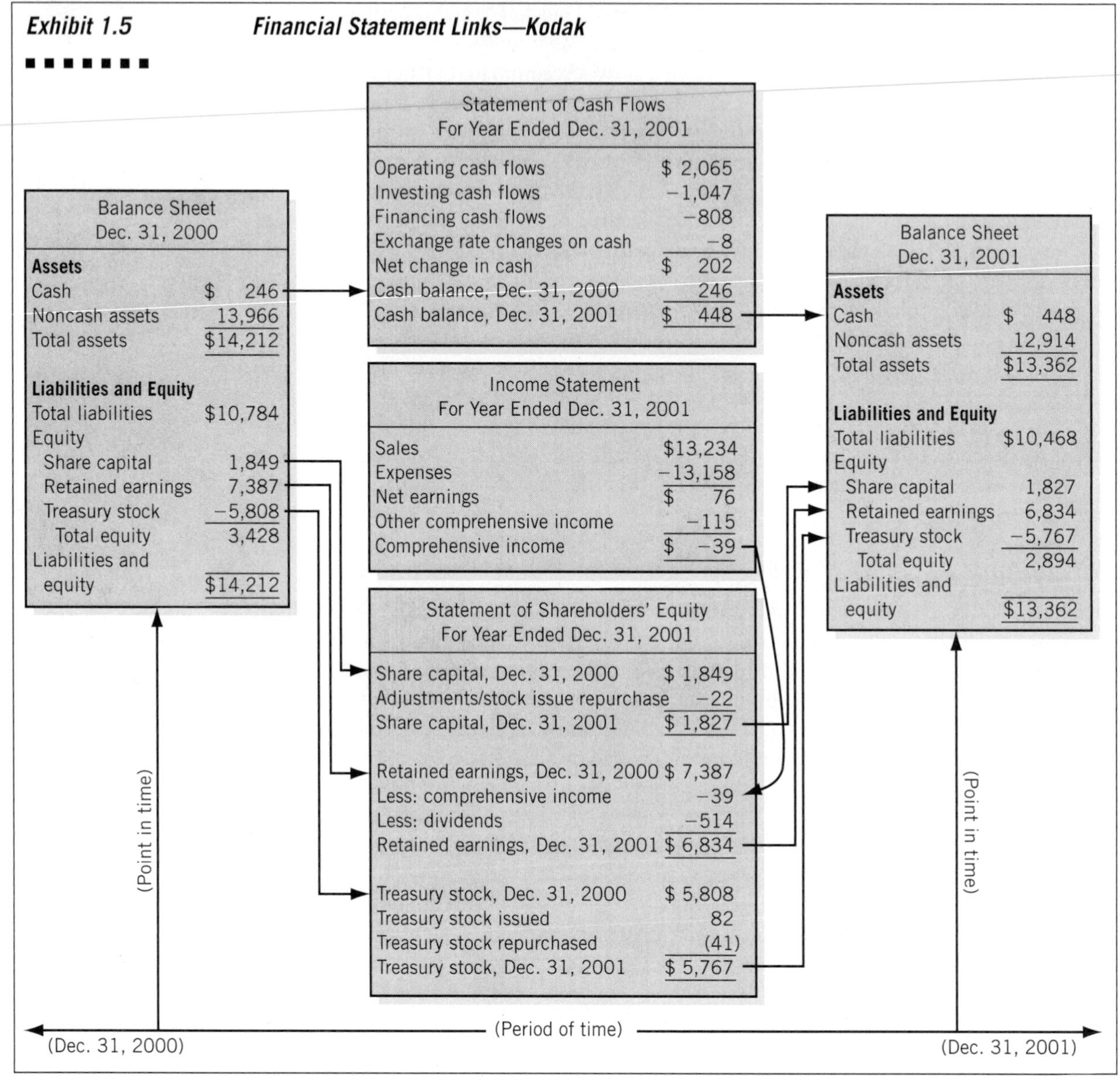

feature of how earnings help explain successive shareholders' equity balances is called **clean surplus** accounting.

To recap, Kodak's balance sheet is a listing of its investing and financing activities at a *point in time.* The three statements that report on (1) cash flows, (2) income, and (3) shareholders' equity, explain changes (typically from operating activities) over a *period of time* for Kodak's investing and financing activities. Every transaction captured in these three latter statements impacts the balance sheet. Examples are (1) revenues and expenses affecting earnings and their subsequent reporting in retained earnings, (2) cash transactions in the statement of cash flows that are summarized in the cash balance on the balance sheet, and (3) all revenue and expense accounts that affect one or more balance sheet accounts. In sum, financial statements are linked by design: the period-of-time statements (income statement, statement of cash flows, and statement of shareholders' equity) explain point-in-time balance sheets. This is known as the *articulation* of financial statements.

ANALYSIS VIEWPOINT ***. . . YOU ARE THE INVESTOR***

You are considering buying Kodak stock. As part of your preliminary review of Kodak, you examine its financial statements. What information are you attempting to obtain from each of these statements to aid in your decision?

Answer–p. 45

Additional Information

Financial statements are not the sole output of a financial reporting system. Additional information about a company is also communicated. A thorough financial statement analysis involves examining this additional information.

- **Management's Discussion and Analysis (MD&A).** Companies with publicly traded debt and equity securities are required by the Securities and Exchange Commission to file a Management's Discussion and Analysis (MD&A). Management must highlight any favorable or unfavorable trends and identify significant events and uncertainties that affect a company's liquidity, capital resources, and results of operations. They must also disclose prospective information involving material events and uncertainties known to cause reported financial information to be less indicative of future operating activities or financial condition. The MD&A for Kodak shown in Appendix A includes a year-by-year analysis along with an evaluation of its liquidity and capital resources by business activities.
- **Management Report.** The purposes of this report are to reinforce: (1) senior management's responsibilities for the company's financial and internal control system and (2) the shared roles of management, directors, and the auditor in preparing financial statements. Kodak's report, titled Management's Responsibility for Financial Statements, discusses its policies and procedures to enhance the reliability of its financial records. Its report also highlights the role of its audit committee of the board of directors in providing added assurance for the reliability of financial statements.
- **Auditor Report.** An external auditor is an independent certified public accountant hired by management to provide an opinion on whether or not the company's financial statements are prepared in conformity with generally accepted accounting principles. Financial statement analysis requires a review of the auditor's report to ascertain whether the company received an unqualified opinion. Anything less than an unqualified opinion increases the risk of analysis. Kodak's Report of Independent Accountants, prepared by PricewaterhouseCoopers, is reproduced in Appendix A. Kodak received an unqualified opinion. We discuss audit reports in Appendix 2A.
- **Explanatory Notes.** Explanatory notes that accompany financial reports play an integral part in financial statement analysis. Notes are a means of communicating additional information regarding items included or excluded from the body of the statements. The technical nature of notes creates a need for a certain level of accounting knowledge on the part of financial statement analysts. Explanatory notes include information on: (1) accounting principles and methods employed; (2) detailed disclosures regarding individual financial statement items; (3) commitments and contingencies; (4) business combinations; (5) transactions with related parties; (6) stock option plans; (7) legal proceedings; and (8) significant customers. The notes for Kodak follow its financial statements in Appendix A.

EDGAR WHO?
EDGAR is the database of documents that public companies are required to file electronically with the SEC. Several websites offer easy-to-use interfaces (most are free), making it a snap to find most public info on a company—see www.freeedgar.com, or www.edgar-online.com.

DOUBLE TROUBLE
PricewaterhouseCoopers earned $13 million from audit fees and $18 million from tax fees it charged to scandal-ridden Tyco International Ltd. in 2001. Such a dual role of auditor and tax adviser is under scrutiny by politicians and social activitists.

- **Supplementary Information.** Supplemental schedules to the financial statement notes include information on: (1) business segment data; (2) export sales; (3) marketable securities; (4) valuation accounts; (5) short-term borrowings; and (6) quarterly financial data. Several supplemental schedules appear in the annual report of Kodak. An example is the information on segment operations included as note 21 in Kodak's financial statements.
- **Proxy Statements.** Shareholder votes are solicited for the election of directors and for corporate actions such as mergers, acquisitions, and authorization of securities. A **proxy** is a means whereby a shareholder authorizes another person to act for him or her at a meeting of shareholders. A **proxy statement** contains information necessary for shareholders in voting on matters for which the proxy is solicited. Proxy statements contain a wealth of information regarding a company including the identity of shareholders owning 5 or more percent of outstanding shares, biographical information on the board of directors, compensation arrangements with officers and directors, employee benefit plans, and certain transactions with officers and directors.

GREEN REPORT CARD
In 2002, 45% of the 250 largest global companies produced corporate responsibility reports, compared with 35% three years ago.

FINANCIAL STATEMENT ANALYSIS PREVIEW

A variety of tools designed to fit specific needs are available to help users analyze financial statements. In this section, we introduce some basic tools of financial analysis and apply them to Kodak's annual report. Specifically, we apply comparative financial statement analysis, common-size financial statement analysis, and ratio analysis. We also briefly describe cash flow analysis. This preview to financial analysis is mainly limited to some common analysis tools, especially as pertaining to ratio analysis. Later chapters describe more advanced, state-of-the-art techniques, including accounting analysis, that considerably enhance financial statement analysis. This section concludes with an introduction to valuation models.

Analysis Tools

This section gives preliminary exposure to five important sets of tools for financial analysis:

1. Comparative financial statement analysis
2. Common-size financial statement analysis
3. Ratio analysis
4. Cash flow analysis
5. Valuation

Comparative Financial Statement Analysis

Individuals conduct **comparative financial statement analysis** by reviewing consecutive balance sheets, income statements, or statements of cash flows from period to period. This usually involves a review of changes in individual account balances on a year-to-year or multiyear basis. The most important information often revealed from comparative financial statement analysis is trend. A comparison of statements over several periods can reveal the direction, speed, and extent of a trend. Comparative analysis also compares trends in related items. For example, a year-to-year 10 percent sales increase accompanied by a 20 percent increase in freight-out costs requires investigation and explanation. Similarly, a 15 percent increase in accounts receivable along with a sales increase of only 5 percent calls for investigation. In both cases we look for reasons behind differences in these interrelated rates and any implications for our analysis. Comparative financial statement analysis also is referred to as *horizontal analysis* given the left-right (or right-left) analysis of account balances as we review comparative statements. Two techniques of comparative analysis are especially popular: year-to-year change analysis and index-number trend analysis.

Year-to-Year Change Analysis. Comparing financial statements over relatively short time periods–two to three years–is usually performed with analysis of year-to-year changes in individual accounts. A year-to-year change analysis for short time periods is manageable and understandable. It has the advantage of presenting changes in absolute dollar amounts as well as in percentages. Change analyses in both amounts and percentages are relevant since different dollar bases in computing percentage changes can yield large changes inconsistent with their actual importance. For example, a 50 percent change from a base amount of $1,000 is usually less significant than the same percentage change from a base of $100,000. Reference to dollar amounts is necessary to retain a proper perspective and to make valid inferences on the relative importance of changes.

Computation of year-to-year changes is straightforward. Still, a few rules should be noted. When a negative amount appears in the base and a positive amount in the next period (or vice versa), we cannot compute a meaningful percentage change. Also, when there is no amount for the base period, no percentage change is computable. Similarly, when the base period amount is small, a percentage change can be computed but the number must be interpreted with caution. This is because it can signal a large change merely because of the small base amount used in computing the change. Also when an item has a value in the base period and none in the next period, the decrease is 100 percent. These points are underscored in Illustration 1.1.

ANALYSIS RESOURCES

www.adr.com
www.bigcharts.com
www.bridge.com
www.cbsmarketwatch.com
www.financenter.com
www.freeedgar.com
www.ipomaven.com
www.marketguide.com
www.morningstar.net
www.nasdaq.com
www.quote.com
www.personalwealth.com
www.10kwizard.com
www.wallstreetcity.com

ILLUSTRATION 1.1

Complications in comparative analysis and how we confront them are depicted in the following five cases:

			CHANGE ANALYSIS	
Item (in millions)	**Period 1**	**Period 2**	**Amount**	**Percent**
Net income (loss)	$(4,500)	$1,500	$ 6,000	—
Tax expense	2,000	(1,000)	(3,000)	—
Cash	10	2,010	2,000	20,000%
Notes payable	—	8,000	8,000	—
Notes receivable	10,000	—	(10,000)	(100%)

Comparative financial statement analysis typically reports both the cumulative total for the period under analysis and the average (or median) for the period. Comparing yearly amounts with an average, or median, computed over a number of periods helps highlight unusual fluctuations.

Exhibit 1.6 shows a year-to-year comparative analysis using Kodak's income statements. This analysis reveals several items of note. First, while sales decreased by 5.4%, Kodak's cost of goods sold increased by 3.5%. This yields an 18.8% decrease in gross profit that is greater than the percentage decrease in sales. Moreover, despite the decrease in gross profit, selling, general, and administrative expenses increased by 4.4%. That increase, combined with additional restructuring expenses, resulted in a decrease of 84.4% in earnings from operations. We also note that as part of its cost-cutting measures, Kodak cut research and development spending by 0.6%. Cuts in research and development spending rarely bode well for future performance.

Exhibit 1.6 **Kodak's Comparative Income Statements**

	2001	2000	Change (in $mil)	Change %
Sales	$13,234	$13,994	$ (760)	−5.4%
Cost of goods sold	8,670	8,375	295	3.5
Gross profit	4,564	5,619	(1,055)	−18.8
Operating expenses:				
Selling, general, and administrative exp.	2,781	2,665	116	4.4
Research and development	779	784	(5)	−0.6
Restructuring costs (credits)	659	(44)	703	—
Operating profit	345	2,214	(1,869)	−84.4
Interest expense and other	237	82	155	189.0
Earnings before income taxes	108	2,132	(2,024)	−94.9
Total income taxes	32	725	(693)	−95.6
Net earnings	76	1,407	(1,331)	−94.6

Index-Number Trend Analysis. Using year-to-year change analysis to compare financial statements that cover more than two or three periods is sometimes cumbersome. A useful tool for long-term trend comparisons is *index-number trend analysis.* Analyzing data using index-number trend analysis requires choosing a base period, for all items, with a preselected index number usually set to 100. Since the base period is a frame of reference for all comparisons, it is best to choose a normal year with regard to business conditions. As with computing year-to-year percentage changes, certain changes, like those from negative amounts to positive amounts, cannot be expressed by means of index numbers.

When using index numbers, we compute percentage changes by reference to the base period as shown in Illustration 1.2.

ILLUSTRATION 1.2

CenTech's cash balance (in thousands) at December 31, Year 1 (the base period), is $12,000. Its cash balance at December 31, Year 2, is $18,000. Using 100 as the index number for Year 1, the index number for Year 2 equals 150 and is computed as:

$$\frac{\text{Current year balance}}{\text{Base year balance}} \times 100 = \frac{\$18{,}000}{\$12{,}000} \times 100 = 150$$

The cash balance of CenTech at December 31, Year 3, is $9,000. The index for Year 3 is 75 and is computed as:

$$\frac{\$9{,}000}{\$12{,}000} \times 100 = 75$$

The change in cash balance between Year 1 and Year 2 for this illustration is 50 percent (150 − 100), and is easily inferred from the index numbers. However, the change from Year 2 to Year 3 is not 75 percent (150 − 75), as a direct comparison might suggest. Instead, it is 50 percent, computed as $9,000/$18,000. This involves computing the Year 2 to Year 3 change by reference to the Year 2 balance. The percentage change is, however, computable using index numbers only. For example, in computing this change, we take 75/150 = 0.50, or a change of 50 percent.

For index-number trend analysis, we need not analyze every item in financial statements. Instead, we want to focus on significant items. We also must exercise care in using index-number trend comparisons where changes might be due to economy or industry factors. Moreover, interpretation of percentage changes, including those using index-number trend series, must be made with an awareness of potentially inconsistent applications of accounting principles over time. When possible, we adjust for these inconsistencies. Also, the longer the time period for comparison, the more distortive are effects of any price-level changes. One outcome of trend analysis is its power to convey insight into managers' philosophies, policies, and motivations. The more diverse the environments constituting the period of analysis, the better is our picture of how managers deal with adversity and take advantage of opportunities.

Results of index-number trend analysis on selected financial statement items for Kodak are reported in Exhibit 1.7. Data used in this analysis are taken from the Summary of Operating Data in Kodak's annual report. Sales have been generally flat or declining since 1997 and have been matched by a decline in total operating expenses, reflecting the results of Kodak's restructuring efforts–the 2001 amount includes additional restructuring costs. Overall, the index-number trend analysis suggests some concern with Kodak's growth prospects. Namely, while cost reduction can boost short-run profits, long-run profitability for Kodak likely depends on whether or not its initiatives yield sales increases. The analysis presented above uses 1997 as the base year. To illustrate the sensitivity of inferences to the choice of base year, the following graphic reports similar indices using 1998 as the base year. The trends look significantly different from those with 1997 used as the base year. This exercise emphasizes the importance of both proper base year selection and caution in the interpretation of evidence.

Exhibit 1.7

Kodak's Index-Number Trend—Sales and Operating Expenses

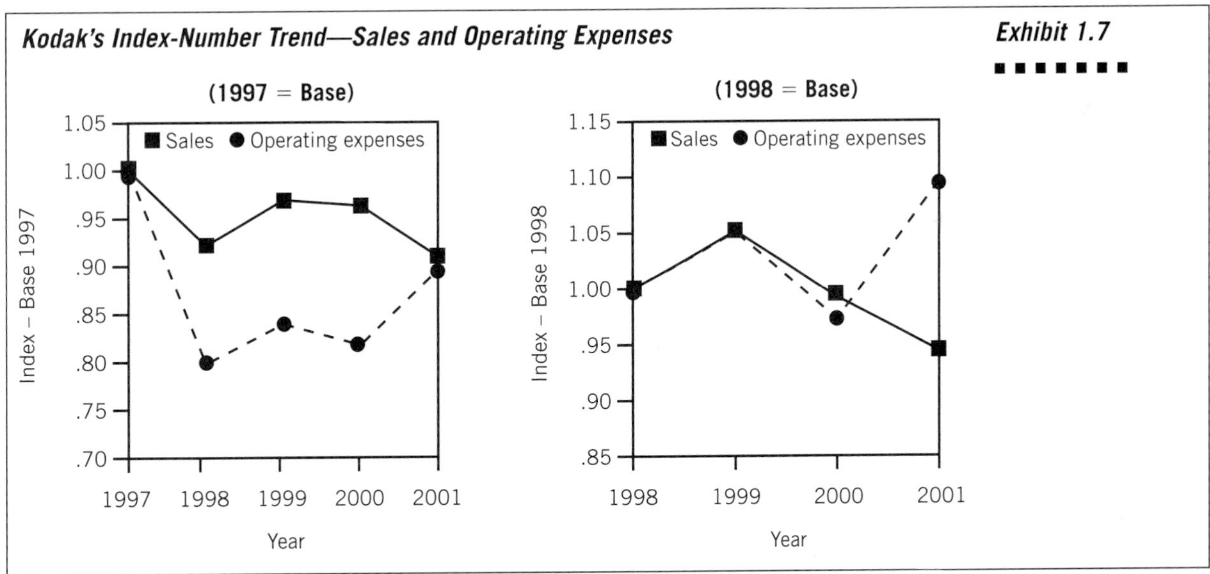

Common-Size Financial Statement Analysis

Financial statement analysis can benefit from knowing what proportion of a group or subgroup is made up of a particular account. Specifically, in analyzing a balance sheet, it is common to express total assets (or liabilities plus equity) as 100 percent. Then, accounts within these groupings are expressed as a percentage of their respective total. In analyzing an income statement, sales are often set at 100 percent with the remaining income statement accounts expressed as a percentage of sales. Since the sum of individual accounts within groups is 100 percent, this analysis is said to yield **common-size**

financial statements. This procedure also is called *vertical analysis* given the up-down (or down-up) evaluation of accounts in common-size statements. Common-size financial statement analysis is useful in understanding the internal makeup of financial statements. For example, in analyzing a balance sheet, a common-size analysis stresses two factors:

1. Sources of financing–including the distribution of financing across current liabilities, noncurrent liabilities, and equity.
2. Composition of assets–including amounts for individual current and noncurrent assets.

Common-size analysis of a balance sheet is often extended to examine the accounts that make up specific subgroups. For example, in assessing liquidity of current assets, it is often important to know what proportion of current assets is composed of inventories, and not simply what proportion inventories are of total assets. Common-size analysis of an income statement is equally important. An income statement readily lends itself to common-size analysis, where each item is related to a key amount such as sales. To varying degrees, sales impact nearly all expenses, and it is useful to know what percentage of sales is represented by each expense item. An exception is income taxes, which is related to pre-tax income and not sales.

Temporal (time) comparisons of a company's common-size statements are useful in revealing any proportionate changes in accounts within groups of assets, liabilities, expenses, and other categories. Still, we must exercise care in interpreting changes and trends as shown in Illustration 1.3.

ILLUSTRATION 1.3

The recent three years' account balances for both Patents and Total Assets of Meade Co. are:

	2003	2002	2001
Patents	$ 50,000	$ 50,000	$ 50,000
Total assets	$1,000,000	$750,000	$500,000
Patents/Total assets	5%	6.67%	10%

While the dollar amount for patents remains unchanged for this period, increases in total assets progressively reduce patents as a percent of total assets. Since this percent varies with both the change in the absolute dollar amount of an item and the change in the total balance for its category, interpretation of common-size analysis requires examination of both the amounts for the accounts under analysis and the bases for their computations.

Common-size statements are especially useful for intercompany comparisons because financial statements of different companies are recast in common-size format. Comparisons of a company's common-size statements with those of competitors, or with industry averages, can highlight differences in account makeup and distribution. Reasons for such differences should be explored and understood. One key limitation of common-size statements for intercompany analysis is their failure to reflect the relative sizes of the companies under analysis. A comparison of selected accounts using common-size statements along with industry statistics is part of the comprehensive case following Chapter 12.

Kodak's common-size income statements are shown in Exhibit 1.8. These common-size statements give us a better perspective for evaluating Kodak's cost reduction efforts. Gross profit margins have declined steadily over the past five years, reflecting the increasingly competitive market in which Kodak participates. Cost control is, therefore, of paramount importance. Prior to the recession of 2001, selling, general, and administrative expenses had declined as a percentage of sales as well. This probably reflects the results of its cost-cutting efforts, although it is possible that Kodak has reduced operating expenses such as marketing, training, and maintenance, all of which will provide short-term gains as a longer-term cost. The decrease in research and development costs also raises concerns about Kodak's future prospects. Overall, this preliminary common-size analysis reveals that, while Kodak did cut operating costs, we cannot be confident that it did not do so at the expense of future sales and profitability.

Common-size analysis of Kodak's balance sheets is in Exhibit 1.9. Kodak has been successful in reducing receivables and inventories. Overall, current assets have declined by 3.6 percentage points. This has been accompanied by an equal decline in current liabilities. Notice, however, that total current assets are less than total current liabilities. This suggests possible liquidity problems. We extend our analysis of Kodak's liquidity in the next section using ratio analysis.

Ratio Analysis

Ratio analysis is among the most popular and widely used tools of financial analysis. Yet its role is often misunderstood and, consequently, its importance often overrated. A ratio expresses a mathematical relation between two quantities. A ratio of 200 to 100 is expressed as 2:1, or simply 2. While computation of a ratio is a simple arithmetic operation, its interpretation is more complex. To be meaningful, a ratio must refer to an economically important relation. For example, there is a direct and crucial relation between an item's sales price and its cost. Accordingly, the ratio of cost of goods sold to sales is

Exhibit 1.8

Kodak's Common-Size Income Statements

	2001	2000	1999	1998	1997
Sales	100	100	100	100	100
Cost of goods sold	65.5	59.9	57.4	54.4	54.9
Gross profit	34.5	40.1	42.6	45.6	45.1
Operating expenses:					
Selling, general, and administrative exp.	21.0	19.0	20.2	24.6	26.9
Research and development	5.9	5.6	5.8	6.9	8.4
Restructuring costs (credits)	5.0	(0.3)	2.5	0.0	8.9
Operating profit	2.6	15.8	14.1	14.1	0.9
Interest expense and other costs (credits)	1.8	0.6	(0.9)	(1.6)	0.6
Earnings before income taxes	0.8	15.2	15.0	15.7	0.3
Total income taxes	0.2	5.2	5.1	5.3	0.3
Net earnings	0.6	10.0	9.9	10.4	0.0

Exhibit 1.9 ***Kodak's Common-Size Balance Sheets***

	2001	2000
Current assets		
Cash and cash equivalents	3.3	1.7
Receivables, net	17.5	18.7
Inventories, net	8.5	12.1
Other current assets	5.7	6.2
Total current assets	35.0	38.7
Property, plant, and equipment, net	42.4	41.6
Other long-term assets	22.6	19.7
Total assets	100.0	100.0
Current liabilities		
Accounts payables and other	24.5	23.9
Short-term borrowings	11.5	15.5
Accrued income taxes	4.1	4.3
Total current liabilities	40.1	43.7
Long-term debt and other	12.5	8.2
Postemployment liabilities	20.4	19.2
Deferred tax liabilities	5.4	4.8
Total liabilities	78.3	75.9
Share capital	13.7	13.0
Retained earnings (less treasury stock)	8.0	11.1
Total liabilities and stockholders' equity	100.0	100.0

important. In contrast, there is no obvious relation between freight costs and the balance of marketable securities. The example in Illustration 1.4 highlights this point.

ILLUSTRATION 1.4

Consider interpreting the ratio of gasoline consumption to miles driven, referred to as miles per gallon (mpg). On the basis of the ratio of gas consumption to miles driven, person X claims to have the superior performer, that is, 28 mpg compared to person Y's 20 mpg. Is person X's vehicle superior in minimizing gas consumption? To answer that question there are several factors affecting gas consumption that require analysis before we can properly interpret these results and identify the superior performer. These factors include: (1) weight load, (2) type of terrain, (3) city or highway driving, (4) grade of fuel, and (5) travel speed. Numerous as the factors influencing gas consumption are, evaluating a gas consumption ratio is a simpler analysis than evaluating financial statement ratios. This is because of the interrelations in business variables and the complexity of factors affecting them.

We must remember that ratios are tools to provide us with insights into underlying conditions. They are one of the starting points of analysis, not an end point. Ratios, properly interpreted, identify areas requiring further investigation. Analysis of a ratio can reveal important relations and bases of comparison in uncovering conditions and trends difficult to detect by inspecting the individual components that make up the ratio. Still, like other analysis tools, ratios often are most useful when they are future oriented. This means we often adjust the factors affecting a ratio for their probable future trend and magnitude. We also must assess factors potentially influencing future ratios. Therefore, the usefulness of ratios depends on our skillful application and interpretation of them, and these are the most challenging aspects of ratio analysis.

Factors Affecting Ratios. Beyond the internal operating activities that affect a company's ratios, we must be aware of the effects of economic events, industry factors, management policies, and accounting methods. Our discussion of accounting analysis later in the book highlights the influence of these factors on the measurements underlying ratios. Any limitations in accounting measurements impact the effectiveness of ratios.

Prior to computing ratios, or similar measures like trend indices or percent relations, we use accounting analysis to make sure the numbers underlying ratio computations are appropriate. For example, when inventories are valued using LIFO (see Chapter 4) and prices are increasing, the current ratio is understated because LIFO inventories (the numerator) are understated. Similarly, certain pension liabilities are often unrecorded and disclosed in notes only (see Chapter 3). We usually want to recognize pension liabilities when computing ratios like debt to equity. We also must recognize that when making adjustments for one ratio, consistency often requires they be made for other ratios. For example, the omission of a pension liability implies understated pension expenses. Accordingly, net income numbers often require adjustment in ratio computations when assets or liabilities are adjusted. We also need to remember that the usefulness of ratios depends on the reliability of the numbers. When a company's internal accounting controls or other governance and monitoring mechanisms are less reliable in generating credible figures, the resulting ratios are equally less reliable.

SEC CHARGES
The SEC recently charged nearly 100 individuals and companies with fraud and/or abuses of financial reporting. The SEC chairman said, "Our enforcement team will continue to root out and aggressively act on abuses of the financial reporting process."

Ratio Interpretation. Ratios must be interpreted with care because factors affecting the numerator can correlate with those affecting the denominator. For instance, companies can improve the ratio of operating expenses to sales by reducing costs that stimulate sales (e.g., research and development). However, reducing these types of costs is likely to yield long-term declines in sales or market share. Thus, a seemingly short-term improvement in profitability can damage a company's future prospects. We must interpret such changes appropriately. Many ratios have important variables in common with other ratios. Accordingly, it is not necessary to compute all possible ratios to analyze a situation. Ratios, like most techniques in financial analysis, are not relevant in isolation. Instead, they are usefully interpreted in comparison with (1) prior ratios, (2) predetermined standards, and (3) ratios of competitors. Finally, the variability of a ratio across time is often as important as its trend.

Illustration of Ratio Analysis. We can compute numerous ratios using a company's financial statements. Some ratios have general application in financial analysis, while others are unique to specific circumstances or industries. This section presents ratio analysis as applied to three important areas of financial statement analysis:

1. **Credit (Risk) Analysis**
   a. **Liquidity.** To evaluate the ability to meet short-term obligations.
   b. **Capital structure and solvency.** To assess the ability to meet long-term obligations.
2. **Profitability Analysis**
   a. **Return on investment.** To assess financial rewards to the suppliers of equity and debt financing.
   b. **Operating performance.** To evaluate profit margins from operating activities.
   c. **Asset utilization.** To assess effectiveness and intensity of assets in generating sales, also called *turnover.*

Exhibit 1.10 ***Financial Statement Ratios for Kodak***

Liquidity

$$\text{Current ratio} = \frac{\text{Current assets}}{\text{Current liabilities}} = \frac{\$4{,}683}{\$5{,}354} = 0.87$$

$$\text{Acid-test ratio} = \frac{\text{Cash + Cash equivalents + Marketable securities + Accounts receivable}}{\text{Current liabilities}}$$

$$= \frac{\$448 + \$2{,}337}{\$5{,}354} = 0.52$$

$$\text{Collection period} = \frac{\text{Average accounts receivable}}{\text{Sales/360}} = \frac{(\$2{,}337 + \$2{,}653)/2}{\$13{,}234/360} = 68 \text{ days}$$

$$\text{Days to sell inventory} = \frac{\text{Average inventory}}{\text{Cost of sales/360}} = \frac{(\$1{,}137 + \$1{,}718)/2}{\$8{,}670/360} = 59 \text{ days}$$

Capital Structure and Solvency

$$\text{Total debt to equity} = \frac{\text{Total liabilities}}{\text{Shareholders' equity}} = \frac{\$10{,}468}{\$2{,}894} = 3.62$$

$$\text{Long-term debt to equity} = \frac{\text{Long-term liabilities}}{\text{Shareholders' equity}} = \frac{(\$1{,}666 + \$2{,}728 + \$720)}{\$2{,}894} = 1.77$$

$$\text{Times interest earned} = \frac{\text{Interest before income taxes and interest expense}}{\text{Interest expense}} = \frac{(\$108 + \$219)}{\$219} = 1.49$$

Return on Investment

$$\text{Return on assets} = \frac{\text{Net income + Interest expense (1 - Tax rate)}}{\text{Average total assets}} = \frac{(\$76 + \$219(1 - 0.35))}{(\$13{,}362 + \$14{,}212)/2} = 1.58\%$$

$$\text{Return on common equity} = \frac{\text{Net income}}{\text{Average shareholders' equity}} = \frac{\$76}{(\$2{,}894 + \$3{,}428)/2} = 2.40\%$$

Operating Performance

$$\text{Gross profit margin} = \frac{\text{Sales - Cost of Sales}}{\text{Sales}} = \frac{\$4{,}564}{\$13{,}234} = 34.49\%$$

$$\text{Operating profit margin} = \frac{\text{Income from operations}}{\text{Sales}} = \frac{\$345}{\$13{,}234} = 2.61\%$$

$$\text{Pretax profit margin} = \frac{\text{Income before income taxes}}{\text{Sales}} = \frac{\$108}{\$13{,}234} = 0.82\%$$

$$\text{Net profit margin} = \frac{\text{Net income}}{\text{Sales}} = \frac{\$76}{\$13{,}234} = 0.57\%$$

(continued)

3. **Valuation**
   a. To estimate the intrinsic value of a company (stock).

Exhibit 1.10 reports results for selected ratios having applicability to most companies. A more complete listing of ratios is located on the book's inside cover. Data used in this illustration are from Kodak's annual report in Appendix A.

***Financial Statement Ratios for Kodak** (concluded)*

Asset Utilization

$$\text{Cash turnover} = \frac{\text{Sales}}{\text{Average cash and equivalents}} = \frac{\$13{,}234}{(\$448 + \$246)/2} = 38.14$$

$$\text{Accounts receivable turnover} = \frac{\text{Sales}}{\text{Average accounts receivable}} = \frac{\$13{,}234}{(\$2{,}337 + \$2{,}653)/2} = 5.30$$

$$\text{Sales to inventory} = \frac{\text{Sales}}{\text{Average inventory}} = \frac{\$13{,}234}{(\$1{,}137 + \$1{,}718)/2} = 9.27$$

$$\text{Working capital turnover} = \frac{\text{Sales}}{\text{Average working capital}} = \frac{\$13{,}234}{(\$4{,}683 - \$5{,}354) + (\$5{,}491 - \$6{,}215)/2} = \text{n/a*}$$

$$\text{Fixed asset turnover} = \frac{\text{Sales}}{\text{Average fixed assets}} = \frac{\$13{,}234}{(\$5{,}659 + \$5{,}919)/2} = 2.29$$

$$\text{Total assets turnover} = \frac{\text{Sales}}{\text{Average total assets}} = \frac{\$13{,}234}{(\$13{,}362 + \$14{,}212)/2} = 0.96$$

Market Measures

$$\text{Price-to-earnings ratio} = \frac{\text{Market price per share}}{\text{Earnings per share}} = \frac{\$29.43}{\$0.26} = 113.19$$

$$\text{Earnings yield} = \frac{\text{Earnings per share}}{\text{Market price per share}} = \frac{\$0.26}{\$29.43} = 0.88\%$$

$$\text{Dividend yield} = \frac{\text{Cash dividends per share}}{\text{Market price per share}} = \frac{\$2.21}{\$29.43} = 7.51\%$$

$$\text{Dividend payout rate} = \frac{\text{Cash dividends paid per share}}{\text{Earnings per share}} = \frac{\$2.21}{\$0.26} = 850\%$$

$$\text{Price-to-book} = \frac{\text{Market price per share}}{\text{Book value per share}} = \frac{\$29.43}{\$9.95} = 2.96$$

*Since Kodak's working capital is negative, this ratio is noninterpretable.

- **Credit analysis.** First, we focus on *liquidity*. An important liquidity ratio is the *current ratio*–current assets available to satisfy current liabilities. Kodak's current ratio of 0.87 implies there are $0.87 of current assets available to meet each $1 of currently maturing obligations. A more stringent test of short-term liquidity, based on the *acid-test ratio,* uses only the most liquid current assets–cash, short-term investments, and accounts receivable. Kodak has $0.52 of liquid assets to cover each $1 of current liabilities. Both of these ratios suggest a tight liquidity situation at Kodak. Still, we need more information to draw definite conclusions about liquidity. One additional piece of information useful in assessing liquidity is the length of time needed for conversion of receivables and inventories to cash. Kodak's *collection period* for receivables is approximately 68 days. Also, there are approximately 59 days between production and sale of inventories. These figures imply an operating (cash-to-cash) cycle of 127 (68 + 59) days. Results of this preliminary liquidity analysis suggest that Kodak has little cushion in meeting its current obligations out of current assets.

Second, to assess Kodak's long-term financing structure and credit risk, we examine its *capital structure and solvency*. Its *total debt-to-equity ratio* of 3.62 indicates that

DEBT TRIGGER

Due to big write-offs, Tyco International Ltd.'s debt-to-assets ratio neared 52.5%—the level at which the company will be in default on much of its more than $25 billion debt.

for each $1 of equity financing, another $3.62 of financing is provided by creditors. Its *long-term debt-to-equity ratio* is 1.77, revealing $1.77 of long-term creditor financing to each $1 of equity financing. These two ratios suggest some degree of solvency risk given the relatively large amount of creditor financing in Kodak's capital structure. The times-interest-earned ratio shows Kodak's 2001 earnings are only 1.49 times its fixed (interest) commitments. The times-interest-earned ratio for 2001 has been impacted significantly by the recession in that year coupled with $659 million of restructuring costs. Historically, its interest coverage has been much greater. Nevertheless, its low interest coverage and rising debt burden, together with a low level of liquidity, is a source of concern.

- **Profitability analysis.** We begin by assessing different aspects of *return on investment.* Kodak's *return on total assets* of 1.58% implies that a $1 asset investment generates $0.015 of annual earnings prior to subtracting after-tax interest. Since equity holders are especially interested in management's performance based on equity financing, we also look at the return on equity. Kodak's *return on common equity* of 2.40% suggests it earns $0.024 annually for each $1 contributed by equity holders. Both of these ratios have been significantly affected by the recession of 2001. Historically, Kodak's return on investment has been in the 10% range and its return on common equity in the 35% range.

  Another part of profitability analysis is evaluation of *operating performance* ratios that typically link income statement line items to sales. Many of these ratios are comparable to results from common-size income statement analysis. The operating performance ratios for Kodak in Exhibit 1.10 all reflect the difficult operating environment in 2001.

  Asset utilization analysis is closely linked with profitability analysis. Asset utilization ratios, which relate sales to different asset categories, are important determinants of return on investment. These ratios for Kodak indicate mediocre performance. For example, Kodak's total asset turnover of 0.96 is less than the average of 1.21 for all publicly traded companies. Note that Kodak's negative working capital makes the sales-to-working-capital ratio uninterpretable.

- **Valuation.** Exhibit 1.10 also includes five market measures. Kodak's price-earnings ratio of 113.19 has been distorted by the effects of recession and restructuring costs. Historically, its P/E ratio has been in the range of 15. While 2001 results for the remaining market measures are lower than normal, historically Kodak has been in the middle of the pack for comparable companies. Later chapters will return to these and many other ratios of financial position and performance to assess Kodak in much greater detail.

Ratio analysis yields many valuable insights as is apparent from our preliminary analysis of Kodak. We must, however, keep in mind that these computations are based on numbers reported in Kodak's financial statements. We stress in this book that our ability to draw useful insights and make valid intercompany comparisons is enhanced by our adjustments to reported numbers prior to their inclusion in these analyses. We also must keep in mind that ratio analysis is only one part of financial analysis. An analyst must dig deeper to understand the underlying factors driving ratios and to effectively integrate different ratios to evaluate a company's financial position and performance.

Cash Flow Analysis

Cash flow analysis is primarily used as a tool to evaluate the sources and uses of funds. Cash flow analysis provides insights into how a company is obtaining its financing and deploying its resources. It also is used in cash flow forecasting and as part of liquidity analysis.

Kodak's statement of cash flows in Appendix A is a useful starting point for cash flow analysis. It shows Kodak generated $2,065 million from operating activities. It then used $1,047 million for investing activities, primarily for the acquisition of new PP&E and for the cash portion of acquisitions of other companies. The remaining excess operating cash flow was primarily used for the payment of dividends as debt inflows and outflows were about a wash. Netting cash inflows and outflows, and taking into account an $8 million cash outflow from exchange rate changes, results in a net increase in cash of $202 million. This preliminary analysis shows Kodak had considerable cash inflows from its operating activities that have been used to a large extent for new investing activities.

While this simple analysis of the statement of cash flows conveys much information about the sources and uses of funds, it is important to analyze cash flows in more detail. For example, operating cash flows declined by $779 million due to research and development costs expensed in the income statement. Are these expenditures a decline in operating cash flow or an investment in the future? Also, while over $1 billion was spent in investing activities, what portion of this amount is mere capital maintenance and what portion is investment in future growth opportunities? These types of questions are answerable only through a detailed analysis of the statement of cash flows along with knowledge of a company's business environment and strategies. We return to these questions and explain cash flow analysis in Chapters 7 and 10.

Specialized Analysis Tools

Beyond the usual multipurpose tools of financial statement analysis are a variety of special-purpose tools. These special-purpose tools include those directed at specific financial statements or segments of statements, or at a particular industry (e.g., occupancy-capacity analysis for hotels, hospitals, or airlines). Special-purpose tools also include some types of cash forecast analyses, statements of variation in gross profit, and earning power analysis. We describe these tools later in the book.

Valuation Models

Valuation is an important outcome of many types of business and financial statement analysis. **Valuation** normally refers to estimating the intrinsic value of a company or its stock. The basis of valuation is **present value theory.** This theory states the value of a debt or equity security (or for that matter, any asset) is equal to the sum of all expected future payoffs from the security that are discounted to the present at an appropriate *discount rate*. Present value theory uses the concept of *time value of money*–it simply states an entity prefers present consumption more than future consumption. Accordingly, to value a security an investor needs two pieces of information: (1) expected future payoffs over the life of the security and (2) a discount rate. For example, future payoffs from bonds are principal and interest payments. Future payoffs from stocks are dividends and capital appreciation. The discount rate in the case of a bond is the prevailing interest rate (or more precisely, the *yield to maturity*), while in the case of a stock it is the risk-adjusted *cost of capital* (also called the *expected rate of return*).

This section begins with a discussion of valuation techniques as applied to debt securities. Because of its simplicity, debt valuation provides an ideal setting to grasp key valuation concepts. We then conclude this section with a discussion of equity valuation.

IPO MISDEALS
Citigroup, CSFB, and Goldman Sachs were investigated for allegedly allocating hot-selling IPO shares to favored executives to cut more investment-banking deals instead of selling them to the highest bidders.

Debt Valuation

The value of a security is equal to the present value of its future payoffs discounted at an appropriate rate. The future payoffs from a debt security are its interest and principal payments. A bond contract precisely specifies its future payoffs along with the investment horizon. The value of a bond at time t, or B_t, is computed using the following formula:

$$B_t = \frac{I_{t+1}}{(1+r)^1} + \frac{I_{t+2}}{(1+r)^2} + \frac{I_{t+3}}{(1+r)^3} + \cdots + \frac{I_{t+n}}{(1+r)^n} + \frac{F}{(1+r)^n}$$

MUTUAL FUNDS
The mutual-fund industry has more than $6 trillion in equity, bond, and money-market funds.

where I_{t+n} is the interest payment in period $t + n$, F is the principal payment (usually the debt's face value), and r is the interest rate. The interest rate is the yield to maturity. When valuing bonds, we determine the expected (or desired) yield based on factors such as current interest rates, expected inflation, and risk of default. Illustration 1.5 offers an example of debt valuation.

ILLUSTRATION 1.5

On January 1, Year 1, a company issues $100 of eight-year bonds with a year-end interest (coupon) payment of 8 percent per annum. On January 1, Year 6, we are asked to compute the value of this bond when the yield to maturity on these bonds is 6 percent per annum.
Solution: These bonds will be redeemed on December 31, Year 8. This means the remaining term to maturity is three years. Each year-end interest payment on these bonds is $8, computed as 8% × $100, and the end of Year 8 principal payment is $100. The value of these bonds as of January 1, Year 6, is computed as:

$$\$8/(1.06) + \$8/(1.06)^2 + \$8/(1.06)^3 + \$100/(1.06)^3 = \$105.35$$

Equity Valuation

Basis of Equity Valuation. The basis of equity valuation, like debt valuation, is the present value of future payoffs discounted at an appropriate rate. Equity valuation, however, is more complex than debt valuation. This is because, with a bond, the future payoffs are specified. With equity, the investor has no claim on predetermined payoffs. Instead, the equity investor looks for two main (uncertain) payoffs–dividend payments and capital appreciation. Since capital appreciation denotes change in equity value, which in turn is determined by future dividends, we can simplify this task to state that the value of an equity security at time t, or V_t, equals the sum of the present values of all future expected dividends:

$$V_t = \frac{E(D_{t+1})}{(1+k)^1} + \frac{E(D_{t+2})}{(1+k)^2} + \frac{E(D_{t+3})}{(1+k)^3} + \cdots + \frac{E(D_{t+n})}{(1+k)^n} + \cdots$$

DECIMAL PRICING
Wall Street has long counted money in the same units that 17th century pirates used—pieces of eight. But fractional pricing—pricing stocks in eighths, sixteenths, and the occasional thirty-second of a dollar—has finally gone the way of Spanish doubloons, as stock and options markets now use decimal pricing.

where D_{t+n} is the dividend in period $t + n$, and k is the cost of capital. This model is called the **dividend discount model.** This equity valuation formula is in terms of *expected* dividends rather than *actual* dividends. We use expectations instead of actual dividends because, unlike interest and principal repayments in the case of a bond, future dividends are neither specified nor determinable with certainty. This means our analysis must use forecasts of future dividends to get an estimate of value.

Alternatively, we might define value as the present value of future cash flows. This definition is problematic for at least two reasons. First, the term *cash flows* is vague. There are many different types of cash flows: operating cash flows, investing cash flows, financing cash flows, and net cash flows (change in cash balance). Hence, which type of cash flows should one use? Second, while we can rewrite the equity valuation formula in terms of one type of cash flows, called *free cash flows*, it is incorrect to define value in terms of cash flows. This is because dividends are the actual payoffs to equity investors and, therefore, the only appropriate valuation attribute. Any other formula is merely a derived form of this fundamental formula. While the free cash flow formula is technically exact, it is simply one derived formula from among several. One can also derive an exact valuation formula using accounting variables independent of cash flows.

Practical Considerations in Valuation. The dividend discount model faces practical obstacles. One main problem is that of infinite horizon. Practical valuation techniques must compute value using a finite forecast horizon. However, forecasting dividends is difficult in a finite horizon. This is because dividend payments are discretionary, and different companies adopt different dividend payment policies. For example, some companies prefer to pay out a large portion of earnings as dividends, while other companies choose to reinvest earnings. This means actual dividend payouts are not indicative of company value except in the very long run. The result is that valuation models often replace dividends with earnings or cash flows. This section introduces two such valuation models–the free cash flow model and the residual income model.

The **free cash flow to equity model** computes equity value at time t by replacing expected dividends with expected free cash flows to equity:

$$V_t = \frac{E(FCFE_{t+1})}{(1+k)^1} + \frac{E(FCFE_{t+2})}{(1+k)^2} + \frac{E(FCFE_{t+3})}{(1+k)^3} + \cdots + \frac{E(FCFE_{t+n})}{(1+k)^n} + \cdots$$

where $FCFE_{t+n}$ is free cash flow to equity in period $t + n$, and k is cost of capital. *Free cash flows to equity* are defined as cash flows from operations less capital expenditures and adjustments for changes in debt. They are cash flows that are free to be paid to equity investors and, therefore, are an appropriate measure of equity investors' payoffs.

Free cash flows also can be defined for the *entire* firm. Specifically, free cash flows to the firm (or simply *free cash flows*) equal operating cash flows (adjusted for interest expense and revenue) less investments in operating assets. Then, the value of the entire firm equals the discounted expected future free cash flows using the weighted average cost of capital. (Note, the value of equity equals the value of the entire firm less the value of debt.)

The **residual income model** computes value using accounting variables. It defines equity value at time t as the sum of current book value and the present value of all future expected residual income:

$$V_t = BV_t + \frac{E(RI_{t+1})}{(1+k)^1} + \frac{E(RI_{t+2})}{(1+k)^2} + \frac{E(RI_{t+3})}{(1+k)^3} + \cdots + \frac{E(RI_{t+n})}{(1+k)^n} + \cdots$$

where BV_t is book value at the end of period t, RI_{t+n} is residual income in period $t + n$, and k is cost of capital. **Residual income** at time t is defined as comprehensive net income minus a charge on beginning book value, that is, $RI_t = NI_t - (k \times BV_{t-1})$.

While both of these models overcome some problems in using dividends, they still are defined in terms of an infinite horizon. To derive value using a finite horizon (say, 5 or 10 years), we must replace the present value of future dividends beyond a particular future date by an estimate of **continuing value** (also called **terminal value**). Unlike forecasts of payoffs for the finite period that often are derived using detailed prospective analysis, a forecast of continuing value is usually based on simplifying assumptions for growth in payoffs. While forecasting continuing value often is a source of much error, its estimation is required in equity valuation.

Note that all three models–dividend discount, free cash flow to equity, and residual income–are identical and exact in an infinite horizon. Therefore, choosing a valuation model is based on practical considerations in a finite horizon setting. Moreover, an important criterion is to choose a valuation model least dependent on continuing value. While the free cash flow to equity and dividend discount models work well under certain circumstances in finite horizons, the residual income model usually outperforms

DISAPPEARING DIVIDEND

A recent study found that in 1978, more than 65% of companies paid dividends. By 2000, that percentage had fallen to near 20%.

both. Illustration 1.6 shows the mechanics of applying the dividend discount model and the residual income model. Still, a complete understanding of these valuation models, the implications of finite horizons, and the practical considerations of alternative models is beyond the scope of this chapter. We return to these issues in Chapter 12.

ILLUSTRATION 1.6

At the end of year 2000, Pitbull Co. owns 51 percent of the equity of Labrador, an entirely equity-financed company. By agreement with Labrador's shareholders, Pitbull agrees to acquire the remaining 49 percent of Labrador shares at the end of year 2005 at a price of $25 per share. Labrador also agrees to maintain annual cash dividends at $1 per share through 2005. An analyst makes the following projections for Labrador:

(in $ per share)	2000	2001	2002	2003	2004	2005
Dividends	—	$1.00	$1.00	$1.00	$1.00	$1.00
Operating cash flows	—	1.25	1.50	1.50	2.00	2.25
Capital expenditures	—	—	—	1.00	1.00	—
Net income	—	1.20	1.30	1.40	1.50	1.65
Book value	$5.00	5.20	5.50	5.90	6.40	7.05

At this same time (end of year 2000), we wish to compute the intrinsic value of the remaining 49 percent of Labrador's shares using the alternative valuation models (assume a cost of capital of 10 percent).

Solution: Since Pitbull will acquire Labrador at the end of 2005 for $25 per share, the terminal value is set–this spares us the task of estimating continuing (or terminal) value. Using the **dividend discount model,** we determine intrinsic value at the end of year 2000 as:

$$\text{Intrinsic value} = \frac{\$1}{(1.1)^1} + \frac{\$1}{(1.1)^2} + \frac{\$1}{(1.1)^3} + \frac{\$1}{(1.1)^4} + \frac{\$1}{(1.1)^5} + \frac{\$25}{(1.1)^5} = 19.31$$

Next, to apply the residual income model, we compute the following amounts for Labrador:

(in $ per share)	2001	2002	2003	2004	2005
Operating cash flows*	$1.25	$1.50	$1.50	$2.00	$2.25
− Capital expenditures*	—	—	1.00	1.00	—
= Free cash flow to equity	$1.25	$1.50	$0.50	$1.00	$2.25
Net income*	$1.20	$1.30	$1.40	$1.50	$1.65
− Capital charge (10% of beg. book value*)	0.50	0.52	0.55	0.59	0.64
= Residual income	$0.70	$0.78	$0.85	$0.91	$1.01
+ Gain on sale of equity to Pitbull (terminal value)					$17.95 ($25 − $7.05)

*Amounts taken from analyst's projections.

Using the **residual income model,** we compute intrinsic value at the end of year 2000 as:

$$\text{Intrinsic value} = \$5.00 + \frac{\$0.70}{(1.1)^1} + \frac{\$0.78}{(1.1)^2} + \frac{\$0.85}{(1.1)^3} + \frac{\$0.91}{(1.1)^4} + \frac{\$1.01}{(1.1)^5} + \frac{\$17.95}{(1.1)^5} = \$19.31$$

The residual income model yields the same intrinsic value as the dividend discount model–where the gain on sale of equity is treated as terminal value.

Analysis in an Efficient Market

This section explains market efficiency and its implications for financial statement analysis.

Market Efficiency

The **efficient market hypothesis,** or EMH for short, deals with the reaction of market prices to financial and other information. There are three common forms of EMH. The *weak form* EMH asserts that prices reflect fully the information contained in historical price movements. The *semistrong form* EMH asserts that prices reflect fully all publicly available information. The *strong form* EMH asserts that prices reflect *all* information including inside information. There is considerable research on EMH. Early evidence so strongly supported both weak and semistrong form EMH that efficiency of capital markets became a generally accepted hypothesis. More recent research, however, questions the generality of EMH. A number of stock price anomalies have been uncovered suggesting investors can earn excess returns using simple trading strategies. Nevertheless, as a first approximation, current stock price is a reasonable estimate of company value.

BEATING THE (FOOTBALL) ODDS

A recent article in *Journal of Business* looks at the efficiency of the pro football-betting market. Efficiency tests are applied to movements in point spreads. Results show it's possible to make some money by adopting a contrarian strategy—that is, waiting till the last minute and then betting against point-spread shifts. But such a strategy is only marginally profitable after accounting for the casinos' fee. That is, the football-betting market appears inefficient, but not enough for investors to capitalize on its inefficiencies.

Market Efficiency Implications for Analysis

EMH assumes the existence of competent and well-informed analysts using tools of analysis like those described in this book. It also assumes analysts are continually evaluating and acting on the stream of information entering the marketplace. Extreme proponents of EMH claim that if all information is instantly reflected in prices, attempts to reap consistent rewards through financial statement analysis is futile. This extreme position presents a paradox. On one hand, financial statement analysts are assumed capable of keeping markets efficient, yet these same analysts are assumed as unable to earn excess returns from their efforts. Moreover, if analysts presume their efforts in this regard are futile, the efficiency of the market ceases.

Several factors might explain this apparent paradox. Foremost among them is that EMH is built on aggregate, rather than individual, investor behavior. Focusing on aggregate behavior highlights average performance and ignores or masks individual performance based on ability, determination, and ingenuity, as well as superior individual timing in acting on information. Most believe that relevant information travels fast, encouraged by the magnitude of the financial stakes. Most also believe markets are rapid processors of information. Indeed, we contend the speed and efficiency of the market are evidence of analysts at work, motivated by personal rewards.

EMH's alleged implication regarding the futility of financial statement analysis fails to recognize an essential difference between information and its proper interpretation. That is, even if all information available at a given point in time is incorporated in price, this price does not necessarily reflect value. A security can be under- or overvalued, depending on the extent of an incorrect interpretation or faulty evaluation of available information by the aggregate market. Market efficiency depends not only on availability of information but also on its correct interpretation. Financial statement analysis is complex and demanding. The spectrum of financial statement users varies from an institutional analyst who concentrates on but a few companies in one industry to an unsophisticated chaser of rumors. All act on information, but surely not with the same

Analysis Research

IS THE STOCK MARKET EFFICIENT?

The efficient markets hypothesis (EMH) has driven many investment strategies for the past three decades. While Wall Street has not embraced EMH as wholeheartedly as the academic community, it has won many converts. While no one maintains that markets are *strong form* efficient, there is a wealth of evidence suggesting that the stock markets (at least in the U.S.) are both *weak form* and *semistrong form* efficient. That is, stock prices are serially uncorrelated–meaning there are no predictable patterns in prices. Stock markets seemingly respond rapidly to information, such as earnings announcements and dividend changes. The markets also seem to filter information, making it difficult to fool the market with cosmetic accounting changes. For example, the markets seem to understand the implications of alternative accounting choices, such as LIFO and FIFO. Probably the strongest evidence in favor of market efficiency is the dismal performance of investment managers. A majority of investment funds underperform market indexes such as the S&P 500. Moreover, even those managers who outperform the indexes show little consistency over time. Further evidence that Wall Street has embraced EMH is the popularity of *buy-and-hold* (which assumes you can't time the market) and *indexing* (which assumes you can't identify winning stocks) strategies.

Still, there is growing evidence suggesting the market is not as efficient as presumed. This evidence on market efficiency, called *anomalies* by EMH believers, began surfacing in the past decade. Consider some of the more intriguing bits of evidence. First, stock markets exhibit some *weak form inefficiency*. For example, the market exhibits systematic "calendar" patterns. The well-known *January effect,* where stock prices (especially those of small companies) increase abnormally in the month of January, is the best known example. Another example is that the average return on the Dow Jones Industrial Average for the six months from November through April is more than four times the return for the other six-month period. Still another is that stock returns show patterns based on the day of the week–Monday is the worst day, while Wednesday and Friday are best. Second, there is evidence of *semistrong form inefficiency*. The P/E anomaly and the price-to-book effects–where stocks with low price-to-earnings or price-to-book ratios outperform those with high ratios–suggest the potential of value-based strategies to beat the market. Also, there are a number of accounting-based market anomalies. The best known is the post-earnings announcement drift, where stock prices of companies with good (bad) earnings news continue to drift upward (downward) for months after the earnings announcements. Recent evidence also suggests that managers might be able to "fool" the market with accrual manipulations–a strategy of buying stocks with low accruals and selling stocks with high accruals beats the market. Furthermore, evidence suggests the residual income valuation model can identify over- and undervalued stocks (as well as over- and undervaluation of the market as a whole). Evidence also suggests that investment strategies using analysts' consensus ratings can beat the market.

These findings of market inefficiency give rise to an alternative paradigm, called *behavioral finance,* suggesting that markets are prone to irrationalities and emotion. While the proliferation of evidence suggesting inefficiency does not necessarily imply that markets are irrational and chaotic, it does suggest that blind faith in market efficiency is misplaced.

insight and competence. A competent analysis of information entering the marketplace requires a sound analytical knowledge base and an information mosaic–one to fit new information to aid in evaluation and interpretation of a company's financial position and performance. Not all individuals possess the ability and determination to expend the efforts and resources to create an information mosaic. Also, timing is crucial in the market.

SELLING SHORT
A short-seller sells shares that are borrowed, either from an institutional investor or from a retail brokerage firm, and then hopes to replace the borrowed shares at a lower price, pocketing the difference.

Movement of new information, and its proper interpretation, flows from the well-informed and proficient segment of users to less-informed and inefficient users. This is consistent with a gradual pattern of processing new information. Resources necessary for competent analysis of a company are considerable and imply that certain market segments are more efficient than others. Securities markets for larger companies are more efficient (informed) because of a greater following by analysts due to potential rewards from information search and analysis compared to following smaller, less-prominent companies. Extreme proponents of EMH must take care in making sweeping generalizations. In the annual report of Berkshire Hathaway, its chairman and famed investor Warren Buffett expresses amazement that EMH is still embraced by some scholars and analysts. This, Buffett maintains, is because by observing correctly that the market is frequently efficient, they conclude incorrectly it is *always* efficient. Buffett declares, "the difference between these propositions is night and day."

BOOK ORGANIZATION

This book is organized into 12 chapters in three parts, see Exhibit 1.11. Part I, covering Chapters 1–2, introduces financial statement analysis. Chapter 1 examines business analysis and provides a preview of selected financial statement analysis techniques. Chapter 2 focuses on financial accounting–its objectives and its primary characteristics. It also explains the importance of accrual accounting, its superiority over cash flow accounting, and provides an overview of accounting analysis. Part II, covering Chapters 3–6, emphasizes accounting analysis. It describes accounting analysis for financing, investing, and operating activities. Part III, covering Chapters 7–12, focuses on financial analysis. Chapter 7 explains the analysis of cash flows, while Chapters 8 and 9 describe profitability analysis. Chapter 10 discusses forecasting and pro forma analysis, and Chapters 11–12 highlight two major applications of financial statement analysis–credit analysis and equity analysis.

Organization of the Book ***Exhibit 1.11***

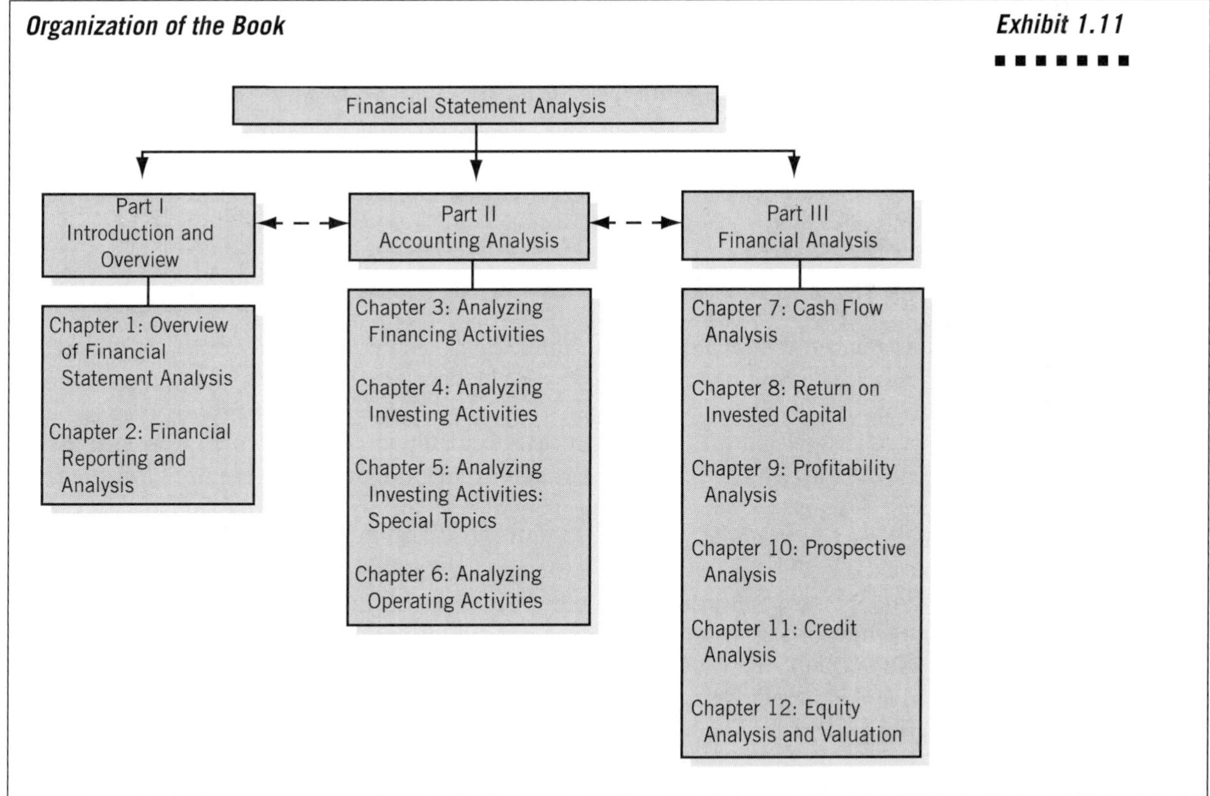

The book concludes with a comprehensive case analysis of the financial statements of Campbell Soup Company. We apply and interpret many of the analysis techniques described in the book using this case. Appendix A reproduces annual report excerpts from three companies that are often referred to in the book: Kodak, Campbell Soup, and Quaker Oats. Throughout this book, the relation of new material to topics covered in earlier chapters is described to reinforce how the material fits together in an integrated structure for financial statement analysis.

APPENDIX 1A INVESTMENT THEORY AND FINANCIAL STATEMENT ANALYSIS

The practice of financial statement analysis is dynamic and challenging. Scholars actively scrutinize this practice and challenge conventional techniques and analyses. Various theories exist and are designed to provide insight into financial statement analysis processes. We briefly review some of the major theories.

PORTFOLIO THEORY

Considerable work is directed at portfolio construction. **Portfolio theory** maintains that both risk and return must be considered–provided a formal framework for quantifying both exists–in portfolio construction. In its basic form, portfolio theory begins by assuming future security returns are estimable and then equates risk with the variance of the returns distribution. Under certain assumptions, portfolio theory produces a linear relation between risk and return. In this framework, it suggests how much of each security to hold in constructing a portfolio. The two-dimensional risk-return approach reinforces to an investor the trade-off between risk and return. Portfolio theory assumes **rational investors** resist increases in risk without commensurate increases in expected returns. Proper diversification can lower risk while preserving expected returns. The relation between the risk accepted and the return expected is fundamental to modern investing and lending decisions. It is worth emphasizing that the greater the perceived risk of an investment or a loan, the greater is the required rate of return to compensate for this risk.

Risk

Risk is linked with uncertainty surrounding outcomes of future events. While many investors and creditors make subjective evaluations of risk, scholars offer statistical measures of risk arising from beta coefficient theory. **Beta coefficient theory** asserts that total risk associated with an investment is made up of two elements: **systematic risk,** the risk attributed to prevailing market movements, and **unsystematic risk,** the risk unique to a specific security. This theory offers a quantitative expression of systematic risk (referred to as **beta**). A beta of 1 implies security price moves with the volatility of the market. The higher (lower) a security's beta, the higher (lower) is its expected return. Treasury bills have a beta of zero because they are essentially riskless. A stock with a beta of 1.20 is expected to rise and fall 20 percent more than (but in the same direction as) the market. A stock with a beta of 0.90 is expected to rise and fall 10 percent less in amplitude than the market. This implies we expect higher returns from higher beta stocks in a bull market but larger than average declines in a bear market.

Unsystematic risk is the residual risk unexplained by market movements–by definition, no unsystematic risk exists for the market. By this reasoning, as portfolios become larger and more diversified, their unsystematic risk approaches zero. Portfolio theorists assert the market does not reward exposure to unsystematic risk when it is removable by proper diversification. They believe the implication of this theory for an investor is to diversify, and if an investor expects the market to rise, to then increase the beta of the portfolio, and vice versa. Experimental studies indicate as much as 30 percent or more of a stock's price movements are due to market (systematic) risk and this influence is as high as 85 percent or more in a well-diversified portfolio of 30 or more stocks.

A portfolio manager who does not wish to rely only on market movements for returns, or who does not wish to forecast market movements, should seek **nondiversification**–that is, exposure to the amount of unsystematic risk required for achieving the desired rate of return. This strategy emphasizes analysis of individual securities, as emphasized in this book, as opposed to overall portfolio risk balancing. Reaping the rewards of exposure to unsystematic risk depends on our ability to identify misvalued securities and to properly assess their risk.

Unsystematic Risk Components

Those wishing to reap rewards from exposure to unsystematic or nonmarket risk through analysis of individual securities must focus on the components of this risk. While these components are interrelated and subject to the influence of such elements of systematic risk as political, economic, and social factors, we can usefully classify them as follows:

- **Economic risk.** Economic risks are inherent in a company's operating environment, including general economic risk (fluctuations in business activity), capital market risk (including changes in interest rates), and purchasing power risk.
- **Business risk.** Business risk is the uncertainty regarding a company's ability to earn a satisfactory return on its investments in light of cost and revenue factors, including factors of competition, product mix, and management ability.
- **Financial risk.** This refers to risks of capital structure and a company's ability to meet fixed and senior charges and claims.
- **Accounting risk.** Accounting risk is inherent in the selection and application of accounting methods, including management latitude in influencing the output of the accounting process.

Beta theorists assume investors are averse to risk and seek to diversify away a security's unsystematic risk, exposing investors only to market risk. Yet these theorists must recognize that historical betas for individual securities are quite unstable over time and, consequently, historical betas are seemingly imperfect predictors (at best) of a security's future betas. While such theories often readily apply to stock aggregates, they are less reliable and sometimes inaccurate for individual stock investment purposes.

Another, and perhaps more troublesome, issue is the assumption by beta theorists that past volatility is a sufficient measure of risk without reference to a security's current price. Namely, is a security that trades above its true value, as determined by some method of fundamental analysis, no more risky than a security of equal volatility (beta) that trades below its true value? We know paying an excessive price for a stable, high-quality security is potentially as risky as investing in an unseasoned speculative security. While theorists have yet to effectively address this issue, they have braved the question of how the market values securities.

Accounting and Market Risk

Research shows accounting measures of risk such as dividend payout rates, capitalization ratios, coverage ratios, and asset growth are reflected in market risk measures like beta. This implies that selecting and ranking portfolios on accounting risk measures is similar to portfolio formation using market-determined risk measures. Research also evidences a relation between systematic risk and a company's leverage (and other accounting risk measures). Moreover, research suggests some value to *fundamental betas,* where this beta is a function of a company's changing fundamentals like earnings, asset structure, financial structure, and growth rates. An important implication of all this research is that many of the same economic (accounting) determinants causing a stock to be more risky also cause it to have high systematic risk (beta).

CAPITAL ASSET PRICING MODEL

The capital asset pricing model (CAPM) extends portfolio theory in a manner intended to explain how prices of assets are determined–in short, by providing greater return for greater risk. This model assumes investors desire to hold securities in efficient portfolios providing maximum return for a given risk level. Several simplifying assumptions underlie this model, including:

- A riskless security exists.
- Investors can borrow or lend unlimited amounts at the riskless rate.
- Investors have identical investment horizons and act on the basis of identical expectations.

ART OF THE CHART
Most analysts dismiss technical analysis as hooey. Technical analysts—also called chartists—try to predict price patterns by looking at graphs of recent prices. A recent study suggests that technical analysis may sometimes work in currency markets. A key pattern in currency trading is the tendency for trades to cluster near round numbers because traders often enter orders to buy or sell currencies when they hit certain specified levels. These levels are usually numbers ending in 0 or 5, which means that currencies have a greater likelihood of peaking or hitting bottom at those levels.

Using these assumptions, the expected return on an individual security *i,* or $E(R_i)$, relates to its systematic risk, β_i, in the following linear form:

$$E(R_i) = E(R_o) + [E(R_M) - E(R_o)] \times \beta_i$$

This formula suggests, under conditions of equilibrium, a security's (or any asset's) expected return equals the expected return of a riskless security, $E(R_0)$, plus a premium for risk taking. The risk premium consists of a constant, $[E(R_M) - E(R_0)]$–defined as the difference between the market expected return and the riskless security return–multiplied by a security's systematic risk (β_i). CAPM implies each security's expected return is related to its risk. Risk is measured as the security's systematic movements with the market that cannot be eliminated by portfolio diversification. A major implication is the market rewards systematic (beta) risk, whereas holding unsystematic risk (potentially removable through diversification) earns no additional return.

Abnormal Return and Jensen's Alpha

The CAPM specifies risk-adjusted expected return for a security (or portfolio). Yet, it is naive to assume that the return for each security in every period is exactly equal to the expected return specified by CAPM. This means the *ex post* return on a security will differ from the expected return as follows:

$$R_i = E(R_i) + \alpha_i = E(R_o) + [E(R_M) - E(R_o)] \times \beta_i) + \alpha_i$$

The deviation of ex post return from the expected return is called abnormal return, and is often referred to as *Jensen's Alpha* in a portfolio context:

$$\alpha_i = R_i - E(R_i) = R_i - E(R_o) - [E(R_M) - E(R_o)] \times \beta_i$$

Jensen's Alpha can be different from zero for the following reasons:

- New information enters the market.
- Beta (systematic risk) is incorrectly measured.
- CAPM is the inappropriate model for expected returns.
- Market has underpriced or overpriced the security.

Equity Analysis

Equity investment strategies demand effective equity analysis. There are two basic approaches to equity investing–passive and active. **Passive investing** assumes the market is efficient and takes stock prices as given. Under this approach, an investor holds a diversified portfolio of stocks and debt securities. The objective is to allocate an investor's wealth to different types of securities based on the investor's risk propensity and investment horizon. A mix of risky and riskless securities determines the optimal allocation. Such investment strategies are called *beta strategies* because they merely involve determining the optimal risk, or beta, of an investor's portfolio. Since there is no attempt to evaluate the investment potential of individual stocks with passive investing, there is no need for business analysis. Passive investing underlies a popular type of investing known as *indexing*.

Active investing involves beating the market in one form or another. An investor adopting this approach believes he or she can, through superior analysis, identify investment opportunities not yet reflected in prices. This implies the investor can buy (or sell) stocks at bargain prices and earn above normal returns. Active investing strategies are called *alpha strategies*, where alpha refers to *Jensen's alpha*, which is the difference between expected and actual return. Active investing is popular on Wall Street and on many other global securities exchanges. It is applied by most mutual and hedge funds and by a growing number of individual investors.

Analysis Research

TITANIC EFFICIENCY

If the market's reaction to the sinking of the *Titanic* in 1912 is any guide, investors were pretty sharp even in the pre-"efficient market" era. The *Titanic* was owned by White Star Line, a subsidiary of International Mercantile Marine (IMM) that was traded on the NYSE. The ship cost $7.5 million and was insured by Lloyd's for $5 million, so the net loss to IMM was about $2.5 million. The two-day market-adjusted returns on IMM's stock (covering the day the news of the tragedy broke and the day after) reflect a decline of $2.6 million in the value of IMM–uncannily close to the $2.5 million actual net loss.

Source: Business Week (December 7, 1998)

GUIDANCE ANSWERS TO ANALYSIS VIEWPOINTS

CREDITOR A creditor (or banker) is concerned about Kodak's ability to satisfy its loan obligations. Concern about the composition of Kodak's financing sources is twofold. First, the greater the owner financing, the lower the credit risk. This is because interest and principal payments must be paid, whereas dividends to owners (shareholders) are optional. Also, in event of liquidation, creditors are paid before owners. Second, creditors concern themselves with a company's current and future creditor obligations. This means that creditors often write *debt covenants* to either restrict a company's future lending, or require collateral, or limit the amount of dividends. For Kodak, about 70 percent of its financing is from shareholders. Accordingly, with adequate protection from debt covenants, you can confidently make the loan.

INVESTOR As a potential investor, your review of financial statements focuses on Kodak's ability to create and sustain net income. Each of the statements is important in this review. The income statement is especially important as it reveals management's current and past success in creating and sustaining income. The cash flow statement is important in assessing management's ability to meet cash payments and the company's cash availability. The balance sheet shows the asset base from which future income is generated, and it reports on liabilities and their due dates.

[Superscript A denotes assignments based on Appendix 1A.]

QUESTIONS

1–1. Describe business analysis and identify its objectives.

1–2. Explain the claim: *Financial statement analysis is an integral part of business analysis.*

1–3. Describe the different types of business analysis. Identify the category of users of financial statements that applies to each different type of business analysis.

1–4. What are the main differences between credit analysis and equity analysis? How do these impact the financial statement information that is important for each type of analysis?

1–5. What is fundamental analysis? What is its main objective?

1–6. What are the various component processes in business analysis? Explain with reference to equity analysis.

1–7. Describe the importance of accounting analysis for financial analysis.

1–8. Describe financial statement analysis and identify its objectives.

1–9. Identify at least five different internal and external users of financial statements.

1–10. Identify and discuss the four major activities of a business enterprise.

1–11. Explain how financial statements reflect the business activities of a company.

1–12. Identify and discuss the four primary financial statements of a business.

1–13. Explain why financial statements are important to the decision-making process in financial analysis. Also, identify and discuss some of their limitations for analysis purposes.

1–14. Identify at least seven additional sources of financial reporting information (beyond financial statements) that are useful for analysis.

1–15. Identify and discuss at least two areas of financial analysis.

1–16. Identify and describe at least four categories of financial analysis tools.

1–17. Comparative analysis is an important tool in financial analysis.
a. Explain the usefulness of comparative financial statement analysis.
b. Describe how financial statement comparisons are effectively made.
c. Discuss the necessary precautions an analyst should take in performing comparative analysis.

1–18. Is past trend a good predictor of future trend? Justify your response.

1–19. Compare the "absolute amount of change" with the percent change as an indicator of change. Which is better for analysis?

1–20. Identify conditions that prevent computation of a valid percent change. Provide an example.

1–21. Describe criteria in selecting a base year for index-number trend analysis.

1–22. Explain what useful information is derived from index-number trend analysis.

1–23. Common-size analysis is an important tool in financial analysis.
a. Describe a common-size financial statement. Explain how one is prepared.
b. Explain what a common-size financial statement report communicates about a company.

1–24. What is a necessary condition for usefulness of a ratio of financial numbers? Explain.

1–25. Identify and describe limitations of ratio analysis.

1–26. Ratio analysis is an important tool in financial analysis. Identify at least four ratios using:
a. Balance sheet data exclusively.
b. Income statement data exclusively.
c. Both balance sheet and income statement data.

1–27. Identify four specialized financial analysis tools.

1–28. What is meant by "time value of money"? Explain the role of this concept in valuation.

1–29. Explain the claim: *While we theoretically use the effective interest rate to compute a bond's present value, in practice it is the other way around.*

1–30. What is amiss with the claim: *The value of a stock is the discounted value of expected future cash flows?*

1–31. Identify and describe a technique to compute equity value only using accounting variables.

1–32. Explain how the efficient market hypothesis (EMH) depicts the reaction of market prices to financial and other data.

1–33. Discuss implications of the efficient market hypothesis (EMH) for financial statement analysis.

1–34. Differentiate between systematic risk and unsystematic risk. Discuss components of unsystematic risk.

1–35. Define the capital asset pricing model (CAPM) and describe how it depicts security valuation by the market.

1–36. Explain the concept of trade-off between risk and return and its significance to portfolio construction.

1–37. Discuss implications of the capital asset pricing model (CAPM) for financial statement analysis.

EXERCISES

EXERCISE 1–1
Discretion in Comparative Financial Statement Analysis

The preparation and analysis of comparative balance sheets and income statements are commonly applied tools of financial statement analysis and interpretation.

Required:

a. Discuss the inherent limitations of analyzing and interpreting financial statements for a single year. Include in your discussion the extent that these limitations are overcome by use of comparative financial statements computed over more than one year.

b. A year-to-year analysis of comparative balance sheets and income statements is a useful analysis tool. Still, without proper care, such analysis can be misleading. Discuss factors or conditions that contribute to such a possibility. How can additional information and supplementary data (beyond financial statements) help prevent this possibility?

EXERCISE 1–2
Computing Common-Size Percents

Express the following income statement information in common-size percents and assess whether this company's situation is favorable or unfavorable.

HARBISON CORPORATION
Comparative Income Statement
For Years Ended December 31, 2003 and 2002

	2003	2002
Sales	$720,000	$535,000
Cost of goods sold	475,200	280,340
Gross profit	244,800	254,660
Operating expenses	151,200	103,790
Net income	$ 93,600	$150,870

EXERCISE 1–3
Evaluating Short-Term Liquidity

Mixon Company's year-end balance sheets show the following:

	2003	2002	2001
Cash	$ 30,800	$ 35,625	$ 36,800
Accounts receivable, net	88,500	62,500	49,200
Merchandise inventory	111,500	82,500	53,000
Prepaid expenses	9,700	9,375	4,000
Plant assets, net	277,500	255,000	229,500
Total assets	$518,000	$445,000	$372,500
Accounts payable	$128,900	$ 75,250	$ 49,250
Long-term notes payable secured by mortgages on plant assets	97,500	102,500	82,500
Common stock, $10 par value	162,500	162,500	162,500
Retained earnings	129,100	104,750	78,250
Total liabilities and equity	$518,000	$445,000	$372,500

Required:

Compare the year-end short-term liquidity position of this company at the end of 2003, 2002, and 2001 by computing the: (*a*) current ratio and (*b*) acid-test ratio. Comment on the ratio results.

EXERCISE 1–4
Common-Size Percents

Refer to Mixon Company's balance sheets in Exercise 1–3. Express the balance sheets in common-size percents. Round to the nearest one-tenth of a percent.

EXERCISE 1–5
Evaluating Short-Term Liquidity

Refer to the information in Exercise 1–3 about Mixon Company. The company's income statements for the years ended December 31, 2003 and 2002 show the following:

	2003		2002	
Sales		$672,500		$530,000
Cost of goods sold	$410,225		$344,500	
Other operating expenses	208,550		133,980	
Interest expense	11,100		12,300	
Income taxes	8,525		7,845	
Total costs and expenses		(638,400)		(498,625)
Net income		$ 34,100		$ 31,375
Earnings per share		$ 2.10		$ 1.93

Required:

For the years ended December 31, 2003 and 2002, assume all sales are on credit and then compute the following: (*a*) days' sales in receivables, (*b*) accounts receivable turnover, (*c*) inventory turnover, and (*d*) days' sales in inventory. Comment on the changes in the ratios from 2002 to 2003.

EXERCISE 1–6
Evaluating Risk and Capital Structure

Refer to the information in Exercises 1–3 and 1–5 about Mixon Company. Compare the long-term risk and capital structure positions of the company at the end of 2003 and 2002 by computing the following ratios: (*a*) total debt ratio and (*b*) times interest earned. Comment on these ratio results.

EXERCISE 1–7
Evaluating Efficiency and Profitability

Refer to the financial statements of Mixon Company in Exercises 1–3 and 1–5. Evaluate the efficiency and profitability of the company by computing the following: (*a*) net profit margin, (*b*) total asset turnover, and (*c*) return on total assets. Comment on these ratio results.

EXERCISE 1–8
Evaluating Profitability

Refer to the financial statements of Mixon Company in Exercises 1–3 and 1–5. The following additional information about the company is known:

Common stock market price, December 31, 2003	$15.00
Common stock market price, December 31, 2002	14.00
Annual cash dividends per share in 2003	0.30
Annual cash dividends per share in 2002	0.15

To help evaluate the profitability of the company, compute the following for 2003 and 2002: (*a*) return on common stockholders' equity, (*b*) price-earnings ratio on December 31, and (*c*) dividend yield.

EXERCISE 1–9
Determining Income Effects from Common-Size and Trend Percents

Common-size and trend percents for JBC Company's sales, cost of goods sold, and expenses follow:

	COMMON-SIZE PERCENTS			TREND PERCENTS		
	2003	2002	2001	2003	2002	2001
Sales	100.0%	100.0%	100.0%	104.4%	103.2%	100.0%
Cost of goods sold	62.4	60.9	58.1	112.1	108.2	100.0
Expenses	14.3	13.8	14.1	105.9	101.0	100.0

Determine whether net income increased, decreased, or remained unchanged in this three-year period.

EXERCISE 1–10
Analyzing Short-Term Financial Conditions

Huff Company and Mesa Company are similar firms that operate in the same industry. The following information is available:

	HUFF			MESA		
	2003	2002	2001	2003	2002	2001
Current ratio	1.6	1.7	2.0	3.1	2.6	1.8
Acid-test ratio	0.9	1.0	1.1	2.7	2.4	1.5
Accounts receivable turnover	29.5	24.2	28.2	15.4	14.2	15.0
Inventory turnover	23.2	20.9	16.1	13.5	12.0	11.6
Working capital	$60,000	$48,000	$42,000	$121,000	$93,000	$68,000

Write a one-half page report comparing Huff and Mesa using the available information. Your discussion should include their ability to meet current obligations and to use current assets efficiently.

EXERCISE 1–11
Computing Trend Percents

Compute index-number trend percents for the following accounts, using Year 1 as the base year. State whether the situation as revealed by the trends appears to be favorable or unfavorable.

	Year 5	Year 4	Year 3	Year 2	Year 1
Sales	$283,880	$271,800	$253,680	$235,560	$151,000
Cost of goods sold	129,200	123,080	116,280	107,440	68,000
Accounts receivable	19,100	18,300	17,400	16,200	10,000

EXERCISE 1–12
Computing Percent Changes

Compute the percent of increase or decrease for each of the following account balances:

	Year 2	Year 1
Short-term investments	$217,800	$165,000
Accounts receivable	42,120	48,000
Notes payable	57,000	0

EXERCISE 1–13
Debt Valuation (annual interest)

Compute the present value for each of the following bonds:

a. Priced at the end of its fifth year, a 10-year bond with a face value of $100 and a contract (coupon) rate of 10 percent per annum (payable at the end of each year) with an effective (required) interest rate of 14 percent per annum.

b. Priced at the beginning of its 10th year, a 14-year bond with a face value of $1,000 and a contract (coupon) rate of 8 percent per annum (payable at the end of each year) with an effective (required) interest rate of 6 percent per annum.

c. What is the answer to *b* if bond interest is payable in equal semiannual amounts?

EXERCISE 1–14
Valuation of Bonds (semiannual interest)

On January 1, Year 1, you are considering the purchase of $10,000 of Colin Company's 8 percent bonds. The bonds are due in 10 years, with interest payable semiannually on June 30 and effective December 31. Based on your analysis of Colin, you determine that a 6 percent (required) interest rate is appropriate.

Required:

a. Compute the price you will pay for the bonds using the present value model (round the answer to the nearest dollar).

b. Recompute the price in *a* if your required rate of return is 10 percent.

c. Describe risk and explain how it is reflected in your required rate of return.

EXERCISE 1–15
Residual Income Equity Valuation

On January 1, Year 1, you are considering the purchase of Nico Enterprises' common stock. Based on your analysis of Nico Enterprises, you determine the following:

1. Book value at January 1, Year 1, is $50 per share.
2. Predicted net income per share for Year 1 through Year 5 is $8, $11, $20, $40, and $30, respectively.
3. For Year 6 and continuing for all years after, predicted residual income is $0.
4. Nico is not expected to pay dividends.
5. Required rate of return (cost of capital) is 20 percent.

Required:
Determine the purchase price per share of Nico Enterprises' common stock as of January 1, Year 1, using the residual income valuation model (round your answer to the nearest cent). Comment on the strengths and limitations of this model for investment decisions.

PROBLEMS

PROBLEM 1–1
Analyzing Efficiency and Financial Leverage

Kampa Company and Arbor Company are similar firms that operate in the same industry. Arbor began operations in 1998 and Kampa in 1992. In 2003, both companies pay 7 percent interest on their debt to creditors. The following additional information is available:

	KAMPA COMPANY			ARBOR COMPANY		
	2003	2002	2001	2003	2002	2001
Total asset turnover	3.0	2.7	2.9	1.6	1.4	1.1
Return on total assets	8.9%	9.5%	8.7%	5.8%	5.5%	5.2%
Profit margin	2.3%	2.4%	2.2%	2.7%	2.9%	2.8%
Sales	$400,000	$370,000	$386,000	$200,000	$160,000	$100,000

Write a one-half page report comparing Kampa and Arbor using the available information. Your discussion should include their ability to use assets efficiently to produce profits. Also comment on their success in employing financial leverage in 2003.

PROBLEM 1–2

Calculation and Analysis of Trend Percents

Selected comparative financial statements of Cohorn Company follow:

COHORN COMPANY
Comparative Income Statement ($000)
For Years Ended December 31, 1997–2003

	2003	2002	2001	2000	1999	1998	1997
Sales	$1,594	$1,396	$1,270	$1,164	$1,086	$1,010	$828
Cost of goods sold	1,146	932	802	702	652	610	486
Gross profit	448	464	468	462	434	400	342
Operating expenses	340	266	244	180	156	154	128
Net income	$ 108	$ 198	$ 224	$ 282	$ 278	$ 246	$214

COHORN COMPANY
Comparative Balance Sheet ($000)
For Years Ended December 31, 1997–2003

	2003	2002	2001	2000	1999	1998	1997
Assets							
Cash	$ 68	$ 88	$ 92	$ 94	$ 98	$ 96	$ 99
Accounts receivable, net	480	504	456	350	308	292	206
Merchandise inventory	1,738	1,264	1,104	932	836	710	515
Other current assets	46	42	24	44	38	38	19
Long-term investments	0	0	0	136	136	136	136
Plant and equipment, net	2,120	2,114	1,852	1,044	1,078	960	825
Total assets	$4,452	$4,012	$3,528	$2,600	$2,494	$2,232	$1,800
Liabilities and Equity							
Current liabilities	$1,120	$ 942	$ 618	$ 514	$ 446	$ 422	$ 272
Long-term liabilities	1,194	1,040	1,012	470	480	520	390
Common stock	1,000	1,000	1,000	840	840	640	640
Other contributed capital	250	250	250	180	180	160	160
Retained earnings	888	780	648	596	548	490	338
Total liabilities and equity	$4,452	$4,012	$3,528	$2,600	$2,494	$2,232	$1,800

CHECK
2003, Total assets trend, 247.3%

Required:

a. Compute trend percents for the individual items of both statements using 1997 as the base year.

b. Analyze and comment on the financial statements and trend percents from part *a.*

PROBLEM 1–3
Comparative Income Statement Analysis

Perform a comparative analysis of Eastman Corporation by completing the analysis below. Describe and comment on any significant findings in your comparative analysis.

CHECK
Average net income, $563

EASTMAN CORPORATION
Income Statement ($ millions)
For Years Ended December 31

	Year 6	Year 5	Year 4	Cumulative Amount	Annual Average Amount
Net sales	$ ____	$3,490	$2,860	$ ____	$ ____
Cost of goods sold	3,210	____	____	____	2,610
Gross profit	3,670	680	1,050	____	1,800
Operating expenses	____	____	____	____	____
Income before taxes	2,740	215	105	____	____
Net income	$1,485	$ 145	$ 58	____	____

PROBLEM 1–4
Index-Number Trend Analysis

Compute increases (decreases) in percents for both Years 6 and 7 by entering all the missing data in the table below. Analyze and interpret any significant results revealed from this trend analysis.

CHECK
Year 6 income percent, 33.3%

	YEAR 7		YEAR 6		YEAR 5
Statement Item	Index No.	Change in Percent	Index No.	Change in Percent	Index No.
Net sales	____	29%	100	____%	90
Cost of goods sold	139	____	100	____	85
Gross profit	126	____	100	____	80
Operating expenses	____	20	100	____	65
Income before tax	____	14	100	____	70
Net income	129	____	100	____	75

PROBLEM 1–5
Understanding Financial Statement Relations: Balance Sheet Construction

Assume you are an analyst evaluating Mesco Company. The following data are available in your financial analysis (unless otherwise indicated, all data are as of December 31, Year 5):

Retained earnings, December 31, Year 4	$98,000	Days' sales in receivables	18 days
Gross profit margin ratio	25%	Shareholders' equity to total debt	4 to 1
Acid-test ratio	2.5 to 1	Sales (all on credit)	$920,000
Noncurrent assets	$280,000	Common stock: $15 par value; 10,000 shares issued and outstanding; issued at $21 per share	
Days' sales in inventory	45 days		

Required:

Using these data, construct the December 31, Year 5, balance sheet for your analysis. Operating expenses (excluding taxes and cost of goods sold for Year 5) are $180,000. The tax rate is 40 percent. Assume a 360-day year in ratio computations. No cash dividends are paid in either Year 4 or Year 5. Current assets consist of cash, accounts receivable, and inventories.

CHECK
Total assets, $422,500

PROBLEM 1–6
Understanding Financial Statement Relations: Balance Sheet Construction

You are an analyst reviewing Foxx Company. The following data are available for your financial analysis (unless otherwise indicated, all data are as of December 31, Year 2):

Current ratio	2	Days' sales in inventory	36 days
Accounts receivable turnover	16	Gross profit margin ratio	50%
Beginning accounts receivable	$50,000	Expenses (excluding cost of goods sold)	$450,000
Return on end-of-year common equity	20%	Total debt to equity ratio	1
Sales (all on credit)	$1,000,000	Noncurrent assets	$300,000

Required:

Using these data, construct the December 31, Year 2, balance sheet for your analysis. Current assets consist of cash, accounts receivable, and inventory. Balance sheet classifications include cash, accounts receivable, inventory, total noncurrent assets, total current assets, total current liabilities, total noncurrent liabilities, and equity.

CHECK
Total assets, $500,000

PROBLEM 1–7
Understanding Financial Statement Relations: Dividend and Balance Sheet Construction

You are planning to analyze Voltek Company's December 31, Year 6, balance sheet. The following information is available:

1. Beginning and ending balances are identical for both accounts receivable and inventory.
2. Net income is $1,300.
3. Times interest earned is 5 (income taxes are zero). Company has 5 percent bonds outstanding and issued at par.
4. Net profit margin is 10 percent. Gross profit margin is 30 percent. Inventory turnover is 5.
5. Days' sales in receivables is 72 days.
6. Sales to end-of-year working capital is 4. Current ratio is 1.5.
7. Acid-test ratio is 1.0 (excludes prepaid expenses).
8. Plant and equipment (net) is $6,000. It is one-third depreciated.
9. Dividends paid on 8 percent nonparticipating preferred stock are $40. There is no change in common shares outstanding during Year 6. Preferred shares were issued two years ago at par.
10. Earnings per common share are $3.75.
11. Common stock has a $5 par value and was issued at par.
12. Retained earnings at January 1, Year 6, are $350.

Required:

a. Given the information available, prepare this company's balance sheet as of December 31, Year 6 (include the following account classifications: cash, accounts receivable, inventory, prepaid expenses, plant and equipment (net), current liabilities, bonds payable, and stockholders' equity).

CHECK
Total assets, $15,750

b. Determine the amount of dividends paid on common stock in Year 6.

PROBLEM 1–8
Financial Statement Ratio Analysis

The balance sheet and income statement for Chico Electronics are reproduced below (tax rate is 40 percent).

CHICO ELECTRONICS
Balance Sheet ($ thousands)
As of December 31

	Year 4	Year 5
Assets		
Current assets:		
Cash	$ 683	$ 325
Accounts receivable	1,490	3,599
Inventories	1,415	2,423
Prepaid expenses	15	13
Total current assets	3,603	6,360
Property, plant and equipment, net	1,066	1,541
Other assets	123	157
Total assets	$4,792	$8,058
Liabilities and Shareholders' Equity		
Current liabilities:		
Notes payable to bank	$ —	$ 875
Current portion of long-term debt	38	116
Accounts payable	485	933
Estimated income tax liability	588	472
Accrued expenses	576	586
Customer advance payments	34	963
Total current liabilities	1,721	3,945
Long-term debt	122	179
Other liabilities	81	131
Total liabilities	1,924	4,255
Shareholders' equity:		
Common stock, $1.00 par value; 1,000,000 shares authorized; 550,000 and 829,000 outstanding, respectively	550	829
Preferred stock, Series A 10%; $25 par value; 25,000 authorized; 20,000 and 18,000 outstanding, respectively	500	450
Additional paid-in capital	450	575
Retained earnings	1,368	1,949
Total shareholders' equity	2,868	3,803
Total liabilities and shareholders' equity	$4,792	$8,058

CHICO ELECTRONICS
Income Statement ($ thousands)
For Years Ending December 31

	Year 4	Year 5
Net sales	$7,570	$12,065
Other income, net	261	345
Total revenues	7,831	12,410
Cost of goods sold	4,850	8,048
General, administrative, and marketing expense	1,531	2,025
Interest expense	22	78
Total costs and expenses	6,403	10,151
Net income before tax	1,428	2,259
Income tax	628	994
Net income	$ 800	$ 1,265

Required:

Compute and interpret the following financial ratios of the company for Year 5:

a. Acid-test ratio.
b. Return on assets.
c. Return on common equity.
d. Earnings per share.
e. Gross profit margin ratio.
f. Times interest earned.
g. Days to sell inventory.
h. Long-term debt to equity ratio.
i. Total debt to equity.
j. Sales to end-of-year working capital.

CHECK
EPS, $1.77

(CFA Adapted)

PROBLEM 1–9
Financial Statement Ratio Computation and Interpretation

As a consultant to MCR Company, you are told it is considering the acquisition of Lakeland Corporation. MCR Company requests that you prepare certain financial statistics and analysis for Year 5 and Year 4 using Lakeland's financial statements that follow:

LAKELAND CORPORATION
Balance Sheet
December 31, Year 5 and Year 4

	Year 5	Year 4
Assets		
Current assets:		
Cash	$ 1,610,000	$ 1,387,000
Marketable securities	510,000	—
Accounts receivable, less allowance for bad debts:		
Year 5, $125,000; Year 4, $110,000	4,075,000	3,669,000
Inventories, at lower of cost or market	7,250,000	7,050,000
Prepaid expenses	125,000	218,000
Total current assets	13,570,000	12,324,000
Plant and equipment, at cost:		
Land and buildings	13,500,000	13,500,000
Machinery and equipment	9,250,000	8,520,000
Total plant and equipment	22,750,000	22,020,000
Less: Accumulated depreciation	13,470,000	12,549,000
Total plant and equipment—net	9,280,000	9,471,000
Long-term receivables	250,000	250,000
Deferred charges	25,000	75,000
Total assets	$23,125,000	$22,120,000
Liabilities and Shareholders' Equity		
Current liabilities:		
Accounts payable	$ 2,950,000	$ 3,426,000
Accrued expenses	1,575,000	1,644,000
Federal taxes payable	875,000	750,000
Current maturities on long-term debt	500,000	500,000
Total current liabilities	5,900,000	6,320,000
Other liabilities:		
5% sinking fund debentures, due January 1,		
Year 16 ($500,000 redeemable annually)	5,000,000	5,500,000
Deferred taxes on income, due to depreciation	350,000	210,000
Total other liabilities	5,350,000	5,710,000
Shareholders' equity:		
Capital stock:		
Preferred stock, $1 cumulative, $20 par, preference		
on liquidation $100 per share (authorized: 100,000 shares;		
issued and outstanding: 50,000 shares)	1,000,000	1,000,000
Common stock, $1 par (authorized: 900,000 shares;		
issued and outstanding: Year 5, 550,000 shares;		
Year 4, 500,000 shares)	550,000	500,000
Capital in excess of par value on common stock	3,075,000	625,000
Retained earnings	7,250,000	7,965,000
Total shareholders' equity	11,875,000	10,090,000
Total liabilities and shareholders' equity	$23,125,000	$22,120,000

LAKELAND CORPORATION
Statement of Income and Retained Earnings
For Years Ended December 31, Year 5 and Year 4

	Year 5	Year 4
Revenues:		
Net sales	$48,400,000	$41,700,000
Royalties	70,000	25,000
Interest	30,000	—
Total revenues	$48,500,000	$41,725,000
Costs and expenses:		
Cost of sales	$31,460,000	$29,190,000
Selling, general, and administrative	12,090,000	8,785,000
Interest on 5% sinking fund debentures	275,000	300,000
Provision for Federal income taxes	2,315,000	1,695,000
Total costs and expenses	$46,140,000	$39,970,000
Net income	$ 2,360,000	$ 1,755,000
Retained earnings, beginning of year	7,965,000	6,760,000
Subtotal	$10,325,000	$ 8,515,000
Dividends paid:		
Preferred stock, $1.00 per share in cash	50,000	50,000
Common stock:		
Cash—$1.00 per share	525,000	500,000
Stock—(10%)—50,000 shares at market value of $50 per share	2,500,000	—
Total dividends paid	$ 3,075,000	$ 550,000
Retained earnings, end of year	$ 7,250,000	$ 7,965,000

Additional Information:

1. Inventory at January 1, Year 4, is $6,850,000.
2. Market prices of common stock at December 31, Year 5 and Year 4, are $73.50 and $47.75, respectively.
3. Cash dividends for both preferred and common stock are declared and paid in June and December of each year. The stock dividend on common stock is declared and distributed in August of Year 5.
4. Plant and equipment disposals during Year 5 and Year 4 are $375,000 and $425,000, respectively. Related accumulated depreciation is $215,000 in Year 5 and $335,000 in Year 4. At December 31, Year 3, the plant and equipment asset balance is $21,470,000, and its related accumulated depreciation is $11,650,000.

Required:

Compute the following financial ratios and figures for both Year 5 and Year 4. Identify and discuss any significant year-to-year changes.

At December 31:	For year ended December 31:
a. Current ratio.	*d.* Gross profit margin ratio.
b. Acid-test ratio.	*e.* Days to sell inventory.
c. Book value per common share.	*f.* Times interest earned.
	g. Common stock price-to-earnings ratio (end-of-year value).
	h. Gross capital expenditures.

CHECK
Year 5 PE, 17.5

(AICPA Adapted)

PROBLEM 1–10

Identifying Industries from Financial Statement Data

Selected ratios for three different companies that operate in three different industries (merchandising, pharmaceuticals, utilities) are reported in the table below:

Ratio	Co. A	Co. B	Co. C
Gross profit margin ratio	18%	53%	n.a.
Net profit margin ratio	2%	14%	8%
Research and development to sales	0%	17%	0.1%
Advertising to sales	7%	4%	0.1%
Interest expense to sales	1%	1%	15%
Return on assets	11%	12%	7%
Accounts receivable turnover	95 times	5 times	11 times
Inventory turnover	9 times	3 times	n.a.
Long-term debt to equity	64%	45%	89%

n.a. = not applicable

Required:

Identify the industry that each of the companies, A, B, and C, operate in. Give at least two reasons supporting each of your selections.

PROBLEM 1–11

Ratio Interpretation–Industry Comparisons

The Tristar Mutual Fund manager is considering an investment in the stock of Best Computer and asks for your opinion regarding the company. Best Computer is a computer hardware sales and service company. Approximately 50 percent of the company's revenues come from the sale of computer hardware. The rest of the company's revenues come from hardware service and repair contracts. Below are financial ratios for Best Computer and comparative ratios for Best Computer's industry. The ratios for Best Computer are computed using information from its financial statements.

	Best Computer	Industry Average
Liquidity ratios:		
Current ratio	3.45	3.10
Acid-test ratio	2.58	1.85
Collection period	42.19	36.60
Days to sell inventory	18.38	18.29
Capital structure and solvency:		
Total debt to equity	0.674	0.690
Long-term debt to equity	0.368	0.400
Times interest earned	9.20	9.89
Return on investment:		
Return on assets	31.4%	30.0%
Return on common equity	52.6%	50.0%

	Best Computer	Industry Average
Operating performance:		
Gross profit margin	36.0%	34.3%
Operating profit margin	16.7%	15.9%
Pre-tax profit margin	14.9%	14.45%
Net profit margin	8.2%	8.0%
Asset utilization:		
Cash turnover	40.8	38.9
Accounts receivable turnover	6.90	8.15
Sales to inventory	29.9	28.7
Working capital turnover	8.50	9.71
Fixed asset turnover	15.30	15.55
Total assets turnover	3.94	3.99
Market measures:		
Price-to-earnings ratio	27.8	29.0
Earnings yield	8.1%	7.9%
Dividend yield	0%	0.5%
Dividend payout rate	0%	2%
Price-to-book	8.8	9.0

Required:

a. Interpret the ratios of Best Computer and draw inferences about the company's financial performance and financial condition—ignore the industry ratios.

b. Repeat the analysis in (*a*) with full knowledge of the industry ratios.

c. Indicate which ratios you consider to deviate from industry norms. For each Best Computer ratio that deviates from industry norms, suggest two possible explanations.

CHECK
Acct. recble., Above norm

PROBLEM 1–12
Equity Valuation

Ace Co. is to be taken over by Beta Ltd. at the end of year 2007. Beta agrees to pay the shareholders of Ace the book value per share at the time of the takeover. A reliable analyst makes the following projections for Ace (assume cost of capital is 10% per annum):

($ per share)	2002	2003	2004	2005	2006	2007
Dividends	—	$1.00	$1.00	$1.00	$1.00	$1.00
Operating cash flows	—	2.00	1.50	1.00	0.75	0.50
Capital expenditures	—	—	—	1.00	1.00	—
Net income	—	1.45	1.10	0.60	0.25	(0.10)
Book value	9.00	9.45	9.55	9.15	8.40	7.30

Required:

a. Estimate Ace Co.'s value per share at the end of year 2002 using the dividend discount model.

b. Estimate Ace Co.'s value per share at the end of year 2002 using the residual income model.

c. Attempt to estimate the value of Ace Co. at the end of year 2002 using the free cash flow to equity model.

CHECK
Value using RI, $8.32

CASES

CASE 1–1
Comparative Analysis: Return on Invested Capital

CHECK
Nike ROI, 7.4%

Key comparative figures ($ millions) for both **NIKE** and **Reebok** follow:

NIKE Reebok

Key Figures	NIKE	Reebok
Financing (liabilities + equity)	$5,397.4	$1,756.1
Net income (profit)	399.6	135.1
Revenues (sales)	9,553.1	3,637.4

Required:

a. What is the total amount of assets invested in (*a*) NIKE and (*b*) Reebok?

b. What is the return on investment for (*a*) NIKE and (*b*) Reebok? NIKE's beginning assets equal $5,361.2 (in millions) and Reebok's beginning assets equal $1,786.2 (in millions).

c. How much are expenses for (*a*) NIKE and (*b*) Reebok?

d. Is return on investment satisfactory for (*a*) NIKE and (*b*) Reebok [assume competitors average a 4% return]?

e. What can you conclude about NIKE and Reebok from these computations?

CASE 1–2
Comparative Analysis: Comparison of Balance Sheet and Income Statement

Key comparative figures ($ millions) for both **NIKE** and **Reebok** follow:

NIKE Reebok

Key Figures	NIKE	Reebok	Key Figures	NIKE	Reebok
Cash and equivalents	$ 108.6	$ 209.8	Income taxes	$ 253.4	$ 12.5
Accounts receivable	1,674.4	561.7	Revenues (Nike)	9,553.1	—
Inventories	1,396.6	563.7	Net sales (Reebok)	—	3,643.6
Retained earnings	3,043.4	1,145.3	Total assets	5,397.4	1,756.1
Costs of sales	6,065.5	2,294.0			

Required:

a. Compute common-size percents for both companies using the data provided.

b. Which company incurs a higher percent of their revenues (net sales) in income taxes?

c. Which company retains a higher portion of cumulative net income in the company?

d. Which company has a higher gross margin ratio on sales?

e. Which company holds a higher percent of its total assets as inventory?

CASE 1–3
Comparative Analysis: Credit and Equity Analysis

Two companies competing in the same industry are being evaluated by a bank that can lend money to only one of them. Summary information from the financial statements of the two companies follows:

	Datatech Company	Sigma Company		Datatech Company	Sigma Company
Data from the current year-end balance sheet:			Data from the current year's income statement:		
Assets			Sales	$660,000	$780,200
Cash	$ 18,500	$ 33,000	Cost of goods sold	485,100	532,500
Accounts receivable, net	36,400	56,400	Interest expense	6,900	11,000
Notes receivable (trade)	8,100	6,200	Income tax expense	12,800	19,300
Merchandise inventory	83,440	131,500	Net income	67,770	105,000
Prepaid expenses	4,000	5,950	Basic earnings per share	1.94	2.56
Plant and equipment, net	284,000	303,400			
Total assets	$434,440	$536,450			

	Datatech Company	Sigma Company
Liabilities and Stockholders' Equity		
Current liabilities	$ 60,340	$ 92,300
Long-term notes payable	79,800	100,000
Common stock, $5 par value	175,000	205,000
Retained earnings	119,300	139,150
Total liabilities and equity	$434,440	$536,450

	Datatech Company	Sigma Company
Beginning-of-year data:		
Accounts receivable, net	$ 28,800	$ 53,200
Notes receivable (trade)	0	0
Merchandise inventory	54,600	106,400
Total assets	388,000	372,500
Common stock, $5 par value	175,000	205,000
Retained earnings	94,300	90,600

Required:

a. Compute the current ratio, acid-test ratio, accounts (including notes) receivable turnover, inventory turnover, days' sales in inventory, and days' sales in receivables for both companies. Identify the company that you consider to be the better short-term credit risk and explain why.

CHECK
Accounts receivable turnover, Sigma, 13.5 times

b. Compute the net profit margin, total asset turnover, return on total assets, and return on common stockholders' equity for both companies. Assuming that each company paid cash dividends of $1.50 per share and each company's stock can be purchased at $25 per share, compute their price-earnings ratios and dividend yields. Identify which company's stock you would recommend as the better investment and explain why.

CASE 1–4
Business Decisions Using Financial Ratios

Jose Sanchez owns and operates Western Gear, a small merchandiser in outdoor recreational equipment. You are hired to review the three most recent years of operations for Western Gear. Your financial statement analysis reveals the following results:

	2003	2002	2001
Sales index-number trend	137.0	125.0	100.0
Selling expenses to net sales	9.8%	13.7%	15.3%
Sales to plant assets	3.5 to 1	3.3 to 1	3.0 to 1
Current ratio	2.6 to 1	2.4 to 1	2.1 to 1
Acid-test ratio	0.8 to 1	1.1 to 1	1.2 to 1
Merchandise inventory turnover	7.5 times	8.7 times	9.9 times
Accounts receivable turnover	6.7 times	7.4 times	8.2 times
Total asset turnover	2.6 times	2.6 times	3.0 times
Return on total assets	8.8%	9.4%	10.1%
Return on owner's equity	9.75%	11.50%	12.25%
Net profit margin	3.3%	3.5%	3.7%

Required:

Use these data to answer each of the following questions with explanations:

a. Is it becoming easier for the company to meet its current debts on time and to take advantage of cash discounts?

b. Is the company collecting its accounts receivable more rapidly over time?

c. Is the company's investment in accounts receivable decreasing?

d. Are dollars invested in inventory increasing?

CHECK
Plant assets are increasing

e. Is the company's investment in plant assets increasing?

f. Is the owner's investment becoming more profitable?

g. Is the company using its assets efficiently?

h. Did the dollar amount of selling expenses decrease during the three-year period?

CASE 1–5
Comparative Financial Statement Ratio Analysis

Quaker Oats Company

Refer to **Quaker Oats Company's** financial statements in Appendix A.

Required:

a. Compute the following ratios for both Year 11 and Year 10.

Liquidity ratios:
- Current ratio
- Acid-test ratio
- Days to sell inventory
- Collection period

Capital structure and solvency ratios:
- Total debt to total equity
- Long-term debt to equity
- Times interest earned

Return on investment ratios:
- Return on total assets
- Return on common equity

Operating performance ratios:
- Gross profit margin ratio
- Operating profits margin ratio
- Pretax profit margin ratio
- Net profit margin ratio

Asset utilization ratios:*
- Cash turnover
- Accounts receivable turnover
- Sales to inventories
- Working capital turnover
- Fixed assets turnover
- Total assets turnover

Market measures (Quaker's stock prices per share are 56½ and 52½ for Years 10 and 11, respectively):
- Price-to-earnings ratio
- Earnings yield
- Dividend yield
- Dividend payout rate
- Price-to-book ratio

* *For simplicity in computing utilization ratios, use end-of-year values and not average values.*

CHECK
ROI rates improve

b. Comment on and interpret any significant year-to-year changes identified in part *a.*

CASE 1–6
Describe and Interpret Business Activities

Explain and interpret the major business activities–namely, planning, financing, investing, and operating. Aim your report at a general audience such as shareholders and employees. Include concrete examples for each of the business activities.

CASE 1–7
Equity Valuation

You are an analyst and investment advisor for a pension fund. You are reviewing Chatsworth Co. as a potential stock to include in the fund's equity portfolio. Chatsworth is a regional supermarket chain and exhibits growth in both earnings and cash flows. The company is making considerable capital investments, both by acquiring smaller supermarkets and opening new stores. The company pays regular dividends, and its stock traded between $22 and $24 per share in the past quarter. At these prices, the company's price-to-earnings and price-to-book ratios are about 15 and 1.9, respectively–both slightly lower than industry norms. After analyzing the company's business prospects and financial statements, you prepare forecasted financial statements for a five-year horizon. Selected forecasts are shown here:

	Actual	FORECAST				
($ per share)	Year 0	Year 1	Year 2	Year 3	Year 4	Year 5
Operating cash flows	$ 1.87	$ 2.00	$ 2.25	$ 2.50	$ 3.25	$ 3.50
Capital expenditures	1.02	1.00	1.00	2.00	2.00	2.50
Net income	1.39	1.45	1.45	1.50	2.30	2.60
Book value	11.00	11.95	12.90	13.80	15.50	17.40
Dividends	0.50	0.50	0.50	0.60	0.60	0.70
Stock price	23.50					

You find it difficult to speculate about the prospects of the company beyond the five-year horizon. While you expect moderate earnings and cash flow growth of around 4 percent thereafter, you consider this long-term expectation unreliable. You are more inclined to examine alternative growth assumptions as sensitivity analyses. You estimate the cost of capital of Chatsworth at 10 percent per annum.

Required:

a. Compute the intrinsic value per share using the dividend discount model, free cash flow to equity model, and residual income model at the end of Year 0. To determine terminal value, take the last year's forecast of the relevant variable (either dividend, free cash flow to equity, or residual income) and project it indefinitely using an assumed growth rate of (1) zero, (2) 4 percent, and (3) 7 percent.

CHECK
Value using RI and 4% growth, $23.24

b. What is your investment recommendation? Explain.

c. Which valuation model (dividend discount, free cash flow to equity, or residual income) do you recommend? Explain.

CASE 1–8
Ethics Challenge

As controller of Tallman Company, you are responsible for keeping the board of directors informed about the company's financial activities. At the recent board meeting, you presented the following financial data:

	2003	2002	2001
Sales trend percent	147.0%	135.0%	100.0%
Selling expenses to net sales	10.1%	14.0%	15.6%
Sales to plant assets	3.8 to 1	3.6 to 1	3.3 to 1
Current ratio	2.9 to 1	2.7 to 1	2.4 to 1
Acid-test ratio	1.1 to 1	1.4 to 1	1.5 to 1
Merchandise inventory turnover	7.8 times	9.0 times	10.2 times
Accounts receivable turnover	7.0 times	7.7 times	8.5 times
Total asset turnover	2.9 times	2.9 times	3.3 times
Return on total assets	9.1%	9.7%	10.4%
Return on stockholders' equity	9.75%	11.50%	12.25%
Profit margin	3.6%	3.8%	4.0%

After the meeting, the company's CEO held a press conference with analysts in which she mentions the following ratios:

	2003	2002	2001
Sales trend percent	147.0%	135.0%	100.0%
Selling expenses to net sales	10.1%	14.0%	15.6%
Sales to plant assets	3.8 to 1	3.6 to 1	3.3 to 1
Current ratio	2.9 to 1	2.7 to 1	2.4 to 1

Required:

a. Why do you think the CEO decided to report these 4 ratios instead of the 11 ratios that you prepared?

b. Comment on the possible consequences of the CEO's reporting decision.

WEB ACTIVITIES

The Web Activities are located on the book's website at www.mhhe.com/wild8e.

2

FINANCIAL REPORTING AND ANALYSIS

A LOOK BACK

We began our study of financial statement analysis with an overview in Chapter 1. We saw how financial statements reflect business activities—financing, investing, and operating activities. We also performed a preliminary analysis of Kodak.

A LOOK AT THIS CHAPTER

This chapter focuses on financial reporting and its analysis. We describe the financial reporting environment, including the principles underlying accounting standards. The advantages and disadvantages of accrual versus cash flow measures are discussed. We also explain the need for accounting analysis and introduce its techniques.

A LOOK AHEAD

Chapters 3 through 6 of this book are devoted to accounting analysis. Chapter 3 focuses on financing activities. Chapters 4 and 5 extend this to investing activities. Each of these chapters describes adjustments of accounting numbers that are useful for financial statement analysis.

ANALYSIS OBJECTIVES

- Explain the financial reporting and analysis environment.
- Identify what constitutes generally accepted accounting principles (GAAP).
- Describe the objectives of financial accounting and identify primary and secondary qualities of accounting information.
- Define principles and conventions that determine accounting rules.
- Describe the relevance of accounting information to business analysis and valuation.
- Identify limitations of accounting data and their importance for financial statement analysis.
- Explain the importance of accrual accounting and its advantages and limitations.
- Describe the need for and techniques of accounting analysis.
- Explain the relevance of auditing and the audit report (opinion) for financial statement analysis (Appendix 2A).
- Analyze and measure earnings quality and its determinants (Appendix 2B).

Cash Is King . . . without Clothes

Bentonville, AR–There is a children's fable about the king who was deceived into believing he wore clothes made of special fabric when in actuality he was naked. All of his subjects were afraid to tell him and, instead, praised the king on his magnificent clothes. All, that is, except a child who dared to speak the truth. The king was quick to recognize the reality of the child's words and, eventually, rewarded him handsomely.

Cash is the king–without clothes (accruals)–in this children's fable. Information users know cash alone is incomplete, but many too often mindlessly act as if it is sufficient. Just as the dressing of robes, crown, and staff better reflects the reality of the king, so does the dressing of accruals better reflect the reality of a company's financial position and performance. Yet, we too often witness the naive use of accruals. Accounting analysis overcomes this failing. As with the king, if the clothes of accruals fail to reflect reality, the aim of accounting analysis is to adjust those clothes to better reflect reality.

> **. . . cash and accruals play supporting roles . . .**

The upshot is that neither cash nor accruals is king. Instead, both cash and accruals play supporting roles, where adjusted or recasted information from accounting and financial analyses plays the lead role. As in the fable, recognition of this reality is richly rewarded.

This chapter takes data from two retailers, Wal-Mart [**www.Wal-Mart.com**] and Kmart [**www.Kmart.com**], to explore the relative importance of cash and accruals in explaining stock prices. Findings show the power of accrual income in explaining stock prices. We also link the relative explanatory power of cash and income to a company's life cycle. This linkage highlights different roles that each play at different times. This knowledge provides an advantage in analyzing and interpreting information for business decisions. We must learn from the king in the fable and not be deceived into believing cash or income is an all-encompassing, idyllic measure of financial performance. Otherwise, we are destined to be caught with our pants down.

Sources: Wal-Mart website, May 2003, and Kmart website, May 2003

PREVIEW OF CHAPTER 2

Chapter 1 introduced financial statements and discussed their importance for business analysis. Financial statements are the products of a financial reporting process governed by accounting rules and standards, managerial incentives, and enforcement and monitoring mechanisms. It is important for us to understand the financial reporting environment along with the objectives and concepts underlying

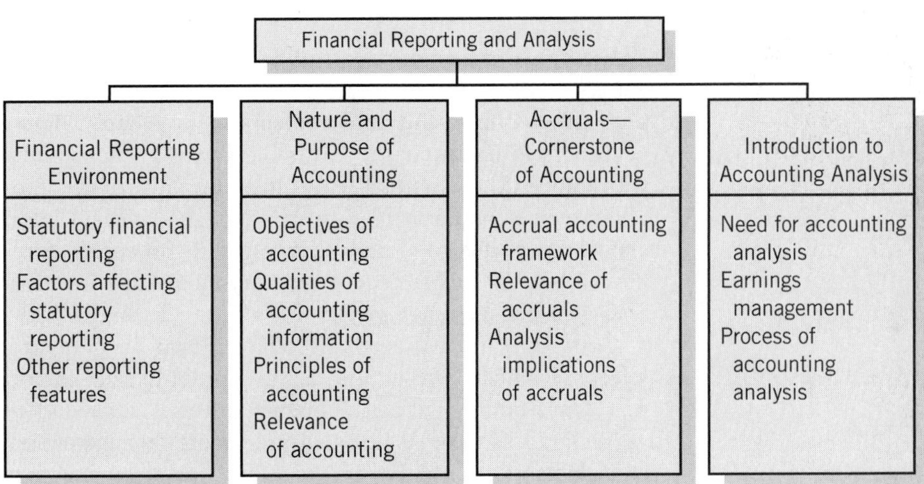

the accounting information presented in financial statements. This knowledge enables us to better infer the reality of a company's financial position and performance. In this chapter we discuss the concepts underlying financial reporting, with special emphasis on accounting rules. We begin by describing the financial reporting environment. Then we discuss the purpose of financial reporting–its objectives and how these objectives determine both the quality of the accounting information and the principles and conventions that underlie accounting rules. We also examine the relevance of accounting information for business analysis and valuation, and we identify limitations of accounting information. We conclude with a discussion of accruals–the cornerstone of modern accounting. This includes an appraisal of accrual accounting in comparison with cash flow accounting and the implications for financial statement analysis.

FINANCIAL REPORTING ENVIRONMENT

Statutory financial reports–primarily the financial statements–are the most important product of the financial reporting environment. Information in financial statements is judged relative to (1) the information needs of financial statement users and (2) alternative sources of information such as economic and industry data, analyst reports, and voluntary disclosures by managers. It is important to understand the factors that affect the nature and content of financial reports to appreciate the financial accounting information reported in them. The primary factors are *accounting rules* (GAAP), *manager motivations, monitoring and enforcement mechanisms, regulators, industry practices,* and *other information sources.* We examine these and other components of the financial reporting environment in this section.

Statutory Financial Reports

Statutory financial reports are the most important part of the financial reporting process. While we are familiar with financial statements–especially the annual report–there are other important statutory financial reports that an analyst needs to review. We examine three categories of these reports in this section: financial statements, earnings announcements, and other statutory reports.

Financial Statements

We described the components of an annual report in Chapter 1. Strictly speaking, the annual report is not a statutory document. It often serves to publicize a company's products, services, and achievements to its shareholders and others. The statutory equivalent to the annual report is the **Form 10-K**, which public companies must file with the SEC. The annual report includes most of the information in the Form 10-K. Still, because the Form 10-K usually contains relevant information beyond that in the annual report, it is good practice to regularly procure a copy of it. Both current and past Form 10-Ks–as well as other regulatory filings–are downloadable from EDGAR at the SEC website [**www.sec.gov**].

Companies are also required to file a **Form 10-Q** quarterly with the SEC to report selected financial information. It is important to refer to Form 10-Q for *timely* information. Unfortunately, most companies release very condensed quarterly information, which limits its value. When analyzing quarterly information, we need to recognize two crucial factors:

1. **Seasonality.** When examining trends, we must consider effects of *seasonality.* For example, retail companies make much of their revenues and profits in the

fourth quarter of the calendar year. This means analysts often make comparisons with the same quarter of the prior year. However, these comparisons are imperfect, as research shows that quarterly numbers (in particular, earnings) are correlated with the preceding quarters as well as with the same quarter of the prior year.

2. **Year-end adjustments.** Companies often make adjustments (for example, inventory write-offs) in the final quarter. Many of these adjustments relate to the entire year. This renders quarterly information less reliable for analysis purposes.

Earnings Announcements

Annual and quarterly financial statements are made available to the public only after the financial statements are prepared and audited. This time lag usually spans one to six weeks. Yet, companies almost always release key summary information to the public earlier through an **earnings announcement.** An earnings announcement is made available to traders on the stock exchange through the broad tape and is often reported in the financial press such as *The Wall Street Journal.* Earnings announcements provide key summary information about company position and performance for both quarterly and annual periods.

While financial statements provide detailed information that is useful in analysis, research shows that much of the immediate stock price reaction to quarterly financial information (at least earnings) occurs on the day of the earnings announcement instead of when the full financial statements are released. This means an investor is unlikely to profit by using summary information that was previously released. The detailed information in financial statements can be analyzed to provide insights about a company's performance and future prospects that are not available from summary information in earnings announcements.

Recently, companies have focused investors' attention on **pro forma earnings** in their earnings announcements. Beginning with GAAP income from continuing operations (excluding discontinued operations, extraordinary items, and changes in accounting principle), the additional transitory items (most notably, restructuring charges) remaining in income from continuing operations are now routinely excluded in computing pro forma income. In addition, companies are also excluding expenses arising from acquisitions, compensation expense in the form of stock options, income (losses) from equity method investees, research and development expenditures, and others. Companies view the objective of this reformulation as providing the analyst community with an earnings figure closer to "core" earnings, purged of transitory and nonoperating charges, which should have the highest relevance for determining stock price.

Significant differences between GAAP and pro forma earnings are not uncommon. For example, the Associated Press recently analyzed earnings reports of the 100 largest technology companies in northern California. The wire service calculated that, under GAAP standards, the 100 companies have reported combined losses of around $71 billion. Using pro forma figures, however, these same companies reported a profit of $10 billion. (Source: **http://www.CFO.com**, 10/02/01)

It is generally acknowledged that additional disclosures by management can help investors understand the core drivers of shareholder value. These provide insight into the way companies analyze themselves and can be useful in identifying trends and predicting future operating results. The general effect of pro forma earnings is purportedly to eliminate transitory items to enhance year-to-year comparability. Although this might be justified on the basis that the resulting earnings have greater predictive ability, important information has been lost in the process. Accounting is beneficial in reporting how effective management has been in its stewardship of invested capital. Asset write-offs, liability accruals, and other charges that are eliminated in this process may

AUDIT PRESS

A recent survey of CFOs found that auditors challenged the company's financial results in less than 40% of audits. Of the CFOs challenged, most refused to back down—specifically, 25% persuaded the auditor to agree to the practice in question, and 32% convinced the auditor that the results were immaterial. Only 43% made changes to win the auditor's approval.

EARLY BIRDS

More companies are issuing a warning or *earnings preannouncement* to avoid nasty negative surprises when they report bad-news earnings.

reflect the outcomes of poor investment decisions or poor management of corporate invested capital. Investors should not blindly eliminate the information contained in nonrecurring, or "noncore," items by focusing solely on pro forma earnings. A systematic definition of operating earnings and a standard income statement format might offer helpful clarification, but it could not be a substitute for the due diligence and thorough examination of the footnotes that constitute comprehensive financial statement analysis.

Other Statutory Reports

Beyond the financial statements, companies must file other reports with the SEC. Some of the more important reports are the **proxy statement,** which must be sent along with the notice of the annual shareholders' meeting; **Form 8-K,** which must be filed to report unusual circumstances such as an auditor change; and the **prospectus,** which must accompany an application for an equity offering. Exhibit 2.1 lists many of the key statutory reports and their content.

Exhibit 2.1 ***Key SEC Filings***

Title	Description	Important Contents from Analysis Perspective
Form 10-K	Annual report	Audited annual financial statements and management discussion and analysis.
Form 10-Q	Quarterly report	Quarterly financial statements and management discussion and analysis.
Form 20-F	Registration statement or annual report by foreign issuers	Reconciliation of reports using non-U.S. GAAP to one using U.S. GAAP.
Form 8-K	Current report	Report filed within 15 days of the following events: (1) change in management control; (2) acquisition or disposition of major assets; (3) bankruptcy or receivership; (4) auditor change; (5) director resignation.
Regulation 14-A	Proxy statement	Details of board of directors, managerial ownership, managerial remuneration, and employee stock options.
	Prospectus	Audited financial statements, information about proposed project or share issue.

Factors Affecting Statutory Financial Reports

The main component of financial statements (and many other statutory reports) is financial accounting information. While much of financial accounting information is determined by GAAP, other determinants are preparers (managers) and the monitoring and enforcement mechanisms that ensure its quality and integrity.

Generally Accepted Accounting Principles (GAAP)

Financial statements are prepared in accordance with **GAAP,** which are the rules and guidelines of financial accounting. These rules determine measurement and recognition policies such as how assets are measured, when liabilities are incurred, when revenues and gains are recognized, and when expenses and losses are incurred. They also dictate what information must be provided in the notes. Knowledge of these accounting principles is essential for effective financial statement analysis.

GAAP Defined. GAAP are a collection of standards, pronouncements, opinions, interpretations, and practice guidelines. Various professional and quasistatutory bodies such as the Financial Accounting Standards Board (FASB), the SEC, and the American Institute of Certified Public Accountants (AICPA) set GAAP. From an analysis viewpoint, the most important types of accounting rules and guidelines are:

- *Statements of Financial Accounting Standards (SFAS)*. *Statements of Financial Accounting Standards* are the most authoritative. These rules and interpretations are issued by the FASB after a due process and are the accounting equivalent of a law. Once an *SFAS* is issued on a topic, it overrules any earlier accounting rule or practice on that topic.
- *APB Opinions.* The predecessor to the FASB is the Accounting Principles Board (APB). The APB issued a number of rules and guidelines called *APB Opinions. APB Opinions* continue to serve the role of a standard unless superseded by a subsequent FASB pronouncement.
- *Accounting Research Bulletins (ARB)*. *ARBs* predate *APB Opinions.* Most *ARBs* have been superseded by later standards, but a few still constitute authoritative rules on certain matters.
- *AICPA pronouncements.* AICPA plays a largely advisory role in standard setting. However, the AICPA issues guidelines for certain topics yet to be addressed by the FASB in its *Statements of Position (SOP)* or for those involving industry-specific matters in its *Industry Audit and Accounting Guidelines.*
- *EITF Bulletins. EITF Bulletins* are issued by the FASB's Emerging Issues Task Force. These bulletins deal with emerging issues on the FASB's agenda for future standards. The EITF bulletins are useful for an analyst as they provide clues to current limitations in statutory reports.
- Industry practices. Industry practices often determine acceptable accounting. From an analyst's viewpoint, industry practices serve as a benchmark to evaluate the degree of conservatism or aggressiveness of a company's accounting.

Setting Accounting Standards. Standard setting in the U.S. (unlike many other nations) is mainly the responsibility of the private sector, with close ties to the accounting profession. The FASB currently serves as the standard-setting body in accounting. It consists of seven full-time paid members, who represent various *interest groups* such as investors, managers, accountants, and analysts. Before issuing a standard, the FASB issues, in most cases, a discussion memorandum for public comment. Written comments are filed with the board, and oral comments can be voiced at public hearings that generally precede the issuance of an *Exposure Draft* of the proposed standard. After further exposure and comment, the FASB usually issues a final version of an *SFAS.* It also sometimes issues interpretations of pronouncements.

FASB RAP
The rap on FASB from business includes (1) too many costly rule changes, (2) unrealistic and confusing rules, (3) bias toward investors, not companies, and (4) resistance to global standards.

Standard setting by the FASB is a political process, with increasing participation by financial statement users. While logical reasoning and empirical research play a part in setting standards, a final standard is the product of the political process. Different groups lobby to protect their interests. It is hoped that this process allows the FASB to better balance costs and benefits of proposed standards. Still, from an analysis viewpoint, this political process often results in standards that are compromise solutions that fall short of requiring the most relevant information. Controversy surrounding executive stock options (ESOs) is a case in point. Even after the FASB voted to include the cost of ESOs in reported earnings, fierce lobbying by Silicon Valley companies forced the FASB to retreat. It eventually issued a watered-down standard (*SFAS 123*) that failed to require companies to recognize the cost of options in earnings. Instead, companies are allowed to bury this expense in notes to the financial statements.

CHIEF PAY
The annual salary of an FASB member exceeds $425,000.

SHAME ON SEC
In his firm's proxy, Warren Buffett writes: "The SEC should be shamed by the fact that they have long let themselves be muscled by business executives."

Role of the Securities and Exchange Commission. The SEC is an independent, quasi-judicial government agency that administers the Securities Acts of 1933 and 1934. These acts pertain to disclosures related to public security offerings. The SEC plays a crucial role both in regulating information disclosure by companies with publicly traded securities and in monitoring and enforcing compliance with accepted practices.

The SEC can override, modify, or introduce accounting reporting and disclosure requirements. It can be viewed as the final authority on financial reporting. However, the SEC respects the accounting profession and understands the difficulties in developing accepted accounting standards. Consequently, it has rarely used its regulatory authority, but has become increasingly aggressive in modifying FASB standards. Current public attitudes toward, and confidence in, financial reporting in large part determine the SEC involvement in accounting practice. SEC involvement is also affected by the aggressiveness of its chief accountant.

FOREIGN GAINS
The NYSE chairman predicts a 20 percent increase in NYSE capitalization—more than $2 trillion—if the SEC allows the listing of foreign companies using IAS.

International Accounting Standards. International Accounting Standards (IAS) are formulated by the International Accounting Standards Board, which is a body representing accountants and other interested parties from different countries. While the IAS are currently not applicable in the U.S.–for example, foreign companies listed on U.S. exchanges need to reconcile IAS-based numbers with U.S. GAAP–there is mounting pressure on the SEC to accept these standards in one form or another. We need to be aware of the growing influence of the IAS outside the U.S. and the possibility that soon these standards may be acceptable in the U.S.

Managers

Primary responsibility for fair and accurate financial reporting rests with managers. Managers have ultimate control over the integrity of the accounting system and the financial records that make up financial statements. We know judgment is necessary in determining financial statement numbers. While accounting standards reduce subjectivity and arbitrariness in these judgments, they do not eliminate it. The exercise of managerial judgment arises both because accounting standards often allow managers to choose among alternative accounting methods and because of the estimation involved in arriving at accounting numbers.

Judgment in financial accounting involves *managerial discretion.* Ideally, this discretion improves the economic content of accounting numbers by allowing managers to exercise their skilled judgment and to communicate their private information through their accounting choices and estimates. For example, a manager could decrease the allowance for bad debts based on inside information such as the improved financial status of a major customer. Still, in practice, too many managers abuse this discretion to manage earnings and window-dress financial statements. This *earnings management* can reduce the economic content of financial statements and can reduce confidence in the reporting process. Identifying earnings management and making proper adjustments to reported numbers are important tasks in financial statement analysis.

RISKY MANAGERS
An executive-search firm conducted profiles of more than 1,400 managers of large companies. The results indicated that one out of eight execs can be termed *high-risk*—they believe the rules do not apply to them, lack concern for others, and rarely possess feelings of guilt. (*Business Week,* August 26, 2002.)

Managers also can indirectly affect financial reports through their collective influence on the standard-setting process. As evident from the ESO situation, managers are a powerful force in determining accounting standards. Managers also provide a balancing force to the demands of users in standard setting. While users focus on the benefits of a new standard or disclosure, managers focus on its costs. Typically, managers oppose a standard that: (1) decreases reported earnings; (2) increases earnings volatility; or (3) discloses competitive information about segments, products, or plans.

Monitoring and Enforcement Mechanisms

Monitoring and enforcement mechanisms ensure the reliability and integrity of financial reports. Some of these, such as the SEC, are set by fiat. Other mechanisms, such as auditing, evolved over time. The importance of these mechanisms for the credibility and survival of financial reporting cannot be overemphasized.

Securities and Exchange Commission. The SEC plays an active role in monitoring and enforcing accounting standards. All public companies must file audited financial statements (10-Ks and 10-Qs) with the SEC. The SEC staff checks these reports to ensure compliance with statutory requirements, including adherence to accounting standards. While a clean audit report is a sign of confidence in financial statements, auditors make mistakes. The SEC has brought enforcement actions against hundreds of companies over the years for accounting violations, despite a clean audit report. These violations range from misinterpretation of standards to outright fraud and falsification of accounts. Enforcement actions against companies and their managers range from restatement of financial statements to fines and imprisonment. Recently, the SEC has been actively attempting to curb earnings management.

An analyst needs to investigate whether the company has a history of problems with the SEC. Any enforcement actions or restatements of numbers can reveal a managerial propensity towards aggressive or misleading reports. This must be considered, especially when we evaluate earnings quality.

HOT SEAT
It's been a difficult period for auditor PricewaterhouseCoopers and its clients—some examples: Tyco International Ltd.'s CEO Dennis Kozlowski and CFO Mark Swartz allegedly looted $600 million from the company. Software maker MicroStrategy settled an SEC suit alleging it had violated accounting rules and overstated its results. Telecom giant Lucent Technologies has been under scrutiny for its accounting practices.

Auditors. External auditing is an important mechanism to help ensure the quality and reliability of financial statements. All public companies' financial statements must be audited by an independent certified public accountant (CPA). The product of an audit is the auditor's report, which is an integral part of financial statements. The centerpiece of an audit report is the **audit opinion.** An auditor can (1) issue a clean opinion, (2) issue one or more types of qualified opinions, or (3) disclaim expressing any opinion.

Analysis of audit reports is an important part of financial statement analysis. The analyst should examine the audit history, including all auditor changes. The 8-K forms–required filing by the SEC whenever an auditor is changed–provides some information on reasons for such changes. An auditor change due to auditor resignation or a disagreement between the auditor and the company often indicates accounting problems. An analyst also should investigate whether the auditor is engaged in providing consulting services for the company. While most auditors do provide some consulting services, an auditor's independence can be compromised if consulting services are substantial. Indeed, consulting revenues often substantially exceed audit fees.

ANALYSIS VIEWPOINT ***. . . YOU ARE THE AUDITOR***

Your audit firm accepts a new audit engagement. How can you use financial statement analysis in the audit of this new client?

Answer–p. 106

TWISTED BOARDS
Some boards don't get it. After all the recent concern with corporate governance, the board of Conseco—the financial services giant—gave an $8 million bonus to CEO Gary Wendt even though he presided over only one profitable quarter in the previous two years.

Corporate Governance. Another important monitor of financial reports is corporate governance mechanisms within a company. Financial statements need approval by a company's *board of directors*. Many companies appoint an *audit committee*–a subcommittee of the board–to oversee the financial reporting process. An audit committee is appointed by the board and is represented by both managers and outsiders. Audit committees are often entrusted with wide-ranging powers and responsibilities relating to many aspects of the reporting process. This includes oversight of accounting methods, internal control procedures, and internal audits. Many believe that an independent and powerful audit committee is a crucial corporate governance feature that contributes

TOP BOARDS
Attributes of a good board include:
Independence—CEO cronies are out. Eliminate insiders and cross-directorships.
Quality—Meetings include real, open debate. Appoint directors familiar with managers and the business.
Accountability—Directors hold stakes in the company and are willing to challenge the CEO.

substantially to the quality of financial reports. An analyst needs to investigate whether an audit committee exists, what its composition is, how qualified its members are, how sufficient its representation of outsiders is, and what its powers and responsibilities are. Most companies also perform *internal audits*, which are another defense against fraud and misrepresentation of financial records.

An analyst needs to learn of the corporate governance mechanisms in place. Poor corporate governance suggests the possibility of poor earnings and accounting quality.

Litigation. Another important monitor of managers (and auditors) is the threat of litigation. The amount of damages relating to accounting irregularities paid by companies, managers, and auditors in the past decade is estimated in the billions of dollars. The threat of litigation influences managers to adopt more responsible reporting practices both for statutory and voluntary disclosures.

ANALYSIS VIEWPOINT ***. . . YOU ARE THE DIRECTOR***

You are named a director of a major company. Your lawyer warns you about litigation risk and the need to constantly monitor both management and the financial health of the company. How can financial statement analysis assist you in performing your director duties?

Answer–p. 106

Alternative Information Sources

Financial statements have long been regarded as a major source of information for users. However, financial statements increasingly compete with alternative sources of information. One major source of alternative information is analysts' forecasts and recommendations. Another source is economic, industry, and company-specific news. With continued development of the Internet, information availability for investors will increase. In this section we discuss some of the major alternative information sources: (1) economy, industry, and company news; (2) voluntary disclosures; and (3) information intermediaries (analysts).

Economic, Industry, and Company Information. Investors use economic and industry information to update company forecasts. Examples of macroeconomic news that affects the entire stock market include data on economic growth, employment, foreign trade, interest rates, and currency exchanges. The effects of economic information vary across industries and companies based on the perceived exposure of an industry's or a company's profits and risks to that news. Investors also respond to industry news such as commodity price changes, industry sales data, changes in competitive position, and government regulation. Moreover, company-specific information impacts user behavior–examples are news of acquisitions, divestitures, management changes, and auditor changes.

Stock markets respond almost instantaneously to economic, industry, and company news. After the initial response, there is a period of consolidation, when the impact of the news on company prospects is evaluated. The market reaction often is complete only after the news is fully reported in company earnings announcements and financial statements.

Voluntary Disclosure. Voluntary disclosure by managers is an increasingly important source of information. One important catalyst for voluntary disclosure is the Safe Harbor Rules. Those rules provide legal protection against genuine mistakes by managers who make voluntary disclosures.

There are several motivations for voluntary disclosure. Probably the most important motivation is *legal liability*. Managers who voluntarily disclose important news, especially of an adverse nature, have a lower probability of being sued by investors. Another motivation is that of *expectations adjustment.* It suggests managers have incentives to disclose information when they believe the market's expectations are sufficiently different from their own. Still another motivation is that of *signaling,* where managers are said to disclose good news to increase their company's stock price. A more recent motivation advanced for voluntary disclosures is the intent to *manage expectations.* Specifically, managers are said to manage market expectations of company performance so that they can regularly "beat" market expectations.

Information Intermediaries. Information intermediaries, or analysts, play an important and unique role in financial reporting. On one hand, they represent a sophisticated and active group of users. On the other hand, they constitute the single most important source of alternative information. As such, standard setters usually respond to analysts' demands as well as the threat they pose as a competing source of information.

ANALYST REPORT
Supervisory analysts and compliance officers scour every word of a Wall Street investment research report.

Information intermediaries represent an industry involved in collecting, processing, interpreting, and disseminating information about the financial prospects of companies. This industry includes security analysts, investment newsletters, investment advisers, and debt raters. Security analysts constitute the largest segment of information intermediaries, which include both buy-side analysts and sell-side analysts. Buy-side analysts are usually employed by investment companies or pension funds such as *TIAA-CREF, Vanguard,* or *Fidelity.* These analysts do their analysis for in-house use. Sell-side analysts provide analysis and recommendations to the public for a fee, for example *Value Line* and *Standard & Poors,* or privately to their clients, for example analysts at *Salomon Smith Barney* and *Charles Schwab.* In short, sell-side analysts' reports are used by outsiders while buy-side analysts' reports are used internally. Another large component of information intermediaries includes investment newsletters such as *Dow Theory Forecasts* and *Smart Money.* Credit rating agencies such as Moody's also are information intermediaries whose services are aimed at credit agencies.

ANALYST BIAS?
Evidence is mixed on whether analysts' forecasts tend to overestimate or underestimate earnings. If they overestimate, they risk alienating a company and losing access. If they underestimate, a company comes out looking good.

Information intermediaries are not directly involved in making investment and credit decisions. Instead, their objective is to provide information useful for those decisions. Their outputs, or products, are forecasts, recommendations, and research reports. Their inputs are financial statements, voluntary disclosures, and economic, industry, and company news. Information intermediaries create value by processing and synthesizing raw and diverse information about a company and output it in a form useful for business decisions. They are viewed as performing one or more of at least four functions:

1. **Information gathering.** This involves researching and gathering information about companies that is not readily available. The ability to garner private information about a company often differentiates a good analyst from a mediocre one–whether from company sources or through their own investigations.
2. **Information interpretation.** A crucial task of an intermediary is the interpretation of information in an economically meaningful manner. Analysts must use skills of business and financial statement analysis. An important part of interpretation is the ability to judge the import of economic events not yet reflected in accounting numbers. The output is often an investment research report or commentary.
3. **Prospective analysis.** This is the final and most visible task of an information intermediary–involving both business analysis and financial statement analysis. The output includes earnings and cash flow forecasts and debt ratings.
4. **Recommendation.** Analysts also often make specific recommendations, such as buy/hold/sell recommendations for stocks and bonds.

PHONY INFO
Regulators allege that Merrill Lynch and Citigroup's Smith Barney issued upbeat research to win investment-banking clients. Also under investigation were CSFB and Morgan Stanley.

By providing timely information that is often of a prospective nature and readily amenable to investment decision making, investment intermediaries perform an

EARNINGS SEER
According to a recent study, 1,025 of 6,000 companies beat analysts' earnings forecasts in at least 9 of the past 12 quarters.

important service. Arguably, the growth of information intermediaries has reduced the importance of financial statements to capital markets. Still, information intermediaries depend significantly on financial statements, while at the same time they view financial statements as a competing information source.

Given their unique role in the financial reporting environment, information intermediaries markedly influence the development of accounting standards as follows:

- Intermediaries are regarded as reflective of the investing community. This means standard setters look to them for feedback on accounting methods and disclosures.
- Intermediaries contribute to increased complexity in financial statements. Recent standards, such as those involving pensions and foreign currency translation, require disclosures that demand considerable skill and effort (like that provided by analysts) to analyze and interpret.
- Intermediaries increase the tendency to report information in notes rather than convert that information into numbers presented in financial statements. This reflects analysts' preference to estimate the impact of information on firm value using their models, rather than have accountants quantify its impact.

Analysts also attempt to directly influence standard setting, most visibly through the *Association of Investment Management and Research (AIMR)*, an organization for analysts. Their behavior reveals a desire to both enhance and limit the scope of financial statements–that is, analysts favor disclosure of historical information but seek to curtail prospective information that competes with analysts' services.

NATURE AND PURPOSE OF FINANCIAL ACCOUNTING

In this section we discuss the objectives, desirable qualities, principles, and conventions underlying financial accounting. Much of our discussion relies on the FASB's *conceptual framework.* Knowledge of this framework allows us to grasp what financial accounting is seeking to achieve, how it aims to attain these objectives, and how effective it is in achieving its objectives. With this insight, we can evaluate the strengths and weaknesses of accounting and its relevance to effective analysis and decision making.

Objectives of Financial Accounting

Stewardship

The concept of stewardship has dominated financial accounting for years. From this perspective, the manager is a steward entrusted with the responsibility of safeguarding assets, increasing the wealth of equity investors, and protecting creditors. Stewardship is a backward-looking concept, utilizing the balance sheet and the income statement in order to evaluate the extent to which managers have been effective stewards of invested capital. While stewardship remains an important dimension of financial accounting–especially with *contracting* such as in determining manager bonuses and debt covenant provisions–its importance has declined.

Information for Decisions

The shift in accounting to a more practical *information perspective* emphasizes relevant information for business decisions, and increases the emphasis of accounting standards on predictability and decision usefulness rather than on accountability and performance measurement. The idea of providing information to users and allowing them to assess its impact moves standard setting away from measuring the effects of transactions on financial statements (*measurement*) to reporting useful information in notes (*disclosure*). The FASB's information perspective has major implications for financial analysis. First, the emphasis on investment decisions increases the usefulness of financial statements for financial analysis. Second, the shift from measurement to disclosure increases both the need for and scope of the accounting analysis skills of financial statement users.

Desirable Qualities of Accounting Information

Relevance is the capacity of information to affect a decision and is the first of two primary qualities of accounting information. Information can be relevant in two ways. First, information can directly help a decision maker predict future outcomes. Such information is relevant because it has *predictive value*. Second, information can help users confirm or revise beliefs or expectations. Such information is relevant because it has *feedback value*. Also realize that information can have feedback value even when it merely confirms investor's beliefs. Earnings reports often do not deviate substantially from analysts' forecasts. Yet these reports are nearly always relevant because of high credibility. We also must recognize that for information to be relevant it must be reported before it loses its capacity to affect decisions. This implies that *timeliness* is a desirable characteristic of accounting information. Interim (quarterly) financial reports are largely motivated by timeliness.

Reliability is a second important quality of financial information. For information to be reliable it must be verifiable, representationally faithful, and neutral. *Verifiability* means the information is confirmable. *Representational faithfulness* means the information reflects reality, and *neutrality* means it is truthful and unbiased.

Accounting information often demands a trade-off between relevance and reliability. For example, reporting forecasts increase relevance but reduce reliability. Also, while analysts' forecasts are relevant, they are less reliable than actual figures based on historical data. Standard setters often struggle with this trade-off.

Both relevance and reliability, and their inherent trade-offs, are important for analysis. An analyst can be frustrated when financial statement information falls short on one or the other dimension. For example, an analyst may be frustrated with the decreased reliability from estimates of bad debts and their susceptibility to manipulation. However, the reliable alternative is to not make an estimate (or account for sales on a cash basis), which reduces the relevance of this information. Our analysis must sometimes restate reported numbers in financial statements depending on whether the analysis stresses reliability or relevance.

Comparability and consistency are secondary qualities of accounting information. *Comparability* implies that information is measured in a similar manner across companies. *Consistency* implies the same method is used for similar transactions across time. Both comparability and consistency are required for information to be relevant and reliable. Accounting standards encourage comparability in accounting practices. However, the complexity and diversity of business activities make this difficult. An analyst must therefore be careful when making comparisons across companies. Financial statements give details of accounting policies adopted by companies and an analyst can restate numbers to increase comparability. Accounting standards also encourage consistency over time. However, the changing nature of business activities and the financial reporting environment make this difficult. A company that changes an accounting method must disclose the effects of this change on both current and past income–sometimes, the company must restate its income statement for the past three years. Changes in underlying measurement assumptions or estimates are less visible. An analyst must review notes to detect such changes and restate the numbers when appropriate.

Important Principles of Accounting

The desirable qualities of accounting information serve as conceptual criteria for accounting principles. Skillful use of accounting numbers for financial analysis requires an understanding of the accounting framework underlying their computation. This includes the principles governing measurement of assets, liabilities, equity, revenues, expenses, gains, and losses.

Double Entry

The *principle of double entry* governs the recording function. Understanding double-entry accounting aids analysis of financial statements because it helps in reconstructing business transactions. The double-entry system uses the duality of every business transaction. To illustrate, if a company borrows $1,000, it acquires both an asset (cash) and a claim against its assets (a liability) in equal amounts. This duality and balance prevails in all transactions. At all times, a company's assets equal the sum of the claims from its creditors and equity providers (this is the accounting equation discussed in Chapter 1). Under double entry, all transactions are recorded, classified, and summarized using account designations. Financial statements are condensed data outputs derived from these accounts.

Historical Cost

Accounting systems aim to report *fair and objective* information. Since the value of an asset determined through arm's-length bargaining is usually fair and objective, *historical cost* values from actual transactions are commonly reported in financial statements. Accounting practice adheres, with some exceptions, to this concept. Historical cost values enjoy objectivity surpassing any other values. The impact of this objectivity when values subsequently change is to impair the usefulness of financial statements. This is because historical costs do not, in most cases, reflect current values. Yet, users of financial statements desire a balance between objectively determined values and estimates of current values of assets and liabilities. Therefore, while we sometimes adjust historical cost values, we recognize that historical cost values are a compromise between reliability and relevance.

Accrual Accounting

Modern accounting adopts the accrual basis over the more primitive cash flow basis. Under accrual accounting, revenues are recognized when earned and expenses when incurred, regardless of the receipt or payment of cash. The accrual basis is arguably the most important, but also controversial, feature of modern accounting. We focus on accrual accounting later in this chapter.

Full Disclosure

The *full disclosure principle* recognizes that information reported in financial statements reflects a trade-off between providing (1) sufficient detail so that information makes a difference (is relevant) to users and (2) sufficient summarization and simplification so that information is understandable and cost beneficial. To be included in financial statements, an item must be relevant, reliable, and measurable with sufficient certainty. Still, an analyst often desires details of how the numbers are determined. These details are conveyed through disclosure–both in notes and supplementary schedules. The principle of full disclosure is important to financial analysis. There often is a wealth of information available in notes and other schedules that can be used to further understand financial statement numbers and to restate them according to the analysis objectives. This restatement process is the focus of Chapters 3 through 6.

Materiality

Materiality, according to the FASB, is "the magnitude of an omission or misstatement of accounting information that, in the light of surrounding circumstances, makes it possible that the judgment of a reasonable person relying on the information would be changed or influenced by the omission or misstatement." One problem with materiality is a concern that some preparers of financial statements and their auditors use it to avoid unwanted disclosures. This is compounded by the fact there is no set criteria guiding either the preparer or user of information in distinguishing between material and nonmaterial items.

Conservatism

Conservatism involves reporting the least optimistic view when faced with uncertainty in measurement. Conservatism reduces both the reliability and relevance of accounting information in at least two ways. First, conservatism understates both net assets and net income. A second point is that conservatism results in selectively delayed recognition of good news in financial statements, while immediately recognizing bad news. Conservatism has important implications for analysis. If the purpose of analysis is equity valuation, it is important to estimate the conservative bias in financial reports and make suitable adjustments so that net assets and net income are better measured. In the case of credit analysis, conservatism provides an additional margin of safety. Conservatism also is a determinant of earnings quality. While conservative financial statements reduce earnings quality, many users (e.g., Warren Buffett) view conservative accounting as a sign of superior earnings quality. This apparent contradiction is explained by conservative accounting reflecting on the responsibility, dependability, and credibility of management.

TIMING
Recording revenues early inflates short-run sales and earnings. Industries such as software sales and services, where service contracts and upgrades can stretch revenue out for years, are especially vulnerable to manipulation.

Relevance and Limitations of Accounting

Relevance of Financial Accounting Information

Business decisions such as equity investing and extending credit require a variety of data that vary in reliability and relevance. These data include information on economic conditions and industry trends, as well as information on intangibles such as the integrity and motivations of managers. Financial statements are measurable indices of past performance and financial conditions. While the importance of qualitative information vis-à-vis quantified financial statements varies, few users would want to make business decisions without analysis of the quantified financial statements.

Financial statements are important because they are objective and they measure and report on economic consequences of business activities. The attribute of measurability endows financial statements with a special characteristic: common monetary unit. Since activities are expressed in the common denominator of money, we can add and combine data, relate them to other data, and work with them arithmetically.

Accounting for business activities is imperfect and has limitations. It is easy to focus on these imperfections and limitations. However, there is no comparable substitute. Financial accounting is and remains the only relevant and reliable system for recording, classifying, and summarizing business activities. Improvement rests with refinements in this time-tested system. It is incumbent on anyone who desires to perform effective financial analysis to understand accounting, its terminology, and its practices, including its imperfections and limitations.

Analysis of financial statements is a crucial part of most business decisions. Its role varies in any particular case. For example, financial statement analysis of a borrower is

Analysis Research

ACCOUNTING INFORMATION AND STOCK PRICES

Do summary accounting numbers such as earnings (net income) explain a company's stock prices and returns? The answer is yes. Evidence from research shows a definite link between the type of *news* or *surprise* conveyed in earnings and a company's stock returns. Good earnings news (positive surprise) is accompanied by positive stock returns, whereas bad earnings news (negative surprise) is associated with negative returns. The more good or bad the earnings news (i.e., the greater the magnitude of the earnings surprise), the greater is the accompanying stock price reactions.

A substantial portion of the stock returns associated with earnings news occurs prior to the earnings announcement, indicating that the stock market is able to infer much of the earnings news well before it is announced. This evidence suggests that accounting information, to a large extent, plays a *feedback role* wherein it confirms prior beliefs of the market. Interestingly, stock returns after the earnings announcement also appear to be associated with the earnings news. This phenomenon, called the *post-earnings-announcement-drift*, is arguably a form of stock market inefficiency and is exploited by several *momentum* based investing strategies.

Research shows us that many factors influence the relationship between accounting earnings and stock prices. These include company factors such as risk, size, leverage, and variability that decrease the influence of earnings on stock prices, and factors, such as earnings growth and persistence that increase their impact. Our analysis must recognize those influences that impact the relevance of accounting numbers for security analysis.

Research also shows the importance of earnings information to the market has declined over time, especially in the past two decades. Some of the suggested reasons for this decline are increased reporting of losses, increased magnitude of one-time charges and other special items, and increased importance of R&D and intangible assets. However, research reveals that while the ability of earnings to explain prices has declined over time, this has been offset to a large extent by the increasing importance of book value.

an important part of the lending decision since a lender's profit derives from a borrower's ability to pay interest and principal. Financial statement analysis plays a different role in equity investing. An equity investor looks to two sources for profit–dividends and capital appreciation. Dividends depend on profitability, growth, and liquidity–elements assessable with financial statement analysis. Capital appreciation often is the larger profit, which derives from other investors' future demand to pay more for the stock than we did. While the demand of investors depends on earning power and growth, it also can depend on the psychology of the market, the valuation of earnings retained, and other factors such as the return available on alternative investments. Generally, the importance of financial statement analysis for equity investing is greater when market valuations are lower. Its importance also is larger when analysis is directed at risk assessment, the detection of vulnerable areas, defensive investing, and avoidance of losses.

Exactly how relevant is financial accounting information for analysis? One way to answer this question is to examine how well financial accounting numbers reflect or explain stock prices. Exhibit 2.2 tracks the ability of earnings and book value to explain stock prices, both separately and in combination, for a large cross-section of companies over a recent 30-year period. The exhibit shows that earnings and book value (combined) are able to explain between 50 percent and 75 percent of stock price behavior. This occurs even though the analysis stacks the deck against accounting numbers in several ways. First, we do not control for many other factors that affect stock prices such as interest rates. Second, we consider only two summary numbers–arguably the two most important–from the wealth of information available in financial statements. Finally, we impose an identical relation between accounting numbers and stock prices

Relation between Accounting Numbers and Stock Prices* **Exhibit 2.2**

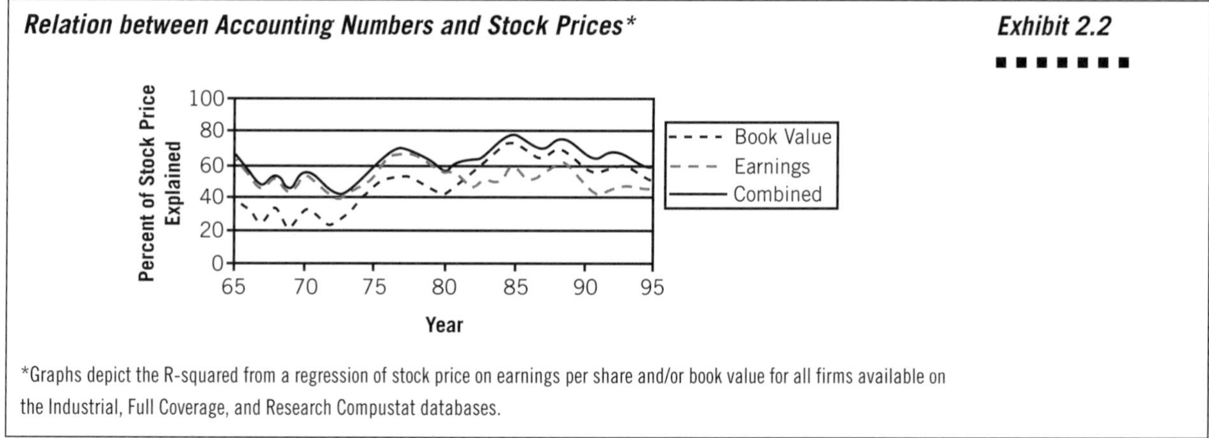

*Graphs depict the R-squared from a regression of stock price on earnings per share and/or book value for all firms available on the Industrial, Full Coverage, and Research Compustat databases.

across all companies–that is, we do not consider differences across companies such as industry effects and expected growth rates.

Exhibit 2.2 does not establish causation. That is, we cannot establish the extent that accounting numbers directly determine stock prices. This is because of the presence of alternative information such as analyst forecasts and economic statistics used in setting stock prices. Still, recall that one element of the relevance of accounting information is feedback value for revising or confirming investor beliefs. At a minimum, this analysis supports the feedback value of accounting information by revealing the strong link between accounting numbers and stock prices.

Limitations of Financial Statement Information

Analyst forecasts, reports, and recommendations along with other alternative information sources are a major competitor for accounting information. What are the advantages offered by these alternative sources? We can identify at least three:

1. **Timeliness.** Financial statements are prepared as often as every quarter and are typically released from three to six weeks after the quarter-end. In contrast, analysts update their forecasts and recommendations on a nearly real-time basis–as soon as information about the company is available to them. Other alternative information sources, such as economic, industry, or company news, are also readily available in many forms including via the Internet.
2. **Frequency.** Closely linked to timeliness is frequency. Financial statements are prepared periodically, typically each quarter. However, alternative information sources, including analysts' reports, are released to the market whenever business events demand their revision.
3. **Forward-looking.** Alternative information sources, particularly analysts' reports and forecasts, use much forward-looking information. Financial statements contain limited forecasts. Further, historical-cost-based accounting (and conservatism) usually yields *recognition lags*, where certain business activities are recorded at a lag. To illustrate, consider a company that signs a long-term contract with a customer. An analyst will estimate the impact of this contract on future earnings and firm value as soon as news about the signing is available. Financial statements only recognize this contract in future periods when the goods or services are delivered.

Despite these drawbacks, financial statements continue to be an important source of information to financial markets.

ACCRUALS—CORNERSTONE OF ACCOUNTING

Financial statements are primarily prepared on an accrual basis. Accounting standards espouse the accrual concept. Supporters strongly believe that accrual accounting is superior to cash accounting, both for measuring performance and financial condition. *Statement of Financial Accounting Concepts No. 1* states that "information about enterprise earnings based on accrual accounting generally provides a better indication of enterprises' present and continuing ability to generate cash flows than information limited to the financial aspects of cash receipts and payments."

Accrual accounting invokes a similarly strong response from its detractors. For detractors, accrual accounting is a medley of complex and imperfect rules that obscure the purpose of financial statements–providing information about cash flows and cash-generating capacity. For extreme critics, accrual accounting is a diversion, a red herring, that undermines the process of information dissemination. These critics claim the purpose of financial analysis is to remove the veil of accrual accounting and get to the underlying cash flows. They are troubled by the intricacy of accruals and their susceptibility to manipulation by managers.

This section presents a critical evaluation of accrual accounting. We discuss the relevance and importance of accruals, their drawbacks and limitations, and the implications of the accruals-versus-cash-flow debate for financial statement analysis. Our aim is not to take sides in this debate. We believe that cash flows and accruals serve different purposes and that both are important for financial analysis. Yet, we caution against a disregard of accruals. It is crucial for an analyst to understand accrual accounting for effective financial analysis.

Accrual Accounting Framework

Accrual Concept

An appealing feature about cash flows is simplicity. Cash flows are easy to understand and straightforward to compute. There also is something tangible and certain about cash flows. They seem like the real thing–not the creation of accounting methods. But unfortunately, when it comes to measuring cash-generating capacity of a company, cash flows are of limited use.

Most business transactions are on credit. Further, companies invest billions of dollars in inventories and long-term assets, the benefits of which occur over many future periods. In these scenarios, cash flow accounting (no matter how reliable it is) fails to provide a relevant picture of a company's financial condition and performance.

Accrual accounting aims to inform users about the consequences of business activities for a company's future cash flows as soon as possible with a reasonable level of certainty. This is achieved by recognizing revenue earned and expenses incurred, regardless of whether or not cash flows occur contemporaneously. This separation of revenue and expense recognition from cash flows is facilitated with *accrual adjustments,* which adjust cash inflows and cash outflows to yield revenues and expenses. Accrual adjustments are recorded after making reasonable assumptions and estimates, without materially sacrificing the reliability of accounting information. Accordingly, judgment is a key part of accrual accounting, and rules and institutional mechanisms exist to ensure reliability.

The next section begins by defining the exact relationship between accruals and cash flows. We show that accrual and cash accounting differ primarily because of timing differences in recognizing cash flow consequences of business activities and events. We then explain the accrual process of revenue and expense recognition and discuss two types of accruals, short term and long term.

Accruals and Cash Flows. To explore the relation between accruals and cash flows, it is important to recognize alternative types of cash flows. *Operating cash flow* refers to cash from a company's ongoing operating activities. *Free cash flow* reflects the added effects of investments and divestments in operating assets. The appeal of free cash flow is that it represents cash that is free to be paid to debt and equity holders. When economists refer to cash flow, they are usually referring to free cash flow, a convention we adopt in this book. Bottom line cash flow is *net cash flow*, which also is the change in the cash account balance (note, cash includes cash equivalents for all these definitions).

Strictly defined, *accruals* are the sum of accounting adjustments that make net income different from net cash flow. These adjustments include those that affect income when there is no cash flow impact (e.g., credit sales) and those that isolate cash flow effects from income (e.g., asset purchases). Because of double entry, accruals affect the balance sheet by either increasing or decreasing asset or liability accounts by an equal amount. Namely, an accrual that increases (decreases) income will also either increase (decrease) an asset or decrease (increase) a liability.

What is included in accruals depends on the definition of cash flow. The most common meaning of accruals is accounting adjustments that convert operating cash flow to net income. This yields the following identity: **Net income = Operating cash flow + Accruals.** Under this definition, accruals are of two types: short-term accruals, which are related to working capital items, and long-term accruals, such as depreciation and amortization. We discuss these two types of accruals later in this chapter. Note that this definition of accruals does not include accruals that arise through the process of capitalization and asset creation.

Accrual Accounting Reduces Timing and Matching Problems. The difference between accrual accounting and cash accounting is one of timing and matching. Accrual accounting overcomes both the timing and the matching problems that are inherent in cash accounting. *Timing* problems refer to cash flows that do not occur contemporaneously with the business activities yielding the cash flows. For example, a sale occurs in the first quarter, but cash from the sale arrives in the second quarter. *Matching* problems refer to cash inflows and cash outflows that occur from a business activity but are not matched in time with each other, such as fees received from consulting that are not linked in time to wages paid to consultants working on the project.

Timing and matching problems with cash flows arise for at least two reasons. First, our credit economy necessitates that transactions, more often than not, do not involve immediate transfer of cash. Credit transactions reduce the ability of cash flows to track business activities in a timely manner. Further, increasing technological and business innovations (such as the Internet and e-commerce) along with more complex credit instruments suggest that credit transactions will continue to grow and fuel this problem. Second, costs often are incurred before their benefits are realized, especially when costs involve investments in plant and equipment. Thus, measuring costs when cash outflows occur often fails to reflect financial condition and performance. This problem is exacerbated by the shift in business toward fixed investments in plant assets, technology, and R&D and away from variable manufacturing costs.

Note that over the life of a company, cash flows and accrual income are equal. This is because once all business activities are concluded, the timing and matching problems are resolved. Yet, as economist John Maynard Keynes once remarked, "In the long run we are all dead." This is meant to stress the importance of measuring financial condition and performance in the short run, typically at periodic points over the life of a company. The shorter these intervals, the more evident are the limitations of cash flow accounting.

Accrual Process—Revenue Recognition and Expense Matching. While accrual accounting impacts the balance sheet and statement of cash flows, it has special importance for the income statement through revenue recognition and expense matching:

1. **Revenue recognition.** Revenues are recognized when both earned and either realized or realizable. Revenues are *earned* when the company delivers its products or services. This means the company has carried out its part of the deal. Revenues are *realized* when cash is acquired for products or services delivered. Revenues are *realizable* when an asset acquired for products or services delivered (often receivables) is convertible to cash or cash equivalents. Deciding when revenues are recognized is sometimes difficult. While revenues are usually recognized at point-of-sale (when delivered), they also can be recognized, depending on the circumstances, when a product or service is being readied, when it is complete, or when cash is received. We further discuss revenue recognition in Chapter 6.
2. **Expense matching.** Accrual accounting dictates that expenses are matched with their corresponding revenues. This matching process is different for two major types of expenses. Expenses that arise in production of a product or service, called *product costs*, are recognized when the product or service is delivered. All product costs are lumped together in *cost of sales* but remain as inventory until matched with revenues. The other type of expenses, called *period costs*, usually are matched with revenues of the period. Some period costs relate to marketing the product or service and are matched with revenues. Other period costs, such as administrative expenses, do not directly relate to production or sale of products or services. They are expensed in the period they occur, which is not necessarily when cash outflows occur. We further discuss matching criteria in Chapter 6.

SALES SCAM
McKesson HBOC's stock price fell by nearly half when it admitted more than $44 million in recorded revenues were not, in fact, realized. One warning sign: Operating cash flow fell early and well below earnings.

Short- and Long-Term Accruals. *Short-term accruals* refer to short-term timing differences between income and cash flow. These accruals generate working capital items in the balance sheet (current assets and current liabilities) and are also called *working capital accruals*. Short-term accruals arise primarily from inventories and credit transactions that give rise to all types of receivables and payables such as trade debtors and creditors, prepaid expenses, and advances received. *Long-term accruals* arise from capitalization. Asset *capitalization* is the process of deferring costs incurred in the current period whose benefits are expected in future periods. This process generates long-term assets such as plant, machinery, and goodwill. Costs of these assets are allocated over their benefit periods and make up a large part of long-term accruals–we provide further discussion in Chapter 4. Accounting for long-term accruals is more complex and subjective than that for short-term accruals (with the possible exception of inventories). Cash flow implications of short-term accruals are more direct and readily determinable. Accordingly, analysis research finds short-term accruals more useful in company valuation. (Dechow, 1994)

Relevance and Limitations of Accrual Accounting

This section gives a critical appraisal of the effects accrual accounting has on financial statements. We then discuss the conceptual and empirical strengths and weaknesses of accrual accounting relative to cash accounting for measuring performance and predicting future cash flows.

Relevance of Accrual Accounting

Conceptual Relevance of Accrual Accounting. The conceptual superiority of accrual accounting over cash flows arises because the accrual-based income statement (and balance sheet) is more relevant for measuring a company's present and future cash-generating capacity. Both short-term and long-term accruals are important for the relevance of income vis-à-vis cash flows as described here:

- **Relevance of short-term accruals.** Short-term accruals improve the relevance of accounting by helping record revenues when earned and expenses when incurred. These accruals yield an income number that better reflects profitability and also creates current assets and current liabilities that provide useful information about financial condition.
- **Relevance of long-term accruals.** To see the import of long-term accruals, note that free cash flow is computed by subtracting investments in long-term operating assets from operating cash flow. Such investments pose problems for free cash flow. First, these investments are usually large and occur infrequently. This induces volatility in free cash flow. Second, free cash flow treats capital growth and capital replacement synonymously. Investments in new projects often bode well for a company and the market usually reacts positively to such capital expenditures. Yet all capital expenditures reduce free cash flow. This problem with free cash flow is evident from typical patterns of operating, investing, and financing cash flows over a company's life cycle as shown in Exhibit 2.3. Investing cash flows are negative until late maturity, and these outflows dominate operating cash inflows during most of the growth phase. This means free cash flow tends to be negative until the company's business matures. In late maturity and decline, a company divests its assets, generating positive investing cash flows and, hence, positive free cash flow. This means free cash flow is negative in the growth stage but positive in the decline stage, sending a *reverse* message about a company's prospects. Operating cash flows are not affected by operating investments as they ignore them.

Cash Flows and Income over a Company's Life Cycle ***Exhibit 2.3***

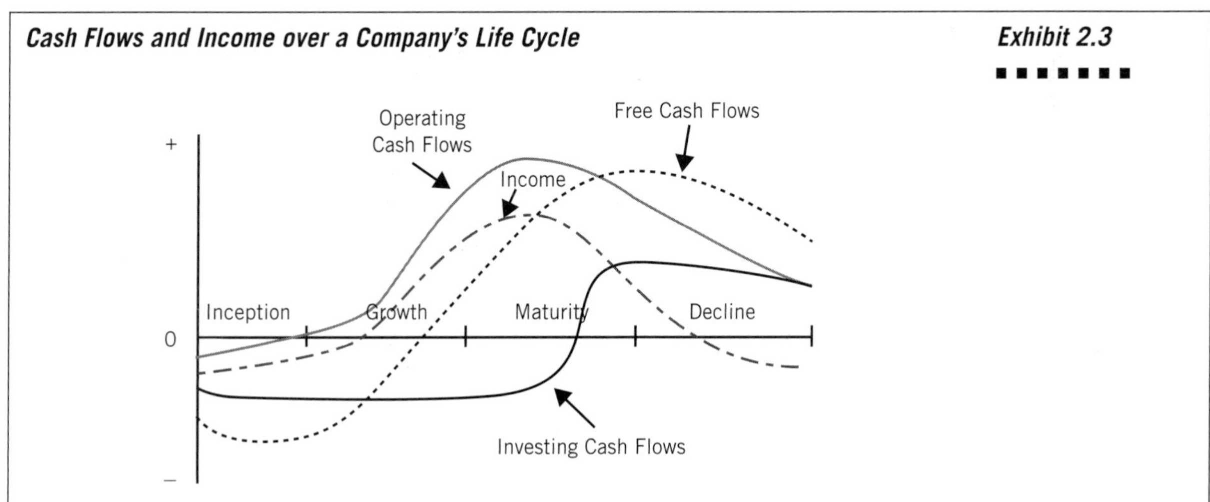

Accrual accounting overcomes these limitations in free cash flow by capitalizing investments in long-term assets and allocating their costs over future benefit periods. This process of capitalization and allocation improves the relevance of income both by reducing its volatility and by matching costs of long-term investments to their benefits. The superiority of accruals in providing relevant information about a company's financial performance and condition, and for predicting future cash flows, is explained as follows:

SALES WATCH
If accounts receivables are rising faster than sales, special scrutiny is warranted.

- **Financial performance.** Revenue recognition and expense matching yields an income number superior to cash flows for evaluating financial performance. Revenue recognition ensures all revenues earned in a period are accounted for. Matching ensures that only expenses attributable to revenues earned in a period are recorded.
- **Financial condition.** An accounting system based on cash flows produces a balance sheet that fails to reflect the financial condition of a company. Accrual accounting produces relevant balance sheet figures.
- **Predicting future cash flows.** Current cash flows are *not* the best predictor of future cash flows. Indeed, accrual income is a superior predictor of future cash flows for at least two reasons. First, through revenue recognition, it reflects future cash flow consequences. For example, a credit sale today forecasts cash to be received from the customer in the future. Second, accrual accounting better aligns inflows and outflows over time through the matching process. This means income is a more stable and dependable predictor of cash flows.

CASH WATCH
A company posting strong income growth but negative or low operating cash flow warrants special scrutiny.

Empirical Relevance of Accrual Accounting. Critics of accrual accounting decry its lower reliability and prefer reliable cash flows. Supporters assert the added relevance of accrual accounting compensates for lower reliability. They also point to institutional mechanisms, such as GAAP and auditing, that ensure at least a minimum acceptable reliability. To see whether accrual accounting works, examine how well accrual income and cash flows measure a company's financial performance.

Consider the two retailers, Wal-Mart and Kmart. Exhibit 2.4 shows split-adjusted per-share stock price, net income, and free cash flow numbers for both companies over the 10-year period 1989-1998. Wal-Mart and Kmart present an interesting contrast for this period. Wal-Mart is a growth company that has seen its market capitalization grow fivefold in this period. Kmart is arguably in decline and has experienced a 60 percent fall in market capitalization from 1994 to 1998. Since 1994, Kmart has struggled to restructure and focus its business, mainly through divesting unprofitable divisions.

Exhibit 2.4

Comparison of Stock Price, Net Income, and Free Cash Flow—Wal-Mart and Kmart

	FISCAL YEAR									
	1989	1990	1991	1992	1993	1994	1995	1996	1997	1998
Wal-Mart										
Stock price	4.22	5.33	8.25	13.47	16.28	13.25	11.44	10.19	11.87	19.91
Net income	0.18	0.24	0.28	0.35	0.44	0.51	0.58	0.60	0.67	0.78
Free cash flow	0.04	(0.01)	(0.05)	(0.17)	(0.48)	(0.50)	(0.19)	(0.21)	0.84	0.60
Kmart										
Stock price	18.94	16.62	15.50	24.50	23.25	19.63	13.63	5.88	11.13	11.00
Net income	2.00	0.81	1.89	2.02	2.07	(2.13)	0.64	(1.24)	(0.45)	0.51
Free cash flow	1.76	(2.26)	0.20	(0.47)	(2.15)	1.29	2.71	0.48	0.61	1.35

All figures are split-adjusted dollars per share from Compustat.

Wal-Mart's income pattern is striking–the company's net income per share has grown fourfold in these 10 years, with a minimum growth of 10 percent each year. This growth pattern in net income is consistent with Wal-Mart's underlying business performance, as reflected in its stock price. In contrast, Kmart's net income per share peaked in 1993 and has declined since. The net income pattern reflects the underlying economics of Kmart's business, especially the reversal of fortunes since 1994.

Unlike net income, free cash flow is not informative about either company's activities. Wal-Mart's free cash flow is markedly negative between 1990 and 1996, a period when its market capitalization doubled. From 1997, however, its free cash flow increased. The free cash flow of Kmart reveals an even more perverse relationship between its performance and stock prices. Kmart's free cash flow is negative in three out of four years from 1990 to 1993, a period in which Kmart's stock increased almost 50 percent. However, since 1994 Kmart's free cash flow is consistently positive, while its market capitalization decreased 60 percent. Free cash flow appears to be a reverse indicator of performance–when free cash flow is negative, Kmart is profitable and growing, but when free cash flow turns positive, Kmart is in decline or growth is slowing.

What drives the reverse relation between free cash flow and performance for both Wal-Mart and Kmart? For an answer we need to look back at Exhibit 2.3 and the related discussion on cash flow patterns over a company's life cycle. Wal-Mart is probably nearing the end of its growth cycle and is entering maturity. Until recently, it generated negative free cash flow as it consistently spent more cash on growth than it was earning from operations. Wal-Mart's free cash flow surged in recent years both because its growth cooled and its earlier investments are now yielding operating cash flows. Notice that Wal-Mart's cash flow patterns are consistent with the life cycle model for a company transitioning from growth to maturity. In contrast, Kmart is probably in decline. As predicted by the life cycle model, Kmart's investing cash flows since 1994 are positive, reflecting its downsizing as it sells assets. Cash flows generated from Kmart's divestments yield large positive free cash flow, even though its operating cash flows decline during this period.

To appreciate the limitation of free cash flow and the power of accrual income to measure financial performance, try to predict the performance of both Wal-Mart and Kmart using the pattern in net income and free cash flow for this period. For Wal-Mart, free cash flow portrays a dismal company–one that, until recently, bled cash. On the other hand, Wal-Mart's net income series shows a picture of consistent growth and profitability. Turning to Kmart, free cash flow reveals a marked upturn in business with positive free cash flow since 1994. Yet, Kmart's net income series suggests looming financial difficulties for the past five years. Which measure, accrual income or free cash flow, better reflects reality? Which measure would have been more useful to you as an equity investor in predicting stock prices? To answer these questions, compare these performance measures with the companies' actual stock prices over this period. This comparison shows the power of net income in tracking stock prices relative to free cash flow.

One case does not make a rule. Could the Wal-Mart and Kmart cases be unique in that free cash flow is otherwise superior to net income as a value indicator? To pursue this question, let's look at the relation between alternative income and cash flow measures with stock prices for a large sample of firms for a recent 10-year period. This evidence is shown in Exhibit 2.5. Here we see measures of R-squared that reflect the ability of performance measures in explaining stock prices. Note that both income measures (NI and NIBX) are better than either operating cash flow (OCF) or free cash flow (FCF) in explaining stock prices. Also, net cash flow (change in cash balance) is entirely uninformative.

A main difference between accrual accounting and cash flow accounting is timeliness in recognizing business activities. Accrual income recognizes the effects of most business activities in a more timely manner. For evidence of this, let's look at the relation between stock returns, net income, and operating cash flow over different time horizons. If we assume stock prices impound the effects of business activities in a timely

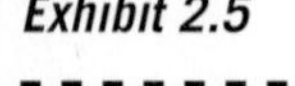

Exhibit 2.5

Relation between Stock Prices and Various Income and Cash Flow Measures

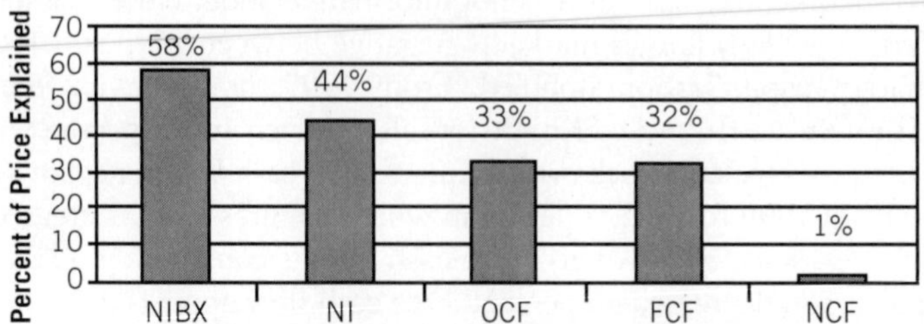

Analysis using 2,300 firms for the period 1987–1997 from Compustat. Graph depicts R-squared of regressions between and-of-period price and various cash flow and income measures. NIBX = Net income before extraordinary items and discontinued operations; NI = Net income; OCF = Operating cash flow; FCF = Free cash flow; NCF = Net cash flow (change in cash).

manner, then the relation between stock returns and alternative performance measures reflects on the timeliness of these measures. Exhibit 2.6 shows evidence of the ability of net income and operating cash flow to explain stock returns over quarterly, annual, and four-year horizons. Net income dominates operating cash flows over all horizons. While net income's timeliness is less impressive for shorter horizons, its superiority over operating cash flow is maintained. Operating cash flow's ability to explain stock returns over short horizons (quarterly and annual) is especially poor. This evidence supports the notion that accrual income reflects the effects of business activities in a more timely manner than do cash flows.

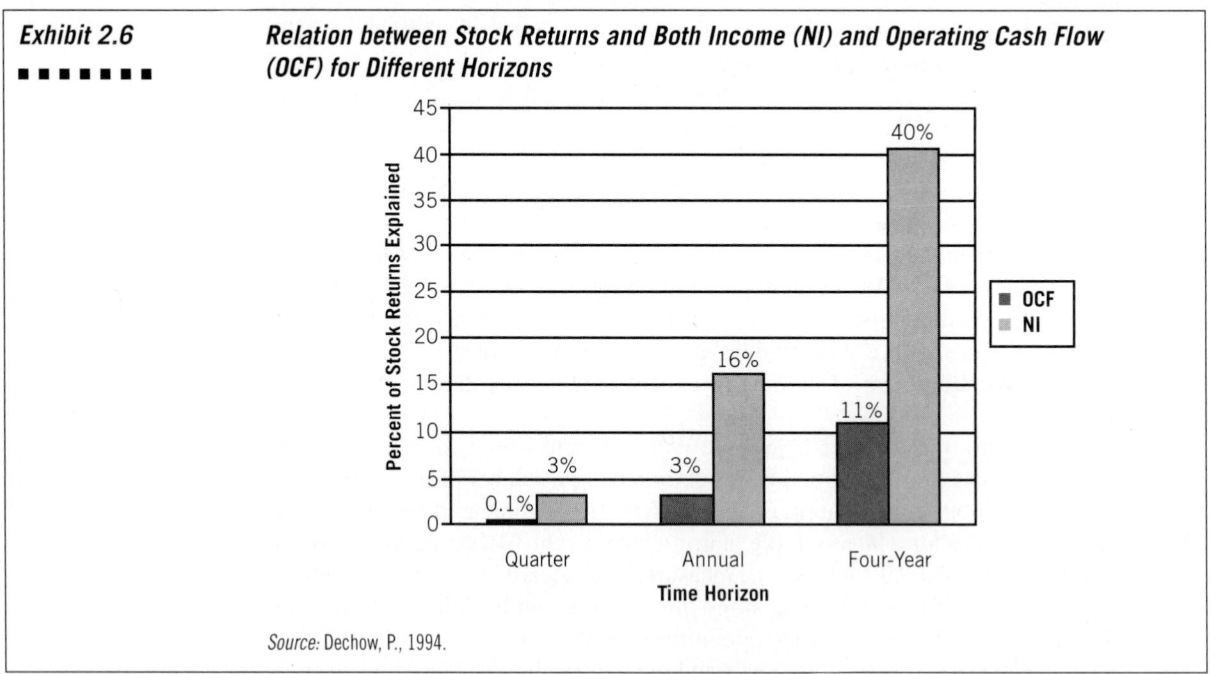

Source: Dechow, P., 1994.

Accruals Can Be a Double-Edged Sword

While accrual accounting is conceptually and empirically more relevant than cash flows, it can be a double-edged sword. Accrual accounting introduces judgment into accounting with various estimations and adjustments. Ideally, allowing managerial judgment should increase the relevance of accounting information. Yet, practice often falls short of the ideal. Use of judgment can reduce comparability and consistency of financial statements, leading to accounting distortions

Most criticism of accrual accounting involves the sacrifice of relevance for reliability. Some advocate more aggressive accrual accounting to estimate the economic consequences of business activities with less stringent reliability criteria. Examples are a move away from historical cost in favor of market values, more aggressive capitalization of R&D and intangibles, disclosing numerical ranges in notes when estimates are uncertain, and including income and cash flow forecasts in annual reports.

Analysis Implications of Accrual Accounting

Accrual accounting is ingrained in modern business. Wall Street focuses on accrual income, not cash flows. We know that accrual accounting is superior to cash accounting in measuring performance and financial condition, and in forecasting future cash flows. Still, accrual accounting has limitations. Consequently, should accrual accounting numbers always be used in business analysis and valuation, or should they sometimes be abandoned in favor of hard cash flows? If accrual accounting is used, how does one deal with its limitations? What is the role of cash flows in a world of accrual accounting? This section provides some answers to these questions. We begin with the myths and truths of both accrual and cash accounting. Then, we discuss the role of accruals and cash flows in financial statement analysis.

Myths and Truths about Accruals and Cash Flows

Several assertions exist regarding accruals and cash flows–both positive and negative. It is important for an analyst to know which assertions are true and which are not.

Accruals and Cash Flows—Myths. There are several myths and misconceptions about accrual accounting, income, and cash flow:

- Myth: *Since company value depends on future cash flows, only current cash flows are relevant for valuation.* Even if we accept that company value depends only on future cash flows, there is no reason to necessarily link current cash flows with future cash flows. We already showed that current income is a better predictor of future cash flows than is current cash flow. We also showed that income better explains stock prices than does cash flow.
- Myth: *Company value is equal to discounted future cash flows.* The ostensible truth of this statement conceals several problems (see Chapter 1). First, while there are many definitions of cash flow, not all of them determine company value. For example, company value is not equal to the present value of future operating cash flows. Second, the basic formula for company value is the present value of discounted future *dividends.* The present value of free cash flow is a derivative of this formula, but many other cash flow definitions are not. Third, Chapter 1 showed we also can express company value as the sum of current book value and discounted future residual income, independent of cash flows.
- Myth: *All cash flows are value relevant.* Many types of cash flows do not affect company value–for example, cash collected from customers on account. Also, certain types of cash flows are negatively related to company value–for example, capital expenditures reduce free cash flow but usually increase company value. Exhibit 2.7 provides additional examples.
- Myth: *All accrual accounting adjustments are value irrelevant.* It is true that "cosmetic" accounting adjustments such as alternative accounting methods for the same underlying business activity do not yield different valuations. However, not all accounting adjustments are cosmetic. A main goal of accrual accounting is to make

Exhibit 2.7 **Effects of Transactions on Income, Free Cash Flow, and Company Value**

Transaction	Income Effect	Free Cash Flow Effect	Company Value Effect (Present Value of Future Dividends)
Sales on credit	Increase	Nil	Increase
Cash collections on credit sales	Nil	Increase	Nil
Inventory markdowns	Decrease	Nil	Decrease
Change depreciation from straight-line to declining balance	Decrease	Nil	Nil
Cash purchase of plant asset	Nil	Decrease	Nil*

*If the plant asset produces a return on investment in excess of the cost of capital it will increase company value.

adjustments for transactions that have future cash flow implications, even when no cash inflows or cash outflows occur contemporaneously–an example is a credit sale as shown in Exhibit 2.7.

- Myth: *Cash flows cannot be manipulated.* Not only is this statement false, it is probably easier to manipulate cash flows than to manipulate income. For example, cash flows can be increased by delaying either capital expenditures or the payment of expenses. They can be decreased by accelerating cash collections from customers.

Analysis Research

RELATIVE PERFORMANCE OF CASH FLOWS AND ACCRUALS

The relative ability of cash flows and accruals in providing value-relevant information is the focus of much research. One line of research addresses this issue by examining the relative ability of cash flows and accruals in explaining stock returns, under the assumption that stock price is the best indicator of a company's intrinsic value. Evidence reveals that both operating cash flows and accruals provide incremental value-relevant information. Yet, net income (which is the sum of accruals and operating cash flows) is superior to operating cash flows in explaining stock returns. The superiority of income is especially evident for short horizons; recall that the difference between income and cash flows is mainly timing and, thus, over long horizons–say, five or more years–income and operating cash flows tend to converge. Operating cash flows tend to perform poorly for companies where the timing and matching problems of cash flows are more pronounced.

The use of stock price as an indicator of intrinsic value is questioned by recent evidence that the market might be attaching more weight than warranted to the accrual component of income, possibly because of a *fixation* on bottom line income. This evidence indicates that operating cash flows are more persistent than accruals and that the market overestimates the ability of accruals to predict future profitability. That is, abnormal returns can be earned from a strategy of buying stocks of companies with the lowest accruals and shorting those with the highest accruals.

Research also shows income is superior to operating cash flow in predicting future income. However, evidence relating to the relative ability of income and operating cash flow in predicting future cash flow is mixed. While operating cash flow is superior to income in predicting operating cash flow, especially over the short run, both income and operating cash flow are useful in this task. This research also reveals the usefulness of investing and financing cash flows for prediction purposes.

In sum, while the preponderance of research shows the superiority of accruals over cash flows in providing value-relevant information, *both* accruals and cash flows are incrementally useful. This suggests that accruals income and cash flow should be viewed as complements rather than substitutes. Research also shows that the relative importance of accruals and cash flows depends on characteristics such as industry membership, operating cycle, and the point in a company's life cycle.

- Myth: *All income is manipulated.* Some managers do manage income, and the frequency of this practice may be increasing. However, not all companies manage income all of the time.
- Myth: *It is impossible to consistently manage income upwards in the long run.* Some users assert it is impossible to manage income upwards year after year because accounting rules dictate that accruals eventually reverse–that is, accrual accounting and cash accounting coincide in the long run. Still, most companies can aggressively manage income upward for several years at a time. Further, a growth company can manage income upward for an even longer period because current period upward adjustments likely exceed the reversal of smaller adjustments from prior years. Also, some companies take a "big bath" when they experience a bad period to recognize delayed expenses or aggressively record future expenses. This enables a company to more easily manage income upward in future periods because of fewer reversals from prior accruals.
- Myth: *Accounting rules are irrelevant for valuation.* The truth in this statement relates to the reversal, or catch-up, of accruals. Also, while true over the long run, the statement is false in the short run. From a practical standpoint, accounting rules affect a wide range of measures–such as current income, income forecasts, and book values–and can therefore affect an estimate of company value. Accordingly, it is important to do accounting analysis and make any needed accounting adjustments before doing prospective analysis and valuation.

Accruals and Cash Flows—Truths. Logic and evidence point to several notable truths about accrual accounting, income, and cash flow:

- Truth: *Accrual accounting (income) is more relevant than cash flow.* Both conceptually and practically, accrual income is more relevant than cash flow in measuring financial condition and performance and in valuation. Note this statement does not challenge the obvious relevance of *future* cash flows. Instead, it points out that *current* cash flow is less relevant than current income.
- Truth: *Cash flows are more reliable than accruals.* This statement is true and it suggests cash flows can and do play an important complementary role with accruals. However, extreme statements, such as "cash flows cannot be manipulated," are untrue. When analyzing cash flows, we also must remember they are more volatile than income.
- Truth: *Accrual accounting numbers are subject to accounting distortions.* The existence of alternative accounting methods along with earnings management reduces both comparability and consistency of accrual accounting numbers. Also, arbitrary accounting rules and estimation errors can yield accounting distortions. A financial analysis or valuation that ignores these facts, and accounting adjustments, is likely to produce erroneous results. For example, a valuation method that simply uses price-to-earnings ratios computed using reported income is less effective.
- Truth: *Company value can be determined by using accrual accounting numbers.* Some individuals wrongly state that value is determined *only* on the basis of discounted cash flows. Chapter 1 showed that we also can determine value as the sum of current book value and discounted future residual income. Chapter 12 extends this analysis to show that practically an accounting-based valuation model is more effective than the discounted cash flow model.

Should We Forsake Accruals for Cash Flows?

Some advocate abandoning valuation models based on accrual income in favor of a cash flow model. Often underlying this position is an attitude that accrual accounting is unscientific and irrelevant. Cash, as they say, is king. Yet, this is an attitude of extremism.

We know accrual accounting is imperfect, and that arbitrary rules, estimation errors, and earnings management distort its usefulness. We also know that accrual accounting is better than cash flows in many respects–it is conceptually superior and works practically. Consequently, abandoning accrual accounting because of its limitations and focusing only on cash flows, is throwing the baby out with the bath water. There is an enormous amount of valuable information in accrual accounting numbers.

This book takes a constructive view toward accrual accounting. That is, despite its quirks, it is useful and important for financial analysis. Our approach to analysis is to be aware of the limitations in accrual accounting and to evaluate and adjust reported numbers in financial statements through a process of accounting analysis. By this process an analyst is able to exploit the richness of accrual accounting and, at the same time, reduce its distortions and limitations. Cash flows also are important for analysis. They provide a reliability check on accrual accounting–income that consistently deviates from cash flows is usually of lower quality. Also, as we note in Chapter 1, analysis of the sources and uses of funds (or cash flows) is crucial for effective financial analysis.

INTRODUCTION TO ACCOUNTING ANALYSIS

Accounting analysis is the process of evaluating the extent to which a company's accounting numbers reflect economic reality. Accounting analysis involves a number of different tasks, such as evaluating a company's accounting risk and earnings quality, estimating earning power, and making necessary adjustments to financial statements to both better reflect economic reality and assist in financial analysis.

Accounting analysis is an important precondition for effective financial analysis. This is because the quality of financial analysis, and the inferences drawn, depends on the quality of the underlying accounting information, the raw material for analysis. While accrual accounting provides insights about a company's financial performance and condition that is unavailable from cash accounting, its imperfections distort the economic content of financial reports. Accounting analysis is the process an analyst uses to identify and assess accounting distortions in a company's financial statements. It also includes the necessary adjustments to financial statements that reduce distortions and make the statements amenable to financial analysis.

In this section, we explain the need for accounting analysis, including identifying the sources of accounting distortions and discussing important analysis needs. We also introduce two alternative concepts of income that are important in analysis. Then we discuss earnings management, its motivations and strategies, and its implications for analysis. We conclude by examining accounting analysis methods and processes.

Need for Accounting Analysis

The need for accounting analysis arises for two reasons. First, accrual accounting improves upon cash accounting by reflecting business activities in a more timely manner. But accrual accounting yields some accounting distortions that need to be identified and adjusted so accounting information better reflects business activities. Second, financial statements are prepared for a diverse set of users and information needs. This means accounting information usually requires adjustments to meet the analysis objectives of a particular user. We examine each of these factors and their implications to financial statement analysis in this section.

Accounting Distortions

Accounting distortions are deviations of reported information in financial statements from the underlying business reality. These distortions arise from the nature of accrual accounting–this includes its standards, errors in estimation, the trade-off between relevance and reliability, and the latitude in application. We separately discuss each of these sources of distortion.

Accounting Standards. Accounting standards are sometimes responsible for distortions. At least three sources of this distortion are identifiable. First, accounting standards are the output of a political process. Different user groups lobby to protect their interests. In this process, standards sometimes fail to require the most relevant information. One example is accounting for employee stock options (ESOs).

A second source of distortion from accounting standards arises from certain accounting principles. For example, the historical cost principle can reduce the relevance of the balance sheet by not reflecting current market values of assets and liabilities. Also, the transaction basis of accounting results in inconsistent goodwill accounting wherein purchased goodwill is recorded as an asset but internally developed goodwill is not. Additionally, double entry implies that the balance sheet articulates with the income statement–meaning that many transactions impact both statements. However, an accounting rule that improves one statement often does so to the detriment of the other. For example, FIFO inventory rules ensure the inventory account in the balance sheet reflects current costs of unsold inventory. Yet, LIFO inventory rules better reflect current costs of sales in the income statement.

A third source of distortion is conservatism. For example, accountants often write down or write off the value of impaired assets, but very rarely will they write up asset values. Conservatism leads to a pessimistic bias in financial statements that is sometimes desirable for credit analysis but problematic for equity analysis.

Estimation Errors. Accrual accounting requires forecasts and other estimates about future cash flow consequences. Use of these estimates improves the ability of accounting numbers to reflect business transactions in a timely manner. Still, these estimates yield errors that can distort the relevance of accrual accounting numbers. To illustrate, consider credit sales. Whenever goods or services are sold on credit, there is a possibility the customer will default on payment. There are two approaches to confront this uncertainty. One approach is to adopt cash accounting that records revenue only when cash is eventually collected from the customer. The other approach, followed by accrual accounting, is to record credit sales as revenue when they are earned and then make an allowance for bad debts based on collection history, customers' credit ratings, and other facts. While accrual accounting is more relevant, it is subject to distortions from errors in estimation of bad debts.

Reliability versus Relevance. Accounting standards trade off reliability and relevance. An emphasis on reliability often precludes recognizing the effects of certain business events and transactions in financial statements until their cash flow consequences can be reasonably estimated. One example is loss contingencies. Before a loss contingency is recorded as a loss, it must be reasonably estimable. Because of this criterion, many loss contingencies are not reported in financial statements even several years after their existence is established beyond reasonable doubt. Another example of distortion due to the reliability emphasis is accounting for research and development costs. While R&D is an investment, current accounting standards require writing it off as an expense because payoffs from R&D are less certain than payoffs from investments in, say, plant and equipment.

SUNBEAM ME UP
Sunbeam's former CEO Albert "Chainsaw Al" Dunlap and former CFO Russell Kersh received lifetime bans from serving as officers or directors of any public companies. Dunlap and Kersh are alleged to have used accounting hocus-pocus to hide the true financial state of Sunbeam from investors.

Earnings Management. Earnings management is probably the most troubling outcome of accrual accounting. Use of judgment and estimation in accrual accounting allows managers to draw on their inside information and experience to enhance the usefulness of accounting numbers. However, some managers exercise this discretion to manage accounting numbers, particularly income, for personal gain, thereby reducing their quality. Earnings management occurs for several reasons, such as to increase compensation, avoid debt covenants, meet analyst forecasts, and impact stock prices. Earnings management can take two forms: (1) changing accounting methods, which is a visible form of earnings management, and (2) changing accounting estimates and policies that determine accounting numbers, which is a hidden form of earnings management. Earnings management is a reality that most users reluctantly accept as part of accrual accounting. While it is important we recognize that earnings management is not as widespread as the financial press leads us to believe, there is no doubt it hurts the credibility of accounting information.

Analysis Objectives

Information needs of users differ based on their objectives and analysis. In equity analysis, accounting information should give an unbiased view of the company's financial position and performance. It should also facilitate the determination of the company's future earnings potential. However, in the case of credit analysis, it is okay for accounting information to reflect conservatively on the company's financial position and performance. This is because of its emphasis on downside risk and cautious assessment of a company's ability to repay its obligations.

The diverse information needs of users means it is impossible for a single set of numbers to satisfy all. This implies that accounting adjustments are necessary to satisfy analysis objectives and needs of particular users. The need for these adjustments arises independent of distortions in accounting information. For example, both comparative analysis (both cross-sectional and time-series) and income measurement require accounting analysis.

Comparative Analysis. Financial analysis often involves making comparisons across companies or across time. Before making such comparisons, it is important to ensure that the information across companies (or time) is prepared using comparable principles. For example, before comparing debt-to-equity ratios across two companies, it is important to ensure that both companies account for leases in a comparable manner. If one company capitalizes its leases while the other company keeps leases off the balance sheet, then debt-to-equity ratio comparisons between these two companies are less meaningful unless accounting adjustments are made to treat leases in a similar manner. Similarly, it is inappropriate to compare information about a company across time, such as in charting its income trend, if the company changes one or more accounting principles during the comparison period. *Comparability* refers to the quality of accounting information for comparative analysis across companies. *Consistency* refers to the quality of accounting information for comparative analysis across time. It is important that appropriate adjustments are made to accounting data to ensure comparability, consistency, or both, depending on the needs of analysis.

Income Measurement. Income serves two different but equally important roles: (1) it measures the net change in shareholders' wealth for a period, and (2) it indicates the ability of a company to generate profits, that is, its earning power. These two roles of income correspond to two alternative concepts of income. *Economic income* (or more properly, *distributable income*) is equal to cash flow plus the change in the market value of net assets. It represents the change in shareholder wealth. *Permanent income* (also called *sustainable earning power*) is the constant cash flow, when earned in perpetuity, that equates to the present value of actual future cash flows. It represents average earnings potential of the company and is an indicator of value (rather than change in value). Both concepts of income are important for financial statement analysis. However, the adjustments necessary for determining each are different. For determining economic income we need to take an inclusive, balance sheet oriented approach–meaning all changes in equity not arising from owner sources (dividend and capital contributions) are included. For determining sustainable income, we need to take an exclusive approach–meaning we include only recurring and persistent components of income. Understanding these alternative income measures is important for accounting analysis. We discuss this in Chapter 6.

Earnings Management

Earnings management can be defined as the "purposeful intervention by management in the earnings determination process, usually to satisfy selfish objectives" (Schipper, 1989). It often involves window-dressing financial statements, especially the bottom line earnings number. Earnings management can be *cosmetic*, where managers manipulate accruals without any cash flows consequences. It also can be *real*, where managers take actions with cash flow consequences for purposes of managing earnings.

Cosmetic earnings management is a potential outcome of the latitude in applying accrual accounting. Accounting standards and monitoring mechanisms reduce this latitude. Yet, it is impossible to eliminate this latitude given the complexity and variation in business activities. Moreover, accrual accounting requires estimates and judgments. This yields some managerial discretion in determining accounting numbers. While this discretion provides an opportunity for managers to reveal a more informative picture of a company's business activities, it also allows them to window-dress financial statements and manage earnings.

Managers also take actions with cash flow consequences, often adverse, for purposes of managing earnings. For example, managers sometimes use the FIFO method of inventory valuation to report higher income even when use of the LIFO method could yield tax savings. Earnings management incentives also influence investing and financing decisions of managers. Such real earnings management is more troubling than cosmetic earnings management because it reflects business decisions that often reduce shareholder wealth.

This section focuses on cosmetic earnings management because accounting analysis can overcome many of the distortions it causes. Distortions from real earnings management usually cannot be overcome by accounting analysis alone.

Earnings Management Strategies

There are three typical strategies to earnings management. (1) Managers increase current period income. (2) Managers take a big bath by markedly reducing current period income. (3) Managers reduce earnings volatility by income smoothing. Managers sometimes apply these strategies in combination or singly at different points in time to achieve long-term earnings management objectives.

Increasing Income. One earnings management strategy is to increase a period's reported income to portray a company more favorably. It is possible to increase income in this manner over several periods. In a growth scenario, the accrual reversals are smaller than current accruals that increase income. This leads to a case where a company can report higher income from aggressive earnings management over long periods of time. Also, companies can manage earnings upward for several years and then reverse accruals all at once with a one-time charge. This one-time charge is often reported "below the line" and, therefore, might be perceived as less relevant.

BATH BUSTER
SEC is increasingly concerned about big-bath write-offs such as Motorola's recent $1.98 billion restructuring charge.

Big Bath. A big bath strategy involves taking as many write-offs as possible in one period. The period chosen is usually one with markedly poor performance (often in a recession when most other companies also report poor earnings) or one with unusual events such as a management change, a merger, or a restructuring. The big bath strategy also is often used in conjunction with an income-increasing strategy for other years. Because of the unusual and nonrecurring nature of a big bath, users tend to discount its financial effect. This affords an opportunity to write off all past sins and also clears the deck for future earnings increases.

Income Smoothing. Income smoothing is a common form of earnings management. Under this strategy, managers decrease or increase reported income so as to reduce its volatility. Income smoothing involves not reporting a portion of earnings in good years through creating reserves or earnings "banks," and then reporting these earnings in bad years. Many companies use this form of earnings management.

Motivations for Earnings Management

There are several reasons for managing earnings, including increasing manager compensation tied to reported earnings, increasing stock price, and lobbying for government subsidies. We identify the major incentives for earnings management in this section.

NUMBER CRUNCH
Bausch & Lomb execs say that maintaining double-digit sales and earnings growth in the 90s was all-important, creating pressures that led to unethical behavior in reporting earnings.

Contracting Incentives. Many contracts use accounting numbers. For example, managerial compensation contracts often include bonuses based on earnings. Typical bonus contracts have a lower and an upper bound, meaning that managers are not given a bonus if earnings fall below the lower bound and cannot earn any additional bonus when earnings exceed the upper bound. This means managers have incentives to increase or decrease earnings based on the *unmanaged* earnings level in relation to the upper and lower bounds. When unmanaged earnings are within the upper and lower bounds, managers have an incentive to increase earnings. When earnings are above the maximum bound or below the minimum bound, managers have an incentive to decrease earnings and create reserves for future bonuses. Another example of a contractual incentive is debt covenants that often are based on ratios using accounting numbers such as earnings. Since violations of debt covenants are costly for managers, they will manage earnings (usually upwards) to avoid them.

Stock Price Effects. Another incentive for earnings management is the potential impact on stock price. For example, managers may increase earnings to temporarily boost company stock price for events such as a forthcoming merger or security offering, or plans to sell stock or exercise options. Managers also smooth income to lower market perceptions of risk and to decrease the cost of capital. Still another related incentive for earnings management is to beat market expectations. This strategy often takes the following form: Managers lower market expectations through pessimistic voluntary disclosures (preannouncements) and then manage earnings upward to beat market expectations. The growing importance of momentum investors and their ability to brutally punish stocks that don't meet expectations has created increasing pressure on managers to use all available means to beat market expectations.

Other Incentives. There are several other reasons for managing earnings. Earnings sometimes are managed downward to reduce political costs and scrutiny from government agencies such as antitrust regulators and the IRS. In addition, companies may manage earnings downward to gain favors from the government, including subsidies and protection from foreign competition. Companies also decrease earnings to combat labor union demands. Another common incentive for earnings management is a change in management. This usually results in a big bath for several reasons. First, it can be blamed on incumbent managers. Second, it signals that the new managers will make tough decisions to improve the company. Third, and probably most important, it clears the deck for future earnings increases. One of the largest big baths occurred when Louis Gerstner became CEO at IBM. Gerstner wrote off nearly $4 billion in the year he took charge. While a large part of this charge comprised expenses related to the turnaround, it also included many items that were future business expenses. Analysts estimate that the earnings increases reported by IBM in subsequent years were in large part attributed to this big bath.

Mechanics of Earnings Management

This section explains the mechanics of earnings management. Areas that offer maximum opportunities for earnings management include revenue recognition, inventory valuation, estimates of provisions such as bad debts expense and deferred taxes, and one-time charges such as restructuring and asset impairments. This section does not provide examples of every conceivable method of managing earnings. Many additional details and examples of earnings management are discussed in Chapters 3–6. In this section, we describe two major methods of earnings management–income shifting and classificatory earnings management.

Income Shifting. Income shifting is the process of managing earnings by moving income from one period to another. Income shifting is achieved by accelerating or delaying the recognition of revenues or expenses. This form of earnings management usually results in a reversal of the effect in one or more future periods, often in the next period. For this reason, income shifting is most useful for income smoothing. Examples of income shifting include the following:

NIFTY SHIFTY
WorldCom execs boosted earnings by shifting (capitalizing) costs that should have been expensed to future periods.

- Accelerating revenue recognition by persuading dealers or wholesalers to purchase excess products near the end of the fiscal year. This practice, called *channel loading,* is common in industries such as automobile manufacturing and cigarettes.
- Delaying expense recognition by capitalizing expenses and amortizing them over future periods. Examples include interest capitalization and capitalization of software development costs.
- Shifting expenses to later periods by adopting certain accounting methods. For example, adopting the FIFO method for inventory valuation (versus LIFO) and the straight-line depreciation (versus accelerated) can delay expense recognition.
- Taking large one-time charges such as asset impairments and restructuring charges on an intermittent basis. This allows companies to accelerate expense recognition and, thus, make subsequent earnings look better.

Classificatory Earnings Management. Earnings are also managed by selectively classifying expenses (and revenues) in certain parts of the income statement. The most common form of this classificatory earnings management is to move expenses below the line, meaning report them along with unusual and nonrecurring items that usually are given less importance by analysts. An extreme case of this form of earnings management is making direct adjustments to equity without running the item through the income statement. This process is usually not possible under U.S. GAAP. Still, managers attempt to classify expenses in the nonrecurring parts of the income statement as these examples illustrate:

- When a company discontinues a business segment, the income from that segment must be separately reported as income (loss) from discontinued operations. This item is properly ignored in analysis because it pertains to a business unit that no longer impacts the company. But some companies load a larger portion of common costs (such as corporate overhead) to the discontinued segment, thereby increasing income for the rest of the company.
- Use of special charges such as asset impairments and restructuring charges has skyrocketed (almost 40 percent of companies report at least one such charge). The motivation for this practice arises from the habit of many analysts to ignore special charges because of their unusual and nonrecurring nature. By taking special charges periodically and including operating expenses in these charges, companies cause analysts to ignore a portion of operating expenses.

KODAK MOMENT
In the '90s, Kodak took six extraordinary write-offs totaling $4.5 billion, which is more than its net earnings for the decade.

Analysis Implications of Earnings Management

Since earnings management distorts financial statements, identifying and making adjustments for it is an important task in financial statement analysis. Still, despite the alarming increase in earnings management, it is less widespread than presumed. The financial press likes to focus on cases of earnings management because it makes interesting reading. This gives many users the incorrect impression that earnings are managed all the time.

Before concluding a company is managing earnings, an analyst needs to check the following:

- **Incentives for earnings management**. Earnings will not be managed unless there are incentives for managing them. We have discussed some of the incentives, and an analysis should consider them.
- **Management reputation and history**. It is important to assess management reputation and integrity. Perusal of past financial statements, SEC enforcements, audit reports, auditor change history, and the financial press provides useful information for this task.
- **Consistent pattern**. The aim of earnings management is to influence a summary bottom line number such as earnings or key ratios such as the debt-to-equity or interest coverage. It is important to verify whether different components of income (or the balance sheet) are consistently managed in a certain direction. For example, if a company appears to be inflating earnings through, say, revenue recognition policies while simultaneously decreasing earnings through an inventory method change, it is less likely the company is managing earnings.
- **Earnings management opportunities**. The nature of business activities determines the extent to which earnings can be managed. When the nature of business activities calls for considerable judgment in determining financial statement numbers, greater opportunities exist to manage earnings.

Process of Accounting Analysis

Accounting analysis involves several interrelated processes and tasks. We discuss accounting analysis under two broad areas–evaluating earnings quality and adjusting financial statements. Although separately discussed, the two tasks are interrelated and complementary. We also discuss earnings quality in more detail in Appendix 2B and adjustments to financial statements throughout Chapters 3–6.

Evaluating Earnings Quality

Earnings quality (or more precisely, accounting quality) means different things to different people. Many analysts define earnings quality as the extent of conservatism adopted by the company–a company with higher earnings quality is expected to have a higher price-earnings ratio than one with lower earnings quality. An alternative definition of earnings quality is in terms of accounting distortions–a company has high earnings quality if its financial statement information accurately depicts its business activities. Whatever its definition, evaluating earnings quality is an important task of accounting analysis. We briefly describe the steps in evaluating earnings quality in this section.

Steps in Evaluating Earnings Quality. Evaluating earnings quality involves the following steps:

- **Identify and assess key accounting policies.** An important step in evaluating earnings quality is identifying key accounting policies adopted by the company. Are the policies reasonable or aggressive? Is the set of policies adopted consistent with industry norms? What impact will the accounting policies have on reported numbers in financial statements?
- **Evaluate extent of accounting flexibility.** It is important to evaluate the extent of flexibility available in preparing financial statements. The extent of accounting flexibility is greater in some industries than others. For example, the accounting for industries that have more intangible assets, greater volatility in business operations, a larger portion of its production costs incurred prior to production, and unusual revenue recognition methods requires more judgments and estimates. Generally, earnings quality is lower in such industries than in industries where the accounting is more straightforward.
- **Determine the reporting strategy.** Identify the accounting strategy adopted by the company. Is the company adopting aggressive reporting practices? Does the company have a clean audit report? Has there been a history of accounting problems? Does management have a reputation for integrity, or are they known to cut corners? It is also necessary to examine incentives for earnings management and look for consistent patterns indicative of it. Analysts need to evaluate the quality of a company's disclosures. While disclosures are not substitutes for good quality financial statements, forthcoming and detailed disclosures can mitigate weaknesses in financial statements.
- **Identify and assess red flags.** One useful step in evaluating earnings quality is to beware of red flags. Red flags are items that alert analysts to potentially more serious problems. Some examples of red flags are:

  Poor financial performance–desperate companies are prone to desperate means.

  Reported earnings consistently higher than operating cash flows.

  Reported earnings consistently higher than taxable income.

  Qualified audit report.

  Auditor resignation or a nonroutine auditor change.

  Unexplained or frequent changes in accounting policies.

  Sudden increase in inventories in comparison to sales.

  Use of mechanisms to circumvent accounting rules, such as operating leases and receivables securitization.

  Frequent one-time charges and big baths.

Answer–p. 106

ANALYSIS VIEWPOINT . . . YOU ARE THE BOARD MEMBER

You are a new member of the board of directors of a merchandiser. You are preparing for your first meeting with the company's independent auditor. A stockholder writes you a letter raising concerns about earnings quality. What are some questions or issues that you can raise with the auditor to address these concerns and fulfill your fiduciary responsibilities to shareholders?

Adjusting Financial Statements

The final and most involved task in accounting analysis is making appropriate adjustments to financial statements, especially the income statement and balance sheet. As discussed earlier, the need for these adjustments arises both because of distortions in the reported numbers and because of specific analysis objectives. The main emphasis of the next four chapters of this book is the proper identification and adjustment of accounting numbers. Some common adjustments to financial statements include:

- Capitalization of long-term operating leases, with adjustments to both the balance sheet and income statement.
- Recognition of ESO expense for income determination.
- Adjustments for one-time charges such as asset impairments and restructuring costs.
- Capitalization of R&D if necessary.
- Recognition of the economic (funded) status of pension and other postretirement benefit plans on the balance sheet.
- Removal of the effects of selected deferred income tax liabilities and assets from the balance sheet.

APPENDIX 2A AUDITING AND FINANCIAL STATEMENT ANALYSIS

Financial statements of a company are the representations of its management, who bear the primary responsibility for the fairness of presentation and the information disclosed. Because of the importance of financial statements, there is demand for their independent verification. Public accounting meets this demand through attestation, or auditing, services. This appendix provides an overview of the relevance of auditing for our analysis. It also discusses the types of audit reports and their analysis implications.

AUDIT PROCESS

Analysts must understand what the audit opinion implies for users of financial statements and must also appreciate the limitations of the opinion and their implications for analysis of financial statements. To obtain this understanding, we must consider the standards governing auditors' behavior and the nature of audit work.

Generally Accepted Auditing Standards

Auditors typically refer to an audit made in accordance with **generally accepted auditing standards.** Audit standards are the measuring sticks assessing the quality of audit procedures. These standards are intended to ensure the auditor's responsibilities are clearly and unequivocally stated and that the degree of responsibility assumed is made clear to users.

Auditing Procedures

The basic objective of a financial statement audit is to identify errors and irregularities, which if undetected would materially affect these statements' fairness of presentation or their conformity with GAAP. To be economically feasible and justifiable, auditing aims for a reasonable level of assurance about the data under review. This means that, under a testing system, assurance is never absolute. Audit reports are subject to this inherent probability of error.

AUDIT REPORT

There is considerable debate among auditors, users, and other interested parties (courts, regulators) concerning the phrase *present fairly* in the auditor's report. Most auditors maintain that financial statements are fairly presented when they conform to accepted accounting principles and fairness is meaningful only when measured against this standard. Yet in several court cases, financial statements supposedly prepared in accordance with accounting principles were found to be misleading.

The audit report's language has been revised to narrow the gap between the responsibility auditors intend to assume and the responsibility the public believes them to assume. The language is intended to be nontechnical and to more explicitly address the responsibility the audit firm assumes, the procedures it performs, and the assurance it provides. The report indicates:

- Financial statements are audited. This is intended to be descriptive of the process.
- Financial statements are the responsibility of management and expressing an opinion on them is the auditor's responsibility. This gives users notice of responsibilities assumed by each party.
- The audit is conducted in accordance with generally accepted auditing standards and is designed to obtain reasonable assurance the financial statements are free of material misstatement.
- Auditors apply procedures to reasonably assure the financial statements are free of material misstatement, including: (1) examining on a test basis evidence supporting the amounts and disclosures in financial statements, (2) assessing accounting principles used and estimates made by management, and (3) evaluating overall financial statement presentation.
- Whether financial statements present fairly in all material respects the financial position, results of operations, and cash flows of the company for the period reported on.

Types of Audit Qualifications

There are several major types of qualifications that an auditor can express.

"Except for" Qualification

"Except for" qualifications express an opinion on the financial statements *except for* repercussions stemming from conditions that must be disclosed. They may arise from limitations in the scope of the audit that, because of circumstances beyond the auditor's control or because of restrictions imposed by the audited company, result in a failure to obtain reasonably objective and verifiable evidence. They can also arise from a lack of conformity of the financial statements to accepted accounting principles. When there are uncertainties about future events that cannot be resolved or whose

Companies with Uncertainties in the Audit Report

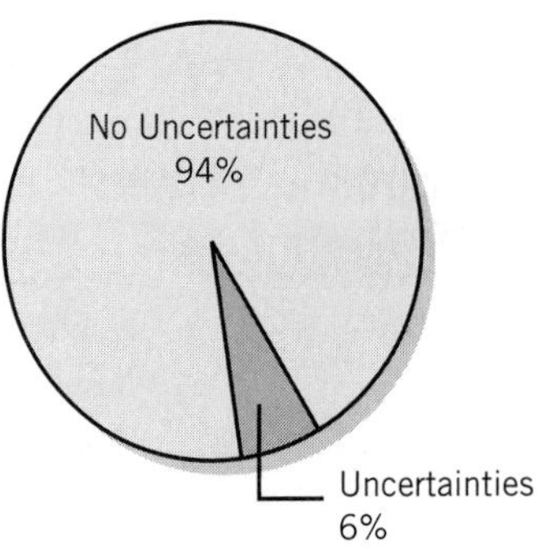

effects cannot be estimated or reasonably provided for at the time an opinion is rendered, a separate paragraph is added. An example is a company with operating losses or in financial distress calling into question the company's ability to continue operating as a going concern. This paragraph refers users to the note in the financial statements providing details about the uncertainty. In cases of pervasive uncertainty that cannot be adequately measured, an auditor can, but is not required to, issue a disclaimer of opinion rather than merely call the user's attention to the uncertainty.

Types of Uncertainties

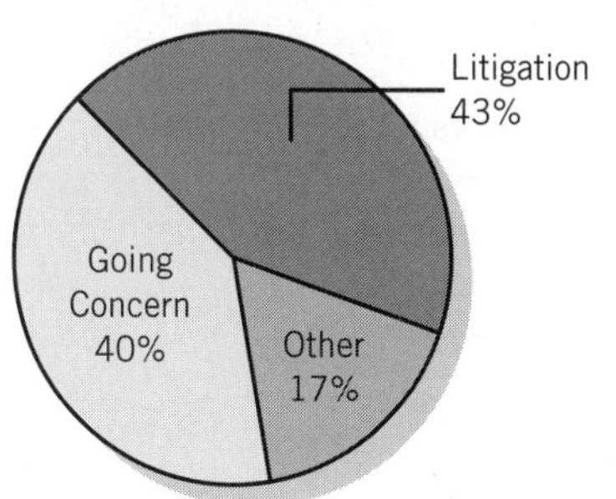

Adverse Opinion

Auditors render adverse opinions in cases where financial statements are not prepared in accordance with accepted accounting principles, and this has a material effect on the fair presentation of the statements. An adverse opinion results generally from a situation where the audit firm is unable to convince its client to either amend the financial statements so that they reflect the auditor's estimate about the outcome of future events or adhere to accepted accounting principles. An adverse opinion must always be accompanied by the reasons for this opinion.

Disclaimer of Opinion

A disclaimer of opinion is a statement of inability to express an opinion. It must be rendered when, for whatever reason, insufficient competent evidential matter is available to the audit firm to enable it to form an opinion on the financial statements. It can arise from limitations in the scope of the audit as well as from the existence of uncertainties, the ultimate impact of which cannot be estimated. Material departures from accepted accounting principles do not justify a disclaimer of opinion. The difference between adverse opinions and disclaimers of opinion is best understood in terms of the difference existing between exceptions affecting the quality of financial statements on one hand, and those expressing uncertainties affecting the auditor's opinion on the other. For example, a situation calling for an "except for" opinion can in certain cases result in major disagreements with management requiring an adverse opinion.

ANALYSIS IMPLICATIONS FROM AUDITING

This section describes the analysis implications related to auditing activities.

Analysis Implications of the Audit Process

Auditing is based largely on a *sampling approach* to the data and information under audit. Sample size is limited by the costs of auditing practice. Users must recognize the audit firm does not aim at, nor can ever achieve, complete certainty. Even a review of every single transaction–a process economically unjustifiable–does not achieve complete assurance.

QB SACKED
Former Minnesota Vikings quarterback Fran Tarkenton paid a $100,000 fine to settle charges that, as former CEO of KnowledgeWare, he helped inflate earnings with $8 million in phony software sales.

While audited financial statements provide us some assurance about the results of the audit process, we must remember there are varying risks to our relying on audit results. These risks relate to many factors, including (1) the auditor's inability and/or unwillingness to detect fraud at the highest level and to apply necessary audit tests to this end, (2) the auditor's inability to grasp the extent of a deteriorating situation, (3) the auditor's conception of the extent of responsibilities to probe and disclose, and (4) overall audit quality. We must be aware the entire audit process is a probabilistic one subject to risks. Flawless application does not yield complete assurance and cannot ensure the auditor has elicited all the facts. This is especially the case if high-level management collusion is involved. Dependence of the auditing process on human judgment also yields varying degrees of audit quality.

Audit Risk and Its Implications

We already discussed accounting risk. Audit risk, while related, is of a different dimension and represents an equal danger to users of audited financial statements. While it is impossible for us to substitute our judgment for that of the auditor, we can use our understanding of the audit process and its limitations to make a better assessment of the degree of audit risk. The following are attributes pointing to potential areas of vulnerability:

- Growth industry or company with pressure to maintain a high market price or pursue acquisitions.
- Company in financial distress requiring financing.
- Company with high market visibility issuing frequent progress reports and earnings estimates.
- Management dominated by one or more strong-willed individuals.
- Signs of personal financial difficulties by members of management.
- Deterioration in operating performance or profitability.
- Management compensation or stock options dependent on reported earnings.
- Deterioration in liquidity or solvency.
- Capital structure too complex for the company's operations or size.
- Management compensation or stock options dependent on reported earnings.

Analysis Implications of Auditing Standards

In relying on audited financial statements, our analysis must be aware of limitations in the audit process. Moreover, we must understand what the auditor's opinion means and does not mean. The audit firm asserts it reviews the financial statements presented to it by management and ascertains whether they are in agreement with the records it audits. The audit firm also determines whether accepted principles of accounting are employed in preparing the financial statements, but does not claim to represent they are the best principles.

Does it make a difference whether the audit firm prepared the statements or not, so long as it expresses an unqualified opinion on them? The profession does not precisely explain what the implications of this distinction are for users of financial statements. However, a number of possible implications should be recognized in our analysis:

1. An auditor's knowledge of business activities underlying financial statements is not as strong as the preparer's. The audit firm knows only what it can discern on the basis of a sampling process and does not know all the facts.
2. Many financial statement items are incapable of exact measurement and the auditor merely reviews these measurements for reasonableness. Unless the auditor can show otherwise (e.g., estimating asset service lives), management's determination prevails.
3. While the audit firm is often consulted in selecting accounting principles, it is the preparer that selects and applies the principles. Auditors cannot insist on using the "best" principle any more than they can insist on a degree of disclosure above the minimum acceptable.
4. There exist limitations in the auditor's ability to audit certain areas. For example, is the audit firm able to audit the value of inventory work in progress? Can it

competently evaluate the adequacy of insurance reserves? Can it estimate the value of problem loans? Can it second-guess the client's estimate of the percentage of completion of a large contract? While these questions are rarely raised in public, they present important challenges to the profession.

5. The auditor's error tolerance is higher. The auditor looks to the concept of *materiality* implying that the audit firm need not concern itself with trivial or unimportant matters. What is important or significant is a matter of judgment, and the profession has yet to precisely define the concept nor set established criteria of materiality. This yields reporting latitude.

An auditor's reference to generally accepted accounting principles in its opinion should also be understood by users of financial statements. This reference means the auditor is satisfied that principles, or standards, have authoritative support and they are applied "in all material respects." Aside from understanding the concept of materiality, our analysis must understand that the definition of what constitutes *generally accepted* is often vague and subject to latitude in interpretation and application. For example, auditing standards state "when criteria for selection among alternative accounting principles have not been established to relate accounting methods to circumstances (e.g., as in case of inventory and depreciation methods), the auditor may conclude that more than one accounting principle is appropriate in the circumstances."

Similarly ambiguous are standards relating to disclosure. While minimum standards are increasingly established in professional and SEC pronouncements, accountants do not always adhere to them. The degree to which lack of disclosure impairs fair presentation of financial statements remains subject to the auditor's judgment and discretion. There are no definite standards indicating the point where lack of disclosure is material enough to impair fairness of presentation, requiring a qualified audit report.

Analysis Implications of Auditor Opinions

When an audit firm qualifies its opinion, our analysis is faced with a problem of interpretation. That is, what is the meaning and intent of the qualification? Also, what effect does qualification have for our reliance on financial statements? The usefulness of this qualification for our analysis depends on the extent supplementary information and data enable us to assess its impact. An added dimension of confusion and difficulty of interpretation arises when the audit firm includes explanatory information in its report, merely for emphasis, without a statement of conclusions or of a qualification. We are often left wondering why the matter is emphasized and whether the auditor is attempting to express an unstated qualification or reservation.

When an audit firm is *not* satisfied with the fairness in presentation of financial statements, it issues an "except for" type of qualification, and when there are *uncertainties* that cannot be resolved, it adds explanatory language after the opinion paragraph. At some point, the size and importance of items under qualification are so large to result in an adverse opinion or disclaimer of opinion. Where is this point? At what point is a qualification no longer meaningful and an overall disclaimer of opinion necessary? Our analysis will not find any explicit guidelines in auditing standards. We must rely on the auditor's judgment with appropriate caveats.

Analysis Implications of the SEC

The SEC has moved more aggressively to monitor auditor performance and to strengthen the auditor's position in dealings with clients. Disciplinary proceedings against auditors were expanded with innovative remedies in consent decrees to include requirements for improvements in internal administration procedures, professional education, and reviews of a firm's procedures by outside professionals (peer review). In moving to strengthen the auditor's position, the SEC requires increased disclosure of the relationship between auditors and their clients, particularly in cases where changes in auditors take place. Disclosure must include details of past disagreements including those resolved to the satisfaction of the prior auditor, and note disclosure of the effects on financial statements of methods of accounting advocated by a former auditor but not followed by the client. The SEC has also moved to discourage "opinion shopping," a practice where companies allegedly canvass audit firms to gain acceptance of accounting alternatives they desire to use before hiring auditors.

This appendix shows our analysis must carefully consider the auditor's opinion and the supplementary information it refers to. While our analysis can place some reliance on the audit, we must maintain an independent and guarded view toward assurances conveyed in the auditor's report.

ACCOUNTING WATCHDOG
The new Public Company Accounting Oversight Board (PCAOB—dubbed "Peek-a-Boo") is expected to serve as a watchdog for wayward auditors.

APPENDIX 2B EARNINGS QUALITY

Earnings quality refers to the relevance of earnings in measuring company performance. Its determinants include a company's business environment and its selection and application of accounting principles. This appendix focuses on measuring earnings quality, describing income statement and balance sheet analysis of earnings quality, and explaining how external factors impact earnings quality.

DETERMINANTS OF EARNINGS QUALITY

We know earnings (income) measurement and recognition involve estimation and interpretation of business transactions and events. Our prior analysis of earnings emphasized that accounting earnings is not a unique amount but depends on the assumptions used and principles applied.

The need for estimation and interpretation in accrual accounting has led some individuals to question the reliability of *all* accrual measures. This is an extreme and unwise reaction because of the considerable wealth of relevant information communicated in accrual measures.

We know accrual accounting consists of adjusting cash flows to reflect universally accepted concepts: earned revenue and incurred expenses. What our analysis must focus on are the assumptions and principles applied, and the adjustments appropriate for our analysis objectives. We should use the information in accruals to our competitive advantage and to help us better understand current and future company performance. We must also be aware of both *accounting and audit risks* to rely on earnings. Improvements in both accounting and auditing have decreased the incidence of fraud and misinterpretation in financial statements. Nevertheless, management fraud and misrepresentation is far from eliminated, and audit failures do occur (e.g., Enron, WorldCom, and Xerox). Our analysis must always evaluate accounting and audit risk, including the character and propensities of management, in assessing earnings.

Measuring earnings quality arose out of a need to compare earnings of different companies and a desire to recognize differences in quality for valuation purposes. There is not complete agreement on what constitutes earnings quality. This section considers three factors typically identified as determinants of earnings quality and some examples of their assessment.

FRAUD ALERT
Many financial frauds are spotted by short-sellers long before regulators and the press pick them up.

1. **Accounting principles.** One determinant of earnings quality is the discretion of management in *selecting accepted accounting principles.* This discretion can be aggressive (optimistic) or conservative. The quality of conservatively determined earnings is perceived to be higher because they are less likely to overstate current and future performance expectations compared with those determined in an aggressive manner. Conservatism reduces the likelihood of earnings overstatement and retrospective changes. However, excessive conservatism, while contributing temporarily to earnings quality, reduces the reliability and relevance of earnings in the longer run. Examining the accounting principles selected can provide clues to management's propensities and attitudes.
2. **Accounting application.** Another determinant of earnings quality is management's discretion in *applying* accepted accounting principles. Management has discretion over the amount of earnings through their application of accounting principles determining revenues and expenses. Discretionary expenses like advertising, marketing, repairs, maintenance, research, and development can be *timed* to manage the level of reported earnings (or loss). Earnings reflecting timing elements unrelated to operating or business conditions can detract from earnings quality. Our analysis task is to identify the implications of management's accounting application and assess its motivations.
3. **Business risk.** A third determinant of earnings quality is the relation between earnings and business risk. It includes the effect of cyclical and other business forces on earnings level, stability, sources, and variability. For example, earnings variability is generally undesirable and its increase harms earnings quality. Higher earnings quality is linked with companies more insulated from business risk. While business risk is not primarily a result of management's discretionary actions, this risk can be lowered by skillful management strategies.

INCOME STATEMENT ANALYSIS OF EARNINGS QUALITY

Important determinants of earnings quality are management's selection and application of accounting principles. This section focuses on several important discretionary accounting expenditures to help us to assess earnings quality. *Discretionary expenditures* are outlays that management can vary across periods to conserve resources and/or influence reported earnings. For this reason, they deserve special attention in our analysis. These expenditures are often reported in the income statement or its notes, and hence, evaluation of these items is referred to as an income statement analysis of earnings quality. Two important examples are:

1. **Advertising expense.** A major portion of advertising outlays has effects beyond the current period. This yields a weak relation between advertising outlays and short-term performance. This also implies management can in certain cases cut advertising costs with no immediate effects on sales. However, long-run sales are likely to suffer. Analysis must look at year-to-year variations in advertising expenses to assess their impact on future sales and earnings quality.
2. **Research and development expense.** Research and development costs are among the most difficult expenditures in financial statements to analyze and interpret. Yet they are important, not necessarily because of their amount but because of their effect on future performance. Interestingly, research and development costs have acquired an aura of productive potential in analysis exceeding what is often warranted by experience. There exist numerous cases of successful research and development activities in areas like genetics, chemistry, electronics,

photography, and biology. But for each successful project there are countless failures. These research failures represent vast sums expensed or written off without measurable benefits. Our intent is to determine the amount of current research and development costs having future benefits. These benefits are often measured by relating research and development outlays to sales growth and new product development.

Analysis of Other Discretionary Costs

There are other discretionary future-directed outlays. Examples are costs of training, selling, managerial development, and repairs and maintenance. While these costs are usually expensed in the period incurred, they often have future utility. To the extent that these costs are separately disclosed in the income statement or the notes to the financial statements, analysis should recognize their effects in assessing current earnings and future prospects.

BALANCE SHEET ANALYSIS OF EARNINGS QUALITY

Conservatism in Reported Assets

The relevance of reported asset values is linked (with few exceptions like cash, held-to maturity investments, and land) with their ultimate recognition as reported expenses. We can state this as a general proposition:

When assets are *overstated*, cumulative earnings are *overstated*.

This is true because earnings are relieved of charges necessary to bring these assets down to realizable values. Examples include the delay in recognizing impaired assets, such as obsolete inventories or unproductive plant and equipment, and the understatement of allowance for uncollectible accounts receivable. The converse is also true: When assets are *understated*, cumulative earnings are *understated*. An example is the unrecognized appreciation on an acquired business that is recorded at original purchase price.

Conservatism in Reported Provisions and Liabilities

Our analysis must be alert to the proposition relating provisions and liability values to earnings. In general,

When provisions and liabilities are *understated*, cumulative earnings are *overstated*.

This is true because earnings are relieved of charges necessary to bring the provisions or liabilities up to their market values. Examples are understatements in provisions for product warranties and environmental liabilities that yield overstatement in cumulative earnings. Conversely, an *overprovision* for current and future liabilities or losses yields an *understatement* of earnings (or overstatement of losses). An example is overestimation of severance costs of a planned restructuring.

We will describe in Chapter 6 how provisions for future costs and losses that are excessive shift the burden of costs and expenses from future income statements to the current period. Bearing in mind our propositions regarding the earnings effects from reported values of assets and liabilities, the critical analysis of these values represents an important factor in assessing earnings quality.

EXTERNAL FACTORS AND EARNINGS QUALITY

Earnings quality is affected by factors external to a company. These external factors make earnings more or less reliable. One factor is the quality of *foreign earnings*. Foreign earnings quality is affected by the difficulties and uncertainties in repatriation of funds, currency fluctuations, political and social conditions, and local customs and regulation. In certain countries, companies lack flexibility in dismissing personnel which essentially converts labor into a fixed cost. Another factor affecting earnings quality is *regulation*. For example, the regulatory environment confronting a public utility affects its earnings quality. An unsympathetic or hostile regulatory environment can affect costs and selling prices and thereby diminish earnings quality due to increased uncertainty of future profits. Also, the stability and reliability of *earnings sources* affect earnings quality. Government defense-related revenues are dependable in times of high international tensions, but affected by political events in peacetime. *Changing price levels* affect earnings quality. When price levels are rising, "inventory profits" or understatements in expenses like depreciation lower earnings quality. Finally, because of uncertainties due to *complexities of operations,* earnings of certain conglomerates are considered of lower quality.

GUIDANCE ANSWERS TO ANALYSIS VIEWPOINTS

AUDITOR

An auditor's main objective is an expression of an opinion on the fairness of financial statements according to generally accepted accounting principles. As auditor, you desire assurance on the absence of errors and irregularities in financial statements. Financial statement analysis can help identify any errors and irregularities affecting the statements. Also, this analysis compels our auditor to understand the company's operations and its performance in light of prevailing economic and industry conditions. Application of financial statement analysis is especially useful as a preliminary audit tool, directing the auditor to areas of greatest change and unexplained performance.

DIRECTOR

As a member of a company's board of directors, you are responsible for oversight of management and the safeguarding of shareholders' interests. Accordingly, a director's interest in the company is broad and risky. To reduce risk, a director uses financial statement analysis to monitor management and assess company profitability, growth, and financial condition. Because of a director's unique position, there is near unlimited access to internal financial and other records. Analysis of financial statements assists our director in: (1) recognizing causal relationships among business activities and events; (2) helping directors focus on the company and not on a maze of financial details; and (3) encouraging proactive and not reactive measures in confronting changing financial conditions.

BOARD MEMBER

Your concern with earnings quality is to ensure earnings accurately reflect the company's return and risk characteristics. Low earnings quality implies *inflated earnings* (returns) and/or *deflated risk* not reflecting actual return or risk characteristics. Regarding inflated earnings (returns), you can ask the auditor for evidence of management's use of liberal accounting principles or applications, aggressive behavior in discretionary accruals, asset overstatements, and liability understatements. Regarding deflated risk, you can ask about earnings sources, stability, variability, and trend. Additional risk-related questions can focus on the character or propensities of management, the regulatory environment, and overall business risk.

[Superscript A (B) denotes assignments based on Appendix 2A (2B).]

QUESTIONS

2-1. Describe the U.S. financial reporting environment including the following:
   a. Forces that impact the content of statutory financial reports
   b. Rule-making bodies and regulatory agencies that formulate GAAP used in financial reports
   c. Users of financial information and what alternative sources of information are available beyond statutory financial reports
   d. Enforcement and monitoring mechanisms to improve the integrity of statutory financial reports

2-2. Why are earnings announcements made in advance of the release of financial statements? What information do they contain and how are they different from financial statements?

2-3. Describe the content and purpose of at least four financial reports that must be filed with the SEC.

2-4. What constitutes contemporary GAAP?

2-5. Explain how accounting standards are established.

2-6. Who has the main responsibility for ensuring fair and accurate financial reporting by a company?

2-7. Describe factors that bring about managerial discretion for preparing financial statements.

2-8. Describe forces that serve to limit the ability of management to manage financial statements.

2-9. Describe alternative information sources beyond statutory financial reports that are available to investors and creditors.

2-10. Describe tasks that financial intermediaries perform on behalf of financial statement users.

2-11. Explain the materiality and conservatism constraints of financial accounting.

2-12. Describe empirical evidence showing that financial accounting information is relevant for decision making.

2-13. Describe at least four major limitations of financial statement information.

2-14. It is difficult to measure the business performance of a company in the short run using only cash flow measures because of timing and matching problems. Describe each of these problems and cite at least one example for each.

2-15. Describe the criteria necessary for a business to record revenue.

2-16. Explain when costs should be recognized as expenses.

2-17. Distinguish between short-term and long-term accruals.

2-18. Explain why cash flow measures of performance are less useful than accrual-based measures.

2-19. What factors give rise to the superiority of accrual accounting over cash accounting? Explain.

2-20. Accrual accounting information is conceptually more relevant than cash flows. Describe empirical findings that support this superiority of accrual accounting.

2-21. Accrual accounting information, cash flow information, and analysts' forecasts are information for investors. Compare and contrast each of these sources in terms of relevance and reliability.

2-22. Explain how accounting principles can, in certain cases, create differences between financial statement information and economic reality.

2-23. Explain how estimates and judgments of financial statement preparers can create differences between financial statement information and economic reality.

2-24. What is accounting analysis? Explain.

2-25. What is the process to carry out an accounting analysis?

2-26. What gives rise to accounting distortions? Explain.

2-27. Why do managers sometimes manage earnings?

2-28. What are popular earnings management strategies? Explain.

2-29. Explain what is meant by the term *earnings management* and what incentives managers have to engage in earnings management.

2-30. Describe the role that accrual accounting information and cash flow information play in your own models of company valuation.

2-31. Explain how accounting concepts and standards, and the financial statements based on them, are subject to the pervasive influence of individual judgments and incentives.

2-32. Would you be willing to pay more or less for a stock, on average, when the accounting information provided to you about the firm is unaudited? Explain.

2-33[A]. What are generally accepted auditing standards?

2-34[A]. What are auditing procedures? What are some basic objectives of a financial statement audit?

2-35[A]. What does the opinion section of the auditor's report usually cover?

2-36[A]. What are some implications to financial analysis stemming from the audit process?

2-37[A]. An auditor does not prepare financial statements but instead samples and investigates data to render a professional opinion on whether the statements are "fairly presented." List the potential implications of the auditor's responsibility to users that rely on financial statements.

2-38[A]. What does the auditor's reference to generally accepted accounting principles imply for our analysis of financial statements?

2-39[A]. What are some circumstances suggesting higher audit risk? Explain.

2-40[A]. **Citigroup** is currently audited by KPMG Peat Marwick. Who pays KPMG for its audit of Citigroup? To whom is KPMG providing assurance regarding the fair presentation of the Citigroup financial statements? List two market forces faced by KPMG that increase the probability that the firm effectively performed an audit with the interests of financial statement users in mind.

2-41[A]. Public accounting firms are being implored to assess a company's reported earnings per share relative to the market expectation of earnings per share (e.g., consensus analysts' forecast) when establishing the level of misstatement that is considered acceptable (the materiality threshold). Explain why a $.01 misstatement can be insignificant for one firm but significant to another otherwise comparable firm.

2-42[B]. What is meant by earnings quality? Why do users assess earnings quality? What major factors determine earnings quality?

2-43[B]. What are discretionary expenses? What is the importance of discretionary expenses for analysis of earnings quality?

2-44[B]. What is the relation between the reported value of assets and reported earnings? What is the relation between the reported values of liabilities, including provisions, and reported earnings?

2-45[B]. How does a balance sheet analysis provide a check on the validity and quality of earnings?

2-46[B]. What is the effect of external factors on earnings quality?

2-47[B]. Explain how earnings management affects earnings quality. How is earnings management distinguished from fraudulent reporting?

2-48[B]. Identify and explain three types of earnings management that can reduce earnings quality.

2-49[B]. What factors and incentives motivate companies (management) to engage in earnings management? What are the implications of these incentives for financial statement analysis?

EXERCISES

EXERCISE 2-1
Uniformity in Accounting

Some financial statement users maintain that despite its intrinsic intellectual appeal, uniformity in accounting seems unworkable in a complex modern society that relies, at least in part, on economic market forces.

Required:

a. Discuss at least three disadvantages of national or international accounting uniformity.

b. Explain whether uniformity in accounting necessarily implies comparability.

(CFA Adapted)

EXERCISE 2-2
Earnings Announcements and Market Reactions

Announcements of goods news or bad news earnings for the recently completed fiscal quarter usually create fairly small abnormal stock price changes on the day of the announcement.

Required:

a. Discuss how stock price changes over the preceding days or weeks help explain this phenomenon.

b. Discuss the types of information that the market might have received in advance of the earnings announcement.

c. How does the relatively small price reaction at the time of the earnings announcement relate to the price changes that are observed in the days or weeks prior to the announcement?

EXERCISE 2-3
Timeliness of Financial Statements

Some financial statement users criticize the timeliness of annual financial statements.

Required:

a. Explain why summary information in the income statement is not new information when the annual report is issued.

b. Describe the types of information in the income statement that are new information to financial statement users when the annual report is issued.

EXERCISE 2-4
Reliability of Quarterly Reports

The SEC requires companies to submit statutory financial reports on both a quarterly and an annual basis. The quarterly report is called the 10-Q.

Required:

What are two factors about quarterly financial reports that can be misleading if the analyst does not consider them when performing analysis of quarterly reports?

EXERCISE 2-5
Information in SEC Reports

The SEC requires various statutory reports from companies with publicly traded securities.

Required:

Identify which SEC report is the best place to find the following information.

a. Management's discussion of the financial results for the fiscal year.

b. Terms of the CEO's compensation and the total compensation paid to the CEO in the prior fiscal year.

c. Who is on the board of directors and are they from within or outside of the company?

d. How much are the directors paid for their services?

e. Results of operations and financial position of the company at the end of the second quarter.

f. Why a firm changed its auditors.

g. Details for the upcoming initial public offering of stock.

EXERCISE 2-6
Mechanisms to Monitor Financial Reporting

Managers are responsible for ensuring fair and accurate financial reporting. Managers also have inside information that can aid their estimates of future outcomes. Yet, managers face incentives to strategically report information in their best interests.

Required:

Assume a manager of a publicly traded company is intending to recognize revenues in an inappropriate and fraudulent manner. Explain the penalty(ies) that can be imposed on a manager by the monitoring and enforcement mechanisms in place to restrict such activity.

EXERCISE 2-7
Incentives for Voluntary Disclosure

There are various motivations for managers to make voluntary disclosures. Identify whether you believe managers are likely to release the following information in the form of voluntary disclosure (examine each case independently):

a. A company plans to sell an underperforming division for a substantial loss in the second quarter of next year.

b. A company is experiencing disappointing sales and, as a result, expects to report disappointing earnings at the end of this quarter.

c. A company plans to report especially strong earnings this quarter.

d. Management believes the consensus forecast of analysts is slightly higher than managers' forecasts.

e. Management strongly believes the company is undervalued at its current stock price.

EXERCISE 2-8
Financial Statement Information versus Analysts Forecasts

Financial statements are a major source of information about a company. Forecasts, reports, and recommendations from analysts are popular alternative sources of information.

Required:

a. Discuss the strengths of financial statement information for business decision makers.

b. Discuss the strengths of analyst forecast information for business decision makers.

c. Discuss how the two information sources in (*a*) and (*b*) are interrelated.

EXERCISE 2-9
Accrual Accounting versus Cash Flows

a. Identify at least two reasons why an accrual accounting income statement is more useful for analyzing business performance than a cash flow based income statement.

b. Describe what would be reported on the asset side of a cash flow based balance sheet versus the asset side of an accrual accounting balance sheet.

c. A strength of accrual accounting is its relevance for decision making. The strength of cash flow information is its reliability. Explain what makes accrual accounting more relevant and cash flows more reliable.

EXERCISE 2-10
Analyst Forecasts versus Financial Statements

Analysts produce forecasts of accounting earnings along with other forward-looking information. This information has strengths and weaknesses versus financial statement information.

Required:

a. Discuss whether you believe analysts forecasts are more relevant for business decision making than financial statement information.

b. Discuss whether you believe analysts forecasts are more reliable than financial statement information.

EXERCISE 2-11
Accrual Accounting Measurement Error

Accrual accounting requires estimates of future outcomes. For example, the reserve for bad debts is a forecast of the amount of current receivables that will ultimately prove uncollectible.

Required:

Identify and explain three reasons why accounting information might deviate from the underlying economic reality. Cite examples of transactions that might give rise to each of the reasons.

EXERCISE 2-12
Accounting for Hidden Reserves

The Chairman of the SEC refers to hidden reserves on the balance sheet as "cookie-jar" reserves. These reserves are built up in periods when earnings are strong and drawn down to bolster earnings in periods when earnings are weak.

Required:

Reserves for (1) bad debts and (2) inventory, along with the (3) large accruals associated with restructuring charges, are transactions that sometimes yield hidden reserves.

a. For each of these transactions, explain when and how a hidden reserve is created.

b. For each of these transactions, explain when and how a hidden reserve is drawn down to boost earnings.

EXERCISE 2-13
Banks and Hidden Reserves

Citicorp

In the past decade, several large "money center" banks recorded huge additions to their loan loss reserve. For example, **Citicorp** recorded a one-time addition to its loan loss reserve totaling about $3 billion. These additions to loan loss reserves led to large net losses for these banks. While most analysts agree that additional reserves were warranted, many speculated the banks recorded more reserve than necessary.

Required:

a. Why might a bank choose to record more loan loss reserve than necessary?

b. Explain how overstated loan loss reserves can be used to manage earnings in future years.

PROBLEMS

PROBLEM 2-1
Financial Statement Analysis and Standard Setting

Financial statement users often liken accounting standard setting to a political process. One user asserted that: *My view is that the setting of accounting standards is as much a product of political action as of flawless logic or empirical findings. Why? Because the setting of standards is a social decision. Standards place restrictions on behavior; therefore, they must be accepted by the affected parties. Acceptance may be forced or voluntary or some of both. In a democratic society, getting acceptance is an exceedingly complicated process that requires skillful marketing in a political arena.* Many parties affected by proposed standards intervene to protect their own interests while disguising their motivations as altruistic or theoretical. People often say, "If you like the answer, you'll love the theory." It is also alleged that those who are regulated by the standard-setting process have excessive influence over the regulatory process. One FASB member declared: "The business community has much greater influence than it's ever had over standard setting. I think it's unhealthy. It is the preparer community that is really being regulated in this process, and if we have those being regulated having a dominant role in the regulatory process, that's asking for major trouble."

Required:

Discuss the relevance of the accounting standard-setting process to analysis of financial statements.

PROBLEM 2-2
Neutrality of Measurements in Financial Statements

Financial reporting has been likened to cartography:

> Information cannot be neutral–it cannot therefore be reliable–if it is selected or presented for the purpose of producing some chosen effect on human behavior. It is this quality of neutrality which makes a map reliable; and the essential nature of accounting, I believe, is cartographic. Accounting is financial mapmaking. The better the map, the more completely it represents the complex phenomena that are being mapped. We do not judge a map by the behavioral effects it produces. The distribution of natural wealth or rainfall shown on a map may lead to population shifts or changes in industrial location, which the government may like or dislike. That should be no concern of the cartographer. We judge his map by how well it represents the facts. People can then react to it as they will.

Required:

a. Explain why neutrality is such an important quality of financial statements.

b. Identify examples of the lack of neutrality in accounting reports.

PROBLEM 2-3

Analysts' Information Needs and Accounting Measurements

An editor of the *Financial Analysts Journal* reviewed an earlier edition of this book and asserted:

> Broadly speaking, accounting numbers are of two types: those that can be measured and those that have to be estimated. Investors who feel that accounting values are more real than market values should remember that, although the estimated numbers in the accounting statements often have a greater impact, singly or together, than the measured numbers, accountants' estimates are rarely based on any serious attempt by accountants at business or economic judgment.
>
> The main reason accountants shy away from precise statements of principle for the determination of asset values is that neither they nor anyone else has yet come up with principles that will consistently give values plausible enough that, if accounting statements were based on these principles, users would take them seriously.

Required:

a. Describe what is meant by measurement in accounting.

b. According to this editor, what are the kinds of measurements investors want?

c. Discuss whether the objectives of accountants and investors regarding accounting measurement are reconcilable.

PROBLEM 2-4

Standard Setting and Politics

A FASB member expressed the following view:

> Are we going to set accounting standards in the private sector or not? . . . Part of the answer depends on how the business community views accounting standards. Are they rules of conduct, designed to restrain unsocial behavior and arbitrate conflicts of economic interest? Or are they rules of measurement, designed to generalize and communicate as accurately as possible the complex results of economic events? . . . Rules of conduct call for a political process . . . Rules of measurement, on the other hand, call for a research process of observation and experimentation . . . Intellectually, the case is compelling for viewing accounting as a measurement process . . . But the history of accounting standard setting has been dominated by the other view–that accounting standards are rules of conduct. The FASB was created out of the ashes of predecessors burned up in the fires of the resulting political process.

Required:

a. Discuss your views on the difference between "rules of conduct" and "rules of measurement."

b. Explain how accounting standard setting is a political process. Identify arguments for and against viewing accounting standard setting as political.

PROBLEM 2-5

Accounting in Society

Consider the following excerpt from the *Financial Analysts Journal:*

> Strictly speaking, the objectives of financial reporting are the objectives of society and not of accountants and auditors, as such. Similarly, society has objective law and medicine–namely, justice and health for the people–which are not necessarily the objectives of lawyers and doctors, as such, in the conduct of their respective "business."
>
> In a variety of ways, society exerts pressure on a profession to act more nearly as if it actively shared the objectives of society. Society's pressure is to be measured by the degree of accommodation on the part of the profession under pressure, and by the degree of counterpressure applied by the profession. For example, doctors accommodate society by getting better educations than otherwise and reducing incompetence in their ranks. They apply counterpressure and gain protection by forming medical associations.

Required:

a. Describe ways in which society has brought pressure on accountants to better serve its needs.

b. Describe how the accounting profession has responded to these pressures. Could the profession have better responded?

PROBLEM 2-6
Financial Reporting or Financial Subterfuge

Consider the following claim from a business observer:

> An accountant's job is to conceal, not to reveal. An accountant is not asked to give outsiders an accurate picture of what's going on in a company. He is asked to transform the figures on a company's operations in such a way that it will be impossible to recreate the original figures.
>
> An income statement for a toy company doesn't tell how many toys of various kinds the company sold, or who the company's best customers are. The balance sheet doesn't tell how many of each kind of toy the company has in inventory, or how much is owed by each customer who is late in paying his bills.
>
> In general, anything that a manager uses to do his job will be of interest to some stockholders, customers, creditors, or government agencies. Managerial accounting differs from financial accounting only because the accountant has to hide some of the facts and figures managers find useful. The accountant simply has to throw out most of the facts and some of the figures that the managers use when he creates the financial statements for outsiders.
>
> The rules of accounting reflect this tension. Even if the accountant thought of himself as working only for the good of society, he would conceal certain facts in the reports he helps write. Since the accountant is actually working for the company, or even for the management of the company, he conceals many facts that outsiders would like to have revealed.

Required:

a. Discuss this observer's misgivings on the role of the accountant in financial reporting.

b. Discuss what type of omitted information the business observer is referring to.

PROBLEM 2-7
Contemporary Valuation

Equity valuations in today's market are arguably too high. Many analysts assert that price-earnings ratios are so high as to constitute an irrational valuation "bubble" that is bound to burst and drag valuations down. Skeptics are especially wary of the valuations for high-tech and Internet companies. Proponents of the "new paradigm" argue that the unusually high price-earnings ratios associated with many high-tech and Internet companies are justified because modern business is fundamentally different. In fact, many believe these companies are still, on average, undervalued. They argue that these companies have invested great sums in intangible assets that will produce large future profits. Also, research and development costs are expensed. This means they reduce income each period and are not reported as assets on the balance sheet. Consequently, earnings appear lower than normal and this yields price-earnings ratios that appear unreasonably high.

Required:
Assess and critique the positions of both the skeptics and proponents of this new paradigm.

PROBLEM 2-8
Income Measurement and Interpretation

In a discussion of corporate income, a user of financial statements alleges that "One of the real problems with income is that you never really know what it is. The only way you can find out is to liquidate a company and reduce everything to cash. Then you can subtract what went into the company from what came out and the result is income. Until then, income is only a product of accounting rituals."

Required:

a. Do you agree with the above statement? Explain. What problems do you foresee in measuring income in the manner described?

b. What assumptions underlie periodic measurement of income under accrual accounting? Which income approach do you think is more reasonable? Explain.

PROBLEM 2-9
Specialized Accounting Information

Polygram

According to an article in the December 20, 1999, *Wall Street Journal,* a European filmmaking studio, **Polygram,** is considering funding movie production by selling securities. These securities will yield returns to investors based on the actual cash flows of the movies that are financed from the sale of these securities.

Required:

a. What information would you suggest the filmmakers provide to investors to encourage them to invest in the production of a particular movie or movies (i.e., what information is relevant to your decision to invest in a movie)?

b. What kind of evidence can be included to support claims in the prospectus (i.e., what can maximize the reliability of the information released)?

PROBLEM 2-10
Politics and Promulgation of Standards

The FASB in *SFAS No. 123,* "Accounting for Stock-Based Options," encourages (but does not require) companies to recognize compensation expense based on the fair value of stock options awarded to their employees and managers. Early drafts of this proposal *required* the recognition of the fair value of the options. But the FASB met opposition from companies and chose to only *encourage* the recognition of fair value.

Required:

a. Discuss the role you believe the following parties should play in the accounting standard promulgation process:

(1) FASB (5) Companies (CEO)
(2) SEC (6) Accounting firms
(3) AICPA (7) Investors
(4) Congress

b. Discuss which parties likely lobbied for the change from requiring expense recognition to only encouraging the expensing of stock options.

PROBLEM 2-11
Relations between Income, Cash Flow, and Stock Price

Lands' End

The following information is extracted from the annual report of **Lands' End** (in millions, except per share data):

Fiscal year	Year 9	Year 8	Year 7	Year 6	Year 5	Year 4
Net income	$31.2	$64.2	$ 51.0	$30.6	$36.1	$43.7
Cash from (used by) operations	74.3	(26.9)	121.8	41.4	34.5	22.4
Net cash flow	0.03	(86.5)	75.7	11.8	(16.1)	(1.2)
Free cash flow*	27.5	(74.6)	103.3	27.5	2.4	5.1
Market price per share (end of fiscal year)	32.375	39.312	28.375	14.625	16.125	24.375
Common shares outstanding	30.1	31.0	32.4	33.7	34.8	35.9

**Defined as: Cash flow from operations − Capital expenditures − Dividends.*

Required:

a. Calculate and graph the following separate relations:
   (1) Net income per share (EPS) and market price per share
   (2) Cash from operations per share and market price per share
   (3) Net cash flow per share and market price per share
   (4) Free cash flow per share and market price per share

b. Which of the measures extracted from the annual report appear to best explain changes in stock price? Discuss the implications of this for stock valuation.

c. Choose another company and prepare similar graphs. Do your observations from Lands' End generalize?

CHECK
EPS performs best

PROBLEM 2-12
Earnings Management Strategies

Marsh Supermarkets

The following information is taken from **Marsh Supermarkets** fiscal 20X7 annual report:

> During the first quarter, we made several decisions resulting in a $13 million charge to earnings. A new accounting pronouncement, *FAS 121,* required the Company to take a $7.5 million charge. *FAS 121* dictates how companies are to account for the carrying values of their assets. This rule affects all public and private companies.
>
> The magnitude of this charge created a window of opportunity to address several other issues that, in the Company's best long term interest, needed to be resolved. We amended our defined benefit retirement plan, and took significant reorganization and other special charges. These charges, including *FAS 121,* totaled almost $13 million. The result was a $7.1 million loss for the quarter and a small net loss for the year. Although these were difficult decisions because of their short term impact, they will have positive implications for years to come.

Marsh Supermarkets' net income for fiscal 20X5 and 20X6 is $8.6 million and $9.0 million, respectively.

Required:

What earnings management strategy appears to have been used by Marsh in fiscal 20X7 in conjunction with the *FAS 121* charge (note, the $7.5 million charge from adoption of *FAS 121* is not avoidable)? Why do you think Marsh pursued this strategy?

CHECK
Big bath strategy

PROBLEM 2-13
Earnings Management Strategies

Emerson Electric

Emerson Electric is engaged in design, manufacture, and sale of a broad range of electrical, electromechanical, and electronic products and systems. The following shows Emerson's net income and net income before extraordinary items for the past 20 years (in millions):

Year	Net Income	Net Income before Extraordinary Items	Year	Net Income	Net Income before Extraordinary Items	Year	Net Income	Net Income before Extraordinary Items
Y1	$201.0	$201.0	Y8	$408.9	$408.9	Y15	$ 708.1	$ 708.1
Y2	237.7	237.7	Y9	467.2	467.2	Y16	788.5	904.4
Y3	273.3	273.3	Y10	528.8	528.8	Y17	907.7	929.0
Y4	300.1	300.1	Y11	588.0	588.0	Y18	1,018.5	1,018.5
Y5	302.9	302.9	Y12	613.2	613.2	Y19	1,121.9	1,121.9
Y6	349.2	349.2	Y13	631.9	631.9	Y20	1,228.6	1,228.6
Y7	401.1	401.1	Y14	662.9	662.9			

Emerson has achieved consistent earnings growth for over 160 straight quarters (over 40 years).

Required:

CHECK
Income smoothing strategy

a. What earnings strategy do you think Emerson has applied over the years to maintain its record of earnings growth?

b. Describe the extent you believe Emerson's earnings record reflects business activities, excellent management, and/or earnings management.

c. Describe how Emerson's earnings strategy is applied in good years and bad.

d. Identify years where Emerson likely built hidden reserves and the years it probably drew upon hidden reserves.

PROBLEM 2-14
Usefulness of Accrual Accounting

A finance textbook likens accrual accounting information to "nail soup." The recipe for nail soup includes the usual soup ingredients such as broth and noodles, but it also includes nails. This means with each spoonful of nail soup, one gets nails with broth and noodles. Accordingly, to eat the soup, one must remove the nails from each spoonful. The textbook went on to say that accountants include much valuable information in financial reports but one must remove the accounting accruals (nails) to make the information useful.

Required:
Critique the analogy of accrual accounting to "nail soup."

PROBLEM 2-15
Relevance of Accruals

Consider the following: *While accrual accounting information is imperfect, ignoring it and making cash flows the basis of all analysis and business decisions is like throwing the baby out with the bath water.*

Required:

a. Do you agree or disagree with this statement? Explain.

b. How does accrual accounting provide superior information to cash flows?

c. What are the imperfections of accrual accounting? Is it possible for accrual accounting to depict economic reality? Explain.

d. What is the prudent approach to analysis using accrual accounting information?

PROBLEM 2-16[B]
Earnings Quality

American Express

The following is an excerpt from a quarterly earnings announcement by **American Express:**

American Express reports record quarterly net income of $648 million

($ millions except per share amounts)	QUARTER ENDED SEPTEMBER 30 20X9	20X8	Percentage Inc./(Dec.)
Net income	$ 648	$ 574	13.0%
Net revenues	$4,879	$4,342	12.4%
Per share net income (Basic)	$1.45	$1.27	14.2%
Average common shares outstanding	446.0	451.6	(1.2%)
Return on average equity	25.3%	23.9%	

($ millions except per share amounts)	NINE MONTHS ENDED SEPTEMBER 30 20X9	20X8	Percentage Inc./(Dec.)
Net income	$ 1,869	$ 1,611	16.0%
Net revenues	$14,211	$12,662	12.2%
Per share net income (Basic)	$4.18	$3.53	18.4%
Average common shares outstanding	447.0	456.2	(2.0%)
Return on average equity	25.3%	23.9%	

Due to a change in accounting rules, the company is required to capitalize software costs rather than expense them as they occur. For the third quarter of 20X9, this amounted to a pre-tax benefit of $68 million (net of amortization). Also, the securitization of credit card receivables produced a gain of $55 million ($36 million after tax) in the current quarter.

Required:

Evaluate and comment on both (a) the earnings quality and (b) the relative performance of American Express in the most recent quarter relative to the same quarter of the prior fiscal year.

CHECK
Adjust for unusual items

CASES

CASE 2-1
Analysis of Kodak's Statements

Answer the following questions using the annual report of **Kodak** in Appendix A.

Kodak

a. Who is responsible for the preparation and integrity of Kodak's financial statements and notes? Where is this responsibility stated in the annual report?

b. In which note does Kodak report its significant accounting policies used to prepare financial statements?

c. What type of audit opinion is reported in its annual report and whose opinion is it?

d. Is any of the information in its annual report based on estimates? If so, where does Kodak discuss this?

e. Did Kodak make any changes that affect the comparability of this annual report with that of the prior year?

f. What forward-looking information is contained in this annual report?

g. What cautions does the company make to the financial statement user about forward-looking information?

h. The company reports its health, safety, and environmental report along with its workforce diversity highlights. Do you believe this is required or voluntary disclosure?

i. How many internal and how many external members comprise the board of directors for Kodak? (*Note:* For parts *i* and *j*, you must access Kodak's 10-K from either the company's website or the SEC EDGAR database [**www.sec.gov**].)

CHECK
(*i*) Three internal

j. What committees are established by the board of directors to oversee the company?

CASE 2-2
Industry Accounting and Analysis: Historical Case

Two potential methods of accounting for the cost of oil drilling are full cost and successful efforts. Under the *full-cost method,* a drilling company capitalizes costs both for successful wells and dry holes. This means it classifies all costs as assets on its balance sheet. A company charges these costs against revenues as it extracts and sells the oil. Under the *successful-efforts method,* a company expenses the costs of dry holes as they are incurred, resulting in immediate charges against earnings. Costs of only successful wells are capitalized. Many small and midsized drilling companies use the full-cost method and, as a result, millions of dollars of drilling costs appear as assets on their balance sheets.

The SEC imposes a limit to full-cost accounting. Costs capitalized under this method cannot exceed a ceiling defined as the present value of company reserves. Capitalized costs above the ceiling are expensed. Oil companies, primarily smaller ones, have been successful in prevailing on the SEC to keep the full-cost accounting method as an alternative even though the accounting profession took a position in favor of the successful-efforts method. Because the imposition of the ceiling rule occurred during a time of relatively high oil prices, the companies accepted it, confident that it would have no practical effect on them.

With a subsequent decline in oil prices, many companies found that drilling costs carried as assets on their balance sheets exceeded the sharply lower ceilings. This meant they were faced with write-offs. Oil companies, concerned about the effect that big write-offs would have on their ability to conduct business, began a fierce lobbying effort to change SEC accounting rules so as to avoid sizable write-offs that threatened to lower their earnings as well as their equity capital. The SEC staff supported a suspension of the rules because, they maintained, oil prices could rise and because companies would still be required to disclose the difference between the market value and book value of their oil reserves. The proposal would have temporarily relaxed the rules pending the results of a study by the SEC on whether to change or rescind the ceiling test. The proposal would have suspended the requirement to use current prices when computing the ceiling amount in determining whether a write-off of reserves is required. The SEC eventually rejected the proposal that would have enabled 250 of the nation's oil and gas producing companies to postpone write-downs on the declining values of their oil and gas reserves while acknowledging that the impact of the decision could trigger defaults on bank loans. The SEC chairman said "the rules are not stretchable at a time of stress."

Tenneco Co. found a way to cope with the SEC's refusal to sanction postponement of the write-offs. It announced a switch to successful-efforts accounting along with nearly $1 billion in charges against prior years' earnings. In effect, Tenneco would take the unamortized dry-hole drilling costs currently on its balance sheet and apply them against prior years' revenues. These costs would affect prior year results only and would not show up as write-offs against currently reported income.

Required:

a. Discuss what conclusions an analyst might derive from the evolution of accounting in the oil and gas industry.

b. Explain the potential effect Tenneco's proposed change in accounting method would have on the reporting of its operating results over the years.

CASE 2-3[B]

Earnings Quality and Accounting Changes

Canada Steel Co. produces steel casting and metal fabrications for sale to manufacturers of heavy construction machinery and agricultural equipment. Early in Year 3, the company's president sent the following memorandum to the financial vice president:

TO: Robert Kinkaid, Financial Vice President
FROM: Richard Johnson, President
SUBJECT: Accounting and Financial Policies

Fiscal Year 2 was a difficult year for us, and the recession is likely to continue into Year 3. While the entire industry is suffering, we might be hurting our performance unnecessarily with accounting and business policies that are not appropriate. Specifically:

(1) We depreciate most fixed assets (foundry equipment) over their estimated useful lives on the "tonnage-of-production" method. Accelerated methods and shorter lives are used for income tax purposes. A switch to straight-line for financial reporting purposes could (a) eliminate the deferred tax liability on our balance sheet, and (b) leverage our profits if business picks up in Year 4.

(2) Several years ago you convinced me to change from the FIFO to LIFO inventory method. Since inflation is now down to a 4 percent annual rate, and balance sheet strength is important in our current environment, I estimate we can increase shareholders' equity by about $2.0 million, working capital by $4.0 million, and Year 3 earnings by $0.5 million if we return to FIFO in Year 3. This adjustment is real–these profits were earned by us over the past several years and should be recognized.

(3) If we make the inventory change, our stock repurchase program can be continued. The same shareholder who sold us 50,000 shares last year at $100 per share would like to sell another 20,000 shares at the same price. However, to obtain additional bank financing, we must maintain the current ratio at 3:1 or better. It seems prudent to decrease our capitalization if return on assets is unsatisfactory and our industry is declining. Also, interest rates are lower (11 percent prime) and we can save $60,000 after taxes annually once our $3.00 per share dividend is resumed.

These actions would favorably affect our profitability and liquidity ratios as shown in the *pro forma* income statement and balance sheet data for Year 3 ($ millions).

	Year 1	Year 2	Year 3 Estimate
Net sales	$50.6	$42.3	$29.0
Net income (loss)	$ 2.0	$ (5.7)	$ 0.1
Net profit margin	4.0%	—	0.3%
Dividends	$ 0.7	$ 0.6	$ 0.0
Return on assets	7.2%	—	0.4%
Return on equity	11.3%	—	0.9%
Current assets	$17.6	$14.8	$14.5
Current liabilities	$ 6.6	$ 4.9	$ 4.5
Long-term debt	$ 2.0	$ 6.1	$ 8.1
Shareholders' equity	$17.7	$11.4	$11.5
Shares outstanding (000s)	226.8	170.5	150.5
Per common share:			
Book value	$78.05	$66.70	$76.41
Market price range	$42–$34	$65–$45	$62–$55*

**Year to date.*

Please give me your reaction to my proposals as soon as possible.

Required

Assume you are Robert Kinkaid, the financial vice president. Appraise the president's rationale for each of the proposals. You should place special emphasis on how each accounting or business decision affects earnings quality. Support your response with ratio analysis.

CHECK
Sig. incr. in debt-to-equity

WEB ACTIVITIES

The Web Activities are located on the book's website at www.mhhe.com/wild8e.

CHAPTER THREE

3

ANALYZING FINANCING ACTIVITIES

A LOOK BACK <

Chapters 1 and 2 presented an overview of financial statement analysis and financial reporting. We showed how financial statements report on financing, investing, and operating activities. We also introduced accounting analysis and explained its importance for financial statement analysis.

A LOOK AT THIS CHAPTER •

This chapter describes accounting analysis of financing activities—both creditor and equity financing. Our analysis of creditor financing considers both operating liabilities and financing liabilities. Analysis of operating liabilities includes extensive study of postretirement benefits. Analysis of financing liabilities focuses on topics such as leasing and off-balance-sheet financing, along with conventional forms of debt financing. We also analyze components of equity financing and the relevance of book value.

A LOOK AHEAD >

Chapters 4 and 5 extend our accounting analysis to investing activities. We analyze operating assets such as current assets and property, plant, and equipment, along with investments in securities and intercorporate acquisitions. Chapter 6 analyzes operating activities.

ANALYSIS OBJECTIVES

- Identify and assess the principal characteristics of liabilities and equity.
- Analyze and interpret lease disclosures and explain their implications and the adjustments to financial statements.
- Analyze postretirement disclosures and assess their consequences for firm valuation and risk.
- Analyze contingent liability disclosures and describe their risks.
- Identify off-balance-sheet financing and its consequences to risk analysis.
- Analyze and interpret liabilities at the edge of equity.
- Explain capital stock and analyze and interpret its distinguishing features.
- Describe retained earnings and their distribution through dividends.

SPEs and the Fall of Enron

In October 2001, Enron announced a $1 billion after-tax charge to its third quarter earnings and a $1.2 billion reduction of stockholders' equity. The following month, Enron announced its intentions to restate annual reports for 1997–2000 and record $569 million of additional charges. Those losses eroded investor confidence in the company and triggered acceleration clauses in its debt, resulting in Enron's bankruptcy. In all, over $60 billion in market capitalization was destroyed.

Enron had used a financing technique called *special purpose entities (SPEs)* to conceal hundreds of millions of dollars of debt from investors and to avoid recognition of losses on investments. SPEs have been used for decades as a legitimate financing technique and are very much in use today. Many retailers, for example, sell private label credit card receivables to an SPE that purchases them with funds raised from the sale of bonds to the investing public. Investors receive a quality investment and the company receives needed cash.

Enron provides an extraordinary example of the misuse of SPEs. It created shell companies that were thinly capitalized and used them to purchase assets at inflated prices, thus allowing it to prop up earnings. Even worse, Enron used these SPEs as counterparties for hedging activities to protect its investment portfolio. Those SPEs issued guarantees to Enron to protect its investments from a decline in value. Since the SPEs were so thinly capitalized and managed by Enron executives, Enron was essentially insuring itself.

. . . do not invest in a firm that you cannot understand.

In its annual report, Enron treated the SPEs as independent companies not consolidated with Enron, thus allowing it to hide unrealized losses from investors. The company did disclose the SPEs in its related party footnote. However, as Sharon Watkins put it in her now-famous whistleblower memo to Chairman Kenneth Lay: "My concern is that the footnotes don't adequately explain the transactions. If adequately explained, the investor would know that the 'Entities' described in our related party footnote are thinly capitalized, [and] the equity holders have [little at risk] . . . I am incredibly nervous that we will implode in a wave of accounting scandals."

Enron's failure and the resulting losses to investors have prompted cries for additional disclosures. Regardless of future legislative response, at least one lesson for investors is clear: read and understand the footnotes before investing and do not invest in a firm you cannot understand.

Source: Watkins internal memo to Kenneth Lay, 2001; Enron 2000 10-K; Powers report to Enron board of directors, February 2002.

PREVIEW OF CHAPTER 3

Business activities are financed with either liabilities or equity, or both. **Liabilities** are financing obligations that require future payment of money, services, or other assets. They are outsiders' claims against a company's present and future assets and resources. Liabilities can be either financing or operating in nature and are usually senior to those

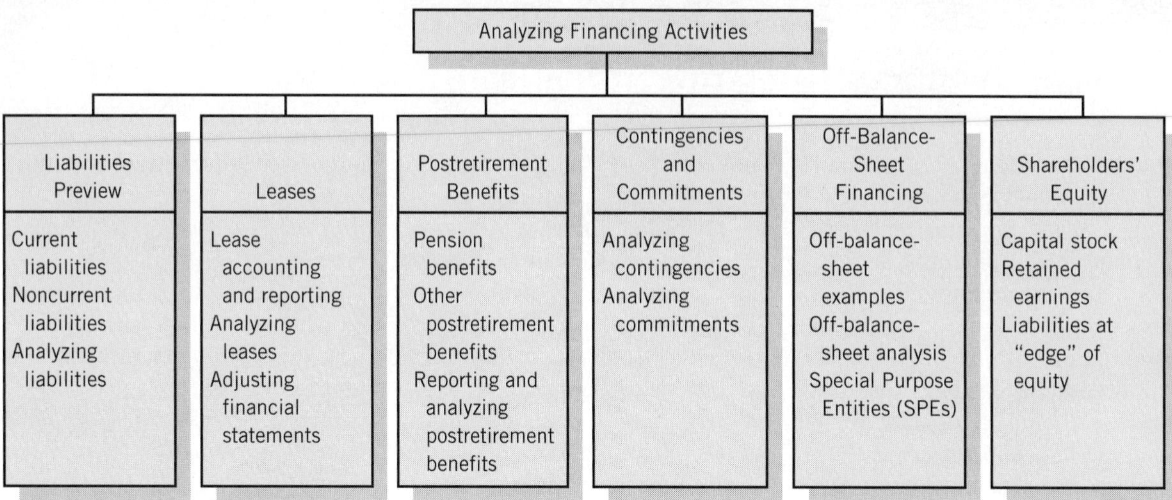

of equity holders. **Financing liabilities** are all forms of credit financing such as long-term notes and bonds, short-term borrowings, and leases. **Operating liabilities** are obligations that arise from operations such as trade creditors, deferred credits, and postretirement obligations. Liabilities are commonly reported as either **current** or **noncurrent**–usually based on whether the obligation is due within one year or not. **Equity** refers to claims of owners on the net assets of a company. Claims of owners are junior to creditors, meaning they are residual claims to all assets once claims of creditors are satisfied. Equity holders are exposed to the maximum risk associated with a company but also are entitled to all residual returns of a company. Certain other securities, such as convertible bonds, straddle the line separating liabilities and equity and represent a hybrid form of financing. This chapter describes these different forms of financing, how companies account and report for them, and their implications for analysis of financial statements.

LIABILITIES

We describe both current and noncurrent liabilities in this section. We also discuss their implications to financial statement analysis.

Current Liabilities

Current (or **short-term**) **liabilities** are obligations whose settlement requires the use of current assets or the incurrence of another current liability. The period over which companies expect to settle current liabilities is the longer of one year or the operating cycle. Conceptually, companies should record all liabilities at the present value of the cash outflow required to settle them. In practice, current liabilities are recorded at their maturity value, and not their present value, due to the short time period until their settlement. Moreover, the availability of current assets for paying current liabilities does not justify offsetting one against another for reporting purposes.

Current liabilities are of two types. The first type arises from operating activities and includes taxes payable, unearned revenues, advance payments, accounts payable, and other accruals of operating expenses. The second type of current liabilities arises from financing activities and includes short-term borrowings and any current portion of long-term debt.

Companies classify short-term obligations as noncurrent when they intend to refinance them on a long-term basis and can demonstrate the ability to do so. Refinancing on a long-term basis means replacing short-term obligations with either long-term obligations or equity securities or renewing them for a period extending beyond one year from the balance sheet date. A company demonstrates its ability to refinance on a long-term basis by either: (1) having issued long-term obligations or equity securities to replace the short-term obligations after the balance sheet date but before its release, or (2) having entered into an agreement with a financing source permitting the refinancing of short-term obligations when due. Financing agreements that are cancelable for violation of a provision that can be evaluated differently by the parties to the agreement (such as "a material adverse change" or "failure to maintain satisfactory operations") do not meet these conditions.

DEBT CLASS
Improper classification of liabilities can affect key ratios in financial analysis.

Many borrowing agreements include covenants to protect creditors. A violation of a noncurrent debt covenant, such as a minimum level of working capital, does not require reclassification of the noncurrent liability as current provided one of the following conditions is met:

1. The lender either waives or loses the right to demand repayment for more than a year from the balance sheet date–for example, a lender might lose the right to demand repayment if a company subsequently cures a violation existing at the balance sheet date and the debt is no longer callable at the time of issuing financial statements.
2. The obligation is not callable because it is probable that the company will cure a violation existing at the balance sheet date within a specified grace period (these circumstances are typically disclosed).

TYING DYING?
Regulators are investigating "tying" by commercial banks—the illegal practice of granting loans only if customers sign on for other services.

BMC Industries provides an example of reclassification of noncurrent debt to current:

ANALYSIS EXCERPT

The third quarter loss . . . placed the Company in default of net worth covenants under both its revolving credit and subordinated debt agreements. Because the defaults triggered a technical acceleration of the Company's senior (revolving credit) debt and allow the subordinated lenders to accelerate, the related debt has been classified as current at December 31. The Company intends to eliminate defaults under its debt agreements by restructuring the agreements through the use of proceeds from divestitures. Until the Company is able to reduce its debt through divestitures and achieve a related restructuring of its debt agreements, it will remain in default of, and subject to the lenders' rights of acceleration under those agreements.

WALKING AWAY
Some high-profile companies have turned their backs on debt obligations, including Iridium World Communications (a satellite mobile-phone company with debt exceeding $1 billion), the restaurant chain Planet Hollywood, and clothing retailer Loehmann's.

Noncurrent Liabilities

Noncurrent (or **long-term**) **liabilities** are obligations not payable within the longer of one year or the operating cycle. They include loans, bonds, debentures, and notes. Noncurrent liabilities can take various forms, and their assessment and measurement requires disclosure of all restrictions and covenants. Disclosures include interest rates, maturity dates, conversion privileges, call features, and subordination provisions. They also include pledged collateral, sinking fund requirements, and revolving credit provisions. Companies must disclose defaults of any liability provisions, including those for interest and principal repayments.

BOWIE BONDS
David Bowie issued more than $50 million in bonds backed by future royalties from 25 of his albums, including *Ziggy Stardust*, *Thin White Duke*, and *Let's Dance.*

A bond is a typical noncurrent liability. The bond's par (or face) value along with its coupon (contract) rate determines cash interest paid on the bond. Bond issuers sometimes sell bonds at a price either below par (at a discount) or in excess of par (at a premium). The discount or premium reflects an adjustment of the bond price to yield the market's required rate of return. A discount is amortized over the life of the bond and increases the effective interest rate paid by the borrower. Conversely, any premium is also amortized but it decreases the effective interest rate incurred. Non-interest-bearing obligations, or those bearing unreasonable rates of interest, are recorded at an amount reflecting the imputation of a reasonable interest rate. This not only shows the debt at an amount comparable to other interest-bearing debt obligations, but also provides for the computation of a realistic interest charge. If debt results from acquisition of assets, this computation helps ensure that a reasonable cost is assigned to these assets.

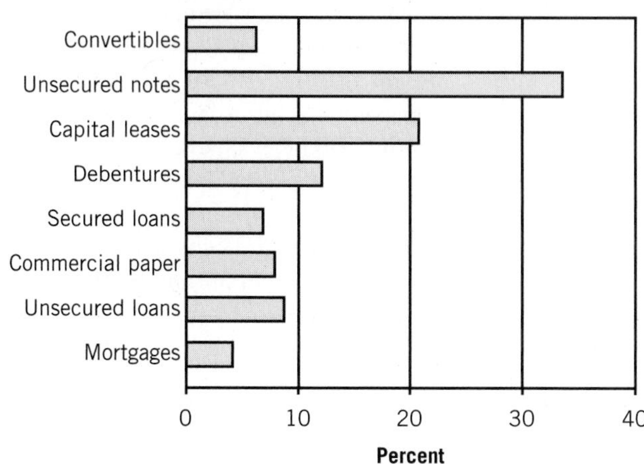

Source: *Accounting Trends and Techniques*

JUNK BONDS
Junk bond issuances in default fell from about 30% in the 80s to under 10% in the 90s.

Bond issuers offer a variety of incentives to promote the sale of bonds and reduce the interest rate required. These include convertibility features and attachments of warrants to purchase the issuer's common stock. A company can offer holders of its convertible debt an incentive to exercise their rights to convert it to equity securities. We refer to this offer as a *convertible debt sweetener.* A company is required to recognize this conversion incentive as an expense and cannot report it as extraordinary.

CONVERTIBLES
In the past decade, convertible bonds yielded about 80% of the return of stock funds but with only 65% of the price volatility.

Another common liability is purchase commitments. Companies frequently agree to buy inventory months or even years in advance. Disclosure is required for these types of commitments when they are unconditional purchase obligations that provide financing to suppliers and are not recognized on the purchaser's balance sheet. For those purchase obligations that are recognized on the balance sheet, the purchasing company must disclose its payments for each of the next five years.

Disclosure is also required for future payments on long-term borrowings and for any redeemable stock. This would include:

- Maturities and any sinking funds requirements for each of the next five years.
- Redemption requirements for each of the next five years.

Examples of disclosures for current and noncurrent liabilities are in Notes 7 through 10 of the financial statements of Kodak in Appendix A. Note 10 for Kodak, under "other commitments and contingencies," describes its purchase agreements with several

Analysis Research

ACCOUNTING-BASED LIABILITY RESTRICTIONS

Do all bonds offer holders the same degree of security for safeguarding their investments? Are all bonds of equal risk? How might we choose among bonds with identical payment schedules and coupon rates? Analysis research on liabilities provides us with some insight into these questions. Namely, bonds are not of equal risk, and an important factor of this risk relates to restrictions, or lack thereof, in liability agreements. Creditors establish liability restrictions (or covenants) to safeguard their investments. These restrictions often limit management behavior that might harm the interests of creditors. Violating any restriction is usually grounds for "technical default," providing creditors legal grounds to demand immediate repayment. Liability restrictions can reduce creditors' risk exposure.

Restrictions on management behavior take many forms, including:

- Dividend distribution restrictions.
- Working capital restrictions.
- Debt-to-equity ratio restrictions.
- Seniority of asset claim restrictions.
- Acquisition and divestment restrictions.
- Liability issuance restrictions.

These restrictions limit the dilution of net assets by constraining management's ability to distribute assets to new or continuing shareholders, or to new creditors. Details of these restrictions are often available in a liability's prospectus, a company's annual report, SEC filings, and various creditor information services (e.g., *Moody's Manuals*). Many restrictions are in the form of accounting-based constraints. For example, dividend payment restrictions are often expressed in the form of a minimum level of retained earnings that companies must maintain. This means the selection and application of accounting procedures are, therefore, potentially affected by the existence of liability restrictions.

companies to deliver products and services. This note includes the minimum payment amounts for these agreements for the next six years.

Analyzing Liabilities

Since liabilities are claims against companies, we need assurance that companies account for them. This includes disclosure of their amounts and due dates, including any conditions, encumbrances, and limitations they impose on a company. We need to recognize that many companies attempt to reduce the amount of liabilities reported on their financial statements. We must also recognize that certain liabilities are more apt to be misclassified or inadequately described.

DEBT LOADED
Nissan Motor Co. admits its mishandling of debts drove Japan's No. 2 automaker into financial distress.

Auditors are one source of assurance in our identification and measurement of liabilities. Auditors use techniques like direct confirmation, review of board minutes, reading of contracts and agreements, and questioning of those knowledgeable about company obligations to satisfy themselves that companies record all liabilities. Another source of assurance is double-entry accounting, which requires that for every asset, resource, or cost acquired, there is a counterbalancing entry for the obligation or resource expended. However, there is *no* entry required for most commitments and contingent liabilities. In this case, our analysis often must rely on notes to financial statements and on management commentary in annual reports and related documents. We also can check on the accuracy and reasonableness of debt amounts by reconciling them to a company's disclosures for interest expense and interest paid in cash. Any significant unexplained differences require further analysis or management explanation.

When liabilities are understated, we must be aware of a likely overstatement in income due to lower or delayed expenses. The SEC censure of various companies reinforces financial statement users' concerns with full disclosure of liabilities as described here:

ANALYSIS EXCERPT

The SEC determined Ampex failed to fully disclose (1) its obligations to pay royalty guarantees totaling in excess of $80 million; (2) its sales of substantial amounts of prerecorded tapes that were improperly accounted for as "degaussed," or erased, to avoid payment of royalty fees; (3) income overstatements from inadequate allowances for returned tapes; and (4) multimillion dollar understatements in both its allowance for doubtful accounts receivable and its provisions for losses from royalty contracts.

WHOLE TRUTH
The Truth-in-Lending Act requires lenders to give borrowers info about loan costs, including finance charges and interest rate.

We must also analyze the descriptions of liabilities along with their terms, conditions, and encumbrances. Results of this analysis can impact our assessments of both risk and return for a company. Exhibit 3.1 lists some important features we should review in an analysis of liabilities.

Exhibit 3.1 ***Important Features in Analyzing Liabilities***

- Terms of indebtedness (e.g., maturity, interest rate, payment pattern, amount).
- Restrictions on deploying resources and pursuing business activities.
- Ability and flexibility in pursuing further financing.
- Obligations for working capital, debt to equity, and other financial figures.
- Dilutive conversion features that liabilities are subject to.
- Prohibitions on disbursements such as dividends.

Minimum disclosure requirements as to debt provisions vary, but we should expect disclosure of any breaches in loan provisions that potentially limit a company's activities or increase its risk of insolvency. Accordingly, we must be alert to any explanations or qualifications in the notes or in an auditor's report such as the following from American Shipbuilding:

ANALYSIS EXCERPT

The credit agreement was amended . . . converting the facility from a revolving credit arrangement to a demand note. Under the amended agreement, the Company is required to satisfy specified financial conditions and is also required to liquidate its indebtedness to specified maximum limits . . . the Company had satisfied all these requirements except for the working capital covenant. Subsequent to that date, the Company has not maintained its compliance as to maximum indebtedness. In addition, the tangible net worth requirement was not met . . . The Company has given notices to the agent bank of its failure to satisfy these requirements . . . In addition to the restrictions described above, this credit facility places restrictions on the Company's ability to acquire or dispose of assets, make certain investments, enter into leases and pay dividends . . . the credit agreement disallowed the payment of dividends.

We wish to foresee problems such as these. One effective tool for this purpose is a comparative analysis of the terms of indebtedness with the *margin of safety*. Margin of safety refers to the extent to which current compliance exceeds minimum requirements.

LEASES

Leasing is a popular form of financing, especially in certain industries. A **lease** is a contractual agreement between a *lessor* (owner) and a *lessee* (user). It gives a lessee the right to use an asset, owned by the lessor, for the term of the lease. In return, the lessee makes rental payments, called *minimum lease payments* (or MLP). Lease terms obligate the lessee to make a series of payments over a specified future time period. Lease contracts can be complex, and they vary in provisions relating to the lease term, the transfer of ownership, and early termination.[1] Some leases are simply extended rental contracts, such as a two-year computer lease. Others are similar to an outright sale with a built-in financing plan, such as a 50-year lease of a building with automatic ownership transfer at the end of the lease term.

The two alternative methods for lease accounting reflect the differences in lease contracts. A lease that transfers substantially all the benefits and risks of ownership is accounted for as an asset acquisition and a liability incurrence by the lessee. Similarly, the lessor treats such a lease as a sale and financing transaction. This type of lease is called a **capital lease**. All other types of leases are accounted for as **operating leases.** In the case of operating leases, the lessee (lessor) accounts for the minimum lease payment as a rental expense (revenue).

Frequencies of Different Lease Types—Lessee

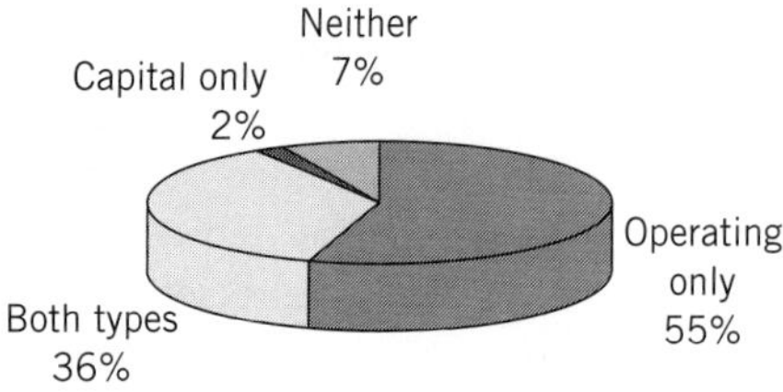

Source: *Accounting Trends and Techniques*

Lessees often structure a lease so that it can be accounted for as an operating lease even when the economic characteristics of the lease are more in line with a capital lease. By doing so, a lessee is engaging in off-balance-sheet financing. *Off-balance-sheet financing* refers to the fact that neither the leased asset nor its corresponding liability are recorded on the balance sheet when a lease is accounted for as an operating lease even though many of the benefits and risks of ownership are transferred to the lessee. The decision to account for a lease as a capital or operating lease can significantly impact financial statements. Analysts must take care to examine the economic characteristics of a company's leases and reclassify them when necessary.

Leasing has grown in frequency and magnitude. Estimates indicate that almost one-third of plant asset financing is in the form of leasing. Leasing is the major form of financing plant assets in the retail, airline, and railroad industries. Lease financing is popular for several reasons. For one, sellers use leasing to promote sales by providing financing to buyers. Interest income from leasing is often a major source of revenue to those sellers. In turn, leasing often is a convenient means for a buyer to finance its asset purchases. Tax considerations also play a role in leasing. Namely, overall tax payments can be reduced when ownership rests with the party in the higher marginal tax bracket. Moreover, as described, leasing can be a source of off-balance-sheet financing. Used in this way, leasing is said to *window-dress* financial statements.

Our discussion of lease financing for the lessee begins with an explanation of the effects of lease classification on both the income statement and balance sheet. Next, we analyze lease disclosures with reference to those of Best Buy. We then provide a method for reclassifying operating leases as capital leases when the economic characteristics support it. Our discussion also examines the impact of lease classification on financial statements and the importance of reclassifying leases for financial statement analysis. We limit our discussion to the analysis of leases for the lessee. Appendix 3A provides an overview of lease accounting and analysis for the lessor.

[1] Some leases are cancelable, but the majority of the long-term leases are noncancelable. The power of the lessee to cancel the lease is an important factor determining the economic substance of the lease. We focus discussion on noncancelable leases.

Accounting and Reporting for Leases

Lease Classification and Reporting

A lessee classifies and accounts for a lease as a capital lease if, at its inception, the lease meets *any* of four criteria: (1) the lease transfers ownership of the property to the lessee by the end of the lease term; (2) the lease contains an option to purchase the property at a bargain price; (3) the lease term is 75% or more of the estimated economic life of the property; or (4) the present value of the rentals and other minimum lease payments at the beginning of the lease term is 90% or more of the fair value of the leased property less any related investment tax credit retained by the lessor. A lease can be classified as an operating lease only when *none* of these criteria are met. The criteria for classification appear comprehensive. Condition (4), in particular, is difficult to avoid. Yet, despite these criteria, companies often effectively structure leases so that they can be classified as operating leases.

When a lease is classified as a capital lease, the lessee records it (both asset and liability) at an amount equal to the present value of the minimum lease payments over the lease term, excluding **executory costs** (if determinable) such as insurance, maintenance, and taxes paid by the lessor that are included in the MLP. The leased asset must be depreciated over the lease term in a manner consistent with the lessee's normal depreciation policy. However, if the lease transfers title or contains a bargain purchase option, depreciation is computed over the estimated economic life. In accounting for an operating lease, the lessee charges rentals (MLPs) to expense as they are incurred.

The accounting rules require that all lessees disclose, usually in notes to financial statements: (1) future minimum lease payments separately for capital leases and operating leases for each of the five succeeding years and the total amount thereafter, and (2) rental expense for each period that an income statement is reported.

Accounting for Leases—An Illustration

This section compares the effects of accounting for a lease as either a capital or an operating lease. Specifically, we look at the effects on both the income statement and the balance sheet of the lessee given the following information:

- A company leases an asset on January 1, 2000–it has no other assets or liabilities.
- Estimated economic life of the leased asset is five years with an expected salvage value of zero at the end of five years. The company will depreciate this asset on a straight-line basis over its economic life.
- The lease has a fixed noncancelable term of five years with annual minimum lease payments of $2,505 paid at the end of each year.
- Interest rate on the lease is 8% per year.

We begin the analysis by preparing an amortization schedule for the leased asset as shown in Exhibit 3.2. The initial step in preparing this schedule is to determine the present (market) value of the leased asset (and the lease liability) on January 1, 2000. Using the interest tables near the end of the book, the present value is $10,000 (computed as 3.992 × $2,505). We then compute the interest and the principal amortization for each year. Interest equals the beginning-year liability multiplied by the interest rate (for year 2000 it is $10,000 × 0.08). The principal amount is equal to the total payment less interest (for year 2000 it is $2,505 − $800). The schedule reveals the interest pattern mimics that of a fixed-payment mortgage with interest decreasing over time as the principal balance decreases. Next we determine depreciation. Since this company uses straight line, the depreciation is $2,000 per year (computed as $10,000/5 years). We now have

Lease Amortization Schedule

Exhibit 3.2

Year	Beginning-Year Liability	INTEREST AND PRINCIPAL COMPONENTS OF MLP: Interest	Principal	Total	Year-End Liability
2000	$10,000	$ 800	$ 1,705	$ 2,505	$8,295
2001	8,295	664	1,841	2,505	6,454
2002	6,454	517	1,988	2,505	4,466
2003	4,466	358	2,147	2,505	2,319
2004	2,319	186	2,319	2,505	0
Totals		$2,525	$10,000	$12,525	

the necessary information to examine the effects of this lease transaction on both the income statement and balance sheet for the two alternative lease accounting methods.

Let's first look at the effects on the income statement. When a lease is accounted for as an operating lease, the minimum lease payment is reported as a periodic rental expense. This implies a rental expense of $2,505 per year for this company. However, when a lease is accounted for as a capital lease, the company must recognize both periodic interest expense (see the amortization schedule in Exhibit 3.2) and depreciation expense ($2,000 per year in this case). Exhibit 3.3 summarizes the effects of this lease transaction on the income statement for these two alternative methods. Note that over the entire five-year period, total expense for both methods is identical. But, the capital lease method reports more expense in the earlier years and less expense in later years. This is due to declining interest expense over the lease term. Consequently, net income under the capital lease method is lower (higher) than under the operating lease method in the earlier (later) years of a lease.

Income Statement Effects of Alternative Lease Accounting Methods

Exhibit 3.3

Year	OPERATING LEASE: Rent Expense	CAPITAL LEASE: Interest Expense	Depreciation Expense	Total Expense
2000	$ 2,505	$ 800	$ 2,000	$ 2,800
2001	2,505	664	2,000	2,664
2002	2,505	517	2,000	2,517
2003	2,505	358	2,000	2,358
2004	2,505	186	2,000	2,186
Total	$12,525	$2,525	$10,000	$12,525

We next examine the effects of alternative lease accounting methods on the balance sheet. First, let's consider the operating lease method. Since this company does not have any other assets or liabilities, the balance sheet under the operating lease method shows zero assets and liabilities at the beginning of the lease. At the end of the first year, the company pays its MLP of $2,505, and cash is reduced by this amount to yield a negative balance. Equity is reduced by the same amount because the MLP is recorded as rent expense. This process continues each year until the lease expires. At the end of the lease, the cumulative amount expensed, $12,525 (as reflected in equity), is equal to the cumulative cash payment (as reflected in the negative cash balance). This amount also equals the total MLP over the lease term as seen in Exhibit 3.2.

Let's now examine the balance sheet effects under the capital lease method (see Exhibit 3.4). To begin, note the balance sheet at the end of the lease term is identical under both lease methods. This result shows that the net accounting effects under the two methods are identical by the end of the lease. Still, there are major yearly differences before the end of the lease term. Most notable, at the inception of the lease, an asset and liability equal to the present value of the lease ($10,000) is recognized under the capital lease method. At the end of the first year (and every year), the negative cash balance reflects the MLP, which is identical under both lease methods–recall that alternative accounting methods do not affect cash flows. For each year of the capital lease, the leased asset and lease liability are not equal, except at inception and termination of the lease. These differences occur because the leased asset declines by the amount of depreciation ($2,000 annually), while the lease liability declines by the amount of the principal amortization (for example, $1,705 in year 2000, per Exhibit 3.2). The decrease in equity in year 2000 is $2,800, which is the total of depreciation and interest expense for the period (see Exhibit 3.3). This process continues throughout the lease term. Note the leased asset is always lower than the lease liability during the lease term. This occurs because accumulated depreciation at any given time exceeds the cumulative principal amount.

Exhibit 3.4 ***Balance Sheet Effects of Capitalized Leases***

Month/Day/Year	Cash	Leased Asset	Lease Liability	Equity
1/1/2000	$ 0	$10,000	$10,000	$ 0
12/31/2000	(2,505)	8,000	8,295	(2,800)
12/31/2001	(5,010)	6,000	6,454	(5,464)
12/31/2002	(7,515)	4,000	4,466	(7,981)
12/31/2003	(10,020)	2,000	2,319	(10,339)
12/31/2004	(12,525)	0	0	(12,525)

This illustration reveals the important impacts that alternative lease accounting methods can have on financial statements. While the operating lease method is simpler, the capital lease method is conceptually superior, both from a balance sheet and an income statement perspective. From a balance sheet perspective, capital lease accounting recognizes the benefits (assets) and obligations (liabilities) that arise from a lease transaction. In contrast, the operating lease method ignores these benefits and obligations and fully reflects these impacts only by the end of the lease term. This means the balance sheet under the operating lease method fails to reflect the lease assets and obligations of the company.

Lease Disclosures

Accounting rules require a company with capital leases to report both leased assets and lease liabilities on the balance sheet. Moreover, all companies must disclose future lease commitments for both their capital and noncancellable operating leases. These disclosures are useful for analysis purposes.

We will analyze the lease disclosures in the Best Buy Co., Inc., 2001 annual report. As of its year-end, and despite the use of leasing as a financing alternative, Best Buy reports no capital lease liability on its balance sheet. As a result, none of its leased properties are recorded, and the company does not recognize on its balance sheet any of its lease obligations. Exhibit 3.5 reproduces the leasing footnote from the annual report and is typical of leasing disclosures. Best Buy leases portions of its corporate offices, essentially all of its retail locations, a majority of its distribution facilities, and some of its equipment. Lease terms generally range from 3 to 16 years. In addition to rental payments, the leases also require Best Buy to pay **executory costs** (real estate taxes, insurance, and maintenance). It is important to note that, in the present value computations that follow, only the minimum lease payments, and not the executory costs, are considered.

Lease Disclosures of Best Buy

Exhibit 3.5

6. Operating Lease Commitments

The Company currently both owns and leases portions of its corporate facilities and conducts essentially all of its retail and the majority of its distribution operations from leased locations. The terms of the lease agreements generally range from three to 16 years for Best Buy stores and three to 20 years for Musicland stores. The leases require payment of real estate taxes, insurance and common area maintenance in addition to rent. Most of the leases contain renewal options and escalation clauses, and the majority of the Musicland stores and several Best Buy stores require contingent rents based on specified percentages of sales. Certain Musicland store leases provide the Company with an early cancellation option if sales for a designated period do not reach a specified level as defined in the lease. Certain leases contain covenants related to maintenance of financial ratios. Also, the Company leases various equipment under operating leases. Transaction costs associated with the sale and leaseback of properties and any gain or loss are recognized over the terms of the lease agreements. Proceeds from the sale and leaseback of properties are included in the net change in recoverable costs from developed properties.

The composition of total rental expenses for all operating leases during the past three fiscal years, including leases of buildings and equipment, was as follows:

	2001	2000	1999
Minimum rentals	$299,090	$227,500	$186,100
Percentage rentals	615	500	500
	$299,705	$228,000	$186,600

Future minimum lease obligations by year (not including percentage rentals) for all operating leases of March 3, 2001, were as follows:

Fiscal Year	
2002	$ 388,000
2003	377,000
2004	346,000
2005	315,000
2006	289,000
Thereafter	2,282,000

The company classifies all of its leases as operating and provides a schedule of future lease payments in its notes to the financial statements. Best Buy will make $388 million in payments on its leases in 2002, $377 million in 2003, and so on.

Analyzing Leases

This section looks at the impact of operating versus capital leases for financial statement analysis. It gives specific guidance on how to adjust the financial statements for operating leases that should be accounted for as capital leases.

Impact of Operating Leases

While accounting standards allow alternative methods to best reflect differences in the economics underlying lease transactions, this discretion is too often misused by lessees who structure lease contracts so that they can use the operating lease method. This practice reduces the usefulness of financial statements. Moreover, because the proportion of capital leases to operating leases varies across companies, lease accounting affects our ability to compare different companies' financial statements.

Lessees' incentives to structure leases as operating leases relate to the impacts of operating leases versus capital leases on both the balance sheet and the income statement. These impacts on financial statements are summarized as follows:

- Operating leases understate liabilities by keeping lease financing off the balance sheet. Not only does this conceal liabilities from the balance sheet, it also inflates solvency ratios (such as debt to equity) that are often used in credit analysis.
- Operating leases understate assets. This can inflate return on investment ratios, especially the return on total assets.
- Operating leases delay recognition of expenses in comparison to capital leases. This means operating leases overstate income in the early term of the lease but understate income late in the lease term.
- Operating leases understate current liabilities by keeping the current portion of the principal payment off the balance sheet. This inflates the current ratio and other liquidity measures.
- Operating leases include interest with the lease rental (an operating expense). Consequently, operating leases understate both operating income and interest expense. This inflates interest coverage ratios such as times interest earned.

Analysis Research

MOTIVATIONS FOR LEASING

Finance theory suggests that leases and debt are perfect substitutes. However, there is little empirical evidence supporting this *substitution hypothesis*. Indeed, evidence appears to contradict this hypothesis. Namely, companies with leases carry a higher proportion of additional debt financing than those without leases. This gives rise to the so-called leasing puzzle. Further, there is considerable variation across companies on the extent of leasing as a form of financing. What then are the motivations for leasing?

One answer relates to taxes. Ownership of an asset provides the holder with tax benefits. This suggests that the entity with the *higher* marginal tax rate would hold ownership of the asset to take advantage of greater tax benefits. The entity with the *lower* marginal tax would lease the asset. Empirical evidence supports this tax hypothesis. Other economic factors that motivate leasing include: (1) an expected use period that is less than the asset's economic life; (2) a lessor that has an advantage in reselling the asset or has market power to force buyers to lease; and (3) an asset that is not specialized to the company or is not sensitive to misuse.

Financial reporting factors also explain the popularity of leasing over other forms of debt financing. While financial accounting and tax reporting need not be identical, use of operating leases for financial reports creates unnecessary obstacles when claiming capital lease benefits for tax purposes. This explains the choice of capital leasing for some financial reports. Still, the choice of operating leasing seems largely dictated by managers' preference for off-balance-sheet financing. Capital leasing yields deterioration in solvency ratios and creates difficulties in raising additional capital. For example, there is evidence that capital leasing increases the tightness of debt covenants and, therefore, managers try to loosen debt covenants with operating leases. While there is some evidence that private debt agreements reflect different lease accounting choices, the preponderance of the evidence suggests that creditors do not fully compensate for alternative lease accounting methods.

Fortunately, lessees cannot entirely conceal lease liabilities because the relevant information is disclosed in notes. Still, the ability of operating leases to inflate key ratios used in credit and profitability analysis provides a major incentive for lessees to pursue this off-balance-sheet-financing. Lessees also believe that classifying leases as operating leases helps them meet debt covenants and improve their prospects for additional financing.

Because of the impacts from lease classification on financial statements and ratios, an analyst must make adjustments to financial statements prior to analysis. Many analysts convert all operating leases to capital leases. Others are more selective. We suggest reclassifying leases when necessary and caution against indiscriminate adjustments. Namely, we recommend reclassification only when the lessee's classification appears inconsistent with the economic characteristics of the lease as explained next.

Converting Operating Leases to Capital Leases

This section provides a method for converting operating leases to capital leases. The specific steps are illustrated in Exhibit 3.6 using data from Best Buy's leasing note. It must be emphasized that while this method provides reasonable estimates, it does not precisely quantify all the effects of lease reclassification for financial statements.

Determining the Present Value of Projected Operating Lease Payments and Lease Amortization

Exhibit 3.6

Year	Payment	Discount Factor	Present Value	Interest	Lease Obligation	Lease Balance
2001						$2,381
2002	$ 388	$0.917	$ 356	$214	$174	2,207
2003	377	0.842	317	199	178	2,029
2004	346	0.772	267	183	163	1,866
2005	315	0.708	223	168	147	1,719
2006	289	0.650	188	155	134	1,585
2007	289	0.596	172	143	146	1,438
2008	289	0.547	158	129	160	1,279
2009	289	0.502	145	115	174	1,105
2010	289	0.460	133	99	190	915
2011	289	0.422	122	82	207	708
2012	289	0.388	112	64	225	483
2013	289	0.356	103	43	246	238
2014	259	0.326	84	21	238	0
Total	$3,997		$2,381			

The first step is to assess whether or not Best Buy's classification of operating leases is reasonable. To do this, we must estimate the length of the remaining period beyond the five years disclosed in the notes–titled "Thereafter" in the Best Buy notes of Exhibit 3.5. Specifically, we divide the reported MLP for the later years by the MLP for the last year that is separately reported. For Best Buy, we divide the total MLP for the later years of $2.282 billion (for its 2001 operating leases) by the MLP reported in 2006, or $289 million, to arrive at 7.9 years beyond 2002. Adding this number to the 5 years already reported gives us an estimate of about 13 years for the remaining lease term.

These results suggest a need for us to reclassify Best Buy's operating leases as capital leases–that is, its 13-year commitment for operating leases is too long to ignore. In particular, whenever the remaining lease period (commitments) is viewed as significant, we need to capitalize the operating leases.

To convert operating leases to capital leases, we need to estimate the present value of Best Buy's operating lease liability. The process begins with an estimate of the interest rate that we will use to discount the projected lease payments. Determining the interest rate on operating leases is challenging. For companies that report both capital and operating leases, we can estimate the implicit interest rate on the capital leases and assume operating leases have a similar interest rate. The implicit rate on capital leases can be inferred by trial and error and is equal to that interest rate that equates the projected capital lease payments with the present value of the capital leases, both of which are disclosed in the leasing footnote.

Two problems can arise when inferring the interest rate from capital lease disclosures. First, it is impossible to use this method for companies that do report capital lease details. In such a case, we need to determine the yield on the company's long-term debt or debt with a similar risk profile and then use it as a proxy for the interest rate on operating leases. A second problem can arise when the interest rates on capital and operating leases are markedly different (this can arise when operating and capital leases are entered into at different times when the interest rates are different). In this scenario, we need to adjust the capital lease interest rate to better reflect the interest rate on operating leases.

Best Buy's recent long-term debt is unsecured and carries an interest rate of about 9%. Since the leases are secured borrowings, their interest rate is probably not significantly higher. For the example that follows, we use 9% as a discount rate to determine the present value of the projected operating lease payments. This analysis is presented in Exhibit 3.6. Lease payments for 2002–2006 are provided in the leasing footnote as required. The estimated payments after 2006 are assumed equal to the 2006 payment and continue for the next seven years with a final lease payment of $259 million in the 13th year (2014). Discounting these projected lease payments at 9% yields a present value of $2.381 billion. This is the amount that should be added to Best Buy's reported liabilities.

HEAVY LUGGAGE

To obtain cushy tax breaks, many large companies invested hundreds of millions of dollars in aircraft leased to major carriers—through so-called leveraged leases. As skies darken for airlines, these lease holders could be in for a rough ride. For example, Pitney Bowes has over $500 million invested in these leases and reports that eventually it could take a $100 million write-down. Electronic Data Systems already has written off $23 million to cover its US Airways leases. AT&T and Whirlpool both report investing over $65 million in these risky liabilities.

The next step in our analysis is to compute the value of the operating lease asset. Recall that the asset value of a capital lease is always lower than its corresponding liability, but how much lower is difficult to estimate because it depends on the length of the lease term, the economic life of the asset, and the lessee's depreciation policy. Consequently, for analysis of operating leases, we assume that the leased asset value is equal to the estimated liability. For Best Buy, this means both the leased asset and lease liability are estimated at $2.381 billion for 2001. We also can split the operating lease liability into its current and noncurrent components of $174 million and $2.207 billion, respectively.

Once we determine the operating lease liability and asset, we then must estimate the impact of lease reclassification on reported income. There are two expenses relating to capitalized leases–interest and depreciation. Interest expense is determined by applying the interest rate to the present value of the lease (the lease liability). For Best Buy, this is estimated at $214 million for 2002, or 9% of $2.381 billion (see Exhibit 3.6). Depreciation expense is determined by dividing the value of the leasehold asset by the remaining lease term. Assuming no residual value, depreciation of the $2.381 billion in leased assets on a straight-line basis over the 13-year remaining lease term yields an annual depreciation expense of $183 million. Total expense, then, is estimated at $397 million for 2002, compared with $388 million in projected rent expense, an increase of $9 million pretax.

Restating Financial Statements for Lease Reclassification

Exhibit 3.7 shows the restated balance sheet and income statement for Best Buy before and after operating lease reclassification using the results in Exhibit 3.6. The operating lease reclassification has a limited effect on Best Buy's income statement:

- Operating expenses decrease by $205 million (elimination of $388 million rent expense and addition of $183 million of depreciation expense)
- Interest expense increases by $214 million (from interest income of $37 million to interest expense of $177 million)
- Net income decreases by $6 million [$9 million pretax × (1 − .35), the assumed marginal corporate tax rate] in 2002.

Exhibit 3.7

Restated Balance Sheet after Converting Operating Leases to Capital Leases—Best Buy 2001

Income Statement	Before	After
Sales	$15,327	$15,327
Operating expenses	14,723	14,518
Operating income before interest and taxes	604	809
Interest expense (income)	(37)	177
Income taxes	246	243
Net income	$ 395	$ 389

Balance Sheet	Before	After		Before	After
Current assets	$2,929	$2,929	Current liabilities	$2,715	$2,889
Fixed assets	1,911	4,292	Long-term liabilities	303	2,510
			Stockholders' equity	1,822	1,822
Total assets	$4,840	$7,221	Total liabilities and equity	$4,840	$7,221

The balance sheet impact is more substantial. Total assets and total liabilities both increase markedly–by $2.381 billion at the end of 2002, which is the present value of the operating lease liability. The increase in liabilities consists of increases in both current liabilities ($174 million) and noncurrent liabilities ($2.207 billion).

Exhibit 3.8 shows selected ratios for Best Buy before and after lease reclassification. The current ratio slightly declines from 1.08 to 1.01. However, reclassification adversely affects Best Buy's solvency ratios. Total debt to equity increases by 78% to 2.96, and the

Exhibit 3.8

Effect of Converting Operating Leases to Capital Leases on Key Ratios—Best Buy 2001

Financial Ratios	Before	After
Current ratio	1.08	1.01
Total debt to equity	1.66	2.96
Long-term debt to equity	0.17	1.38
Return on common equity	21.7%	21.4%
Return on assets	8.16%	5.39%
Times interest earned	n.a.	4.57

long-term debt to equity ratio jumps from 0.17 to 1.38. Best Buy's interest coverage (times interest earned ratio) increases from n.a. (since it is recording net interest *income* prior to the reclassification) to 4.57 and remains very strong even after the operating lease adjustment.

Return on equity is largely unaffected because of the small change in after-tax income (meaning equity is not markedly affected by reclassification). Profitability components, however, are significantly affected. Return on assets decreases from 8.16% to 5.39% due to the increase in reported assets and its consequent effect on total asset turnover. Financial leverage has increased to offset this decrease, leaving return on equity unchanged. Although ROE is unaffected, our inferences about how this return is achieved are different. Following lease capitalization, Best Buy is seen as requiring significantly more capital investment (resulting in lower turnover ratios), and is realizing its ROE as a result of a higher level of financial leverage than was apparent from its unadjusted financial statements.

Analysis Research

OPERATING LEASES AND RISK

Analysis research encourages capitalizing noncancelable operating leases. The main impact of capitalizing these operating leases is an increase in the debt to equity and similar ratios with a corresponding increase in the company's risk assessment. An important question is whether off-balance-sheet operating leases actually do increase risk. Research has examined this question by assessing the effect of operating leases on *equity risk*, defined as variability in stock returns. Evidence shows that the present value of noncapitalized operating leases increases equity risk from its impact on both the debt to equity ratio and the variability of return on assets (ROA). This implies that analysts take a 'property rights' perspective to lease liabilities rather than a 'legal ownership' perspective.

Analysis research also shows that only the present value of future MLPs impacts equity risk. Further, it shows that the contingent fee included in rental payments is not considered by analysts. This evidence favors the lease capitalization method adopted by accounting standards, instead of an alternative method that involves multiplying the lease rental payments by a constant.

POSTRETIREMENT BENEFITS

Employers often provide benefits to their employees after retirement. These **postretirement benefits** come in two forms: (1) **pension benefits**, where the employer promises monetary benefits to the employee after retirement, and (2) **other postretirement employee benefits (OPEB)**, where the employer provides other (usually nonmonetary) benefits after retirement–primarily health care and life insurance. Both types of benefits pose conceptually similar challenges for accounting and analysis. Current accounting standards require that the costs of providing postretirement benefits be recognized when the employee is in active service, rather than when the benefits are actually paid. The estimated present value of accrued benefits is reported as a liability for the employer. Because of the uncertainty regarding the timing and magnitude of these benefits, postretirement costs (and liabilities) need to be estimated based on *actuarial assumptions* regarding life expectancy, employee turnover, compensation, health care costs, expected rates of return, and interest rates.

Pensions and other postretirement benefits make up a major part of many companies' liabilities. Moreover, pensions constitute a large portion of the economy's savings and investments. Current estimates are that pension plans, with assets exceeding $4 trillion (about 20% of U.S. assets), cover nearly 50 million individuals. Also, pension funds control about 25% of the value of NYSE stock, and account for nearly one-third of daily trading volume. While somewhat smaller in magnitude, OPEB, in particular health care costs, is an important component of companies' employee costs. Nearly one-third of U.S. workers participate in postretirement health care plans, with a total unfunded liability in the $1 to $2 trillion range. Both pension and OPEB liabilities are likely to grow because of changing demographics and increased life expectancy.

While accounting for pensions and other postretirement benefits is specified in separate standards (primarily *SFAS 87* and *SFAS 112*, respectively), the current reporting and disclosure requirements are specified jointly in *SFAS 132*. Accordingly, we first explain the accounting for pensions and other postretirement benefits separately, and then jointly discuss disclosure requirements and analysis implications.

Pension Benefits

Pension accounting requires an understanding of the economics underlying pension transactions and events. Consequently, we first discuss the nature of pension transactions and events along with the economics underlying pension accounting before discussing pension accounting requirements.

Nature of Pension Obligations

Pension commitments by companies are formalized through pension plans. A **pension plan** is an agreement by the employer to provide pension benefits to the employee, and it involves three entities: the employer, who contributes to the plan; the employee, who derives benefits; and the pension fund. The **pension fund** is independent of the employer and is administered by *trustees*. The pension fund receives contributions, invests them in an appropriate manner, and disburses pension benefits to employees. This pension plan process is diagrammed in Exhibit 3.9.

Elements of the Pension Process ***Exhibit 3.9***

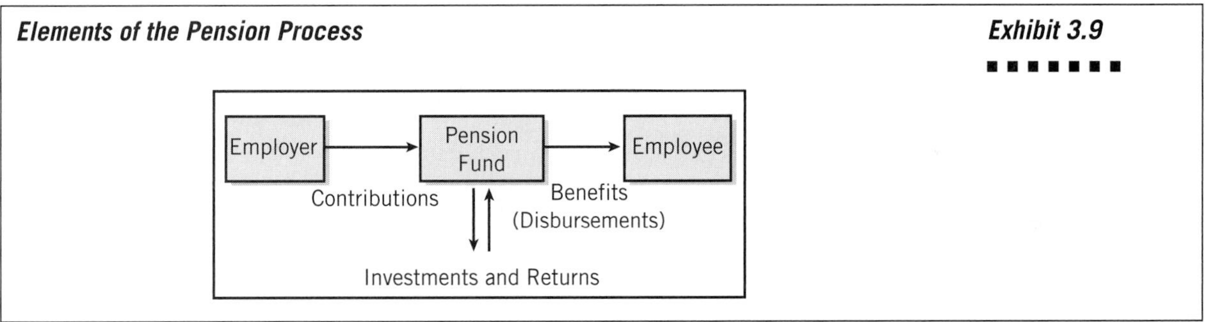

Pension plans precisely specify the benefits and the rights and responsibilities of the employer and employee. Pension plans can be divided into two basic categories. **Defined benefit** plans specify the amount of pension *benefits* that the employer promises to provide to retirees. Under defined benefit plans, the *employer* bears the risk of pension fund performance. **Defined contribution** plans specify the amount of pension *contributions* that the employer makes to the pension plan. In this case, the actual amount of pension benefits to retirees depends on the pension fund performance. Under defined contribution plans, the *employee* bears the risk of pension fund performance. While defined contribution plans are growing in popularity, defined benefit plans still constitute the major share of pension plans.

In both plans, employee benefits are usually determined through a formula linked to employee wages. Defined contribution plans *immediately* obligate the employer to pay some fixed proportion of the employees' current compensation, whereas defined benefit plans require the employer to periodically pay the employee a predetermined sum of money *after retirement* until the employee's death.

POST GAME
Major league baseball players need only play a quarter of a season to receive some pension. A fully vested MLB pension is about $120,000 a year.

Pension payments are also affected by vesting provisions. **Vesting** is an employee's right to pension benefits regardless of whether the employee remains with the company or not. This right is usually conferred after the employee has served some minimum specified period with the employer.

Once the pension liability is determined, **funding** the expense becomes a managerial decision for defined benefit plans that is influenced by legal and tax considerations. Tax law specifies minimum funding requirements to ensure the security of retirees' benefits. It also has tax deductibility limitations for overfunded pension plans. Minimum funding requirements also exist under the Employee Retirement Income Security Act (ERISA). A company has the option to fund the plan exactly (by providing assets to the plan trustee that equal the pension liability) or it can overfund or underfund the plan.

We focus attention on defined benefit plans because of the challenge they pose to analysis of financial statements.[2] Exhibit 3.10 depicts the time line for a simple defined benefit plan. This case involves a single employee who is expected to retire in 15 years and is paid an annual fixed pension of $20,000 for 10 years after retirement. The discount (interest) rate is assumed to be 8% per year. We also assume the employer exactly funds the plan. While a simplification, this exhibit reflects the economics underlying defined pension plans. These plans involve current investments by the employer for future payments of benefits to the employee. The challenges for accounting are estimating the employer's pension plan exposure and determining the pension cost for the period, which is different from the funding (actual contributions made) by the employer. For this purpose, accountants rely on assumptions made by specialists known as actuaries.

Exhibit 3.10 ***Pension Accumulation and Disbursement for a Defined Benefits Plan***

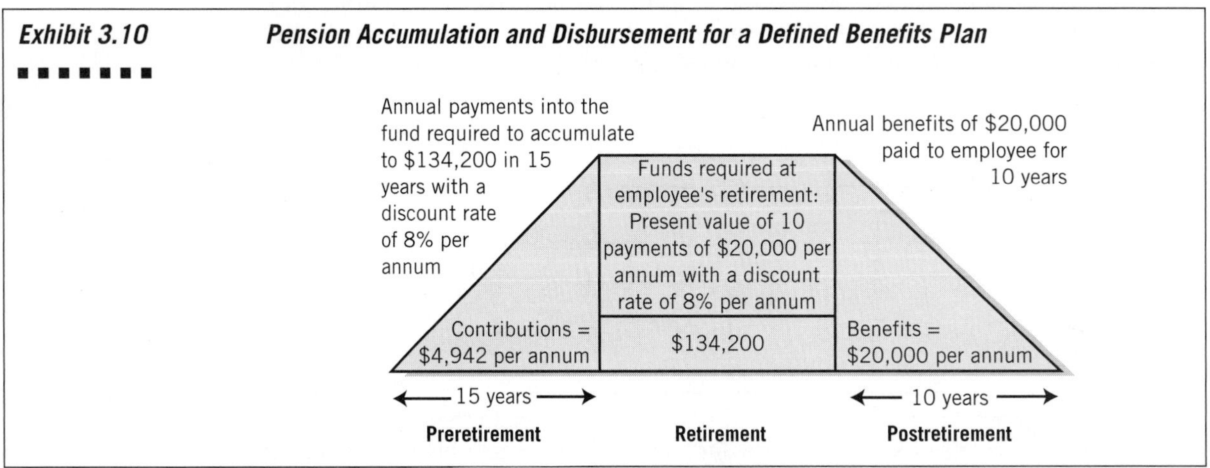

Economics of Pension Accounting

In this section, we examine the economics underlying accounting for defined benefit pension plans. The following example is used to illustrate the discussion:

- Consider a pension plan with a single employee, J. Smith, who joined the plan exactly five years ago on January 1, 1996. Smith is due to retire on December 31, 2020, and is expected to live for 10 years after retirement.
- J. Smith's current compensation is $10,000 per annum. Actuarial estimates indicate that compensation is expected to increase by 4% per annum over the next 20 years.

SIX-DAY WORKWEEK
Of the world's industrialized nations only South Korea still has a six-day workweek.

[2] Accounting for, and analysis of, defined contribution plans is straightforward. That is, the periodic contribution by the employer is recognized as an expense in the period when it is due. There are no other liabilities of serious note.

- The pension plan specifies the following formula for determining the employee's pension benefit: "The annual pension is equal to one week's compensation at the time of retirement multiplied by the number of years worked under the plan." Employees vest four years after joining the plan.
- At December 31, 2000, the fair value of assets in the pension fund is $2,000. In 2001, the employer contributes $200 to the pension fund.
- Return on pension assets is 22% in 2001. The long-term return is expected to be 10% per annum.
- Discount rate is 7% per annum.

Pension Obligation

Exhibit 3.11 explains the computation of the pension obligation, under alternative assumptions, for the J. Smith example. We first determine the pension obligation as of December 31, 2000. This computation is explained in the two columns headed "2000 Formula." We describe two alternative definitions for the pension obligation:

Exhibit 3.11

Determining Pension Obligations under Different Assumptions— J. Smith Example

	2000 FORMULA		2001 FORMULA		
				ASSUMPTION CHANGE	
	Actual	Projected	Projected	Actuarial	Plan
At December 31, 2020 (Retirement)					
Salary per year	$10,000	$21,911	$21,911	$26,533	$26,533
Pension per year	962	2,107	2,528	3,061	4,592
Present value of pension	6,753	14,798	17,757	21,503	32,254
At December 31, 2000					
Present value of pension	1,745	3,824			
At December 31, 2001					
Present value of pension		4,091	4,910	5,946	8,919

1. **Accumulated benefit obligation (ABO)** is the actuarial present value of the future pension benefits payable to employees at retirement based on their *current* compensation and service to date. (The term *actuarial* signifies it is based on assumptions such as life expectancy and employee turnover.) This present value is equivalent to an employer's current obligation if the plan is discontinued immediately. The computation of ABO for the J. Smith example is illustrated in the column headed "Actual" in Exhibit 3.11. Since J. Smith has been with the plan for five years, the annual pension benefit, given current compensation, is $962 (5/52 × $10,000). This pension benefit can be viewed as a fixed annuity of $962 per annum for 10 years. Given a discount rate of 7% per annum, the value of these pension benefits at retirement is $6,753 [7.0236 (from interest tables) × $962]. This means the entire stream of future pension benefits is represented by a single lump sum payment of $6,753 on December 31, 2020. The present value of this amount as of the end of 2000, or $1,745 [computed as $6,753 × 0.2584 (from interest tables)], is the accumulated benefit obligation (ABO).
2. **Projected benefit obligation (PBO)** is the actuarial estimate of future pension benefits payable to employees on retirement based on *expected future* compensation and service to date. This estimate is a more realistic estimate of the pension obligation. In our example, J. Smith's salary is expected to increase by 4% per annum. The computation of PBO for the J. Smith example is shown in

the column headed "Projected" in Exhibit 3.11. The PBO at December 31, 2000, is $3,824. The only difference between the ABO and PBO is that we consider the expected salary at retirement ($21,911) instead of Smith's current salary ($10,000) when determining periodic pension payment. Expected salary is estimated using the annual compensation growth of 4% [computed as $10,000 $\times$ $(1.04)^{20}$]. By using current salary, the ABO would understate the pension obligation.

Pension Assets and Funded Status

The market value of plan assets at December 31, 2000, in the J. Smith example is given as $2,000. While the assets' value exceeds the ABO, it is lower than the PBO. The difference between the value of the plan assets and the PBO is called the **funded status** of the plan. A plan is said to be *overfunded* when the value of pension assets exceeds the PBO. It is *underfunded* when the value of pension assets is less than the PBO. The funded status of the plan reflects its **net economic position**–defined as the PBO less the value of the plan assets. The J. Smith plan is underfunded by $1,824 ($3,824 – $2,000).

There are various reasons for overfunding, including tax-free accumulation of funds, outstanding company performance, or better-than-expected fund investment performance. Company raiders sometimes consider overfunded pension plans as sources of funds to help finance their acquisitions. The implications of overfunded pension plans include:

- Companies can discontinue or reduce contributions to the pension fund until pension assets equal or fall below the PBO. Reduced or discontinued contributions have income statement and cash flow implications.
- Companies can withdraw excess assets. Recaptured amounts are subject to income taxes. Since companies often use pension funding as a tax shelter, reversion excise taxes are often imposed.

LABOR PAINS
In a recent 5-year period, the Labor Dept. [www.dol.gov/dol/pwba] opened 24,523 civil and 660 criminal investigations of pension plans suspected of misusing employees' money.

There also are reasons for underfunding, including poor investment performance, changes in pension rules such as granting of retroactive benefits, and inadequate contributions by the employer. However, employers are subject to certain minimum funding requirements by law.

Pension Cost

Economic pension cost (or expense) is the net cost arising from changes in net economic position for the period.[3] Economic pension cost includes both recurring (or normal) and nonrecurring (or abnormal) components. Any return on pension plan assets is used to offset these costs in arriving at a net economic pension cost.

Recurring pension cost consists of two components:

1. **Service cost** is the actuarial present value of the pension benefit earned by employees based on the pension benefit formula. It is the increase in the projected benefit obligation that arises when employees work another period. Service cost arises only for plans where the pension amount is based on periods of service.

[3] We refer to this cost as the *economic* pension cost to distinguish it from the *reported* pension cost determined under GAAP that is discussed in the next section.

2. **Interest cost** is the increase in the projected benefit obligation that arises when the pension payments are one period closer to being made. This cost arises because the PBO is the present value of the future pension benefits, which increases over time due to the *time value of money*. Interest cost is computed by multiplying beginning-period PBO by the discount rate.

These recurring costs can be explained by returning to the J. Smith example. See the column headed "Projected" under the main heading "2001 Formula" in Exhibit 3.12. The PBO at the end of 2001 is $4,910–an increase of $1,086 from 2000 (recall PBO in 2000 was $3,824). What drives this increase? There are two factors. First, while Smith's compensation is unchanged, the pension benefit per year increases in 2001 (from $2,107 to $2,528). This increase occurs because Smith's pension in 2001, as per the formula, is

Articulation of Net Economic Position (Funded Status) and Economic Pension Cost: J. Smith Example

Exhibit 3.12

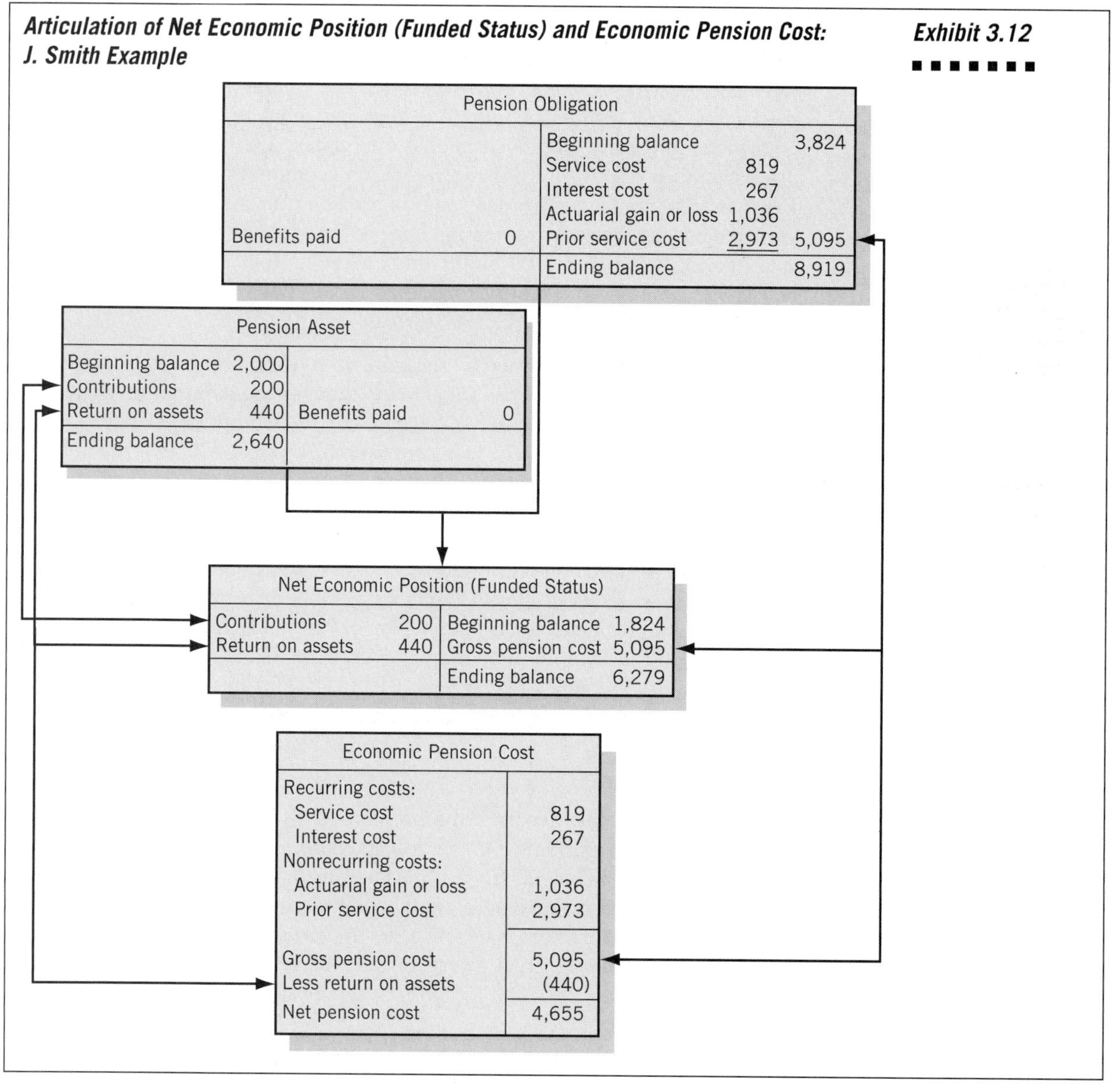

based on six weeks' compensation rather than on five weeks' compensation (as in 2000). The effect of this change is determined by comparing the present values of pension benefits at December 31, 2001, using the 2000 formula versus the 2001 formula. Specifically, the present value using the 2000 formula is $4,091, which is $819 lower than the present value using the 2001 formula. This means the PBO increases by $819 in 2001 because Smith serves an additional year–hence, the term *service* cost. Next, compare the present values using the 2000 formula at the end of 2000 and 2001. The present values of identical future benefits–represented by the identical lump sum of $14,798 at the end of 2020–increases from $3,824 in 2000 to $4,091 in 2001. This $267 increase is because of the time value of money; hence, the term *interest* cost (interest cost also is computed as 7% × $3,824).

Nonrecurring pension cost, arising from events such as changes in actuarial assumptions or plan rules, consists of two components:

1. **Actuarial gain or loss** is the change in PBO that occurs when one or more actuarial assumptions are revised in estimating PBO. A revised discount rate is the most frequent source of revision as it depends on the prevailing interest rate in the economy. Other assumptions that can change are mortality rates, employee turnover, and compensation growth rates. Altering these assumptions can have major effects on PBO and, hence, on economic pension cost.
2. **Prior service cost** arises from changes in pension plan rules on PBO. Prior service cost includes retroactive pension benefits granted at the initiation of a pension plan or benefits created by plan amendments typically occurring during collective bargaining or labor negotiations. These changes are often retroactive and give credit for employees' prior services.

These nonrecurring costs are explained by returning to the J. Smith example. First, let's consider an actuarial change: Assume the actuary changes the assumption regarding compensation growth rate from 4% to 5%. Because of this assumption change, Smith's estimated compensation at retirement increases from $21,911 to $26,533 (see column headed "Assumption Change–Actuarial" in Exhibit 3.11). This change also increases the PBO at the end of 2001 by $1,036 (from $4,910 to $5,946), representing an actuarial loss.

Additionally, let's assume the pension formula changes to one-and-one-half weeks' compensation per year of service (instead of one week per year of service). This effect is shown in the column headed "Assumption Change–Plan" in Exhibit 3.11. This results in the pension benefit per annum increasing by 50% from $3,061 to $4,592. This also yields a corresponding increase of $2,973 ($8,919 − $5,946) in the PBO. Since this change compensates Smith for any prior service, it represents a prior service cost.

The final component in arriving at the net economic pension cost is to adjust for the actual return on plan assets:

- **Actual return on plan assets** is the pension plan's earnings. Earnings on the plan's assets consist of: *investment income*–capital appreciation and dividend and interest received, less management fees, plus *realized and unrealized appreciation* (or minus depreciation) of other plan assets. The return on plan assets usually reduces pension cost (unless the return is negative, in which case it increases pension cost). In the J. Smith example, actual return on plan assets in 2001 is $440 (22% of $2,000).

To summarize, the net economic pension cost for a period consists of the following components (with amounts from the J. Smith example):

Recurring costs:	
Service cost	$ 819
Interest cost	267
Nonrecurring costs:	
Actuarial gain or loss	1,036
Prior service cost	2,973
Gross economic pension cost	5,095
Less return on plan assets	(440)
Net economic pension cost	$4,655

Articulation of Pension Cost and Funded Status

This section explains the articulation of economic pension cost and the funded status. Articulation arises from the linkage of the balance sheet, the income statement, and the statement of cash flows that is inherent in accrual accounting. Understanding this articulation improves analysis of pension accounting.

Exhibit 3.12 shows this articulation for the J. Smith example using T-accounts. For 2001, assume both the actuarial and the prior service cost changes are in effect. The beginning balance on the pension obligation is $3,824 (which is the PBO at the end of 2000–see Exhibit 3.11) and the closing balance is $8,919 (which is the PBO at the end of 2001 after both actuarial and prior service cost effects). The change in the pension obligation is entirely explained by the gross pension cost. Benefits paid reduce the pension obligation, but no benefits are paid in this example.

The pension asset opening balance of $2,000 increases to $2,640 at the end of 2001. Employer's contributions ($200) and actual return on assets ($440) make up this change. Any benefits paid would decrease pension assets, but again, no benefits are paid in this example. The net economic position (or funded status) is the difference between the value of pension assets and the projected benefit obligation. The net economic position deteriorates from $1,824 underfunded to $6,279 underfunded. Note that benefits paid would not affect funded status because they reduce both the pension obligation and the pension asset by an equal amount. The change in funded status is explained as follows (negative amounts represent liabilities):

Beginning funded status	$(1,824)
Add contributions	200
Less net pension cost	(4,655)
Closing funded status	$(6,279)

Understanding the articulation of net economic position and economic pension cost is useful in analyzing pension disclosures, which is the topic of the next section.

Pension Accounting Requirements

The framework for pension accounting is specified under *SFAS 87* (note, *SFAS 132* alters pension disclosure requirements but leaves the framework intact). The focus of *SFAS 87* is obtaining a stable, and permanent, measure of pension cost. Accordingly, this standard smooths reported pension cost by delaying recognition of economic effects on pension cost. This smoothing achieves its purpose of reducing volatility in reported pension cost (and reported income). However, this smoothing can distort analysis of the underlying economic reality of pensions, especially for the balance sheet.

Reported Pension Cost. Pension obligations (and assets) often are a major part of a company's liabilities (and assets). As shown in the J. Smith example, pension obligations are sensitive to changes in actuarial assumptions and plan rules. The value of plan assets, in turn, is subject to market fluctuations. Because of these factors, changes in pension assets and liabilities can be large in comparison to a company's net income. Moreover, many nonrecurring pension costs tend to reverse themselves over time. This means that listing economic pension cost in the income statement could induce unnecessary volatility in reported income, often to the extent of obscuring other economic effects. Also, some argue that prior service costs are attributed to the employee's entire expected service period with the company, and not to the current period alone.

PENSION BOOST
Pension income constituted 40% of USX-US Steel's recent operating income.

Given an objective of reducing unnecessary volatility in reported pension cost, *SFAS 87* prescribes a smoothing process. This involves deferring certain economic costs (and income) that are presumed to be of an unusual or nonrecurring nature and then amortizing them over the expected service period of the employee. Before explaining these details, it is useful to understand the overall smoothing process.

Exhibit 3.13 compares the economic and the reported pension costs for the J. Smith example (in practice, note that **reported pension cost** is often titled **net periodic pension cost**). Three differences are immediately apparent: (1) expected rather than actual return on plan assets is reported; (2) the full effects of actuarial changes and prior service cost are excluded (deferred) from reported pension cost (the arrow lines highlight these deferrals); and (3) the deferred components are amortized over the remaining service of the employee.

Exhibit 3.13 ***Economic versus Reported Pension Costs—J. Smith Example***

Economic Pension Cost		Smoothing	Reported Pension Cost*	
Service cost	$ 819	—	Service cost	$ 819
Interest cost	267	—	Interest cost	267
Actual return	(440)	$ (240)	Expected return	(200)
Actuarial gain or loss	1,036	1,036		—
Net gain or loss	—	796 →		—
Prior service cost	2,973	2,973 →		—
			Amortization:	
		(21)	→ Net gain or loss	21
		(149)	→ Prior service cost	149
Total	$4,655	$3,599		$1,056

* This also is referred to as *net periodic pension cost*.

We review each deferral (and amortization) below:

- **Expected return on plan assets** reduces reported pension cost. While capital markets are volatile in the short run, long-term returns are more predictable. Since pension plans invest for the long run, pension costs are reduced by the expected (rather than actual) return on plan assets. Use of actual return subjects pension costs to the fluctuations of financial markets and to a concern that pension costs would be too volatile. Gains or losses from the difference between expected and actual returns are deferred and amortized to reduce this volatility. As we discuss below (under amortization of net unrecognized gains or losses), these deferred gains or losses on plan assets are amortized over an appropriate period of time and included in reported pension cost. Expected return on plan assets is computed by multiplying the expected long-term rate of return on plan assets by the market-related value of plan assets at the beginning of the period. The pension trustee estimates long-term rate of return on plan assets. The market-related value of plan assets is either the fair value or a calculated value recognizing changes in fair value in a systematic manner over five years. The expected return in the J. Smith example is computed as $200 (10% of $2,000).

- **Deferral and amortization of net gains and losses** arise from the delayed recognition of deviations from expectations for both pension obligations and pension assets. Net gains and losses consist of (1) the difference between actual and expected return on plan assets and (2) actuarial gains and losses. Pension accounting specifies both a minimum value and a systematic method of amortizing net unrecognized gains and losses. A *corridor* approach shields unrecognized gains and losses falling within a corridor from required amortization. This corridor is the greater of 10% of plan asset value or 10% of the PBO at the beginning of the year. This means only the *excess* of unrecognized gains and losses above 10% of the plan assets or PBO, whichever is larger, is amortized over the average service period of plan employees. The 10% corridor is applied each year on the net cumulative deferral (i.e., cumulative deferral less cumulative amortization). In the J. Smith example, the deferred net gains or losses is $796 ($1,036 actuarial loss less $240 abnormal return), of which $21 (1/20 of the excess of $796 over 10% of $3,824) is amortized in 2001.
- **Deferral and amortization of prior service cost** delay recognition of prior service cost effects on reported pension cost. Pension accounting does not require immediate recognition of costs for retroactive benefits granted. These costs, however, do increase PBO and are recognized as expense over the remaining employment of the existing employees in the plan. Deferred recognition allows these costs of retroactive benefits to be matched against future economic benefits expected to be realized from their granting. Amortization is based on the future service period of employees and is applied on a straight-line basis. In the J. Smith example, the prior service cost of $2,973 is deferred and $149 (1/20 × $2,973) is amortized.
- **Deferral and amortization of transition loss or gain** arise when a plan is initially adopted. In pension accounting, a company determines: (1) the PBO (from the actuary); (2) the fair value of plan assets (from the trustee); and (3) previously recognized unfunded or prepaid pension cost (from company records). The difference between the PBO and the sum of (2) and (3) is not recognized immediately. Instead, it is designated as *unrecognized transition loss or gain* and amortized on a straight-line basis over the average remaining service period of qualified employees. There is no transition gain or loss in the J. Smith example.

Reported Status on the Balance Sheet. While the main purpose for smoothing reported pension cost is to reduce volatility, pension accounting specifies that the **net position** of the pension plan reported in the balance sheet should articulate exactly with the reported pension cost in the income statement. This requirement means that all deferred items are *unrecognized* (i.e., not disclosed) on the balance sheet. This also means the balance sheet is likely misleading about the real economic status of the pension plan.

Exhibit 3.14 illustrates the net reported position for the J. Smith example. The reported status in the balance sheet (referred to as accrued or prepaid pension cost) is $2,680 underfunded. This is much lower than the actual funded status, which is $6,279 underfunded. The difference arises because of unrecognized amounts–$775 net gain or loss ($796 deferral less $21 amortization) and $2,824 prior service cost ($2,973 deferral less $149 amortization). The reported status on the balance sheet articulates with reported pension cost as follows:

Beginning balance	$(1,824)
Reported pension cost	(1,056)
Contributions	200
Ending balance	$(2,680)

The reported status on the balance sheet can be viewed as the cumulative reported pension cost net of cumulative contributions, as opposed to the difference between assets and obligations of the pension fund. For this reason, the liability (or asset) reported in the balance sheet is called **accrued (or prepaid) pension cost**.

Exhibit 3.14 ***Reported Status of Pension Fund in Balance Sheet—J. Smith Example***

Projected benefit obligation	$(8,919)
Plan assets	2,640
Funded status	(6,279)
Unrecognized transition asset	0
Unrecognized net gain or loss	775
Unrecognized prior service cost	2,824
Reported status (accrued pension cost)	$(2,680)

Additional Minimum Liability. Pension accounting specifies an **additional minimum pension liability** in excess of the amount of the reported status (accrued pension cost) that must be recognized under certain conditions. The amount of this additional liability depends on the minimum liability required for the balance sheet. The **minimum pension liability** that an employer must record in the balance sheet is the amount by which the accumulated benefit obligation exceeds the fair value of plan assets. This minimum liability is based on the ABO rather than the PBO–the rationale being that the employer's liability is the ABO and not the PBO in the event of plan termination. No minimum liability is required when the fair value of plan assets exceeds the ABO. The *additional* minimum pension liability is recorded whenever the accrued pension cost is less than the minimum pension liability. The purpose of this additional minimum liability is to ensure that the pension liability recorded in the balance sheet is never *below* the minimum liability. Exhibit 3.15 illustrates the computation of the additional minimum

Exhibit 3.15 ***Additional Minimum Pension Liability Computations****

	Case 1	Case 2	Case 3	Case 4
(1) Accumulated benefit obligation (ABO)—given	$(1,000)	$(1,000)	$(1,000)	$(1,000)
(2) Fair market value of plan assets (FMV)—given	700	700	700	1,400
(3) Excess of FMV above ABO—[(2) − (1)]	(300)	(300)	(300)	400
(4) Minimum liability—[lower of (3) or zero]	(300)	(300)	(300)	0
(5) Prepaid (accrued) pension cost—given	0	(400)	100	(200)
(6) Additional minimum liability—[lower of (4) − (5) or zero]	(300)	0	(400)	0
(7) Reported liability on balance sheet—[(5) + (6)]	$ (300)	$ (400)	$ (300)	$ (200)

*Positive (negative) numbers denote assets (liabilities).

pension liability for four different cases. For reporting purposes, companies usually combine the additional minimum pension liability with the accrued or prepaid pension cost.

When the fair value of pension assets exceeds the ABO, no asset is recorded. Note that the minimum liability requirement is prescribed on a plan-by-plan basis. If an employer has multiple pension plans (as many do), then the minimum liability for one plan cannot be offset by the excess of plan assets over ABO for another plan. However, the final liability (or asset) recognized in the balance sheet is the cumulative liability of *all* plans, both underfunded and overfunded.

Other Postretirement Employee Benefits (OPEBs)

Postretirement benefits other than pensions (referred to as **other postretirement employee benefits,** or OPEBs) are benefits provided by employers to retirees and their designated dependents. Examples are life insurance, health care, housing assistance, and legal and tax services.

Until recently, recognition of these postretirement obligations ranged from inadequate to nonexistent. Companies had historically charged outlays for these postretirement costs on a pay-as-you-go basis. IBM, for example, followed a policy of "terminal accrual" by providing for this liability only when an employee retired; that is, it did not accrue any costs for active employees. When IBM ultimately recognized these liabilities, it yielded a $2.3 billion charge. Current accounting substantially improves these reporting practices.

HEALTH GAIN
Technology affects postretirement benefit assumptions. For example, life expectancy at birth in the Western world grew from 45 years in 1900 to over 75 years in 2000.

While these other postretirement obligations pose accounting challenges similar to those for pensions, there are some major differences. One difference is funding. Because no legal requirements exist for these postretirement benefits (in contrast with ERISA requirements for pensions) and because funding them is not tax deductible (unlike pension contributions), few companies fund these postretirement liabilities. This results in large unfunded liabilities. While companies often back these liabilities with assets on their balance sheets, independent trustees have no control over the assets. Another major difference is that these other postretirement benefits are often in the form of promised *services,* such as health care benefits, rather than monetary compensation. Accordingly, estimating these benefit obligations is especially difficult and requires a different set of actuarial assumptions, including trends in health care cost and usage and Medicare policies. Estimation of OPEB costs also must consider employee participation (cost sharing) and maximum eligibility (caps).

Features of OPEB Accounting

Accounting for other postretirement employee benefits is prescribed by *SFAS 106.* While differences exist, the basic features of pension accounting are retained when accounting for OPEBs. These features include:

- **Net cost reporting.** Consequences of events and transactions affecting OPEBs are reported as a single amount. This amount includes at least three components: (1) present value of the accrued cost of deferred compensation promised in exchange for employee service; (2) interest cost accruing from the passage of time until these benefits are paid; and (3) returns from investments in the plan's assets–these returns do not reduce the cost of most plans because most are unfunded.
- **Delayed recognition.** Certain changes in OPEBs, including those arising as a result of a plan initiation or amendment, and certain changes in the value of plan assets that are set aside to meet these obligations are recognized systematically over future periods. This is done through a process of deferral and amortization aimed at insulating current costs from excessive volatility.

- **Offsetting.** Plan assets restricted for payment of OPEBs offset the accumulated postretirement benefit obligation in determining amounts recognized in the balance sheet.

OPEB Obligations and Costs

The employer's obligation under *SFAS 106* is called the **accumulated postretirement benefit obligation** (APBO). The total actuarially determined costs of providing future benefits, the **expected postretirement benefit obligation** (EPBO), are gradually recognized over the employee's expected service period. The APBO is that portion of the EPBO "earned" by employee services as of a given date–that is, the accumulated benefits recognized to date. The funded status of OPEBs is the difference between APBO and the fair value of assets designated to meet this obligation.

Reported OPEB costs include these components:

- **Service costs**–actuarial present value of benefits earned by employees during the period, the portion of EPBO attributable to the current year. EPBO is typically allocated to each year in the service period (usually on a straight-line basis).
- **Interest costs**–imputed growth in APBO during a period using an assumed discount rate. Interest is compounded because APBO is recognized on a present value basis.
- **Amortization of net gains and losses**–amounts arising when actual experience of the plan differs from initial estimates or, alternatively stated, if the expected return on assets differs from actual return. Because these resulting gains and losses can fluctuate, they are deferred. If the cumulative net amount of previously unrecognized gains or losses exceeds 10% of APBO, the excess portion is amortized to income over the average remaining service period.
- **Amortization of prior service costs**–costs arising from plan amendments that change benefits and are attributed to employee service rendered prior to the amendment date. These costs are deferred and amortized by assigning equal amounts to the remaining future service periods.
- **Amortization of transition obligation**–costs arising from initial adoption. At adoption, an unfunded postretirement obligation, called *transition obligation,* is identified and measured as the difference between APBO and plan assets (if any) minus any postretirement liabilities previously recorded. If a company does not immediately recognize the transition obligation with a charge to income (as a cumulative effect of an accounting change), periodic postretirement expense is increased by the amortization of this unrecognized transition obligation. This obligation can be amortized over the remaining employee service period or an optional 20-year period.
- **Expected return on plan assets**–this return reduces the net annual postretirement expense if the plan is funded. The difference between actual and expected return is deferred and included in the unrecognized portion of net gains and losses.

The balance sheet reflects the accrued reported cost of OPEBs to date less cumulative benefit payments. This means the balance sheet liability excludes unrecognized components such as: (1) unrecognized transition obligation measured on the date of adoption less amortization, if any, to date; (2) unamortized net gain or loss; and (3) unamortized prior service cost. The **additional minimum liability** is *not recognized* on the balance sheet, although it is reported in a note.

Exhibit 3.16 summarizes, with the use of hypothetical values, the interrelation between the OPEB expense, liability, and other related balance sheet accounts. Also, the APBO is reconciled to the accrued postretirement expense reported.

Interrelation between Other Postretirement Employee Benefits (OPEB) Accounts* **Exhibit 3.16**

	Accumulated Postretirement Benefit Obligation (APBO)	UNRECOGNIZED[a]			Accrued OPEB Cost[c]	Net Annual OPEB Cost
		Transition Obligation	Prior Service Cost	Net (Gain) or Loss[b]		
Balance—on adoption of *SFAS 106* or beginning-year	$(20,000)	$20,000				
Activity in period:						
Service cost	(1,600)					$1,600
Interest cost	(2,200)					2,200
Liability gain or loss	(200)			$200		
Plan amendments	(3,000)		$3,000			
Amortization of:						
Unrecognized prior service costs			(200)			200
Unrecognized transition obligation		(1,000)[d]				1,000
Net annual OPEB cost					$(5,000)	$5,000
Benefit payments	1,600				1,600[e]	
Balance at year-end	$(25,400)	$19,000	$2,800	$200	$ 3,400	

*This plan is unfunded.

[a]Unrecognized liabilities reflect unrecorded deferred charges offsetting the APBO.

[b]Net gains and losses on assumptions or plan experience deemed below level requiring amortization.

[c]Balance sheet liability for OPEB costs.

[d]Transition obligation is amortized over 20 years.

[e]Benefit payments reflect a discharge of plan obligation—they also reflect the cash basis OPEB outlay.

Reporting of Postretirement Benefits

Reporting requirements for postretirement benefits (pensions and OPEBs) are specified in *SFAS 132,* which prescribes similar disclosure formats for both OPEBs and pension benefits. While companies rarely separately report either the current or accrued benefit cost (pension or OPEB) in the financial statements, the standard mandates extensive note disclosure. This includes details about both economic and reported amounts relating to liabilities, assets, and costs of postretirement benefits–separately for both OPEBs and pensions. The notes also must give details about actuarial assumptions and, in the case of OPEBs, the effect of changes in these assumptions on both the income statement and balance sheet.

Exhibit 3.17 shows excerpts of the note for pensions and other postretirement benefits from the 2001 annual report of Merck & Co., Inc. Merck reports details for both pensions and OPEBs in identical formats. The note consists of three main parts: (1) an explanation of the reported position in the balance sheet; (2) details of net periodic benefit costs; and (3) information regarding actuarial and other assumptions. Recognize that while a single set of numbers is reported for pension and OPEB plans, in reality these numbers are aggregations of many different plans. To explain the reported position in the balance sheet (accrued benefit cost), Merck reports the funded status (net economic position) and then shows the necessary adjustments in the form of unrecognized assets and liabilities to arrive at the reported net position in the balance sheet. Merck's funded status in 2001 is $(747) million underfunded for its pension and $(358) million underfunded for its OPEB plans. The pension plan is primarily reported

Exhibit 3.17 *Postretirement Benefits Footnote—Merck & Co., Inc.*

The net cost for the Company's pension plans consisted of the following components:

Years Ended December 31	**2001**	2000	1999
Service cost	$190.4	$171.2	$159.4
Interest cost	217.4	199.7	179.0
Expected return on plan assets	(287.9)	(266.6)	(299.4)
Net amortization	27.9	11.5	27.0
Net pension cost	$147.8	$115.8	$136.0

The net pension cost attributable to international plans included in the above table was $67.3 million in 2001, $73.3 million in 2002 and $66.9 million in 1999. The net cost of postretirement benefits other than pensions consisted of the following components:

Years Ended December 31	**2001**	2000	1999
Service cost	$ 52.7	$ 36.5	$ 39.4
Interest cost	77.4	62.0	58.8
Expected return on plan assets	(84.6)	(94.5)	(73.2)
Net amortization	(11.4)	(29.5)	(18.7)
Net postretirement benefit cost	$ 34.1	$ (25.5)	$ 6.3

The cost of health care and life insurance benefits for active employees was $307.2 million in 2001, $263.0 million in 2000 and $212.7 million in 1999. Summarized information about the changes in plan assets and benefit obligation is as follows:

	PENSION BENEFITS		OTHER POSTRETIREMENT BENEFITS	
	2001	2000	**2001**	2000
Fair value of plan assets at January 1	$3,121.3	$3,368.9	$ 861.3	$948.6
Actual return on plan assets	(258.1)	(195.8)	(56.5)	(80.8)
Company contributions	250.2	169.0	—	—
Benefits paid from plan assets	(255.0)	(228.3)	(7.9)	(6.5)
Other	6.1	7.5	—	—
Fair value of plan assets at December 31	$2,864.5	$3,121.3	$796.9	$861.3
Benefit obligation at January 1	$3,166.8	$2,820.9	$909.8	$818.6
Service cost	190.4	171.2	52.7	36.5
Interest cost	217.4	199.7	77.4	62.0
Actuarial losses (gains)	283.0	220.5	177.1	36.4
Benefits paid	(272.5)	(252.0)	(50.9)	(43.7)
Plan amendments	26.6	13.4	(11.5)	—
Other	0.1	(6.9)	—	—
Benefit obligation at December 31	$3,611.8	$3,166.8	$1,154.6	$909.8

A reconciliation of the plans' funded status to the net asset (liability) recognized at December 31 is as follows:

	PENSION BENEFITS		OTHER POSTRETIREMENT BENEFITS	
	2001	2000	**2001**	2000
Plan assets less than benefit obligation	$ (747.3)	$ (45.5)	$(357.7)	$ (48.5)
Unrecognized net loss (gain)	1,331.2	538.3	215.6	(101.3)
Unrecognized plan changes	84.4	72.9	(100.7)	(102.2)
Unrecognized transitional net asset	(6.3)	(15.8)	—	—
Net asset (liability)	$ 662.0	$549.9	$(242.8)	$(252.0)
Recognized as:				
Other assets	$ 853.2	$713.1	$ —	$ —
Accounts payable and accrued liabilities	(17.1)	(2.8)	(24.9)	(24.8)
Deferred income taxes and noncurrent liabilities	(412.2)	(280.4)	(217.9)	(227.2)
Accumulated other comprehensive loss	238.1	120.0	—	—

Assumptions used in determining U.S. plan information are as follows:

	PENSION AND OTHER POSTRETIREMENT BENEFITS		
December 31	**2001**	**2000**	**1999**
Discount rate	7.25%	7.50%	7.75%
Expected rate of return on plan assets	10.0	10.0	10.0
Salary growth rate	4.5	4.5	4.5

Unrecognized net loss (gain) amounts, which reflect experience differentials, primarily relating to differences between expected and actual returns on plan assets as well as the effects of changes in actuarial assumptions, are amortized over the average remaining service period of employees. The health care cost trend rate for other postretirement benefit plans was 9.0% at December 31, 2001. The rate is expected to decline to 5.0% over a 7-year period. A one percentage point change in the health care cost trend rate would have had the following effects:

	ONE PERCENTAGE POINT	
	Increase	**Decrease**
Effect on total service and interest cost components	$ 26.0	$ (21.4)
Effect on benefit obligation	186.8	(160.4)

on the balance sheet, however, as a $662 million net *asset*, prepaid pension cost, and is reported in other assets. This is because some of the pension liability contributing to the underfunded status is deferred and not recognized on the balance sheet at this time. Due to deferrals, only $243 of the $(358) million of underfunded status for the other retirement benefits appears on the balance sheet as a liability.

The beginning and ending funded status are reconciled through explanation of changes to both the obligation and the plan assets (similar to Exhibit 3.12 for the J. Smith example). The change in benefit obligation is explained by recurring and nonrecurring costs less benefits paid. In 2001, Merck's gross benefit costs (service cost, interest cost, actuarial gain or loss, and other) totaled $717.5 million ($295.7 million) for pensions (OPEBs), while the company paid pension (OPEB) benefits of $273 million ($51 million).

The change in plan assets increases as a result of contributions and decreases due to a negative return on plan investments and benefits paid. In 2001, Merck contributed $250 million to its pension plans, the plan investments realized a negative return of $(258) million, and the company paid benefits of $255 million. OPEB investments also suffered a negative return of $(57) million and were also reduced as a result of benefits paid in the amount of $8 million. Merck did not make a contribution to its OPEB plan during the year.

Merck also explains how net periodic (reported) benefit cost for both pensions and OPEBs is computed. Reported pension (and OPEB) costs include recurring costs (service cost and interest cost), less the *expected* return on plan investments. In 2001, Merck's service and interest cost for pension (OPEB) plans are $190 million ($53 million) and $217 million ($77 million), respectively, while its expected return on pension assets is $288 million ($85), respectively. Nonrecurring items are deferred and recognized through amortization. The net amortization expense (gain) for pension (OPEB) plans is $28 million [$(11) million] in 2001.

The final part of the note provides details of actuarial assumptions used in the computation of both the benefit obligations and the reported expenses. The discount rate, the rate of return on plan assets, and the annual rate of increase in compensation are some of these assumptions. Merck reduced its discount rate in 2001 from 7.5% to 7.25% to reflect the decrease in interest rates. Return on assets and compensation growth rates are unchanged at 10% and 4.5%, respectively. The note also reports assumptions regarding growth rates in health care costs and the sensitivity of both benefit expense and liability to changes in health care cost assumptions.

Analyzing Postretirement Benefits

Analysis of postretirement benefit disclosures is an important task, both because of the magnitude of these obligations and because of the distortions introduced by accounting rules. We give a three-step procedure for analyzing postretirement benefits: (1) determine and reconcile the reported and economic benefit cost and liability (or asset); (2) make necessary adjustments to financial statements, especially the balance sheet; and (3) evaluate actuarial assumptions and their effects on financial statements.

Reconciling Economic and Reported Numbers

Exhibit 3.18 provides a reconciliation between economic and reported costs separately for pensions and OPEBs, and in total. The economic pension cost for Merck is $943 million. Compare this with its reported pension cost of $148 million. The difference arises mainly through deferrals of unrealized losses on pension investments and increases in the pension liability due to changes in actuarial assumptions, primarily the interest rate used to discount projected payments. For example, Merck's pension plan

Exhibit 3.18 ***Economic and Reported Postretirement Costs—Merck***

	Economic	Deferred	Amortized	Reported
Pension Expense				
Service cost	$190			$190
Interest cost	217			217
Losses (gains) in investments	258	$(546)		(288)
Actuarial losses (gains)	283	(283)		
Other losses (gains)	(6)	6		
Amortization			$28	28
Total costs (gains)	$943	$(823)	$28	$148
OPEB				
Service cost	$ 53			$53
Interest cost	77			77
Losses (gains) in investments	57	$(141)		(85)
Actuarial losses (gains)	177	(177)		
Other	0			
Amortization			$(11)	(11)
Total costs (gains)	$364	$(318)	$(11)	$34
Total				
Service cost	$ 243			$243
Interest cost	295			295
Losses (gains) in investments	315	$ (687)		(373)
Actuarial losses (gains)	460	(460)		
Other losses (gains)	(6)	6		
Net amortization			$17	17
Total costs (gains)	$1,307	$(1,141)	$17	$182

lost $258 million on its investments during the year, but it reported an expected return of $287 million as a reduction of pension cost. This is because $545 million of the loss was deferred and will not be recognized in the financial statements unless the accumulated gains (losses) from all sources (returns on plan assets and affects of changes in actuarial assumptions) exceeds the threshold level required for recognition under GAAP (10% of the larger of beginning-of-year plan assets or PBO). In that event, the cumulative unrealized gain (loss) will be recognized in the balance sheet and income statement over time. Net amortization of deferred losses, included in pension expense, is $28 million for the year.

The difference between the economic and reported costs for OPEBs is $330 million. This relates to the deferral of losses on OPEB assets and actuarial losses, similar to the deferrals in its pension plans, less the amortization of those deferred losses. In total, the economic costs for all of Merck's postretirement benefits are $1.3 billion, compared to its reported figure for pension cost of $182 million, included in general and administrative expenses in its income statement.

Exhibit 3.19 compares the net economic position (funded status) to the reported accrued benefit cost in the balance sheet. The reported amount of Merck's pension obligation in its balance sheet significantly understates the true liability. In 2001, Merck reports a net *asset*, prepaid pension cost of $662 million [$853.2 prepaid pension cost, less liabilities (credits) and equity reductions (debits) of $191.2 million, net] when, in reality, Merck's pension plans are underfunded by $747 million. Similarly, Merck reports

Economic and Reported Postretirement Benefits—Merck

Exhibit 3.19

	Pension	OPEB	Total
Benefit obligations	$3,612	$1,155	$4,766
Plan assets	2,865	797	3,661
Funded status	(747)	(358)	(1,105)
Unrecognized net loss (gain)	1,331	216	1,547
Unrecognized plan amendments	84	(101)	(16)
Unrecognized transition assets	(6)	0	(6)
Net asset (liability) recognized	662	(243)	419

an OPEB liability of $243 million, less than its true net liability of $358 million, reflecting its underfunded status. This means Merck's 2001 balance sheet reports a total net pension and OPEB net assets of $419 million in comparison to the net economic liability of $1.105 billion. In total, then, $1.524 billion of net liabilities are unrecognized, thus understating Merck's true liabilities.

Adjusting the Income Statement and Balance Sheet

Exhibit 3.20 demonstrates the adjustments for Merck's income statement and balance sheet from our analysis of its pension and OPEB disclosures. The use of economic

Reconciliation of Economic and Reported Changes—Merck

Exhibit 3.20

	Reported	Economic
Income Statement		
Sales	$47,716	$47,716
Operating expenses	36,972	38,113
Operating income	10,744	9,603
Interest	342	342
Income before taxes	10,402	9,261
Income taxes	3,121	2,779
Net income	$ 7,281	$ 6,482
Balance Sheet		
Assets		
Current	$12,962	$12,962
Noncurrent	31,045	30,192
Total assets	$44,007	$43,154
Liabilities and equity		
Current	$11,544	$11,544
Noncurrent	16,413	17,089
Stockholders' equity	16,050	14,521
Total liabilities and equity	$44,007	$43,154
Ratios		
Total debt to equity	1.74	1.97
Long-term debt to equity	1.02	1.18
Return on assets	16.5%	15.0%
Return on common equity	45.4%	44.6%

benefit costs rather than reported costs results in net income that is $799 million lower. This 11% decline in income is mainly driven by a $1.141 billion increase in operating expenses offset by a decrease in deferred taxes of $342 million.

The balance sheet effects are even more pronounced. Using the net economic position (funded status) instead of the reported position (accrued benefit cost) yields a decline in noncurrent assets (reported prepaid pension cost) of $853 million and an increase in noncurrent liabilities of $676 million in 2001. Correspondingly, equity decreases by $1.529 billion, or 9.5%.

Using net economic position (funded status) instead of the reported position (prepaid pension cost) would inflate the total debt to equity ratio by 13% (from 1.74 to 1.97) and the long-term debt to equity ratio by 16% (from 1.02 to 1.18). Using economic-based ratios reduces Merck's return on equity slightly (from 45.4% to 44.6%). The difference in the return on assets (16.5% to 15.0%), however, is more significant as Merck's prepaid pension cost asset disappears, only partially offsetting the reduction in profitability. Still, the inference is that analyzing the economic status (versus reported status) of Merck's postretirement benefits has a substantial impact on our evaluation of the company's overall financial position and performance.

To this point, we have examined the effects of reflecting the economic status of postretirement benefits on financial statements. Yet, an analyst must address at least three additional questions: What is the postretirement benefit cost that should be charged to income? What is the liability that should be reflected on the balance sheet, and in what format? What are the effects of actuarial assumptions on both the income statement and balance sheet? We answer the first two questions in this section. The third question is addressed in the next section.

At first glance it seems the appropriate cost to be reflected in the income statement should be the economic benefit cost. Further analysis suggests the answer is not so obvious. Recall that reported benefit cost differs from economic cost because transitory effects, such as actuarial gains and losses, prior service cost, and abnormal return on assets, are amortized to reported cost through the smoothing process. The purpose of this smoothing is to obtain a more stable or permanent component of postretirement benefit cost. Accordingly, the proper benefit cost depends on the objectives of the analysis. If the analyst is attempting to measure permanent income (see Chapters 2 and 6), then reported cost is probably a more useful measure. In fact, measuring the permanent component of benefit cost is a major aim of accounting standards in this area. However, if the objective of the analysis is to determine economic income, then an analyst should consider all transitory elements in income, which implies that the more useful measure of benefit cost is economic cost.

A related issue is whether benefit cost is part of operating or nonoperating income. Presumably, postretirement benefits are an integral part of employee compensation packages and should be classified as operating. However, further analysis reveals that not all components of these benefits are operating items. Certainly, service cost and its nonrecurring components such as prior service cost and changes in actuarial assumptions (except discount rate changes) are operating items. But what about interest cost and the return on plan assets? Before classifying them as operating or nonoperating, we must understand why they are included in the benefit cost. To illustrate, let's look at the pension for the J. Smith case. We know the pension obligation that is expected to arise in the future is larger than PBO (recall that PBO is the present value of a future expected payment). For J. Smith, the lump sum obligation on the date of retirement (using the 2000 formula) is $14,798, while its present value at the end of 2000 (the PBO) is $3,824. Under what assumption can an obligation of $14,798 20 years hence be represented by $3,824 today? The answer is we assume the company sets aside $3,824 immediately and invests it at 7% per annum (the discount rate) for 20 years. If the company does set aside this amount, it incurs an opportunity cost equal to the interest it could have earned on that amount. This is the interest cost. The return on plan assets (actual or expected) denotes the amount the company actually earns (or expects to earn) from its investments. The amount by which interest cost exceeds (is less than) the return on plan assets represents a nonoperating expense (revenue).

For the second question, we turn to the balance sheet and see that reported status (accrued benefit cost) on the balance sheet distorts the economic position of the benefit plans. Recall that funded status is determined using the projected benefit obligation (PBO). To the extent an analyst is interested in evaluating the liquidating value of a company's net assets, a better measure of the liability is accumulated benefit obligation (ABO). Unfortunately, *SFAS 132* discontinues the required reporting of ABO. This means an analyst must concede that the obligation is overstated when determining liquidating value and is left to make subjective downward adjustments to this obligation.

An analyst must also assess whether the proper balance sheet preparation is the netting of plan assets against its liabilities or the separate disclosure of plan assets and plan liabilities. This issue is more than one of mere presentation. For example, if plan assets are not netted against liabilities, Merck's total debt to equity and long-term debt to equity ratios at the end of 2001 would be significantly greater. Proper presentation depends on the underlying economics of the benefit plans. Specifically, three questions must be addressed: (1) Is the benefit fund separate from the employer? (2) What is the true indebtedness of the employer? (3) What is the nature of the plan assets?

Answers to these questions are interrelated. A benefit fund is separate from the employer when independent trustees administer it. While the employer is ultimately responsible for benefit obligations, its indebtedness is limited to the extent that plan assets are inadequate to cover benefit obligations. This is because plan assets are not under the control of the employer–an employer cannot use these assets for other purposes unless the plan is grossly overfunded. Consequently, the liability of the employer equals the extent of underfunding (if any) of its benefit plans, and not the total

Analysis Research

MARKET VALUATION OF PENSION LIABILITY AND EXPENSE

Analysis methods involve several adjustments to better reflect the economic reality of pension plans. For example, we suggest that the funded status of a plan is its economic position instead of its reported accrued benefit or cost. Also, we suggest the proper pension liability for a going concern is its PBO and that its correct balance sheet presentation is one that nets pension liabilities and plan assets. While these adjustments are reasonable, it is important to assess whether they are valid. Research attempts to address their validity by examining stock price behavior.

There is evidence that the stock market views the unfunded pension obligation (instead of the reported accrued benefit or cost) as the liability. This applies both when determining company value and when assessing systematic risk. The market also views pension assets and obligations separately as assets and liabilities of the company, rather than simply a net amount. We also find that the market values all components of the PBO–indicating the PBO is the proper measure of the pension obligation. However, the market appears to attach more than one dollar of value for every one dollar of PBO. Research to date has been unable to explain this latter result.

Analysis research also examines the market valuation of pension expense and its components. Results show the market attaches a higher value to pension expense than nonpension expense. This is probably because pension expense is more persistent and/or predictable. Furthermore, interest cost and the expected (and actual) return on pension expense is valued as expected, while amortization components are not valued at all. One anomalous market result is the positive value placed on service cost–even though it is an expense and should yield a negative correlation with company value.

obligation. This implies that the proper balance sheet presentation is the netting of plan assets against its liabilities.

Actuarial Assumptions and Sensitivity Analysis

It is tempting to think of the net economic position (or the economic cost) of a company's benefit plans as a reliable estimate of its underlying economic fundamentals. In reality, this is not so. While the value of plan assets is based on verifiable numbers (typically market values), the benefit obligation is estimated using a number of actuarial assumptions. Guidelines for determining actuarial assumptions leave room for discretion by an employer who might wish to window dress the financial statements. Even if we ignore managerial manipulation, both the PBO and the value of plan assets are sensitive to volatile economic factors such as interest rates and stock market performance. Hence, both net economic position and economic cost are volatile numbers not necessarily reflective of economic fundamentals.

Moreover, both the reported position (accrued benefit or cost) and reported cost (net periodic benefit cost), although less volatile than their economic counterparts, are also sensitive to actuarial assumptions. In addition, the reported numbers (especially the reported cost) often reflect managerial window-dressing.

Accordingly, an important task in analysis of postretirement benefits is evaluating the reasonableness of actuarial assumptions used by the employer. This includes examining the effects of changes in assumptions (or market values) on both the economic and reported numbers. Exhibit 3.21 provides a chart that identifies the effects of changes in actuarial assumptions for the discount rate, expected rate of return, and compensation (and health care) growth on both the reported and the economic position and cost numbers.

Exhibit 3.21 ***Effect of Actuarial Assumptions on Benefit Obligation and Cost***

		DIRECTION OF EFFECT ON*			
		ECONOMIC		REPORTED	
Assumption	Direction of Change	Position	Cost	Position	Cost
Discount rate	+	+	–	Indefinite	Indefinite
	–	–	+	Indefinite	Indefinite
Expected return	+	No effect	No effect	+	–
	–	No effect	No effect	–	+
Growth rate†	+	–	+	–	+
	–	+	–	+	–

*Economic position refers to funded status and reported position refers to accrued benefit or cost.

†Growth rate pertains to both compensation and health care costs.

A crucial assumption is the discount rate estimate. Changes in discount rate affect the magnitude of both the PBO and the economic benefit cost. A lower discount rate increases PBO and, hence, reduces funded status–although the smoothing process removes these effects from the balance sheet. The discount rate also affects the reported cost, although the direction of its impact is indefinite. An increase (decrease) in discount rate potentially decreases (increases) service cost but increases (decreases) interest cost. This means the direction of the overall effect on reported cost depends on the relative magnitude of the effects of a discount rate change on interest cost and service cost. In most cases, the effect on interest cost exceeds the effect on service cost. In such a scenario, the discount rate has opposite effects on the reported and economic numbers.

RATE GAFFE
An incorrect discount rate assumption shortchanged 7,130 GTE employees to the tune of $18 million—it was subsequently fixed.

While the company needs to determine the discount rate based on the prevailing interest rate for a company with similar risk, there is some latitude in its determination. The discount rate is a favorite tool for earnings management, with lower discount rates generally indicating more aggressive accounting practices.

The expected rate of return assumption affects the reported numbers–it does not impact the economic cost or economic position numbers. The expected rate of return depends on many factors, such as the composition of the plan assets and the long-term returns on different asset classes. The expected rate of return also can be used to manage earnings, with higher expected rates of return indicating more aggressive accounting practices.

The growth rate assumption is probably of less concern than either the discount rate or the expected return assumptions. It tends to be more stable and predictable. Still, companies worry about changing compensation growth rates because they can affect labor negotiations. The charts on this page reflect the distribution of actuarial assumptions for a large sample of companies.

Discount Rate

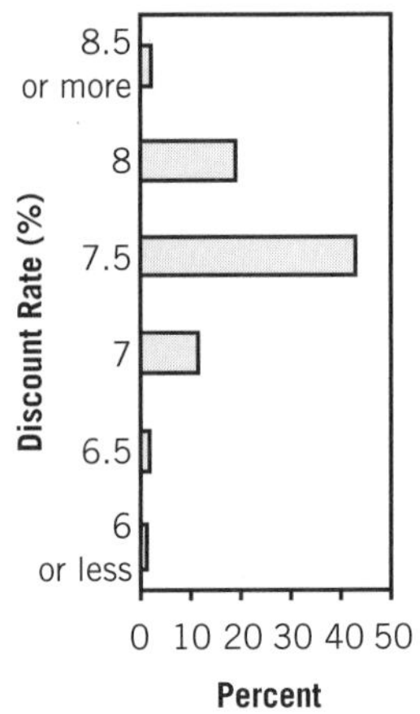

Compensation Growth

8
7.5
7
6.5
6
5.5
5
4.5 or less
Compensation Growth (%)
0 10 20 30 40
Percent

Cash Flow Implications of Postretirement Benefits

Cash flow implications of postretirement benefits are straightforward. That is, cash outflow is equal to the contribution made to the plan by the company. In 2001, Merck's cash outflow on its pension plans was $250 million, while it was $0 on its OPEB plans (see Exhibit 3.17). The current period's cash flow number is not especially useful for evaluating either the profitability or the financial position of a company. Instead, the information provided by accrual accounting is more useful in estimating future cash outflows pertaining to postretirement benefits.

To illustrate, although Merck's cash contributions to its pension plans ($250 million in 2001) are nearly equal to the benefits paid ($255 million), in 2000 the shortfall was $59 million. Current and future cash contributions are related to the degree to which the

Expected Rate of Return

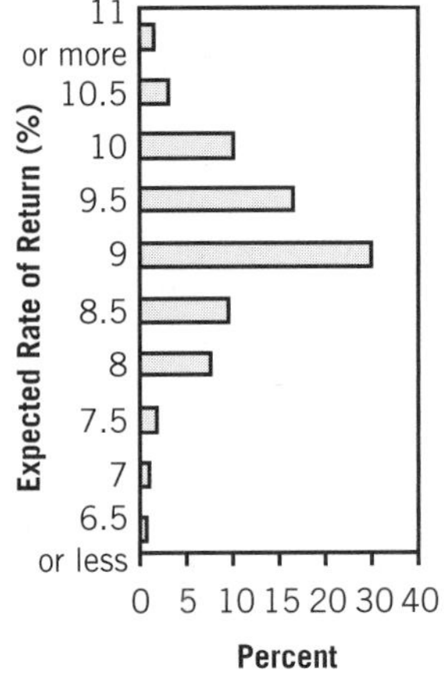

Analysis Research

DO MANAGERS MANIPULATE PENSION ASSUMPTIONS?

Do managers manipulate pension assumptions to window-dress financial statements? Research reveals that managers strategically select (or adjust) pension assumptions to window-dress both the reported values on balance sheets and the funded status of pensions. Specifically, managers strategically select the discount rate to reduce the level of pension underfunding and, therefore, the debt-to-equity ratio. Also, the discount rate selected is typically slightly higher than the prevailing interest rate on securities of similar risk. This suggests an attempt to understate the pension obligation. Moreover, the discount rate and health care cost trend rates on OPEBs show evidence of underreporting of the OPEB obligation. This is especially apparent in situations where companies are close to violating debt covenants. Also, there is little relation between the expected rate of return assumption and (1) the asset composition (a higher proportion of equity should imply a higher expected rate of return) and (2) the actual fund performance. Overall, there is evidence of managerial manipulation of pension assumptions to window-dress financial statements.

pension plans have been underfunded in the past and the current and expected returns on the plan assets. Companies with significantly overfunded pension plans can reduce current contributions and are not as dependent on current year returns on plan assets. For Merck whose pension plans are underfunded, however, cash contributions will be higher, especially in those years when market returns are not strong. An analyst must consider these factors when forecasting Merck's future cash flows.

ANALYSIS VIEWPOINT ... YOU ARE THE LABOR NEGOTIATOR

As the union negotiator on a labor contract, you request that management increase postretirement benefits to employees. Management responds with no increase in benefits but does offer a guarantee to fund a much larger portion of previously committed postretirement benefits. These funds would be dispensed to an independent trustee. You are confused since a large postretirement obligation already exists on the balance sheet. Does this benefit offer seem legitimate?

Answer–p. 176

CONTINGENCIES AND COMMITMENTS

Contingencies

Frequency of Contingent Liabilities

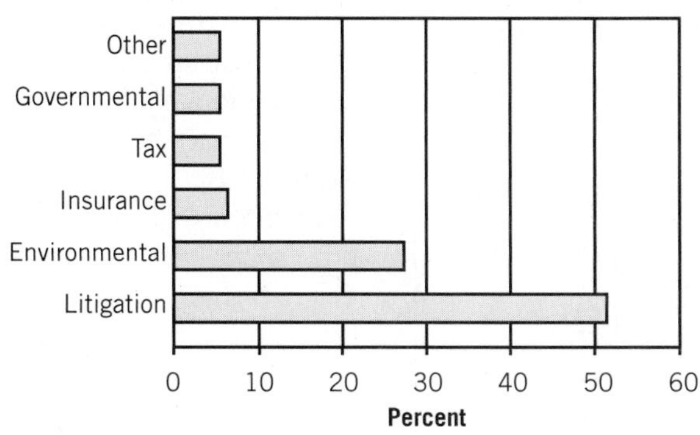

Source: *Accounting Trends and Techniques*

Contingencies are potential gains and losses whose resolution depends on one or more future events. Loss contingencies are potential claims on a company's resources and are known as **contingent liabilities.** Contingent liabilities can arise from litigation, threat of expropriation, collectibility of receivables, claims arising from product warranties or defects, guarantees of performance, tax assessments, self-insured risks, and catastrophic losses of property.

WARRANTIES
Zenith recently reported over $30 million in Warranty Liabilities.

A loss contingency must meet two conditions before a company records it as a loss. First, it must be *probable* that an asset will be impaired or a liability incurred. Implicit in this condition is that it must be probable that a future event will confirm the loss. The second condition is the amount of loss must be *reasonably estimable.* Examples that usually meet these two conditions are losses from uncollectible receivables and the obligations related to product warranties and defects. For these cases, both an estimated liability and a loss are recorded in the financial statements. However, losses from self-insurance risks (injury to others or damage to others' properties) or business interruption losses are not usually recorded until these losses actually occur.

GLOBAL
Accounting for contingencies varies across countries. Germany, for example, allows recording of contingent liabilities that are 'reasonably possible.'

Other examples involving contingent losses such as expropriations, litigation, claims, and assessments depend on the facts in each case. If a company does not record a loss contingency because one or both of the conditions are not met, the company must disclose the contingency in the notes when there is at least a *reasonable possibility* that it will incur a loss. Such a note reports the nature of the contingency and offers an estimate of the possible loss or range of loss–or reports that such an estimate cannot be made.

Consistent with conservatism in financial reporting, companies do not recognize gain contingencies in financial statements. They can, however, disclose gain contingencies in a note if the probability of realization is high.

Analyzing Contingent Liabilities

Reported contingent liabilities for items such as service guarantees and warranties are estimates. Our analysis of these liabilities is only as accurate as the underlying estimates, which companies often determine on the basis of prior experience or future expectations. We must exercise care in accepting management's estimates for these and other contingent liabilities. For instance, recall that Manville argued it had substantial defenses to legal claims against it until the year it declared bankruptcy due to asbestos-related lawsuits.

We also need to analyze note disclosures of all loss (and gain) contingencies. For example, note disclosure of indirect guarantees of indebtedness, such as advancing funds or covering fixed charges of another entity is important for our analysis. Note disclosure for contingencies typically includes:

- A description of the contingent liability and the degree of risk.
- The potential amount of the contingency and how participation of others is treated in determining risk exposure.
- The charges, if any, against income for the estimates of contingent losses.

Our analysis must recognize that companies sometimes underestimate or fail to recognize these liabilities.[4] One example of disclosure for a contingent liability follows:

ANALYSIS EXCERPT

There are various libel and other legal actions that have arisen in the ordinary course of business and are now pending against the Company. Such actions are usually for amounts greatly in excess of the payments, if any, that may be required to be made. It is the opinion of management after reviewing such actions with counsel that the ultimate liability which might result from such actions would not have a material adverse effect on the consolidated financial statements.

—*New York Times*

Another example of a contingent liability involves frequent flyer mileage. Unredeemed frequent flyer mileage entitles airline passengers to billions of miles of free travel. Frequent flyer programs ensure customer loyalty and offer marketing benefits that are not cost-free. Yet airlines tend to underestimate these obligations.

FLYER DEBT
American Airlines estimates its 2000 year-end frequent-flyer liabilities at nearly $900 million.

Reserves for future losses are another type of contingency requiring our scrutiny. Conservatism in accounting calls for companies to recognize losses as they determine or foresee them. Still, companies tend, particularly in years of very poor performance, to overestimate their contingent losses. This behavior is referred to as a *big bath* and often includes recording losses from asset disposals, relocation, and plant closings. Overestimating these losses shifts future costs to the current period and can serve as a means for companies to manage or smooth income. Only in selected reports filed with the SEC are details of these loss estimates (also called *loss reserves*) sometimes disclosed, and even here there is no set requirement for detailed disclosure. Despite this, our analysis should attempt to obtain details of loss reserves by category and amount.

ECO COPS
Contingent Valuation is a means of measuring environmental contingent liabilities. In this case people are surveyed and asked to assign value to environmental damage.

Two sources of useful information are (1) note disclosures in financial statements and (2) information in the Management's Discussion and Analysis section. Also, under the U.S. Internal Revenue Code, only a few categories of anticipated losses are tax deductible. Accordingly, a third source of information is analysis of deferred taxes. This

[4] A recent study reports that of 126 lawsuits lost by publicly traded companies, nearly 40% were not disclosed in years preceding the loss. The implication is that companies are reluctant to disclose pending litigation, even when the risk of loss due to litigation is high.

analysis can reveal undisclosed provisions for future losses, because any undeductible losses should appear in the adjustments for deferred (prepaid) taxes. We also must remember that loss reserves do not alter risk exposure, have no cash flow consequences, and do not provide an alternative to insurance.

Cigna, a property and casualty insurer, shows us how tenuous the reserve estimation process is. In a recent year, Cigna claimed it could look back on 10 years of a very stable pattern of claims (insurance reserves are designed to provide funds for claims). However, in the very next year, the incidence and severity of claims worsened. Cigna claimed that the year was an aberration and it did not increase reserves for future claims. Yet, within two years, Cigna announced a more than $1 billion charge to income to bring insurance reserves to proper levels with claims. Consequently, Cigna's reserves for these earlier years were obviously understated and its net income overstated.

DIFFERENCES
Managers and auditors often differ on whether a contingency should be recorded, disclosed, or ignored.

The auditor's report gives us another perspective on contingencies. Still, auditors exhibit an inability to express an opinion on the outcome of contingencies. For example, the auditor's report for the years involving the Cigna case described above was unqualified. Another typical example, when they do comment on contingencies, is from the auditor's report of Harsco shown here:

ANALYSIS EXCERPT

The Company is subject to the Government exercising an additional option under a certain contract. If the Government exercises this option, additional losses could be incurred by the Company. Also, the Company has filed or is in the process of filing various claims against the Government relating to certain contracts. The ultimate outcome of these matters cannot presently be determined. Accordingly, no provision for such potential additional losses or recognition of possible recovery from such claims (other than relating to the Federal Excise Tax and related claims) has been reflected in the accompanying financial statements.

Notice the intentional ambiguity of this auditor's report.

Banks especially are exposed to large contingent losses that they often underestimate or confine to note disclosure. One common example relates to losses on international loans where evidence points to impairments of assets, but banks and their auditors fail to properly disclose the impact. Another example is off-balance-sheet commitments of banks. These include such diverse commitments as standby letters of credit, municipal bond and commercial paper guarantees, currency swaps, and foreign exchange contracts. Unlike loans, these commitments are promises banks expect (but are not certain) they will not have to bear. Banks do not effectively report these commitments in financial statements. This further increases the danger of not fully identifying risk exposures of banks.

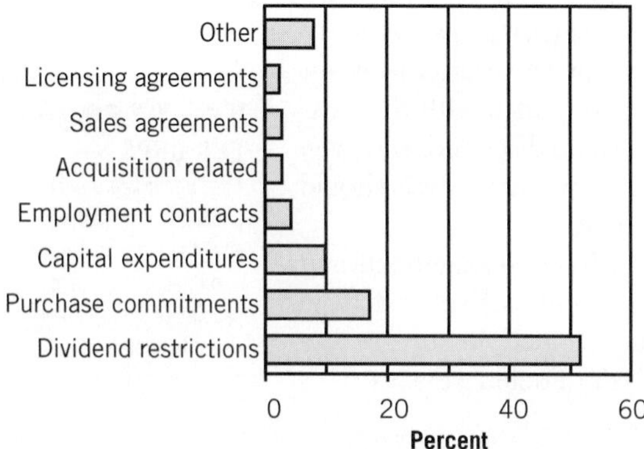

Source: *Accounting Trends and Techniques*

Commitments

Commitments are potential claims against a company's resources due to future performance under contract. They are not recognized in financial statements since events such as the signing of an executory contract or issuance of a purchase order is not a completed transaction. Additional examples are long-term noncancelable contracts to purchase products or services at specified prices and purchase contracts for fixed assets calling for payments during construction. An example of a commitment for Intermec Co. is shown here:

ANALYSIS EXCERPT

The Company signed a patent license agreement with its former principal supplier of hand-held laser scanning devices. This agreement provides that the Company may manufacture and sell certain laser scanning products of its own design and that the Company pay minimum royalties and purchase minimum quantities of other products from that supplier.

A lease agreement is also, in many cases, a form of commitment.

All commitments call for disclosure of important factors surrounding their obligations including the amounts, conditions, and timing. An example of how far-reaching the commitments can be is illustrated in the following note from Wells Fargo:

WOOLLY LOAN
Execs of the insurer Conseco borrowed $480 million to acquire its stock. But when prices plunged, the likelihood of default soared. Conseco guaranteed the loans and must pay if the execs don't. The loan guarantees are disclosed only in notes.

ANALYSIS EXCERPT

Commitments and Contingent Liabilities. In the normal course of business, there are various commitments outstanding and contingent liabilities that are properly not reflected in the accompanying financial statements. Losses, if any, resulting from these commitments are not anticipated to be material. The approximate amounts of such commitments are summarized below ($ in millions):

Standby letters of credit	$ 2,400
Commercial and similar letters of credit	400
Commitments to extend credit*	17,300
Commitments to purchase futures and forward contracts	5,000
Commitments to purchase foreign and U.S. currencies	1,500

*Excludes credit card and other revolving credit loans.

Standby letters of credit include approximately $400 million of participations purchased and are net of approximately $300 million of participations sold. Standby letters of credit are issued to cover performance obligations, including those which back financial instruments (financial guarantees).

OFF-BALANCE-SHEET FINANCING

Off-balance-sheet financing refers to the nonrecording of certain financing obligations. We already examined transactions that fit this mold–such as operating leases that are indistinguishable from capital leases. In addition to leases, there are other off-balance-sheet financing arrangements ranging from the simple to the highly complex. These arrangements are part of an ever-changing landscape, where as one accounting requirement is brought in to better reflect the obligations from a specific off-balance-sheet financing transaction, new and innovative means are devised to take its place.

Off-Balance-Sheet Examples

One way to finance property, plant, and equipment is to have an outside party acquire them while a company agrees to use the assets and provide funds sufficient to service the debt. Examples of these arrangements are *through-put agreements,* where a company agrees to run a specified amount of goods through a processing facility, or *take-or-pay arrangements,* where a company guarantees to pay for a specified quantity of goods whether needed or not. A variation on these arrangements involves creating separate entities and then providing financing not to exceed 50% ownership–such as joint ventures or limited partnerships. Companies carry these variations as an investment in equity and do not consolidate them with the company's financial statements. This means they are excluded from liabilities. Consider the following two practices:

ANALYSIS EXCERPT

Avis Rent-A-Car set up a separate trust to borrow money to finance the purchase of automobiles that they then leased to Avis for its rental fleet. Because the trust is separate from Avis and its parent, the debt of about $400 million is kept off their balance sheets. The chief accounting officer of its parent company proclaimed: "One of the big advantages of off-balance-sheet financing is that it permits us to make other borrowings from banks for operating capital that we could not otherwise obtain." Two major competitors, Hertz and National Car Rental, bought rather than leased their rental cars.

ANALYSIS EXCERPT

Oil companies often resort to less-than-50%-owned joint ventures as a means to raise money for building and operating pipelines. While the debt service is the ultimate responsibility of the oil company, its notes simply report that the company might have to advance funds to help the pipeline joint venture meet its debt obligations if sufficient crude oil needed to generate the necessary funds is not shipped.

Another case involves companies financing inventory without reporting the inventory or its related liability on the buyer's balance sheet. These are referred to as *product financing arrangements,* where a company sells and agrees either to repurchase inventory at a price equal to the original selling price plus carrying and related costs or to guarantee a selling price to third parties. There are criteria for determining when these arrangements are "in substance" financing arrangements that are accounted for as a borrowing, with repurchase costs treated as financing or holding expenses. A typical inventory financing agreement from Seagram's is disclosed as follows:

ANALYSIS EXCERPT

The Company entered into a five-year contract whereunder it agreed to purchase Scotch whiskey from a subsidiary of a British bank. The amount of the commitment is $28,279,000.

Special Purpose Entities (SPEs)

Special purpose entities, now made infamous in the wake of Enron's bankruptcy, have been a legitimate financing mechanism for over two decades and are an integral part of corporate finance today. The concept is straightforward:

- A special purpose entity is formed by the sponsoring company and is capitalized with equity investment, some of which must be from independent third parties.
- The SPE leverages this equity investment with borrowings from the credit markets and purchases earnings assets from or for the sponsoring company.
- The cash flow from the earnings assets is used to repay the debt and provide a return to the equity investors.

This structure has been used for legitimate transactions for decades. Some examples are:

• A company sells accounts receivable to the SPE. These receivables may arise, for example, from the company's proprietary credit card that it offers its customers to attempt to ensure their future patronage (the Sears credit card, for example). The company removes the receivables from its balance sheet and receives cash that can be invested in other earning assets. The SPE collateralizes bonds that it sells in the credit markets with the receivables and uses the cash to purchase additional receivables on an ongoing basis as the company's credit card portfolio grows. This process is called *securitization.* Consumer finance companies like Capital One are significant issuers of receivable-backed bonds. Exhibit 3.22 provides an illustration of the flow of funds in this use of SPEs.

Illustration of SPE Transaction to Sell Accounts Receivable ***Exhibit 3.22***

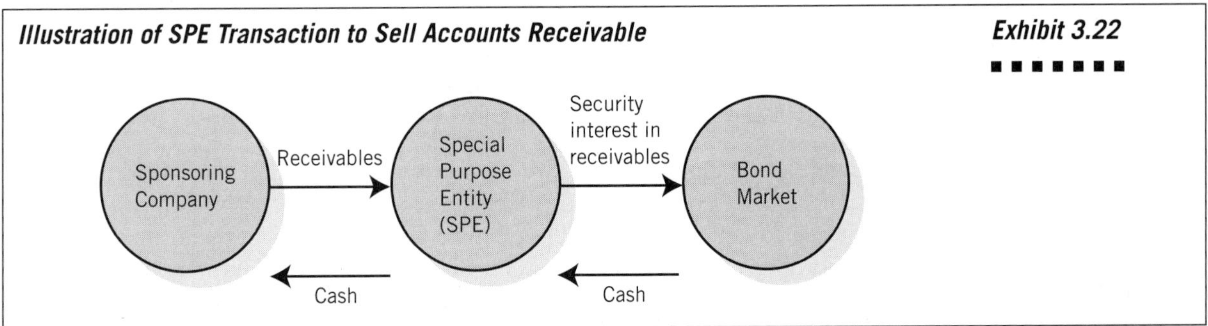

• A company desires to construct a manufacturing facility. It executes a forward contract to purchase output from the plant. A SPE uses the contract to collateralize bonds that it sells to finance the plant's construction. The company obtains the benefits of the manufacturing plant, but does not recognize either the asset or the liability on its balance sheet since executory contracts (commitments) are not recorded under GAAP and are also not considered derivatives that would require balance sheet recognition (see Chapter 5).

• A company desires to construct an office building. It has sufficient profitability to benefit from tax deductions for interest on the mortgage and depreciation of the building but does not want to record either the asset or the liability on its balance sheet. A SPE agrees to finance and construct the building and lease it to the company under an operating lease. If structured properly, neither the leased asset nor the lease obligation are reflected on the company's balance sheet. Surprisingly, the company can be considered an owner of the property and borrower under the mortgage for tax purposes and realize all of the consequent tax benefits. This type of transaction is called a *synthetic lease.*

There are two primary reasons for the popularity of SPEs:

1. SPEs may provide a lower-cost financing alternative than borrowing from the credit markets directly. This is because the activities of the SPE are restricted and, as a result, investors purchase a well-secured cash flow stream that is not subject to the range of business risks inherent in providing capital directly to the sponsoring company.
2. Under present GAAP, so long as the SPE is properly structured, the SPE is accounted for as a separate entity, unconsolidated with the sponsoring company (see Chapter 5 for a discussion of consolidations). The company thus is able to use SPEs to achieve off-balance-sheet transactions to remove assets, liabilities,

or both from its balance sheet. Since the company continues to realize the economic benefits of the transactions, operating performance ratios (like return on assets, asset turnover ratios, leverage ratios, and so on) improve significantly.

FUTURE GAAP
Regulators continue to debate the reporting standards for consolidation.

GAAP provides little guidance relating to the accounting for SPEs and the rules for their consolidation with the sponsoring company. Accountants generally do not require consolidation so long as the SPE is capitalized with outside equity from independent third-party investors of at least 10% of total capitalization. (This percentage was originally 3%, but was increased following publicity in the wake of the Enron bankruptcy.) For an SPE to be an arm's-length entity not consolidated into the sponsor's financial statements, the third-party investor must bear the risk of its investment.

Problems stemming from the accounting for SPEs generally arise when companies seek to shelter the risk of the SPE's outside investors. If investors contribute equity as a note payable to the SPE or secure the investment by a letter of credit, insurance or other form of guarantee, the investment is not considered at risk and consolidation will result, completely negating the original intent of the SPE.

We close our discussion of SPEs with three examples of their use.

Capital One Financial Corporation. We begin with Capital One Financial Corporation, the consumer finance company with $28 billion in total assets, consisting mostly of consumer loans and credit card receivables. Capital One uses SPEs in the form of trusts to purchase portions of its consumer loan portfolio. The trusts, in turn, finance the purchase by selling bonds collateralized by the receivables.

Capital One manages over $45 billion in consumer loans, yet only $21 billion is reported on its balance sheet. The other $24 billion have been sold to the trust/SPE. In 2001, Capital One reported a net increase in consumer loans of just over $18 billion. It also reported cash inflows of nearly $12 billion relating to the securitization of these loans.

Capital One is an example of a company using SPEs for a legitimate financial purpose and with full disclosure. Receivables are removed from the balance sheet only when the SPE has been properly structured with sufficient third-party equity and when Capital One has sold the assets without recourse, meaning that it is relieved of all risk of loss on the receivables. Furthermore, the company fully discloses its off-balance-sheet financing activities so that analysts can consider their effects in the evaluation of the company's financial condition. Excerpts from the annual report of Capital One follow.

ANALYSIS EXCERPT

The Company actively engages in off-balance-sheet consumer loan securitization transactions. Securitizations involve the transfer of a pool of loan receivables by the Company to an entity created for securitizations, generally a trust or other special purpose entity ("the trusts"). . . . Securities ($24.3 billion outstanding as of December 31, 2001) representing undivided interests in the pool of consumer loan receivables are sold to the public through an underwritten offering or to private investors in private placement transactions. The Company receives the proceeds of the sale. In certain securitizations, the Company retains an interest in the trust ("seller's interest") equal to the amount of the outstanding receivables transferred to the trust in excess of the principal balance of the securities outstanding. . . . A securitization accounted for as a sale in accordance with *SFAS 140* generally results in the removal of the receivables, other than any applicable seller's interest, from the Company's balance sheet for financial and regulatory accounting purposes. . . . As of December 31, 2001, we had $27.4 billion, or approximately 60%, of our total loans subject to securitization transactions.

eBay, Inc. On March 1, 2000, eBay constructed office facilities in San Jose, California, at a total cost of $126.4 million. The property was owned by a separate entity, eBay Realty Trust, and leased to eBay. The structure of this transaction was unique in that it allowed eBay to be the lessee of an operating lease for financial reporting purposes, but the owner of the property for federal tax purposes, thus allowing it to treat as deductions both the interest on the lease and the depreciation of the property. These synthetic leases have become increasingly popular because they provide off-balance-sheet financing yet allow the organization to retain all of the tax benefits of ownership.

eBay Realty Trust was formed with a nominal investment. It then agreed to construct a building for eBay, which leased the property upon completion. Financing of the building came from lenders, with Chase Manhattan Bank serving as agent. The loan was secured by a mortgage on the property and an assignment of the lease. In addition, eBay agreed to place $126.4 million in a cash collateral account and also guaranteed the owner-lessor a minimum residual amount upon termination of the lease and sale of the property. Exhibit 3.23 provides a summary of the lease terms and an excerpt relating to its treatment for book and tax purposes. Particularly interesting from the accounting point of view is the treatment of the lease as an operating lease for financial reporting purposes, and of eBay as the owner of the property for federal tax purposes.

Exhibit 3.23

eBay, Inc. Synthetic lease

Summary of the terms of the lease:

Term:	5 years with two 5-year renewal options
Rent:	Based on the London Interbank Offering Rate (LIBOR) plus 0.394% applied to the $126.4 million cost of the facility funded by the lessor
Transfer of title:	None
Purchase option:	At appraised value

Lease Provision:

7.1 Ownership of the Property. (a) Lessor and Lessee intend that (i) for financial accounting purposes with respect to Lessee (A) this Lease will be treated as an "operating lease" pursuant to *Statement of Financial Accounting Standards (SFAS) No. 13,* as amended, (B) Lessor will be treated as the owner and lessor of the Property and (C) Lessee will be treated as the lessee of the Property, but (ii) for federal, state and local income tax and all other purposes (A) this Lease will be treated as a financing arrangement, (B) the Lenders will be treated as senior lenders making loans to Lessee in an amount equal to the Loans, which Loans will be secured by the Property, (C) Investor will be treated as a subordinated lender making a loan to Lessee in an amount equal to the Investor Contribution, which loan is secured by the Property, and (D) Lessee will be treated as the owner of the Property and will be entitled to all tax benefits ordinarily available to an owner of property like the Property for such tax purposes.

This treatment of the lease as operating, together with the associated tax benefits, had the following effects on eBay's financial condition:

1. Total asset turnover increased and financial leverage decreased due to the fact that the lease was not capitalized.
2. Treatment of the lease as a capital lease for tax purposes resulted in a tax savings since depreciation and interest are greater than rent expense in the initial years, thus increasing cash flow.

3. Reported profitability was higher in the initial years since rent expense is less than depreciation plus interest.

The financial statement and cash flow benefits of a synthetic lease are significant. A synthetic lease, though within the confines of GAAP, uses the lease structure to avoid capitalization and does not abide by the spirit of the accounting standards. It is an example, therefore, of SPE use that realizes cosmetic, rather than economic, benefits.

Following Enron, investors have demanded greater transparency in financial reporting and have been critical of companies perceived as using financial engineering. In response, Krispy Kreme issued the following statement in its recent annual report:

ANALYSIS EXCERPT

In the current economic climate, investors are understandably paying closer attention to the financial strength of companies and the way they conduct business. We have taken the position that there is no reason for us to do anything that could be misinterpreted, regardless of how legal and acceptable it may be. The confidence of our investors and customers is more important than the propriety of any business practice. For that reason, immediately after our experience with the press and its probe of synthetic leases, an experience that in many cases was frankly neither responsible nor constructive, we called a meeting of our Board of Directors to discuss any business practices or situations that could possibly be misunderstood or misinterpreted. On April 26, 2001, the Company entered into a synthetic lease agreement in which the lessor, a bank, had agreed to fund up to $35 million for construction of the Company's new mix and distribution facility. . . . On February 12, 2002, a commitment letter was signed with the bank to terminate the synthetic lease and purchase the Facility from the bank.

Enron. Our third example, Enron, demonstrates the misuse of special purpose entities. According to its CFO, Enron's substantial growth could not be sustained through issuing common stock because of near-term dilution and also the company could not increase its financial leverage through debt issuance for fear of jeopardizing its debt rating. As a result, the company sought to conceal massive amounts of debt and to significantly overstate its earnings with SPEs.

Enron's hedge of its investment in Rhythms NetConnections was the first of several such SPEs that the company established in order to avoid recognition of asset impairments and serves as an appropriate example of the misuse of this financial technique. Enron invested $10 million ($1.85 per share) in Rhythms in 1998. The following year, Rhythms went public and its stock rose to $69 per share. Enron was prohibited from selling its investment due to a prior agreement and wished to shelter its $300 million unrealized gain from potential loss.

Although the transaction is quite complicated, in essence Enron formed an SPE and capitalized it with its own stock, covered by forward contracts to preserve its value from potential decline. The SPE, in turn, acted as the counterparty (an insurance company) to hedge Enron's investment in Rhythms and protect the company from possible decline in its value. If the investment declined in value, Enron, theoretically, would be able to call on the guaranty issued by the SPE to make up the loss.

PARTNER PROBLEMS

Investment banks including CFSB and Merrill Lynch earned tens of millions of dollars helping Enron disguise billions of dollars in debt by selling the company's off-balance-sheet partnerships to institutional investors.

If this transaction was conducted with a third party with sufficient equity of its own, Enron would have effectively hedged its investment and would not be required to report a loss if the investment declined in value. As structured, however the SPE had no outside equity of its own and its assets consisted solely of Enron stock. The hedge was a sham. Furthermore, Enron took the position that these SPEs did not need to be consolidated in its annual report. This meant that any liabilities of the SPE would not be reflected on Enron's consolidated balance sheet.

Consolidation rules require that the SPEs be truly independent in order to avoid consolidation. That means that they should be capitalized with outside equity and effective control should remain with outside parties. Enron violated both of these requirements. First, in many cases Enron guaranteed the investment of its "outside" investors. That meant that the investors did not have the required risk of loss. And second, the management of the SPEs was often Enron employees with outside investors not serving in a management capacity. In the restatement of its 1997–2000 financial statements in the third quarter of 2001, Enron consolidated the SPEs. The effect was to recognize on-balance-sheet hundreds of millions of dollars of debt, to record asset impairments of approximately \$1 billion, and to reduce stockholders' equity by \$1.2 billion. The restatement eroded investor confidence and triggered violations of debt covenants that ultimately resulted in the bankruptcy of the company.

ENRON UNDERWRITER
From 1999 to 2001, Merrill Lynch earned \$38 million in fees from Enron for its stock and bond deals and advice.

How much could investors have learned about these SPE activities from Enron's annual report? Exhibit 3.24 contains an excerpt from Enron's 2000 annual report, the year before its bankruptcy. The only mention of the SPEs was in a related party footnote. Enron described the hedging of its investment (merchant) portfolio and revealed that the SPEs had been capitalized with Enron common stock. It also disclosed that the managing partner of the SPE was an executive of Enron and highlighted the disclosures in a separate "Related Party" footnote. In hindsight, the disclosures proved more significant than they first appeared. Analysts are now paying much more attention to these details following the billions of dollars of losses that resulted from Enron's collapse.

THEY'RE HISTORY
Merrill Lynch fired two of its highest ranking investment bankers who refused to cooperate with investigations into Merrill's role in the collapse of Enron.

Enron Related Party Transactions Footnote

Exhibit 3.24

In 2000 and 1999, Enron entered into transactions with limited partnerships (the Related Party) whose general partner's managing member is a senior officer of Enron. The limited partners of the Related Party are unrelated to Enron. Management believes that the terms of the transactions with the Related Party were reasonable compared to those which could have been negotiated with unrelated third parties.

In 2000, Enron entered into transactions with the Related Party to hedge certain merchant investments and other assets. As part of the transactions, Enron (i) contributed to newly-formed entities (the Entities) assets valued at approximately \$1.2 billion, including \$150 million in Enron notes payable, 3.7 million restricted shares of outstanding Enron common stock and the right to receive up to 18.0 million shares of outstanding Enron common stock in March 2003 (subject to certain conditions) and (ii) transferred to the Entities assets valued at approximately \$309 million, including a \$50 million note payable and an investment in an entity that indirectly holds warrants convertible into common stock of an Enron equity method investee. In return, Enron received economic interests in the Entities, \$309 million in notes receivable, of which \$259 million is recorded at Enron's carryover basis of zero, and a special distribution from the Entities in the form of \$1.2 billion in notes receivable, subject to changes in the principal for amounts payable by Enron in connection with the execution of additional derivative instruments. Cash in these Entities of \$172.6 million is invested in Enron demand notes. In addition, Enron paid \$123 million to purchase share-settled options from the Entities on 21.7 million shares of Enron common stock. The Entities paid Enron \$10.7 million to terminate the share-settled options on 14.6 million shares of Enron common stock outstanding. In late 2000, Enron entered into share-settled collar arrangements with the entities on 15.4 million shares of Enron common stock. Such arrangements will be accounted for as equity transactions when settled.

In 2000, Enron entered into derivative transactions with the Entities with a combined notional amount of approximately \$2.1 billion to hedge certain merchant investments and other assets. Enron's notes receivable balance was reduced by \$36 million as a result of premiums owed on derivative transactions. Enron recognized revenues of approximately \$500 million related to the subsequent change in the market value of these derivatives, which offset market value changes of certain merchant investments and price risk management activities. In addition, Enron recognized \$44.5 million and \$14.1 million of interest income and interest expense, respectively, on the notes receivable from and payable to the Entities.

SHAREHOLDERS' EQUITY

Equity refers to owner (shareholder) financing of a company. It is viewed as reflecting the claims of owners on the net assets of the company. Holders of equity securities are typically subordinate to creditors, meaning that creditors' claims are settled first. Also, typically variation exists across equity holders on seniority for claims on net assets. Equity holders are exposed to the maximum risk associated with a company. At the same time, they have the maximum return possibilities as they are entitled to all returns once creditors are covered.

Our analysis of equity must take into account several measurement and reporting standards for shareholders' equity. Such analysis would include:

- Classifying and distinguishing among major sources of equity financing.
- Examining rights for classes of shareholders and their priorities in liquidation.
- Evaluating legal restrictions for distribution of equity.
- Reviewing contractual, legal, and other restrictions on distribution of retained earnings.
- Assessing terms and provisions of convertible securities, stock options, and other arrangements involving potential issuance of shares.

It is important for us to distinguish between liability and equity instruments given their differences in risks and returns. This is especially crucial when financial instruments have characteristics of both. Some of the more difficult questions we must confront are:

- Is a financial instrument such as mandatory redeemable preferred stock or a put option on a company's common stock–obligating a company to redeem it at a specified amount–a liability or equity instrument?
- Is a financial instrument such as a stock purchase warrant or an employee stock option–obligating a company to issue its stock at specified amounts–a liability or equity instrument?
- Is a right to issue or repurchase a company's stock at specified amounts an asset or equity instrument?
- Is a financial instrument having features of both liabilities and equity sufficiently different from both to warrant separate presentation? If yes, what are the criteria for this presentation?

GLOBAL
Countries vary in preference given to creditors vs. shareholders; e.g., Germany, France, and Japan give preference to shareholders.

The following sections help us answer these and other issues confronting our analysis of financial statements. We will return to these questions at other points in the book to further describe the analysis implications. This section first considers capital stock and then retained earnings–the two major components of equity.

Capital Stock

Reporting of Capital Stock

Reporting of capital stock includes an explanation of changes in the number of capital shares. This information is disclosed in the financial statements or related notes. The following partial list shows reasons for changes in capital stock, separated according to increases and decreases.

Sources of increases in capital stock outstanding:

- Issuances of stock.
- Conversion of debentures and preferred stock.
- Issuances pursuant to stock dividends and splits.

- Issuances of stock in acquisitions and mergers.
- Issuances pursuant to stock options and warrants exercised.

Sources of decreases in capital stock outstanding:

- Purchases and retirements of stock.
- Stock buybacks.
- Reverse stock splits.

Another important aspect of our analysis of capital stock is the evaluation of the options held by others that, when exercised, cause the number of shares outstanding to increase and thus dilute ownership. These options include:

- Conversion rights of debentures and preferred stock into common.
- Warrants entitling holders to exchange them for stock under specified conditions.
- Stock options with compensation and bonus plans calling for issuances of capital stock over a period of time at fixed prices–examples are qualified stock option plans and employee stock ownership plans.
- Commitments to issue capital stock–an example is merger agreements calling for additional consideration contingent on the occurrence of an event such as achieving a specific earnings level.

The importance of analyzing these disclosures is to alert us to the potential increase in the number of shares outstanding. The extent of dilution in earnings and book value per share depends on factors like the amount received or other rights given up when converting securities. We must recognize that dilution is a real cost (cash outflow) for a company–a cost that is given little formal recognition in financial statements. We examine the impact of dilution on earnings per share in the appendix to Chapter 6.

Contributed Capital. **Contributed (or paid-in) capital** is the total financing received from shareholders in return for capital shares. Contributed capital is usually divided into two parts. One part is assigned to the par or stated value of capital shares: **common** and/or **preferred stock** (if stock is no-par, then it is assigned the total financing). The remainder is reported as **contributed** (or **paid-in**) **capital in excess of par or stated value** (also called *additional* (or *paid-in*) *capital.* When combined, these accounts reflect the amounts paid in by shareholders for financing business activities. Other accounts in the contributed capital section of shareholders' equity arise from charges or credits from a variety of capital transactions, including (1) sale of treasury stock, (2) capital changes arising from business combinations, (3) capital donations, often shown separately as donated capital, (4) stock issuance costs and merger expenses, and (5) capitalization of retained earnings by means of stock dividends.

Treasury Stock. **Treasury stock** (or *buybacks*) are the shares of a company's stock reacquired after having been previously issued and fully paid for. Acquisition of treasury stock by a company reduces both assets and shareholders' equity. Consistent with this transaction, treasury stock is not an asset, it is a *contra-equity account.* Treasury stock is typically recorded at *cost,* and the most common method of presentation is to deduct treasury stock cost from the total of shareholders' equity. When companies record treasury stock at par, they typically report it as a contra to its related class of stock.

Classification of Capital Stock

Capital stock are shares issued to equity holders in return for assets and services. There are two basic types of capital stock: preferred and common. There also are a number of different variations within each of these two classes of stock.

MERGER-DADDY
The biggest-ever merger was America Online Inc.'s $166 billion, all-stock bid for Time Warner, Inc. in 2000.

MERGER DISCLOSURE
New accounting rules require companies to explain in more detail why they are making an acquisition. They must tell what assets, including intangible ones such as goodwill and patents, they are getting for their money.

Preferred Stock. **Preferred stock** is a special class of stock possessing preferences or features not enjoyed by common stock. The more typical features attached to preferred stock include:

- Dividend distribution preferences including participating and cumulative features.
- Liquidation priorities–especially important since the discrepancy between par and liquidation value of preferred stock can be substantial. For example, General Aniline & Film Corp. had a preferred stock par value of $3.9 million versus a liquidation value of $85.7 million.
- Convertibility (redemption) into common stock–the SEC requires separate presentation of these shares when preferred stock possesses characteristics of debt.
- Nonvoting rights–which can change with changes in items such as arrearages in dividends.
- Call provisions–usually protecting preferred shareholders against premature redemption (call premiums often decrease over time).

While preferred shareholders are usually senior to common shareholders, the preferred shareholders' rights to dividends are usually fixed. Yet, their dividend rights can be cumulative, meaning they are entitled to arrearages (prior years) of dividends before common shareholders receive any dividends.

Among preferred stock classes, we find a variety of preferences relating to dividend and liquidation rights. These features, and the fixed nature of their dividends, often give preferred stock the appearance of liabilities. An important distinction between preferred shareholders and creditors is that preferred stockholders are typically not entitled to demand redemption of their shares. Nevertheless, some preferred stocks possess set redemption dates that can include sinking funds–funds accumulated for expected repayment. Characteristics of preferred stock that would make them more akin to common stock include dividend participation rights, voting rights, and rights of conversion into common stock. Preferred stock often has a par value, but it need not be the amount at which it was originally issued.

SQUEEZE PLAY
A recent $1.6 billion lawsuit alleges five telecom execs, including WorldCom's Bernard Ebbers and Qwest Communications's Philip Anschutz, essentially took bribes when they shared in highly sought initial public offerings. In return they steered business to investment bankers at Citigroup's Salomon Smith Barney unit, where analysts arranged payoffs by issuing flattering research reports to pump up the price of shares the execs held. The lawsuit argues that by not disclosing these arrangements, the execs defrauded ordinary shareholders.

Common Stock. **Common stock** is a class of stock representing ownership interest and bearing ultimate risks and rewards of company performance. Common stock represents **residual interests**–having no preference, but reaping residual net income and absorbing net losses. Common stock can carry a par value; if not, it is usually assigned a stated value. The par value of common stock is a matter of legal and historical significance–it usually is unimportant for modern financial statement analysis.

There is sometimes more than one class of common stock for major companies. The distinctions between common stock classes typically are differences in dividend, voting, or other rights.

Analyzing Capital Stock

Items that constitute shareholders' equity usually do not have a marked effect on income determination and, as a consequence, do not seriously impact analysis of income. The more relevant information for analysis relates to the composition of capital accounts and to their applicable restrictions. Composition of equity is important because of provisions that can affect residual rights of common shares and, accordingly, the rights, risks, and returns of equity investors. Such provisions include dividend participation rights, conversion rights, and a variety of options and conditions that characterize complex securities frequently issued under merger agreements–most of which dilute common equity. It is important that we reconstruct and explain changes in these capital accounts.

ANALYSIS VIEWPOINT ***. . . YOU ARE THE MONEY MANAGER***

You are searching for an investment opportunity. You narrow your search to a company with two different securities: common stock and 10% preferred stock. The returns for both securities (including dividends and price appreciation) in the past few years are consistently around 10%. In which security do you invest?

Answer–p. 177

Retained Earnings

Retained earnings are the earned capital of a company. The Retained Earnings account reflects the accumulation of undistributed earnings or losses of a company since its inception. This contrasts with the Capital Stock and Additional Paid-In Capital accounts that constitute capital contributed by shareholders. Retained earnings are the primary source of dividend distributions to shareholders. While some states permit distributions to shareholders from additional paid-in capital, these distributions represent capital (not earnings) distributions.

Cash and Stock Dividends

A **cash dividend** is a distribution of cash to shareholders. It is the most common form of dividend and, once declared, is a liability of a company. Another form of dividend is the *dividend in kind,* or property dividend. These dividends are payable in the assets of a company, in goods, or in the stock of another corporation. Such dividends are valued at the market value of the assets distributed.

ANALYSIS EXCERPT

Ranchers Exploration and Development Corp. distributed a dividend in kind using gold bars. Also, Dresser Industries paid a dividend in kind with "a distribution of one INDRESCO share for every five shares of the Company's common stock."

A **stock dividend** is a distribution of a company's own shares to shareholders on a pro rata basis. It represents, in effect, a permanent capitalization of earnings. Shareholders receive additional shares in return for reallocation of retained earnings to capital accounts. Accounting for *small* (or *ordinary*) *stock dividends,* typically less than 20% to 25% of shares outstanding, requires the stock dividend be valued at its market value on the date of declaration. This requirement is presumably designed to limit the frequency of stock dividends. *Large stock dividends* (or "split-ups effected in the form of a dividend"), typically exceeding 25% of shares outstanding, require that the stock dividend be valued at the par value of shares issued. We must not be misled into attaching substantive value to stock dividends. Companies sometimes encourage such inferences for their own self-interests as shown here:

ANALYSIS EXCERPT

Wickes Companies announced a stock dividend "in lieu of the quarterly cash dividend." Its management asserted this stock "dividend continues Wickes' 88-year record of uninterrupted dividend payments."

Prior Period Adjustments

Prior period adjustments are mainly corrections for errors in prior periods' financial statements. Companies exclude them from the income statement and report them as an adjustment (net of tax) to the beginning balance of retained earnings.

Appropriations of Retained Earnings

Appropriations of retained earnings are reclassifications of retained earnings for specific purposes. Through management action, and with board of director approval in compliance with legal requirements, companies can appropriate retained earnings. Appropriations of retained earnings (sometimes referred to as reserves) recognize that a company does not intend to distribute these amounts as dividends, but rather to reserve them for litigation, plant expansion, self-insurance, and other business contingencies. We must remember that appropriations do not set aside cash. Also, appropriations do not relieve the income statement of potential charges. Appropriations are reclassified as unappropriated retained earnings when their purpose is achieved. An appropriation of retained earnings at an amount equal to the cost of treasury stock purchased is an example of an appropriation established under legal requirements in certain states. This appropriation is reclassified as retained earnings once the treasury stock is sold, retired, or otherwise disposed of.

Restrictions on Retained Earnings

Restrictions (or covenants) on retained earnings are constraints or requirements on the retention of a certain retained earnings amount. An important restriction involves limitations on a company's distribution of dividends. Bond indentures and loan agreements are typical sources of these restrictions. Companies often disclose such restrictions in notes. One example of note disclosure stemming from debt indentures follows:

ANALYSIS EXCERPT

Under the most restrictive of these agreements, approximately $33,000,000 was available for distribution of earnings to shareholders. Presently, the Company has no plans to declare any dividends.

—Leslie Fay Companies

Another case involving restrictions on retained earning involves Allied Van Lines and is reported as follows in its notes:

ANALYSIS EXCERPT

Restrictive loan covenants. The various loans include restrictive covenants which provide as follows: That the Company must maintain consolidated tangible net worth of $28,000,000 plus 50% of cumulative net income . . . ; current assets not less than 115% of current liabilities at all times and 120% year-end; long-term debt not more than 35% of consolidated tangible net worth; income available for fixed charges not less than 125% of fixed charges; guarantees of loans made to or leases entered into by agents or owner-operators cannot exceed $3,500,000; . . . net working capital of not less than $6,000,000; and the sum of cash flow (principally working capital provided from operations) plus current notes receivable must be at least 130% of current maturities of long-term debt.

ANALYSIS VIEWPOINT **. . . YOU ARE THE SHAREHOLDER**

You own common stock in a company. This company's stock price doubled in the past 12 months, and it is currently selling at $66. Today, the company announces a 3-for-1 'stock split effected in the form of a dividend.' How do you interpret this announcement?

Answer–p. 177

Analyzing Retained Earnings

Our analysis of restrictions imposed on distributions of retained earnings by loan or other agreements usually reveals a company's latitude in areas like dividend distributions or in maintaining required levels of working capital. These restrictions also reveal a company's bargaining strength and standing in credit markets. Knowledge of restrictive covenants enables us to assess a company's risk of default on these provisions.

Book Value per Share

Computation of Book Value per Share

Book value per share is the per share amount resulting from a company's liquidation at amounts reported on its balance sheet. *Book value* is conventional terminology referring to net asset value–that is, total assets reduced by claims against them. The *book value of common stock* is equal to the total assets less liabilities and claims of securities senior to common stock (such as preferred stock) at amounts reported on the balance sheet (but can also include unbooked claims of senior securities). A simple means of computing book value is to add up the common stock equity accounts and reduce this total by any senior claims not reflected in the balance sheet (including preferred stock dividend arrearages, liquidation premiums, or other asset preferences to which preferred shares are entitled).

The shareholders' equity section of Kimberly Corp. for periods ending in Years 4 and 5 is reproduced below as an example of the measurement of book value per share:

	Year 5	Year 4
Preferred stock, 7% cumulative, par value $100 (authorized 4,000,000 shares; outstanding 3,602,811 shares)	$ 360,281,100	$ 360,281,100
Common stock, par value $16.67 (authorized 90,000,000 shares; outstanding 54,138,137 shares at December 31, Year 5, and 54,129,987 shares at December 31, Year 4)	902,302,283	902,166,450
Retained earnings	2,362,279,244	2,220,298,288
Total shareholder's equity	$3,624,862,627	$3,482,745,838

Note: Preferred stock is nonparticipating and callable at 105. Dividends for Year 5 are in arrears.

Our calculation of book value per share for both common and preferred stock at the end of Year 5 follows:

	Preferred	Common	Total
Preferred stock* (at $100 par)	$360,281,100		$ 360,281,100
Dividends in arrears (7%)	25,219,677		25,219,677
Common stock		$ 902,302,283	902,302,283
Retained earnings (net of amount attributed to dividend in arrears)		2,337,059,567	2,337,059,567
Total	$385,500,777	$3,239,361,850	$3,624,862,627
Divided by number of shares outstanding	3,602,811	54,138,137	
Book value per share	$107.00	$59.84	

*The call premium does not normally enter into computation of book value per share because the call provision is at the option of the company.

Relevance of Book Value per Share

Book value plays an important role in analysis of financial statements. Applications can include the following:

- Book value, with potential adjustments, is frequently used in assessing merger terms.
- Analysis of companies composed of mainly liquid assets (finance, investment, insurance, and banking institutions) relies extensively on book values.
- Analysis of high-grade bonds and preferred stock attaches considerable importance to asset coverage.

These applications must recognize the accounting considerations entering into the computation of book value per share such as the following:

- Carrying values of assets, particularly long-lived assets like property, plant, and equipment, are usually reported at cost and can markedly differ from market values.
- Internally generated intangible assets often are not reflected in book value, nor are contingent assets with a reasonable probability of occurrence.

Also, other adjustments often are necessary. For example, if preferred stock has characteristics of debt, it is appropriate to treat it as debt at the prevailing interest rate. In short, book value is a valuable analytical tool, but we must apply it with discrimination and understanding.

Liabilities at the "Edge" of Equity

This section describes two items straddling liabilities and equity–redeemable preferred stock and minority interest.

Redeemable Preferred Stock

Analysts must be alert for equity securities (typically preferred stock) that possess mandatory redemption provisions making them more akin to debt than equity. These securities require a company to pay funds at specific dates. A true equity security does not impose such requirements. Examples of these securities, under the guise of preferred stock, exist for many companies including Lockheed and Koppers. Tenneco's annual report refers to its preferred stock redemption provision as follows:

> **ANALYSIS EXCERPT**
>
> The aggregate maturities applicable to preferred stock issues outstanding at December 31, 20X1, are none for the Year 20X2, $10 million for Year 20X3, and $23 million for each of the Years 20X4, 20X5, and 20X6.

The SEC asserts that redeemable preferred stocks are different from conventional equity capital and should *not* be included in shareholders' equity nor combined with nonredeemable equity securities. The SEC also requires disclosure of redemption terms and five-year maturity data. Accounting standards require disclosure of redemption requirements of redeemable stock for each of the five years subsequent to the balance sheet date. Companies whose shares are not publicly traded are not subject to SEC requirements and can continue to report redeemable preferred stock as equity. Still, our analysis should treat them for what they are–an obligation to pay cash at a future date.

Minority Interest

Minority interest in consolidated companies is typically listed on the balance sheet between liabilities and equity. Yet, minority interest is not an immediate claim on company resources. Instead, minority interest represents the proportionate stake of minority shareholders in a company's majority-owned subsidiary that is consolidated. Since the parent includes all net assets (assets less liabilities) of a consolidated subsidiary in its financial statements, it reports the minority's interest as a credit, or financing component, on the balance sheet.

APPENDIX 3A LEASE ACCOUNTING AND ANALYSIS—LESSOR

Many manufacturing companies lease their products rather then sell them outright. Examples are IBM and Caterpillar Tractor. Other companies, like General Electric, act as financial intermediaries, purchasing the assets from manufacturers and leasing them to the ultimate user. Leasing has become an important ingredient in the sales of products and is now also a significant factor in the analysis of financial statements. This appendix briefly describes the accounting and analysis of leases from the perspective of a lessor. The accounting for leases by the lessor is similar to that for lessees. With minor exceptions, the lessor categorizes the lease as operating or capital to parallel the classification by the lessee. If classified as an operating lease, the leased asset remains on the lessor's balance sheet, and the rent payments are treated as income when received. The lessor continues to record depreciation expense on the leased asset. The difference between the rent income and the depreciation expense is the lessor's profit on the lease.

If the lease is classified as capital, the lessor removes the leased asset from its balance sheet and records a receivable equal to the sum of the expected minimum lease payments. The difference between the receivable and the asset removed from the balance sheet is classified as a liability, unearned income, which is reduced and recorded as earned income periodically over the life of the lease. Two types of leases are important from the lessor's point of view:

1. **Sales-type lease.** In this case, the cost of the leased asset is different from its fair market value at the date it is leased. This situation might arise, for example, with a company like IBM that manufactures computers and leases them to its customers. In this case, accountants take the view that the asset has been sold and IBM has entered into a subsequent financing transaction with the lessee. As a

result, IBM records a sale, cost of goods sold, and gross profit at the time the lease is executed. IBM, therefore, records gross profit upon the lease of the computer and lease revenue over the life of the lease equal to its unearned revenue when the lease is signed. Furthermore, since the leased asset has been removed from the balance sheet, IBM no longer records depreciation expense.

2. **Direct financing lease.** Companies like General Electric Capital Corporation engage in direct financing leases. In this case, GECC is acting like a bank. It purchases the asset from the manufacturer and leases it directly to the customer. In this case, the value of the lease (present value of the lease payments receivable) is equal to the cost of the asset purchased and no sale or gross profit is recorded. Instead, GECC recognizes lease income gradually over the life of the lease.

ANALYSIS IMPLICATIONS

The analysis implications of leasing are similar to those involving any extension of credit. Be aware of the risks inherent in any extension of credit. An analysis of the adequacy of the reserve for uncollectible lease receivables in comparison with the loss experience of the lessor is required. And second, recognize that lease receivables will be collected over a period of years and compare the average life of the lease portfolio with that of the company's liabilities. That is, it is inappropriate to finance fixed-rate leases of intermediate duration with short-term floating rate debt.

Lessors often package service contracts with leases to gain additional revenue. Under GAAP, income from the service contract must be recognized ratably over the life of the contract. In an effort to boost current period sales and profits, companies have attempted to accelerate the revenue recognition from service contracts by recording relatively more of the initial contract in the lease itself, thus increasing sales and gross profit and reducing the future payments under the service contract. Xerox is a company under investigation by the SEC for this practice. Analysts must be aware of this possibility and examine carefully the relative components of lease income and service revenue mix in the company's total sales.

SALE-LEASEBACK

A **sale-leaseback** transaction involves the sale of an owned asset and execution of a lease on the same asset. Companies often use sale-leasebacks to free up cash from existing assets, primarily real estate. Generally, any profit realized on the value of the asset sold must be deferred and recognized over the life of the lease as a reduction of lease expense.

GUIDANCE ANSWERS TO ANALYSIS VIEWPOINTS

LABOR NEGOTIATOR

We first must realize that while postretirement benefits are recorded as liabilities on the balance sheet (and as expenses on the income statement), their funding is less than guaranteed. It is clear from management's counteroffer that this company does not fully fund postretirement benefits–note, funding is not required in accounting for these benefits. This lack of funding can yield substantial losses for employees if the company is insolvent and it cannot be forced to fund these obligations. As labor negotiator, you sometimes must trade off higher current wages for rewards such as postretirement benefits *and* a guarantee to fund those benefits. From the company's perspective, it wishes to limit recorded liabilities and its funding commitments as it depletes resources. Your task as labor's representative is to obtain both postretirement benefits and funding for those benefits. Accordingly, while you need to weigh the pros and cons of the details, management's offer should be viewed seriously as a real employee benefit.

MONEY MANAGER
Your decision involves aspects of both risk and return. From the perspective of risk, preferred stock is usually a senior claimant to the net assets of a company. This means that in the event of liquidation, preferred stock receives preference before any funds are paid to common shareholders. From the perspective of return, the decision is less clear. Your common stock return involves both cash dividends and price appreciation, while preferred stock return relates primarily to cash dividends. If recent returns are reflective of future returns, then your likely preference is for preferred stock given its equivalence in returns along with its reduced risk exposure.

SHAREHOLDER
Your interpretation of this stock split is likely positive. This derives from the 'information signal' usually embedded in this type of announcement. Also, a lower price usually makes the stock more accessible to a broader group of buyers and can reduce transaction costs in purchasing it. Yet, too low a price can create its own problems. Consequently, a split is perceived as a signal of management's expectation (forecast) that the company will perform at the same or better level into the future. We must recognize there is no tangible shareholder value in a split announcement–namely, there is no income to shareholders. However, there is transfer of an amount from retained earnings to common stock.

[Superscript ^{A} identifies assignment material based on Appendix 3A.]

QUESTIONS

3–1. Identify and describe the two major sources (as linked with business activities) of current liabilities.

3–2. Identify the major disclosure requirements for financing-related current liabilities.

3–3. Describe the conditions necessary to demonstrate the ability of a company to refinance its short-term debt on a long-term basis.

3–4. Explain how bond discounts and premiums usually arise. Describe how they are accounted for.

3–5. Both convertibility and warrants attached to debt aim at increasing the attractiveness of debt securities and lowering their interest cost. Describe how the costs of these two features affect income and equity.

3–6. Explain how the issuance of convertible debt and warrants can affect the valuation analysis conducted by current and potential stockholders.

3–7. Describe the major disclosure requirements for long-term liabilities.

3–8. Debt contracts usually place restrictions on the ability of a company to deploy resources and to pursue business activities. These are often referred to as debt covenants.
   a. Identify where information about such restrictions is found.
   b. Define margin of safety as it applies to debt contracts and describe how the margin of safety can impact assessment of the relative level of company risk.

3–9. Explain how analysis of financial statements is used to evaluate a company's liabilities, both existing and contingent.

3–10. *a.* Describe the criteria for classifying leases by a *lessee.*
   b. Prepare a summary of accounting for leases by a *lessee.*

3–11.^{A} *a.* Identify the different classifications of leases by a *lessor.* Describe the criteria for classifying each lease type.
   b. Explain the accounting procedures for leases by a *lessor.*

3–12.^{A} Describe the provisions concerning leases involving real estate.

3–13. Discuss the implications of lease accounting for the analysis of financial statements.

3–14. When a lease is considered an operating lease for both the lessor and the lessee, describe what amounts will be found on the balance sheets of both the lessor and the lessee related to the lease obligation and the leased asset.

3–15. When a lease is considered a capital lease for both the lessor and the lessee, describe what amounts will be found on the balance sheets of both the lessor and the lessee related to the lease obligation and the leased asset.

3–16. Discuss how the lessee reflects the cost of leased equipment in the income statement for (*a*) assets leased under operating leases and (*b*) assets leased under capital leases.

3–17.[A] Discuss how the lessor reflects the benefits of leasing in the income statement under (*a*) an operating lease and (*b*) a capital lease.

3–18. Companies use various financing methods to avoid reporting debt on the balance sheet. Identify and describe some of these off-balance-sheet financing methods.

3–19. Explain the following amounts according to current accounting standards for pensions: (*a*) accumulated benefit obligation, and (*b*) projected benefit obligation.

3–20. The projected benefit obligation in excess of the pension fund assets is an estimate of the net economic obligation of the pension plan. However, the pension liability reported on the balance sheet often is a different amount. Describe the types of items that create this difference and explain how these items can be treated from a financial statement analysis viewpoint.

3–21. Why is the expected (rather than actual) return on pension plan assets treated as a reduction of periodic pension expense?

3–22. How does pension accounting serve to smooth pension expense? Under what circumstances will this relatively smooth expense not reflect the underlying economics?

3–23. Discuss key estimates in accounting for pension and other postretirement benefits and how these estimates affect net income and total liabilities.

3–24. How can management exercise latitude over the amount of pension expense recorded?

3–25. Where do pension costs appear in the financial statements?

3–26. Accounting for OPEBs draws on the accounting for pensions, with some important differences. Explain these differences.

3–27. Discuss the required accounting disclosures for OPEBs.

3–28. Explain why estimation of OPEB costs is more difficult than for pension costs.

3–29. *a.* Explain a loss contingency. Provide examples.
b. Explain the two conditions necessary before a company can record a loss contingency against income.

3–30. Define the term *big bath.* Explain when a manager would consider "taking a big bath" and how analysis of current financial position and future profitability might be adjusted if one suspects that a company has taken a big bath.

3–31. Define a commitment and provide three examples of commitments for a company.

3–32. Explain when a commitment becomes a recorded liability.

3–33. Define off-balance-sheet financing and provide three examples.

3–34. Describe the required financial statement disclosures for financial instruments with off-balance-sheet risk of loss. How might these disclosures be used to assist financial analysis?

3–35. Describe the criteria a company must meet before a transfer of receivables with recourse can be booked as a sale rather than as a loan.

3–36. Explain how off-balance-sheet financing items should be treated for financial analysis purposes.

3–37. Identify types of equity securities that are similar to debt.

3–38. Identify and describe several categories of reserves, allowances, and provisions for expenses and losses.

3–39. Explain why analysis must be alert to the accounting for future loss reserves.

3–40. Distinguish between different kinds of deferred credits on the balance sheet. Discuss how to analyze these accounts.

3–41. Identify objectives of the classifications and note disclosures associated with the equity section of the balance sheet. Explain the relevance of these disclosures to analysis of financial statements.

3–42. Identify features of preferred stock that make it similar to debt. Identify the features that make it more like common stock.

3–43. Explain the importance of disclosing the liquidation value of preferred stock, if different from par or stated value, for analysis purposes.

3–44. Explain why the accounting for small stock dividends requires that market value, rather than par value, of the shares distributed be charged against retained earnings.

3–45. Identify what items are treated as prior period adjustments.

3–46. Many companies report "minority interests in subsidiary companies" between the long-term debt and equity sections of a consolidated balance sheet; others present them as part of shareholders' equity.

a. Describe minority interest.

b. Indicate where on the consolidated balance sheet it best belongs. Discuss what different points of view these differing presentations represent.

EXERCISES

EXERCISE 3–1
Interpreting and Analyzing Debt Disclosures

Refer to the financial statements of **Quaker Oats** in Appendix A. **Quaker Oats**

Required:

a. Determine the amount paid toward long-term debt during Year 11.

b. The *liquidity and capital resources* section of the MD&A discusses how total debt increased by $217 million in Year 10. Describe the major cause for this increase.

c. Does any of the debt outstanding at the end of Year 11 appear to be a candidate for early extinguishment and replacement with less expensive debt or equity?

d. Analyze and discuss the relative mix of debt financing for Quaker Oats. Do you think Quaker Oats has any solvency or liquidity problems? Do you think the company should have more or less debt relative to equity (or is its current financing strategy proper)? Do you think that Quaker Oats would encounter difficulty if they wanted to issue additional debt to fund an especially attractive business opportunity?

CHECK
a. $39.1 mil.

EXERCISE 3–2
Evaluating Accounting for Leases by the Lessee

On January 1, Year 8, Von Company entered into two noncancelable leases of new machines for use in its manufacturing operations. The first lease does not contain a bargain purchase option and the lease term is equal to 80% of the estimated economic life of the machine. The second lease contains a bargain purchase option and the lease term is equal to 50% of the estimated economic life of the machine.

Required:

a. Explain the justification for requiring lessees to capitalize certain long-term leases. Do not limit your discussion to the specific criteria for classifying a lease as a capital lease.

b. Describe how a lessee accounts for a capital lease at inception.

c. Explain how a lessee records each minimum lease payment for a capital lease.

d. Explain how Von should classify each of the two leases. Provide justification.

(AICPA Adapted)

EXERCISE 3–3
Distinguishing between Capital and Operating Leases

Capital leases and operating leases are two major classifications of leases.

Required:

a. Describe how a lessee accounts for a capital lease both at inception of the lease and during the first year of the lease. Assume the lease transfers ownership of the property to the lessee by the end of the lease.

b. Describe how a lessee accounts for an operating lease both at inception of the lease and during the first year of the lease. Assume the lessee makes equal monthly payments at the beginning of each month during the lease term. Describe any changes in the accounting when rental payments are not made on a straight-line basis.

Note: Do not discuss the criteria for distinguishing between capital and operating leases.

(AICPA Adapted)

EXERCISE 3–4[A]
Analyzing and Interpreting Sales-Type and Financing Leases

Sales-type leases and direct financing leases are two common types of leases from a lessor's perspective.

Required:

Compare and contrast a sales-type lease with a direct-financing lease on the following dimensions:

a. Gross investment in the lease.

b. Amortization of unearned interest income.

c. Manufacturer's or dealer's profit.

Note: Do not discuss the criteria for distinguishing between sales-type, direct financing, and operating leases.

(AICPA Adapted)

EXERCISE 3–5
Recognizing Unrecorded Liabilities for Analysis

Consider the following excerpt from an article published in **Forbes:** **Forbes**

> **The Supersolvent**–No longer is it a mark of a fuddy-duddy to be free of debt. There are lots of advantages to it. One is that you always have plenty of collateral to borrow against if you do get into a jam. Another is that if a business investment goes bad, you don't have to pay interest on your mistake. . . . debt-free, you don't have to worry about what happens if the prime rate goes to 12% again. You might even welcome it. You could lend out your own surplus cash at those rates.

The article went on to list 92 companies reporting no more than 5% of total capitalization in noncurrent debt on their balance sheets.

Required:

Explain how so-called debt-free companies (in the sense used by the article) can possess substantial long-term debt or other unrecorded noncurrent liabilities. Provide examples.

(CFA Adapted)

EXERCISE 3–6
Interpreting Disclosures for Loss Contingencies

Nearly all companies confront loss contingencies of various forms.

Required:

a. Describe what conditions must be met for a loss contingency to be accrued with a charge to income.

b. Explain when disclosure is required, and what disclosures are necessary, for a loss contingency that does not meet the criteria for accrual of a charge to income.

EXERCISE 3–7
Analyzing Loss Contingencies

Lawsuits are one type of contingent loss, where the loss is contingent upon an adverse settlement or verdict in the case. Domestic tobacco companies are currently facing lawsuits from several states. The tobacco litigation loss contingency should be accrued if a loss is probable and can be estimated. Probable and estimable are difficult concepts that offer managers a fair degree of discretion.

Required:

a. List two reasons why the managers in this case might resist quantification and accrual of a loss liability.

b. Describe a circumstance when managers might be willing to accrue a contingent loss that they had earlier resisted accruing.

Refer to the financial statements of **Campbell Soup** in Appendix A.

Campbell Soup

EXERCISE 3–8
Analyzing Equity and Book Value

Required:

a. Identify the cause of the $101.6 million increase in shareholders' equity for Year 11.

b. Compute the average price at which treasury shares were repurchased during Year 11.

c. Compute the book value of common stock at the end of Year 11.

d. Compare the book value per share of common stock and the average price at which treasury shares were repurchased during the year (a measure of average market value per share during the year). What are some reasons why these figures are different?

CHECK
c. $14.12

Refer to the financial statements of **Quaker Oats** in Appendix A.

Quaker Oats

EXERCISE 3–9
Analyzing Shareholders' Equity and Computing Book Value

Required:

a. Explain the cause of the $116.5 million decrease in shareholders' equity for Year 11 and the $119.6 million decrease in Year 10.

b. Compute the book value of both common stock and preferred stock at the end of Year 11.

c. Compare the book value per share of common and preferred stock and the average price at which treasury shares were repurchased during the year. What might cause these figures to be different for Quaker Oats?

CHECK
b. $11.80 and $3.77

It is often asserted that using the LIFO inventory costing method during an extended period of rising prices and the expensing of all human resource costs are among the accepted accounting practices helping create "secret reserves."

EXERCISE 3–10
Interpreting Secret Reserves and Watered Stock

Required:

a. Describe a secret reserve. Explain how companies create or increase such reserves.

b. Explain the basis for saying the two specific practices cited create secret reserves.

c. Discuss the possibility of creating a secret reserve in connection with accounting for a liability. Explain and give an example.

d. Describe objections to the creation of secret reserves.

e. "Watered stock" is arguably the opposite of a secret reserve.
(1) Explain the nature of watered stock.
(2) Describe the circumstances where watered stock can arise.
(3) Discuss steps that can be taken to eliminate "water" from a firm's capital structure.

(AICPA Adapted)

Ownership interests in a corporation are reported both in the balance sheet under shareholders' equity and in the statement of shareholders' equity.

EXERCISE 3–11
Interpreting Shareholders' Equity Transactions

Required:

a. List the principal transactions and events reducing the amount of retained earnings. (Do not include appropriations of retained earnings.)

b. The shareholders' equity section of the balance sheet makes a distinction between contributed capital and retained earnings. Discuss why this distinction is important.

c. There is frequently a difference between the purchase price and sale price of treasury stock. Yet, practitioners agree that a corporation's purchase or sale of its own stock cannot result in a profit or loss to the corporation. Explain why corporations do not recognize the difference between the purchase and sale price of treasury stock as a profit or loss.

EXERCISE 3–12
Interpreting Capital Stock

Capital stock is a major part of a corporation's equity. The term *capital stock* embraces both common and preferred stock.

Required:

a. Identify the basic rights inherent in ownership of common stock and explain how owners exercise them.

b. Describe preferred stock. Discuss various preferences often afforded preferred stock.

c. In the analysis and interpretation of equity securities of a corporation, it is important to understand certain terminology. Define and describe the following equity items:
(1) Treasury stock (2) Stock right (3) Stock warrant

EXERCISE 3–13
Dividends and Capital Stock

Presidential Realty Corporation

Presidential Realty Corporation reports the following regarding its distributions paid on common stock: "Cash distributions on common stock were charged to Paid-In Surplus because the parent company has accumulated no earnings (other than its equity in undistributed earnings of certain subsidiaries) since its formation."

Required:

a. Explain whether these cash distributions are dividends.

b. Speculate as to why Presidential Realty made such a distribution.

EXERCISE 3–14
Dividends versus Treasury Stock

The purchase of treasury stock (commonly called stock buybacks) is being done with increasing frequency in lieu of dividend payments.

Required:

a. Explain why stock buybacks are similar to dividends from the company's viewpoint.

b. Explain why managers might prefer the purchase of treasury shares to the payment of dividends.

c. Explain why investors might prefer that firms use excess cash to purchase treasury shares rather than pay dividends.

EXERCISE 3–15
Cash Balance Pension Plan

IBM

IBM recently announced its intention to begin offering a cash balance pension plan. A cash balance pension plan is a form of defined contribution pension plan. IBM is not alone as there is a distinct trend in favor of defined contribution pension plans.

Required:

a. Describe the ramifications for analysis of the level and variability of both earnings and cash flows for defined benefit versus defined contribution pension plans.

b. Why do you think managers prefer the defined contribution pension plan?

c. Under what circumstances would employees favor defined benefit versus defined contribution plans?

EXERCISE 3–16
Understanding Defined Benefit Pension Plans

Carson Company sponsors a defined benefit pension plan. The plan provides pension benefits determined by age, years of service, and compensation. Among the components included in the recognized net pension cost for a period are service cost, interest cost, and actual return on plan assets.

Required:

a. Identify at least two accounting challenges of the defined benefit pension plan. Why do these challenges arise?

b. How does Carson determine the service cost component of the net pension cost?

c. How does Carson determine the interest cost component of the net pension cost?

d. How does Carson determine the actual return on plan assets component of the net pension cost?

(AICPA Adapted)

EXERCISE 3–17
Analyzing Postretirement Benefits

The accounting treatment for postretirement benefits other than pensions requires that companies offering these benefits adopt accrual accounting (similar to the requirements for pension plans)–that is, pay-as-you-go accounting is not acceptable. Assume you are considering an investment in one of two companies that both offer postretirement benefits. The two companies are of equal size and have identical retiree medical plans. However, one company is more labor intensive, and has a greater ratio of retirees to workers along with an older, more strongly unionized work force than the other company.

Required:

a. Compare the relative impacts of accounting for postretirement benefits on the:
   (1) Size of the postretirement benefit obligation recognized by each of the two firms.
   (2) Size of the postretirement benefit cost reported by each of the two firms.

b. For each of the three forms of the efficient market hypothesis, explain the effect that adoption of this accounting has on the per share price of a firm. Comment on the applicability of these implications to actual markets.

(CFA Adapted)

PROBLEMS

PROBLEM 3–1
Interpreting Notes Payable and Lease Disclosures

Campbell Soup Company

Refer to the financial statements of **Campbell Soup Company** in Appendix A.

Required:

a. Campbell Soup Company has zero coupon notes payable outstanding.
   (1) Indicate the total amount due noteholders on the maturity date of these notes.
   (2) The liability for these notes is lower than the maturity value. Describe the pattern in the reported amounts for this liability in future years.
   (3) Ignoring dollar amounts, prepare the annual journal entry that Campbell Soup Company makes to record the liability for accrued interest.

b. Campbell Soup reports long-term debt on the balance sheet totaling $772.6 million. Conceptually, what does the amount $772.6 represent? Over what years will cash outflows occur as related to this debt?

c. The note on leases reports future minimum lease payments under capital leases as $28.0 million and the present value of such payments as $21.5 million. Identify which amount is actually paid in future years.

d. Identify where in the financial statements that Campbell Soup reports the payment obligation for operating leases of $71.9 million.

e. Predict what interest expense will be in Year 12 assuming no substantial change in the debt structure (Hint: Identify the substantial interest-bearing obligations of the company and multiply that balance times an appropriate estimate of the effective rate for that debt).

CHECK
e. Rate is 11.53%

PROBLEM 3–2
Capital Lease Implications for Financial Statements

On January 1, Year 1, Burton Company leases equipment from Nelson Company for an annual lease rental of $10,000. The lease term is five years, and the lessor's interest rate implicit in the lease is 8%. The lessee's incremental borrowing rate is 8.25%. The useful life of the equipment is five years, and its estimated residual value equals its removal cost. Annuity tables indicate that the present value of an annual lease rental of $1 (at 8% rate) is $3.993. The fair value of leased equipment equals the present value of rentals. (Assume the lease is capitalized.)

Required:

a. Prepare accounting entries required by Burton Company for Year 1.

b. Compute and illustrate the effect on the income statement for the year ended December 31, Year 1, and for the balance sheet as of December 31, Year 1.

CHECK
Interest is $2,649.95 for Year 2

c. Construct a table showing payments of interest and principal made every year for the five-year lease term.

d. Construct a table showing expenses charged to the income statement for the five-year lease term if the equipment is purchased. Show a column for (1) amortization, (2) interest, and (3) total expenses.

e. Discuss the income and cash flow implications from this capital lease.

PROBLEM 3–3
Explaining and Interpreting Leases

On January 1, Borman Company, a lessee, entered into three noncancelable leases for new equipment identified as: Lease J, Lease K, and Lease L. None of the three leases transfers ownership of the equipment to Borman at the end of the lease term. For each of the three leases, the present value at the beginning of the lease term of the minimum lease payments, excluding that portion of the payments representing executory costs such as insurance, maintenance, and taxes to be paid by the lessor, including any profit thereon, is 75% of the excess of the fair value of the equipment to the lessor at the inception of the lease over any related investment tax credit retained by the lessor and expected to be realized by the lessor. The following additional information is distinct for each lease:

- Lease J does not contain a bargain purchase option; the lease term is equal to 80% of the estimated economic life of the equipment.
- Lease K contains a bargain purchase option; the lease term is equal to 50% of the estimated economic life of the equipment.
- Lease L does not contain a bargain purchase option; the lease term is equal to 50% of the estimated economic life of the equipment.

Required:

a. Explain how Borman Company should classify each of these three leases. Discuss the rationale for your answer.

CHECK
Leases J and K are capital leases

b. Identify the amount, if any, Borman records as a liability at inception of the lease for each of the three leases.

c. Assuming that Borman makes the minimum lease payments on a straight-line basis, describe how Borman should record each minimum lease payment for each of these three leases.

d. Assess accounting practice in accurately portraying the economic reality for each lease.

(AICPA Adapted)

PROBLEM 3–4
Interpreting Accounting for Bonds

One means for a corporation to generate long-term financing is through issuance of noncurrent debt instruments in the form of bonds.

Required:

a. Describe how to account for proceeds from bonds issued with detachable stock purchase warrants.

b. Contrast a serial bond with a term (straight) bond.

c. Interest expense, under the generally accepted effective interest method, equals the book value of the debt (face value plus unamortized premium or minus unamortized discount) multiplied by the effective rate of the debt. Any premium or discount is amortized to zero over the life of the bond. Explain how both interest expense and the debt's book value will differ from year-to-year for debt issued at a premium versus a discount.

d. Describe how to account for and classify any gain or loss from reacquisition of a long-term bond prior to its maturity.

e. Assess accounting for bonds in the analysis of financial statements.

PROBLEM 3–5
Interpreting Accounting for Bonds

On November 1, Year 5, Abbott Company sells its five-year, $1,000 face value, 11% term bonds dated October 1, Year 5, at a discount yielding an effective annual interest rate (yield) of 12%. Interest is payable semiannually, and the first interest payment date is April 1, Year 6. Abbott amortizes the bond discount. It also incurs bond issue costs in preparing and selling the bond issue. In another, unrelated transaction, dated December 1, Year 5, Abbott issues six-year, $1,000 face value, 9% nonconvertible bonds with detachable stock warrants at an amount exceeding the sum of the face value of the bonds and the fair value of the warrants.

Required:

a. Identify what factors determine that the 11% term bonds are sold at a discount. Explain.

b. Describe how all items related to the 11% term bonds (except cash) are reported/disclosed (1) in a balance sheet prepared immediately after the term bond issue is sold, and (2) for a balance sheet prepared at December 31, Year 5.

c. Identify the period of time over which Abbott amortizes the bond discount.

d. Describe how Abbott should account for the proceeds from sale of the 9% nonconvertible bonds with detachable stock purchase warrants.

(AICPA Adapted)

PROBLEM 3–6
Interpreting Stock Prices and Their Link to Financial Statements

Assume the stock of Superior Oil Corporation is being traded on the New York Stock Exchange for $1,492 per share, while Getty Oil Company stock is trading at $64 per share.

Required:

a. Explain how Superior Oil stock could be selling for a much larger price than Getty stock.

b. Indicate whether you can conclude anything about the relative profitability of these two companies from their stock prices.

c. On the previous day, Superior Oil stock was selling at $1,471 per share, while Getty Oil sold for $62. Indicate which stock experienced the greater return.

CHECK
Getty's return is higher

d. If you (as an investor) purchased Getty Oil at $62 per share and sold it the next day for $64, describe what effect your purchase and sale of stock would have on the financial statements of Getty Oil Company.

PROBLEM 3–7
Leases, Pensions, and Receivables Securitization

Westfield Capital Management Co.'s equity investment strategy is to invest in companies with low price-to-book ratios, while considering differences in solvency and asset utilization. Westfield is considering investing in the shares of either Jerry's Departmental Stores (JDS) or Miller Stores (MLS). Selected financial data for both companies follow:

SELECTED FINANCIAL DATA AS OF MARCH 31, 2003

($ millions)	JDS	MLS
Sales	$21,250	$18,500
Fixed assets	5,700	5,500
Short-term debt		1,000
Long-term debt	2,700	2,500
Equity	6,000	7,500
Outstanding shares (in millions)	250	400
Stock price ($ per share)	51.50	49.50

Required:

a. Compute each of the following ratios for both JDS and MLS:
(1) Price-to-book ratio (2) Total-debt-to-equity ratio (3) Fixed-asset-utilization (turnover)

b. Select the company that better meets Westfield's criteria.

c. The following information is from these companies' notes as of March 31, 2003:

(1) JDS conducts a majority of its operations from leased premises. Future minimum lease payments (MLP) on noncancelable operating leases follow:

MLP	
2004	$ 259
2005	213
2006	183
2007	160
2008	155
2009 and later	706
Total MLP	$1,676
Less interest	(676)
Present value of MLP	$1,000
Interest rate	10%

(2) MLS owns all of its property and stores.

(3) During the fiscal year ended March 31, 2003, JDS sold $800 million of its accounts receivable with recourse, all of which was outstanding at year-end.

(4) Substantially all of JDS's employees are enrolled in company-sponsored defined contribution plans. MLS sponsors a defined benefits plan for its employees. The MLS pension plan assets' fair value is $3,400 million. No pension cost is accrued on its balance sheet as of March 31, 2003. The details of MLS's pension obligations follow:

($ millions)	**ABO**	**PBO**
Vested	$1,550	$1,590
Nonvested	40	210
Total	$1,590	$1,800

CHECK
Price-to-Adjusted-Book, JDS = $2.14, MLS = $2.02

Compute all three ratios in part (*a*) after making necessary adjustments using the note information. Again, select the company that better meets Westfield's criteria. Comment on your decision in part (*b*) relative to the analysis here.

(CFA Adapted)

PROBLEM 3–8
Analyzing Environmental Liability Disclosures

Exxon

The U.S. government actively seeks the identification and cleanup of sites that contain hazardous materials. The Environmental Protection Agency (EPA) identifies contaminated sites under the Comprehensive Environmental Response Compensation and Liability Act (CERCLA). The government will force parties responsible for contaminating the site to pay for cleanup whenever possible. Also, companies face lawsuits for persons injured by environmental pollution. Potentially responsible parties include current and previous owners and operators of hazardous waste disposal sites, parties who arranged for disposal of hazardous materials at the site, and parties who transported the hazardous materials to the site. Potentially responsible parties should accrue a contingent environmental liability if the outcome of pending or potential action is probable to be unfavorable and a reasonable estimate of costs can be made. Amounts for environmental liabilities can be large. For example, **Exxon** paid damages totaling $5 billion for the highly publicized Exxon Valdez tanker accident. Estimates to clean up sites identified by the EPA range as high as $500 billion to $750 billion. The 'superfund' sites are sites with the highest priority for cleanup under CERCLA. Estimates to clean up these sites alone total $150 billion. The responsible parties face additional lawsuits as well and these potential losses are not included in these totals.

Required:

a. Discuss why environmental liabilities are especially difficult to measure.

b. Discuss how you would adjust the financial analysis of companies that are predisposed to environmental legal action but have not accrued any contingent loss amounts. For example, how might you adjust your beliefs about the financial position of Union Carbide and its competitors following the Bhopal tragedy?

c. Identify three industries that you consider as likely to face significant environmental risk. Explain.

PROBLEM 3–9
Analyzing Pension Plan Disclosures

Campbell Soup Company

Refer to the financial statements of **Campbell Soup** in Appendix A. The Note on Pension Plans and Retirement Benefits describes computation of pension expense, projected benefit obligation (PBO), and other elements of the pension plan (all amounts in millions).

Required:

a. Explain what the service cost of $22.1 for Year 11 represents.

b. What discount rate did the company assume for Year 11? What is the effect of Campbell's change from the discount rate used in Year 10?

c. How is the "interest on projected benefit obligation" computed?

d. Actual return on assets is $73.4. Does this item enter in its entirety as a component of pension cost? Explain.

e. Campbell shows an accumulated benefit obligation (ABO) of $714.4. What is this obligation?

f. Identify the PBO amount and explain what accounts for the difference between it and the ABO.

g. Has Campbell funded its pension expense at the end of Year 11?

CHECK
b. Year 11 rate, 8.75%

PROBLEM 3–10
Predicting Pension Expense

The weighted-average discount rate used in determining General Energy Co.'s actuarial present value of its projected benefit obligation (PBO) is 8.5%, and the assumed rate of increase in future compensation is 7.5%. The expected long-term rate of return on its plan assets is 11.5%. Its PBO at the end of Year 6 is $2,212,000, and its accumulated benefit obligation is $479,000. Fair value of its assets is $3,238,000, and a transition asset of $581,000 remains.

Required:

Predict General Energy Co.'s Year 7 net periodic pension expense given a 10% growth in service cost, the amortization of deferred loss over 30 years, and no change in the other assumed rates. Show calculations.

CHECK
Predicted expense, $444 mil.

CASES

CASE 3–1
Analyzing and Interpreting Pension Disclosures

Campbell Soup

Refer to the **Campbell Soup** annual report in Appendix A.

Required:

a. What type of pension plan does Campbell Soup offer its employees?

b. Does Campbell Soup have a net pension asset or a net pension liability at July 28, Year 11? What is the amount?

c. Identify the amounts of the vested, accumulated, and projected benefit obligations at July 28, Year 11. What do those amounts represent?

d. What is the amount of the assets currently held by the pension plan?

e. What types of assets are held by the pension plan?

f. What is the net economic position of the pension plan?

g. What creates the difference between the net pension asset (liability) and the net economic position of the pension plan?

CHECK
f. $30 mil. overfunded

h. How much unrecognized prior service cost is left to amortize to pension expense?

i. Comment on the reasonableness of the expected return on plan assets.

j. Comment on the reasonableness of the long-term rate of compensation increase for employees. Comment from the viewpoint of an equity analyst and the viewpoint of a potential employee.

CASE 3–2
Analyzing and Interpreting Liabilities

Refer to the annual report of **Kodak** in Appendix A. **Kodak**

Required:

a. Identify Kodak's major categories of liabilities. Identify which of these liabilities require recognition of interest expense.

b. Reconcile activity in the long-term borrowing account for 2001.

c. Determine the fair value of Kodak's long-term borrowings according to its note 11. Identify factors that might change this value.

d. Identify Kodak's arrangements to borrow funds.

e. Describe the composition of Kodak's other long-term liabilities account using its note 9.

f. Examine Kodak's note 10 regarding commitments and contingencies. What is the nature of Kodak's contingencies? Identify any probable future cash outflows not recorded on Kodak's balance sheet.

CASE 3–3
Analyzing and Interpreting Pension and OPEB Liabilities

CHECK
b. Adjusted ratio, 84.5%

Refer to the annual report of **Kodak** in Appendix A. **Kodak**

Required:

a. Examine Kodak's pension and OPEB liabilities using its notes 15 and 16. What are the reported amounts from its balance sheet and income statement that relate to its U.S. and foreign plans in each of 2001 and 2000?

b. Determine the economic position of the pension and OPEB plans for 2001 and 2000. Restate the balance sheet accordingly and examine the effect of the adjusted position on the debt to total assets ratio.

c. What is the true economic pension cost for 2001? Reconcile it with the reported pension expense. Determine the pension expense you would consider when determining Kodak's permanent income.

d. Evaluate the reasonableness of its key actuarial assumptions. Do you think that Kodak is using its pension plans to manage its earnings and/or financial position?

CASE 3–4
Analyzing and Interpreting Equity

Refer to the annual report of **Kodak** in Appendix A. **Kodak**

Required:

a. Determine the book value per share and price-to-book ratio of Kodak's common stock for its fiscal year-end 2001. What does the observed price-to-book ratio indicate about investors' expectations regarding future profitability? (Hint: Answer this question with reference to the accounting-based equity valuation model described in Chapter 1.)

b. From analysis of Kodak's statement of shareholders' equity, identify reasons for it issuing additional common shares in each of 2001, 2000, and 1999. Determine at what per share amounts Kodak issued the shares in 2001.

c. Identify the par value of Kodak's common shares. Determine the number of common shares authorized, issued, and outstanding at the end of each fiscal year 2001 and 2000.

CHECK
d. 2001 repurchase price, $43.29

d. Determine how many common shares Kodak repurchased as treasury stock for each of the three years 2001, 2000, and 1999. Determine the price at which Kodak repurchased the shares.

CASE 3–5
Leasing in the Airline Industry

The airline industry is one of the more volatile industries. During lean years in the early 1990s, the industry wiped out the earnings it had reported during its entire history. Pan American Airlines and Eastern Airlines ceased operations, while Continental Airlines, TWA, and US Air filed for bankruptcy protection. The industry bounced back in the mid-1990s, riding on the wings of the U.S. economic prosperity and lower energy prices. The airlines have been especially profitable since 1996, with returns on equity often in excess of 25%. The stock market has recognized the stellar growth in profitability as market capitalization of many airlines has tripled since then.

Volatility in airlines' earnings arises from a combination of demand volatility, cost structure, and competitive pricing. Air travel demand is cyclical and sensitive to the economy's performance. The cost structure of airlines is dominated by fixed costs, resulting in high operating leverage. While most airlines break even at 60% flight occupancy, deviations from this can send earnings soaring upward or downward. Also, the airline industry is price competitive. Because of their cost structure (low variable but high fixed costs), airlines tend to reduce fares to increase market share during a downturn in demand. These fare reductions often lead to price wars, which reduces average unit revenue. Hence, airfares are positively correlated with volume of demand, resulting in volatile revenues. When this revenue variability is combined with fixed costs, it yields volatile earnings.

Airline companies lease all types of assets–aircraft, airport terminal, maintenance facilities, property, and operating and office equipment. Lease terms range from less than a year to as much as 25 years. While many companies report some capital leases on the balance sheet, most companies are increasingly structuring their leases, long-term and short-term, as operating leases. The condensed balance sheets and income statements along with excerpts of lease notes from the 1998 and 1997 annual reports for **AMR (American Airlines), Delta Airlines,** and **UAL (United Airlines)** follow.

	AMR		DELTA		UAL	
	Year 8	Year 7	Year 8	Year 7	Year 8	Year 7
Balance Sheets ($ millions)						
Assets						
Current assets	$ 4,875	$ 4,986	$ 3,362	$ 2,867	$ 2,908	$ 2,948
Freehold assets (Net)	12,239	11,073	9,022	7,695	10,951	9,080
Leased assets (Net)	2,147	2,086	299	347	2,103	1,694
Intangibles and other	3,042	2,714	1,920	1,832	2,597	1,742
Total assets	**$22,303**	**$20,859**	**$14,603**	**$12,741**	**$18,559**	**$15,464**
Liabilities and equity						
Current liabilities:						
Current portion of capital lease	$ 154	$ 135	$ 63	$ 62	$ 176	$ 171
Other current liabilities	5,485	5,437	4,514	4,021	5,492	5,077
Long-term liabilities:						
Lease liability	1,764	1,629	249	322	2,113	1,679
Long-term debt	2,436	2,248	1,533	1,475	2,858	2,092
Other long-term liabilities	5,766	5,194	4,046	3,698	3,848	3,493
Preferred stock			175	156	791	615
Shareholder's equity:						
Contributed capital	3,257	3,286	3,299	2,896	3,518	2,877
Retained earnings	4,729	3,415	1,776	812	1,024	300
Treasury stock	(1,288)	(485)	(1,052)	(701)	(1,261)	(840)
Total liabilities and equity	**$22,303**	**$20,859**	**$14,603**	**$12,741**	**$18,559**	**$15,464**
Income Statement ($ millions)						
Operating revenue	$19,205	$18,184	$14,138	$13,594	$17,561	$17,378
Operating expenses	(16,867)	(16,277)	(12,445)	(12,063)	(16,083)	(16,119)
Operating income	**2,338**	**1,907**	**1,693**	**1,531**	**1,478**	**1,259**
Other income and adjustments	198	137	141	91	133	551
Interest expense*	(372)	(420)	(197)	(216)	(361)	(291)
Income before tax	**2,164**	**1,624**	**1,637**	**1,406**	**1,250**	**1,519**
Tax provision	(858)	(651)	(647)	(561)	(429)	(561)
Continuing income	**$ 1,306**	**$ 973**	**$ 990**	**$ 845**	**$ 821**	**$ 958**

**Includes preference dividends.*

($ millions)	AMR Capital	AMR Operating	DELTA Capital	DELTA Operating	UAL Capital	UAL Operating
Excerpts from Lease Notes (Year 8)						
MLP Due:						
Year 9	$ 273	$ 1,012	$100	$ 950	$ 317	$ 1,320
Year 10	341	951	67	950	308	1,329
Year 11	323	949	57	940	399	1,304
Year 12	274	904	57	960	341	1,274
Year 13	191	919	48	960	242	1,305
Year 14 and after	1,261	12,480	71	10,360	1,759	17,266
Total MLP due	2,663	$17,215	400	$15,120	3,366	$23,798
Less interest	(745)		(88)		(1,077)	
Present value of MLP	$1,918		$312		$2,289	
Excerpts from Lease Notes (Year 7)						
MLP Due:						
Year 8	$ 255	$ 1,011	$101	$ 860	$ 288	$ 1,419
Year 9	250	985	100	860	262	1,395
Year 10	315	935	68	840	241	1,402
Year 11	297	931	57	830	314	1,380
Year 12	247	887	57	850	277	1,357
Year 13 and after	1,206	13,366	118	9,780	1,321	19,562
Total MLP due	2,570	$18,115	501	$14,020	2,703	$26,515
Less interest	(806)		(117)		(853)	
Present value of MLP	$1,764		$384		$1,850	

Both the capital and operating leases are noncancelable. Interest rates on the leases vary from 5% to 14%. (Assume a 35% marginal tax rate for all three companies.)

Required:

a. Compute key liquidity, solvency, and return on investment ratios for Year 8 (current ratio, total debt to equity, long-term debt to equity, times interest earned, return on assets, return on equity). Comment on the financial performance, financial position, and risk of these three companies—both as a group and individually.

b. To understand the effect of high operating leverage on the volatility of airlines' earnings, prepare the following sensitivity analysis: Assume that 25% of airline costs are variable—that is, for a 1% increase (decrease) in operating revenues, assume operating costs increase (decrease) by only 0.25%. Recast the income statement assuming operating revenues decrease by two alternative amounts: 5% and 10%. What happens to earnings at these reduced revenue levels? Also, compute key ratios at these hypothetical revenue levels. Comment on the risk of these companies' operations.

c. Why do you think the airline industry relies so heavily on leasing as a form of financing? What other financing options could airlines consider? Discuss their advantages and disadvantages versus leasing.

d. Examine the lease notes. Do you think the lease classification adopted by the companies is reasonable? Explain.

e. Reclassify all operating leases as capital leases and make necessary adjustments to both the balance sheet and income statement for Year 8. [Hint: (1) Use the procedures described in the chapter. (2) Assume identical interest rates for operating and capital leases. (3) Do not attempt to articulate the income statement with the balance sheet, i.e., make balance sheet and income statement adjustments separately without "tallying" the effects on the two statements. (4) Make adjustments to the tax provision using a 35% marginal tax rate. Since all leases are accounted for as operating leases for tax purposes, converting operating leases to capital leases will create deferred tax liabilities. However, since we are not articulating the income statement with the balance sheet, the deferred tax effects on the balance sheet can be ignored.]

CHECK

e. AMR restated Year 8 continuing income, $1,244

f. What assumptions did you make when reclassifying leases in (*e*)? Evaluate the reasonableness of these assumptions and suggest alternative methods you could use to improve the reliability of your analysis.

g. Repeat the ratio analysis in (*a*) using the restated financial statements from (*e*). Comment on the effect of the lease classification for the ratios and your interpretation of the companies' profitability and risk (both collectively and individually).

h. Using the results of your analysis in (*g*), explain the reliance of airline companies on lease financing and their lease classifications. What conclusions can you draw about the importance of accounting analysis for financial analysis in this case?

General Electric

CASE 3–6
Analyzing Post Retirement Benefits

Condensed financial statements of **General Electric,** along with note information regarding postretirement benefits, are shown here:

INCOME STATEMENTS

($ millions)	Year 8	Year 7	Year 6
Revenues	$100,469	$90,840	$79,179
Cost of goods and services	(42,280)	(40,088)	(34,591)
Interest, insurance, and financing	(20,970)	(18,083)	(15,615)
Other expenses	(23,477)	(21,250)	(17,898)
Minority interest	(265)	(240)	(269)
Earnings before tax	13,477	11,179	10,806
Tax provision	(4,181)	(2,976)	(3,526)
Net earnings	$ 9,296	$ 8,203	$ 7,280

BALANCE SHEETS

	Year 8	Year 7
Assets		
Current assets	$243,662	$212,755
Plant assets	35,730	32,316
Intangible assets	23,635	19,121
Other	52,908	39,820
Total assets	$355,935	$304,012
Liabilities and equity		
Current liabilities	$141,579	$120,668
Long-term borrowing	59,663	46,603
Other liabilities	111,538	98,621
Minority interest	4,275	3,683
Equity share capital	7,402	5,028
Retained earnings	31,478	29,410
Total liabilities and equity	$355,935	$304,013

POSTRETIREMENT BENEFITS—NOTES

	PENSION BENEFITS			RETIREE HEALTH AND LIFE BENEFITS		
($ millions)	Year 8	Year 7	Year 6	Year 8	Year 7	Year 6
Effect on Operations						
Expected return on plan assets	$ 3,024	$ 2,721	$2,587	$ 149	$ 137	$ 132
Service cost for benefits earned	(625)	(596)	(550)	(96)	(107)	(93)
Interest cost on benefit obligation	(1,749)	(1,686)	(1,593)	(319)	(299)	(272)
Prior service cost	(153)	(145)	(99)	(8)	11	31
SFAS 87 "transition gain"	154	154	154	—	—	—
Net actuarial gain recognized	365	295	210	(39)	(32)	(43)
Special early retirement cost	—	(412)	—	—	(165)	—
Post retirement benefit income/(cost)	$ 1,016	$ 331	$ 709	$ (313)	$ (455)	$(245)

($ millions)	Pension Benefits Year 8	Pension Benefits Year 7	Pension Benefits Year 6	Retiree Health and Life Benefits Year 8	Retiree Health and Life Benefits Year 7	Retiree Health and Life Benefits Year 6
Benefit Obligation (as of Dec. 31)						
Balance at January 1	$25,874	$23,251		$ 4,775	$ 3,954	
Service cost for benefits earned	625	596		96	107	
Interest cost on benefit obligation	1,749	1,686		319	299	
Participant contributions	112	120		24	21	
Plan amendments	—	136		—	369	
Actuarial loss	1,050	1,388		268	301	
Benefits paid	(1,838)	(1,715)		(475)	(441)	
Special early retirement cost	—	412		—	165	
Balance at Dec. 31	$27,572	$25,874		$ 5,007	$ 4,775	
Fair Value of Plan Assets (as of Dec. 31)						
Balance at January 1	$38,742	$33,686		$ 1,917	$ 1,682	
Actual return on plan assets	6,363	6,587		316	343	
Employer contributions	68	64		339	312	
Participant contributions	112	120		24	21	
Benefits paid	(1,838)	(1,715)		(475)	(441)	
Balance at Dec. 31	$43,447	$38,742		$ 2,121	$ 1,917	
Prepaid Pension Asset (as of Dec. 31)						
Fair value of plan assets	$43,447	$38,742		$ 2,121	$ 1,917	
Add/deduct unrecognized balances:						
SFAS 87 transition gain	(308)	(462)		—	—	
Net actuarial gain	(9,462)	(7,538)		358	296	
Prior service cost	850	1,003		108	116	
Benefit obligation	(27,572)	(25,874)		(5,007)	(4,775)	
Pension liability	797	703		—	—	
Prepaid pension asset	$ 7,752	$ 6,574		$(2,420)	$(2,446)	
Actuarial Assumptions (as of Dec. 31)						
Discount rate	6.75%	7.00%	7.50%	6.75%	7.00%	7.50%
Compensation increase	5.00	4.50	4.50	5.00	4.50	4.50
Return on assets	9.50	9.50	9.50	9.50	9.50	9.50
Health care cost trend				7.80	7.80	8.00

CHECK
Restated Year 8 D/E and ROE are 6.0 and 18.29%

Required:

a. Determine the economic position of the postretirement plans for each of Year 8 and Year 7. Restate the balance sheets and examine the effect of reflecting the true position on key ratios (debt to equity, long-term debt to equity, return on equity).

b. What is economic pension cost for each of Year 8 and Year 7? Reconcile it with the reported pension expense. Determine the pension expense you would consider when determining GE's permanent income and economic income.

c. Evaluate the key actuarial assumptions. Is there any hint of earnings management?

d. In its editorial, *Barron's* hinted GE was using pensions to manage its earnings growth:

> In Year 7, pension income chipped in $331 million of GE's total earnings of $8.2 billion. In Year 8, pension income accounted for $1.01 billion of the company's total earnings of $9.3 billion. Okay, let's suppose that there was no contribution to earnings in either years (these are not, in any case, actual cash additions). Minus the noncash contributions from the pension plans, GE's Year 7 net was $7.9 billion; its Year 8 net amounted to $8.3 billion. On this basis, the rise in

> earnings last year was roughly $400 million, or about 5.1%. And 5.1%, while respectable, is a good cut below the 13% the company triumphantly announced . . . GE's shares, as we observed, are selling at some 40 times last year's earnings.

Do you agree with *Barron's* editorial? In what manner, if any, might GE be managing its earnings through pensions?

e. Note the reference to cash flows in the *Barron's* editorial—"these are not, in any case, actual cash additions." Is it true that every earnings effect that does not necessarily have an equal and contemporaneous cash flow effect is tainted in some manner? Answer this question with respect to GE's pension disclosures. What are the cash flows relating to GE's postretirement plans? How useful are these cash flows for understanding the economics of postretirement benefit plans—are they more meaningful than the pension expense (income) number?

CASE 3–7

Analysis of Contingent Liabilities–Philip Morris

Philip Morris

Much of the litigation against **Philip Morris** is related to exposure of persons to environmental tobacco smoke. This is addressed by Philip Morris in the following excerpts from its Year 8 annual report:

> Pending claims related to tobacco products generally fall within three categories: (i) smoking and health cases alleging personal injury brought on behalf of individual plaintiffs, (ii) smoking and health cases alleging personal injury and purporting to be brought on behalf of a class of individual plaintiffs, and (iii) health care cost recovery cases brought by governmental and non-governmental plaintiffs seeking reimbursement for health care expenditures allegedly caused by cigarette smoking. Governmental plaintiffs have included local, state, and certain foreign governmental entities. Non-governmental plaintiffs in these cases include union health and welfare trust funds, Blue Cross/Blue Shield groups, HMO's, hospitals, Native American tribes, taxpayers, and others. Damages claimed in some of the smoking and health class actions and health care cost recovery cases range into the billions of dollars. Plaintiffs' theories of recovery and the defenses raised in those cases are discussed below.
>
> In recent years, there has been a substantial increase in the number of smoking and health cases being filed. As of December 31, Year 8, there were approximately 510 smoking and health cases filed and served on behalf of individual plaintiffs in the United States against PM Inc. and, in some cases, the Company, compared with approximately 375 such cases on December 31, Year 7, and 185 such cases on December 31, Year 6. Many of these cases are pending in Florida, West Virginia and New York. Fifteen of the individual cases involve allegations of various personal injuries allegedly related to exposure to environmental tobacco smoke ("ETS").
>
> In addition, as of December 31, Year 8, there were approximately 60 smoking and health putative class actions pending in the United States against PM Inc. and, in some cases, the Company (including eight that involve allegations of various personal injuries related to exposure to ETS), compared with approximately 50 such cases on December 31, Year 7, and 20 such cases on December 31, Year 6. Most of these actions purport to constitute statewide class actions and were filed after May Year 6 when the Fifth Circuit Court of Appeals, in the *Castano* case, reversed a federal district court's certification of a purported nationwide class action on behalf of persons who were allegedly "addicted" to tobacco products.
>
> During Year 7 and Year 8, PM Inc. and certain other United States tobacco product manufacturers entered into agreements settling the asserted and unasserted health care cost recovery and other claims of all 50 states and several commonwealths and territories of the United States. The settlements are in the process of being approved by the courts, and some of the settlements are being challenged by various third parties. As of December 31, Year 8, there were approximately 95 health care cost recovery actions pending in the United States (excluding the cases covered by the settlements), compared with approximately 105 health care cost recovery cases pending on December 31, Year 7, and 25 such cases on December 31, Year 6.
>
> There are also a number of tobacco-related actions pending outside the United States against PMI and its affiliates and subsidiaries including, as of December 31, Year 8, approximately 27 smoking and health cases initiated by one or more individuals (Argentina (20), Brazil (1), Canada (1), Italy (1), Japan (1), Scotland (1) and Turkey (2)), and six smoking and health class actions (Brazil (2), Canada (3) and Nigeria (1)). In addition, health care cost recovery actions have been brought in Israel, the Republic of the Marshall Islands and British Columbia, Canada, and, in the United States, by the Republics of Bolivia, Guatemala, Panama and Nicaragua.
>
> ***Pending and upcoming trials:*** As of January 22, Year 9, trials against PM Inc. and, in one case, the Company, were underway in the *Engle* smoking and health class action in Florida

(discussed below) and in individual smoking and health cases in California and Tennessee. Additional cases are scheduled for trial during Year 9, including three health care cost recovery actions brought by unions in Ohio (February), Washington (September) and New York (September), and two smoking and health class actions in Illinois (August) and Alabama (August). Also, twelve individual smoking and health cases against PM Inc. and, in some cases, the Company, are currently scheduled for trial during Year 9. Trial dates, however, are subject to change.

Verdicts in individual cases: During the past three years, juries have returned verdicts for defendants in three individual smoking and health cases and in one individual ETS smoking and health case. In June Year 8, a Florida appeals court reversed a $750,000 jury verdict awarded in August Year 6 against another United States cigarette manufacturer. Plaintiff is seeking an appeal of this ruling to the Florida Supreme Court. Also in June Year 8, a Florida jury awarded the estate of a deceased smoker in a smoking and health case against another United States cigarette manufacturer $500,000 in compensatory damages, $52,000 for medical expenses and $450,000 in punitive damages. A Florida appeals court has ruled that this case was tried in the wrong venue and, accordingly, defendants are seeking to set aside the verdict and retry the case in the correct venue. In Brazil, a court in Year 7 awarded plaintiffs in a smoking and health case the Brazilian currency equivalent of $81,000, attorneys' fees and a monthly annuity of 35 years equal to two-thirds of the deceased smoker's last monthly salary. Neither the Company nor its affiliates were parties to that action.

Litigation settlements: In November Year 8, PM Inc. and certain other United States tobacco product manufacturers entered into a Master Settlement Agreement (the "MSA") with 46 states, the District of Columbia, the Commonwealth of Puerto Rico, Guam, the United States Virgin Islands, American Samoa and the Northern Marianas to settle asserted and unasserted health care cost recovery and other claims. PM Inc. and certain other United States tobacco product manufacturers had previously settled similar claims brought by Mississippi, Florida, Texas and Minnesota (together with the MSA, the "State Settlement Agreements") and an ETS smoking and health class action brought on behalf of airline attendants. The State Settlement Agreements and certain ancillary agreements are filed as exhibits to various of the Company's reports filed with the Securities and Exchange Commission, and such agreements and the ETS settlement are discussed in detail therein.

PM Inc. recorded pre-tax charges of $3,081 million and $1,457 million during Year 8 and Year 7, respectively, to accrue for its share of all fixed and determinable portions of its obligations under the tobacco settlements, as well as $300 million during Year 8 for its unconditional obligation under an agreement in principle to contribute to a tobacco growers trust fund, discussed below. As of December 31, Year 8, PM Inc. had accrued costs of its obligations under the settlements and to tobacco growers aggregating $1,359 million, payable principally before the end of the year Year 10. The settlement agreements require that the domestic tobacco industry make substantial annual payments in the following amounts (excluding future annual payments contemplated by the agreement in principle with tobacco growers discussed below), subject to adjustment for several factors, including inflation, market share and industry volume: Year 9, $4.2 billion (of which $2.7 billion related to the MSA and has already been paid by the industry); Year 10, $9.2 billion; Year 11, $9.9 billion; Year 12, $11.3 billion; Year 14 through Year 17, $8.4 billion; and thereafter, $9.4 billion. In addition, the domestic tobacco industry is required to pay settling plaintiff's attorneys' fees, subject to an annual cap of $500 million, as well as additional amounts as follows: Year 9, $450 million; Year 10, $416 million; and Year 11 through Year 12, $250 million. These payment obligations are the several and not joint obligations of each settling defendant. PM Inc.'s portion of the future adjusted payments and legal fees, which is not currently estimable, will be based on its share of domestic cigarette shipments in the year preceding that in which the payment is made. PM Inc.'s shipment share in Year 8 was approximately 50%.

The State Settlement Agreements also include provisions relating to advertising and marketing restrictions, public disclosure of certain industry documents, limitations on challenges to tobacco control and underage use laws and other provisions. As of January 22, Year 9, the MSA had been approved by courts in 41 states and in the District of Columbia, Puerto Rico, Guam, the United States Virgin Islands, American Samoa and Northern Marianas. If a jurisdiction does not obtain final judicial approval of the MSA by December 31, Year 11, the agreement will be terminated with respect to such jurisdiction.

As part of the MSA, the settling defendants committed to work cooperatively with the tobacco grower community to address concerns about the potential adverse economic impact of the MSA on that community. To that end, in January Year 9, the four major domestic tobacco product manufacturers, including PM Inc., agreed in principle to participate in the establishment of a $5.15 billion trust fund to be administered by the tobacco growing states. It is currently contemplated that the trust will be funded by industry participants over twelve years, beginning in Year 9. PM Inc. has agreed to pay $300 million into the trust in Year 9, which amount has been charged to Year 8 operating income. Subsequent annual industry payments are to be adjusted for several factors, including inflation and United States cigarette consumption, and are to be allocated based on each manufacturer's market share.

The Company believes that the State Settlement Agreements may materially adversely affect the business, volume, results of operations, cash flows or financial position of PM Inc. and the Company in future years. The degree of the adverse impact will depend, among other things, on the rates of decline in United States cigarette sales in the premium and discount segments, PM Inc.'s share of the domestic premium and discount cigarette segments, and the effect of any resulting cost advantage of manufacturers not subject to the MSA and the other State Settlement Agreements. As of January 22, Year 9, manufacturers representing almost all domestic shipments in Year 8 had agreed to become subject to the terms of the MSA.

Required:

a. Philip Morris classifies pending tobacco lawsuits against the company into three general categories. What are these three categories? What is the number of claims for each of these categories at the end of Year 8?

b. Can you determine how much liability is recorded for each of these categories as of December 31, Year 8? Explain.

c. Can you determine what amount is charged against earnings in Year 8 for contingent tobacco litigation losses? Explain.

d. Do you believe the eventual losses will exceed the losses currently recorded on the balance sheet? Explain.

e. Describe adjustments to PM's financial statements, and to an investor's financial analysis of PM, to reflect estimates of under- or over-accrued losses.

WEB ACTIVITIES

The Web Activities are located on the book's website at www.mhhe.com/wild8e.

4

ANALYZING INVESTING ACTIVITIES

A LOOK BACK <
Our discussion of accounting analysis began with the analysis and interpretation of financing activities. We studied the interaction of financing activities with operating and investing activities and the importance of creditor versus equity financing.

A LOOK AT THIS CHAPTER •
Our discussion of accounting analysis extends to investing activities in this chapter. We analyze assets such as securities, receivables, derivatives, inventories, property, equipment, and intangibles. We show how these numbers reflect company performance and financing requirements, and how adjustments to these numbers can improve our analysis.

A LOOK AHEAD >
Chapter 5 extends our analysis of investing activities to intercompany and international activities. Analyzing and interpreting a company's investing activities requires consideration of these institutional and economic aspects. Chapter 6 focuses on operating activities and income measurement.

ANALYSIS OBJECTIVES

- Define current assets and their relevance for analysis.
- Explain cash management and its implications for analysis.
- Analyze receivables, allowances for bad debts, and securitization.
- Interpret the effects of alternative inventory methods under varying business conditions.
- Analyze financial statement disclosures for investment securities.
- Describe derivative securities and their implications for analysis.
- Explain the concept of long-lived assets and its implications for analysis.
- Interpret valuation and cost allocation of plant assets and natural resources.
- Describe and analyze intangible assets and their disclosures.
- Analyze financial statements for unrecorded and contingent assets.

Covering One's Assets

NEW YORK–Risk management of assets is an important part of modern business. One important aim of risk management activities is to insulate a company from fluctuations in world financial markets. An important tool of risk management is use of derivatives. Bristol-Meyers Squibb Company [**www.bms.com**], with total assets of just over $27 billion, is one example among thousands of companies that use interest rate and foreign exchange contracts to hedge market risks.

Current accounting standards require companies to report the fair market value of derivatives on the balance sheet. In 2001, Bristol reported $27 million on its balance sheet relating to its derivative contracts. These reported amounts, however, are small in relation to the notional (face) amount of the derivatives, and recognized gains and losses on changes in their market value do not suffice for a comprehensive evaluation of the company's exposure risk.

Effective analysis must go beyond the financial statements to include analysis of its notes. Such analysis in this case reveals that Bristol reports foreign exchange contracts with a notional amount of $1.4 billion to hedge against foreign currency denominated assets and liabilities in the amount of $2.1 billion. The company faces currency exposure to fluctuations in the Japanese yen, Mexican peso, the Canadian dollar, and the euro and has not completely hedged all of its foreign exchange risk.

. . . effective analysis must go beyond the financial statements.

Bristol is also hedging its cash flow volatility with interest rate derivatives with a notional amount of $2 billion. These hedges cover less than one-third of its exposure of nearly $6 billion in debt issued for two acquisitions.

Only an analysis of derivative investments would reveal Bristol's entire exposure to potential gains and losses from hedging. Analysis of derivative investments, however, is just one part of a complete analysis of a company's investing activities. A thorough analysis would extend to all assets, including their composition and amounts, and would require evaluation of financial statement notes. Similar to reading relevant information when using a Bristol medical product for health purposes, we must understand information in financial statement notes for our financial health.

Source: Bristol-Meyers Squibb Company website and 2001 annual report.

PREVIEW OF CHAPTER 4

Assets are resources controlled by a company for the purpose of generating profit. They can be categorized into two groups–current and noncurrent. **Current assets** are resources or claims to resources readily convertible to cash within the *operating cycle* of the company. Major classes of current assets include cash, cash equivalents, marketable securities, receivables, derivatives, inventories, and prepaid expenses. **Long-lived** (or **noncurrent**) **assets** are resources or claims to resources expected to benefit the company for periods beyond the current period. Major long-lived assets include property, plant, equipment, intangibles, investments, and deferred charges. An alternative distinction often useful for analysis is to designate assets as either financial assets or operating assets. **Financial assets** consist mainly of marketable securities and investments. They usually are valued at fair (market) value and are expected to yield returns equal to their risk-adjusted cost of capital. **Operating assets** constitute most of a company's assets. They usually are valued at cost and are productive operating assets expected to yield above normal profits. This chapter discusses accounting issues involving the valuation of assets and their subsequent cost allocation. We explain the implications of asset accounting for credit and profitability analysis and for equity valuation. The content and organization of this chapter follows:

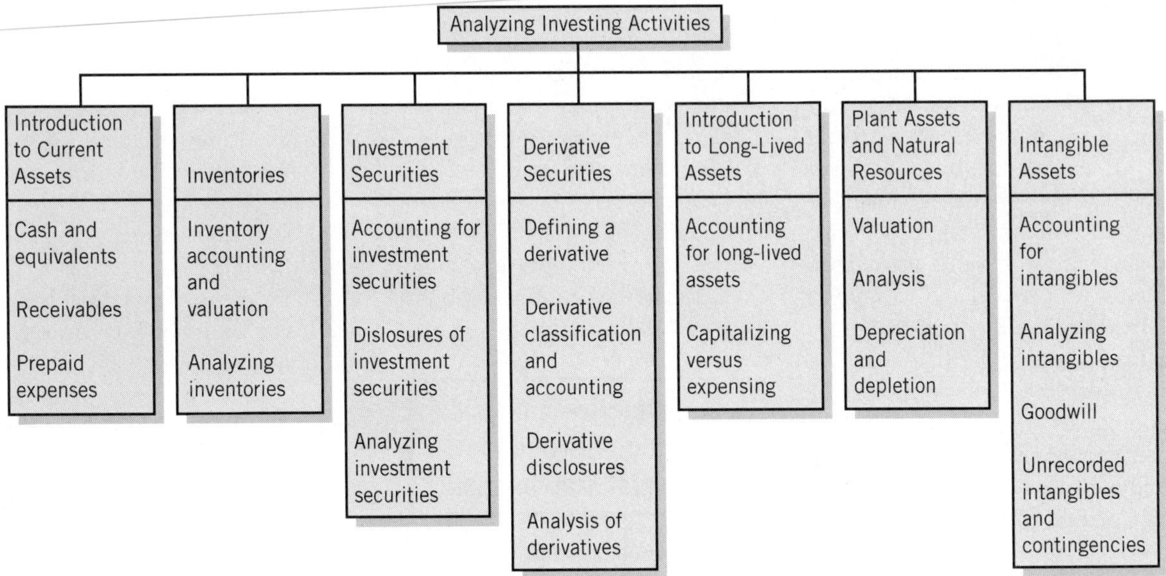

INTRODUCTION TO CURRENT ASSETS

Current assets are resources or claims to resources that are readily convertible to cash, usually within the operating cycle of the company. An **operating cycle,** shown in Exhibit 4.1, is the amount of time from commitment of cash for purchases until the collection of cash resulting from sales of goods or services. It is the process by which a company converts cash into short-term assets and back into cash as part of its ongoing operating activities. For a manufacturing company, this would entail purchasing raw materials, converting them to finished goods, and then selling and collecting cash from receivables. Cash represents the starting point, and the end point, of the operating cycle. The operating cycle is used to classify assets (and liabilities) as either current or noncurrent. Current assets are expected to be sold, collected, or used within one year or the operating cycle, whichever is longer.[1] Typical examples are cash, cash equivalents, short-term receivables, short-term securities, inventories, and prepaid expenses.

Exhibit 4.1 *Operating Cycle*

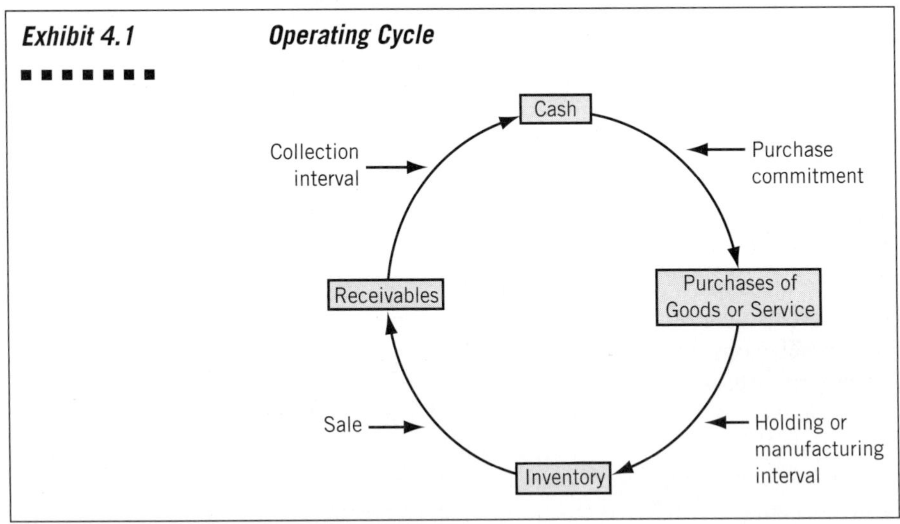

[1] Similarly, current liabilities are obligations due to be paid or settled within the longer of one year or the operating cycle.

The excess of current assets over current liabilities is called **working capital**. Working capital is a double-edged sword–companies need working capital to effectively operate, yet working capital is costly because it takes away from more profitable investments. Many companies attempt to improve profitability by reducing investment in current assets through methods such as just-in-time inventory management. Other companies try to finance their current assets through current liabilities, such as accounts payable, in an attempt to reduce working capital. Current assets, however, are mainly liquid assets. This means that while reducing current assets improves expected profitability, it also increases liquidity risk. Managers must adopt working capital management practices that balance profitability and liquidity risk.

DELL-OCITY
Dell Computer claims its operating cycle is less than 24 hours and its days' sales in inventory is under 13 days.

Because of the impact of current assets (and current liabilities) on liquidity and profitability, analysis of current assets (and current liabilities) is very important in both credit analysis and profitability analysis. We shall discuss these issues at length later in the book. In this chapter, we limit analysis to the accounting aspects of current assets, specifically their valuation and expense treatment.

Cash and Cash Equivalents

The vast majority of companies classify their most liquid assets in the cash and cash equivalents category. **Cash**, the most liquid asset, includes currency, funds on deposit, money orders, and certified and cashier checks. **Cash equivalents** are highly liquid, short-term investments that are (1) readily convertible into cash and (2) so near maturity that they have minimal risk of price changes due to interest rate movements. These investments usually carry maturities of three months or less. Examples of cash equivalents are short-term treasury bills, commercial paper, and money market funds. Cash equivalents often serve as temporary repositories of excess cash.

The concept of **liquidity** is important in financial statement analysis. By liquidity, we mean the amount of cash or cash equivalents the company has on hand and the amount of cash it can raise in a short period of time. Liquidity provides flexibility to take advantage of changing market conditions and to react to strategic actions by competitors. Liquidity also relates to the ability of a company to meet its obligations as they mature. Many companies with strong balance sheets run into serious difficulties because of illiquidity.

GLOBAL
A company must disclose restrictions on cash for accounts located in foreign countries.

Companies differ widely in the amount of liquid assets they carry on their balance sheets. As the graphic indicates, cash and cash equivalents as a percentage of total assets ranges from 2% (Kodak) to 19% (Texas Instruments). These differences can result from a number of factors. In general, companies in a dynamic industry require increased liquidity to take advantage of opportunities or to react to a quickly changing competitive landscape.

Cash and Cash Equiuvalents as a Percentage of Total Assets

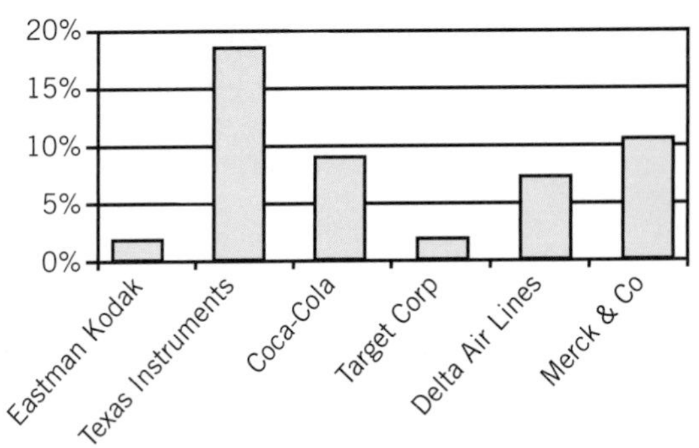

In addition to examining the amount of liquid assets available to the company, analysts must also consider the following:

1. To the extent that cash equivalents are invested in equity securities, companies risk a reduction in liquidity should the market value of those investments decline.
2. Cash and cash equivalents are sometimes required to be maintained as compensating balances to support existing borrowing arrangements or as collateral for indebtedness. For example, eBay, Inc. was required under the terms

of a lease to place $126 million out of its $400 million in cash and investment securities as collateral for the term of the lease. These investments were, therefore, not available to meet normal operating needs of the company.

Receivables

Receivables are amounts due that arise from the sale of products or services, or from the loaning of money. These include amounts due from activities such as rent and interest. **Accounts receivable** refer to oral promises of indebtedness due from sales of products and services. **Notes receivable** refer to formal written promises of indebtedness due. Certain other receivables often require separate disclosure by source, including receivables from affiliated companies, corporate officers, company directors, and employees. Companies can establish receivables without the formal billing of a debtor. For example, costs accumulated under a cost-plus-fixed-fee contract or some other types of contracts are usually recorded as receivables when earned. Also, claims for tax refunds often are classified as receivables provided no substantial question of compliance exists. Receivables classified as current assets are expected to be realized or collected within a year or the operating cycle, whichever is longer.

Valuation of Receivables

It is important to analyze receivables because of their impact on a company's asset position and income stream. These two impacts are interrelated. Experience shows that companies do not collect all receivables. While decisions about collectibility can be made at any time, collectibility of receivables as a group is best estimated on the basis of past experience, with suitable allowance for current economy, industry, and debtor conditions. The risk in this analysis is that past experience might not be an adequate predictor of future loss, or that we fail to fully account for current conditions. Losses with receivables can be substantial and affect both current assets and current and future net income.

In practice, companies report receivables at their **net realizable value**–total amount of receivables less an allowance for uncollectible accounts. Management estimates the allowance for uncollectibles based on experience, customer fortunes, economy and industry expectations, and collection policies. Uncollectible accounts are written off against the allowance (often reported as a deduction from receivables in the balance sheet), and the expected loss is included in current operating expenses. Our assessment of earnings quality is often affected by an analysis of receivables and their collectibility. Analysis must be alert to changes in the allowance account–computed relative to sales, receivables, or industry and market conditions.

Analyzing Receivables

While an unqualified opinion of an independent auditor lends assurance to the validity and valuation of receivables, our analysis must recognize the possibility of error in audit procedure or judgment. We also must be alert to management's (and the auditor's) incentives in reporting income and assets. In this respect, two important questions confront our analysis of receivables.

Collection Risk. Most provisions for uncollectible accounts are based on past experience, although they make allowance for current and emerging economic, industry, and debtor circumstances. In practice, management likely attaches more importance to past experience–for no other reason than economic and industry conditions are difficult to predict. Our analysis must bear in mind that while a formulaic approach to calculating the provision for bad debts is convenient and practical, it reflects a mechanical judgment that yields errors. Analysis must rely on our knowledge of industry conditions to reliably assess the provision for uncollectibles.

Full information to assess *collection risk* for receivables is not usually included in financial statements. Useful information must be obtained from other sources or from the company. Analysis tools for investigating collectibility include:

- Comparing competitors' receivables as a percentage of sales with those of the company under analysis.
- Examining customer concentration–risk increases when receivables are concentrated in one or a few customers.
- Investigating the age pattern of receivables (overdue and for how long).
- Determining the portion of receivables that are renewals of prior accounts or notes receivable.

An interesting case involving valuation of receivables and its importance for analysis is that of Brunswick Corp. In a past annual report, Brunswick made a "special provision for possible losses on receivables" involving a write-off of $15 million after taxes. Management asserted circumstances revealed themselves that were not apparent to management or the auditor at the end of the previous year when a substantial amount of these receivables were reported as outstanding. Management explained these write-offs as follows (dates adapted):

ANALYSIS EXCERPT

Delinquencies in bowling installment payments, primarily related to some of the large chain accounts, continued at an unsatisfactory level. Nonchain accounts, which comprise about 80% of installment receivables, are generally better paying accounts . . . In the last quarter of 20X3, average bowling lineage per establishment fell short of the relatively low lineage of the comparable period of 20X2, resulting in an aggravation of collection problems on certain accounts. The bowling business may have felt the competition of outdoor activities associated with the unseasonably warm weather during the latter part of 20X3. Some improvement in bowling lineage was noted in the early months of 20X4, which tends to confirm this view. However, the fact that collections were lower in late 20X3 contributed to management's decision to increase reserves. After the additional provision of $15 million, total reserves for possible future losses on all receivables amounted to $66 million.

While it is impossible to precisely define the moment when collection of a receivable is sufficiently doubtful to require a provision, the relevant question is whether our analysis can warn us of an inadequate provision. In year 20X2 of the Brunswick case, our analysis should have revealed the inadequacy of the bad debt provision in light of known industry conditions. Possibly not coincidentally, Brunswick's income peaked in 20X2–the year benefiting from the insufficient provision.

Our analysis of current financial position and a company's ability to meet current obligations as reflected in measures like the current ratio also must recognize the importance of the operating cycle in classifying receivables as current. The operating cycle can result in installment receivables that are not collectible for several years or even decades being reported in current assets (e.g., wineries). Our analysis of current assets, and their relation to current liabilities, must recognize and adjust for these timing risks.

CEO EXCESS

A recent study found that CEO pay at 23 companies under investigation for accounting irregularities was 70% more than the typical CEO at a large company. Specifically, the scandal-ridden CEO averaged $62 million in pay compared with $36 million for the typical CEO. The four highest paid were Tyco's Dennis Kozlowski ($467 million), Qwest Communications's Joseph Nacchio ($266 million), Enron's Kenneth Lay ($251 million), and AOL Time Warner's Gerald Levin ($178 million).

ANALYSIS VIEWPOINT ... **YOU ARE THE AUDITOR**

Your client reports preliminary financial results showing a 15% growth in earnings. This growth meets earlier predictions by management. In your audit, you discover management reduced its allowance for uncollectible accounts from 5% to 2% of gross accounts receivable. Absent this change, earnings would show 9% growth. Do you have any concern about this change in estimate?

Answer–p. 247

Authenticity of Receivables. The description of receivables in financial statements or notes is usually insufficient to provide reliable clues as to whether receivables are genuine, due, and enforceable. Knowledge of industry practices and supplementary sources of information are used for added assurance. One factor affecting authenticity of receivables is a company's *credit policy.* Stringent credit policies imply higher quality, or lower risk, receivables. A company sometimes reports its credit policy in notes to the statements. Another factor affecting authenticity is the *right of merchandise return.* Customers in certain industries, like the compact disk, textbook, or toy industries, enjoy a substantial right of merchandise return. Our analysis must allow for return privileges. Liberal return privileges can impair quality of receivables.

Receivables also are subject to various contingencies. Analysis can reveal whether contingencies impair the value of receivables. A note to the financial statements of O. M. Scott & Sons reveals several contingencies:

ANALYSIS EXCERPT

Accounts receivable: Accounts receivable are stated net after allowances for returns and doubtful accounts of $472,000. Accounts receivable include approximately $4,785,000 for shipments made under a deferred payment plan whereby title to the merchandise is transferred to the dealer when shipped; however, the Company retains a security interest in such merchandise until sold by the dealer. Payment to the Company is due from the dealer as the merchandise is sold at retail. The amount of receivables of this type shall at no time exceed $11 million under terms of the loan and security agreement.

Under these conditions, a receivable might not represent an actual sale but, rather, a merchandise or service advance. Receivables like these cannot be valued like receivables without contingencies.

Securitization of Receivables. Another important analysis issue arises when a company sells all or a portion of its receivables to a third party. Such practice is called **factoring** or **securitization**. Receivables can be sold with or without recourse to a buyer (*recourse* refers to guarantee of collectibility). Sale of receivables *with recourse* does not effectively transfer risk of ownership of receivables from the seller.

Receivables can be kept off the balance sheet only when the company selling its receivables surrenders all control over the receivables to the buyer. This means as long as a buyer has any type of recourse, the company selling receivables has to record both an asset and a compensating liability for the amount factored.

ILLUSTRATION 4.1

Syntex Co. securitizes its entire receivables of $400 million with no recourse by selling the portfolio to a trust that finances the purchase by selling bonds. As a result, the receivables are removed from the balance sheet and the company receives $400 million in cash. The balance sheet and key ratios of Syntex are shown below under three alternative scenarios: (1) before securitizing the receivables; (2) after securitizing receivables with off-balance-sheet financing (as reported under GAAP); and (3) after securitizing receivables *but* reflecting the securitization as a borrowing (reflecting the analyst's adjustments). Notice how scenario 2, compared to the true economic position of scenario 3, window-dresses the balance sheet by not reporting a portion of current liabilities.

Balance Sheet

	Before	After	Adjusted		Before	After	Adjusted
Assets				**Liabilities**			
Cash	$ 50	$ 450	$ 450	Current liabilities	$ 400	$ 400	$ 800
Receivables	400	0	400	Noncurrent liabilities	500	500	500
Other current assets	150	150	150	**Equity**	600	600	600
Total current assets	600	600	1,000				
Noncurrent assets	900	900	900				
Total assets	$1,500	$1,500	$1,900	Total liabilities and equity	$1,500	$1,500	$1,900

Key ratios			
Current ratio	1.50	1.50	1.25
Total debt to equity	1.50	1.50	2.17

The securitization of receivables is often accomplished by establishing a special purpose entity (SPE), such as the trust in Illustration 4.1, to purchase the receivables from the company and finance the purchase via sale of bonds into the market. Capital One Financial Corporation (discussed in Chapter 3) provides an excellent example of a company securitizing a significant portion of its receivables. The consumer finance company has sold $24 billion of its $45 billion loan portfolio and acknowledges that securitization is a significant source of its financing.

Sears, Roebuck and Company also has employed this technique to remove a sizable portion of its receivables from its balance sheet and provides an example of off-balance-sheet effects of securitization that have been negated under current accounting standards. The sale of receivables to a SPE only removes them from the balance sheet so long as the SPE is not required to be consolidated with the company selling the receivables. Consolidation (covered in Chapter 5) results in an adding together of the balance sheets of the company and the SPE, thus eliminating the benefits of the securitization.

The consolidation rules regarding SPEs are complicated, and if the SPEs are not properly structured, can result in consolidation of the SPE with the selling company. *SFAS 140,* "Accounting for Transfers and Servicing of Financial Assets and Extinguishments of Liabilities," changed the requirements for an entity to qualify as a SPE and established new conditions for a securitization to be accounted for as a sale of receivables. Essentially, to avoid consolidation, the company selling the receivables cannot have any recourse or other continuing involvement with the receivables after the sale. As a result of the standard, Sears now consolidates its receivable trusts, thus recognizing on its balance sheet $8 billion of previously unconsolidated credit card receivables and related borrowings. The company now accounts for the securitizations as secured borrowings. In addition, the company will no longer be able to recognize gains on the sales of these receivables, amounting to over $100 million.

RISKY LENDING

Securitization often involves lenders that package loans and sell them to investors, then use the freed-up capital to make new loans. Yet lenders often retain the riskiest piece of the loans because it is the hardest to sell—meaning they could still be on the hook if the loans go bad.

Prepaid Expenses

Prepaid expenses are advance payments for services or goods not yet received. Examples are advance payments for rent, insurance, utilities, and property taxes. Modest supplies of stationery or stamps often are included in prepaid expenses. Prepaid expenses usually are classified in current assets because they reflect services due that would otherwise require use of current assets. Our analysis should be aware, for reasons of expediency and lack of materiality, that services due beyond one year usually are included among prepaid expenses classified as current. These items typically represent a small portion of current assets. Yet, when their magnitude is large, or when substantial changes occur, they warrant our scrutiny.

INVENTORIES

Inventory Accounting and Valuation

Inventories are goods held for sale as part of a company's normal business operations. With the exception of certain service organizations, inventories are essential and important assets of companies. We scrutinize inventories because they are a major component of operating assets and directly affect determination of income.

Inventories as a Percentage of Total Assets

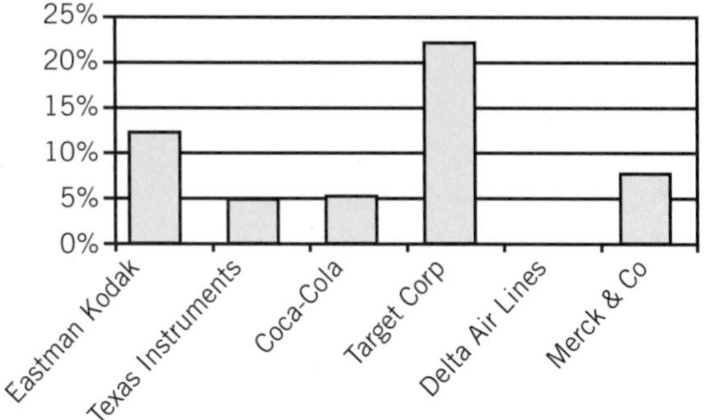

The importance of costing methods for inventory valuation is due to their impact on net income and asset valuation. Inventory costing methods are used to allocate cost of goods available for sale (beginning inventory plus net purchases) between either cost of goods sold (an income deduction) or ending inventory (a current asset). Accordingly, assigning costs to inventory affects both income and asset measurements.

The **inventory equation** is useful in understanding inventory flows. For a merchandising company:

$$\text{Beginning inventories} + \text{Net purchases} - \text{Cost of goods sold} = \text{Ending inventories}$$

This equation highlights the flow of costs within the company. It can be expressed alternatively as,

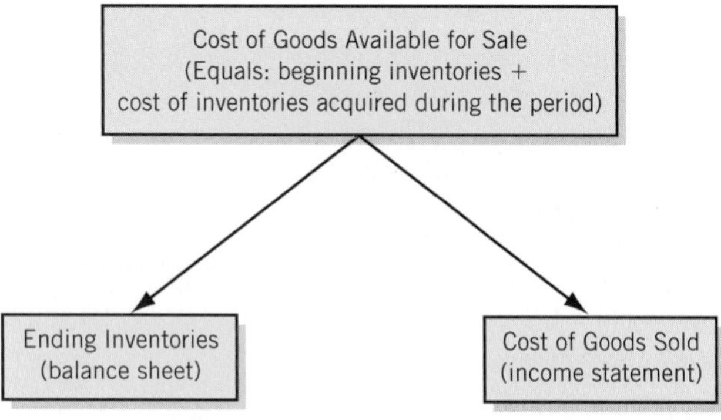

The costs of inventories are initially recorded on the balance sheet. As the inventories are sold, these costs are removed from the balance sheet and flow into the income statement as cost of goods sold (COGS). Costs cannot be in two places as the same time; either they remain on the balance sheet (as a future expense) or are recognized currently in the income statement and reduce profitability to match against sales revenue.

An important concept in inventory accounting is the flow of costs. If all inventories acquired or manufactured during the period are sold, then COGS is equal to the cost of the goods purchased or manufactured.

When inventories remain at the end of the accounting period, however, it is important to determine which inventories have been sold and which costs remain on the balance sheet. GAAP allows companies several options to determine the order in which costs are removed from the balance sheet and recognized as COGS in the income statement.

Inventory Cost Flows

To illustrate the available cost-flow assumptions, assume that the following reflects the inventory records of a company:

Inventory on January 1, Year 2	40 units @ $500 each	$20,000
Inventories purchased during the year	60 units @ $600 each	36,000
Cost of goods available for sale	100 units	$56,000

Now, assume that 30 units are sold during the year at $800 each for total sales revenue of $24,000. GAAP allows companies three options in determining which costs to match against sales:

First-In, First-Out (FIFO). This method assumes that the first units purchased are the first units sold. In this case, these units are the units on hand at the beginning of the period. Under FIFO, the company's gross profit is as follows

Sales	$24,000
COGS (30 @ $500 each)	15,000
Gross profit	$ 9,000

Also, since $15,000 of inventory cost has been removed, the remaining inventory cost to be reported on the balance sheet at the end of the period is $41,000.

Last-In, First-Out. Under the LIFO inventory costing assumption, the last units purchased are the first to be sold. Gross profit is, therefore, computed as

Sales	$24,000
COGS (30 @ $600 each)	18,000
Gross profit	$ 6,000

And since $18,000 of inventory cost has been removed from the balance sheet and reflected in COGS, $38,000 remains on the balance sheet to be reported as inventories.

Average Cost. This method assumes that the units are sold without regard to the order in which they are purchased and computes COGS and ending inventories as a simple weighted average as follows:

Sales	$24,000
COGS (30 @ $560 each)	16,800
Gross profit	$ 7,200

COGS is computed as a weighted average of the total cost of goods available for sale divided by the number of units available for sale ($56,000/100 = $560). Ending units reported on the balance sheet are $39,200 (70 units × $560 per unit).

Companies Employing Various Inventory Costing Methods

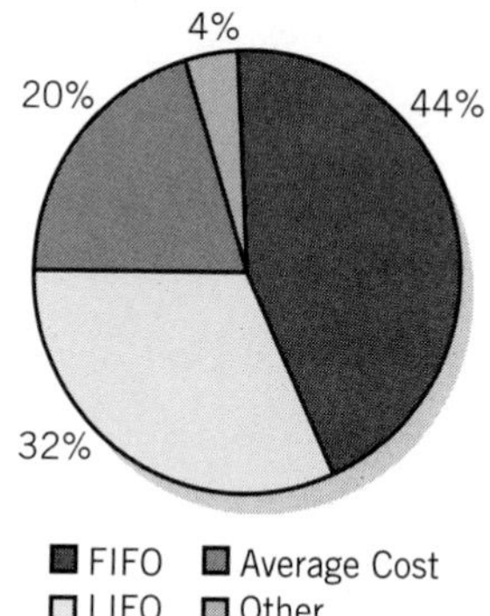

Source: Accounting Trends and Techniques

Analyzing Inventories

Inventory Costing Effects on Profitability

To summarize, the financial results of using each of the three alternative methods are:

	Beginning Inventory	Purchases	Ending Inventory	Cost of Goods Sold
FIFO	$20,000	$36,000	$41,000	$15,000
LIFO	20,000	36,000	38,000	18,000
Average cost	20,000	36,000	39,200	16,800

The income statements under the three methods, then, are as follows:

	Sales	Cost of Goods Sold	Gross Profit
FIFO	$24,000	$15,000	$9,000
LIFO	24,000	18,000	6,000
Average cost	24,000	16,800	7,200

As the examples presented above highlight, gross profit can be affected by the company's choice of its inventory costing method. *In periods of rising prices,* FIFO produces higher gross profits than LIFO because lower cost inventories are matched against sales revenues at current market prices. This is sometimes referred to as *FIFO's phantom profits* as the gross profit is actually a sum of two components: an **economic profit** and a **holding gain**. The economic profit is equal to the number of units sold multiplied by the difference between the sales price and the replacement cost of the inventories (approximated by the cost of the most recently purchased inventories):

$$\text{Economic profit} = 30 \text{ units} \times (\$800 - \$600) = \$6{,}000$$

The holding gain is the increase in replacement cost since the inventories were acquired and is equal to the number of units sold multiplied by the difference between the current replacement cost and the original acquisition cost:

$$\text{Holding gain} = 30 \text{ units} \times (\$600 - \$500) = \$3{,}000$$

Of the $9,000 in reported gross profit, $3,000 relates to the inflationary gains realized by the company on inventories it purchased some time ago at prices lower than current prices.

Holding gains are a function of the inventory turnover (e.g., how long the goods remain on the shelves) and the rate of inflation. Once a serious problem, these gains have been mitigated during the past decade due to lower inflation and management scrutiny of inventory quantities through improved manufacturing processes and better inventory controls. In countries with higher inflation rates than the United States, however, FIFO holding gains can still be an issue.

Inventory Costing Effects on the Balance Sheet

In periods of rising prices, and assuming that the company has not previously liquidated older layers of inventories, LIFO reports ending inventories at prices that can be significantly lower than replacement cost. As a result, balance sheets for LIFO companies do not accurately represent the current investment that the company has in its inventories. Kodak, for example, reports inventories under LIFO costing at $1.1 billion. Had these inventories been valued under FIFO, the reported amount would have been $1.5 billion, nearly a 40% increase. Over $400 million of invested capital is omitted from its balance sheet.

Analysis Research

PREDICTIONS USING INVENTORY LEVELS

Can our analysis use changes in a company's inventory levels to predict future sales and earnings? From one perspective, evidence of increased inventory can reveal management's expected increase in sales. From another, increased inventory can suggest excess inventory due to an unexpected sales decrease. Analysis research indicates we must cautiously interpret changes in inventory levels, even within industries and types of inventories.

For *manufacturing* companies, an increase in finished goods inventory is a predictor of increased sales but with decreased earnings–that is, evidence suggests companies reduce prices to dispose of undesirable inventory at lower profit margins. Periods subsequent to this increase in finished goods inventory do not appear to fully recover, meaning future sales and earnings do not rebound to previous levels. In contrast, an increase in raw materials or work-in-process inventory tends to foreshadow both increased sales and earnings that persist.

Evidence with *merchandising* companies suggests a slightly different pattern. Specifically, an increase in merchandise inventory implies future increased sales but with reduced earnings. This pattern is consistent with less demand, subsequently followed by reduced inventory prices to dispose of undesirable inventory–yielding lower profit margins.

These research insights can be useful in our analysis of inventory. Yet we must not ignore the role of inventory methods and estimates in determining inventory dollar levels. We must jointly consider these latter factors and adjust for them, in light of these research implications.

Inventory Costing Effects on Cash Flows

The increase in gross profit under FIFO also results in higher pretax income and, consequently, higher tax liability. In periods of rising prices, companies can get caught in a cash flow squeeze as they pay higher taxes and must replace the inventories sold at replacement costs higher than the original purchase costs. This can lead to liquidity problems, an issue that was particularly acute in the high inflationary period of the 1970s.

One of the reasons frequently cited for the adoption of LIFO is the reduction of tax liability in periods of rising prices. The IRS requires, however, that companies using LIFO inventory costing for tax purposes also use it for financial reporting. This is the **LIFO conformity rule**.

Companies using LIFO inventory costing are required to disclose the amount at which inventories would have been reported had the company used FIFO inventory costing. The difference between these two amounts is called the **LIFO reserve.** Analysts can use this reserve to compute the amount by which cash flow has been affected both cumulatively and for the current period by the use of LIFO. For example, Kodak reports the following in its 2001 annual report:

Note 3: Inventories, net (in millions)	2001	2000
At FIFO or average cost (approximates current cost)		
Finished goods	$ 851	$1,155
Work in process	318	423
Raw materials and supplies	412	589
	1,581	2,167
LIFO reserve	(444)	(449)
Total	$1,137	$1,718

LIFO inventories are reported on the balance sheet at $1,137 million. Had the company used FIFO inventory costing, inventories would have been reported at $1,581 million. The difference of $444 million is the LIFO reserve. This is the amount by which inventories and pretax income have been reduced since the company adopted LIFO. Assuming a 35% tax rate, Kodak has saved over $155 million through the use of LIFO inventory costing. During 2001, however, the LIFO reserve decreased by $5 million ($449 million to $444 million). This is most likely due to *deflation* in the cost of its inventories during the year. For 2001, then, LIFO inventory costing actually *increased* taxes by $1.75 million ($5 million × 35% tax rate).

Analysis Research

LIFO RESERVE AND COMPANY VALUE

What is the relation between the LIFO reserve and company value? A common assumption is that the LIFO reserve represents an unrecorded asset. Under this view, the magnitude of the LIFO reserve reflects a current value adjustment to inventory. Analysis research has investigated this issue, with interesting results.

Contrary to the "unrecorded asset theory," evidence from practice is consistent with a *negative* relation between the LIFO reserve and company market value. This implies the higher the LIFO reserve is, the lower the company value. Why this negative relation? An "economic effects theory" suggests that companies adopt LIFO if the present value of expected tax savings exceeds the costs of adoption (such as administrative costs). If we assume the present value of tax savings is related to the anticipated effect of inflation on inventory costs (a reasonable assumption), a negative relation might reflect the decline in the real value of a company due to anticipated inflation. Our analysis must therefore consider the possibility that companies using LIFO and companies using FIFO are inherently different and that adjustments using the LIFO reserve reflect this difference.

Other Issues in Inventory Valuation

LIFO Liquidations. Companies are required to maintain each cost level as a separate inventory pool (e.g., the $500 and $600 units in our initial example). When a *reduction* in inventory quantities occurs, which can occur as a company becomes leaner or downsizes, companies dip into earlier cost layers to match against current selling prices. For FIFO inventory costing, this does not present a significant problem as ending inventories are reported at the most recently acquired costs and earlier cost layers do not differ significantly from current cost. For LIFO inventories, however, ending inventories can be reported at much older costs that may be significantly lower or higher than current costs. In periods of rising prices, this reduction in inventory quantities, known as **LIFO liquidation**, results in an increase in gross profit that is similar to the effect of FIFO inventory costing. In periods of declining prices, however, the reduction of inventory quantities can lead to a decrease in reported gross profit as higher cost inventories are matched against current sales.

The effect of LIFO liquidation can be seen in the inventory footnote of a recent Stride Rite Corporation annual report. The company indicates that reductions in inventory quantities resulted in the sale of products carried at prior years' costs that were different from current costs. As a result of these inventory reductions, net income *decreased* by $373,000 and *increased* by $235,000 in the current and prior year, respectively. Analysts need to be aware of the effects on profitability of these LIFO liquidations.

Analytical Restatement of LIFO to FIFO. When financial statements are available using LIFO, and if LIFO is the method preferred in our analysis, the income statement requires no major adjustment since cost of goods sold approximates current cost. The LIFO method, however, leaves inventories on the balance sheet at less recent, often understated costs. This can impair the usefulness of various measures like the current ratio or inventory turnover ratio. We already showed that LIFO understates inventory values *when prices rise.* Consequently, LIFO understates the company's debt-paying ability (as measured, for example, by the current ratio), overstates inventory turnover, and provides a means of earnings management. To counter this we use an analytical technique for adjusting LIFO statements to approximate a pro forma situation assuming FIFO. This balance sheet adjustment is possible when a company discloses the amount by which current cost exceeds reported cost of LIFO inventories, the LIFO reserve. The following three adjustments are necessary:

(1) Inventories = Reported LIFO inventory + LIFO reserve
(2) Increase deferred tax payable by: (LIFO reserve × Tax rate)
(3) Retained earnings = Reported retained earnings
+ [LIFO reserve × (1 − Tax rate)]

We illustrate these adjustments to restate LIFO inventories to FIFO using Campbell Soup's financial statements from Appendix A–see Illustration 4.2

ILLUSTRATION 4.2

Campbell's Soup Note 14 reports "adjustments of inventories to LIFO basis" (the LIFO reserve) are $89.6 million in Year 11 and $84.6 million in Year 10. To restate Year 11 LIFO inventories to a FIFO basis we use the following analytical entry (an analytical entry is an adjustment aid for purposes of accounting analysis):

Inventories[(a)]	89.6	
Deferred Tax Payable[(b)]		30.5
Retained Earnings[(c)]		59.1

[(a)]*Inventories increase by $89.6 to approximate current cost (note: a low turnover ratio can result in inventories of FIFO not reflecting current cost).*

[(b)]*Since inventories increase, a provision for taxes payable in the future is made, using a tax rate of 34% (from Note 9)—computed as $89.6 × 34%. The reason for tax deferral is this analytical entry reflects an accounting method different from that used for tax purposes.*

[(c)]*Higher ending inventories imply lower cost of goods sold and higher cumulative net income flowing into retained earnings (net of tax)—computed as $89.6 × (1 − 34%).*

Similarly, to adjust Year 10 LIFO inventories to FIFO, we use the following analytical entry:

Inventories	84.6	
Deferred Tax Payable		28.8
Retained Earnings		55.8

We also can readily compute income statement impacts from the adjustment of LIFO inventories to FIFO inventories, see Illustration 4.3.

ILLUSTRATION 4.3

To assess the impact on Year 11 income from restatement of inventories from LIFO to FIFO for Campbell Soup, we make the following computations:

	YEAR 11		
	Under LIFO	**Difference**	**Under FIFO**
Beginning inventory	\$819.8[a]	\$84.6[b]	\$904.4
+ Purchases (P)[c]	P	—	P
− Ending inventory	(706.7)[d]	(89.6)[b]	(796.3)
= Cost of goods sold	P + \$113.1	\$ (5.0)[d]	P + \$108.1

[a] As reported per balance sheet, see Note 14.

[b] Per financial statement Note 14.

[c] Since purchases (P) are unaffected by using either LIFO or FIFO, purchases need not be adjusted to arrive at the effect on cost of goods sold or income. If desired, we can compute purchases for Year 11 as: \$4,095.5 (cost of goods per income statement) + \$706.7 (ending inventory) − \$819.8 (beginning inventory) = \$3,982.4.

[d] Restatement to FIFO decreases cost of goods sold by \$5.0 and, therefore, increases income by \$5.0 × (1 − 0.34), or \$3.3 using a 34% tax rate.

Illustration 4.3 shows us that the income restatement (net of tax) from LIFO to FIFO for Campbell Soup for Year 11 is \$3.3. This amount is reconciled with the adjustments to retained earnings (balance sheet restatement) as implied from the analytical entries (see Illustration 4.2) for Years 10 and 11:

Year 10 Credit to Retained Earnings	−	Year 11 Credit to Retained Earnings	=	Increase in Year 11 Income
\$55.8		\$59.1		\$3.3

Generally, when prices rise, LIFO income is less than FIFO income. However, the net effect of restatement in any given year depends on the combined effects of the change in beginning and ending inventories and other factors including liquidation of LIFO layers.

Analytical Restatement of FIFO to LIFO. The adjustment from FIFO to LIFO, unfortunately, involves an important assumption and may, therefore, be prone to error. Remember that FIFO profits include a holding gain on beginning inventory. It is helpful to think of this gain as the beginning inventory (BI_{FIFO}) multiplied by an inflation rate for the particular lines of inventory that the firm carries. Let us call this rate *r*. Then, current FIFO profits include a holding gain equal to BI × *r*. This means that cost of goods sold (FIFO) is understated by $BI_{FIFO} \times r$. Therefore, to compute LIFO cost of goods sold ($COGS_{LIFO}$), simply add $BI_{FIFO} \times r$ to $COGS_{FIFO}$ as follows:

$$COGS_{LIFO} = COGS_{FIFO} + (BI_{FIFO} \times r)$$

Note that this inflation factor, *r*, is not a general rate of inflation like the CPI or the producer's price index. It is an inflation index relating to the specific lines of inventory carried by the firm. To the extent that the firm carries a number of product lines, these must each be estimated separately.

How does one estimate *r*? There are several possibilities. First, the analyst might use indices published by the U.S. Department of Commerce for the firm's particular industry. Second, to the extent that the firm is involved in a commodity-based business, commodity indices might be used under the assumption that other cost components of its inventory vary proportionately with that of its raw materials. Third, the analyst can

Analysis Research

INVENTORY METHOD CHOICE

Why are all firms not using LIFO? Or FIFO? Or another method? Can a company's choice of inventory method help direct our analysis of a company? Analysis research on inventory provides answers to some of these questions. Specifically, information on inventory method choice for a company can give us insights into the company and its environment.

For companies choosing LIFO, the following characteristics are common:

- Greater expected tax savings.
- Larger inventory balances.
- Less tax loss carryforwards.
- Lower variability in inventory balances.
- Less likelihood of inventory obsolescence.
- Larger in size.
- Less leveraged.
- Higher current ratios.

Accordingly, knowledge of inventory method choice can reveal information about a company's characteristics or circumstances otherwise obscured by the complexity of data or operations.

examine rates of inflation for the firm's competitors. To the extent that a company carrying similar lines of products can be found that uses LIFO inventory costing, the rate of inflation can be estimated as the increase in the LIFO reserve divided by the competitor's FIFO inventories at the end of the previous year as follows:

$$r = \frac{\text{Change in LIFO reserve}}{\text{FIFO inventories from previous year-end}}$$

Inventory Costing for Manufacturing Companies and the Effect of Production Increases

The cost of inventories for manufacturing consists of three components:

1. Raw materials–the cost of the basic materials used to manufacture the product.
2. Labor–the cost of the direct labor required to transform the product to a finished state.
3. Overhead–the indirect costs incurred in the manufacturing process, such as depreciation of the manufacturing equipment, supervisory wages, and utilities.

Companies can estimate the first two components fairly accurately from design specifications and time and motion studies on the assembly line. Overhead is often the largest component of product cost and the most difficult to measure at the product level. In total, overhead must be allocated to all products produced. But which products get what portion of the total? Accountants generally subscribe to the notion that those products consuming most of the resources (e.g., requiring the most costly production machinery or the most engineering time) should be allocated most of the overhead. Inventory costing for manufacturing companies is generally covered in managerial accounting courses and is beyond the scope of this text. Analysts need to be aware, however, that overhead cost allocation is not an exact science and is highly dependent on the assumptions used.

Analysts also need to understand the effect of production levels on profitability. Overhead is allocated to all units produced, and instead of expensing these costs as period expenses, they are included in the cost of inventories and remain on the balance sheet until the inventories are sold, at which time they are reflected as cost of goods sold in the income statement. If an increase in production levels causes ending inventories to increase, more of the overhead costs remain on the balance sheet and profitability increases. Later, if inventory quantities decrease, the income statement is burdened by not only the current overhead costs, but also previous overhead costs that have been

EBAY TO THE RESCUE

At least 71 large companies, including Bloomingdale's, Dell Computer, Home Depot, IBM, and Motorola, now sell outdated inventory, ranging from tractors to laptops, on eBay. The reason: They can recoup 45¢ on the dollar instead of the 15¢ to 20¢ they would get otherwise from liquidators.

removed from inventories in the current year, thus lowering profits. Analysts need to be aware, therefore, of the effect of changing production levels on reported profits.

Lower of Cost or Market

The generally accepted principle of inventory valuation is to value at the **lower of cost or market**. This simple phrase masks the complexities and variety of alternatives to which it is subject. It can significantly affect periodic income and inventory values. The lower-of-cost-or-market rule implies that if inventory declines in market value below its cost for any reason, including obsolescence, damage, and price changes, then inventory is written down to reflect this loss. This write-down is effectively charged against revenues in the period the loss occurs. Since write-ups from cost to market are prohibited (except for recovery of losses up to the original cost), inventory is conservatively valued.

Market is defined as current replacement cost through either purchase or reproduction. However, market value must not be higher than net realizable value nor less than net realizable value reduced by a normal profit margin. The upper limit of market value, or net realizable value, reflects completion and disposal costs associated with sale of the item. The lower limit ensures that if inventory is written down from cost to market, it is written down to a figure that includes realization of a normal gross profit on subsequent sale. **Cost** is defined as the acquisition cost of inventory. It is computed using one of the accepted inventory costing methods–for example, FIFO, LIFO, or average cost. Our analysis of inventory must consider the impact of the lower-of-cost-or-market rule. When prices are rising, this rule tends to *undervalue* inventories regardless of the cost method used. This depresses the current ratio. In practice, certain companies voluntarily disclose the current cost of inventory, usually in a note.

ANALYSIS EXCERPT

Toro Company's initial venture into snowblowers was less than successful. Toro reasoned that snowblowers were a perfect complement to its lawnmower business, especially after higher than normal snowfall in recent years. Toro reacted and produced snowblowers as if snow was both a growth business and fell reliably as grass grows. When, in its launch year, winter yielded a less than normal snowfall, both Toro and its dealers were bursting with excess inventory. Many dealers were so financially pressed that they were unable to finance lawnmower inventories for the summer season.

ANALYSIS EXCERPT

Regina Company recently experienced an unusually high rate of returns due to poor product quality. Early analytical clues to this problem included a near twofold increase in both finished goods inventories and receivables when sales increases were much less than expected. Yet many investors, creditors, and others were seemingly surprised when news of this problem became public.

ANALYSIS VIEWPOINT ***. . . YOU ARE THE BUYING AGENT***

You are trying to reach agreement with a supplier on providing materials for manufacturing. To make its case for a higher price, the supplier furnishes an income statement revealing a historically low 20% gross margin. In your analysis of this statement, you discover a note stating that market value of inventory declined by $2 million this period and, therefore, ending inventory is revalued downward by that amount. Is this note relevant for your price negotiations?

Answer–p. 247

INVESTMENT SECURITIES

Companies also invest assets in **investment securities** (also called *marketable securities*). Investment securities vary widely in terms of the type of securities that a company invests in and the purpose of such investment. Some investments are temporary repositories of excess cash held as marketable securities. They also can include funds awaiting investment in plant, equipment, and other operating assets, or can serve as funds for payment of liabilities. The purpose of these temporary repositories is to deploy idle cash in a productive manner. Other investments, for example equity participation in a foreign affiliate, are often an integral part of the company's core activities.

Investment securities can be in the form of either debt or equity. **Debt securities** are securities representing a creditor relationship with another entity–examples are corporate bonds, government bonds, notes, and municipal securities. **Equity securities** are securities representing ownership interest in another entity–examples are common stock and nonredeemable preferred stock. Companies classify investment securities among their current and/or noncurrent assets, depending on the investment horizon of the particular security.

For most companies, investment securities constitute a relatively minor share of total assets and, with the exception of investments in equity of subsidiaries or affiliates, these investments are in financial, rather than operating, assets. This means these investments usually are *not* an integral part of the operating activities of the company. However, for financial institutions and insurance companies, investment securities constitute the primary operating assets.

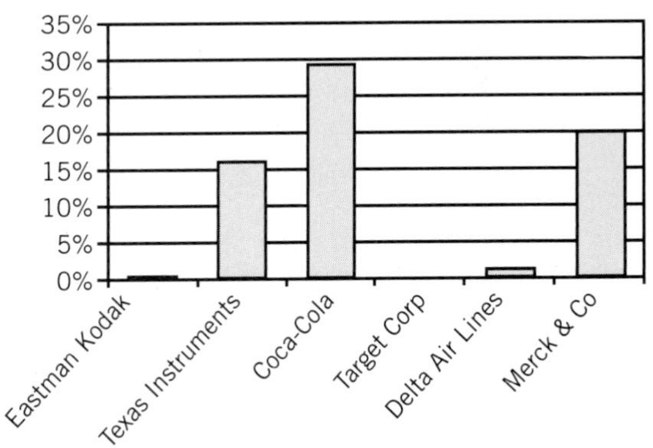

In this section we first explain the classification and accounting for investment securities. We then examine disclosure requirements for investment securities, using pertinent disclosures from Coca-Cola Company's annual report. We conclude the section by discussing analysis of investment securities.

Accounting for Investment Securities

The accounting for investment securities is prescribed under *SFAS 115*. This standard departs from the traditional lower-of-cost-or-market principle by prescribing that investment securities be reported on the balance sheet at cost or fair (market) value, depending on the type of security and the purpose of investment. This means investment securities can be valued at market even when market value exceeds the acquisition cost.

Fair value of an asset is the amount the asset can be exchanged for in a current, normal transaction between willing parties. When an asset is regularly traded, its fair value is *readily determinable* from its published market price. If no published market price exists for an asset, fair value is determined using historical cost.

Accounting for an investment security is determined by its classification. Exhibit 4.2 presents the classification possibilities for investment securities. Investment securities are broadly classified as either debt or equity securities. Debt securities, in turn, are further classified based on the purpose of the investment. Equity securities, on the other hand, are classified on the extent of interest–that is, the extent of investor ownership in the investee. Equity securities reflecting no significant ownership interest in the investee are further classified on the purpose of the investment. Since the accounting for investments in debt and equity securities are different, we explain each separately.

Exhibit 4.2 ***Classification of Investment Securities***

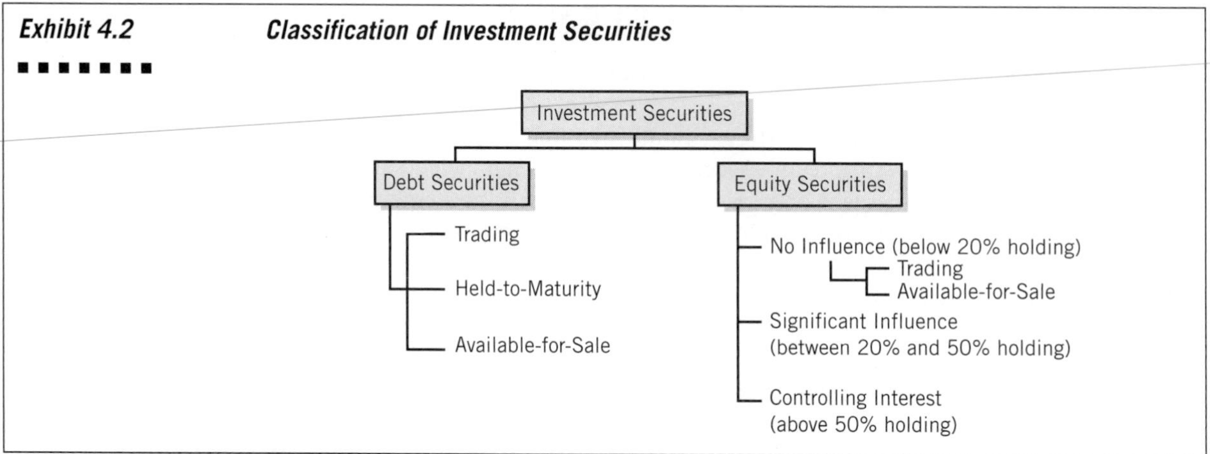

Debt Securities

Debt securities represent creditor relationships with other entities. Examples are government and municipal bonds, company bonds and notes, and convertible debt. Debt securities are classified as trading, held-to-maturity, or available-for-sale. Since classification is based on the intent (purpose) of the investment, there is some discretion in classification. Accounting guidelines for debt securities differ depending on the type of security. Exhibit 4.3 describes the criteria for classification and the accounting for each class of debt securities.

Trading Securities. **Trading securities** are debt (or noninfluential equity) securities purchased with the intent of actively managing them and selling them for profit in the near future. Trading securities are current assets. Companies report them at aggregate fair value at each balance sheet date. Unrealized gains or losses (changes in fair value of the securities held) and realized gains or losses (gains or losses on sales) are included in net income. Interest income from the trading securities held in the form of debt is recorded as it is earned. (Dividend income from the trading securities held in the form of equity is recorded when earned.)

Held-to-Maturity Securities. **Held-to-maturity securities** are debt securities that management has both the ability and intent to hold to maturity. They could be either short term (in which case they are classified as current assets) or long term (in which case they are classified as noncurrent assets). Companies report short-term (long-term) held-to-maturity securities on the balance sheet at cost (amortized cost). No unrealized gains or losses from these securities are recognized in income. Interest income and realized gains and losses, including amortization of any premium or discount on long-term securities, are included in income.

Available-for-Sale Securities. **Available-for-sale securities** are debt (or noninfluential equity) securities not classified as either trading or held-to-maturity securities. These securities are included among current or noncurrent assets, depending on their maturity and/or management's intent regarding their sale. These securities are reported at fair value on the balance sheet. However, changes in fair value are excluded from net income and, instead, are included in comprehensive income (Chapter 6 defines comprehensive income). With available-for-sale debt securities, interest income, including amortization of any premium or discount on long-term securities, is recorded when earned. (With available-for-sale equity securities, dividends are recorded in income

Classification and Accounting for Debt Securities *Exhibit 4.3*

		ACCOUNTING		
			INCOME STATEMENT	
Category	**Description**	**Balance Sheet**	**Unrealized Gains/Losses**	**Other**
Trading	Securities acquired mainly for short-term or trading gains (usually less than three months)	Fair value	Recognize in net income	Recognize realized gains/losses and interest income in net income
Held-to-Maturity	Securities acquired with both the intent and ability to hold to maturity	Amortized cost	Not recognized in either net income or comprehensive income	Recognize realized gains/losses and interest income in net income
Available-for-Sale	Securities neither held for trading nor held-to-maturity	Fair value	Not recognized in net income, but recognized in comprehensive income	Recognize realized gains/losses and interest income in net income

when earned.) Realized gains and losses on available-for-sale securities are included in income.

Transfers between Categories. When management's intent or ability to carry out the purpose of investment securities significantly changes, securities usually must be reclassified (transferred to another class). Normally, debt securities classified as held-to-maturity cannot be transferred to another class except under exceptional circumstances such as a merger, acquisition, divestiture, a major deterioration in credit rating, or some other extraordinary event. Also, transfers from available-for-sale to trading are normally not permitted. However, whenever transfers of securities between classes do occur, the securities must be adjusted to their fair value. This fair value requirement ensures that a company transferring securities immediately recognizes (in its income statement) changes in fair value. It also reduces the likelihood a company could conceal changes in fair value by transferring securities to another class that does not recognize fair value changes in income. Exhibit 4.4 summarizes the accounting for transfers between various classes.

Accounting for Transfers between Security Classes *Exhibit 4.4*

TRANSFER			
From	**To**	**Effect on Asset Value in Balance Sheet**	**Effect on Income Statement**
Trading	Available-for-Sale	No effect	Unrealized gain or loss on date of transfer included in net income
Available-for-Sale	Trading	No effect	Unrealized gain or loss on date of transfer included in net income
Available-for-Sale	Held-to-Maturity	No effect at transfer; however, asset reported at (amortized) cost instead of fair value at future dates	Unrealized gain or loss on date of transfer included in comprehensive income
Held-to-Maturity	Available-for-Sale	Asset reported at fair value instead of (amortized) cost	Unrealized gain or loss on date of transfer included in comprehensive income

Equity Securities

Equity securities represent ownership interests in another entity. Examples are common and preferred stock and rights to acquire or dispose of ownership interests such as warrants, stock rights, and call and put options. Redeemable preferred stock and convertible debt securities are not considered equity securities (they are classified as debt securities). The two main motivations for a company to purchase equity securities are (1) to exert influence over the directors and management of another entity (such as suppliers, customers, subsidiaries) or (2) to receive dividend and stock price appreciation income. Companies report investments in equity securities according to their ability to influence or control the investee's activities. Evidence of this ability is based on the percentage of voting securities controlled by the investor company. These percentages are guidelines and can be overruled by other factors. For example, a minority interest (say 15%) can provide effective control if other owners are widely dispersed and unorganized. Exhibit 4.5 summarizes the classification and accounting for equity securities.

Exhibit 4.5 ***Classification and Accounting for Equity Securities***

	NO INFLUENCE			
Attribute	**Available-for-Sale**	**Trading**	**Significant Influence**	**Controlling Interest**
Ownership	Less than 20%	Less than 20%	Between 20% and 50%	Above 50%
Purpose	Long- or intermediate-term investment	Short-term investment or trading	Considerable business control	Full business control
Valuation basis	Fair value	Fair value	Equity method	Consolidation
Balance sheet Asset value	Fair value	Fair value	Acquisition cost adjusted for proportionate share of investee's retained earnings and appropriate amortization	Consolidated balance sheet
Income statement: Unrealized gains	In comprehensive income	In net income	Not recognized	Not recognized
Income statement: Other income effects	Recognize dividends and realized gains and losses in net income	Recognize dividends and realized gains and losses in net income	Recognize proportionate share of investee's net income less appropriate amortization in net income	Consolidated income statement

IPO NO-NO
Raising cash for new companies through initial public offerings is rife with conflicts. Investment banks push their analysts to give IPO clients sky-high ratings. And banks routinely underprice IPOs so they can use shares in a hot new stock to reward friends and woo potential banking clients.

No Influence—Less than 20% Holding. When equity securities are nonvoting preferred or less than 20% of an investee's voting stock, they are considered noninfluential. In these cases, investors are assumed to possess minimal influence over the investee's activities. These investments are classified as either trading or available-for-sale securities, based on the intent and ability of management. Accounting for these securities is already described under debt securities that are similarly classified.

Significant Influence—Between 20% and 50% Holding. Security holdings, even when below 50% of the voting stock, can provide an investor the ability to exercise significant influence over an investee's business activities. Evidence of an investor's ability to exert significant influence over an investee's business activities is revealed in several ways, including management representation and participation. In the absence of evidence to the contrary, an investment (direct or indirect) of 20% or more (but less than 50%) in the voting stock of an investee is presumed to possess significant influence. The investor accounts for this investment using the equity method.

The **equity method** requires investors initially to record investments at cost and later adjust the account for the investor's proportionate share in both the investee's income (or loss) since acquisition and decreases from any dividends received from the investee. Any difference between acquisition cost and the proportionate share purchased of an investee's equity is no longer amortized. We explain the mechanics of this process when we cover intercorporate investments in Chapter 5. While holdings in convertible preferred stock count toward the percentage of ownership, they do not count in adjusting for the proportionate share of income, as shown in Illustration 4.4.

ILLUSTRATION 4.4

Company A owns 15% of the common stock of Company B. Through additional holdings of convertible preferred stock, the total percent of voting power held is 20%. Total holdings imply Company A will account for its investment in Company B using the equity method. Yet, Company A can record only 15% of Company B's income since this is the percentage of ownership in B's common stock.

Controlling Interest—Holdings of More than 50%. Holdings of more than 50% are referred to as **controlling interests**–where the investor is known as the *holding company* and the investee as the *subsidiary. Consolidated financial statements* are prepared for holdings of more than 50%. We explain consolidation in Chapter 5 under the topic of intercorporate investments.

ANALYSIS VIEWPOINT ***. . . YOU ARE THE COMPETITOR***

Toys 'R' Us, a retailer in toys and games, is concerned about a recent transaction involving a competitor. Specifically, Marvel Entertainment, a comic book company, obtained 46% of equity securities in Toy Biz by granting Toy Biz an exclusive worldwide license to use all of Marvel's characters (such as Spider-Man, Incredible Hulk, Storm) for toys and games. What is the primary concern of Toys 'R' Us? What is Marvel's motivation for its investment in Toy Biz's equity securities?

Answer–p. 247

Disclosures for Investment Securities

This section focuses on the disclosures required under *SFAS 115.* We use Microsoft as an example. This discussion is confined to disclosures for debt and noninfluential (and marketable) equity securities. We do not examine disclosures relating to intercorporate investments, which are covered in Chapter 5.

Exhibit 4.6 provides excerpts from Microsoft Corporation's notes relating to debt and marketable equity securities (holdings below 20%). Microsoft classifies the majority of its debt and equity investment as available for sale and reports acquisition cost, fair value, and unrealized gain/loss details for each class of its investments. On June 30, 2001, the estimated fair value of Microsoft's available-for-sale securities is $14,141 million, of which $8,560 million is equity and $5,581 million debt. The cost of these securities is $13,225 million, implying a cumulative unrealized gain of $916 million (consisting of a $2,042 million gross unrealized gain and a $1,126 million gross unrealized loss), which is included in its accumulated other comprehensive income figure (OCI). In addition, Microsoft reports that it owns restricted or nonpublicly traded securities that it records at cost as prescribed by GAAP. The excess of the estimated (by Microsoft) fair market value of these securities over their reported cost is $161 million ($2.7 billion in the prior year). This unrealized gain is not reflected either on the balance sheet or in OCI since the securities are reported at cost.

Exhibit 4.6

Financial Instruments

The Company considers all liquid interest-earning investments with a maturity of three months or less at the date of purchase to be cash equivalents. Short-term investments generally mature between three months and six years from the purchase date. All cash and short-term investments are classified as available for sale and are recorded at market value using the specific identification method; unrealized gains and losses are reflected in other comprehensive income (OCI). Equity and other investments include debt and equity instruments. Debt securities and publicly traded equity securities are classified as available for sale and are recorded at market using the specific identification method. Unrealized gains and losses (excluding other-than-temporary losses) are reflected in other comprehensive income. All other investments, excluding those accounted for using the equity method, are recorded at cost.

EQUITY AND OTHER INVESTMENTS (IN MILLIONS—JUNE 30, 2001)

	Cost Basis	Unrealized Gains	Unrealized Losses	Recorded Basis
Debt securities recorded at market, maturing:				
Within one year	$ 500	$ —	$ —	$ 500
Between 2 and 10 years	643	12	(3)	652
Between 10 and 15 years	513	—	(9)	504
Beyond 15 years	4,754	—	(829)	3,925
Debt securities recorded at market	6,410	12	(841)	5,581
Common stock and warrants	5,555	2,030	(285)	7,300
Preferred stock	881	—	—	881
Other investments	379	—	—	379
Equity and other investments	$13,225	$2,042	$(1,126)	$14,141

Debt securities include corporate and government notes and bonds and derivative securities. Debt securities maturing beyond 15 years are composed entirely of AT&T 5% convertible preferred debt with a contractual maturity of 30 years. The debt is convertible into AT&T common stock on or after December 1, 2000, or may be redeemed by AT&T upon satisfaction of certain conditions on or after June 1, 2002. Equity securities that are restricted for more than one year or not publicly traded are recorded at cost. At June 30, 2000 and 2001, the estimated fair value of these investments in excess of their recorded basis was $2.70 billion and $161 million, based on publicly available market information or other estimates determined by management. Realized gains and (losses) from equity and other investments (excluding impairments discussed previously) were $786 million and $(2) million in 1999, $1.94 billion and $(10) million in 2000, and $3.03 billion and $(23) million in 2001.

In fiscal 2001, the Company reported an investment loss of $36 million, a decrease in investment income of $3.36 billion versus fiscal 2000. Net recognized losses were $2.22 billion in fiscal 2001, reflecting $4.80 billion in impairments of certain investments, primarily in the cable and telecommunication industries, and $592 million of net losses attributable to derivative instruments. These losses were partially offset by higher net gains from the sales of investments, including a gain from Microsoft's investment in Titus Communications (which was merged with Jupiter Telecommunications) and the closing of the sale of Transpoint to CheckFree Holdings Corp. Interest and dividend income increased $591 million from the prior year, reflecting a larger investment portfolio. In fiscal years 2000 and 1999, investment income increased primarily as a result of a larger investment portfolio generated by cash from operations coupled with realized gains from the sale of securities.

The components of investment income/(loss) are as follows:

INVESTMENT INCOME/(LOSS) (IN MILLIONS—YEAR ENDED JUNE 30)

	1999	2000	2001
Dividends	$ 118	$ 363	**$ 377**
Interest	1,030	1,231	**1,808**
Net recognized gains/(losses) on investments	803	1,732	**(2,221)**
Investment income/(loss)	$1,951	$3,326	**$ (36)**

The company's income statement reports an investment loss for the year of $36 million. The notes to the financial statement reveal that this loss is composed of the following:

(in $millions)	
Realized gains on the sale of investments	$3,171
Unrealized losses on derivative investments	(592)
Write-down of investments in telecommunications and cable industries	(4,800)
Net recorded loss	(2,221)
Dividend income	377
Interest income	1,808
Net investment loss	$ (36)

Analyzing Investment Securities

Analysis of investment securities has at least three main objectives: (1) to separate operating performance from investing (and financing) performance; (2) to evaluate investment performance and risk; and (3) to analyze accounting distortions due to accounting rules and/or earnings management involving investment securities. We limit our analysis to debt securities and noninfluential (and marketable) equity securities. Analysis of the remaining equity securities is in Chapter 5 under intercorporate investments.

Separating Operating from Investing Assets and Performance

The operating and investing performance of a company must be separately analyzed. This is because a company's investing performance can distort its true operating performance. For this purpose, it is important for an analyst to remove all gains (losses) relating to investing activities–including dividends, interest income, and realized and unrealized gains and losses–when evaluating operating performance. An analyst also needs to separate operating and nonoperating assets when determining the operating return on investment.

While evaluation of operating performance is discussed in detail when we take up profitability analysis in Chapters 8 and 9, we discuss the evaluation of investment performance in this section. However, before we turn to this evaluation, we provide guidelines for classifying securities (and associated income) as either operating or investing.

As a rule of thumb, all debt securities and marketable noninfluential equity securities, and their related income streams, are viewed as investing activities. Still, an analyst must review the nature of a company's business and the objectives behind different investments before classifying them as operating or investing. Here is a short list of cases where the rule of thumb does not always apply:

- Financial institutions focus on financing and investing activities. This implies that all financing and investing income and assets are operating-related for financial institutions.
- Some nonfinancial institutions derive a substantial portion of their income from investing activities. For example, finance subsidiaries are sometimes the most profitable business units for companies such as General Electric, Sears, and General Motors. For such companies it is important to separate the performance of the financing (and investing) units from these companies' core operations–although income from such important activities should not be considered secondary.

BANK FAVORS

Big banks allegedly dole out favorable loans to corporations to gain investment-banking business. Despite growing defaults, banks have largely avoided losses by securitizing many of the loans and selling them off to pension funds and insurance companies.

- Noninfluential equity investments (below a 20% holding) are normally considered pure investments made with the objective of realizing dividends and capital gains. Still, using percentage of holding as an indicator of investing intentions can be deceptive. For example, Coca-Cola has substantial investments in bottling companies that fall below the 20% holding threshold. Are these investments part of Coca-Cola's business strategy or simply attractive investment opportunities? Another example arises when analyzing multinational investments because investment holdings of a parent are often artificially low to circumvent national laws and restrictions.

There are no "cookbook" solutions for determining whether investment securities (and related income streams) are investing or operating in nature. This classification must be made based on an assessment of whether each investment is a strategic part of operations or made purely for the purpose of investment.

Analyzing Accounting Distortions from Securities

SFAS 115 takes an important step towards fair value accounting for investment securities. However, this standard does not fully embrace fair value accounting. Instead, the standard is a compromise between historical cost and fair value, leaving many unresolved issues along with opportunities for earnings management. This means an analyst must examine disclosures relating to investment securities to identify potential distortions due to both accounting methods and earnings management. This analysis is especially important when analyzing financial institutions and insurance companies because investing activities constitute the core of their operations and provide the bulk of their income. We list some of the potential distortions caused by the accounting for investment securities that an analyst must watch for:

- **Opportunities for gains trading:** The standard allows opportunities for *gains trading* with available-for-sale and held-to-maturity securities. Since unrealized gains and losses on available-for-sale and held-to-maturity securities are excluded from net income, companies can increase net income by selling those securities with unrealized gains and holding those with unrealized losses. However, the standard requires unrealized gains and losses on available-for-sale securities be reported as part of comprehensive income. An analyst must therefore examine comprehensive income disclosures to ascertain unrealized losses (if any) on unsold available-for-sale securities. Still, examining comprehensive income disclosures will only partly alleviate problems with gains trading in held-to-maturity securities. That is, when a company sells any held-to-maturity securities, it has to classify the entire set of those securities as available-for-sale. To the extent there are unrealized losses on unsold securities in a similar class, they will be reported in comprehensive income. Moreover, it is impossible to detect gains trading across security classes. Also, in evaluating sales of securities, we must be aware of the methods for determining securities' cost (such as specific identification, FIFO, LIFO, average cost) that can affect income and assets.
- **Liabilities recognized at cost:** Accounting for investment securities is arguably one-sided. That is, if a company reports its investment securities at fair value, why not its liabilities? For many companies, especially financial institutions, asset positions are not managed independent of liability positions. As a result, accounting can yield earnings volatility exceeding what the true underlying economics suggest. This consideration led regulators to exclude unrealized holding gains and losses on available-for-sale securities from income. Excluding holding gains and losses from income affects our analysis of the income statement, but does not affect

OUT OF LUCK
Defrauded investors have many avenues for relief—but none that promises much restitution. For example, class-action cases against solvent companies return an average of only 6% of claimed losses.

analysis of the balance sheet. Still, unrealized holding gains and losses on available-for-sale securities are reported in comprehensive income.

- **Inconsistent definition of equity securities:** There is concern the definition of equity securities is arbitrary and inconsistent. For instance, convertible bonds are excluded from equity securities. Yet convertible bonds often derive all or most of their value from the conversion feature and are more akin to equity securities than debt. This means an analyst should question the exclusion of convertible securities from equity. Redeemable preferred stocks also are excluded from equity securities and, accordingly, our analysis must review their characteristics to validate this classification.
- **Classification based on intent:** Classification of (and accounting for) investment securities depends on management intent, which refers to management's objectives regarding disposition of securities. This intent rule can result in identical debt securities being separately classified into one or any combination of all three classes of trading, held-to-maturity, and available-for-sale securities. This creates ambiguities in how changes in market values of securities are accounted for. An analyst should assess the credibility of management intent by reviewing "premature" sale of held-to-maturity securities. If premature sales occur, they undermine management's credibility. Also, there is some concern that the rules for determining whether companies report changes in market values in income or not depends on securities classification. While companies presumably record transfers of marketable securities from one category to another at market value, the accounting still permits some leeway. Further, companies are *not* required to disclose the classification of specific investment securities on the balance sheet. Analysis must examine notes to make this determination. For both available-for-sale and held-to-maturity securities, companies are encouraged to report aggregate fair value and unrealized holding gains and losses. Moreover, for analysis of the income statement effects of marketable securities, we must look at required disclosures on sales, gains and losses from transfers, and unrealized holding gains and losses.

CONVERTIBLES
Evidence shows that convertible bonds earn about 80% of the returns of diversified stock funds but with only 65% of the price volatility.

Analysis Research

DO FAIR VALUE DISCLOSURES EXPLAIN STOCK PRICES AND RETURNS?

Researchers have investigated whether fair value disclosures of investment securities are helpful in explaining variation in stock prices and/or stock returns. The evidence suggests that fair value disclosures do provide useful information beyond book values in explaining stock prices. This is especially apparent with financial institutions. Research also suggests that disclosures for unrealized gains and losses of marketable investment securities provide information beyond net income in explaining stock prices and stock returns.

DERIVATIVE SECURITIES

Companies are exposed to different types of *market risks.* These risks arise because the profitability of business operations is sensitive to fluctuations in several areas such as commodity prices, foreign currency exchange rates, and interest rates. Market forces determine these factors. For example, a gold mining company can control the volume and, at least partially, the cost of gold it produces. However, its profitability depends on the spot price of gold, a price it can neither control nor reliably forecast–*commodity price risk.* As another example, a U.S. equipment manufacturer can contract to supply machinery to a foreign buyer in its local currency. If the dollar strengthens against the local currency before the buyer makes payment, the U.S. manufacturer loses–*foreign currency risk.* As still another example, a real estate financier can offer a fixed-rate mortgage to a homebuyer. If interest rates increase, the financier may find it difficult to fund the mortgage in a profitable manner–*interest rate risk.*

EARNINGS GUARANTEE
A New York company recently launched a radical insurance product that covers any operating earnings shortfall due to events beyond management's control. The least risky customer can pay as little as 5% of estimates to guard against a 20% fluctuation in earnings—the bigger the risk, the bigger the retention.

To lessen these market risks, companies enter into *hedging transactions,* or hedges for short. **Hedges** are contracts that seek to insulate companies from market risks. A hedge is similar in concept to an insurance policy, where the company enters into a contract that ensures a certain payoff regardless of market forces. A hedge is possible because different parties are affected in different ways by market risks. For example, while a gold mining company is concerned with a drop in gold prices, a jewelry maker is concerned with an increase in gold prices. This means a gold miner and a jewelry maker are potentially interested in a contract to sell (buy) gold at a future date for a fixed price. This is called a *forward contract,* and often is transacted in a commodities market.

Financial instruments such as futures, options, and swaps are commonly used as hedges. These financial instruments are called *derivative financial instruments,* or simply *derivatives.* A **derivative** is a financial instrument whose value is derived from the value of another asset, class of assets, or economic variable such as a stock, bond, commodity price, interest rate, or currency exchange rate. However, a derivative contracted as a hedge can expose companies to considerable risk. This is either because it is difficult to find a derivative that entirely hedges the risk exposure or because the parties to the derivative contract fail to understand the potential risks from the instrument. Companies also use derivatives to speculate. Counterparties that bear risk in a derivative contract are called *speculators.*

ANALYSIS EXCERPT

We have established strict counterparty credit guidelines and enter into transactions only with financial institutions of investment grade or better. We monitor counterparty exposures daily and any downgrade in credit rating receives immediate review. If a downgrade in the credit rating of a counterparty were to occur, we have provisions requiring collateral in the form of U.S. Government securities for substantially all our transactions.

—Coca-Cola Co.

Derivative use has exploded in the past decade. The value of derivative contracts is now in the multitrillion dollar range. This increased use of derivatives, along with their complexity and risk exposure, has led the FASB to place derivative accounting at the forefront of its agenda, yielding a number of rulings in quick succession. The SEC also has called for additional disclosures in annual reports relating to risk exposure from derivatives. The accounting and disclosure requirements for derivatives are prescribed under *SFAS 133.* This section defines and classifies derivatives, describes the accounting and disclosure requirements, and concludes with a discussion of the analysis of derivatives.

Defining a Derivative

A **futures contract** is an agreement between two or more parties to purchase or sell a certain commodity or financial asset at a future date (called *settlement date*) and at a definite price. Futures exist for most commodities and financial assets. It also is possible to buy a futures contract on indexes such as the S&P 500 stock index.

A **swap contract** is an arrangement between two or more parties to exchange future cash flows. It is common for hedging risks, especially interest rate and foreign currency risks. In its basic form, a swap hedges both balance sheet and cash flow exposures. To illustrate, let's consider an *interest-rate swap*. A company issues $200 million, 8%, 10-year notes to finance installment sales of its products. Since most installment agreements are short term with implicit interest based on prevailing interest rates, this company worries about the fixed 8% interest commitment to its note holders, especially if interest rates decline. A company can hedge this risk by retiring its notes and replacing them with a variable-rate loan. However, this can be costly and cumbersome. Instead, a company can enter into a swap, in this case a *fixed-for-floating interest-rate swap* (also called *fixed-to-variable*). That is, a company contacts a *swap dealer,* who is a financial intermediary. The swap dealer identifies a *counterparty* that wishes to substitute its variable interest-rate exposure with a fixed-rate exposure, and then arranges a deal whereby the two parties agree to exchange (or swap) their interest payments. This swap benefits both parties. The first company hedges its risk by matching its interest payments to its interest receipts from installment sales, and the counterparty hedges its variable interest-rate exposure by switching to fixed payments. A *foreign currency swap* is similar to an interest-rate swap, except its purpose is to hedge foreign currency risk rather than interest-rate risk. Both futures and swaps obligate all parties to execute the transaction.

An **option contract** gives a party the right–not the obligation–to execute a transaction. To illustrate, an option to purchase a security at a specific contract price at a future date is likely to be exercised only if the security price on that future date is higher than the contract price. An option also can be either a call or a put. A *call option* is a right to buy a security (or commodity) at a specific price on or before the settlement date. A *put option* is an option to sell a security (or commodity) at a specific price on or before the settlement date. An *American option* can be exercised before its settlement date, while a *European option* can be exercised only on its settlement date. However, both options can be traded in an options market before their settlement dates. Unlike a futures contract, an option contract allows a party to specify its downside risk–namely, the maximum loss from an option is limited to its purchase price.

CREDIT DEFAULT SWAPS

Banks use these derivatives to insure against losses on corporate loans or bonds. The market has grown nearly 50% in the past year, to $1.5 trillion in face value. Yet the risk does not disappear—it is absorbed by the sellers of protection such as insurance companies (and other banks).

An important derivative often not covered under *SFAS 133* is a **forward contract**. One example is the purchase or sale of inventory with forward contracts as a part of normal business operations, where a net settlement is not possible. This contract is not a derivative for accounting purposes. In addition, employee compensation agreements and insurance contracts are not classified as derivatives. However, to prevent financial engineering to circumvent accounting requirements, these exclusions do not apply when a contract or security in the nature of a derivative is *embedded* in the host contract. That is, when the contract ostensibly appears to be a normal contract but implicitly includes a derivative contract.

Accounting for Derivatives

Exhibit 4.7 shows the classification of derivatives for accounting purposes. All derivatives, regardless of their nature or purpose, are recorded at fair value on the balance sheet. This is an important requirement that increasingly affects balance sheets of companies, both because of the growing magnitude of derivatives and their volatile nature. However, unlike fair-value accounting for investment securities, where only assets and not corresponding liabilities are marked to market, the accounting for derivatives affects *both* sides of transactions (wherever applicable) by marking to market. This means if a derivative is an effective hedge, the effects of changes in fair values usually should cancel

Exhibit 4.7 ***Classification of Derivatives for Accounting***

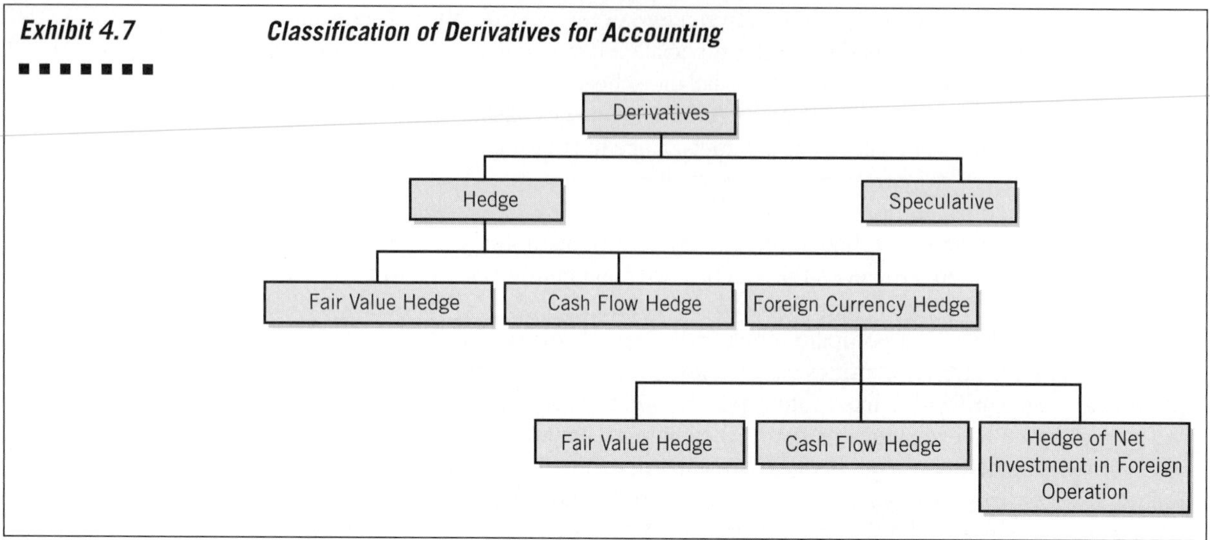

out and have a minimal effect on financial statements. Exhibit 4.8 summarizes the accounting for different derivatives.

Exhibit 4.8 ***Accounting for Derivatives***

Derivative	Balance Sheet	Income Statement
Speculative	Derivative recorded at fair value	Unrealized gains and losses included in net income
Fair value hedge	Both derivative and hedged asset and/or liability recorded at fair value	Unrealized gains and losses on both derivative and hedged asset and/or liability included in net income
Cash flow hedge	Derivative recorded at fair value (offset by accumulated comprehensive income)	Unrealized gains and losses on effective portion of derivative are recorded in other comprehensive income until settlement date, after which transferred to net income; unrealized gains and losses on the ineffective portion of derivative are included in net income
Foreign currency fair value hedge	Same as fair value hedge	Same as fair value hedge
Foreign currency cash value hedge	Same as cash flow hedge	Same as cash flow hedge
Foreign currency hedge of net investment in foreign operation	Derivative (and cumulative unrealized gain or loss) recorded at fair value (part of cumulative translation adjustment in accumulated comprehensive income)	Unrealized gains and losses reported in other comprehensive income as part of translation adjustment

Unrealized gains and losses on fair-value hedges (fixed-for-floating interest-rate swaps, futures contracts or options to hedge the fair value of a security, and the hedge of a fixed future commitment to sell a commodity at a specified price) as well as on the related asset or liability are recorded in income and affect current profitability. As long as the hedge is effective, this accounting does not affect the financial statements in a material manner as balance sheet and income statement effects are largely offsetting. Illustration 4.5 provides an example of fair-value hedge accounting.

ILLUSTRATION 4.5

Helix Co. owns 5,000 shares of Prima as part of its available-for-sale securities. On October 1, 2000, Helix purchases 5,000 March 2001 put options (50 contracts) of Prima at an exercise price of $50 (market price of Prima on October 1, 2000, is $58) for $5 per option. On December 31, 2000, Prima's stock trades at $53 and its put option is valued at $7 per option. The balance sheet and income statement effects on Helix for the fourth quarter of 2000 follow:

BALANCE SHEET

	10/1/00	12/31/00
Investment securities	$290,000	$265,000
Put option	25,000	35,000
Effect on total assets	$315,000	$300,000

INCOME STATEMENT

Unrealized loss on securities	$(25,000)
Unrealized gain on put option	10,000
Effect on net income	$(15,000)

The net effect in the fourth quarter of 2000 is a charge of $15,000 to net income, which is matched by a corresponding decrease in total asset value. Notice that this put option is not a perfect hedge.

Alternatively, unrealized gains and losses arising from cash flow hedges, floating-for-fixed interest-rate swaps, and hedges of forecasted sales of commodities are reported as part of other comprehensive income (as a component of stockholders' equity and not in current income) until the effective date of the transaction, after which they are transferred to income and are offset by the effect of the transaction itself. (Note that unrealized gains and losses on speculative hedges are reported immediately in income.) Illustration 4.6 provides an example of cash flow hedge accounting.

ILLUSTRATION 4.6

Ace Co. took a $5 million, five-year floating-interest-rate loan from a bank on January 1, 2000 (interest payable annually on December 31). On January 1, 2001, Ace swaps its future variable interest payments on this loan for fixed 8% interest payments. On December 31, 2001, Ace pays $400,000 (8% of $5 million) on the swap instrument–its interest payment on the original loan would have been $300,000 (6% of $5 million). This means the swap results in an excess annual interest payment of $100,000 for 2001. The present value of this expected excess interest payment from the swap as of December 31, 2001, is $267,300 (computed as $100,000 per year for three additional years discounted at 6% per annum). Ace's balance sheet effects as of December 31, 2000 and 2001, related to this swap are:

	12/31/00	12/31/01
Fair value of swap liability	$0	$267,300
Accumulated other comprehensive income	0	(267,300)
Effect on total liabilities and equity	$0	$ 0

Ace's income statement effects from the swap for year 2001 are:

Net income effect (interest expense)*	$(100,000)
Other comprehensive income effect (unrealized loss on marketable securities)†	(267,300)

**Realized loss for the year—excess interest payment for 2001.*

†Unrealized loss for the year—change in present value of future excess interest payments reflected in accumulated comprehensive income.

Disclosures for Derivatives

Companies are required to disclose qualitative and quantitative information about derivatives both in notes to financial statements and elsewhere (usually in the Management's Discussion and Analysis section). The purpose of these disclosures is to inform analysts about potential risks underlying derivative securities.

Qualitative Disclosures

Exhibit 4.9 provides a typical example of the note disclosure relating to derivative use by Campbell Soup Company. Disclosures generally outline the types of hedging activities conducted by the company and the accounting methods employed. Campbell Soup, for example, uses derivatives primarily to hedge interest-rate and foreign currency risks. All derivatives are recognized on the balance sheet at fair market value, although, as is typical, they are often immaterial and are not recognized as a separate line item. Also, changes in fair values of fair-value hedges (and the related asset or liability) are included in current income while fair-value changes for cash flow hedges are included in other comprehensive income until the forecasted transaction occurs.

Exhibit 4.9 ***Example Note Disclosure***

Note 18 Financial Instruments

The company utilizes certain derivative financial instruments to enhance its ability to manage risk, including interest rate, foreign currency and certain equity-linked employee compensation exposures which exist as part of ongoing business operations. Derivative instruments are entered into for periods consistent with related underlying exposures and do not constitute positions independent of those exposures. The company does not enter into contracts for speculative purposes, nor is it a party to any leveraged derivative instrument.

All derivatives are recognized on the balance sheet at fair value. On the date the derivative contract is entered into, the company designates the derivative as (1) a hedge of the fair value of a recognized asset or liability or of an unrecognized firm commitment (fair-value hedge), (2) a hedge of a forecasted transaction or of the variability of cash flows to be received or paid related to a recognized asset or liability (cash-flow hedge), (3) a foreign-currency fair-value or cash-flow hedge (foreign-currency hedge), or (4) a hedge of a net investment in a foreign operation. Some derivatives may also be considered natural hedging instruments (changes in fair value are recognized to act as economic offsets to changes in fair value of the underlying hedged item and do not qualify for hedge accounting under *SFAS No. 133*).

Changes in the fair value of a fair-value hedge, along with the loss or gain on the hedged asset or liability that is attributable to the hedged risk (including losses or gains on firm commitments), are recorded in current period earnings. Charges in the fair value of a cash-flow hedge are recorded in other comprehensive income, until earnings are affected by the variability of cash flows. Changes in the fair value of a foreign-currency hedge are recorded in either current-period earnings or other comprehensive income, depending on whether the hedge transaction is a fair-value hedge (e.g., a hedge of a firm commitment that is to be settled in foreign currency) or a cash-flow hedge (e.g., a hedge of a foreign-currency-denominated forecasted transaction). If, however, a derivative is used as a hedge of a net investment in a foreign operation, its changes in fair value, to the extent effective as a hedge, are recorded in the cumulative translation adjustments account within Shareowners' equity.

Quantitative Disclosures

Campbell Soup also provides quantitative information relating to its interest rate and foreign exchange hedging activities in the MD&A section of the annual report. These disclosures are provided in Exhibit 4.10.

Interest Rate Risk Exposure

Campbell Soup's hedging activities relating to interest rates employ swap agreements in order to maintain a desired relation between fixed- and floating-rate debt. The company indicates that it has entered into $250 million of fixed-to-variable swaps in order to increase the level of variable-rate debt. The debt maturity schedule reveals that $1.8 billion of variable-rate debt is maturing in 2002, leaving $1.72 billion of fixed-rate debt

Campbell Soup Market Risk Sensitivity Section—MD&A *Exhibit 4.10*

Market Risk Sensitivity
The principal market risks to which the company is exposed are changes in interest rates and foreign currency exchange rates. In addition, the company is exposed to equity price changes related to certain employee compensation obligations. The company manages its exposure to changes in interest rates by optimizing the use of variable-rate and fixed-rate debt and by utilizing interest rate swaps in order to maintain its variable-to-total debt ratio within targeted guidelines. International operations, which accounted for approximately 25% of 2001 net sales, are concentrated principally in Germany, France, the United Kingdom, Canada and Australia. The company manages its foreign currency exposures by borrowing in various foreign currencies and utilizing cross-currency swaps, forward contracts, and options. Swaps and forward contracts are entered into for periods consistent with related underlying exposures and do not constitute positions independent of those exposures. The company does not enter into contracts for speculative purposes and does not use leveraged instruments.

The company principally uses a combination of purchase orders and various short- and long-term supply arrangements in connection with the purchase of raw materials, including certain commodities and agricultural products. On occasion, the company may also enter into commodity futures contracts, as considered appropriate, to reduce the volatility of price fluctuations for commodities such as corn, soybean meal and cocoa. At July 29, 2001 and July 30, 2000, the notional values and unrealized gains or losses on commodity futures contracts held by the company were not material.

The information below summarizes the company's market risks associated with debt obligations and other significant financial instruments as of July 29, 2001. Fair values included herein have been determined based on quoted market prices. The information presented below should be read in conjunction with Notes 16 and 18 to the Consolidated Financial Statements.

The table below presents principal cash flows and related interest rates by fiscal year of maturity for debt obligations. Variable interest rates disclosed represent the weighted-average rates of the portfolio at the period end. Notional amounts and related interest rates of interest rate swaps are presented by fiscal year of maturity. For the swaps, variable rates are the average forward rates for the term of each contract.

EXPECTED FISCAL YEAR OF MATURITY

(US$ equivalents in millions)	2002	2003	2004	2005	2006	Thereafter	Total	Fair Value
Debt								
Fixed rate	$ 6	$300	$400[1]	$ 1	$ 1	$1,013	$1,721	$1,795
Weighted average interest rate	5.79%	6.15%	4.97%	9.0%	9.0%	7.23%	6.51%	
Variable rate	$1,800		$ 528				$2,328	$2,328
Weighted average interest rate	4.35%		4.68%				4.43%	
Interest Rate Swaps								
Fixed to variable						$ 250[2]	$ 250[2]	$ 5
Average pay rate						6.47%	6.47%	
Average receive rate						6.75%	6.75%	

[1] $100 million callable in 2002.
[2] Hedges 6.75% notes due 2011.

As of July 30, 2000, fixed-rate debt of approximaely $1.3 billion with an average interest rate of 6.47% and variable-rate debt of approximately $1.8 billion with an average rate of 6.57% were outstanding. There were no interest rate swaps outstanding at July 30, 2000.

The company is exposed to foreign currency exchange risk related to its international operations, including net investments in subsidiaries and subsidiary debt which is denominated in currencies other than the functional currency of those businesses. The following table summarizes the cross-currency swap outstanding as of July 29, 2001, which hedges such an exposure. The notional amount of the currency and the related weighted-average forward interest rate are presented in the Cross-Currency Swap table.

CROSS-CURRENCY SWAP

(US$ equivalents in millions)	Expiration	Interest Rate	Notional Value	Fair Value
Pay variable FrF		4.88%		
Receive variable US$	2003	4.21%	$110	$25

The cross-currency contracts outstanding at July 30, 2000 also included a pay fixed DM/received fixed US$ contract with a notional value of $107 million. This contract matured in 2001. The aggregate fair value of contracts was $22 million as of July 30, 2000.

The company is also exposed to foreign exchange risk as a result of transactions in currencies other than the functional currency of certain subsidiaries, including subsidiary debt. The company utilizes foreign currency forward purchase and sale contracts in order to hedge these exposures. The table below summarizes the foreign currency forward contracts outstanding and the related weighted-average contract exchange rates as of July 29, 2001.

FORWARD EXCHANGE CONTRACTS

(US$ equivalents in millions)	Contract Amount	Average Contractual Exchange Rate
Receive USD/Pay GBP	$424	1.41
Receive USD/Pay Euro	$292	0.86
Receive USD/Pay SEK	$ 90	10.63
Receive CAD/Pay USD	$ 35	0.65
Receive Euro/Pay GBP	$ 17	0.62
Receive USD/Pay JPY	$ 6	118
Receive AUD/Pay NZD	$ 5	0.83
Receive GBP/Pay AUD	$ 5	2.66

The company had an additional $6 million in a number of smaller contracts to purchase or sell various other currencies, such as the euro, Australian dollar, Japanese yen, and Swiss franc, as of July 29, 2001. The aggregate fair value of all contracts was $(7) million as of July 29, 2001. Total forward exchange contracts outstanding as of July 30, 2000 were $236 million with a fair value of $(3) million.

(76.5% of the total) and $528 million of variable-rate debt (23.5% of the total) after this maturity. The fixed-to-variable interest-rate swap lowers the fixed rate debt after 2002 to $1.465 ($1.721 − $0.006 − $0.250) and increases the floating-rate debt to $778 ($2.328 − $1.8 + $0.250), or 34.6% of the total.

Why would Campbell want to increase its percentage of floating-rate debt? Generally speaking, variable-rate debt carries a lower interest rate than fixed-rate debt. So, the company can lower its interest costs with this swap. It is also taking on interest-rate risk, however. This may not be as problematic as it may first appear. The amount of floating-rate debt the company can safely absorb depends on the covariance of EBITDA with interest rates. The higher this covariance, the greater percentage of debt the company can borrow on a floating-rate basis and not incur significant risk to reported profits should interest rates fluctuate in the future. Campbell Soup's target level of floating-rate debt referenced in the MD&A disclosure is determined on this basis.

Foreign Exchange Exposure

Campbell Soup reports that it has foreign exchange risk relating to investments in subsidiaries and subsidiary debt denominated in foreign currencies. The nature of these risks is discussed more fully in Chapter 5. In general, these risks relate to assets or liabilities denominated in foreign currencies that ultimately will be translated into or require U.S. currency for payment. Fluctuations in the value of the U.S. dollar relative to these currencies could, therefore, affect the ultimate value realized on those assets or paid on those liabilities.

Campbell Soup utilizes cross-currency swaps to hedge its risk on liabilities denominated in foreign currencies and indicates that it has outstanding $110 million of swaps on variable-rate loans denominated in foreign currencies. In addition, Campbell Soup has receivables and payables denominated in various currencies and has executed $874 million in forward contracts to hedge this risk.

Analysis of Derivatives

Objectives for Using Derivatives

The first aim in analysis of derivatives is to learn a company's objectives for use of derivatives. Most companies allegedly use derivatives for hedging. Still, some companies use derivatives for trading and/or speculative purposes. Sometimes, these trading or speculative activities arise as part of risk-management services offered by the company. For example, the Williams Companies' structured risk division offers price-risk management services for energy-related commodities such as natural gas and crude oil with a variety of financial instruments. Also, some managers use derivatives to speculate about movements in underlying market variables.

Identifying a company's objectives for use of derivatives is important because risk associated with derivatives is much higher for speculation than for hedging. In the case of hedging, risk does not arise through strategic choice. Instead it arises from problems with the hedging instrument, either because the hedge is imperfect or because of unforeseen events. In the case of speculation, a company is making a strategic choice to bear the risk of market movements. Some companies take on such risk because they are in a position to diversify the risk (in a manner similar to that of an insurance company). More often, managers speculate because of "informed hunches" about market movements. We must realize that many companies (implicitly) speculate even when they suggest derivatives are used for hedging. One reason for this is that when a company hedges specific exposures it does not always hedge overall company risk (see discussion below).

Risk Exposure and Effectiveness of Hedging Strategies

Once an analyst concludes a company is using derivatives for hedging, the analyst must evaluate the underlying risks for a company, the company's risk management strategy, its hedging activities, and the effectiveness of its hedging operations. Unfortunately, disclosures currently mandated under *SFAS 133* do not always provide meaningful information to conduct a thorough analysis. For example, Campbell Soup uses fixed-to-variable swaps to achieve a targeted percentage of variable-rate debt and takes on interest-rate risk in the process. The company does not, however, provide information to describe the method by which it arrives at this targeted percentage, nor does it describe the level of interest-rate risk that it is undertaking in the process. Likewise, the company does not provide information on the degree of foreign exchange exposure and the extent to which this has been mitigated by the use of cross-currency swaps and forward contracts.

SFAS 133 was principally designed to provide readers with current values of derivative instruments and the effect of changes in these values on reported profitability. Oftentimes, however, the fair market values are immaterial and the notional amounts do not provide information necessary to evaluate the effectiveness of the company's hedging activities. Companies are not required to quantify, for example, the extent to which exposures have been mitigated via hedging activities which would, if disclosed, provide investors and creditors with a greater understanding of the effectiveness of the hedging strategy.

Transaction-Specific versus Companywide Risk Exposure

Companies hedge specific exposures to transactions, commitments, assets, and/or liabilities. While hedging specific exposures usually reduces overall risk exposure of the company to an underlying economic variable, companies rarely use derivatives with an aim to hedge overall companywide risk exposure. Moreover, accounting rules disallow hedge accounting unless the hedge is specifically linked to an identifiable asset, liability, transaction, or commitment. This raises a broader question: What is the ultimate purpose of hedging? If the purpose of hedging is to reduce overall business risk by reducing the sensitivity of a company's cash flows (or net asset values) to a specific risk factor, then does hedging individual risk exposures achieve this? It probably does, but not necessarily. To see this, Illustration 4.7 shows how hedging a specific risk exposure *increases* a company's overall exposure to this risk.

FUTURE HEDGES?
Honeywell is bundling much of its foreign-exchange exposure with other risks under a blanket insurance policy with one deductible arranged by AIG—it may expand this to include interest-rate hedges, weather, and commodity prices.

ILLUSTRATION 4.7

Dynamics Co. takes government contracts on a cost plus basis. This means Dynamics is allowed to add a profit margin equal to a fixed percentage of its cost. A major allowable element of its cost is interest. Dynamics finances its operations largely with variable interest rate loans. In a move to reduce volatility of its interest payments, Dynamics enters into a floating-for-fixed interest-rate swap. What is the impact of this hedge on Dynamics' overall cash flow volatility? To help answer this, recall that Dynamics' profit margin is a fixed percentage of cost, and that cost includes interest. This implies any increase in interest is automatically hedged through the cost-plus-basis contract, and that its profit margin is *positively* related to interest. Consequently, if Dynamics hedged its variable interest with a variable-for-fixed interest-rate swap, then its cash flow risk exposures to changes in interest rates *increase*.

The relevant analysis question is whether rational managers enter into derivative contracts that increase overall companywide risk. In some cases the answer is yes. Such actions can arise because of the size and complexity of modern businesses and the difficulty of achieving *goal congruence* across different divisions of a company. For example, the treasury department of a company might be responsible for controlling financing cash flows and then enter into interest-rate swaps to reduce volatility of interest payments even though these interest payments could be negatively correlated with the company's operating cash flows. Similarly, the American and European divisions of a

SNOW SHIELD
Toro Co. recently entered into a $400,000 insurance policy to cover up to $9.5 million in refunds for a snowfall-related promotion. The cost of this policy is based on projected sales and snowfall.

company might hedge currency risk exposures with conflicting aims because each division is attempting to manage its specific risk exposure without considering overall companywide risk. An analyst must evaluate overall companywide effects of derivatives and be aware that hedging specific risk exposures does not necessarily ensure hedging of companywide risk.

Inclusion in Operating or Nonoperating Income

GLOBAL
British Aerospace PLC recently bought a $70 million policy to guarantee $3.7 billion in revenue from aircraft leasing until the end of 2013—taking a volatile business off its books.

Another analysis issue is whether to view unrealized (and realized) gains and losses on derivative instruments as part of operating or nonoperating income. To the extent derivatives are hedging instruments, then unrealized and realized gains and losses should not be included in operating income. Also, the fair value of such derivatives should be excluded from operating assets. This classification is clear for derivative instruments that hedge interest-rate movements since the underlying exposure (usually interest expense or interest income) is itself a nonoperating item. For hedging of other types of risks, such as foreign currency and commodity price risks, classification is less clear. That is, gains and losses (and fair values) from derivatives are nonoperating when: (1) hedging activities are not a central part of a company's operations and (2) including effects of hedging in operating income conceals the underlying volatility in operating income or cash flows. However, when a company offers risk management services as a central part of its operations (as many financial institutions do), we must view all speculative gains and losses (and fair values) as part of operating income (and operating assets or liabilities).

Analysis Research

DO DERIVATIVES REDUCE RISK?

Researchers have investigated managerial motivations for using derivatives, along with the impacts of derivative use, for company risk. While there is mixed evidence about whether derivatives are used for hedging or speculative purposes, the preponderance of evidence suggests that managers use derivatives to hedge overall companywide risk. Companies that invest in derivatives reveal a marked decline in risk as reflected in reduced stock returns' volatility. The reduction in risk exposure to the underlying risk type (such as interest-rate exposure and foreign currency exposure) is even more striking. Overall, evidence shows that, on average, managers use derivatives for hedging specific risk exposures that ultimately reduce overall companywide risk.

INTRODUCTION TO LONG-LIVED ASSETS

GLOBAL HEDGE
By locating plants in countries where it does business, so its costs are in the same currency as its revenues, IBM reduces the impact of currency swings without hedging.

To this point, we have explained the analysis of current assets along with that of investment and derivative securities. These latter assets share many characteristics with those of current assets including their ready convertibility to cash. The remainder of this chapter (and parts of Chapter 6) focuses on long-lived assets. Long-lived assets are resources that are used to generate operating revenues (or reduce operating costs) for more than one period. The most common type of long-lived asset is *tangible fixed assets* such as property, plant, and equipment. Long-lived assets also include *intangible assets* such as patents, trademarks, copyrights, goodwill, and *natural resources.* This section discusses conceptual issues pertaining to long-lived assets. We then separately discuss accounting and analysis issues relating to fixed assets (tangible assets and natural resources), intangible assets, and unrecorded assets.

Accounting for Long-Lived Assets

This section explains the concept of long-lived assets and the processes of capitalization, allocation, and impairment.

Concept of Long-Lived Assets

Assets are "probable future economic benefits obtained or controlled by a particular entity as a result of past transactions or events" (*SFAC 6*). Simply put, an asset carries an expected future benefit or, more precisely, an *unexpired cost.* Under this view, an asset is a creation of accrual accounting and the *matching principle*–that is, it is a cost not expensed in the current period because its expected benefits (against which its cost will later be matched) are in future periods. This implies accounting for long-lived assets is not a *valuation* concept. Instead, it is a *cost allocation* process over time. For this reason, reporting long-lived assets at fair (market) value makes little sense since asset value arises from use in operating activities, which may not relate to their fair value.

Capitalization, Allocation, and Impairment

The process of long-lived asset accounting involves three distinct activities: capitalization, allocation, and impairment. **Capitalization** is the process of deferring a cost that is incurred in the current period, but whose benefits are expected to extend to one or more future periods. It is capitalization that creates an asset account. **Allocation** is the process of periodically expensing a deferred cost (asset) to one or more future expected benefit periods. This allocation process is called *depreciation* for tangible assets, *amortization* for intangible assets, and *depletion* for natural resources. **Impairment** is the process of writing down the book value of the asset when its expected cash flows are no longer sufficient to recover the remaining cost reported on the balance sheet. This section discusses each of these three accounting activities.

GLOBAL
Many countries including Switzerland, Brazil, the Netherlands, and the United Kingdom permit upward and downward asset revaluations under certain conditions.

Capitalization. A long-lived asset is created through the process of capitalization. Capitalization is a deliberate decision to defer costs, usually occurring when an asset is acquired or a cost is incurred. The growth of both technology and service companies increasingly makes the capitalization decision more controversial and important. That is, more and more companies are moving from *hard assets,* such as plant and machinery, to *soft assets* such as software, R&D, and intellectual capital. Unlike hard assets, where the capitalization (and allocation) decision is relatively straightforward, soft assets create challenging issues regarding capitalization.

Accounting rules for capitalization are framed to meet the objectives of relevance and reliability. The reliability objective has meant that capitalization rules are conservative and, in some cases, inconsistent. Generally, for a cost to be capitalized, it must meet each of the following criteria:

- It must arise from a past transaction or event. This criterion yields inconsistent treatment of purchased versus internally generated intangible assets. For example, purchased goodwill is capitalized but internally generated goodwill (which is much larger in amount) is not.
- It must yield identifiable and reasonably probable future benefits. This criterion results in immediate expensing of most R&D expenditures, which is one of the most valuable assets for high-tech companies.
- It must allow the owner (restrictive) control over future benefits. This criterion (among others) precludes capitalizing technology or human capital where ownership is not legally enforceable.

BONUS AIDS
When management's compensation is tied to income, evidence indicates this can impact the decision to capitalize or expense costs.

An analyst must be cognizant of these criteria, and their emphasis on reliability, for the potential distortions they can have on financial statements. Analysts must make adjustments for any distortive effects, such as capitalizing R&D expense when appropriate.

One area that has been particularly troublesome for the accounting profession has been the capitalization of software development costs. GAAP differentiates between two types of costs: the cost of software developed for internal use and the cost of software that is developed for sale or lease. The cost of computer software developed for internal use should be capitalized and amortized over its expected useful life. An important factor bearing on the determination of software's useful life is expected obsolescence. Software that is developed for sale or lease to others is capitalized and amortized only after it has reached *technological feasibility*. Prior to that stage of development, the software is considered to be R&D and is expensed accordingly.

Allocation. Allocation is the periodic assignment of asset cost to expense over its expected benefit period. Allocation of costs is called **depreciation** when applied to tangible fixed assets, **amortization** when applied to intangible assets, and **depletion** when applied to natural resources. Each refers to cost allocation. We must remember that cost allocation is a process to match asset cost with its benefits–it is not a *valuation* process. Asset carrying value (capitalized value less cumulative cost allocation) need not reflect fair value.

Three factors determine the cost allocation amount: benefit period (often called useful life), salvage value, and allocation method. We discuss these factors shortly. However, each of these factors requires estimates–estimates that involve managerial discretion. Analysis must consider the effects of these estimates on financial statements, especially when estimates change.

Impairment. When the expected (undiscounted) cash flows are less than the asset's carrying amount (cost less accumulated depreciation), the asset is deemed to be impaired and is written down to its fair market value (the discounted amount of expected cash flows). The effect is to reduce the carrying amount of the asset on the balance sheet and to reduce profitability by a like amount. The fair value of the asset, then, becomes the new cost and is depreciated over its remaining useful life. It is not written up if expected cash flows subsequently improve. From our analysis perspective, two distortions arise from asset impairment:

1. Conservative biases distort long-lived asset valuation because assets are written down but not written up.
2. Large transitory effects from recognizing asset impairments distort net income while potentially increasing the usefulness of asset values in the balance sheet.

Note that asset impairment is still an allocation process, not a move toward valuation. That is, an asset impairment is recorded when managers' expectations of future benefits from the asset fall below carrying value. This yields an immediate write-off in a desire to better match future cost allocations with future benefits.

Capitalizing versus Expensing: Financial Statement and Ratio Effects

Capitalization is an important part of modern accounting. It affects both financial statements and their ratios. It also contributes to the superiority of earnings over cash flow as a measure of financial performance. This section examines the effects of capitalization (and subsequent allocation) versus immediate expensing for income measurement and ratio computation.

Effects of Capitalization on Income

Capitalization has two effects on income. First, it postpones recognition of costs. This means capitalization yields higher income in the acquisition period but lower income in subsequent periods as compared with expensing of costs. Second, capitalization yields a smoother income series. Why does immediate expensing yield a volatile income series? The answer is volatility arises because capital expenditures are often 'lumpy'–occurring in spurts rather than continually–while revenues from these expenditures are earned steadily over time. In contrast, allocating asset cost over benefit periods yields an accrual income number that is a more stable and meaningful measure of company performance.

PRO FORMA
The SEC now requires an explanation of how pro forma earnings numbers are computed and how they relate to earnings as computed under GAAP.

Effects of Capitalization for Return on Investment

Capitalization decreases volatility in income measures and, similarly, return on investment ratios. It affects both the numerator (income) and denominator (investment bases) of the return on investment ratios. In contrast, expensing asset costs yields a lower investment base and increases income volatility. This increased volatility in the numerator (income) is magnified by the smaller denominator (investment base), leading to more volatile and less useful return ratios. Expensing also introduces bias in income measures, as income is understated in the acquisition year and overstated in subsequent years.

Effects of Capitalization on Solvency Ratios

Under immediate expensing of asset costs, solvency ratios, such as debt to equity, reflect more poorly on a company than warranted. This occurs because the immediate expensing of costs understates equity for companies with productive assets.

Effects of Capitalization on Operating Cash Flows

When asset costs are immediately expensed, they are reported as operating cash outflows. In contrast, when asset costs are capitalized, they are reported as investing cash outflows. This means that immediate expensing of asset costs both overstates operating cash outflows and understates investing cash outflows in the acquisition year in comparison to capitalization of costs.

PLANT ASSETS AND NATURAL RESOURCES

Property, plant, and equipment (or plant assets) are noncurrent tangible assets used in the manufacturing, merchandising, or service processes to generate revenues and cash flows for *more than one period*. Accordingly, these assets have expected benefit periods (useful lives) extending over more than one period. These assets are intended for use in operating activities and are not acquired for sale in the ordinary course of business. Their value or service potential diminishes with use, and they are typically the largest of all operating assets. *Property* refers to the cost of real estate; *plant* refers to buildings and operating structures; and *equipment* refers to machinery used in operations. Property, plant, and equipment are also referred to as *productive assets, capital assets,* and *fixed assets.*

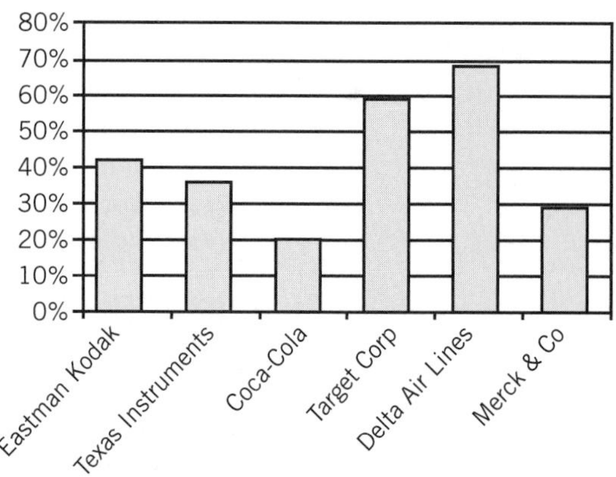

Valuing Plant Assets and Natural Resources

This section describes the valuation of plant assets and natural resources.

Valuing Property, Plant, and Equipment

The historical cost principle is applied when valuing property, plant, and equipment. Historical cost valuation implies a company initially records an asset at its fair value or the fair value of the asset(s) given up. This cost includes any expenses necessary to bring the asset to a usable or serviceable condition and location such as freight, installation, taxes, and set-up. All costs of acquisition and preparation are capitalized in the asset's account balance. Justification for historical cost includes:

- **Conservatism**–in not anticipating subsequent replacement costs.
- **Accountability**–in dollar amounts for management.
- **Objectivity**–in cost determination.

Historical cost valuation of plant assets, if consistently applied, usually does not yield serious distortions. However, this is not the case when determining a benefit period and a depreciation schedule, which are important to our analysis and are considered in Chapter 6. This section considers some special concerns that arise when valuing assets.

Valuing Natural Resources

Natural resources, also called **wasting assets,** are rights to extract or consume natural resources. Examples are purchase rights to minerals, timber, natural gas, and petroleum. Natural resources possess two important characteristics: (1) removal or consumption of the asset and (2) replacement of the asset only by natural progression. Cutting and replanting can replenish timberland. Yet, most natural resources once exhausted cannot be replenished (oil, coal, iron ore, and sulfur). Companies report natural resources at historical cost plus costs of discovery, exploration, and development. Also, there often are substantial costs subsequent to discovery of natural resources that usually are not given immediate recognition. Instead, these costs are expensed only when the resource is later removed, consumed, or sold. Companies typically allocate costs of natural resources over the total units of estimated reserves available. This allocation process is called *depletion* and is discussed in Chapter 6.

Companies Employing Various Depreciation Methods

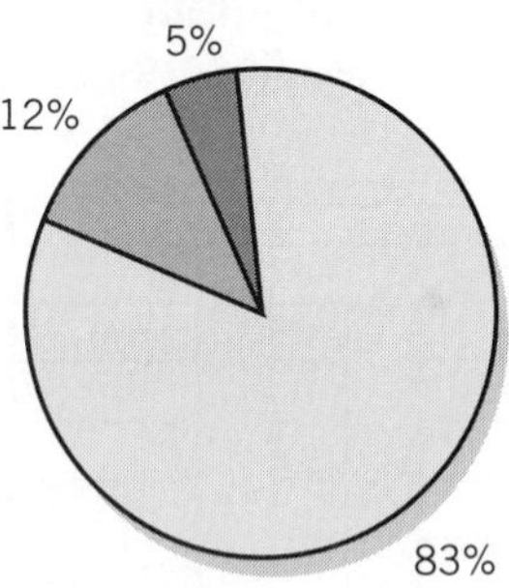

Source: Accounting Trends and Techniques.

Depreciation

A basic principle of income determination is that income benefiting from use of long-lived assets must bear a proportionate share of their costs. Depreciation is the allocation of the costs of property, plant, and equipment over their useful lives. If operations are unprofitable, depreciation becomes an unrecovered cost, that is, it adds to the loss. This is as true for depreciation as it is for all costs not recovered due to inadequate revenues. Also, depreciation does *not* provide funds for replacement of an asset. Funding is achieved through financing activities. There is little dispute about the principles of depreciation accounting. Still, depreciation is an expense subject to some confusion among analysts. This confusion stems from the methods and assumptions used to allocate asset costs to operations.

Rate of Depreciation

The rate of depreciation depends on two factors: useful life and allocation method.

Useful Life. The useful lives of assets vary greatly. Assumptions regarding useful lives of assets are based on economic conditions, engineering studies, experience, and information about an asset's physical and productive properties. Physical deterioration is an important factor limiting useful life, and nearly all assets are subject to it.[2] The frequency and quality of maintenance bear on physical deterioration. Maintenance can extend useful life but cannot prolong it indefinitely. Another limiting factor is obsolescence, which impacts useful life through technological developments, consumption patterns, and economic forces. Ordinary obsolescence occurs when technological developments make an asset inefficient or uneconomical before its physical life is complete. Extraordinary obsolescence occurs when revolutionary changes occur or radical shifts in demand ensue. High-tech equipment is continually subject to rapid obsolescence. The integrity of depreciation, and that of income determination, depends on reasonably accurate estimates and timely revisions of useful lives. These estimates and revisions are ideally not influenced by management's incentives regarding timing of income recognition.

Allocation Method. Once the useful life of an asset is determined, periodic depreciation expense depends on the allocation method. Depreciation varies significantly depending on the method chosen. We consider the two most common classes of methods: straight-line and accelerated.

- **Straight-line.** The straight-line method of depreciation allocates the cost of an asset to its useful life on the basis of equal periodic charges. Exhibit 4.11 illustrates depreciation of an asset costing \$110,000, with a useful life of 10 years and a salvage value of \$10,000 (salvage value is the amount for which the asset is expected to be sold at the end of its useful life). Each of the 10 years is charged with one-tenth of the asset's cost less the salvage value–computed as (\$110,000 − \$10,000)/10 years.

Straight-Line Depreciation ***Exhibit 4.11***

End of Year	Depreciation	Accumulated Depreciation	Asset Book Value
			\$110,000
1	\$10,000	\$ 10,000	100,000
2	10,000	20,000	90,000
⋮	⋮	⋮	⋮
9	10,000	90,000	20,000
10	10,000	100,000	10,000

The rationale for straight-line depreciation is the assumption that physical deterioration occurs uniformly over time. This assumption is likely more valid for fixed structures such as buildings than for machinery where utilization is a more important factor. The other determinant of depreciation, obsolescence, is not necessarily uniformly applicable over time. Yet in the absence of information on probable rates of depreciation, the straight-line method has the advantage of simplicity. This attribute, perhaps more than any other, accounts for its popularity.

Our analysis must be aware of conceptual flaws with straight-line depreciation. Straight-line depreciation implicitly assumes that depreciation in early years is identical to that in later years when the asset is likely less efficient and requires increased maintenance. Another flaw with straight-line depreciation, and one of special interest for

[2] The general exception is land, which is not subject to depreciation. Yet, even land, which has an indefinite life span, is not resistant to valuation losses. Such losses on land are not provided for by depreciation but are instead recognized as and when it occurs via asset impairments.

analysis, is the resulting distortion in rate of return. Namely, straight-line depreciation yields an increasing bias in the asset's rate of return pattern over time. To illustrate, assume the asset in Exhibit 4.11 yields a constant income of $20,000 per year before depreciation. Straight-line depreciation yields an increasing bias in the asset's rate of return as shown here:

End of Year	Income before Depreciation	Depreciation	Net Income	Beginning Year Book Value	Return on Book Value
1	$20,000	$10,000	$10,000	$110,000	9.1%
2	20,000	10,000	10,000	100,000	10.0
3	20,000	10,000	10,000	90,000	11.1
⋮	⋮	⋮	⋮	⋮	⋮
10	20,000	10,000	10,000	10,000	100.0

While increasing maintenance costs can decrease income before depreciation, they do not negate the overall effect of an increasing return over time. Certainly, an increasing return on an aging asset is not reflective of most businesses.

MACRS
U.S. tax rules use a Modified Accelerated Cost Recovery System (MACRS) for asset depreciation. MACRS assigns assets to classes where depreciable life and rate are defined.

- **Accelerated.** Accelerated methods of depreciation allocate the cost of an asset to its useful life in a decreasing manner. Use of these methods is encouraged by their acceptance in the Internal Revenue Code. Their appeal for tax purposes is the acceleration of cost allocation and the subsequent deferral of taxable income. The faster an asset is written off for tax purposes, the greater the tax deferral to future periods and the more funds immediately available for operations. The conceptual support for accelerated methods is the view that decreasing depreciation charges over time compensate for (1) increasing repair and maintenance costs, (2) decreasing revenues and operating efficiency, and (3) higher uncertainty of revenues in later years of aged assets (due to obsolescence).

GLOBAL
German accounting permits accelerated depreciation of up to three times the straight-line rate.

The two most common accelerated depreciation methods are declining-balance and sum-of-the-years'-digits. The *declining-balance method* applies a constant rate to the declining asset balance (carrying value). In practice, an approximation to the exact rate of declining-charge depreciation is to use a multiple (often two times) of the straight-line rate. For example, an asset with a 10-year useful life is depreciated at a double-declining-balance rate of 20% computed as $[2 \times (1/10)]$. The *sum-of-the-years'-digits method* applies a decreasing fraction to asset cost less salvage value. For example, an asset depreciated over a five-year period is written off by applying a fraction whose denominator is the sum of the five years' digits $(1 + 2 + 3 + 4 + 5 = 15)$–also computed as $n(n + 1)/2$ where n equals the useful life–and whose numerator is the remaining life from the beginning of the period. This yields a fraction of $5/15$ for the first year, $4/15$ for the second year, progressing to $1/15$ in the fifth and final year.

Exhibit 4.12 illustrates these accelerated depreciation methods applied to an asset costing $110,000, with a salvage value of $10,000 and a useful life of 10 years. Since an asset is never depreciated below its salvage value, companies take care to ensure that declining-balance methods do not violate this. When depreciation expense using the declining-balance method falls below the straight-line rate, it is common practice to use the straight-line rate for the remaining periods.

GLOBAL
Qualifying Canadian real estate companies are permitted to use an "increasing charge" depreciation method—the opposite of accelerated depreciation.

- **Special.** Special methods of depreciation are found in certain industries like steel and heavy machinery. The most common of these methods link depreciation charges to *activity* or intensity of asset use. For example, if a machine has a useful life of 10,000 running hours, the depreciation charge varies with hours of running time rather than the period of time. It is important when using *activity methods* (also called unit-of-production methods) that the estimate of useful life be periodically reviewed to remain valid under changing conditions. Bethlehem Steel reports its use of an activity method as follows:

ANALYSIS EXCERPT

Steel and most raw materials producing assets are depreciated on a straight-line basis adjusted by an activity factor. This factor is based on the ratio of production and shipments for the current year to the average production and shipments for the five preceding years at each operating location. Annual depreciation after adjustment for this activity factor is not less than 75% nor more than 125% of straight-line depreciation. The costs of blast furnace linings are depreciated on a unit-of-production basis.

Accelerated Depreciation

Exhibit 4.12

	DEPRECIATION		CUMULATIVE DEPRECIATION	
End of Year	Double-Declining	Sum-of-the Years'-Digits	Double-Declining	Sum-of-the Years'-Digits
1	$22,000	$18,182	$ 22,000	$ 18,182
2	17,600	16,364	39,600	34,546
3	14,080	14,545	53,680	49,091
4	11,264	12,727	64,944	61,818
5	9,011	10,909	73,955	72,727
6	7,209	9,091	81,164	81,818
7	5,767	7,273	86,931	89,091
8	4,614	5,455	91,545	94,546
9	4,228*	3,636	95,773	98,182
10	4,228*	1,818	100,000	100,000

*Reverts to straight-line.

Depletion

Depletion is the allocation of the cost of natural resources on the basis of rate of extraction or production. The difference between depreciation and depletion is that depreciation usually is an allocation of the cost of a productive asset over time, while depletion is an allocation of cost based on unit exploitation of natural resources like coal, oil, minerals, or timber. Depletion depends on production–no production yields no depletion. To illustrate, if an ore deposit costs $5 million and contains an estimated 10 million recoverable tons, the depletion rate per ton of ore mined is $0.50. Production and sale of 100,000 tons yields a depletion charge of $50,000 and a net balance in the asset account at year-end of $4.95 million. Our analysis must be aware that, like depreciation, depletion can produce complications. One is reliability, or lack thereof, of the estimate of recoverable resources. Companies must periodically review this estimate to ensure it reflects all information. Another is the definition of cost. For example, companies must assess the necessity of costs for resources under development. Still another is the composition of the asset. In the case of oil fields, depletion could be based on individual wells or an entire field.

Analyzing Plant Assets and Natural Resources

Valuation of plant assets and natural resources emphasizes objectivity of historical cost, the conservatism principle, and accounting for the monies invested in these assets. There is no clear recognition of user needs in valuing these assets. Instead, preparers often argue that balance sheets do not purport to reflect market values. Unfortunately, historical costs are not especially relevant in assessing replacement values or in determining future need for operating assets. Also, they are not comparable across different companies' reports and are not particularly useful in measuring opportunity costs of disposal or in assessing alternative uses of funds. Further, in times of changing price levels, they represent a collection of expenditures reflecting different purchasing power.

Analysis Research

WRITE-DOWN OF ASSET VALUES

Asset write-downs are increasingly conspicuous due to their escalating number and frequency in recent years. Are these write-downs good or bad signals about current and future prospects of a company? What are the implications of these asset write-downs for financial analysis? Are write-downs relevant for security valuation? Do write-downs alter users' risk exposures? Analysis research is beginning to provide us insights into these questions.

Evidence shows that companies that previously recorded write-downs are more likely to report current and future write-downs. This result adds further complexity to our analysis and interpretation of earnings. Research also examines whether companies take advantage of the discretionary nature of asset write-downs to manage earnings toward a target figure. Evidence on this question shows management tends to time asset write-downs for a period when the company's financial performance is already low relative to competitors. While this evidence is consistent with companies loading additional charges against income in years when earnings are unfavorable (referred to as a *big bath*), it is also consistent with management taking an appropriate reduction in asset value due to decreasing earnings potential. Regardless, our analysis of a company's financial statements that include write-downs must consider their implications in light of current business conditions and company performance.

Yet, historical costs of plant assets and natural resources reflect (at some level) a company's capacity to produce goods and services. It is sometimes argued that the value of assets derives from their ability to earn a return and, consequently, the value rests with their impact on the income statement. While true in many ways, this argument is not the only means to evaluating an asset's value. Asset value also is tied to its productive capacity (balance sheet) and the skill of management. Indeed, one of management's primary tasks is to effectively and efficiently manage these operating assets.

Write-up of plant assets to market is not acceptable accounting. Yet, conservatism permits a write-down if a permanent impairment in value occurs. A write-down relieves future periods of charges related to operating activities. Amerada Hess Corp. reports the following asset write-down in its annual report:

ANALYSIS EXCERPT

The Corporation recorded a special charge to earnings of $536,692,000 ($432,742,000 after income taxes, or $5.12 per share). The special charge consists of a $146,768,000 write-down in the book value of certain ocean-going tankers and a $389,924,000 provision for marine transportation costs in excess of market rates.

GLOBAL
International accounting standards encourage use of the cost principle for plant assets. Yet, plant asset revaluation (downward and upward) is permitted provided it is consistently applied across periods.

While realities of business dictate numerous uncertainties, including accounting estimation errors, our analysis demands scrutiny of such special charges. Accounting rules for impairments of long-lived assets require companies to periodically review events or changes in circumstances for possible impairments. Nevertheless, companies can still defer recognition of impairments beyond the time when management first learns of them. In this case, subsequent write-downs can distort reported results. Under current rules, companies use a "recoverability test" to determine whether an impairment exists. That is, a company must estimate future net cash flows expected from the asset and its eventual disposition. If these expected net cash flows (undiscounted) are less than the asset's carrying amount, it is impaired. The impairment loss is measured as the excess of the asset's carrying value over fair value, where fair value is the market value or present value of expected future net cash flows.

A concern in our analysis of natural resources (as it is with other assets) is the increasing use of write-downs. Examples are Diamond Shamrock's $600 million write-down of its oil and gas properties and Standard Oil's $200 million write-down of its gas and oil reserves. Similarly, and less apparent for our analysis, is a change in the estimated benefit period that can act like a form of write-down that is extended over more than one period as shown here.

ANALYSIS EXCERPT

The Company reduced the estimated useful lives of its New Wales uranium plant assets because of the uncertainty whether sales contracts, covering most of the production, will be renewed when they expire . . . and whether the market price of uranium oxide will be favorable enough to warrant continued operation of the plant beyond that date . . . depreciation expense increased $4.3 million because of this change.

IMC Fertilizer Group

Asset valuation issues also arise with public utilities when operating assets are impaired due to reasons like cost overruns and inefficient operations. In assessing the value of operating assets after recent deregulation, AT&T recorded a $7.3 billion pretax write-down of network facilities and telephone equipment. Still, there is an increasing reluctance of regulatory bodies to allow recovery of such costs through utility rate increases.

Analyzing Depreciation and Depletion

Most companies use long-lived productive assets in their operating activities and, in these cases, depreciation is usually a major expense. Managers make decisions involving the depreciable base, useful life, and allocation method. These decisions can yield substantially different depreciation charges. Our analysis should include information on these factors both to effectively assess earnings and to compare analysis of companies' earnings.

One focus of analysis is on any revisions of useful lives of assets. While such revisions can produce more reliable allocations of costs, our analysis must approach any revisions with concern, because such revisions are sometimes used to shift or smooth income across periods. The following General Motors' revision had a major earnings impact:

ANALYSIS EXCERPT

The corporation revised the estimated service lives of its plants and equipment and special tools . . . These revisions, which were based on . . . studies of actual useful lives and periods of use, recognized current estimates of service lives of the assets and had the effect of reducing . . . depreciation and amortization charges by $1,236.6 million or $2.55 per share.

In this case, GM's "studies of actual useful lives" were less than precise since three years later GM took a $2.1 billion charge to cover expenses of closing several plants and for other plants not to be closed for several years. Further analysis suggests evidence of earnings management by a newly elected chairman who explained this as "a major element in GM's long-term strategic plan to improve the competitiveness and profitability of its North American operations." That is, by charging $2.1 billion of plant costs to current earnings that otherwise would be depreciated in future periods, GM reduces future expenses and increases future income.

The quality of information in annual reports regarding allocation methods varies widely and is often less complete than disclosures in SEC filings. More detailed information typically includes the method or methods of depreciation and the range of useful lives for various asset categories. However, even this information is of limited usefulness. It is difficult to infer much from allocation methods used without quantitative information on the extent of their use and the assets affected. Basic information on ranges of useful lives and allocation methods contributes little to our analysis as evidenced in the following disclosure from Homasote, which is typical:

ANALYSIS EXCERPT

Estimated useful lives and depreciation methods are as follows:

	Estimated Useful Lives	Predominant Methods in Use
Buildings and additions	10–50 years	Straight-line
Machinery and equipment	5–20 years	Sum-of-the-years'-digits
Office equipment	10 years	Sum-of-the-years'-digits
Automotive equipment	3–5 years	Declining-balance

There is usually no disclosure on the relation between depreciation rates and the size of the asset pool, nor between the rate used and the allocation method. While use of the straight-line method enables us to approximate future depreciation, accelerated methods make this approximation less reliable unless we can obtain additional information often not disclosed.

Another challenge for our analysis arises from differences in allocation methods used for financial reporting and for tax purposes. Three common possibilities are:

1. Use of straight-line for both financial reporting and tax purposes.
2. Use of straight-line for financial reporting and an accelerated method for tax. The favorable tax effect resulting from higher tax depreciation is offset in financial reports with interperiod tax allocation discussed in Chapter 6–the favorable tax effect derives from deferring tax payments, yielding cost-free use of funds.
3. Use of an accelerated method for both financial reporting and tax. This yields higher depreciation in early years, which can be extended over many years with an expanding company.

GLOBAL
Several countries require the depreciation method for financial reporting to match the method for tax reporting.

Disclosures about the impact of these differing possibilities are not always adequate. Adequate disclosures include information on depreciation charges under the alternative allocations. If a company discloses deferred taxes arising from accelerated depreciation for tax, our analysis can approximate the added depreciation due to acceleration by dividing the deferred tax amount by the current tax rate. We discuss how to use these expanded disclosures for the composition of deferred taxes in Chapter 6.

In spite of these limitations, our analysis should not ignore depreciation information, nor should it focus on income before depreciation. Note, depreciation expense derives from cash spent *in the past*–it does not require any current cash outlay. For this reason, a few analysts refer to income before depreciation as *cash flow.* This is an unfortunate oversimplification because it omits many factors constituting cash flow. It is, at best, a poor estimate since it includes only selected inflows without considering a company's commitment to outflows like plant replacement, investments, or dividends. Another misconception from this cash flow simplification is that depreciation is but a 'bookkeeping expense' and is different from expenses like labor or material and, thus, can be dismissed or accorded less importance than other expenses. Our analysis must not make this mistake. One reason for this misconception is the absence of any current cash outflow. Purchasing a machine with a five-year useful life is, in effect, a prepayment for five years of services. For example, take a machine and assume a worker operates it for eight hours a day. If we contract with this worker for services over a five-year period and pay for them in advance, we would allocate this pay over five years of work. At the end of the first year, one-fifth of the pay is expensed and the remaining four-fifths of pay is an asset for a claim on future services. The similarity between the labor contract and the machine is apparent. In Year 2 of the labor contract, there is no cash outlay, but there is no doubt about the reality of labor costs. Depreciation of machinery is no different.

Analyzing depreciation requires evaluation of its adequacy. For this purpose we use measures such as the ratio of depreciation to total assets or the ratio of depreciation to other size-related factors. In addition, there are several measures relating to plant asset age that are useful in comparing depreciation policies over time and across companies, including the following:

Average total life span = Gross plant and equipment assets/Current year depreciation expense.

Average age = Accumulated depreciation/Current year depreciation expense.

Average remaining life = Net plant and equipment assets/Current year depreciation expense.

These measures provide reasonable estimates for companies using straight-line depreciation but are less useful for companies using accelerated methods. Another measure often useful in our analysis is:

Average total life span = *Average age* + *Average remaining life*

Each of these measures can help us assess a company's depreciation policies and decisions over time. Average age of plant and equipment is useful in evaluating several factors including profit margins and future financing requirements. For example, capital-intensive companies with aged facilities often have profit margins not reflecting the higher costs of replacing aging assets. Similarly, the capital structures of these companies often do not reflect the financing necessary for asset replacement. Finally, when these analytical measures are used as bases of comparison across companies, care must be exercised since depreciation expense varies with the allocation method and assumptions of useful life and salvage value.

INTANGIBLE ASSETS

Intangible assets are rights, privileges, and benefits of ownership or control. Two common characteristics of intangibles are high uncertainty of future benefits and lack of physical existence. Examples of important types of intangibles are shown in Exhibit 4.13. Intangible assets often (1) are inseparable from a company or its segment, (2) have

GLOBAL
Japan permits recording costs of both externally purchased and internally developed patents as intangible assets.

Selected Categories of Intangible Assets — ***Exhibit 4.13***

- Goodwill
- Patents, copyrights, tradenames, and trademarks
- Leases, leaseholds, and leasehold improvements
- Exploration rights and natural resource development costs
- Special formulas, processes, technologies, and designs
- Licenses, franchises, memberships, and customer lists

indefinite benefit periods, and (3) experience large valuation changes based on competitive circumstances. Historical cost, including costs necessary to ready the asset for its intended use, is the valuation rule for *purchased* intangibles. Still, there is an important difference between accounting for tangible and intangible assets. That is, if a company uses materials and labor in constructing a tangible asset, it capitalizes these costs and depreciates them over the benefit period. In contrast, if a company spends monies advertising a product or training a sales force–creating *internally generated* intangibles–it cannot usually capitalize these costs even when benefits for future periods are likely. This accounting treatment is due to conservatism–presumably from increased uncertainty of realizing the benefits of intangibles such as advertising and training vis-à-vis the benefits of tangible assets such as buildings and equipment.

Intangibles as a Percentage of Total Assets

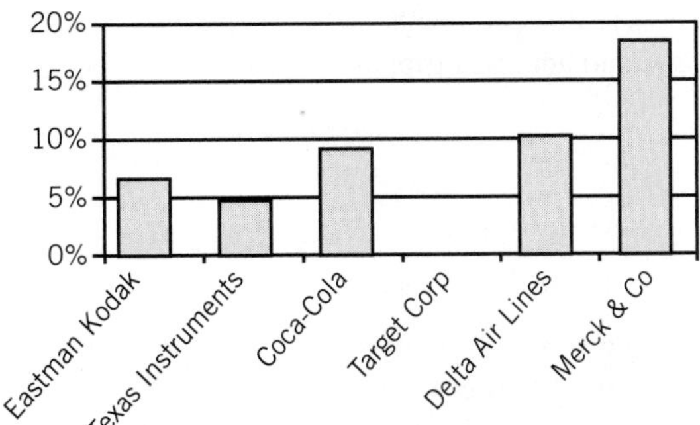

Accounting for Intangibles

Identifiable Intangibles

Identifiable intangibles are intangible assets that are separately identified and linked with specific rights or privileges having limited benefit periods. Candidates are patents, trademarks, copyrights, and franchises. Identifiable intangibles can be developed internally or acquired singly or in combination with a group of assets. Companies record them at cost and amortize them over their benefit periods. The writing off to expense the entire cost of identifiable intangibles at acquisition is prohibited.

Unidentifiable Intangibles

SUNDRY OR NOT?
IBM's recent balance sheet includes *Investments and Sundry Assets.* A note reports this includes more than $1 billion in goodwill.

Unidentifiable intangibles are assets that are either developed internally or purchased but are not identifiable and often possess indefinite benefit periods. Examples include R&D activities, advertising, and goodwill. Companies must expense as incurred the costs of developing, maintaining, and restoring unidentifiable intangibles other than goodwill.

When one company acquires another company or segment, it needs to allocate the amount paid to all identifiable net assets and liabilities according to their fair market values. Any excess remaining after this allocation is called goodwill. Goodwill can be a sizable asset, but it is recorded only upon purchase of another entity or segment (internally developed goodwill is not recorded on the balance sheet). Its makeup varies considerably–it can refer to an ability to attract and retain customers or to qualities inherent in business activities such as organization, efficiency, and effectiveness. Goodwill implies earning power. Stated differently, goodwill translates into future excess earnings, where this excess is the amount above normal earnings. Excess earnings are similar to *residual income (abnormal earnings)* described in Chapter 1.

Amortization of Intangibles

LEASEHOLD
A leasehold implies future benefits that the lessee controls because of prepayment. It meets the definition of an asset.

When costs are capitalized for identifiable and unidentifiable intangible assets, they must be subsequently amortized over the benefit periods for these assets. The length of a benefit period depends on the type of intangible; demand conditions; competitive circumstances; and any other legal, contractual, regulatory, or economic limitations. For example, patents are exclusive rights conveyed by governments to inventors for a specific period. Similarly, copyrights and trademarks convey exclusive rights for specific periods. Leaseholds and leasehold improvements are benefits of occupancy that are contractually set by the lease. In any case, accounting limits the benefit period for amortization of intangibles to a maximum of 40 years. Also, if an intangible materially declines in value (applying the recoverability test), it is written down. As discussed in Chapter 5, under current accounting standards goodwill is not amortized but is tested annually for impairment.

Analyzing Intangibles

Analysts often treat intangibles with suspicion when analyzing financial statements. Many analysts associate intangibles with riskiness. We encourage caution and understanding when evaluating intangibles. Intangibles often are one of the more valuable assets a company owns, and they can be seriously misvalued.

Analysis of goodwill reveals some interesting cases. Since goodwill is recorded only when acquired, most goodwill likely exists off the balance sheet. Yet, we know that goodwill is eventually reflected in superearnings. If superearnings are not evident, then goodwill, whether purchased or not, is of little or no value. To illustrate this point, consider the write-off of goodwill reported by Inter City Gas:

ANALYSIS EXCERPT

As a result of the losses incurred by KeepRite in the past two years, the Company has reassessed its investment in KeepRite Inc. As a result of this reassessment, it has been determined that the value of the underlying assets in KeepRite have been impaired by an amount of $4,697,000. Accordingly, the Company has written off goodwill of $4,697,000 as an extraordinary charge against income.

Our analysis of intangibles other than goodwill also must be alert to management's latitude in amortization. Since less amortization increases reported earnings, management might amortize intangibles over periods exceeding their benefit periods. We are probably confident in assuming any bias is in the direction of a lower rate of amortization. We can adjust these rates if armed with reliable information on intangibles' benefit periods.

In analyzing intangibles, we must be prepared to form our own estimates regarding their valuation. We must also remember that goodwill does not require amortization and that auditors have a difficult time with intangibles, especially goodwill. They particularly find it difficult to assess the continuing value of unamortized intangibles.

Our analysis must be alert to the composition, valuation, and disposition of goodwill. Goodwill is written off when the superior earning power justifying its existence disappears. Disposition, or write-off, of goodwill is frequently timed by management for a period when it has the least impact on the market. This is often a period of loss or reduced earnings. An example of such a write-off of goodwill explanation follows:

ANALYSIS EXCERPT

As a result of *Book Digest Magazine*'s continuing losses, management concluded that there had been a substantial reduction in the value of the magazine's net assets. Accordingly . . . Excess of Cost over Net Assets of Businesses Acquired was reduced by $9,400,000.

—Dow Jones & Company

ANALYSIS VIEWPOINT **. . . YOU ARE THE ENVIRONMENTALIST**

You are testifying at congressional hearings demanding substantially tougher pollution standards for paper mills. The industry's spokesperson insists tougher standards cannot be afforded and continually points to an asset to liability ratio of slightly above 1.0 as indicative of financial vulnerability. You counter by arguing the existence of undervalued and unrecorded intangible assets for this industry. The spokesperson insists any intangibles are worthless apart from the company, that financial statements are fairly presented and certified by an independent auditor, and that intangible assets are irrelevant to these hearings. How do you counter the spokesperson's arguments?

Answer–p. 247

Unrecorded Intangibles and Contingencies

Our discussion of assets is not complete without tackling intangible and contingent assets not recorded in a balance sheet. One important asset in this category is internally generated goodwill. In practice, expenditures toward creating goodwill are expensed when incurred. To the extent goodwill is created and is salable or generates superior earning power, a company's current income is understated due to expenses related to goodwill development. Similarly, its assets would fail to reflect this future earning power. Our analysis must recognize these cases and adjust assets and income accordingly.

Another important category of unrecorded assets relates to service or idea elements. Examples are television programs carried at amortized cost (or nothing) but continuing to yield millions of dollars in licensing fees (e.g., *M*A*S*H, Star Trek*) and current drugs taking years to develop but whose costs were written off many years earlier. Other examples are developed brands (trade names) like Coca-Cola, McDonald's, Nike, Kodak, and Pepsi. Exhibit 4.14 shows value estimates for some major brands.

GLOBAL
Some Australian and United Kingdom companies value brand names separately on their balance sheets.

Exhibit 4.14 ***Valuation of Brands***

	Value ($billions)	Percent of Firm Value		Value ($billions)	Percent of Firm Value
Starbucks	$ 1,757	19	Nokia	$35,035	34
Coca-Cola	69,945	61	Nike	7,589	71
Budweiser	10,838	32	Intel	34,655	17
Microsoft	65,068	17	Disney	32,591	54
Wrigley's	4,530	59	Kellogg's	7,005	61
Dell	8,269	7	Ford	30,092	66
Jack Daniels	1,583	41	Mercedes	21,728	48
IBM	52,752	27	Citibank	19,005	7
Barbie	2,037	41	Gucci	5,363	53
GE	42,396	9			

Source: Interbrand website

APPENDIX 4A INVESTMENT RETURN ANALYSIS

ADJUSTMENTS TO FINANCIAL STATEMENTS

What adjustments due to investment securities must we make when determining economic income and permanent income? Recall that economic income includes all changes to shareholder wealth. This means all components of investing income (interest, dividends, and realized and unrealized gains and losses) for all classes of investment securities must be included when determining economic income. Since comprehensive income includes unrealized gains and losses only from trading and available-for-sale securities, we must adjust comprehensive income to include unrealized gains and losses from held-to-maturity securities.[3] Unrealized gains and losses on held-to-maturity securities are disclosed in the notes.

Determining permanent income is more involved and is computed as follows:

$$\text{Permanent investment income} = \text{Expected ROI} \times (\text{Beginning fair value of investment} + \text{Ending fair value of investment})/2$$

The expected return on investment (ROI) for the portfolio of securities held by the company is computed as follows: Expected ROI = Required ROI + Historical deviation of the Realized ROI less the Required ROI. Required ROI is the weighted-average cost of capital for the company's investment portfolio given its risk and asset composition. The historical deviation component reflects the performance of the company's investments. It is important to consider a sufficiently long history to purge transitory effects from this component (we discuss the computation of realized ROI in the next section).

Next, what adjustments should be made to the balance sheet? Trading and available-for-sale securities are presently reported at fair value, while held-to-maturity securities are reported at cost. For analysis purposes, we want all investment securities (including held-to-maturity) reported at fair value in the balance sheet. Accordingly, we want to adjust held-to-maturity securities to fair value. Remember that offsetting adjustments must be made to equity to reflect any adjustments to the fair value.

EVALUATING INVESTMENT PERFORMANCE

Evaluating investment performance is an important analysis task. This task is especially important for companies where investment income constitutes a large portion of their income. For example, investment performance is one of the most important factors for success with banks, insurance companies, and other financial institutions. The performance of investment securities is evaluated using a return on investment (ROI) metric, which we loosely define as the "realized" investment income for the period divided by the average investment base:

$$\text{Realized ROI} = \frac{\text{Investment income}}{(\text{Beginning fair value of investment} + \text{Ending fair value of investment})/2}$$

The investment income, or numerator, is made up of three parts: Interest (and dividend) income + Realized gains and losses + Unrealized gains and losses. Note that ROI for investment securities is based on fair values, both for determining investment income (by including unrealized gains and losses) and for measuring average investment base (by using fair values of investments). This means evaluation of investment performance is not limited to analysis of only realized amounts.

[3] Some argue that including unrealized gains and losses from held-to-maturity securities in income is incorrect because the company does not intend to sell these securities till maturity and, thus, fluctuations in market values of those securities are of no consequence. This argument is erroneous. It is true that *future realizations* from a security that is not expected to be sold will remain constant. However, the *present value* of these future realizations will change with changes in expected interest rates, which is what is reflected in the securities' current market prices.

Exhibit 4A.1 ***Evaluating Investment Performance—Coca-Cola***

	Held to Maturity	Available for Sale	Total
Investment Income (1998)			
Interest and dividend income	$ 219	$ —	$ 219
Realized gains and losses	—	—	—
Unrealized gains and losses	—	(70)	(70)
Total before tax	$ 219	$ (70)	$ 149
Tax adjustment (33%)	(72)	23	(49)
Total after tax	$ 147	$ (47)	$ 100
Average Investment Base (1998)			
1997 Fair value	$1,591	$526	$2,117
1998 Fair value	1,431	422	1,853
Average	$1,511	$474	$1,985
Return on Investment (ROI)			
Before tax	14.5%	−14.8%	7.5%
After tax	9.7%	−9.9%	5.0%

We compute Coca-Cola's return on investment for 1998 in Exhibit 4A.1. First, we determine Coca-Cola's investment income as follows: interest and dividend income as reported in the income statement *plus* realized gains and losses (reported in its notes to be immaterial) *plus* unrealized gains and losses as reported in comprehensive income.[4] We also adjust for taxes using the company's effective tax rate of 33%. Next, the average investment base is computed from the beginning and ending fair values. Finally, Coca-Cola's ROI is computed. For its total securities it is 7.5% before tax and 5% after tax. The total ROI pretax return of 7.5% is made up of a pretax return of 14.5% (negative 14.8%) on its held-to-maturity (available-for-sale) securities. The loss on its available-for-sale securities is mainly due to its equity investments in bottling companies. Also, its pretax return of 14.5% on held-to-maturity securities appears especially high, particularly when most of these securities are of extremely short maturity. This might be explained by one or both of the following: (1) interest income as reported on the income statement may include interest income from other sources, and/or (2) the fair value of held-to-maturity securities on the current balance sheet may be much lower than the daily balance. The second possibility is more likely given seasonality in Coca-Cola's business, especially since securities in this class are predominantly short term.

How do we evaluate Coca-Cola's, or any company's, investment performance? One approach is to compare the realized ROI with the required ROI (weighted-average cost of capital) based on the composition and risk of the asset classes in the portfolio. However, this approach attributes transitory market movements to investment performance. Another approach is to compare the realized ROI against a benchmark ROI–where the benchmark ROI is the realized ROI for a portfolio with a similar risk profile for the period under analysis.

[4] Note that comprehensive income does not include unrealized gains and losses from held-to-maturity securities. Since Coca-Cola does not report any unrealized gains and losses on its held-to-maturity securities, we use the unrealized gains and losses reported in comprehensive income. If a company reports unrealized gains and losses from held-to-maturity securities, we need to include those when determining the return on investment. The unrealized gains and losses from held-to-maturity securities can be obtained by determining the difference between the ending and beginning unrealized gains and losses from held-to-maturity securities disclosed in the notes.

GUIDANCE ANSWERS TO ANALYSIS VIEWPOINTS

AUDITOR

Yes, as an auditor you are concerned about changes in estimates, especially when those changes exactly coincide with earlier predictions from management. An auditor must be certain the estimate of uncollectible accounts is reasonable in light of current industry, economic, and customer conditions.

BUYING AGENT

Yes, a buying agent should not necessarily compensate suppliers for potentially poor purchasing decisions. The supplier's 20% reported gross margin 'buries' the $2 million market adjustment in its cost of goods sold. The buyer should remove the market adjustment from cost of goods sold and place it among operating expenses in the income statement. Accordingly, the supplier's gross margin would be $2 million greater and, hence, the buyer has a legitimately stronger negotiating position for a lower price.

COMPETITOR

Toys 'R' Us is concerned about the threat of the Marvel/Toy Biz agreement for its future sales in toys and games. Financial statement disclosure of this agreement is useful not only for those interested in Marvel and Toy Biz, but also (and in some cases markedly more so) to competitors like Toys 'R' Us. Because of this agreement, Marvel character-based toys are one of the leading boys' action figure lines, and Toy Biz recently introduced Marvel Interactive CD-ROM comics. Toy Biz is now arguably one of the fastest-growing toys and games companies and lists its securities on the New York Stock Exchange. The motivation for Marvel's acquisition of 46% of the equity securities in Toy Biz is to retain some influence on the business activities of Toy Biz–especially as it relates to Marvel-related products. It is also an opportunity for Marvel to expand its operations using the existing expertise of Toy Biz and, thus, to reduce its investment risk.

ENVIRONMENTALIST

This is a challenging case. On one hand, the spokesperson's claim that intangibles are irrelevant is in error–intangible assets confer substantial economic benefits to companies and often make up a major part of assets. Moreover, the spokesperson's reliance on auditors to certify the fairness of financial statements according to accepted accounting principles is misguided. Since accounting principles do not permit capitalization of internally generated intangibles, and do not require adjustment of intangibles to market values, and do not value many intangibles (human resources, customer/buyer relationships), an auditor's certification is insufficient evidence on the worth of intangibles. On the other hand, the spokesperson is correct in questioning the value of intangibles apart from the company. Absent the sale of a company or a segment, the cash inflow from intangibles is indirect–from above-normal earnings levels. Also, most lending institutions do not accept intangibles as collateral in making credit decisions. In sum, resolution of these hearings must recognize the existence of intangibles, the sometimes high degree of uncertainty regarding value and duration of intangibles, the limited worth of intangibles absent liquidation of all or part of a company, and finally the need for a 'political' decision reflecting the needs of society.

QUESTIONS

4–1. Companies typically report compensating balances that are required under a loan agreement as unrestricted cash classified within current assets.
- *a.* For purposes of financial statement analysis, is this a useful classification? Explain.
- *b.* Describe how you would evaluate compensating balances.

4–2.
- *a.* Explain the concept of a company's operating cycle and its meaning.
- *b.* Discuss the significance of the operating cycle to classification of current versus noncurrent items in a balance sheet. Cite examples.
- *c.* Is the operating cycle concept useful in measuring the current debt-paying ability of a company and the liquidity of its working capital components?
- *d.* Describe the impact of the operating cycle concept for classification of current assets in the following industries: (1) tobacco, (2) liquor, and (3) retailing.

4–3. Discuss the gaps and inconsistencies in accounting for debt and equity securities that we must be aware of when analyzing financial statements.

4–4. *a.* Identify the main concerns in analysis of accounts receivable.
b. Describe information, other than that usually available in financial statements, that we should collect to assess the risk of noncollectibility of receivables.

4–5. *a.* What is meant by the factoring or securitization of receivables?
b. What does selling receivables with recourse mean? What does it mean to sell them without recourse?
c. How does selling receivables (particularly with recourse) potentially distort the balance sheet?

4–6. *a.* Discuss the consequences for each of the acceptable inventory methods in recording costs of inventories and in determination of income.
b. Comment on the variation in practice regarding the inclusion of costs in inventories. Give examples of at least two sources of such cost variations.

4–7. *a.* Describe the importance of the level of activity on the unit cost of goods produced by a manufacturer.
b. Allocation of overhead costs requires certain assumptions. Explain and illustrate cost allocations and their links to activity levels with an example.

4–8. Explain the major objective(s) of LIFO inventory accounting. Discuss the consequences of using LIFO in both measurement of income and the valuation of inventories for the analysis of financial statements.

4–9. Discuss current disclosures for inventory valuation methods and describe how these disclosures are useful in our analysis. Identify additional types of inventory disclosures that would be useful for analysis purposes.

4–10. Companies typically apply the lower-of-cost-or-market (LCM) method for inventory valuation.
a. Define *cost* as it applies to inventory valuation.
b. Define *market* as it applies to inventory valuation.
c. Discuss the rationale behind the LCM rule.
d. Identify arguments against the use of LCM.

4–11. Compare and contrast the effects of LIFO and FIFO inventory costing methods on earnings in an inflationary period.

4–12. Manufacturers report inventory in the form of raw materials, work-in-process, and finished goods. For each category, discuss how an increase might be viewed as a positive or a negative indicator of future performance depending on the circumstances that led to the inventory build up.

4–13. Describe accounting procedures governing valuation and presentation of noncurrent investments. Distinguish between accounting for investments in equity securities of an investee when holding (*a*) less than 20% of voting shares outstanding and (*b*) 20% or more of voting shares outstanding.

4–14. *a.* Evaluate the accounting for investments when holding between 20 and 50% of equity securities of an investee from the view of an analyst of financial statements.
b. When are losses in noncurrent security investments recognized? Evaluate the accounting governing recognition of these losses.

4–15. Describe weaknesses and inconsistencies in accounting for noncurrent security investments that are relevant for analysis purposes.

4–16. Many investors view noninfluential stock investments (stock purchased to earn return versus stock purchased to gain influence over another entity for strategic purposes) as a signal to sell a stock. Why might a noninfluential stock investment be perceived as a negative signal about the prospects of a company?

4–17. Distinguish between hedging and speculative activities with regard to derivatives.

4–18. Describe a futures contract.

4–19. Describe a swap contract. How are swaps typically used by companies?

4–20. Describe an option contract. When is an option likely to be exercised?

4–21. What is a hedge transaction?

4–22. When does a derivative security qualify for hedge accounting under *SFAS 133?*

4–23. Give an example of a cash flow hedge and an example of a fair value hedge.

4–24. Describe the accounting treatment for both fair value hedges and cash flow hedges.

4–25. Describe the accounting treatment for speculative derivatives.

4–26. Comment on the following: Depreciation accounting is imperfect for analysis purposes.

4–27. Analysts cannot unequivocally accept the depreciation amount. One must try to estimate the age and efficiency of plant assets. It is also useful to compare depreciation, current and accumulated, with gross plant assets, and to make comparisons with similar companies. While an analyst cannot adjust earnings for depreciation with precision, an analyst doesn't require precision. Comment on these statements.

4–28. Identify analytical tools useful in evaluating deprecation expense. Explain why they are useful.

4–29. Analysts must be alert to what aspects of goodwill valuation and amortization?

4–30. Explain when an expenditure should be capitalized versus when it should be expensed.

4–31. Distinguish between a "hard asset" and a "soft asset." Cite several examples.

4–32. The net income of companies that explore for natural resources can sometimes bear little relation to the asset amounts reported on the balance sheet for natural resources.
  a. Explain how the lack of a relation between income and natural resource assets can occur.
  b. Describe circumstances when a more economically sensible relation is likely to exist.

4–33. From the view of a user of financial statements, describe objections to using historical cost as the basis for valuing tangible assets.

4–34. *a.* Identify the basic accounting procedures governing valuation of intangible assets.
  b. Distinguish between accounting for internally developed and purchased goodwill (and intangibles).
  c. Discuss the importance of distinguishing between identifiable intangibles and unidentifiable intangibles.
  d. Explain the principles underlying amortization of intangible assets.

4–35. Describe analysis implications for goodwill in light of current accounting procedures.

4–36. Identify five types of deferred charges and describe the rationale of deferral for each.

4–37. *a.* Describe at least two assets not recorded on the balance sheet.
  b. Explain how an analyst evaluates unrecorded assets.

EXERCISES

EXERCISE 4–1
Analyzing Allowances for Uncollectible Receivables

On December 31, Year 1, Carme Company reports its accounts receivable from credit sales to customers. Carme Company uses the allowance method, based on credit sales, to estimate bad debts. Based on past experience, Carme fails to collect about 1% of its credit sales. Carme expects this pattern to continue.

Required:

a. Discuss the rationale for using an allowance method based on credit sales to estimate bad debts. Contrast this method with an allowance method based on the accounts receivable balance.

b. How should Carme report its allowance for bad debts account on its balance sheet at December 31, Year 1? Describe the alternatives, if any, for presentation of bad debt expense in Carme's Year 1 income statement.

c. Explain the analysis objectives when evaluating the reasonableness of Carme's allowance for bad debts.

(AICPA Adapted)

EXERCISE 4–2
Assessing Inventory Cost and Market Values

K2 Sports, a wholesaler that has been in business for two years, purchases its inventories from various suppliers. During these two years, each purchase has been at a lower price than the previous purchase. K2 uses the lower-of-(FIFO)cost-or-market method to value its inventories. The original cost of the inventories exceeds its replacement cost, but it is below the net realizable value (also, the net realizable value less a normal profit margin is lower than replacement cost for the inventories).

Required:

a. What criteria should be used in determining costs to include in inventory?

b. Why is the lower-of-cost-or-market rule used in valuing inventory?

c. At what amount should K2 report its inventories on the balance sheet? Explain the application of the lower-of-cost-or-market rule in this situation.

d. What would be the effect on ending inventories and net income for the second year had K2 used the lower-of-(average) cost-or-market inventory method instead of the lower-of-(FIFO)cost-or-market inventory method? Explain.

(AICPA Adapted)

EXERCISE 4–3
Explaining Inventory Measurement Methods

Cost for inventory purposes should be determined by the inventory cost flow method best reflecting periodic income.

Required:

a. Describe the inventory cost flow assumptions of (1) average-cost, (2) FIFO, and (3) LIFO.

b. Discuss management's usual reasons for using LIFO in an inflationary economy.

c. When there is evidence the value of inventory, through its disposal in the ordinary course of business, is less than cost, what is the accounting treatment? What concept justifies this treatment?

(AICPA Adapted)

EXERCISE 4–4
Usefulness of LIFO and FIFO Inventory Disclosures

Inventory and cost of goods sold figures prepared under the LIFO cost flow assumption versus the FIFO cost flow assumption can differ dramatically.

Required:

a. Would an analyst consider ending inventory asset value more useful if computed using LIFO or FIFO? Explain.

b. Would an analyst consider cost of goods sold more useful if computed using LIFO or FIFO? Explain.

c. Assume a company uses the LIFO cost flow assumption. Identify any FIFO-computed values that are useful for analysis purposes, and explain how they are determined using financial statement information.

EXERCISE 4–5
Restating Inventory from LIFO to FIFO

Campbell Soup Company

Refer to the financial statements of **Campbell Soup Company** in Appendix A.

Required:

a. Compute Year 10 cost of goods sold and gross profit under the FIFO method. (*Note:* At the end of Year 9, LIFO inventory is $816.0 million, and the excess of FIFO inventory over LIFO inventory is $88 million.)

b. Explain the potential usefulness of the LIFO to FIFO restatement in *a*.

CHECK
c. Year 11 FIFO Inventory, $796.3 mil.

c. Compute ending inventory under the FIFO method for both Years 10 and 11.

d. Explain why the FIFO inventory computation in *c* might be useful for analysis.

EXERCISE 4–6
LIFO and FIFO Financial Effects

During a period of rising inventory costs and stable output prices, describe how net income and total assets would differ depending upon whether LIFO or FIFO is applied. Explain how your answer would change if the company is experiencing declining inventory costs and stable output prices.

(CFA Adapted)

EXERCISE 4–7
Identifying Unrecorded Assets

A balance sheet, which is intended to present fairly the financial position of a company, frequently is criticized for not reflecting all assets under the control of a company.

Required:

Cite five examples of assets that are not presently included on the balance sheet. Discuss the implications of unrecorded assets for financial statement analysis.

(CFA Adapted)

EXERCISE 4–8
Expensing versus Capitalizing Costs

An analyst must be familiar with the determination of income. Income reported for a business entity depends on proper recognition of revenues and expenses. In certain cases, costs are recognized as expenses at the time of product sale; in other situations, guidelines are applied in capitalizing costs and recognizing them as expenses in future periods.

Required:

a. Under what circumstances is it appropriate to capitalize a cost as an asset instead of expensing it? Explain.

b. Certain expenses are assigned to specific accounting periods on the basis of systematic and rational allocation of asset cost. Explain the rationale for recognizing expenses on such a basis.

(AICPA Adapted)

EXERCISE 4–9
Motivation for Classification of Investment Securities

An important element in accounting for investment securities concerns the distinction between its noncurrent and current classification.

Required:

a. Why do most companies maintain an investment portfolio consisting of both current and noncurrent securities?

b. What factors should an analyst consider when evaluating whether investments in marketable equity securities are properly classified as current or noncurrent? How do these factors affect the accounting treatment for unrealized losses?

EXERCISE 4–10
Analysis of Microsoft Investments

Microsoft Corporation

Refer to Exhibit 4.6 to answer the following questions about **Microsoft Corporation** investments.

a. Microsoft reports unrealized gains and unrealized losses on securities totaling $2.042 billion and $1.126 billion, respectively. Accordingly, the investment cost basis is marked to market. What type of account is increased or decreased as a result (asset account, liability account, other gain account, other loss account, or equity account)?

b. If Microsoft investments were trading securities, what type of account would have been increased or decreased when the investment account is marked to market?

c. Given that Microsoft designates its securities portfolio as available-for-sale, what possibilities exist for the company to manage earnings using its investments?

EXERCISE 4–11
Investment Securities

A company can have passive interest (noninfluencial) investments, significant influential investments, or controlling interests. Passive interest investments can be trading, available-for-sale, or held-to-maturity securities.

Required:

a. Describe the valuation basis at which each of these types of investments is reported on the balance sheet.

b. If the investment type is reported at fair value, indicate where any value fluctuation is reported (net income or comprehensive income).

c. What is the rationale for reporting held-to-maturity securities at cost? Does this rationale make economic sense?

(CFA Adapted)

EXERCISE 4–12
Analytical Measures of Plant Assets

Quaker Oats Company

Refer to the financial statements of **Quaker Oats Company** in Appendix A.

Required:

a. Compute the following analytical measures applied to Quaker Oats for both Years 10 and 11:
   (1) Average total life span of plant and equipment.
   (2) Average age of plant and equipment.
   (3) Average remaining life of plant and equipment.

b. Discuss the importance of these ratios for analysis of Quaker Oats.

CHECK
a. (1) Year 11, 15.04 years

EXERCISE 4–13
Analytical Measures of Plant Assets

Refer to the financial statements of **Campbell Soup Company** in Appendix A.

Campbell Soup Company

Required:

a. Compute the following analytical measures applied to Campbell Soup for both Years 10 and 11:
(1) Average total life span of plant and equipment.
(2) Average age of plant and equipment.
(3) Average remaining life of plant and equipment.

b. Discuss the importance of these ratios for analysis of Campbell Soup.

CHECK
a. (3) Year 11, 7.23 years

EXERCISE 4–14
Identifying Assets

Which of the following items are classified as assets on a typical balance sheet?

a. Depreciation.
b. CEO salary.
c. Cash.
d. Deferred income taxes.
e. Installment receivable (collectible in 3 years).
f. Capital withdrawal (dividend).
g. Inventories.
h. Prepaid expenses.
i. Deferred charges.
j. Work-in-process inventory.
k. Depreciation expense.
l. Bad debts expense.
m. Loan to officers.
n. Loan from officers.
o. Fully trained sales force.
p. Common stock of a subsidiary.
q. Trade name purchased.
r. Internally developed goodwill.
s. Franchise agreements obtained at no cost.
t. Internally developed e-commerce system.

EXERCISE 4–15
Classifying and Accounting for Derivatives

Explain how the following transactions and events are classified under *SFAS 133* (covering derivatives and hedges) and describe their effects on financial statements:

a. A company enters into a long-term contract with a customer to supply 1,000 pieces of made-to-order equipment at a fixed price. There exists no ready market for this product. The company expects to deliver the contracted quantity.

b. An oil company sold forward 10,000 barrels of crude oil at a fixed price of $18 per barrel.

c. An oil refiner purchases forward 20,000 barrels of crude oil at a fixed price of $16 per barrel.

d. The oil refiner in *c* partially reverses the above forward purchase by selling forward 6,000 barrels of crude oil at $16 per barrel.

e. An investment company, fearing the stock market may plunge, purchases put options on its equity holdings.

f. A company discovers its cash flows highly depend on the U.S. GDP growth rate—the higher the growth rate, the higher its cash flows. To reduce its business risk, the company decides to purchase an option whose value is linked to the term structure of interest rates (note that an inverted term-structure of interest rates is a predictor of recession).

PROBLEMS

PROBLEM 4–1
Restating and Analyzing Inventory from LIFO to Average Cost

Refer to the financial statements of **Quaker Oats Company** in Appendix A.

Quaker Oats Company

Required:

a. Quaker Oats mainly uses the LIFO cost assumption in determining its cost of goods sold and inventory amounts. Compute both ending inventory and gross profit of Quaker Oats for the following years if average cost is used for all inventory items (see its note 1 and assume a 34% tax rate):
(1) For Year 11.
(2) For Year 10.

CHECK
Year 11 Gross Profit, $2,651.5 mil.

b. Compute the net income effect of using LIFO instead of average cost. Comment on this difference for analysis of Quaker's financial statements.

c. Give the restatements for adjusting the financial statements from LIFO to the average cost basis for Year 11. How do these restatements help for analysis purposes?

PROBLEM 4–2
Interpreting and Restating Inventory from FIFO to LIFO

Assume you are analyzing the financial statements of ABEX Chemicals. Your analysis raises concerns with certain accounting procedures that potentially distort its operating results.

Required:

a. Data for ABEX Corp. is reported in Case 11–8. Using the data in Exhibit I of that case, describe how ABEX's use of the FIFO method in accounting for its petrochemical inventories affects its division's operating margin for each of the following periods:
   (1) Years 5 through 7.
   (2) Years 7 through 9.

b. ABEX is considering adopting the LIFO method of accounting for its petrochemical inventories in either Year 10 or Year 11. Recommend an adoption date for LIFO and justify your choice.

(CFA Adapted)

CHECK
a. (2) FIFO increases margins

PROBLEM 4–3
Restating Inventory from LIFO to FIFO

BigBook.Com uses LIFO inventory accounting. Notes to BigBook.Com's Year 9 financial statements disclose the following (it has a marginal tax rate of 35%):

Inventories	Year 8	Year 9
Raw materials	$392,675	$369,725
Finished products	401,342	377,104
	$794,017	$746,829
Less LIFO reserve	(46,000)	(50,000)
	$748,017	$696,829

Required:

a. Determine the amount by which Year 9 retained earnings of BigBook.Com changes if FIFO is used.

b. Determine the amount by which Year 9 net income of BigBook.Com changes if FIFO is used for both Years 8 and 9.

c. Discuss the usefulness of LIFO to FIFO restatements in an analysis of BigBook.Com.

(AICPA Adapted)

CHECK
b. $2,600

PROBLEM 4–4
Analysis of Inventory and Related Adjustments

Lands' End

Excerpts from the annual report of **Lands' End** follow ($ in thousands):

	Jan. 29, 1999	Jan. 30, 1998
Inventory	$219,686	$241,154
Cost of sales	754,661	675,138
Net income	31,185	64,150
Tax rate	37%	37%

Note 1: If the first-in, first-out (FIFO) method of accounting for inventory had been used, inventory would have been approximately $26.9 million and $25.1 million higher than reported at January 29, 1999, and January 30, 1998, respectively.

Required:

CHECK
b. $32,319

a. What would ending inventory have been at January 29, 1999, and January 30, 1998, had FIFO been used?

b. What would net income for the year ended January 29, 1999, have been had FIFO been used?

c. Discuss the usefulness of LIFO to FIFO restatements for analysis purposes.

PROBLEM 4–5
T-Account Analysis of Plant Assets

Campbell Soup

Refer to the financial statements of **Campbell Soup** in Appendix A.

Required:

a. By means of T-account analysis, explain the changes in Campbell's Property, Plant, and Equipment account for Year 11. Provide as much detail as the disclosures enable you to provide. (*Hint:* Utilize information disclosed on the Form 10-K schedule attached at the end of its annual report in Appendix A.)

b. Explain the usefulness of this type of analysis.

PROBLEM 4–6
T-Account Analysis of Plant Assets

Quaker Oats

Refer to the financial statements of **Quaker Oats** in Appendix A.

Required:

a. By means of a T-account analysis, explain changes in Quaker's Property, Plant, and Equipment account for both Years 10 and 11. Provide as much detail as the disclosures enable you to provide.

b. Explain the usefulness of this analysis.

PROBLEM 4–7
Investment Disclosures

Munger.Com began operations on January 1, 2003. The company reports the following information about its investments at December 31, 2003:

Current assets ***($ in thousands)***	**Cost**	**Market**
Investments in marketable debt securities:		
Able Corp. bonds (held-to-maturity)	$ 330	$ 290
Bryan Co. bonds (available-for-sale)	800	825
Caltran, Inc. bonds (trading)	550	515
Investments in marketable equity securities:		
Available-for-sale	1,110	1,600
Trading	1,500	950

Required:

CHECK
Total of securities, $4,220

a. Show how each of these investments are reported on the Munger.Com balance sheet.

b. For assets that are marked to market, indicate where the unrealized value fluctuation is reported (in net income and/or in comprehensive income).

PROBLEM 4–8
Capitalizing versus Expensing of Costs

Trimax Solutions develops software to support e-commerce. Trimax incurs substantial computer software development costs as well as substantial research and development (R&D) costs related to other aspects of its product line. Under GAAP, if certain conditions are met, Trimax capitalizes software development costs but expenses the other R&D costs. The following information is taken from Trimax's annual reports ($ in thousands):

	1996	**1997**	**1998**	**1999**	**2000**	**2001**	**2002**	**2003**
R&D costs	$ 400	$ 491	$ 216	$ 212	$ 355	$ 419	$ 401	$ 455
Net income	312	367	388	206	55	81	167	179
Total assets (at year-end)	3,368	3,455	3,901	4,012	4,045	4,077	4,335	4,650
Equity (at year-end)	2,212	2,460	2,612	2,809	2,889	2,915	3,146	3,312
Capitalized software costs:								
Unamortized balance (at year-end)	20	31	27	22	31	42	43	36
Amortization expense	4	7	9	12	13	15	15	14

Required:

a. Compute the total expenditures for software development costs for each year.

b. R&D costs are expensed as incurred. Compare and contrast computer software development costs with the R&D costs and discuss the rationale for expensing R&D costs but capitalizing some software development costs.

c. Based on the information provided, when do successful research efforts appear to produce income for Trimax?

d. Discuss how income and equity are affected if Trimax invests more in software development versus R&D projects (focus your response on the accounting, and not economic, implications).

e. Compute net income, return on assets, and return on equity for year 2003 while separately assuming (1) Software development costs are expensed as incurred and (2) R&D costs are capitalized and amortized using straight line over the following four years.

f. Discuss how the two accounting alternatives in *e* would affect cash flow from operations for Trimax.

CHECK
a. Year 2003, $7

CHECK
e. (2) ROE, 6.6%

PROBLEM 4–9
Alternative Depreciation Methods

Sports Biz, a profitable company, built and equipped a $2,000,000 plant brought into operation early in Year 1. Earnings of the company (before depreciation on the new plant and before income taxes) is projected at: $1,500,000 in Year 1; $2,000,000 in Year 2; $2,500,000 in Year 3; $3,000,000 in Year 4; and $3,500,000 in Year 5. The company can use straight-line, double-declining-balance, or sum-of-the-years'-digits depreciation for the new plant. Assume the plant's useful life is 10 years (with no salvage value) and an income tax rate of 50%.

Required:

Compute the separate effect that *each* of these three methods of depreciation would have on:

a. Depreciation

b. Income taxes

c. Net income

d. Cash flow (assumed equal to net income before depreciation)

(CFA Adapted)

CHECK
Year 1 net income ($000s), SL: $650, DDB: $550, SYD: $568.2

PROBLEM 4–10
Analyzing Depreciation for Rates of Return

Assume that a machine costing $300,000 and having a useful life of five years (with no salvage value) generates a yearly income before depreciation and taxes of $100,000.

Required:

Compute the annual rate of return on this machine (using the beginning-of-year book value as the base) for each of the following depreciation methods (assume a 25% tax rate):

a. Straight-line

b. Sum-of-the-years' digits

CHECK
Year 2 return, SL: 12.5%, SYD: 7.5%

PROBLEM 4–11
Analyzing and Interpreting Marketable Equity Securities

Cited below are four unrelated cases involving marketable equity securities:

1. A noncurrent portfolio of available-for-sale equity securities with an aggregate market value in excess of cost; includes one particular security whose market value has declined to less than one-half of the original cost.
2. The balance sheet of a company does not classify assets and liabilities as current and noncurrent. The portfolio of available-for-sale equity securities includes securities normally considered current that have a net cost in excess of market value of $2,000. The remainder of the portfolio has a net market value in excess of cost of $5,000.
3. An available-for-sale marketable equity security, whose market value is currently less than cost, is classified as noncurrent but is to be reclassified as current.
4. A company's noncurrent portfolio of marketable equity securities consists of the common stock of one company. At the end of the prior year, the market value of the security was 50% of original cost, and this effect was properly reflected in a Valuation Adjustment account. However, at the end of the current year, the market value of the security had appreciated to twice the original cost. The security is still considered noncurrent at year-end.

Required:

For each of the cases, describe how the information provided affects the classification, carrying value, and income reported for that company's investment securities.

PROBLEM 4–12
Analyzing Investment Securities Transactions

The following data are taken from the December 31 annual report of Bailey Company:

($ in thousands)	2001	2002	2003
Sales	$50,000	$60,000	$70,000
Net income	2,000	2,200	2,500
Dividends paid	1,000	1,200	1,500

Bailey had 1,000,000 common shares outstanding during this entire period and there is no public market for Bailey Company shares. Also during this period, Simpson Corp. bought Bailey shares for cash, as follows:

January 1, 2001	10,000 shares at $10 per share
January 1, 2002	290,000 shares at $11 per share, increasing ownership to 300,000 shares
January 1, 2003	700,000 shares at $15 per share, resulting in 100% ownership of Bailey Company

Simpson assumed significant influence over Bailey's management in 2002. Ignore income tax effects and the opportunity costs of making investments in Bailey for the requirements below.

Required:

a. Compute the effects of these investments on Simpson's reported sales, net income, and cash flows for each of the years 2001 and 2002.

b. Compute the carrying (book) value of Simpson's investment in Bailey as of December 31, 2001, and December 31, 2002.

c. Identify the U.S. GAAP-based accounting method Simpson would use to account for its intercorporate investment in Bailey for 2003. Give two reasons this accounting method must/should be used.

(CFA Adapted)

CHECK
b. Book value, 12/31/2002, $3,600,000

PROBLEM 4–13
Property, Plant, and Equipment Accounting and Analysis

Among the crucial events in accounting for property, plant, and equipment are acquisition and disposition.

Required:

a. What expenditures should be capitalized when a company acquires equipment for cash?

b. Assume the market value of equipment acquired is not determinable by reference to a similar purchase for cash. Describe how the acquiring company should determine the capitalizable cost of equipment for each of the following separate cases when it is acquired in exchange for:
(1) Bonds having an established market price.
(2) Common stock not having an established market price.
(3) Dissimilar equipment having a determinable market value.

c. Describe the factors that determine whether expenditures toward property, plant, and equipment already in use should be capitalized.

d. Describe how to account for the gain or loss on sale of property, plant, and equipment for cash.

e. Discuss the important considerations in analyzing property, plant, and equipment.

PROBLEM 4–14
Capitalization, Depreciation, and Return on Investment

Mirage Resorts, Inc., recently completed construction of Bellagio Hotel and Casino in Las Vegas. Total cost of this project was approximately $1.6 billion. The strategy of the investors is to build a gambling environment for "high rollers." As a result, they paid a premium for property in the "high rent" district of the Las Vegas Strip and built a facility inspired by the drama and elegance of fine art. The investors are confident that if the facility attracts high volume and high stakes gaming, the net revenues will justify the $1.6 billion investment several times over. If the facility fails to attract high rollers, this investment will be a financial catastrophe. Mirage Resorts depreciates its fixed assets using the straight-line method over the estimated useful lives of the assets. Assume construction of Bellagio is completed and the facility is opened for business on January 1, 2001. Also assume annual net income before depreciation and taxes from Bellagio is $50 million, $70 million, and $75 million for 2001, 2002, and 2003, and that the tax rate is 25%.

Required:

Compute the return on assets for the Bellagio segment for years 2001, 2002, and 2003, assuming management estimates the useful life of Bellagio to be:

a. 25 years. *b.* 15 years. *c.* 10 years. *d.* 1 year.

CHECK
a. ROA, 2001: −0.68%, 2002: 0.31%, 2003: 0.59%

PROBLEM 4–15
Analyzing Self-Constructed Assets

Jay Manufacturing, Inc., began operations five years ago producing probos, a new medical instrument it hoped to sell to doctors and hospitals. The demand for probos far exceeded initial expectations, and the company was unable to produce enough probos to meet demand. The company was manufacturing this product using self-constructed equipment at the start of operations. To meet demand, it needed more efficient equipment. The company decided to design and self-construct this new, more efficient equipment. A section of the plant was devoted to development of the new equipment and a special staff was hired. Within six months, a machine was developed at a cost of $170,000 that successfully increased production and reduced labor costs substantially. Sparked by the success of this new machine, the company built three more machines of the same type at a cost of $80,000 each.

Required:

a. In addition to satisfying a need that outsiders could not meet within the desired time, why might a company self-construct fixed assets for its own use?

b. Generally, what costs should a company capitalize for a self-constructed fixed asset?

c. Discuss the propriety of including in the capitalized cost of self-constructed assets:
   (1) The increase in overhead caused by the self-construction of fixed assets.
   (2) A proportionate share of overhead on the same basis as that applied to goods manufactured for sale.

d. Discuss the accounting treatment for the $90,000 amount ($170,000 − $80,000) by which the cost of the first machine exceeded the cost of subsequent machines.

(AICPA Adapted)

PROBLEM 4–16
Analyzing Intangible Assets (Patents)

On June 30, Year 1, your client, the Vandiver Corp., is granted two patents covering plastic cartons that it has been producing and marketing profitably for the past three years. One patent covers the manufacturing process, and the other covers related products. Vandiver executives tell you that these patents represent the most significant breakthrough in the industry in three decades. The products have been marketed under the registered trademarks Safetainer, Duratainer, and Sealrite. Your client has already granted licenses under the patents to other manufacturers in the U.S. and abroad and is receiving substantial royalties. On July 1, Year 1, Vandiver commenced patent infringement actions against several companies whose names you recognize as those of substantial and prominent competitors. Vandiver's management is optimistic that these suits will result in a permanent injunction against the manufacture and sale of the infringing products and collection of damages for loss of profits caused by the alleged infringement. The financial vice president has suggested that the patents be recorded at the discounted value of expected net royalty receipts.

Required:

a. Explain what an intangible asset is.

b. (1) Explain what is meant by "discounted value of expected net royalty receipts."
   (2) How would such a value be calculated for net royalty receipts?

c. What basis of valuation for Vandiver's patents is generally accepted in accounting? Give supporting reasons for this basis.

d. (1) Assuming no problems of implementation and ignoring generally accepted accounting principles, what is the preferable basis of evaluation for patents? Explain.
   (2) Explain what would be the preferable conceptual basis of amortization.

e. What recognition or disclosure, if any, is Vandiver likely to make for the infringement litigation in its financial statements for the year ending September 30, Year 1? Explain.

(AICPA Adapted)

CASES

CASE 4–1

Inventory Valuation in the Film Industry

Columbia Pictures Industries

Financial statements of **Columbia Pictures Industries** include the following note:

> **Inventories.** The costs of feature films and television programs, including production advances to independent producers, interest on production loans and distribution advances to film licensors, are amortized on bases designed to write off costs in proportion to the expected flow of income.
>
> The cost of general release feature productions is divided between theatrical ion and television ion, based on the proportion of net revenues expected to be derived from each source. The portion of the cost of feature productions allocated to theatrical ion is amortized generally by the application of tables which write off approximately 62% in 26 weeks, 85% in 52 weeks, and 100% in 104 weeks after release. Costs of two theatrical productions first released on a reserved-seat basis are amortized in the proportion that rentals earned bear to the estimated final theatrical and television rentals. Because of the depressed market for the licensing of feature films to television and poor acceptance by the public of a number of theatrical films released late in the year, the company made a special provision for additional amortization of recent releases and those not yet licensed for television to reduce such films to their currently estimated net realizable values.

Required:

a. Identify the main determinants for valuation of feature films, television programs, and general release feature productions by Columbia Pictures.

b. Are the bases of valuation reasonable? Explain.

c. Indicate additional information on inventory valuation that an unsecured lender to Columbia would wish to obtain and any analyses the lender would wish to conduct.

CASE 4–2

Financial Statement Consequences of LIFO and FIFO

Falcon.Com purchases its merchandise at current market costs and resells the product at a price 20 cents higher. Its inventory costs are constant throughout the current year. Data on the number of units in inventory at the beginning of the year, unit purchases, and unit sales are shown below:

Number of units in inventory—beginning of year (@ $1 per unit cost)	1,000 units
Number of units purchased during year @ $1.50 per unit cost	1,000 units
Number of units sold during year @ $1.70 per unit selling price	1,000 units

The beginning-of-year balance sheet for Falcon.Com reports the following:

Inventory (1,000 units @ $1)	$1,000
Total equity	$1,000

Required:

a. Compute the after-tax profit of Falcon.Com separately for both the (1) FIFO and (2) LIFO methods of inventory valuation assuming the company has no expenses other than cost of goods sold and its income tax rate is 50%. Taxes are accrued currently and paid the following year.

CHECK
b. Total assets, FIFO: $1,700, LIFO: $1,200

b. If all sales and purchases are for cash, construct the balance sheet at the end of this year separately for both the (1) FIFO and (2) LIFO methods of inventory valuation.

c. Describe the significance of each of these methods of inventory valuation for income determination and financial position in a period of increasing costs.

d. What problem does the LIFO method pose in constructing and analyzing interim financial statements?

(CFA Adapted)

CASE 4–3
Financial Statement Effects of Alternative Inventory Methods

Droog Co. is a retailer dealing in a single product. Beginning inventory at January 1 of this year is zero, operating expenses for this same year are $5,000, and there are 2,000 common shares outstanding. The following purchases are made this year:

	Units	Per Unit	Cost
January	100	$10	$ 1,000
March	300	11	3,300
June	600	12	7,200
October	300	14	4,200
December	500	15	7,500
Total	1,800		$23,200

Ending inventory at December 31 is 800 units. End-of-year assets, excluding inventories, amount to $75,000, of which $50,000 of the $75,000 are current. Current liabilities amount to $25,000, and long-term liabilities equal $10,000.

Required:

a. Determine net income for this year under each of the following inventory methods. Assume a sales price of $25 per unit and ignore income taxes.
   (1) FIFO
   (2) LIFO
   (3) Average cost

b. Compute the following ratios under each of the inventory methods of FIFO, LIFO, and average cost.
   (1) Current ratio
   (2) Debt-to-equity ratio
   (3) Inventory turnover
   (4) Return on total assets
   (5) Gross margin as a percent of sales
   (6) Net profit as a percent of sales

c. Discuss the effects of inventory accounting methods for financial statement analysis given the results from parts *a* and *b*.

CHECK
a. Income, FIFO: $8,500, LIFO: $5,900, AC: $7,112

CASE 4–4
Analysis of Investing Activities

Refer to the annual report of **Kodak** in Appendix A. **Kodak**

a. Compute Kodak's working capital at the end of 2001.

b. Kodak carries investments in marketable securities and other investments. Into what classifications did it categorize these investments and what are the accounting ramifications of these classifications?

c. Kodak reports net receivables totaling over $2.3 billion. To whom has it extended credit and how much bad debt reserve is provided against these receivables? What percentage of total receivables is considered uncollectible?

d. What cost flow assumption does Kodak use for inventories? What is its inventory write-down policy?

e. Kodak is a manufacturing company and carries raw materials, work-in-process, and finished goods inventories. What percent of total assets is in each type of inventory? How do these percentages compare with the previous year? What might an analyst do to determine if Kodak's investment in inventory is efficient?

f. The inventory turnover ratio (cost of goods sold/average inventory) is a measure of inventory management efficiency and effectiveness. Compute the inventory turnover ratio for Kodak and comment on ways that it might improve the ratio.

g. How much is the LIFO reserve for Kodak? What are the total tax benefits realized by Kodak as of the end of fiscal 2001 because it chose the LIFO inventory cost flow assumption?

h. What would Kodak's net income have been in 2001 if it had chosen FIFO?

i. What percentage of total assets is Kodak's investment in property, plant, and equipment? What depreciation method does it use for fixed assets? What useful life assumptions are used for fixed assets? What percentage of historical cost is the accumulated depreciation amount associated with these assets? What can the percentage depreciated calculation reveal to an analyst about fixed assets?

CHECK
f. Inventory turnover, 5.85; FIFO income, $1,361.6 mil.

j. Kodak reports goodwill totaling about $948 million at the end of 2001. What major transaction(s) gave rise to this amount? How does Kodak determine if this asset is impaired?

k. Many analysts consider investments in research and development to be the key to a company's future. How does Kodak account for its investment in research and development?

l. Kodak reports on its risk management activities. Describe these activities of Kodak that are designed to manage the company's exposures to changes in commodity prices, interest rates, and foreign currency exchange rates as well as credit risk.

m. For each asset reported on the balance sheet, comment on the extent to which you believe the amount reported represents future benefits for Kodak.

CASE 4–5
Analyzing Depreciation

Toro Manufacturing is organized on January 1, Year 5. During Year 5, financial reports to management use the straight-line method of depreciating plant assets. On November 8, you (as consultant) hold a conference with Toro's officers to discuss the depreciation method for both tax and financial reporting. Toro's president suggests the use of a new method he feels is more suitable than straight line during this period of predicted rapid expansion of production and capacity. He shows an example of his proposed method as applied to a fixed asset with an original cost of $32,000, estimated useful life of five years, and a salvage value of $2,000, as follows:

End of Year	Years of Life Used	Fraction Rate	Depreciation Expense	Accumulated Depreciation at Year-End	Book Value at Year-End
1	1	1/15	$ 2,000	$ 2,000	$30,000
2	2	2/15	4,000	6,000	26,000
3	3	3/15	6,000	12,000	20,000
4	4	4/15	8,000	20,000	12,000
5	5	5/15	10,000	30,000	2,000

Toro's president favors this new method because he asserts it:

1. Increases funds recovered in years near the end of the assets' useful lives when maintenance and replacement costs are high.
2. Increases write-offs in later years and thereby reduce taxes.

Required:

a. What are the purpose of and the principle behind accounting for depreciation?

b. Is the president's proposal within the scope of GAAP? Discuss the circumstances, if any, where this method is reasonable and those, if any, where it is not.

c. The president requests your advice on the following additional questions:
(1) Do depreciation charges recover or create cash? Explain.
(2) Assuming the IRS accepts the proposed depreciation method, and it is used for both financial reporting and tax purposes, how does it affect availability of cash generated by operations?

CASE 4–6
Derivatives-Hedging Strategies, Accounting, and Economic Effects

Newmont Mining

Newmont Mining is the largest gold producer in North America and second largest in the world, with mining interests in the U.S., Mexico, Peru, Uzbekistan, and Indonesia. In 1998, Newmont produced 4.07 million ounces of gold and its proven and probable reserves total 52.6 million ounces.

The price of gold is usually inversely related to the performance of financial assets such as stocks and bonds. Gold mining shares often provide a leveraged exposure to movements in gold price and, thus, are a convenient hedge against downturns in financial markets, especially those precipitated by inflation. However, gold prices have been in a secular downtrend for the past 18 years and especially in the past 3 years–gold prices fell from around $400 an ounce in early 1996 to around $250 an ounce by mid-1998. The prolonged bear market in gold has driven many gold-mining companies out of business. Many other companies have attempted to mitigate their exposure to the decline in gold prices with a variety of derivative instruments such as forward sales, and the purchase and sale of gold options. Some large companies such as Barrick Gold, Placer Dome, and Ashanthi Gold Fields have hedged major portions (upwards of 50% in some cases) of their gold reserves. While these hedging strategies reduce downside risk, they also limit gains from a sustained rally in the price of gold.

Newmont's management has avoided hedging its production because of its philosophy of providing its shareholders with the maximum exposure to gold price movements. Until recently, the only hedging by Newmont pertained to a minor quantity of its production from an Indonesian mine. The absence of hedging combined with the steep decline in gold prices adversely affected Newmont's profitability. This decline in profitability is despite Newmont's success at cost reduction–its less than $180 an ounce cost of production is one of the lowest in the industry. As gold prices continued to fall, Newmont's stock price declined from a high of $60 in 1996 to under $20 in 1998. Its creditors became increasingly uncomfortable with the exposure of the company to falling gold prices. Accordingly, in July and August 1999 (when the gold price was near its 20-year low of $250 an ounce) Newmont decided to hedge part of its reserves, although the proportion of reserves hedged is still one of the lowest in the industry.

Newmont's hedging program is designed to protect near-term cash flows in case of any further decline in gold price but to preserve leverage for any gold price increase. Details of its hedging program and accounting treatment follows:

1. *Forward sales commitments and associated call options from Indonesian mine:* The company agreed to sell 125,000 ounces of gold per year through 2000 from an Indonesian mine at a price of $454 per ounce. According to the company, the purpose of this hedge is to accelerate income and mitigate country risk. The accounting treatment for this contract is hedge accounting—all unrealized gains and losses on the contracts are deferred until the delivery date of the associated ounces. At the time of delivery, the contract price is recognized in income. As a result, the accounting numbers should reflect the spirit of the investment, which is to lock-in the price of gold. The proceeds from sale of gold will be supplemented or offset by gains and losses on the related hedge contract. Outstanding sales commitments as of September 30, 1999, are:

	1999	**2000**
Ounces	31,250	125,000
Average price	$454	$454

Coincident with the forward sales contracts, the company purchased call options on 50,000 ounces of gold per year for the same time period. These options give the company the right, but not the obligation, to purchase gold at $454 per ounce. The effect of these options is to allow the company, in a rising gold price environment, to realize the market price above $454 per ounce on 40% of the ounces subject to the forward sales contracts. The accounting treatment for the call options is the same as the related forward sales contracts (hedge accounting—all unrealized gains and losses on the contracts are deferred until the delivery date of the associated ounces). In combination, the forward sales and associated calls allow Newmont to create a floor price for its future production without entirely losing out on the upside potential. Outstanding call options at September 30, 1999, are:

	1999	**2000**
Ounces	12,500	50,000
Average price	$454	$454

2. *Prepaid forward sales and purchases in July 1999:* In July 1999, the company entered into a prepaid forward sale agreement covering 483,333 ounces of gold for delivery in 2005, 2006, and 2007 and received $137.2 million. The proceeds were used to pay down its debt. The initial proceeds received on this sale were based on a $300 per ounce gold price. If gold price exceeds $300 per ounce at the time of delivery, the company will receive additional proceeds subject to a ceiling of $380 per ounce. The initial proceeds were recorded as deferred revenue. As gold is delivered against this contract, a proportionate amount of the deferred revenue will be recognized as sales income. The company also agreed to deliver 35,900 ounces per year from 2000 to 2007 in a prepaid manner. To facilitate contracting for a fixed price without losing the benefit of upside potential, the company simultaneously signed forward purchase contracts for like quantities at prices increasing from $263 per ounce in 2000 to $354 per ounce in 2007. The accounting treatment for this transaction involves increasing or reducing the sales income from the forward sales contracts by the difference between the market price and forward purchase price at the scheduled future delivery dates.

3. *Purchased put and call options in August 1999:* In August 1999, with the price of gold at a 20-year low, the company sought to establish a floor price for a portion of its production with the purchase of put options. These options gave the company the right, but not the obligation, to sell 2.85 million ounces of gold at $270 per ounce. If the gold price is above $270, the options expire unexercised and the company sells gold at the higher market price. To avoid paying cash for the put options, the company sold call options on 2.35 million ounces for delivery in 2004 to 2009 at prices ranging from $350 to $392 an ounce. The sales proceeds from the call options exactly offset the purchase cost of the put options. The call options give the purchaser the right to buy the specified amount of gold at the stated strike price. If the market price is above the strike price at the time of maturity, the company can deliver the contracted quantity of gold to the option holder or roll the contracts over to a future delivery date. If the market price is below the strike price at the time of maturity, the options expire unexercised. Alternatively, the company can buy back the calls before they become exercisable. The written calls did not involve any margin-call risk or lease rates.

   The accounting treatment for the put options is hedge accounting. As such, any gains and losses on the contracts are deferred until the exercise date. If the gold price is below $270, the company exercises the put option and recognizes $270 per ounce as sales income. If the gold price is above $270 the company sells gold at the higher market price. Although no cash was paid for the put options, the fair value of the options at the time of purchase (approximately $37 million) is recorded as a prepaid asset and amortized over the term of the put options (the amortization is accounted for as an offset against revenue).

   Because the call options are longer term, an interpretation of GAAP requires the call options to be marked to market at the end of each quarter. The market value of the calls reflects the approximate price for which the options could be sold on the last day of each quarter. The initial fair value of the call options (the proceeds that would have been received if sold outright) is $37 million. Depending on the gold price and other factors that affect option pricing, the fair value can vary significantly from one quarter to the next, and the change in fair value is recognized as a gain or loss each quarter. By the end of the options' term, if gold price is below the strike price on the calls, the option value will be $0 and the initial $37 million fair value would have been included in income.

Subsequent Events:

While well-conceived hedging strategies reduce risk, in retrospect, the timing of the Newmont's hedging activities was unfortunate. In late September 1999 (just after the purchase of puts and writing of calls) the Consortium of European Central Banks, whose selling had contributed largely to the decline in the price of gold during the past 3 years, announced a moratorium on gold sales for the next 5 years. As a result, gold prices shot up from around $250 per ounce to over $300 per ounce in just a few days. Newmont was forced to recognize an unrealized loss on the written calls in its financial statements for the quarter ended September 1999 because the upward spike in gold price increased the fair value of the call options.

For the quarter ended September 1999, Newmont earned $2.3 million, or 2 cents per share, before noncash, hedge-related accounting charges. The average realized gold price for the period was $271 per ounce. This compares with earnings of $6.1 million, or 4 cents per share, at an average realized gold price of $295 per ounce in the corresponding quarter of 1998. In the quarter ended September 1999, gold production rose 4% to 1,043,000 ounces, while total cash costs were reduced 6% to $174 per ounce and total production costs declined 10% to $228 per ounce. As a result of the amortization of the put options and holding loss on the written long-dated calls, an after-tax noncash charge of $41.3 million is recorded in the September 1999 quarter. Given these holding losses, the company's net loss for the quarter is $39 million, or 23 cents per share.

Newmont believes the accounting applied to the long-dated call options is inappropriate and does not reflect the economic fundamentals of the hedging transaction. First, the company believes that marking only the written calls to market is inconsistent and distorts the economic reality of the company's underlying economic position. As a largely unhedged producer, the company's cash flow per quarter is expected to increase by $1 million for each $1 increase per ounce in the price of gold. Moreover, the company cannot mark its 52.6 million ounces of gold reserves to market value. Interestingly, the company points out that if the price of gold fell precipitously near the end of the next quarter, the company's fundamental value would decline but it would get to book a gain on its written call options. Second, the company argues that it has no cash flow exposure from the written calls unless it reverses the transaction. The written calls are not subject to margin-calls or lease rates. The company has the necessary gold reserves to meet the committed quantities of gold, and the strike price of the calls is well above its cost of production. The company will incur an opportunity cost to the extent the prevailing gold price on the expiration of the calls is above the strike price. The company also notes that the accounting treatment is different from the long-standing industry practice of recording gains and losses only when realized and it induces unnecessary volatility to reported income.

NEWMONT MINING CORPORATION AND SUBSIDIARIES

Statement of Consolidated Operations

For quarter ended September 30

(in $millions)	1999	1998
Sales	$ 340.2	$ 349.9
Amortization of put option	(12.2)	—
Other income	9.8	2.7
	337.8	352.6
Cost of sales	(206.5)	(206.5)
Depreciation, depletion and amortization	(60.7)	(72.9)
Exploration and research	(14.3)	(18.9)
General administrative	(12.5)	(11.7)
Other expenses	(4.2)	1.0
Interest (net)	(14.6)	(19.5)
Unrealized loss on written call options	(51.3)	—
Tax provision	7.8	3.3
Minority interest and equity loss	(20.5)	(21.3)
Net income	$ (39.0)	$ 6.1

BALANCE SHEET

As of September 30

(in $millions)	1999	1998		1999	1998
Assets			**Liabilities and Equity**		
Fair value of put options	$ 23.1	$ —	Current liabilities	$ 193.1	$ 212.5
Other current assets	467.9	513.1	Long-term debt	1,073.5	1,201.1
			Deferred revenue	137.2	—
Total current assets	491.0	513.1	Fair value of written calls	88.9	—
Noncurrent assets	2,792.2	2,673.7	Other liabilities	263.5	240.9
			Minority interest	117.6	92.8
			Liabilities	1,873.8	1,747.3
			Equity	1,409.4	1,439.5
Total assets	$3,283.2	$3,186.8	Total liabilities and equity	$3,283.2	$3,186.8

Required:

a. Describe and analyze the hedging transactions of Newmont. What is Newmont's motivation for each of its hedging transactions?

b. Since *SFAS 133* is effective for fiscal years beginning June 15, 1999, Newmont's September 1999 quarterly financials are not subject to the standard. Explain how each of the hedging transactions entered into by Newmont will be classified and accounted for under *SFAS 133*.

c. Examine the underlying economics for each of its hedging transactions. Does the accounting (both under *SFAS 133* and the earlier method employed by Newmont) reflect economic reality?

d. Newmont is not allowed to use hedge accounting for the written calls. Is this appropriate?

e. Evaluate Newmont's criticisms of the accounting for its written calls. Is Newmont's criticism justified?

f. What is the underlying economic reality of the sudden increase in gold price for Newmont? Do its financial statements reflect economic reality? Would marking all assets and liabilities to fair value improve the presentation of its balance sheet and income statement?

WEB ACTIVITIES

The Web Activities are located on the book's website at www.mhhe.com/wild8e.

5

ANALYZING INVESTING ACTIVITIES: SPECIAL TOPICS

A LOOK BACK <

Chapters 3 and 4 focused on accounting analysis of financing and investing activities. We explained and analyzed these activities as reflected in financial statements and interpreted them in terms of expectations for company performance.

A LOOK AT THIS CHAPTER •

This chapter extends our analysis to special investing activities—intercompany and international. We analyze both intercorporate investments and business combinations from the perspective of the parent company. We also examine international investments and their impact for financial statements. We show the importance of interpreting disclosures on intercompany and international activities for analysis of financial statements.

A LOOK AHEAD >

Chapter 6 extends our analysis to operating activities. We analyze the income statement as a means to understand and predict future company performance. We also introduce and explain important concepts and measures of income.

ANALYSIS OBJECTIVES

- Analyze financial reporting for intercorporate investments.
- Interpret consolidated financial statements.
- Analyze implications of both the purchase and pooling methods of accounting for business combinations.
- Interpret goodwill arising from business combinations.
- Describe international accounting and auditing practices.
- Analyze foreign currency translation disclosures.
- Distinguish between foreign currency translation and transaction gains and losses.

The Goodwill Plunge

In the first quarter of 2002, AOL Time Warner wrote off about $54 billion goodwill it recorded in the $106 billion merger of these two media conglomerates. That expense exceeded the total revenues of 483 of the Fortune 500 companies. In the previous year, JDS Uniphase announced a restatement of its March 2001 results and recorded a $44 billion write-off of goodwill. Angry investors are now suing the company, alleging that it misrepresented the success of previous acquisitions.

These write-offs are the result of an accounting standard passed in 2001 relating to business combinations. Previously, companies had two options to account for acquired businesses: the pooling method, under which acquired assets were recorded at book value, and the purchase method, which requires assets to be recorded at fair market value and the recognition of goodwill for the difference between the purchase price and the value of the assets acquired. Goodwill was subsequently amortized over a period of up to 40 years, resulting in an earnings drag that company managements complained compromised their ability to compete globally.

Under current accounting standards, only the purchase option is available. Instead of being amortized, however, goodwill is tested annually for impairment. Initial results of this impairment test started rolling in during the first quarter of 2002 and estimates range up to $1 trillion in initial goodwill write-offs. "We are going to get confirmation that hundreds of billions of dollars in shareholder capital has been wasted or destroyed," says David Tice, manager of the Prudent Bear fund.

. . . sporadic write-offs of unprecedented proportions.

While companies and Wall Street analysts generally stress that goodwill write-downs are one-time, noncash charges that have no impact on underlying operations or cash flow, many accounting experts argue they are significant–an admission that the investments that companies previously made are no longer worth as much.

Believing their own growth stories and enjoying high stock valuations that gave them pricey stock to swap for acquisitions, several companies engaged in an unprecedented number of acquisitions. Many of the prices paid now look excessive. "The serial acquisitions many companies made are not going to generate the revenues they anticipated. That suggests management made some bad deals," says Lehman Bros. accounting expert Robert Willens. These mistakes will show up, not as orderly amortization of goodwill, but in sporadic write-offs of unprecedented proportions.

Sources: "The Profit Plunge . . . ; It was a record drop for the 500," Fortune, April 15, 2002; "The Law Firm of Scott + Scott, LLC Announces Class Action Lawsuit Against JDS UNIPHASE CORPORATION," PR Newswire, April 19, 2002; "Buying Binge Could Cost Corporate America $1 Trillion; Accounting Change Forces Goodwill Write-Downs," USA Today, April 5, 2002.

PREVIEW OF CHAPTER 5

Intercompany and international activities play an increasing role in business activities. Companies pursue intercompany activities for several reasons such as diversification, expansion, and competitive opportunities and returns. International activities provide similar opportunities but offer unique and often riskier challenges. This chapter considers the analysis and interpretation of these business activities as reflected in financial statements. We consider current reporting requirements from an analysis perspective–both for what they do and do not tell us. We describe how current disclosures are relevant for analysis, and how we might usefully apply analytical adjustments to these

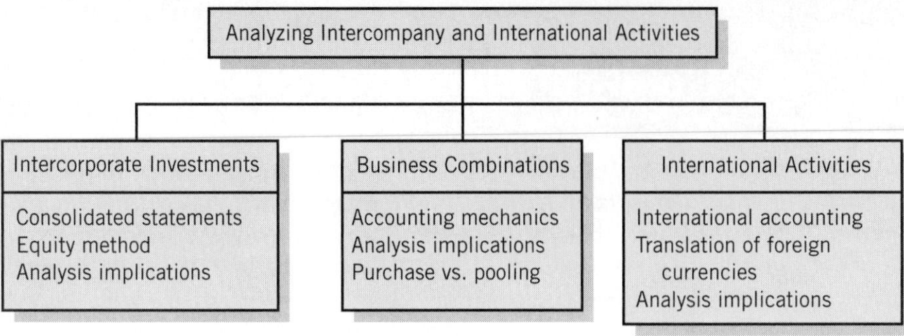

disclosures. We direct special attention to the unrecorded assets and liabilities in intercompany investments, the interpretation of international operations, and the risks with intercompany and international activities.

SECTION 1: INTERCOMPANY ACTIVITIES

Section 1 considers intercorporate investments and business combinations. We consider international activities in Section 2.

INTERCORPORATE INVESTMENTS

Intercorporate investments are investments by one corporation in the equity securities of another corporation. A **parent** corporation is one who controls, generally through ownership of equity securities, the activities of another separate legal entity known as a **subsidiary.** A **parent-subsidiary** relation exists when one corporation owns all or a majority of the voting equity securities of another corporation. A parent corporation also often invests in **affiliates.** Although a parent might exercise influence over affiliates' activities, it does not control them.

Reasons why one company pursues intercorporate investments, or buys control of another company, are many and varied. They include superior sources of supplies, growth in market share, entry into new lines of business, tax advantages, reduced risk exposure, government support, and technological and strategic advantages.

There are two basic methods for a parent company to account for its ownership in a subsidiary: consolidated financial statements and equity method accounting. We consider these methods in this section. From an analysis perspective, these methods differ substantially in the amount of information they provide about the financial condition and results of operations for the combined parent-subsidiary entity. We discuss implications of these methods for analysis. Chapter 4 described investments where one company holds a minority of the voting securities of another company, and we do not discuss them here.

GLOBAL BIZ
Intercorporate investments permeate the music industry as shown here:

Label	Parent	Hot Act
Columbia	Sony	Mariah Carey
Universal	Universal	98 Degrees
Arista	BMG	Santana
Warner	Warner	Red Hot Chili Peppers
Jive	BMG	Backstreet Boys

Consolidated Financial Statements

Consolidated financial statements report the results of operations and financial condition of a parent corporation and its subsidiaries in one set of statements. A parent company's financial statements evidence ownership of stock in a subsidiary through an investment account. From a legal point of view, a parent company owns the stock of its subsidiary. A parent does not own the subsidiary's assets nor is it usually responsible for the subsidiary's debts, although it frequently guarantees them. Consolidated financial statements disregard the separate legal identities of the parent and its subsidiary in favor of its "economic substance." That is, consolidated financial statements reflect a business entity controlled by a single company–the parent. There is a presumption in practice that consolidated financial statements are more meaningful than separate financial statements in reporting on this parent-subsidiary relation.

Basic Technique of Consolidation

Consolidation involves two steps: *aggregation* and *elimination*. First, consolidated financial statements aggregate the assets, liabilities, revenues, and expenses of subsidiaries with their corresponding items in the financial statements of the parent company. To the extent the parent does not own 100 percent of a subsidiary's equity securities, the **minority interest** of outsiders is recognized. Minority interest represents the portion of a subsidiary's equity securities owned by other than the parent company. If the parent owns all of a subsidiary's equity securities, the subsidiary is referred to as a *wholly owned subsidiary*.

BEDFELLOWS
World Championship Wrestling is a subsidiary of Turner Broadcasting System.

The second step is to eliminate *intercompany transactions* (or reciprocal accounts) to avoid double counting or prematurely recognizing income. For example, a parent's account payable to its subsidiary and its subsidiary's account receivable from the parent are both eliminated when preparing a consolidated balance sheet. Likewise, sales and cost of goods sold are eliminated for intercompany inventory sales.

The net effect of the consolidation on the balance sheet is to report the subsidiary acquired at its fair market value as of the date of acquisition. That is, all of the subsidiary's tangible and separately identifiable intangible assets are reported at their appraised values. Any excess of the purchase price over the fair market values of these identifiable assets is recorded as goodwill.

The consolidated income statement begins by adding together the income statements of the parent and subsidiary companies after elimination of intercompany transactions. Then, additional depreciation/amortization expense is recorded by the parent to allocate the excess of the purchase price over the net book value of the assets acquired. As discussed more fully below, in a significant departure from previous financial reporting standards, under present GAAP goodwill is no longer amortized but is tested annually for impairment.

ANALYSIS VIEWPOINT . . . YOU ARE THE LAWYER

One of your clients calls on you with a legal matter. Your client has nearly all of her savings invested in the common stock of NY Research Labs, Inc. Her concern stems from the financial statements of NY Research Labs that were released yesterday. These financial statements are, for the first time, consolidated statements involving a subsidiary, Boston Chemicals Corp. Your client is concerned her investment in NY Research Labs is now at greater risk due to several major lawsuits against Boston Chemicals—some have the potential to bankrupt Boston Chemicals. How do you advise your client? Should she be more concerned about her investment in NY Research Labs because of the consolidation?

Answer–p. 296

Principles Governing Consolidation

Accounting practice presumes consolidated statements are more meaningful than separate parent and subsidiary statements. Consequently, consolidation is considered the preferred method of reporting the financial statements of a parent and its subsidiaries. Accounting requires consolidation of a majority-owned subsidiary (that is, when the parent owns more than 50% of the voting stock) even if it has nonhomogeneous operations (such as credit, insurance, and leasing divisions), a large minority interest, or a foreign location. Practice requires that summarized information about the assets, liabilities, and operating results (or separate statements) of previously unconsolidated majority-owned subsidiaries continues to be reported after these subsidiaries are consolidated. There are two conditions where a subsidiary should not be consolidated for reporting purposes:

1. *Control is incomplete or temporary.* To consolidate a subsidiary, a parent should have ownership or **effective management control** of a subsidiary. Ownership of over 50% of the voting stock is generally required for consolidation, and consolidation is inappropriate when control is temporary, does not rest with the majority owner, or when the subsidiary is to be disposed of.
2. *Income is uncertain.* When there is substantial uncertainty about whether an increase in equity from a subsidiary has actually accrued to the parent, consolidation is inappropriate. Substantial uncertainty can arise, particularly with international subsidiaries, when there are restrictions on conversion of foreign currencies or on remittance of foreign earnings.

Exposure Draft on Consolidation

Recently, the FASB issued a revised *Exposure Draft* (ED), "Consolidated Financial Statements: Purpose and Policy," to address concerns that many constituents raised with an earlier ED involving consolidation. The revised ED proposes a "control framework" that represents a major departure from current practice. The ED establishes presumption of control if a company meets one or more of the following conditions:

- Has a majority voting interest in or a right to appoint a majority of another company's governing body.
- Has a large minority voting interest and no other party or organized group of parties has a significant voting interest.
- Has a unilateral ability to (1) obtain a majority voting interest in or (2) obtain a right to appoint a majority of the other company's governing body through the present ownership of convertible securities or other rights that are currently exercisable at the option of the holder and the expected benefit from converting those securities or exercising that right exceeds its expected cost.
- Is the only general partner in a limited partnership and no other partner or organized group of partners has the current ability to dissolve the limited partnership or otherwise remove the general partner.

Control of another company is defined as the ability to direct and manage the policies that guide its ongoing activities to increase the benefits and limit losses from those activities. Consequently, some companies that are less than 50% owned will be consolidated under these control criteria. More entities will be consolidated than are presently. Consolidation will not be required if control is incomplete or temporary, or if income is uncertain. The FASB continues to deliberate the proposal.

ANALYSIS VIEWPOINT . . . YOU ARE THE ANALYST

Coca-Cola Company has three types of bottlers: (1) independently owned bottlers, in which the Company has no ownership interest; (2) bottlers in which the Company has invested and has noncontrolling ownership; and (3) bottlers in which the Company has invested and has controlling ownership. In line with its long-term bottling strategy, the Company periodically considers options for reducing ownership in its consolidated bottlers. In Note 2 of its annual report, Coca-Cola reports that it owns equity interest of 24% to 38% in some of the largest bottlers in the world. Will these bottlers be consolidated in its future annual reports if the ED becomes effective? How would the consolidation of these bottlers affect its solvency ratios?

Answer–p. 297

Equity Method Accounting

Equity method accounting reports the parent's investment in the subsidiary and the parent's share of the subsidiary's profits as line items in the parent's financial statements.

Accordingly, the equity method is sometimes referred to as a *one-line consolidation*. Equity method accounting is used in consolidated financial statements for investments in equity securities of all unconsolidated subsidiaries (international or domestic) where, for reasons described in the prior section, consolidation is inappropriate. Equity method accounting is not a valid substitute for consolidation and should not be used to justify exclusion of a subsidiary when consolidation is appropriate. Equity method accounting is generally used for investments representing 20% to 50% of the voting stock of a company's equity securities. It can, in certain cases, be appropriate for investments representing an interest of less than 20% if the parent has effective control. The primary difference between consolidation and equity method accounting rests in the level of detail reported in the financial statements.

There is wide application of equity method accounting for investments in subsidiaries, joint ventures, and less than majority-owned investees. Practice in this area emphasizes the need to consider substance over form in determining accounting for intercorporate investments. SEC regulations specifically address the possible need to consolidate a less than majority-owned subsidiary and to employ equity method accounting to achieve fair presentation.

GLOBAL LINKS

Although handled by RCA in the United States, 'N Sync's contract is with a German BMG subsidiary. The band claims this led to smaller royalties because the United States is treated as a "foreign" market.

Equity Method Mechanics

We begin with a discussion of the mechanics of equity method accounting. Assume that Global Corp. acquires for cash a 25% interest in Synergy, Inc. for $500,000, representing one-fourth of Synergy's stockholders' equity as of the acquisition date. The investment is, therefore, acquired at book value. Synergy's condensed balance sheet as of the date of the acquisition is

Current assets	$ 700,000
Property, plant and equipment	5,600,000
Total assets	$6,300,000
Current liabilities	$ 300,000
Long-term debt	4,000,000
Stockholders' equity	2,000,000
Total liabilities and equity	$6,300,000

The initial investment is recorded on Global's books as,

Investment	500,000	
Cash		500,000

Global reports the investment account as a noncurrent asset on its balance sheet. This $500,000 investment represents a 25% interest in an investee company with total assets of $6,300,000 and liabilities of $4,300,000.

Subsequent to the date of the acquisition, Synergy reports net income of $100,000 and pays dividends of $20,000. Global records its proportionate share of Synergy's earnings and the receipt of dividends as follows,

Investment	25,000	
Equity in earnings of investee company		25,000
To record proportionate share of investee company earnings		
Cash	5,000	
Investment		5,000
To record receipt of dividends		

Global's earnings have increased by its proportionate share of the net income of Synergy. This income will be reported in the other income section of the income statement as it is treated similarly to interest income. In contrast to the accounting for available-for-sale and trading securities described in Chapter 4, the dividends received are not recorded as income. Instead, they are treated as a return of the capital invested in Synergy, and the investment account is reduced accordingly.

Note the symmetry between Global's investment accounting and Synergy's stockholders' equity:

	Global Corp. Investment Account			Synergy, Inc. Stockholders' Equity	
Beg.	500,000			2,000,000	Beg.
	25,000	5,000	20,000	100,000	
End	520,000			2,080,000	End

Global's investment remains at 25% of Synergy's stockholders' equity.

There are a number of important points relating to equity method accounting:

- The investment account represents the proportionate share of the stockholders' equity of the investee company. Substantial assets and liabilities may, therefore, not be recorded on balance sheet unless the investee is consolidated. This can have important implications for the analysis of the investor company.
- Investment earnings (the proportionate share of the earnings of the investee company) should be distinguished from core operating earnings in the analysis of the earnings of the investor company.
- Contrary to the reporting of available-for-sale and trading securities discussed in Chapter 4, investments accounted for under the equity method are reported at adjusted cost, not at market value. Substantial unrealized gains may, therefore, not be reflected in assets or stockholders' equity. Losses in value that are deemed to be other than temporary, however, must be reflected as a write-down in the carrying amount of the investment with a related loss recorded in the income statement.
- An investor should discontinue equity method accounting when the investment is reduced to zero (such as due to investee losses) and should not provide for additional losses unless the investor has guaranteed the obligations of the investee or is otherwise committed to providing further financial support to the investee. Equity method accounting only resumes once all cumulative deficits have been recovered via investee earnings.
- If the amount of the initial investment exceeds the proportionate share of the book value of the investee company, the excess is allocated to identifiable tangible and intangible assets that are depreciated/amortized over their respective useful lives. Investment income is reduced by this additional expense. The excess not allocated in this manner is treated as goodwill and is no longer amortized.

Analysis Implications of Intercorporate Investments

Our analysis continues with several important considerations relating to intercorporate investments. This section discusses the more important implications.

Recognition of Investee Company Earnings

Both consolidation and equity method accounting assume a dollar earned by a subsidiary is equivalent to a dollar earned for the parent, even if not received in cash. While disregarding the parent's potential tax liability from remittance of earnings by a subsidiary, the dollar-for-dollar equivalence of earnings cannot be taken for granted. Reasons include:

- A regulatory authority can sometimes intervene in a subsidiary's dividend policy.
- A subsidiary can operate in a country where restrictions exist on remittance of earnings or where the value of currency can deteriorate rapidly. Political risks can further inhibit access to earnings.
- Dividend restrictions in loan agreements can limit earnings accessibility.
- Presence of a stable or powerful minority interest can reduce a parent's discretion in setting dividend or other policies.

Our analysis must recognize these factors in assessing whether a dollar earned by a subsidiary is the equivalent of a dollar earned by the parent.

Unrecognized Capital Investment

The investment account is often referred to as a one-line consolidation. This is because it represents the investor's percentage ownership in the investee company stockholders' equity. Behind this investment balance are the underlying assets and liabilities of the investee company. There can be a significant amount of unrecorded assets and liabilities of the investee company that are not reflected on the balance sheet of the investor.

Consider the case of Coca-Cola presented in the Analysis Viewpoint on page 268. Coca-Cola owns approximately 38% of Coca-Cola Enterprises (CCE), one of its bottling companies. It accounts for this investment under the equity method and reports an investment balance as of December 31, 2001, of $788 million, approximately its proportionate share of the $2.8 billion stockholders' equity of CCE. The balance sheet of CCE reports total assets of $23.7 billion and total liabilities of $20.9 billion. The investment balance on Coca-Cola's balance sheet, representing 3.5% of its reported total assets, belies a much larger investment and financial leverage.

The concern facing the analyst is how to treat this sizable off-balance-sheet investment. Should financial ratio analysis be conducted solely on the reported financial statements of Coca-Cola? Should CCE be consolidated with Coca-Cola by the analyst and financial ratios computed on the consolidated financial statements? Should only Coca-Cola's proportionate interest in the assets and liabilities of CCE be included in place of the investment account for purposes of analysis? These are important issues that must be addressed before beginning the analysis process.

Provision for Taxes on Undistributed Subsidiary Earnings

When the undistributed earnings of a subsidiary are included in the pretax accounting income of a parent company (either through consolidation or equity method accounting), it can require a concurrent provision for taxes. This provision depends on the action and intent of the parent company. Current practice assumes all undistributed earnings transfer to the parent and, thus, a provision for taxes is made by the parent in the current period. This assumption is overcome, however, if persuasive evidence exists that the subsidiary either has or will invest undistributed earnings permanently or will remit earnings through a tax-free liquidation. In analysis, we should be aware that the decision on whether taxes are provided on undistributed earnings is primarily that of management.

BUSINESS COMBINATIONS

Business combinations refer to the merger, acquisition, reorganization, or restructuring of two or more businesses to form another business entity. Business combinations

Companies Reporting Business Combinations

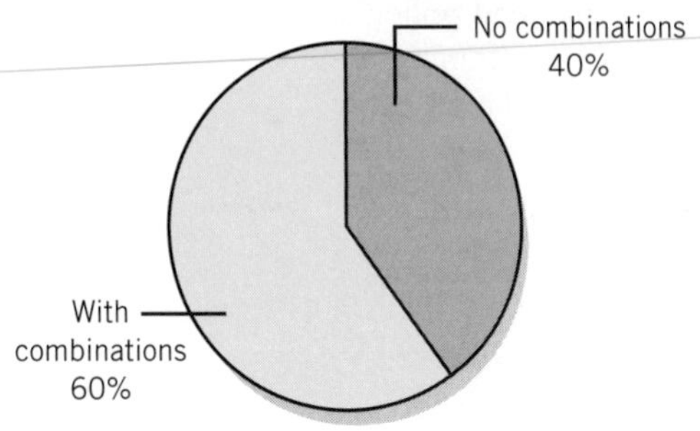

Source: Accounting Trends & Techniques.

alter the ownership and control of the acquired or divested businesses. They occur when one company acquires or divests itself of a substantial part of one or more other companies' equity securities. Business combinations require that subsequent financial statements report on the combined activities of this new entity. Accounting for a business combination requires a decision on how to value the assets and liabilities of the new entity. This decision can involve a complete revaluation to market value of all assets and liabilities acquired, with substantial effects extending to current and future financial statements. This accounting decision is different from the intercorporate activities discussion in the prior section that focused not on the accounting for the "combination" but on the extent a subsidiary is viewed as an integral part of the parent. Analysis of business combinations must recognize management's incentives, the accounting implications, and the need to evaluate and interpret financial statements of the new entity.

Business combinations with sound economic motivations have a long history. Among the economic reasons for business combinations are (1) acquiring valuable sources of materials, productive facilities, technology, marketing channels, or market share; (2) securing financial resources or access to them; (3) strengthening management; (4) enhancing operating efficiency; (5) encouraging diversification; (6) rapidity in market entry; (7) achieving economies of scale; and (8) acquiring tax advantages. We should also recognize certain intangible reasons for business combinations. In certain cases these intangibles are the best explanation for the high costs incurred. They include management prestige, compensation, and perquisites. Management's accounting choices in recording business combinations are often better understood when considering these motivations.

WORST BOARD
Apple Computer, Inc. is known to have one of business's worst boards. Some reasons: Recently departed director Larry Ellison had missed more than 25% of meetings in the past five years. The CEO of Micro Warehouse, which accounted for nearly 3% of Apple's net sales in 2001, sits on the compensation committee. Since 2000, the board has awarded founder Steve Jobs 27.5 million stock options and a $90 million jet. And there is an interlocking directorship—Gap CEO Mickey Drexler and Jobs sit on each other's boards.

However, business combinations also can arise as a means to enhance a company's image, its perceived growth potential, or its prosperity, and it is a means of increasing reported earnings. Specifically, financial engineers can utilize methods in accounting for business combinations to deliver a picture of earnings growth that is, in large part, illusory. The means to achieve illusionary earnings growth include:

- Merging a growth company having a high price-earnings ratio with a company having lesser growth prospects, and using payment in the high-growth company's stock. This transaction can contribute to further earnings per share growth and can reinforce and even increase the acquiring company's high price-earnings ratio. Markets sometimes fail to fully account for the potential lower quality of acquired earnings. This is primarily a transitory problem inherent in the market evaluation mechanism, and it is not easily remedied by regulators.
- Using latitude in accounting for business combinations. This is distinct from genuine economic advantages arising from combinations. We consider alternative accounting methods for business combinations in the next section.
- Issuing convertible securities with limited or no recognition given to their potential dilutive effects on common shareholders' equity.

Accounting for Business Combinations

The Financial Accounting Standards Board recently enacted two significant pronouncements (*SFAS 141,* "Business Combinations," and *SFAS 142,* "Goodwill and Other Intangible Assets") relating to accounting and reporting for business combinations (effective for fiscal periods beginning December 15, 2001, and after). These standards mandate a number of major changes in financial reporting:

1. The purchase method of accounting is required for all business combinations, thus prohibiting future use of pooling accounting. However, previous combinations that qualified for pooling treatment continue to be accounted for as poolings in consolidated financial reports.
2. Companies must record the fair market value of previously unrecognized purchased intangible assets before recording goodwill.
3. Goodwill will no longer be amortized. Instead, it will be subject to an annual test for impairment.
4. The standard requires disclosure of the primary reasons for a business combination and expanded purchase price allocation information.

Under the purchase method of accounting, companies are required to recognize on their balance sheets the fair market value of the tangible and intangible assets acquired. Furthermore, the tangible assets are depreciated and the identifiable intangible assets amortized over their estimated useful lives. In a significant departure from prior practice, however, *SFAS 142* mandates that goodwill will no longer be amortized. This non-amortization approach will be applied to both previously recognized and newly acquired goodwill. Instead, goodwill will be subject to an annual test for impairment. When the carrying amount of goodwill exceeds its implied fair value, an impairment loss will be recognized equal to that excess.

Although financial statements will reflect these new provisions for acquisitions initiated after June 30, 2001, acquisitions previously accounted for as poolings remain as such. Analysts must, therefore, understand the effects on balance sheets and income statements of these two approaches.

Mechanics of Consolidations

To illustrate the impact of these new standards we now consider the following case:

On December 31, Year 1, Synergy Corp. purchases 100% of Micron Company by exchanging 10,000 shares of its common stock ($5 par value, $77 market value) for all of the common stock of Micron, which will remain in existence as a wholly owned subsidiary of Synergy. On the date of the acquisition, the book value of Micron is $620,000. Synergy is willing to pay the market price of $770,000 because it feels that Micron's property, plant, and equipment (PP&E) is undervalued by $20,000, it has an unrecorded trademark worth $30,000, and intangible benefits of the business combination (corporate synergies, market position, and the like) are valued at $100,000. The purchase price is, therefore, allocated as follows:

Purchase price	$770,000
Book value of Micron	620,000
Excess	$150,000

Excess allocated to		Useful Life	Annual Depreciation/Amortization
Undervalued PP&E	$ 20,000	10	$2,000
Trademark	30,000	5	6,000
Goodwill	100,000	Indefinite	0
	$150,000		

Goodwill can only be recorded following the recognition of the fair market values of all tangible (PP&E) and identifiable intangible (trademark) assets acquired. Under current GAAP, Synergy will make the following entry to record the acquisition,

Investment in Micron	770,000	
Common stock		50,000 (at par value)
Additional Paid-in-capital		720,000

During Year 2, Micron earns $150,000. The investment, accounted for under the equity method, has a balance on Synergy's books at December 31, Year 2, as follows:

Beginning balance (12/31/Y1)	$770,000
Investment income	150,000
Dividends	0
Amortization of excess (above)	(8,000)
Ending balance (12/31/Y2)	$912,000

Under current GAAP, goodwill is not amortized and the net investment income recognized by Synergy is $142,000, including its proportionate share of Micron's earnings and only the expense relating to depreciation of the excess PP&E ($2,000) and the amortization of the trademark ($6,000). The individual company trial balances for both Synergy and Micron at the end of Year 2 are presented below together with the consolidation worksheet and consolidated totals.

SYNERGY CORP. AND SUBSIDIARY
Trial Balances and Consolidated Financial Statements
For Year Ended December 31, Year 2
Prepared under the Purchase Accounting Method

	Synergy	Micron	Debits	Credits	Consolidated
Revenues	$ 610,000	$ 370,000			$ 980,000
Operating expenses	(270,000)	(140,000)			(410,000)
Depreciation expense	(115,000)	(80,000)	[4] $ 2,000		(197,000)
Amortization expense	0	0	[4] 6,000		(6,000)
Investment income	142,000	0	[3] 142,000		0
Net income	$ 367,000	$ 150,000			$ 367,000
Retained earnings, 1/1/Y1	$ 680,000	$ 490,000	[1] 490,000		$ 680,000
Net income	367,000	150,000			367,000
Dividends paid	(90,000)				(90,000)
Retained earnings, 12/31/Y2	$ 957,000	$ 640,000			$ 957,000
Cash	$ 105,000	$ 20,000			$ 125,000
Receivables	380,000	220,000			600,000
Inventory	560,000	280,000			840,000
Investment in Micron	912,000	0		[1] $620,000 [2] 150,000 [3] 142,000	0
Plant, property and equipment (net)	1,880,000	720,000	[2] 20,000	[4] 2,000	2,618,000
Trademark	0	0	[2] 30,000	[4] 6,000	24,000
Goodwill			[2] 100,000		100,000
Total assets	$3,837,000	$1,240,000			$4,307,000
Liabilities	$ 780,000	$ 470,000			$1,250,000
Common stock	800,000	100,000	[1] 100,000		800,000
Additional paid-in capital	1,300,000	30,000	[1] 30,000		1,300,000
Retained earnings	957,000	640,000			957,000
Total liabilities and equity	$3,837,000	$1,240,000	$920,000	$920,000	$4,307,000

The original balance of the investment account on the purchase date ($770,000) represents the market value of Micron. It includes the market value of Micron's reported net assets plus fair market value of the previously unrecognized trademark and the goodwill purchased in the acquisition. The four consolidation entries are:

1. Replace $620,000 of the investment account with the book value of the assets acquired. If less than 100% of the subsidiary is owned, the credit to the investment account is equal to the percentage of the book value owned and the remaining credit is to a liability account, *minority interest.*
2. Replace $150,000 of the investment account with the fair value adjustments required to fully record Micron's assets at fair market value.
3. Eliminate the investment income recorded by Synergy and replace that account with the income statement of Micron. If less than 100% of the subsidiary is owned, the investment income reported by the Synergy is equal to its proportionate share and an additional expense is reported for the *minority interest* in Micron's earnings.
4. Record the depreciation of the fair value adjustment for Micron's PP&E and the amortization of the trademark. Note, there is no amortization of goodwill under current GAAP.

There are several important points to understand about the consolidation process:

- The consolidated balance sheet includes the book value of Synergy and the fair market value of Micron as of the acquisition date, less depreciation/amortization of the excess of the Micron market value over its book value.
- The consolidated income statement includes the income statements of both Synergy and Micron. The investment income recorded by Synergy on its books is replaced by the income statement of Micron. In addition, depreciation expense includes the depreciation expense that Micron recorded on the book value of its depreciable assets plus the depreciation of the excess of fair market value over book value recorded upon acquisition of Micron. Second, the newly created trademark asset is amortized over its useful life, resulting in additional expense of $6,000. The goodwill recognized in the acquisition is not amortized.
- Goodwill is only recorded after recognizing the fair market values of all tangible and intangible assets acquired. Companies are required to identify any intangible assets acquired. These intangibles are deemed to have an identifiable useful life and are, therefore, subject to annual amortization.

Impairment of Goodwill

Goodwill recorded in the consolidation process has an indefinite life and is, therefore, not amortized. It is, however, subject to annual review for impairment. This review is a two step process. In the first step, the fair market value of Micron is compared with the book value of its associated investment account on Synergy's books ($912,000 as of December 31, Year 2). The fair market value of Micron can be determined using a number of alternative methods, such as quoted market prices of comparable businesses, or a discounted free cash flow valuation method. If the current market value is less than the investment balance, goodwill is deemed to be impaired and an impairment loss must be recorded in the consolidated income statement.

Assume that the fair market value of Micron is estimated to be $700,000 as of December 31, Year 2, and that the fair market value of the net tangible and identifiable intangible assets is $660,000. This results in an impairment loss of $60,000 as follows:

Fair market value of Micron		$ 700,000
Current assets	$ 520,000	
PP&E	570,000	
Trademark	20,000	
Liabilities	(450,000)	
Net assets		660,000
Implied goodwill		40,000
Current balance goodwill		(100,000)
Impairment loss		$ 60,000

The resulting entry on Synergy 's books is:

Goodwill impairment loss	60,000	
Investment in Micron		60,000

The impairment loss will be reported as a separate line item in the operating section of Synergy's consolidated income statement. In addition, a portion of the goodwill contained in Synergy's investment account is written off, and the balance of goodwill in the consolidated balance sheet is reduced accordingly. Disclosures are also required detailing the facts and circumstances resulting in the impairment, and the method by which Synergy determines the fair market value of Micron.

Issues in Business Combinations

Valuing the Consideration

A major problem in purchase accounting is determining the total cost of the acquired entity. The same accounting principles apply whether determining the cost of assets acquired individually, in a group, or in a business combination. It is the nature of the transaction that determines the accounting principles to apply in arriving at total cost of assets acquired. No problems usually arise in determining the total cost of assets acquired for cash, since the amount of cash disbursed is the cost of acquired assets. Allocation of this cost to the individual assets acquired, however, is more difficult. If a company acquires assets by incurring liabilities, the total cost of acquired assets is the present value of the amounts to be paid in the future. If the debt security is issued at an interest rate substantially above or below the current effective rate for a similar security, an appropriate amount for premium or discount is recorded. In some cases, the characteristics of a preferred stock are so similar to a debt security that it is valued in the same manner.

If a company acquires assets in exchange for stock, the total cost of the acquired assets is the fair value of the stock given or the fair value of the net assets received, whichever is more evident. The fair value of securities traded in an organized market is typically preferred over estimating the fair value of the acquired company. Quoted market price serves as a guide in determining total cost of an acquired company. If the quoted market price is not reliable, the fair value of net assets received, including goodwill, must be determined. In these cases, the best available means of estimation are used, including a detailed review of the negotiations leading up to the purchase and the use of independent appraisals.

Contingent Consideration

A company usually records the amount of any contingent consideration payable in accordance with a purchase agreement when the contingency is resolved and the consideration is issued or issuable. Two common types of contingencies are based on either earnings or security prices. Guidelines for accounting for contingent consideration include: (1) disclose a contingent issuance of additional consideration, but not as a liability or as outstanding securities unless the outcome of the contingency is determinable beyond a reasonable doubt; (2) record a contingent issuance of additional consideration based on future earnings as additional cost of the acquisition when the contingency is resolved; and (3) adjust the amount originally recorded for securities at the date of acquisition for a contingent issuance of additional consideration based on future security prices.

Allocating Total Cost

Once a company determines the total cost of an acquired entity, it is necessary to allocate this cost to individual assets. All identifiable assets acquired and liabilities assumed in a business combination are assigned a portion of the total cost, normally equal to their fair value at date of acquisition. Identifiable assets include intangible as well as tangible assets. *SFAS 141* requires companies to identify and value specific categories of intangible assets. These include the following:

1. Trademarks and other marketing-related assets.
2. Noncompetition agreements.
3. Customer lists, contracts, and other customer-related assets.
4. Artistic-related intangible assets such as literary or music works, and video and audiovisual material, including television programs and music videos.
5. Intangible assets relating to contractual relationships such as licensing, royalty, advertising, and management contracts, lease or franchise agreements, broadcast rights, employment contracts, and the like.
6. Patents, computer software, databases, trade secrets or formulae, and other technology-based intangible assets.

Only after the purchase price has been allocated to the fair market value of all tangible and identifiable intangible assets, less the market value of all liabilities assumed, can any of the purchase price be assigned to goodwill. The reason is that all assets other than goodwill have an identifiable useful life, resulting in depreciation and amortization expense. Goodwill, however, is deemed to have an indefinite life and is not amortized.

It is possible that market or appraisal values of identifiable assets acquired, less liabilities assumed, exceed the cost of the acquired company (*negative goodwill*). In those rare cases, values otherwise assignable to noncurrent assets acquired (except long-term investments in marketable securities) are reduced by this excess. Then, the remainder, if any, is recorded in the income statement as an extraordinary gain net of tax.

Types of Intangible Assets Reported by Companies

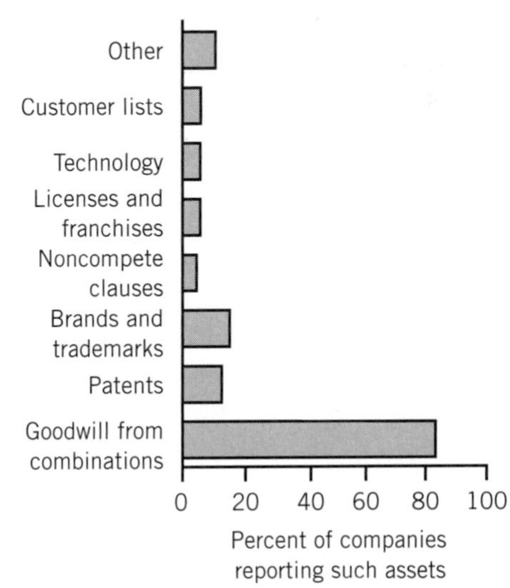

Source: Accounting Trends & Techniques.

In-Process Research and Development (IPR&D)

Some companies write off a large portion of an acquisition's costs as purchased research and development. Moreover, there has been a dramatic increase in such write-offs within the past decade, especially in the high-tech industry. Under prior GAAP, this practice was attractive as it allowed acquiring companies to reduce or even eliminate any allocation of the purchase price to goodwill and, thus, lower or avoid future earnings charges from the resulting goodwill amortization.

R&D SPENDING AND CEOS

A recent study reports that companies spend on average of $8,300 per employee on R&D. However, CEOs with law degrees spent just $5,600 while those from operations spent $6,900. On the other hand, CEOs with marketing backgrounds spent $10,300, and those from R&D and engineering backgrounds spent the most: $10,500.

In the IPR&D write-off situation, companies value the IPR&D assets of the acquired companies before writing them off. However, there is no guidance on how to value IPR&D. Given the incentive to avoid recognizing IPR&D as goodwill, companies are alleged to value IPR&D as high as possible to increase the write-off and reduce or eliminate subsequent goodwill amortization. Such a write-off creates quality-of-earnings concerns if IPR&D is overstated since it would understate assets and overstate return on equity (and assets).

The SEC recently announced an initiative to investigate this accounting practice. As a result, recent merging companies have reduced the size of their IPR&D write-offs. Further, several companies have restated the size of their initial IPR&D write-offs. In a study of SEC filings, the average size of the IPR&D write-off as a percentage of purchase price declined to 45% compared with an average of 72% for the decade prior to the SEC initiative–this is despite a more than 200% increase in average purchase price. The implication here is that managers were too aggressive in their accounting practices.

A side note: In its initial Exposure Draft, the FASB concluded that IPR&D should be capitalized. Later, the FASB concluded that it was impossible to address IPR&D costs separately from other R&D costs. As a result, the FASB decided to postpone reconsideration of the accounting treatment for IPR&D until some unspecified future date when all R&D costs can be considered in a comprehensive manner. The accounting for IPR&D has not been affected by *SFAS 141* and *SFAS 142.*

Debt in Consolidated Financial Statements

Liabilities in consolidated financial statements do not operate as a lien upon a common pool of assets. Creditors, whether secured or unsecured, have recourse in the event of default only to assets owned by the specific corporation that incurred the liability. If a parent company guarantees a liability of a subsidiary, then the creditor has the guarantee as additional security with potential recourse provisions. The consolidated balance sheet does not help us assess the margin of safety enjoyed by creditors. To assess the security of liabilities, our analysis must examine the individual financial statements of each subsidiary. We must also remember that legal constraints are not always effective measures of liability. For example, American Express recently covered the obligations of a warehousing subsidiary not because of any legal obligation, but because of concern for its own reputation.

Gains on Subsidiary IPOs

Recently, Tycom, Ltd., a wholly owned subsidiary of Tyco International, Ltd. sold previously unissued shares to outside parties in an initial public offering (IPO). As a result of the sale, Tyco International Ltd.'s percentage ownership in Tycom Ltd. decreased from 100% to 89% and the parent company recorded a pretax gain of $2.1 billion ($1.01 billion after tax) in its consolidated statement of income. IPOs by subsidiaries are becoming increasingly common as companies seek to capture unrecognized gains in the value of their subsidiary stock holdings while, at the same time, retaining control over their subsidiaries.

The rationale for the gain treatment can be seen from this example: assume that Synergy owns 100% of Micron with a book value of stockholders' equity of $1,000,000 and records an investment in Micron account of $1,000,000. Micron sells previously unissued shares for $500,000 and, thereby, reduces Synergy's ownership to 80%. Synergy now owns 80% of a subsidiary with a book value of $1,500,000 for an investment equivalent of $1,200,000. The value of its investment account has thus risen by $200,000. The FASB formally supports the treatment of this "gain" as an increase in additional paid-in capital. The SEC, however, in *Staff Accounting Bulletin 51,* allows companies to record the credit to either additional paid-in capital or to earnings. The effect on stockholder's equity of Synergy is the same. But in the first alternative, stockholders' equity is increased by an increase in additional paid-in capital. In the second alternative, stockholders' equity is increased via the closure of net income to retained earnings and a gain is recorded in the statement of income.

Preacquisition Sales and Income

When an acquisition of a subsidiary occurs in midyear companies only report their equity in subsidiary income from the acquisition date forward. There are, however, two methods available under GAAP (*Accounting Research Bulletin 51*), to accomplish this:

1. The company can issue a consolidated income statement with sales, expenses, and income of the subsidiary from the acquisition date forward.
2. The company can report in its consolidated income statement subsidiary sales and expenses for the entire year and back out preacquisition earnings so that only post-acquisition earnings are included in consolidated net income.

The effect on consolidated net income is the same for either method, that is, only net income of the acquired company subsequent to the acquisition date is included in consolidated earnings. Top line (sales) growth, however, can be dramatically different depending on the acquisition date and magnitude of the acquired company's sales. Companies whose growth occurs primarily via acquisitions (vs. "organic," or internal, growth) can be particularly troublesome for analysts.

The amount of preacquisition income is likely to be deemed immaterial and included in other expense categories rather than reported as a separate line item. One hint into the accounting method employed is to examine the pro forma disclosures required in the acquisitions footnote. Companies are required to report pro forma sales and income as if the investees had been included for the entire year. A comparison of these pro forma sales against reported consolidated sales can provide insight into the accounting choice made by management in this area.

Push-Down Accounting

Purchase accounting requires the assets and liabilities of an acquired company to be included in the consolidated financial statements of the purchaser at their market values. A controversial issue is how the acquired company reports these assets and liabilities in its separate financial statements (if that company survives as a separate entity). The SEC requires that purchase transactions resulting in an entity's becoming substantially wholly owned (as defined in Regulation S-X) establish a new basis of accounting for the purchased assets and liabilities if the acquired company issues securities in public markets. For example, if Company A acquires substantially all the common stock of Company B in one or a series of purchase transactions, Company B's financial statements must reflect the new basis of accounting arising from its acquisition by Company A. When ownership is under control of the parent, the basis of accounting for purchased assets and liabilities should be the same regardless of whether the entity continues to exist or is merged into the parent's operations. That is, Company A's cost of acquiring Company B is "pushed down" and used to establish a new accounting basis in Company B's separate financial statements. The SEC recognizes that the existence of outstanding public debt, preferred stock, or significant minority interest in a subsidiary can impact a parent's ability to control ownership. In these cases, the SEC has not insisted on push-down accounting.

Additional Limitations of Consolidated Financial Statements

Consolidated financial statements often are meaningful representations of the financial condition and results of operations of the parent-subsidiary entity. Nevertheless, there are limitations in addition to those already discussed.

- Financial statements of the individual companies composing the larger entity are not always prepared on a comparable basis. Differences in accounting principles, valuation bases, amortization rates, and other factors can inhibit homogeneity and impair the validity of ratios, trends, and other analyses.
- Consolidated financial statements do not reveal restrictions on use of cash for individual companies. Nor do they reveal intercompany cash flows or restrictions placed on those flows. These factors obscure the relation between liquidity of assets and the liabilities they aim to meet.
- Companies in poor financial condition sometimes combine with financially strong companies, thus obscuring our analysis–since assets of one member of the consolidated entity cannot necessarily be seized to pay liabilities of another.
- Extent of intercompany transactions is unknown unless the procedures underlying the consolidation process are reported–consolidated statements generally reveal only end results.
- Accounting for the consolidation of finance and insurance subsidiaries can pose several problems for analysis. Aggregation of dissimilar subsidiaries can distort ratios and other relations–for example, current assets of finance subsidiaries are not generally available to satisfy current liabilities of the parent. Assets and liabilities of separate entities are not interchangeable, and consolidated financial statements obscure the priorities of creditors' claims.

Excess of Cost over Fair Value of Net Assets Acquired

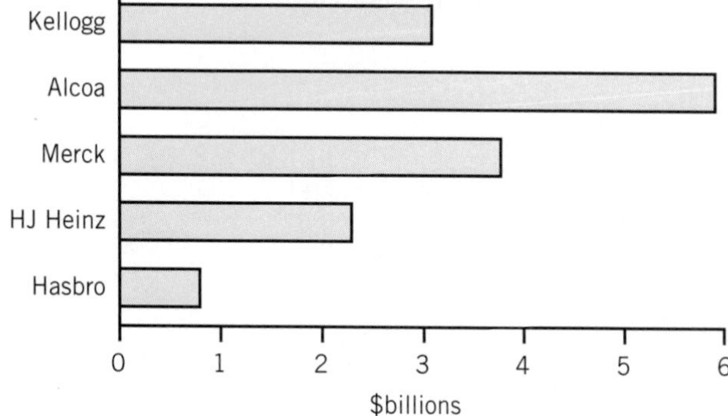

Source: Annual reports.

Consequences of Accounting for Goodwill

The excess of the purchase price over the market value of identifiable net assets acquired represents payment for super (abnormal) earnings. Superearnings are attributed to brand names and other items offering superior competitive position. Superior competitive position is subject to change from a myriad of economic and environmental forces. With effort and opportunity, a company can maintain a superior position. Nevertheless, goodwill is not permanent.

The residual measurement of goodwill gives rise to potential measurement problems. For example, payments resulting from errors of estimation, of intense bidding contests, or of carelessness with owner or creditor resources get swept into goodwill. These payments can even include finder's fees, legal costs, investment banker fees, and interim financing costs. Warren Buffett, chairman of Berkshire Hathaway, recognized this residual measurement of goodwill in writing to his shareholders: "When an overexcited management purchases a business at a silly price . . . silliness ends up in the goodwill account. Considering the lack of managerial discipline that created the account, under the circumstances it might better be labeled no-will." The crux of this issue is: Does goodwill represent superior earnings power and do its benefits extend to future periods? Our analysis must realize that in too many cases the answer is no.

If companies do write off goodwill in the face of substantial losses by purchased subsidiaries, the timing of the write-off seldom reflects prompt recognition of this loss in value. The following case reflects this.

ANALYSIS EXCERPT

Bangor Punta Corporation acquired Piper Aircraft for payment that included a substantial amount for goodwill. Ultimately, time revealed that this payment was for superlosses rather than superearnings. In one period, Bangor Punta earned $3.1 million on a consolidated basis, while Piper Aircraft lost $22.4 million. Only when confronting a subsequent operating loss of $38.5 million by Piper Aircraft and an overall consolidated loss did Bangor Punta write off the Piper Aircraft goodwill of $54.7 million. It also appears that Bangor Punta did so with a "big bath." That is, recognition of the write-off was delayed until its impact was diminished by Bangor Punta's own loss (it took all the hits at one time). This write-off also yielded the beneficial side effect of relieving Bangor Punta's future income of goodwill amortization charges.

To help in our analysis, we might better understand goodwill and its implications for analysis if we compare the accounting definition of goodwill to the usual analyst's definition:

Accounting definition of goodwill. Goodwill is the excess of cost over fair market value of net assets acquired in a purchase transaction. No attempt is made to explicitly identify components of this asset or the economic values assigned to them. Whatever has been paid for and that cannot be separately identified is assigned to goodwill.

Analyst's definition of goodwill. Goodwill reflects real economic value such as that due to brand names requiring costly development and maintenance. Goodwill can also reflect overpayments attributed to unrealistic expectations, undisciplined zeal, or lack of sound judgment and proper analysis. Evaluation of goodwill requires careful analysis of a company's competitive market position and superior earning power with respect to its operations. Goodwill represents a nonpermanent advantage that must manifest itself in superior earning power; if not, it does not exist.

Analysis of goodwill continues to be challenging. Billions of dollars in goodwill are on corporate balance sheets. In certain companies, it represents a substantial part of net assets or even exceeds total equity. Payment for superior earning power is warranted. Still, analysis must be aware that in many cases goodwill is nothing more than mechanical application of accounting rules giving little consideration to value received in return. The process by which billions of dollars in goodwill are placed on balance sheets is illustrated by a prior battle for control of RJR Nabisco:

ANALYSIS EXCERPT

Prior to the bidding battle for RJR Nabisco, the market (dominated by financial institutions holding 40 percent of its stock) valued the company at about $12 billion. A group, led by RJR Nabisco's CEO, started the bidding by offering $17 billion for the company—$5 billion more than the value assigned to it by the market. RJR Nabisco was eventually sold for $25 billion, including $13 billion in goodwill. Undoubtedly swept into this account were significant costs of financing, professional and investment banking talent, and other expenses involved in this costly bidding war. A reasonable analysis concern is the extent to which goodwill reflects, or does not reflect, the present value of future residual income (superearnings).

Finally, our analysis must also realize that goodwill on corporate balance sheets typically fails to reflect a company's entire intangible earning power (due to market position, brand names, or other proprietary advantages). That is, under generally accepted accounting principles, internally developed goodwill cannot be recorded as an asset. This is evidenced in the case of Philip Morris:

ANALYSIS EXCERPT

Philip Morris acquired General Foods for $5.8 billion, of which about $2.8 billion was payment for goodwill. General Foods' brand names arguably justify this premium. On Philip Morris's balance sheet, goodwill makes up nearly 80% of equity. Yet, it does not include the considerable value of Philip Morris's own brand names.

Pooling Accounting for Business Combinations

Although disallowed for business combinations initiated subsequent to June 30, 2001, companies may continue the use of pooling accounting for acquisitions accounted for under that method prior to the effective date of the standard. Pooling accounting was widely used and will continue to impact financial statements for many years to come. It is important, therefore, for analysts to understand the accounting for business combinations under this method. This section describes the mechanics of pooling accounting and follows with a discussion of the analysis implications.

The difference between the pooling and purchase accounting methods lies in the amount recorded as the initial investment in the acquired company. Under the purchase method, as we have seen, the investment account is debited for the purchase price, that is, the fair market value of the acquired company on the date of acquisition. Under the pooling method, this debit is in the amount of the book value of the acquired company. Assets are not written up from the historical cost balances reported on the investee company balance sheet, no new intangible assets are created in the acquisition, and no goodwill is reported. The avoidance of goodwill was the principle attraction of this method as companies would thereby avoid the subsequent earnings drag from goodwill amortization.

Mechanics of Pooling-of-Interest Accounting

Continuing with our previous example, under pooling accounting, the initial investment is recorded as follows:

Investment in Micron	620,000	
Common Stock		50,000 (at par value)
Additional Paid-in Capital		80,000
Retained earnings		490,000

The investment account is $150,000 less than in our previous example as the assets of the acquired company are recorded at book value rather than market value. In addition, Synergy records beginning retained earnings and paid-in capital (common stock and additional paid-in capital) equal to that of Micron as of the beginning of the year.

During the year, Micron earns $150,000. The investment is accounted for under the equity method and has a balance on Synergy's books at December 31, Year 2, as follows:

Beginning balance (12/31/Y1)	$620,000
Investment income	150,000
Dividends	0
Ending balance (12/31/Y2)	$770,000

The consolidated balance sheet under pooling accounting is as follows:

SYNERGY CORP. AND SUBSIDIARY
Trial Balances and Consolidated Financial Statements
For Year Ended December 31, Year 2
Prepared under the Pooling Accounting Method

	Synergy	Micron	Debits	Credits	Consolidated
Revenues	$ 610,000	$ 370,000			$ 980,000
Cost of goods sold	(270,000)	(140,000)			(410,000)
Depreciation expense	(115,000)	(80,000)			(195,000)
Amortization expense	0	0			0
Investment income	150,000	0	[2] $150,000		0
Net income	$ 375,000	$ 150,000			$ 375,000
Retained earnings, 1/1/Y1	$1,170,000	$ 490,000	[1] 490,000		$1,170,000
Net income	375,000	150,000			375,000
Dividends paid	(90,000)				(90,000)
Retained earnings, 12/31/Y2	$1,455,000	$ 640,000			$1,455,000
Cash	$ 105,000	$ 20,000			$ 125,000
Receivables	380,000	220,000			600,000
Inventory	560,000	280,000			840,000
Investment in Micron	770,000	0		[1] $620,000 [2] 150,000	0
Plant, property and equipment (net)	1,880,000	720,000			2,600,000
Total assets	$3,695,000	$1,240,000			$4,165,000
Liabilities	$ 780,000	$ 470,000			$1,250,000
Common stock	800,000	100,000	[1] 100,000		800,000
Additional paid-in capital	660,000	30,000	[1] 30,000		660,000
Retained earnings	1,455,000	640,000			1,455,000
Total liabilities and equity	$3,695,000	$1,240,000	$770,000	$770,000	$4,165,000

The original balance of the investment account on the purchase date ($620,000) represents the book value of Micron's stockholder's equity. It consists of the beginning of the year retained earnings plus Micron's paid-in capital (common stock plus additional paid-in capital). In contrast to the purchase method, however, the investment balance does not include the fair market value of the tangible assets, the previously unrecognized trademark, and the goodwill purchased in the acquisition. The two consolidation entries accomplish the following:

1. Replace $620,000 of the investment account with the book value of the assets acquired.
2. Eliminate the investment income recorded by Synergy and replace that account with the income statement of Micron.

There are several important points to understand about the consolidation process using the pooling method:

- The consolidated balance sheet includes the book value of both Synergy and Micron.
- The consolidated income statement includes the income statements of both Synergy and Micron. Depreciation is only computed on the historical book values of both companies, not the acquisition price. Net income is, therefore, higher.
- There is no recognition of the unrecorded trademark or goodwill. Consequently, prior to the passage of the current business accounting standards, this would have avoided amortization of goodwill.

MURKY POOL

In a recent pooling, Applied Materials paid $1.8 billion to take over Etec Systems, a maker of laser gear. Etic's book value was $249 million—meaning that $1.5 billion of the purchase price is not recorded on the books.

- The income of Micron is included for the entire year in the year of acquisition, not subsequent to the acquisition date.

MICKEY'S PROFITS IMPROVE
Changes in the accounting for goodwill have increased Walt Disney Company's earnings. Disney's acquisition of CapitalCities/ABC resulted in goodwill of $19.2 billion. The $480 million annual hit to Disney's earnings from goodwill amortization is no longer present under current accounting rules.

The difference in net income between purchase and pooling is due to pooling's reporting of fixed assets at $720,000 (their historical cost to Micron) and the consequent omission of the excess depreciation/amortization expense. This example emphasizes that reporting of income for the combined company at either $367,000 or $375,000 depends on how the acquisition is accounted for. Note that revaluation of assets and liabilities, or absence thereof, is the fundamental difference between pooling and purchase accounting. Pooling potentially understates assets and overstates income in current and future periods. This heightens our concern with potentially inflated earnings from pooling accounting.

For analysis, we summarize likely consequences from pooling accounting for the combined company that markedly distinguish it from purchase accounting:

- Assets are acquired and carried at book value and not the market value of the consideration given. To the extent goodwill or other identifiable intangible assets are purchased, the acquiring company does not report them on its balance sheet.
- Understatement of assets yields understatement in combined company equity.
- Understatement of assets (including inventory, property, plant, equipment, goodwill, and intangibles) yields understatement of expenses (such as cost of goods sold, depreciation, and amortization) and overstatement of income.
- Understatement of assets yields likely overstatement of gains on asset disposition.
- Understatement of equity or overstatement of income yields overstatement in return on investment ratios.
- Income statements and balance sheets of the combined entity are restated for all periods reported. (Under purchase accounting, they are combined and reported *postacquisition*–although pro forma statements showing preacquisition combined results are typically furnished.)

Restating prior periods' statements can lead to a type of double counting similar in effect to an acquirer of a pooled company reporting gains on the sale of undervalued acquired (pooled) assets. Such a case is evidenced in the following.

ANALYSIS EXCERPT

Blockbuster Entertainment enhanced earnings by means of acquisitions accounted for as poolings. This arguably inflated its stock price—used to consummate additional poolings. Blockbuster acquired its largest franchisee, Video Superstore, for stock. Blockbuster's past sales of video tapes to Video Superstore contributed greatly to Blockbuster's profits. When Video Superstore was pooled, the revenues and profits related to the intercompany video tape sales were eliminated in comparative statements. With these prior sales and profits reported at now lower levels, Blockbuster's growth curve appeared all the more impressive.

One crude adjustment for omitted values in a pooling transaction is to estimate the difference between reported amounts and the market value of assets acquired. This difference would then be amortized against reported income on some reasonable basis to arrive at results comparable to those achieved under purchase accounting. Generally, purchase accounting is designed to recognize the acquisition to which a buyer and seller in a business acquisition agree. As such, it is more relevant for our analysis needs provided we are interested in market values at the date of a business combination rather than the original costs of the seller.

> ***ANALYSIS VIEWPOINT . . . YOU ARE THE INVESTMENT BANKER***
>
> Your client, LA Delivery, requests your services in offering common stock to potential shareholders. You are excited about this engagement for, among other reasons, you are offered a 7% fee for services. Prior to accepting the engagement, you perform an analysis of the company and its financial statements. One matter concerns you. You discover LA Delivery recently acquired Riverside Trucking. LA Delivery accounts for this acquisition using pooling accounting. Your concern stems from pooling accounting and its potential to understate assets of Riverside Trucking. This would imply a corresponding overstatement in income due to lower expenses attributed to less depreciation with the understated assets. Since Riverside Trucking's income is pooled with that of LA Delivery's income, the income number and financial ratios based on income are *inflated.* The pooling accounting used by LA Delivery is acceptable practice and is fully disclosed in the financial statements. Do you accept this engagement?

Answer–p. 297

SECTION 2: INTERNATIONAL ACTIVITIES

REPORTING OF INTERNATIONAL ACTIVITIES

When we analyze the financial statements of a company with international investments and operations, we must recognize obstacles unique to companies operating in more than one country. These obstacles subdivide into at least two categories:

1. Obstacles due to differences in accounting practices peculiar to a country where operations exist.
2. Obstacles arising from translation of assets, liabilities, and equities into the home-country measuring unit.

This section considers both of these obstacles for analysis of international activities.

International Accounting and Auditing Practices

Accounting practices vary considerably across countries. There are several reasons for cross-country variation in accounting, including lack of agreement on objectives of financial statements, differences in legal requirements, disparities in taxation laws, and variation in authority and maturity of local professional bodies (such as securities exchanges). Recent years have seen serious attempts at more conformity in international accounting practices. Establishment of international accounting standards through the International Accounting Standards Board (IASB) is a major step toward uniformity. IASB's objective is to "formulate and publish in the public interest, basic standards to be observed in the presentation of audited accounts and financial statements and to promote their worldwide acceptance and observance." IASB continues to release standards for accounting and reporting on a number of important topics (such as changing prices, taxes, contingencies, pensions, earnings per share). These standards represent important steps toward narrowing differences in accounting practices across countries.

COMPETITION
Many foreign companies won't list on Wall Street if they must meet U.S. GAAP—they want the United States to accept IASB GAAP. As such, the NYSE and Nasdaq face fierce competition, both from electronic markets at home and from foreign exchanges such as Deutsche Bourse. The latter has applied to put its terminals in New York to let U.S. investors trade on European markets.

Perspectives on International Accounting

A key premise of this book is that analysis of financial statements requires an understanding of the accounting underlying their preparation. When confronting analysis of international companies, we must possess a working familiarity with international accounting practices. Variation in international accounting is linked to differences in financial reporting objectives across countries. Accounting is a social science and its objectives are determined within societal settings. A country's history, culture, politics, geography, legal system, economic environment, and religion all affect financial reporting. For this reason, harmonization of international accounting practices is difficult. In the United States, financial statements are prepared with an emphasis on the interests of security holders. In Germany, the interests of creditors tend to dominate, while in France, the government and taxing authorities' interests take precedence. Moreover, in countries like Switzerland and Germany, the emphasis is on conservatism where reserves, including some unreported, are used to understate both assets and income or to overstate liabilities. We must recognize that not all countries share the view that accounting is a means to communicate economic data for investment and credit decisions.

R&D COSTS
Under U.S. accounting, research and development must be subtracted from current earnings. International standards allow companies to spread out some development expenses, which can permit them to smooth earnings growth.

Due to variations across these systems and societies, differences in accounting practices across countries can be substantial. Exhibit 5.1 lists a few key differences indicative of international practices. Our analysis must use up-to-date sources in identifying significant international accounting differences. In consolidating international subsidiaries, U.S.-based multinationals usually require their subsidiaries' accounting to conform to the parent company.

Exhibit 5.1 ***Key Sources of Differences in International Accounting Practices***

- Inventory reserves and other unrecorded ("hidden") reserves permitted.
- Restatements of property accounts due to price-level changes.
- Legal reserves amounting to a fixed percent of income recorded.
- Tax allocation not practiced.
- Stock dividends recorded using the par value of stock issued.
- Pooling of interests accounting not sanctioned.
- Consolidation of parent and subsidiary financial statements not required.
- Pension liabilities not fully recognized.
- Provisions (reserves) and subsequent reversals used to manage income.
- Capitalization of lease obligations not generally acceptable.
- Certain assets (research and development) not recorded on financial statements.
- Little significance attached to consistency in accounting.
- Disclosure of accounting policies not fully required.

Perspectives on International Auditing and Governance

Auditing and governance activities are concerned with the reliability of financial reporting and ensuring managerial accountability. There is a variety of international auditing and governance practices. In countries like the United Kingdom, Australia, and Canada, the auditing function is important and highly regarded, while in others its standing is weak and, consequently, the reliability of financial statements is reduced. An auditing firm of international repute can enhance the credibility of a company's financial statements. Our analysis must assess the reliability of financial statements with knowledge of auditing and governance mechanisms in place.

ANALYSIS VIEWPOINT ***. . . YOU ARE THE BOND RATER***

Your supervisor assigns you the task of rating an international bond issue. Your analysis follows the usual procedures, including examination of numerous measures of both risk and return for the bonds involved. Upon completion, you submit your bond rating to the supervisor. Your supervisor responds with several questions as to how you dealt with international auditing and governance concerns. How do you satisfy your supervisor's concerns?

Answer–p. 297

Translation of Foreign Currencies

Consolidation of, and equity accounting for, foreign subsidiaries (and affiliates) requires translation of their financial statements into dollar equivalents. This is necessary before the accounts of foreign subsidiaries are combined with the parent company. We now turn to a discussion of this important topic and examine both the mechanics of the translation process and its implications for analysis of consolidated financial statements that include operations conducting business activities in foreign currencies.

Methods of Foreign Currency Translation

Many non-U.S. subsidiaries conduct business activities in their local currencies. That is, sales are made, assets are purchased, and debts are created and paid in the local currency. Their financial statements, therefore, are reported in the local currency. Before a non-U.S. subsidiary can be consolidated with its U.S. parent, however, the local-currency-denominated financial statements must be converted into U.S. dollars. This conversion is called **foreign currency translation.**

The accounting for foreign currency translation is governed by *SFAS 52,* issued in 1981. This standard prescribes two translation approaches, the **current rate method** (most commonly used) and the **temporal method**. To determine which method is appropriate for a particular subsidiary, the standard created the concept of a **functional currency**. The functional currency is the primary currency employed by the subsidiary. It can be either the $U.S. or local currency. Once the functional currency is determined, the prescribed translation method is as follows:

Companies Reporting Foreign Currency Translation Adjustments

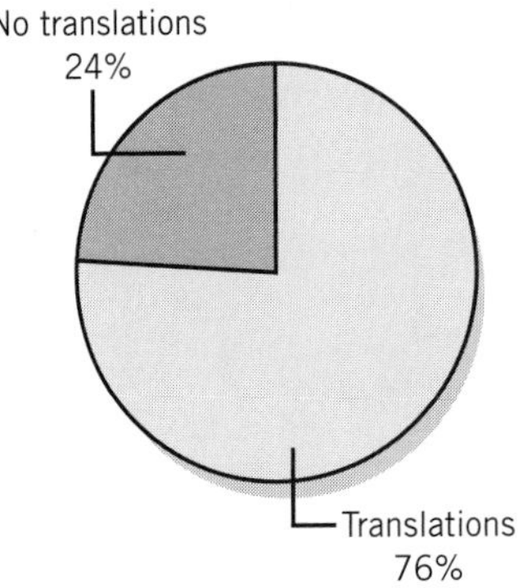

Source: Accounting Trends & Techniques.

Functional Currency	Translation Method
Local currency	Current rate method
$U.S.	Temporal method

The choice of the functional currency is related to the degree of independence of the subsidiary from its parent. If the subsidiary is relatively independent, the local currency is the functional currency and the current rate method is employed. These companies use the local currency to conduct their business activities. If the subsidiary is closely integrated with the parent, conducting most of their transactions in U.S. currency, for example, the functional currency is the U.S. dollar and the temporal method is employed. *SFAS 52* provides a number of indicators that may be used in the determination of the functional currency of the subsidiary. There is some leeway, however, available to management in the selection process. One final note, subsidiaries located in highly inflationary economies (cumulative three-year inflation rates in excess of 100%) are required to employ the temporal method.

FIXED ASSETS
International standards allow companies to revalue buildings and equipment when appropriate, creating an opportunity to boost equity if asset values increase. U.S. rules value assets at cost.

There are important implications of the choice of the translation method. If the current rate method is employed, **translation adjustments** are reported in other comprehensive income (OCI) and do not affect current income. If the temporal method is employed, however, these adjustments are reported as **remeasurement** gains and losses in the income statement. The majority of multinational corporations employ the current rate method and, thereby, defer these translation gains and losses for as long as they continue to own the foreign subsidiary.

Translation of financial statements involves four exchange rates:

1. **Historical**–the exchange rate in effect when the transaction originally occurred.
2. **Current**–the exchange rate in effect at the end of the accounting period.
3. **Specific**–the exchange rate in effect when specific transactions occur.
4. **Weighted average**–the weighted-average exchange rate in effect during the accounting period.

A comparison of the current and temporal methods is illustrated by the following table:

	EXCHANGE RATE USED FOR TRANSLATION	
	Current Rate Method	Temporal Method
Account		
Cash and securities	Current	Current
Inventory	Current	Historical
PP&E and intangibles	Current	Historical
Current liabilities	Current	Current
Long-term liabilities	Current	Current
Capital stock	Historical	Historical
Retained earnings	Derived	Derived
Dividends	Specific	Specific
Revenues	Average	Average
Expenses	Average	Average
COGS	Average	Historical
Depreciation/amortization	Average	Historical
Translation adjustment	Other comprehensive income	
Remeasurement gains (losses)		Income statement

Under the current method, all assets and liabilities are translated at the current rate, or spot rate, in effect as of the statement date. Stockholders' equity accounts are translated at historical rates with dividends translated at the specific rate in effect when the dividends are declared. Income statement items that are deemed to have occurred evenly throughout the period are translated at the weighted-average exchange rate, with specific exchange rates for nonrecurring items like gains or losses on the sale of assets. Finally, the cumulative translation adjustment is reported in other comprehensive income and does not affect current profitability. It is, in effect, deferred until the foreign subsidiary is sold.

The temporal method requires *monetary* assets and liabilities (cash, receivables, and short-term and long-term debt) to be translated at the current exchange rate. All other assets and stockholders' equity accounts are translated at the historical exchange rate, with dividends translated at the specific date the dividends are declared. Revenues and expenses occurring evenly throughout the period are translated at the weighted-average exchange rate, but expenses relating to assets translated at historical exchange rates are reported at those exchange rates. For example, depreciation is computed based on the originally capitalized cost of the fixed asset and is, therefore, a function of the exchange rate in effect when the asset was acquired. Likewise, since inventories are translated at the historical rates in effect when acquired, cost of goods sold is computed using those capitalized costs and the cost flow assumption (e.g., LIFO/FIFO) used by the company. Finally, remeasurement gains and losses as a result of the translation process are reflected in current income and, thereby, affect the current profitability of the company.

Companies Reporting Foreign Currency Translation Gains or Losses

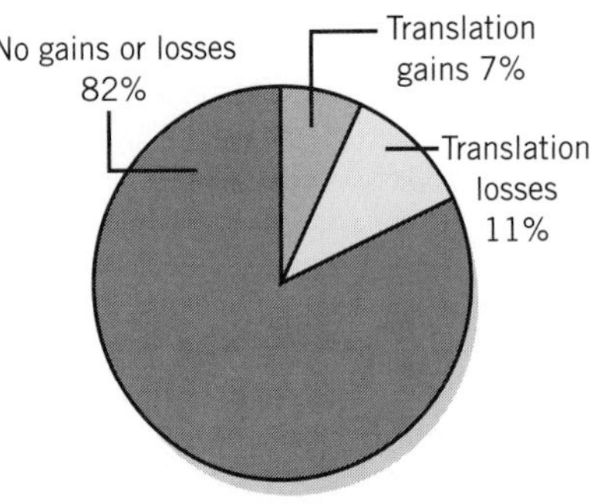

Source: Accounting Trends & Techniques.

Accounting for Foreign Currency Translation

We now illustrate the mechanics of foreign currency translation under the current method as it is the most commonly used. The major provisions of accounting for foreign currency translation are:

- Translation requires identifying the functional currency of the entity. It is generally the currency of the country in which the subsidiary is located. All financial statement elements of the foreign entity are measured using the functional currency, in conformity with the parent's accounting practices.
- Translation from the functional currency into U.S. currency is required prior to consolidation. This translation generally occurs at the *current* exchange rate (reporting date), except for revenues and expenses that are translated at the *average* current exchange rate during the period.
- Translation adjustments are not included in net income. Rather, they are reported and accumulated as a separate component of equity (in comprehensive income) until such time as the parent sells or completely or substantially liquidates the net investment in the foreign entity. The cumulative translation adjustments are removed from equity and included as gains or losses in determining income for the period when such sale or liquidation occurs.
- Once the financial statements of the subsidiary have been translated into U.S. dollars, the subsidiary is consolidated with the parent as described earlier in this chapter.

Illustration of Foreign Currency Translation

BritCo, a wholly owned British subsidiary of DollarCo, incorporates when the exchange rate is £1 = US$1.10. No capital stock changes have occurred since incorporation. The trial balance of BritCo at December 31, Year 6, expressed in units is reproduced in Step (5) as follows:

Additional Information for Translation:

1. BritCo's trial balance is adjusted to conform to DollarCo's accounting principles. The pound (£) is the functional currency of BritCo.
2. The Cumulative Foreign Exchange Translation Adjustment account at December 31, Year 5, is $30,000 (credit).
3. The dollar balance of Retained Earnings at December 31, Year 5, is $60,000.
4. Exchange rates are as follows:

January 1, Year 6	£1 = US$1.20
December 31, Year 6	£1 = US$1.40
Average for Year 6	£1 = US$1.30

5. All accounts receivable, payables, and noncurrent liability amounts are denominated in the local currency. BritCo's December 31, Year 6, trial balance is:

	Debit	Credit
Cash	£ 100,000	
Accounts receivable	300,000	
Inventories, at cost	500,000	
Prepaid expenses	25,000	
Property, plant, and equipment (net)	1,000,000	
Long-term note receivable	75,000	
Accounts payable		£ 500,000
Current portion of long-term debt		100,000
Long-term debt		900,000
Capital stock		300,000
Retained earnings, January 1, Year 6		50,000
Sales		5,000,000
Cost of sales	4,000,000	
Depreciation	300,000	
Other expenses	550,000	
Totals	£6,850,000	£6,850,000

6. Sales, purchases, and all operating expenses occur evenly throughout the year. Accordingly, use of the average exchange rate produces results as if each individual month's revenues and expenses are translated using the rate in effect during each month. In this case, cost of goods sold is also convertible by use of the average rate.
7. Income tax consequences, if any, are ignored in this illustration.

Exhibit 5.2 reports the translation of the trial balance into both a balance sheet and income statement. The balance sheet highlights the reporting of translation adjustments as a separate component of shareholders' equity–usually this is simply reported in a more general component titled Accumulated Other Comprehensive Income (Loss). A review of the translated financial statements of BritCo reveals the following:

1. The company converts all income statement items using the average rate of exchange during the year.
2. All assets and liabilities are translated at the current rate of exchange as of the balance sheet date. Capital stock is translated at the historical rate. If all of a foreign entity's assets and liabilities are measured in its functional currency and are translated at the current exchange rate, then the net accounting effect of a change in the exchange rate is the effect on the entity's net assets. This accounting result is compatible with the concept of economic hedging, which is the basis of the net investment view. That is, no gains or losses arise from hedged assets and liabilities, and the dollar equivalent of the unhedged net investment increases or decreases as the functional currency strengthens or weakens.
3. Notice that after the translated net income for Year 6 of $195,000 is added to the retained earnings in the balance sheet, a translation adjustment of $85,000 must be inserted to balance the statement. When this current year translation adjustment (credit) of $85,000 is added to the $30,000 beginning credit balance of the Cumulative Foreign Exchange Translation Adjustment account, the ending balance equals a credit of $115,000. This is the beginning balance of this equity account for January 1, Year 7.

Exhibit 5.2

BRITCO

Translated Balance Sheet and Income Statement
Year Ended December 31, Year 6

	£	Exchange Rate	Translation Code or Explanation*	US $
Balance Sheet				
Cash	100,000	1.4	C	140,000
Accounts receivable	300,000	1.4	C	420,000
Inventories, at cost	500,000	1.4	C	700,000
Prepaid expenses	25,000	1.4	C	35,000
Property, plant, and equipment (net)	1,000,000	1.4	C	1,400,000
Long-term note receivable	75,000	1.4	C	105,000
Total assets	2,000,000			2,800,000
Accounts payable	500,000	1.4	C	700,000
Current portion of long-term debt	100,000	1.4	C	140,000
Long-term debt	900,000	1.4	C	1,260,000
Total liabilities	1,500,000			2,100,000
Capital stock	300,000	1.1	H	330,000
Retained earnings:				
Balance, 1/1/Year 6	50,000		B	60,000
Current year net income	150,000		F	195,000
Balance, 12/31/Year 6	200,000			255,000
Cumulative foreign exchange translation adjustment:				
Balance, 1/1/Year 6			B	30,000
Current year translation adjustment			G	85,000
Balance, 12/31/Year 6				115,000
Total stockholders' equity	500,000			700,000
Total liabilities and equity	2,000,000			2,800,000
Income Statement				
Sales	5,000,000	1.3	A	6,500,000
Cost of sales	(4,000,000)	1.3	A	(5,200,000)
Depreciation	(300,000)	1.3	A	(390,000)
Other expenses	(550,000)	1.3	A	(715,000)
Net income	150,000			195,000

**Translation code or explanation:*
C = Current rate.
H = Historical rate.
A = Average rate.
B = Balance in U.S. dollars at the beginning of the period.
F = Per income statement.
G = Amount needed to balance the financial statements.

Analysis of Translation Gain or Loss. Use of the current rate translation yields a balancing figure of $85,000 in the translated balance sheet. This translation gain of $85,000 for BritCo is added to the Cumulative Foreign Exchange Translation Adjustment

GLOBAL BURNS
Accounting helps reveal risks of global operations such as the following: Credit Suisse took an earnings hit of about $700 million in Russia; Barclays Bank expects to write off $542 million in emerging markets; Deutsche Bank has an estimated $8 billion exposure (about 3% of total lending) to Asia, Latin America, and Russia; Dresdner Bank is owed about $5.8 billion by borrowers in Asia, Latin America, and Russia.

account in equity. Exchange rate changes do not affect accounts translated at historical rates because such accounts are assigned the dollar amount prevailing at their origination. Accordingly, exchange gains and losses arise from translation of assets and liabilities at the current rate. Since companies translate equity accounts at historical rates, it is the remaining net assets translated at current rates that are exposed to risk of changes in exchange rates. If the dollar strengthens against the foreign currency, the dollar value of foreign net assets declines and yields exchange losses. If the dollar weakens against the foreign currency, the dollar value of foreign net assets increases and yields exchange gains–this is the case with BritCo in Year 6.

The $85,000 translation gain for BritCo, that we computed indirectly, is also computable directly. We start with the beginning net asset position of £350,000 (capital stock of £300,000 + retained earnings of £50,000). Then we multiply the beginning balance of net assets by the change in exchange rate between the beginning and end of the year–in our illustration, this is a strengthening of $0.20 ($1.40 − $1.20) per pound. Since net assets increase in Year 6, the entire beginning balance is exposed to the change in exchange rate for the year, yielding a gain of $70,000 for this part of net assets (computed as £350,000 × $0.20). The second part involves the *change* in net assets during the year. Here we multiply the change by the difference between the year-end rate ($1.40) and the rate prevailing at the date or dates when change(s) occur. We know in the BritCo example that the change occurs due to income earned. Revenue and expense items are translated at the average exchange rate ($1.30). Therefore, we multiply the increase in net assets by the difference between the year-end rate and the average rate ($1.40 − $1.30) or $0.10. We can directly compute the translation gain as follows:

Translation gain on beginning net assets (£350,000 × [$1.40 − $1.20])	$70,000
Translation gain on increase in net assets for Year 6 (£150,000 × [$1.40 − $1.30])	15,000
Total translation gain	$85,000

When the cause of a change in net assets for the year is due to reasons other than those related to operations, the company needs to identify the reasons along with the rate of exchange for translation. These adjustments enter the computation of translation gain or loss consistent with the above procedures.

Disclosing Foreign Currency Translation

Practice requires disclosure of the aggregate transaction gain or loss in income for the period. It also requires disclosure of the analysis of changes during the period as a separate component of equity for cumulative translation adjustments. The SEC is concerned about the adequacy of disclosures for the effects of translating international operations. They encourage additional disclosure in Management's Discussion and Analysis section to supplement financial statements, including:

- Explaining how rate changes affect reported operating results (such as the depressing effect of weakening foreign currencies on reported sales).
- Identifying functional currencies used in measuring foreign operations.
- Describing the degree of exposure to exchange rate risks.
- Determining availability of cash flows from foreign operations in meeting company demands.
- Describing net investments by major functional currency.
- Identifying the company's intracompany financing practices.
- Interpreting the nature of translation components of equity.
- Analyzing the translation components of equity by functional currency or geographical region.

Accounting for Foreign Investment by Parent Company

When the parent company accounts for the investment in a foreign subsidiary by using the equity method, the parent records its proportionate share of the translation adjustment. In our illustration, DollarCo makes the following entries in Year 6 (in US$):

Investment in BritCo	195,000	
Equity in Earnings of Subsidiary		195,000
To record equity in BritCo's earnings (£150,000 × 1.3).		

Investment in BritCo	85,000	
Translation Adjustment		85,000
To record current year translation adjustment.		

If DollarCo sells its investment in BritCo on January 1, Year 7, then DollarCo: (1) records a gain or loss on the difference between the proceeds of the sale and the reported (book) value of the investment and (2) transfers the Cumulative Foreign Exchange Translation Adjustment account, with a credit balance of $115,000, to income.

Analysis Implications of Foreign Currency Translation

Accounting for foreign currency translation is controversial, partly due to the difficulty and complexity of translation. Our analysis requires an understanding of both the economic underpinnings and the accounting mechanics to evaluate and predict effects of currency rate changes on a company's financial position.

The temporal method of translation is most faithful to and consistent with the historical cost accounting model. Under this method, nonmonetary items like property, plant, equipment, and inventories are stated at translated dollar amounts at date of acquisition. Similarly, companies translate depreciation and cost of goods sold on the basis of these historical-dollar costs. Since fluctuations in exchange rates do not affect the reported amounts of these nonmonetary assets, exposure to balance sheet translation gains and losses is measured by the excess (or deficit) of monetary assets over monetary liabilities (which are translated at current rates). For example, under the temporal method, if a foreign subsidiary has an excess of monetary liabilities over monetary assets (*high debt position*), then the following relations prevail:

Dollar Versus Local Currency	Balance Sheet Translation Effect
Dollar strengthens	Gain
Dollar weakens	Loss

If a foreign subsidiary has an excess of monetary assets over monetary liabilities (*high equity position*), then the following relations ensue:

Dollar Versus Local Currency	Balance Sheet Translation Effect
Dollar strengthens	Loss
Dollar weakens	Gain

Companies generally do not like translation gains and losses subjected to variation in economic environments as with the temporal method. They dislike even more the recording of these unpredictable gains and losses in net income, yielding earnings volatility. Admittedly, company criticism is not as strong when the translation process results in gains rather than losses.

Current practice does *not* follow the temporal method *except* in two cases:

NATURAL HEDGE

One solution to fluctuating currencies is "natural hedges," in which revenues and expenses are in the same currencies. For instance, by using locally earned revenues to fund production of local products, a company reduces the hit to earnings that come from exporting products from a strong-currency country to one with a weak currency. As one example, Coca-Cola reinvests in local bottling operations instead of repatriating earnings in devalued foreign currencies.

1. When a foreign entity is merely an extension of the parent and, thus, the functional currency is that of the parent.
2. When hyperinflation causes translation of nonmonetary assets to unrealistically low reported values because of using the current rate. The foreign currency thus loses its usefulness and a more stable currency is used.

Current practice uses the current exchange rate method. This approach selectively introduces current value accounting. It also allows gains and losses to bypass the net income statement (reported, instead, in comprehensive income). This removes from current operations certain risk effects of international activities and the risks of changes in exchange rates. Yet, while insulating income from balance sheet translation gains and losses, the current rate method introduces a different translation exposure. Namely, while translation exposure for the temporal method is measured by the difference between monetary assets and monetary liabilities, the translation exposure for the functional currency approach is measured by the *size of the net investment.* This is because all balance sheet items, except equity, are translated at the current rate. We illustrate this as follows.

SwissCo, a subsidiary of AmerCo, started operations on January 1, Year 1, with a balance sheet in euros (€) as follows:

	€		€
Assets		**Liabilities and Equity**	
Cash	100	Accounts payable	90
Receivables	120	Capital stock	360
Inventory	90		
Fixed assets	140		
Total assets	450	Total liabilities and equity	450

The income statement for the year ended December 31, Year 1, is:

	€
Sales	3,000
Cost of sales (including depreciation of SF 20)	(1,600)
Other expenses	(800)
Net income	600

The December 31, Year 1, balance sheet is:

	€		€
Assets		**Liabilities and Equity**	
Cash	420	Accounts payable	180
Receivables	330	Capital stock	360
Inventory	270	Retained earnings	600
Fixed assets (net)	120		
Total assets	1,140	Total liabilities and equity	1,140

The following exchange rates are applicable:

January 1, Year 1	$1 = €2.0
December 31, Year 1	$1 = €3.0
Year 1 average	$1 = €2.5

The beginning and ending balance sheets are translated into dollars as follows:

	JANUARY 1, YEAR 1			DECEMBER 31, YEAR 1		
	€	Conversion	$	€	Conversion	$
Assets						
Cash	100	÷2.0	50	420	÷3.0	140
Receivables	120	÷2.0	60	330	÷3.0	110
Inventory	90	÷2.0	45	270	÷3.0	90
Fixed assets (net)	140	÷2.0	70	120	÷3.0	40
Total assets	450		225	1,140		380
Liabilities and Equity						
Accounts payable	90	÷2.0	45	180	÷3.0	60
Capital stock	360	÷2.0	180	360	÷2.0	180
Retained earnings	—		—	600	*	240
Translation adjustment						(100)
Total liabilities and equity	450		225	1,140		380

**Per income statement—since each individual income statement item is translated at the average rate, net income in dollars is €600 ÷ 2.5 = $240.*

The translation adjustment account (a component of equity as reported in comprehensive income) is independently calculated as:

	€	$
Total equity (equals net assets):		
In € at December 31, Year 1	€960	
Converted into dollars at year-end rate (÷3.0)		$ 320
Less:		
Capital stock at December 31, Year 1, per converted balance sheet (in dollars)		(180)
Retained earnings balance at December 31, Year 1, per converted balance sheet (in dollars)		(240)
Translation adjustment—loss		$(100)

We can derive several analysis insights from this illustration. First, the translation adjustment (loss of $100 in Year 1) is determined from the net investment in SwissCo at end of Year 1 (€960) multiplied by the change in exchange rates. The exchange rate declines from €2.0 per dollar for capital stock, and from €2.5 per dollar for retained earnings, to the year-end exchange rate of €3.0 per dollar. Consequently, the € investment expressed in dollars suffers a loss of $100. This is intuitive–when an investment is expressed in a foreign currency and that currency weakens in relation to the dollar, then the investment value (in dollars) declines. The reverse occurs if that currency strengthens.

Second, under the current rate method, currency translation affects equity (but not income). As such, this approach affects, among other ratios, the debt-to-equity ratio (potentially endangering debt covenants) and book value per share for the translated balance sheet (but not for the foreign currency balance sheet). Since equity capital represents the measure of exposure to balance sheet translation gain or loss under this approach, that exposure is potentially more substantial than under the temporal method, especially with a subsidiary financed with low debt and high equity. Our analysis can estimate the translation adjustment impact by multiplying year-end equity by the estimated change in the period-to-period rate of exchange.

Third, we can examine the effect of a change in exchange rates on the translation of the income statement. If we assume in Year 2 that SwissCo reports the same income but the € further *weakens* to €3.5 (average for year) per dollar, then the translated income totals €600 ÷ 3.5 = $171, or a decline of $69 from the Year 1 level of $240. This loss would be reflected in the translated income statement. In contrast, if the € *strengthens* to €2.0 per dollar (average for year), the translated income totals €600 ÷ 2.0 = $300, or a gain of $60 from the Year 1 level of $240. This gain is reflected in net income and recognizes that income earned in € is worth more dollars. Under the current rate method, translated income varies directly with changes in exchange rates. This makes our estimation of the income statement translation effect easier.

Our analysis must be aware that net income also includes the results of completed foreign exchange transactions. Further, any gain or loss on translation of a current payable by the subsidiary to the parent (which is not of a long-term nature) flows through net income.

A substantial drop in the dollar relative to many important currencies has the effect of increasing the reported net income of consolidated foreign subsidiaries. It also often increases equity, in certain cases by substantial amounts. This effect lowers measures such as return on equity. Should the dollar recover its value, the results are the opposite and yield lower reported net income.

While current practice yields smaller fluctuations in net income relative to the fluctuations in exchange rates, it yields substantial changes in equity because of changes in the cumulative translation adjustment (CTA) account. For companies with a large equity base, these changes are arguably insignificant. But for companies with a small equity base these changes, which further reduce equity, yield potentially serious effects on debt-to-equity and other ratios. This can put a company at risk of violating its debt covenants or other accounting-based restrictions. Exposure to changes in the CTA depends on the degree of exposure in foreign subsidiary net assets to changes in exchange rates. Companies can reduce this exposure by reducing the net assets of their foreign subsidiaries. This can be achieved by withdrawing foreign investment through dividends or by substituting foreign debt for equity. We must recognize that an increasing debit balance in the CTA is often symptomatic of a failure to manage properly the foreign exchange exposure. This can result from investments denominated in persistently weak currencies, among other reasons.

GUIDANCE ANSWERS TO ANALYSIS VIEWPOINTS

LAWYER

Your client needs to be informed about a distinction between "economic substance" and "legal responsibility." Consolidated financial statements are meant to recognize the entire business entity under a centralized control. Economic substance suggests that all subsidiaries under a parent's control are its responsibility and should be reported as such–yielding consolidated statements. Legal responsibility is *not* the same. Shareholders like your client (and NY Research Labs) are *not* responsible for any losses incurred by lawsuits against Boston Chemicals Corporation. Shareholders' risks generally extend only to their investment in a corporation's stock. In sum, NY Research Labs is not responsible for lawsuits of Boston Chemicals because of consolidation. But the amount of NY Research Labs' investment in common stock of Boston Chemicals is subject to the risk presented from these lawsuits.

ANALYST

It appears the ED would require consolidation of many of the bottlers in category (3)—those in which Coca-Cola has controlling ownership. It is difficult to precisely gauge the impact of consolidation on its solvency ratios. Still, it is likely that consolidation would yield solvency ratios that reflect less favorably on Coca-Cola.

INVESTMENT BANKER

There are two important aspects to this case. First, you require complete and accurate disclosure of your client's stock offering according to accepted practices. This includes your analysis of LA Delivery's financial statements to ensure adherence to accepted accounting principles. On this dimension, you are entirely assured. Second, and not unrelated to the first point, you require that your client is not misrepresenting its financial position. This is important for your reputation and future business opportunities as an investment banker. Here is the dilemma. LA Delivery properly reports its financial statements using pooling accounting for its acquisition of Riverside Trucking. Yet you know from your analysis that pooling does not entirely reflect the economic substance of this transaction. More specifically, you expect its common stock will fetch a price considerably higher than what its fundamentals suggest. To accept this engagement you would like to report pro forma statements for LA Delivery assuming *purchase accounting* for Riverside Trucking. In this way you are comfortable in fairly representing the economic substance of your client's financial position. If LA Delivery refuses to disclose any additional information than that required under acceptable practices, you might be forced to decline this engagement.

BOND RATER

Analyzing auditing and governance factors for international bond issue rating decisions is demanding and crucial. You must decide on the role played by particular firms and institutions, and then assign a measure of reliance to their responsibility in safeguarding company assets. The less rigorous are auditing and governance mechanisms, the greater risk assigned to a bond issue. For example, bond covenants are of little value when auditors fail to encourage compliance or disclosure of violations. Audit firms and governance mechanisms do differ in quality and responsibility across countries, and bond ratings must reflect these. The supervisor is wise in questioning a rating's reliance on these factors.

QUESTIONS

5–1. Evaluate the following statement from an analysis viewpoint: "A parent company is not responsible for the liabilities of its subsidiaries nor does it own the assets of its subsidiaries. As such, consolidated financial statements distort legal realities."

5–2. Describe important information potentially disclosed in the individual parent and subsidiary companies' financial statements that is not found in their consolidated statements.

(CFA Adapted)

5–3. Identify and explain some of the important limitations of consolidated financial statements.

5–4. The note below appears in the financial statements of Best Company for the period ending December 31, Year 1:

> Event subsequent to December 31, Year 1: In January Year 2, Best Company acquired Good Products, Inc., and its affiliates by the issuance of 48,063 shares of common stock. Net assets of the combined companies amount to $1,016,198, and net income for Year 1 is $150,000. To the extent the acquired companies earn in excess of $1,000,000 over the next five years, Best Company is required to issue additional shares not to exceed 151,500, and limited to a market value of $2,000,000.

a. Explain whether this disclosure is necessary and adequate.

b. If Good Products, Inc., is acquired in December Year 1, at what price does Best Company record this acquisition? (*Note:* Best Company's shares traded at $22 on the acquisition date.)

c. Explain the contingency for additional consideration.
d. If the contingency materializes to the maximum limit, how does Best Company record this investment?

5–5. Describe how you determine the valuation of assets acquired in a purchase when:
a. Assets are acquired by incurring liabilities.
b. Assets are acquired in exchange of common stock.

5–6. Identify which of the cases require consolidated financial statements.
a. Parent company has a two-fifths ownership of a subsidiary.
b. Parent company has temporary but absolute control over a subsidiary.
c. Parent company has a controlling interest in a subsidiary but plans to dispose of it.
d. Parent company is to relinquish control of a subsidiary in the near future because of a minority shareholder's legal suit.
e. A conglomerate parent company has majority interest in diversified subsidiaries.
f. Parent company has a 100% interest in a foreign subsidiary located in a country where government authorities severely restrict conversion of currencies and the transfer of funds.
g. Parent company has a 100% interest in a subsidiary whose principal business is leasing properties to the parent company and its affiliates.

5–7. From an analysis point of view, is pooling accounting or purchase accounting for a business combination preferable? Explain with reference to the balance sheet and income statement.

5–8. Assume a company appropriately determines the total cost of a purchased entity. Explain how the company allocates this total cost to the following assets.
a. Goodwill.
b. Negative goodwill (bargain purchase).
c. Marketable securities.
d. Receivables.
e. Finished goods.
f. Work in process.
g. Raw materials.
h. Plant and equipment.
i. Land and mineral reserves.
j. Payables.
k. Goodwill recorded by acquired company.

5–9. Describe the analysis procedure available to adjust an income statement using pooling accounting so as to be comparable with an income statement using purchase accounting.

5–10. When an acquisition accounted for as a purchase is effected for stock or other equity securities, discuss what our analysis should be alert to.

5–11. Resources, Inc., is engaged in an aggressive program of acquiring competing companies through the exchange of common stock.
a. Explain how an acquisition program might contribute to the rate of growth in earnings per share of Resources, Inc.
b. Explain how the income statements of prior years might be adjusted to reflect the potential future earnings trend of the combined companies.

(CFA Adapted)

5–12. When a balance sheet reports a substantial dollar amount for goodwill, discuss what we should be concerned with in our analysis.

5–13. Indicate factors that can alter estimates for the benefit periods of intangible assets.

5–14. When a consolidated financial statement includes foreign operations, discuss what information and background an analyst should acquire to perform an effective analysis.

5–15. Identify at least two significant problem areas in the accounting for and the analysis of foreign operations.

5–16. Identify and discuss the major provisions of accounting for foreign currency translation.

5–17. Discuss the major objectives of current accounting practice involving foreign currency translation.

5–18. Identify and discuss at least three implications for analysis of financial statements that result from the accounting for foreign currency translation.

5–19. Describe two circumstances where a company must employ the temporal method of translating foreign currency.

EXERCISES

EXERCISE 5–1
Interpreting Accounting for Business Combinations

Spellman Company acquires 90% of Moore Company in a business combination. The total consideration is agreed upon, but the exact nature of Spellman's payment is not yet fully specified. This business combination is accounted for as a purchase. It is expected that at the date of the business combination, the fair value will exceed the book value of Moore's assets minus liabilities.

Spellman desires to prepare consolidated financial statements that include the financial statements of Moore.

Required:

a. Explain how the method of accounting for a business combination affects whether goodwill is reported.

b. If goodwill is recorded, explain how to determine the amount of goodwill.

c. From a conceptual standpoint, explain why consolidated financial statements should be prepared.

d. From a conceptual standpoint, identify the first necessary condition before consolidated financial statements are prepared.

EXERCISE 5–2
Analyzing and Interpreting Intercorporate Investments

The diagram below portrays Company X (the parent or investor company), its two subsidiaries C1 and C2, and its "50 percent or less owned" affiliate C3. Each of the companies has only one type of stock outstanding, and there are no other significant shareholders in either C2 or C3. All four companies engage in commercial and industrial activities.

X

C1 — 100% owned | C2 — 80% owned | C3 — 30% owned

Required:

a. Explain whether or not each of the separate companies maintains distinct accounting records.

b. Identify the type of financial statements each company prepares for financial reporting.

c. Assume you have the ability to enforce your requests of management, describe the type of financial statement information about these companies (separate or consolidated) that you would request.

d. Explain what Company X reports among its assets regarding subsidiary C1.

e. If C1 is legally dissolved into Company X, describe how Company X's balance sheet would change.

f. If C1 is legally dissolved into Company X, describe how the consolidated balance sheet would change.

g. In the consolidated balance sheet, explain how the 20 percent of C2 that is *not* owned by Company X is reported.

h. Identify the transaction that is necessary before C3 is included line by line in the consolidated financial statements.

i. If combined statements are reported for C1 and C2, discuss the need for any elimination entries.

j. Suppose Company X sold its entire investment in C2 to C1 (C2 then is 80 percent owned by C1). Explain how the consolidated balance sheet changes.

k. If C1 sold additional common stock to Company X for cash, describe how the consolidated balance sheet changes.

EXERCISE 5–3
Analyzing Companies with International Operations

Assume your firm is considering investing in the equity securities of companies operating in several different countries. After a preliminary review of financial statements, you realize there is a range of international accounting practices that can materially affect net income and other financial data relevant for equity valuation purposes.

Required:

a. Discuss at least two plausible approaches for comparing companies operating in different countries and using different accounting principles.

b. Discuss how international variations in accounting for each of the following items can affect reported net income:
(1) Revaluation of fixed assets. (2) Treatment of acquired goodwill. (3) Discretionary reserves.

EXERCISE 5–4
Interpreting the Effects of Functional Currency

Bethel Company uses the U.S. dollar as its functional currency worldwide. Home Brite Company uses the local currency for each country in which it operates as its functional currency.

Required:

Explain how the choice of functional currency affects each of the following:

a. Reported sales.

b. Computation of translation gains and losses.

c. Reporting of translation gains and losses.

(CFA Adapted)

EXERCISE 5–5
Interpreting Foreign Currency Translation

Accounting rules for foreign currency translation are intended to apply to foreign currency transactions and financial statements of foreign branches, subsidiaries, partnerships, and joint ventures that are consolidated, combined, or reported under the equity method.

Required:

a. Explain the following key concepts in accounting for foreign currency translation:
(1) Functional currency. (2) Translation.

b. Describe the accounting problem for foreign currency translation of a multinational company located in a highly inflationary country.

PROBLEMS

PROBLEM 5–1
Intercorporate Investments under the Equity Method

Burry Corporation acquires 80% of Bowman Company for $40 million on January 1, Year 6. At the time of acquisition, Bowman has total net assets with a fair value of $25 million. For the years ended December 31, Year 6, and December 31, Year 7, Bowman reports net income (loss) and pays dividends as shown below:

	Net Income (loss)	Dividends Paid		Net Income (loss)	Dividends Paid
Year 6	$2,000,000	$1,000,000	Year 7	$(600,000)	$800,000

The excess of the acquisition price over the fair value of net assets acquired is assigned to goodwill. Since goodwill has an indefinite life, it is not amortized.

Required:

CHECK
Investment at Dec. 31, Year 7, $39,680

a. Compute the value of Burry's investment in Bowman Co. as of December 31, Year 7, under the equity method.

b. Discuss the strengths and weaknesses of the income statement and balance sheet in reflecting the economic substance of this transaction and subsequent business activities using the equity method.

(CFA Adapted)

PROBLEM 5–2
Analyzing Financial Statement Effects of Intercorporate Investments

The following data are from the annual report of Francisco Company, a specialized packaging manufacturer:

	Year 6	Year 7	Year 8
Sales	$25,000	$30,000	$35,000
Net income	2,000	2,200	2,500
Dividends paid	1,000	1,200	1,500
Book value per share (year-end)	11	12	13

Note: Francisco had 1,000 common shares outstanding during the entire period. There is no public market for Francisco shares.

Potter Company, a manufacturer of glassware, made the following acquisitions of Francisco common shares:

January 1, Year 6	10 shares at $10 per share
January 1, Year 7	290 shares at $11 per share, increasing ownership to 300 shares
January 1, Year 8	700 shares at $15 per share, yielding 100% ownership of Francisco

Ignore income tax effects and the effect of lost income on funds used to make these investments.

Required:

a. Compute the effects of these investments on Potter Company's reported sales, net income, and cash flows for each of the Years 6 and 7.

b. Calculate the carrying value of Potter Company's investment in Francisco as of December 31, Year 6, and December 31, Year 7.

c. Discuss how Potter Company accounts for its investment in Francisco during Year 8. Describe any additional information necessary to calculate the impact of this acquisition on Potter Company's financial statements for Year 8.

(CFA Adapted)

CHECK
(*b*) $3,600 at Dec. 31, Year 7

PROBLEM 5–3
Interpreting Pro Forma Balance Sheets under Purchase and Pooling

Your supervisor asks you to analyze the potential purchase of Drew Company by your firm, Pierson, Inc. You are provided the following information (in millions):

	Pierson, Inc., Historical Cost-Based	DREW COMPANY Historical Cost-Based	DREW COMPANY Fair Value
Current assets	$ 70	$ 60	$ 65
Land	60	10	10
Buildings, net	80	40	50
Equipment, net	90	20	40
Total assets	$300	$130	$165
Current liabilities	$120	$ 20	$ 20
Shareholders' equity	180	110	—
Total liabilities and equity	$300	$130	

Required:

a. Prepare a pro forma combined balance sheet using purchase accounting. Note that Pierson pays $180 million in cash for Drew where the cash is obtained by issuing long-term debt.

b. Discuss how differences between pooling and purchase accounting for acquisitions affect future reported earnings of the Pierson/Drew business combination.

(CFA Adapted)

CHECK
(*a*) Total assets, $500

PROBLEM 5–4
Analyzing Intercorporate and International Investments

Campbell Soup Company

Refer to the financial statements of **Campbell Soup Company** in Appendix A.

Required:

a. As of July 28, Year 11, Campbell owned 33% of Arnotts Limited. Explain where Campbell reports the amounts representing this investment.

b. Note 18 contains disclosures regarding the market value of the company's investment in Arnotts Limited. Explain whether this market value is reflected in Campbell's financial statements beyond the disclosures referred to.

c. In July of Year 11, Campbell acquired the remaining shares of Campbell Canada. This is in addition to one other acquisition during Year 11. Describe what the difference between the purchase price paid for these acquisitions and the fair market value of the acquired net assets implies for analysis purposes.

d. Prepare a composite journal entry recording the total Year 11 acquisitions.

e. Explain the likely causes of changes in the cumulative translation adjustment accounts for (1) Europe and (2) Australia.

CHECK
(*d*) Cr. Cash for 180.1

PROBLEM 5–5
Interpreting Intercorporate Investments and Foreign Operations

Quaker Oats Company

Refer to the financial statements of **Quaker Oats Company** in Appendix A.

Required:

a. The financial statements of fiscal Year 10 and earlier years reflect the company's decision to discontinue (divest) the operations of Fisher-Price. Identify where in the financial statements the assets and liabilities of Fisher-Price are reflected in Year 10.

b. Quaker Oats reports no acquisitions in Years 10 and 11. Yet goodwill amortization, which Quaker Oats is amortizing on a straight-line basis, increases in both years. Explain how these events are reconcilable.

c. Quaker Oats has forward contracts to purchase and sell currencies so as to hedge balance sheet exposure. Describe where gains and losses on these contracts are reported.

d. The company reports on hyper-inflationary conditions in Brazil. Explain where in the financial statements the gains and losses on translation of Brazilian subsidiaries are reflected.

CASES

CASE 5–1
Accounting Entries for Consolidation of Intercorporate Investments

Axel Corporation acquires 100% of the stock of Wheal Company on December 31, Year 4. The following information pertains to Wheal Company on the date of acquisition:

	Book Value	Fair Value
Cash	$ 40,000	$ 40,000
Accounts receivable	60,000	55,000
Inventory	50,000	75,000
Property, plant, and equipment (net)	100,000	200,000
Secret formula (patent)	—	30,000
Total assets	$250,000	$400,000
Accounts payable	$ 30,000	$ 30,000
Accrued employee pensions	20,000	22,000
Long-term debt	40,000	38,000
Capital stock	100,000	—
Other contributed capital	25,000	—
Retained earnings	35,000	—
Total liabilities and equity	$250,000	$ 90,000

Axel Corporation issues $110,000 par value ($350,000 market value on December 31, Year 4) of its own stock to the shareholders of Wheal Company to consummate the transaction, and Wheal Company becomes a wholly owned, consolidated subsidiary of Axel Corporation.

Required:

a. Prepare journal entries for Axel Corp. to record the acquisition of Wheal Company stock assuming (1) pooling accounting and (2) purchase accounting.

b. Prepare the worksheet entries for Axel Corp. to eliminate the investment in Wheal Company stock in preparation for a consolidated balance sheet at December 31, Year 4 assuming (1) pooling accounting and (2) purchase accounting.

c. Calculate consolidated retained earnings at December 31, Year 4 (Axel's retained earnings at this date are $150,000), assuming:
(1) Axel Corp. uses the pooling method for this business combination.
(2) Axel Corp. uses the purchase method for acquisition of Wheal Company.

CHECK
(*b*) Cr. Investment in Wheal for $110,000 in (1), and $350,000 total in (2)

The December 31, Year 8, trial balance of SwissCo Ltd., a Swiss company, follows (in euros, €).

CASE 5–2
Analyzing Translated Financial Statements and Intercorporate Investments

	Debit	Credit
Cash	€ 50,000	
Accounts receivable	100,000	
Allowance for doubtful accounts		€ 10,000
Inventory, January 1, Year 8	150,000	
Property, plant, and equipment (net)	800,000	
Accounts payable		80,000
Notes payable		20,000
Capital stock		100,000
Retained earnings, January 1, Year 8		190,000
Sales		2,000,000
Purchases (of inventory)	1,000,000	
Depreciation expense	100,000	
Other expenses (including taxes)	200,000	
	€2,400,000	€2,400,000

Additional Information:

1. SwissCo uses the periodic inventory system along with the FIFO costing method for inventory and cost of goods sold. On December 31, Year 8, the inventory balance is €120,000—it is carried at FIFO cost.
2. SwissCo capital stock was issued six years ago when the company was established; the exchange rate at that time was €1 = $0.30. The company purchased plant and equipment five years ago when the exchange rate was €1 = $0.35; also, the note payable was made out to a local bank at the same time.
3. Revenues are earned and expenses (including cost of goods sold) are incurred uniformly throughout Year 8. Inventory available at December 31, Year 8, is purchased throughout the second half of Year 8.
4. The December 31, Year 7, balance sheet (in U.S. dollars) of SwissCo shows Retained Earnings of $61,000.
5. The spot rates for € in Year 8 are:

January 1, Year 8	$0.32
Average for Year 8	$0.37
Average for second half of Year 8	$0.36
December 31, Year 8	$0.38

6. Management determined the functional currency of SwissCo is the euro.

Required:

a. Prepare a trial balance in U.S. dollars for SwissCo as of December 31, Year 8.

b. Prepare an income statement for the year ended December 31, Year 8, and the balance sheet at December 31, Year 8 (both in U.S. dollars) for SwissCo.

CHECK
(*b*) Net income, $247,900; Total assets, $402,800

c. Assume Unisco Corporation, a U.S. firm, purchases a 75% ownership interest in SwissCo at book value on January 1, Year 8. Prepare the entry Unisco makes at December 31, Year 8, to record its equity in SwissCo's Year 8 earnings. Unisco Corp. uses the equity method in accounting for its investment in SwissCo.

CASE 5–3
Analyzing Translated Financial Statements

On December 31, Year 8, U.S. Dental Supplies (USDS) created a wholly owned foreign subsidiary, Funi, Inc. (FI), located in the country of Lumbaria. The condensed balance sheet of Funi as of December 31, Year 8, reported in local currency (the pont), follows:

FUNI, INC.
Balance Sheet
December 31, Year 8

	Ponts (millions)
Assets	
Cash	180
Fixed assets (net)	420
Total assets	600
Liabilities and Equity	
Capital stock	600

Funi initially adopted the U.S. dollar as its functional currency and translated its Year 9 balance sheet and income statement in accordance with U.S. accounting practice. These statements are reproduced below:

FUNI, INC.
Balance Sheet
December 31, Year 9

	Ponts (millions)	Exchange Rate (ponts/US$)	US$ (millions)
Assets			
Cash	82	4.0	$ 20.5
Accounts receivable	700	4.0	175.0
Inventory	455	3.5	130.0
Fixed assets (net)	360	3.0	120.0
Total assets	1,597		$445.5
Liabilities and Equity			
Accounts payable	532	4.0	$133.0
Capital stock	600	3.0	200.0
Retained earnings	465		112.5
Total liabilities and equity	1,597		$445.5

FUNI, INC.
Income Statement
For Year Ended December 31, Year 9

	Ponts (millions)	Exchange Rate (ponts/US$)	US$ (millions)
Sales	3,500	3.5	$1,000.0
Cost of sales	(2,345)	3.5	(670.0)
Depreciation expense	(60)	3.0	(20.0)
Selling expense	(630)	3.5	(180.0)
Translation gain (loss)	—		(17.5)
Net income	465		$ 112.5

USDS subsequently instructed Funi to change its functional currency to the pont. The following exchange rates (pont per U.S. dollar) are applicable:

January 1, Year 9	3.0
Average for Year 9	3.5
December 31, Year 9	4.0

Required:

a. Prepare a pro forma balance sheet as of December 31, Year 9, and an income statement for the year ending December 31, Year 9, for Funi. Both statements should be prepared in U.S. dollars, using the pont as the functional currency for Funi.

CHECK
(*a*) Total assets, $399.25; Net income, $132.86

b. Analyze and describe the comparative effects of selecting the dollar versus the pont as the functional currency for Funi:
(1) U.S. dollar balance sheet as of December 31, Year 10.
(2) U.S. dollar income statement for year ended December 31, Year 10.
(3) U.S. dollar financial ratios for Year 10.

(CFA Adapted)

CASE 5–4
Analysis of in-Process R&D Write-Off

Sapient Corporation

Sapient Corporation is a provider of management consulting services, Internet commerce solutions, and systems implementation services. Using a fixed-price model designed to ensure on-budget and on-time delivery, Sapient helps clients achieve their business objectives. Sapient has experienced consistent revenue growth for the past decade. It has more than 1,400 employees in eight U.S. offices and one London office.

Sapient recently acquired Studio Archetype, a leader in the integration of brand strategy, design, and interactive technology. Studio Archetype has 10 years of experience in brand consulting and user-centered design. With its acquisition, Sapient has expanded its Internet and e-business services capabilities to offer Internet consulting services that integrate technology, brand, business strategy, and user-centered design. The acquisitions note from Sapient's annual report follows:

On August 25, 1998, the Company acquired Studio Archetype for approximately $25.3 million in stock and cash, including direct acquisition costs of approximately $2.3 million, pursuant to which the Company issued 498,314 shares of Sapient Common Stock and paid $250,000 in cash to the former Studio stockholders. The acquisition was accounted for as a purchase, and accordingly, the purchase price was allocated to the assets acquired and liabilities assumed based on their respective fair values.

In connection with the acquisition of Studio Archetype in the third quarter of 1998, Sapient allocated $11.1 million to in-process technology and recorded a corresponding income tax benefit of $4.2 million. This allocation represents the estimated fair value of such technology based on risk-adjusted cash flows related to the development of projects that had not reached technological feasibility at the time of the acquisition and with respect to which the in-process research and development had no alternative future uses. Accordingly, these costs were expensed as of the acquisition date.

Sapient allocated values to the in-process research and development projects by identifying significant research projects for which technological feasibility had not been established, including development, engineering, and testing activities associated with the introduction of Studio's Archetype next-generation enterprisewide suite of development, scheduling, bug tracking, and content management applications. The integrated solution will be a comprehensive enterprise scale system, allowing developers and clients to access prototypes and trial deliverables. It will fully integrate user interface tools with client server, advanced database, and legacy systems.

The value assigned to purchased in-process technology was determined by estimating the costs to develop the purchased in-process technology into commercially viable products, estimating the resulting net cash flows from the projects and discounting the net cash flows to their present value. The revenue projection used to value the in-process research and development is based on estimates of relevant market sizes and growth factors, expected trends in technology, and the nature and expected timing of new product introductions by Studio Archetype and its competitors. The estimated revenues for the projects are expected to be realized over a six-year period through 2004 when other new products are expected to enter the market. Studio Archetype projected revenues are dependent upon successful introduction of the in-process projects.

The nature of the efforts to develop the acquired in-process technology into commercially viable products and services principally relate to the completion of all planning, designing, prototyping, verification, and testing activities that are necessary to establish that the proposed technologies meet their design specifications including functional, technical, and economic performance requirements. The efforts to develop the purchased in-process technology also include testing of the technology for compatibility and interoperability with other applications. Expenditures on these projects to date have been approximately $2.5 million, and estimated costs to complete these projects are expected to total approximately $625,000 through 2001. These estimates are subject to change, given the uncertainties of the development process, and no assurance can be given that deviations from these estimates will not occur. Several milestones have been or are near completion including a comprehensive needs analysis mapping data, technical and information architectures and building an integrated prototype.

The rates utilized to discount the net cash flows to their present value are based on venture capital rates of return. Due to the nature of the forecast and the risks associated with the projected growth, profitability and developmental projects, discount rates of 25.0% to 30.0% were utilized for the business enterprise and for the in-process research and development. Sapient believes that these discount rates are commensurate with Studio's stage of development, the uncertainties in the economic estimates described above, the inherent uncertainty surrounding the successful development of the purchased in-process technology, the useful life of such technology, the profitability levels of such technology, and the uncertainty of technological advances that are unknown at this time.

The forecasts used by Sapient in valuing in-process research and development were based upon assumptions that the Company believes to be reasonable but which are inherently uncertain and unpredictable. Sapient's assumptions may be incomplete or inaccurate, and unanticipated events and circumstances are likely to occur. For these reasons, actual results may vary materially from the assumed results and could have a material adverse effect on Sapient's business, results of operations and financial condition.

Sapient believes that the assumptions used in the forecasts were reasonable. No assurance can be given, however, that the underlying assumptions used to estimate expected project sales, development costs or profitability, or the events associated with such projects, will transpire as estimated. For these reasons, actual results may vary from the assumed results and could have a material adverse effect on Sapient's business, results of operations and financial condition.

Sapient expects to continue its support of these efforts and believes Studio Archetype has a reasonable chance of successfully completing the research and development programs. However, there is risk associated with the completion of the projects and there is no assurance that any of the projects will meet with either technological or commercial success.

If these projects are not successfully developed, the sales and profitability of Studio Archetype may be adversely affected in future periods. Additionally, the value of the other intangible assets acquired may become impaired. Studio expects to benefit from the purchased in-process technology beginning in 1999.

Other intangible assets of $14.4 million consists of $3.8 million for marketing assets, $1.6 million for assembled workforce, and approximately $9.0 million of goodwill comprising the reputation of Studio Archetype, all of which have estimated useful lives of approximately 7 years. However there are no assurances that the value of these intangible assets acquired will not become impaired.

Required:

a. Sapient allocated about 44% of the $25.3 million purchase price to in-process R&D (IPR&D). What constitutes IPR&D and how are these amounts reported on its financial statement at the acquisition date?

CHECK
(*b*) Discount rate, 25%–30%

b. What process did Sapient use to value IPR&D? What discount rate was used in its valuation process? What does the magnitude of this rate tell you about the uncertainty in this process?

c. Since the acquisition date, what expenditures have been made on these projects? What estimated costs remain to bring these projects to completion? How are these costs accounted for on its financial statements?

d. What inconsistency do you see in accounting for IPR&D? Why do you believe that the FASB asserts that accounting for IPR&D should be addressed within the context of a project that considers the accounting for all R&D costs?

TYCO International

CASE 5–5
Analyzing TYCO: Aggressive or Out of Line?

TYCO International was featured in a November 1999, article in *Business Week* for its accounting methods related to acquisitions. In mid-October 1999, Tyco's market value declined by 23% amid allegations by an analyst that the company was inflating its growth picture using accounting gimmicks along with rumors that Tyco's auditors would resign. Tyco has spent $30 billion on deals in the past three years alone–$23 billion paid with stock. It has focused on mundane technologies–including security systems, electronic connectors, industrial valves, and health-care products. Tyco reported that its fiscal 1999 net income before special charges more than doubled to $2.6 billion, and sales jumped 83%, to $22.5 billion. Before the allegations, Tyco's market value was over $80 billion, up from just $1.7 billion in 1992.

Some analysts allege Tyco aggressively managed its earnings using acquisitions to produce eye-popping numbers. Wall Street's short-sellers have long whispered about Tyco's accounting. Tyco is known as a "rollup" company–one that uses its lofty stock price to snap up companies with lower PE multiples–whose acquisitions strategy is now at risk given its stock price decline. Tyco's problems center around aggressive merger-related accounting, including restating downward the results of acquired companies before the deals close to make its future results look better. Most of Tyco's biggest acquisitions are accounted for using pooling accounting. This means Tyco restates its financials, effectively pretending the acquired company was part of Tyco long before the deal closed. These restatements make it difficult to compare one period to the next. Adding to the confusion, Tyco has taken $4 billion in merger-related charges in recent years, changed the end of its fiscal year from December to September, and moved its headquarters from the U.S. to Bermuda for a lower tax rate. One analyst claims that Tyco is using huge charges to create "cookie jars" of reserves against future operating expenses.

Indeed, Tyco's earnings look anything but stellar once the massive charges are taken into account. With these charges, Tyco shows huge net losses in both fiscal 1996 and 1997 and an 83 percent drop in net income in the first nine months of fiscal 1999. However, Wall Street convention is to overlook such charges, figuring that pro-forma earnings provides a better picture of "normalized" earnings.

Tyco rejects all allegations. Its CEO says the SEC conducted full legal and accounting reviews of filings for Tyco's three largest deals over the past two years. The CEO also says only 6 of the 120 recent deals involved pooling, although it was applied to some of its biggest deals. Accounting questions aside, Tyco is adept at cutting costs. For example, Tyco has cut annual operating costs by $200 million at U.S. Surgical since its acquisition in 1988. However, former U.S. Surgical execs and competitors say Tyco may have lost some of the innovation needed to ensure its future in an evolving medical supply business. Said one exec, "They had a lot of interesting products in the pipeline, but [Tyco] pulled the plugs on all of that."

Required:

a. Describe how merger-related accounting inhibits a user's ability to use accounting reports to make period-to-period comparisons. Is this true for both the purchase method and the pooling method? Explain.

b. Explain why a high price-to-earnings ratio is crucial to Tyco's acquisitions strategy.

c. How do merger-related charges potentially enable a company to inflate future operating earnings? How can a user of financial statements assess whether this is occurring?

d. Many short-term gains in acquisition come from cutting costs. What potential long-term harm can cost-cutting create?

e. Tyco's controversy is arguably a quality of earnings concern, where Tyco strategically used the discretion in GAAP. Why is the market's reaction to this alleged behavior so severe?

f. Many companies report pro-forma earnings that exclude one-time acquisition costs and, increasingly, goodwill amortization. Critique the use of pro-forma earnings for financial statement analysis.

WEB ACTIVITIES

The Web Activities are located on the book's website at www.mhhe.com/wild8e.

6

ANALYZING OPERATING ACTIVITIES

A LOOK BACK <

The previous three chapters analyzed the accounting numbers describing financing and investing activities. We focused on their evaluation and interpretation. We also analyzed these activities for future operations.

A LOOK AT THIS CHAPTER •

This chapter extends our analysis to operating activities. We analyze accrual measures of both revenues and expenses in determining net income. Understanding recognition methods for both revenues and expenses is emphasized. We also interpret the income statement and its components for financial analysis.

A LOOK AHEAD >

Chapter 7 extends our analysis to cash measures of operating and other business activities. We analyze the cash flow statement for interpreting these activities. We show how both accrual and cash measures of business activities enhance our analysis of financial statements.

ANALYSIS OBJECTIVES

- Explain the concepts of income measurement and their implications for analysis of operating activities.
- Describe and analyze the impact of nonrecurring items, including extraordinary items, discontinued segments, accounting changes, write-offs, and restructuring charges.
- Analyze revenue and expense recognition and its risks for financial statement analysis.
- Analyze deferred charges, including expenditures for research, development, and exploration.
- Explain supplementary employee benefits and analyze the disclosures for employee stock options (ESOs).
- Describe and interpret interest costs and the accounting for income taxes.
- Analyze and interpret earnings per share data (Appendix 6A).

Spin City of Earnings

NEW YORK–In today's markets, companies adhere to accounting standards. Auditors scour the books to keep management honest. Regulators ensure "sunshine" through disclosure. And analysts parse the numbers for investors. Or at least that's the way the checks and balances are supposed to work. But lately, concerns have been raised about the integrity of financial markets.

Companies that push the accounting limits, auditors who are AWOL, and analysts who are too enmeshed with their investment-banking brethren to give objective advice drive this concern. Even investors bear responsibility: They were so eager to cash in on the bull market of the 1990s that they often ignored or optimistically interpreted restructuring charges, write-downs, and other disclosures that mask true earnings. As risk returns to the market with a vengeance, smart players are educating themselves and applying more discrimination.

Restructuring charges and write-downs are two main culprits. Too often the aim of such charges is to front-load costs to boost future years' earnings. Meanwhile, others have taken so many "extraordinary" charges year in and year out that the only thing truly out of the ordinary is a year without them. For example, Kellogg, AT&T, and GM have all taken a remarkable number of restructuring write-offs in the past decade–leading critics to question how "extraordinary" they are.

. . . write-offs are increasingly distorting earnings . . .

Of course, companies have always taken such charges. But nervous investors fear that huge multiyear write-offs are increasingly distorting earnings–so much so, that some question whether the meaning of earnings numbers and their value as a measure of performance is getting trampled.

Fueling this behavior are stock traders that tend to ignore big "one-time" charges, focusing instead on prospects. So even if total dollars spent are the same, companies have an incentive to take one big charge rather than stretch expenses out as the money is actually spent. That has investors worried that companies are burying all sorts of normal operating expenses in these charges. "Somebody woke up to the fact that if you take something as a restructuring charge, investors will forgive you immediately," says Robert S. Miller, the nonexecutive chairman hired to clean up Waste Management. "We've almost lost the notion of what are earnings and what are one-time charges."

Sources: Business Week, July 2002, May and November 2001, and April 2000.

PREVIEW OF CHAPTER 6

Income is the net of revenues and gains *less* expenses and losses. Income is one measure of operating activities and it is determined using the accrual basis of accounting. The income statement reports net income for a period of time along with the income components: revenues, expenses, gains, and losses. We analyze income and its components to assess company performance and risk exposures, and to predict the amounts, timing, and uncertainty of future cash flows. While "bottom line" net income frames our analysis, income components provide the crucial pieces of a mosaic revealing the economic portrait of a company's operating activities. This chapter describes the analysis and interpretation of income components. We consider current reporting requirements and their implications for analysis of income components. We describe how we might usefully apply analytical adjustments to income components and related disclosures to enhance the analysis. We direct special attention to revenue recognition and the recording of major expenses and costs. The content and organization of this chapter are as follows:

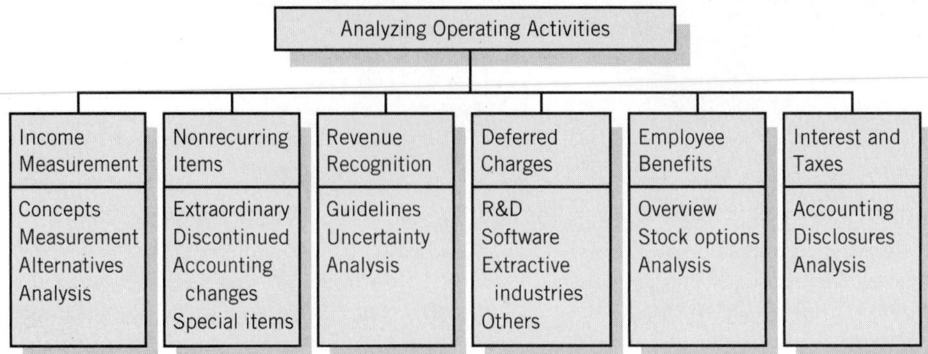

INCOME MEASUREMENT

This section describes the concept of income measurement, the alternative measures available, and the interpretation of income.

Concept of Income

Income (also referred to as **earnings** or **profit**) summarizes in financial terms the operating activities of a business. It is the most demanded piece of company information in the financial markets. Determining and explaining a business's income for a period is the main purpose of the **income statement**. As discussed in prior chapters, income provides both a measure of the change in shareholders' wealth (change in value) for a period and an estimate of a company's future earning power. Understanding this dual role of income is important for analysis of financial statements.

Accounting, or *reported*, income is different from *economic* income. Also, income measurement is complex, both conceptually and practically. To illustrate these points, consider a company with $100,000 in cash. This company uses the $100,000 to buy a condominium, which it rents out for $12,000 per year. At the end of the first year the company still owns the condominium, which is valued at $125,000. Let's begin our analysis by deriving free cash flow and operating cash flow. Net (free) cash flow for the year is $(88,000), while operating cash flow is $12,000. Next, let's compute income, both economic and accounting. The rental income of $12,000 is part of both income measures. Further, since the condominium is worth $125,000 at year-end, there is a $25,000 holding gain. This holding gain plus the rental income yields the economic income of $37,000. Accounting income, which is based on accrual accounting, depends on the depreciation policy for the condominium. Namely, if the condominium's useful life is 50 years and its salvage value is $75,000 (consisting primarily of the land value), then yearly straight-line depreciation is $500 [computed as ($100,000 − $75,000)/50 years]. This yields an accounting income of $11,500 (rental income of $12,000 less $500 depreciation) for the year.

This illustration shows that economic income differs from accounting income, and both differ from the cash flow measures. We might also notice that the $37,000 economic income is probably not sustainable. That is, we can't count on a 25% annual appreciation in the condominium's value year after year. This implies the economic income of $37,000 is less useful for forecasting future earnings. Accounting income of $11,500 is probably closer to permanent income–at least in this case.

Understanding alternative income concepts and relating these concepts to accounting income is helpful in financial statement analysis. As we saw in Chapter 2, a major task in financial statement analysis is evaluating and making necessary adjustments to income to improve its ability to reflect business performance. In this section, we discuss alternative concepts of income, in particular, permanent income and economic income. We also distinguish them from cash flows. Then, we discuss accounting income, relate it to the alternative income concepts, and describe the analysis implications.

Economic Concept of Income

This section describes two important income measures: economic income and permanent income.

Economic Income. *Economic income* is typically measured as cash flow plus the change in the fair value of net assets. Under this definition, income includes both realized (cash flow) and unrealized (holding gain or loss) components. This concept of income is similar to how we measure the return on a security or a portfolio of securities–that is, return includes both dividends and capital appreciation.

Economic income measures *change* in shareholder value. As such, economic income is useful when the objective of analysis is determining the exact return to the shareholder for the period (without recourse to market price). In a sense, economic income is the bottom line indicator of company performance–measuring the financial effects of all events for the period in a comprehensive manner. However, because of its comprehensive nature, economic income includes both recurring and nonrecurring components and is therefore less useful for forecasting future earnings potential.

Permanent Income. *Permanent income* (also called *sustainable or normalized income*) is the stable average income that a company is expected to earn over its life. Exhibit 6.1 presents a hypothetical example of a company's permanent income and economic income for a 50-year period. For simplicity, we assume permanent income is constant over this period. In reality, permanent income can change when the long-term earnings prospects of a company are altered.

Economic Income and Permanent Income ***Exhibit 6.1***

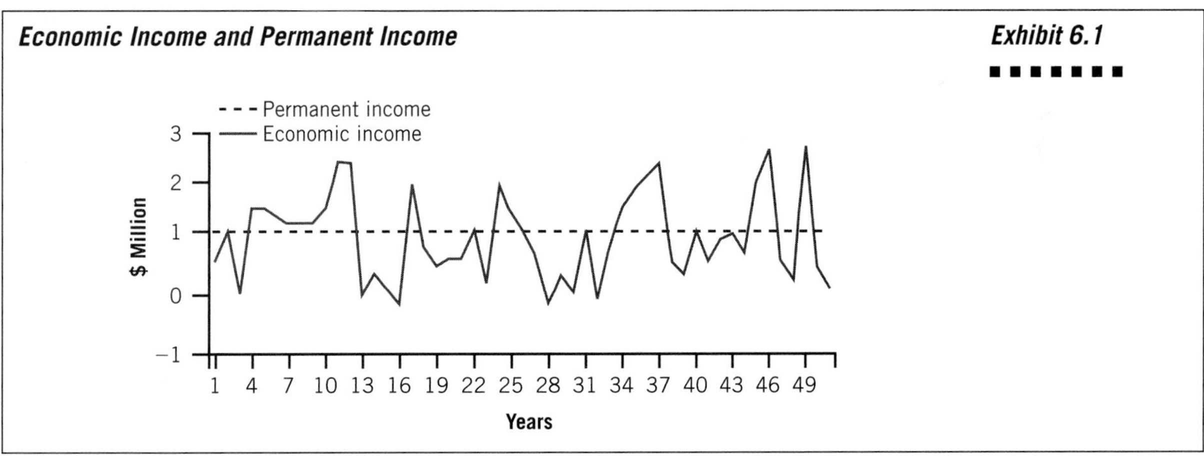

Permanent income reflects a long-term focus. Accordingly, permanent income is often referred to as *sustainable earning power*, which is an important concept for both equity valuation and credit analysis. Benjamin Graham, the mentor of investing guru Warren Buffett and the father of fundamental analysis, maintained that the single most important indicator of a company's value is its sustainable earning power. Permanent income's usefulness arises because of its direct relation to this concept and company value. Unlike economic income, which measures *change* in company value, permanent income is directly proportional to company value. In particular, for a going concern, company value can be expressed by dividing permanent income by the cost of capital.

Because of this relation, determining a company's permanent income is a major quest for many analysts.

Accounting Concept of Income

Accounting income is based on the concept of accrual accounting. While accounting income does capture aspects of both economic income and permanent income, it does not directly measure either income concept. Also, as noted in Chapter 2, accounting income suffers from measurement problems that reduce its ability to reflect economic reality. Consequently, a major task in financial statement analysis is adjusting accounting income to better reflect alternative income concepts. This section describes the process by which accountants determine income. It then discusses analysis implications, including conceptual approaches to adjusting income for analysis purposes.

Revenue Recognition and Matching. A main purpose of accrual accounting is income measurement. The two major processes in income measurement are revenue recognition and expense matching. Revenue recognition is the starting point of income measurement. The two necessary conditions for recognition are that revenues must be:

- **Realized or realizable.** For revenue to be recognized, a company should have received cash or a reliable commitment to remit cash, such as a valid receivable.
- **Earned**. The company must have completed all of its obligations to the buyer; that is, the earning process must be complete.

Once revenues are recognized, related costs are matched with recognized revenues to yield income. Note that an expense is incurred when the related economic event occurs, not when the cash outflow occurs.

Accounting versus Economic Income. Conceptually, accrual accounting converts cash flow to a measure that, in principle, approximates the economic concepts of income. Recall that economic income differs from cash flow because it includes not only the current cash flow but also changes in the present value of future cash flows. Similarly, recall that accrual accounting attempts to obtain an income measure that considers not only current cash flow but also future cash flow implications of current transactions. For example, accrual accounting recognizes future cash flows of credit sales by reporting revenue when the sale is consummated and before cash is received.

Accounting income may seem similar to economic income. However, accounting income is a product of the financial reporting environment that involves accounting standards, enforcement mechanisms, and managers' incentives. It is governed by accounting rules, many of which are economically appealing and some of which are not. These rules often require estimates, giving rise to differential treatment of similar economic transactions and allowing opportunities for managers to window-dress numbers for personal gain. This means accounting income can diverge from economic income (Chapter 2 referred to these divergences as *accounting distortions*). Some reasons why accounting income differs from economic income include:

- **Alternative income concepts.** The concept of economic income is very different from the concept of permanent income. Accounting standard setters are faced with a dilemma involving which concept to emphasize. While this problem is partially resolved by reporting alternative measures of income (which we discuss subsequently), this dilemma sometimes results in inconsistent measurement of accounting income. Some standards, for example *SFAS 87* on pensions, adopt the permanent income concept, while other standards, for example *SFAS 115* on marketable securities, adopt the economic income concept.

- **Historical cost.** The historical cost basis of income measurement introduces divergence between accounting and economic income. The use of historical cost affects income in two ways: (1) the current cost of sales is not reflected in the income statement, such as under the FIFO inventory method; and (2) unrealized gains and losses on fixed assets are not recognized.
- **Transaction basis.** Accounting income usually reflects effects of transactions. Economic effects unaccompanied by an arm's-length transaction often are not considered. For example, purchase contracts are not recognized in the financial statements until the transactions occur.
- **Conservatism.** Conservatism results in recognizing income-decreasing events immediately, even if there is no transaction to back it up–for example, inventory write-downs. However, the effect of an income-increasing event is delayed until realized. This creates a conservative (income decreasing) bias in accounting income.
- **Earnings management.** Earnings management causes distortions in accounting income that has little to do with economic reality. However, one form of earnings management–income smoothing–can sometimes improve the ability of accounting income to reflect permanent income.

Permanent, Transitory, and Value Irrelevant Components. We note that accounting income attempts to capture elements of both permanent income and economic income, but with measurement error. Accordingly, it is useful to view accounting income as consisting of three components:

1. **Permanent component.** The permanent (or *recurring*) component of accounting income is expected to persist indefinitely. It has characteristics identical to the economic concept of permanent income. For a going concern, each dollar of the permanent component is equal to $1/r$ dollar of company value, where r is the cost of capital.
2. **Transitory component.** The transitory (or *nonrecurring*) component of accounting income is not expected to recur–it is a one-time event. It has a dollar-for-dollar effect on company value. The concept of economic income includes both permanent and transitory components.
3. **Value irrelevant component.** Value irrelevant components have no economic content–they are accounting distortions. They arise from the imperfections in accounting. Value irrelevant components have zero effect on company value.

Analysis Implications. Adjusting accounting income is an important task in financial analysis. Before making any adjustments it is necessary to specify the analysis objectives. In particular, it is important to determine whether the objective is determining economic income or permanent income of the company. This determination is crucial because economic income and permanent income differ in both nature and purpose, and accordingly, the adjustments necessary to determine each measure can differ substantially.

We already noted that determining a company's permanent income (sustainable earning power) is a major quest in analysis. For this purpose, an analyst needs to determine the permanent component of current period income by identifying recurring (permanent) and nonrecurring (transitory) components of accounting income and making appropriate adjustments. Determining the permanent component of current period income is useful for determining and interpreting a company's "true" P/E ratio and makes P/E ratio comparisons more meaningful. It is also useful in formal forecasting, by giving a meaningful "starting point" for the forecasting exercise and in helping derive assumptions for profit margins and asset turnovers.

To adjust accounting income in determining economic income, we need to adopt an inclusive approach whereby we include all income components whether recurring or nonrecurring. One way to view economic income is the net change in shareholders' wealth that arises from nonowner sources–hence it includes everything that changes the net wealth of shareholders. When we make adjustments to obtain economic income, we need to realize the adjusted numbers are not faithful representations of economic income because we cannot determine the change in the fair value of fixed assets, which are recorded at historical cost. It is also more difficult to justify the need for making adjustments to determine economic income than for determining permanent income. However, economic income serves as a comprehensive measure of change in shareholder wealth and is thus useful as the bottom-line indicator of income for the period.

Measuring Accounting Income

As described earlier, accounting income is determined by recognizing revenues and matching costs. Hence, revenues (and gains) and expenses (and losses) are the two major components of accounting income. This section discusses these two components. Exhibit 6.2 shows a typical income statement with major line items along with some alternative income measures.

Exhibit 6.2 ***Income Statement***

AMBER CORP. AND SUBSIDIARIES
Consolidated Income Statement ($ millions)

	2003	2002	2001
Revenues	**$14,314**	$12,716	$13,033
Cost of goods sold	**(8,270)**	(7,454)	(7,943)
Gross profit	**6,044**	5,262	5,090
Expenses:			
Selling and administrative	**(2,964)**	(2,478)	(2,396)
Research and development	**(1,234)**	(899)	(855)
Restructuring charge	—	(1,016)	—
Interest expense	**(725)**	(715)	(654)
Income before taxes	**1,121**	154	1,185
Income taxes	**(336)**	(351)	(355)
Income from continuing operations	**785**	(197)	830
Gain from extinguishment of debt	**38**	—	—
Loss from operating discontinued segment	—	0	(23)
Gain from sale of discontinued segment	—	—	66
Net income	**$ 823**	$ (197)	$ 873
Foreign currency translation adjustments	**82**	(54)	(31)
Unrealized holding gain on available-for-sale securities	**24**	22	6
Additional minimum pension liability adjustment	**0**	(4)	—
Comprehensive income	**$ 929**	$ (233)	$ 848

Revenues and Gains

Revenues are earned inflows or prospective earned inflows of cash that arise from a company's ongoing business activities. These include cash inflows such as cash sales, and prospective cash inflows such as credit sales. **Gains** are earned inflows or prospective earned inflows of cash arising from transactions and events unrelated to a company's ongoing business activities. Exhibit 6.2 provides an example of a gain–specifically, a gain on sale of a discontinued segment. The distinction between revenues and gains is based on the ongoing business activities that produce revenues. Revenues, or at least activities that yield revenues, are expected to persist indefinitely for a going concern. In contrast, gains are nonrecurring. This distinction is important for analysis, especially when determining sustainable income.

Revenue recognition methods can significantly affect reported income. Revenue recognition is becoming more complex, as it is increasingly linked with e-commerce activity. It is also an area with minimal guidance from accounting standards. This permits opportunities for earnings management. Accordingly, analyzing revenue recognition practices is crucial in financial statement analysis. For this reason we devote a section to revenue recognition later in the chapter.

Expenses and Losses

Expenses are incurred outflows, prospective outflows, or allocations of past outflows of cash that arise from a company's ongoing business operations. **Losses** are decreases in a company's net assets arising from peripheral or incidental operations of a company. This implies expenses and losses are resource and service potentials consumed, spent, or lost in pursuing or producing revenues and gains. Accounting for expenses and losses often involves assessing the amount and timing of their allocation to reporting periods. Timing is a matter of when they are incurred, often based on matching them with revenues generated.

Another important issue is that of cost *deferral* (or multiperiod allocation). Accountants capitalize costs whose benefits are realized over many periods. These costs are systematically allocated to future periods. In contrast, many costs are incurred in the same period in which they are recognized. (It is not necessary that cash outflows for expenses and losses occur at the same time they are recognized.)

Alternative Income Classifications and Measures

Proper income classification is important in analysis. Income can be classified along two major dimensions: (1) operating versus nonoperating and (2) recurring versus nonrecurring. Many times, these two dimensions of classification are used synonymously. For example, certain analysts (and even certain companies) refer to an income measure that excludes all nonrecurring items as operating income. While it may be true that a majority of operating income components tend to be recurring, it must be understood that these two classifications are distinct, both in nature and purpose. For example, a nonrecurring item such as loss of inventory from fire is an operating loss. Similarly, a nonoperating item such as interest income may be recurring in nature. The operating versus nonoperating classification depends primarily on the source of the revenue or expense–namely, whether it arises from the ongoing operations of the company or from its investing or financing activities. The recurring versus nonrecurring classification depends primarily on the behavior of the revenue or expense–namely, whether it is expected to persist or it is a one-time event. It is important for an analyst to appreciate the differences between these alternative classifications. Exhibit 6.3 stresses the distinction in these dimensions of classifying income.

Exhibit 6.3 **Operating vs. Nonoperating and Recurring vs. Nonrecurring Dimensions for Classifying Income**

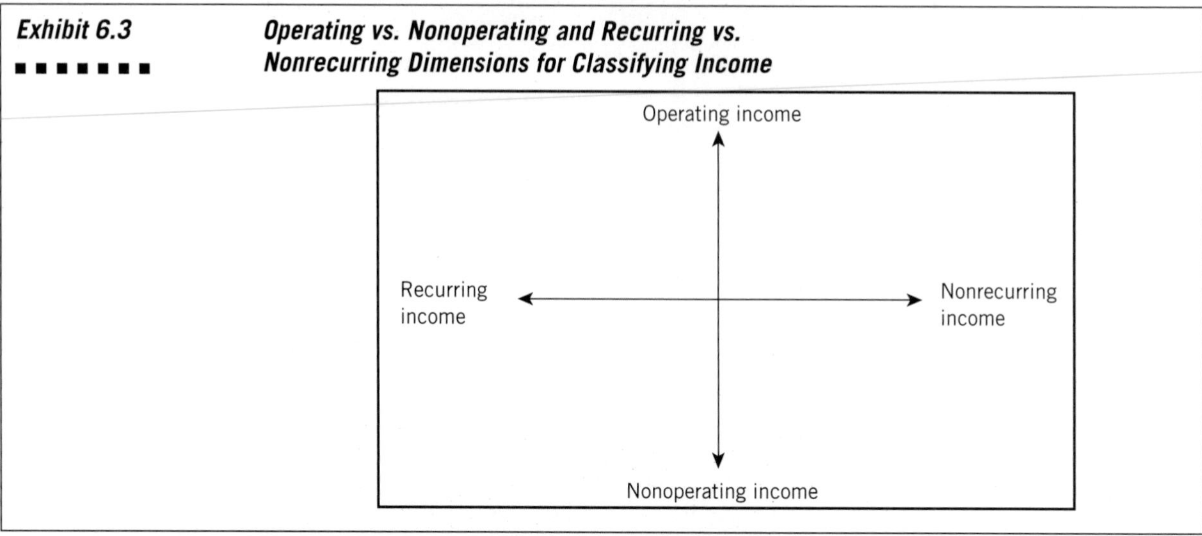

Recurring and Nonrecurring Income

The importance of classifying income components as recurring or nonrecurring arises from the need to determine the permanent and transitory components of income. This helps in estimating permanent income. In this section, we discuss alternative income measures reported in financial statements and their implications for analysis.

Alternative Measures of Accounting Income. Income statements typically report three alternative income measures: (1) net income; (2) comprehensive income; and (3) continuing income. **Net income** is regarded as the bottom line measure of income. In reality, it is not. GAAP allows a number of direct adjustments to equity, called *dirty surplus* items, that by-pass the income statement. *SFAS 130* attempts to remedy this problem with an alternative measure of income called *comprehensive income.* **Comprehensive income** reflects nearly all changes to equity, other than those from owner activities (such as dividends and share issuances). This implies that comprehensive income is the bottom-line measure of income and is the accountant's proxy for economic income. Unfortunately, companies are allowed to report comprehensive income in the statement of changes in equity instead of the income statement. The income statement in Exhibit 6.2, however, does include both measures of income. Note that comprehensive income differs from net income in that it reflects certain unrealized holding gains and losses.

Accountants also report an intermediate measure of income called *continuing income.* **Continuing income** is a measure that excludes extraordinary items, cumulative effects of accounting changes, and the effects of discontinued operations. For this reason, continuing income is often called *income before extraordinary items, income before discontinued operations,* or *income before cumulative effect of accounting change,* or any combination as appropriate. Companies without these components need not report continuing income. Exhibit 6.2 includes income from continuing operations as a separate line item.

Many analysts compute another measure of income that we refer to as *core income.* (This is because core income, which excludes all nonrecurring and unusual items, can better reflect the results of current operations. However, as we noted earlier, the distinction between operating and nonoperating income is separate from the sustainability of income components.) **Core income** is a measure that excludes all nonrecurring items that are reported as separate line items on the income statement. In Exhibit 6.2, core income equals the continuing income reported in 2003 and 2001. Yet in 2002, core income is different–it excludes the after-tax effect of the restructuring charge of $1,016 million. In this case, core income equals continuing income *plus* the restructuring charge that is multiplied by one minus the 35% marginal tax rate, or $463 [computed as $(197) plus the quantity $1,016 × 0.65].

Analysis Implications. Accounting standards require alternative income measures so users can identify sustainable and nonsustainable income components. Many analysts prefer an income measure that corresponds to one of the reported measures or some variation that excludes (or includes) certain line items. Debates rage over what constitutes the "correct" measure of income. We caution against such debates for two reasons.

First, a correct measure of income is not possible without specifying analysis objectives. As already noted, income serves two important but different roles: to measure the net change in equity and to provide an estimate of sustainable earning power. It is impossible for a single income measure to satisfy both objectives at the same time.

Second, the alternative accounting income measures result from merely including, or excluding, certain line items. This means they are still *accounting measures* of income and are subject to accounting distortions. At best, these alternative accounting income measures are starting points for more detailed accounting analysis necessary to estimate sustainable income. For example, comprehensive income is a natural starting point to determine economic income.

Operating and Nonoperating Income

Operating income is a measure of company income from ongoing operating activities. There are three important aspects of operating income. First, operating income pertains only to income generated from operating activities. Therefore, any revenues (and expenses) not related to business operations are not part of operating income. Second, and related to the first, operating income focuses on income for the company as a whole rather than for equity holders. This means that financing revenues and expenses (mainly interest expense) are excluded when measuring operating income. Third, operating income pertains only to ongoing business activities. This means any income or loss pertaining to discontinued operations is excluded from operating income.

Nonoperating income includes all components of income not included in operating income. It is sometimes useful when analyzing nonoperating income to separate components pertaining to financing activities from those pertaining to discontinued operations.

Analysis Implications. The usefulness of operating income arises from an important goal in corporate finance. That is, the desire to separate investing (and operating) decisions such as capital budgeting, from those of financing decisions such as dividend policy. Because of this goal, it is necessary to determine a comprehensive measure of company income that is independent of a company's financing decisions. Operating income is one such measure. Note that operating income before taxes is similar to earnings before interest and taxes (EBIT), while operating income after taxes is similar to net operating profit after taxes (NOPAT).

In most cases, operating income can be determined by rearranging the income statement and making proper adjustments for taxes. Still, it is sometimes necessary to draw on more detailed adjustments using information in notes. For example, when a company has operating leases, the entire lease rental is included as an operating expense even though the lease payment includes an interest component. In this case, operating income is understated unless the analyst estimates the interest component and makes the necessary adjustments using note information. It is beyond the scope of this chapter to show how to compute operating income. We return to this topic in the financial analysis part of the book.

Comprehensive Income

GAAP has long espoused the comprehensive, or all-inclusive, concept of income, where the bottom-line income number articulates with equity in successive balance sheets–that is, the bottom-line income reflects all changes in shareholders' equity arising from other than owner transactions. This articulation is called *clean surplus.* Nevertheless, standard setters have over time allowed certain components of comprehensive income to bypass the income statement as direct adjustments to equity. These adjustments, called *dirty surplus*, have increased in importance and magnitude in recent years. The motivation for these dirty surplus items comes from concerns about excessive income volatility if all changes to equity flow through the income statement. Still, many users are concerned that allowing changes to equity to bypass the income statement will reduce the reliability of accounting income. To address these concerns, companies are required to report a measure of comprehensive income in addition to net income.

Measuring Comprehensive Income. As defined by *SFAS 130,* comprehensive income is computed by adjusting net income for dirty surplus items, collectively called *other comprehensive income.* We show the determination of comprehensive income from a typical company:

Net income		$1,205
Other comprehensive income:		
+/− Unrealized holding gain (loss) on marketable securities	$305	
+/− Foreign currency translation adjustment	(12)	
+/− Additional minimum pension liability adjustment	(17)	
+/− Unrealized holding gain or loss on derivative instruments	945	1,221
Comprehensive income		$2,426

The other comprehensive income for this company consists of four components: (1) unrealized holding gains or losses that result from changes in the fair (market) value of available-for-sale investment securities; (2) foreign currency translation gains and losses; (3) any increase or decrease in the additional minimum pension liability; and (4) unrealized holding gains or losses arising from the effective portion of cash flow hedges (derivatives). These amounts are expressed on an after-tax basis. Note all four components are in the nature of unrealized (holding) gains or losses. The components arise from changes in the value of assets and liabilities that do not originate from arm's-length transactions. A few analysts maintain that the transaction basis of net income is an important distinction between net income and comprehensive income. We show that this distinction is neither important nor necessarily true.

Analysis Implications. The importance of comprehensive income for financial statement analysis arises because it is the accountant's proxy for economic income. Comprehensive income is preferred to net income, where the latter measure purports to estimate neither economic nor sustainable income.

A few analysts argue the importance of net income vis-à-vis comprehensive income relates to the notion that net income is transaction-based while comprehensive income is not. However, this argument is not entirely correct. Namely, net income has many components in the nature of unrealized gains or losses that are not transaction-based. For example, net income includes holding gains or losses from trading securities, from fair-value hedges, and from the ineffective portion of cash flow hedges. Moreover, the fact that some income components arise through arm's-length transactions is a distinction that is irrelevant from an economic point of view since unrealized gains or losses are a legitimate part of economic income.

It is important to recognize that comprehensive income must be adjusted in determining economic income. We confine discussion in this section to evaluating the appropriateness of the four usual items included in other comprehensive income. In particular, unrealized gains and losses arising from investment and/or derivative securities are a legitimate part of economic income. However, note that unrealized holding gains on investment securities reported as part of other comprehensive income excludes holding gains on held-to-maturity securities. Similarly, foreign currency translation adjustments must be included when determining economic income. The additional minimum pension liability adjustment, however, must be excluded when determining economic income. The additional minimum pension liability arises from an artificial accounting distinction that has little economic meaning. The appropriate pension expense to include when determining economic income is the change in the funded status (see Chapter 3).

Some analysts argue that all components of other comprehensive income are irrelevant because they do not persist. Research shows the only component of other comprehensive income that is relevant for equity valuation is the unrealized holding gain or loss on marketable securities, and even that applies only to financial institutions (Dhaliwal, Subramanyam, and Trezevant, 2000). This implies the components of comprehensive income are irrelevant for determining permanent income, which is probably a more important measure for equity valuation than is economic income. Still, as we already pointed out, economic income is an important measure that has a role distinct from sustainable income. The components of other comprehensive income are important in determining economic income.

NONRECURRING ITEMS

This section describes several nonrecurring items–including extraordinary items, discontinued segments, accounting changes, restructuring charges, and special items–along with their analysis and interpretation.

Extraordinary Items

Extraordinary items are distinguished by their unusual nature and by the infrequency of their occurrence. The vast majority of extraordinary items relate to gains and losses from early retirement of debt. Extraordinary items are classified separately in the income statement. Because of the stringent criteria for classification, extraordinary items are uncommon. Exhibit 6.4 reports the frequency and magnitude of extraordinary items. We see that the proportion of companies reporting extraordinary items is typically less than 8%. Extraordinary items, when they occur, usually constitute less than 3% of sales. The proportion of negative and positive extraordinary items is about the same.

The significant increase in extraordinary items in 1993 is interesting. This period corresponds to a cyclical decline in long-term interest rates together with a significant decline in income before extraordinary items. The decline in interest rates resulted in an increase in the market price of corporate bonds above the carrying amount of the bonds on company balance sheets (see Chapter 1). As these bonds were refinanced, a loss on their retirement, therefore, occurred. One possibility for the increase, then, is that companies, already facing a decline in profitability, chose to refinance their long-term debt with lower rate bonds and to record a loss on the retirement. This further depressed current period profitability (known as the "Big Bath") and increased future period profitability. Companies, therefore, shifted profitability from an already poor

Exhibit 6.4 ***Magnitude and Frequency of Extraordinary Items***

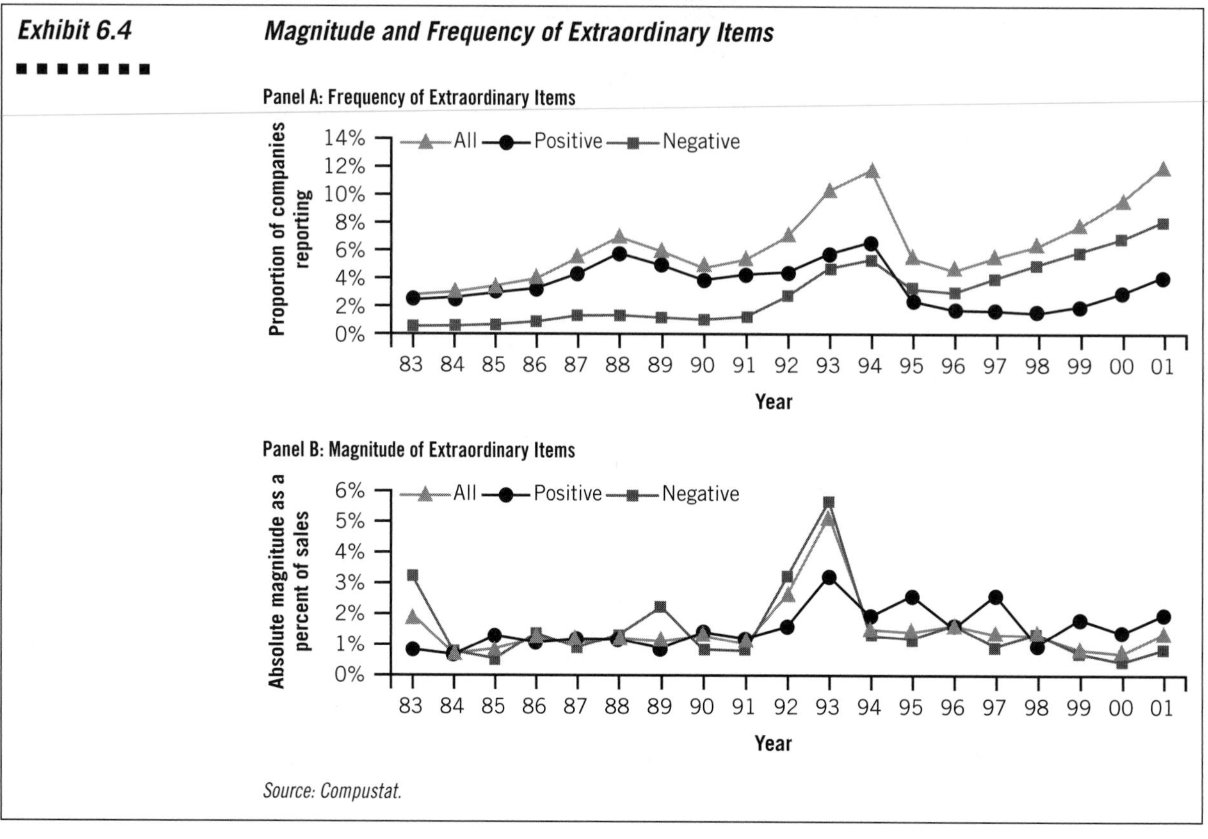

Source: Compustat.

earnings year into the future. An example of such debt retirement is provided in Illustration 6.1.

ILLUSTRATION 6.1

Sears, Roebuck & Co. recently paid off 6% debentures with a face value of $300 million. The transaction yielded an extraordinary loss of $37 million and a related income tax benefit of $13 million, resulting in an after-tax loss of $24 million. This extraordinary loss, resulting mainly from the write-off of the unamortized discount, is discussed in the company's financial statement notes and reported in the income statement as follows ($ millions):

Income before extraordinary loss	$1,072
Extraordinary loss on early extinguishment of debt, net of tax	(24)
Net income	$1,048

Accounting for Extraordinary Items

To qualify as extraordinary, an item must be *both* unusual in nature and infrequent in occurrence. These terms are defined as follows:

- **Unusual nature.** An event or transaction that has a high degree of abnormality and is unrelated to, or only incidentally related to, the ordinary and typical activities of the company.
- **Infrequent occurrence.** An event or transaction that is not reasonably expected to recur in the foreseeable future.

Extraordinary items are reported, net of tax, as separate line items in the income statement after continuing income. When a company reports extraordinary items, continuing income is called *income before extraordinary items*. Any item that is either unusual or infrequent (not both) cannot be classified as an extraordinary item.

Practice also requires companies to *not* report certain gains and losses as extraordinary items because they are not unusual in nature and are expected to recur as a consequence of customary and continuing business activity. Examples include:

- Write-down or write-off of receivables, inventories, equipment leased to others, deferred R&D costs, or other intangible assets.
- Gains or losses on disposal of a business segment.
- Gains or losses from sale or abandonment of property, plant, or equipment.
- Effects of a strike, including those against competitors and major suppliers.
- Adjustment of accruals on long-term contracts.

Analyzing Extraordinary Items

Extraordinary items are nonrecurring in nature. An analyst, therefore, excludes extraordinary items when computing permanent income. Extraordinary items also are excluded from income when making comparisons over time or across companies. Yet, while extraordinary items are transitory, they yield a cost (or benefit) on the company, dollar for dollar. An analyst must therefore include the entire amount of the extraordinary item when computing economic income.

Extraordinary items often are operating in nature. However, they differ from normal operating revenues or expenses since they are nonrecurring. For example, a loss of inventory from fire arises as a part of the company's operations (and reveals the nature of operating risks inherent in the company's business) but it is not expected to occur on a regular basis. Thus, extraordinary items that arise from a company's business operations are included when computing operating income but excluded when determining permanent income. Extraordinary items also reveal risk exposures of a company. While these risks may be remote, their occurrence suggests the possibility of recurrence at some future date. The large magnitude of most extraordinary losses also encourages analysis even when their occurrence is infrequent. In some cases, extraordinary items may recur, although infrequently. For example, a warehouse by the beach in an area susceptible to hurricanes may incur flood damage every few years. An analyst must consider this when evaluating sustainable earning power.

ANALYSIS VIEWPOINT **. . . YOU ARE THE SUPPLIER**

Your company supplies raw materials to Chicago Construction Corp. Your job is to annually assess customers for credit terms and policies. Chicago Construction's net income for this year is down by 12%. Your analysis of its financial statements shows this decrease is due to an extraordinary loss attributed to a construction site fire. Absent this extraordinary loss, income is up by 23%. What is your credit assessment of Chicago Construction?

Answer–p. 362

Discontinued Operations

Companies sometimes dispose of entire divisions or product lines. When these dispositions pertain to separately identifiable business segments, they are accorded special accounting treatment in the income statement. Exhibit 6.5 shows the magnitude and frequency of discontinued operations over the past two decades. Through the mid-1990s, approximately 2% of publicly traded companies reported discontinued operations in their income statements. Since that time, the frequency of these items has increased significantly to about 8% in 2001. Similarly, the magnitude of discontinued

Exhibit 6.5 **Magnitude and Frequency of Discontinued Operations**

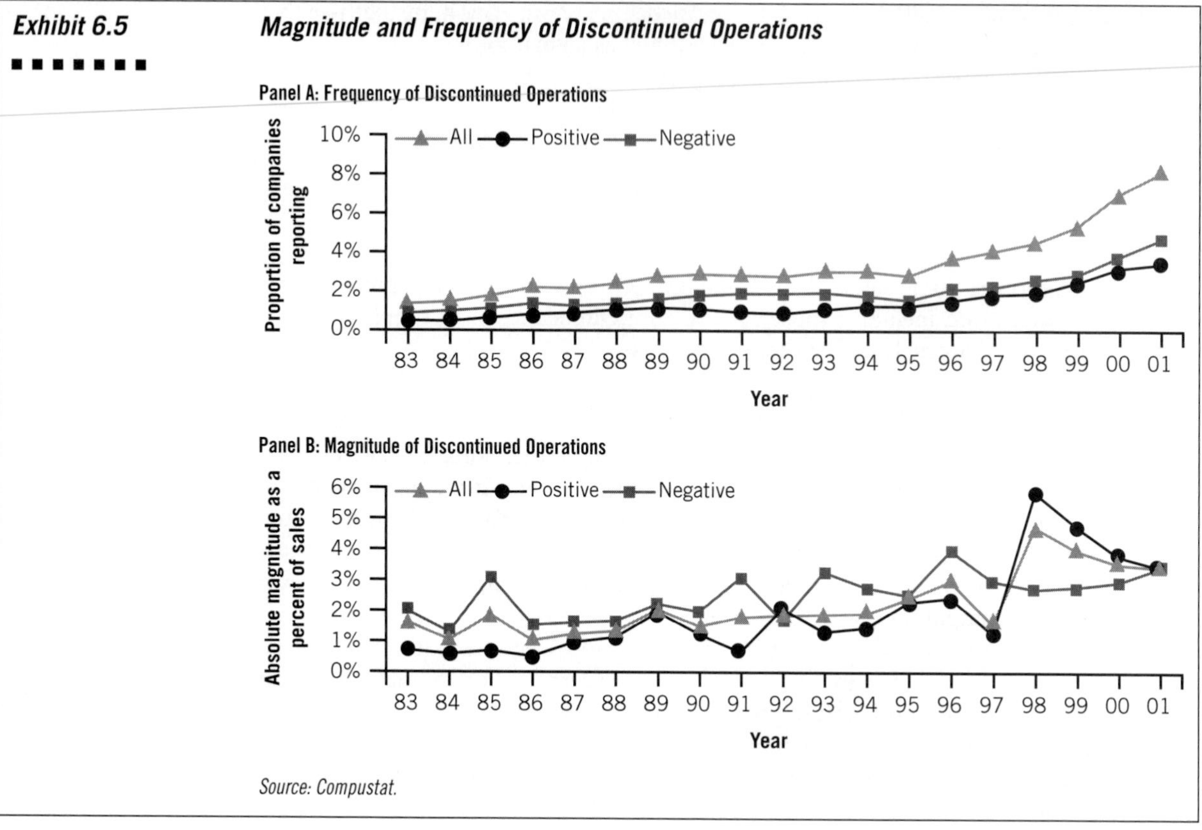

Source: Compustat.

operations as a percentage of sales remained fairly constant at about 2% of sales, but has now nearly doubled in the past decade. Discontinued operations, when they occur, are a significant component of net income.

Accounting for Discontinued Operations

To qualify as discontinued operations, the assets and business activities of the divested segment must be clearly distinguishable (both physically and operationally) from the assets and business activities of the remaining entity. For example, discontinuance of an entire line of products will usually qualify as a discontinued operation, but not the discontinuance of a particular brand. Judgment is involved in deciding what constitutes a discontinued operation since it depends on the nature and scale of a company's business–what constitutes a discontinued operation for one company may not for another. Companies also record gains or losses from discontinued operations when they sell their stake (either fully or partially) in a consolidated subsidiary.

Accounting and reporting for discontinued operations is twofold. First, the income statements for the current and prior two years are restated after excluding the effects of the discontinued operations from the line items that determine continuing income. Second, gains or losses pertaining to the discontinued operations are reported separately, net of their related tax effects and are excluded from continuing income. Continuing income is called *income before discontinued operations* when discontinued operations are reported.

A company reports gains or losses from discontinued operations (for the current and two prior years) in two categories: (1) operating income or loss from discontinued operations until the management commits to the disposal date and (2) gains and losses on disposal, including operating income or loss during the phase-out period. We provide an example of the reporting for discontinued operations in Illustration 6.2.

ILLUSTRATION 6.2

Kmart agreed to sell a majority stake in its consolidated subsidiary, Builders Square. Accordingly, Kmart recorded an after-tax loss on disposal of discontinued operations of $385 million in Year 6 and restated its prior two years' income statements to reflect this discontinuance. This restatement resulted in a loss of $260 million in the prior year, which was the operating loss of Builders Square for that year. The left-side of the excerpt below shows the lower part of Kmart's income statements (from its Year 6 annual report). The right side shows the original and restated income statements for Year 5 and an explanation of the $260 million loss on discontinued operations. Note that the loss on disposal of discontinued operations includes $61 million ($446 million less $385 million) in Year 6 and $30 million in Year 5 related to discontinuances *other than* Builders Square.

LOWER PORTION OF INCOME STATEMENT

	Year 6	Year 5
Net income (loss) from continuing operations before extraordinary item	$231	$(230)
Loss from discontinued operations, net of taxes	(5)	(260)
Loss on disposal of discontinued operations, net of taxes	(446)	(30)
Extraordinary item	—	(51)
Net income (loss)	$(220)	$(571)

ORIGINAL AND RESTATED INCOME STATEMENT FOR YEAR 5

	Original	Restated (Builders)	Difference
Net income (loss) from continuing operations before extraordinary item	$(490)	$(230)	$(260)
Loss from discontinued operations, net of taxes		(260) ←	↑
Loss on disposal of discontinued operations, net of taxes	(30)	(30)	
Extraordinary item	(51)	(51)	
Net income (loss)	$(571)	$(571)	

Analyzing Discontinued Operations

Analysis is futuristic and decision oriented. Therefore, for purposes of analysis, all effects of discontinued operations must be removed from current and past income. This rule applies regardless of whether the objective is determining economic or permanent income or in determining operating or nonoperating income. The adjustment is straightforward for the current and past two years because companies are required to restate their income statements and report the income or loss on discontinued operations separately. Such ready information does not exist for prior years. Some companies restate summary financial information, including income, for the past 10 years, which we can then use. Also, some companies report several prior years' information about discontinued operations separately. Yet, in most cases this information is unavailable. In such situations, an analyst must be careful when conducting intertemporal analysis, such as evaluating income patterns over time.

With regard to a company's financial condition, an analyst must remove the assets and liabilities of the discontinued operations from the balance sheet (if they are not already removed). The cumulative gains or losses from discontinued operations should not, however, be removed from equity.

Accounting Changes

Companies can change accounting methods and assumptions underlying financial statements for certain reasons. Sometimes, accounting methods are changed because of a new accounting standard. Other times, accounting methods and/or assumptions are changed to better reflect changing business activities or conditions. Also, managers sometimes change accounting methods and/or assumptions to window-dress financial statements, particularly for managing earnings. To discourage managers from unjustified switching from one accounting method to another, accounting standards require that "in the preparation of financial statements there is a presumption that an accounting principle once adopted should not be changed in accounting for events and transactions of a similar type . . . the presumption that an entity should not change an accounting principle may be overcome only if the enterprise justifies the use of an alternative acceptable accounting principle on the basis that it is preferable."

Accounting standards distinguish among four types of accounting changes: (1) a change in accounting principle, (2) a change in accounting estimate, (3) a change in reporting entity, and (4) correction of an error. We discuss reporting requirements pertaining to each type and examine analysis implications.

Reporting of Accounting Changes

Change in Accounting Principle. A change in accounting principle occurs when a company switches from one generally accepted accounting principle to another generally accepted accounting principle. The phrase *accounting principle* refers to both the accounting standards and practices used and the methods of applying them. An example of a change in accounting principle is a change in depreciation method from straight-line to accelerated.

When a change occurs, current period income is computed using the new principle. The cumulative effect of this change in principle (net of tax) on retained earnings as of the beginning of the period when the change occurs is computed. This cumulative effect is reported in the income statement after extraordinary items, but before net income. This computation is a "catch-up" adjustment, since previously published financial statements are not revised. Companies also disclose the following information in notes to financial statements when an accounting principle change occurs:

- Nature of and justification for the change in principle.
- Effect of the new principle on both net income and income before extraordinary items for the period of change, including effects on earnings per share.
- Pro forma (as if) effects of retroactive application of the accounting change on net income and income before extraordinary items (and related earnings per share) for the years for which income statements are shown (usually two prior years).

When pro forma effects are not determinable, the company discloses the reasons. A change in the method of allocating costs of long-lived assets, if adopted only for newly acquired assets, does not require this catch-up adjustment. We provide an example of an accounting principle change in Illustration 6.3.

Change in Accounting Estimate. Accrual accounting requires estimates of items such as useful lives of assets, warranty costs, inventory obsolescence, pension assumptions, and uncollectible receivables. These are known as *accounting estimates.* Accounting estimates are approximations based on unknown future conditions. As such, accounting estimates can change. There exist certain accounting and disclosure requirements when changes occur in accounting estimates. These are:

- **Prospective application**–a change is accounted for in the period of change and, if applicable, future periods as and when any effects occur (there is no retroactive restatement).
- **Note disclosure**–disclose the effects of the change on both net income and income before extraordinary items (including earnings per share) for the current period only, even when a change affects future periods.

ILLUSTRATION 6.3

The following excerpt is an example of the reporting for a change in accounting principle:

SEABOARD CORPORATION—CONSOLIDATED STATEMENT OF EARNINGS

($ thousands)	Year 6	Year 5	Year 4
Earnings before cumulative effect of a change in accounting principle	$2,840	$20,202	$35,201
Cumulative effect of changing accounting for inventory (net of $1,922 tax)	3,006	—	—
Net earnings	$5,846	$20,202	$35,201

Note 5: Inventories
During the fourth quarter of Year 6, the company changed its method of accounting for spare parts and supplies used in poultry and pork processing operations retroactively effective January 1, Year 6. Previously these spare parts and supplies were expensed when purchased. Under the new method such purchases will be recorded as inventory and charged to operations when used. The company believes this method is preferable as it provides a better matching of revenues and expenses. The cumulative effect of this accounting change at January 1, Year 6, was to increase net income by $3,006 thousand or $2.02 per common share. The effect of this accounting change was to increase income before cumulative effect of change in accounting principle by $788,000 or $0.53 per common share for the year ended December 31, Year 6. The pro forma effect of retroactive application of this new method of accounting would not materially affect the results of operations for years ended December 31, Year 5 and Year 4.

Illustration 6.4 identifies one example of a change in accounting estimate.

ILLUSTRATION 6.4

Delta Airlines previously depreciated its flight equipment over 15 years using a salvage value of 10%. In the fourth quarter of a recent year, Delta changed its depreciation policy to one that assumes a life of 20 years with a salvage value of 5%. This change decreased Delta's depreciation expense by $36 million in that fourth quarter and, consequently, increased its fiscal year net income by $22 million.

Change in Reporting Entity. A change in reporting entity can arise in several ways, including:

- Initial publication of consolidated financial statements.
- Change in consolidation policy regarding subsidiaries.

In this case, accounting practice requires restating all prior periods' financial statements and disclosing the nature of the change in reporting entity and its rationale.

Correction of an Error. Errors in financial statements can arise from arithmetic mistakes, mistakes in application of accounting principles, or mistakes of information disclosure. The correction of an error is not considered an accounting change. Instead, the correction of an error is treated as a *prior period adjustment* to the beginning balance of retained earnings for the period when it is discovered. Disclosure includes the nature of the error and the effect on net income and income before extraordinary items (and related earnings per share).

Analyzing Accounting Changes

There are several points an analyst must consider when analyzing accounting changes. First, accounting changes are "cosmetic" and yield no cash flow consequences–either present or future. This means the financial condition of a company is not affected by a change in accounting.

Second, while an accounting change is cosmetic, it can sometimes better *reflect* economic reality. For example, a company's decision to extend the depreciable lives of its machinery might be an attempt to better match costs with actual usage patterns. In principle, a necessary condition for a change in accounting methods is that the change better reflect the underlying economics.

PRICEY D&O
Providers of directors and officers (D&O) liability coverage are demanding full disclosure from clients. The alternative is vastly higher premiums or no coverage at all. Companies are being rejected for dubious revenue-recognition practices, poor internal controls, and financial restatements. Last year a company might have paid a few hundred thousand dollars per year for D&O coverage that now costs more than $1 million.

Third, an analyst must be alert to earnings management. Earnings management is less of an issue in the adoption of new standards–although, managers may time its adoption for a period when its effect is most favorable (or least detrimental). However, in the case of voluntary accounting changes, earnings management is a likely motivation. While managers sometimes manage earnings through changes in accounting principles, the more popular and shrewd method of earnings management is by changing accounting estimates. Unlike a change in accounting principle, where the cumulative effect is highlighted in the income statement, information about changes in estimates often are buried in the notes. To illustrate, the motive for Delta Airlines' change in depreciation policy, described in Illustration 6.4, is apparent when we examine its pattern in operating losses around that time: Year 2–$(675) million; Year 3–$(575) million; Year 4–$(447) million. This pattern depicts a marked improvement over time–a compounded decrease in losses of 13% per annum. However, when we restate reported numbers as per the original depreciation methods, we see the following pattern in operating losses: Year 2–$(675) million; Year 3–$(609) million; Year 4–$(583) million. This shows the accounting change increases income by $34 million in Year 3 and by $136 million in Year 4. The decline in operating losses using the original data is, thus, a mere 5% per annum.

Another concern with accounting changes is earnings manipulation. Unlike earnings management, which is window dressing within the confines of GAAP, earnings manipulation arises when companies stray beyond acceptable practices. When the SEC staff spots such accounting practices, the company is asked to restate its financial statements. Such restatements are reported in *Accounting Enforcement Releases* (or *AERs*), suggest that a company is adopting excessively aggressive accounting practices. While honest errors do arise, an analyst should be concerned when a company is forced by the SEC to restate its financial statements. At a minimum, this reflects poor earnings quality, and an analyst must take extra care when analyzing financial statements of such companies.

Fourth, an analyst must assess the impact of accounting changes on comparisons across time. It is important for an analyst to compare "apples with apples." This means making sure any comparisons (especially across time) are made with a consistent set of accounting rules. If the company reports the effects of accounting changes for prior years' data in its notes, the income history can be adjusted. If no such information is reported, an analyst must be aware of the potential limitations for any comparisons across time. This is important because companies sometimes change accounting estimates to window-dress earnings' history.

Finally, an analyst would want to evaluate the effect of an accounting change on both economic income and permanent income. For estimating permanent income, the analyst can use the reported numbers under the new method and ignore the cumulative effect. For estimating economic income of the current period, both the current and cumulative effect are included. More generally, an analyst must evaluate the ability of the change to better reflect economic reality. If the change is arbitrary or seems to impair the ability of the numbers to reflect economic reality, then we can undo the effects of the change using note information.

Special Items

Special items refer to transactions and events that are unusual or infrequent, but not both. These items are typically reported as separate line items on the income statement *before* continuing income. Often, special items are nonroutine items that do not meet the criteria for classification as extraordinary.

Special items constitute the most common and important class of nonrecurring items. As reported in Exhibit 6.6, their frequency and magnitude are increasing. The frequency of special items has increased dramatically, from 1% of reporting companies through the 1980s to over 40% today. Most of this increase has been concentrated in special items that reduce income, primarily restructuring expenses. The magnitude of special items has also increased substantially to over 5% of sales. These items, when they occur, have a significant impact on reported profits, often turning a profitable year into a loss. They are generally the most transitory item in income from continuing operations.

Exhibit 6.6

Frequency and Magnitude of Special Items

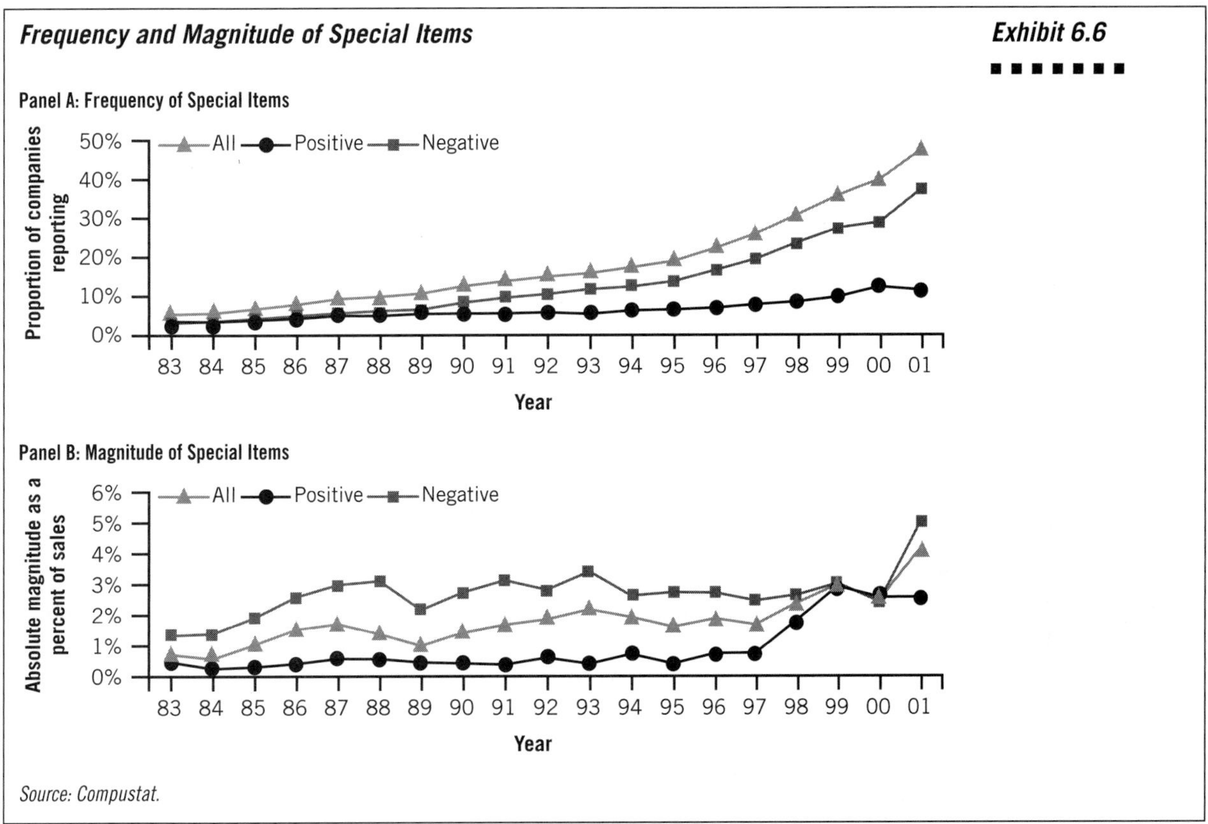

Source: Compustat.

Exhibit 6.7 shows the makeup of one-time special charges both by frequency and by dollar value. Restructuring charges and asset write-offs of goodwill, inventory, and property, plant, and equipment (PP&E) form the bulk of such charges. Of these, impairment of long-lived assets and restructuring charges constitute the two major categories of special items. There are two differences between them. First, restructuring charges are associated with major reorganizations of a company as a whole or within a division. Restructuring often involves a change in business strategy, financing, or physical reorganization of the business. On the other hand, asset impairments are narrower in scope, involving the write-down or write-off of a class of assets. A second major difference is that asset impairments are mainly accrual accounting adjustments, while restructuring charges often involve substantial cash flow commitments either contemporaneously or in the future.

Exhibit 6.7 ***Makeup of One-Time Charges (Special Items)***

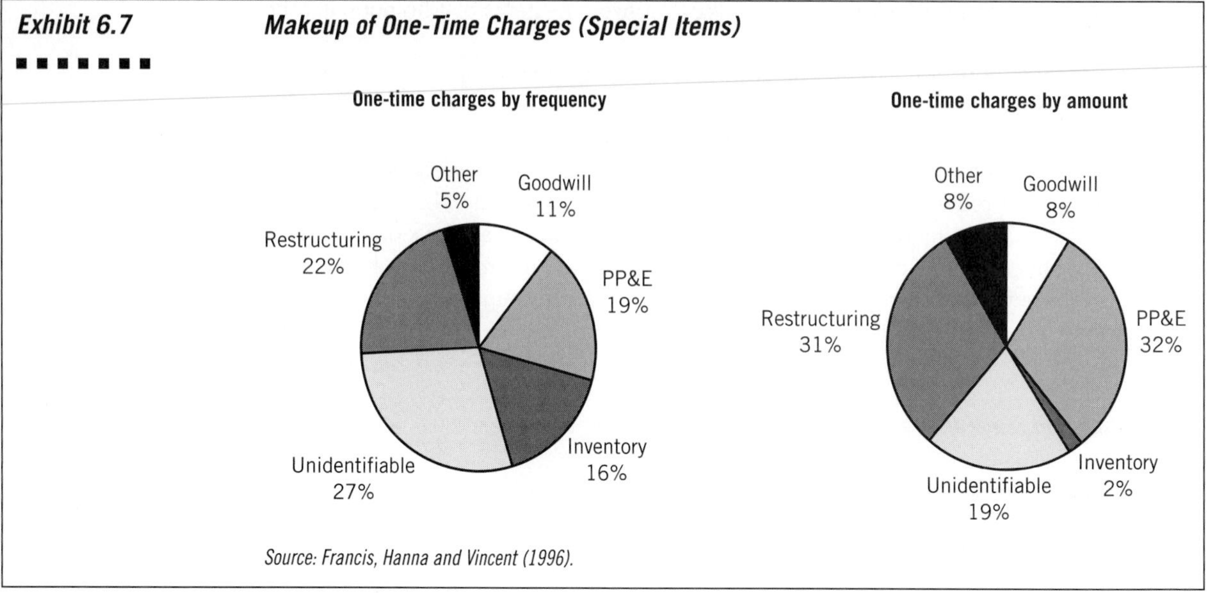

Source: Francis, Hanna and Vincent (1996).

Special items pose challenges for analysis. First, unlike other nonrecurring items, there often is no clear GAAP guidance regarding special items. Second, the economic implications of special items such as restructuring charges are complex. Third, many special items are discretionary and, hence, serve earnings management aims. The remainder of this section focuses on the two major types of special items: asset impairments and restructuring charges. We describe the accounting and reporting for these items, and discuss the analysis implications.

Asset Impairments

Impairment of Long-Lived Assets. A long-lived asset is said to be impaired when its fair value (market value or value from use within the company) is below its carrying value (book value in the balance sheet). Asset impairments occur for many reasons, these include a decline in the asset market value, a decline in market demand for the output from the asset, technological obsolescence, and changes in the company's business strategy. Asset impairments are a byproduct of conservatism–report at the lower of cost or market. GAAP does not permit writing up asset values.

Asset impairments must be distinguished from both restructurings and disposals of segments. We have already discussed differences between a restructuring and an asset impairment. An asset impairment is also different from a disposal of a business segment, both in its accounting treatment and in its economic implications. In a disposal, a company sells one or more assets, or a business segment, and ceases to operate the disposed assets. In contrast, an impaired asset, while it can be sold or disposed of in any manner, is often retained in the company and operated at a reduced level, made idle, or abandoned. From an accounting point of view, disposal of a business segment is treated as discontinued operations that we discussed earlier, while asset impairments are recorded as special items.

SFAS 121 prescribes a two-step procedure for determining the amount of impairment. First, an asset impairment is recognized when the carrying value of the asset is below the *undiscounted* value of future expected cash flows from the asset. Second, once this condition is satisfied, the amount of loss is measured as the difference between the asset carrying value and its fair value, which equals the *discounted* value of future expected cash flows from the asset if its fair value cannot be determined from the market.

This standard does not require disclosure about the determination of the impairment amount, nor does it require disclosure about probable asset impairments. The standard also allows flexibility in determining when and how much of an asset's value to write off and does not require a plan for disposal of the asset. Illustration 6.5 gives a typical disclosure of asset impairment.

ILLUSTRATION 6.5

Chiron Corp. reported an impairment loss of $31.3 million in its income statement pertaining to its manufacturing facility in Puerto Rico. The company discloses the following information in its notes: "The cumulative impact on the company's manufacturing needs of recent product developments prompted management to conclude that Chiron currently has excess manufacturing capacity relative to its projected needs. Specifically, management concluded that the company's need for its idle pharmaceutical fill and finishing facility in Puerto Rico (the "Puerto Rico facility"), originally outfitted as a second manufacturing site of Betaseron, was eliminated due to manufacturing process improvements and cumulative impact of the introduction of a competing product . . . [later] management determined that it could not find a suitable use for the Puerto Rico facility consistent with its previous expectations for the facility's use as a contract manufacturing plant. As a result, the company reviewed the carrying amount of the Puerto Rico facility and related machinery and equipment assets for impairment in accordance with *SFAS 121*. Consequently, . . . the Company recorded a $31.3 million impairment loss to record the Puerto Rico facility and related machinery and equipment at their individual estimated fair market values determined on the basis of independent appraisals."

Impairment of Other Assets. In addition to impairment of long-lived assets, companies sometimes write off other types of assets such as receivables, inventories, and goodwill. There are no specific standards relating to the write-off of such assets. While the values of inventory and receivables are determinable with reasonable accuracy, the write-off of goodwill is the result of a valuation process and is, therefore, somewhat subjective (see Chapter 5).

Restructuring Charges

Unlike asset impairments, restructuring charges are usually associated with major changes in a company's business and strategy. Restructuring usually entails extensive reorganization including divestment of business units, termination of contractual agreements, discontinuation of product lines, worker retrenchment, change in management, and writing off of assets often combined with new investments in plant, technology, and manpower. Restructuring comes at a cost. Divested business units often are sold at a loss, laid-off employees demand compensation, written-off fixed assets and inventory yield losses, foreclosed leases are costly, and new investments and improvements must be paid for. Companies usually make a provision for the cost of the restructuring program, including severance accruals and accruals for asset write-downs, among others. This provision is created through a restructuring charge, which is entirely charged to the current income statement as a special item. When the restructuring program is implemented, sometimes over many years, actual costs are charged against the provision as and when incurred. The remaining balance in the provision is shown as a restructuring reserve. Any remaining balance in the reserve at the completion of the program is reversed by recording it back to income.

To illustrate, Kodak extensively restructured its operations in 2001, taking cumulative charges in excess of $600 million. In 2001, Kodak reported a net income of just $76 million, compared to yearly income of over $1 billion in the previous two years. Kodak's

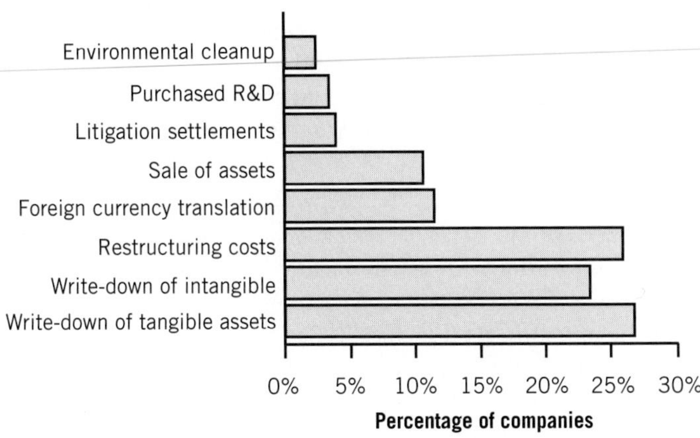

Source: Accounting Trends & Techniques

financial statements, including notes and discussion pertaining to its restructuring program, are provided in Appendix A at the end of the text.

As mentioned in its MD&A, Kodak's main motivation for its restructuring program is cost reduction. This cost reduction is achieved by (1) streamlining and consolidating its manufacturing operations, (2) severing employment with 7,200 employees, and (3) exiting nonstrategic operations. The company provided for its restructuring program by taking a charge against earnings for the entire cost estimate of $698 million, although only $380 million is actually incurred in 2001. The remaining accrual of $318 million is reported as a current liability. Of the $698 million of total cost, $399 million relates to employee severance and exit costs and, most likely, involves the payment of cash. The $298 million relating to inventory and fixed asset write-offs, however, are a noncash expense.

Analyzing Special Items

Analyzing special items is a challenging and important task in accounting analysis. The challenge arises from the lack of guidance in accounting standards. This lack of guidance creates opportunities for managing earnings. Also challenging is understanding the underlying economics of special items, especially restructuring charges. The importance of special items arises because of their frequency and impact on net income of past, present, and future periods. In this section, we explain why special items are a popular tool for earnings management. We then describe the implications of special charges and the adjustments necessary for financial statements.

Earnings Management and Special Charges. Exhibit 6.6 showed that a large proportion of special items, both in frequency and in magnitude, is income-decreasing. Further, the proportion of companies reporting income-decreasing items is increasing over time. This increase in special charges is troubling and has gained the attention of the SEC. The SEC warns that earnings management techniques such as the use of "big-bath restructuring charges" are eroding confidence in financial reporting. (Remarks by SEC Chairman, Arthur Levitt, delivered at the NYU Center for Law and Business, September 28, 1998.)

What is the motivation for reporting special charges? The answer is that one-time charges are of less concern to investors under the assumption they are nonrecurring and do not persist into the future. Many well-known Wall Street analysts, for example Abby Cohen of Goldman Sachs, favor use of "operating earnings" in equity analysis, instead of bottom-line net income–where "operating earnings" excludes special charges (and other nonrecurring items). This encourages managers to reclassify legitimate operating expenses as one-time charges. When analysts ignore such reclassified special charges, it leads to underestimating operating expenses and overestimating company value.

To illustrate, consider a company earning $2 per share in perpetuity. Given a cost of capital of 10%, the value of this company is $20 ($2/0.10). Now, alternatively, assume this company overstates earnings by $1 per share for four consecutive periods and then reverses them with a single charge in the final year as follows:

($ per share)	Year 1	Year 2	Year 3	Year 4
Recurring earnings	$3	$3	$3	$ 3
Special charge	0	0	0	(4)
Net income	$3	$3	$3	$(1)

This pattern of net income suggests a permanent component of $3 per share and a transitory component of a negative $4 per share in Year 4. (Recall the impact of a dollar of permanent earnings to company value is equal to that dollar divided by its cost of capital, whereas the impact of a dollar of transitory earnings to company value is a dollar.) Accordingly, many analysts would naively value this company's stock at $26 [($3/0.10) − $4]. Further, if the analyst entirely ignores this one-time charge (as some analysts suggest), then this company's stock is valued at $30 ($3/0.10). These amounts are substantially different than the correct value of $20.

Exhibit 6.8 graphically illustrates this point. The recast line reflects a constant "true" earnings of $2 per share from Year −9 to Year 0. The reported line shows reported earnings that are progressively managed upward, with a massive charge taken in Year −3. At the end of Year 0, both cumulative reported and cumulative "true" earnings are, in reality, equal because all earnings management has been reversed. The dotted lines indicate forecasts of both "true" earnings and reported earnings trends beyond Year 0 based on past earnings' time series. It can be seen that an illusion of higher permanent earnings and earnings growth can be created by regularly managing earnings upward and reversing the accruals with special one-time charges.

Managing Earnings Level and Growth Perceptions with a One-Time Charge ***Exhibit 6.8***

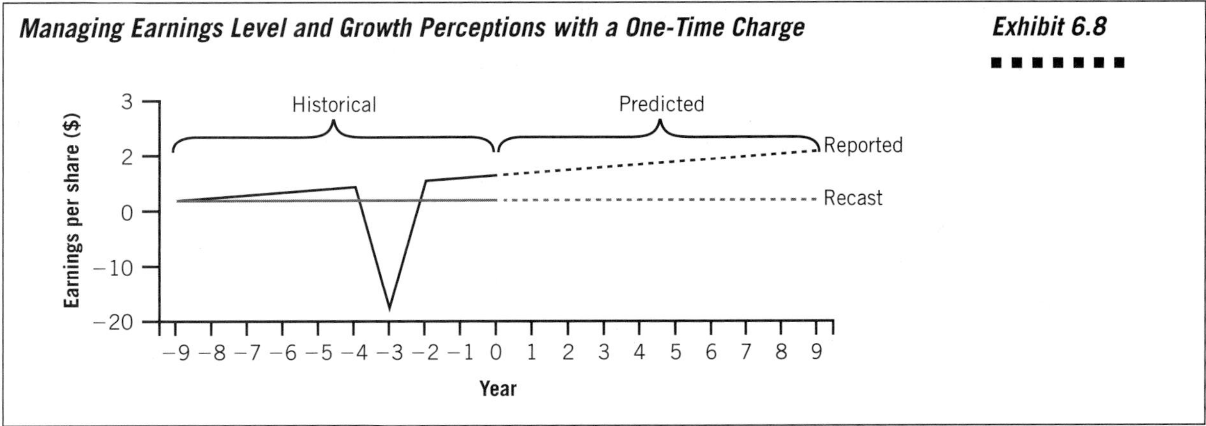

This graphical illustration shows that when analysts focus on only recurring components of earnings and ignore nonrecurring charges, managers are motivated to manage earnings in this manner. The illustration also shows we should be wary of special charges. It is important to investigate companies that repeatedly take one-time charges to determine if these charges are the result of an earnings management strategy.

Income Statement Adjustments. As Exhibit 6.8 reveals, one-time charges can seriously distort earnings patterns and trends. It is important for an analyst to make adjustments for determining the effect of special charges, especially on permanent income. This section discusses adjustments to determine a company's permanent income and then discusses adjustments to determine economic income. Permanent income should reflect the profitability of a company under normal circumstances. Most special charges constitute operating expenses that need to be reflected in permanent income. At a basic level, special charges reflect either understatements of past expenses or "investments" for improved future profitability.

To illustrate, consider a company that invests $40 million in machinery to manufacture a drug. The company expects the drug to be sold over the remaining life of its patent, which is eight years. Accordingly, the company depreciates the machinery (on a straight-line basis with no salvage value) over an eight-year period–depreciation expense is $5 million per year. At the end of the fourth year, however, a competing, revolutionary product eliminates the market for this company's drug. Consequently, the company stops producing the drug at the end of the fourth year. Also, the machinery is scrapped and the company recognizes an asset impairment charge of $20 million (which is the machine's carrying value at the end of the fourth year). The company reports the impairment as a one-time charge that is not expected to occur again. Do we concur with this company's assessment? Well, let's begin by looking at the cause of the asset impairment. Basically, the impairment arose because the company overestimated the economic life of the drug and, hence, the machine. This led to undercharging depreciation expense over the four-year period when the machine was used. The proper analysis for this case would be to adjust depreciation expense assuming a four-year life and restate past (and current) earnings. Specifically, we would decrease current period earnings (along with each of the prior three years' earnings if we are analyzing earnings trend) by $5 million.

An actual example of such a scenario is the $31.3 million write-down of the Puerto Rico manufacturing facility by Chiron (see Illustration 6.5). This facility is idled because of process improvements and the introduction of a competing product, which led to recognizing an impairment loss. It is important to note that the costs of the Puerto Rico facility are normal operating expenses and that these costs must be allocated to the entire period during which the facility has been operational–this period often can be determined by examining past financial reports. If it cannot be determined, these costs can be distributed over an arbitrary prior period of, say, five years.

Sometimes special charges are "investments" for improving future profitability. To illustrate, consider a company that streamlines its procurement procedures. This streamlining results in reducing the workforce in the procurement department by 20%, which is expected to save the company $1.3 million per year in the future. The laid-off workers are paid $4.2 million as retrenchment compensation. The company decides to expense this entire amount as a one-time charge. On the surface, this accounting treatment seems reasonable. However, note the worker retrenchment is expected to reduce future expenses by $1.3 million per year. Consequently, the $4.2 million retrenchment compensation is similar to an investment in a long-term asset that is expected to generate net revenues (or reduced costs) of $1.3 million per year in the future. This means the proper accounting is to allocate the $4.2 million over current and future periods when the benefits are expected to be realized. If this period cannot be determined, then we can use an estimate–say, a period of five years.

Most restructuring charges are, at least in part, in the form of an investment. One objective of restructuring programs is streamlining a company's operations so as to improve future profitability. A restructuring program that consists of cash outflows such as retrenchment compensation and accrual adjustments such as asset write-offs is a type of investment for improving future profitability. Accordingly, our analysis should allocate that portion of the restructuring charge over future periods expected to reap the benefits from the restructuring program.

As an actual example, recall the $698 million restructuring charge taken by Kodak (Appendix A). Its restructuring charge consists of four major categories: $351 million for employee severance; $215 million relating to the write-down of long-term assets; $84 million in inventory write-downs; and $48 million for the costs of exiting nonstrategic businesses. These restructuring costs include investments for future cost reduction. Moreover, Kodak reports that the aim of its restructuring program is mainly cost reduction. Given the long-term nature of its restructuring program, it is reasonable to allocate the $698 million over, for example, a 10-year period (the current year and next 9 years). An analyst following Kodak might adopt a more detailed adjustment, where in-depth knowledge of Kodak's business can be used to write off certain costs and amortize the remainder over different periods of time corresponding to the expected benefit periods.

One caveat: because restructuring charges usually impact several different years, an analyst often needs to examine prior years' reports so as to estimate the impact of allocating past restructuring charges in determining permanent income. Also, unlike permanent income, where an analyst must determine normal profitability for a company, the determination of economic income involves measuring the effects on equity of all events that occur in the period. This means the entire amount of any special charges is included when determining economic income. Restructuring charges often include a provision for the estimated future cost of the restructuring program. This entire charge is taken in the year the program is initiated, although the actual costs are incurred over several later periods. In this situation, an alternative approach in determining economic income is to only adjust for amounts actually incurred for each year, rather than the entire charge. For example, while Motorola took a $698 million charge in 2001, only $380 million was actually incurred in 2001. The remaining $318 million will be charged to future years. When such a method is adopted, it is important to remember to also include actual costs related to past restructuring programs.

Adjustments to Balance Sheet. A major focus of the asset impairment standard, *SFAS 121,* is the balance sheet. Consequently, unlike income that is distorted by one-time charges, these charges (especially inventory and long-term asset write-downs) improve the ability of the balance sheet to reflect business reality by reporting assets closer to net realizable values.

Still, two points demand attention. First, as already noted, a portion of most restructuring charges is often in the form of a provision. This means the effects on assets and liabilities are reflected gradually over time when the actual costs are incurred. A question that arises is should the balance sheet include the entire provision or should the remaining balance in the restructuring reserve (reflecting costs yet incurred) be netted against equity? The answer depends on the analysis objectives. If the analysis is considering a going-concern scenario, it is better to keep the provision in the balance sheet because it reflects a more realistic picture of the long-term assets and liabilities. However, if the analysis objective is to determine the liquidating value of a company, it is better to offset the restructuring provision against equity. Care must be taken to ensure that determination of economic income is consistent with the balance sheet treatment. The second main point is that asset write-offs introduce a conservative bias in the reporting of assets and liabilities. Since asset write-ups are not permitted in the U.S. (they are, for example, allowed in the U.K.), the balance sheet is conservatively distorted from asset impairments.

REVENUE AND GAIN RECOGNITION

Revenues are defined in practice as "inflows or other enhancements of assets of an entity or settlements of its liabilities" resulting from a company's "ongoing major or central operations." **Gains,** on the other hand, are increases in net assets (equity) resulting from "peripheral or incidental transactions" of a company. Distinguishing between revenues and gains depends on the usual business activities of a company. Since our analysis treats these items differently (that is, revenues are expected to persist, while gains are not), their distinction is important. It is also important to understand when a company

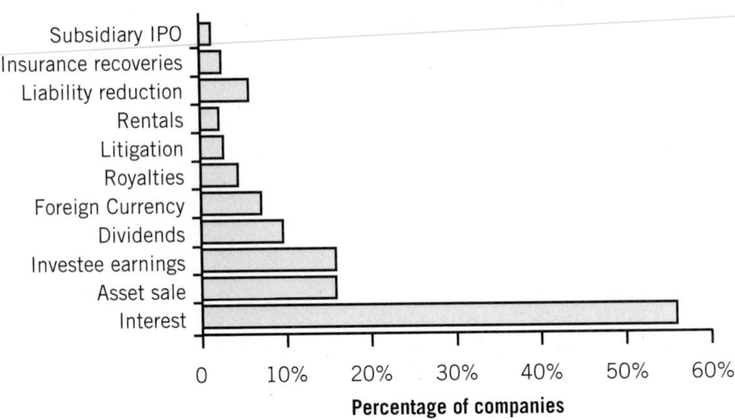

Source: Accounting Trends & Techniques.

recognizes revenues and gains. Our analytical adjustments sometimes modify income numbers using revenue recognition information. An important question is when, or at what point, in the sequence of revenue-earning activities in which a company is engaged, is it proper to recognize revenues and gains as earned? This section addresses this question.

Guidelines for Revenue Recognition

From our analysis perspective, inappropriate accrual recognition of revenues (and gains) can have one of two undesirable consequences:

1. If a company records revenue prematurely or belatedly, then revenue is assigned to the wrong period.
2. If a company records revenue prior to reasonable certainty of realization, then revenue might be recorded in one period and later canceled or reversed in another–this overstates income in the first period and understates it in the latter period.

These two effects adversely affect income measurement. To counter this, accounting applies strict and conservative rules regarding revenue recognition. Generally, revenue is recognized when it is both realized (or realizable) and earned. Exhibit 6.9 lists criteria that must be satisfied for revenue recognition. While these criteria are seemingly straightforward, they are subject to certain exceptions and have, in practice, been interpreted in different ways. To understand these variations for analysis purposes, the next section considers the application of these criteria under special circumstances.

Exhibit 6.9 **Revenue Recognition Criteria**

- Earning activities creating revenue are substantially complete, and no significant effort is necessary to complete the transaction.
- Risk of ownership in sales is effectively passed to the buyer.
- Revenue and the associated expense are measured or estimated with reasonable accuracy.
- Revenue recognized normally yields an increase in cash, receivables, or securities. Under certain conditions it yields an increase in inventories or other assets, or a decrease in liabilities.
- Revenue transaction is at arm's length with an independent party(ies) (not with controlled parties).
- Revenue transaction is not subject to revocation (such as a right of return).

Uncertainty in Revenue Collection

Companies use a provision for doubtful (uncollectible) accounts to reflect uncertainty in the collectibility of receivables from credit sales. A company makes a judgment, based on the circumstances, when it can no longer reasonably assure the collectibility of receivables. This judgment can be conservative or it might use liberal or optimistic assumptions. When collectibility is no longer reasonably assured, practice follows a general procedure to defer recognition of revenue until cash is collected.

Revenue When Right of Return Exists

When the buyer has a right of return, revenue is recognized at the time of sale *only* if the following conditions are met:

- Price is substantially fixed or determinable at the sale date.
- Buyer pays the seller or is obligated to pay the seller (not contingent on resale).
- Buyer's obligation to seller is unchanged in event of theft or damage to product.
- Buyer has economic substance apart from the seller.
- Seller has no significant obligations for future performance related to the sale.
- Returns are reasonably estimated.

If these conditions are met, sales revenue and cost of sales are recorded but reduced to reflect estimated returns and related expenses; if not met, revenue recognition is postponed.

Franchise Revenues

Revenue from franchises is approximately $1 trillion per year. Franchises employ nearly 10 million individuals and make up one-third of all retail sales. Accounting standards for franchisors require that franchise fee revenue from franchise sales be recognized only when all material services or conditions relating to the sale are substantially performed or satisfied by the franchisor. This also applies to continuing franchise fees, continuing product sales, agency sales, repossessed franchises, franchising costs, commingled revenue, and relationships between a franchisor and a franchisee. A typical franchise fee arrangement follows:

ANALYSIS EXCERPT

Application, License, and Royalty Fees. All fees from licensed operation are included in revenue as earned. Management accelerated the revenue recognition for application fees from the time the site was approved or construction began to the time cash is received. Management believes this method will more accurately relate the income recognition to performance of the related service . . . License fees are earned when the related store opens. Unearned license fees which have been collected are included in current liabilities. Royalty fees are based on licensee revenues and are recognized in the period the related revenues are earned.

Churchs Chicken

Product Financing Arrangements

A *product financing arrangement* is an agreement involving the transfer or sponsored acquisition of inventory that (although it sometimes resembles a sale of inventory) is in substance a means of financing inventory. For example, if a company transfers ("sells") inventory to another company and concurrently agrees to repurchase the inventory at a later date, this transaction is likely a product financing arrangement and not a sale and subsequent purchase of inventory. In essence, if a party bearing the risks and rewards of ownership transfers inventory to a purchaser and in a related transaction agrees to repurchase the product at a specified price over a specified time, or guarantees some specified resale price for sales of the product to outside parties, the arrangement is a product financing arrangement and is accounted for as such. In this case the inventory remains on the seller's statements and the seller recognizes no revenue.

Revenue under Contracts

Accounting for *long-term* construction contracts for items like buildings, aircraft, ships, or heavy machinery poses conceptual problems for the determination of revenue and profit. GAAP requires companies to use the **percentage-of-completion method** when reasonable estimates exist for both costs to complete a contract and progress toward completion of the contract. A common basis of profit estimation is to record part of the estimated total profit based on the ratio of costs incurred to date divided by expected total costs. Other acceptable methods of estimation are based on units completed, engineering estimates, or units delivered. Under this method, current or anticipated losses are fully recognized in the period when they are initially identified. Johnson Controls describes its revenue recognition as follows:

ANALYSIS EXCERPT

Revenue Recognition. The Company recognizes revenue from long-term systems installation contracts of the Controls Group over the contractual period under the percentage-of-completion method of accounting (see "Long-Term Contracts"). In all other cases, the Company recognizes revenue at the time products are shipped and title passes to the customer or as services are performed.

Long-Term Contracts. Under the percentage-of-completion method of accounting used for long-term contracts, sales and gross profit are recognized as work is performed based on the relationship between actual costs incurred and total estimated costs at completion. Sales and gross profit are adjusted prospectively for revisions in estimated total contract costs and contract values. Estimated losses are recorded when identified. Claims against customers are recognized as revenue upon settlement. The amount of accounts receivable due after one year is not significant.

Analysis Implications of Revenue Recognition

The income statement is important to the analysis and valuation of a company. This statement is also important to management for these same reasons and others, including its role in accounting-based contractual agreements, management pressure to achieve income-based results, management compensation linked to income, and the value of stock options. Given management's incentives, we rationally expect management to select and apply accounting principles that best meet their own interests but are still within acceptable accounting practice. The objectives of income reporting do not always align with management's incentives in this area. Our analysis must be alert to management propensities in this area and the accounting discretion available.

ANALYSIS EXCERPT

Datapoint Corporation recorded a significant amount of sales that sales representatives booked by asking customers to order millions of dollars of computer equipment months in advance with payment to be made later. In many of these cases, Datapoint recorded sales when it had not even manufactured such equipment. It is reported that its sales representatives were under intense pressure to achieve unreasonable or unattainable goals. Datapoint subsequently reversed these sales and consented to an SEC order barring it from such future violations.

Recording of revenue is a critical event in income determination. Our analysis must take aim at the accounting methods to ascertain whether they properly reflect economic reality. For example, if a manufacturer records profits on sale to a dealer, our analysis must inquire about dealer inventories and market conditions–because real earnings activity consists of selling to the ultimate consumer.

Managers' propensities and incentives to manage revenue yields many pronouncements on the subject of revenue recognition by accounting regulatory agencies. In spite of these, our analysis must remain alert to accounting approaches skirting the spirit, if not the letter, of these pronouncements. The following excerpt provides an example:

ANALYSIS EXCERPT

Prime Motor Inns earns a major portion of its income, not from core operations, but rather from hotel sales, construction fees, and interest. In recording these nonrecurring revenues, Prime Motor Inns stretched recognition criteria by accepting notes and receivables of dubious value, and by guaranteeing to buyers of their hotels, and their bankers, certain levels of future income. While they recorded revenues, they did not record contingent liabilities associated with these revenues.

Aware of these revenue recognition problems, the SEC expressed its belief that significant uncertainties regarding a seller's ability to realize noncash proceeds received in transactions often arise when the purchaser is thinly capitalized, or highly leveraged, or when the purchaser's assets consist primarily of those purchased from the seller. These characteristics raise doubt as to whether revenue recognition is appropriate. Circumstances fueling questions about revenue recognition include:

- Lack of substantial equity capital in the purchasing entity other than that provided by the seller.
- Existence of contingent liabilities such as debt guarantees or agreements requiring the seller to infuse cash into the purchasing entity under certain conditions.
- Sale of assets or operations that have historically not produced operating cash flows sufficient to fund future debt service and dividend expectations.

Even when a company receives cash proceeds, any guarantees or other agreements requiring the company to infuse cash into the purchasing entity impacts the validity of revenue recognition. Revenue should not be recognized until: (1) cash flows from operating activities are sufficient to fund debt service and dividend requirements (on an accrual basis), or (2) the company's investment in the purchasing entity is or can be readily converted to cash and the company has no further obligations under any debt guarantees or other agreements requiring it to make additional investments in the purchasing entity. Amounts of any deferred revenue, including deferral of interest or dividend revenue, are generally disclosed in a balance sheet as a deduction from the related asset account. Notes to the financial statements usually offer a description of such transactions including any commitments and contingencies, and the accounting methods applied.

Current practice generally does not allow for recognition of revenue in advance of sale. For example, it is not typical to recognize increases in the market value of property such as land, equipment, or buildings; the accretion of values in timber or natural resources; or increases in the value of inventories. Yet the timing of sales is an important item that is partly within the discretion of management. This gives management certain latitude in revenue recognition as evidenced in the following:

ANALYSIS EXCERPT

Thousand Trails, a membership campground operator, recorded revenue from membership fees when a new member initially signed even though these fees were nearly 90% financed and many canceled within days of signing. When their revenue recognition practices became public, Thousand Trails' stock price sharply declined.

ANALYSIS VIEWPOINT **. . . YOU ARE THE BANKER**

Playground Equipment Company calls on you for a long-term loan to expand operations. Although you are its banker, they are a recent client with new management. In reviewing financial statements as part of its application, you notice it recognizes revenue *during production.* The statements report: "revenue is recognized during production because production activity is the critical event in the company's earning process . . . and deferring revenue substantially impairs the usefulness of the financial statements." You ask a colleague for her opinion, and she feels its revenue recognition method is too liberal. She voices a preference for revenue recognition at point of sale or, possibly, when cash is received. Do you require Playground Equipment to restate its statements? What risks do you see in acting on this loan?

Answer–p. 362

DEFERRED CHARGES

Deferred charges are costs incurred that are deferred because they are expected to benefit future periods. The increasing complexities of business activities are expanding the number and types of deferred charges. Examples are research and development costs and computer software expenditures. The distinction between deferred charges and intangible assets is often vague. In most cases, costs arising from operating activities are classified as deferred charges, while those arising from investing activities are classified as intangible assets.

The motivation for deferral of costs is to better match costs with expected benefits. This motivation underlies the capitalization of all long-lived assets and was discussed in Chapter 4. If a cost incurred in the current period benefits a future period by either a contribution to revenues or reduction in costs, then a company defers this cost until the future period(s). For example, if a company incurs start-up costs in operating new, better, or more efficient facilities, it can defer these costs and match (amortize) them to expected future benefit periods.

Research and Development

Companies undertake research, exploration, and development activities for several reasons. Some of these activities are directed at maintaining existing products, while others aim at developing new products and processes. Research activities aim at discovery, and development activities are a translation of research. R&D activities exclude routine or periodic alterations in ongoing operations, market research, and testing activities.

Accounting for Research and Development

Accounting for R&D expenses is problematic. Reasons for difficulties in R&D accounting include:

- High uncertainty of ultimate benefits derived from R&D activities.
- An often significant lapse of time between initiation of R&D activities and determination of their success.
- Evaluation problems due to the intangible nature of most R&D activities.

These characteristics of R&D activities cause difficulties in accounting for them. Consequently, U.S. accounting requires companies to expense R&D costs when incurred. Only costs of materials, equipment, and facilities having *alternative future uses* (in R&D projects or otherwise) are capitalized as tangible assets.

Analysis Research

VALUING R&D EXPENDITURES

Are R&D expenditures assets? Do R&D expenditures benefit periods other than the period of the outlay? Analysis research implies R&D expenditures are valued much like other long-lived assets. For expenditures benefiting the current period only, the market immediately reduces the value of the company. Examples include rent, utilities, and taxes. If an expenditure benefits future periods, and those benefits exceed its costs, the market does not reduce the value of the company–in fact, the expenditure *increases* company value. Research indicates the market assesses R&D expenditures in a manner similar to many long-lived assets like property, plant, and equipment. In several cases, the market is found to value R&D expenditures as possessing greater future value than many long-lived assets. This market assessment accorded R&D expenditures is inconsistent with the accounting treatment for them. R&D expenditures are generally expensed as incurred. Why the discrepancy? The accounting treatment is a convenient solution to a difficult valuation problem. More research is needed to precisely estimate the net benefits of R&D expenditures before capitalization of their costs is likely. More important, we need research on a measurement system to better assess the future benefits of *specific* R&D expenditures. R&D expenditures are not all equal, and advances in accounting for R&D depend on better techniques to recognize these differences and appropriately account for them.

Costs identified with R&D activities include:

- Materials, equipment, and facilities acquired or constructed for a *specific* R&D project, or purchased intangibles having *no* alternative future uses (in R&D projects or otherwise).
- Materials consumed in R&D activities; and depreciation of equipment or facilities, and amortization of intangible assets used in R&D activities having alternative future uses.
- Salaries and other related costs of personnel engaged in R&D activities.
- Services performed by others in connection with R&D activities.
- Allocation of indirect costs, excluding general and administrative costs not directly related to R&D activities.

Analyzing Research and Development

Analysis of R&D expenditures is challenging. They are often of sufficient magnitude to warrant scrutiny in an analysis of a company's current and future income. Accounting for R&D expenditures is a simple solution to a complex phenomenon. Future benefits are undoubtedly created by many R&D activities and, conceptually, these R&D expenditures should not be expensed as incurred. It is the uncertainty of these benefits that limits R&D capitalization. Yet expensing R&D costs impairs the usefulness of income. For example, when a company incurs a major R&D outlay in a desire for future benefits, there is a decline in income at the same time the market often revalues upward the company's stock price. Our analysis recognizes that while current accounting virtually assures no overstatement in R&D assets, it is at the loss of reasonable measures of expenditures to match with revenues arising from R&D activities. Accounting ignores the productive experience of many ongoing R&D activities. It does, however, achieve a uniformity of accounting for R&D activities and avoids difficult judgments with a policy of capitalization and deferral. Nevertheless, current "nonaccounting" for R&D activities fails to effectively serve the needs and interests of users of financial statements.

In spite of accounting problems, it is reasonable to assume companies pursue R&D projects with expectations of positive returns. Companies often have specific return expectations, and their realization or nonrealization can be monitored and estimated as R&D projects progress. A policy of deferral of R&D costs affords managements and their independent auditors, who regularly work with uncertainties and estimates, an opportunity to convey useful information of R&D outlays. Currently, R&D outlays are treated as if they have no future benefits. Consequently, our analysis does not benefit from the insights of those in the best position to provide them.

To assess the quality and potential value of R&D outlays, our analysis needs to know more than the periodic R&D expense. We desire information on the types of research performed, the R&D outlays by category, technical feasibility, commercial viability, and the potential of projects periodically assessed and reevaluated. We also desire information on a company's success/failure experience with R&D activities to date. Current accounting does not provide us this basic information. Except in cases of voluntary disclosure, or an investor or lender with sufficient influence, we are unable to obtain this information.

What our analysis can safely assume is that expensing of R&D outlays yields more conservative balance sheets. There are likely fewer "bad" news surprises from R&D activities with this accounting treatment. Still, our analysis must realize that with a lack of information about potential benefits, we are also unaware of potential disasters befalling a company tempted or forced to spend added funds in R&D projects whose promise is great but whose failure is imminent.

ANALYSIS VIEWPOINT ***. . . YOU ARE THE ANALYST***

The announcement of net income for California Technology Corporation shows an increase of 10%. Your analysis of its operating activities reveals the increase in income is due to a decrease in research and development expenditures. If R&D expenditures for California Technology equaled that for the previous year, income would be down by more than 15%. What is your assessment of the future profitability of California Technology Corporation based on its income announcement?

Answer–p. 363

Computer Software Expenses

Development of computer software is a specialized activity that does not fit the usual expenditures of R&D activities. Development of software for marketing purposes is an ongoing activity leading directly to current or future revenues. At some point in the software's development cycle, its costs need to be deferred and matched against future revenues. Current practice in accounting for expenditures of computer software to be sold, leased, or otherwise marketed identifies a point referred to as *technological feasibility* where these costs are capitalized and matched against future revenues. Until the establishment of the point of technological feasibility, all expenditures are expensed as incurred (similar to R&D). Expenditures incurred after technological feasibility, and until the product is ready for general release to customers, are capitalized as an intangible asset. Additional costs to produce software from the masters and package it for distribution are inventoried and charged against revenue as a cost of the product sold.

HIDDEN-WARE
Microsoft has never capitalized its software development costs.

Exploration and Development Costs in Extractive Industries

The search for new deposits of natural resources is important to companies in extractive industries. These industries include oil, natural gas, metals, coal, and nonmetallic minerals. The importance of these industries and their special accounting problems deserve our separate attention. As with R&D activities, the search for and development of natural resources is characterized by high risk. Risk involves uncertainty; and for income determination, uncertainty yields measurement and recognition problems. For extractive industries, the problem is whether exploration and development costs that are reasonably expected to be recovered from sale of natural resources are expensed as incurred or capitalized and amortized over the expected future benefit period. While many companies expense exploration and development costs as incurred, some charge off a portion and capitalize the remainder. Few companies capitalize all exploration and development costs.

Accounting for Extractive Industries

Accounting regulators have made various attempts to curtail these divergent practices. The FASB prescribed *successful efforts accounting* for oil and gas producing companies. This directs that exploration costs, except costs of drilling exploratory wells, are capitalized when incurred. These costs are later expensed if the resource is unsuccessful *or* reclassified as an amortizable asset if proved oil or gas reserves are discovered. The SEC disagreed with this approach and instead favored *reserve recognition accounting* (a current value method). This led the FASB to reconsider and, in effect, permitted the same alternatives to continue. The SEC subsequently requested the FASB to develop supplementary disclosures, including value-based disclosures. The FASB responded with the following required supplementary *disclosures* for publicly traded oil and gas producers:

- Proved oil and gas reserve quantities.
- Capitalized costs related to oil and gas producing activities.
- Costs incurred in acquisition, exploration, and development activities.
- Results of operations for oil and gas producing activities.
- Measures of discounted future net cash flows for proved reserves.

Both publicly traded and other companies are required to disclose the method of accounting for costs incurred in oil and gas producing activities and the manner of disposing of related capitalized costs.

Disclosure is one thing and accounting measurement is another. The successful efforts accounting method has not received general support. Yet, in sanctioning use of full-cost accounting, the SEC provided that costs under this method are capitalized up to a ceiling. This ceiling is determined by the present value of company reserves. Capitalized costs exceeding this ceiling are expensed. When falling oil prices lower this ceiling, companies have and likely will continue to pressure the SEC to suspend or modify the rules.

Analysis Implications for Extractive Industries

The variety of acceptable methods of treating exploration and development costs in extractive industries hampers our comparison of results across companies. Accounting in this industry continues to exhibit diversity. The two methods in common use, and the variations on these methods, can yield significantly different results. Our analysis must be aware of this. Many analysts favor successful efforts accounting over full-cost accounting because it better matches costs with related revenues and is more consistent with current accounting practices. Successful efforts accounting requires a direct relation between costs incurred and specific reserves discovered before these exploration and development costs are capitalized. In contrast, full-cost accounting permits companies to label unsuccessful exploration and development activities as assets.

Other Deferred Charges

Companies often capitalize start-up costs as a deferred charge and amortize them over an expected future benefit period. Neptune International describes its deferral of start-up costs as follows:

ANALYSIS EXCERPT

Other assets. The Corporation has incurred costs prior to attaining normal levels of production in connection with the start-up of two new manufacturing facilities and the start-up of a new foundry. These costs are being amortized over three-year periods.

Relocation costs are another item often capitalized as a deferred charge. Willcox & Gibbs, Inc., includes the following note in its annual report:

ANALYSIS EXCERPT

The Company has deferred approximately $782,000 related to moving expenses and start-up costs associated with new facilities placed into operation. It is the Company's intention to amortize these costs over a five-year period.

There is disagreement on the merits of deferring start-up and relocation costs in practice. Increasing complexities in both technology and business practices have expanded the Deferred Charges account. Since deferred charges often represent intangible future benefits, they are very similar in nature to intangible assets. While we focus on the validity of these costs as deferred charges, we must remember it is not the existence but the timing of expense recognition that is most relevant here.

Deferred charges are often substantial and present challenges in our understanding and interpretation of financial statements. We can readily understand certain deferred charges like start-up costs or debt issue costs. Other deferred charges, like organization costs, are more difficult to justify and their amortization periods are arbitrary. Many users are not supportive of capitalization of software costs. They are concerned with rapid obsolescence of software and unjustified deferring of expenses. Users are also concerned that the balance sheet excludes capitalizing more important assets like research and development. Validating many deferred charges such as relocation costs, promotional costs, and initial operating losses depends on estimates. Similarly, assessing the benefit period over which companies amortize deferred charges demands attention. Our analysis must be alert to deferred charges that do not represent future benefits. Experience shows that costs are sometimes carried forward under the guise of deferred charges so as not to burden current operating results with additional expenses. While an auditor's opinion and a company's description of deferred costs are helpful in our analysis, we must be prepared to evaluate evidence and information regarding deferrals on our own. We must also be aware that deferred charges are generally incapable of satisfying creditors' claims. Overall, our analysis of financial statements must examine the propensity of management to defer the costs of today into tomorrow. This is symptomatic of certain behavior in practice. Following is a classic case in point.

ANALYSIS EXCERPT

Lockheed Corporation experienced a time of unprofitable activity in its TriStar Jetliner program. Yet, management repeated its forecasts of future favorable developments while new orders consistently proved overly optimistic. Management deferred "initial planning and tooling and unrecovered production start-up costs" and adopted a policy of amortizing these deferred charges over a 10-year period. By the middle of this 10-year period, deferred costs grew to more than $280 million. Two-thirds into this period, Lockheed abandoned TriStar and recognized the inevitable—the necessity of writing off the deferred charges that had overstated operating results for the past several years. Inventory write-downs added further to the losses with this program.

SUPPLEMENTARY EMPLOYEE BENEFITS

This section describes the accounting, analysis, and interpretation of supplementary employee benefits, with an emphasis on employee stock options.

Overview of Supplementary Employee Benefits

Societal pressures, competition, and scarcity of employee talent have led to a proliferation of employee benefits supplementary to salaries and wages. Some fringe benefits like vacation pay, bonuses, profit sharing, and paid health or life insurance are identifiable with the period when earned or granted. These identifiable expenses do not pose problems of accounting recognition and accrual. Other supplementary benefits, due to their tentative or contingent nature, are not accorded full or timely accounting recognition. Some of these benefits and the accounting for them are described here:

- **Deferred compensation contracts** are promises to pay employees in the future, some with contingencies. A company often grants them to key executives it wishes to retain or who desire deferring income to postretirement or lower tax years. These contracts often include noncompete clauses or specify an employee's availability for consulting services. Accounting generally requires that at least the present value of deferred compensation is accrued in a systematic and rational manner over the period of active employment starting when the contract is entered into.
- **Stock appreciation rights (SARs)** are stock rights granted to an employee on a specified number of shares. SAR awards are based on the increase in market value of the company's stock since date of grant and can be awarded in cash, stock, or a combination of both. Under these plans, a company records compensation expense at the end of each period. Expense is computed as the difference between the award market price of the shares and their grant date option price. Accounting provides a method for apportioning expense over the service period–changes in market price from period to period are reflected as adjustments to compensation expense.
- **Junior stock plans** allow employees to buy shares of a special class of stock at a fair market value (determined by independent appraisal) that is less than the company's common stock price because of reduced voting, dividend, or liquidation rights. At a future date, junior stock is exchangeable for regular common stock if certain performance goals are achieved (such as sales or income increases). Accounting requires that junior stock plans be treated like stock appreciation rights. That is, expense is measured by the difference between the amount the company receives for the junior stock and the market price of common stock on

GOLDEN PARACHUTES

Most CEOs get two to three years' severance pay, plus generous bonuses. The severance pay guaranteed to 100 CEOs follows:

35%	3 years
26	Between 2 and 3 years
12	Between 1 and 2 years
14	Until end of employment contract
1	Less than 1 year
12	Unavailable

the date conversion is certain. Companies recognize expense when it becomes probable that performance targets will be met and the junior stock will be converted to regular common. Periodic charges to income are based on end-of-period common stock prices and are subject to change until the final amount is set at the date conversion is certain.

Employee Stock Options

Employee stock options (ESOs), also referred to as *stock-based compensation,* are arguably the most popular form of incentive compensation. There are many reasons for this popularity. First, companies contend ESOs enhance performance by giving employees a stake in the business and thereby align employee and company incentives. Second, ESOs are viewed by employees as means to riches. Thousands of managers, scientists, accountants, engineers, programmers, and secretaries have become millionaires with ESOs in the past decade. Because of this, ESOs have emerged as a tool to attract talented and enterprising workers. Third, although ESOs are a form of employee compensation, they do not have direct cash flow effects. Fourth, ESOs provide employee benefits without requiring the recording of costs. The opposition of companies to the FASB's proposal in the mid-90s to deduct the cost of ESOs from income is testimony to the importance of this factor. This section explains characteristics of ESOs and defines key terms. We then discuss the economics underlying ESOs with specific emphasis on costs and benefits. This discussion includes the accounting and reporting for ESOs. We conclude with a discussion of analyzing ESOs.

Characteristics of Employee Stock Options

An employee stock option is a contractual opportunity granted by a company to an employee whereby the employee can purchase a fixed number of shares of the company at a specified price on or after a specified future date. Exhibit 6.10 illustrates an option granted to an employee. The *exercise price* is the price for which the employee has the right to purchase the shares. Exercise price often is set equal to the stock price on the *grant date.* The *vesting date* is the earliest date the employee can exercise the option–the employee can exercise the option at any date after the vesting date. Most ESOs have *vesting periods* of between 2 and 10 years. When the stock price is higher than the exercise price, the option is said to be *in-the-money.* It is *out-of-the-money* when the stock price is less than the exercise price.

Employee stock options fit two broad categories: incentive and nonqualified. *Incentive,* or *tax-favored qualified, stock options* are not taxed until the stock is sold by the employee. These options must be granted at fair market value and the stock must be

Exhibit 6.10 ***Illustration of an Option Granted to an Employee***

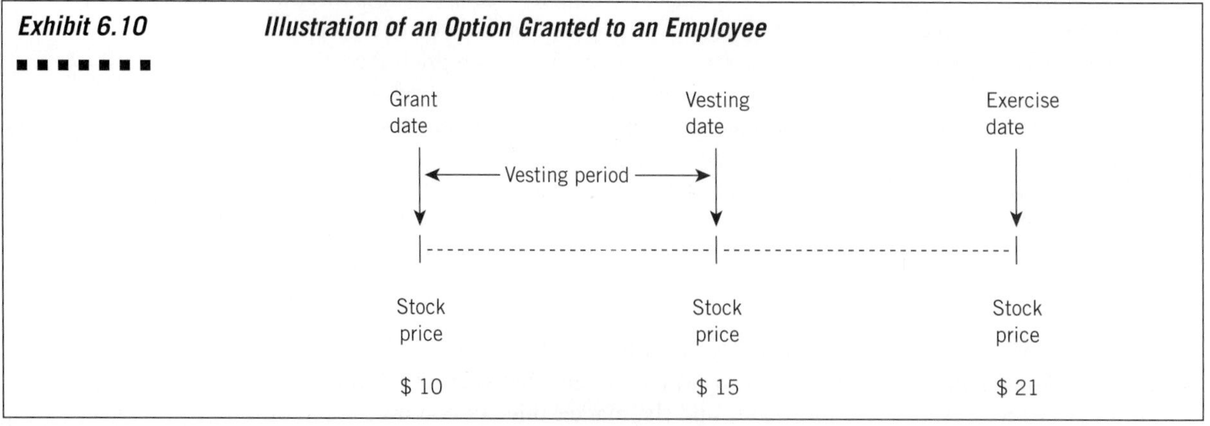

held for two years from the date of the grant and another one year from the date they are exercised. The difference between the exercise price and the selling price is usually taxed as ordinary income. *Nonqualified stock options* do not have the tax benefits of qualified options. These options are sometimes granted at a discount from fair market value and employees are taxed at the time of exercise on the difference between the exercise price and the stock's fair market value. In this case, the company benefits from a tax deduction equal to the amount of income recognized by the employee.

There are no direct cash flow effects from ESOs. No ESO related expense is recorded as long as the exercise price is equal to or greater than the stock price on the grant date. This means ESOs have no financial statement effects even though they are a form of employee compensation. For this reason, ESOs often are called *stealth* or *off-balance-sheet* compensation. Sometimes ESOs are *repriced* when the stock price falls below the exercise price–repricing refers to adjusting downward the exercise price on the ESOs. Companies contend that repricing is important to both motivate and retain employees. Accounting records an expense to the extent to which ESOs are repriced.

Economics of Employee Stock Options

In the absence of incentive effects (resulting in improved performance), ESOs constitute a net transfer of wealth from shareholders to employees. This section describes both the economic benefits and costs of ESOs.

Benefits of Employee Stock Options. The main benefit of ESOs is the potential increase in company value that can arise through incentive effects on employee behavior. ESOs aim to align incentives of employees and the company by providing employees an ownership stake in the company. The idea of *incentive alignment* has its origins in *agency theory* and is explained in Illustration 6.6.

ILLUSTRATION 6.6

A manager of a company is planning a business trip to China. The manager can either travel coach for $1,000 round-trip or first class for $4,000. By traveling coach, the manager saves the shareholders of the company $3,000. Assume the manager is paid a fixed salary of $80,000 per year. The manager probably prefers the comfort of traveling first class to traveling coach and saving $3,000 for shareholders. Alternatively, the manager can be granted a 20% stake in the company's common stock. In this case the manager loses $600 (20% of $3,000) by traveling first class rather than coach. The manager may value the $600 savings more than the comfort of traveling first class and, thereby, travel coach and save the company $3,000. The manager's motivation to select this shareholder-value-enhancing action arises because his incentives are better aligned with that of the company through the 20% ownership stake.

While strong arguments support the incentive effects of providing employee stock options, it is debatable whether ESOs actually contribute to improved employee performance. U.S. evidence of the incentive effects of ESOs is mixed, and evidence from other countries suggests there may be other, more important, factors affecting employee motivation. Still, ESOs are a popular and powerful factor in attracting talented employees. ESOs also may increase the *risk propensity* of managers. That is, ESOs may motivate managers to venture into more risky projects because managers can share in the increased upside potential but have the benefit of the downside protection offered by the option. Such behavior usually is harmful to shareholders because they do not have downside protection. Still, ESOs often are granted to managers in growth and innovative industries to induce more risk taking.

Cost of Employee Stock Options. The cost of employee stock options is their potential dilutive effects. That is, when exercised, ESOs transfer wealth from shareholders to employees by diluting current shareholders' stake in the company. But does the company incur a cost when the exercise price equals the stock price on the grant date? The *intrinsic value approach* to this question implies there is no cost. This approach measures cost as the extent to which the exercise price is lower than the stock price. It is based on the erroneous logic that granting ESOs, with exercise price equal to stock price, is similar to issuing stock at the prevailing market price. This leads to the nonrecognition of cost provided the exercise price is equal to or greater than current stock price. Accounting follows this intrinsic value approach when determining accounting income.

A main flaw with the intrinsic value approach is it ignores two types of costs–costs that arise even when the exercise price is equal to current stock price. The first is *interest cost,* which arises because the ESO is exercisable at a future date for the current stock price. The second is *option cost,* which is the cost of providing an employee the option to purchase (or not purchase) the company's stock. The option cost should not be confused with the intrinsic value of the option itself–the value of an option is determined by several factors that include both interest cost and option cost. We explain both interest cost and option cost in Illustration 6.7.

ILLUSTRATION 6.7

A company with 100 outstanding shares issues its CEO 40 stock options that vest 10 years later with exercise price equal to current stock price. Assume the value of the company at the end of 10 years is expected to be either $38,000 or $2,000 with equal likelihood. Also assume that company value is not affected by any incentive effects from the options. What is the cost of these ESOs to the company (current shareholders) if the cost of capital is 10% per annum? To help answer this, let's first compute the company's current stock price without considering the ESOs as follows:

	Scenario 1	Scenario 2	Expected
Likelihood of occurrence	50%	50%	
Stock price without ESOs exercised (10 years hence):			
Value of company	$2,000	$38,000	
Number of shares	100	100	
Stock price without ESOs exercised*	$20.00	$380.00	$200.00†
Present value of stock price			$ 77.11

*Computed as (Market value of company/Number of shares).
†Computed as (50% × $20) plus (50% × $380).

The expected stock price of the company 10 years hence is $200. This is equal to a stock price of $77.11 today (computed as the present value of $200, 10 years hence, discounted at 10% per annum). This means the exercise price of the ESO is set at $77.11. Let's now consider what would happen if the ESOs were exercised under both scenarios:

	Scenario 1	Scenario 2	Expected
Stock price if ESOs exercised (10 years hence):			
Value of company without ESOs	$2,000	$38,000	
Proceeds of ESOs issue*	$3,084	$ 3,084	
Value of company with ESOs	$5,084	$41,084	
Number of shares (100 + 40)	140	140	
Stock price if ESOs exercised	$36.31	$293.46	$164.89
Present value of stock price			$ 63.57

*Computed as $77.11 × 40 stock options.

(continued)

Note that while there is an implicit cost arising from the ESOs, there are no direct cash flow effects. However, there are indirect cash flow effects because many companies repurchase stock to offset the dilution from ESOs. This means, in an indirect manner, ESOs have cash flow effects.

Accounting and Reporting for ESOs

There are two major accounting issues related to ESOs: (1) dilution of earnings per share (EPS) and (2) recognizing the cost of the employee stock option. This section discusses both issues.

Dilution of Earnings per Share. *SFAS 128* recognizes the potential dilution from ESOs when determining **diluted earnings per share**. The treasury stock method determines the extent of dilution based on both the exercise price and the current stock price. ESOs in-the-money are considered *dilutive securities* and affect diluted EPS. ESOs out-of-the-money are considered *antidilutive securities* and do not affect diluted EPS.

ILLUSTRATION 6.7 *(concluded)*

The value of the company 10 years hence increases by $3,084 (40 shares × $77.11) because of proceeds from the exercise of the ESOs. However, the share price 10 years hence declines to $164.89, compared with $200 per share without the ESOs exercised. This decline is due to the CEO purchasing shares that are on average worth $164.89 for only $77.11 each–a discount of $87.78 per share. The company's (current shareholders') loss is $3,511, computed as ($200 − $164.89) × 100 shares. This loss equals the CEO's gain of $3,511, computed as $87.78 × 40 shares. In present value terms, the company loss is $1,354, computed as ($77.11 − $63.57) × 100 shares. This is the *interest cost* and arises because the CEO can exercise the option 10 years hence at today's price.

Holders of ESOs enjoy the upside potential without the downside risk. This means that under Scenario 1, the CEO will not exercise ESOs at $77.11 when a share is worth $36.31. This behavior implies the following:

	Scenario 1	Scenario 2	Expected
Stock price after considering decision to exercise:			
Stock price without ESOs exercised	$20.00	$380.00	
Stock price if ESOs exercised	$36.31	$293.46	
Exercise price	$77.11	$ 77.11	
Decision—Exercise ESOs?	No	Yes	
Stock price after decision to exercise	$20.00	$293.46	$156.73
Present value of stock price			$ 60.43

Since the CEO has the option of selectively exercising the right to purchase shares, the CEO is able to enjoy the upside potential of Scenario 2 without the downside risk of Scenario 1. The loss to the company (current shareholders) from providing the CEO this option is $3.14 per share ($63.57 − $60.43) or $314 total. This is the *option cost* of the ESOs. Accordingly, total cost to the company along with reconciliation of value with and without the ESOs follows:

	Per Share	Total
Interest cost	$13.54	$1,354
+ Option cost	3.14	314
= Total cost of ESOs	16.68	1,668
+ Value with ESOs	60.43	6,043
= Value without ESOs	$77.11	$7,711

Illustration 6.8 provides an example. Appendix 6A gives a detailed explanation of EPS terminology and computations.

ILLUSTRATION 6.8

A Company's net income is $100,000, and its weighted-average shares outstanding are 10,000. During the year, the company issues 2,000 ESOs at an exercise price of $20. We compute both basic and diluted EPS below under two separate scenarios: (1) average stock price during the year is $40, and (2) average stock price during the year is $10.

	Scenario 1	**Scenario 2**
Number of ESOs outstanding	2000 shares	2000 shares
Exercise price	$20	$20
Proceeds of ESOs issuance	$40,000	$40,000
Average stock price	$40	$10
Treasury shares that can be purchased	1,000 shares	4,000 shares
Number of ESOs less treasury shares *(a)*	1,000 shares	(2,000) shares
Average number of shares outstanding *(b)*	10,000 shares	10,000 shares
Number of diluted shares *(c) = (a + b)*	11,000 shares	8,000 shares
Net income *(d)*	$100,000	$100,000
Compute *(d)/(c)*	$9.09	$12.50
Basic EPS ($100,000/10,000 shares)	**$10.00**	**$10.00**
Dilutive or antidilutive?	Dilutive	Antidilutive
Diluted EPS	**$9.09**	**$10.00**

Compensation Expense. Accounting and reporting for ESOs are prescribed under *SFAS 123*. This standard reflects a compromise–*SFAS 123 does not require* companies to recognize the cost of ESOs in accounting income; instead companies are *encouraged* to recognize this cost. As expected, most companies do not recognize the cost of ESOs. *SFAS 123* allows companies to account for ESOs using the intrinsic value method prescribed by the earlier standard, *APB 25*. This compromise was precipitated by opposition to an FASB proposal to require recognition of the cost of ESOs in income–especially from Silicon Valley companies. *SFAS 123* does, however, require companies to disclose in a note the *pro forma* net income (and EPS) that reflects *compensation expense* arising from ESOs.

Determining the ESOs compensation expense for a period is a two-step process: (1) determining the cost of ESOs granted and (2) amortizing this cost over the vesting period of the option to determine compensation expense for each period. We discuss each step:

- **Determining ESO cost.** The cost of ESOs is determined at the time of the grant. ESO cost is the product of the fair value of each individual option and the number of options expected to vest. The fair value of the ESO is determined by applying an option pricing model (usually Black-Scholes model) as of the grant date. Exhibit 6.11 identifies the factors affecting the fair value of an option. While we do not give the details of how the option value is determined, note that the expected life of the option is based on the expected exercise date, not the vesting date. The number of options expected to vest is determined by adjusting the number of options granted for the expected employee turnover over the expected life of the option. As already noted, ESO cost is determined only once, at the time of the grant. No adjustments to this cost are made, even if the fair value of the ESO changes.

Exhibit 6.11

Factors Affecting the Fair Value of an Option

Factor	Effect on fair value
Exercise price	−
Stock price on date of grant	+
Expected life of option	+
Risk-free rate of interest	+
Expected volatility of stock	+
Expected dividends of stock	−

- **Amortizing ESO cost.** While companies hope ESOs motivate employees to work in the interest of shareholders, they also specify minimum vesting periods to further align employee and company incentives over the long run. This ESO benefit is expected to persist at least until the employee is free to exercise the option. Accordingly, the fair value of granted ESOs is amortized on a straight-line basis over the vesting period. Compensation expense for a period is based on the cumulative amortization of all past and current ESOs that are yet to vest. However, since *SFAS 123* took effect in 1995, all option grants prior to January 1, 1995, are ignored in computing compensation expense.

Disclosures of Employee Stock Options

Exhibit 6.12 provides excerpts from the notes of Pfizer, Inc. Beyond the disclosure of pro forma income and EPS, the note gives details on options granted, outstanding, and exercisable, along with assumptions used for computing the fair value of options granted.

At December 31, 2001, Pfizer had 413.9 million outstanding options (both vested and nonvested) and 276.3 million options vested but not yet exercised. The weighted-average exercise price on outstanding options is $28.05 (Pfizer's stock price was $39.85 on December 31, 2001). Between January 1, 2000, and December 31, 2001, Pfizer granted over 78 million options to its employees. In 2001, the weighted-average fair value per option granted was $15.12, which is determined using the following assumptions: dividend yield of 1.41%, risk-free interest rate of 5%, expected life of 5.50 years, and stock price volatility of 31.45%.

Pfizer discloses its pro forma income (both total income and EPS) after considering the ESO compensation expense and compares it to reported net income (EPS). In 2001, Pfizer's pro forma income (basic EPS) is $7,228 million ($1.16) compared to reported net income (basic EPS) of $7,788 million ($1.25)–the compensation expense attributed to ESOs is $560 million (9 cents per share).

Analyzing Employee Stock Options

This section explains the analysis of both the income statement and balance sheet effects of ESOs.

Income Effects. The cost of ESOs is real. Accounting income, however, does not recognize this cost (recall *SFAS 123* recommends, but does not require, recognition of amortized option cost in accounting income). An analyst must consider this cost when evaluating a company's income (both permanent income and economic income). This task appears straightforward in that the information is readily available in pro forma income disclosures. Specifically, recognizing the effect of ESOs reduces Pfizer's net

Exhibit 6.12 Disclosure of Excerpts for Employee Stock Options—Pfizer

18 Stock Option and Performance Unit Awards

We have stock and incentive plans related to employees which allow for stock options, performance unit awards and stock awards.

We may grant stock options to employees, including officers, under the plans. Options are exercisable after five years or less, subject to continuous employment and certain other conditions, and expire 10 years after the grant date. Once exercisable, the employee can purchase shares of our common stock at the market price on the date we granted the option. The 1996 Stock Plan, a former Warner-Lambert plan, provided that, in the event of a change in control of Warner-Lambert, stock options already granted became exercisable immediately.

Shares available for award (in thousands) at:

- December 31, 1999 198,423
- December 31, 2000 137,248
- December 31, 2001 249,572

The table below summarizes information concerning options outstanding under the plans at December 31, 2001:

(THOUSANDS OF SHARES)	OPTIONS OUTSTANDING			OPTIONS EXERCISABLE	
Range of Exercise Prices	Number Outstanding at 12/31/01	Weighted Average Remaining Contractual Term (years)	Weighted Average Exercise Price	Number Exercisable at 12/31/01	Weighted Average Exercise Price
$ 0–$ 5	7,683	2.1	$ 4.03	7,683	$ 4.03
5– 10	57,754	2.9	6.66	57,747	6.66
10– 15	48,747	4.9	11.59	48,505	11.59
15– 20	42,798	5.8	17.91	41,446	17.90
20– 30	20,298	7.1	24.92	20.099	24.83
30– 40	100,077	7.5	33.65	75,804	33.76
over 40	136,566	8.3	43.68	26,066	42.07

The following table summarizes the activity for the plans:

	UNDER OPTION	
(thousands of shares)	Shares	Weighted Average Exercise Price Per Share
Balance January 1, 1999	454,325	11.97
Granted	94,168	37.32
Exercised	(75,872)	7.81
Cancelled	(5,641)	25.63
Balance December 31, 1999	466,980	17.59
Granted	65,863	32.49
Exercised	(130,756)	8.79
Cancelled	(6,473)	34.23
Balance December 31, 2000	395,614	22.71
Granted	79,155	45.34
Exercised	(54,082)	14.41
Cancelled	(6,764)	39.23
Balance December 31, 2001	413,923	28.05

Options granted in 1999 include options for 450 shares granted to every eligible pre-merger Pfizer employee worldwide in celebration of our 150th Anniversary.

The tax benefits related to certain stock option transactions were $395 million in 2001, $1,306 million in 2000 and $470 million in 1999.

The weighted-average fair value per stock option granted was $15.12 for 2001, $11.12 for 2000 and $11.79 for 1999. We estimated the fair values using the Black-Scholes option pricing model, modified for dividends and using the following assumptions:

	2001	2000	1999
Expected dividend yield	**1.41%**	1.54%	1.26%
Risk-free interest rate	**5.00%**	6.65%	5.06%
Expected stock price volatility	**31.45%**	30.68%	26.22%
Expected term until exercise (years)	**5.50**	5.35	5.75

The following table summarizes our results as if we had recorded compensation expense for 2001, 2000 and 1999 option grants:

(millions of dollars, except per share data)	**2001**	2000	1999
Net Income:			
As reported	**$7,788**	$3,726	$4,952
Pro forma	**7,228**	2,919	4,433
Basic earnings per share:			
As expected	**$ 1.25**	$ .60	$ .81
Pro forma	**1.16**	.47	.72
Diluted earnings per share:			
As reported	**$ 1.22**	$ .59	$ .78
Pro forma	**1.14**	.46	.70

In 2001, our shareholders approved a new Performance-Contingent Share Award Plan (the Plan) allowing a maximum of 12.5 million shares to be awarded. The Plan replaces the Performance-Contingent Share Award Program (the Program) that was established and became effective in 1993 to provide executives and other key employees the right to earn common stock awards. Similar to the previous Program, determination of award payouts under the Plan is made after the performance period ends, based upon specific performance criteria. Under the previous Program, up to 120 million shares could be awarded. The actual number of shares awarded and pending under the previous Program since its approval is approximately 20 million shares. At December 31, 2001, participants had the right to earn up to 11.0 million additional shares under the old Program. All awards beginning in 2002 and later will be made under the new Plan and all previous awards that may have extended performance periods will be made under the previous Program. Under the previous Program, we awarded approximately 1.7 million shares in 2001, approximately 2.3 million shares in 2000, and approximately 2.3 million shares in 1999. We did not award any shares under the new Plan as of December 31, 2001. Compensation expense related to the previous Program was $94 million in 2001, $170 million in 2000 and $64 million in 1999.

income by about 7%. Four observations are of note. First, although the percentage effect may not be great, the dollar amount is substantial (for example, $560 million in 2001). Second, as Pfizer notes, the pro forma income does not reflect the entire effect of ESOs because the cost of options issued before 1995 is ignored. Third, it is important to understand that the ESO effect is insidious in the sense that it is a permanent effect that is expected to persist indefinitely. A permanent reduction of around 10% in income is substantial as it implies a corresponding 10% reduction in the market value of the company! Fourth, many companies and industries are affected in a more significant manner than Pfizer.

Balance Sheet Effects. Our analysis has focused on the income statement, but what about the impact of ESOs on the balance sheet? Accounting standards are silent about the impact of ESOs on the balance sheet. Yet, it is important for an analyst to evaluate the effect of ESOs on the net economic position of a company. To illustrate, let's consider Pfizer. At the end of 2001, Pfizer had 413.9 million outstanding ESOs at an average exercise price of $28.05 per share (see Exhibit 6.12). Pfizer's stock price at the end of 2001 is $39.85. Do these outstanding options affect the net economic position of Pfizer? It depends on their potential cost and benefits. The potential cost of the outstanding options to current shareholders is equal to the fair value of outstanding ESOs at the end of 1998. Each option, *at a minimum,* is worth $11.80 (stock price of $39.85 less $28.05 average exercise price). This value reflects the extent to which ESOs on average are in-the-money and does not include either the interest or option cost discussed in Illustration 6.8. This means the potential cost to current shareholders is conservatively estimated at $4.884 billion. This amount is often referred to as the *option overhang.* What about the potential benefit? The potential benefit is the present value of future income that arises from the incentive effects of the ESOs. It is impossible to determine these benefits. If these incentive effects are separately considered in forecasts of future operating income (either explicitly or implicitly, for example, through a sales forecast) then the potential benefits of ESOs can be ignored in the analysis as they are reflected in the forecasts.

OPTION VALUE
Many analysts use the Black-Scholes model to value options. Another method is the binomial tree model that is more sensitive to the underlying variables and arguably more accurate.

The other issue that needs consideration is whether or not the net potential cost to current shareholders constitutes a liability for the company. The answer is unclear. While the outstanding options (in the absence of incentive effects) do constitute a net potential cost to current shareholders, they neither impose a fixed cash flow commitment on the company, nor do they involve any resource allocation away from shareholders. Specifically, ESOs do not affect either total liabilities or shareholder's equity: any wealth transfer occurs only between current shareholders and prospective shareholders (employees). The analysis implication is that while the potential reduction in the value of current equity shares must be considered (e.g., in equity analysis), it can be ignored for evaluating solvency and liquidity (e.g., in credit analysis).

INTEREST COSTS

Interest is compensation for use of money. It is the *excess* cash paid or collected beyond the money (principal) borrowed or loaned. Interest is determined by several factors, and one of the most important is credit (nonpayment) risk of the borrower. *Interest expense* is determined by the interest rate, principal, and time.

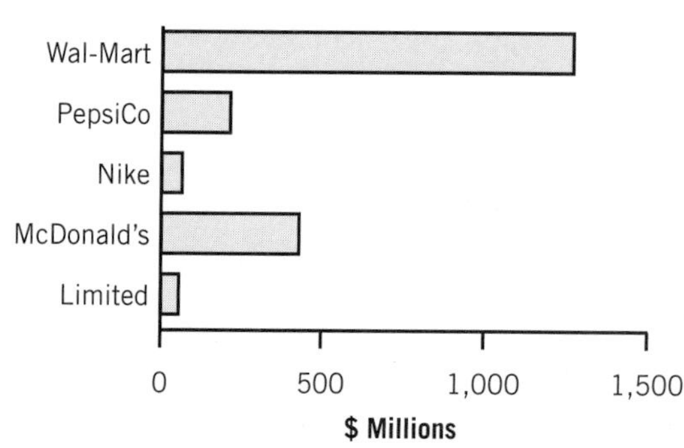

Interest Computation

Interest expense for a company is the nominal rate paid on debt financing including, in the case of bonds, the amortization of any discount or premium. A complication arises when companies issue convertible debt or debt with warrants. These situations yield a nominal rate below the cost of similar debt not enjoying these added features. In the case of convertible debt, accounting practice considers the debt and equity features inseparable. Therefore, no portion of the proceeds from issuance of convertible debt is accounted for as attributable to the conversion feature. In the case of debt issued with attached stock warrants, the proceeds attributable to the value of the warrants are accounted for as paid-in capital. The corresponding charge is to a debt discount account that is amortized over the life of the debt issue, increasing the effective interest cost.

Interest Capitalization

Capitalization of interest is required as part of the cost of assets constructed or otherwise produced for a company's *own use* (including assets constructed or produced for a company by others where deposits or progress payments are made). The objectives of interest capitalization are to (1) measure more accurately the acquisition cost of an asset and (2) amortize acquisition cost against revenues generated by an asset. An example follows:

> In connection with various construction projects, interest of approximately $19,118,000, $30,806,000 and $17,393,000 was capitalized as property, plant and equipment
>
> –New York Times Company

Analyzing Interest

Our analysis must realize that current accounting for interest on convertible debt is controversial. Many contend that ignoring the value of a conversion privilege and using the coupon rate as the measure of interest ignores the real interest cost. Somewhat contrary to this position, computation of diluted earnings per share uses the number of shares issuable *in the event of conversion of convertible debt.* This in effect creates an additional charge to the coupon rate through diluting earnings per share.

Accounting for interest capitalization is also disputable. Some analysts take the position that interest represents a period cost and is not capitalizable. Whatever one's views, our analysis must realize that accounting for interest capitalization is vague, leading to variations in practice. We must remember that capitalized interest is included in assets' costs and enters expense via depreciation and amortization. To assess the impact of interest capitalization on net income, our analysis must know the amount of capitalized interest currently charged to income via depreciation and amortization. We also need this amount to accurately compute the fixed-charge coverage ratio (see Chapter 11). Unfortunately, practice does not require disclosure of these amounts, so our analysis is often handicapped. One potential source of this information is Form 10-K disclosures.

INCOME TAXES

Income tax expense is a substantial cost of business. Understanding accounting for income taxes is important to successful analysis of financial statements. The discussion here focuses on the accounting and analysis of periodic income tax expense, and not on tax law.

Accounting for Income Tax

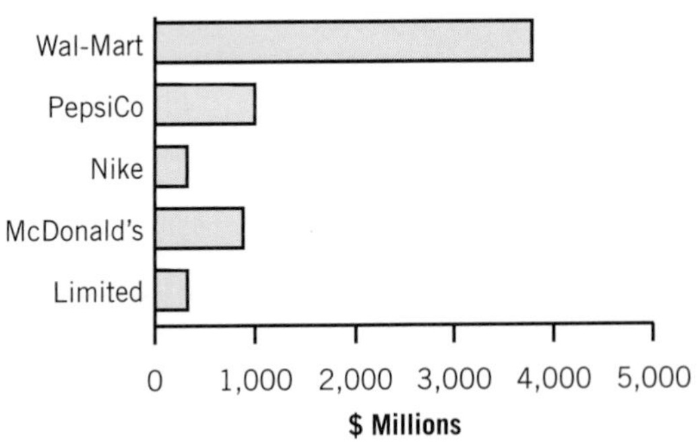

Source: Annual reports.

The accounting and reporting standards for income taxes require both an asset and a liability approach. Specifically, deferred taxes are determined separately for each tax-paying component (an individual entity or group of entities consolidated for tax purposes) in each tax jurisdiction. Determination includes the following procedures:

- Identifying the types and amounts of temporary differences (discussed below) and the nature and amount of each type of operating loss and tax credit carryforward including the remaining length of the carryforward period.
- Measuring total deferred tax liability for taxable temporary differences using the applicable tax rate.
- Computing the total deferred tax asset for deductible temporary differences and the operating loss carryforwards using the applicable tax rate.
- Measuring deferred tax assets for each type of tax credit carryforward.
- Reducing deferred tax assets by a valuation allowance if, based on the weight of available evidence, it is more likely than not (a more than 50% probability) some portion or all of deferred tax assets will not be realized.

The valuation allowance must be sufficient to reduce deferred tax assets to the amount likely to be realized. Deferred tax assets and deferred tax liabilities are adjusted for effects of changes in tax rates and laws. These effects are reflected in income from continuing operations for that period. One notable provision of current practice is allowing a parent company to not recognize a liability for deferred taxes due to a subsidiary's unremitted earnings. Taxes paid on taxable income are governed by regulations. Net income computed using accepted accounting principles is often different from taxable income computed using tax regulations.

Temporary Income Tax Differences

Companies maintain two sets of books: one for computation of the annual report and another for taxes. Income and expense in the income statement are determined in accordance with GAAP on the accrual basis. Taxable income reported to state and federal taxing authorities is generally computed on a cash basis. As a result there will be temporary differences between the two that ultimately must reverse.[1] For example, consider a company depreciating a $1,000 asset over 10 years (with zero salvage value) on a straight-line basis. To conserve cash, the company elects for tax purposes to use double-declining-balance depreciation. In Year 1, accounting depreciation is $100 while tax depreciation is $200. Years later, accounting depreciation will eventually exceed tax depreciation because under either method total depreciation equals $1,000. Consequently, this tax difference reverses and is temporary. We summarize the types of book/tax differences and their financial statement effects as follows:

[1] There may also be *permanent* differences, like interest received on tax-exempt bonds that is reflected in reported income but will never be taxable and fines that will never be deductible for tax purposes. Permanent differences do not give rise to deferred taxes and are, therefore, ignored in this discussion.

	REPORTED ON		INITIAL INCOME TAX JOURNAL ENTRIES	
Category of Transaction	Income Statement	Tax Return	Income Tax Expense	Balance Sheet Deferred Tax Accounts*
Revenue or gain	Earlier	Later	Debit	Credit
Expenses or loss	Later	Earlier	Debit	Credit
Revenue or gain	Later	Earlier	Credit	Debit
Expenses or loss	Earlier	Later	Credit	Debit

*These can reverse later.

While all four categories exist in practice, the desirable temporary differences from a company's perspective are those yielding credits to the deferred tax account–thus postponing taxes paid. The third and fourth categories are least desirable in this regard (they yield "early" tax payments).

A balance sheet separately reports deferred tax liabilities and deferred tax assets into current and noncurrent amounts. Deferred tax liabilities and deferred tax assets are classified as current or noncurrent depending on the classification of the related asset or liability for financial reporting. A deferred tax liability or deferred tax asset not related to an asset or liability for financial reporting, including deferred tax assets related to carryforwards, is classified according to the expected reversal period of the temporary difference. When a valuation allowance measuring the likelihood of realizing deferred tax assets is used, it is allocated between current and noncurrent deferred tax assets on a pro rata basis.

A basic problem with temporary differences is the disparity between income before tax reported in the income statement and the taxable income on the tax return. If actual tax paid is considered a period expense, it will not fit with pretax income on the income statement. This violates the basic accounting principle of matching income and related expenses. **Interperiod tax allocation** is designed to ensure income reported on financial statements is charged with the tax applicable to it regardless of how this income is reported for tax purposes. This achieves the basic objective of recognizing tax consequences of an event in the same period it is recognized in financial statements.

Case 6.1. Consider a case illustrating the principles of *interperiod tax allocation.* A retailer sells mountain bikes on installment. On January 1, Year 1, it sells a bike for \$720 payable at the rate of \$20 a month for 36 months. Ignoring finance charges, the gross profit to the retailer is 20 percent, and the tax rate is 50 percent. For financial reporting, the retailer recognizes in Year 1 the total gross profit of \$144 (20 percent of \$720). For tax purposes it recognizes profit based on actual cash collections as follows:

	Cash Collection	Taxable Gross Profit (20%)	Actual Tax Payable (50%)
Year 1	\$240	\$48	\$24
Year 2	240	48	24
Year 3	240	48	24
Total	\$720	\$144	\$72

With no interperiod tax allocation the retailer reports the following financial results:

	Pretax Profit	Tax Payable	Net Profit (Loss)
Year 1	$144	$24	$120
Year 2	—	24	(24)
Year 3	—	24	(24)
Total	$144	$72	$72

The potential for misinterpretation from these reports is apparent. The financial reporting profit of Year 1 does not bear its proper share of tax. This yields a profit "overstatement" of $48. This misrepresentation carries over to Years 2 and 3, where profits are understated by $24 each since they bear a tax payment unrelated to any revenues from those years. These reports can mislead one to believe that in Year 1 this retailer conducted business activities that yielded a profit of $120. In reality, this retailer sells a mountain bike for cash ($720), realizes a gross profit of $144, pays tax of $72, and reports an after-tax profit of $72. Interperiod tax allocation is designed to remedy these distortions by means of a deferred tax account. This account is used to better match tax expense reported with revenue reported as follows:

	Pretax Profit	TAX EXPENSE Payable	Deferred	Total	After-Tax Profit	Deferred Tax Account
Year 1	$144	$24	$48	$72	$72	$48
Year 2	—	24	(24)	—	—	24
Year 3	—	24	(24)	—	—	—

This deferred tax account ($48 in Year 1) is a liability in this case and adjusts for temporary differences. The provision for deferred taxes does not require cash, and the tax credit arising from the reversal of deferred taxes is not a source of cash.

This installment sales case is a simplification of a complex process. While the tax deferral on the mountain bike is, as shown in the case, entirely reversed at the end of Year 3, the aggregate tax deferral account usually does not entirely reverse. For example, if another mountain bike is sold in Year 2, the aggregate deferred tax account remains the same. Moreover, if the retailer sells an increasing number of mountain bikes, the deferred tax account actually grows. In the case of differences in financial reporting and tax attributed to depreciation, and where assets are long lived, the deferred tax account typically increases over time or at least is stable.

Tax Loss Carrybacks and Carryforwards

A company incurring an operating loss can generally carry it back for a refund on taxes paid. If a loss cannot be entirely covered within the preceding 2 years, it can be carried forward for 20 years to apply against future taxes payable. The status of a tax loss carryback is usually simple to determine–it is either available or not. An asset is recognized for the amount of taxes paid in prior years that is refundable by carryback of an operating loss or unused tax credit. The value of a tax loss carryforward depends on a company's ability to earn taxable income in the future, which is not a certainty. An operating loss or tax credit carryforward is recognized as a reduction of a deferred tax liability for temporary differences expected to yield taxable amounts in the carryforward period. The tax benefit of an operating loss or tax credit carryforward that cannot be recognized as a reduction of a deferred tax liability is instead reported as a deferred tax asset. This asset then is reduced by a valuation allowance if, based on available evidence, it is more likely than not that all or part of the deferred tax asset will not be realized. In the year of a loss when both a net operating loss (NOL) carryback *and* carryforward are available, a company makes the following entry:

Income Tax Refund Receivable	xxx	
Future Benefit from NOL Carryforward	xxx	
Income Tax Benefit from NOL Carryback		xxx
Income Tax Benefit from NOL Carryforward		xxx

Tax reductions resulting from tax loss carryforwards show up in the reconciliation of tax expense to the amount based on applying domestic federal statutory rates to pretax income from continuing operations. Our analysis of this reconciliation often yields insights into a company's future effective tax rates.

Income Tax Disclosures

Exhibit 6.13 presents the income tax footnote from the Wal-Mart 2001 annual report. Wal-Mart reports tax expense of $3,897 million. Of that amount, $3,712 million represents cash payments (the current portion) and $185 million is the portion of the expense arising from *changes* in deferred taxes. Wal-Mart also provides a summary of the components of its deferred tax liabilities and assets. Its $1,913 million of deferred tax liabilities arises primarily from PP&E and relates to the use of accelerated depreciation in its tax returns and straight-line depreciation for book purposes. Its $1,613 million of deferred tax assets arise as a result of the accrual of expenses in its income statement that have not yet been paid and are, therefore, not deductible for tax purposes. Also, Wal-Mart has not set up a valuation allowance for its deferred tax assets as it expects all of these benefits to be realized. The net deferred tax liability of $300 million is reported on its balance sheet. Finally, Wal-Mart provides a reconciliation of the statutory corporate income tax rate of 35% with the 36.25% it actually paid. Most of this difference is due to state taxes paid.

Analyzing Income Taxes

Our analysis must understand the relation between pretax income and income tax expense. We should remember that procedures applied to loss carryforwards differ from those applied to carrybacks. Tax loss carrybacks result in a tax refund in the loss year and are recognized as an asset. A loss carryforward results in a *deferred* asset. This deferred tax asset is reduced by a valuation allowance to the extent "it is more likely than not" that all or part of it will not be realized by a reduction of taxes payable (on taxable income) during the carryforward period.

In spite of disagreements on tax allocation, the accounting yields a reasonable tax accrual and, hence, reasonable income numbers. Practice distinguishes tax strategy from financial reporting of income. It tempers management motivation to adjust results through accounting techniques. Interperiod tax allocation is also sound from an analytical perspective. That is, assets whose future tax deductibility is reduced are not worth as much as those having greater tax deductibility. For example, consider two companies

Wal-Mart Income Tax Footnote

Exhibit 6.13

The income tax provision consists of the following (in millions):

Fiscal years ended January 31,	**2002**	2001	2000
Current			
Federal	**$3,021**	$2,641	$2,920
State and local	**310**	297	299
International	**381**	412	257
Total current tax provision	**3,712**	3,350	3,476
Deferred			
Federal	**230**	457	(71)
State and local	**17**	34	(3)
International	**(62)**	(149)	(183)
Total deferred tax provision (benefit)	**185**	342	(257)
Total provision for income taxes	**$3,897**	$3,692	$3,219 (a)

(a) Total provision for income tax includes a provision on income before the cumulative effect of accounting change of $3,338 million and a tax benefit of $119 million resulting from the cumulative effect of the accounting change.

Earnings before income taxes are as follows (in millions):

Fiscal years ended January 31,	**2002**	2001	2000
Domestic	**$ 9,523**	$ 9,203	$8,414
International	**1,228**	913	669
Total earnings before income taxes	**$10,751**	$10,116	$9,083

Items that give rise to significant portions of the deferred tax accounts at January 31 are as follows (in millions):

	2002	2001	2000
Deferred tax liabilities			
Property, plant, and equipment	**$ 906**	$ 751	$ 748
Inventory	**368**	407	393
International, principally asset basis difference	**448**	398	348
Acquired asset basis difference	**53**	65	314
Other	**138**	87	66
Total deferred tax liabilities	**1,913**	1,708	1,869
Deferred tax assets			
Amounts accrued for financial reporting purposes not yet deductible for tax purposes	**832**	865	1,098
Capital leases	**26**	74	193
International, asset basis and loss carryforwards	**459**	352	402
Deferred revenue	**137**	142	181
Other	**159**	153	215
Total deferred tax assets	**1,613**	1,586	2,089
Net deferred tax liabilities (assets)	**$ 300**	$ 122	$ (220)

A reconciliation of the significant differences between the effective income tax rate and the federal statutory rate on pretax income follows:

Fiscal years ended January 31,	**2002**	2001	2000
Statutory tax rate	**35.00%**	35.00%	35.00%
State income taxes, net of federal income tax benefit	**1.98%**	2.13%	2.18%
International	**(1.01%)**	(0.84%)	(0.74%)
Other	**0.28%**	0.21%	0.31%
	36.25%	36.50%	36.75%

Federal and state income taxes have not been provided on accumulated but undistributed earnings of certain foreign subsidiaries aggregating approximately $1 billion at January 31, 2002, as such earnings have been reinvested in the business. The determination of the amount of the unrecognized deferred tax liability related to the undistributed earnings is not practicable.

depreciating an identical asset costing $100,000 under different tax methods of depreciation resulting in first-year depreciation amounts of $10,000 and $20,000, respectively. At the end of Year 1, one company has an asset it can depreciate for tax purposes to the amount of $90,000. The other company can depreciate its asset only to the amount of $80,000. These two assets do not possess equal value. The tax deferral adjustment recognizes this economic reality.

A weakness with interperiod tax allocation is its lack of recognition of the present value of a future obligation or loss of benefits. These values should be discounted rather than reported at their entire amounts as currently done in companies' deferred tax accounts. The FASB ignored the time value of money because of its alleged complexity, both in implementation and interpretation. Yet present value computations appear in many other areas including accounting for leases and pensions. Failure to discount these values hinders our analysis. This can contribute to the often steady increase of deferred tax liabilities that, while reducing income, do not represent a legal obligation. The FASB also bowed to pressure from various constituencies when it retained earlier provisions allowing parent companies to avoid providing deferred taxes on unremitted earnings of subsidiaries.

Analysis of tax expense also must guard against a common error in this area. It is sometimes incorrectly assumed that deferred tax accounting acts as an entire offset to differences between tax and financial accounting methods. Rather, if we assume, for example, that accelerated depreciation for tax purposes is more realistic than straight-line or financial reporting, the effect of deferred taxes is to remove only about one-third of the overstatement in income resulting from straight-line depreciation for financial reporting.

Income tax disclosures provide an explanation of why the effective tax expense rate differs from the current statutory rate. This is an important tool in analysis of whether present tax benefits or extra costs that a company enjoys or incurs are expected to continue. More reliable information can improve our predictions of cash flows and earnings. Benefits like the research and development credit, foreign tax shelters, depletion allowances, and capital gains treatment depend on legislative sanction and are subject to change, repeal, or expiration. Other differences, such as those arising from foreign tax differentials and tax loss carryforwards, depend on economic and legal conditions that also demand our attention. Some tax benefits may or may not remain in tax laws. The long-standing and substantial benefit of the investment tax credit was repealed in 1986–but is likely to return again. Other benefits, such as capital expenditures, depend on the company's ability to take advantage of them to earn investment tax credits when available.

A low effective tax rate leads us to investigate the likelihood of recurrence of tax benefits, as a higher than normal tax rate similarly demands our scrutiny. For example, a higher than normal effective tax rate can be due to subsidiary losses that a company might not be able to offset on its tax return. A source of useful information is the analysis of the effective tax rate reconciliation. If, for example, our analysis indicates tax-free interest reduced taxes by $144,000, we can determine the amount of tax-free income by dividing $144,000 by 0.35 (assumed statutory tax rate)–$411,429. Our analysis of *components* of deferred income tax expense can also yield insights. Through evaluation of components we can learn about capitalization of costs, early recognition of revenues, and other discretionary accrual adjustments. We can also acquire information about expected future reductions in deferred income taxes. These reductions can foretell higher tax (cash) outlays and are valuable predictors of liquidity. For example, whenever a deferred tax credit "reverses," accounting tax expense is reduced by the amount of the reversal. However, the actual tax payment is higher than the net expense reported in the income statement. The implication is a cash decrease.

APPENDIX 6A EARNINGS PER SHARE: COMPUTATION AND ANALYSIS

Earnings per share (EPS) data are widely used in evaluating the operating performance and profitability of a company. This appendix describes the principles governing earnings per share computation and interpretation. A key feature in earnings per share computation is recognition of the potential impact of dilution. **Dilution** is the reduction in earnings per share (or increase in net loss per share) resulting from dilutive securities being converted into common stock, the exercise of options and warrants, or the issuance of additional shares in compliance with contracts. Since these adverse effects on earnings per share can be substantial, the earnings per share computation serves to call attention to the potentially dilutive effects of a firm's capital structure.

The computation and reporting requirements (see *SFAS 128*) for earnings per share are consistent with international accounting standards. *SFAS 128* requires dual presentation of *basic EPS* and *diluted EPS* on income statements of companies with complex capital structures and requires a reconciliation of the numerator and denominator of basic EPS to diluted EPS. To understand these computations and their interpretation, this appendix (1) explains simple and complex capital structures, (2) describes the various earnings per share measures, and (3) provides several case examples.

SIMPLE CAPITAL STRUCTURE

A **simple capital structure** consists only of common stock and nonconvertible senior securities and does not include potentially dilutive securities. For companies with simple capital structures, a single presentation of earnings per share is required and is computed as follows:

$$\text{Basic earnings per share} = \frac{\text{Net income} - \text{Preferred dividends}}{\text{Weighted-average number of common shares outstanding}}$$

In the numerator of this computation, dividends of cumulative senior equity securities, whether earned or not, are deducted from net income or added to net loss. The precise computation of weighted-average number of common shares is the sum of shares outstanding each day, divided by the number of days in the period.

COMPLEX CAPITAL STRUCTURE

A company is viewed as having a **complex capital structure** if it has outstanding potentially dilutive securities such as convertible securities, options, warrants, and other similar stock issue agreements. More than 25% of publicly traded companies have potentially dilutive securities. The relation between basic and diluted earnings per share for these companies is depicted as:

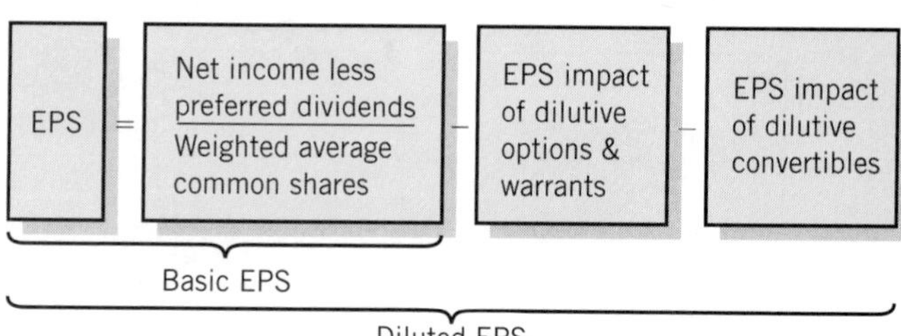

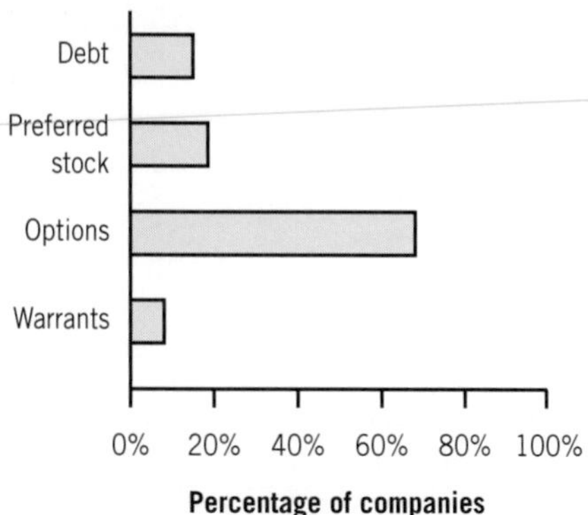

Source: Accounting Trends & Techniques.

This dual presentation warns users of the potential for dilution in earnings per share. Both of these earnings per share figures are reported with equal prominence on income statements of companies with complex capital structures. These companies need not report diluted earnings per share when its potential common shares are antidilutive. **Antidilutive securities** are those that increase earnings per share when exercised or converted.

Basic Earnings per Share

The basic earnings per share computation for companies with complex capital structures is identical to that for companies with simple capital structures.

Diluted Earnings per Share

Companies with complex capital structures must report both basic and diluted EPS figures. Exhibit 6A.1 portrays the computation of earnings per share for complex capital structures. Diluted EPS reflects *all* potential common shares that decrease earnings per share. We consider only the more familiar types of potentially dilutive securities–stock options and warrants, and convertible preferred stocks and bonds.

Diluted EPS is computed on an *as if* basis, that is, we assume that all convertible securities are converted and options exercised at the earliest possible opportunity (e.g., the beginning of the year if the securities are outstanding on that date). The numerator

Exhibit 6A.1 ***EPS Computations***

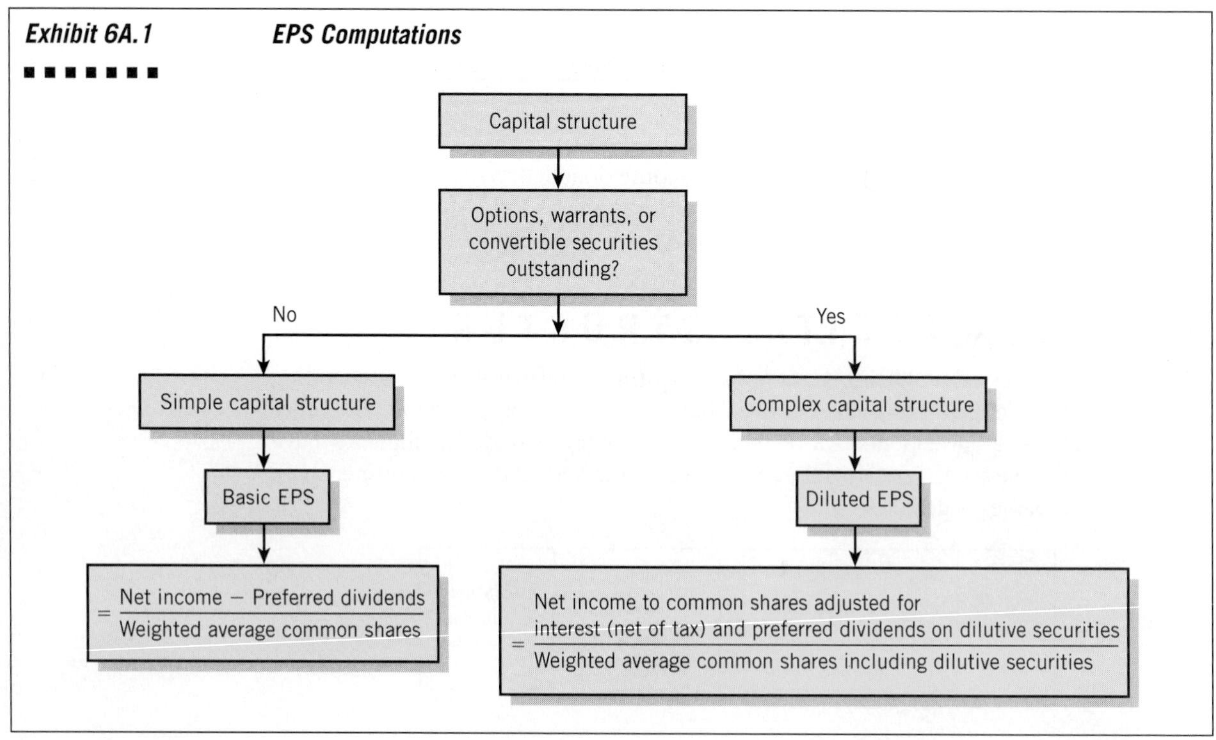

for diluted EPS adjusts net income for the following effects of the exercise of convertible securities or options:

1. If preferred shares have been converted into common, any preferred dividends must be removed as we are assuming that the preferred shares are no longer outstanding.
2. If bonds are converted, any interest expense must be backed out of net income. This is accomplished by adding back the after-tax amount of the interest accrued.

The denominator adds the additional shares issued as a result of conversion or exercise of options. For convertible bonds, the amount of shares to be issued upon conversion is added directly. For options, we assume that the proceeds from the exercise of the option are used to repurchase shares in the open market at the average stock price. Only the net shares issued are added to the denominator.

To illustrate the computation of EPS, consider a company with the following securities outstanding:

- *Common stock:* 1,000,000 shares outstanding for the entire year.
- *Preferred stock:* 500,000 shares outstanding for the entire year.
- *Convertible bonds:* \$5,000,000 6% bonds, sold at par, convertible into 200,000 shares of common stock.
- *Employee stock options:* options to purchase 100,000 shares at \$30 have been outstanding for the entire year. The average market price of the company's common stock during the year is \$40.
- *Net income:* \$3,000,000
- *Preferred dividends: \$50,000*
- *Marginal tax rate:* 35%

$$\text{Basic EPS} = \frac{\$3{,}000{,}000 - \$50{,}000}{1{,}000{,}000} = \$2.95$$

$$\text{Diluted EPS} = \frac{\$3{,}000{,}000 - \$50{,}000 + [(\$5{,}000{,}000 \times 6\%)(1 - .35)]}{1{,}000{,}000 + 200{,}000 + 25{,}000} = \$2.57$$

Basic EPS is computed as net income less preferred shares divided by the weighted-average (by fraction of the year outstanding) number of shares outstanding during the year.

Diluted EPS assumes conversion of all convertible securities and exercise of all dilutive options at their earliest possible opportunity, in this case the beginning of the year. The third term in the numerator is the add-back of after-tax interest that would not have been paid had the bonds converted into common stock. The tax adjustment is necessary since pretax income would have increased by the amount of forgone interest expense. The additional shares assumed to be issued upon conversion of the bonds are added into the denominator. The third term in the denominator relates to the exercise of the options. This is computed as follows:

Shares purchased upon exercise of option	100,000
Exercise price	× \$30
Proceeds received upon exercise	\$3,000,000
Average market price of common stock	÷ \$40
Shares repurchased with option proceeds	75,000

Net increase in shares due to exercise of options = 100,000 − 75,000 = 25,000

ANALYSIS IMPLICATIONS OF EARNINGS PER SHARE

Earnings per share requirements in accounting are often criticized because they extend to areas outside the usual realm of accountancy. Accounting for earnings per share relies on pro forma presentations influenced in large measure by market fluctuations. It also involves itself with areas of financial statement analysis. Whatever the merits of these criticisms, our analysis must welcome this initiative by the accounting profession. Factors considered in computation of earnings per share are varied and require considerable proprietary data, so it is appropriate to place this responsibility on management and its auditors. Our analysis must, however, bring a thorough understanding of the bases on which earnings per share are computed so that we can draw reliable inferences. The earnings per share disclosures require a reconciliation of the numerators and denominators of basic and diluted earnings per share computations. This entails disclosure of the individual income and common share effects of all securities that affect earnings per share. Such disclosure provides us additional insights into companies' complex capital structures.

Despite these improvements in earnings per share computations and disclosures, serious barriers to effective analysis remain:

- Computation of basic earnings per share ignores the potential effects of dilution from options and warrants. This can "boost" the earnings per share of certain companies by 10% to 20% or more, while potentially obscuring the risk from issuances of new shares. Our analysis must study diluted earnings per share to avoid this pitfall.
- There are inconsistencies in treating certain securities as the equivalent of common stock for computing earnings per share while not considering them as part of shareholders' equity. Consequently, it is difficult in analysis to effectively link reported earnings per share with the debt-leverage position pertaining to those earnings.
- The dilutive effects of options and warrants depend on the company's common stock price. This can yield a "circular effect," in that reporting of earnings per share can influence stock prices that, in turn, influence earnings per share. Hence, reported earnings per share can be affected by stock price and not solely reflect the economic fundamentals of the company. This also suggests that our projection of reported earnings per share consider not only future earnings but also future stock prices.

GUIDANCE ANSWERS TO ANALYSIS VIEWPOINTS

Supplier

Your credit assessment of Chicago Construction is likely positive. While the company's extraordinary loss is real, it is not recurring. This implies the 23% increase in net income is more representative of the ongoing business activities of Chicago Construction than the 12% decrease after the extraordinary loss. You must also assess the extent to which the fire loss is extraordinary. That is, this loss might be more than what extraordinary implies, or it might signal a new risk exposure for Chicago Construction. Nevertheless, on the information provided, the credit terms should be at least as good and perhaps better in the coming year.

Banker

Playground Equipment's recognition of revenue during production is probably too liberal. Recognizing revenue during production is acceptable only when total revenues and expenses are estimated with reasonable certainty *and* when realization (payment) is reasonably assured. For most companies, these conditions are not met. Unless we are highly confident that Playground Equipment's earnings process meets these stringent conditions, we should require restatement (or an alternative statement) using point of sale as the basis for revenue recognition. If Playground Equipment has considerable collection risks or costs, we might require restatement using revenue recognition when cash is received. The more conservative the statements used in our analysis, the less risky should be our loan agreement with Playground Equipment. The primary risk we are exposed to in acting on its loan is risk of nonpayment or default. Additional risks include interest rate changes, renegotiation potential, delayed payments, industry changes, and personal employment/promotion.

Analyst

All corporations wish to minimize expenses. When net income increases due to decrease in expenditures, this is generally good news. Nevertheless, our analysis must examine the source of the expenditure decrease *and* assess its potential ramifications. In the case of California Technology, our analysis reveals a less than comfortable situation. Since most R&D outlays are expensed as incurred, we know that each dollar decrease in R&D outlays increases current net income by a dollar. But since R&D is the essence of a high technology corporation, our analysis of California Technology is troubling. Unless R&D costs have generally fallen in the industry (which is unlikely), California Technology's decrease in R&D expenditures hints at a less than optimistic future. While short-term income rises from decreases in R&D outlays, long-run income is likely to suffer.

[Superscript ^{A} denotes assignments based on Appendix 6A]

QUESTIONS

6–1 Explain why an analyst attaches great importance to evaluation of the income statement.

6–2 Define income. Distinguish income from cash flow.

6–3 What are the two basic economic concepts of income? What implications do they have for analysis?

6–4 Economic income measures change in value while permanent income is proportional to value itself. Explain this statement.

6–5 Explain how accountants measure income.

6–6 Accounting income has elements of both permanent income and economic income. Explain this statement.

6–7 Distinguish between the permanent and transitory components of income. Cite an example of each and discuss how each component affects analysis.

6–8 Define and cite an example of a value irrelevant component of income.

6–9 Distinguish between net income, comprehensive income, and continuing income. Cite examples of items that create differences between these three income measures.

6–10 Although comprehensive income is the bottom line income number, it is rarely reported in the income statement. Where will you typically find details regarding comprehensive income?

6–11 Analysts often refer to the core income of a company. What is meant by the term *core income*?

6–12 Distinguish between operating and nonoperating income. Cite examples of items that are typically included in each category.

6–13 Operating vs. nonoperating and recurring vs. nonrecurring are two distinct dimensions of classifying income. Explain this statement and discuss whether or not you agree with it.

6–14 How does accounting define an *extraordinary* item? Cite three examples of such an item. What are the analysis implications of such an item?

6–15 Describe the accounting treatment for discontinued operations. How should an analyst treat discontinued operations?

6–16 What conditions are necessary for an item to qualify as a prior period adjustment?

6–17 Identify some accounting sources of income distortion.

6–18 For each of the three items, (1) depreciation, (2) inventory, and (3) installment sales, explain:
a. Two acceptable accounting methods for reporting purposes.
b. How each of the two acceptable accounting methods identified affect current period income.

(CFA Adapted)

6–19 Accounting practice distinguishes among different types of accounting changes. Identify three different types of accounting changes.

6–20 Explain what special items are. Give three examples of special items.

6–21 How do companies use special charges to influence investors' perceptions regarding company value?

6–22 How should an analyst treat special items?

6–23 Describe the conditions that are usually required before revenue is considered realized.

6–24 Identify the conditions that are usually required before a sale with right of return is recognized as a sale and the resulting receivable is recognized as an asset.

6–25 An ability to estimate future returns (when right of return exists) is an important consideration in revenue recognition. Identify factors impairing the ability to predict future returns.

6–26 Explain how accounting practice defines a product financing arrangement.

6–27 Distinguish between the two major methods used to account for revenue under long-term contracts.

6–28 Describe aspects of revenue recognition that an analyst must be especially alert to.

6–29 Discuss the accounting standards that govern R&D costs. What are the disclosure requirements?

6–30 What information does our analysis need regarding R&D outlays, especially in light of the limited disclosure requirements in practice?

6–31 What aspects of the valuation and the amortization of goodwill must analysts be alert to?

6–32 Contrast the computation of total interest costs of a bond issue with warrants attached to an issue of convertible debt.

6–33 *a.* What is the main provision of accounting for capitalization of interest, and what are its objectives?
b. How is interest to be computed, and how is the interest rate to be ascertained?
c. What restrictions to capitalization are imposed in practice and when does the capitalization period begin?

6–34 Distinguish between the intrinsic value and the fair value of an option.

6–35 List and discuss the factors that affect the fair value of an option.

6–36 Describe the calculation of compensation expense associated with employee stock options. Is it necessary for a company to charge option-related compensation expense to income?

6–37 Net income computed on the basis of financial reporting often differs from taxable income due to permanent differences. What are permanent differences and how do they arise?

6–38 What factors cause the effective tax rate to differ from the statutory rate?

6–39 What are the main requirements of accounting for income taxes?

6–40 List four general cases giving rise to temporary differences between financial reporting and tax reporting.

6–41 What are the disclosure requirements when accounting for income taxes?

6–42 Identify and explain at least one flaw to which tax allocation procedures are subject.

6–43[A] Why is a thorough understanding of the principles governing computation of EPS important to our analysis?

6–44[A] Discuss uses of EPS and reasons or objectives for the current method of reporting EPS.

6–45[A] What is the purpose underlying the reporting of diluted EPS?

6–46[A] How does the payment of dividends on preferred stock affect the EPS computation?

6–47[A] EPS can affect a company's stock prices. Can a company's stock prices affect EPS?

6–48[A] Accounting for earnings per share has certain weaknesses that our analysis must consider for interpreting EPS data. Identify and discuss at least two weaknesses.

6–49[A] In estimating the value of common stock, the amount of EPS is considered an important element.
a. Explain why EPS is important in the valuation of common stock.
b. Is EPS equally important in valuing a preferred stock? Why or why not?

(CFA Adapted)

EXERCISES

EXERCISE 6–1

Analyzing Discontinued Operations

Quaker Oats

Refer to the financial statements of **Quaker Oats** in Appendix A. In note 2, Discontinued Operations, various transactions are discussed concerning the operations and disposal of certain lines of business.

Required:

a. What is your best estimate of the summary journal entry recording the disposal of discontinued operations in Year 11?

b. What are the expenses of discontinued operations in Year 10?

c. Discuss the importance of discontinued operations in analyzing Quaker Oats.

d. What is the rationale for separately reporting the results of discontinued operations?

EXERCISE 6–2
Analyzing Accounting Reserves

The following quote is taken from an article (by L. Bernstein) scrutinizing use of reserves to recognize future costs and losses.

> The growing use of reserves for future costs and losses impairs the significance of periodically reported income and should be viewed with skepticism by the analyst of financial statements. That is especially true when the reserves are established in years of heavy losses, when they are established in an arbitrary amount designed to offset an extraordinary gain, or when they otherwise appear to have as their main purpose the relieving of future income or expenses properly chargeable to it. The basic justification in accounting for the recognition of future losses stems from the doctrine of conservatism that, according to one popular application, means that one should anticipate no gains, but take all the losses one can clearly see as already incurred.

Required:

a. Discuss the merits of Bernstein's arguments and apprehensions regarding reserves.

b. Explain how this perspective can be factored into an analysis of past earnings trends, estimates of future earnings, and the valuation of common stock.

c. Cite examples of such reserves—you can draw on those in the chapter.

(CFA Adapted)

EXERCISE 6–3
Interpreting Disclosures of Accounting Changes

There are various types of accounting changes requiring different types of reporting treatments. Understanding the different changes is important to analysis of financial statements.

Required:

a. Under what category of accounting changes is the change from sum-of-the-years'-digits method of depreciation to the straight-line method for previously recorded assets classified? Under what circumstances does this type of accounting change occur?

b. Under what category of accounting changes is the change in expected service life of an asset (due to new information) classified? Under what circumstances does this type of accounting change occur?

c. Regarding changes in accounting principle:
(1) How does a company compute the effect of such changes?
(2) How does a company report the effect of these changes?

Note: Do not discuss earnings per share requirements.

d. Why are accounting principles, once adopted, normally consistently applied over time?

e. What is the rationale for disclosure of a change from one accounting principle to another?

f. Discuss how your analysis of mandatory accounting changes might differ from that of voluntary accounting changes.

g. Discuss how companies might time the adoption of mandatory accounting changes for their own benefit.

h. Discuss how the adoption of mandatory accounting changes can create an opportunity to establish a hidden reserve. Cite examples.

(AICPA Adapted)

EXERCISE 6–4
Computing Comprehensive Income

Harvatin Group reported net income totaling $1,000,000 for the year 2003. The following is additional information obtained from the Harvatin Group's financial reports:

- The Company purchased 100,000 shares of Micron Specialists for $10 per share during the fourth quarter of 2003. The investment is considered a "no influence" investment and the shares are declared to be "available for sale." The value of the shares is $9 at the end of 2003.

- The Company purchased 10,000 shares of Sunswept Properties for $20 per share during the fourth quarter of 2003. The investment is considered a "no influence" investment and the shares are declared to be "trading" securities. The value of the shares is $22 at the end of 2003.
- The company began operations in the Baltic region of Europe during the year and reports a foreign currency translation gain at the end of 2003 totaling $50,000.
- The actual return on assets in its pension fund total $150,000. The expected return was $110,000.
- The company has substantial prior service cost associated with its employee pension plan. As a result, the company had to record an additional minimum pension liability during the year totaling $25,000.
- The company reported unrealized holding losses on derivative instruments totaling $12,000.

Required:

a. Compute comprehensive income for Harvatin Group.

b. For each item in comprehensive income, discuss balance sheet accounts affected by the item.

EXERCISE 6–5
Analysis of Revenue Recognition and Timing

Revenue is usually recognized at the point of sale. Under special circumstances, dates other than the point of sale are used for timing of revenue recognition.

Required:

a. Why is point of sale usually used as the basis for the timing of revenue recognition?

b. Disregarding special circumstances when bases other than the point of sale are used, discuss the merits of both of the following objections to the sale basis of revenue recognition:
(1) It is too conservative because revenue is earned throughout the entire process of production.
(2) It is too liberal because accounts receivable do not represent disposable funds, sales returns and allowances can occur, and collection and bad debt expenses can be incurred in a later period.

c. Revenue can be recognized (1) during production and (2) when cash is received. For each of these two bases of timing revenue recognition, give an example of the circumstances where it is properly used and discuss the accounting merits of its use in lieu of the sales basis.

(AICPA Adapted)

EXERCISE 6–6
Analyzing Percentage-of-Completion Figures

Michael Company accounts for a long-term construction contract using the percentage-of-completion method. It is a four-year contract currently in its second year. Recent estimates of total contract costs indicate the contract will be completed at a profit to Michael Company.

Required:

a. What theoretical justification is there for Michael Company's use of the percentage-of-completion method?

b. How are progress billings accounted for? Include in your discussion the classification of progress billings in the Michael Company financial statements.

c. How is income computed in the second year of the four-year contract using the cost method of determining percentage of completion?

d. What is the effect on earnings in the second year of the four-year contract when using the percentage-of-completion method instead of the completed-contract method? Discuss.

(AICPA Adapted)

EXERCISE 6–7
Interpreting Revenue Recognition for Leases (book and tax effects)

Crime Control Co. accounts for a substantial part of its alarm system sales under the sales-type (capitalized) lease method. Under this method the company computes the present value of the total receipts it expects to get (over periods as long as eight years) from a lease and records this present value amount as sales in the first year of the lease. Justification for this accounting is that the 8-year lease extends over more than 75% of the 10-year useful life of the equipment. While the sales-type lease method is used for financial reporting, for tax purposes the company reports revenues only when received. Since first-year expenses of a lease are particularly large, the company reports substantial tax losses on these leases.

Required:

a. Critics maintain the sales-type lease method "front loads" income and that reported earnings may not be received in cash for several years. Comment on this criticism.

b. Will financial reporting income be improved from the company's tax benefit?

c. The company insists it can achieve earnings results similar to those achieved by the sales-type lease method by selling the lease receivables to third-party lessors or financial institutions. Comment on this assertion.

(AICPA Adapted)

EXERCISE 6–8
Revenue Recognition in Dot.Com Companies

Lookhere.Com and StopIn.Com enter into a reciprocal agreement whereby (1) StopIn.Com is given valuable advertising space on the home page of Lookhere.Com and (2) Lookhere.Com is given valuable advertising space on the home page of StopIn.Com. The main source of revenue for both StopIn.Com and Lookhere.Com is sales of advertising on their respective websites. Both companies recognize advertising revenue received from the other company and recognize advertising expense paid to the other company. Accounting regulators express support for the accounting treatment applied by these companies.

Required:

a. Do you believe these companies should be allowed to recognize revenue in conjunction with the advertising agreements described above?

b. Why do you believe these companies want to record revenue along with its offsetting expense for these transactions?

c. How would you assess such transactions in an analysis of these companies?

EXERCISE 6–9
Expensing vs. Capitalization of Costs

An analyst must be familiar with the concepts involved in determining income. The amount of income reported for a company depends on the recognition of revenues and expenses for a given time period. In certain cases, costs are recognized as expenses at the time of product sale; in other situations, guidelines are applied in capitalizing costs and recognizing them as expenses in future periods.

Required:

a. Explain the rationale for recognizing costs as expenses at the time of product sale.

b. What is the rationale underlying the appropriateness of treating costs as expenses of a period instead of assigning the costs to an asset? Explain.

c. Under what circumstances is it appropriate to treat a cost as an asset instead of as an expense? Explain.

d. Certain expenses are assigned to specific accounting periods on the basis of systematic and rational allocation of asset cost. Explain the underlying rationale for recognizing expenses on this basis.

e. Identify the conditions necessary to treat a cost as a loss.

(AICPA Adapted)

EXERCISE 6–10
Analyzing Research and Development Costs

The annual research and development costs for Frontier Biotech for years 1999 through 2003 are shown below ($ millions):

1999	2000	2001	2002	2003
$5.1	$5.9	$6.0	$6.2	$3.3

Required:

a. Comment on the manner in which research and development costs impact net income in both the current year and in future years.

b. How would you assess the reduced research and development expenditure in year 2003?

EXERCISE 6–11
Analyzing Employee Stock Option Disclosures

SFAS 123 encourages companies to recognize the fair value of employee stock options as an operating expense. Options pricing models are used to estimate the fair value of the options. Yet, the FASB only *encourages* the adoption of *SFAS 123*. Companies have the choice to continue to apply *APB 25,* which uses the intrinsic value of the options. Under the intrinsic value approach, companies need to record an expense only if the exercise price of the option is lower than the prevailing stock price–since most companies grant options with exercise price equal to the current stock price, no stock option expense is recorded. If companies choose to apply *APB 25*, they must disclose, in a note, the fair value of options and its effect on reported income.

Required:

a. Discuss whether an analyst would prefer financial information prepared using the rules of *SFAS 123* or *APB 25*.
b. If you prefer *SFAS 123* rules, describe how you can use the pro forma disclosures to recast your analysis for the impact of employee stock options.
c. Identify at least four ratios in your financial analysis that are impacted by the *SFAS 123* versus *APB 25* choice.

EXERCISE 6–12
Interpreting Employee Stock Options

On August 1, 1999, the board of directors of Incent.Com approved a stock option plan for its middle managers and software design professionals (100 employees). The plan awards 1,000 shares of $5 par value common stock to each employee. The grant date is January 1, 2000. The option (exercise) price of the shares is the opening stock price on January 1, 2000 ($20). The options are nontransferable and are exercisable after December 31, 2004. The options expire when the employee leaves the company or on December 31, 2011, whichever is first. Management estimates annual forfeitures will be 4% and that the expected life of the options is 6 years. The fair value of the options based on the Black-Scholes Options Pricing Model is $8 per option. On the first exercise date, 50,000 options are exercised when the stock price is $60 per share.

Required:

a. Is this a compensatory or noncompensatory stock option plan? Explain.
b. Why would Incent.Com offer such a plan to its employees?
c. What is the grant date, vesting date, and exercise date for this ESO plan?
d. Are the stock options "in-the-money" at the grant date? Explain.
e. When should total compensation cost be measured? Explain.
f. How much compensation cost should be recognized in total in relation to this stock option plan?
g. In which periods should total compensation cost be allocated to as compensation expense?
h. Explain how this ESO plan transfers wealth from stockholders to employees.

EXERCISE 6–13
Information Disclosures and Employee Stock Options

Some research shows that the price of stock is likely to fall in the days leading up to the fixing of the exercise price for employee stock options. It is suggested that the price decreases are the result of selective news releases from managers. Specifically, managers are asserted to delay the release of good news until after the ESO grant date and, instead, selectively release bad news before the date that the stock option exercise price is fixed.

Required:

a. Why do you believe managers are willing to announce bad news but not good news in advance of the stock option grant date?
b. How might you adjust your reaction to news announcements (or lack thereof) around the date when employee stock option exercise prices are set?

EXERCISE 6–14
Interpreting Deferred Income Taxes

Primrose Co. uses the deferred method for interperiod tax allocation. Primrose reports depreciation expense for machinery purchases for the current year using the modified accelerated cost recovery system (MACRS) for income tax purposes and the straight-line basis for financial reporting. The tax deduction is the larger amount this year. Primrose also received rent revenues in advance this year. It included these revenues in this year's taxable income. For financial reporting, rent revenues are reported as unearned revenues, a current liability.

Required:

a. What is the conceptual underpinning for deferred income taxes?
b. How does Primrose determine and account for the income tax effect for both depreciation and rent? Explain.
c. How does Primrose classify the income tax effect of both depreciation and rent on its balance sheet and income statement? Explain.

EXERCISE 6–15
Earnings Management Motives

Companies sometimes use earnings management techniques to increase reported earnings per share by as little as $0.01.

Required:

Explain why a $0.01 change in reported earnings per share would be insignificant for some companies but significant for other companies. Include in your answer reference to at least two earnings targets that a company might be managing earnings per share toward.

EXERCISE 6–16[A]
Analyzing Earnings per Share

Publicly traded companies are required to report earnings per share data on the face of the income statement.

Required:

Compare and contrast basic earnings per share with diluted earnings per share for each of the following:

a. The effect of dilutive stock options and warrants on the number of shares used in computing earnings per share.

b. The effect of dilutive convertible securities on the number of shares used in computing earnings per share data.

c. The effect of antidilutive securities in computing earnings per share.

(CFA Adapted)

EXERCISE 6–17[A]
Interpreting Earnings per Share

Accounting requires presentation of earnings per share data along with the income statement.

Required:

a. Explain the meaning of basic earnings per share.

b. Explain how diluted earnings per share differs from basic earnings per share.

(CFA Adapted)

EXERCISE 6–18[A]
Earnings per Share Computations (multiple choice)

CHECK
(1) b

Champion had 2 million shares outstanding on December 31, Year 7. On March 31, Year 8, Champion paid a 10% stock dividend. On June 30, Year 8, Champion sells $10 million of 5% convertible debentures, convertible into common shares at $5 per share. The AA bond rate on the issue date is 10%.

1. Basic earnings per share for Year 8 is computed on the following number of shares:
   a. 2,050,000 *c.* 3,200,000
   b. 2,200,000 *d.* 4,200,000
2. Assume that Champion also has outstanding warrants to purchase 1 million shares at $5 per share. The price of Champion common shares is $8 per share at December 31, Year 8, and the average share price for Year 8 is $4. For the computation of basic earnings per share, how many *additional* shares must be assumed to be outstanding because of the warrants?
   a. Zero *c.* 625,000
   b. 375,000 *d.* 1,000,000
3. Given the same facts as in (*2*), how many *additional* shares must be assumed to be outstanding because of the warrants when computing diluted earnings per share?
   a. Zero *c.* 625,000
   b. 375,000 *d.* 1,000,000

(CFA Adapted)

PROBLEMS

PROBLEM 6–1
Disclosing Discontinued Operations

The *unaudited* income statements of Disposo Corporation are reproduced below.

	Year 8	Year 7
Sales	$1,100	$900
Costs and expenses	990	860
Loss on asset disposal	10	—
Income before taxes	100	40
Tax expense	50	20
Net income	$ 50	$ 20

Note: On August 15, Year 8, the company decided to discontinue its Metals Division. The business was sold on December 31, Year 8, at book value except for a factory building with a book value of $25 that was sold for $15. Operations of the Metals Division were:

	Sales	Income (Loss)
Year 7	$300	$8
Jan. 1 to Aug. 15, Year 8	250	(3)
Aug. 16 to Dec. 31, Year 8	75	(1)

CHECK
Year 8 Continuing income, $59

Required:
Correct the Year 7 and Year 8 income statements to reflect the proper reporting of discontinued operations.

PROBLEM 6–2
Revenue Recognition (multiple choice)

1. In preparing its Year 9 adjusting entries, the Singapore Company neglected to adjust rental fees received in advance for the amount of rental fees earned during Year 9. What is the effect of this error?
   a. Net income is understated, retained earnings are understated, and liabilities are overstated.
   b. Net income is overstated, retained earnings are overstated, and liabilities are unaffected.
   c. Net income, retained earnings, and liabilities all are understated.
2. The Sutton Construction Company entered into a contract in early Year 8 to build a tunnel for the city at a price of $11 million. The company estimated total cost of the project at $10 million and three years to complete. Actual costs incurred (on budget) and billings to the city are as follows:

	Costs Incurred	Billings to City
Year 8	$2,500,000	$2,000,000
Year 9	4,000,000	3,500,000
Year 10	3,500,000	5,500,000

   Using the percentage-of-completion method for revenue recognition, what does Sutton Construction report for revenues and profit for Year 9?

	Revenues	Profit		Revenues	Profit
a.	$4,000,000	$300,000	*c.*	$3,850,000	$350,000
b.	$4,400,000	$400,000	*d.*	$3,500,000	$500,000

CHECK
(2) b

3. Using the percentage-of-completion method in accounting for long-term projects, a company can increase reported earnings by:
   a. Accelerating recognition of project expenditures.
   b. Delaying recognition of project expenditures.
   c. Switching to completed-contract accounting.
   d. Overestimating the total cost of the project.
4. Revenue can be recognized at the time of:
   a. Production.
   b. Sale.
   c. Collection.
   d. All of the above.
5. In October, a company shipped a new product to retailers. Which one of the following conditions would prohibit immediate recognition of revenue?
   a. Terms of the sale require the company to provide extensive promotional materials to retailers before December 1.
   b. Retailers are not obligated to pay the purchase price until February, after their holiday sales are collected.
   c. On the basis of past performance, reliable estimates are that 20% of the product is returned.
   d. The company is unable to enforce agreements concerning discounting of the retail sales of the product.
6. In accounting for long-term contracts, how does the percentage-of-completion method of revenue recognition differ from the completed contract method? (Choose one answer from *a, b, c,* or *d* below.)
   i. Present value of income tax payments is minimized.
   ii. Revenue for each period reflects more closely the results of construction activity during the period.
   iii. Current status of uncompleted contracts is reported more accurately.
   iv. Percentage-of-completion method relies less on estimates for both the degree of completion and the extent of future costs to be incurred.
   a. *i* and *ii.*
   b. *i* and *iii.*
   c. *ii* and *iii.*
   d. *ii* and *iv.*

7. R. Lott Corporation, which began business on January 1, Year 7, uses the installment sales method of accounting. The following data are available for December 31, Year 7 and Year 8:

	Year 7	Year 8
Balance of deferred gross profit on sales account:		
Year 7	$300,000	$120,000
Year 8	—	$440,000
Gross profit on sales	30%	40%

The installment accounts receivable balance at December 31, Year 8, is:

a. $1,000,000 *c.* $1,400,000
b. $1,100,000 *d.* $1,500,000

(CFA Adapted)

CHECK
(7) d

PROBLEM 6–3
Revenue Recognition and Fraudulent Behavior

Cendant

Cendant was formed on December 18, 1997, via the merger of CUC International and HFS Inc. The company owns the rights to franchises and brands including Avis, Century 21 Real Estate, Coldwell Banker, Days Inn, Howard Johnson, and Ramada. The consolidated entity got off to a bad start when it was revealed that CUC International executives had been committing "widespread and systemic" accounting fraud with intent to deceive investors. When the company announced that it had discovered "potential accounting irregularities" the stock dropped from $36 to $19 per share. Eventually the stock would fall to as low as $6 per share as the company struggled to convince investors about management's integrity. According to the company's own investigation, CUC executives had inflated earnings by over $650 million over a three-year period using several tactics, including: (1) failing to timely record returned credit card purchases and membership cancellations, (2) improperly capitalizing and amortizing expenses related to attracting new members, and (3) recording fictitious sales.

Required:

a. For each of three fraudulent tactics employed by CUC, identify an analysis technique that could have identified the accounting improprieties.

b. Both the investors and the management of HFS had relied on audited financial statements in making decisions regarding CUC International. What do you believe was the external auditor's culpability in not detecting these fraudulent practices?

PROBLEM 6–4
Analyzing Income Tax Disclosures

Campbell Soup Company

Refer to the financial statements of **Campbell Soup Company** in Appendix A.

Required:

a. Estimate the amount of depreciation expense reported on Campbell's tax returns for each of the Years 11, 10, and 9. Use a tax rate of 34%.

CHECK
(a) Year 11, $211.9 mil.

b. Identify the amounts and sources in each of the Years 11, 10, and 9 for the following (*note:* combine federal, foreign, and state taxes).
(1) Earnings before income taxes.
(2) Expected income tax at 34%.
(3) Total income tax expense.
(4) Total income tax due.
(5) Total income tax due and not yet paid at end of Years 11, 10, and 9.

c. Why does the effective tax rate for Years 11, 10, and 9 differ from 34% of income before taxes? Answer with a reconciliation including explanations.

d. There is a small tax benefit derived from the divestiture and restructuring charges in Year 10. Can you estimate the cash outlays for these charges in Year 10?

CHECK
(d) $110 mil.

PROBLEM 6–5
Analyzing Income Tax Disclosures

Refer to the financial statements of **Quaker Oats Company** in Appendix A.

Quaker Oats Company

Required:

a. Estimate the amount of depreciation expense reported on Quaker Oats' tax returns for each of the Years 11, 10, and 9. Use a tax rate of 34%.

b. Identify the amounts and sources in each of the Years 11, 10, and 9 for the following (*note:* combine federal, foreign, and state taxes).
(1) Earnings before income taxes.
(2) Expected income tax at 34%.
(3) Total income tax expense.
(4) Total income tax due.
(5) Total income tax due and not yet paid at the end of Years 11, 10, and 9.

CHECK
(b) 5. Year 11, $45.1 mil.

c. Why does the effective tax rate for Years 11, 10, and 9 differ from 34% of income before taxes? Answer with a reconciliation including explanations. Is it likely that the effective tax rate will continue to be high in the future?

d. Is the company's effective tax rate in Year 11 different from that in Year 10? If it is, what is the main reason?

e. What is the increase or decrease in deferred tax (current) for each of the Years 11, 10, and 9?

f. What is the increase or decrease in deferred tax (noncurrent) for each of the Years 11, 10, and 9?

PROBLEM 6–6
Understanding Revenue Recognition and Deferred Income Taxes

Big-Deal Construction Company specializes in building dams. During Years 3, 4, and 5, three dams were completed. The first dam was started in Year 1 and completed in Year 3 at a profit before income taxes of $120,000. The second and third dams were started in Year 2. The second dam was completed in Year 4 at a profit before income taxes of $126,000, and the third dam was completed in Year 5 at a profit before income taxes of $150,000. The company uses percentage-of-completion accounting for financial reporting and the completed-contract method of accounting for income tax purposes. The applicable income tax rate is 50% for each of the Years 1 through 5. Data relating to progress toward completion of work on each dam as reported by the company's engineers are below:

Dam	Year 1	Year 2	Year 3	Year 4	Year 5
1	20%	60%	20%		
2		30	60	10%	
3		10	30	50	10%

Required:

For each of the five years, Year 1 through Year 5, compute:

a. Financial reporting (book) income.

b. Taxable income.

c. Change in deferred income taxes.

CHECK
Year 2, Increase in Def. Inc. Taxes, $62,400; Year 5, Decrease in Def. Inc. Taxes, $67,500

PROBLEM 6–7
Analyzing Preoperating Costs and Deferred Income Taxes

Stead Corporation is formed in Year 4 to take over the operations of a small business. This business proved very stable for Stead, as is evidenced below ($ in thousands):

	Year 4	Year 5	Year 6
Sales	$10,000	$10,000	$10,000
Expenses (except taxes)	9,000	9,000	9,000
Income before taxes	$ 1,000	$ 1,000	$ 1,000

Stead also expends $1,400,000 on preoperating costs for a new product during Year 4 (not included in the above figures). These costs are deferred for financial reporting purposes but are deducted in calculating Year 4 taxable income. During Year 5, the new product line is delayed; and in Year 6, Stead abandons the new product and charges the deferred cost of $1,400,000 to the Year 6 income statement. The applicable tax rate is 50%.

Required:

a. Prepare comparative income statements for Years 4, 5, and 6. Identify all tax amounts as either current or deferred.

b. Compute both current and deferred taxes payable for the balance sheet for each of the Years 4, 5, and 6 (assume all tax payments and refunds occur in the year following the reporting year).

CHECK
Year 5 income, $500;
Year 6 loss, $(200)

PROBLEM 6–8
Accounting for Income Tax Expense

Playgrounds, Inc., is granted a distribution franchise by Shady Products in Year 1. Operations are profitable until Year 4 when some of the company's inventories are confiscated and large legal expenses are incurred. Playgrounds' tax rate is 50% each year (all expenses and costs are tax deductible). Relevant income statement data are (in thousands):

	Year 1	Year 2	Year 3	Year 4	Year 5	Year 6	Year 7	Year 8
Sales	$50	$80	$120	$ 100	$200	$400	$500	$600
Cost of sales	20	30	50	300	50	120	200	250
General and administrative	10	15	20	100	20	30	40	50
Net income before tax	$20	$35	$ 50	$(300)	$130	$250	$260	$300

Required:

Compute tax expense for each of the Years 1 through 8, and present comparative income statements for these years (assume a 3-year carryback period and a 20-year carryforward period for any losses).

CHECK
Year 4 loss, $(247.5);
Year 8 income, $150

PROBLEM 6–9[A]
Earnings per Share Computations (multiple choice)

The financial data below should be used to answer the following two questions.

WRESTLING FEDERATION OF AMERICA, INC.
Capital Structure and Earnings for Year 7

Number of common shares outstanding on December 31, Year 7	2,700,000
Number of common shares outstanding during Year 7 (weighted average)	2,500,000
Market price per common share on December 31, Year 7	$25
Weighted-average market price per share during Year 7	$20
Options outstanding during Year 7:	
Number of shares issuable on exercise of options	200,000
Exercise price	$15
Convertible bonds outstanding (December 31, Year 3, issue date):	
Number of convertible bonds	10,000
Shares of common issuable on conversion (per bond)	10
Coupon rate	5.0%
Proceeds per bond at issue (at par value)	$1,000
Net income for Year 7	$6,500,000
Tax rate for Year 7	40.0%

1. Basic earnings per share for Year 7 is (choose one of the following):
   a. $2.41
   b. $2.57
   c. $2.60
   d. $2.50

2. Diluted earnings per share for Year 7 is (choose one of the following):
   a. $2.43
   b. $2.55
   c. $2.54
   d. $2.60

(CFA Adapted)

PROBLEM 6–10[A]
Computing Earnings per Share

Ace Company's net income for the year is $4 million and the number of common shares outstanding is 3 million (there is no change in shares outstanding during the year). Ace has options and warrants outstanding to purchase 1 million common shares at $15 per share.

Required:

a. If the average market value of the common share is $20, year-end price is $25, interest rate on borrowings is 6%, and the tax rate is 50%, then compute both basic and diluted EPS.

b. Do the same computations as in *a* assuming net income for the year is only $3 million, the average market value per common share is $18, and year-end price is $20 per share.

CHECK
(b) Diluted EPS, $0.95

CASES

CASE 6–1
Understanding Revenue Recognition

BIKE Company starts with $3,000 cash to finance its business plan of producing bike helmets using a simple assembly process. During the first month of business, the company signs sales contracts for 1,300 units (sales price of $9 per unit), produces 1,200 units (production cost of $7 per unit), ships 1,100 units, and collects in full for 900 units. Production costs are paid at the time of production. The company has only two other costs: (1) sales commissions of 10% of selling price when the company collects from the customer, and (2) shipping costs of $0.20 per unit paid at time of shipment. Selling price and all costs per unit have been constant and are likely to remain the same.

Required:

a. Prepare comparative (side-by-side) balance sheets and income statements for the first month of BIKE Company for each of the following three alternatives:
(1) Revenue is recognized at the time of shipment.
(2) Revenue is recognized at the time of collection.
(3) Revenue is recognized at the time of production.

Note: Net income for each of these three alternatives is (1) $990, (2) $810, and (3) $1,080, respectively.

b. The method where revenue is recognized at time of collection, known as the *installment method,* is acceptable for financial reporting in unusual and special cases. Why is BIKE Company likely to prefer this method for tax purposes?

c. Comment on the usefulness of the installment method for a credit analyst in using both the balance sheet and income statement.

CASE 6–2
Analyzing Operating Activities

Refer to the annual report of **Kodak** in Appendix A. **Kodak**

Required:

a. Compute all of the items that constitute earnings from operations as a percentage of sales for each of the three years shown. Analyze and comment on the percentages computed.

b. Comment on the extent to which each component in (*a*) is expected to persist into future years.

c. The provision for income taxes makes up what percent of earnings before income taxes? What percent of total taxes is made up of (1) U.S. federal income taxes, and (2) income taxes outside the U.S.?

d. What potentially dilutive security is included in Kodak's capital structure that creates a difference between the number of shares used to compute basic earnings per share and diluted earnings per share?

e. Kodak announced operational restructuring programs in December 2001. What amount of restructuring charges is recorded in association with these programs?

f. At the end of 2001, how much restructuring liability remains associated with Kodak's 2001 restructuring?

g. Of the $698 million restructuring charge, $351 million is for restructuring costs such as severance payments. The motivation for incurring these costs is ongoing cost reduction. As such, the $351 million accrual can be thought of as an investment in ongoing lower costs. Discuss how one might adjust the balance sheet and income statement to reflect this concept.

h. How might large liabilities such as Kodak's restructuring liabilities be used to manage earnings?

i. Kodak reports an income tax valuation allowance of $56 million at the end of 2001. Comment on the reasonableness of this provision based on the company's explanation of the allowance. Explain how the income tax valuation allowance could be used to manage earnings.

j. Kodak reports net income of $76 million and basic earnings per share of $0.26 for 2001. What would net income and basic earnings per share have been had Kodak adopted *SFAS 123* that requires the fair value of employee stock options to be recognized as compensation expense? How might this information be used in your valuation models?

CASE 6–3
Analyzing Comprehensive Income

Kodak

Refer to the annual report of **Kodak** in Appendix A.

Required:

a. Comprehensive income is a required disclosure. Where does Kodak report its comprehensive income and its related adjustments? Why do you believe the company chose to disclose comprehensive income in that manner?

b. How much is Kodak's comprehensive income for 2001? Identify the items that create the difference between net income and comprehensive income.

c. What is Kodak's comprehensive income or loss for the previous two years?

d. How do comprehensive income items affect your valuation analysis?

CHECK
Comp. Inc. 2001, $(39) mil.

CASE 6–4
Analyzing Restructuring Activities

Toys 'R' Us

On September 16, 1998, **Toys 'R' Us** [ToysRUs.Com], the world's largest toy-seller announced strategic initiatives to restructure its business. The total cost to implement these initiatives yielded a charge of $508 million, which exceeded operating earnings from the prior year. The $508 million charge consisted of costs to close and/or downsize stores, distribution centers, and administrative functions to streamline store formats, inventories and supply chains; and for changes in accounting estimates and provisions for legal settlements. These initiatives included the closing of 50 toy stores in the international division, predominantly in continental Europe, and 9 in the U.S. that did not meet the company's return on investment goals. It also closed 31 Kids 'R' Us stores and converted 28 nearby U.S. toy stores into combination stores. Combination stores sell toys and apparel. These initiatives were expected to save more than $75 million in 1999 and even more in subsequent years. At the time of the restructuring announcement, the company had 116,000 employees and 1,145 stores worldwide. Of the 1,145 stores, 697 are in the U.S. The company also ran 214 Kids 'R' Us stores, 101 Babies 'R' Us stores, and 2 KidsWorld stores. It hoped to reverse a trend of losing sales to Wal-Mart and other discount retailers. Toys 'R' Us had an 18.4% U.S. toy market share in 1997, down from 18.9% in 1996. Wal-Mart's share and Target's share rose from 15.3% to 16.4%, and 6.4% to 7.1%, respectively, during that time. Toys 'R' Us selected financial reports follow:

Letter to Stockholders

To Our Stockholders

1998 was indeed a year of enormous challenge and change. We've spent the year intensively reviewing every aspect of our business and making some tough calls aimed at repositioning our worldwide business. Key elements of our strategic plan include a Total Solutions Strategy focused on our C-3 plan, which includes the reformatting and repositioning of our toy stores; development of a customer-driven culture; expanding product development; improving our customer value proposition; accelerating our supply chain management program; and expanding our channels of selling. In conjunction with these restructuring efforts, we have been proactively rebuilding and reshaping a stronger management team which will serve to build the foundation for repositioning your Company in the years ahead. We believe that the sum total of these efforts will serve as the springboard toward implementing our expanded vision for the future: to position Toys'R'Us as the worldwide authority on kids, families and fun.

1998 Restructuring Benefits

We ended 1998 a much healthier and vibrant company. This was attributable to some tough strategic decisions that will shape the Company's future. We recorded restructuring and other charges of $508 million net of taxes, which caused the Company to incur a net loss in 1998. The impact of making these tough calls will be evident in our future operations, growth and financial performance. These charges are the result of an exhaustive review of all our operations in 1998 from both a strategic and an Economic Value Added (EVA®) perspective. These reviews prompted the following significant actions:

- The closing and/or downsizing of approximately 50 toy stores in the International arena, predominantly in continental Europe, and about 9 U.S. toy stores which do not meet the Company's strategic or financial objectives. This will free our management to focus on higher return opportunities;
- The conversion of 28 existing U.S. toy stores into "combo" stores, which will enable us to close 31 nearby Kids'R'Us stores. In addition to reducing operating costs and releasing working capital, this will allow us to enhance our productivity by further expanding kids' apparel into additional Toys'R'Us stores;
- The consolidation of several distribution centers and over half a dozen administrative offices. These actions will reduce administrative support functions in the U.S. and Europe, which will not only generate selling, general and administrative efficiencies, but "flatten" our organization and bring our management even closer to our stores and customers;
- The continuation of taking aggressive markdowns on clearance product to optimize inventory levels, accommodate new product offerings and accelerate our store reformatting. In conjunction with the initial stages of our supply chain re-engineering, we have already been able to reduce same store inventories in all our divisions by over $560 million or 24% at year end 1998, with roughly $480 million or 31% of this favorable swing coming from reduced inventory in the U.S. toy stores division alone. This brought us into the new year with heightened merchandise flexibility and increased "open to buy" as we begin the rollout of the initial phase of our store reformat program in 1999.

One of our other key priorities in 1998 was to build a strong executive team, and we are well on our way towards assembling a truly outstanding management team. Since the beginning of 1998, more than 50 percent of our officer team has either joined the company from the outside, or has been promoted or transferred to new assignments, bringing fresh perspectives and proven skills to our business.

It is obvious our 1998 sales and earnings were not what we wanted them to be. However, we've spent a year making tough calls and hard decisions, and we're now ready to move forward stronger and more focused than ever.

Total Solutions Strategy

Our restructuring program, in September 1998, was the first step required to launch a winning strategy for Toys'R'Us–a strategy which will realign our assets, organization and thinking based on customer-driven priorities in a more competitive marketplace. In the 'R'Us brand, we have one of the best-known brand names in the world: our challenge is to more effectively develop this strong customer franchise potential. Today's retail marketplace demands stores that are exciting, easy to shop and customer-friendly. While our selection is still superior to our competitors, that alone is not compelling enough to rebuild market share and brand loyalty. We must become more focused on developing greater everyday customer value in terms of price, service and the total shopping experience.

Management's Discussion and Analysis

Results of Operations and Financial Condition

During 1998 the Company announced strategic initiatives to reposition its worldwide business and other charges including the customer-focused reformatting of its toy stores into the new C-3 format, as well as the restructuring of its International operations which resulted in a charge of $353 million ($279 million net of tax benefits, or $1.05 per share). The strategic initiatives resulted in a restructuring charge of $294 million. The other charges of $59 million primarily consist of changes in accounting estimates and provisions for legal settlements. The Company is closing and/or downsizing underperforming stores and consolidating distribution centers and administrative offices. As a result, approximately 2,600 employees will be terminated worldwide. Stores expected to be closed had aggregate store sales and net operating losses of approximately $322 million and $5 million, respectively, for the year ended January 30, 1999. The write-down of property, plant and equipment relating to the above mentioned closures and downsizings were based on both internal and independent appraisals. Unused reserves at January 30, 1999, should be utilized in 1999, with the exception of long-term lease commitments, which will be utilized in 1999 and thereafter. Details on the components of the charges are described in the Notes to the Consolidated Financial Statements and are as follows:

* References to 1998, 1997 and 1996, are for the 52 weeks ended January 30, 1999, January 31, 1998 and February 1, 1997.

Description	Charge	Utilized	Reserve Balance at 1/30/99
Closings/Downsizings:			
Lease commitments	$ 81	$ —	$ 81
Severance and other closing costs	29	4	25
Write-down of property, plant & equipment	155	155	—
Other	29	5	24
Total Restructuring	$294	$164	$130
Changes in accounting estimates and Provisions for legal settlements	$ 59	$ 20	$ 39

In 1998 the Company also announced markdowns and other charges of $345 million ($229 million net of tax benefits, or $.86 per share). Of this charge, $253 million relates to markdowns required to clear excess inventory from stores. These markdowns should enable the Company to achieve its optimal inventory assortment and streamline systems so that it can proceed with the C-3 conversions on an accelerated basis. The Company's objective with its new C-3 concept is to provide customers with a better shopping experience leading to increased sales and higher inventory turns. In addition, the Company recorded $29 million in markdowns related to the store closings discussed previously. The Company also recorded charges to cost of sales of $63 million related to inventory system refinements and changes in accounting estimates. Unused reserves at January 30, 1999 are expected to be utilized in 1999. Details of the markdowns and other charges are as follows:

Description	Charge	Utilized	Reserve Balance at 1/30/99
Markdowns			
Clear excess inventory	$253	$179	$ 74
Store closings	29	2	27
Change in accounting estimates & other	63	57	6
Total Cost of Sales	$345	$238	$107

The strategic initiatives, markdowns and other charges described above are expected to improve the Company's free cash flow and increase operating earnings.

CONSOLIDATED STATEMENTS OF EARNINGS

Toys 'R' Us, Inc. and Subsidiaries

(In millions except per share data)	Year Ended January 30, 1999	January 31, 1998	February 1, 1997
Net sales	$11,170	$11,038	$9,932
Cost of sales	8,191	7,710	6,892
Gross profit	2,979	3,328	3,040
Selling, advertising, general and administrative expenses	2,443	2,231	2,020
Depreciation, amortization and asset write-offs	255	253	206
Restructuring and other charges	294	—	60
Total operating expenses	2,992	2,484	2,286
Operating income (loss)	(13)	844	754
Interest expense	102	85	98
Interest and other income	(9)	(13)	(17)
Interest expense, net	93	72	81
Earnings (loss) before income taxes	(106)	772	673
Income taxes	26	282	246
Net earnings (loss)	$ (132)	$ 490	$ 427
Basic earnings (loss) per share	$ (0.50)	$ 1.72	$ 1.56

CONSOLIDATED BALANCE SHEETS

Toys 'R' Us, Inc. and Subsidiaries

(In millions)	January 30, 1999	January 31, 1998
Assets		
Current assets:		
Cash and cash equivalents	$ 410	$ 214
Accounts and other receivables	204	175
Merchandise inventories	1,902	2,464
Prepaid expenses and other current assets	81	51
Total current assets	2,597	2,904
Property and equipment:		
Real estate, net	2,354	2,435
Other, net	1,872	1,777
Total property and equipment	4,226	4,212
Goodwill, net	347	356
Other assets	729	491
	$7,899	**$7,963**

LIABILITIES AND STOCKHOLDERS' EQUITY

Current liabilities:		
Short-term borrowings	$ 156	$ 134
Accounts payable	1,415	1,280
Accrued expenses and other current liabilities	696	680
Income taxes payable	224	231
Total current liabilities	2,491	2,325
Long-term debt	1,222	851
Deferred Income taxes	333	219
Other liabilities	229	140
Stockholders' equity:		
Common stock	30	30
Additional paid-in capital	459	467
Retained earnings	4,478	4,610
Foreign currency translation adjustments	(100)	(122)
Treasury shares, at cost	(1,243)	(557)
Total stockholders' equity	3,624	4,428
	$7,899	**$7,963**

Financial Statement Footnote

Restructuring and Other Charges

On September 16, 1998, the Company announced strategic initiatives to reposition its worldwide business. The cost to implement these initiatives, as well as other charges resulted in a total charge of $333 ($266 net of tax benefits, or $1.00 per share). The Company determined that the strategic initiatives required a restructuring charge of $294 to close and/or downsize stores, distribution centers and administrative functions. This worldwide plan includes the closing of 50 toy stores in the International division, predominantly in continental Europe, and 9 in the United States that do not meet the Company's return on investment objectives. The Company will also close 31 Kids'R'Us stores and convert 28 nearby U.S. toy stores into combination stores in the new C-3 format discussed below. Combination stores include toys and an apparel selling space of approximately 5,000 square feet. Other charges consist primarily of changes in accounting estimates and provisions for legal settlements of $39 recorded in selling, general and administrative expenses. Of the total restructuring and other charges, $149 relates to domestic operations and $184 relates to International operations. Remaining reserves of $149 should be utilized in 1999, with the exception of long-term lease commitments, which will be utilized in 1999 and thereafter.

Also on September 16, 1998, the Company announced mark-downs and other charges to cost of sales of $345 ($229 net of tax benefits, or $.86 per share). The Company has designed a new store format called C-3. The Company plans to convert approximately 200 U.S. toy stores to the new C-3 format in 1999. Of this charge, $253 related to markdowns required to clear excess inventory from its stores so the Company can proceed with its new C-3 store format on an accelerated basis. Another component of the charge was inventory markdowns of $29 related to the closing and/or downsizing of stores discussed above. The Company also recorded charges to cost of sales of $63 related to inventory system refinements and changes in accounting estimates. Of these charges, $288 relate to domestic operations and $57 relate to International operations. Remaining reserves of $107 are expected to be utilized in 1999.

Additionally, in the fourth quarter of 1998 the Company recorded a charge of $20 ($13 net of tax benefits, or $.05 per share), related to the resolution of third party claims asserted from allegations made by the Federal Trade Commission. This charge was in addition to a $15 charge relating to the same matter, included in the charges mentioned above. (See Other Matters.)

At January 30, 1999, the Company had approximately $45 of liabilities remaining for its restructuring program announced in 1995 primarily relating to long-term lease obligations.

The Company believes that reserves are adequate to complete the restructuring and other programs described previously.

On July 12, 1996, an arbitrator rendered an award against the Company in connection with a dispute involving rights under a 1982 license agreement for toy store operations in the Middle East. Accordingly, the Company recorded a provision of $60 during 1996 ($38 net of tax benefits, or $.14 cents per share), representing all costs in connection with this matter.

Required:

Refer to the Toys 'R' Us financial information to answer the following questions.

1. What is the total amount that Toys 'R' Us spent for its restructuring plan? Analyze the breakdown of charges and identify where the charge is reported in the income statement.
2. Recast the income statement without the restructuring charge and analyze operating performance for 1999 by comparing with 1998 performance.
3. Identify the major elements of its restructuring strategy and their economic effects. What will be the effect on future income and how are the savings expected to arise?
4. Discuss how the restructuring liability could be used by Toys 'R' Us as a vehicle for earnings management. In your opinion is Toys 'R' Us managing earnings through this charge?
5. Describe how an analyst would recast the balance sheet and income statement of Toys 'R' Us to reflect the restructuring costs as an investment to create future cost savings.
6. How can the relative success of these restructuring activities be measured?

CASE 6–5[A]
Analyzing Earnings per Share with Convertible Debentures

The officers of Environmental, Inc., considered themselves fortunate when the company sold a $9,000,000 subordinated convertible debenture issue on June 30, Year 1, with a 6% coupon. They had the alternative of refunding and enlarging the outstanding term loan, but the interest cost would have been one-half point above the AA bond rate. The AA bond rate was as high as 8½% until March 29, Year 1, when it was lowered to 8%, the rate that prevailed until September 21, Year 1, when it was lowered again to 7½%. As of December 31, Year 1, Environmental, Inc., had the following capital structure:

7% term loan*	$3,000,000
6% convertible subordinated debentures†	9,000,000
Common stock, $1 par, authorized 2,000,000 shares, issued and outstanding	900,000
900,000 warrants, expiring July 1, Year 6‡	—
Additional Paid-In Capital	1,800,000
Retained earnings	4,500,000

**Term loan (originally $5,000,000) is repayable in semiannual installments of $500,000.*

†Convertible subordinated debentures, sold June 30, Year 1, are convertible any time at $18 until maturity. Sinking fund of $300,000 per year to start in Year 6.

‡Warrants entitle holder to purchase one share for $10 to expiration on July 1, Year 6.

Additional data for Year 1:

Interest expense	$ 500,000
Net income	1,500,000
Dividends paid	135,000
Earnings retained	900,000

Market prices December 31, Year 1 (averages for Year 1):	
Convertible debentures 6%	$107
Common Stock	$13
Stock Warrants	$4.5
Treasury bills interest rate at 12/31/Year 1	6%

Required:

a. Calculate and show computations for basic and diluted earnings per share figures for common stock for the Year 1 annual report (assume a 50% tax rate).

CHECK
Diluted EPS, $1.20

b. What is the times-interest-earned ratio for Year 2 assuming net income before interest and taxes is the same as in Year 1 (a 50% income tax rate applies)?

(CFA Adapted)

CASE 6–6[A]
Determining Earnings per Share

Part I. Information concerning the capital structure of Dole Corporation is reproduced below:

	DECEMBER 31	
	Year 5	**Year 6**
Common stock	90,000 shares	90,000 shares
Convertible preferred stock	10,000 shares	10,000 shares
8% convertible bonds	$1,000,000	$1,000,000

During Year 6, Dole pays dividends of $1 per share on its common stock and $2.40 per share on its preferred stock. The preferred stock is convertible into 20,000 shares of common stock. The 8% convertible bonds are convertible into 30,000 shares of common stock. Net income for the year ended December 31, Year 6, is $285,000. The income tax rate is 50%.

Required:

a. Compute basic earnings per share for the year ended December 31, Year 6.

b. Compute diluted earnings per share for the year ended December 31, Year 6.

CHECK
Diluted EPS, $2.32

Part II. The R. Lott Company's net income for the year ended December 31, Year 6, is $10,000. During Year 6, R. Lott declares and pays $1,000 cash dividends on preferred stock and $1,750 cash dividends on common stock. At December 31, Year 6, 12,000 shares of common stock are issued and outstanding–10,000 of which were issued and outstanding throughout the entire year and 2,000 of which were issued on July 1, Year 6. There are no other common stock transactions during the year, and there is no potential dilution of earnings per share.

Required:

Compute the Year 6 basic earnings per common share of R. Lott Company.

WEB ACTIVITIES

The Web Activities are located on the book's website at www.mhhe.com/wild8e.

7

CASH FLOW ANALYSIS

A LOOK BACK <

In Chapter 6 we analyzed operating activities using accrual measures. We examined revenue and expense recognition methods for interpretation of operations. Per share figures for income were also examined.

A LOOK AT THIS CHAPTER •

In this chapter we analyze cash flow measures for insights into all business activities, with special emphasis on operations. Attention is directed at company and business conditions when interpreting cash flows. We also consider alternative measures of cash flows.

A LOOK AHEAD >

The next chapter begins our focus on a more strategic application and analysis of financial statements. We analyze return on investment, asset utilization, and other measures of performance that are relevant to a wide class of financial statement users. We describe several tools of analysis to assist in evaluation of company performance and return.

ANALYSIS OBJECTIVES

- Explain the relevance of cash flows in analyzing business activities.
- Describe the reporting of cash flows by business activities.
- Describe the preparation and analysis of the statement of cash flows.
- Interpret cash flows from operating activities.
- Analyze cash flows under alternative company and business conditions.
- Describe alternative measures of cash flows and their usefulness.
- Illustrate an analytical tool in evaluating cash flows (Appendix 7A).

Rite Aid's Bad Case of Cash Woes

HARRISBURG, PA–Rite Aid's financial problems began with an overly aggressive store construction and acquisition binge by former CEO Martin Grass that drained cash. As soon as Grass took over, he built more than 1,600 new stores, shelled out $1.4 billion for Thrifty PayLess, a 1,000-store West Coast chain that proved a drag on earnings, and paid $1.5 billion for pharmacy-benefits manager PCS Health Systems.

The fallout: for the next five years, Rite Aid's cash outflows for investing activities totaled $5 billion. At the same time, its cash inflows from operating activities totaled $800 million. This means Rite Aid financed most of its investments and working capital increases with debt–as reflected by a five-fold increase in total liabilities from $1,738 million to $9,393 million as of 2000.

The crushing debt load impacted the company's ability to obtain supplier credit for inventory purchases and strapped the company of much-needed cash for operating activities. Store sales suffered as a result of inventory shortages, reductions in advertising expenditures, and the inability to be price competitive. The consequent reduction in stock price also prohibited the company from selling common stock to refinance its debt and resulted in a downgrade in its credit rating.

Analysis of cash flows would have exposed these ills.

The company is now in turnaround mode under the leadership of its new CEO, Bob Miller. The company has sold the PCS Health Systems investment for a net cash inflow of $480 million that it used to reduce its indebtedness. It has also renegotiated store leases to allow them to be reclassified as operating, thereby reducing its on-balance-sheet lease liabilities by $850 million, and convinced many of its bond holders to accept common stock in exchange for approximately $580 million of indebtedness.

Analysis of cash flows would have exposed these potential ills. Adds T. D. Barrett, an analyst at Massachusetts Financial Services, "This company clearly got in way over its head." The prescription for Rite Aid's ills must include sensible checks on its excessive cash outflows for investing activities–checks that can be monitored by analysis of its statement of cash flows.

Source: Rite Aid website and 2002 10-K, and Business Week, *November 1999 and January 2000.*

PREVIEW OF CHAPTER 7

Cash is the residual balance from cash inflows *less* cash outflows for all prior periods of a company. Net cash flows, or simply *cash flows,* refers to the current period's cash inflows less cash outflows. Cash flows are different from accrual measures of performance. Cash flow measures recognize inflows when cash is received but not necessarily earned, and they recognize outflows when cash is paid but the expenses not necessarily incurred. The statement of cash flows reports cash flow measures for three primary business activities: operating,

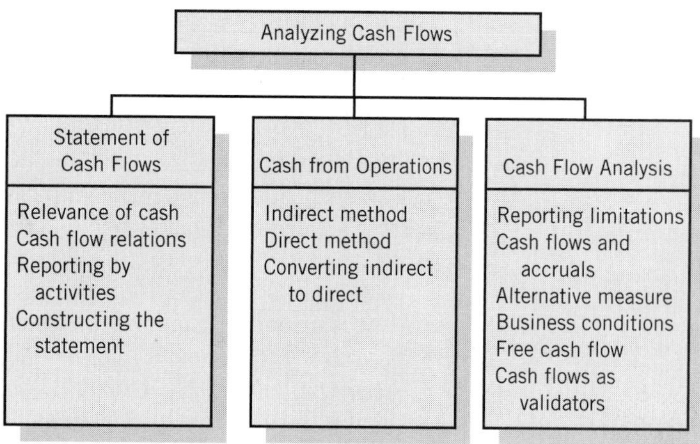

investing, and financing. Operating cash flows, or cash flows from operations, are the cash basis counterpart to accrual net income. More generally, information on cash flows helps us assess a company's ability to meet obligations, pay dividends, increase capacity, and raise financing. It also helps us assess the quality of earnings and the dependence of income on estimates and assumptions regarding future cash flows. This chapter describes cash flows and their relevance to analysis of financial statements. We describe current reporting requirements and their implications for analysis of cash flows. We explain useful analytical adjustments to cash flows using financial data. We direct special attention to transaction reconstruction, and to T-account and conversion analyses.

STATEMENT OF CASH FLOWS

The purpose of the statement of cash flows is to provide information on cash inflows and outflows for a period. It also distinguishes among the source and uses of cash flows by separating them into operating, investing, and financing activities. This section discusses important cash flow relations and the layout of the cash flow statement.

Relevance of Cash

Cash is the most liquid of assets and offers a company both liquidity and flexibility. It is both the beginning and the end of a company's operating cycle. A company's operating activities involve cash conversion into various assets (such as inventories) that are used to yield receivables from credit sales. The operating cycle is complete when the collection process returns cash to the company, enabling a new operating cycle to begin.

Our analysis of financial statements recognizes that accrual accounting, where companies recognize revenue when earned and expenses when incurred, differs from cash basis accounting. Yet net cash flow is the end measure of profitability. It is cash, not income, that ultimately repays loans, replaces equipment, expands facilities, and pays dividends. Accordingly, analyzing a company's cash inflows and outflows, and their operating, financing, or investing sources, is one of the most important investigative exercises. This analysis helps in assessing liquidity, solvency, and financial flexibility. **Liquidity** is the nearness to cash of assets and liabilities. **Solvency** is the ability to pay liabilities when they mature. **Financial flexibility** is the ability to react and adjust to opportunities and adversities.

Useful but incomplete information on sources and uses of cash is available from comparative balance sheets and income statements. However, a comprehensive picture of cash flows is derived from the **statement of cash flows** (SCF). This statement is important to analysis and provides information to help users address questions such as:

- How much cash is generated from or used in operations?
- What expenditures are made with cash from operations?
- How are dividends paid when confronting an operating loss?
- What is the source of cash for debt payments?
- What is the source of cash for redeeming preferred stock?
- How is the increase in investments financed?
- What is the source of cash for new plant assets?
- Why is cash lower when income increased?
- What is the use of cash received from new financing?

Users of financial statements analyze cash flow to answer these and many similar questions. The statement of cash flows is key to the reconstruction of many transactions, which is an important part of the analysis. Analysis of this statement requires our understanding of the accounting measures underlying its preparation and presentation. This chapter focuses first on these important accounting fundamentals and then on the analytical uses for the statement of cash flows.

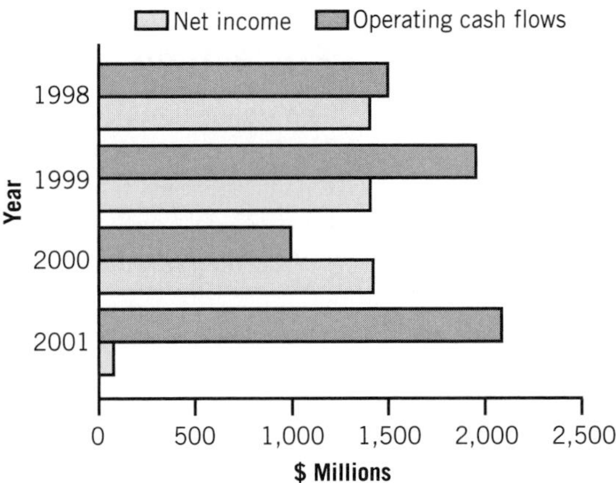

Reporting by Activities

The statement of cash flows reports cash receipts and cash payments by operating, financing, and investing activities–the primary business activities of a company.

Operating activities are the earning-related activities of a company. Beyond revenue and expense activities represented in an income statement, they include the net inflows and outflows of cash resulting from related operating activities like extending credit to customers, investing in inventories, and obtaining credit from suppliers. Operating activities relate to income statement items (with minor exceptions) and to balance sheet items relating to operations–usually working capital accounts like receivables, inventories, prepayments, payables, and accrued expenses. Practice also requires operating activities to include transactions and events that do not fit into investing or financing activities (such as settlements in lawsuits).

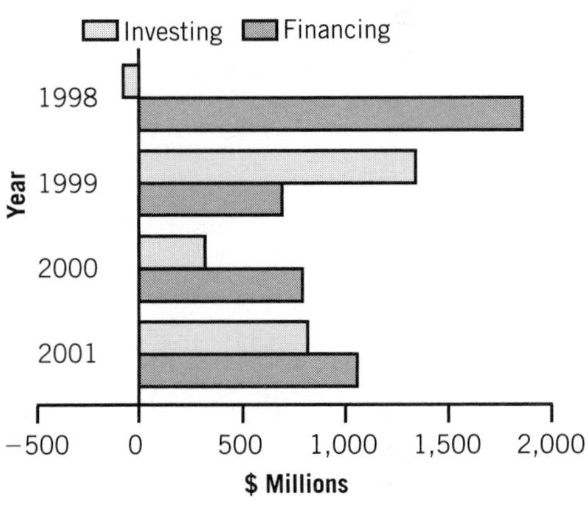

Investing activities are means of acquiring and disposing of noncash (and noncash equivalent) assets. These activities involve assets expected to generate income for a company. They also include lending funds and collecting the principal on these loans.

Financing activities are means of contributing, withdrawing, and servicing funds to support business activities. They include resources from creditors and repaying of principal amounts borrowed. They also include contributions and withdrawals by owners and their return (dividends) on investment. Major investing and financing activities not involving cash are reported separately in either narrative or summary form.

Constructing the Cash Flow Statement

There are two acceptable methods for reporting cash flows from operations (CFO): the indirect and direct methods. While both methods yield identical results, their format differs. With the **indirect method,** net income is adjusted for noncash income (expense) items and accruals to yield cash flows from operations. An advantage of this method is the disclosure of a reconciliation of differences between net income and operating cash flows. This can aid some users that predict cash flows by first predicting income and then adjusting income for leads and lags between income and cash flows–that is, using the noncash accruals. The indirect method is most commonly employed in practice and we use it initially to illustrate preparation of the statement of cash flows. Computation of the statement of cash flows using the **direct method** is provided subsequently for comparison. This method adjusts each income item for its related accruals and, arguably, provides a better format to assess the amount of operating cash inflows (outflows). The format for computing net cash provided by investing and financing activities is the same for both methods. Only the preparation of net cash flows from operations differs.

Preparation of the Statement of Cash Flows

The statement of cash flows is a blend of the income statement and the balance sheet. Net income is first adjusted for noncash income and expense items to yield cash profits which are, then, further adjusted for cash generated and used by balance sheet transactions to yield cash flows from operations, as well as investing and financing activities.

Consider first the net cash from operations. Its computation is as follows:

Net income
\+ Depreciation and amortization expense
± Gains (losses) on sales of assets
± Cash generated (used) by current assets and liabilities

Net cash flows from operating activities

The starting point for the statement of cash flows is net income which we first adjust for noncash depreciation and amortization expense. To better understand this add-back, consider that cash outflow occurs when tangible and intangible assets are purchased. The depreciation process, then, allocates that cost over their useful lives to match the expense against the revenues generated by those assets with the following accounting entries,

Depreciation expense	XXX	
Accumulated depreciation		XXX
Amortization expense	XXX	
Intangible asset		XXX

Since the statement of cash flows focuses on cash flows, we need to eliminate these noncash expenses that are recognized in the computation of net income, hence the add-back of depreciation and amortization expense. Adding depreciation and amortization expense does not increase operating cash flow, it merely zeros out the expense subtracted in the computation of net income. This can easily be seen by expanding net income as follows:

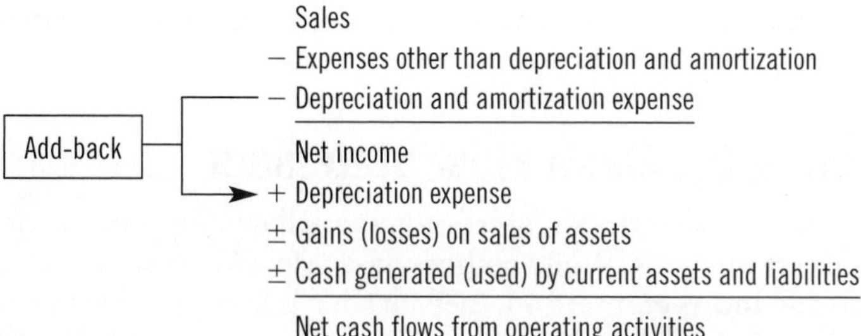

We also adjust net income for gains (losses) on the sales of assets in a similar fashion. The purpose of the adjustment, however, is not to eliminate these investment gains (losses) in their entirety, but to move them out of the operating section of the statement of cash flows. The cash inflows from the sales of these assets are reflected in net cash flows from investing activities.

The final adjustments involve analysis of cash generated and used by changes in current assets and liabilities. To see these effects, consider the simple example of a $100 sale on account:

Sales	100	
Accounts receivable		100

In the period of sale, net income is increased by $100, but no cash has been generated as the receivable has not yet been collected. The statement of cash flows at this point reports net income of $100 and net cash from operations of $0 as follows:

Net income	100
Depreciation and amortization expense	0
Gains (losses) on sale of assets	0
Change in accounts receivable	(100)
Net cash flow from operations	0

In the following period, the receivable is collected and the statement of cash flows looks like this:

Net income	0
Depreciation and amortization expense	0
Gains (losses) on sale of assets	0
Change in accounts receivable	100
Net cash flow from operations	100

The reduction in accounts receivable has generated a $100 cash inflow and is, therefore, reported as a positive amount in the statement of cash flows.

The adjustments for changes in balance sheet accounts can be summarized as follows:

	Increase	Decrease
Assets	(Outflow)	Inflow
Liabilities	Inflow	(Outflow)

Once net income has been adjusted for depreciation and amortization expense and gains (losses) on the sales of assets, the final step in the preparation of cash flows from operations is to examine changes in current assets (liabilities) and, using the matrix presented above, to reflect these changes as cash inflows (outflows), coded as positive (negative) amounts, respectively.

We now apply these concepts in the preparation of the statement of cash flows for Gould Corporation, whose balance sheet and income statement are presented in Exhibits 7.1 and 7.2, respectively. The following additional information about Gould for Year 2 is available:

1. The company purchased a truck during the year at a cost of $30,000 that was financed in full by the manufacturer.
2. A truck with a cost of $10,000 and a net book value of $2,000 was sold during the year for $7,000. There were no other sales of depreciable assets.
3. Dividends paid during the Year 2 are $51,000.

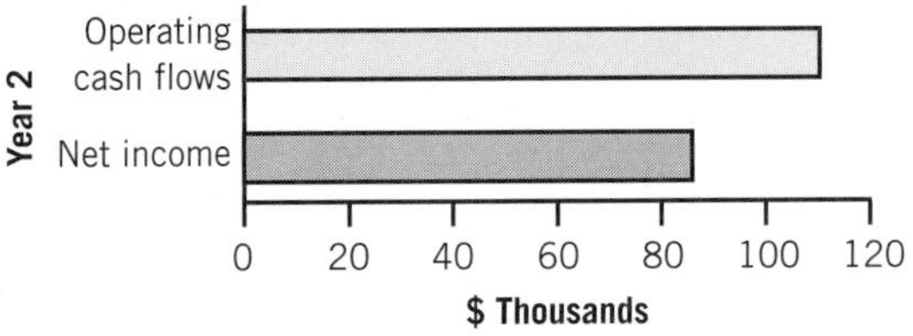

Gould's statement of cash flows is presented in Exhibit 7.3. The operating section begins with net income of $84,000, which is then adjusted for noncash depreciation and amortization expense. Next, the gain on sale of assets is subtracted to zero it out (the proceeds will be reflected in net cash flows from investing activities). Finally, changes in current assets and liabilities are reflected as

Exhibit 7.1

GOULD CORPORATION
Comparative Balance Sheet
As of December 31, Year 2

	Year 2	Year 1	Absolute Value of Change
Cash	$ 75,000	$ 51,000	$ 24,000
Receivables	48,000	39,000	9,000
Inventory	54,000	60,000	6,000
Prepaid expenses	6,000	9,000	3,000
Plant assets	440,000	350,000	90,000
Accumulated depreciation	(145,000)	(125,000)	20,000
Intangibles	51,000	58,000	7,000
	$529,000	$442,000	
Accounts payable	$ 51,000	$ 56,000	5,000
Accrued expenses	18,000	14,000	4,000
Long-term note payable	30,000	0	30,000
Mortgage payable	0	150,000	150,000
Preferred stock	175,000	0	175,000
Common stock	200,000	200,000	0
Retained earnings	55,000	22,000	33,000
	$529,000	$442,000	

Exhibit 7.2

GOULD CORPORATION
Income Statement
For the Year Ended December 31, Year 2

Sales	$660,000
Cost of sales	(363,000)
Gross profit	297,000
Operating expenses	(183,000)
Depreciation & intangibles amort.	(35,000)
Gain on sale of asset	5,000
Net income	$ 84,000

cash inflows (outflows) using the matrix presented above. Gould realized $113,000 in net cash flow from operations in Year 2.

Net cash flows from investing activities include purchases and sales of plant assets. Purchases can be inferred from the T-account for plant assets (PP&E):

Plant Assets

	Debit	Credit	
	350,000		
(p)	100,000	10,000	(s)
	440,000		

Exhibit 7.3

GOULD CORPORATION
Statement of Cash Flows
For the Year Ended December 31, Year 2

Net income	$ 84,000	
Add (deduct):		
Depreciation and amortization expense	35,000	
Gain on sale of assets	(5,000)	
Accounts receivable	(9,000)	
Inventories	6,000	
Prepaids	3,000	
Accounts payable	(5,000)	
Accrued expenses	4,000	
Net cash flow from operating activities		$113,000
Purchase of equipment	(70,000)	
Sale of equipment	7,000	
Net cash flows from investing activities		(63,000)
Mortgage payable	(150,000)	
Preferred stock	175,000	
Dividends	(51,000)	
Net cash flows from financing activities		(26,000)
Net increase in cash		24,000
Beginning cash		51,000
Ending cash		$ 75,000

Note: assets costing $30,000 were purchased during Year 2 and were financed in whole by the manufacturer.

Beginning with a balance of $350,000, PP&E was reduced by the cost of the asset sold (s). Net purchases (p), then, can be inferred as the amount necessary to yield the ending balance of $440,000. Of the $100,000 increase in PP&E, only $70,000 was paid in cash as the remainder was financed by the manufacturer. Thus, the $70,000 cash payment appears as purchases in the statement of cash flows. The $30,000 equipment purchase is a noncash investing and financing activity and is not reflected in the body of the statement of cash flows. Instead, it is referenced in an explanatory footnote.

The journal entry for the sale of the asset is:

Cash	7,000	
Accumulated depreciation	8,000	
Asset (cost)		10,000
Gain on sale		5,000

The gain on sale of $5,000 is deducted from net income to zero it out of the operating section and the $7,000 cash proceeds are reported in the investing section of the statement of cash flows. Net cash flows from investing activities reflect a net cash outflow of $(63,000).

Net cash flows from financing activities reflect changes in long-term liability and equity accounts. Here, the repayment of the mortgage ($150,000), issuance of preferred stock ($175,000) and payment of dividends ($51,000) are included. The net cash flows from financing activities reflect a net outflow of $(26,000).

The net change in cash is equal to the sum of the net cash flows from operations, investing, and financing activities:

Net cash flow from operations	$113,000
Net cash flows from investing activities	(63,000)
Net cash flows from financing activities	(26,000)
Net change in cash	24,000
Beginning cash (Year 1)	51,000
Ending cash (Year 2)	$ 75,000

The statement of cash flows also provides explanatory notes detailing any noncash investing and financing activities. In our example, this includes the purchase of a truck financed by the manufacturer.

ANALYSIS VIEWPOINT ***. . . YOU ARE THE BOARD MEMBER***

You are a school board member. Your district has received contributions from a publishing company to support educational programs. New management recently took control of the publishing company and reported a $1.2 million annual loss. Net cash flows were an equally dismal $1.1 million decrease—with reported decreases in investing and financing equaling $1.9 million and $0.7 million, respectively. The new management warns you that its contributions to educational programs are ending due to the company's financial distress, including this period's $1.3 million extraordinary loss. What is your course of action?

Answer–p. 403

Special Topics

This section presents several special circumstances that commonly arise in connection with the statement of cash flows and warrant discussion.

Equity Method Investments

Under equity method accounting, the investor records as income its percentage interest in the income of the investee company and records dividends received as a reduction of the investment balance (see Chapter 5). The portion of undistributed earnings, then, is noncash income and should be eliminated from the statement of cash flows, leaving only that portion of earnings that has been received in cash. This is accomplished by subtracting from net income the percentage interest in earnings of the investee company net of dividends received. For example, assume that Gould Corp. owns a 40% interest in Netcom Inc. Netcom reports net income of $100,000 and distributes $60,000 as dividends. Gould includes $40,000 ($100,000 × 40%) as equity earnings on its investment in its net income and reduces its investment balance by $24,000 (dividends received). The $16,000 of reported investment earnings not received in cash must be deducted from net income in computing net cash received from operations.

Acquisitions of Companies with Stock

When one company purchases another with stock, consolidated assets and liabilities increase together with equity accounts as discussed in Chapter 5. Only those changes in balance sheet accounts resulting from cash transactions, however, are reported in the statement of cash flows. As a result, the balance sheet adjustments reported to compute operating cash flows do not equal the changes in balance sheet accounts themselves. Instead, noncash changes in balance sheet accounts are reported in the notes to the statement of cash flows as noncash investing and financing activities, similar to the acquisition of the truck by Gould Corporation that was financed by the manufacturer in the example presented above.

Postretirement Benefit Costs

Pension and other post employment benefit plans accrue expense for service costs and interest, net of expected returns on plan assets, as discussed in Chapter 3. Benefits paid are recorded as a reduction in the investment balance and the liability. The excess of net benefit expense reported in net income over the cash benefits paid, then, must be added to net income in computing net cash flows from operating activities.

Securitization of Accounts Receivable

Companies are increasingly utilizing securitization of accounts receivable via SPEs as a method of improving cash flow (see Chapter 3). Securitization involves the transfer of receivables to a SPE that purchases them with the proceeds of bonds sold in the capital markets. Many companies account for the reduction in receivables as an increase in cash flow from operations since that relates to a current asset. Others, however, treat the cash inflows as a financing activity. Analysts need to be cognizant of the source of receivables reductions and question whether they represent true improvement in operating performance or a disguised borrowing.

Direct Method

The **direct** (or **inflow-outflow) method** reports gross cash receipts and cash disbursements related to operations–essentially adjusting each income statement item from accrual to cash basis. A majority of respondents to the accounting *Exposure Draft* preceding current requirements for reporting cash flows, especially creditors, preferred the direct method. The direct method reports total amounts of cash flowing in and out of a company from operating activities. This offers most analysts a better format to readily assess the amount of cash inflows and outflows for which management has discretion. The risks to lenders are typically greater for fluctuations in cash flows from operations vis-à-vis fluctuations in net income. Information on the individual amounts of operating cash receipts and payments is important in assessing such fluctuations and risks. These important analytical considerations at first convinced regulators to require the direct method of reporting cash flows. But partly because preparers of information claimed this method imposes excessive implementation costs, regulators decided to only encourage the direct method and to permit the indirect method. When companies report using the direct method, they must disclose a reconciliation of net income to cash flows from operations in a separate schedule. They also, at a minimum, must report the following cash receipts and payments:

Receipts

- Cash from customers, including lessees and licensees.
- Interest and dividend payments received.
- Other operating cash receipts, if any.

Payments

- Cash paid to employees and suppliers of goods or services, including suppliers of insurance and advertising.
- Interest paid.
- Income taxes paid.
- Other important operating cash payments, if any.

Converting from Indirect to Direct Method

We now show how to convert cash flows from operations reported under the indirect method to the direct method. Accuracy of conversion depends on adjustments using data available from external accounting records. The method of conversion we describe is sufficiently accurate for most analytical purposes.

Conversion from the indirect to the direct format is portrayed in Exhibit 7.4 using values from Gould Corporation. We begin by disaggregating net income ($84,000) into total revenues ($660,000) and total expenses ($576,000). Next, our conversion adjustments are applied to relevant categories of revenues or expenses. From these adjustments we report the direct format of Gould Corporation's cash flows from operations. The gain from sale of equipment (transferred to investing activities) is omitted from the direct method presentation.

Exhibit 7.4 ***Cash Flows from Operations Section***

GOULD CORPORATION
Cash Flows from Operations
For Year Ended December 31, Year 2
($ in thousands)

Cash flows from operating activities:	
Cash receipts from customers[a]	$651,000
Cash paid for inventories[b]	(362,000)
Cash paid for operating expenses[c]	(176,000)
Net cash flows from operations	$113,000

Computations
[a]Sales of $660,000 less increase in accounts receivables of $9,000.
[b]Cost of goods sold of $363,000 less decrease in inventories of $6,000 plus decrease in accounts payable of $5,000.
[c]General, selling, and administrative expenses of $218,000 less (noncash) depreciation and amortization of $35,000, less decrease in prepaid expenses of $3,000, less increase in accrued expenses of $4,000.

ANALYSIS VIEWPOINT ***. . . YOU ARE THE INVESTOR***

You are considering investing in D. C. Bionics. Earlier today D. C. Bionics announced a $6 million annual loss; however, net cash flows were a positive $10 million. How are these results possible?

Answer–p. 403

ANALYSIS IMPLICATIONS OF CASH FLOWS

Cash flow information yields several implications for our financial analysis. We discuss the more significant implications in this section.

Limitations in Cash Flow Reporting

The FASB argues that a "more comprehensive and presumably more useful approach would be to use the direct method in the statement of cash flows and to provide a reconciliation of net income and net cash flow from operating activities in a separate schedule–thereby reaping the benefit of both methods while maintaining the focus of the statement of cash flows in cash receipts and payments." Yet, it did *not* require the direct method. This is a limitation that we can in most cases overcome by restating the statement from the indirect format to the direct format.

Other limitations of cash flow reporting include:

- Practice does not require separate disclosure of cash flows pertaining to either extraordinary items or discontinued operations.
- Interest and dividends received and interest paid are classified as operating cash flows. Many users consider interest paid a financing outflow, and interest and dividends received as cash inflows from investing activities.
- Income taxes are classified as operating cash flows. This classification can distort analysis of the three individual activities if significant tax benefits or costs are attributed to them in a disproportionate manner.
- Removal of pretax (rather than after-tax) gains or losses on sale of plant or investments from operating activities distorts our analysis of both operating and investing activities. This is because their related taxes are *not* removed, but left in total tax expense among operating activities.

Interpreting Cash Flows and Net Income

Our analysis of Gould Corporation focused on the two primary financial statements directed to operating activities: the statement of cash flows and the income statement. In spite of practitioners' best efforts to explain the combined usefulness of both operating statements, not all users understand the dual information roles of cash flows and accrual net income. A recurrent misunderstanding among users is the meaning of *operations* and, also, the comparative relevance of cash flows and accrual net income in providing insights into operating activities. More simply, what different insights into operating activities do these two statements provide?

To help us understand their combined usefulness, we return to our analysis of Gould Corporation. Exhibit 7.5 lists amounts side by side from both operating statements and indicates their measurement objectives. We recognize the function of an income statement is to measure company profitability for a period. An income statement records revenues when earned and expenses when incurred. No other statement measures profitability in this manner. Yet an income statement does *not* show us the timing of cash inflows and outflows, nor the effect of operations on liquidity and solvency. This information is available to us in the statement of cash flows, shown separately for operating, investing, and financing activities.

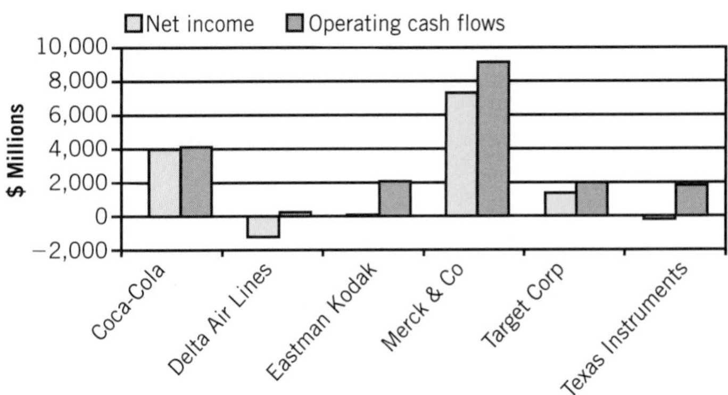

Cash flows from operations is a broader view of operating activities than is net income. Cash flows from operations encompass all earning-related activities of a company. This measure concerns not

Exhibit 7.5

GOULD CORPORATION

Comparison of Accrual and Cash Reporting

	Income Statement	Operating Cash Flows	
Sales	$660,000	$651,000	Cash collections from customers
Gain on sale of asset	5,000		
	665,000	651,000	Total cash collections
Cost of goods sold	(363,000)	(362,000)	Payments to suppliers
Operating expenses	(183,000)	(176,000)	Payments for expenses
Depreciation and amortization	(35,000)		
Net income	$ 84,000	$113,000	Cash from operations

only revenues and expenses but also the cash demands of these activities. They include investing in customer receivables and inventories, and the financing provided by suppliers of goods and services. This difference is evident in Exhibit 7.5 where we arrive at operating cash receipts and disbursements by analyzing changes in operating assets and liabilities to adjust income statement items. Cash flow from operations focuses on the liquidity aspect of operations. It is *not* a measure of profitability because it does not include important costs like the use of long-lived assets in operations nor revenues like the noncash equity in earnings of subsidiaries or nonconsolidated affiliates.

We must bear in mind that a *net* measure, be it net income or cash flows from operations, is of limited usefulness. Whether our purpose of analysis is evaluation of prior performance or prediction of future performance, the key is information about **components** of these net measures. Our discussion in Chapter 12 emphasizes our evaluation of operating performance, and future earning power depends not on net income but on its components.

Accounting accruals determining net income rely on estimates, deferrals, allocations, and valuations. These considerations sometimes allow more subjectivity than do the factors determining cash flows. For this reason we often relate cash flows from operations to net income in assessing its quality. Some users consider earnings of higher quality when the ratio of cash flows from operations divided by net income is greater. This

Analysis Research

USEFULNESS OF CASH FLOWS

Are cash flow measures useful for users of financial statements? Do cash flow measures offer any additional information beyond accrual measures? Do securities markets react to cash flow information? Analysis research provides valuable insights into these important questions. Several studies of users identify a market shift away from traditional accrual measures like net income in favor of cash flow measures. Cash flow measures are increasingly used for credit analysis, bankruptcy prediction, assigning loan terms, earnings quality assessments, solvency forecasts, and setting dividend and expansion policies. Users of these measures include investors, analysts, creditors, auditors, and management.

Capital market studies provide evidence consistent with the use of cash flow measures. Namely, cash flows from operations explain changes in stock prices beyond those explained by net income. Research also suggests the usefulness of cash flow measures depends on the company and economic conditions prevailing. Evidence indicates the *components* of cash flows, and not the aggregate figure, are what drive the usefulness of cash flow data.

derives from a concern with revenue recognition or expense accrual criteria yielding high net income but low cash flows. Cash flows from operations effectively serve as a check on net income, but not a substitute for net income. Cash flows from operations include a financing element and are useful for evaluating and projecting both short-term liquidity and longer-term solvency.

Cash flows from operations exclude, by definition, elements of revenues and expenses not currently affecting cash. Our analysis of operations and profitability should not proceed without considering these elements. Both the income statement and the statement of cash flows are designed to meet different needs of users. The income statement uses accrual accounting in recognizing revenues earned and expenses incurred. Cash flows from operations report revenues received in cash and expenses paid. It is not an issue of which statement is superior to another–only a matter of our immediate analysis needs. Our use of these statements requires that we bear in mind the statements' objectives and limitations.

ANALYSIS EXCERPT

Coca-Cola recently marketed a large initial share offering, not on the basis of traditional measures like price-earnings ratio (which was near 100), but on the basis of operating cash flows (specifically, earnings before taxes, depreciation, interest, and goodwill amortization). This latter measure substantially exceeded net income that was depressed due to heavy noncash charges.

ANALYSIS OF CASH FLOWS

Since conditions vary from company to company, it is difficult to formulate a standard analysis of cash flows. Nevertheless, certain commonalities exist. First, our analysis must establish the major past sources of cash and their uses. A common-size analysis of the statement of cash flows aids in this assessment. In estimating trends, it is useful to total the major sources and uses of cash over a period of a few years since annual or quarterly reporting periods are often too short for meaningful inferences. For example, financing of major projects often spans several years. In evaluating sources and uses of cash, the analyst should focus on questions like:

- Are asset replacements financed from internal or external funds?
- What are the financing sources of expansion and business acquisitions?
- Is the company dependent on external financing?
- What are the company's investing demands and opportunities?
- What are the requirements and types of financing?
- Are managerial policies (such as dividends) highly sensitive to cash flows?

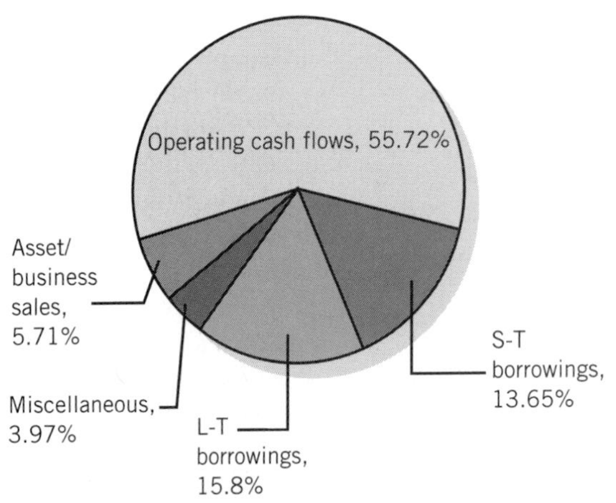

Case Analysis of Cash Flows of Campbell Soup

We illustrate the analysis of prior years' statements of cash flows for Campbell Soup Company in the Comprehensive Case following Chapter 12. Our analysis covers the six-year period ending July 28, Year 11. Exhibit CC.10 presents these statements in common-size format.

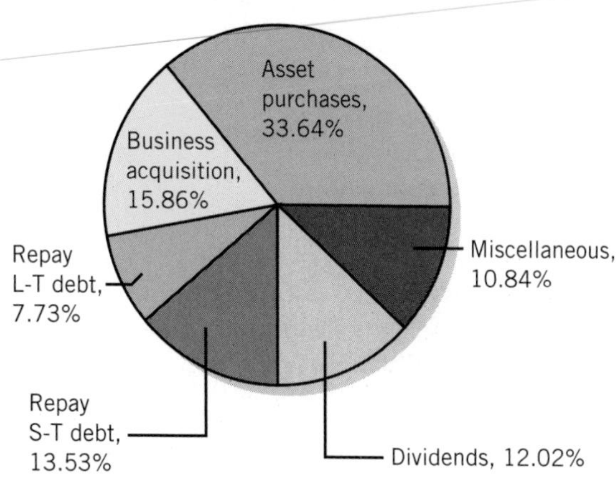

Our analysis of these statements reveals several insights. During this six-year period the major sources of cash are operations ($3,010 million), long-term debt ($854 million), and short-term debt ($737 million)—see Exhibit CC.4 and Campbell's statements in Appendix A. Major uses are plant purchases (net of sales) of $1,647 million, business acquisitions (net of sales) of $718 million, and cash dividends of $649 million. During this six-year period, cash and cash equivalents increased by $24 million. Sources of cash from operations as a percentage of total sources average 55.7%, with a low of 31.3% in Year 9—see Exhibit CC.10. Year 11 is the most profitable of the six, reflecting a recovery after two years of poor performance and restructuring activities. For this six-year period, cash from operations covered net cash used in investing activities and nearly all dividends paid. Cash flows are partially insulated from the sharp declines in earnings for Years 9 and 10 because restructuring charges of $682 million involved no cash outlays.

Inferences from Analysis of Cash Flows

The Campbell Soup case illustrates the range of useful insights drawn from this analysis. An overall analysis of financial statements then either corroborates or refutes the inferences from the analysis of cash flows.

There are useful generalizations we can make about potential inferences from analysis of the statement of cash flows. First, our analysis of the statement of cash flows enables us to appraise the quality of management's decisions over time and their impact on the company's results of operations and financial position. When our analysis covers a long time period, it can yield insights into management's success in responding to changing business conditions and their ability to seize opportunities and overcome adversities.

Inferences from our analysis of cash flows include where management committed its resources, where it reduced investments, where additional cash was derived from, and where claims against the company were reduced. Inferences also pertain to the disposition of earnings and the investment of discretionary cash flows. Analysis also enables us to infer the size, composition, pattern, and stability of operating cash flows.

We previously described patterns of cash flows through a company. Cash flows are used for labor, material, and overhead. They are also used for long-term assets like plant and equipment where conversion through the product-cost stream is at a slower rate. Eventually, all uses of cash enter the sales process and are converted into receivables or cash. Profitable operations yield cash recoveries exceeding amounts invested and, consequently, increase cash inflows. Losses yield a reverse effect.

Inferences must also include explanations for the variation in cash flow segmentation. Most view operating cash flows as an index of management's ability to redirect funds away from unprofitable opportunities to those of greater profit potential. Yet not all operating cash flows can be so judged because of commitments for items like debt retirements, stock redemptions, equipment replacements, and dividend payments. Nor are operating cash flows the only potential inflow since management can draw on external financing sources. We must also examine the components of operating cash flows. Components often hold important clues about the stability of cash sources. For example, depreciation is a stable component representing a "recovery" of investments in fixed assets from sales. Cash recovered from depreciation is normally reinvested in maintaining productive assets.

Our inferences from analysis of cash flows include earnings quality assessments. One factor in the quality of earnings is the impact of changes in business conditions for cash flows. The statement of cash flows also reveals noncash income components bearing on our inferences of earnings quality. Inferences can involve assessments of future earnings potential implying demands for additional financing. Our analysis of the statement of cash flows can provide us insights into likely sources of this needed cash and its potential impacts, including any dilution of earnings per share.

Alternative Cash Flow Measures

Accrual accounting permits a variety of alternative accounting treatments and the potential for earnings management. Users sometimes use a crude measure of cash flows, defined as **net income plus major noncash expenses** (typically depreciation and amortization), to bypass these influences. This crude measure fails to provide for several important elements of cash flows and is an unreliable surrogate for cash flows. There is, however, at least one legitimate use of this measure–preferably these numbers are tax adjusted. Comparisons using this measure avoid differences arising from dissimilar depreciation methods and inconsistencies in estimates (useful life, salvage value).

The usefulness of this measure is demonstrated in the following case. Assume two companies (A and B) each invest $50,000 in machinery yielding $45,000 per year cash flows before depreciation. Assuming a five-year useful life and no salvage value for the machinery, results for the entire five-year period are:

	Five-Year Period
Cash provided by operations ($45,000 × 5 years)	$225,000
Cost of the machine	(50,000)
Income from operating machine	175,000
Average yearly net income	$ 35,000

Under accrual accounting, the $175,000 five-year income is reported differently depending on the depreciation method adopted. Assuming company A adopts straight-line depreciation and company B adopts sum-of-the-years'-digits depreciation, annual income before and after depreciation (ignoring taxes) is:

		COMPANY A: STRAIGHT-LINE DEPRECIATION		COMPANY B: SUM-OF-THE-YEARS'-DIGITS DEPRECIATION	
Year	Income before Depreciation	Depreciation	Net Income	Depreciation	Net Income
1	$ 45,000	$10,000	$ 35,000	$16,667	$ 28,333
2	45,000	10,000	35,000	13,334	31,666
3	45,000	10,000	35,000	10,000	35,000
4	45,000	10,000	35,000	6,667	38,333
5	45,000	10,000	35,000	3,332	41,668
Total	$225,000	$50,000	$175,000	$50,000	$175,000

Income before depreciation (or the "crude" cash flows measure) for these two companies is identical. This faithfully reveals identical earning power. However, income after depreciation, while identical for the entire five-year period, is considerably different for individual years. Accordingly, income before depreciation is a useful analytical tool provided we know its relevance and recognize its limitations.

Usefulness of cash flows is sometimes harmed by its misuse. Management dissatisfied with the reported income occasionally asserts cash flows are a better measure of performance. This is like asserting depreciation, or any costs not requiring immediate use of cash, are not genuine. When asked about cash flow measures, value-based investor Warren Buffett replied:

ANALYSIS EXCERPT

We believe those numbers are frequently used by marketers of businesses and securities in attempts to justify the unjustifiable; and thereby to sell what should be unsalable.

Net income is properly regarded as our measure of operating performance and is consistently linked with equity. If we add back depreciation to net income and compute return on investment, we are also in effect confusing the return *on* investment with return *of* investment in fixed assets. We should also realize that with inflation the depreciation allocated to sales is not likely to be sufficient for asset replacement because costs are probably higher. The primary source of cash from operations is sales to customers. It is from sales that companies pay expenses and make profits. If sales are insufficient to cover cash and accrual expenses, depreciation is not entirely covered.

Company and Economic Conditions

A balance sheet describes the assets of a company at a point in time and the manner in which those assets are financed. An income statement portrays the results of operations for a period of time. Income increases assets, including cash and noncash (both current and noncurrent) assets. Expenses are the consumption of assets (or incurrence of liabilities). Accordingly, net income is linked to cash flows through adjustments in balance sheet accounts.

It is conceivable that a profitable company can find it difficult to meet current obligations and need cash for expansion. Success through increasing sales can yield liquidity problems and restrict cash due to a growing asset base. Accordingly, there might be insufficient cash to cover maturing obligations. It is also important for us to distinguish performance across business activities. It is especially important to separate operating performance and profitability from those of investing and financing activities. All activities are essential and interconnected, but they are not identical and reflect on different aspects of a company. A statement of cash flows reveals the implications of earnings activities for cash. It reveals assets acquired and how they are financed. It describes how net income and cash flows from operations are different. The ability to generate cash flows from operations is vital to financial health. No business survives in the long run without generating cash from operations. Yet we must interpret cash flows and trends with care and an understanding of economic conditions.

CLEAR CARDS
Several companies, including Reliance Insurance and Western Union, have issued the new Clear Cards as a benefit to employees. When employees buy items with their Clear Cards, the cost is automatically deducted from their paychecks. Credit is normally limited to 2.5% of their salaries, no interest is charged, and employees pay a $29 annual fee.

While both successful and unsuccessful companies can experience problems with cash flows from operations, the reasons are markedly different. A successful company confronting increasing investments in receivables and inventories to meet expanding customer demand often finds its growing profitability useful in obtaining additional financing from both debt and equity suppliers. This profitability (positive accrual income) ultimately yields positive cash flows. An unsuccessful company experiences cash shortages from slowdowns in receivable and inventory turnovers, losses in operations, or combinations of these and other factors. The unsuccessful company can increase cash flows by reducing receivables and inventories, but usually this is done at the expense of services to customers, further depressing profits. These factors are signs of current and future crises and cash shortages, including declining trade credit. Decreasing cash flows for an unsuccessful company have entirely different implications than they do for a successful one. Even if an unsuccessful manager borrows money, the costs and results of borrowing only magnify the ultimate loss. Profitability is our key variable; without it a company is doomed to failure.

We must also interpret changes in operating working capital items in light of economic circumstances. An increase in receivables can imply expanding consumer demand for products or it can signal an inability to collect amounts due in a timely fashion. Similarly, an increase in inventories (and particularly of raw materials) can imply anticipation of increases in production in response to consumer demand, or it can imply an inability to accurately anticipate demand or sell products (especially if finished goods inventory is increased).

Inflationary conditions add to the financial burdens and challenges of companies. The more significant challenges include replacing plant assets at costs exceeding depreciation expense, increasing investments in inventories and receivables, and dividend policies based on profits that do not provide for current costs of resources used in operations. While managerial decisions are not necessarily based on financial statements, we cannot dismiss their importance and implications. We look to the statement of cash flows for information on the effects, in current dollars, of how management copes under inflationary conditions. This yields a focus on cash flows from operations after capital expenditures and dividends.

Free Cash Flow

A useful analytical derivative of the statement of cash flows in the computation of **free cash flow.** As with other analytical measures, we must pay attention to components of the computation. Ulterior motives in reporting the components used in computing free cash flow can sometimes affect its usefulness. While there is not agreement on its exact definition, one of the more useful measures of free cash flow is:

Cash flows from operations
− Net capital expenditures required to maintain productive capacity
− Dividends on preferred stock and common stock (assuming a payout policy)

Free cash flow (FCF)

Positive free cash flow reflects the amount available for business activities after allowances for financing and investing requirements to maintain productive capacity at current levels. Growth and financial flexibility depend on adequate free cash flow. We must recognize that the amount of capital expenditures needed to maintain productive capacity is generally not disclosed. Rather it is part of total capital expenditures, which are disclosed, but can include outlays for expansion of productive capacity. Separating capital expenditures between these two components is problematic. The statement of cash flows rarely separates capital expenditures into maintenance and expansion components.

ANALYSIS VIEWPOINT ***. . . YOU ARE THE CREDIT ANALYST***

You are a credit analyst at a credit-rating agency for industrial companies. A company you are rating has a strong history of positive (1) net cash flows and (2) cash flows from operations. However, its free cash flow has recently turned negative and you expect it to remain negative into the foreseeable future. Do you change your credit rating of the company?

Answer–p. 403

Cash Flows as Validators

The statement of cash flows is useful for prediction of operating results on the basis of acquired and planned productive capacity. It is also of use in assessment of a company's future expansion capacity, its capital requirements, and its sources of cash inflows. The statement of cash flows is an essential bridge between the income statement and the balance sheet. It reports a company's cash inflows and outflows, and a company's ability to meet current obligations. Moreover, the statement of cash flows provides us with important clues on:

- Feasibility of financing capital expenditures.
- Cash sources in financing expansion.
- Dependence on external financing (liabilities versus equity).
- Future dividend policies.
- Ability in meeting debt service requirements.
- Financial flexibility to unanticipated needs and opportunities.
- Financial practices of management.
- Quality of earnings.

The statement of cash flows is useful in identifying misleading or erroneous operating results or expectations. Further discussion of earnings quality and the usefulness of cash flows as validators appears in Chapter 12. Nevertheless, like other statements, the statement of cash flows is a reliable and credible source of a company's actions and intentions–more so than are predictions and press releases of management.

We must take care to examine relations among items in a statement of cash flows. Certain transactions are related–for example, purchasing assets by issuing debt. Yet our analysis must be careful not to infer relations among items where none exist. A change in cash, whether positive or negative, cannot be judged solely by the statement of cash flows. It must be analyzed in relation to other variables in a company's financial structure and operating results. For example, an increase in cash can arise from sacrificing a company's future earning power by selling valuable assets, or by taking on debt at high costs or unfavorable terms. Relations among financial statement items and their implications are important for the reliability of our analysis.

SPECIALIZED CASH FLOW RATIOS

The following two ratios are often useful in analyzing a firm's flow of funds.

Cash Flow Adequacy Ratio

The **cash flow adequacy ratio** is a measure of a company's ability to generate sufficient cash from operations to cover capital expenditures, investments in inventories, and cash dividends. To remove cyclical and other random influences, a three-year total is typically used in computing this ratio. The cash flow adequacy ratio is calculated as:

$$\frac{\text{Three-year sum of cash from operations}}{\text{Three-year sum of capital expenditures, inventory additions, and cash dividends}}$$

Investment in other important working capital items like receivables is omitted because they are financed primarily by short-term credit (such as growth in accounts payable). Accordingly, only additions to inventories are included. Note in years where inventories decline, the downward change is treated as a zero change in computing the ratio. Using the financial statement data from Campbell Soup Company in Appendix A, we compute its (three-year) cash flow adequacy ratio as:

$$\frac{\$1,610.9^{(a)}}{\$1,390.3^{(b)} + \$113.2^{(c)} + \$348.5^{(d)}} = 0.87$$

[a]Cash from operations–item 64.
[b]Property additions–items 65 and 67.
[c]Inventory additions–item 62.
[d]Cash dividends–item 77.

Proper interpretation of the cash flow adequacy ratio is important. A ratio of 1 indicates the company exactly covered these cash needs without a need for external financing. A ratio below 1 suggests internal cash sources were insufficient to maintain dividends and current operating growth levels. For Campbell Soup Company, the ratio indicates that for the three years ending in Year 11, Campbell's operating cash flows fell short of covering dividends and operating growth. While not illustrated here, if we compute a six-year ratio, a more favorable ratio emerges. The cash flow adequacy ratio also reflects on the inflationary effects for funding requirements of a company. As with other analyses, inferences drawn from this ratio should be supported with further analysis and investigation.

Cash Reinvestment Ratio

The **cash reinvestment ratio** is a measure of the percentage of investment in assets representing operating cash retained and reinvested in the company for both replacing assets and growth in operations. This ratio is computed as:

$$\frac{\text{Operating cash flow} - \text{Dividends}}{\text{Gross plant} + \text{Investment} + \text{Other assets} + \text{Working capital}}$$

A reinvestment ratio in the area of 7% to 11% is generally considered satisfactory. Using the financial statements of Campbell Soup Company, we compute the cash reinvestment ratio for Year 11:

$$\frac{\$805.2^{(e)} - \$137.5^{(f)}}{(\$2,921.9 + \$477.6)^{(g)} + 404.6^{(h)} + (\$1,518.5 - \$1,278.0)^{(i)}} = 16.5\%$$

[e]Cash from operations–item 64.
[f]Cash dividends–item 77.
[g]Gross plant assets–items 158 thru 161; plus: intangibles–items 163 and 164.
[h]Other assets–item 39.
[i]Total current assets–item 36; less: total current liabilities–item 45.

APPENDIX 7A ANALYTICAL CASH FLOW WORKSHEET

This appendix provides a usable worksheet to facilitate the conversion of financial data to the direct (inflow-outflow) format for cash flows from operations. We often desire to convert a company's indirect format for cash flows from operations to an analytically more useful direct format. Exhibit 7A.1 displays a worksheet designed to simplify this conversion.

Exhibit 7A.1

WORKSHEET TO COMPUTE CASH FLOW FROM OPERATIONS (CFO)

Direct Presentation ($ in ______________)
Company: ______________
Year Ended ______________

		YEAR		
		______	______	______
Cash receipts from operations:				
Net sales and revenues[(a)]	*1	$	$	$
Other revenue and income (see also lines 22 and 25)	*2			
(I) D in current receivables	3			
(I) D in noncurrent receivables[(b)]	4			
Other adjustments[(c)]	5			
Total cash receipts	6			
Cash disbursements for operations:				
Total expenses (include interest and taxes)[(a)]	*7			
Less expenses and losses not using cash:				
Depreciation and amortization	8			
Noncurrent deferred income taxes	9			
Other ______	10			
Other ______	11			
Other ______	12			
Changes in current operating assets and liabilities:				
I (D) in inventories	13			
I (D) in prepaid expenses	14			
(I) D in accounts payable	15			
(I) D in taxes payable	16			
(I) D in accruals	17			
I or D other ______	18			
I or D other ______	19			
I or D in noncurrent accounts[(b)]	20			
Total cash disbursements[(d)]	21			
Dividends received:				
Equity in income of unconsolidated affiliates	*22			
Less Undistributed equity in income of affiliates	23			
Dividends from unconsolidated affiliates	24			
Other cash receipts (disbursements) [(e)]	*25			
Describe ______________ [(a)]	25			
______________ [(a)]	25			
Total cash flow from operations[(f)]	26			

Footnote all amounts that are composites or that are not self-evident. Indicate all sources for figures. I(D) refers to increases (decreases) in accounts.

* *The sum of the five lines denoted by asterisks must equal reported net income per income statement.*

[(a)] *Including adjustment (grossing up) of revenue and expense of discontinued operations disclosed in footnote(s). Describe computation. Include other required adjustments and explain.*

[(b)] *That relating to operations—describe in notes.*

[(c)] *Such as removal of gains included above—describe in notes.*

[(d)] *That include (from supplemental disclosures):*

Cash paid for interest (net of amount capitalized)	$______	______	______
Cash paid for income taxes	$______	______	______

[(e)] *These include extraordinary items, discontinued operations, and any other item not included above. The amount in line 25 is after adjustment to cash basis while the * refers to item(s) included in income before such adjustment. (Present details in notes.)*

[(f)] *Reconcile to amount reported by company. If not reported, reconcile to change in cash for period along with investing and financing activities.*

GUIDANCE ANSWERS TO ANALYSIS VIEWPOINTS

Board Member

Your initial course of action is to verify management's claim of financial distress. A $1.2 million loss along with a $1.1 million decrease in net cash flows seemingly supports their claim. However, you should be suspicious of management's motives and its aversion to community activism. Consequently, you scrutinize the financial results, and your findings reveal a markedly different picture. You note cash flows from operations increased $1.5 million (−$1.1 = CFO − $1.9 − $0.7). You note that net income *before* the extraordinary loss is a positive $100,000. This is sufficient and powerful information with which to confront management. A serious and directed discussion is likely to yield reconsideration of this company's support of your educational programs.

Investor

Several factors can account for an increase in net cash flows when a loss is reported. Possibilities include: (1) early recognition of expenses relative to revenues generated (such as research and development), (2) valuable long-term sales contracts not yet recognized in income, (3) issuances of debt or equity to finance expansion, (4) selling of assets, (5) delayed cash payments, and (6) prepayment on sales. Our analysis of D.C. Bionics needs to focus on the components of both net income and net cash flows, and their implications for future performance.

Credit Analyst

The downward turn in free cash flow is an ominous sign. Free cash flow is the cash remaining after providing for commitments necessary to maintain operations at current levels. These commitments include a company's continuing operations, interest payments, income taxes, net capital expenditures, and dividends. A negative free cash flow implies a company must either sell assets or acquire financing (debt or equity) to maintain current operations. A significant change in free cash flow must be seriously scrutinized in assigning a new credit rating.

[Superscript ^{A} denotes assignments based on Appendix 7A.]

QUESTIONS

7–1 What is the meaning of the term *cash flow?* Why is this term subject to confusion and misrepresentation?

7–2 What information can a user of financial statements obtain from the statement of cash flows?

7–3 Describe the three major activities the statement of cash flows reports. Cite examples of cash flows for each activity.

7–4 Explain the three categories of adjustments in converting net income to cash flows from operations.

7–5 Describe the two methods of reporting cash flow from operations.

7–6 Contrast the purpose of the income statement with that of cash flow from operations.

7–7 Discuss the importance to analysis of the statement of cash flows. Identify factors entering into the interpretation of cash flows from operations.

7–8 Describe the computation of free cash flow. What is its relevance to financial analysis?

7–9 List insights that the statement of cash flows can provide to our analysis.

EXERCISES

EXERCISE 7–1
Interpreting Differences between Income and Cash from Operations

Campbell Soup Company

Refer to the financial statements of **Campbell Soup Company** in Appendix A.

Required:

Explain how Campbell Soup Company can have net income of $401.5 million, but generate $805.2 million in cash from operations in Year 11. Explain this in language understood by a general businessperson. Illustrate your explanation by reference to the major reconciling items.

EXERCISE 7–2
Relations in the Statement of Cash Flows

It is important that an analyst understand the activities that comprise the statement of cash flows, including the disclosure of their individual elements.

Required:

a. Practice requires the classification of cash inflows and outflows into three categories. Identify and describe those categories.

b. Which noncash activities are reported in the statement of cash flows and how are they reported?

c. Assume First Corporation retains you to consult with them on preparation of the statement of cash flows using the indirect method for the year ended December 31, Year 8. Advise them on how the following separate items affect the statement of cash flows and how they are shown on the statement:
(1) Net income for the fiscal year is $950,000, including an extraordinary gain of $60,000.
(2) Depreciation expense of $80,000 is included in the income statement.
(3) Uncollectible accounts receivable of $50,000 are written off against the allowance for uncollectible accounts. Bad debts expense of $24,000 is included in determining earnings for the year, and the same $24,000 amount is added to the allowance for uncollectible accounts.
(4) Accounts receivable increase by $140,000 during the year and inventories decline by $60,000.
(5) Taxes paid to governments amount to $380,000.
(6) A gain of $5,000 is realized on the sale of a machine; it originally cost $75,000 and $25,000 is undepreciated on the date of sale.
(7) On June 5, Year 8, buildings and land are purchased for $600,000; First Corp. gave in payment $100,000 cash, $200,000 in market value of its unissued common stock, and a $300,000 mortgage note.
(8) On August 8, Year 8, First Corp. converts $700,000 face value of its 6 percent convertible debentures into $140,000 par value of its common stock. The bonds are originally issued at face value.
(9) The board of directors declares a $320,000 cash dividend on October 30, Year 8, payable on January 15, Year 9, to stockholders of record on November 15, Year 8.
(10) On December 15, Year 8, First Corp. declares a 2-for-1 stock split payable on December 25, Year 8.

EXERCISE 7–3
Analyzing Operating Cash Flows

The following data are taken from the records of Saro Corporation and subsidiaries for Year 1:

Net income	$10,000
Depreciation, depletion, and amortization	8,000
Disposals of property, plant, and equipment (book value) for cash	1,000
Deferred income taxes for Year 1 (noncurrent)	400
Undistributed earnings of unconsolidated affiliates	200
Amortization of discount on bonds payable	50
Amortization of premium on bonds payable	60
Decrease in noncurrent assets	1,500
Cash proceeds from exercise of stock options	300
Increase in accounts receivable	900
Increase in accounts payable	1,200
Decrease in inventories	850
Increase in dividends payable	300
Decrease in notes payable to banks	400

Required:

a. Determine the amount of cash flows from operations for Year 1 (use the indirect format).

CHECK
CFO, $19,340

b. For the following items, explain their meaning and implications, if any, in adjusting net income to arrive at cash flows from operations.
(1) Issuance of treasury stock as employee compensation.
(2) Capitalization of interest incurred.
(3) Amount charged to pension expense differing from the amount funded.

EXERCISE 7–4
Deriving Cash Flows from Financial Statements

The balance sheets of Barrier Corporation as of December 31, Year 2, and Year 1, and its statement of income and retained earnings for the year ended December 31, Year 2, follow:

BARRIER CORPORATION
Balance Sheets
As of December 31, Year 2 and Year 1

	Year 2	Year 1	Increase (decrease)
Assets			
Cash	$ 275,000	$ 180,000	$ 95,000
Accounts receivable	295,000	305,000	(10,000)
Inventories	549,000	431,000	118,000
Investment in Ort Inc., at equity	73,000	60,000	13,000
Land	350,000	200,000	150,000
Plant and equipment	624,000	606,000	18,000
Less: accumulated depreciation	(139,000)	(107,000)	(32,000)
Goodwill	16,000	20,000	(4,000)
Total assets	$2,043,000	$1,695,000	$348,000
Liabilities and Stockholders' Equity			
Accounts payable	$ 604,000	$ 563,000	$ 41,000
Accrued expenses	150,000	—	150,000
Bonds payable	160,000	210,000	(50,000)
Deferred income taxes	41,000	30,000	11,000
Common stock, par $10	430,000	400,000	30,000
Additional paid-in capital	226,000	175,000	51,000
Retained earnings	432,000	334,000	98,000
Treasury stock, at cost	—	(17,000)	17,000
Total liabilities and equity	$2,043,000	$1,695,000	$348,000

BARRIER CORPORATION
Statement of Income and Retained Earnings
For Year Ended December 31, Year 2

Net sales		$1,937,000
Undistributed income from Ort Inc.		13,000
Total net revenue		$1,950,000
Cost of sales		(1,150,000)
Gross income		$ 800,000
Depreciation expense	$ 32,000	
Amortization of goodwill	4,000	
Other expenses (including income taxes)	623,000	(659,000)
Net income		$ 141,000
Retained earnings, January 1, Year 2		334,000
		$ 475,000
Cash dividends paid		(43,000)
Retained earnings, December 31, Year 2		$ 432,000

Additional information:

- Capital stock is issued to provide additional cash.
- All accounts receivable and payable relate to operations.
- Accounts payable relate only to items included in cost of sales.
- There are no noncash transactions.

Required:

Determine the following amounts:

CHECK
(b) $1,227,000

a. Cash collected from sales during Year 2.

b. Cash payments on accounts payable during Year 2.

c. Cash receipts during Year 2 *not* provided by operations.

d. Cash payments for noncurrent assets purchased during Year 2.

EXERCISE 7–5
Interpreting Cash Flows

Indicate if each transaction and event is (1) a source of cash, (2) a use of cash, and/or (3) an adjustment leading to a source or use of cash (assume an indirect format). List also its placement in the statement of cash flows: operations (O), financing (F), investing (I), noncash significant (NCS), noncash nonsignificant (NCN), or no effect (NE).

Example

Transaction or Event	Source	Use	Adjustment	Category in Statement of Cash Flows
Cash dividend received	X			0

a. Increase in accounts receivable.

b. Pay bank note.

c. Issue common stock.

d. Sell marketable securities.

e. Retire bonds.

f. Declare stock dividend.

g. Purchase equipment.

h. Convert bonds to preferred stock.

i. Pay dividend.

j. Increase in accounts payable.

EXERCISE 7–6
Interpreting Cash Flows

Indicate if each transaction and event is (1) a source of cash, (2) a use of cash, and/or (3) an adjustment leading to a source or use of cash (assume an indirect format). List also its placement in the statement of cash flows: operations (O), financing (F), investing (I), noncash significant (NCS), noncash nonsignificant (NCN), or no effect (NE).

Example

Transaction or Event	Source	Use	Adjustment	Category in Statement of Cash Flows
Issue bonds for cash	X			F

a. Decrease in inventory.

b. Paid current portion of long-term debt.

c. Retire treasury stock.

d. Purchase marketable securities (noncurrent).

e. Issue bonds for property.

f. Declare stock dividend.

g. Sell equipment for cash.

h. Convert bonds to preferred stock.

i. Purchase inventory on credit.

j. Decrease in accounts payable from return of merchandise.

EXERCISE 7–7
Interpreting Economic Impacts of Transactions

During a meeting of the management committee of Edsel Corporation, a number of proposals are made to alleviate its weak cash position and improve income. Evaluate and comment on both the immediate *and* long-term effects of the following proposals on the measures indicated. Indicate increase (+), decrease (−), or no effect (NE).

	EFFECT ON		
Proposal	**Net Income**	**Cash from Operations**	**Cash Position**
1. Substitute stock dividends for cash dividends.			
2. Delay needed capital expenditures.			
3. Reduce repair and maintenance outlays.			
4. Increase the provision for depreciation:			
a. For GAAP books only.			
b. For tax only.			
c. For both GAAP books and tax.			
5. Require earlier payment from clients.			
6. Delay payment to suppliers and pass up cash discounts.			
7. Borrow money short term.			
8. Switch from sum-of-the-years'-digits to straight-line depreciation for books only.			
9. Pressure dealers to buy more.			
10. Reduce funding of pension plan to the minimum legal level.			
11. Reduce inventories by implementing a just-in-time inventory system.			
12. Sell trading securities that have declined by $1,000 in the current period but are still valued at $3,000 above cost.			
13. Reissue treasury shares.			

CHECK
(12) −, NE, +

EXERCISE 7–8
Depreciation as a Source of Cash

An economics book has the following statement: "For the business firm there are, typically, three major sources of funds. Two of these, depreciation reserves and retained earnings, are internal. The third is external, consisting of funds obtained either by borrowing, or by the sale of new equities."

Required:

a. Is depreciation a source of cash? (Exclude all considerations pertaining to depreciation differences between taxable income and accounting income.)

b. If depreciation is not a source of cash, what might explain the belief by some that depreciation is a source of cash?

c. If depreciation is a source of cash, explain the manner in which depreciation provides cash to the business.

EXERCISE 7–9
Analyzing the Statement of Cash Flows

Quaker Oats Company

Refer to the financial statements of **Quaker Oats Company** in Appendix A.

Required:

a. How much cash does Quaker Oats collect from customers during Year 10?

b. How much is paid in cash dividends on its common stock during Year 11?

CHECK
(c) $2,788.1 mil.

c. How much is the cost of goods and services produced and otherwise generated in Year 11? (*Hint:* Consider all inventories.)

d. If the company acquires property by issuing common stock, where in the statement of cash flows is this reported?

e. How much is the deferred tax provision for Year 11? What effect did it have on current liabilities?

f. What effect did the Year 11 depreciation expense have on cash from operations? Discuss as fully as you can.

g. What does the ($97.8) adjustment for receivables in the Year 11 statement of cash flows mean?

h. Does the cash flows from operations amount of $532.4 reported in Year 11 include discontinued operations?

i. How is it possible for Quaker Oats Company to have a Year 11 net income of $205.8 million but generate $532.4 million cash from operations? (Describe in general terms using selected figures; do not merely repeat the calculations shown in the statement.)

j. Where is the provision for uncollectible accounts probably included? How can this affect the presentation of the statement of cash flows?

k. Of the $532.4 million reported in Year 11 as cash flows from operations, what is your best estimate of cash provided by continuing operations?

CHECK
(l) Year 11, $168.8 mil.

l. Compute free cash flows for all years shown.

m. How does Quaker Oats use its free cash flows?

EXERCISE 7–10
Analyzing the Statement of Cash Flows

Campbell Soup Company

Refer to the financial statements of **Campbell Soup Company** in Appendix A.

Required:

a. How much cash does Campbell Soup collect from customers during Year 10? (*Hint:* Use the statement of cash flows to derive the beginning balance of receivables.)

b. How much is paid in cash dividends on common stock during Year 11?

CHECK
(c) $3,982.4 mil.

c. How much is the total cost of goods and services produced and otherwise generated in Year 11? Consider all inventories.

d. How much is the deferred tax provision for Year 11? What effect did it have on current liabilities?

e. What effect does Year 11 depreciation expense have on cash from operations?

f. Why are the "Divestitures & restructuring" provisions in the statement of cash flows for Year 10 added back to net income in arriving at cash from operations?

g. What does the adjustment "Effect of exchange rate changes on cash" represent?

h. Note 1 to the financial statements discusses the accounting for disposal of property. Where is the adjustment for any gain or loss reported in the statement of cash flows?

CHECK
(i) Year 11, $306.6 mil.

i. Compute free cash flows for all years shown.

j. Campbell is an established manufacturer. How would you expect the free cash flows of a start-up competitor in this industry to differ from Campbell?

k. If Campbell launched a new product line in Year 12, how would you expect the three sections of the statement of cash flows to be affected?

EXERCISE 7–11
Linking Operating Cash Flows with Earnings Quality

In reviewing the financial statements of NanoTech Co., you discover that net income increased while operating cash flows decreased for the most recent two consecutive years.

Required:

a. Explain how net income could increase for NanoTech while its operating cash flows decrease. Your answer should include three illustrative examples.

b. Describe how operating cash flows can serve as one indicator of earnings quality.

(CFA Adapted)

EXERCISE 7–12
Relation of Cash Flows to Company Life Cycle

Analysts often exploit the relation between a company's life cycle and its cash flows to better understand company performance and financial condition.

Required:

a. Explain how a company's transition from the growth stage to "cash cow" is reflected in the statement of cash flows.

b. Describe how the decline of a "cash cow" is reflected in the statement of cash flows.

EXERCISE 7–13
Financial Analysis Using Cash Flow Ratios

Quaker Oats Company

Refer to the financial statements of **Quaker Oats Company** in Appendix A.

Required:

a. Compute Quaker's cash flow adequacy ratio for Year 11. To remove cyclical and random influences, use a *three-year* total in computing this ratio for Quaker.

b. Discuss the importance and significance of the cash flow adequacy ratio. Interpret this ratio for Quaker Oats.

c. Compute the cash reinvestment ratio for both Years 10 and 11.

d. Discuss the importance and significance of the cash reinvestment ratio.

CHECK
(a) 1.069
(c) Year 11, 14.77%

PROBLEMS

PROBLEM 7–1[A]
Converting Cash from Operations under Indirect Method to Direct

Campbell Soup Company

Refer to **Campbell Soup Company's** statement of cash flows in Appendix A.

Required:

Convert Campbell's statement of cash flows for Year 11 to show cash flows from operations (CFO) using the direct method.

For purposes of this problem only, *assume* the following:

a. Net change in other current assets and current liabilities of $30.6 consists of:

Decrease in prepaid expenses	$(25.3)
Decrease in accounts payable	42.8
Increase in taxes payable	(21.3)
Increase in accruals and payrolls	(26.8)
	$(30.6)

b. Campbell disposed of a division in Year 11 reporting revenues of $7.5 million and an after-tax loss of $5.3 million. The loss is included in expenses. The CFO presentation should include revenues and expenses of the discontinued operations in Year 11.

PROBLEM 7–2A
Converting the Statement of Cash Flows to Alternative Formats

Campbell Soup Company

Refer to **Campbell Soup Company's** statement of cash flows in Appendix A.

Required:

Convert Campbell's statement of cash flows for Year 10 to report its cash from operations under the direct method. (For purposes of this assignment only, assume Campbell disposed of a division in Year 10 that had revenues of $7.5 million and an after-tax loss of $5.3 million. The loss is included in expenses. The CFO presentation should include revenues and expenses of discontinued operations in Year 10.)

PROBLEM 7–3A
Computing Cash from Operations (Direct)

Quaker Oats Company

Refer to the financial statements of **Quaker Oats Company** in Appendix A.

Required:

Determine cash flows from operations for Years 11, 10, and 9 using the direct approach. Use a worksheet to compute cash flows from operations and include revenues and expenses of discontinued operations.

PROBLEM 7–4
Preparing and Analyzing the Statement of Cash Flows (Indirect)

A colleague who is aware of your understanding of financial statements asks for help in analyzing the transactions and events of Zett Corporation. The following data are provided:

ZETT CORPORATION
Balance Sheet
At December 31, Year 1 and Year 2

	Year 1	Year 2
Cash	$ 34,000	$ 34,500
Accounts receivable (net)	12,000	17,000
Inventory	16,000	14,000
Investments (long term)	6,000	—
Fixed assets	80,000	93,000
Accumulated depreciation	(48,000)	(39,000)
Total assets	$100,000	$119,500
Accounts payable	$ 19,000	$ 12,000
Bonds payable	10,000	30,000
Common stock	50,000	61,000
Retained earnings	21,000	28,000
Treasury stock	—	(11,500)
Total liabilities and equity	$100,000	$119,500

Additional data for the period January 1, Year 2, through December 31, Year 2, are:

1. Sales on account, $70,000.
2. Purchases on account, $40,000.
3. Depreciation, $5,000.
4. Expenses paid in cash, $18,000 (including $4,000 of interest and $6,000 in taxes).
5. Decrease in inventory, $2,000.
6. Sales of fixed assets for $6,000 cash; cost $21,000 and two-thirds depreciated (loss or gain is included in income).
7. Purchase of fixed assets for cash, $4,000.
8. Fixed assets are exchanged for bonds payable of $30,000.
9. Sale of investments for $9,000 cash.

10. Purchase of treasury stock for cash, $11,500.
11. Retire bonds payable by issuing common stock, $10,000.
12. Collections on accounts receivable, $65,000.
13. Sold unissued common stock for cash, $1,000.

Required:

a. Prepare a statement of cash flows (indirect method) using the T-account approach for the year ended December 31, Year 2.

b. Prepare a side-by-side comparative statement contrasting two bases of reporting: (1) net income and (2) cash flows from operations.

c. Which of the two financial reports in (b) better reflects profitability? Explain.

CHECK
Year 2 CFO, $0

PROBLEM 7–5
Analyzing the Statement of Cash Flows (Indirect)

Dax Corporation's genetically engineered flowers have rapidly gained market acceptance and shipments to customers have increased dramatically. The company is preparing for significant increases in production. Management notes that despite increasing profits the cash balance has declined, and it is forced to nearly double its debt financing in the current year. You are hired to advise management as to specific causes of the cash deficiency and how to remedy the situation. You are given the following balance sheets of Dax Corporation for Years 1 and 2 ($ thousands):

DAX CORPORATION
Balance Sheet
At December 31, Year 2 and Year 1

($ thousands)		Year 2		Year 1
Cash		$ 500		$ 640
Accounts receivable (net)		860		550
Inventories		935		790
Prepaid expenses		25		—
Total current assets		$2,320		$1,980
Patents	$ 140			
Less accumulated amortization	(10)	130		—
Plant and equipment	2,650		$1,950	
Less accumulated depreciation	(600)	2,050	(510)	1,440
Other assets	200		175	
Less accumulated depreciation	(30)	170	(25)	150
Total assets		$4,670		$3,570
Accounts payable		$ 630		$ 600
Deferred income tax		57		45
Other current liabilities		85		78
Total current liabilities		$ 772		$ 723
Long-term debt		1,650		850
Common stock, $1 par		2,000		1,800
Retained earnings		248		197
Total liabilities and equity		$4,670		$3,570

In addition, the following information is available:

1. Net income for Year 2 is $160,000 and for Year 1 it is $130,000.
2. Cash dividends paid during Year 2 are $109,000 and during Year 1 they are $100,000.

3. Depreciation expense charged to income during Year 2 is $95,000, and the provision for bad debts (expense) is $40,000. Expenses include cash payments of $28,000 in interest costs and $70,000 in income taxes.
4. During Year 2 the company purchases patents for $140,000 in cash. Amortization of patents during the year amount to $10,000.
5. Deferred income tax for Year 2 amounts to $12,000 and for Year 1 it amounts to $15,000.

Required:

CHECK
Year 2 CFO, $(166,000)

a. Prepare a statement of cash flows (indirect method) for Year 2 using the T-account approach.
b. Explain the discrepancy between net income and cash flows from operations.
c. Describe options available to management to remedy the cash deficiency.

PROBLEM 7–6
Preparing the Statement of Cash Flows (Direct)

Using the income statement and balance sheets of Niagara Company below, prepare a statement of cash flows for the year ended December 31, Year 9, using the direct method.

NIAGARA COMPANY
Income Statement
For Year Ended December 31, Year 9

Sales	$1,000
Cost of goods sold	(650)
Depreciation expense	(100)
Sales and general expense	(100)
Interest expense	(50)
Income tax expense	(40)
Net income	$ 60

NIAGARA COMPANY
Balance Sheets
As of December 31, Year 9 and Year 8

	Year 8	Year 9
Assets		
Cash	$ 50	$ 60
Accounts receivable	500	520
Inventory	750	770
Current assets	$1,300	$1,350
Fixed assets	500	550
Total assets	$1,800	$1,900
Liabilities and Equity		
Notes payable to banks	$ 100	$ 75
Accounts payable	590	615
Interest payable	10	20
Current liabilities	$ 700	$ 710
Long-term debt	300	350
Deferred income tax	300	310
Capital stock	400	400
Retained earnings	100	130
Total liabilities and equity	$1,800	$1,900

CHECK
CFO, $165

(CFA adapted)

PROBLEM 7–7
Interpreting Cash Flow Effects of Transactions

An ability to visualize quickly the effect of a transaction on the cash resources of a company is a useful analytical skill. This visualization requires an understanding of the economics underlying transactions and how they are accounted for. Expressing transactions in entry form can help one understand business activities.

Required:

A schematic statement of cash flows is reproduced below. The titles of lines in the schematic are given labels (letters). Several business activities are listed below the schematic. For each of the activities listed, identify the lines affected and by what amount. Each activity is separate and unrelated to another. The company closes its books once each year on December 31. Do not consider subsequent activities. Use the labels (letters) shown below. Do not indicate the effect on any line not given a label. If a transaction has no effect, write none. In indicating effects for lines labeled *Y* and *C*, use a + to indicate an increase and a – to indicate a decrease. (*Hint:* Every activity with an effect, affects at least two lines–equal debits and credits. An analytical entry can aid in arriving at a solution.)

Schematic Statement of Cash Flows

SOURCES OF CASH:

(Y)	Net income	______	(Y)
(YA)	Additions and addbacks of expenses and losses not using cash	______	(YA)
(YS)	Subtractions for revenues and gains not generating cash	______	(YS)
	Changes in current operating assets and liabilities:		
(CC)	Add credit changes	______	(CC)
(DC)	Deduct debit changes	______	(DC)
(NC)	Add (deduct) changes in noncurrent operating accounts	______	(NC)
	Cash flow from operations Y + YA – YS + CC – DC + or – NC	______	
(DE)	Proceeds of debt and equity issues	______	(DE)
(IL)	Increase in nonoperating current liabilities	______	(IL)
(AD)	Proceeds of long-term assets dispositions	______	(AD)
(OS)	Other sources of cash	______	(OS)
	Total sources of cash	______	

USES OF CASH:

(ID)	Income distributions	______	(ID)
(R)	Retirements of debt and equity	______	(R)
(DL)	Decreases in nonoperating current liabilities	______	(DL)
(AA)	Long-term assets acquisitions	______	(AA)
(OU)	Other uses of cash	______	(OU)
	Total uses of cash		
(C)	Increase (decrease) in cash	______	(C)

SCHEDULE OF NONCASH INVESTING AND FINANCING ACTIVITIES:

(NDE)	Issue of debt or equity	______	(NDE)
(NCR)	Other noncash-generating credits	______	(NCR)
(NAA)	Acquisitions of assets	______	(NAA)
(NDR)	Other noncash-requiring debts	______	(NDR)

Examples:

a. Sales of $10,000 are made on credit.

b. Cash dividends of $4,000 are paid.

c. Entered into long-term capital lease obligation (present value $60,000).

Answers in the form [Line, Amount]:

a. [DC, $10,000], [+ Y, $10,000]

b. [ID, $4,000], [− C, $4,000]

c. [NAA, $60,000], [NDE, $60,000]

Business activities:

a. Provision for bad debts of $11,000 for the year is included in selling expenses.

b. Depreciation of $16,000 is charged to cost of goods sold.

c. Company acquires a building by issuance of a long-term mortgage note for $100,000.

d. Treasury stock with a cost of $7,000 is retired and canceled.

e. The company has outstanding 50,000 shares of common stock with par value of $1. The company declares a 20 percent stock dividend at the end of the year when the stock is selling for $16 a share.

f. Inventory costing $12,000 is destroyed by fire. The insurance company pays only $10,000 toward this loss, although the market value of the inventory is $15,000.

g. Inventories originally costing $25,000 are used by production departments in producing finished goods that are sold for $35,000 in cash and $5,000 in accounts receivable.

h. Accounts receivable of $8,000 are written off. There is an allowance for doubtful accounts balance of $5,000 prior to the write off.

i. Long-lived assets are acquired for $100,000 cash on January 1. The company decides to depreciate $20,000 each year.

j. A machine costing $15,000 with accumulated depreciation of $6,000 is sold for $8,000 cash.

PROBLEM 7–8

Interpreting Cash Flow Effects of Transactions

Complete the requirements of Problem 7–7 using the business activities listed below:

Part I

a. An annual installment of $100,000 due on long-term debt is paid on its due date.

b. Equipment originally costing $12,000 with $7,000 of accumulated depreciation is sold for $4,000 cash.

c. Obsolete inventory costing $75,000 is written down to zero.

d. Treasury stock costing $30,000 is sold for $28,000 cash.

e. A plant is acquired by issuing a $300,000 mortgage payable due in equal installments over six years.

f. The company's 30 percent-owned unconsolidated subsidiary earns $100,000 and pays dividends of $20,000. The company recorded its 30 percent share of these items using the equity method.

g. A product is sold for $40,000, to be paid with $10,000 down plus $10,000 each year for three years. Interest at 10 percent of the outstanding balance is due. Consider only the effect at the time of sale (the company's operating cycle is less than one year).

h. The company uses a periodic inventory method. Certain inventory is mistakenly valued at $1,000—it should have been valued at $10,000. Show the effect of correcting the error.

i. Cash of $400,000 is used to acquire 100 percent of ZXY Manufacturing Company. At date of acquisition, ZXY has current assets of $300,000 (including $40,000 in cash); plant and equipment of $670,000; current liabilities of $160,000; and long-term debt of $410,000.

j. A provision for bad debt expense of $60,000 is made (calculated as a percent of sales for the period).

Part II

a. Cash of $120,000 is invested in a 30-percent-owned company.

b. A 30 percent-owned subsidiary earns $25,000 (in total) and pays no dividends.

c. A 30 percent-owned subsidiary earns $30,000 (in total) and pays dividends of $10,000 (in total).

d. Equipment with an original cost of $15,000 and accumulated depreciation of $12,000 is sold for $4,000 cash.

e. The company borrows $60,000 from its banks on November 30 payable on June 30 of next year.

f. Convertible bonds with a face value of $9,000 are converted into 1,000 shares of common stock with a par value of $2 per share.

g. Treasury stock with a cost of $4,000 is sold for $6,000 cash.

h. Common stock (par value $2) with a fair market value of $100,000 plus $100,000 cash are given to acquire 100 percent of ZYX Mfg. Co. At date of acquisition ZYX had current assets of $120,000 (including $40,000 cash); plant and equipment of $180,000; current liabilities of $60,000; and long-term debt of $40,000.
  (1) Identify the effect on the parent's statement.
  (2) Identify the effect on the consolidated statement.

i. The minority's share of income is $4,000.

j. Inventory with a cost of $80,000 is written down to its market value of $30,000.

k. Accounts receivable for $1,200 are written off. The company uses an allowance for doubtful accounts.

l. A noncancelable lease of equipment for 10 years with a present value of $120,000 is capitalized.

m. A 15 percent stock dividend is declared. The 60,000 shares of common stock issued to cover the dividend have a par value of $2 per share and a fair market value of $3 per share.

n. A provision of $27,000 for uncollectible accounts is made (calculated as a percent of sales for the period).

PROBLEM 7–9
Reconstructing a Balance Sheet from Cash Flows

While on assignment you discover that you have misplaced the balance sheet of Bird Corporation as of January 1, Year 1. However, you do have the following data on Bird Corporation:

BIRD CORPORATION
Postclosing Trial Balance
December 31, Year 1

Debit balances:	
Cash	$ 100,000
Accounts receivable	120,000
Inventory	130,000
Property, plant, and equipment	550,000
Other noncurrent investments	200,000
Total	$1,100,000
Credit balances:	
Accounts payable	$ 100,000
Current portion of long-term debt	80,000
Accumulated depreciation	270,000
Long-term debt	200,000
Common stock	300,000
Retained earnings	150,000
Total	$1,100,000

BIRD CORPORATION
Statement of Cash Flows
For Year Ended December 31, Year 1

Cash flows from operations:			
Net income			$150,000
Add (deduct) adjustment to cash basis:			
Depreciation		$ 85,000	
Loss on sale of equipment		5,000	
Gain on sale of noncurrent investments		(50,000)	
Increase in accounts receivable		(30,000)	
Increase in inventories		(20,000)	
Increase in accounts payable		40,000	30,000
Cash from operations			$180,000
Cash flows from investing activities:			
Additions to property and equipment		$(150,000)	
Sale of equipment		10,000	
Sale of investments		95,000	
Cash used for investing activities			(45,000)
Cash flows from financing activities:			
Issuance of common stock		$ 10,000	
Additions to long-term debt	$15,000		
Decrease in current portion of long-term debt	(30,000)	(15,000)	
Cash dividends		(80,000)	
Cash used for financing activities			(85,000)
Increase in cash			$ 50,000

Required:

Using the available data and information, prepare the balance sheet of Bird Corporation as of January 1, Year 1. T-accounts can be helpful in reconstructing the individual accounts. (*Note:* Equipment sold had accumulated depreciation of $50,000.)

CHECK
Total assets, $725,000

PROBLEM 7–10
Analyzing Economic Impacts of Transactions

Indicate whether the following independent transactions increase (+), decrease (−), or do not affect (NE) the current ratio, the amount of working capital, and cash from operations. Also indicate the amounts of any effects. The company presently has a current ratio of 2 to 1 along with current liabilities of $160,000.

	Current Ratio Effect	Working Capital Effect $___	Cash from Operations Effect $___
a. Paid accrued wages of $1,000.			
b. Purchased $20,000 worth of material on account.			
c. Received judgment notice from the court that the company must pay $70,000 damages for patent infringement within six months.			
d. Collected $8,000 of accounts receivable.			
e. Purchased land for factory for $100,000 cash.			
f. Repaid currently due bank note payable of $10,000.			
g. Received currently due note receivable of $15,000 from customer as consideration for sale of land.			
h. Received cash of $90,000 from stockholders as donated capital.			
i. Purchased machine costing $50,000; $15,000 down and the balance to be paid in seven equal annual installments.			
j. Retired bonds maturing five years hence at par of $50,000. Bonds have unamortized premium of $2,000.			
k. Declared dividends of $10,000 payable after year-end.			
l. Paid the dividends in *k* in cash.			
m. Declared a 5% stock dividend.			
n. Paid the stock dividend in *m*.			
o. Signed a long-term purchase contract of $100,000 to commence a year from now.			
p. Borrowed $40,000 cash for one year.			
q. Pays accounts payable of $20,000.			
r. Purchases a patent for $20,000.			
s. Write off $15,000 of current marketable securities that became worthless.			
t. $8,500 of organization expenses are written off.			
u. Depreciation expense of $70,000 is recorded.			
v. Sold $28,000 of merchandise on account.			
w. A building is sold for $90,000. It has a book value of $45,000.			
x. A machine is sold at cost for $5,000; $2,500 down and the balance receivable in six months.			
y. Income tax expense is booked at $80,000, half of which is deferred (long term).			

PROBLEM 7–11
Analyzing Operating Flow Measures

Your banker confides to you after looking at a number of financial statements that she is confused about the difference between two operating measures, net income and cash from operations.

Required:

a. Explain the purpose and significance of these two operating measures.

b. Several financial transactions or events follow. For each transaction or event, indicate whether it yields an increase (+), decrease (−), or no effect (NE) on each of the two measures.

	EFFECT OF TRANSACTION/EVENT ON:	
	Net Income	Cash from Operations
1. Sales of marketable securities for cash at more than their carrying value.		
2. Sale of merchandise with deferred payments (one-half within one year and one-half after one year).		
3. Reclassify noncurrent receivable as current receivable.		
4. Payment of current portion of long-term debt.		
5. Collection of an account receivable.		
6. Recording the cost of goods sold.		
7. Purchase of inventories on account (credit terms).		
8. Accrual of sales commissions (to be paid at a later date).		
9. Payment of accounts payable (resulting from purchase of inventory).		
10. Provision for depreciation on a sales office.		
11. Borrowing cash from a bank on a 90-day note payable.		
12. Accrual of interest on a bank loan.		
13. Sale of partially depreciated equipment for cash at less than its book value.		
14. Flood damage to merchandise inventories (no insurance coverage).		
15. Declaration and payment of a cash dividend on preferred stock.		
16. Sale of merchandise on 90-day credit terms.		
17. Provision for uncollectible accounts receivable.		
18. Write-off of an uncollectible receivable.		
19. Provision for income tax expense (to be paid the following month).		
20. Provision for deferred income taxes (set up because depreciation for tax reporting exceeded depreciation for financial reporting).		
21. Purchase of a machine (fixed asset) for cash.		
22. Payment of accrued salary expense to employees.		

PROBLEM 7–12

Preparing and Interpreting the Statement of Cash Flows

Kraft
Philip Morris Companies

Following the acquisition of **Kraft** during Year 8, the **Philip Morris Companies** released its Year 8 financial statements. The Year 8 financial statements and other data are reproduced on the next page.

PHILIP MORRIS COMPANIES, INC.

Balance Sheets ($ millions)
As of December 31, Year 8 and Year 7

	Year 8	Year 7
Assets		
Cash and cash equivalents	$ 168	$ 90
Accounts receivable	2,222	2,065
Inventories	5,384	4,154
Current assets	$ 7,774	$ 6,309
Property, plant, and equipment (net)	8,648	6,582
Goodwill (net)	15,071	4,052
Investments	3,260	3,665
Total assets	$34,753	$20,608
Liabilities and Stockholders' Equity		
Short-term debt	$ 1,259	$ 1,440
Accounts payable	1,777	791
Accrued liabilities	3,848	2,277
Income taxes payable	1,089	727
Dividends payable	260	213
Current liabilities	$ 8,233	$ 5,448
Long-term debt	17,122	6,293
Deferred income taxes	1,719	2,044
Stockholders' equity	7,679	6,823
Total liabilities and stockholders' equity	$34,753	$20,608

PHILIP MORRIS COMPANIES, INC.

Income Statement ($ millions)
For Year Ending December 31, Year 8

Sales	$31,742
Cost of goods sold	(12,156)
Selling and administrative expenses	(14,410)
Depreciation expense	(654)
Goodwill amortization	(125)
Interest expense	(670)
Pre-tax income	$ 3,727
Income tax expense	(1,390)
Net income	$ 2,337

Note: Dividends declared, $941 million.

PHILIP MORRIS PURCHASE OF KRAFT

Allocation of Purchase Price ($ millions)

Accounts receivable	$ 758
Inventories	1,232
Property, plant, and equipment	1,740
Goodwill	10,361
Short-term debt	(700)
Accounts payable	(578)
Accrued liabilities	(530)
Long-term debt	(900)
Purchase price (net of cash acquired)	$11,383

Required:

a. Prepare a statement of cash flows (indirect method) for Philip Morris. (*Hint:* Acquisition of Kraft requires you to remove the assets acquired and liabilities incurred as a result of that acquisition from the balance sheet before computing changes used in preparing the statement of cash flows. Philip Morris pays $11.383 billion for Kraft, net of cash acquired—see the Allocation of Purchase Price table.)

CHECK
CFO, $5,205 mil.

b. Calculate cash flows from operations using the direct method for Philip Morris.

CHECK
(c) $3,331

c. Based on your answer to *a*, compute Philip Morris's free cash flow for Year 8. Discuss how free cash flow impacts the company's future earnings and financial condition.

(CFA Adapted)

PROBLEM 7–13
Analyzing Cash from Operations (Direct)

Refer to the financial statements of ZETA Corporation reproduced in Case CC–2 of the Comprehensive Case (following Chapter 12).

Required:

a. Prepare a schedule computing cash flows from operations using the direct method. Include revenues and expenses of discontinued operations. Include a list of important assumptions and weaknesses as a note to your cash statement. Support all amounts shown. (*Hint:* Discontinued operations cannot be separated from continuing operations, but unadjusted income and expense of discontinued operations can be.)

CHECK
Year 6 CFO, $6,400

b. ZETA's statement of cash flows reports income taxes paid in Year 6 of $2,600. Verify this amount independently.

c. Reconcile the change in "accounts payable and accruals" reported in the statement of cash flows with the number derived from the balance sheet. Explain the reason(s) for any difference. (*Hint:* Refer to notes 3 and 4.)

PROBLEM 7–14
Analyzing Common-Size Statements of Cash Flows

Quaker Oats Company

Refer to financial statements of **Quaker Oats Company** in Appendix A.

Required:

Using common-size statements (where the total of all positive cash sources (gross) = 100%), prepare and analyze the annual statements of cash flows for Quaker Oats for each of the three years–Year 11, Year 10, and Year 9. Arrange the common-size statements into two parts: (1) sources of cash, and (2) uses of cash. Include in your analysis the interpretation and discussion of the major sources and uses of cash.

CHECK
Year 11 total net sources, 86.56%

CASES

CASE 7–1
Analysis of Cash Flows

Kodak

Refer to the annual report of **Kodak** in Appendix A:

Required:

a. Explain how the following items create differences between Kodak's earnings from continuing operations and its net cash provided by operating activities:
   (1) Depreciation and amortization
   (2) Gain on sale of assets
   (3) Increase in receivables
   (4) Increase in inventories
   (5) Decrease in liabilities excluding borrowings

b. Explain why net income is much less than cash from operations in 2001. When will the cash outflows occur for the major reconciling item between net income and operating cash flows?

c. Calculate Kodak's free cash flows for each of the past three years.

d. How has Kodak used its free cash flows during the past three years?

e. How much cash has Kodak returned to shareholders during the past three years?

CASE 7–2
Cash Flow and Free Cash Flow Analysis

The statement of cash flows for **Lands' End** is reproduced here:

Lands' End

LANDS' END, INC. & SUBSIDIARIES
Consolidated Statements of Cash Flows
($ in thousands)

	FOR THE PERIOD ENDED		
	Year 9	**Year 8**	**Year 7**
Cash flows from operating activities:			
Net income	$31,185	$ 64,150	$ 50,952
Adjustments to reconcile net income to net cash flows from operating activities—			
Pre-tax non-recurring charge	12,600	—	—
Depreciation and amortization	18,731	15,127	13,558
Deferred compensation expense	653	323	317
Deferred income taxes	(5,948)	(1,158)	994
Pre-tax gain on sale of subsidiary	—	(7,805)	—
Loss on disposal of fixed assets	586	1,127	325
Changes in assets and liabilities excluding the effects of divestitures:			
Receivables	(5,640)	(7,019)	(675)
Inventory	21,468	(104,545)	22,371
Prepaid advertising	(2,844)	(7,447)	4,758
Other prepaid expenses	(2,504)	(1,366)	(145)
Accounts payable	4,179	11,616	14,205
Reserve for returns	1,065	944	629
Accrued liabilities	6,993	8,755	4,390
Accrued profit sharing	(2,030)	1,349	1,454
Income taxes payable	(5,899)	(1,047)	8,268
Other	1,665	64	394
Net cash flows from (used for) operating activities	74,260	(26,932)	121,795
Cash flows from (used for) investing activities:			
Cash paid for capital additions	(46,750)	(47,659)	(18,481)
Proceeds from sale of subsidiary	—	12,350	—
Net cash flows used for investing activities	(46,750)	(35,309)	(18,481)

(continued)

CASE 7–2
(concluded)

	FOR THE PERIOD ENDED		
	Year 9	Year 8	Year 7
Cash flows from (used for) financing activities:			
Proceeds from short-term debt	$ 6,505	$ 21,242	$ 1,876
Purchases of treasury stock	(35,557)	(45,899)	(30,143)
Issuance of treasury stock	1,845	409	604
Net cash flows used for financing activities	(27,207)	(24,248)	(27,663)
Net increase (decrease) in cash and cash equiv.	$ 303	$ (86,489)	$ 75,651
Beginning cash and cash equivalents	6,338	92,827	17,176
Ending cash and cash equivalents	$ 6,641	$ 6,338	$ 92,827

Required:

a. Lands' End recently implemented a strategy of filling nearly all orders when the order is placed. In what year do you believe the company implemented this strategy and how is the strategy reflected in the information contained in the statement of cash flows?

b. Explain how the following items reconcile net income to net cash flows from operating activities:
(1) Depreciation (2) Receivables (3) Inventory (4) Reserve for returns

c. Calculate free cash flows for each year shown.

d. How does Lands' End use its free cash flow? Do you think its use of free cash flows reflects good financial strategy?

CASE 7–3
Analysis of Cash Flows for a Dot.Com

The statement of cash flows for **Yahoo!** is reproduced here: **Yahoo!**

YAHOO! INC.
Consolidated Statements of Cash Flows
(in thousands)

	YEAR ENDED DECEMBER 31,		
	Year 8	Year 7	Year 6
Cash flows from operating activities:			
Net income (loss)	$ 25,588	$(25,520)	$ (6,427)
Adjustments to reconcile net income (loss) to net cash provided by (used in) operating activities:			
Depreciation and amortization	10,215	2,737	639
Tax benefits from stock options	17,827	—	—
Non-cash charges related to stock option grants and warrant issuances	926	1,676	197
Minority interests in operations of consolidated subsidiaries	(68)	(727)	(540)
Purchased in-process research and development	17,300	—	—
Other non-cash charge	—	21,245	—

(continued)

CASE 7–3
(concluded)

	YEAR ENDED DECEMBER 31,		
	Year 8	Year 7	Year 6
Changes in assets and liabilities:			
Accounts receivable, net	$(13,616)	$ (5,963)	$ (4,269)
Prepaid expenses	2,144	(6,110)	(386)
Accounts payable	515	2,425	1,386
Accrued expenses and other current liabilities	16,688	7,404	4,393
Deferred revenue	33,210	2,983	1,665
Due to related parties	(451)	330	948
Net cash provided by (used in) operating activities	110,278	480	(2,394)
Cash flows from investing activities:			
Acquisition of property and equipment	(11,911)	(6,722)	(3,442)
Cash acquired in acquisitions	199	—	—
Purchases of marketable securities	(471,135)	(58,753)	(115,247)
Proceeds from sales and maturities of marketable securities	158,350	86,678	43,240
Other investments	(5,445)	(1,649)	(729)
Net cash provided by (used in) investing activities	(329,942)	19,554	(76,178)
Cash flows from financing activities:			
Proceeds from issuance of Common Stock, net	280,679	7,516	42,484
Proceeds from issuance of Convertible Preferred Stock	—	—	63,750
Proceeds from minority investors	600	999	1,050
Other	—	1,106	(128)
Net cash provided by financing activities	281,279	9,621	107,156
Effect of exchange rate changes on cash and cash equivalents	288	(380)	(63)
Net change in cash and cash equivalents	$ 61,903	$ 29,275	$ 28,521
Cash and cash equivalents at beginning of year	63,571	34,296	5,775
Cash and cash equivalents at end of year	$125,474	$ 63,571	$ 34,296

Required:

a. Yahoo!'s operations did not produce significant cash flows during Year 6 and Year 7. How does Yahoo! finance its growth in the absence of sufficient operating cash flows?

b. What appears to drive the operating cash flows of Yahoo!?

c. Yahoo! engages in purchases and sales of marketable securities. Why do you believe Yahoo! pursues this activity?

d. Yahoo! reports $33.21 million of deferred revenue. Based on your understanding of Yahoo!'s operations, what do you believe this amount represents?

CHECK
(a) Equity financing

CASE 7–4
Credit Analysis for a Leveraged Buyout

The management of Wyatt Corporation is frustrated because its parent company, SRW Corporation, repeatedly rejects Wyatt's capital spending requests. These refusals led Wyatt's management to conclude its operations play a limited role in the parent's long-range plans. Acting on this assumption, Wyatt's management approaches a merchant banking firm about the possibility of a leveraged buyout of itself. In their proposal, Wyatt management stresses the stable, predictable cash flows from Wyatt's operations as more than adequate to service the debt required to finance the proposed leveraged buyout. As a partner in the merchant banking firm, you investigate the feasibility of their proposal. You receive the following balance sheet and supplementary information for Wyatt Corporation. The management of Wyatt further discloses that, following their proposed purchase, they intend to acquire machinery costing $325,000 in each of the next three years to overcome the previous low level of capital expenditures while a subsidiary of SRW Corporation. Management argues these expenditures are needed for competitive reasons.

CHECK
CFO, $269,000

Required:

a. Using information in the balance sheet and the supplementary disclosures, prepare a statement of cash flows (indirect method) for the year ended December 31, Year 10.

b. Using the statement of cash flows from *a* and assuming that debt service is $300,000 per year after the leveraged buyout, evaluate the feasibility of management's proposal.

WYATT CORPORATION
Balance Sheet
As of December 31, Year 10 and Year 9

	Year 9	Year 10
Assets		
Current assets:		
Cash	$ 175,000	$ 192,000
Accounts receivable	248,000	359,000
Inventory	465,000	683,000
Total current assets	888,000	1,234,000
Land	126,000	138,000
Building and machinery	3,746,000	3,885,000
Less accumulated depreciation	(916,000)	(1,131,000)
Total assets	$3,844,000	$4,126,000
Liabilities and Shareholders' Equity		
Current liabilities:		
Accounts payable	$ 156,000	$ 259,000
Taxes payable	149,000	124,000
Other short-term payables	325,000	417,000
Total current liabilities	630,000	800,000
Bonds payable	842,000	825,000
Total liabilities	1,472,000	1,625,000
Shareholders' equity:		
Common stock	846,000	863,000
Retained earnings	1,526,000	1,638,000
Total shareholders' equity	2,372,000	2,501,000
Total liabilities and equity	$3,844,000	$4,126,000

Supplementary Information:

1. Dividends declared and paid in Year 10 were $74,000.
2. Depreciation expense for Year 10 was $246,000.
3. Machinery originally costing $61,000 was sold for $34,000 in Year 10.

(CFA Adapted)

CASE 7–5
Analyzing a Management Buyout Using the Statement of Cash Flows

The management of Dover Corporation claims that the securities market undervalues shares of its company. They propose to take it private by means of a leveraged buyout. Management's proposal contains the following features:

1. The leveraged buyout is expected to yield additional after-tax annual interest costs of $200,000.
2. To make Dover Corporation competitive, management plans to undertake:
   a. Annual investments in equipment of $180,000.
   b. Annual buildups in inventory of $60,000.

3. Management expects no additional financing demands beyond that listed in (1) and plans to use cash generated by operations as the primary financing source.

At the end of Year 8, management requests you to analyze the feasibility of their proposal. They provide you with the financial data listed below to assist in your analysis.

	DECEMBER 31		
	Year 8	**Year 7**	**Net Change**
Assets			
Cash	$ 471,000	$ 307,000	$ 164,000
Marketable equity securities, at cost	150,000	250,000	(100,000)
Allowance to adjust securities to market	(10,000)	(25,000)	15,000
Accounts receivable, net	550,000	515,000	35,000
Inventories	810,000	890,000	(80,000)
Investment in Top Corp., at equity	420,000	390,000	30,000
Property, plant, and equipment	1,145,000	1,070,000	75,000
Less accumulated depreciation	(345,000)	(280,000)	(65,000)
Patents, net	109,000	118,000	(9,000)
Total assets	$3,300,000	$3,235,000	$ 65,000
Liabilities and Stockholders' Equity			
Accounts payable and accrued liabilities	$ 845,000	$ 960,000	$(115,000)
Note payable, long-term	600,000	900,000	(300,000)
Deferred income taxes	190,000	190,000	—
Common stock, $10 par value	850,000	650,000	200,000
Additional paid-in capital	230,000	170,000	60,000
Retained earnings	585,000	365,000	220,000
Total liabilities and stockholders' equity	$3,300,000	$3,235,000	$ 65,000

Additional Information:

1. On January 2, Year 8, Dover sold equipment costing $45,000, with a carrying amount of $28,000, for $18,000 cash.
2. On March 31, Year 8, Dover sold one of its marketable equity securities for $119,000 cash. There are no other transactions involving marketable equity securities.
3. On April 15, Year 8, Dover issues 20,000 shares of its common stock for cash at $13 per share.
4. On July 1, Year 8, Dover purchases equipment for $120,000 cash.
5. Dover's net income for Year 8 is $305,000. Dover pays a cash dividend of $85,000 on October 26, Year 8.
6. Dover acquires a 20 percent interest in Top Corporation's common stock during Year 5. There is no goodwill attributable to the investment, which is accounted for using the equity method. Top reports net income of $150,000 for the year ended December 31, Year 8. No dividend is paid on Top's common stock during Year 8.

Required:

Prepare an analysis evaluating the financial feasibility of management's plans. (*Hint:* Prepare a statement of cash flows. Use the indirect method.)

CHECK
CFO, $272,000

WEB ACTIVITIES

The Web Activities are located on the book's website at www.mhhe.com/wild8e.

8

RETURN ON INVESTED CAPITAL

A LOOK BACK

Chapter 7 examined cash flow measures of business activities and showed how this information complements our study of accrual measures in earlier chapters. We also demonstrated how reconstruction of transactions assists in the use of cash flow data.

A LOOK AT THIS CHAPTER

This chapter focuses on return. We emphasize return on invested capital and explain variations in its measurement. Special attention is directed at return on assets and return on common shareholders' equity. We explore disaggregations of both these return measures and describe their relevance to our analysis. Financial leverage is explained and analyzed using the return measures in this chapter.

A LOOK AHEAD

Chapter 9 extends our analysis of return to focus on profitability. We analyze operating activities using several techniques, including component analysis and gross profit analysis. We describe operating leverage and its implications for profitability.

ANALYSIS OBJECTIVES

- Describe the usefulness of return measures in financial statement analysis.
- Explain return on invested capital and variations in its computation.
- Analyze return on total assets and its relevance for analysis.
- Describe disaggregation of return on assets and the importance of its components.
- Analyze return on common shareholders' equity and its role in analysis.
- Describe disaggregation of return on common shareholders' equity and the relevance of its components.
- Explain leverage and how to assess a company's success in trading on the equity across financing sources.

Trends That Gap Missed

SAN FRANCISCO–Gap, Inc., once the consummate marketer has fallen on hard times. Old Navy, launched in 1993, posted huge sales gains for years, but that was partly because it cannibalized customers from Gap. Ultimately, Old Navy contributed to the woes of the entire company as its image blurred with Gap's and combined sales slowed. The Gap recently reported its first loss in a decade and has found itself out of touch with its customer base and heavily laden with debt. The rating on the Gap's bonds has been downgraded to just above junk status, reflecting its declining ability to service debt, and its stock has plummeted 80%.

The Gap's financial problems were evident from a review of its financial ratios. As the costs of new stores continued to mount, its continued expansion ballooned assets well ahead of increases in sales. As a result, its total asset turnover decreased by 25%. In addition, financing its expansion with debt instead of equity increased its financial leverage by 33%. Interestingly, none of the Gap's store leases are capitalized. Adjusting its liabilities for lease obligations would increase its liabilities by $3.5 billion and its financial leverage by nearly 50%.

The Gap's . . . misguided expansion.

The Gap's return on equity reached a high of 59% in fiscal 1999 as a result of a 9.7% net profit margin, total asset turnover of 2.5 times and financial leverage of 2.4, not including capitalization of operating leases. Each component of its ROE had increased steadily. When its markets weakened, however, its financial leverage worked against it and its long-run viability has been questioned. "Who in their right mind would have expanded like the Gap in the face of such terrible results?" asks Howard Davidowitz, chairman of retail consulting firm Davidowitz & Associates Inc. The Gap's problems should not have been a surprise for those conducting a thorough analysis of its financial ratios as they told the story of misguided expansion.

Source: Business Week, *February and May 2002; Gap, Inc. 2001 10-K and 2003 website*

PREVIEW OF CHAPTER 8

Financial statement analysis involves assessing both risk and return. *Return on invested capital* refers to a company's earnings relative to both the level and source of financing. It is a measure of a company's success in using financing to generate profits. It also is an excellent measure of a company's solvency risk. This chapter describes return on invested capital and its relevance to financial statement analysis. We explain variations in measurement of return on invested capital and their interpretation. We also disaggregate return on invested capital into important components for additional insights into

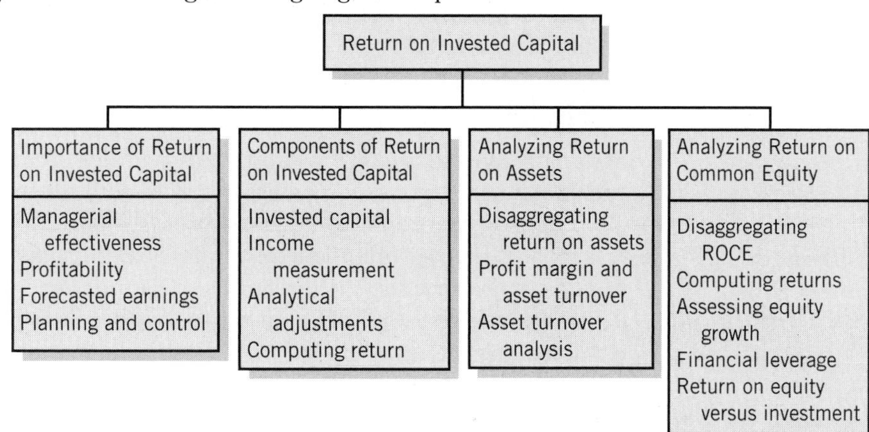

company performance and future operations. The role of financial leverage and its importance for returns analysis is examined. This chapter demonstrates each of these analysis techniques using actual financial statement data, including those of Campbell Soup Company.

IMPORTANCE OF RETURN ON INVESTED CAPITAL

We can analyze company performance in several ways. Revenue, gross profit, and net income are performance measures in common use. Yet none of these measures *individually* are useful as a comprehensive measure of company performance. The reason stems from their interdependency and the interdependency of business activities. For example, increases in revenue are desirable only if they increase profits. The same applies to sales volume. To assess gross profit or net income we must relate them to invested capital. For example, a profit of $1 million is assessed differently if a company's invested capital is $2 million or $200 million.

Analysis of company performance demands *joint* analysis, where we assess one measure relative to another. The relation between income and invested capital, referred to as **return on invested capital** or *return on investment (ROI),* is probably the most widely recognized measure of company performance. It allows us to compare companies on their success with invested capital. It also allows us to assess a company's return relative to its capital investment risk, and we can compare the return on invested capital to returns of alternative investments. Government treasury bonds reflect a minimum return due to their low risk. Riskier investments are expected to yield higher returns. Analysis of return on invested capital compares a company's income, or other performance measure, to the company's level and source of financing. It determines a company's ability to succeed, attract financing, repay creditors, and reward owners. We use return on invested capital in several areas of our analysis including: (1) managerial effectiveness, (2) level of profitability, (3) earnings forecasting, and (4) planning and control.

MATTER OF RESPECT

A recent survey of investors reports the most and least trustworthy corporate leaders:

Most Trustworthy
Warren Buffett—Berkshire Hathaway
Jeffrey Immelt—General Electric
Bill Gates—Microsoft
Michael Dell—Dell Computer

Least Trustworthy
Steve Case—AOL Time Warner
Larry Ellison—Oracle
Sanford Weill—Citigroup
John Chambers—Cisco Systems

Measuring Managerial Effectiveness

The level of return on invested capital depends primarily on the skill, resourcefulness, ingenuity, and motivation of management. Management is responsible for a company's business activities. It makes financing, investing, and operating decisions. It selects actions, plans strategies, and executes plans. Return on invested capital, especially when computed over intervals of a year or longer, is a relevant measure of a company's managerial effectiveness.

Measuring Profitability

Return on invested capital is an important indicator of a company's long-term financial strength. It uses key summary measures from both the income statement (profits) and the balance sheet (financing) to assess profitability. This profitability measure has several advantages over other long-term measures of financial strength or solvency that rely on only balance sheet items (such as debt to equity ratio). It can effectively convey the return on invested capital from varying perspectives of different financing contributors (creditors and shareholders). It is also helpful in short-term liquidity analysis.

Measure of Forecasted Earnings

Return on invested capital is useful in earnings forecasting. This measure effectively links past, current, and forecasted earnings with total invested capital. Its use in our analysis and forecasting of earnings adds discipline and realism. It identifies overly optimistic or pessimistic forecasts relative to competitors' returns on invested capital, and it yields managerial assessments of financing sources when forecasts are different from expectations. Expectations are determined from historical and incremental rates of return, projected changes in company and business conditions, and expected returns for new projects. Return on invested capital is used as either a primary or supplementary means of earnings forecasting and to evaluate the reasonableness of forecasts from other sources.

Measure for Planning and Control

Return on invested capital serves an important role in planning, budgeting, coordinating, evaluating, and controlling business activities. This return is composed of the returns (and losses) achieved by the company's segments or divisions. These segment returns are also made up of the returns achieved by individual product lines, projects, and other components. A well-managed company exercises control over returns achieved by each of its profit centers and rewards its managers on these results. In evaluating investing alternatives, management assesses performance relative to expected returns. Out of this assessment come strategic decisions and action plans for the company.

DELL HURDLE
Dell Computer has its marketing department compute return on investment for *each* equipment sale.

ANALYSIS VIEWPOINT ... YOU ARE THE AUDITOR

You are the audit manager responsible for substantive audit tests of a manufacturing client. Your analytical procedures reveal a 3% increase in sales from \$2 to \$2.06 (millions) and a 4% decrease in total expenses from \$1.9 to \$1.824 (millions). Both changes are within your "reasonableness" criterion of ±5%. Accordingly, you do not expand audit tests of these accounts. The audit partner in charge questions your lack of follow-up on these deviations and expressly mentions *joint* analysis. What is the audit partner referring to?

Answer–p. 448

COMPONENTS OF RETURN ON INVESTED CAPITAL

Analyzing company performance using return on invested capital is conceptually sound and appealing. **Return on invested capital** is computed as:

$$\frac{\text{Income}}{\text{Invested capital}}$$

There is, however, not complete agreement on the computation of either the numerator or denominator in this relation. These differences are valid and stem from the diverse perspectives of financial statement users. This section describes these differences and explains how different computations are relevant to different users or analyses. We begin with a discussion of invested capital, followed by consideration of income.

Invested Capital for a Typical Company

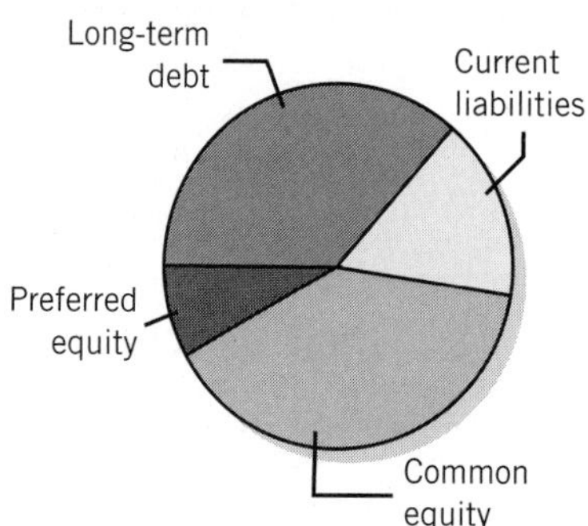

Defining Invested Capital

There is no universal measure of invested capital from which to compute rate of return. Return on invested capital reflects fundamental and accepted concepts of income and financing levels. The different measures of invested capital used reflect users' different perspectives. In this section we describe different measures of invested capital and explain their relevance to different users and interpretations.

Net Income to Total Assets

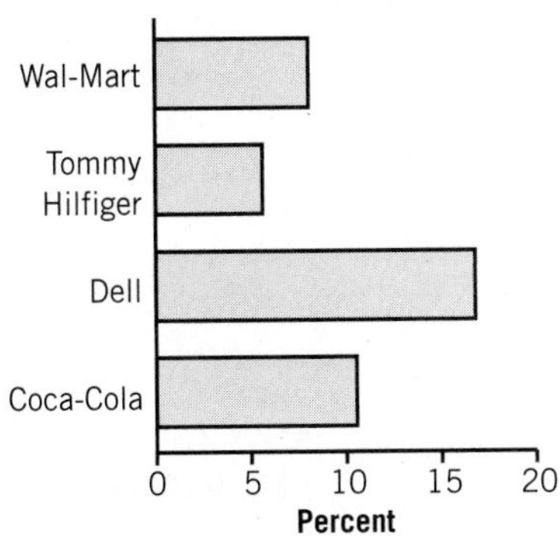

Total Assets

A company's return can be assessed from the perspective of its total financing base–*liabilities plus equity*, or simply *total assets*. This **return on total assets** is a relevant measure of operating efficiency. It reflects a company's return from all assets (or financing) entrusted to it. This measure does not distinguish return by financing sources. By removing the effect of the financing source of assets, the analysis can concentrate on evaluating or forecasting operating performance. Still, the total asset base for computing return on invested capital is sometimes subject to adjustments. We describe three types of adjustments below.

Nonoperating Asset Adjustment. One type of adjustment relates to nonoperating assets. The nonoperating asset adjustment removes investments in marketable securities and excess cash from the invested capital base. These exclusions focus the analysis on operating assets and segregate the analysis of operations from that of the financial activities of the company. This can be a useful perspective for companies with significant investment in financial assets.

Intangible Asset Adjustment. Another type of adjustment excludes intangible assets from invested capital. This adjustment derives from skepticism regarding their value or the assumption that their intangible nature is of a different character than that of tangible assets. Under current GAAP, intangible assets are subject to periodic review for impairment (Chapter 5). Adjustments should be made to the carrying amount of the asset prior to the analysis process if information can be brought to bear that it is incorrect. Excluding intangible assets from invested capital in their entirety, however, is not justified as they represent valid investments by company management despite their intangible nature.

Accumulated Depreciation Adjustment. A third adjustment relates to whether the invested capital base includes an addback for accumulated depreciation on depreciable assets (note that earnings are still reported *net* of depreciation). Advocates argue that since plant assets are maintained in prime working condition during their useful life, it is inappropriate to assess return relative to *net* assets. They also argue if accumulated depreciation is not added back, then earnings in succeeding periods relate to an ever-decreasing investment base. Accordingly, even with stable earnings, return on investment continually rises and would fail to reveal true company performance.

In evaluating this adjustment, we must remember its focus on the internal control of separate productive units and of operating management. Our analysis is different, focusing on the operating performance of an entire company. For analysis of an entire company, it is better to not add back accumulated depreciation to invested capital. This is consistent with computation of income net of depreciation expense. The increase in return due to decreasing depreciable assets is offset by the acquisition of new depreciable assets. These new assets must also earn a return. We also must recognize that maintenance and repair costs commonly increase as assets age, tending to offset the reduction (if any) in the invested capital base.

Equity Capital

The use of equity capital as the definition of invested capital gives us a measure of the return on shareholders' equity. This implies a focus on the return to equity holders. As we will subsequently show, return on equity captures the effect of leveraged (debt) capital on shareholders' return. Since preferred stock typically receives a fixed return, we exclude it from the calculation of equity capital.

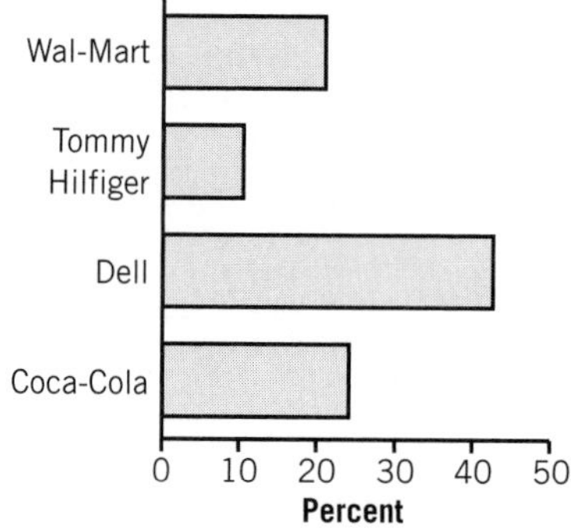

Book versus Market Value of Invested Capital

Return on invested capital is typically computed using reported values from financial statements rather than market values. Yet market values are sometimes more relevant for analysis because certain assets are not recognized in financial statements (for example, internally developed trademarks, reputation, and human resources). Additionally, earnings by companies are sometimes delayed due to overly conservative accounting recognition criteria. One adjustment is to use the market value of invested capital. This adjustment substitutes the market value of invested capital (debt and equity) for its reported value in computing return.

Investor versus Company Invested Capital

In computing return on invested capital, we must distinguish between a company's invested capital and an investor's invested capital. An investor's invested capital is the price paid for a company's securities. Except when an investor acquires securities at book value, an investor's invested capital differs from the company's invested capital. Our analysis of return on invested capital focuses on the company and not on individual shareholders. Later in this chapter we come back to this issue and focus on shareholder return.

Computing Invested Capital for the Period

Regardless of our *invested capital* definition, we compare the return for the period with its investment base. The invested capital for the period is typically computed using the *average* capital available to a company during the period. An average is used to reflect changes in invested capital during the period. The most common method is adding beginning and ending year invested capital and dividing by 2. We must use care in applying averaging. Companies in certain industries choose a "natural" rather than calendar business year. For example, in retailing the natural business year ends when inventories and sales are low (for example, January 31 after the holiday season). In this case, averaging year-ends yields the lowest rather than the average invested capital during the period. A more accurate method is to average interim amounts–for example, adding quarter-end invested capital amounts and dividing by 4.

Defining Income

The analysis of return on invested capital requires a measure of **income.** The definition of *income,* or *return,* depends on the definition of *invested capital.* If *invested capital* is defined as assets, then income *before* interest expense is used. Excluding interest from income is necessary because interest is viewed as payment to suppliers of debt capital. Similar reasoning is used to exclude dividends–viewed as payments to suppliers of equity capital. Hence, income *before* interest expense and dividends is used when computing return on assets.

The income of a consolidated company that includes a subsidiary that is partially owned by a minority interest typically reflects a deduction for the minority's share of income. The company's consolidated balance sheet, however, includes the subsidiary's assets. Since invested capital (denominator) includes assets of the consolidated company, the income (numerator) should include total company income (or loss), not just the parent's share. For this reason we add back the minority's share of earnings (or loss) to income when computing return on assets. When we define *invested capital* (denominator) as equity capital excluding minority interest, we need *not* add back the minority's share of earnings (or loss) to income.

CLEANING UP

Insurance companies are placing increasing demands on corporations such as:

- Access to outside auditors' reports
- More grilling of the CEO and CFO
- Increased scrutiny of financials by specialists
- Reviews of execs' track records and how involved the board is
- Up-to-tenfold hike in deductibles and co-liability for coverage beyond that

Return on common equity capital uses income defined as net income *after* deductions for interest and preferred dividends. If preferred dividends are cumulative, they are deducted in computing income whether these dividends are declared or not. This is because common shareholders' claims are junior to preferred shareholders.

Measures of income in computing return on invested capital must reflect all applicable expenses including income taxes. Some users exclude income taxes in their computations. These users claim it is to isolate the effects of tax management from operating performance. Others claim changes in tax rates impair comparability across years. Still others claim that companies with tax loss carryforwards add confusion and complications to return on invested capital computations. Nevertheless, we must recognize that income taxes reduce a company's income and we should include them in measuring income, especially for the return on shareholders' equity. Later in the chapter we disaggregate return on invested capital where one component reflects the company's tax situation.

Adjustments to Invested Capital and Income

Our analysis of return on invested capital uses reported financial statement numbers as a starting point. As we discussed in several prior chapters, many accounting numbers call for analytical adjustment. Also, several numbers not reported in financial statements need to be included. Some adjustments, like those relating to inventory, affect both the numerator and denominator of return on invested capital, moderating their effect. Whatever their impacts, the analysis of return on invested capital should use the appropriately adjusted financial statement numbers as described in earlier chapters.

Computing Return on Invested Capital

This section applies our discussion to an analysis of return on invested capital. We illustrate the different measures of both income and invested capital for the computations. For this purpose, we draw on the financial statements of Excell Corporation reproduced in Exhibits 8.1 and 8.2. Our return on invested capital computations are for Year 9 and use amounts rounded to the nearest million.

Return on Total Assets

Return on assets (both debt and equity capital) of Excell Corporation for Year 9 is computed as:

$$\frac{\text{Net Income} + \text{Interest expense } (1 - \text{Tax rate}) + \text{Minority interest in income}}{(\text{Beginning total assets} + \text{Ending total assets}) \div 2}$$

$$\frac{\$64{,}569 + \$20{,}382(1 - 0.40) + \$0}{(\$1{,}333{,}982 + \$1{,}371{,}621) \div 2} = 5.677\%$$

Our tax adjustment of interest expense recognizes that interest is tax deductible. This implies that if interest expense is excluded, the related tax benefit must be excluded from income. We assume a *marginal* corporate tax rate of 40%–the tax incidence with respect to any one item (like interest expense) can be measured by the marginal tax rate. There is no minority interest in the income of Excell, and the assets are averaged using year-end figures.

Exhibit 8.1

EXCELL CORPORATION
Income Statement
For Years Ended December 31, Year 8 and Year 9

($ in thousands)	Year 8	Year 9
Net sales	$1,636,298	$1,723,729
Costs and expenses	1,473,293	1,579,401
Operating income	163,005	144,328
Other income, net	2,971	1,784
Income before interest and taxes	165,976	146,112
Interest expense*	16,310	20,382
Income before taxes	149,666	125,730
Less federal and other income taxes	71,770	61,161
Net income	$ 77,896	$ 64,569
Less cash dividends:		
Preferred stock	2,908	2,908
Common stock	39,209	38,898
Net income reinvested in the business	$ 35,779	$ 22,763

* *In Year 9, interest on long-term debt is $19,695.*

Return on Common Shareholders' Equity

Return on common equity typically excludes from invested capital all but common shareholders' equity. The **return on common equity** of Excell Corporation for Year 9 is computed as:

$$\frac{\text{Net income} - \text{Preferred dividends}}{\text{Average common shareholders' equity}}$$

$$\frac{\$64{,}569 - \$2{,}908}{(\$674{,}363 + \$698{,}917) \div 2} = 8.98\%$$

Excell's higher return on common shareholders' equity as compared to its return on total assets reflects the favorable effects of financial leverage. That is, Excell is successfully trading on the equity. There is another method to compute the return on common shareholders' equity using a ratio of two often reported figures as follows:

$$\frac{\text{Basic earnings per share}}{\text{Book value per share}}$$

The return from this latter computation is often slightly different due to rounding. Also, note that when *convertible* debt sells at a substantial premium above par and is held by investors primarily for its conversion feature, there is justification for treating it as an equivalent of equity capital. This is especially true when a company has the right to force conversion by calling it in.

Exhibit 8.2

EXCELL CORPORATION
Balance Sheet
At December 31, Year 8 and Year 9

($ in thousands)	Year 8	Year 9
Assets		
Current assets:		
Cash	$ 25,425	$ 25,580
Marketable securities	38,008	28,910
Accounts and notes receivable—net	163,870	176,911
Inventories	264,882	277,795
Total current assets	492,185	509,196
Investments in and receivables from nonconsolidated subsidiaries	33,728	41,652
Miscellaneous investments and receivables	5,931	6,997
Funds held by trustee for construction	6,110	—
Land, buildings, equipment, and timberlands—net	773,361	790,774
Deferred charges to future operations	16,117	16,452
Goodwill and other intangible assets	6,550	6,550
Total assets	$1,333,982	$1,371,621
Liabilities		
Current liabilities:		
Notes payable to banks	$ 7,850	$ 13,734
Accounts payable and accrued expenses	128,258	144,999
Dividends payable	10,404	10,483
Federal and other taxes on income	24,370	13,256
Long-term indebtedness payable within one year	9,853	11,606
Total current liabilities	180,735	194,078
Long-term indebtedness	350,565	335,945
Deferred taxes on income	86,781	101,143
Total liabilities	618,081	631,166
Equity		
Preferred, 7% cumulative and noncallable, par value $25 per share; authorized 1,760,000 shares	41,538	41,538
Common, par value $12.50 per share; authorized 30,000,000 shares	222,245	222,796
Capital in excess of par value—common	19,208	20,448
Retained earnings	436,752	459,515
Less: Common treasury stock	(3,842)	(3,842)
Total equity	715,901	740,455
Total liabilities and equity	$1,333,982	$1,371,621

ANALYZING RETURN ON ASSETS

Return on invested capital is useful in management evaluation, profitability analysis, earnings forecasting, and planning and control. Our use of return on invested capital for these tasks requires a thorough understanding of this return measure. This is because the return measure includes components with the potential to contribute to an understanding of company performance. This section examines this return when invested capital is viewed independently of its financing sources, using debt and equity capital (total assets), commonly referred to as **return on assets (ROA).**

Disaggregating Return on Assets

Recall that the return on assets (or return on total capital) in its most *simplified form* is computed as:

$$\frac{\text{Income}}{\text{Assets}}$$

We can disaggregate this return into meaningful components relative to sales. We do this because these component ratios are useful in analysis of company performance. Sales is an important criterion to judge company profitability and is a major indicator of company activity. This disaggregation of return on assets is:

Return on assets = Profit margin × Asset turnover

$$\frac{\text{Income}}{\text{Assets}} = \frac{\text{Income}}{\text{Sales}} \times \frac{\text{Sales}}{\text{Assets}}$$

Return on Assets for Selected Industries

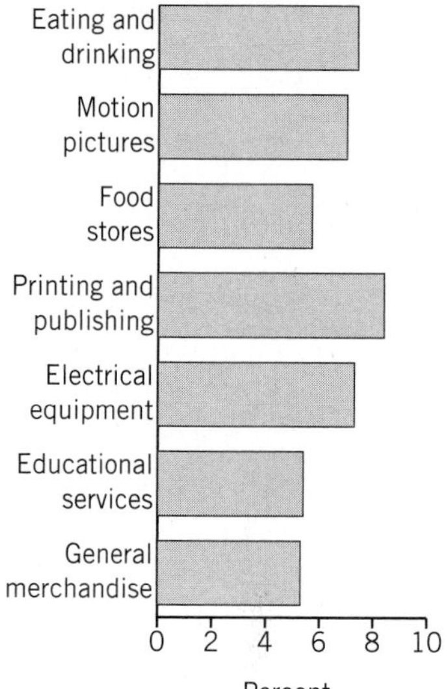

Source: Dun & Bradstreet.

The income to sales relation is called **profit margin** and measures a company's profitability relative to sales. The sales to assets relation is called **asset turnover** and measures a company's effectiveness in generating sales from assets. This decomposition highlights the role of these components, both profit margin and asset turnover, in determining return on assets. Profit margin and asset turnover are useful measures that require analysis to gain further insights into a company's profitability. We describe the major components determining return on assets in Exhibit 8.3. The first level of analysis

Disaggregating Return on Assets ***Exhibit 8.3***

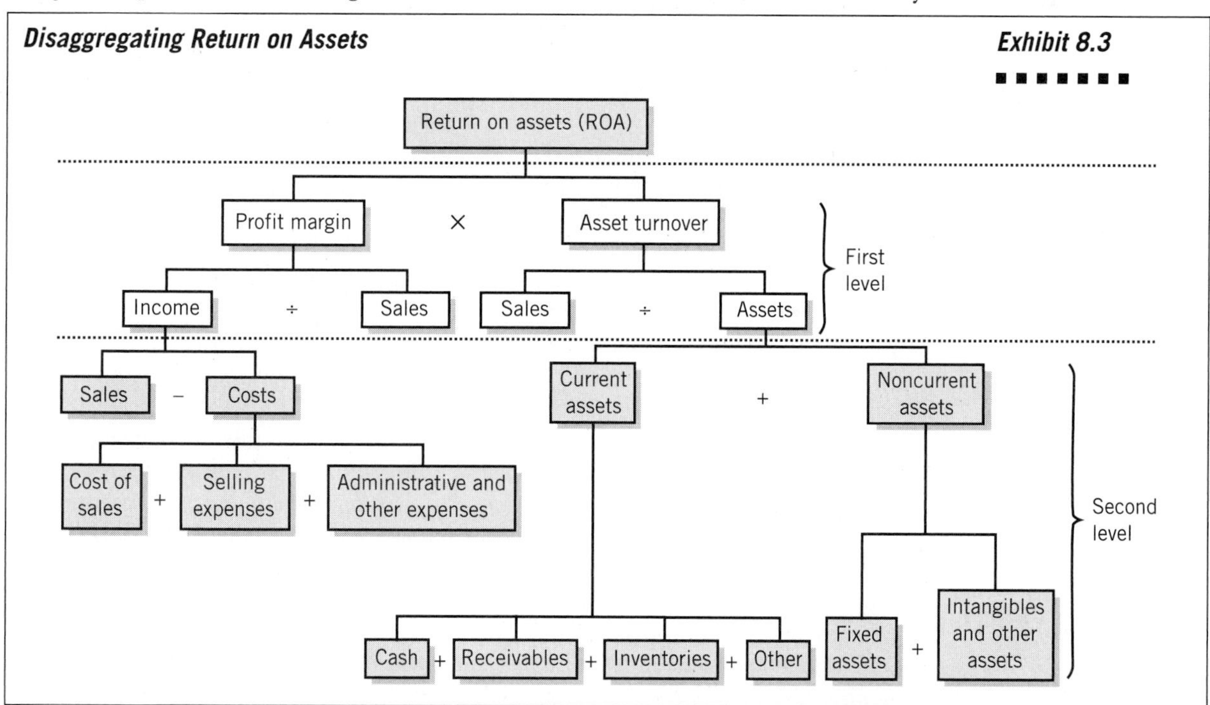

focuses on the interaction of profit margin and asset turnover. The second level of analysis highlights other important factors determining profit margin and asset turnover. This section emphasizes the first level of analysis. Two later chapters explore the second level–Chapter 9 with analysis of operating results and Chapter 12 with analysis and forecasting of earnings.

Relation between Profit Margin and Asset Turnover

The relation between profit margin and asset turnover is illustrated in Exhibit 8.4. As defined, return on assets (in percent) equals profit margin (in percent) multiplied by asset turnover. As Exhibit 8.4 shows, Company X achieves a 10% return on assets with a relatively high profit margin and a low asset turnover. In contrast, Company Z achieves the same return on assets but with a low profit margin and high asset turnover. Company Y's margin and turnover is between these two companies. Namely, Company Y has a 10% return with a profit margin one-half that of Company X and an asset turnover double that of Company X. This exhibit indicates there are many combinations of profit margins and asset turnovers yielding a 10% return on assets.

Exhibit 8.4 ***Analysis of Return on Assets***

	Company X	Company Y	Company Z
Sales	$5,000,000	$10,000,000	$10,000,000
Income	$ 500,000	$ 500,000	$ 100,000
Assets	$5,000,000	$ 5,000,000	$ 1,000,000
Profit margin	10%	5%	1%
Asset turnover	1	2	10
Return on assets	10%	10%	10%

We can generalize the returns analysis of Exhibit 8.4 to show a continuous range of possible combinations of profit margins and asset turnovers yielding a 10% return on assets. Exhibit 8.5 portrays graphically this relation between profit margin (horizontal axis) and asset turnover (vertical axis). The curve drawn in this exhibit traces all combinations of profit margin and asset turnover yielding a 10% return on assets. This curve slopes from the upper left corner of low profit margin and high asset turnover to the lower right corner of high profit margin and low asset turnover. We plot the data from Companies X and Y (from Exhibit 8.4) in Exhibit 8.5–designated points X and Y, respectively. The remaining points A through P are combinations of profit margins and asset turnovers of other companies. Graphing returns of companies within an industry around the 10% return on asset curve (or other applicable return curve) is a valuable method of comparing profitability. More important, such graphing reveals the relation between profit margin and asset turnover determining ROA and is extremely useful in company analysis.

Disaggregating return on assets as in Exhibit 8.5 provides insights in assessing companies' strategic actions to increase returns. For example, Companies B and C must concentrate on restoring profitability. Moreover, assuming the industry represented in Exhibit 8.5 has a representative profit margin and asset turnover, the evidence suggests Company P should focus on improving asset turnover while Company A should focus on increasing profit margin. Other companies like H and I best concentrate on both profit margin and asset turnover. Our analysis to this point treats profit margin and asset turnover as independent. Yet profit margin and asset turnover are *interdependent.* Specifically, when fixed expenses are substantial, a higher level of asset turnover increases

Relation between Profit Margin, Asset Turnover, and Return on Assets **Exhibit 8.5**

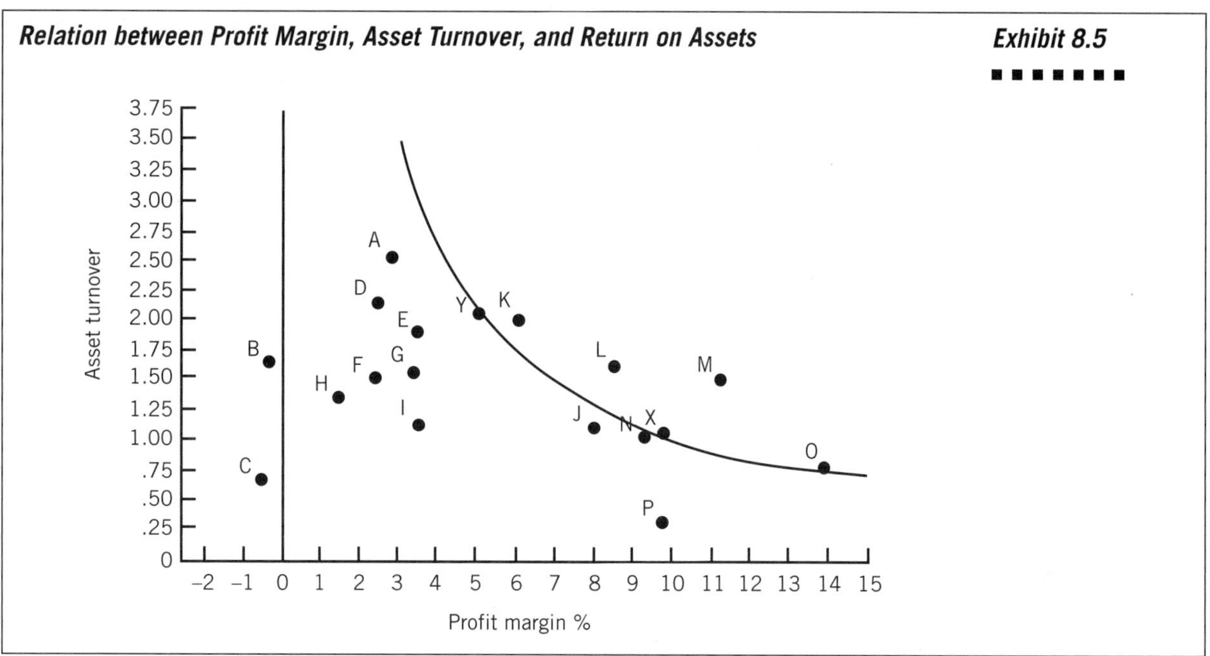

profit margin. This is because in a certain range of activity, costs increase proportionally less than sales. In comparing companies in an industry, we must consider companies with low asset turnovers having the potential to increase return through increased asset turnover (sales expansion).

Analysis of return on assets can reveal additional insights into strategic activity. As another example, consider two companies in the same industry with identical returns on assets.

	Company AA	Company BB
Sales	$ 1,000,000	$20,000,000
Income	$ 100,000	$ 100,000
Assets	$10,000,000	$10,000,000
Profit margin	10%	0.5%
Asset turnover	0.1	2.0
Return on assets	1%	1%

Both companies' returns on assets are poor. Yet, the strategically corrective action for each is different. Our analysis of such cases must evaluate the likelihood of managerial success and other factors in improving performance. In particular, Company AA has a 10% profit margin (near the industry average) while Company BB's is considerably lower. On the other hand, a dollar invested in assets yields only $0.10 in sales for Company AA, whereas Company BB achieves $2 in sales for each dollar invested. Accordingly, one part of our analysis focuses on Company AA's assets, asking questions such as: Why is turnover so low? Are there assets yielding little or no return? Are there idle assets requiring disposal? Are assets inefficiently or ineffectively utilized? We would expect that Company AA can achieve immediate improvements by concentrating on increasing turnover (by increasing sales, reducing investment, or both). It is likely more difficult for Company AA to increase profit margin much beyond the industry norm.

Company BB confronts a much different scenario. Our analysis suggests Company BB should focus on correcting its low profit margin. Reasons for low profit margins are varied but often include inefficient equipment or production methods, unprofitable product lines, excess capacity with high fixed costs, or excessive selling and administrative expenses. Companies with low profit margins sometimes discover that changes in tastes and technology require increased investment in assets to finance sales. This implies that to maintain its return on assets, a company must increase its profit margin or else production is no longer moneymaking.

There is a tendency to view a high profit margin as a sign of high earnings quality. Yet we must emphasize the importance of return on invested capital (however defined) as the ultimate test of profitability. A supermarket is content with a profit margin of 1% or less because of its high asset turnover owing to a relatively low asset investment and a high proportion of leased assets (like stores and fixtures). Similarly, a discount store accepts a low profit margin to generate high asset turnover (primarily in inventories). In contrast, capital-intensive industries like steel, chemicals, and automobiles having large asset investments and low asset turnovers must achieve higher profit margins to be successful. Exhibit 8.6 portrays graphically the relation between profit margin and asset turnover for several industries. We graph the 5% return on assets curve in Exhibit 8.6 as a reference point for analysis.

Exhibit 8.6 ***Profit Margin, Asset Turnover, and Return on Assets for Selected Industries***

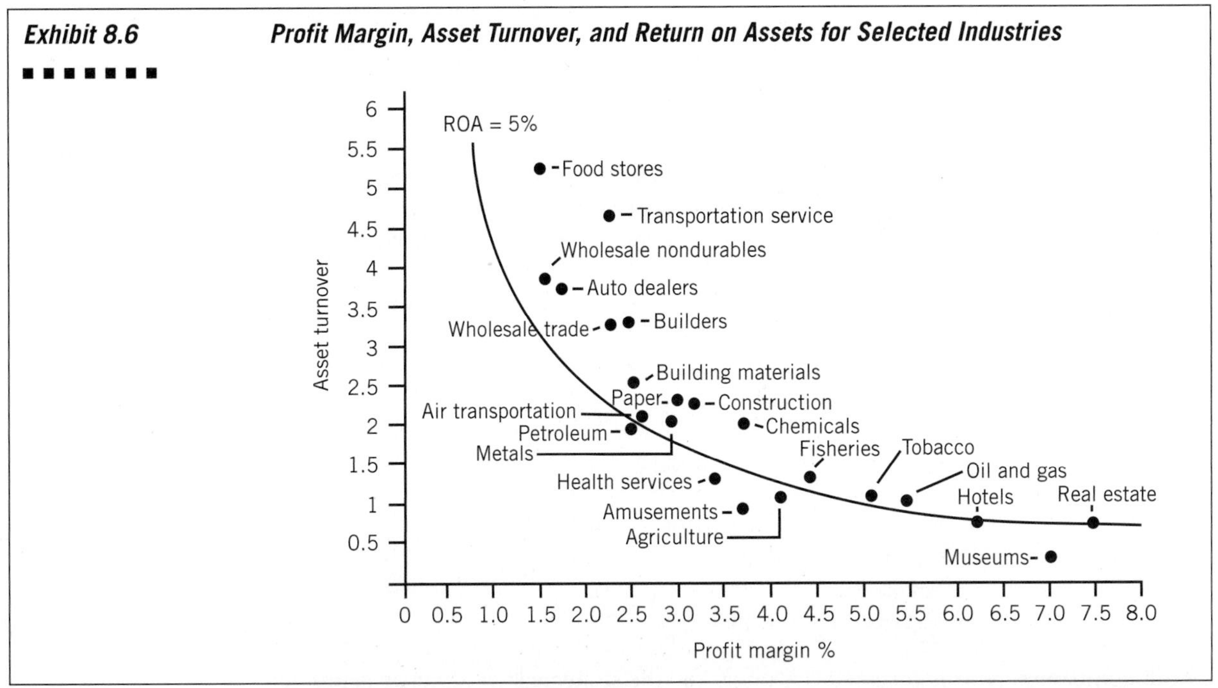

We must remember that analysis of returns for a single year is potentially misleading. The cyclical nature of many industries yields swings in profit margins where some years' profits can be excessive while others are not. Companies must be analyzed using returns computed over several years and spanning a business cycle.

Asset Turnover Analysis

Asset turnover measures the intensity with which companies utilize assets. The most relevant measure of asset utilization is sales, since sales are essential to profits. In special cases like start-up or development companies, our analysis of turnover must recognize that most assets are committed to *future* business activities. Also, unusual supply problems or work stoppages are conditions affecting asset utilization and require special evaluation and interpretation. This section describes various analyses using disaggregation of asset turnover.

Disaggregation of Asset Turnover

The standard measure of asset turnover in determining return on assets is:

$$\frac{\text{Sales}}{\text{Assets}}$$

Further evaluation of changes in turnover rates for individual assets can be useful in a company analysis. This section examines asset turnover for *component asset accounts.*

Sales to Cash. Cash and cash equivalents are held primarily for purposes of meeting day-to-day transactions and as a liquidity reserve to prevent shortages arising from imbalances in cash inflows and outflows. All businesses have and must maintain a relation between sales and cash. A too high cash turnover can be due to a cash shortage that might signal a liquidity crisis if a company has no ready source of cash. A low cash turnover might signal idle or excess cash. Cash accumulated for specific purposes or known contingencies often yields temporary decreases in turnover. The basic trade-off is between liquidity and accumulation of funds yielding little or no return.

Sales to Receivables. A company selling on credit knows that the level of its receivables is a function of sales. A low receivables turnover is likely due to overextending credit, an inability of customers to pay, or poor collection activity. A high receivables turnover can imply a strict credit policy, or a reluctance or inability to extend credit. Receivables turnover often involves a trade-off between increased sales and accumulation of funds in receivables.

Sales to Inventories. Maintaining sales typically requires inventories. The sales-to-inventories relation varies across industries depending on the variety of types, models, varieties, and other inventory classes necessary to lure and retain consumers. Both the length of production cycle and type of item (luxury versus necessity, or perishable versus durable) has a bearing on inventory turnover. A low inventory turnover often suggests overstocked, slow-moving, or obsolete inventories. It can also signal overestimation of sales. Temporary conditions like work stoppages or slowdowns with important customers can yield low turnover. A high turnover can imply underinvestment in inventory, threatening customer relations and future sales. Inventory turnover involves a trade-off between funds accumulated in inventory and the potential loss of customers and future sales (and inventory obsolescence).

Sales to Fixed Assets. The relation between sales and property, plant, and equipment is long term and fundamental to most companies. There are temporary conditions affecting this relation. Temporary conditions include excess capacity, inefficient plants, obsolete equipment, demand changes, and interruptions in raw materials supply. Our analysis must remember increases in fixed assets are typically *not* gradual, but occur in large increments. This process can create changes in fixed asset turnover. Leased facilities and equipment, often not appearing on the balance sheet, can distort this turnover. The fixed asset turnover involves a trade-off between fixed asset investments having high break-even points vis-à-vis more efficient, productive investments with high sales potential.

Sales to Current Liabilities. The relation between sales and current trade liabilities is a predictable one. A company's short-term trade liabilities depend on its sales (demand for its goods and services). Short-term credit is relatively cost free and reduces a company's funds accumulated in working capital. Also, a company's available credit line depends on its sales and income.

Factors in Asset Turnover

The analysis of return on assets involves several additional factors. In Chapter 12 we consider extraordinary gains and losses and how our analysis adjusts for them. The effect of discontinued operations must be similarly evaluated. An analysis of the trend in return on assets must consider the effects of acquisitions accounted for as poolings of interest (Chapter 5) and their likelihood of recurrence. An internal analysis (by managers, auditors, consultants) can often obtain return data by segments, product lines, and divisions. These disaggregated data increase the reliability of and insights from the analysis. Where bargaining power or position permits, an external analysis can sometimes obtain and then analyze disaggregated data. A problem arises when the level of individual assets (or total assets) changes during a period and adversely affects the turnover computation. Accordingly, we use averages of individual and total asset levels. Specifically, the *denominator in computing asset turnover is an average of beginning and ending balances.* Provided data are available, an average can be computed using monthly or quarterly balances.

A consistently high return on assets is the earmark of effective management. Such management can distinguish a growth company from one experiencing merely a cyclical or seasonal pickup in business. Examining all factors constituting return on assets usually reveals the sources and limitations of a company's return. Neither profit margin nor asset turnover can increase indefinitely. Increasing assets through external financing and/or internal earnings retention is necessary for further earnings growth.

ANALYZING RETURN ON COMMON EQUITY

Return on common shareholders' equity (ROCE), or simply return on common equity, is of great interest to the shareholders of a company. Return on common shareholders' equity differs from return on assets due primarily to what is excluded from invested capital. Return on common shareholders' equity excludes assets financed by creditors and preferred shareholders. Creditors usually receive a fixed return on their financing. Preferred shareholders usually receive a fixed dividend. Yet common shareholders are provided no fixed or promised returns. These shareholders have claims on the *residual* earnings of a company only after all other financing sources are paid. Accordingly, the return on shareholders' equity is most important to common shareholders. The relation between return on shareholders' equity and return on assets is also important as it bears on the analysis of a company's success with financial leverage.

Return on common shareholders' equity serves a key role in equity valuation. Recall the accounting-based stock valuation formula from Chapter 1:

$$V_t = BV_t + \frac{NI_{t+1} - (k \times BV_t)}{(1+k)} + \frac{NI_{t+2} - (k \times BV_{t+1})}{(1+k)^2} + \cdots + \frac{NI_{t+n} - (k \times BV_{t+n-1})}{(1+k)^n} + \cdots$$

Through algebraic simplification, the formula can be restated in terms of *future* returns on common shareholders' equity:

$$V_t = BV_t + \frac{(ROCE_{t+1} - k)BV_t}{(1+k)} + \frac{(ROCE_{t+2} - k)BV_{t+1}}{(1+k)^2} + \cdots + \frac{(ROCE_{t+n} - k)BV_{t+n-1}}{(1+k)^n} + \cdots$$

where ROCE is equal to net income available to common shareholders (*after* preferred dividends) divided by the beginning-of-period balance of common equity. This formula is intuitively appealing. Namely, it implies that companies with ROCE greater than the investors' required rate of return (k) increase value in excess of that implied by book value alone.

Disaggregating Return on Common Equity

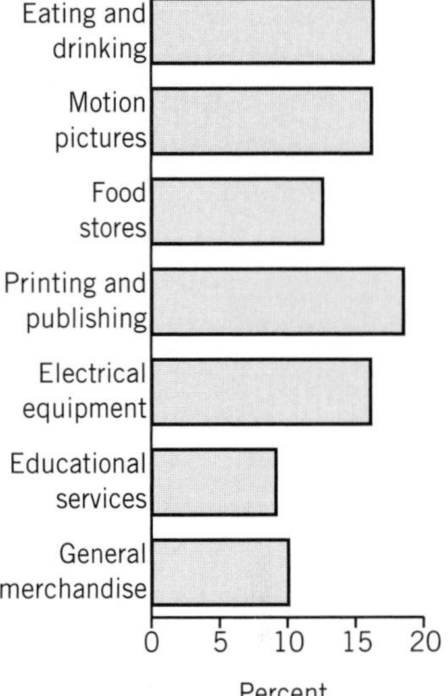

Source: Dun & Bradstreet.

While ROCE in the above formula is computed using the beginning-of-period balance of common equity, in practice we use the *average* balance for the period under analysis. As with return on assets, disaggregating return on common equity into components is extremely useful for analysis purposes. Recall that the return on common shareholders' equity is computed as:

$$\frac{\text{Net income} - \text{Preferred dividends}}{\text{Average common shareholders' equity}}$$

We can disaggregate return on common shareholders' equity to obtain:

ROCE = Adjusted profit margin × Asset turnover × Leverage

$$\frac{\text{Net income} - \text{Preferred dividends}}{\text{Average common equity}} = \frac{\text{Net income} - \text{Preferred dividends}}{\text{Sales}} \times \frac{\text{Sales}}{\text{Average assets}} \times \frac{\text{Average assets}}{\text{Average common equity}}$$

Adjusted profit margin reflects the portion of every sales dollar remaining for common shareholders after providing for all costs and claims (including preferred dividends). Asset turnover is exactly as defined above for return on assets, and **leverage** (or *financial leverage*) is the common shareholders' leverage ratio measuring the proportion of assets financed by common shareholders. The larger the leverage ratio, the smaller the proportion of assets financed by common shareholders and the greater the financial leverage. These components are useful in both an analysis of company performance and in assessing returns to shareholders.[1]

Drawing on the financial statements of Excell Corporation in Exhibits 8.1 and 8.2, we can compute the disaggregated ROCE for Year 9 as (in \$ millions):

$$\frac{\$65 - \$3}{(\$674 + \$699) \div 2} = \frac{\$65 - \$3}{\$1{,}724} \times \frac{\$1{,}724}{(\$1{,}334 + \$1{,}372) \div 2} \times \frac{(\$1{,}334 + \$1{,}372) \div 2}{(\$674 + \$699) \div 2}$$

or

ROCE = Adjusted profit margin × Asset turnover × Leverage

$$8.98\% = 3.577\% \times 1.274 \times 1.970$$

We can compute additional variations on the disaggregated ROCE of Excell Corporation to provide further insights into different aspects of its business. One variation is to merge asset turnover and leverage. In Excell's operations, each dollar of common equity

[1]An alternative disaggregation of return on common equity is a variant of the return on assets (ROA). This disaggregation is:

ROCE = ROA × Earnings leverage × Common leverage

$$\frac{\text{Net income} - \text{Preferred dividends}}{\text{Average common shareholders' equity}} = \frac{\text{Net income} + \text{Interest}(1 - \text{Tax rate}) + \text{Minority interest in earnings}}{\text{Average assets}} \times \frac{\text{Net income} - \text{Preferred dividends}}{\text{Net income} + \text{Interest}(1 - \text{Tax rate}) + \text{Minority interest in earnings}} \times \frac{\text{Average assets}}{\text{Average common shareholders' equity}}$$

Return on assets reflects return independent of financing sources. The two leverage components reflect the effect of using both creditor and preferred shareholder financing to increase return to common shareholders. **Earnings leverage** is the proportion of income available to common shareholders (*after* removing costs of both creditor [interest] and preferred [dividend] financing) relative to income available to creditor and equity financing sources (*before* removing these costs). **Financial leverage** reflects the proportion of assets financed by common shareholders.

is used to obtain an *incremental* \$0.97 of noncommon equity (creditor and preferred equity) financing. The *total* financing of \$1.97 generates \$2.51 in sales. We obtain this insight from recognizing that assets (equaling total debt and equity financing) are turning over (generating sales) at a rate of 1.274–or, in formula form, \$1.97 × 1.274 = \$2.51. This highlights that \$2.51 in sales earn an adjusted profit margin (after all costs and preferred dividends) of 3.577%, yielding a return on common shareholders' equity of 8.98% (\$2.51 × 3.577%).

Another variation of this analysis disaggregates adjusted profit margin into its pretax and tax retention components. When *pre-tax* adjusted profit margin is multiplied by (1 − Effective tax rate), or **retention rate,** of the company, we get adjusted profit margin:

Adjusted profit margin = Pretax adjusted profit margin × Retention rate

$$\frac{\text{Net income} - \text{Preferred dividends}}{\text{Sales}} = \frac{\text{Pretax income} - \text{Preferred dividends}}{\text{Sales}} \times \frac{\text{Net income} - \text{Preferred dividends}}{\text{Pretax income} - \text{Preferred dividends}}$$

The purpose of this profit margin disaggregation is to separate pretax margin, a measure of *operating effectiveness,* from retention rate, a measure of *tax-management effectiveness.* In the case of Excell Corporation, the adjusted profit margin of 3.577% is disaggregated as:

$$3.577\% = \frac{\$126 - \$3}{\$1{,}724} \times \frac{\$65 - \$3}{\$126 - \$3} = 7.125\% \times 50.204\%$$

ANALYSIS VIEWPOINT ***. . . YOU ARE THE CONSULTANT***

You are the management consultant to a client seeking a critical review of its performance. As part of your analysis you compute ROCE and its components (industry norms in parenthesis): asset turnover = 1.5 (1.0); leverage = 2.1 (2.2); pretax adjusted profit margin = 0.05 (0.14); and retention rate = 0.40 (0.24). What does your preliminary analysis of these figures suggest?

Answer–p. 448

Computing Return on Invested Capital

This section applies our analysis of return on invested capital to the financial statements of Campbell Soup Company reproduced in Appendix A.

Return on Assets

Return on assets is measured as (includes reference codes to Campbell's relevant financial statement items):

$$\frac{\text{Net income } \boxed{28} + [\text{Interest expense } \boxed{18} + (1 - \text{Tax rate})] + \text{Minority interest in earnings } \boxed{25}}{\text{Average assets } \boxed{39A}}$$

Computation of this return for Year 11 of Campbell yields (\$ millions):

$$\frac{\$401.5 + \$116.2(1 - 0.34) + \$7.2}{(\$4{,}149.0 + \$4{,}115.6)/2} = \frac{\$485.4}{\$4{,}132.3} = 11.75\%$$

Disaggregated Return on Assets

We can disaggregate Campbell's Year 11 return on assets (ROA) into its profit margin and asset turnover components:

$$\text{Return on assets} = \text{Profit margin} \times \text{Asset turnover}$$

$$= \frac{\text{Net income} + \text{Interest } (1 - \text{Tax rate}) + \text{Minority interest in earnings}}{\text{Sales}} \times \frac{\text{Sales}}{\text{Average assets}}$$

$$11.75\% = \frac{\$485.4}{\$6{,}204.1} \times \frac{\$6{,}204.1}{\$4{,}132.3} = 7.8\% \times 1.5$$

Return on Common Equity

Return on common shareholders' equity is defined as (includes reference codes to Campbell's relevant financial statement items):

$$\frac{\text{Net income } \boxed{28} - \text{Preferred dividends}}{\text{Average common equity}^{*} \ \boxed{54}\ \boxed{176}}$$

*Includes 50% of deferred taxes we assume as equity.

Computation of return on common equity for Year 11 of Campbell yields ($ millions):

$$\frac{\$401.5}{[(\$1{,}793.4 + \$129.3) + (\$1{,}691.8 + \$117.5)]/2} = \frac{\$401.5}{\$1{,}866} = 21.52\%$$

Disaggregated Return on Common Equity

We disaggregate Campbell's Year 11 return on common equity into its components:

$$\text{ROCE} = \text{Adjusted profit margin} \times \text{Asset turnover} \times \text{Leverage}$$

$$\text{ROCE} = \frac{\text{Net income} - \text{Preferred dividends}}{\text{Sales } \boxed{13}} \times \frac{\text{Sales}}{\text{Average assets}} \times \frac{\text{Average assets}}{\text{Average common equity}}$$

$$= \frac{\$401.5}{\$6{,}204.1} \times \frac{\$6{,}204.1}{\$4{,}132.3} \times \frac{\$4{,}132.3}{\$1{,}866.0}$$

$$21.52\% = 6.47\% \times 1.50 \times 2.22$$

Further disaggregation of Campbell's adjusted profit margin into its *pretax* and *tax retention* components yields:

$$\text{Adjusted profit margin} = \text{Pretax adjusted profit margin} \times \text{Retention rate}$$

$$= \frac{\text{Pretax income}}{\text{Sales}} \times \frac{\text{Net income}}{\text{Pretax income}}$$

$$= \frac{\$667.4\ \boxed{26}}{\$6{,}204.1} \times \frac{\$401.5\ \boxed{28}}{\$667.4}$$

$$6.5\% = 10.8\% \times 60.2\%$$

We conduct a comparative analysis of these ratios across time in the section on analysis of return on invested capital for the Comprehensive Case chapter. An analysis of return on invested capital measures across time is often revealing of company performance. If ROCE declines, it is important for us to identify the component(s) responsible for this decline to better assess past and future company performance. We can also then better assess areas of greatest potential improvement in ROCE and the likelihood of a company successfully pursuing this strategy. For example, if leverage is high and not likely to increase, our analysis focuses on adjusted profit margin and asset turnover. An analysis of company strategies and the potential for improvements also depends on industry and economic conditions. We pursue answers to questions such as: Is profit margin high or low in comparison with the industry? What is the potential improvement in asset turnover in this industry? Evaluating returns using the structured approach described in this chapter and interpreting them in their proper context can greatly aid our analysis.

Further Disaggregation of Return on Common Equity

Further disaggregation of return on common equity is sometimes useful for analysis. Specifically, we can separate both *interest* and *tax* components from net income as follows (using numbers from Campbell):

EBIT [$783.6] = Net income [$401.5] + Interest [$116.2] + Taxes [$265.9] **27**

where EBIT is earnings (income) *before* interest and taxes (and *before* preferred dividends, if applicable). We then use these net income components and merge them into the ROCE disaggregation formula as follows:

ROCE = [(EBIT profit margin × Asset turnover) − Interest burden] × Leverage × Retention rate

where *EBIT profit margin* equals EBIT divided by sales, *interest burden* equals interest expense divided by average assets, and the other components are as defined above. Interest burden is sometimes referred to as *interest turnover*. This derives from the notion that the higher the interest burden, the lower the ROCE. Also, the higher the tax retention, the higher the ROCE. Computation of the disaggregation of ROCE for Year 11 of Campbell yields ($ millions):

$$\text{ROCE} = \left[\left(\frac{\$783.6}{\$6{,}204.1} \times \frac{\$6{,}204.1}{\$4{,}132.3}\right) - \frac{\$116.2}{\$4{,}132.3}\right] \times \frac{\$4{,}132.3}{\$1{,}866.0} \times (1.000 - 0.398)$$

$$21.52\% = [(0.126 \times 1.50) - 0.028] \quad \times 2.22 \quad \times 0.602$$

This disaggregation highlights *both* effects of interest and taxes on Campbell's ROCE.

Analysis Research

RETURN ON COMMON SHAREHOLDERS' EQUITY

How does a company's return on common shareholders' equity (ROCE) behave across time? Do certain companies consistently have high or low ROCE? Do companies' ROCEs tend to move toward an average ROCE? Analysis research has addressed these important questions. *On average,* a company's ROCE for the current period is a good predictor of its ROCE for the next period. However, as the time horizon increases, a company's ROCE tends to converge toward the average economywide ROCE. This is usually attributed to the effects of competition. Companies that are able to sustain high ROCEs typically command large premiums over book value.

A large portion of the variability in companies' ROCEs is due to changes in ROA. This is because, on average, leverage factors do not vary significantly over time. Two factors are important in predicting ROCE. First, disaggregating net income into operating and nonoperating components improves forecasts. Second, the conservatism inherent in accounting practice must eventually "reverse." This accounting reversal predictably yields an increase in ROCE.

Assessing Growth in Common Equity

Equity Growth Rate

We can assess the common equity growth rate of a company through earnings retention. This analysis emphasizes equity growth *without* resort to external financing. To assess equity growth, we assume earnings retention *and* a constant dividend payout over time. The **equity growth rate** is computed as:

$$\text{Equity growth rate} = \frac{\text{Net income} - \text{Preferred dividends} - \text{Common dividend payout}}{\text{Average common equity}}$$

The equity growth rate for Year 9 of Excell Corporation, using its financial statements reproduced in Exhibits 8.1 and 8.2, is computed as:

$$3.35\% = \frac{\$65 - \$3 - \$39^*}{(\$674 + \$699) \div 2}$$

* Common stock dividend payout.

This measure implies Excell Corporation can grow 3.35% per year without increasing its current level of financing.

Sustainable Equity Growth Rate

The **sustainable equity growth rate,** or simply sustainable equity growth, recognizes that internal growth for a company depends on *both* earnings retention and the return earned on the earnings retained. Specifically, the **sustainable equity growth rate** is computed as:

$$\text{Sustainable equity growth rate} = \text{ROCE} \times (1 - \text{Payout rate})$$

For Excell Corporation (see Exhibits 8.1 and 8.2), we find the dividend payout rate for Year 9 equals 65% ($41,806/$64,569). We then compute Excell's sustainable equity growth rate for Year 9 as:

$$3.17\% = 8.98\% \times (1 - 0.647)$$

Excell experienced an earnings decline from Year 8 ($77,896) to Year 9 ($64,569). This along with a constant dividend payout produced a decline in its sustainable growth rate. When estimating future equity growth rates it is often advisable to average (or otherwise recognize) sustainable growth rates for several recent years. We should also recognize potential changes in earnings retention and forecasted ROCE.

Financial Leverage and Return on Common Equity

This section analyzes effects of financial leverage for the return on common equity. *Financial leverage* refers to the extent of invested capital from other than common shareholders. For purposes of analysis, we use financial statements of Excell Corporation. The first step is to list the *average* amounts of all financing sources for Excell Corporation taken from its December 31, Year 9 and Year 8, balance sheets ($ thousands):

Current liabilities (excluding current portion of long-term debt)		$ 176,677
Long-term debt	$343,255	
Current portion of long-term debt	10,730	353,985
Deferred taxes		93,962
Preferred stock		41,538
Common shareholders' equity		686,640
Total financing		$1,352,802

We also reproduce relevant financial data from Excell's income statement and its notes for Year 9 ($ thousands):

Income before taxes	$125,730
Income taxes	61,161
Net income	$ 64,569
Preferred dividends	2,908
Income accruing to common shareholders	$ 61,661

Total interest expense	$ 20,382
Interest on short-term notes (5%)	687
Balance of interest on long-term debt	$ 19,695

We then compute Excell Corporation's return on assets as:

$$\text{ROA} = \frac{\text{Net income} + \text{Interest} \times (1 - \text{Tax rate})}{\text{Average assets}}$$

$$5.677\% = \frac{\$64{,}569 + \$20{,}382(1 - 0.40)}{\$1{,}352{,}802}$$

Excell's 5.677% return on assets is relevant for assessing the effects of financial leverage. This implies that if suppliers of capital (other than the common shareholders) receive a less than 5.677% return on their financing, then common shareholders benefit. The reverse occurs when suppliers of capital receive more than a 5.677% return. The greater the difference in returns between common equity and other capital suppliers, the more successful (or unsuccessful) is the *trading on the equity*.

A thorough analysis of Excell's financial leverage appears in Exhibit 8.7. This exhibit shows an analysis of the relative contribution and return for each of the major financing sources. It also shows the influence of each financier's returns on ROCE. A few findings deserve mention. The $9,618 accruing to common shareholders from use of current liabilities is largely due to them being free of interest costs. The $8,279 accruing to common shareholders from long-term debt is primarily due to tax deductibility of interest.

Exhibit 8.7

Analyzing Leverage on Common Equity ($ thousands)

Financing Source	Average Funds Supplied	Earnings on Funds Supplied at Rate of 5.677 Percent	Payment to Suppliers of Funds	Accruing to (Detracting from) Return on Common Equity
Current liabilities	$ 176,677	$10,030	$ 412[(a)]	$ 9,618
Long-term debt	353,985	20,096	11,817[(b)]	8,279
Deferred taxes	93,962	5,334	none	5,334
Preferred stock	41,538	2,358	2,908[(c)]	(550)
Earnings in excess of return to suppliers of funds				$22,681
Add: Common equity	686,640	38,980	—	38,980
Totals	$1,352,802	$76,798	$15,137	
Total return to shareholders				$61,661

[(a)] Short-term interest expense of $687 less 40 percent tax (from Exhibit 8.1).
[(b)] Long-term interest expense of $19,695 less 40 percent tax (from Exhibit 8.1).
[(c)] Preferred dividends (from Exhibit 8.1)—not tax deductible.

The value of tax deferrals is evident where Excell's use of cost-free funds yields an annual advantage of $5,334. Finally, since preferred dividends are *not* tax deductible, the low return on assets (5.677%) yields a leverage disadvantage to common shareholders of $550.

We can further extend the analysis of leverage to its component parts. Excell's return on common shareholders' equity is ($ thousands):

$$\frac{\text{Net income} - \text{Preferred dividends}}{\text{Average common equity}} = \frac{\$61{,}661^{*}}{\$686{,}640} = 8.98\%$$

* Identical to income accruing to common shareholders in Exhibit 8.7.

We know the net benefit to common shareholders from financial leverage is $22,681 (see Exhibit 8.7). As a percent of common equity, this benefit is computed as:

$$\frac{\text{Earnings in excess of return to suppliers of funds}}{\text{Average common equity}} = \frac{\$22{,}681}{\$686{,}640} = 3.303\%$$

Accordingly, our analysis of return on common equity can view return as consisting of two components:

Return on assets	5.677%
Leverage advantage accruing to common equity	3.303
Return on common equity	8.980%

Return on Common Shareholders' Equity versus Investment

Return on common shareholder's equity measures the relation of net income (attributable to common shareholders) to common shareholders' equity. Common shareholders' equity is measured using book values reported in the balance sheet. These values do not necessarily reflect how individual shareholders might fare in terms of return on their personal investment (that is, the price paid for common stock). This is important since shareholders do not typically buy common stock at book value–they often pay a multiple of book value. The price one pays for stock plays an important role in determining **return on shareholders' investment (ROSI),** computed as (using all per share figures):

$$\text{ROSI} = \frac{\text{Dividends} + \text{Market value of earnings reinvested}}{\text{Share price (cost)}}$$

To illustrate, consider the following financial data from Austin Technics, Inc. (per share rounded to nearest dollar):

Net income	$ 6
Cash dividends to common	(2)
Earnings reinvested	$ 4
Book value of common equity	$60
Ratio of market value to book value	2:1
Market valuation of earnings reinvested	$ 4

The return on common shareholders' equity for Austin Technics is 10% ($6/$60). However, since a shareholder must pay the market share price (2 × $60), the shareholders' ROSI is only 5%–computed as:

$$5\% = \frac{\$2 + \$4}{2 \times 60}$$

SUPERMONTAGE
Nasdaq's SuperMontage trading system lets professional traders see how many shares are bid or offered at several price points—not just at the best price.

One assumption in computing shareholders' return on investment is that the market uses earnings reinvested at their reported amount. It is important for the shareholder to consider how the market values earnings reinvested and make an informed assumption. In the case of Austin Technics' earnings of $6 per share, shareholders benefit from: (1) earnings paid out as dividends [$2] and (2) the value the market places on the earnings reinvested [$4]. If we assume the market value of earnings reinvested is more than their reported value, say $5.2 per share, then we can compute a **shareholder multiple** as (in per share):

$$\frac{\$2\text{ (dividend)} + \$5.2\text{ (market valuation of \$4 earnings reinvested)}}{\$6\text{ (earnings)}} = \frac{\$7.2}{\$6} = 1.20$$

This shareholder multiple implies a dollar earned and reinvested by the company enriches shareholders by $1.20 (ignoring tax effects). Evidence in practice suggests a wide variation in the shareholder multiple across companies, where earnings do not always yield increased dividends or higher stock values. There is some evidence that the correlation between ROCE and ROSI is low–recall ROCE does not include the market's valuation of earnings reinvested or other measures. (See B. Ball, "The Mysterious Disappearance of Retained Earnings," *Harvard Business Review,* July–August 1987.) The ROSI critically depends on market valuation. As we discussed in Chapters 1 and 2, our valuation of equity securities must include analysis of both financial statements *and* market prices. This distinction between the value of a company and its stock is extremely important. For example, financial statement analysis might reveal a company is well managed and fundamentally sound. Yet, this company might be a poor investment because its stock is overvalued (unless we can sell it short). Conversely, a poor performing company can be a good investment because its stock is undervalued.

GUIDANCE ANSWERS TO ANALYSIS VIEWPOINTS

Auditor

Joint analysis is the assessment of one measure of company performance relative to another. In the case of our manufacturing client, both *individual* analyses yield percentage changes within the ±5% acceptable range. However, a joint analysis would suggest a more alarming situation. Consider a joint analysis using profit margin (net income/sales). The client's profit margin is 11.46% ($2,060,000 − $1,824,000/ $2,060,000) for the current year compared with 5.0% ($2,000,000 − $1,900,000/ $2,000,000) for the prior year–a 129% increase in profit margin! This is what the audit partner is concerned with, and encourages expanded audit tests including joint analysis to verify or refute the client's figures.

Consultant

Your preliminary analysis highlights deviations from the norm in (1) asset turnover, (2) pretax adjusted profit margin, and (3) retention rate. Asset turnover for your client is better than the norm. Your client appears to efficiently use its assets. One note of warning: we need to be assured all assets are accounted for and properly valued, and we want to know if the company is sufficiently replacing its aging assets. Your client's pretax adjusted profit margin is 60% lower than the norm. This is alarming, especially in light of the positive asset turnover ratio. Our client has considerably greater costs than the norm, and we need to direct efforts to identify and analyze these costs. Retention rate is also considerably worse than competitors. Our client is paying a greater proportion of its income in taxes. We need to utilize tax experts to identify and appropriately plan business activities with tax considerations in mind.

QUESTIONS

8–1 How is return on invested capital used as an internal management tool?

8–2 Why is return on invested capital one of the most relevant measures of company performance? How do we use this measure in our analysis of financial statements?

8–3 Why is interest added back to net income when computing return on total assets?

8–4 Discuss the motivation for excluding "nonproductive" assets from invested capital when computing return. What circumstances justify excluding intangible assets from invested capital?

8–5 Why must minority interest's share in net income be added back when computing return on total assets?

8–6 Why must net income used in computing return on invested capital be adjusted to reflect the capital base (denominator) used in the computation?

8–7 What is the relation between return on invested capital and sales? Consider both net income to sales and sales to total assets in your response.

8–8 Company A acquires Company B because the latter has a profit margin (net income to sales) exceeding the industry norm. After acquisition, a shareholder complains that the acquisition lowered return on invested capital. Discuss possible reasons for this occurrence.

8–9 Company X's profit margin is 2% of sales. Company Y has an asset turnover of 12. Both companies' returns on assets are 6% and are considered unsatisfactory by industry norms. What is the asset turnover of Company X? What is the profit margin for Company Y? What strategic actions do you recommend to the managements of the respective companies?

8–10 What is the purpose of measuring asset turnover for different asset categories?

8–11 What factors (limitations) enter into our evaluation of return on invested capital?

8–12 How is the equity growth rate computed? What does it measure?

8–13 *a.* How do return on assets and return on common equity differ?
b. What are the components of return on common shareholders' equity? What do the components measure?

8–14 *a.* Equity turnover is sales divided by average shareholders' equity. What does equity turnover measure? How is it related to return on common equity? (*Hint:* Look at the components of ROCE.)
b. "Growth in earnings per share from an increase in equity turnover is unlikely to continue indefinitely." Do you agree or disagree with this assertion? Explain your answer and discuss the components of equity turnover for their impact on earnings.

8–15 What circumstances justify including convertible debt as equity capital when computing return on shareholders' equity?

(CFA Adapted)

EXERCISES

EXERCISE 8–1
Analyzing Financial Leverage for Alternative Financing Strategies

FIT Corporation's return on assets is 10% and its tax rate is 40%. Its total assets ($4 million) are financed entirely by common shareholders' equity. Management is considering its options to finance an expansion costing $2 million. It expects return on assets to remain unchanged. There are two alternatives to finance the expansion:

1. Issue $1 million bonds with 12% coupon, and $1 million common stock.
2. Issue $2 million bonds with 12% coupon.

Required:

a. Determine net income and operating income (income before interest and taxes) for each alternative.
b. Compute return on common shareholders' equity for each alternative.
c. Calculate the financial leverage ratio for each alternative.
d. Compute return on assets and explain how the level of leverage interacts with it in helping determine which alternative management should pursue.

CHECK
Plan 1: ROCE = 10.56%,
ROA = 10%,
Leverage = 1.2

EXERCISE 8–2
Analyzing Returns and Strategies of Alternative Financing

Roll Corporation's return on assets is 10% and its tax rate is 40%. Its assets ($10 million) are financed entirely by common shareholders' equity. Management is considering using bonds to finance an expansion costing $6 million. It expects return on assets to remain unchanged. There are two alternatives to finance the expansion:

1. Issue $2 million bonds with 5% coupon and $4 million common stock.
2. Issue $6 million bonds with 6% coupon.

Required:

a. Compute Roll's current net income and operating income (income before interest and taxes).

b. Determine net income and operating income for each alternative financing plan.

c. Compute return on common shareholders' equity for each alternative.

d. Explain any difference in the ROCE for the alternative plans computed in (*c*) Include a discussion of leverage in your response.

CHECK
Plan 2: ROCE = 13.84%, ROA = 10%, Leverage = 1.6

EXERCISE 8–3
Disaggregating Return Measures for Analyzing Leverage

Selected financial information from Syntex Corporation is reproduced below:

1. Asset turnover (average assets equal ending assets) is 2.
2. Adjusted profit margin equals 5%.
3. Leverage ratio (average assets/average common equity) is 1.786.
4. Sales equal $5,000,000.
5. Capital structure consists of $100,000 minority interests; 10% of total financing is current liabilities (average interest expense is 5% for one-half of current liabilities); 30% of total financing is long-term debt (average interest expense is 6%); and common equity makes up the remainder.
6. Tax rate is 40%.
7. Minority interest in earnings equals $1,000.

Required:

a. Compute return on common equity using its three major components.

b. Compute return on assets.

c. Analyze the disaggregation of return on common equity as in Exhibit 8.7. What is the "leverage advantage (in percent return) accruing to common equity"?

CHECK
ROA = 11.27%, Leverage advantage = 6.59%

EXERCISE 8–4
Disaggregating and Analyzing Return on Common Equity

Refer to the financial data in Case 11–6 (on page 584). In analyzing this company, you feel it is important to differentiate between operating success and financing decisions.

Required:

a. Explain the difference between ABEX's ROCE in Year 5 and in Year 9. Your analysis should include computation and discussion of the components determining return on common shareholders' equity.

b. Explain why ABEX's earnings per share nearly doubled between Year 5 and Year 9 despite the decline in its return on common shareholders' equity.

(CFA Adapted)

CHECK
Year 9 ROCE, 9.07%

EXERCISE 8–5
Analyzing Returns and Effects of Leverage

Selected financial information for ADAM Corporation is reproduced below:

1. Asset turnover (average assets equal ending assets) is 3.
2. Net income to sales is 7%.
3. Leverage ratio (average assets to average common equity) is 1.667.
4. Sales equal $12,000,000.
5. Capital structure consists of $200,000 minority interests; 15% of total financing is current liabilities (average interest expense is 4% for one-third of current liabilities); 20% of total financing is long-term debt (average interest expense is 5%); and 60% is common equity.
6. Tax rate is 50%.
7. Minority interest in earnings is $2,000.

Required:

a. Compute return on common equity using its three major components.

b. Compute return on assets.

c. Prepare an analysis of the composition of return on common equity describing the advantage or disadvantage accruing to common shareholders' equity from use of leverage (see Exhibit 8.7).

CHECK
ROA = 21.65%, Leverage advantage = 13.35%

EXERCISE 8–6
Analyzing Financial Leverage for Shareholders' Returns

Rose Corporation's condensed balance sheet for Year 2 is reproduced below:

Assets	
Current assets	$ 250,000
Noncurrent assets	1,750,000
Total assets	$2,000,000
Liabilities and Equity	
Current liabilities	$ 200,000
Noncurrent liabilities (8% bonds)	675,000
Common stockholders' equity	1,125,000
Total liabilities and equity	$2,000,000

Additional Information:

1. Net income for Year 2 is $157,500.
2. Income tax rate is 50%.
3. Amounts for total assets and shareholders' equity are the same for Years 1 and 2.

Required:

a. Determine whether leverage (from long-term debt) benefits Rose's shareholders. (*Hint:* Examine ROCE with and without leverage.)

b. If Rose Corporation achieves a 20% return on assets, compute both its return on common equity and its financial leverage index.

c. What can you conclude from the leverage index computed in (*b*)? Explain the implications for the company's shareholders.

CHECK
(b) ROCE = 33.16%

EXERCISE 8–7
Understanding Return Measures (multiple choice)

1. Which of the following situations best correspond with a ratio of "sales to average net tangible assets" exceeding the industry norm? (Choose one answer.)
   a. A company expanding plant and equipment during the past three years.
   b. A company inefficiently using its assets.
   c. A company with a large proportion of aged plant and equipment.
   d. A company using straight-line depreciation.
2. Return on assets is equivalent to (choose one answer):
   a. Profit margin × Total asset turnover.
   b. Profit margin × Total asset turnover × Leverage /Interest expense.
   c. $\frac{\text{Net income} + \text{Interest expense } (1 - \text{Tax rate}) + \text{Minority interest in earnings}}{\text{Average assets}}$
   d. $\frac{\text{Net income} + \text{Minority interest in earnings}}{\text{Average assets}}$
   e. (*a*) and (*c*)
3. A measure of asset utilization (turnover) is (choose one answer):
   a. Sales divided by fixed assets.
   b. Return on assets.
   c. Return on common equity.
   d. Operating income divided by sales.
4. Return on assets depends on the (choose one answer):
   a. Interest rates and pretax profits.
   b. Debt to equity ratio.
   c. After-tax profit margin and asset turnover.
   d. Sales and fixed assets.

EXERCISE 8–8
Predicting the Components of Return on Assets

Return on assets is a function of both profit margin and asset turnover.

Required:
How do you believe that knowledge of profit margin and asset turnover would contribute to analysis of the reported return on assets for the following companies (that is, if the business reported high return on assets, is it more likely that profit margin is especially high or that asset turnover is especially high or both)? Make your assessments relative to industry norms.

a. BMW
b. Ford
c. Sak's Fifth Avenue
d. Target
e. Wal-Mart
f. McDonald's
g. Amazon.com

EXERCISE 8–9
Analyzing Return on Assets

Two auto dealers, Legend Auto Sales and Reliable Auto Sales, operate and compete in the same area. Both purchase autos for $10,000 each and sell them for $12,000 each. Both maintain 10 cars on the lot at all times. A local basketball legend owns Legend Auto Sales. As a result, Legend sells 100 cars each year, while Reliable sells only 50 cars each year. The dealerships have no other revenues or expenses.

Required:

The town banker has denied Reliable Auto Sales a loan because its return on assets is inferior to its rival. The owner of Reliable Auto Sales has engaged you to help explain why its return on assets is inferior to that of Legend Auto Sales. Please prepare a memorandum for Reliable Auto Sales explaining the problem. Present quantitative support for your conclusions.

EXERCISE 8–10
Analyzing Property, Plant, and Equipment Turnover

A machine that produces hockey pucks costs $20,500 and produces 10 pucks per hour. Two similar companies purchase the machine and begin producing and selling pucks. The first company, Northern Sales is located in International Falls, Minnesota. The second company, Southern Sales is located in Huntsville, Alabama. Northern Sales operates the machine 20 hours per day to meet customer demand. Southern sales operates the machine 10 hours per day to meet customer demand. Sales data for the first month of operations are:

	Northern	Southern
Property, plant, and equipment	$20,500	$20,500
Accumulated depreciation—Property, plant and equipment	$500	$500
Pucks sold	6,000 pucks	3,000 pucks
Sales	$12,000	$6,000

Required:

Calculate the property, plant, and equipment turnover ratio for both Northern Sales and Southern Sales. Explain how this ratio impacts the return on assets of each company (assume the profit margin for each company is the same).

PROBLEMS

PROBLEM 8–1
Determining Return on Invested Capital (conceptual)

Quaker Oats Company

Quaker Oats in its Year 11 annual report (Appendix A) discloses the following:

Financial Objectives: Provide total shareholder returns (dividends plus share price appreciation) that exceed both the cost of equity and the S&P 500 stock index over time. Quaker's total return to shareholders for Year 11 was 34%. That compares quite favorably to our cost of equity for the year, which was about 12%, and to the total return of the S&P 500 stock index, which was 7%. Driving this strong performance, real earnings from continuing operations grew 7.4% over the last five years, return on equity rose to 24.1%. [Quaker Oats' stock price at the beginning and end of Year 11 was $48 and $62, respectively.]

The Benchmark for Investment

We use our cost of capital as a benchmark, or hurdle rate, to ensure that all projects undertaken promise a suitable rate of return. The cost of capital is used as the discount rate in determining whether a project will provide an economic return on its investment. We estimate a project's potential cash flows and discount these cash flows back to present value. This amount is compared with the initial investment costs to determine whether incremental value is created. Our cost of capital is calculated using the approximate market value weightings of debt and equity used to finance the Company.

Cost of equity + Cost of debt = Cost of capital

When Quaker is consistently able to generate and reinvest cash flows in projects whose returns exceed our cost of capital, economic value is created. As the stock market evaluates the Company's ability to generate value, this value is reflected in stock price appreciation.

The cost of equity. The cost of equity is a measure of the minimum return Quaker must earn to properly compensate investors for the risk of ownership of our stock. This cost is a combination of a "risk-free" rate and an "equity risk premium." The risk-free rate (the U.S. Treasury Bond rate) is the sum of the expected rate of inflation and a "real" return of 2 to 3%. For Year 11, the risk-free rate was approximately 8.4%. Investors in Quaker stock expect the return of a risk-free security plus a "risk premium" of about 3.6% to compensate them for assuming the risks in Quaker stock. The risk in holding Quaker stock is inherent in the fact that returns depend on the future profitability of the Company. In Year 11, Quaker's cost of equity was approximately 12%.

The cost of debt. The cost of debt is simply our after-tax, long-term debt rate, which was around 6.4%.

Required:

a. Quaker reports the "return to shareholders" for Year 11 to be 34%.
   (1) How is this return computed (provide calculations)?
   (2) How is this return different from return on common equity?
   (3) Compare Quaker Oats' concept of "return to shareholders" to the concept of return on shareholder's investment (ROSI) discussed in the chapter.
   (4) Can you verify Quaker Oats' computation of 24.1% for return on equity?

CHECK
ROCE = 21.01%

b. Explain how Quaker Oats arrives at a 3.6% "risk premium" needed by common shareholders as compensation for assuming the risks of Quaker Oats' stock.

c. Explain how Quaker Oats determines the 6.4% cost of debt.

PROBLEM 8–2
Analyzing Return Measures for Investment Decisions

Campbell Soup Company

Refer to the financial statements of **Campbell Soup Company** in Appendix A. Assume our analysis reveals that one-half of deferred income taxes should be treated as equity.

Required:

a. Compute the following measures for Year 10 of Campbell Soup:
   (1) Return on assets.
   (2) Return on common equity.
   (3) Equity growth rate.

CHECK
ROA = 2.08%,
ROCE = 0.24%

b. Disaggregate Campbell's return on common equity and interpret the results.

c. Compute Campbell's Year 10 asset turnover for individual asset categories (for this part only, use year-end balances for individual assets).

d. Assume you are considering investing in Campbell's common stock. There is another investment of equal quality and risk having a 12.7% return on common equity. Do you prefer one investment over the other? Is there other information you require to make a decision?

PROBLEM 8–3
Analyzing Company Returns and Proposed Wage Increases

Zear Company produces an electronic processor and sells it wholesale to manufacturing and retail outlets at $10 each. In Zear's Year 8 fiscal period, it sold 500,000 processors. Fixed costs for Year 8 total $1,500,000, including interest costs on its 7.5% debentures. Variable costs are $4 per processor for materials. Zear employs about 20 hourly paid plant employees, each earning $35,000 in Year 8.

Zear is currently confronting labor negotiations. The plant employees are requesting substantial increases in hourly wages. Zear forecasts a 6% increase in fixed costs and no change in either the processor's price or in material costs for the processors. Zear also forecasts a 10% growth in sales volume for Year 9. To meet the necessary increase in production due to sales demand, Zear recently hired two additional hourly plant employees.

The condensed balance sheet for Zear at the end of fiscal Year 8 follows (the tax rate is 50%):

Assets		Liabilities and equity	
Current assets:		Current liabilities	$2,000,000
Cash	$ 700,000	Long-term 7½% debenture	2,000,000
Receivables	1,000,000	6% preferred stock, 10,000	
Other	800,000	shares, $100 par value	1,000,000
Total current assets	2,500,000	Common stock	1,800,000
Fixed assets (net)	5,500,000	Retained earnings	1,200,000
	$8,000,000		$8,000,000

CHECK
a. (1) 5.94%
(2) 11.33%

Required:

a. Compute Zear's return on invested capital for Year 8 where invested capital is:
(1) Assets at end of Year 8. (2) Common equity capital at end of Year 8.

b. Calculate the maximum annual wage increase Zear can pay each plant employee and show a 10% return on assets (invested capital computed using end of Year 8 data).

(CFA Adapted)

PROBLEM 8–4
Disaggregating and Interpreting Return on Common Equity

Selected income statement and balance sheet data from **Merck & Co.** for Year 9 are reproduced below:

Merck & Co.

MERCK & COMPANY, INC.
Year 9 Selected Financial Data ($ in millions)

Income Statement Data:	
Sales revenue	$7,120
Depreciation	230
Interest expense	10
Pretax income	2,550
Income taxes	900
Net income	1,650
Balance Sheet Data:	
Current assets	$4,850
Fixed assets, net	2,400
Total assets	7,250
Current liabilities	3,290
Long-term debt	100
Shareholders' equity	3,860
Total liabilities & shareholders' equity	7,250

Values for each of the components determining return on common equity of Merck & Co. for **Year 4** are reported below. (*Note:* Some of Merck's measures are defined slightly different from those in the chapter.)

Profit margin (Net income/Sales)	0.245
Asset turnover (Sales/Total assets)	0.724
Interest burden (Pretax income/EBIT)	0.989
Leverage (Total assets/Common equity)	1.877
Retention (Net income/Pretax income)	0.628

Required:

a. Calculate each of the five components of ROCE (defined above) for Merck in Year 9.

b. Calculate return on common equity for Year 9 using the five components (in multiplicative form).

CHECK
ROCE = 42.8% (20.7%) for Year 9 (Year 4)

c. Analyze and interpret your calculations in (*a*) and (*b*). Describe how each component contributes to the change in Merck's ROCE between Year 4 and Year 9, and suggest reasons for the change in Merck's ROCE.

PROBLEM 8–5
Disaggregating and Analyzing Return on Invested Capital

As a financial analyst at a debt-rating agency, you are asked to analyze return on invested capital and asset utilization (turnover) measures for ZETA Corporation. Selected financial information for Years 5 and 6 of ZETA Corporation are reproduced in the Comprehensive Case chapter (see Case CC–2). You are provided the following additional account balances (for this problem only) at December 31, Year 4 ($ thousands):

Total assets	$94,500
Long-term debt	11,200
Deferred income taxes (assume is long-term liability)	1,000
Minority interest	800
Shareholders' equity	42,000

Interest expense on long-term debt is $4,000 in Year 6 and $3,000 for Year 5 (tax rate is 50%).

Required:

a. Compute the following return measures for Year 5 and Year 6:
(1) Return on assets. (2) Return on common equity. (3) Equity growth rate.

b. Comment on the year-to-year changes in the measures in part (*a*).

c. Disaggregate ROCE and explain the usefulness of this disaggregation.

d. Analyze and interpret the disaggregation of ROCE for Year 6 as in Exhibit 8.7. What is the relevance of this analysis?

CHECK
Year 6: ROA = 12.51%, ROCE = 19.82%, Growth rate = 13.86%

PROBLEM 8–6
Disaggregating and Analyzing Return on Common Equity

Selected financial statement data from Texas Telecom, Inc., for Years 5 and 9 are reproduced below ($ millions):

	Year 5	Year 9
Income Statement Data:		
Revenues	$542	$979
Operating income	38	76
Depreciation and amortization	3	9
Interest expense	3	0
Pretax income	32	67
Income taxes	13	37
Net income	19	30
Balance Sheet Data:		
Fixed assets	$ 41	$ 70
Total assets	245	291
Working capital	123	157
Total liabilities	16	0
Total shareholders' equity	159	220

Return on common equity can be disaggregated into five components:

1. Profit margin (Net income/Sales).
2. Asset turnover (Sales/Average assets).
3. Interest burden (Interest expense/Average assets).
4. Leverage (Average assets/Average common equity).
5. Effective tax rate (Tax expense/Income before income tax).

Required:

a. Calculate each of the five components of return on common equity (ROCE) for Years 5 and 9. Use end-of-year values for computations requiring an average.

b. Calculate return on common equity for Years 5 and 9 using each of the five components. Use end-of-year values for computations requiring an average. (*Hint:* Set up the disaggregation formula in terms of these components.)

c. Analyze and interpret changes in asset turnover and leverage for the change in ROCE from Year 5 to Year 9.

CHECK
Year 9: ROCE = 12.87%, Leverage = 1.32

CASES

CASE 8–1
Comprehensive Analysis of Return on Invested Capital

Quaker Oats Company

Refer to the financial statements of **Quaker Oats Company** reproduced in Appendix A.

Required:

a. Compute the following return on invested capital ratios of Quaker Oats for Years 11 and 10:
   (1) Return on assets.
   (2) Disaggregated return on assets.
   (3) Return on common equity.
   (4) Equity growth rate.
   (5) Disaggregated return on common equity into adjusted profit margin, asset turnover, and leverage.

b. Compute the following assets turnover ratios for Quaker Oats for Years 11 and 10.
   (1) Sales to cash.
   (2) Sales to receivables.
   (3) Sales to inventories.
   (4) Sales to property, plant, and equipment.
   (5) Sales to "other current assets."
   (6) Sales to total assets.

c. Using your computations in parts (*a*) and (*b*), analyze and evaluate Quaker Oats' return on invested capital and asset turnover for Years 11 and 10.

d. For Year 11, construct a table showing net amounts accruing to (or detracting from) return on common equity from financing sources (including current liabilities). Discuss the results in your table (identify any assumptions you make and use averages for financing suppliers). (*Hint:* Apply the format of Exhibit 8.7.)

e. Compute return on invested capital for Year 11 when invested capital is measured as:
   (1) Gross productive assets (assume 20 percent of "other current assets" are unproductive).
   (2) Market value of common stock (assume market value equals the average market price for Year 11).

CHECK
(*d*) Return to common = $201.5 mil.

(*e*) 1. 8.74%
   2. 4.95%

CASE 8–2
Comprehensive Analysis of Return on Common Equity

While you are an analyst at Investment Counselors, Inc., the senior portfolio manager at your firm makes a decision to increase communication stocks in the firm's managed funds. You are assigned to recommend one stock as an initial investment to meet this long-run objective. You diligently analyze and evaluate all communication stocks and narrow the decision to two newspaper publishers: Thomson Newspapers, Ltd., and Southam, Inc.

Thomson Newspapers Ltd., is one of the largest nondiversified newspaper companies in North America. It owns and publishes predominantly small town daily newspapers. Thomson is usually the dominant newspaper advertising vehicle in individual markets. Its successful record of acquisitions assures future growth opportunities without jeopardizing earnings.

Southam Inc., is a diversified communications company. It derives 70% of income from newspaper publishing, with the remainder from commercial printing, book retailing, and information services in Canada and the United States. Southam is Canada's largest daily newspaper company with publishing operations primarily in large competitive markets. While Southam is diversified into higher growth segments of communications to augment company growth, its more cyclical large city newspapers continue to dominate earnings performance.

The senior portfolio manager requests that you analyze the internal sources of earnings growth for each company. You decide to disaggregate and evaluate the internal growth components for each company to explain any trends in your variable of interest, *return on common equity.* You identify five key components: profit margin, interest turnover, income taxes, asset turnover, and leverage. Summary measures using these components follow:

THOMSON NEWSPAPERS, LTD.

Year	Assets/ Common Equity	Profit Margin	Income Tax Rate	Revenues/ Assets	EBIT†/ Revenues	Interest/ Assets	Return on Common Equity
Year 11*	1.53	21.2%	28.0%	0.61	32.2%	1.9%	–
Year 10	1.31	21.0	38.1	0.77	33.5	0.5	20.5%
Year 9	1.32	19.5	43.8	0.86	35.4	0.6	22.1
Year 8	1.41	19.0	41.6	0.80	34.2	1.5	21.2
Year 7	1.41	18.9	43.0	0.84	34.4	1.0	22.3
Year 6	1.45	17.9	44.3	0.86	33.2	1.0	22.2
Year 5	1.60	14.9	42.9	0.98	28.4	2.2	23.5
Year 4	1.67	15.0	45.7	0.91	30.8	3.2	22.6
Year 3	1.48	14.5	48.5	0.95	30.9	3.0	20.0
Year 2	1.37	19.4	46.9	0.81	38.1	1.3	21.4
Year 1	1.34	18.5	48.0	0.81	37.0	1.4	19.9

† *Earnings before interest and taxes.*
* *Estimated values for that year.*

SOUTHAM, INC.

Year	Assets/ Common Equity	Profit Margin	Income Tax Rate	Revenues/ Assets	EBIT†/ Revenues	Interest/ Assets	Return on Common Equity
Year 11*	2.39	4.6%	43.0%	1.29	7.3%	2.7%	–
Year 10	2.22	5.4	44.7	1.38	8.9	3.1	11.3%
Year 9	2.20	5.6	42.7	1.37	9.4	3.1	12.4
Year 8	2.47	4.2	42.7	1.46	8.9	3.6	13.3
Year 7	2.82	4.1	46.4	1.61	9.9	4.3	17.6
Year 6	2.70	4.5	46.7	1.57	10.2	3.3	18.2
Year 5	2.65	2.3	46.0	1.54	7.9	5.8	9.1
Year 4	2.73	5.4	46.1	1.62	13.5	6.2	23.2
Year 3	2.39	6.1	45.9	1.54	12.9	4.1	20.4
Year 2	2.03	7.0	44.3	1.62	13.0	2.5	21.1
Year 1	1.85	8.2	41.1	1.64	12.2	1.1	20.6

† *Earnings before interest and taxes.*
* *Estimated values for that year.*

Required:

a. Estimate return on common equity for Year 11 for both Thomson and Southam using their disaggregated data.

b. Discuss how the recent 10-year trend in each of the five components affects return on common equity for each company.

CHECK
Thomson ROCE = 19.5%

CASE 8–3
Analyzing Return on Invested Capital

Using the annual report of **Kodak** in Appendix A, answer the following: **Kodak**

a. Compute the following return on invested capital ratios for 2001 and 2000:
(1) Return on assets.
(2) Disaggregated return on assets.
(3) Return on common equity.
(4) Equity growth rate.
(5) Disaggregated return on common equity into adjusted profit margin, asset turnover, and leverage.

b. Compute the following assets turnover ratios for 2001 and 2000:
(1) Sales to cash.
(2) Sales to receivables.
(3) Sales to inventories.
(4) Sales to property, plant, and equipment.
(5) Sales to "other current assets."
(6) Sales to total assets.

c. Using your computations in (*a*) and (*b*), analyze and evaluate Kodak's return on invested capital and its asset turnover for 2001 and 2000.

CASE 8–4
Analyzing Return on Invested Capital

Walt Disney Company

Walt Disney Company (Disney) is a diversified international entertainment company with operations in three business segments. Revenue and operating income data for the three segments are shown below.

Business Segment Data ($ millions)
Years Ending September 30

	YEAR 13		YEAR 9	
Business Segments	**Revenue**	**Operating Income**	**Revenue**	**Operating Income**
Theme Parks and Resorts	$3,441	$ 747	$2,595	$ 785
Film Entertainment	3,673	622	1,588	256
Consumer Products	1,415	355	411	188
	$8,529	$1,724	$4,594	$1,229

The profitability of the leisure-time industry is influenced by various factors including economic conditions, the amount of available leisure time, oil and transportation prices, and weather patterns. Disney management has been very aggressive in raising theme park admission prices. For the 10-year period ending in Year 13, admission prices increased at an annual rate of 8–9% compared to less than 4% for U.S. consumer price inflation. Disney's Film Entertainment business has grown rapidly because of increasing acceptance of The Disney Channel and, importantly, management efforts to exploit the expanding distribution opportunities available for its extensive video library. Disney's Consumer Products revenue has also grown meaningfully as the company has moved its product mix aggressively toward direct publishing and direct retail and away from higher-margined licensing and royalty income sources. During the fourth quarter of fiscal Year 13 (ending September 30, Year 13), Disney wrote off the full carrying value of Euro Disney. The charge was $350 million ($218 million after tax).

WALT DISNEY COMPANY
Selected Financial Statement and Other Data
Years Ending September 30
($ millions except per share data)

	Year 13	Year 9
Income Statement		
Revenue	$ 8,529	$4,594
Operating expenses	(6,805)	(3,365)
Operating income	$ 1,724	$1,229
General, and administrative expenses	(163)	(119)
Interest expense	(158)	(24)
Investment and interest income	186	67
Income (loss) from Euro Disney	(515)	0
Pretax income	$ 1,074	$1,153
Taxes	(403)	(450)
Net income	$ 671	$ 703
Earnings per share	$1.23	$1.27
Dividends per share	$0.23	$0.11

(continued)

Balance Sheet		
Cash	$ 363	$ 381
Receivables	1,390	224
Inventories	609	909
Other	1,889	662
Current assets	$ 4,251	$2,176
Property, plant and equipment, net	5,228	3,397
Other assets	2,272	1,084
Total assets	$11,751	$6,657
Current liabilities	$ 2,821	$1,262
Borrowings	2,386	861
Other liabilities	1,514	1,490
Stockholder's equity	5,030	3,044
Total liabilities and stockholder's equity	$11,751	$6,657
Cash Flow from Operations	$2,145	$1,275
Other Data		
Common shares outstanding (millions)	544	552
Closing price, common stock per share	$37.75	$30.22

Required:

a. Calculate and disaggregate Disney's return on common equity for *each* of the *two* fiscal years ending September 30, Year 9, and September 30, Year 13.

b. Drawing only on your answers to part (*a*) and the data available, identify the *two* components that contributed most to the observed change in Disney's return on common equity between Year 9 and Year 13. State *two* reasons for the observed change in *each* of the *two* components.

CHECK
Year 13: ROCE = 13.3%

(CFA Adapted)

WEB ACTIVITIES

The Web Activities are located on the book's website at www.mhhe.com/wild8e.

9

PROFITABILITY ANALYSIS

A LOOK BACK

The preceding chapter described return on invested capital and explained its relevance for analysis. Return on assets and return on common equity were shown to be useful tools of analysis. We disaggregated both return measures and explained the impact of financial leverage.

A LOOK AT THIS CHAPTER

This chapter expands return analysis to emphasize profitability. Our analysis focuses on the components of income and their evaluation. We direct special attention at sales, cost of sales, taxes, and selling and financing expenses. We demonstrate the use of profitability analysis tools, emphasizing interpretation and adjustments.

A LOOK AHEAD

Chapter 10 extends our focus on analysis tools to include prospective analysis and the forecasting of financial statements. We illustrate forecasting mechanics and demonstrate the application of prospective analysis for valuation of common stock.

ANALYSIS OBJECTIVES

- Describe the importance of profitability analysis and the necessity of analyzing and adjusting income.
- Analyze the sources, persistence, measurement, and recognition of revenues for assessing profitability.
- Explain gross profit and its evaluation using volume, price, and costs of sales.
- Analyze operating and nonoperating expenses using common-size, index number, and ratio analyses.
- Describe the effective tax rate and analyze income tax disclosures.
- Prepare, analyze, and interpret a statement of variations in income and income components.

Cutting the Fat from Home Depot

ATLANTA–Times have been good for Home Depot, the world's largest home improvement retailer. Store counts and sales have been growing at 20% per year and profits by 40% per year. That is, however, until recently. The company is facing increased competition from Lowes Companies and is burdened by a bloated infrastructure. Efficiency is now the name of the game. "This is a company in transition," said Colin McGranahan, an analyst at Sanford C. Bernstein & Co. "The core function that drove Home Depot's performance in the past 20 years is not going to drive it in the future."

Home Depot's basic systems–purchasing, accounting, and logistics–have not been updated in years. Buyers from each of its nine regions deal directly with suppliers, which creates redundancies that reduce operating efficiency. In addition, inventory controls are loose and the company has too many management layers. Although gross profit margins have remained strong, selling, general, and administrative expenses have increased steadily as a percentage of sales for each of the past five years. Net profit margins have flattened as a result.

Analyze operating expenses for signs of inefficiency.

None of these problems are much of a concern as long as the market is growing fast enough. Overhead is spread out over an increasing number of stores. When growth slows as a result of market saturation and increased competition, however, fixed overhead expenses continue to eat away at an ever-increasing percentage of operating profits.

Under the new leadership of Bob Nardelli, formerly an executive at GE, changes are taking place in Home Depot's operations. Store growth has been slowed and management layers thinned. Purchasing and other back-office functions have been centralized in Atlanta and management of store operations decentralized.

Analysis of operating expenses is as important as the analysis of growth opportunities. Analysts must scrutinize selling, advertising, labor, and overhead expenses carefully for signs of inefficiency that can significantly impact financial performance when markets soften.

Source: Business Week, November 2001; Home Depot 2001 10-K; Bloomberg News, August, 2002

PREVIEW OF CHAPTER 9

Profitability analysis is important in analyzing financial statements and it complements the return analysis in the previous chapter. Profitability analysis goes beyond the accounting measures–such as sales, cost of sales, and operating and nonoperating expenses–to assess their sources, persistence, measurement, and key economic relations. Results from this assessment enable us to better estimate both the return and risk characteristics of a company. Profitability analysis also allows us to distinguish between performance primarily attributed to operating decisions and those that are tied to financing and investing decisions. This chapter describes tools of analysis enabling us to make these distinctions. We also describe operating leverage and its importance for profitability. Throughout this chapter we emphasize the application of these analysis tools with illustrative cases.

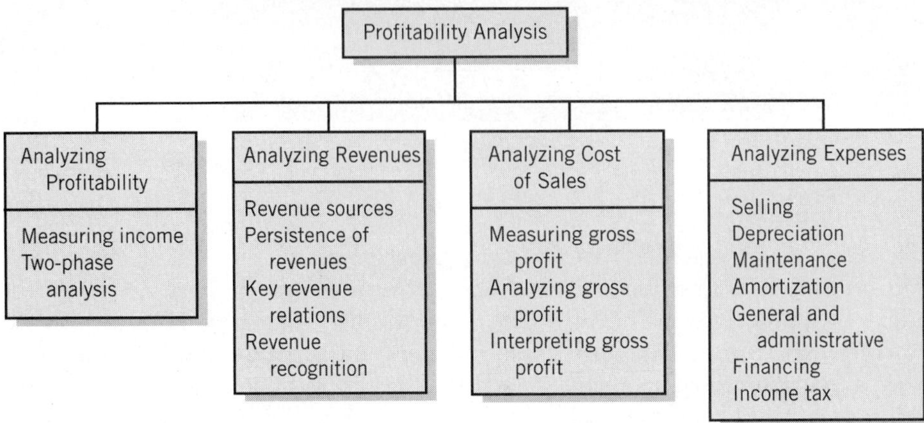

ANALYZING COMPANY PROFITABILITY

Analyzing company profitability is a major part of financial statement analysis. All financial statements are pertinent to profitability analysis, but none is more important than the income statement. The income statement reports a company's operating results over a period of time. Operating results are the primary purpose of a company and play an important role in determining company value, solvency, and liquidity.

Profitability analysis is critically important for all users but especially for equity investors and creditors. For equity investors, income is often the single most important determinant of changes in security values. Measuring and forecasting income are among the most critical tasks of investors. For creditors, income and operating cash flows are common and desirable sources of interest and principal repayments. When we evaluate company profitability, our analysis focuses on several questions such as:

- What is the company's relevant income measure?
- What is the quality of income?
- What income components are most important for income forecasting?
- How persistent (including stability and trend) are income and its components?
- What is a company's earning power?

This chapter will help answer these and similar questions.

Factors in Measuring Company Income

Income is defined as revenues and gains less expenses and losses over a reporting period. This presumably simple concept creates many challenges in practice. Users' frustrations are reflected in questions like: Why is it so difficult to determine income under specific circumstances? What is "true income"? Does accounting identify and measure true income? Chapters 1–6 of this book described why we cannot expect accounting to provide us with a true income measure. Income is not a unique amount awaiting the perfection of a measurement system to precisely value it. The following are a number of practical considerations:

FILING TIME
The SEC is considering cutting the time allotted for filing quarterly reports from 45 days after the period-end to 30 days. Annual reports would need to be filed in 60 days, down from 90.

1. **Estimation issues.** Income measurement depends on estimates of the outcome of future events. These estimates require allocation of revenues and expenses across current and future periods. While we expect the judgments of skilled and experienced professionals to reveal some consensus (less variability), income measurement requires certain discretion.

2. **Accounting methods.** Accounting standards governing income measurement are the result of professional experience, regulatory agendas, business happenings, and other social influences. They reflect a balance in these factors, including compromises on differing interests and views toward income measurement. We discussed some of these factors in Chapters 1 and 2. There is also latitude in the application of accounting to accommodate different business circumstances.
3. **Incentives for disclosure.** Ideally, practitioners are concerned with fairly presenting financial statements. However, pressures of competition, finances, and society all bear on financial statements and income measurement. These incentives create pressure to choose "acceptable" measures rather than "appropriate" measures given the business circumstances. Our analysis must recognize these incentives and evaluate income accordingly.
4. **Diversity across users.** Financial statements are general-purpose reports serving diverse needs of many users. This diversity of views implies that our analysis must use income as an initial measure of profitability. We then use information from financial statements and elsewhere to appropriately adjust income consistent with our interests and objectives.

DISTORTIONS
Multibillion-dollar charges taken by high-tech acquirers, such as Cisco, to write off "in-process" research when they close a deal, distorts financial reports.

SHOW TIME
The Fed and the SEC allege Livent (motion picture company) pumped up income by spreading current production costs over several years and by recording expenses as preproduction costs for other shows, treating them as assets.

This chapter describes analysis tools useful in this task and in evaluating income components. Chapter 12 returns to this task and considers questions regarding the quality of earnings, usefulness of income components for forecasting, persistence of income, and earning power.

Two-Phase Analysis of Income

The analysis of income and its components involves two phases. The first phase is *analysis of accounting and its measurements.* This requires an understanding of the accounting for revenue and expenses. It also requires an understanding of accounting for assets and liabilities since many assets reflect costs deferred and some liabilities represent deferred income. We must understand and assess the implications of using one type of accounting versus another, and its effect on income measurement and comparative analysis. Chapters 3 through 6 of this book emphasized this important phase of financial statement analysis.

The second phase is *applying analysis tools to income (and its components) and interpreting the analytical results.* Applying analysis tools is aimed at achieving our respective objectives in using income. These objectives often include income forecasting, assessing income persistence and quality, and estimating earning power. We devote the remainder of this chapter to describing these tools and interpreting their results.

ANALYSIS VIEWPOINT . . . YOU ARE THE SECURITIES DIRECTOR

You are responsible for setting companies' listing requirements for a regional securities exchange. Several analyst groups request that you increase information disclosure requirements for income, regarding both income components and note disclosures. You also receive requests from certain labor unions, activist groups, and small investors to streamline and condense financial reports and improve the usefulness of aggregate income. What are some reasons for the apparent differences in these groups' requests? How do you balance their information needs?

Answer–p. 477

ANALYZING COMPANY REVENUES

This section focuses on analyzing a company's revenues (also called *sales*). Our analysis of revenues focuses on several questions including:

Kodak's Revenue Sources

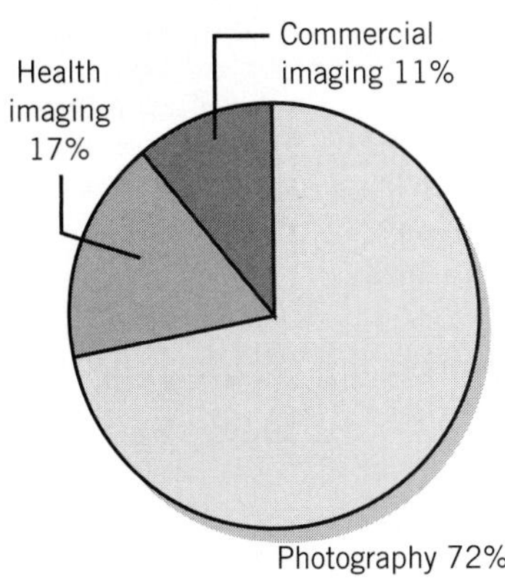

- What are the major sources of revenue?
- How persistent are revenue sources?
- How are revenues, receivables, and inventories related?
- When is revenue recorded and how is it measured?

Major Sources of Revenues

Knowledge of major sources of revenues is important in the analysis of income. This information is especially important if our analysis is of a *diversified* company. With diversified companies, each market or product line often has its own growth pattern, profitability, and future potential. An excellent means to analyze sources of revenues is common-size analysis. A *common-size analysis* shows each major class of revenue as a percentage of the total. Adjacent to this paragraph we show a pie chart presentation of Kodak's total revenues.

Challenges of Diversified Companies

The analysis of financial statements of diversified companies must separate and interpret the impact of individual business segments on the company as a whole. This is challenging because different segments or divisions can experience varying rates of profitability, risk, and growth opportunities. Their existence is an important reason why our analysis requires considerable detailed information by business segment. Our evaluation, projection, and valuation of earnings requires this information be separated into segments sharing characteristics of variability, growth, and risk. Asset composition and financing requirements of segments often vary and demand separate analysis. A creditor is interested in knowing which segments provide cash and which use it. The makeup of investing and financing activities, the size and profitability of segments, and the performance of segment management is important information. We show in Chapter 12 that income forecasting benefits from forecasting by segments.

Reporting by Segments

Information reported on operating results and financial position by segments varies. Full disclosure would provide detailed income statements, balance sheets, and statements of cash flow for each important segment. However, full disclosure by segments is rare in practice because of difficulties in separating segments and management's reluctance to release information that can harm its competitive position.

Types of Segment Disclosures*

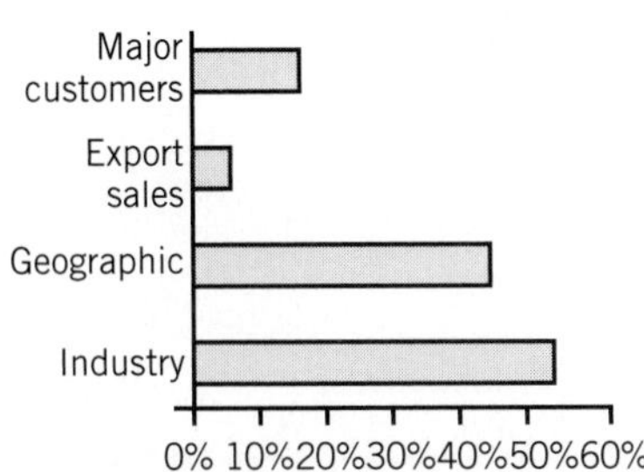

** Total can exceed 100% because companies can report one or more types of segments. Source: Accounting Trends & Techniques.*

Regulatory agencies have established reporting requirements for industry segments, international activities, export sales, and major customers. Evaluating risk and return is a major objective of financial statement analysis, and practice recognizes the value of segment disclosures in this evaluation. Analysis of companies operating across industry segments or geographic areas, which often have different rates of profitability, risk, and growth, is aided by segment data. These data assist us in analyzing uncertainties affecting the timing and amount of expected cash inflows and outflows.

Practice considers a segment significant if its sales, operating income (or loss), *or* identifiable assets are 10% or more of the combined amounts of all the company's operating segments. To ensure that these segments constitute a substantial portion of a company's operations, the combined sales of all segments reported must be at least 75% of the company's combined sales. For each segment, companies must report selected annual financial information (see *SFAS 131*) including: (1) sales–both to other segments and to external customers; (2) operating income–revenues less operating expenses; (3) identifiable assets; (4) interest and tax expenses or benefits; (5) special items' gains and losses; and (6) depreciation, depletion, and amortization expense. Additionally, if a company derives 10% or more of revenues from sales to a single customer, revenues from this customer must be reported. The SEC also requires a narrative description of the company's business by operating segments such as information on competition, customer dependence, principal products and services, backlogs, sources and availability of raw materials, patents, research and development costs, number of employees, and the seasonality of its business. Segment information for Kodak is reported in note 21 of its annual report in Appendix A.

Analysis Implications of Segment Reports

Diversified companies, and the loss of identity for subsidiary companies in consolidated financial statements, create challenges for analysis. While segment information is available, our analysis must be careful in using this information for profitability tests. The more specific and detailed segment information is, the more dependent it is on accounting allocations of revenues and expenses. Allocation of common costs as practiced in internal accounting is often based on notions of fairness, reasonableness, and acceptability to managers. These notions are of little relevance to our profitability analysis. Allocations of joint expenses are often arbitrary and limited in their validity and precision. Examples are research and development costs, promotion expenses, advertising costs, interest, pension costs, federal and state income taxes, and general and administrative costs. There are no accepted principles in allocating or transferring costs of one segment to another. We must recognize these limitations when relying on segment reports.

ANALYSIS EXCERPT

Companies do not typically disclose internal accounting practices unless it is in their interest. Management of Murray Ohio Manufacturing Company felt it advantageous to disclose, in federal court, that its annual report did not reveal the true story of profitability or loss by product line. They admitted to understating losses in the bicycle division by millions of dollars to fend off hostile takeover advances by a Swedish company. Murray Ohio feared that the potential closing of a nonprofitable bicycle division would appeal to a potential acquirer. They therefore chose not to allocate $17 million in overhead to their bicycle division. This case offers us a rare glimpse into the murky area of overhead allocation and the many possibilities companies have to report misleading segment data.

Segment reports are and must be analyzed as "soft" information–information subject to manipulation and preinterpretation by management. It must be treated with uncertainty, and inferences drawn from these data must be subjected to alternative sources of verification. Nevertheless, segment data supported by alternative evidence can be extremely useful for analysis. Specifically, segment data can aid our analysis of:

- *Sales growth.* Analysis of trends in sales by segments is useful in assessing profitability. Sales growth is often the result of one or more factors including: (1) price changes, (2) volume changes, (3) acquisitions/divestitures, and (4) changes in exchange rates. A company's Management's Discussion and Analysis section usually offers insights into the causes of sales growth.
- *Asset growth.* Analysis of trends in identifiable assets by segments is relevant for our profitability analysis. Comparing capital expenditures to depreciation can reveal the segments undergoing "real" growth. When analyzing geographic segment

DISGORGEMENT
One of the government's strongest weapons for going after shady executives is disgorgement. When the SEC wins a court order or settles a case against execs for securities law violations, it can require them to give back their compensation, including stock gains.

reports, our analysis must be alert to changes in foreign currency exchange rates that can significantly affect reported values.

- *Profitability.* Measures of operating income to sales and operating income to identifiable assets by segment are useful in analyzing profitability. Due to limitations with segment income data, our analysis should focus on trends versus absolute levels.

Exhibit CC.1 in the Comprehensive Case chapter reports a summary of segment information for Campbell Soup Company. Note 2 of Campbell Soup's financial statements also reports geographic area information.

Analysis Research

USEFULNESS OF SEGMENT DATA

Analysis research provides evidence that segment disclosures are useful in forecasting future profitability. We know that total sales and earnings of a company equals the sum of the sales and earnings of all segments (less any intercompany transactions). As long as different segments are subject to different economic factors, the accuracy of segment-based forecasts should exceed that of forecasts based on consolidated data.

Combining company-specific segment data with industry-specific forecasts improves the accuracy of sales and earnings forecasts. Evidence shows that the introduction of segment reporting requirements increased the accuracy and reduced the dispersion of earnings forecasts made by professional securities analysts. This implies that our profitability analysis can also benefit from segment data.

Persistence of Revenues

The stability and trend, or *persistence,* of revenues are important to the analysis of profitability. To the extent we can assess the persistence of revenues by segments, profitability analysis is enhanced. This section considers two useful analysis tools for assessing persistence in revenues: (1) trend percent analysis and (2) evaluation of Management's Discussion and Analysis.

Trend Percent Analysis

A useful method in assessing persistence of revenues either in total or by segments is **trend percent analysis.** A five-year trend percent analysis of revenues by product lines for Madison, Inc., is shown in Exhibit 9.1. Year 1 revenues are set equal to 100% and all years' revenues are compared to it (for example, Year 2 percent equals Year 2 revenues divided by Year 1 revenues). Revenue indexes by segments are often correlated and compared to industry norms or to similar measures for competitors. We can also compute *(auto)correlations* for revenues across periods to measure persistence in revenues. Additional considerations bearing on analysis of revenues' persistence include:

- Sensitivity of revenues to business conditions.
- Anticipated demand with new or revised products and services.

Exhibit 9.1

Trend Percent Analysis of Revenues by Product Line for Madison, Inc. (Year 1 = 100)

Segment	Year 1	Year 2	Year 3	Year 4	Year 5
Bridges	100	110	114	107	121
Roadways	100	120	135	160	174
Landscaping	100	98	94	86	74
Engineering	100	101	92	98	105

- Customer analysis–concentration, dependence, and stability.
- Revenues' concentration or dependence on one segment.
- Revenues' reliance on sales staff.
- Geographical diversification of markets.

As an example, analysis of Micron Products yields concern with overreliance on a few major customers as revealed in its notes.

> **ANALYSIS EXCERPT**
>
> Sales to three major customers amounted to approximately 32%, 25%, and 11% of the Company's net sales.

Management's Discussion and Analysis

The Management's Discussion and Analysis (MD&A) of a company's financial condition and operating results is often useful in analysis of persistence in revenues. The SEC requires several disclosures of an interpretative or explanatory nature in MD&A. This information aids us in understanding and evaluating period-to-period changes in financial accounts including revenues. Management is required to report on changes in revenue and expense components relevant for understanding operating activities. These include unusual events affecting operating income, trends or uncertainties affecting or likely to affect operations, and impending changes in revenue and expense relations like increases in material or labor costs. Management must also report on whether they attribute growth in revenues to increases in prices, volume, inflation, or new product introduction. Management is encouraged to describe financial results, report forward-looking information, and discuss trends and forces not evident in the financial statements. The SEC presumes that the MD&A provides information relevant to analyzing financial condition and operating results by evaluating the amounts and uncertainty of cash flows.

Reporting guidelines for management in preparing the MD&A are few. Management has considerable discretion in communicating relevant information. The aim is meaningful disclosure by management in narrative form to supply useful information not typically available in financial statements. Its success in achieving this aim depends on management's attitudes and incentives. While our analysis using information in the MD&A is likely to be "soft," we must remember that management cannot risk being careless or deceptive with this information because of potential SEC and legal-related consequences. Still, this information usually provides useful insights, offers management's perspective, and cannot readily be obtained in other ways. We can use such disclosures as analytical supplements for both the information offered (especially when independently verified) and as insight into management's strategic plans and actions.

BIG BUCKS

The typical CFO earns about $1 million per year. But the best paid CFOs get pay packages that look more like those of CEOs. A sampling (from *Business Week*, September 16, 2002):

	Total Compensation (in mil.)
Michael Lehman—Sun Microsystems	$37.2
Mark Swartz—Tyco International	32.4
Larry Carter—Cisco Systems	29.4
Anthony Thornley—Qualcom	20.3

Relations between Revenues, Receivables, and Inventories

The relations between revenues and accounts receivable, and revenues and inventories, often provide important clues for evaluation of operating results. They also are often useful in predicting future performance.

Revenues and Accounts Receivable

While we will discuss the relation between accounts receivable and revenues in Chapter 11 in the context of short-term liquidity, understanding this relation is important in evaluating earnings quality. For example, if accounts receivable grow at a rate exceeding revenues, we need to analyze this to identify the causes. Such causes might include revenues being driven by increased incentives, generous extension of credit, or an "in-the-door" strategy in anticipation of future revenue. These factors bear on future revenues, both favorably and unfavorably. Additionally, such factors often affect collectibility of receivables–see Illustration 9.1.

ILLUSTRATION 9.1

The relation between revenues and accounts receivable of Toyland, Inc., for a recent five-year period is reflected in the following chart ($ thousands):

	YEAR ENDED				
	Year 6	Year 5	Year 4	Year 3	Year 2
Net revenues	$199	$227	$175	$198	$290
Percent change	−12.3%	29.7%	−11.6%	−31.7%	—
Accounts receivable	$271	$225	$190	$276	$328
Percent change	20.4%	18.4%	−31.2%	−15.9%	—

In Year 6, revenues declined by 12.3% whereas accounts receivable increased by 20.4%. This relation contrasts with relations prevailing in preceding years where increases and decreases in revenues and accounts receivables were met with increases and decreases in the other. Consequently, Year 6's negative correlation warrants special attention and analysis.

Revenues and Inventories

The discussion in Chapter 8 showed how inventory turnover is related to inventory quality and asset turnover. Analysis of inventory components often reveals valuable clues to future revenues and operating activity. For example, when increases in finished goods are accompanied by decreases in raw materials and/or work in process, we expect a decline in production–see Illustration 9.2.

ILLUSTRATION 9.2

The relation between revenues and inventories (and inventory components) for Burroughs Corporation for a recent five-year period is reported in the chart below ($ millions):

	YEAR ENDED				
	Year 6	Year 5	Year 4	Year 3	Year 2
Net revenues	$ 762.7	$ 793.9	$ 689.8	$ 559.0	$ 560.0
Inventories:					
Finished goods	907.1	830.6	631.6	677.9	699.9
Work in process and raw materials	609.0	664.7	561.2	467.7	379.2
Total inventories	$1,516.1	$1,495.3	$1,192.8	$1,145.6	$1,079.1

This table reveals that during the most recent two years, finished goods inventories increase while work in process and raw materials decline. This relation usually foreshadows a production decline. Specifically, an increase in inventories (especially in finished goods) with a decline in revenues is indicative of a failure of revenues to keep up with production.

Revenue Recognition and Measurement

There are various criteria in the recognition and measurement of revenue. We described revenue recognition and measurement in Chapter 6. We know that certain methods are more conservative than others. Our analysis must recognize the revenue recognition methods used by a company and their implications. We must also be aware of potential differences in revenue recognition methods used by different companies in any comparative analysis. When forecasting revenue, one consideration is whether the revenue recognition method used reflects the most relevant measure of business performance and operating activities for our analysis purposes.

TIMING MATTERS
Interpublic Group shares fell 32% in two days after the firm said it would postpone its earnings release by one week.

ANALYSIS VIEWPOINT ***. . . YOU ARE THE BANKER***

You are considering loan requests from two companies. Analysis of both companies' financial statements indicates similar risk and return characteristics, and both are marginal applicants. In discussing these cases with your senior loan officer, it is pointed out that one company's income is dispersed across 10 different segments while the other is concentrated in one industry. Does this additional information influence your loan decision? Does it impact your comparison of these companies?

Answer–p. 477

ANALYZING COMPANY COST OF SALES

Cost of sales or services provided is, as a percent of revenues, the single largest cost item for most companies. We discussed several methods of determining cost of sales in Chapter 4. There is also, especially in unregulated industries, no generally accepted cost classification method yielding a clear distinction between expenses such as cost of sales, administrative, general, selling, and financing. This is particularly true in classifying general and administrative expenses. Our analysis must be ever alert to methods of cost classification and the effect they have on individual cost assessments and comparative analysis within and across companies.

Measuring Gross Profit (Margin)

Gross profit, or *gross margin,* is measured as revenues less cost of sales. It is frequently reported and described as a percent. A recent year's gross profit for New York Jewelry, Inc., is ($ thousands):

Sales	$11,950	100%
Cost of sales	8,604	72
Gross profit	$ 3,346	28%

The gross profit, or gross profit percentage, is a key performance measure. New York Jewelry's gross profit is $3,346,000 or 28% of sales. All other costs must be recovered from this gross profit, and any income earned is the balance remaining after these costs. A company must produce a sufficient gross profit to be profitable. Also, gross profit must be sufficiently large to finance essential future-directed discretionary expenditures like research and development, marketing, and advertising. Gross profits vary across industries depending on factors like competition, capital investment, and the level of remaining costs that must be recovered from gross profit.

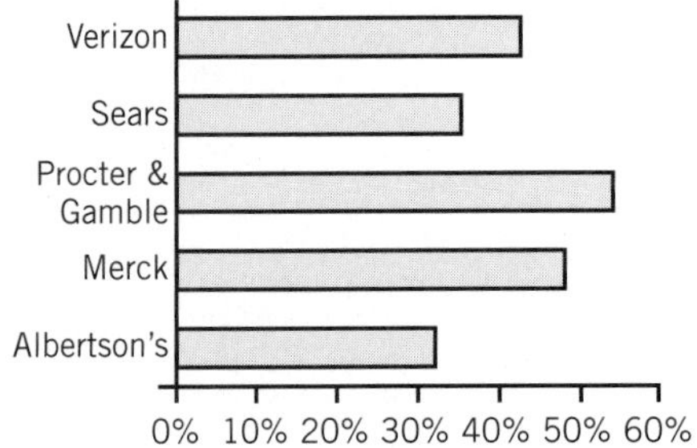

Analyzing Changes in Gross Profit

An analysis of gross profit directs special attention to the factors explaining variations in sales and cost of sales. Analyzing changes in gross profit is usually performed internally because it often requires access to nonpublic data, including number of units sold, unit selling prices, and unit costs. Unless a company sells a single product, this analysis benefits from data by product line. For internal analysis (and for external analysis when data permits), evaluating changes in gross profit reveals useful insights.

Case 9.1. This case shows an analysis of changes in gross profit for Pennsylvania Printers, Inc. (PPI). Selected financial data of PPI for the most recent two years are reproduced below:

	YEAR ENDED DECEMBER 31		YEAR-TO-YEAR CHANGE	
Item	**Year 1**	**Year 2**	**Increase**	**Decrease**
1. Sales ($ millions)	$657.6	$687.5	$29.9	
2. Cost of sales ($ millions)	237.3	245.3	8.0	
3. Gross profit ($ millions)	$420.3	$442.2	$21.9	
4. Units sold (in millions)	215.6	231.5	15.9	
5. Sales price per unit (1 ÷ 4)	$3.05	$2.97		$0.08
6. Cost per unit (2 ÷ 4)	1.10	1.06		0.04

Drawing on these financial data, we prepare an analysis of the change in PPI's gross profit of $21,900,000 from Year 1 to Year 2. Our analysis focuses sequentially on changes in sales and then cost of sales. The following steps underlie our analysis, and the results are reported in Exhibit 9.2.

Exhibit 9.2 ***Analysis Statement of Changes in Gross Profit***

PENNSYLVANIA PRINTERS, INC.
Year 2 versus Year 1 ($ millions)

Analysis of Variation in Sales	
(1) Change in volume of products sold:	
Change in volume (15.9) × Year 1 unit selling price ($3.05)	$48.5
(2) Change in selling price:	
Change in selling price (−$0.08) × Year 1 sales volume (215.6)	−17.2
	$31.3
(3) Combined change in sales volume (15.9) and unit price (−$0.08)	−1.3
Increase in net sales	$30.0*
Analysis of Variation in Cost of Sales	
(1) Change in volume of products sold:	
Change in volume (15.9) × Year 1 cost per unit ($1.10)	$17.5
(2) Change in cost per unit sold:	
Change in cost per unit (−$0.04) × Year 1 sales volume (215.6)	−8.6
	$ 8.9
(3) Combined change in volume (15.9) and cost per unit (−$0.04)	−0.6
Increase in cost of sales	$ 8.3*
Net variation in gross profit	$21.7*

* *Differences are due to rounding.*

Step 1. We focus first on year-to-year change in volume assuming unit selling price remains unchanged from Year 1. The volume change (15.9) is then multiplied by the constant unit selling price ($3.05) yielding a positive change in sales ($48.5).

Step 2. We focus next on year-to-year change in selling price assuming volume is constant. This decrease in selling price (−$0.08) is then multiplied by the constant volume (215.6) yielding a decline in sales (−$17.2).

Step 3. We recognize that the assumptions in steps 1 and 2–that volume is constant while unit price changes and vice versa–are simplifications to highlight causes for change. Our analysis must recognize these assumptions ignore *joint* changes in volume and unit price. Specifically, the positive volume change (15.9) along with the decrease in unit selling price (−$0.08) yields a net decline in sales (−$1.3).

Step 4. The first three steps explain the $29.9 net increase in sales. Namely, adding the effects on sales due to a (1) volume change (48.5), (2) price change (−17.2), and (3) combined volume and price change (−1.3), we obtain the components explaining the sales increase (difference due to rounding).

Our analysis of the increase in cost of sales ($8.0) follows the same four steps. Exhibit 9.2 reports results from analysis of both components of gross profit.

Interpreting Changes in Gross Profit

Analyzing changes in sales and cost of sales is useful in identifying major causes of changes in gross profit. The types of changes often consist of one or a combination of the following factors:

- Increase (decrease) in sales volume.
- Increase (decrease) in unit selling price.
- Increase (decrease) in cost per unit.

The potential for a combined change in volume and unit selling price or a combined change in volume and unit cost poses no particular problem for our analysis.

Interpreting the results of our analysis of changes in gross profit requires identifying the major factors responsible for these changes. It also requires assessing the reasons underlying changes in the factors responsible for gross profit changes. Moreover, we often extend the analysis to focus on strategic activities to remedy or improve (through volume, price, or cost) gross profit. If we determine the reason for a decrease in gross profit is a decline in unit selling prices and this reflects overcapacity in the industry with necessary price cutting, then our analysis of the company is pessimistic given management's lack of strategic actions when confronting this condition. However, if the reason for a decrease in gross profit is an increase in unit costs, then our analysis is more optimistic yielding a wider range of potential strategic activities for management.

When interpreting cost of sales and gross profit, especially for comparative analysis, we must direct attention to potential distortions arising from accounting methods. While this is applicable to all cost analysis, it is especially important with inventories and depreciation accounting. These two items, considered in detail in Chapters 4 and 6, merit special attention because they represent costs that are usually substantial in amount and are subject to alternative accounting methods that can substantially affect their measurement.

ANALYZING COMPANY EXPENSES

Most expenses have an identifiable and measurable relation to revenues. This is because revenues are the primary measure of a company's operating activity. Three useful tools for our analysis are based, in part, on the relation between revenues and expenses:

- *Common-size analysis.* Common-size income statements express expenses in terms of their percentage relation with revenues. This relation between expenses and sales is then traced over several periods or compared with the experience of competitors. Our analysis of Campbell Soup Company (see the Comprehensive Case following Chapter 12) includes common-size income statements spanning several years.
- *Index number analysis.* Index number analysis of income statements expresses income and its components in index numbers that relate to a base period. This analysis highlights relative changes in these items across time, allowing us to trace and assess their significance. Changes in expenses are readily compared with changes in both revenues and related expenses. Using index number analysis *with* common-size balance sheets, we can relate percentage changes in expenses to changes in assets and liabilities. For example, a change in revenues or revenue-related expenses might explain a change in inventories or accounts receivable. Index number analysis is illustrated in the Comprehensive Case analysis of Campbell Soup.
- *Operating ratio analysis.* The operating ratio measures the relation between operating expenses (or its components) and revenues. It equals cost of goods sold plus other operating expenses divided by net revenues. Interest and taxes are normally excluded from this measure due to its focus on operating efficiency (expense control) and not financing and tax management. It is useful for analysis of expenses within or across companies and can be viewed as an intermediate step in a common-size analysis of income. Properly interpreting this measure requires analysis of the reasons for variations in its components, including gross margin, selling, marketing, general, and administrative expenses.

This section applies selected components of these analytical tools to evaluate a company's expenses.

Selling Expenses

The analysis of selling expenses focuses on at least three primary areas:

1. Evaluating the relation between revenues and key expenses.
2. Assessing bad debts expense.
3. Evaluating the trend and productivity of future-directed marketing expenses.

Relation of Selling Expenses to Revenues

The importance of the relation between selling expenses and revenues varies across industries and companies. In certain companies, selling expenses are primarily commissions and are highly variable, while in others they are largely fixed. Our analysis must attempt to distinguish between these variable and fixed components, which can then be usefully analyzed relative to revenues. The more detailed the components, the more meaningful the analysis. A component analysis of selling expenses for Sporting Goods, Inc., is reported in Exhibit 9.3. An analysis of this exhibit reveals that selling expenses are rising faster than revenues from Year 1 to Year 4. Specifically, selling expenses in Year 4 constituted 5.6% more of revenues than in Year 1 ($360/$1,269 versus $180/$791). This is driven by increases, as a percentage of revenue, of 1.0% in sales staff salaries, 3.6% in advertising, and 2.2% in branch expenses. Special attention should be directed at the 3.6 percent increase in advertising to determine its cause–for example, is it due to promotion of new products or development of new branches benefiting future sales? The 1.2% decline in delivery expense is partially offset with a 0.7% increase in freight costs.

FRONT-LOADER

The aim of many write-offs is to front-load expenses. For example, charge off future years' expenses now, and then future earnings will be higher.

Component Analysis of Selling Expenses

Exhibit 9.3

SPORTING GOODS, INC.
Comparative Statement of Selling Expenses ($ thousands)

	YEAR 4		YEAR 3		YEAR 2		YEAR 1	
Sales	$1,269		$935		$833		$791	
Sales trend percent (Year 1 = 100%)		160.0%		118.0%		105.0%		100.0%
Selling expenses*								
Advertising	$ 84	6.6%	$ 34	3.6%	$ 28	3.4%	$ 24	3.0
Branch expenses†	80	6.3	41	4.4	38	4.6	32	4.1
Delivery expense (own trucks)	20	1.6	15	1.6	19	2.3	22	2.8
Freight-out	21	1.7	9	1.0	11	1.3	8	1.0
Sales staff salaries	111	8.7	76	8.1	68	8.1	61	7.7
Sales staff travel expense	35	2.8	20	2.1	18	2.2	26	3.3
Miscellaneous selling expenses	9	0.7	9	1.0	8	0.9	7	0.9
Total selling expense	$ 360	28.4%	$204	21.8%	$190	22.8%	$180	22.8%

* *Selling expenses are reported in both dollars and as a percentage of that year's sales amount.*
† *Includes rent, regional advertising, and promotion.*

When selling expenses as a percentage of revenues show an increase, we should focus attention on the increase in selling expense generating the associated increase in revenues. Beyond a certain level of selling expenses, there are lower marginal increases in revenues. This can be due to market saturation, brand loyalty, or increased expense in new territories. It is important for us to distinguish between the percentage of selling expenses to revenues for new versus continuing customers. This has implications for forecasts of profitability. If a company must substantially increase selling expenses to increase sales, its profitability is limited or can decline.

Bad Debts Expense

Bad debts expense is usually regarded as a marketing expense. Since the level of bad debts expense is related to the level of "allowance for doubtful accounts," it is usefully analyzed by examining the relation between the allowance and (gross) accounts receivable. We illustrate this analysis with interim data from BikeLand, Inc. ($ thousands):

YEAR 3—QUARTERLY	1st Quarter	2nd Quarter	3rd Quarter	4th Quarter
Allowance for doubtful accounts	$ 13,500	$ 12,900	$ 10,600	$ 15,800
Gross receivables	343,319	223,585	179,791	305,700
Allowance as a percentage of gross receivables	3.93%	5.77%	5.90%	5.17%

YEAR 2—QUARTERLY	1st Quarter	2nd Quarter	3rd Quarter	4th Quarter
Allowance for doubtful accounts	$ 16,600	$ 15,000	$ 12,200	$ 18,500
Gross receivables	331,295	215,660	172,427	285,600
Allowance as a percentage of gross receivables	5.01%	6.96%	7.07%	6.48%

Notice the significant decline in BikeLand's Year 3 allowance for doubtful accounts in relation to gross receivables as compared with Year 2. Potential reasons include improved collectibility of receivables or inadequate allowances resulting in understated bad debts expense. Further analysis is necessary to identify the reasons.

CASH COW
Some execs pocketed sizable amounts in bonuses, stock sales, and company loans during periods for which their companies were later under investigation (*Business Week*, August 26, 2002):

Kenneth Lay (Enron)	$184 mil.
Dennis Kozlowski (Tyco)	332 mil.
Scott Sullivan (WorldCom)	45 mil.
Gary Winnick (Global Crossing)	123 mil.

Future-Directed Marketing Expenses

Certain sales promotion expenses, particularly advertising, yield current *and* future benefits. Measuring future benefits from these expenses is extremely difficult. Expenditures for these future-directed marketing activities are largely discretionary, and our analysis must consider year-to-year trends in these expenditures. Beyond the ability of these expenditures to influence future sales, they provide insights into management's tendency to "manage" reported earnings. We consider the effect of these and other discretionary expenses on earnings quality in Chapter 12.

Depreciation Expense

Depreciation expense is often substantial in amount, especially for manufacturing and many service companies. Depreciation is usually considered a fixed cost in that it is often computed based on elapsed time. If its computation uses operating activity, it is a variable cost. In contrast to most expenses, the relation of depreciation to income is not usually meaningful due to its fixed nature. The relation of depreciation to gross plant and equipment is often more meaningful. A measure of this relation is the ratio of depreciation to depreciable assets:

$$\frac{\text{Depreciation expense}}{\text{Depreciable assets}}$$

The purpose of this ratio is to help us detect changes in the composite rate of depreciation. This is useful in evaluating depreciation levels and in detecting any adjustments (smoothing) to income. It is often useful to compute this ratio by asset categories. Analyzing other characteristics of assets is also important and is discussed in Chapter 4.

Maintenance and Repairs Expenses

. . . LIKE IT IS
Some argue a write-off is akin to making 5 years of rent payments at once, then claiming your income is higher in the next 4 years.

Maintenance and repairs expenses vary with investment in plant and equipment and with the level of productive activity. They affect cost of goods sold and other expenses. Maintenance and repairs comprise both variable *and* fixed expenses and therefore do not vary directly with sales. Accordingly, the relation of sales to maintenance and repairs expenses, both across companies and time, must be interpreted with care. To the extent our analysis can distinguish between variable and fixed portions of these expenses, we can better interpret their relation to sales. We also must remember that maintenance and repairs are largely discretionary expenses. Many of these expenses can be timed to not detract from one period's income or to preserve liquid resources. For example, companies can postpone or limit much preventive maintenance and many repairs; there are, of course, certain expenses that cannot be postponed without losses in productivity. Management's decisions in this regard bear on earnings quality. We should also consider a company's maintenance and repairs expenses when evaluating depreciation expense. We estimate assets' useful lives using many assumptions including their upkeep and maintenance. If maintenance and repairs are cut back, assets' useful lives likely decline. We may need to adjust upward the depreciation expense to counter the overstatement in income.

General and Administrative Expenses

Most general and administrative expenses are fixed, largely because these expenses include items like salaries and rent. There is a tendency for increases in these expenses, especially in prosperous times. When analyzing these expenses, our analysis should direct attention at both the trend in these expenses and the percentage of revenues they consume.

> ***ANALYSIS VIEWPOINT ... YOU ARE THE ACTIVIST***
>
> You are the campaign manager for a first-time candidate running for state representative. The incumbent's campaign is financed almost exclusively by a major forest products company in your district. The incumbent fought for and received state and local logging cost benefits for this company in the past two years. One of your candidate's goals is to repeal these benefits if elected. The incumbent counters that this company is the largest employer in the district and points to this company's income *after* these benefits, which is similar to its competition. You look at the financial statements and find gross margin is 40% of sales while the industry norm is 20%. Yet profit margin is at the industry norm of 10%—the difference between gross and profit margin is primarily due to executive compensation. Is this useful information?

Answer–p. 477

Financing Expenses

Financing expenses are largely fixed (an exception is interest on short-term debt). Experience shows most creditor financing is eventually refinanced and not removed unless replaced with equity financing. Interest expense often includes amortization of any premium or discount on the debt along with any issue expenses. A useful tool in our analysis of a company's cost of borrowed money and credit standing is its **average effective interest rate,** which is computed as:

$$\frac{\text{Total interest incurred}}{\text{Average interest-bearing indebtedness}}$$

As an example, we compute Quaker Oats' average effective interest rate for Year 11 using data in Appendix A as ($ millions):

$$\frac{(\$43.3 + \$60.5)^{(a)}}{(\$814.7 + \$1{,}115.8)^{(b)} \div 2} = 10.75\%$$

[a] Total interest costs (before deduction for interest capitalized)–item 156.

[b]	Year 10	Year 11
Short-term debt 147	$ 343.2	$ 80.6
Current portion of long-term debt 148	32.3	32.9
Long-term debt 148	740.3	701.2
Total liabilities subject to interest	$1,115.8	$814.7

The average effective interest rate is usefully compared across years and companies. Quaker Oats includes a good discussion of debt in the Liquidity and Capital Resources section of its MD&A and in its disclosure on weighted-average interest rates of debt (see note 5 to its financial statements). We can also measure a company's sensitivity to interest rate changes by determining the portion of debt tied to market rates like the prime rate. In periods of rising interest rates, a company with debt tied to market rates is exposed to increased risk through higher interest expenses. Conversely, declining interest rates yield less expenses for these companies.

Income Tax Expenses

Income taxes essentially reflect a distribution of profits between a company and governmental agencies. They usually constitute a substantial portion of a company's income before taxes. For this reason our analysis must pay special attention to income

Analysis Research

LEVERAGE AND EQUITY RISK

Analysis research has examined the relation between accounting data and the risk associated with investing in a company's equity securities. In economic terms, *total risk* is related to the riskiness of the company's capital structure (*financial risk*) and its asset structure (operating risk). *Operating risk* is composed of variability in sales and operating leverage.

Evidence indicates the existence of a positive association between operating leverage (extent of fixed expenses) and total risk. There is also evidence of a negative relation between companies' financial leverage (extent of fixed-interest financing) and operating leverage, especially for companies with a high degree of total risk. This implies that companies are strategically attempting to trade off financial risk and operating risk in their business activities.

taxes. Since corporations conduct nearly 10 times more sales activity than other forms of businesses combined, we focus primarily on *corporate* income taxes in this section.

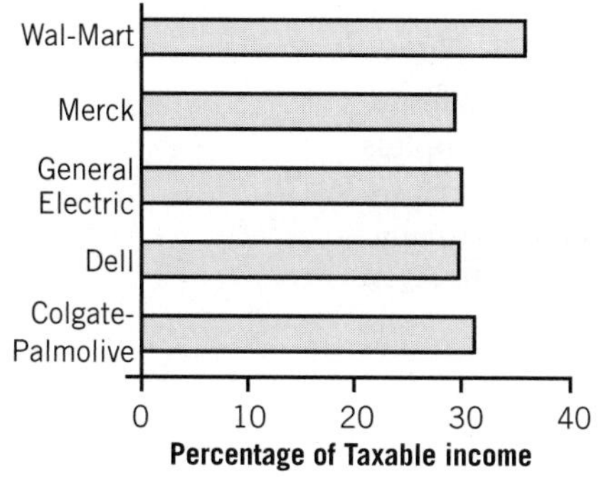

Measuring Effective Tax Rate

Except for a graduated rate on lower levels of income, corporate income is taxed at a uniform rate determined by tax law (35%). Differences in timing of recognition for revenues or expenses between taxable income and accrual income should not influence the effective tax rate. This is because interperiod income tax allocation aims to match tax expense with accrual income regardless of when taxes are paid. The relations between the income tax accrual and the pretax income, referred to as the **effective tax rate** or *tax ratio,* is influenced by *permanent* tax differences. Examples include differences due to state and local taxes, foreign tax rate differentials, various tax credits, untaxed income and nondeductible expenses. We discussed income tax allocation and permanent differences in Chapter 6. The effective tax rate is computed as:

$$\frac{\text{Income tax expense}}{\text{Income before income taxes}}$$

For Quaker Oats the effective tax rate for Year 11 is computed as:

$$\frac{\$175.7^{(a)}}{\$411.5^{(b)}} = 42.7\%$$

(a) Provision for income taxes–item [8] in Appendix A.

(b) Income from continuing operations before income taxes–item [7] in Appendix A.

The 42.7% effective tax rate corresponds to the rate computed by the company (see note 16 of its annual report in Appendix A). Notice the effective tax rate uses income from continuing operations rather than net income. If we want to compute the effective tax rate incurred by the company on *all* items of income during a period, including discontinued operations and extraordinary items, then a different computation is required. We use Quaker Oats to illustrate this:

Income (loss)	Before Tax	Related Tax	After Tax
Income from continuing operations before income taxes and other items	$411.5 [7]	$175.7 [8]	$235.8 [9]
Loss from discontinued operations	(50)	(20) [144]	(30) [10]
Net income	$361.5*	$155.7*	$205.8 [11]

* *Derived amount.*

The effective tax rate using all items in net income is:

$$\frac{\$155.7}{\$361.5} = 43.1\%$$

In evaluating income level, trend, and forecasts, we must identify the reasons why an effective tax rate deviates from the normal or expected rate. Income taxes are of such magnitude that small changes in the effective tax rate can yield major changes in income. Knowledge of the reasons for deviations and changes in the effective tax rate of a company is important to profitability analysis and income forecasting.

GUIDANCE ANSWERS TO ANALYSIS VIEWPOINTS

Securities Director

Differences in users' information requests stem from their expertise and planned applications with financial data. Analysts' compensation depends on their ability to accurately assess and predict future risk and return characteristics of securities. Information that aids them in this task is welcome. Analysts typically possess the necessary expertise and training to effectively use this information. Unions, activists, and less sophisticated investors often do not possess the expertise, time, or motivation to seriously analyze financial statements. These users would prefer one number that captures a company's current financial position and future performance potential. Balancing these information needs (or analysis limitations) is delicate and demands consideration of both economic, political, and social factors. Social factors include public "access" to markets, fairness across users, costs to society, and other resource allocation implications. Establishing information listing requirements demands a broad perspective on fairness and is not unlike environmental or tax law.

Banker

Additional segment information can cause you to reassess risk and return characteristics. The fact that a company's income is derived from 10 different segments generally lowers its riskiness. This is because a downturn in one segment has less of an impact on overall company profitability. In contrast, an economic downturn in the segment of the single industry company can have severe negative consequences. A comparative analysis of these two companies including segment information would favor the multisegment company. The segment information is especially important in this situation given the *marginal* status of both companies and the unlikelihood of accepting additional risk.

Activist

This information is extremely valuable to your candidate. While income for this company is similar to the industry norm, its executive compensation is substantially *higher* than the norm. Logging benefits appear to have substantially lowered this company's cost of sales, as indicated by its high gross margin, but excess profits are being paid to top executives of the company at a rate far exceeding the norm. This information is not only useful in your candidate's campaign, but hints at less than ethical practices.

QUESTIONS

9–1 Why is *income* not a unique, specific quantity? Identify at least three reasons.

9–2 What are the major objectives of profitability analysis?

9–3 Distinguish between appropriate and acceptable measures of income. Explain why acceptable measures are often reported in financial statements rather than more appropriate measures.

9–4 Two main phases are identifiable in an analysis of income. Describe them.

9–5 Why is knowledge of the major sources of sales of a company so crucial in the analysis of income?

9–6 Why are information and detailed segment data for diversified companies important for profitability analysis?

9–7 Disclosure of various types of information by line of business is required. Comment on the value of this segment information and the problems of reporting it in financial statements.

9–8 What are the major disclosure requirements for segment reporting?

9–9 Identify limitations of segment data that we must be aware of in analysis of financial statements.

9–10 Describe important considerations bearing on the quality and persistence of revenue.

9–11 How are disclosures of an interpretive or explanatory nature in MD&A useful for profitability analysis?

9–12 Identify examples of subjects covered in MD&A.

9–13 What are the objectives of MD&A?

9–14 What are two important relations in analyzing gross profit?

9–15 What is a useful measure of the adequacy of current depreciation? What is its purpose?

9–16 Maintenance and repairs expenses can be meaningfully related to what items?

9–17 What are at least two objectives of an analysis of selling expenses?

9–18 How is bad debts expense most meaningfully evaluated? What are potential reasons for a decline in the allowance for doubtful accounts?

9–19 What is the effective tax rate and how is it computed?

9–20 Explain why managers rarely offer information beyond the minimum required disclosures for operating segments (such as product segments or geographic segments).

EXERCISES

EXERCISE 9–1
Analyzing the Relation between Revenues and Expenses

A press report carried the following news item: *General Motors, Ford, and Chrysler are expected to post losses on fourth-quarter operations despite sales gains. Automakers' revenues are based on factory output rather than retail sales by dealers, and last quarter's sales increases were from the bulging inventories at the end of the third quarter, rather than from models produced in the fourth quarter.*

Required:

Discuss likely accounting-based reasons that contribute to these expected fourth-quarter losses of automakers.

EXERCISE 9–2
Analyzing Income for Diversified Companies

The statement of consolidated income for Standard Industries, Inc., is reproduced below:

STANDARD INDUSTRIES, INC.
Statement of Consolidated Income
For the Year Ended March 31, Year 8

Revenue:	
Net sales	$38,040,000
Other revenue	408,600
Total revenue	$38,448,600
Costs and expenses:	
Cost of products sold	$27,173,300
Selling and administrative expenses	8,687,500
Interest expense	296,900
Total costs and expenses	$36,157,700
Income before income taxes	$ 2,290,900
Provision for income taxes	1,005,000
Net income	$ 1,285,900

In its annual report, Standard's president reports the company is engaged in the pharmaceutical, food processing, toy manufacturing, and metal-working industries. Standard does not disclose separately the profit earned in each of its component industries. Also, several items appearing on its statement of consolidated retained earnings are not included on the income statement–specifically, a gain of $633,400 on the sale of its furniture division in early March of the current year and an assessment of additional income taxes of $164,900 resulting from an audit of tax returns covering the years ended March 31, Year 5, and Year 6.

Required:

a. Explain what is meant by the term *diversified* company.

b. Discuss the accounting problems involved in measuring net income by industry segments within a diversified company.

c. With reference to Standard Industries' statement of consolidated income, identify the specific items where we might encounter difficulty in measuring income by each of its industry segments and explain the nature of the difficulty.

d. What criteria should be applied in determining whether a gain or loss that is properly included in net income should be reported in the results of continuing operations or shown separately as an extraordinary item after all other revenues and expenses?

e. How should both the gain on sale of the furniture division and the assessment of additional taxes be reported in Standard's financial statements?

(AICPA adapted)

EXERCISE 9–3
Analyzing Income Tax Disclosures

Quaker Oats Company

Refer to the financial statements of **Quaker Oats Company** in Appendix A.

Required:

What is the effective tax rate for each year shown?

EXERCISE 9–4
Variations in Income and Income Components

Quaker Oats Company

Refer to the financial statements of **Quaker Oats Company** in Appendix A.

Required:

Analyze variations in income and income components for Quaker Oats for Year 11 to Year 10. Analyze and interpret your results. (*Hint:* Management's Discussion and Analysis is useful for this purpose.)

EXERCISE 9–5
Analyzing Income Tax Disclosures

Campbell Soup Company

Refer to the financial statements of **Campbell Soup Company** in Appendix A.

Required:

Explain (with a schedule) how Campbell Soup, with income before tax of $667.4 in Year 11, reports $185.8 of current federal income tax when the statutory tax rate is 34 percent.

EXERCISE 9–6
Analyzing Depreciation Expense

CHECK
(a) 42.3%

Campbell Soup Company

Refer to the financial statements of **Campbell Soup Company** in Appendix A.

Required:

Compute and interpret the following analytical measures for Year 10:

a. Accumulated depreciation as a percent of gross plant assets subject to depreciation.

b. Depreciation expense as a percent of gross plant assets subject to depreciation.

c. Depreciation expense as a percent of sales.

EXERCISE 9–7
Variations in Income and Income Components

Campbell Soup Company

Refer to the financial statements of **Campbell Soup Company** in Appendix A.

Required:

Analyze variations in income and income components for Campbell Soup that compares Year 11 to Year 10. (*Hint:* Management's Discussion and Analysis is useful for this purpose.)

PROBLEMS

PROBLEM 9–1
Analyzing Measures of Company Profitability

CHECK
(a) 2. Year 11, 12.7%
Year 10, 11.0%

Refer to the financial statements of **Quaker Oats Company** in Appendix A.

Quaker Oats Company

Required:

a. Compute the following analytical measures for both Years 11 and 10:
   (1) Ratio of depreciation expense to depreciable assets.
   (2) Effective interest rate on liabilities subject to interest.
   (3) Ratio of tax expense to income before tax (effective tax rate).
   (4) Ratio of cost of goods sold plus other operating expenses to net sales.
   (5) Ratio of net income to total revenues.

b. Comment on both the level and trend of these analytical measures.

PROBLEM 9–2
Analyzing Line-of-Business Data (extending beyond the book)

Selected data from Kemp Corporation are reproduced below:

KEMP CORPORATION
Product-Line Information ($ in thousands)

	Year 1	Year 2	Year 3	Year 4
Data communications equipment:				
Net sales	$4,616	$ 5,630	$ 4,847	$ 6,890
Income contribution	570	876	996	1,510
Inventory	2,615	2,469	2,103	1,897
Time recording devices:				
Net sales	3,394	4,200	4,376	4,100
Income contribution	441	311	34	412
Inventory	1,193	2,234	2,574	2,728
Hardware for electronics industry:				
Net sales	—	—	1,564	1,850
Income contribution	—	—	771	919
Inventory	—	—	331	287
Home sewing products:				
Net sales	1,505	1,436	1,408	1,265
Income contribution	291	289	276	342
Inventory	398	534	449	526
Corporate totals:				
Net sales	9,515	11,266	12,195	14,105
Income contribution	1,302	1,476	2,077	3,183
Inventory	4,206	5,237	5,457	5,438

Required:

a. For Year 4, compute the following ratios:
   (1) Inventory ÷ sales
   (2) Inventory ÷ Income contribution

b. Compute the percentage of each product line's income contribution to the total for each year. Interpret this evidence.

c. Comment on the desirability of an investment in each product line.

PROBLEM 9–3
Analyzing Changes in Gross Margin

Johnson Corporation sells primarily two products: (A) consumer cleaners and (B) industrial purifiers. Its gross margin and components for the past two years are:

	Year 7	Year 6
Sales revenue:		
Product A	$60,000	$35,000
Product B	30,000	45,000
Total	90,000	80,000
Deduct cost of goods sold:		
Product A	50,000	28,000
Product B	19,500	27,000
Total	69,500	55,000
Gross margin	$20,500	$25,000

In Year 6, the selling price of A is $5 per unit, while in Year 7 it is $6 per unit. Product B sells for $50 per unit in both years. Security analysts and the business press expressed surprise at Johnson's 12.5% increase in sales and $4,500 decrease in gross margin for Year 7.

Required:
Prepare an analysis statement of the change in gross margin for Year 7 versus Year 6. Discuss and show the effects of changes in quantities, prices, costs, and product mix on gross margin.

CHECK
Net decrease, $(4,500)

PROBLEM 9–4
Common-Size Analysis of Comparative Income Statements

Comparative income statements of Spyres Manufacturing Company for Years 8 and 9 are reproduced below:

	Year 9	Year 8
Net sales	$600,000	$500,000
Cost of goods sold	490,000	430,000
Gross margin	110,000	70,000
Operating expenses	101,000	51,000
Income before taxes	9,000	19,000
Income taxes	2,400	5,000
Net income	$ 6,600	$ 14,000

Required:

a. Prepare common-size statements showing the percent of each item to net sales for both Year 8 and Year 9. Include a column reporting the percentage increase or decrease for Year 9 relative to Year 8 (round numbers to the tenth of 1%).

b. Interpret the trend shown in your percentage calculations of *a.* What areas identified from this analysis should be a matter of managerial concern?

PROBLEM 9–5
Variations in Income and Income Components

At a meeting of your company's Investment Policy Committee the possibility of investing in ZETA Corporation (see Case CC–2 in the Comprehensive Case chapter) is considered. During discussions, a committee member asked about the major factors explaining the change in ZETA Corporation's income from Year 5 to Year 6.

Required:
Analyze variations in income and income components for ZETA Corporation that compares Year 6 to Year 5. Analyze and interpret your results. (*Hint:* ZETA's notes are useful for this purpose.)

PROBLEM 9–6
Analyzing Income Tax Disclosures
CHECK
$9,200

Refer to the financial statements of ZETA Corporation in Case CC–2 in the Comprehensive Case chapter.

Required:

Estimate the amount of depreciation expense reported for tax purposes.

CASES

CASE 9–1
Analyzing Profitability and Profitability Components

Use the annual report of **Kodak** in Appendix A to answer the following: **Kodak**

Required:

a. Analyze variations in income and income components for 2001 and 2000. Interpret the results.

b. Note 21 to Kodak's financial statements reports segment information.
  (1) How does Kodak segment its operations for decision making?
  (2) Convert the reported segment financial information to common-size form.
  (3) Analyze sales growth, asset growth, and profitability segments. Interpret the results.
  (4) Analyze capital additions as a percentage of segment sales and segment net operating assets.
  (5) Calculate "cash earnings" as a percentage of sales for each segment by adding goodwill amortization back to earnings (loss) from operations.

c. Prepare a trend percent analysis of Kodak's sales from continuing operations and sales by segment for the period 1997 to 2001 (see the summary of operating data). Comment on the relative persistence of these items.

d. Compare Kodak's receivable growth rate to the revenue growth rate for 2001. Interpret any unusual variation.

e. Calculate gross profit as a percentage of sales for each year shown. Interpret any significant variations or trends.

f. Calculate selling, general, and administrative expenses as a percentage of sales for each year shown. Interpret any significant variations or trends.

g. Calculate changes in the finished goods, work in process, and raw materials inventories. Discuss how the results might impact your forecast of 2002 sales.

h. Calculate the ratio of accumulated depreciation to gross assets subject to depreciation. Comment on any significant change.

i. Estimate the average effective interest rate paid by Kodak on its interest-bearing debt in 1999, 2000, and 2001.

j. Estimate the effective income tax rate paid by Kodak for 1999, 2000, and 2001.

k. Prepare a trend percent analysis of research and development costs. Discuss the implications of changes in the level of spending on future prospects.

CASE 9–2
Analysis of Common-Size Profitability Information

The following data are excerpted from the annual report of **Lands' End:** **Lands' End**

For the period ended	Year 9	Year 8	Year 7	Year 6	Year 5
Net sales	100%	100%	100%	100%	100%
Cost of sales	55.0	53.4	54.5	57.0	57.6
Gross profit	45.0	46.6	45.5	43.0	42.4
Selling, general, and admin.	39.7	38.8	37.9	38.0	36.0
Other expenses	3.0	2.7	3.0	2.0	2.8
Net income	2.3%	5.1%	4.6%	3.0%	3.6%

Required:

a. Discuss three factors that determine the level of sales and the level of gross profit as a percentage of sales in the context of the operations of Lands' End.

b. Interpret the gross profit percentage (45% in fiscal Year 9) in simple terms and in the context of Lands' Ends operations.

c. Catalog mailing costs constitute a large percentage of the selling, general, and administrative costs for Lands' End. These costs have risen steadily as a percent of sales (only 32.4% in fiscal Year 4). Discuss drivers (determinants) of total catalog mailing costs and indicate ways that Lands' End can control these costs. With each suggestion, indicate how the level of sales might be affected.

CASE 9–3
Analyzing Line-of-Business Data

Selected financial data for Petersen Corporation's revenue and income (contribution) are reproduced below:

Line of Business	Year 1	Year 2	Year 3	Year 4
Revenue:				
Manufactured and engineered products:				
Engineered equipment	$ 30,341	$ 29,807	$ 32,702	$ 43,870
Other equipment	5,906	5,996	6,824	7,424
Parts, supplies and services	29,801	29,878	33,623	44,223
Total manuf. & engineered products	66,048	65,681	73,149	95,517
Engineering and erecting services	—	—	12,261	36,758
Total environmental systems group	66,048	65,681	85,410	132,275
Frye Copysystems	25,597	28,099	31,214	39,270
Sinclair & Valentine	—	53,763	57,288	60,973
A. L. Garber	16,615	15,223	20,445	24,808
Total graphics group	42,212	97,085	108,947	125,051
Total consolidated revenue	$108,260	$162,766	$194,357	$257,326
Income:				
Manufactured and engineered products	$3,785	$ 3,943	$ 9,209	$10,762
Engineering and erecting services	—	—	1,224	3,189
International operations	2,265	2,269	2,030	2,323
Total environmental systems group	6,050	6,212	12,463	16,274
Frye Copysystems	1,459	2,011	2,799	3,597
Sinclair & Valentine	—	3,723	4,628	5,142
A. L. Garber	(295)	926	1,304	1,457
Total graphics group	1,164	6,660	8,731	10,196
Total divisional income	7,214	12,872	21,194	26,470
Unallocated expenses and taxes	(5,047)	(8,146)	(13,179)	(16,449)
Total income from continuing operations	$2,167	$ 4,726	$ 8,015	$10,021

Required:

a. Use common-size statements to analyze every division's (1) contribution to total consolidated revenue, (2) contribution to total divisional income, and (3) ratio of income to revenue.

b. Interpret and comment on the evidence revealed from your computations in *a.*

WEB ACTIVITIES

The Web Activities are located on the book's website at www.mhhe.com/wild8e.

10 PROSPECTIVE ANALYSIS

A LOOK BACK <

The preceding two chapters dealt with analysis of company returns—both profitability and return on invested capital. Emphasis was on rate of return measures, disaggregation of returns, and accounting analysis of income components. These return-based chapters complement later chapters that focus on risk, including liquidity and solvency.

A LOOK AT THIS CHAPTER •

We study forecasting and pro forma analysis of financial statements in this chapter. We provide a detailed example of the forecasting process to project the income statement, the balance sheet, and the statement of cash flows. We describe the relevance of forecasting for security valuation and provide an example using forecasted financial statements to implement the residual income valuation model. We discuss the concept of value drivers and their reversion to long-run equilibrium levels.

A LOOK AHEAD >

Chapter 11 expands our analysis of a company to short-term liquidity, capital structure, and long-term solvency. We explain liquidity and describe analysis tools such as accounting-based ratios, turnover, and operating activity measures of liquidity. We also analyze capital structure and interpret its implications for company performance and solvency.

LEARNING OBJECTIVES

- Describe the importance of prospective analysis.
- Explain the process of projecting the income statement, balance sheet, and the statement of cash flows.
- Discuss and illustrate the importance of sensitivity analysis.
- Describe the implementation of the projection process in the valuation of equity securities.
- Discuss the concept of value drivers and their reversion to long-run equilibrium levels.

Fundamental Analysis Is Back

NEW YORK–For years, two great armies of investors have done battle on Wall Street. In one camp stand growth investors, willing to pay dearly for companies they believe can generate big profits for years to come. In the other camp are value investors. They'll buy only into companies with real assets and solid earnings in the here and now–and at bargain prices. As yet, value investing is more a framework than a set of codified rules. It relies more on forecasting, even though Benjamin Graham and David Dodd, who laid the principles of value investing, frowned on forecasts.

During the growth and bull markets of the 1990s and the recession and bear market of the early 2000s, the Standard & Poor's 500/Barra Growth index was considerably more volatile than the S&P 500/Barra Value index, reaching higher highs and lower lows. Over the past 10 years, however, the S&P 500/Barra Value index has yielded a 14.97% annualized return, vs. 14.24% for the S&P 500/Barra Growth index–a minuscule gap of just 0.73%. "The outperformance of one over the other is purely random," says Marci Rossell, chief economist at Oppenheimer Funds. "For the smart investor, both should be part of a diversified investment portfolio." Whether you use growth or value criteria, it's more important to pay attention to the fundamentals of a company's business than it is to set investment criteria based solely on ratios like price-to-earnings or p-e to sales growth.

. . . pay attention to the fundamentals of a company's business plan . . .

Value investors' interpretations of the investing style are as varied. But if you listen closely, the bottom line is the same–assessment of fundamentals. In the broadest terms, value investors are looking for companies that trade at less than their real value in the hope that the value will be recognized by other market players and reflected in higher stock prices. To identify such latent value, investors need to examine companies' fundamental business prospects carefully. "You want a company where something is going to change, either externally, like a fundamental change in its industry, or internally, like a change in management," says Chris Leavy, portfolio manager of Oppenheimer Value Fund.

Prospective analysis is a central component of value investing. It relies on a sound understanding of the business's fundamentals and economic environment. From this base, forecasts of future performance are developed that provide the basis for the valuation of stock price. Whichever investing philosophy you subscribe to, the message is clear: understand clearly where the company's business model and strategic plan are taking it.

Sources: Business Week, July 2001, Spring 2002.

PREVIEW OF CHAPTER 10

Prospective analysis is the final step in the financial statement analysis process. It can be undertaken only after the historical financial statements have been properly adjusted to accurately reflect the economic performance of the company. As discussed in previous chapters, these adjustments may include, for example, eliminating transitory items in the income statement or reallocating them to past or future years, capitalizing (expensing) items that have

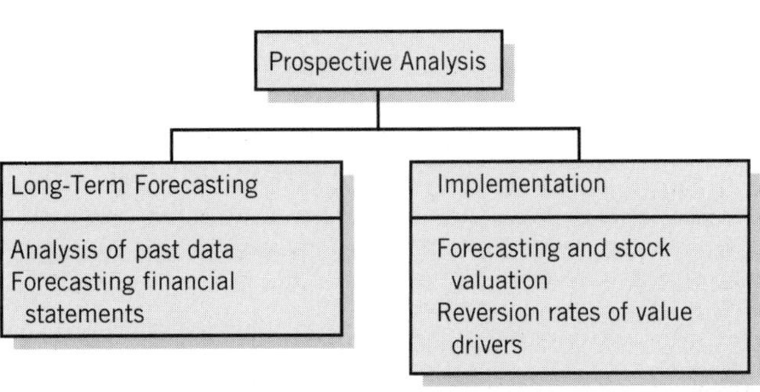

been expensed (capitalized) by management, capitalizing operating leases and other forms of off-balance sheet financing, and so forth. Prospective analysis includes forecasting of the balance sheet, income statement and statement of cash flows.

Prospective analysis is central to security valuation. Both the free cash flow and residual income valuation models described in Chapter 1 require estimates of future financial statements. The residual income model, for example, requires projections of future net profits and book values of equity in order to estimate current stock price. Prospective analysis is also useful to examine the viability of companies' strategic plans. For this, we analyze whether a company will be able to generate sufficient cash flows from operations to finance expected growth or whether it will be required to seek debt or equity financing in the future. We are also interested in analyzing whether current strategic plans will yield the benefits forecasted by company management. And finally, prospective analysis is useful to creditors to assess a company's ability to meet its debt service requirements.

Our discussion of projection mechanics centers on forecasts of the financial statements for Target Corporation. We provide a detailed explanation of the forecasting process in the next section.

THE PROJECTION PROCESS

We begin our discussion with a comprehensive example of the projection process using the financial statements of Target Corporation.

Projecting Financial Statements

The projection process begins with the income statement, followed by the balance sheet and the statement of cash flows.

Projected Income Statement

The income statements of Target as of 1999–2001 are provided in Exhibit 10.1 together with selected ratios. The projection process begins with an expected growth in sales. In this example we use historical trends to predict future levels. A more detailed analysis would incorporate outside information such as the following:

- **Expected level of macroeconomic activity.** Since Target customers' purchases are influenced by the level of personal disposable income, our analysis might incorporate estimates relating to the overall growth in the economy and the expected growth of retail sales in particular. For example, if the economy is in a cyclical upturn, we might be comfortable in projecting an increase in sales greater than that of the recent past.
- **The competitive landscape.** Has the number of competitors increased? Or, have weaker rivals ceased operations? Changes in the competitive landscape will influence our projections of unit sales as well as Target's ability to raise prices. Both of these will impact top line growth.
- **New versus old store mix.** New stores typically enjoy significantly greater sales increases than older stores since they may tap poorly served markets or provide a more up-to-date product mix than existing competitors. Older stores, by comparison, typically grow at the overall rate of growth in the local economy. Our analysis must consider, therefore, expansion plans announced by management.

Target's sales have been growing between 8% and 9.5% per year in the recent past. We begin with an assumption that sales will grow at 8.09% as in 2001. Once the

Target Corporation Income Statement

Exhibit 10.1

	2001	2000	1999
Net sales	$39,888	$36,903	$33,702
Cost of goods sold	27,246	25,295	23,029
Gross profit	12,642	11,608	10,673
Selling, general, and administrative expense	8,883	8,190	7,490
Depreciation and amortization expense	1,079	940	854
Interest expense	464	425	393
Income before tax	2,216	2,053	1,936
Income tax expense	842	789	751
Loss from extraordinary items and discontinued operations	6	0	41
Net income	$ 1,368	$ 1,264	$ 1,144
Outstanding shares	905	898	912
Selected Ratios			
Sales growth	8.09%	9.50%	9.91%
Gross profit margin	31.69	31.46	31.67
Selling, general, and administrative expense/Sales	22.27	22.19	22.22
Depreciation expense/Gross prior year PP&E	6.85	6.80	6.70
Interest expense/Prior-year long-term debt	7.15	8.47	8.35
Income tax expense/Pretax income	38.00	38.43	38.79

projection has been completed, sensitivity analysis will examine the implications of higher and lower growth rates on our forecasts.

Target's gross profit margin has remained steady at 31.5%–31.7% of sales. For our purposes, we assume 31.69%, the most recent gross profit margin. In practice, our estimate of gross profit margin will be influenced, in part, by the strength of the economy and the level of competition in Target's markets. For example, in an increasingly competitive environment we might question the company's ability to increase gross profit margin as selling prices will be difficult to increase. Selling, general, and administrative expenses have also remained constant at about 22% of sales. Our projection of SG&A expense is 22.27% of sales, the most recent experience. In practice, we might examine individual expense items and estimate each individually, incorporating knowledge we have gained from the MD&A section of the financial statements or from outside sources. For a retailing company like Target, trends in wage and occupancy costs and advertising expenses require greater scrutiny.

Depreciation expense is a significant line item and should be projected separately. It is a fixed expense and is a function of the amount of depreciable assets. In recent years, Target has reported depreciation expense of approximately 6.8% of the balance of beginning-of-year gross property, plant, and equipment. Our projection assumes 6.85% of the 2001 PP&E balance.

Similarly, we compute the historical ratio of interest expense relative to beginning-of-year interest-bearing debt. This ratio has recently decreased from 8.47% to 7.15%, primarily as the result of new borrowings and refinancings at lower rates. Our projection assumes 7.15% of the beginning-of-year balance of interest-bearing debt. In practice, our estimates will incorporate projections of future levels of long-term interest rates. Finally, tax expense as a percentage of pretax income has been declining to the most recent level of 38%, used in our projection.

PLANE TRUTH

Unit costs for one seat flown one mile follow (*Business Week*, September 2, 2002):

US Airways	$15.37
United	12.85
American	12.46
Northwest	11.47
Continental	11.09
Delta	10.40
Southwest	7.51
JetBlue	6.69

Given these assumptions, Target's projected income statement for 2002 is presented in Exhibit 10.2. The following are the steps in the projection of this statement:

1. Sales: $43,115 = $39,888 × 1.0809
2. Gross profit: $13,665 = $43,115 × 31.69%
3. Cost of goods sold: $29,450 = $43,115 − $13,665
4. Selling, general and administrative: $9,602 = $43,115 × 22.27%
5. Depreciation: $1,263 = $18,442 (beginning-of-period PP&E gross) × 6.85%
6. Interest: $578 = $8,088 (beginning-of-period interest-bearing debt) × 7.15%
7. Pretax income: $2,222 = $13,665 − $9,602 − $1,263 − $578
8. Tax expense: $844 = $2,222 × 38%
9. Extraordinary and discontinued items: none
10. Net income: $1,378 = $2,222 − $844

Exhibit 10.2 ***Target Corporation Projected Income Statement***

	Forecasting Step	2002 Estimate
Income statement		
Net sales	1	$43,115
Cost of goods sold	2	29,450
Gross profit	2	13,665
Selling, general and administrative expense	4	9,602
Depreciation and amortization expense	5	1,263
Interest expense	6	578
Income before tax	7	2,222
Income tax expense	8	844
Extraordinary items and discontinued operations	9	0
Net income	10	$ 1,378
Outstanding shares		905
Forecasting Assumptions		
Sales growth		8.09%
Gross profit margin		31.69
Selling, general and administrative expense/Sales		22.27
Depreciation expense/Gross prior year PP&E		6.85
Interest expense/Prior-year long-term debt		7.15
Income tax expense/Pretax income		38.00

Projected Balance Sheet

The balance sheets of Target as of 1999–2001 are provided in Exhibit 10.3 together with selected ratios. The forecast of the 2002 balance sheet involves the following steps:

1. Project current assets other than cash, using projected sales or cost of goods sold and appropriate turnover ratios as described below.
2. Project PP&E increases with capital expenditures estimate derived from historical trends or information obtained in the MD&A section of the annual report.
3. Project current liabilities other than debt, using projected sales or cost of goods sold and appropriate turnover ratios as described below.
4. Obtain current maturities of long-term debt from the long-term debt footnote.
5. Assume other short-term indebtedness is unchanged from prior year balance unless they have exhibited noticeable trends.

6. Assume initial long-term debt balance is equal to the prior period long-term debt less current maturities from (4) above.
7. Assume other long-term obligations are equal to the prior year's balance unless they have exhibited noticeable trends.
8. Assume initial estimate of common stock is equal to the prior year's balance.
9. Assume retained earnings are equal to the prior year's balance plus (minus) net profit (loss) and less expected dividends.
10. Assume other equity accounts are equal to the prior year's balance unless they have exhibited noticeable trends.

Target Corporation Balance Sheet

Exhibit 10.3

	2001	2000	1999
Cash	$ 499	$ 356	$ 220
Receivables	3,831	1,941	1,724
Inventories	4,449	4,248	3,798
Other current assets	869	759	741
Total current assets	9,648	7,304	6,483
Property, plant and equipment (PP&E)	18,442	15,759	13,824
Accumulated depreciation	4,909	4,341	3,925
Net property, plant and equipment	13,533	11,418	9,899
Other noncurrent assets	973	768	761
Total assets	$24,154	$19,490	$17,143
Accounts payable	$ 4,160	$ 3,576	$ 3,514
Current portion of long-term debt	905	857	498
Accrued expenses	1,566	1,507	1,520
Income taxes payable	423	361	318
Total current liabilities	7,054	6,301	5,850
Deferred income taxes and other liabilities	1,152	1,036	910
Long-term debt	8,088	5,634	4,521
Total liabilities	16,294	12,971	11,281
Preferred stock	0	0	0
Common stock	75	75	76
Capital surplus	1,098	902	730
Retained earnings	6,687	5,542	5,056
Shareholders' equity	7,860	6,519	5,862
Total liabilities and net worth	$24,154	$19,490	$17,143
Selected Ratios			
Accounts receivable turnover rate	10.41	19.01	19.55
Inventory turnover rate	6.12	5.95	6.06
Accounts payable turnover rate	6.55	7.07	6.55
Accrued expenses turnover rate	25.47	24.49	22.17
Taxes payable/Tax expense	50.24%	45.75%	42.34%
Total assets/Stockholders' equity (financial leverage)	3.07	2.99	2.92
Dividends per share	$0.225	$0.215	$0.214
Capital expenditures (CAPEX)	$3,163	$2,528	$1,918
CAPEX/Sales	7.93%	6.85%	5.69%

The sum of (3)–(10) yields total liabilities and equity. Total assets are, then, set equal to this amount and the resulting cash figure is computed as total assets less (1) and (2). At this point, cash will either be too high or too low. Long-term debt and common stock are then adjusted for issuances (repurchases) as appropriate to yield the desired level of cash and to maintain historical financial leverage. These adjustments indicate the degree of financing required to support the company's growth.

To begin, the projection of receivables, inventories, PP&E, accounts payable, and accrued expenses uses sales and cost of goods sold projections together with turnover rates for these accounts. For example, the receivables turnover rate based on current year's sales is:

$$\text{Accounts receivable turnover rate} = \frac{\text{Sales}}{\text{Accounts receivable balance}}$$

Next, the projected accounts receivables can be computed as:

$$\text{Projected accounts receivable} = \frac{\text{Projected sales}}{\text{Accounts receivable turnover rate}}$$

The accounts receivable turnover rate has declined from 19.55 in 1999 to 10.41 in 2001. This was the result of Target including $800 million of receivables that had previously been sold to a special purpose entity (SPE) and not recognized on the balance sheet. The inclusion of these receivables in the current period balance sheet was required under *SFAS 140* that was effective in 2001 (see Chapter 3). Our projection of accounts receivables assumes that Target will not be able to use SPEs to remove receivables from its balance sheet and we, therefore, use the most recent turnover rate of 10.41.

Inventory turnover rates have ranged from 5.95 to 6.12 over the past three years. Due to the stability of this ratio, and absent any information to indicate a change in turnover, we use the most recent rate of 6.12 together with cost of goods sold to project inventories. A more refined level of analysis might examine inventory turnover rates for seasoned versus new stores and the anticipated growth of new stores. Existing inventories might be projected to grow with the level of anticipated sales growth. Additional inventories required for new stores would be added to this amount.

Property, plant and equipment is estimated as the prior year's gross PP&E balance plus historical capital expenditures as a percentage of sales. Historical capital expenditures are obtained from the statement of cash flows. Over the past three years, capital expenditures as a percentage of sales have increased from 5.69% to 7.93%. We use 7.93% to estimate capital expenditures for 2002. Once the projection is complete, this percentage can be subsequently adjusted to examine the financial implications of higher (lower) levels of capital expenditures.

Accounts payable estimates are based on historical payable turns and cost of goods sold. We use the most recent turnover ratio of 6.55 to estimate 2002 payables. Similarly, accrued expenses as a percentage of sales are estimated with the most recent accrual turn of 25.47. Finally, taxes payable are estimated based on the historical relation of payables to tax expense and we use the most recent level of 50.24% to project 2002 taxes payable.

A schedule of current maturities of long-term debt is provided in the footnotes. We use the amount for 2002 referenced in the schedule. Long-term debt, then, is initially estimated as the previous balance of long-term debt less our estimate of its current maturities. This level of debt will be adjusted to achieve the desired balance of cash and financial leverage once the initial balance sheet is constructed. Likewise, common and treasury stock are assumed to be equal to the prior year's balances.

Given these assumptions, Target's projected balance sheet for 2002 is presented in Exhibit 10.4. The following are the steps in the projection of this statement:

1. Receivables: $4,141 = $43,115 (Sales)/10.41 (Receivable turnover).
2. Inventories: $4,809 = $29,450 (Cost of goods sold)/6.12 (Inventory turnover).
3. Other current assets: no change.
4. PP&E: $21,861 = $18,442 (Prior year's balance) + $3,419 (Capital expenditure estimate).
5. Accumulated depreciation: $6,172 = $4,909 (Prior balance) + $1,263 (Depreciation estimate).
6. Net PP&E: $21,861 − $6,172.
7. Other long-term assets: no change.

Target Corporation Projected Balance Sheet

Exhibit 10.4

	2001	Forecasting Step	Initial 2002 Estimate	Final 2002 Estimate
Cash	$ 499	16	$ (1,574)	$ 626
Receivables	3,831	1	4,141	4,141
Inventories	4,449	2	4,809	4,809
Other current assets	869	3	869	869
Total current assets	9,648		8,245	10,445
Property, plant and equipment	18,442	4	21,861	21,861
Accumulated depreciation	4,909	5	6,172	6,172
Net property, plant and equipment	13,533	6	15,689	15,689
Other noncurrent assets	973	7	973	973
Total assets	$24,154		$ 24,907	$27,107
Accounts payable	$ 4,160	8	$ 4,496	$ 4,496
Current portion of long-term debt	905	9	892	892
Accrued expenses	1,566	10	1,693	1,693
Income taxes payable	423	11	424	424
Total current liabilities	7,054		7,505	7,505
Deferred income taxes and other liabilities	1,152	12	1,152	1,152
Long-term debt	8,088	13	7,196	9,396
Total liabilities	16,294		15,853	18,053
Common stock	75	14	75	75
Capital surplus	1,098	15	1,118	1,118
Retained earnings	6,687	15	7,861	7,861
Shareholders' equity	7,860		9,054	9,054
Total liabilities and net worth	$24,154		$ 24,907	$27,107
Selected Ratios				
Accounts receivable turnover rate	10.41		10.41	
Inventory turnover rate	6.12		6.12	
Accounts payable turnover rate	6.55		6.55	
Accrued expenses turnover rate	25.47		25.47	
Taxes payable/Tax expense	50.24%		50.24%	
Total assets/Stockholders' equity	3.07		2.99	
Dividends per share	$0.225		$0.225	
Capital expenditures (CAPEX)	$3.163		$3,419	
CAPEX/Sales	7.93%		7.93%	

8. Accounts payable: $29,450 (Cost of goods sold)/6.55 (Payable turnover).
9. Current portion of long-term debt: amount reported in long-term debt footnote as the current maturity for 2002.
10. Accrued expenses: $43,115 (Sales)/25.47 (Accrued expense turnover).
11. Taxes payable: $844 (Tax expense) × 50.24% (Tax payable/Tax expense).
12. Deferred income taxes and other liabilities: no change.
13. Long-term debt: $8,088 (Prior year's long-term debt) − $892 (Scheduled current maturities from 9).
14. Common stock: no change.
15. Capital surplus: $1,118 = $1,098 + $20 (reflecting normal ESOP and stock option activity).
16. Retained earnings: $7,861 = $6,687 (Prior year's retained earnings) + $1,378 (Projected net income) − $204 (Estimated dividends of $0.225 per share).
17. Cash: amount needed to balance total liabilities and equity less (1)–(7).

The initial balance sheet estimate yields a cash balance of $(1,574) million. Long-term debt is, then, increased by $2,200 million to yield a final cash balance of $626 million. The final debt balance results in a financial leverage ratio (defined as Total assets/Total equity) of 2.99. This is in line with historical ratios of 2.92 to 3.07. Were this to be out of line, debt and equity could be adjusted to achieve the desired degree of financial leverage.

Projected Statement of Cash Flows

The projected statement of cash flows is computed from the projected income statement and projected balance sheet as discussed in Chapter 7. It is presented in Exhibit 10.5. The projected net cash flows from operations of $2,435 million partially finance

Exhibit 10.5 ***Target Corporation Projected Statement of Cash Flows***

	2002 Estimate
Net income	$1,378
Items to adjust income to cash flows:	
Depreciation	1,263
Accounts receivable	(310)
Inventories	(360)
Accounts payable	336
Accrued expenses	127
Income taxes	1
Net cash flow from operations	2,435
Capital expenditures	(3,419)
Net cash flow from investing activities	(3,419)
Long-term debt	1,295
Additional paid-in capital	20
Dividends	(204)
Net cash flow from financing activities	1,111
Net change in cash	127
Beginning cash	499
Ending cash	$ 626

the capital expenditures of $3,419 and dividends of $204 million. The deficit is made up with a $1,295 million net increase in long-term debt.

Sensitivity Analysis

The projected financial statements are primarily based on expected relations between income statement and balance sheet accounts. In this example, we used the most recent ratios as Target's operations are fairly stable and we are assuming no significant changes in operating strategy.

It is often useful, however, to vary these assumptions in order to analyze their impact on financing requirements, return on assets and equity, and so on. For example, Target's capital expenditures have been steadily increasing as a percentage of sales, from 5.69% three years ago to 7.93% in the previous year. If we assume a similar increase in 2002 to 9%, capital expenditures will rise to $3.88 billion, adding another $500 million of financing requirements. Similar increases would also result from a continued decrease in receivable or inventory turns. Analysts often prepare several projections to examine best (worst) case scenarios in addition to the most likely case. This sensitivity analysis highlights which assumptions have the greatest impact on financial results and, consequently, help to identify those areas requiring greater scrutiny.

Application of Prospective Analysis in the Residual Income Valuation Model

As we stated at the outset of this chapter, prospective analysis is central to security analysis. The residual income valuation model, for example, defines equity value at time t as the sum of current book value and the present value of all future expected residual income:

$$V_t = BV_t + \frac{E(RI_{t+1})}{(1+k)^1} + \frac{E(RI_{t+2})}{(1+k)^2} + \frac{E(RI_{t+3})}{(1+k)^3} + \cdots \frac{E(RI_{t+n})}{(1+k)^n} + \cdots$$

where BV_t is book value at the end of period t, RI_{t+n} is residual income in period $t+n$, and k is cost of capital (see Chapter 1). **Residual income** at time t is defined as comprehensive net income minus a charge on beginning book value, that is, $RI_t = NI_t - (k \times BV_{t-1})$.

The valuation process requires estimates of future net income and the book value of stockholder's equity. Exhibit 10.6 provides an example for the valuation of Syminex Corp. common stock as of 2000. In this relatively simple form, the valuation model requires estimates of six parameters:

- Sales growth.
- Net profit margin (Net income/Sales).
- Net working capital turnover (Sales/Net working capital).
- Fixed-asset turnover (Sales/Fixed assets).
- Financial leverage (Operating assets/Equity).
- Cost of equity capital.

Sales are expected to grow at 8.9% and 9.1% in 2001 and 2002, then trailing off with growth rates of 8%, 7%, and 6% for the next three years. This five-year period is the forecast horizon, the period of time about which we have the greatest confidence in our estimates. We assume that sales will continue to grow with the long-run rate of inflation, 3.5%, thereafter.

Net profit margins are expected to increase to 9.2% and 9.4% over the next two years and to level off at that percentage thereafter. Net working capital and fixed-asset

Exhibit 10.6 *Valuation of Syminex Common Stock*

	HISTORICAL FIGURES		FORECAST HORIZON					TERMINAL YEAR
	1999	2000	2001	2002	2003	2004	2005	2006
Sales growth	8.50%	8.70%	*8.90%*	*9.10%*	*8.00%*	*7.00%*	*6.00%*	*3.50%*
Net profit margin (Net income/Sales)	9.05%	9.16%	*9.20%*	*9.40%*	*9.40%*	*9.40%*	*9.40%*	*9.40%*
Net working capital turnover (Sales/Avg. NWC)	22.74	11.83	*11.83*	*11.83*	*11.83*	*11.83*	*11.83*	*11.83*
Fixed assets turnover (Sales/Avg. fixed assets)	1.83	1.99	*1.99*	*1.99*	*1.99*	*1.99*	*1.99*	*1.99*
Total operating assets/Total equity	2.34	2.52	*2.52*	*2.52*	*2.52*	*2.52*	*2.52*	*2.52*
Cost of equity			*12.5%*					
(in $ thousands)								
Sales	$81,324	$88,396	$96,263	$105,023	$113,425	$121,365	$128,647	$133,149
Net income ($ mil)	7,360	8,093	8,856	9,872	10,662	11,408	12,093	12,516
Net working capital	3,577	7,474	8,139	8,880	9,590	10,262	10,877	11,258
Fixed assets	44,340	44,469	48,427	52,834	57,060	61,054	64,718	66,983
Total operating assets	47,917	51,943	56,566	61,713	66,651	71,316	75,595	78,241
Long-term liabilities	27,406	31,319	34,106	37,210	40,187	43,000	45,580	47,175
Total stockholders' equity ($ mil)	20,511	20,624	22,460	24,503	26,464	28,316	30,015	31,066
Residual Income Computation								
Net income			$ 8,856	$ 9,872	$ 10,662	$ 11,408	$ 12,093	$ 12,516
Beginning equity			$20,624	$ 22,460	$ 24,503	$ 26,464	$ 28,316	$ 30,015
Required equity return			12.5%	12.5%	12.5%	12.5%	12.5%	12.5%
Expected income			$ 2,578	$ 2,807	$ 3,063	$ 3,308	$ 3,540	$ 3,752
Residual income			$ 6,278	$ 7,065	$ 7,599	$ 8,100	$ 8,553	$ 8,764
Discount factor			0.89	0.79	0.70	0.62	0.55	
Present value of residual income			$ 5,581	$ 5,582	$ 5,337	$ 5,057	$ 4,746	
Cumulative present value of residual income			$ 5,581	$ 11,163	$ 16,500	$ 21,557	$ 26,303	
Terminal value of residual income							$ 54,039	
Beginning book value of equity							$ 20,624	
Value of equity							$100,966	
Common shares outstanding (thousands)							1,737	
Value of equity per share							$ 58.13	

turnover rates are expected to remain at present levels of 11.83 and 1.99 times, respectively. Financial leverage is also expected to remain constant at the current level of 2.52. And finally, the cost of equity capital is estimated at 12.5%. (The cost of equity capital is given by the capital asset pricing model discussed in Appendix 1A to Chapter 1.)

Net income is estimated using projected sales and projected net profit margin (Sales × Net profit margin). Net working capital and fixed assets are estimated using projected sales and the estimated turnover rates for net working capital and fixed assets, respectively (Sales/Turnover rate). Finally, equity is projected using the operating assets to equity ratio (Operating assets = Net working capital + Fixed assets).

Given these estimates, residual income for 2001 is estimated as projected net income less beginning of the year equity × the cost of equity capital of 12.5%,

$$\$6,278 = \$8,856 - (\$20,624 \times .125)$$

Reversion of ROE for Quintiles of Firms in the Compustat Database (1982–2000)

Exhibit 10.7

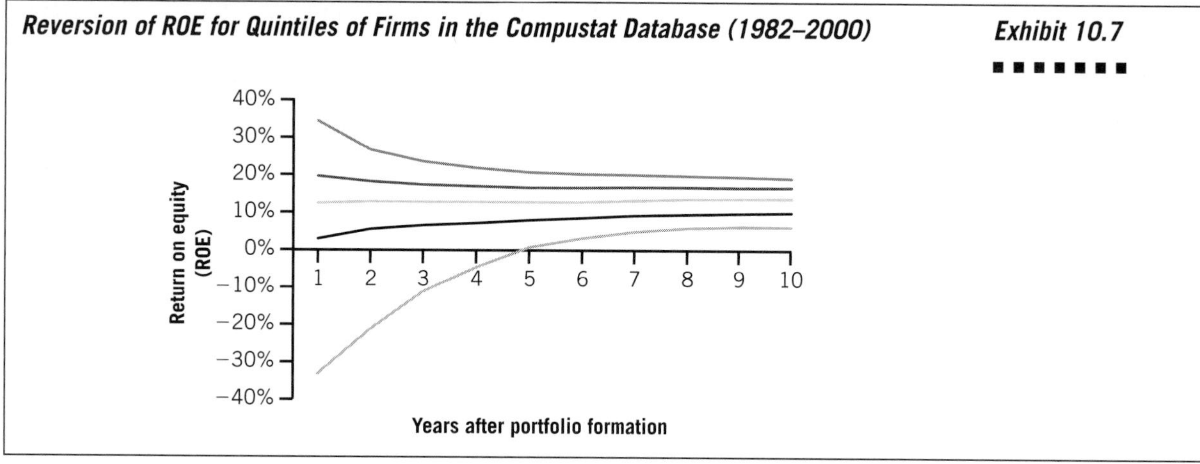

Subsequent years during the forecast horizon are computed similarly. Each year during the forecast horizon is, then, discounted at the cost of equity capital (12.5%). For example, the discount factor for the second year is computed as:

$$0.79 = \frac{1}{1.125^2}$$

Present values for each year in the forecast horizon are summed to yield a cumulative present value through 2005 of $26,303.

The residual income projected in 2006 is assumed to grow at the rate of inflation (3.5%). The present value of this annuity, discounted to 2000 is:[1]

$$54{,}039 = \frac{8{,}764}{(.125 - .035)(1.125)^5}$$

The estimated value of Syminex Corp. common stock as of 2000 is equal to the book value of its stockholder's equity ($20,624) plus the present value of its residual income ($26,303 + $54,039) for a total of $100,966. Given outstanding shares of 1,737, per share value of Syminex Corp. common stock is $58.13.

Valuation of equity shares is critically dependent on the projection process. As discussed above, our valuation should closely examine the sensitivity of share price estimates to underlying assumptions in the projections.

Trends in Value Drivers

The residual income model defines stock price as the book value of stockholders' equity plus the present value of expected residual income (RI), where $RI_t = NI_t - (k \times BV_{t-1})$. Residual income can also be expressed in ratio form as,

$$RI = (ROE_t - k) \times BV_{t-1}$$

where $ROE = NI_t/BV_{t-1}$. This form highlights the fact that stock price is only impacted so long as $ROE \neq k$. In equilibrium, competitive forces will tend to drive rates of return (ROE) to cost (k) so that abnormal profits are competed away. The estimation of stock price, then, amounts to the projection of the reversion of ROE to its long-run value for a particular company and industry.

Exhibit 10.7 presents ROE performance for quintiles of all firms in the Compustat data base. For each year, portfolios of firms in each ROE quintile are formed and the

[1]The present value (PV) of annuity (A) expected to grow at g% per year and discounted at k% is given by $PV = \frac{A}{k-g}$. The remaining term in the denominator (1.125^5) discounts this PV, which occurs in Year 5, back to the present at the 12.5% cost of capital.

ROEs for each firm in the portfolio are tracked for the subsequent 10 years. The graph presents the median value for each portfolio. Two observations are evident:

1. ROEs tend to revert to a long-run equilibrium. This reflects the forces of competition. Furthermore, the reversion rate for the least profitable firms is greater than that for the most profitable firms. And finally, reversion rates for the most extreme levels of ROE are greater than those for firms at more moderate levels of ROE.
2. The reversion is incomplete. That is, there remains a difference of about 12% between the highest and lowest ROE firms even after 10 years. This may be the result of two factors: differences in risk that are reflected in differences in their costs of capital (k); or, greater (lesser) degrees of conservatism in accounting policies.

Exhibit 10.7 reveals that most of the reversion is complete after about 5 years. This lends support to our use of a 5-year forecast horizon for Syminex Corp. as there is little impact on share price after the point at which ROE $= k$ regardless of the growth rate assumption for sales.

ROE is considered a *value driver* since it is the variable that directly affects stock price. ROA is further disaggregated into profit margin and turnover (see Chapter 8). These components are also value drivers and are two of the input items we project in our valuation of Syminex Corp. It is useful, therefore, to understand the reversion rates for these components as well.

Exhibit 10.8 presents a graph highlighting the reversion of net profit margins (NPM) for quintiles of firms in the Compustat database. It has been constructed similarly to the ROE graph in Exhibit 10.7. The significant reversion rates for the highest and lowest NPM firms are evident. In addition, the reversion rate for the lowest profit firms is greater than that for the most profitable firms and the reversion rates for both extreme groups are greater than those for less extreme profit firms. And finally, there remains a difference between the highest and lowest NPM portfolios at the end of 10 years of approximately the same spread as that for ROE. Much of the reversion in ROE, then, appears to be driven by reversion in NPM.

Exhibit 10.8 **Reversion of Net Profit Margin for Quintiles of Firms in the Compustat Database (1982–2000)**

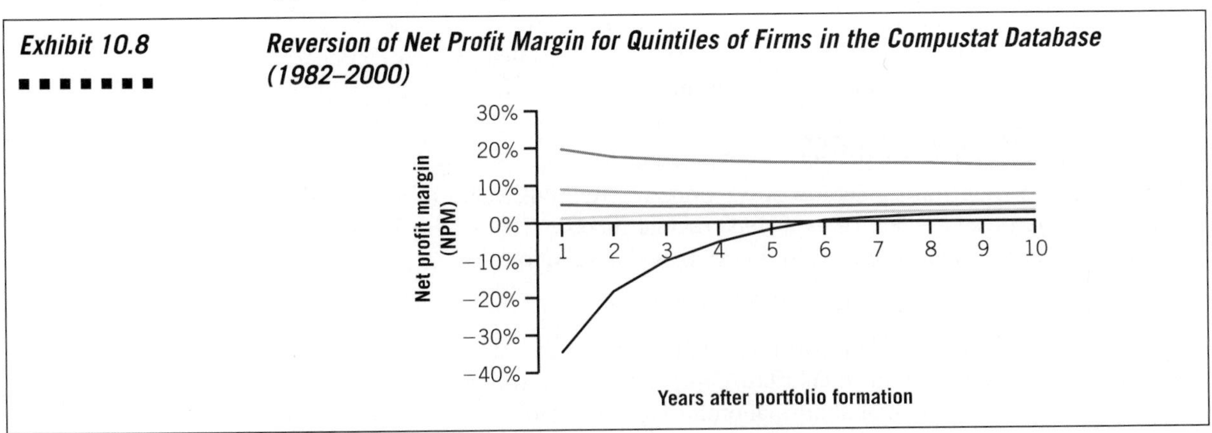

Total asset turnover (TAT) is the second component of ROA. In Exhibit 10.9 we present reversion rates for TAT that are constructed on the same basis as the previous graphs. Although some reversion is evident, it is much less than that of the profitability measures. In addition, there is a wide range of asset turnover rates between the highest and lowest turnover firms. This reflects varying degrees of capital intensity.

Our projection of profit margins and turnover rates needs to consider typical reversion patterns and the level of the drivers from their long-run average at the point when

Reversion of Total Asset Turnover for Quintiles of Firms in the Compustat Database (1982–2000) — Exhibit 10.9

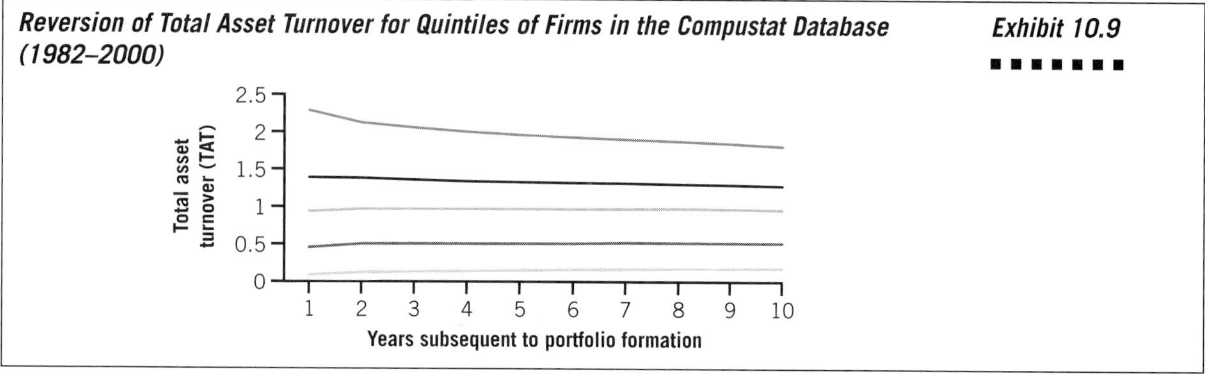

the estimation is made. Furthermore, we need to be mindful of industry characteristics as these exhibit marked differences along the net profit margin–total asset turnover dimension as discussed in Chapter 8. And finally, our projection horizon need not be excessively long as we lose confidence in our estimates and ROE tends to revert to close to the cost of capital over a relatively short period of time.

ANALYSIS VIEWPOINT ... **YOU ARE THE STOCKBROKER**

You are analyzing the long-term cash forecasts of Boston Biotech, Inc., that are reported along with a scheduled initial public offering (IPO) of its common stock for next month. You notice Boston Biotech's forecasts of net cash flows are zero or negative for the next five years. During this same time period, Boston Biotech is forecasting net income at more than 10% of equity. Your co-workers at the securities firm question the reliability of these forecasts. Can you identify potential explanations for the disparity between the five-year forecasts of cash flows and income?

Answer–p. 502

APPENDIX 10A SHORT-TERM FORECASTING

For analysis of short-term liquidity, one of the most useful tools is **short-term cash forecasting.** Short-term cash forecasting is of interest to internal users like managers and auditors in evaluating a company's current and future operating activities. It is also of interest to external users like short-term creditors who need to assess a company's ability to repay short-term loans. Our analysis stresses short-term cash forecasting when a company's ability to meet current obligations is in doubt. The accuracy of cash flow forecasting is inversely related to the *forecast horizon*–the longer the forecast period, the less reliable the forecasts. This is due to the number and complexity of factors influencing cash inflows and outflows that cannot be reliably estimated in the long term. Even in the case of short-term cash forecasting, the information required is substantial. Since cash flow forecasting often depends on publicly available information, our objective is "reasonably accurate" forecasts. By studying and preparing cash flow forecasts, our analysis should achieve greater insights into a company's cash flow patterns.

CASH FLOW PATTERNS

It is important for us to review the nature of cash flow patterns before examining models for cash flow analysis and projection. Cash and cash equivalents (hereafter simply *cash*) are the most liquid of assets. Nearly all management decisions to invest in assets or pay expenses require the immediate or eventual use of cash. This results in management's focus on cash rather than on other concepts of liquid funds. Some users (like creditors) sometimes consider assets like receivables and inventories part of liquid assets given their near-term conversion into cash.

Holding cash provides little or no return and, in times of rising prices, cash (like all monetary assets) is exposed to purchasing power loss. Nevertheless, holding cash represents the least exposure to risk. Management is responsible for the decisions to invest cash in assets or to immediately pay costs. These *cash conversions* increase risk because the ultimate recovery of cash from these activities is less than certain. Risks associated with these cash conversions are of various types and degrees. For instance, risk in converting cash into temporary investments is less than the risk in committing cash to long-term payout assets like plant and equipment. Investing cash in assets or costs aimed at developing and marketing new products often carries more serious cash-recovery risks. Both short-term liquidity and long-term solvency depend on the recovery and realizability of cash outlays.

Cash inflows and outflows are interrelated. A failure of any aspect of the company's business activities to successfully carry out its assigned task affects the entire cash flow system. A lapse in sales affects the conversion of finished goods into receivables and cash, leading to a decline in cash availability. A company's inability to replace this cash from sources like equity, loans, or accounts payable can impede production activities and produce losses in future sales. Conversely, restricting expenditures on items like advertising and marketing can slow the conversion of finished goods into receivables and cash. Long-term restrictions in either cash outflows or inflows can lead to company insolvency.

Our analysis must recognize the interrelations between cash flows, accruals, and profits. Sales is the driving source of operating flows. When finished goods representing the accumulation of many costs and expenses are sold, the company's profit margin produces an inflow of liquid funds through receivables and cash. The higher the profit margin, the greater the growth of liquid funds. Profits often primarily derive from the difference between sales and cost of sales (gross profit) and have enormous consequences to cash flows. Many costs, like those flowing from utilization of plant and equipment or deferred charges, do not require cash outlays. Similarly, items like long-term installment sales of land create noncurrent receivables limiting the relevance of accruals for cash flows. Our analysis must appropriately use these measures in assessing cash flow patterns.

Cash flows are limited in an important respect. As cash flows into a company, management has certain discretion in its disbursement. This discretion depends on commitments to outlays like dividends, inventory accumulation, capital expenditures, or debt repayment. Cash flows also depend on management's ability to draw on sources like equity and debt. With noncommitted cash inflows, referred to as free cash flows, management has considerable discretion in their use. It is this noncommitted cash component that is of special interest and importance for our analysis.

IMPORTANCE OF FORECASTING SALES

The reliability of our cash forecast depends on the *quality of the sales forecast.* With few exceptions, such as funds from financing or funds used in investing activities, most cash flows relate to and depend on sales. Our forecasting of sales includes an analysis of:

- Directions and trends in sales.
- Market share.
- Industry and economic conditions.

- Productive and financial capacity.
- Competitive factors.

These components are typically assessed along product lines potentially affected by forces peculiar to their markets. Later examples illustrate the importance of sales forecasts.

ANALYSIS VIEWPOINT ***. . . YOU ARE THE LOAN OFFICER***

As a recently hired loan officer at Intercontinental Bank you are processing a loan application for a new customer, DEC Manufacturing. In their application materials, DEC submits short-term sales forecasts for the next three periods of $1.1, $1.25, and $1.45 million, respectively. You notice the most recent two periods' sales are $0.8 and $0.65 million, and you ask DEC management for an explanation. DEC's response is twofold: (1) recent sales are misleading due to a work stoppage and an unusual period of abnormally high raw material costs due to bankruptcy of a major supplier; and (2) variations in consumer demand have caused recent industry volatility. Do you use their forecasts in your loan analysis?

Answer–p. 503

CASH FLOW FORECASTING WITH PRO FORMA ANALYSIS

The reasonableness and feasibility of short-term cash forecasts are usefully checked by means of **pro forma financial statements.** We accomplish this by using assumptions underlying cash forecasts to construct a pro forma income statement for the forecast period and a pro forma balance sheet for the end of the forecast period. Financial ratios and other relations are derived from these pro forma financial statements and checked for feasibility against historical relations. These comparisons must recognize adjustments for factors expected to affect them during the cash forecast period.

We illustrate cash flow forecasting using financial data from IT Technologies, Inc. IT Technologies recently introduced a new electronic processor that has enjoyed excellent market acceptance. IT's management estimates sales ($ thousands) for the next six months ending June 30, Year 1, as: $100, $125, $150, $175, $200, and $250 (see the bar graph). The current cash balance at January 1, Year 1, is $15,000. In light of the predicted increase in sales, IT's treasurer hopes to maintain *minimum* monthly cash balances of $20,000 for January; $25,000 for February; $27,000 for March; and $30,000 for April, May, and June. The treasurer foresees a need for additional funds to finance sales expansion. The treasurer expects that new equipment valued at $20,000 will be purchased in February by giving a note payable to the seller. The note will be repaid, beginning in February, at the rate of $1,000 per month. The new equipment is not planned to be operational until August of Year 1.

IT's Forecasted Sales ($ thousands)

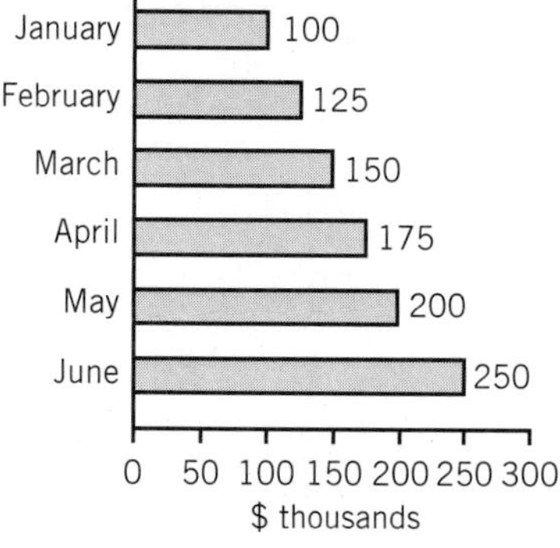

The treasurer plans several further steps to fund these financing requirements. First, she obtains a financing commitment from an insurance company to acquire $110,000 of IT's long-term bonds (less $2,500 issue costs). These bond sales are planned for April ($50,000) and May ($60,000). She plans to sell real estate for additional financing, including $8,000 in May and $50,000 in June, and will sell equipment (originally costing $25,000 with a book value of zero) for $25,000 in June. The treasurer approaches IT's banker for approval of short-term financing to cover additional funding needs. The bank's loan officer requires the treasurer to prepare a *cash forecast* for the six months ending June 30, Year 1, along with *pro forma financial statements* for that period, to process her request. The loan officer also requests that IT Technologies specify its uses of cash and its sources of funds for loan repayment. The treasurer recognizes the importance of a cash forecast and proceeds to compile data necessary to comply with the loan officer's request.

As one of her first steps, the treasurer estimates the pattern of receivables collections. Prior experience suggests the following collection pattern:

Collections	Percent of Total Receivables
In month of sale	40%
In second month	30
In third month	20
In fourth month	5
Written off as bad debts	5
	100%

This collection pattern along with expected product sales allows the treasurer to construct estimates of cash collections shown in Exhibit 10A.1.

Exhibit 10A.1

Estimates of Cash Collections
For Months January–June, Year 1

	January	February	March	April	May	June
Sales	$100,000	$125,000	$150,000	$175,000	$200,000	$250,000
Collections of sales:*						
1st month—40%	$ 40,000	$ 50,000	$ 60,000	$ 70,000	$ 80,000	$100,000
2nd month—30%		30,000	37,500	45,000	52,500	60,000
3rd month—20%			20,000	25,000	30,000	35,000
4th month—5%				5,000	6,250	7,500
Total cash collections	$ 40,000	$ 80,000	$117,500	$145,000	$168,750	$202,500
Write-offs—5%				5,000	6,250	7,500

* *For simplicity, cash collections from sales prior to January are ignored.*

IT's Forecasted Cash ($ thousands) (from Exhibit 10A.4)

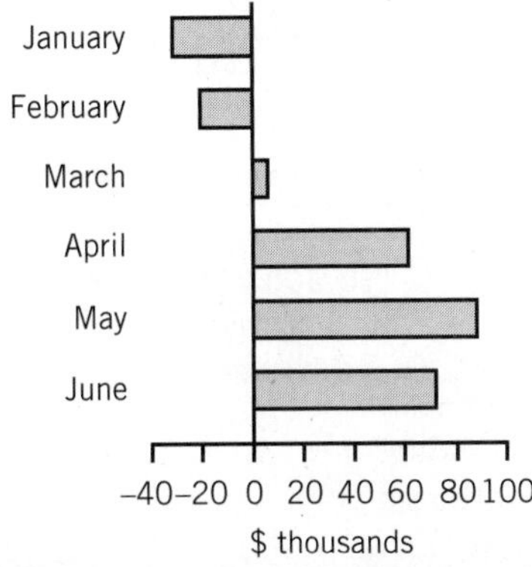

Analyzing expense patterns in prior periods' financial statements yields expense estimates based on either sales or time. Exhibit 10A.2 shows these expense estimates. IT Technologies pays off these expenses (excluding the $1,000 monthly depreciation) when incurred. The only exception is for purchases of materials, where 50% is paid in the month of purchase and 50% in the following month. Materials inventory on January 1, Year 1, is $57,000. The treasurer estimates materials inventory for the end of each month from January to June of Year 1 as: $67,000, $67,500, $65,500, $69,000, $67,000, and $71,000, respectively. She also estimates the pattern of payments on accounts payable for these materials. Exhibit 10A.3 shows these expected payments. Since the electronic processor is manufactured to specific order, no finished goods inventories are expected to accumulate.

The treasurer's resulting cash forecast for each of the six months ending June 30, Year 1, is shown in Exhibit 10A.4. Using these forecasts, Exhibit 10A.5 shows IT Technologies' pro forma income statement for the six months ending June 30, Year 1. Also, both actual and pro forma balance

Exhibit 10A.2

Expense Estimates
For Months January–June, Year 1

Materials	30% of sales
Labor	25% of sales
Manufacturing overhead:	
Variable	10% of sales
Fixed	$8,000 per month (includes $1,000 depreciation per month)
Selling expenses	10% of sales
General and administrative expenses:	
Variable	8% of sales
Fixed	$7,000 per month

Exhibit 10A.3

Estimates of Cash Payments for Materials
For Months January–June, Year 1

	January	February	March	April	May	June
Materials purchases*	$40,000	$38,000	$43,000	$56,000	$58,000	$79,000
Payments:						
1st month—50%	$20,000	$19,000	$21,500	$28,000	$29,000	$39,500
2nd month—50%		20,000	19,000	21,500	28,000	29,000
Total payments	$20,000	$39,000	$40,500	$49,500	$57,000	$68,500

* *Material purchases reconcile with material costs and changes in inventories.*

sheets of IT Technologies as of January 1 and June 30, respectively, of Year 1 are shown in Exhibit 10A.6.

Our prospective analysis should critically examine the pro forma statements and submit them to *feasibility tests* on both their forecasts and their assumptions. We should evaluate both ratios and relations revealed in pro forma financial statements and compare them to historical ratios to determine their reasonableness and feasibility. As an example, IT Technologies' current ratio increases from 2.6 on January 1, Year 1, to 3.5 in the pro forma balance sheet of June 30, Year 1. In addition, for the six months ended June 30, Year 1, the projected return on average equity exceeds 8%. These and other measures such as turnover, trends, and common-size comparisons should be evaluated. Unexpected variations in important relations should be either explained or adjustments made to assumptions and expectations if errors are identified. These steps increase the reliability of pro forma statements for our analysis.

We should recognize that electronic spreadsheet programs are available to assist us in pro forma analysis. The ease of changing variables for sensitivity tests improves the usefulness of pro forma statements. Nevertheless, we should not confuse the ease and flexibility of these programs with the crucial need to develop and verify estimates and

Exhibit 10A.4

IT TECHNOLOGIES, INC.
Cash Forecast
For Months January–June, Year 1

	January	February	March	April	May	June	Six-Month Totals
Cash balance—beginning	$15,000	$ 20,000	$ 25,750	$ 27,250	$ 30,580	$ 30,895	$ 15,000
Add cash receipts for:							
Cash collections (Exh. 10A.1)	40,000	80,000	117,500	145,000	168,750	202,500	753,750
Sale of real estate*	—	—	—	—	8,000	50,000	58,000
Sale of bonds*	—	—	—	47,500	60,000	—	107,500
Sale of equipment*	—	—	—	—	—	25,000	25,000
Total cash available	55,000	100,000	143,250	219,750	267,330	308,395	959,250
Less cash disbursements for:							
Materials (Exh. 10A.3)	20,000	39,000	40,500	49,500	57,000	68,500	274,500
Labor†	25,000	31,250	37,500	43,750	50,000	62,500	250,000
Fixed overhead†	7,000	7,000	7,000	7,000	7,000	7,000	42,000
Variable overhead†	10,000	12,500	15,000	17,500	20,000	25,000	100,000
Selling expenses†	10,000	12,500	15,000	17,500	20,000	25,000	100,000
General and administrative†	15,000	17,000	19,000	21,000	23,000	27,000	122,000
Taxes‡	—	—	—	—	—	19,000	19,000
Purchase of fixed assets*	—	1,000	1,000	1,000	1,000	1,000	5,000
Total cash disbursements	87,000	120,250	135,000	157,250	178,000	235,000	912,500
Tentative cash balance (deficit)	(32,000)	(20,250)	8,250	62,500	89,330	73,395	46,750
Minimum cash required*	20,000	25,000	27,000	30,000	30,000	30,000	—
Borrowing required	52,000	46,000	19,000	—	—	—	117,000
Repayment of loan	—	—	—	30,000	58,000	29,000	(117,000)
Interest paid on balance§	—	—	—	1,920	435	145	2,500
Ending cash balance	$20,000	$ 25,750	$ 27,250	$ 30,580	$ 30,895	$ 44,250	$ 44,250
Loan balance	$52,000	$ 98,000	$117,000	$ 87,000	$ 29,000	—	—

* *Treasurer's expectations taken from information on prior pages.*
† *Estimates computed using information from Exhibit 10A.2.*
‡ *Taxes total a 40% combined state and federal rate. Taxes of $19,000 are paid in June, with the balance accrued.*
§ *Interest is computed at the rate of ½% per month and paid at month-end. Any loan is taken out at the beginning of a month.*

assumptions underlying their output. The reasonableness of important estimates and assumptions, and the usefulness of this analysis, depend on our critical evaluation and judgment and *not* on our technology.

GUIDANCE ANSWERS TO ANALYSIS VIEWPOINTS

Stockbroker
The disparity in Boston Biotech's forecasts of cash flows and income is not necessarily of concern. Many growing companies experience little to no positive cash flows in the near term. Of course, these low near-term cash flows are expected to yield above-average cash flows in the future. Boston Biotech could potentially be recording substantial operating cash flows that are offset by large cash outflows in new investments, debt retirements, or dividends. Our analysis must look to the components of both cash flows and income to address our potential interest in Boston Biotech's IPO of common stock. Instead of spurning the stock of Boston Biotech,

Exhibit 10A.5

IT TECHNOLOGIES, INC.
Pro Forma Income Statement
For Six Months Ended June 30, Year 1

		Source of Estimate
Sales	$1,000,000	Forecasted sales
Cost of sales:		
Materials	300,000	Exhibit 10A.2
Labor	250,000	Exhibit 10A.2
Overhead	148,000	Exhibit 10A.2
Total cost of sales	698,000	
Gross profit	302,000	
Selling expense	100,000	Exhibit 10A.2
Bad debts expense	18,750	Exhibit 10A.1
General and administrative expense	122,000	Exhibit 10A.2
Operating expenses	240,750	
Operating income	61,250	
Gain on sale of equipment	25,000	Treasurer
Interest expense	(2,500)	Exhibit 10A.4 note
Income before taxes	83,750	
Income taxes (40% rate)	33,500	Exhibit 10A.4 note
Net income	$ 50,250	

we might find it a lucrative and underpriced security due to our superior knowledge of accounting in financial statements.

Loan Officer
Your first step is to corroborate or refute management's explanation for decreased sales in recent years. If their explanations are *not* validated with objective evidence, then you should reject DEC's application–hint of unscrupulous behavior is reason enough for immediate nonapproval. If you are able to verify management's explanations, your next step is to assess the *level and uncertainty* of DEC's sales forecasts. Your analysis of sales forecasts should consider important economic factors, including consumer demand, industry competition, supplier costs, and DEC's productive capacity/quality. Perhaps more important given DEC's circumstances is your assessment of uncertainty with sales. For example, sales might be objectively forecasted at $1 million, but the range of likely sales might extend anywhere from $0.5 to $1.5 million. Recent volatility in consumer demand, material costs, and supplier relations suggests substantially greater risk than normal. Your assessment of increased risk can yield a response extending from a slight increase in interest rates or increased collateral demands to ultimate loan rejection. Consequently, while DEC's sales forecasts might be unbiased, we must recognize differences in uncertainty associated with sales forecasts in practice.

[Superscript A denotes assignments based on Appendix 10A.]

QUESTIONS

10–1 What are some of the uses for prospective analysis?

10–2 What steps must usually take place before the forecasting process can begin?

Exhibit 10A.6

IT TECHNOLOGIES, INC.
Balance Sheets

	ACTUAL JANUARY 1, YEAR 1		PRO FORMA JUNE 30, YEAR 1	
Assets				
Current assets:				
Cash	$ 15,000		$ 44,250	
Accounts receivable (net)	6,500		234,000	
Inventories—materials	57,000		71,000	
Total current assets		$ 78,500		$349,250
Real estate	58,000		—	
Fixed assets	206,400		201,400	
Accumulated depreciation	(36,400)		(17,400)	
Net fixed assets		228,000		184,000
Other assets		3,000		3,000
Deferred bond issue costs		—		2,500
Total assets		$309,500		$538,750
Liabilities and Equity				
Current liabilities:				
Accounts payable	$ 2,000		$ 41,500	
Notes payable	28,500		43,500	
Accrued taxes	—		14,500	
Total current liabilities		$ 30,500		$ 99,500
Long-term debt	15,000		125,000	
Common stock	168,000		168,000	
Retained earnings	96,000		146,250	
		279,000		439,250
Total liabilities and equity		$309,500		$538,750

10–3 In addition to recent trends, what other items of information might be brought to bear in the projection of sales?

10–4 What is the forecast horizon?

10–5 What assumption is usually made about sales growth at the end of the forecast horizon?

10–6 Describe the steps in forecasting the income statement.

10–7 Describe the two-step process of forecasting the balance sheet.

10–8 What are value drivers?

10–9 Describe the typical trend of value drivers over time.

10–10[A] Why are short-term cash forecasts important for the analysis of financial statements?

10–11[A] What limitations are associated with short-term cash forecasting?

10–12[A] Describe the relation between inflows of cash and outflows of cash.

10–13[A] It is often asserted: *From an operational point of view, management focuses on cash rather than working capital.* Do you agree with this statement? Why or why not?

10–14[A] Describe the primary difference between "funds flow" analysis and ratio analysis. Which analysis technique is preferred and why?

10–15[A] What is the usual first step in preparing cash forecasts, and what considerations are required in this step?

EXERCISES

EXERCISE 10–1
Forecasting Income and Income Components

Quaker Oats Company

Refer to the financial statements of **Quaker Oats Company** in Appendix A. Prepare a forecasted income statement for Year 12 using the following assumptions ($ millions):

1. Revenues are forecast to equal $6,000.
2. Cost of sales forecast uses the average percent relation between cost of sales and sales for the four-year period ending June 30, Year 11.
3. Selling, general, and administrative expenses are expected to increase by the same percent increase occurring from Year 10 to Year 11.
4. Other expenses are predicted to be 8% higher than in Year 11.
5. A $2 million loss (net of taxes) is expected from disposal of net assets from discontinued operations.
6. Interest expense, net of interest capitalized and interest income, is expected to increase by 6% due to increased financial needs.
7. The effective tax rate is equal to that of Year 11.

CHECK
Forecast NI, $140.1 mil.

EXERCISE 10–2
Forecasting Sales and Net Income

General Electric

Quarterly sales and net income data for **General Electric** for 1991–1999 are shown below (in $ millions).

	Sales	Net Income		Sales	Net Income		Sales	Net Income
Dec. 91	$17,349	$1,263	Sep. 94	$14,442	$1,457	Jun. 97	$21,860	$2,162
Mar. 92	12,278	964	Dec. 94	17,528	1,685	Sep. 97	21,806	2,014
Jun. 92	13,984	1,130	Mar. 95	14,948	1,372	Dec. 97	24,876	2,350
Sep. 92	13,972	996	Jun. 95	17,630	1,726	Mar. 98	22,459	1,891
Dec. 92	16,040	1,215	Sep. 95	17,151	1,610	Jun. 98	24,928	2,450
Mar. 93	12,700	1,085	Dec. 95	19,547	1,865	Sep. 98	23,978	2,284
Jun. 93	14,566	656	Mar. 96	16,931	1,517	Dec. 98	28,455	2,671
Sep. 93	14,669	1,206	Jun. 96	18,901	1,908	Mar. 99	24,062	2,155
Dec. 93	17,892	1,477	Sep. 96	19,861	1,788	Jun 99	27,410	2,820
Mar. 94	12,621	1,219	Dec. 96	22,848	2,067			
Jun. 94	14,725	1,554	Mar. 97	19,998	1,677			

Required:
Use these data and any other historical information available to forecast sales and net income for each of the quarters ending September 1999, December 1999, March 2000, and June 2000. Explain the basis of your forecasts.

EXERCISE 10–3
Forecasting Sales and Net Income

In Year 2000, Cough.com is in its second year of operations. Cough.com produces children's cough medicine. Industry sales of children's cough medicine for 1999 totaled $3 billion. For 1999, Cough.com had sales totaling $2.4 million (.08% market share).

Required:

a. Explain how predictions of the total market and market share can be used in the forecasting process.
b. What data might you seek to enhance your sales forecast and how might such data be gathered?
c. Illustrate what-if scenarios in which market share gained by Cough.com is (1) 5% greater than and (2) 5% worse than the predicted .08% of the Year 2000 expected industry sales of $3.2 billion.
d. For *each* of these two separate scenarios, illustrate what-if analysis when total expected industry sales of $3.2 billion are (1) 10% greater than and (2) 10% worse than expected.

CHECK
(c) 1. $2.688 mil.

EXERCISE 10–4[A]
Preparing a Short-Term Cash Forecast

The Lyon Corporation is a merchandising company. Prepare a short-term cash forecast for July of Year 6 following the format of Exhibit 10A.4. Selected financial data from Lyon Corporation as of July 1 of Year 6 are reproduced below ($ thousands):

Cash on hand, July 1, Year 6	$ 20
Accounts receivable, July 1, Year 6	20
Forecasted sales for July	150
Forecasted accounts receivable, July 31, Year 6	21
Inventory, July 1, Year 6	25
Desired inventory, July 31, Year 6	15
Depreciation expense for July	4
Miscellaneous outlays for July	11
Minimum cash balance desired	30
Accounts payable, July 1, Year 6	18

Additional Information:

1. Gross profit equals 20% of cost of goods sold.
2. Lyon purchases all inventory on the second day of the month and receives it the following week.
3. Lyon pays 75% of payables within the month of purchase and the balance in the following month.
4. Lyons pays all remaining expenses in cash.

CHECK
Cash bal., $54

PROBLEMS

PROBLEM 10–1
Preparing Pro Forma Financial Statements

Comparative income statements and balance sheets for **Coca-Cola** are shown below (in $ millions):

Coca-Cola

	Year 2	Year 1
Income Statement		
Net sales	$20,092	$19,889
Cost of goods	6,044	6,204
Gross profit	14,048	13,685
Selling, general and administrative expense	7,893	9,221
Depreciation and amortization expense	803	773
Interest expense (revenue)	(308)	292
Income before tax	5,660	3,399
Income tax expense	1,691	1,222
Net income	3,969	2,177
Outstanding shares	3,491	3,481
Balance Sheet		
Cash	1,934	1,892
Receivables	1,882	1,757
Inventories	1,055	1,066
Other current assets	2,300	1,905
Total current assets	7,171	6,620
Property, plant and equipment	7,105	6,614
Accumulated depreciation	2,652	2,446
Net property, plant and equipment	4,453	4,168
Other noncurrent assets	10,793	10,046
Total assets	$22,417	$20,834

Balance Sheet—*continued.*	Year 2	Year 1
Accounts payable and Accrued liabilities	$ 3,679	$ 3,905
Short-term debt and current maturities of long-term debt	3,899	4,816
Income tax liabilities	851	600
Total current liabilities	8,429	9,321
Deferred income taxes and other liabilities	1,403	1,362
Long-term debt	1,219	835
Total noncurrent liabilities	2,622	2,197
Common stock	873	870
Capital surplus	3,520	3,196
Retained earnings	20,655	18,543
Treasury stock	13,682	13,293
Shareholders' equity	11,366	9,316
Total liabilities and net worth	$22,417	$20,834

Required:

a. Use the following ratios to prepare a projected income statement, balance sheet, and statement of cash flows for Year 3.

Sales growth	1.02%
Gross profit margin	69.92%
Selling, general and administrative expense/Sales	39.28%
Depreciation expense/Prior-year PPE gross	12.14%
Interest expense/Prior-year long-term debt	5.45%
Income tax expense/Pretax income	29.88%
Accounts receivable turnover	10.68
Inventory turnover	5.73
Accounts payable turnover	1.64
Taxes payable/Tax expense	50.33%
Total assets/Stockholders' equity (financial leverage)	2.06
Dividends per share	$1.37
Capital expenditures/Sales	5.91%

b. Based on your initial projections, how much external financing (long-term debt and/or stockholders' equity will Coca-Cola need to fund its growth at projected increases in sales?

PROBLEM 10–2

Preparing Pro Forma Financial Statements

Best Buy

Comparative income statements and balance sheets for **Best Buy** are shown below (in $ millions):

	Year 2	Year 1
Income Statement		
Net sales	$15,326	$12,494
Cost of goods	12,267	10,101
Gross profit	3,059	2,393
Selling, general and administrative expense	2,251	1,728
Depreciation and amortization expense	167	103
Income before tax	641	562
Income tax expense	245	215
Net income	$ 396	$ 347
Outstanding shares	208	200

Balance Sheet	**Year 2**	**Year 1**
Cash	$ 746	$ 751
Receivables	313	262
Inventories	1,767	1,184
Other current assets	102	41
Total current assets	2,928	2,238
Property, plant and equipment	1,987	1,093
Accumulated depreciation	543	395
Net property, plant and equipment	1,444	698
Other noncurrent assets	466	59
Total assets	$4,838	$2,995
Accounts payable and accrued liabilities	$2,473	$1,704
Short-term debt and current maturities of long-term debt	114	16
Income tax liabilities	127	65
Total current liabilities	2,714	1,785
Long-term liabilities	122	100
Long-term debt	181	15
Total long-term liabilities	303	115
Common stock	20	20
Capital surplus	576	247
Retained earnings	1,225	828
Shareholders' equity	1,821	1,095
Total liabilities and net worth	$4,838	$2,995

Required:

a. Use the following ratios to prepare a projected income statement, balance sheet, and statement of cash flows for Year 3.

Sales growth	22.67%
Gross profit margin	19.96%
Selling, general and administrative expense/Sales	14.69%
Depreciation expense/Prior-year PPE gross	15.28%
Income tax expense/Pretax income	38.22%
Accounts receivable turnover (Sales/Accounts receivable)	48.96
Inventory turnover (Cost of goods sold/Inventory)	6.94
Accounts payable turnover (Cost of goods sold/Accounts payable)	4.96
Taxes payable/Tax expense	51.84%
Total assets/Stockholders' equity (financial leverage)	2.55
Dividends per share	$0.00
Capital expenditures/Sales	6.71%

b. Based on your initial projections, how much external financing (long-term debt and/or stockholders' equity will Best Buy need to fund its growth at projected increases in sales?

PROBLEM 10–3

Preparing Pro Forma Financial Statements

Merck

Comparative income statements and balance sheets for **Merck** (in $ millions) follow:

	Year 2	Year 1
Income Statement		
Net sales	$47,716	$40,343
Cost of goods	28,977	22,444
Gross profit	18,739	17,900
Selling, general and administrative expense	6,531	6,469
Depreciation and amortization expense	1,464	1,277
Interest expense	342	329
Income before tax	10,403	9,824
Income tax expense	3,121	3,002
Net income	7,282	6,822
Outstanding shares	2,976	2,968
Balance Sheet		
Cash	$ 3,287	$ 4,255
Receivables	5,215	5,262
Inventories	3,579	3,022
Other current assets	880	1,059
Total current assets	12,961	13,598
Property, plant and equipment	18,956	16,707
Accumulated depreciation	5,853	5,225
Net property, plant and equipment	13,103	11,482
Other noncurrent assets	17,942	15,075
Total assets	$44,007	$40,155
Accounts payable and accrued liabilities	$ 5,904	$ 5,391
Short-term debt and current maturities of long-term debt	4,067	3,319
Income taxes payable	1,573	1,244
Total current liabilities	11,544	9,954
Deferred income taxes and other liabilities	11,614	11,768
Long-term debt	4,799	3,601
Total noncurrent liabilities	16,413	15,368
Common stock	30	30
Capital surplus	6,907	6,266
Retained earnings	31,500	27,395
Treasury stock	(22,387)	(18,858)
Shareholders' equity	16,050	14,832
Total liabilities and net worth	$44,007	$40,155

Required:

a. Use the following ratios to prepare a projected income statement, balance sheet, and statement of cash flows for Year 3.

Sales growth	18.27%
Gross profit margin	39.27%
Selling, general and administrative expense/Sales	13.69%

Depreciation expense/Prior-year property, plant & equipment (gross)	8.76%
Interest expense/Prior-year long-term debt	4.94%
Income tax expense/Pretax income	30.00%
Accounts receivable turnover (Sales/Accounts receivable)	9.15
Inventory turnover (Cost of goods sold/Inventory)	8.10
Accounts payable turnover (Cost of goods sold/Accounts payable)	4.91
Taxes payable/Tax expense	50.41%
Total assets/Stockholders' equity (financial leverage)	2.35
Dividends per share	$1.06
Capital expenditures/Sales	9.04%

b. Based on your initial projections, how much external financing (long-term debt and/or stockholders' equity) will Merck need to fund its growth at projected increases in sales?

PROBLEM 10–4
Using Prospective Analysis to Value Securities

Following are financial statement information for Welmark Corporation as of Year 2 and Year 3.

WELMARK CORPORATION

	Year 2	Year 3
Sales growth	8.50%	10.65%
Net profit margin (Net income/Sales)	6.71%	8.22%
Net working capital turnover (Sales/Average net working capital)	8.98	9.33
Fixed asset turnover (Sales/Average fixed assets)	1.67	1.64
Total operating assets/Total equity	1.96	2.01
Number of shares outstanding	1,737	1,737
(in $ thousands, except where otherwise noted)		
Sales	$25,423	$28,131
Net income ($ Mil)	1,706	2,312
Net working capital	2,832	3,015
Fixed assets	15,232	17,136
Total operating assets	18,064	20,151
Long-term liabilities	8,832	10,132
Total stockholders' equity ($ Mil)	9,232	10,019

Required:

Using the residual income model, prepare a valuation of the common stock of Welmark Corporation as of Year 3 under the following assumptions:

a. Forecast horizon of five years

b. Sales growth of 10.65% per year over the forecast horizon and 3.5% thereafter.

c. All financial ratios remain at Year 3 levels

d. Cost of equity capital is 12.5%

PROBLEM 10–5[A]
Preparing Pro Forma Financial Statements

Telnet Corporation is a newly formed computer manufacturer. Telnet plans to begin operations on January 1, Year 2. Selected financial information is available for the preparation of Telnet's six-month forecasted performance covering the period January 1 to June 30 of Year 2.

Forecasted *monthly* sales	$250,000
Monthly operating expenses:	
Labor	30,500
Rent for factory	10,000
Variable overhead	22,500
Depreciation on equipment	35,000
Amortization of patents	500
Selling and administrative expenses	47,500
Materials	125,000

Additional Information:

1. Collection period 45 days
2. Purchase terms n/30
3. Ending finished goods inventory $100,000
4. Ending raw material inventory $35,000
5. Effective tax rate 50%
6. Beginning cash balance $60,000
7. Minimum cash balance required $40,000
8. Prepaid expenses on June 30, Year 2 $7,000
9. No inventory is in process on June 30, Year 2.
10. Sales are made evenly throughout the period.
11. Expenses are paid in cash (unless otherwise indicated).
12. Telnet Corporation's balance sheet data on January 1, Year 2, appears as:

Cash	$ 60,000	Patents	$ 40,000
Equipment	1,200,000	Shareholders' equity	1,300,000

Required:

a. Prepare a pro forma income statement to portray the forecasted financial position of Telnet Corporation for the six-month period ended June 30, Year 2.

b. Prepare a pro forma balance sheet as of June 30, Year 2.

c. Prepare a cash forecast analysis as in Exhibit 10A.4 for the six-month period ended June 30, Year 2.

CHECK
(a) NI, $8,000
(b) Total assets, $1,584,000
(c) Borrowing, $143,000

PROBLEM 10–6
Forecasting the Statement of Cash Flows

Quaker Oats Company

Refer to the financial statements of **Quaker Oats Company** in Appendix A. Using Quaker's financial statements and the analysis guidance from the chapter, prepare a forecasted statement of cash flows for Year 12 using the following information:

Selected Forecast Data ($ millions)

Item	Year 12
Sources of cash:	
Assets retirements	$ 20
Uses of cash:	
Repayment of long-term debt	45
Capital expenditures—Property, plant and equipment	300
Cash dividends on capital stock	135
Other cash expenditures	30
Revenue forecast	6,000

CHECK
Forecasted CFO, $477.0
Forecasted net cash increase, $2.8

Additional assumptions for your forecasting task include:

1. Income from continuing operations in Year 12 is expected to equal the average percentage of income from continuing operations to sales for the three-year period ending June 30, Year 11.
2. The depreciation and amortization forecast for Year 12 uses the average percentage relation of depreciation and amortization to income from continuing operations for the period Year 9 through Year 11. The average is computed at 82.33%.
3. Forecasts of deferred income taxes (noncurrent portion) and other items in Year 12 reflect the past three years' relation of deferred taxes (noncurrent) and other items to total income from continuing operations.
4. Provisions for restructuring charges are predicted to be zero for Year 12.
5. Days' sales in receivables is expected to be 42 for Year 12.
6. Days' sales in inventory of 55 and a ratio of cost of sales to sales of 0.51 are forecasted for Year 12.
7. Changes in other current assets are predicted to be equal to the average increase/decrease over the period Year 9 through Year 11.
8. Days' purchases in accounts payable of 45 is forecasted for Year 12, and purchases are expected to increase in Year 12 by 12% over Year 11 purchases of $2,807.20.
9. Change in other current liabilities is predicted to be equal to the average increase/decrease over the period Year 9 through Year 11.
10. There are no more changes expected with Fisher-Price and no expected changes in net current assets of discontinued operations.
11. Decreases in short-term debt are predicted at $40 million each year.
12. No cash inflows are expected from issuance of debt for spin-off and no cash effects from purchases or issuances of common and preferred stock.
13. Predicted year-end cash needs are equal to a level measured by the ratio of cash to revenues prevailing in Year 11.
14. Additions to long-term debt in Year 12 are equal to the amount needed to meet the desired year-end cash balance.

CASES

CASE 10–1
Forecasting Pro Forma Financial Statements

Refer to the annual report for **Kodak** in Appendix A.

Kodak

Required:

Prepare forecasts of its income statement, balance sheet, and statement of cash flows for 2002 under the following assumptions:

a. All financial ratios remain at 2001 levels.

b. Kodak will not record restructuring costs for 2002.

c. There will be no goodwill amortization under current GAAP.

d. Taxes payable are at the 2001 level of $544 million.

CASE 10–2
Preparing and Analyzing Cash Forecasts

Miller Company is planning to construct a two-unit facility for the loading of beverage barrels onto ships. On or before January 1, Year 2, stockholders will invest $100,000 in the company's capital stock to provide the initial working capital. To finance the construction program (total planned cost is $1,800,000) the company will obtain a commitment from a lending organization for a loan of $1,800,000. This loan is to be secured by a 10-year mortgage note bearing interest at 5% per year on the unpaid balance. The principal amount of the loan is to be repaid in equal semiannual installments of $100,000 beginning June 30, Year 3. Since loan proceeds will only be required as construction work progresses, the company agrees to pay a commitment fee beginning January 1, Year 2, equal to 1 percent per year on the unused portion of the loan commitment. This fee is payable when amounts are "drawn down" except for the first draw-down.

Work on the construction of the facility will commence in the fall of Year 1. The first payment to the contractors is due on January 1, Year 2, at which time the commitment and loan agreement become effective and the company will make its first draw-down for payment to the contractors in the amount of $800,000. As construction progresses, additional payments will be made to the contractors by drawing down the remaining loan proceeds as follows (payments to contractors are made on the same dates as the loan proceeds are drawn down):

April 1, Year 2	$500,000	December 31, Year 2	$100,000
July 1, Year 2	300,000	April 1, Year 3	100,000

Because of weather conditions, the facility operates from April 1 through November 30 of each year. The construction program will permit the completion of the first of two plant units (capable of handling 5,000,000 barrels) in time for its use during the Year 2 shipping season. The second unit (capable of handling an additional 3,000,000 barrels) will be completed in time for the Year 3 season. It is expected 5,000,000 barrels will be handled by the facility during the Year 2 season. Thereafter, barrels handled are expected to increase in each subsequent year by 300,000 barrels until a level of 6,500,000 barrels is reached.

The company's revenues are derived by charging the consignees of the beverage for its services at a fixed rate per barrel loaded. All revenues are collected in the month of shipment. Based upon past experience with similar facilities, Miller Company expects operating profit to average $0.04 per barrel before charges for interest, financing fees, and depreciation. Depreciation is $0.03 per barrel.

Required:

Prepare a cash forecast for each of the three calendar years: Year 2, Year 3, and Year 4. Evaluate the sufficiency of cash obtained from the issuance of capital stock, draw-downs on the loan, and the operating facility to cover cash payments to the contractor and the creditor (principal and interest).

CHECK
Ending cash:
Year 2, $1,929,000
Year 3, $254,500

CASE 10–3
Preparing a Cash Forecast for a Company in Distress

Royal Company has incurred substantial losses for several years and is insolvent. On March 31, Year 5, Royal petitions the court for protection from creditors and submits the following balance sheet:

ROYAL COMPANY
Balance Sheet
March 31, Year 5

	Book Value	Liquidation Value
Assets:		
Accounts receivable	$100,000	$ 50,000
Inventories	90,000	40,000
Plant and equipment	150,000	160,000
Total assets	$340,000	$250,000
Liabilities and Stockholders' Equity:		
Accounts payable—general creditors	$600,000	
Common stock	60,000	
Retained earnings	(320,000)	
Total liabilities and equity	$340,000	

Royal's management informed the court that the company developed a new product and a prospective customer is willing to sign a contract for the purchase of (at a price of $90 per unit) 10,000 units during the year ending March 31, Year 6; 12,000 units during the year ending March 31, Year 7; and 15,000 units during the year ending March 31, Year 8. The product can be manufactured using Royal's current facilities. Monthly production with immediate delivery is expected to be uniform within each year. Receivables are expected to be collected during the calendar month following sales. Production costs per unit for the new product are:

Direct materials	$20	Direct labor	$30	Variable overhead	$10

Fixed costs (excluding depreciation) amount to $130,000 per year. Purchases of direct materials are paid during the calendar month following purchase. Fixed costs, direct labor, and variable overhead are paid as incurred. Inventory of direct materials are equal to 60 days' usage. After the first month of operations, 30 days' usage of direct materials is ordered each month.

Creditors have agreed to reduce their total claims to 60% of their March 31, Year 5, balances under two conditions:

1. Existing accounts receivable and inventories are liquidated immediately with the proceeds going to creditors.
2. The remaining balance in accounts payable is paid as cash is produced from future operations—but in no event is it to be paid later than March 31, Year 7. No interest is paid on these obligations.

Under this proposal, creditors would receive $110,000 more than the current liquidation value of Royal's assets. The court engages you to determine the feasibility of this proposal.

Required:

CHECK
Ending cash bal.:
Year 6, $75,000
Year 7, $15,000

Prepare a cash forecast for years ending March 31, Year 6 and Year 7. Ignore any need to borrow and repay short-term funds for working capital purposes and show the cash expected to be available to pay creditors, the actual payments to creditors, and the cash remaining after payments to creditors.

(AICPA Adapted)

CASE 10–4
Comprehensive Analysis of Loan Request

You are a loan officer for Pacific Bank. The senior loan officer submits to you the following selected financial information as of September 30, Year 6, for Union Corporation, which has filed a loan application:

Current assets:	
Cash	$ 12,000
Accounts receivable	10,000
Inventory	63,600
Plant and equipment—net	100,000
Total liabilities	0
Actual sales:	
September, Year 6	$ 40,000
Forecasted sales:	
October, Year 6	48,000
November, Year 6	60,000
December, Year 6	80,000
January, Year 7	36,000

Sales are 75% for cash and 25% on account. Receivables are collected in full in the month following the sale. For example, the accounts receivable balance of $10,000 on September 30, Year 6, equals 25% of the sales from September, of which all $10,000 is paid in October. Gross profit averages 30% of sales *before* purchase discounts. Therefore, the gross invoice cost of goods sold is 70% of sales. Union Corp. carries $30,000 of inventory plus additional inventory sufficient to provide for the anticipated sales of the following month. Purchase terms are 2/10, n/30. Since purchases are made early in each month and all discounts are taken, payments are consistently made in the month of purchase.

Salaries and wages average 15% of sales, rent averages 5% of sales, and all other expenses (except depreciation) average 4% of sales. These expenses are paid in cash when incurred. Depreciation expense is $750 per month, computed on a straight-line basis. Equipment expenditures are forecasted at $600 in October and $400 in November. Depreciation on these new expenditures is not recorded until Year 7.

Union Corp. maintains a minimum cash balance of $8,000. Any borrowings are made at the beginning of the month and any repayments are made at the end of the month, both in multiples of $1,000 (excluding interest). Interest is paid when the principal is repaid, equal to a rate of 6% per year.

Required:

a. The senior loan officer requests you prepare the following schedules for the months of October, November, and December, and for the total three months (quarter) ending in December of Year 6:
  (1) Estimated total cash receipts.
  (2) Estimated cash disbursements for purchases (purchases are 70% of sales for the following month).
  (3) Estimated cash disbursements for operating expenses.
  (4) Estimated total cash disbursements.
  (5) Estimated net cash receipts and disbursements.
  (6) Estimated financing required.

b. For the three months (quarter) ending in December of Year 6, prepare a:
  (1) Forecasted income statement (ignore taxes).
  (2) Forecasted balance sheet.

CHECK
(a) 3. Dec., $19,200
5. Dec., $31,104
(b) 1. NI, $11,314
2. Assets, $195,810

WEB ACTIVITIES

The Web Activities are located on the book's website at www.mhhe.com/wild8e.

11 CREDIT ANALYSIS

A LOOK BACK <

Chapter 10 focused on analysis tools for cash flow prediction and analysis. We illustrated both short- and long-term forecasting procedures and discussed their reliability. We also described cash-based measures in assessing companies' cash requirements.

A LOOK AT THIS CHAPTER •

This chapter begins with tools for assessing short-term liquidity. We explain liquidity and describe analysis tools capturing different aspects of it. Attention is directed at accounting-based ratios, turnover, and operating activity measures of liquidity. This chapter also focuses on capital structure and its implications for solvency. We analyze the importance of financial leverage and its effects on risk and return. We also describe book values and earnings coverage measures and their interpretation.

A LOOK AHEAD >

Chapter 12 emphasizes earnings-based analysis and equity valuation. Our earnings-based analysis focuses on assessing earning power. Discussion of equity valuation focuses on issues in estimating company values and forecasting earnings.

ANALYSIS OBJECTIVES

- Explain the importance of liquidity in analyzing business activities.
- Describe working capital measures of liquidity and their components.
- Interpret the current ratio and cash-based measures of liquidity.
- Analyze operating cycle and turnover measures of liquidity and their interpretation.
- Illustrate what-if analysis for evaluating changes in company conditions and policies.
- Describe capital structure and its relation to solvency.
- Explain financial leverage and its implications for company performance and analysis.
- Analyze adjustments to accounting book values to assess capital structure.
- Describe analysis tools for evaluating and interpreting capital structure composition and for assessing solvency.
- Analyze asset composition and coverage for solvency analysis.
- Explain earnings-coverage analysis and its relevance in evaluating solvency.
- Describe capital structure risk and return and its relevance to financial statement analysis.
- Interpret ratings of organizations' debt obligations (Appendix 11A).
- Describe prediction models of financial distress (Appendix 11B).

Are We Building a Debt Bomb?

NEW YORK–The debt load on companies is bigger than ever. During economic booms, leverage can help companies make the most of their money. But if growth slows appreciably, once-manageable debts become a strain. Faced with big debt payments, a mild downturn can trigger a surge of defaults, leading to a drying up of liquidity and a credit crunch.

There's nothing wrong with borrowing–it's *excessive* borrowing that causes the problems. Tapping outside financing to fund growth is crucial for expansion, especially in a company's early stages. One of the remarkable things about the 1990s, however, was the way most companies relied on borrowing to fund their operations rather than issuing equity to take advantage of high stock prices. Indeed, nonfinancial corporations bought back some $870 billion in equity from 1995 to 2001. Buybacks help reduce outstanding shares, lift earnings-per-share figures, impress Wall Street–and boost share prices.

Credit-rating agencies are now doing their part to raise the cost of credit throughout the economy. Even before the collapse of Enron, they were aggressively slashing corporate credit ratings as the economy deteriorated. Downgrades soared to record levels, raising corporate borrowing costs. Now, ratings agencies have ratcheted up their oversight even further. "We've accelerated and heightened our credit-review process," says Edward Z. Emmer, executive managing director of Standard & Poor's, which, like *BusinessWeek*, is owned by The McGraw-Hill Companies. S&P is spending more time looking over company accounts and broadening its review to include customers and competitors. In the wake of Enron, ratings agencies are also paying more attention to equity and corporate bond prices as early warning signs that a company may be in trouble.

How much debt is too much? First, look at capital, which is long-term debt plus shareholder equity. As a rule of thumb, the debt should be less than 50%. But it's best to compare companies in the same industry. In cyclical industries like paper and chemicals, where revenues can swing wildly, the less debt the better. Industries with stable revenues, like old-fashioned utilities, or those that generate lots of cash, like supermarkets, can service more debt. Lehman Brothers' Willens likes to see companies with total debt burdens that are less than 40%.

Another way to determine if a company can cover interest payments on its debt is to calculate "fixed charge coverage." This is a ratio of earnings before fixed charges divided by the company's fixed charges, such as annual interest payments. "A company should have five times or more interest coverage for a level of comfort," says Kenneth A. Shea, director of equity research at Standard & Poor's. He notes that General Mills has a stiff debt-to-capital ratio of 82%, thanks to its acquisition of Pillsbury. But because the cereal maker generates lots of cash, it can more than meet its debt obligations.

BORROWING GETS PRICIER . . .

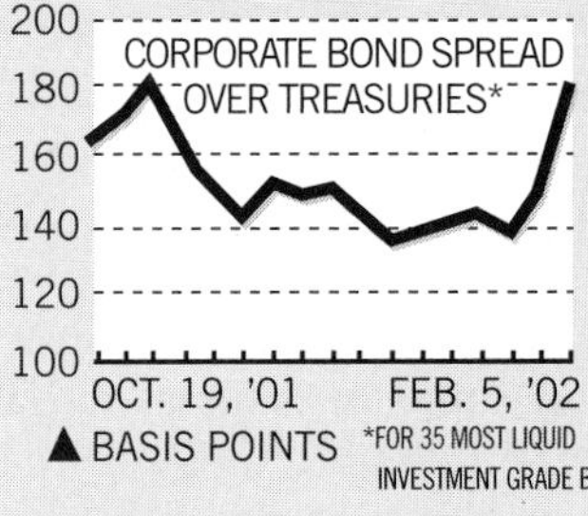

*FOR 35 MOST LIQUID INVESTMENT GRADE BONDS

. . . AS CREDIT QUALITY DETERIORATES . . .

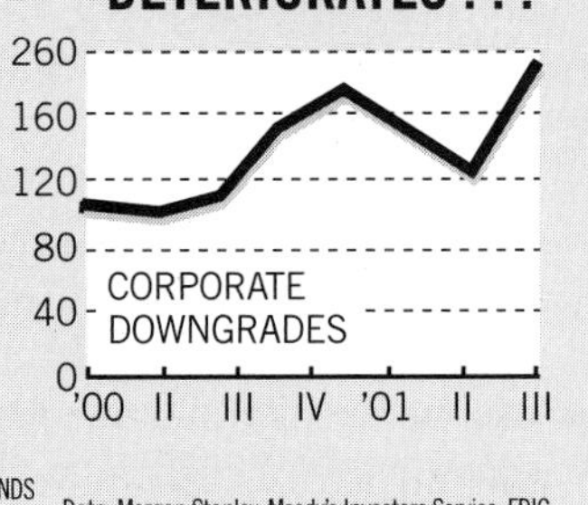

. . . AND TROUBLED LOANS SURGE

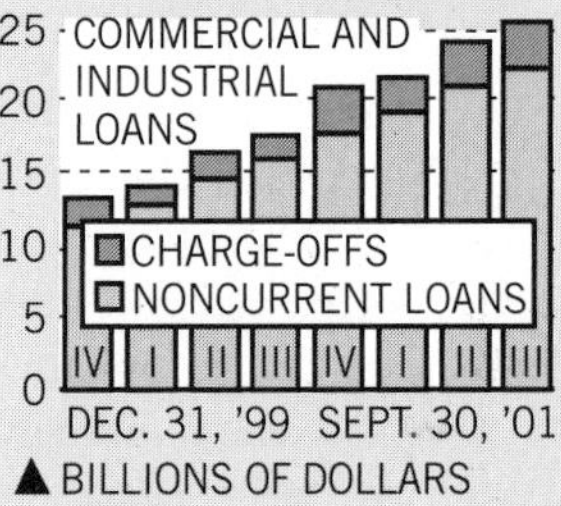

Data: Morgan Stanley, Moody's Investors Service, FDIC

Sources: Business Week, February, April, and July 2002.

PREVIEW OF CHAPTER 11

Liquidity refers to the availability of company resources to meet short-term cash requirements. A company's short-term liquidity risk is affected by the timing of cash inflows and outflows along with its prospects for future performance. Analysis of liquidity is aimed at companies' operating activities, their ability to generate profits from sale of products and services, and working capital requirements and measures. Section 1

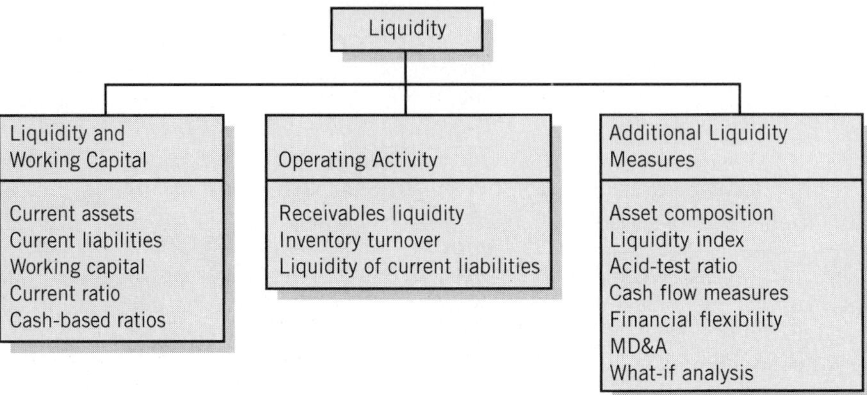

of this chapter describes several financial statement analysis tools used to assess liquidity risk. We begin with a discussion of the importance of liquidity and its link to working capital. We explain and interpret useful ratios of both working capital and a company's operating cycle for assessing liquidity. We also discuss potential adjustments to these analysis tools and the underlying financial statement numbers. What-if analysis of changes in a company's conditions or strategies concludes this section.

Solvency refers to a company's long-run financial viability and its ability to cover long-term obligations. All business activities of a company–financing, investing, and operating–affect a company's solvency. One of the most important components of solvency analysis is the composition of a company's capital structure. **Capital structure** refers to a company's sources of financing and its economic attributes. Section 2 of this chapter describes capital structure and explains its importance to solvency analysis. Since solvency depends on success in operating activities, we examine earnings and the ability of earnings to *cover* important and necessary company expenditures. We describe

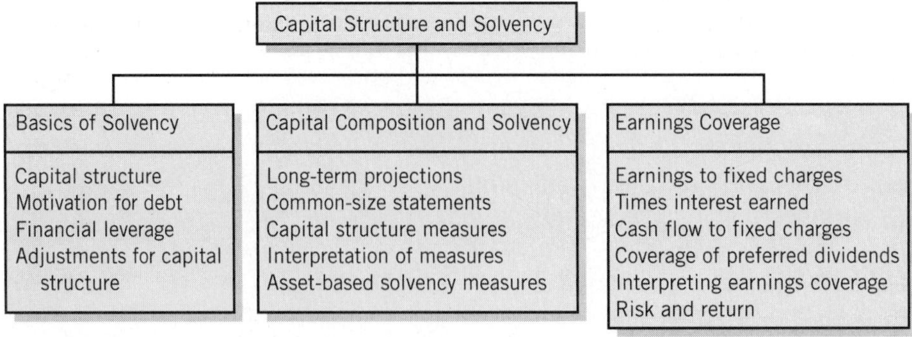

various tools of solvency analysis, including leverage measures, analytical accounting adjustments, capital structure analysis, and earnings-coverage measures. We demonstrate these analysis tools with data from financial statements. We also discuss the relation between risk and return inherent in a company's capital structure and its implications for financial statement analysis.

SECTION 1: LIQUIDITY

Section 1 focuses on liquidity. We consider solvency and capital structure in Section 2.

LIQUIDITY AND WORKING CAPITAL

Liquidity refers to a company's ability to meet short-term obligations. *Liquidity* is the ability to convert assets into cash or to obtain cash. *Short term* is conventionally viewed as a period up to one year, though it is identified with the normal operating cycle of a company (the time period encompassing the buying-producing-selling-collecting cycle).

The importance of liquidity is best seen by considering repercussions stemming from a company's inability to meet short-term obligations. Liquidity is a matter of degree. Lack of liquidity prevents a company from taking advantage of favorable discounts or profitable opportunities. It also implies limited opportunities and constraints on management actions. More extreme liquidity problems reflect a company's inability to cover current obligations. This can lead to forced sale of investments and assets and, in its most severe form, to insolvency and bankruptcy.

For a company's shareholders, a lack of liquidity often precedes lower profitability and opportunity. It can foretell a loss of owner control or loss of capital investment. When a company's owners possess unlimited liability (proprietorships and certain partnerships), a lack of liquidity endangers their personal assets. To creditors of a company, a lack of liquidity can yield delays in collecting interest and principal payments or the loss of amounts due them. A company's customers and suppliers of products and services are affected by short-term liquidity problems. Implications include a company's inability to execute contracts and damage to important customer and supplier relationships.

These scenarios highlight why measures of liquidity are of great importance in our analysis of a company. If a company fails to meet its current obligations, its continued existence is doubtful. Viewed in this light, all other measures of analysis are of secondary importance. While accounting measurements assume indefinite existence of the company, our analysis must always assess the validity of this assumption using liquidity and solvency measures.

Working capital is a widely used measure of liquidity. **Working capital** is defined as the excess of current assets over current liabilities. It is important as a measure of liquid assets that provide a safety cushion to creditors. It is also important in measuring the liquid reserve available to meet contingencies and the uncertainties surrounding a company's balance of cash inflows and outflows.

Current Assets and Liabilities

Current assets are cash and other assets reasonably expected to be (1) realized in cash or (2) sold or consumed within one year (or the normal operating cycle of the company if greater than one year). Balance sheet accounts typically included as current assets are cash, marketable securities maturing within the next fiscal year, accounts receivable, inventories, and prepaid expenses. **Current liabilities** are obligations expected to be satisfied within a relatively short period of time, usually one year. Current liabilities typically include accounts payable, notes payable, short-term bank loans, taxes payable, accrued expenses, and the current portion of long-term debt.

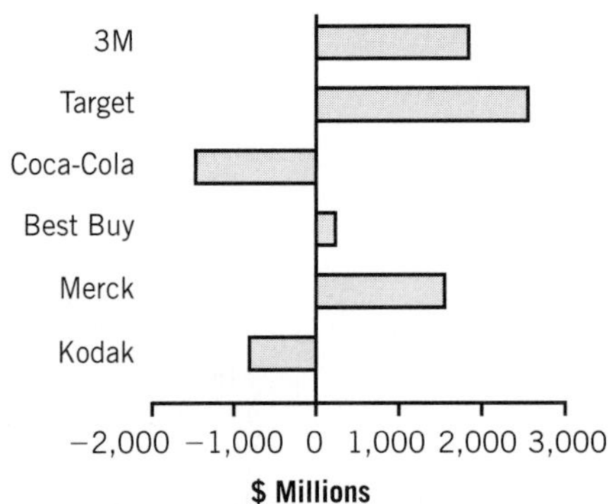

Our analysis must assess whether all current obligations with a reasonably high probability of eventual payment are reported in current liabilities. Their exclusion from current liabilities handicaps analysis of working capital. Three common concerns are:

1. Contingent liabilities associated with loan guarantees. We need to assess the likelihood of this contingency materializing when we compute working capital.
2. Future minimum rental payments under noncancelable operating lease agreements.
3. Contracts for construction or acquisition of long-term assets often call for substantial progress payments. These obligations for payments are reported in the footnotes as "commitments" and *not* as liabilities in the balance sheet. When computing working capital, our analysis should often include these commitments.

We also should recognize that current deferred tax assets (debits) are no more current assets than current deferred tax liabilities (credits) are current liabilities. Current deferred tax assets do not always represent expected cash inflows in the form of tax refunds. These assets usually serve to reduce future income tax expense. An exception is the case of net operating loss carrybacks. Similarly, current deferred tax liabilities do not always represent future cash outflows. Examples are temporary differences of a recurring nature (such as depreciation) that do not necessarily result in payment of taxes because their reversing differences are offset by equal or larger originating differences.

Working Capital Measure of Liquidity

Loan agreements and bond indentures often contain stipulations for maintenance of minimum working capital levels. Financial analysts assess the magnitude of working capital for investment decisions and recommendations. Government agencies compute aggregates of companies' working capital for regulatory and policy actions. And published financial statements distinguish between current and noncurrent assets and liabilities in response to these and other user needs.

Yet the amount of working capital is more relevant to users' decisions when related to other key financial variables like sales or total assets. It is of limited value for direct comparative purposes and for assessing the adequacy of working capital. This is seen in Illustration 11.1.

ILLUSTRATION 11.1

	Company A	Company B
Current assets	$300,000	$1,200,000
Current liabilities	(100,000)	(1,000,000)
Working capital	$200,000	$ 200,000

These companies have an equal amount of working capital. Yet, even a quick comparison of the relation of current assets to current liabilities indicates Company A's working capital position is superior to Company B's.

Current Ratio Measure of Liquidity

The previous illustration highlights the need to consider *relative* working capital. That is, a $200,000 working capital excess yields a different conclusion for a company with $300,000 in current assets than one with $1,200,000 in current assets. A common relative measure in practice is the current ratio. The **current ratio** is defined as:

$$\text{Current ratio} = \frac{\text{Current assets}}{\text{Current liabilities}}$$

In Illustration 11.1, the current ratio is 3:1 ($300,000/$100,000) for Company A and 1.2:1 ($1,200,000/$1,000,000) for Company B. This ratio reveals a different picture for companies A and B. The ability to differentiate between companies on the basis of liquidity helps account for the widespread use of the current ratio.

Relevance of the Current Ratio

Reasons for the current ratio's widespread use as a measure of liquidity include its ability to measure:

- **Current liability coverage.** The higher the amount (multiple) of current assets to current liabilities, the greater assurance we have that current liabilities will be paid.
- **Buffer against losses.** The larger the buffer, the lower the risk. The current ratio shows the margin of safety available to cover shrinkage in noncash current asset values when ultimately disposing of or liquidating them.
- **Reserve of liquid funds.** The current ratio is relevant as a measure of the margin of safety against uncertainties and random shocks to a company's cash flows. Uncertainties and shocks, such as strikes and extraordinary losses, can temporarily and unexpectedly impair cash flows.

While the current ratio is a relevant and useful measure of liquidity and short-term solvency, it is subject to certain limitations we must be aware of. Consequently, before we describe the usefulness of the current ratio for our analysis, we discuss its limitations.

Current Ratios for Selected Companies

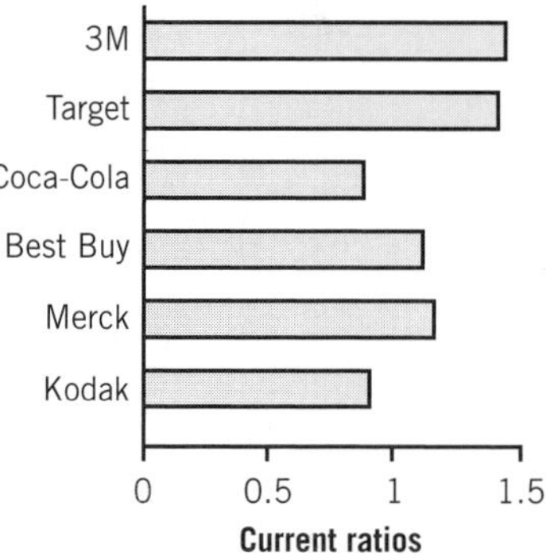

Limitations of the Current Ratio

A first step in critically evaluating the current ratio as a tool for liquidity and short-term solvency analysis is for us to examine both its numerator and denominator. If we define *liquidity* as the ability to meet cash outflows with adequate cash inflows, including an allowance for unexpected decreases in inflows or increases in outflows, then it is appropriate for us to ask: Does the current ratio capture these important factors of liquidity? Specifically, does the current ratio:

- Measure and predict the pattern of future cash inflows and outflows?
- Measure the adequacy of future cash inflows to outflows?

The answer to both these questions is generally no. The current ratio is a static measure of resources available at a point in time to meet current obligations. The current reservoir of cash resources does not have a logical or causal relation to its future cash inflows. Yet future cash inflows are the greatest indicator of liquidity. These cash inflows depend on factors excluded from the ratio, including sales, cash expenditures, profits, and changes in business conditions. To clarify these limitations, we need to examine more closely the individual components of the current ratio.

Numerator of the Current Ratio

We discuss each individual component of current assets and its implications for analysis using the current ratio.

Cash and Cash Equivalents. Cash held by a well-managed company is primarily of a precautionary reserve intended to guard against short-term cash imbalances. For example, sales can decline more rapidly than cash outlays for purchases and expenses in a business downturn, requiring availability of excess cash. Since cash is a nonearning asset and cash equivalents are usually low-yielding securities, a company aims to minimize its investment in these assets. The cash balance has little relation to the existing level of business activity and is unlikely to convey predictive implications. Further, many companies rely on cash substitutes in the form of open lines of credit not entering into the computation of the current ratio.

Marketable Securities. Cash in excess of the precautionary reserve is often spent on investment securities with returns exceeding those for cash equivalents. These investments are reasonably viewed as available to discharge current liabilities. Since investment securities are reported at their fair values (see Chapter 4), much of the guesswork from estimating their net realizable value is removed. Our analysis must recognize that the further removed the balance sheet date is from our analysis date, the greater likelihood for unrecorded changes in these investments' fair values.

Accounts Receivable. A major determinant of accounts receivable is sales. The relation of accounts receivable to sales is governed by credit policies and collection methods. Changes in receivables correspond to changes in sales, though not necessarily on a directly proportional basis. Our analysis of accounts receivable as a source of cash must recognize, except in liquidation, the revolving nature of this asset. That is, the collection of one account is succeeded by a new extension of credit. Accordingly, the level of receivables is not a measure of future net cash inflows.

Inventories. Like receivables, the major determinant of inventories is sales or expected sales–not the level of current liabilities. Since sales are a function of demand and supply, methods of inventory management (such as economic order quantities, safety stock levels, and reorder points) maintain inventory increments varying not in proportion to demand but by lesser amounts. The relation of inventories to sales is underscored by the observation that sales initiate the conversion of inventories to cash. Determination of future cash inflows from the sale of inventories depends on the profit margin that can be realized since inventories are reported at the lower of cost or market. The current ratio does not recognize sales level or profit margin, yet both are important determinants of future cash inflows.

Prepaid Expenses. Prepaid expenses are expenditures for future benefits. Since these benefits are typically received within a year of the company's operating cycle, they preserve the outlay of current funds. Prepaid expenses are usually small relative to other current assets. However, our analysis must be aware of the tendency of companies with weak current positions to include deferred charges and other items of dubious liquidity in prepaid expenses. We should exclude such items from our computation of working capital and the current ratio.

Denominator of the Current Ratio

Current liabilities are the focus of the current ratio. They are a source of cash in the same way receivables and inventories use cash. Current liabilities are primarily determined by sales, and a company's ability to meet them when due is the object of working capital measures. For example, since purchases giving rise to accounts payable are a function of sales, payables vary with sales. As long as sales remain constant or are rising, the payment of current liabilities is a refunding activity. In this case the components of the current ratio provide little, if any, recognition to this activity or to its effects on future cash flows. Also, current liabilities entering into the computation of the current ratio do not include prospective cash outlays–examples are certain commitments under construction contracts, loans, leases, and pensions.

Using the Current Ratio for Analysis

From our discussion of the current ratio, we can draw at least three conclusions.

1. Liquidity depends to a large extent on *prospective* cash flows and to a lesser extent on the level of cash and cash equivalents.
2. No direct relation exists between balances of working capital accounts and likely patterns of future cash flows.
3. Managerial policies regarding receivables and inventories are directed primarily at efficient and profitable asset utilization and secondarily at liquidity.

These conclusions do not bode well for the current ratio as an analysis tool and we might question why it enjoys widespread use in analysis. Reasons for using the current ratio include its understandability, its simplicity in computation, and its data availability. Its use also derives from the creditor's (especially banker's) propensity toward viewing credit situations as conditions of last resort. They ask themselves: What if there were a complete stoppage of cash inflows? Would current assets meet current liabilities? This extreme analysis is not always a useful way of assessing liquidity. Two other points are also pertinent. First, our analysis of short-term liquidity and solvency must recognize the relative superiority of cash flow projections and pro forma financial statements versus the current ratio. These analyses require information not readily available in financial statements, including product demand estimation (see Chapter 10). Second, if our analysis uses the current ratio as a static measure of the ability of current assets to satisfy current liabilities, we must recognize this is a different concept of liquidity from the one described above. In our context, liquidity is the readiness and speed that current assets are convertible to cash and the extent this conversion yields shrinkage in current asset values.

It is not our intent to reject the current ratio as an analysis tool. But it is important for us to know its relevant use. Moreover, there is no "adjustment" to rectify its limitations. Consequently, to what use can we apply the current ratio? The relevant use of the current ratio is only to measure the ability of current assets to discharge current liabilities. In addition, we can consider the excess of current assets, if any, as a liquid surplus available to meet imbalances in the flow of funds and other contingencies. These two applications are applied with our awareness that the ratio assumes company liquidation. This is in contrast to the usual going-concern situation where current assets are of a revolving nature (such as new receivables replacing collected receivables) and current liabilities are of a refunding nature (such as new payables covering payables due).

Provided we apply the current ratio in the manner described, there are two elements that we must evaluate and measure before the current ratio can usefully form a basis of analysis:

1. Quality of both current assets and current liabilities.
2. Turnover rate of both current assets and current liabilities–that is, the time necessary for converting receivables and inventories into cash and for paying current liabilities.

Several adjustments, ratios, and other analysis tools are available to make these evaluations and enhance our use of the current ratio (see subsequent pages). The remainder of this section describes relevant applications of the current ratio in practice.

Comparative Analysis

Analyzing the trend in the current ratio is often enlightening. Changes in the current ratio over time, however, must be interpreted with caution. Changes in this ratio do not necessarily imply changes in liquidity or operating performance. For example, during a recession a company might continue to pay current liabilities while inventory and receivables accumulate, yielding an increase in the current ratio. Conversely, in a successful period, increases in taxes payable can lower the current ratio. Company expansion often accompanying operating success can create larger working capital requirements. This "prosperity squeeze" in liquidity decreases the current ratio and is the result of company expansion unaccompanied by an increase in working capital–see Illustration 11.2.

ILLUSTRATION 11.2

Technology Resources, Inc., experiences a doubling of current assets and a quadrupling of current liabilities with *no change* in its working capital. This yielded a prosperity squeeze evidenced by a 50% decline in the current ratio.

	Year 1	Year 2
Current assets	$300,000	$600,000
Current liabilities	(100,000)	(400,000)
Working capital	$200,000	$200,000
Current ratio	3:1	1.5:1

Ratio Management

Our analysis must look for "management" of the current ratio, also known as *window dressing*. Toward the close of a period, management will occasionally press the collection of receivables, reduce inventory below normal levels, and delay normal purchases. Proceeds from these activities are then used to pay off current liabilities. The effect of these activities is to increase the current ratio–see Illustration 11.3.

ILLUSTRATION 11.3

Technology Resources, Inc., increases its current ratio by making an earlier-than-normal payoff of $50,000 of current liabilities:

	Before Payoff	After Payoff
Current assets	$200,000	$150,000
Current liabilities	(100,000)	(50,000)
Working capital	$100,000	$100,000
Current ratio	2:1	3:1

Our analysis should also go beyond annual measures and use interim measures of the current ratio. Interim analysis makes it more difficult for management to window dress and allows us to gauge seasonal effects on the ratio. For example, a strong current ratio in December can be misleading if a company experiences a credit squeeze at its seasonal peak in July.

Rule of Thumb Analysis

A frequently applied rule of thumb is if the current ratio is 2:1 or better, then a company is financially sound, while a ratio below 2:1 suggests increasing liquidity risks. The 2:1 norm implies there are $2 of current assets available for every $1 of current liabilities or, alternatively viewed, the value of current assets can in liquidation shrink by as much as

50% and still cover current liabilities. A current ratio much higher than 2:1, while implying superior coverage of current liabilities, can signal inefficient use of resources and a reduced rate of return. Our evaluation of the current ratio with any rule of thumb is of dubious value for two reasons:

1. Quality of current assets and the composition of current liabilities are more important in evaluating the current ratio (for example, two companies with identical current ratios can present substantially different risks due to variations in the quality of working capital components).
2. Working capital requirements vary with industry conditions and the length of a company's net trade cycle.

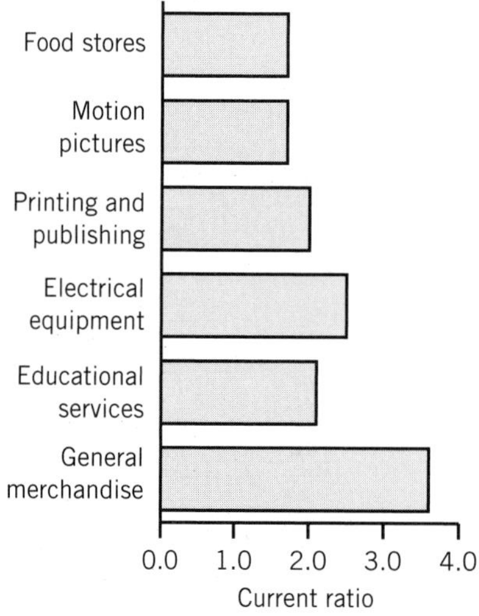

Net Trade Cycle Analysis

A company's working capital requirements are affected by its desired inventory investment and the relation between credit terms from suppliers and those extended to customers. These considerations determine a company's **net trade cycle.** Computation of a company's net trade cycle is described in Illustration 11.4

ILLUSTRATION 11.4

Selected financial information from Technology Resources for the end of Year 1 is reproduced below:

Sales for Year 1	$360,000
Receivables	40,000
Inventories*	50,000
Accounts payable†	20,000
Cost of goods sold (including depreciation of $30,000)	320,000

* *Beginning inventory is $100,000.*
† *These relate to purchases included in cost of goods sold.*

We estimate Technology Resources' purchases per day as:

Ending inventory	$ 50,000
Cost of goods sold	320,000
	$370,000
Less: Beginning inventory	(100,000)
Cost of goods purchased and manufactured	$270,000
Less: Depreciation in cost of goods sold	(30,000)
Purchases	$240,000

Purchases per day = $240,000 ÷ 360 = $666.67

Then, the net trade cycle for Technology Resources is computed as (in days):

$$\text{Accounts receivable} = \frac{\$40{,}000}{\$360{,}000 \div 360} = 40.00 \text{ days}$$

$$\text{Inventories} = \frac{\$50{,}000}{\$320{,}000 \div 360} = \underline{56.24} \text{ days}$$

$$96.24 \text{ days}$$

$$\text{Less: Accounts payable} = \frac{\$20{,}000}{\$666.67} = \underline{30.00} \text{ days}$$

$$\text{Net trade cycle (days)} = \underline{\underline{66.24}} \text{ days}$$

Notice the numerator and denominator in Illustration 11.4 are adjusted on a consistent basis. Specifically, accounts receivable reported in sales dollars are divided by sales per day, inventories reported at cost are divided by cost of goods sold per day, and accounts payable reported in dollars of purchases are divided by purchases per day. Consequently, while the day measures are expressed on different bases, our estimation of the net trade cycle is on a consistent basis. This analysis shows Technology Resources has 40 days of sales tied up in receivables, maintains 56 days of goods available in inventory, and receives only 30 days of purchases as credit from its suppliers. The longer the net trade cycle, the larger is the working capital requirement. Reduction in the number of days' sales in receivables or cost of sales in inventories lowers working capital requirements. An increase in the number of days' purchases as credit received from suppliers lowers working capital needed. Working capital requirements are determined by industry conditions and practices. Comparisons using industry current ratios, and analysis of working capital requirements using net trade cycle measures, are useful in analysis of the adequacy of a company's working capital.

ANALYSIS VIEWPOINT ***. . . YOU ARE THE BANKER***

International Machines Corporation (IMC) calls on you for a short-term one-year $2 million loan to finance expansion in the United Kingdom. As part of your loan analysis of IMC you compute a 4:1 current ratio on current assets of nearly $1.6 million. Analysis of industry competitors yields a 1.9:1 average current ratio. What is your decision on IMC's loan application using this limited information? Would your decision change if IMC's application is for a 10-year loan?

Answer–p. 560

Cash-Based Ratio Measures of Liquidity

Cash and cash equivalents are the most liquid of current assets. In this section, we examine cash-based ratio measures of liquidity.

Cash to Current Assets Ratio

The ratio of "near-cash" assets to the total of current assets is one measure of the degree of current asset liquidity. This measure, known as the **cash to current assets ratio,** is computed as:

$$\frac{\text{Cash} + \text{Cash equivalents} + \text{Marketable securities}}{\text{Current assets}}$$

The larger this ratio, the more liquid are current assets.

Cash to Current Liabilities Ratio

Another ratio measuring cash adequacy is the **cash to current liabilities ratio.** It is computed as:

$$\frac{\text{Cash} + \text{Cash equivalents} + \text{Marketable securities}}{\text{Current liabilities}}$$

This ratio measures the cash available to pay current obligations. This is a severe test ignoring the refunding nature of current assets and current liabilities. It supplements the cash to current assets ratio in measuring cash availability from a different perspective. To view this ratio as an extension of the quick ratio (see later analysis in this chapter) is, except in extreme cases, a too severe test of short-term liquidity. Still the importance of cash as the ultimate form of liquidity should not be underestimated. The record of business failures provides many examples of insolvent companies with sizable noncash assets (both current and noncurrent) and an inability to pay liabilities or to operate.

OPERATING ACTIVITY ANALYSIS OF LIQUIDITY

Operating activity measures of liquidity are important in credit analysis. This section considers three operating activity measures based on accounts receivable, inventory, and current liabilities.

Accounts Receivable Liquidity Measures

For most companies selling on credit, accounts and notes receivable are an important part of working capital. In assessing liquidity, including the quality of working capital and the current ratio, it is necessary to measure the quality and liquidity of receivables. Both quality and liquidity of accounts receivable are affected by their turnover rate. *Quality* refers to the likelihood of collection without loss. A measure of this likelihood is the proportion of receivables within terms of payment set by the company. Experience shows that the longer receivables are outstanding beyond their due date, the lower is the likelihood of collection. Their turnover rate is an indicator of the age of receivables. This indicator is especially useful when compared with an expected turnover rate computed using the permitted credit terms. *Liquidity* refers to the speed in converting accounts receivable to cash. The receivables turnover rate is a measure of this speed.

Receivables Turnover for Selected Industries

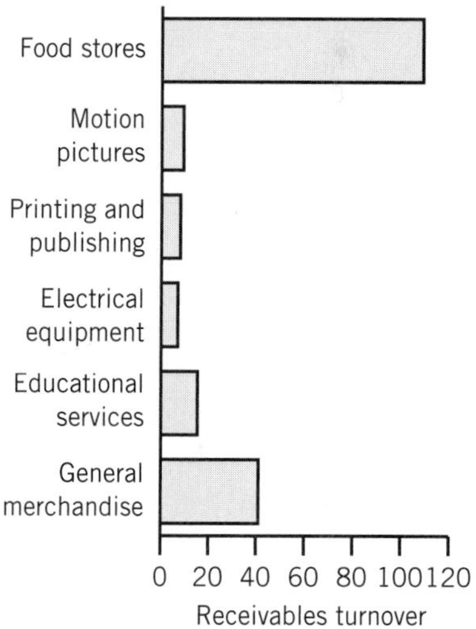

Accounts Receivable Turnover

The **accounts receivable turnover** ratio is computed as:

$$\frac{\text{Net sales on credit}}{\text{Average accounts receivable}}$$

Notes receivable from normal sales should be included when computing accounts receivable turnover. We should also include only credit sales when computing this ratio because cash sales do not create receivables. Since financial statements rarely separately disclose cash and credit sales, our analysis often must compute this ratio using total net sales (that is, assuming cash sales are insignificant). If cash sales are not insignificant, then this ratio is less useful. However, if the proportion of cash sales to total sales is relatively stable, then year-to-year comparisons of changes in the receivables turnover ratio are reliable. The most direct way for us to determine *average* accounts receivable is to add beginning and ending accounts receivable for the period and divide by two. Using monthly or quarterly figures yields more accurate estimates. The more that sales fluctuate, the more likely this ratio is distorted. The receivables turnover ratio indicates how often, on average, receivables revolve–that is, are received and collected during the year. Illustration 11.5 provides an example.

ILLUSTRATION 11.5

Consumer Electronics reports sales of \$1,200,000, beginning receivables of \$150,000, and year-end receivables of \$250,000. Its accounts receivable turnover ratio is computed as:

$$\frac{\$1,200,000}{(\$150,000 + \$250,000) \div 2} = \frac{\$1,200,000}{\$200,000} = 6$$

Collection Period for Selected Industries

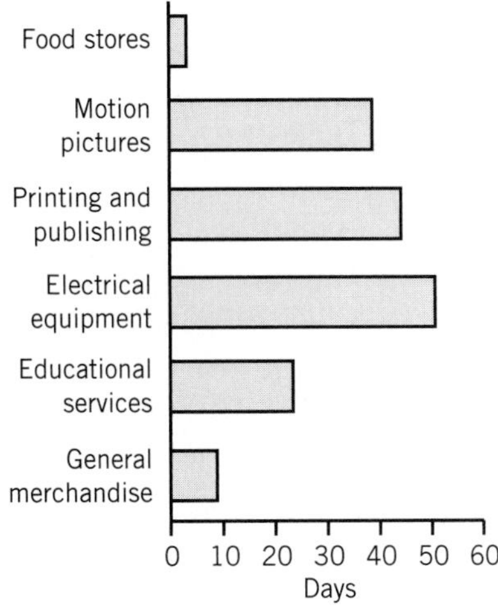

Accounts Receivable Collection Period

While the accounts receivable turnover ratio measures the speed of collections and is useful for comparison purposes, it is not directly comparable to the terms of trade a company extends to its customers. This latter comparison is made by converting the turnover ratio into days of sales tied up in receivables. The **receivables collection period** measures the number of days it takes, on average, to collect accounts (and notes) receivable. It is computed by dividing the accounts receivable turnover ratio into 360 days (an approximate number of days in a year):

$$\text{Collection period} = \frac{360}{\text{Accounts receivable turnover}}$$

Using the figures from Consumer Electronics in Illustration 11.5, the receivables collection period is:

$$\frac{360}{6} = 60 \text{ days}$$

An alternative computation, known as **days' sales in receivables,** is to divide *ending* accounts receivable by average daily sales as follows:

$$\text{Days' sales in receivables} = \text{Accounts receivable} \div \frac{\text{Sales}}{360}$$

This measure differs from the foregoing collection period computation. The accounts receivable collection period uses *average* accounts receivable, while the latter alternative computation uses *ending* accounts receivable. Again, using data from Consumer Electronics, the alternative computation is as follows:

$$\frac{\text{Accounts receivable}}{\text{Average daily sales}} = \frac{\$250{,}000}{(\$1{,}200{,}000/360)} = \frac{\$250{,}000}{\$3{,}333} = 75 \text{ days}$$

Interpretation of Receivables Liquidity Measures

Accounts receivable turnover rates and collection periods are usefully compared with industry averages or with the credit terms given by the company. When the collection period is compared with the terms of sale allowed by the company, we can assess the extent of customers paying on time. For example, if usual credit terms of sale are 40 days, then an average collection period of 75 days reflects one or more of the following conditions:

- Poor collection efforts.
- Delays in customer payments.
- Customers in financial distress.

The first condition demands corrective managerial action, while the other two reflect on both the quality and liquidity of accounts receivable and demand judicious managerial action. An initial step is to determine whether accounts receivable are representative of company sales activity. For example, receivables may be sold to SPEs and, if the SPEs are properly structured, the receivables are removed from the books. Intermittent sales of accounts receivable may, therefore, distort the ratio computations. It is not uncommon for companies to continue to service the accounts for the SPE. In this case the total amount of serviced receivables is provided in the footnotes. These can be added to those reported on the balance sheet to arrive at total outstanding receivables. The turnover ratios are then computed using total outstanding receivables.

Another complication relates to whether the receivable turnover ratios are computed based on gross or net accounts receivable. If the latter, the resulting computations are affected by the company's degree of conservatism in estimating uncollectible accounts. It is generally preferable to compute turnover ratios based on gross receivables to avoid this problem.

Certain trend analyses also merit our study. The trend in collection period over time is important in helping assess the quality and liquidity of receivables. Another trend to watch is the relation between the provision for doubtful accounts and gross accounts receivable, computed as:

$$\frac{\text{Provision for doubtful accounts}}{\text{Gross accounts receivable}}$$

Increases in this ratio over time suggest a decline in the collectibility of receivables. Conversely, decreases in this ratio suggest improved collectibility or the need to reevaluate the adequacy of the doubtful accounts provision. Overall, accounts receivable liquidity measures are important in our analysis. They are also important as measures of asset utilization, a subject we addressed in Chapter 8.

Inventory Turnover Measures

Inventories often constitute a substantial proportion of current assets. The reasons for this often have little to do with a company's need to maintain adequate liquid funds. Inventories are investments made for purposes of obtaining a return through sales to customers. In most companies, a certain level of inventory must be kept. If inventory is inadequate, sales volume declines below an attainable level. Conversely, excessive inventories expose a company to storage costs, insurance, taxes, obsolescence, and physical deterioration. Excessive inventories also tie up funds that can be used more profitably elsewhere. Due to risks in holding inventories, and given that inventories are further removed from cash than receivables are, they are normally considered the least liquid current asset. Our evaluation of short-term liquidity and working capital, which involves inventories, must include an evaluation of the quality and liquidity of inventories. Measures of inventory turnover are excellent tools for this analysis.

Inventory Turnover

The **inventory turnover ratio** measures the average rate of speed at which inventories move through and out of a company. Inventory turnover is computed as:

$$\frac{\text{Cost of goods sold}}{\text{Average inventory}}$$

Consistency requires we use cost of goods sold in the numerator because, like inventories, it is reported at cost. Sales, in contrast, includes a profit margin. Average inventory is computed by adding the beginning and ending inventory balances, and dividing by two. This averaging computation can be refined by averaging quarterly or monthly inventory figures. When we are interested in evaluating the *level* of inventory at a specific date, such as year-end, we compute the inventory turnover ratio using the inventory balance at that date in the denominator.

Sales-Based Inventory Turnover Ratio for Selected Industries

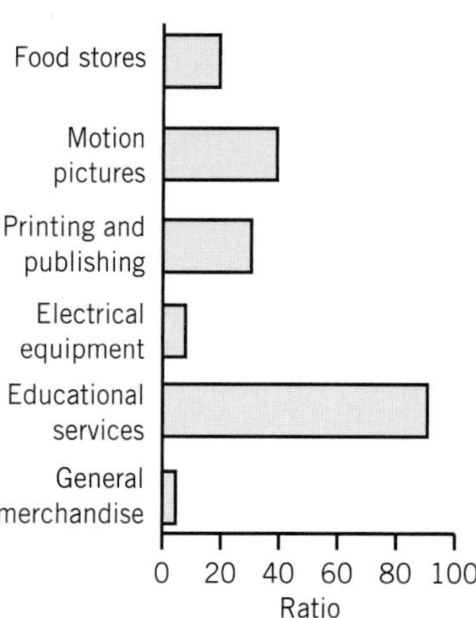

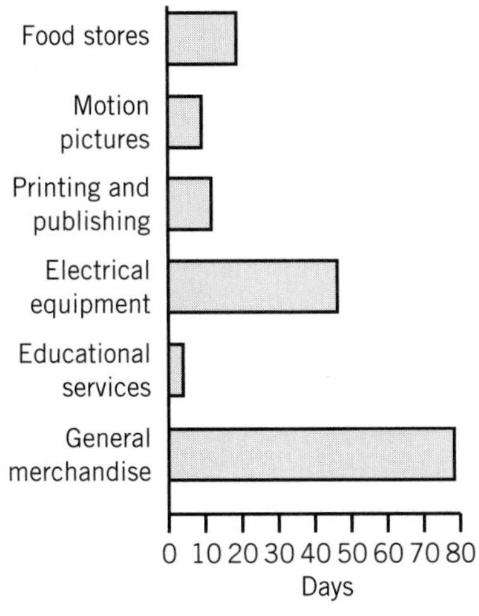

Days to Sell Inventory

Another measure of inventory turnover useful in assessing a company's purchasing and production policy is the number of days to sell inventory. The **days to sell inventory ratio** is computed as:

$$\frac{360}{\text{Inventory turnover}}$$

This ratio tells us the number of days a company takes in selling *average* inventory for that year. An alternative computation, referred to as the **days' sales in inventory,** is computed as:

$$\frac{\text{Ending inventory}}{\text{Cost of average day's sales}}$$

This alternative ratio tells us the number of days required to sell *ending* inventory assuming a given rate of sales. The cost of average days' sales is computed as:

$$\frac{\text{Cost of goods sold}}{360}$$

Illustration 11.6 provides an example.

ILLUSTRATION 11.6 Selected financial information from Macon Resources for Year 8 is reproduced below:

Sales	$1,800,000
Cost of goods sold	1,200,000
Beginning inventory	200,000
Ending inventory	400,000

Inventory turnover ratios using average inventory are computed as:

$$\text{Inventory turnover ratio} = \frac{\$1,200,000}{(\$200,000 + \$400,000) \div 2} = 4$$

$$\text{Days to sell inventory ratio} = \frac{360}{4} = 90 \text{ days}$$

Inventory turnover ratios based on *ending* inventory equal:

$$\text{Cost of average days' sales} = \frac{\$1,200,000}{360} = \$3,333$$

$$\text{Days' sales in inventory} = \frac{\$400,000}{\$3,333} = 120 \text{ days}$$

Interpreting Inventory Turnover

The current ratio views current asset components as sources of funds to potentially pay off current liabilities. Viewed similarly, inventory turnover ratios offer measures of both the quality and liquidity of the inventory component of current assets. *Quality of inventory* refers to a company's ability to use and dispose of inventory. We should recognize, however, that a continuing company does not use inventory for paying current liabilities since any serious reduction in normal inventory levels likely cuts into sales volume.

When inventory turnover decreases over time, or is less than the industry norm, it suggests slow-moving inventory items attributed to obsolescence, weak demand, or nonsalability. These conditions question the feasibility of a company recovering inventory costs. We need further analysis in this case to see if decreasing inventory turnover is due to inventory buildup in anticipation of sales increases, contractual commitments, increasing prices, work stoppages, inventory shortages, or other legitimate reason. We also must be aware of inventory management (such as just-in-time systems) aimed at keeping inventory levels low by integrating ordering, producing, selling, and distributing. Effective inventory management increases inventory turnover.

Another useful inventory liquidity measure is its **conversion period** or **operating cycle.** This measure combines the collection period of receivables with the days to sell inventories to obtain the time interval to convert inventories to cash. Using results computed from our two independent illustrations above, we would compute the conversion period as:

Days to sell inventory	90
Collection period	60
Conversion period	150

This implies it takes 150 days for a company to both sell its inventory and to collect the receivables.

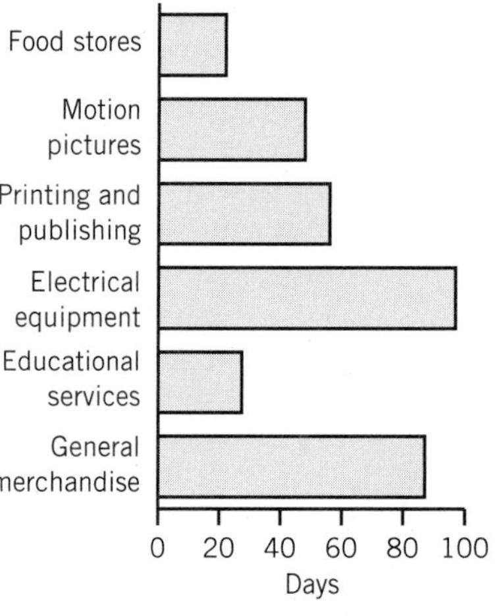

In evaluating inventory turnover, our analysis must be alert to the influence of alternative accounting principles for valuing the ratio's components. Our discussion of accounting for inventory in Chapter 4 is relevant here. Use of the LIFO method of inventory valuation can seriously impair the usefulness of both turnover and current ratios. For example, inventory valuation affects both the numerator and denominator of the current ratio–the latter through its effect on taxes payable. Information is often available in the financial statements enabling us to adjust unrealistically low LIFO inventory values in times of rising prices, making these values useful for inclusion in turnover and current ratios. Notice that even if two companies use the LIFO method for inventory valuation, their inventory-based ratios are likely *not* comparable because their LIFO inventory pools (bases) are almost certainly acquired in different years with different price levels. We also must remember that companies using a "natural year" may have at year-end an atypically low inventory level. This can increase a turnover ratio to an abnormally high level.

ANALYSIS VIEWPOINT ***. . . YOU ARE THE CONSULTANT***

King Entertainment, Inc., engages your services as a management consultant. One of your tasks is to streamline costs of inventory. After studying prior performance and inventory reports, you propose to strategically reduce inventories through improved inventory management. Your proposal expects the current inventory turnover of 20 will increase to 25. Money not invested in inventory can be used to decrease current liabilities—the costs of holding current liabilities average 10% per year. What is your estimate of cost savings if predicted sales are $150 million and predicted cost of sales is $100 million?

Answer–p. 560

Liquidity of Current Liabilities

Current liabilities are important in computing both working capital and the current ratio for two related reasons:

1. Current liabilities are used in determining whether the excess of current assets over current liabilities affords a sufficient margin of safety.
2. Current liabilities are deducted from current assets in arriving at working capital.

In using working capital and the current ratio, the point of view is one of liquidation and *not* of continuing operations. This is because in normal operations current liabilities are not paid off but are of a refunding nature. Provided sales remain stable, both purchases and current liabilities should remain steady. Increasing sales usually yield increasing current liabilities.

Quality of Current Liabilities

The quality of current liabilities is important in analysis of working capital and the current ratio. Not all current liabilities represent equally urgent or forceful payment demands. At one extreme, we find liabilities for various taxes that must be paid promptly regardless of current financial pressures. Collection powers of federal, state, and local government authorities are formidable. At the other extreme are current liabilities to suppliers with whom a company has a long-standing relationship and who depend on and value its business. Postponement and renegotiation of these liabilities in times of financial pressures are both possible and common.

The quality of current liabilities must be judged on their degree of urgency in payment. We should recognize if fund inflows from current revenues are viewed as available for paying current liabilities, then labor and similar expenses requiring prompt payment have a first call on revenues. Trade payables and other liabilities are paid only after these outlays are met. We examined this aspect of funds flow in the prior chapter.

Our analysis also must be aware of unrecorded liabilities having a claim on current funds. Examples are purchase commitments and certain postretirement and lease obligations. When long-term loan acceleration clauses exist, a failure to meet current installments can render the entire debt due and payable.

Days' Purchases in Accounts Payable

A measure of the extent to which accounts payable represent current and not overdue obligations is the **days' purchases in accounts payable ratio.** This ratio is computed as:

$$\text{Days' purchases in accounts payable} = \frac{\text{Accounts payable}}{\text{Purchases} \div 360}$$

One difficulty we often encounter when computing this ratio is that purchases are usually not separately reported in financial statements. For merchandising companies, an approximation of purchases is obtained by adjusting cost of goods sold for any included depreciation, other noncash charges, and changes in inventories as follows:

$$\text{Purchases} = \text{Adjusted cost of goods sold} + \text{Ending inventory} - \text{Beginning inventory}$$

A related measure is **accounts payable turnover.** It is computed as: Purchases ÷ Average accounts payable. This ratio indicates the speed at which a company pays for purchases on account.

ADDITIONAL LIQUIDITY MEASURES

Current Assets Composition

The composition of current assets is an indicator of working capital liquidity. Use of common-size percentage comparisons facilitates our evaluation of comparative liquidity, regardless of the dollar amounts. Consider Illustration 11.7 as a case example.

ILLUSTRATION 11.7

Texas Electric's current assets along with their common-size percentages are reproduced below for Years 1 and 2:

	Year 1		Year 2	
Current assets:				
Cash	$ 30,000	30%	$ 20,000	20%
Accounts receivable	40,000	40	30,000	30
Inventories	30,000	30	50,000	50
Total current assets	$100,000	100%	$100,000	100%

An analysis of Texas Electric's common-size percentages reveals a marked deterioration in current asset liquidity in Year 2 relative to Year 1. This is evidenced by a 10% decline for both cash and accounts receivable.

Acid-Test (Quick) Ratio

A more stringent test of liquidity uses the **acid-test (quick) ratio.** This ratio includes those assets most quickly convertible to cash and is computed as:

$$\frac{\text{Cash} + \text{Cash equivalents} + \text{Marketable securities} + \text{Accounts receivable}}{\text{Current liabilities}}$$

Inventories are often the least liquid of current assets and are not included in the acid-test ratio. Another reason for excluding inventories is that their valuation typically involves more managerial discretion than required for other current assets. Yet we must remember that inventories for some companies are more liquid than slow-paying receivables. Our analysis must assess the merits of excluding inventories in evaluating liquidity. The interpretation of the acid-test ratio is similar to that of the current ratio.

Dun & Bradstreet's Quick Ratio for Selected Industries

(Cash + Account receivables/ Current liabilities)

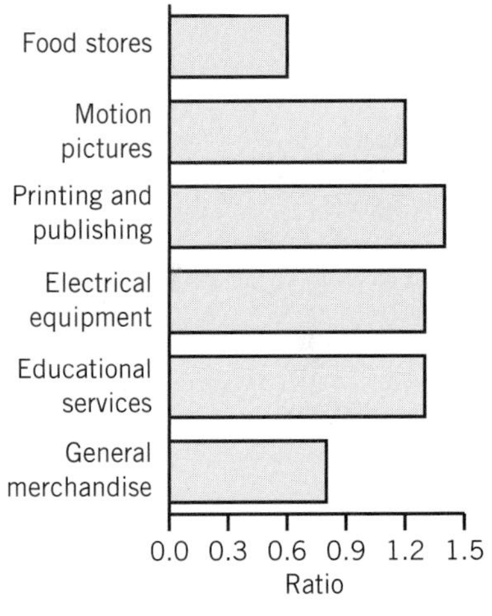

Cash Flow Measures

The static nature of the current ratio and its inability (as a measure of liquidity) to recognize the importance of cash flows in meeting maturing obligations has led to a search for a dynamic measure of liquidity. Since liabilities are paid with cash, a comparison of operating cash flow to current liabilities is important. A ratio comparing operating cash flow to current liabilities overcomes the static nature of the current ratio since its numerator reflects a flow variable. This **cash flow ratio** is computed as:

$$\frac{\text{Operating cash flow}}{\text{Current liabilities}}$$

The cash flow ratio computation for Campbell Soup in Year 11 is (data taken from financial statements reproduced in Appendix A):

$$\frac{\$805.2}{\$1,278} = 0.63$$

A ratio of operating cash flow to current liabilities of 0.40 or higher is common for healthy companies.

Financial Flexibility

There are important *qualitative* considerations bearing on short-term liquidity. These are usefully characterized as depending on the financial flexibility of a company. **Financial flexibility** is the ability of a company to take steps to counter unexpected interruptions in the flow of funds. It can mean the ability to borrow from various sources, to raise equity capital, to sell and redeploy assets, or to adjust the level and direction of operations to meet changing circumstances. A company's capacity to borrow depends on several factors and is subject to change. It depends on profitability, stability, size, industry position, asset composition, and capital structure. It also depends on credit market conditions and trends. A company's capacity to borrow is important as a source of cash and in turning over short-term debt. Prearranged financing or open lines of credit are reliable sources of cash. Additional factors bearing on an assessment of a company's financial flexibility are (1) ratings of its commercial paper, bonds, and preferred stock, (2) any restrictions on its sale of assets, (3) the extent expenses are discretionary, and (4) ability to respond quickly to changing conditions (such as strikes, demand shifts, and breaks in supply sources).

Management's Discussion and Analysis

As we discussed in Chapter 1, the Securities and Exchange Commission requires companies to include in their annual reports an expanded management discussion and analysis of financial condition and results of operations (MD&A). The financial condition section requires a discussion of liquidity–including known trends, demands, commitments, or uncertainties likely to impact the company's ability to generate adequate cash. If a material deficiency in liquidity is identified, management must discuss the course of action it has taken or proposes to take to remedy the deficiency. Internal and external sources of liquidity and any material unused sources of liquid assets must be identified and described. Our analysis benefits from management's discussion and analysis. For example, Kodak includes a useful discussion titled Liquidity and Capital Resources in its MD&A section (see Appendix A).

CRIME SPREE

One in five employees has witnessed fraud in the workplace. Here's what their co-workers are doing:

Taking supplies or shoplifting	37%
Stealing products or cash	25
Claiming extra hours worked	18
Inflating expense accounts	8
Accepting kickbacks from suppliers	6
Phony bookkeeping	3

What-If Analysis

What-if analysis is a useful technique to trace through the effects of changes in conditions or policies on the resources of a company. What-if analysis is illustrated in this section using the following selected financial data from Consolidated Technologies, Inc., at December 31, Year 1:

Cash	$ 70,000
Accounts receivable	150,000
Inventory	65,000
Fixed assets	200,000
Accumulated depreciation	43,000
Accounts payable	130,000
Notes payable	35,000
Accrued tax liability	18,000
Capital stock	200,000

The following additional information is reported for the year ended December 31, Year 1:

Sales	$750,000
Cost of sales	520,000
Purchases	350,000
Depreciation	25,000
Net income	20,000

Consolidated Technologies anticipates 10% growth in sales for Year 2. All revenue and expense items are expected to increase by 10%, except for depreciation, which remains the same. All expenses are paid in cash as they are incurred, and Year 2 ending inventory is projected at $150,000. By the end of Year 2, Consolidated Technologies expects to have notes payable of $50,000 and a zero balance in accrued taxes. The company maintains a minimum cash balance of $50,000 as a managerial policy.

Case 11.1 Consolidated Technologies is considering a change in credit policy where ending accounts receivable reflect 90 days of sales. What impact does this change have on the company's cash balance? Will this change affect the company's need to borrow? Our analysis of this what-if situation is as follows:

CONSOLIDATED TECHNOLOGIES
Cash Forecast
For Year Ended December 31, Year 2

Cash, January 1, Year 2			$ 70,000
Cash collections:			
Accounts receivable, January 1, Year 2		$150,000	
Sales		825,000	
Total potential cash collections		975,000	
Less: Accounts receivable, December 31, Year 2		(206,250)[a]	768,750
Total cash available			838,750
Cash disbursements:			
Accounts payable, January 1, Year 2	$130,000		
Purchases	657,000[b]		
Total potential cash disbursements	787,000		
Accounts payable, December 31, Year 2	(244,000)[c]	543,000	
Notes payable, January 1, Year 2	35,000		
Notes payable, December 31, Year 2	(50,000)	(15,000)	
Accrued taxes		18,000	
Cash expenses[d]		203,500	749,500
Cash, December 31, Year 2			89,250
Cash balance desired			50,000
Cash excess			$ 39,250

Explanations:

(a) $\$825{,}000 \times \frac{90}{360} = \$206{,}250.$

(b)

Year 2 cost of sales: $520,000 × 1.1 =*	*$572,000*
Ending inventory (given)	*150,000*
Goods available for sale	*$722,000*
Beginning inventory	*(65,000)*
Purchases	*$657,000*

* *Excluding depreciation.*

(c) $\text{Purchases} \times \frac{\text{Beg. accounts payable}}{\text{Year 1 purchases}} = \$657{,}000 \times \frac{\$130{,}000}{\$350{,}000} = \$244{,}000$

(d)

Gross profit ($825,000 − $572,000)		*$253,000*
Less: Net income	*$24,500**	
Depreciation	*25,000*	*(49,500)*
Other cash expenses		*$203,500*

* *110% of $20,000 (Year 1 income) + 10% of $25,000 (Year 1 depreciation).*

This change in credit policy would yield an excess in cash and no required borrowing.

Case 11.2 What if Consolidated Technologies worked to achieve an *average* accounts receivable turnover of 4.0 (instead of using *ending* receivables as in the previous case)? What impact does this change have on the company's cash balance? Our analysis of this what-if situation follows:

Excess cash balance as computed above		$39,250
Change from *ending* to *average* accounts receivable turnover increases year-end accounts receivable to:		

$$\text{Average A. R.} = \frac{\$825{,}000}{4} = \$206{,}250$$

$$\text{Ending A. R.} = [\$206{,}250 \times 2] - \$150{,}000 = \$262{,}500^{a}$$

Less: Accounts receivable balance from Case 11.1	(206,250)	56,250 (cash decrease)
Cash to be borrowed		$17,000 (cash deficit)

[a] *Average A. R.* $= \frac{\text{Sales}}{\text{Average A. R. turnover}}$; *Ending A. R. = [(Average A. R.) × 2] − Beginning A. R.*

Consolidated Technologies would be required to borrow funds to achieve expected performance under the conditions specified.

Case 11.3 What if, in addition to the conditions prevailing in Case 11.2, the company's suppliers require payment within 60 days? What is the effect of this payment requirement on the cash balance? Our analysis of this case is as follows:

Cash required to borrow (from Case 11.2)		$ 17,000
Ending accounts payable (from Case 11.1)	$244,000	
Ending accounts payable under 60-day payment:		
Purchases $\times \frac{60}{360} = \$657{,}000 \times \frac{60}{360} =$	(109,500)	
Additional disbursements required		134,500
Cash to be borrowed		$151,500

This more demanding payment schedule from suppliers would place additional borrowing requirements on Consolidated Technologies.

SECTION 2: CAPITAL STRUCTURE AND SOLVENCY

BASICS OF SOLVENCY

Analyzing solvency of a company is markedly different from analyzing liquidity. In liquidity analysis, the time horizon is sufficiently short for reasonably accurate forecasts of cash flows. Long-term forecasts are less reliable and, consequently, analysis of solvency uses less precise but more encompassing analytical measures.

Analysis of solvency involves several key elements. Analysis of capital structure is one of these. *Capital structure* refers to the sources of financing for a company. Financing can range from relatively permanent equity capital to more risky or temporary short-term financing sources. Once a company obtains financing, it subsequently invests it in various assets. Assets represent secondary sources of security for lenders and range from loans secured by specific assets to assets available as general security for unsecured creditors. These and other factors yield different risks associated with different assets and financing sources.

Another key element of long-term solvency is *earnings* (or *earning power*)–implying the recurring ability to generate cash from operations. Earnings-based measures are important and reliable indicators of financial strength. Earnings is the most desirable and reliable source of cash for long-term payment of interest and debt principal. As a measure of cash inflows from operations, earnings is crucial to covering long-term interest and other fixed charges. A stable earnings stream is an important measure of a company's ability to borrow in times of cash shortage. It is also a measure of the likelihood of a company's rebounding from conditions of financial distress.

Lenders guard themselves against company insolvency and financial distress by including loan covenants in the lending agreements. Loan covenants set conditions of *default,* often based on accounting measures, at a level to allow the lender the opportunity to collect on the loan before severe financial distress. Covenants are often designed to (1) emphasize key measures of financial strength like the current ratio and debt to equity ratio, (2) prohibit the issuance of additional debt, or (3) ensure against disbursement of company resources through excessive dividends or acquisitions. Covenants cannot assure lenders against operating losses–invariably the source of financial distress. Covenants and protective provisions also cannot substitute for our alertness and monitoring of a company's results of operations and financial condition. The enormous amount of both public and private debt financing has led to some standardized approaches to its analysis and evaluation. While this chapter explains many of these approaches, Appendix 11A discusses the analysis of debt securities by rating agencies, and Appendix 11B describes the use of ratios as predictors of financial distress.

DEBT LIMIT
Each year, about 40% of small-business owners seek a loan. Banks reject about one-quarter of them.

Importance of Capital Structure

Capital structure is the equity and debt financing of a company. It is often measured in terms of the relative magnitude of the various financing sources. A company's financial stability and risk of insolvency depend on its financing sources and the types and amounts of various assets it owns. Exhibit 11.1 portrays a typical company's asset distribution and its financing sources. This exhibit highlights the potential variety in the investing and financing items that comprise a company–depicted within the accounting framework of assets equal liabilities plus equity.

Capital Structure

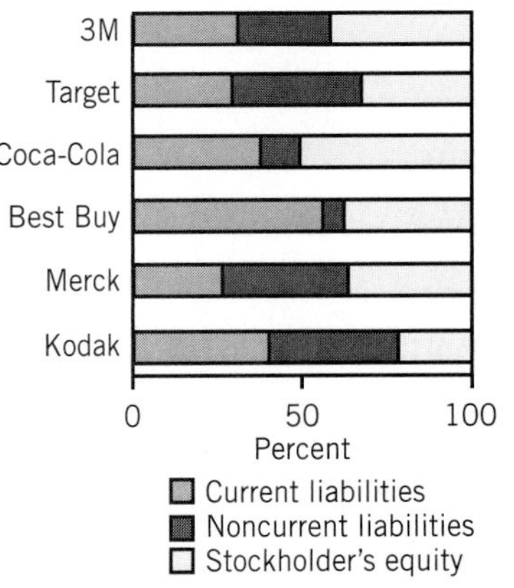

Exhibit 11.1 *A Typical Company's Asset Distribution and Capital Structure*

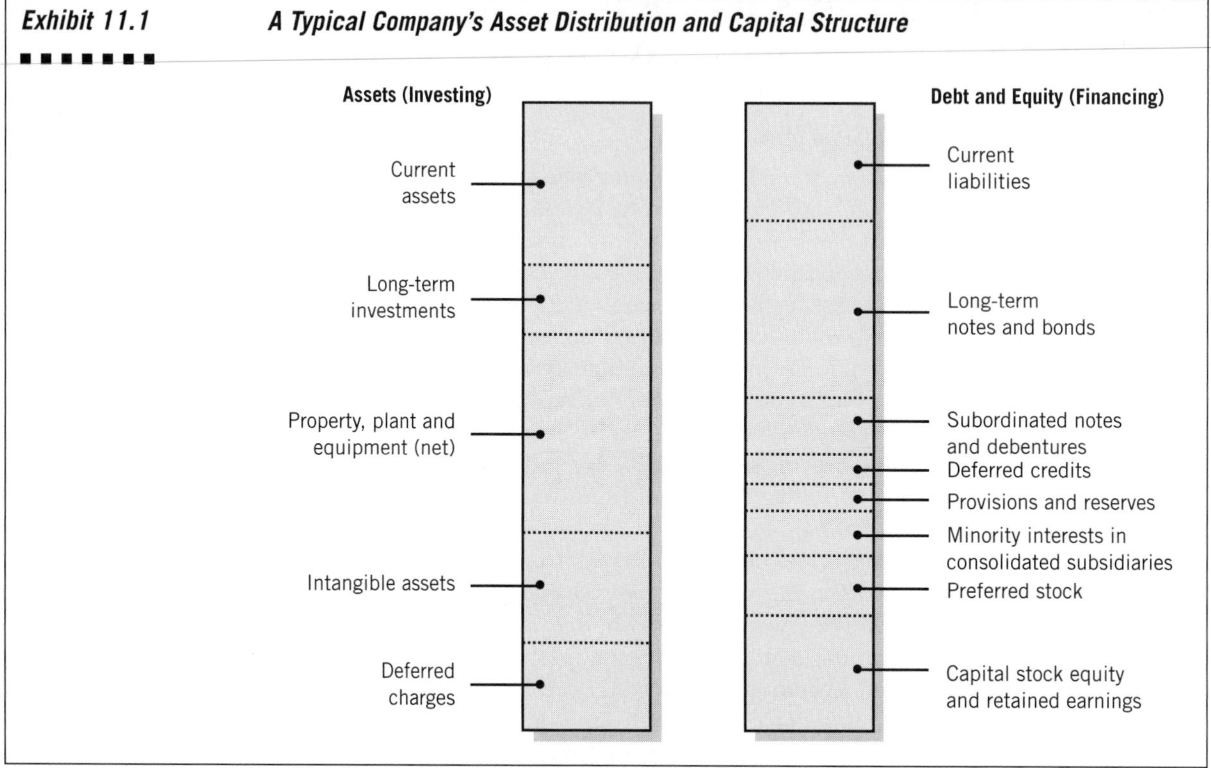

Characteristics of Debt and Equity

The importance of analyzing capital structure derives from several perspectives, not the least is the difference between debt and equity. **Equity** refers to the *risk capital* of a company. Characteristics of equity capital include its uncertain or unspecified return and its lack of any repayment pattern. Equity capital contributes to a company's stability and solvency. It is usually characterized by a degree of permanence, persistence in times of adversity, and a lack of any mandatory dividend requirement. A company can confidently invest equity financing in long-term assets and expose them to business risks without threat of recall.

Unlike equity capital, both short-term and long-term **debt** capital must be repaid. The longer the debt repayment period and the less demanding its repayment provisions, the easier it is for a company to service debt capital. Still, debt must be repaid at specified times regardless of a company's financial condition, and so too must periodic interest on most debt. Failure to pay principal and interest typically results in legal proceedings where common shareholders can lose control of the company and all or part of their investment. When the proportion of debt in the total capital structure of a company is larger, the higher are the resulting fixed charges and repayment commitments. The likelihood of a company's inability to pay interest and principal when due and potential losses for creditors also increases.

For investors in common stock, debt reflects a risk of loss of the investment, balanced by the potential of profits from financial leverage. **Financial leverage** is the use of debt to increase earnings. Leverage magnifies both managerial success (income) and failure (losses). Excessive debt limits management's initiative and flexibility for pursuing profitable opportunities. For creditors, increased equity capital is preferred as protection against losses from adversities. Lowering equity capital as a proportionate share of a company's financing decreases creditors' protection against loss and consequently

Trading on the Equity—Returns for Different Earnings Levels ($ millions) ***Exhibit 11.2***

	Assets	Financing Sources: Debt	Financing Sources: Equity	Income before Interest and Taxes	10% Debt Interest	Taxes*	Net Income	Net Income + [Interest × (1 − Tax Rate)]	Return on Assets†	Return on Equity‡
Year 1:										
Risky, Inc.	$1,000	$400	$ 600	$200	$40	$64	$ 96	$120	12%	16%
Safety, Inc.	1,000	0	1,000	200	0	80	120	120	12	12
Year 2:										
Risky, Inc.	1,000	400	600	100	40	24	36	60	6	6
Safety, Inc.	1,000	0	1,000	100	0	40	60	60	6	6
Year 3:										
Risky, Inc.	1,000	400	600	50	40	4	6	30	3	1
Safety, Inc.	1,000	0	1,000	50	0	20	30	30	3	3

*Tax rate is 40%.

†Return on assets = [Net income + Interest (1 − 0.40)]/Assets.

‡Return on equity = Net income/Shareholders' equity.

increases credit risk. Our analysis task is to measure the degree of risk resulting from a company's capital structure. The remainder of this section looks at the motivation for debt capital and measuring its effects.

Motivation for Debt Capital

A primary motivation for a company financing its business activities through debt is its potential for lower cost. From a shareholder's perspective, debt is *less expensive* than equity financing for at least two reasons:

1. Interest on most debt is fixed and, provided interest is less than the return earned from debt financing, the excess return goes to the benefit of equity investors.
2. Interest is a tax-deductible expense whereas dividends are not.

We discuss each of these factors in this section due to their importance for debt financing and risk analysis.

Concept of Financial Leverage

Companies typically carry both debt and equity financing. Creditors are generally unwilling to provide financing without protection provided by equity financing. Financial leverage refers to the amount of debt financing (that pays a fixed return) in a company's capital structure. Companies with financial leverage are said to be **trading on the equity.** This indicates a company is using equity capital as a borrowing base in a desire to reap excess returns.

Exhibit 11.2 illustrates trading on the equity. This exhibit computes the returns achieved for two companies referred to as Risky, Inc., and Safety, Inc. These two companies have identical assets and income before interest expense. Risky, Inc., derives 40% of its financing from debt while Safety, Inc., is debt-free, or *unlevered.* For Year 1, when the average return on total assets is 12%, the return on stockholders' equity of Risky, Inc., is 16%. This higher return to stockholders is due to the excess return on

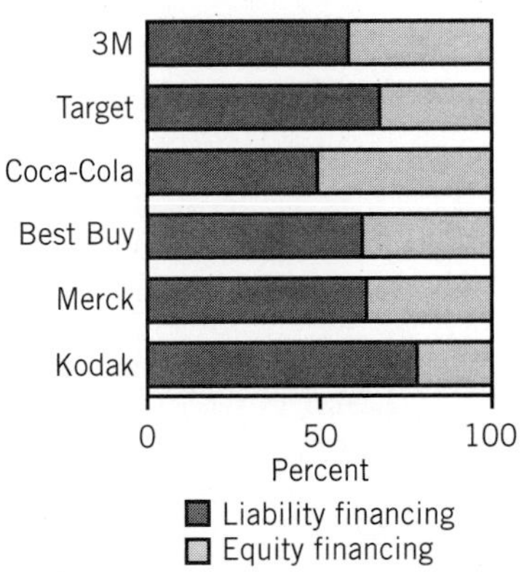

assets over the *after-tax* cost of debt (12% versus 6%, the latter computed as 10% [*1 − 0.40*]). Safety, Inc.'s return on equity always equals the return on assets since there is no debt. For Year 2, the return on assets of Risky, Inc., equals the after-tax cost of debt and, consequently, the effects of leverage are neutralized. For Year 3, leverage is shown to be a double-edged sword. Specifically, when the return on assets is *less* than the after-tax cost of debt, Risky, Inc.'s return on equity is lower than the return on equity for debt-free Safety, Inc. To generalize from this example: (1) an unlevered company's return on assets is identical to its return on equity, (2) a levered company is *successfully* trading on the equity when return on assets exceeds the after-tax cost of debt (alternatively stated, return on assets is less than return on equity), (3) a levered company is *unsuccessfully* trading on the equity when return on assets is less than the after-tax cost of debt (alternatively stated, return on assets exceeds return on equity), and (4) effects of leveraging are magnified in both good *and* bad years (for example, when return on assets drops below the after-tax cost of debt, a levered company's return on equity drops even farther).

Tax Deductibility of Interest

One reason for the advantageous position of debt is the *tax deductibility of interest.* We illustrate this tax advantage by extending the case in Exhibit 11.2. Let us reexamine the two companies' results ($ millions) for Year 2:

Year 2	Risky, Inc.	Safety, Inc.
Income before interest and taxes	$100	$100
Interest (10% of $400)	(40)	0
Income before taxes	$ 60	$100
Taxes (40%)	(24)	(40)
Net income	$ 36	$ 60
Add back interest paid to bondholder	40	0
Total return to security holders (debt and equity)	$ 76	$ 60

Recall the leverage effects are neutral in Year 2. Still, notice that even when the return on assets equals the after-tax cost of debt, the total amount available for distribution to debt and equity holders of Risky, Inc., is $16 higher than the amount available for the equity holders of Safety, Inc. This is due to the lower tax liability for Risky, Inc. We must remember the value of tax deductibility of interest depends on having sufficient income. To generalize from this example: (1) interest is tax deductible while cash dividends to equity holders are not, (2) because interest is tax deductible the income available to security holders can be much larger, and (3) nonpayment of interest can yield bankruptcy whereas nonpayment of dividends does not.

Other Effects of Leverage

Beyond the advantages from excess return to financial leverage and the tax deductibility of interest, a long-term debt position can yield other benefits to equity holders. For example, a growth company can avoid earnings dilution through issuance of debt. In addition, if interest rates are increasing, a leveraged company paying a fixed lower interest rate is more profitable than its nonleveraged competitor. However, the reverse is also true. Finally, in times of inflation, monetary liabilities (like most debt capital) yield price-level gains.

Financial Leverage Ratio

The **financial leverage ratio** measures the relation between total assets and the common equity capital that finances assets. It is expressed as:

$$\frac{\text{Total assets}}{\text{Common equity capital}}$$

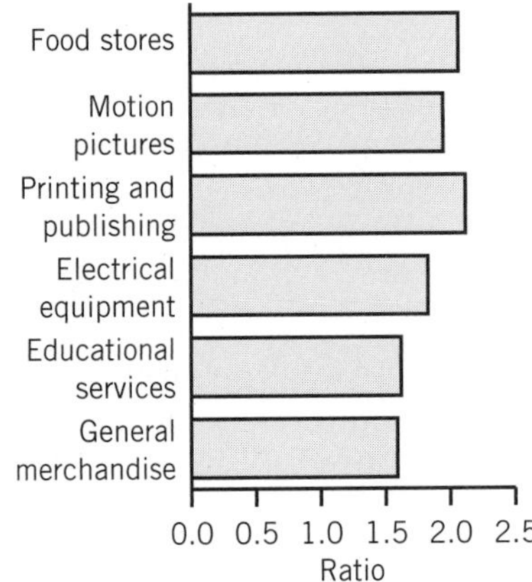

The greater the proportion of assets financed by common equity capital, the lower the financial leverage ratio. For a company successfully utilizing leverage, a higher financial leverage ratio enhances return on equity. Concurrently, the risk inherent in a change in profitability is greater when the financial leverage ratio is higher. The financial leverage ratio of Risky, Inc., (see Exhibit 11.2) at the end of Year 3 is:

$$\frac{\$1{,}000 \text{ mil.}}{\$600 \text{ mil.}} = 1.67$$

This financial leverage ratio indicates that every dollar of common equity commands \$1.67 in assets for the company. We showed in Chapter 8 how the financial leverage ratio can be viewed as a component of the analytical disaggregation of return on equity.

ANALYSIS VIEWPOINT . . . YOU ARE THE ENTREPRENEUR

You are the entrepreneur and sole shareholder of a small, start-up restaurant. Your business is unlevered and doing well. The most recent year's return on assets is 9% on assets of \$200,000 (the tax rate is 40%). You are considering expanding your business but need to take on debt to finance expansion. What is your criterion in deciding whether to expand by adding debt?

Answer–p. 560

Adjustments for Capital Structure Analysis

Measurement and disclosure of liability (debt) and equity accounts in financial statements are governed by the application of accepted accounting principles. We discussed principles governing measurement and disclosure of liability and equity accounts in Chapter 3. Our analysis must remember these principles when analyzing capital structure and its implications for solvency.

Adjustments to Book Values of Liabilities

The relation between liabilities and equity capital, the two major sources of a company's financing, is an important factor in assessing long-term solvency. An understanding of this relation is therefore essential in our analysis. There exist liabilities not fully reflected in balance sheets and there are financing-related items whose accounting classification as debt or equity must not be blindly accepted in our analysis. Our identification and classification of these items depend on a thorough understanding of their economic substance and the conditions to which they are subject. The discussion in this section supplements the important analytical considerations in Chapter 3.

Deferred Income Taxes. An important question is whether we treat deferred taxes as a liability, as equity, or as part debt and part equity. Our answer depends on the nature of the deferral, past experience of the account (such as its growth pattern), and the likelihood of future reversals. In reaching our decision, we must recognize that, under normal circumstances, deferred taxes reverse and become payable when a company's size declines. A company declining in size is usually accompanied by losses rather than by positive taxable income. In this case the drawing down of deferred taxes likely involves credits to tax loss carryforwards or carrybacks rather than payments in cash. To the extent future reversals are a remote possibility, as conceivable with timing differences from accelerated depreciation, deferred taxes should be viewed like long-term financing and treated like equity. However, if the likelihood of a drawing down of deferred taxes in the foreseeable future is high, then deferred taxes (or part of them) should be treated like long-term liabilities.

Operating Leases. Current accounting practice requires that most financing long-term noncancelable leases be shown as debt. Yet companies have certain opportunities to structure leases in ways to avoid reporting them as debt. Operating leases should be recognized on the balance sheet for analytical purposes, increasing both fixed assets and liabilities as discussed in Chapter 3.

Off-Balance-Sheet Financing. In determining the debt for a company, our analysis must be aware that some managers attempt to understate debt, often with new and sometimes complex means. We discuss several means for doing this in Chapter 3 including take or pay contracts, sales of receivables, inventory repurchase agreements, and special purpose entities (SPEs). Our critical reading of notes and management comments, along with inquiries to management, can often shed light on the existence of unrecorded liabilities.

IHOP NOTES
International House of Pancakes (IHOP) allows most of its franchise fee to be paid for with a note.

Contingent Liabilities. Contingencies such as product guarantees and warranties represent obligations to offer future services or goods that are classified as liabilities. Typically, reserves created by charges to income are also considered liabilities. Our analysis must make a judgment regarding the likelihood of commitments or contingencies becoming actual liabilities and then treat these items accordingly. For example, guarantees of indebtedness of subsidiaries or others that are likely to become liabilities should be treated as liabilities.

Minority Interests. Minority interests in consolidated financial statements represent the book value of ownership interests of minority shareholders of subsidiaries in the consolidated group. These are *not* liabilities similar to debt because they have neither mandatory dividend payment nor principal repayment requirements. Capital structure measurements concentrate on the mandatory payment aspects of liabilities. From this point of view, minority interests are more like outsiders' claims to a portion of equity or an offset representing their proportionate ownership of assets.

Convertible Debt. Convertible debt is usually reported among liabilities (or as an item separate from both debt and equity listings). If conversion terms imply this debt will be converted into common stock, then it can be classified as equity for purposes of capital structure analysis.

Preferred Stock. Most preferred stock requires no obligation for payment of dividends or repayment of principal. These characteristics are similar to those of equity. However, as we discussed in Chapter 3, preferred stock with a fixed maturity or subject to sinking fund requirements should, from our analytical perspective, be considered debt. Preferred stock with mandatory redemption requirements is also similar to debt and should be considered as debt in our analysis. This is in spite of certain cases where default by a company on redemption provisions does not carry repercussions as severe as those from nonpayment of debt. An example of financing with redeemable preferred stock is BFGoodrich:

ANALYSIS EXCERPT

BFGoodrich has issued 250,000 shares of $7.85 cumulative preferred stock, series A. In order to comply with sinking-fund requirements, each year on August 15, BFGoodrich must redeem 12,500 shares . . . The redemption price is $100 per share, plus dividends accrued at the redemption date.

ANALYSIS VIEWPOINT ***. . . YOU ARE THE ANALYST***

You are an analyst for a securities firm. Your supervisor asks you to assess the relative risk of two potential *preferred equity* investments. Your analysis indicates these two companies are identical in all aspects of both returns and risks with the exception of their financing composition. The first company is financed 20% by debt, 20% from preferred equity, and 60% from common equity. The second is financed 30% by debt, 10% from preferred equity, and 60% from common equity. Which company presents the greater preferred equity risk?

Answer–p. 561

CAPITAL STRUCTURE COMPOSITION AND SOLVENCY

The fundamental risk with a leveraged capital structure is the risk of inadequate cash under conditions of adversity. Debt involves a commitment to pay fixed charges in the form of interest and principal repayments. While certain fixed charges can be postponed in times of cash shortages, the fixed charges related to debt cannot be postponed without adverse repercussions to a company's shareholders and creditors. This section discusses several measures commonly used to estimate the degree of financial leverage and to evaluate the risk of insolvency.

Common-Size Statements in Solvency Analysis

A common measure of financial risk for a company is its capital structure composition. **Composition analysis** is performed by constructing a **common-size statement** of the liabilities and equity section of the balance sheet. Exhibit 11.3 illustrates a common-size analysis for Tennessee Teletech, Inc. An advantage of common-size analysis of capital structure is in revealing the relative magnitude of financing sources for a company. We see Tennessee Teletech is primarily financed from common (35.6%) and preferred (17.8%) stock and liabilities (41.2%)–and a small amount of earnings is retained in the company (4.5%). Common-size analysis also lends itself to direct comparisons across different companies. A variation of common-size analysis is to perform the analysis using ratios. Another variation focuses only on long-term financing sources, excluding current liabilities.

Common-Size Analysis of Tennessee Teletech's Capital Structure

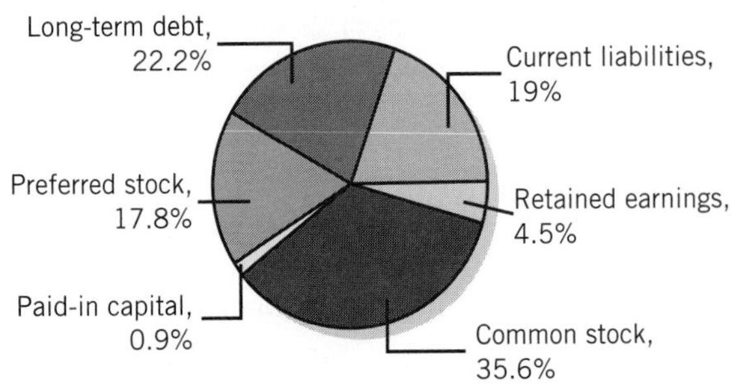

Exhibit 11.3 **Tennessee Teletech's Capital Structure: Common-Size Analysis**

Current liabilities	$ 428,000	19.0%
Long-term debt	500,000	22.2
Equity capital:		
Preferred stock	400,000	17.8
Common stock	800,000	35.6
Paid-in capital	20,000	0.9
Retained earnings	102,000	4.5
Total equity capital	1,322,000	58.8
Total liabilities and equity	$2,250,000	100.0%

Capital Structure Measures for Solvency Analysis

Capital structure ratios are another means of solvency analysis. Ratio measures of capital structure relate components of capital structure to each other or their total. In this section we describe the most common of these ratios. We must take care to understand the meaning and computation of any measure or ratio before applying it.

Total Debt to Total Capital

A comprehensive ratio is available to measure the relation between total debt (Current debt + Long-term debt + Other liabilities as determined by analysis such as deferred taxes and redeemable preferred) and total capital [Total debt + Stockholders' equity (including preferred)]. The **total debt to total capital ratio** (also called **total debt ratio**) is expressed as

$$\frac{\text{Total debt}}{\text{Total capital}}$$

Recall that total capital equals, by definition, total assets. The total debt to total capital ratio for Year 11 of Quaker Oats (financial statements are in Appendix A) is computed as:

$$\frac{\$926.9^{(a)} + \$701.2^{(b)} + \$115.5^{(c)} + \$366.7^{(d)}}{\$99.3^{(e)} + \$806.5^{(f)} + \$2,110.3^{(g)}} = \frac{\$2,110.3}{\$3,016.1} = 0.70$$

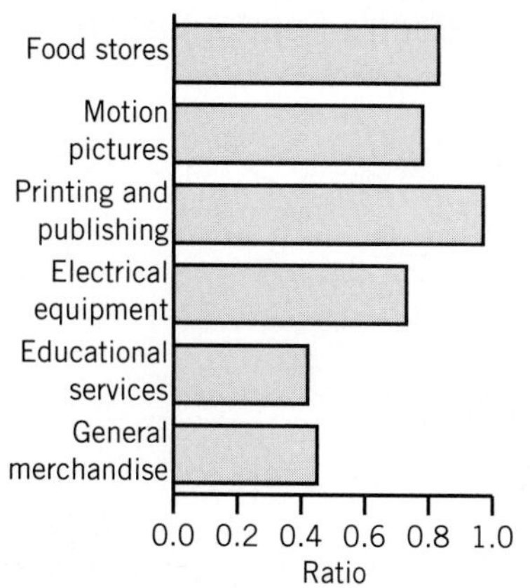

(a) Current liabilities
(b) Long-term debt
(c) Other liabilities
(d) Deferred income taxes
(e) Preferred stock outstanding
(f) Shareholders' equity
(g) Total debt (numerator)

This measure is often expressed in ratio form, such as 0.70, or described as debt constituting 70% of Quaker Oats' capital structure.

Total Debt to Equity Capital

Another measure of the relation of debt to capital sources is the ratio of total debt (as defined above) to *equity* capital. The **total debt to equity capital ratio** is defined as:

$$\frac{\text{Total debt}}{\text{Shareholders' equity}}$$

The total debt to equity capital ratio for Year 11 of Quaker Oats is computed as:

$$\frac{\$2{,}110.3}{\$99.3 + \$806.5} = 2.33$$

This ratio implies that Quaker Oats' total debt is 2.33 times its equity capital. Alternatively stated, Quaker Oats' credit financing equals \$2.33 for every \$1 of equity financing.

Long-Term Debt to Equity Capital

The **long-term debt to equity capital ratio** measures the relation of long-term debt (usually defined as all noncurrent liabilities) to equity capital. A ratio in excess of 1:1 indicates greater long-term debt financing compared to equity capital. This ratio is commonly referred to as the debt to equity ratio and it is computed as:

$$\frac{\text{Long-term debt}}{\text{Shareholders' equity}}$$

For Year 11 of Quaker Oats, the long-term debt to equity ratio equals:

$$\frac{\$2{,}110.3^{(a)} - \$926.9^{(b)}}{\$905.8^{(c)}} = 1.31$$

[a] Total debt

[b] Total current liabilities

[c] Shareholders' equity

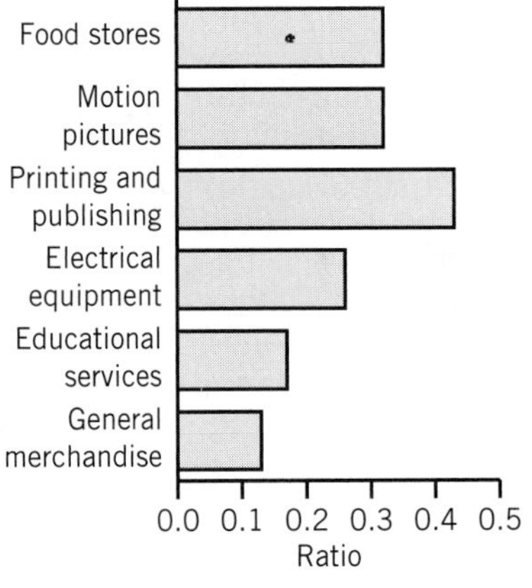

Short-Term Debt to Total Debt

The ratio of debt maturing in the short term relative to total debt is an important indicator of the short-run cash and financing needs of a company. Short-term debt, as opposed to long-term debt or sinking fund requirements, is an indicator of enterprise reliance on short-term (primarily bank) financing. Short-term debt is usually subject to frequent changes in interest rates.

Interpretation of Capital Structure Measures

Common-size and ratio analyses of capital structure are primarily measures of the *risk* of a company's capital structure. The higher the proportion of debt, the larger the fixed charges of interest and debt repayment, and the greater the likelihood of insolvency during periods of earnings decline or hardship. Capital structure measures serve as *screening devices*. For example, when the ratio of debt to equity capital is relatively small (10% or less), there is no apparent concern with this aspect of a company's financial condition–our analysis is probably better directed elsewhere. Should our analysis reveal debt is a significant part of capitalization, then further analysis is necessary. Extended analysis should focus on several different aspects of a company's financial condition, results of operations, and future prospects.

Analysis of short-term liquidity is always important because before we assess long-term solvency we want to be satisfied about the near-term financial survival of the company. We described various analyses of short-term liquidity already in this chapter. Loan and bond indenture covenants requiring maintenance of minimum working capital levels attest to the importance of current liquidity in ensuring a company's long-term solvency. Additional analytical tests of importance include the examination of debt

DEFAULT

A recent study indicates that fewer than 1% of companies that carry the "A" rating have defaulted on their debt. This compares to 35% of companies with the "B" rating that have defaulted.

maturities (as to amount and timing), interest costs, and risk-bearing factors. The latter factors include a company's earnings stability or persistence, industry performance, and composition of assets.

Asset-Based Measures of Solvency

This section describes two categories of asset-based analyses of a company's solvency.

Common-Size Analysis of Tennessee Teletech's Asset Composition

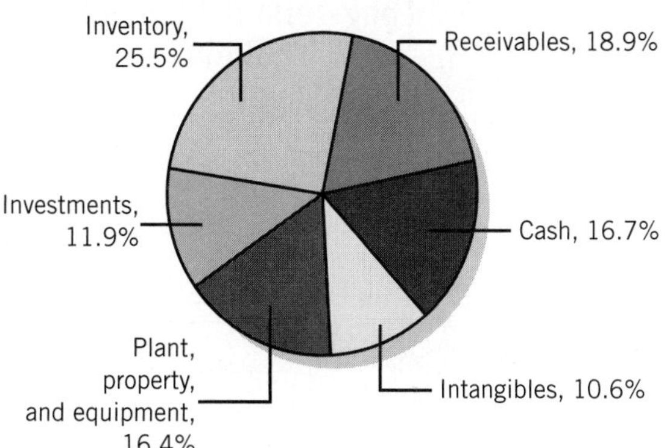

Asset Composition in Solvency Analysis

The assets a company employs in its operating activities determine to some extent the sources of financing. For example, fixed and other long-term assets are typically not financed with short-term loans. These long-term assets are usually financed with equity capital. Debt capital is also a common source of long-term asset financing, especially in industries like utilities where revenue sources are stable.

Asset composition analysis is an important tool in assessing the risk exposure of a company's capital structure. Asset composition is typically evaluated using common-size statements of asset balances. Exhibit 11.4 shows a common-size analysis of Tennessee Teletech's assets (its liabilities and equity are analyzed in Exhibit 11.3). Judging by the distribution of assets and the related capital structure, it appears that since a relatively high proportion of assets is current (61%), a 41% total liabilities position is not excessive. Further analysis and measurements might alter or reinforce this preliminary interpretation.

Exhibit 11.4 ***Tennessee Teletech's Asset Composition: Common-Size Analysis***

Current assets		
Cash	$ 376,000	16.7%
Accounts receivable (net)	425,000	18.9
Merchandise inventory	574,000	25.5
Total current assets	1,375,000	61.1
Investments	268,000	11.9
Plant, property, and equipment (net)	368,000	16.4
Intangibles	239,000	10.6
Total assets	$2,250,000	100.0%

EARNINGS COVERAGE

Our discussion of capital structure measures recognizes their usefulness as screening devices. They are a valuable means of deciding whether risk inherent in a company's capital structure requires further analysis. One limitation of capital structure measures is their inability to focus on availability of cash flows to service a company's debt. As debt is repaid, capital structure measures typically *improve* whereas annual cash requirements for paying interest or sinking funds remain *fixed* or *increase* (examples of the latter include level payment debt with balloon repayment provisions or zero coupon bonds). This limitation highlights the important role of a company's **earnings coverage,** or *earning power*, as the source of interest and principal repayments. While highly profitable companies can in the short term face liquidity problems because of asset composition, we must remember that long-term earnings are the major source of liquidity, solvency, and borrowing capacity.

Relation of Earnings to Fixed Charges

The relation of earnings to fixed charges is part of **earnings coverage analysis.** Earnings coverage measures focus on the relation between debt-related fixed charges and a company's earnings available to meet these charges. These measures are important factors in debt ratings (see Appendix 11A). Bond indentures often specify minimum levels of earnings coverage for additional issuance of debt. Securities and Exchange Commission regulations require that the ratio of *earnings to fixed charges* be disclosed in the prospectus of all debt securities registered. The typical measure of the **earnings to fixed charges ratio** is:

$$\frac{\text{Earnings available for fixed charges}}{\text{Fixed charges}}$$

The concept underlying this measure is straightforward. Yet application of this measure is complicated by what is included in both "earnings available for fixed charges" and "fixed charges."

Computing Earnings Available for Fixed Charges

We previously discussed differences between income determined using accrual accounting and cash from operations (see Chapters 2, 6, and 7). For example, certain revenue items like undistributed subsidiary earnings and sales on extended credit terms do not generate immediate cash inflows (although a parent can determine dividends for controlled subsidiaries). Similarly, certain expenses like depreciation, amortization, depletion, and deferred tax charges do not require cash outflows. These distinctions are important since fixed debt charges are paid out of cash, not earnings. Our analysis must recognize that unadjusted net income is not necessarily a good measure of cash available for fixed charges. Using earnings as an approximation of cash from operations is sometimes appropriate while in others it can misstate the amount available for servicing fixed charges. Our approach to this problem lies not with generalizations but in careful analysis of noncash revenue and expense items that make up income. For example, in analyzing depreciation as a noncash expense, we must remember the long-run necessity of a company's replacing plant and equipment. Our analysis of the earnings available for fixed charges requires consideration of several important factors that are discussed below.

Extraordinary Gains and Losses. As discussed in Chapters 6 and 12, extraordinary gains and losses enter into the determination of long-term average earning power. They must be recognized as a factor that can over the long term contribute to or reduce cash available to pay fixed charges. Our computation of earnings coverage measures using average earnings must recognize extraordinary gains and losses. This is especially true of earnings coverage ratios where we measure the risk of loss of cash sources for paying fixed charges.

Preferred Dividends. Preferred dividends are not deducted from income because paying these dividends is not mandatory. In consolidated financial statements, preferred dividends of a subsidiary whose income is consolidated are deducted because they represent a charge having priority over the distribution of earnings to the parent.

Earnings Attributed to Minority Interests. These earnings are usually deducted from earnings available for fixed charges even though minority shareholders can rarely enforce a cash claim. The coverage ratio should be computed using earnings before deducting minority interests.

Adding Back Fixed Charges. To determine pretax earnings available for fixed charges, add back the fixed charges that were deducted to arrive at pretax earnings in the numerator of earnings coverage ratios.

Income Level. The income level used in computing earnings coverage ratios deserves attention. We must consider the question: What level of income is most representative of the amount actually available in future periods for paying debt-related fixed charges? Average earnings from continuing operations that span the business cycle and are adjusted for likely future changes are probably a good approximation of the average cash available from future operations to pay fixed charges. If one objective of an earnings coverage ratio is to measure a creditor's maximum exposure to risk, an appropriate earnings figure is one that occurs at the low point of the company's business cycle.

Computing Fixed Charges

The second major component in the earnings to fixed charges ratio is fixed charges. In this section we examine the fixed charges typically included in the computation. Analysis of fixed charges requires us to consider several important components.

Interest Incurred. Interest incurred is the most direct and obvious fixed charge arising from debt. Yet reported interest expense includes amortization of any discount or premium. *Discount* and issuance expenses represent an amount by which par value exceeded proceeds from the debt issuance. Discount amortization increases reported interest expense. *Premium* is the reverse of a discount and represents proceeds exceeding par value. Premium amortization reduces reported interest expense. Both discount and premium amortization do not typically affect cash flows and should be removed from fixed charges. They reflect expense or revenue allocations over the debt period. When information is so limited that it precludes the computation of interest incurred from interest capitalized, we can approximate the amount of interest incurred by referring to the mandatory disclosure of *interest paid* in the statement of cash flows. Interest incurred differs from the reported interest paid due to reasons that include (1) changes in interest payable, (2) interest capitalized being netted, and (3) discount and premium amortization. In the absence of information, interest paid is a good approximation of interest incurred.

Interest Implicit in Lease Obligations. We discussed accounting recognition of leases as financing devices in Chapter 3. When a lease is capitalized, the interest portion of the lease payment is included in interest expense on the income statement, while most of the balance is usually considered repayment of the principal obligation. A question arises when our analysis discovers certain leases that should be capitalized but are not. This question goes beyond the accounting question of whether capitalization is appropriate or not. We must remember a long-term lease represents a fixed obligation that must be given recognition in computing the earnings to fixed charges ratio. Long-term leases that conceptually need not be capitalized can consist of fixed charges requiring inclusion in the earnings to fixed charges ratio. One problem is extracting the interest portion from the long-term lease payment. Our analysis can sometimes obtain the rate of interest implicit in a lease from note disclosures. Absent this, a rule of thumb (such as interest is approximately one-third of rental payments) might be our only solution. The

SEC accepts this rule of thumb by registrants if management believes it represents a reasonable approximation of the interest factor.

Preferred Stock Dividend Requirements of Majority-Owned Subsidiaries. These are viewed as fixed charges because they have priority over the distribution of earnings to the parent. Items that would be or are eliminated in consolidation should not be viewed as fixed charges. We must remember that all fixed charges not tax deductible must be tax adjusted. This is done by increasing them by an amount equal to the income tax required to yield an after-tax income sufficient to cover these fixed charges. The preferred stock dividend requirements of majority-owned subsidiaries are an example of a non-tax-deductible fixed charge. We make an adjustment to compute the "gross" amount:

$$\frac{\text{Preferred stock dividend requirements}}{1 - \text{Income tax rate}}$$

The tax rate used should be based on the relation between income tax expense on income from continuing operations and the amount of pretax income from continuing operations (this is a company's *effective tax rate*). We use the effective tax rate rather than the statutory rate since this is the SEC's requirement.

Principal Repayment Requirements. Principal repayment obligations are from a cash outflow perspective as onerous as interest obligations. In the case of rental payments, a company's obligations to pay principal and interest must be met simultaneously. Several reasons are advanced as to why requirements for principal repayments are not given recognition in earnings to fixed charges ratio calculations, including:

- The earnings to fixed charges ratio is based on income. It assumes if the ratio is at a satisfactory level, a company can refinance obligations when they become due or mature. Accordingly, they need not be met by funds from earnings.
- If a company has an acceptable debt to equity ratio it should be able to reborrow amounts equal to principal repayments.
- Inclusion can result in double counting. For example, funds recovered by depreciation provide for debt repayment. If earnings reflect a deduction for depreciation, then fixed charges should not include principal repayments. There is some merit to this argument if debt is used to acquire depreciable fixed assets and if there is some correspondence between the pattern of depreciation and principal repayments. We must recognize that depreciation is recovered typically only from profitable or at least break-even operations. Therefore, this argument's validity is subject to these conditions. We must also recognize the definition of *earnings* in the earnings to fixed charges ratio emphasizes cash from operations as that available to cover fixed charges. Using this concept eliminates the double-counting problem since noncash charges like depreciation would be added back to net income in computing earnings coverage.
- A problem with including debt repayment requirements in fixed charges is that not all debt agreements provide for sinking funds or similar repayment obligations. Any arbitrary allocation of indebtedness across periods would be unrealistic and ignore differences in pressures on cash resources from actual debt repayments across periods. In the long run, maturities and balloon payments must all be met. One solution rests with our careful analysis of debt repayment requirements. This analysis serves as the basis in judging the effect of these requirements for long-term solvency. To assume debt can be refinanced, rolled over, or otherwise paid from current operations is risky. Rather, we must recognize debt repayment requirements and their timing in analysis of long-term solvency. Including sinking fund or

other early repayment requirements in fixed charges is a way of recognizing these obligations. Another way is applying debt repayment requirements over a period of 5 to 10 years into the future and relating these to after-tax funds expected to be available from operations.

Guarantees to Pay Fixed Charges. Guarantees to pay fixed charges of unconsolidated subsidiaries or of unaffiliated persons (entities) should be added to fixed charges if the requirement to honor the guarantee appears imminent.

Other Fixed Charges. While interest payments and principal repayment requirements are the fixed charges most directly related to the incurrence of debt, there is no reason to restrict our analysis of long-term solvency to these charges or commitments. A thorough analysis of fixed charges should include all long-term rental payment obligations[1] (not only the interest portion), and especially those rentals that must be met under noncancelable leases. The reason short-term leases can be excluded from consideration in fixed charges is they represent obligations of limited duration, usually less than three years. Consequently, these leases can be discontinued in a period of financial distress. Our analysis must evaluate how essential these leased items are to the continued operation of the company. Additional charges not directly related to debt, but considered long-term commitments of a fixed nature, are long-term noncancelable purchase contracts in excess of normal requirements.

Computing Earnings to Fixed Charges

The conventional formula, and one adopted by the SEC, for computing the earnings to fixed charges ratio is:

$$\frac{\left[\begin{array}{c}(a)\text{ Pretax income from continuing operations } plus\ (b)\text{ Interest expense } plus\\ (c)\text{ Amortization of debt expense and discount or premium } plus\ (d)\text{ Interest portion of}\\ \text{operating rental expenses } plus\ (e)\text{ Tax-adjusted preferred stock dividend requirements of}\\ \text{majority-owned subsidiaries } plus\ (f)\text{ Amount of previously capitalized interest amortized in the}\\ \text{period } minus\ (g)\text{ Undistributed income of less than 50\%-owned subsidiaries or affiliates}\end{array}\right]}{\left[\begin{array}{c}(h)\text{ Total interest incurred } plus\ (c)\text{ Amortization of debt expense and discount or premium}\\ plus\ (d)\text{ Interest portion of operating rental expenses } plus\ (e)\text{ Tax-adjusted preferred stock}\\ \text{dividend requirements of majority-owned subsidiaries}\end{array}\right]}$$

Individual components in this ratio are labeled *a–h* and are further explained here:

a. Pretax income before discontinued operations, extraordinary items, and cumulative effects of accounting changes.
b. Interest incurred less interest capitalized.
c. Usually included in interest expense.
d. Financing leases are capitalized so the interest implicit in these is already included in interest expense. However, the interest portion of long-term operating leases is included on the assumption many long-term operating leases narrowly miss the capital lease criteria, but have many characteristics of a financing transaction.
e. Excludes all items eliminated in consolidation. The dividend amount is increased to pretax earnings required to pay for it.[2]

[1]Capitalized long-term leases affect income by the interest charge implicit in them and by the amortization of the property right. To consider the "principal" component of these leases as fixed charges (after income is reduced by amortization of the property right) can yield double counting.

[2]Computed as (Preferred stock dividend requirements)/(1 − Income tax rate). The income tax rate is computed as Actual income tax provision/Income before income taxes, extraordinary items, and cumulative effect of accounting changes.

f. Applies to nonutility companies. This amount is not often disclosed.
g. Minority interest in income of majority-owned subsidiaries having fixed charges can be included in income.
h. Included whether expensed or capitalized.

For ease of presentation, two items (provisions) are left out of the ratio above, but they should be reflected in the ratio when they exist:

1. Losses of majority-owned subsidiaries should be considered in *full* when computing earnings.
2. Losses on investments in less than 50%-owned subsidiaries accounted for by the equity method should not be included in earnings *unless* the company guarantees subsidiaries' debts.

Finally, the SEC requires that if the earnings to fixed charges ratio is less than 1.0, the amount of earnings insufficient to cover fixed charges should be reported.

Illustration of Earnings to Fixed Charges Ratio

This section illustrates actual computation of the earnings to fixed charges ratio. Our first case focuses on CompuTech Corp., whose income statement is reproduced in Exhibit 11.5 along with selected notes. Using this information for CompuTech ($ thousands) we compute the earnings to fixed charges ratio as (letter references are to the ratio definition):

$$\frac{\$2{,}200\ (a) + \$700\ (b \text{ and } c) + \$300\ (d) + \$80\ (f) - \$600\ (g) + \$200^*}{\$840\ (h) + \$60\ (c) + \$300\ (d)} = 2.40$$

* *Note:* The SEC permits inclusion in income of the minority interest in the income of majority-owned subsidiaries having fixed charges. This amount is added to reverse a similar deduction from income.

Our second case uses the Year 11 financial statements of Quaker Oats from Appendix A ($ millions). The Year 11 earnings to fixed charges ratio for Quaker Oats is computed as (letter references are to the ratio definition):

$$\frac{(a)\ \$411.5^{(1)} + (b)\ \$101.9^{(2)} + (d)\ \$14.8^{(3)}}{(h)\ \$103.8^{(4)} + (d)\ \$14.8^{(3)}} = 4.45$$

(1) Income from continuing operations before taxes [7].

(2) Interest expense [156].

(3) One-third of operating lease rentals or one-third of $44.5 = $14.8 [154].

(4) Interest incurred $101.9 + $1.9 = $103.8 [156].

Pro Forma Computation of Earnings to Fixed Charges

In situations where fixed charges not yet incurred are recognized in computing the earnings to fixed charges ratio (such as interest costs under a prospective debt issuance), it is acceptable to estimate offsetting benefits expected from these future cash inflows and include them in pro forma earnings. Benefits derived from prospective debt can be measured in several ways, including interest savings from a planned refunding activity, income from short-term investments where proceeds can be invested, or other reasonable estimates of future benefits. When the effect of a prospective refinancing plan changes the ratio by 10% or more, the SEC usually requires a pro forma computation of the ratio reflecting changes to be effected under the plan.

Exhibit 11.5

COMPUTECH CORPORATION

Income Statement

Net sales		$13,400,000
Income of less than 50%-owned affiliates (all undistributed)		600,000
Total revenue		14,000,000
Cost of goods sold	$7,400,000	
Selling, general, and administrative expenses	1,900,000	
Depreciation (excluded from above costs)[1]	800,000	
Interest expense, net[2]	700,000	
Rental expense[3]	800,000	
Share of minority interests in consolidated income[4]	200,000	(11,800,000)
Income before taxes		2,200,000
Income taxes:		
Current	$ 800,000	
Deferred	300,000	(1,100,000)
Income before extraordinary item		1,100,000
Extraordinary gain (net of $67,000 tax)		200,000
Net income		$ 1,300,000
Dividends:		
On common stock	$ 200,000	
On preferred stock	400,000	(600,000)
Earnings retained for the year		$ 700,000

Selected notes to financial statements:

[1] *Depreciation includes amortization of previously capitalized interest of $80,000.*

[2] *Interest expense consists of:*

Interest incurred (except items below)	*$740,000*
Amortization of bond discount	*60,000*
Interest portion of capitalized leases	*100,000*
Interest capitalized	*(200,000)*
Interest expense	*$700,000*

[3] *Interest implicit in noncapitalized leases amounts to $300,000.*

[4] *These subsidiaries have fixed charges.*

Additional information (for the income statement period):

Increase in accounts receivable	*$310,000*
Increase in inventories	*180,000*
Increase in accounts payable	*140,000*
Decrease in accrued taxes	*20,000*

Times Interest Earned Analysis

Another earnings coverage measure is the **times interest earned ratio.** This ratio considers interest as the only fixed charge needing earnings coverage:

$$\frac{\text{Income} + \text{Tax expense} + \text{Interest expense}}{\text{Interest expense}}$$

The times interest earned ratio is a simplified measure. It ignores most adjustments to both the numerator and denominator that we discussed with the earnings to fixed charges ratio. While its computation is simple, it is potentially misleading and not as effective an analysis tool as the earnings to fixed charges ratio.

Relation of Cash Flow to Fixed Charges

Companies must pay fixed charges in cash while net income includes earned revenues and incurred expenses that do not necessarily generate or require immediate cash. This section describes a cash-based measure of fixed-charges coverage to address this limitation.

Cash Flow to Fixed Charges Ratio

The **cash flow to fixed charges ratio** is computed using *cash from operations* rather than earnings in the numerator of the earnings to fixed charges ratio. Cash from operations is reported in the statement of cash flows. The cash flow to fixed charges ratio is defined as:

$$\frac{\text{Pretax operating cash flow} + \text{Adjustments } (b) \text{ through } (g) \text{ on page 550}}{\text{Fixed charges}}$$

Using financial data of CompuTech from Exhibit 11.5 we can compute pretax cash from operations for this ratio as:

Pretax income	$2,200,000
Add (deduct) adjustments to cash basis:	
Depreciation	800,000
Deferred income taxes (already added back)	—
Amortization of bond discount	60,000
Share of minority interest in income	200,000
Undistributed income of affiliates	(600,000)
Increase in receivables	(310,000)
Increase in inventories	(180,000)
Increase in accounts payable	140,000
Decrease in accrued tax	(20,000)
Pretax cash from operations	$2,290,000

Fixed charges needing to be added back to pretax cash from operations are:

Pretax cash from operations	$2,290,000
Interest expensed (less bond discount added back above)	640,000
Interest portion of operating rental expense	300,000
Amount of previously capitalized interest amortized during period*	—
Total numerator	$3,230,000

* Assume included in depreciation (already added back).

Notice the numerator does not reflect a deduction of $600,000 (undistributed income of affiliates) because it, being a noncash source, is already deducted in arriving at pretax cash from operations. Also the "share of minority interests in consolidated income" is already added back in arriving at pretax cash from operations. Fixed charges for the ratio's denominator are:

Interest incurred	$ 900,000
Interest portion of operating rentals	300,000
Fixed charges	$1,200,000

CompuTech's cash flow to fixed charges ratio is computed as:

$$\frac{\$3{,}230{,}000}{\$1{,}200{,}000} = 2.69$$

As another example, we compute Quaker Oats' pretax cash from operations plus fixed charges for the numerator in the cash flow to fixed charges ratio as:

NUMERATOR OF CASH FLOW TO FIXED CHARGES RATIO ($ MILLIONS)	
Cash from operations 31	$532.4
Add back:	
Income tax expense (except deferred)[a] 158	161.4
Interest expense 156	101.9
One-third of operating lease rentals of 44.5[c]	14.8
Amortization of previously capitalized interest (already added back)—presumably included in 20	—
Total numerator of ratio	$810.5

We then compute Quaker Oats' cash flow to fixed charges ratio as:

$$\frac{\$810.5}{\$103.8^{(b)} + \$14.8^{(c)}} = 6.83$$

[a] Deferred tax already added back in computing cash from operations.

[b] Interest incurred 156 ($101.9 + $1.9).

[c] One-third of operating lease rentals of $44.5 154.

Permanence of Cash from Operations

The relation of a company's cash flows from operations to fixed charges is important to an analysis of long-term solvency. Because of this relation's importance, we assess the "permanence" of operating cash flows. We typically do this in evaluating the components constituting operating cash flows. For example, the depreciation add-back to net income is more permanent than net income because recovery of depreciation from sales precedes receipt of any income. For all businesses, selling prices must (in the long run) reflect the cost of plant and equipment used in production. The depreciation add-back assumes cash flow benefits from recovery of depreciation are available to service debt. This assumption is true only in the short run. In the long run, this cash recovery must be dedicated to replacing plant and equipment. An exception can occur with add-backs of items like amortization of goodwill that are not necessarily replaced or depleted. Permanence of changes in the operating working capital (operating current assets less operating current liabilities) component of operating cash flows is often difficult to assess. Operating working capital is linked more with sales than with pretax income and therefore is often more stable than operating cash flows.

Earnings Coverage of Preferred Dividends

Our analysis of preferred stock often benefits from measuring the earnings coverage of preferred dividends. This analysis is similar to our analysis of how earnings cover debt-related fixed charges. The SEC requires disclosure of the ratio of combined fixed charges and preferred dividends in the prospectus of all preferred stock offerings. Computing the earnings coverage of preferred dividends must include in fixed charges all expenditures taking precedence over preferred dividends. Since preferred dividends are not tax deductible, after-tax income must be used to cover them. Accordingly, the **earnings coverage of preferred dividends ratio** is computed as:

$$\frac{\text{Pretax income} + \text{Adjustments } (b) \text{ through } (g) \text{ on page 550}}{\text{Fixed charges} + \left(\dfrac{\text{Preferred dividends}}{1 - \text{Tax rate}}\right)}$$

Using the financial data from CompuTech Corp. in Exhibit 11.5, we can compute its earnings coverage of preferred dividends ratio. This is identical to using CompuTech's ratio of earnings to fixed charges (computed earlier) and adding the tax-adjusted preferred dividend requirement. Computation of the earnings coverage to preferred dividends ratio is ($ thousands):

$$\frac{\$2{,}200\ (a) + \$700\ (b \text{ and } c) + \$300\ (d) + \$80\ (f) - \$600\ (g) + \$200^{*}}{\$840\ (h) + \$60\ (c) + \$300\ (d) + \left(\dfrac{\$400^{\dagger}}{1 - 0.50}\right)} = 1.44$$

Note: Letters refer to components in the earnings to fixed charges ratio (see page 550).

* Minority interest in income of majority-owned subsidiaries (see prior discussion).

† Tax-adjusted preferred dividend requirement.

If there are two or more preferred issues outstanding, the coverage ratio is usually computed for each issue by omitting dividend requirements of junior issues and including all prior fixed charges and senior issues of preferred dividends.

Interpreting Earnings Coverage Measures

Earnings coverage measures provide us insight into the ability of a company to meet its fixed charges out of current earnings. There exists a high correlation between earnings coverage measures and the default rate on debt–that is, the higher the coverage, the lower the default rate. A study of creditor experience with debt revealed the following default and yield rates for debt classified according to times interest earned ratios:

Times Interest Earned	Default Rate	Promised Yield	Realized Yield	Loss Rate
3.0 and over	2.1%	4.0%	4.9%	−0.9%
2.0–2.9	4.0	4.3	5.1	−0.8
1.5–1.9	17.9	4.7	5.0	−0.3
1.0–1.4	34.1	6.8	6.4	0.4
Under 1.0	35.0	6.2	6.0	0.2

Our attention on earnings coverage measures is sensible since creditors place considerable reliance on the ability of a company to meet its obligations and continue operating. An increased yield rate on debt seldom compensates creditors for the risk of losing principal. If the likelihood of a company meeting its obligations through continuing operations is not high, creditors' risk is substantial.

Importance of Earnings Variability and Persistence for Earnings Coverage

An important factor in evaluating earnings coverage measures is the behavior of earnings and cash flows across time. The more stable the earnings pattern of a company or industry, the lower is the acceptable earnings coverage measure. For example, a utility experiences little in the way of economic downturns or upswings and therefore we accept a lower earnings coverage ratio. In contrast, cyclical companies like machinery manufacturers can experience both sharp declines and increases in performance. This uncertainty leads us to impose a higher earnings coverage ratio on these companies. Both *earnings variability* and *earnings persistence* are common measures of this uncertainty across time. Our analysis can use one or both of these measures in determining the accepted standard for earnings coverage. Earnings persistence often is measured as the (auto) correlation of earnings across time.

Importance of Measurements and Assumptions for Earnings Coverage

Determining an acceptable level for earnings coverage depends on the method of computing an earnings coverage measure. We described several earnings coverage measures in this chapter. Many of these measures assume different definitions of *earnings* and *fixed charges*. We expect lower levels for earnings coverage measures employing the most demanding and stringent definitions. Both the SEC and our computation of the earnings to fixed charges coverage ratio use earnings *before* discontinued operations, extraordinary items, and cumulative effects of accounting changes. While excluding these three items yields a less variable earnings stream, it also excludes important components that are part of a company's business activities. Accordingly, we suggest these components be included in computing the *average* coverage ratio over several years. The acceptable level also varies with the measure of earnings–for example, earnings measured as the average, worst, best, or median performance. The quality of earnings is another important factor. We should not compute earnings coverage ratios using shortcuts or purposefully conservative means. For example, using after-tax income in computing coverage ratios where fixed charges are tax deductible is incorrect and uses conservatism improperly. Our acceptable level of coverage must ultimately reflect our willingness and ability to incur risk (relative to our expected return). Appendix 11A refers to acceptable levels of coverage ratios used by rating agencies in analyzing debt securities.

Capital Structure Risk and Return

It is useful for us to consider recent developments in financial innovations for assessing the risk inherent in a company's capital structure. A company can increase risks (and potential returns) of equity holders by increasing leverage. For example, a *leveraged buyout* uses debt to take a company private by buying out equity holders. The acquirors rely on future cash flows to service the increased debt and on anticipated asset sales to reduce debt. Another potential benefit of leverage is the tax deductibility of interest while dividends paid to equity holders are not tax deductible. Still, substitution of debt for equity yields a riskier capital structure. This is why bonds used to finance certain leveraged buyouts are called *junk bonds.* A junk bond, unlike its high-quality counterpart, is part of a high-risk capital structure where its interest payments are minimally covered by earnings. Economic adversities rapidly jeopardize interest payments and principal of junk bonds. Junk bonds possess the risk of equity more so than the safety of debt.

Financial experience continually reminds us of those who forget the relation between risk and return. It is no surprise that highly speculative financial periods spawn risky securities. Our surprise is the refusal by some to appreciate the adjective *junk* when applied to bonds. Similarly, zero coupon bonds defer all payment of interest to maturity and offer several advantages over standard debt issues. However, when issued by companies with less than outstanding credit credentials, the risk with zero coupon bonds is substantially higher than with standard debt–due to the uncertainty of receiving interest and principal many years into the future. Another financial innovation called *payment in kind (PIK) securities* pay interest by issuing additional debt. The assumption is a debtor, possibly too weak to pay interest currently, will subsequently be successful enough to pay it later. While innovations in financing companies' business activities continue, and novel terms are coined, our analysis must focus on substance over form. The basic truth about the relation between risk and return in a capital structure remains.

Factors contributing to risk and our available tools of analysis discussed in this and preceding chapters point to our need for thorough and sound financial analysis. Relying on credit ratings or others' rankings is a delegation of our analysis and evaluation responsibilities. It is risky for us to place partial or exclusive reliance on these sources of analysis. No matter how reputable, these sources *cannot* capture our unique risk and return expectations.

APPENDIX 11A RATING DEBT

A comprehensive and complex system for rating debt securities is established in the world economy. Ratings are available from several highly regarded investment research firms: Moody's, Standard & Poor's (S&P), Duff and Phelps, and Fitch Ratings. Many financial institutions also develop their own in-house ratings.

10-Year Treasury and Corporate Bond Yields—2002

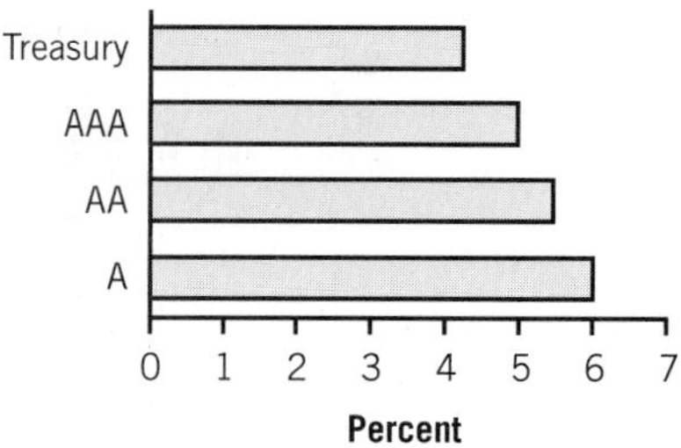

Source: Standard & Poor's

BOND CREDIT RATINGS

The bond credit rating is a composite expression of judgment about the *creditworthiness* of the bond issuer and the quality of the specific security being rated. A rating measures credit risk where *credit risk* is the probability of developments unfavorable to the interests of creditors. This judgment of creditworthiness is expressed in a series of symbols reflecting degrees of credit risk. Specifically, the top four rating grades from Standard & Poor's are:

AAA Bonds rated AAA are highest-grade obligations. They possess the highest degree of protection as to principal and interest. Marketwise, they move with interest rates and provide maximum safety.

AA Bonds rated AA also qualify as high-grade obligations and in the majority of instances differ little from AAA issues. Here, too, prices move with the long-term money market.

A Bonds rated A are regarded as upper-medium grade. They have considerable investment strength but are not free from adverse effects of changes in economic and trade conditions. Interest and principal are regarded as safe. They predominantly reflect money rates in their price behavior, and to some extent economic conditions.

BBB Bonds rated BBB, or medium-grade category, are borderline between sound obligations and those where the speculative element begins to predominate. These bonds have adequate asset coverage and normally are protected by satisfactory earnings. Their susceptibility to changing conditions, particularly economic downturns, necessitates constant monitoring. Marketwise, these bonds are more responsive to business and trade conditions than to interest rates. This grade is the lowest that typically qualifies for commercial bank investment.

There is a lower selection of ratings, including **BB,** lower-medium grade to marginally speculative; **B,** very speculative; and **D,** bonds in default.

A major reason why debt securities are widely rated while equity securities are not is because there is far greater uniformity of approach and homogeneity of analytical measures in analyzing creditworthiness than in analyzing future market performance of equity securities. This wider agreement on what is being measured in credit risk analysis has resulted in acceptance of and reliance on published credit ratings for several purposes.

BOND QUALITY RATINGS

Rating Grades	Standard & Poor's	Moody's
Highest grade	AAA	Aaa
High grade	AA	Aa
Upper medium	A	A
Lower medium	BBB	Baa
Marginally speculative	BB	Ba
Highly speculative	B	B, Caa
Default	D	Ca, C

Criteria determining a specific rating are never precisely defined. They involve both *quantitative* (ratio and comparative analyses) and *qualitative* (market position and management quality) factors. Major rating agencies refuse to disclose their precise mix of factors determining ratings (which is usually a committee decision). They wish to avoid arguments about the validity of qualitative factors in ratings. These rating agencies use the analysis techniques discussed throughout this book. The following description of factors determining ratings is based on published sources and from discussions with officials of rating agencies.

RATING COMPANY BONDS

In rating an industrial bond issue, the rating agency focuses on the issuing company's asset protection, financial resources, earning power, management, and specific provisions of the debt. Also important are company size, market share, industry position, cyclical influences, and general economic conditions.

Asset protection refers to the extent a company's debt is covered by its assets. One measure is net tangible assets to long-term debt. One rating agency uses a rule of thumb where a bond needs a net tangible asset to long-term debt value of 5:1 for a AAA rating; 4:1 for a AA rating; 3 to 3.5:1 for an A rating; and 2.5:1 for a BBB rating. Concern with undervalued assets, especially with companies in the natural resources or real estate industries, leads to adjustments to these rating levels. Another rule of thumb suggests the long-term debt to total capital ratio be under 25% for a AAA, near 30% for a AA, near 35% for an A, and near 40% for a BBB rating. Additional factors entering rating agencies' consideration of asset protection include book value; composition of working capital; the quality and age of property, plant, and equipment; off-balance-sheet financing; and unrecorded liabilities.

IS DEBT TOO HIGH?
To get a sense for whether a company has too much debt, compare its debt level with the average for companies with different ratings. The following table gives ratios (code: [1] is the long-term debt to equity ratio and [2] is the total debt to equity ratio) for different credit ratings:

	[1]	[2]
AAA	4.4%	4.5%
AA	23.0	34.1
A	33.3	42.9
BBB	41.5	47.9
BB	56.4	59.8
B	73.6	76.0

Financial resources refer to liquid resources like cash and working capital accounts. Analysis measures include the collection period of receivables and inventory turnover. Their values are assessed relative to industry and absolute standards. Raters also analyze the issuer's use of both short-term and long-term debt, and their mix.

Future earning power, and the issuer's cash-generating ability, is an important factor in rating debt securities because the level and quality of future earnings determine a company's ability to meet its obligations, especially those of a long-term nature. Earning power is usually a more reliable source of protection than assets. One common measure of protection due to earning power is the earnings to fixed charges coverage ratio. A rule of thumb suggests an acceptable earnings to fixed charges ratio is 5:1 to 7:1 for a AAA rating, over 4:1 for a AA rating, over 3:1 for an A rating, and over 2:1 for a BBB rating. Another measure of debt servicing potential is cash flow from operations to long-term debt. A rule of thumb suggests this ratio be over 65% for a AAA, 45 to 60% for a AA, 35 to 45% for an A, and 25 to 30% for a BBB rating.

Management's abilities, foresight, philosophy, knowledge, experience, and integrity are important considerations in rating debt. Through interviews, site visits, and other analyses, the raters probe management's goals, strategies, plans, and tactics in areas like research and development, product promotion, product planning, and acquisitions.

Debt provisions are usually written in the bond indenture. Raters analyze the specific provisions in the indenture designed to protect interests of bondholders under a variety of conditions. These include analysis of stipulations (if any) for future debt issuances, security provisions like mortgaging, sinking funds, redemption provisions, and restrictive covenants.

LIMITATIONS IN THE RATINGS GAME

Debt ratings are useful to a large proportion of debt issuances. Yet we must understand the inherent limitations of the standardized procedures of rating agencies. As with equity security analysis, our analysis can improve on these ratings. Debt issuances reflect a wide range of characteristics. Consequently, they present us with opportunities to identify differences within rating classes and assess their favorable or unfavorable impact within their ratings class. Also, there is evidence that rating changes lag the market. This lag effect presents us with additional opportunities to identify important changes prior to their being reported by rating agencies.

APPENDIX 11B PREDICTING FINANCIAL DISTRESS

A common use of financial statement analysis is identifying areas needing further investigation and analysis. One of these applications is **predicting financial distress.** Research has made substantial advances in suggesting various ratios as predictors of distress. This research is valuable in providing additional tools for analyzing long-term solvency. Models of financial distress, commonly referred to as **bankruptcy prediction models,** examine the trend and behavior of selected ratios. Characteristics of these ratios are used in identifying the likelihood of future financial distress. Models presume that evidence of distress appears in financial ratios and that we can detect it sufficiently early for us to take actions to either avoid risk of loss or to capitalize on this information.

ALTMAN *Z*-SCORE

Probably the most well-known model of financial distress is **Altman's *Z-score*.** Altman's *Z*-score uses multiple ratios to generate a predictor of distress.[3] Altman's *Z*-score uses a statistical technique (multiple discriminant analysis) to produce a predictor that is a linear function of several explanatory variables. This predictor classifies or predicts the likelihood of bankruptcy or nonbankruptcy. Five financial ratios are included in the *Z*-score: X_1 = Working capital/Total assets, X_2 = Retained earnings/Total assets, X_3 = Earnings before interest and taxes/Total assets, X_4 = Shareholders' equity/Total liabilities, and X_5 = Sales/Total assets. We can view X_1, X_2, X_3, X_4, and X_5 as reflecting (1) liquidity, (2) age of firm and cumulative profitability, (3) profitability, (4) financial structure, and (5) capital turnover rate, respectively. The Altman *Z*-score is computed as:

$$Z = 0.717\, X_1 + 0.847\, X_2 + 3.107\, X_3 + 0.420\, X_4 + 0.998\, X_5$$

[3] See E. Altman, "Financial Ratios, Discriminant Analysis, and the Prediction of Corporate Bankruptcy," *Journal of Finance* 22 (September 1968), pp. 589–609. Also see J. Begley, J. Ming, and S. Watts, "Bankruptcy Classification Errors in the 1980s: An Empirical Analysis of Altman's and Ohlson's Models," *Review of Accounting Studies* (1997).

A Z-score of less than 1.20 suggests a high probability of bankruptcy, while Z-scores above 2.90 imply a low probability of bankruptcy. Scores between 1.20 and 2.90 are in the gray or ambiguous area.[4]

DISTRESS MODELS AND FINANCIAL STATEMENT ANALYSIS

Research efforts identify a useful role for ratios in predicting financial distress. However, we must *not* blindly apply this or any other model without informed and critical analysis of a company's fundamentals. There is no evidence to suggest computation of a Z-score is a better means of analyzing long-term solvency than is the integrated use of the analysis tools described in this book. Rather, we assert the use of ratios as predictors of distress is best in complementing our rigorous analysis of financial statements. Evidence does suggest the Z-score is a useful screening, monitoring, and attention-directing device.

GUIDANCE ANSWERS TO ANALYSIS VIEWPOINTS

Banker

Your decision on IMC's one-year loan application is positive for at least two reasons. First, your analysis of IMC's short-term liquidity is reassuring. IMC's current ratio of 4:1 suggests a considerable margin of safety in its ability to meet short-term obligations. Second, IMC's current assets of $1.6 million and current ratio of 4:1 implies current liabilities of $400,000 and a working capital excess of $1.2 million. This working capital excess totals 60 percent of the loan amount. The evidence supports approval of IMC's loan application. However, if IMC's application is for a 10-year loan, our decision is less optimistic. While the current ratio and working capital suggest a good safety margin, there are indications of inefficiency in operations. First, a 4:1 current ratio is in most cases too excessive and characteristic of inefficient asset use. Second, IMC's current ratio is more than double that of its competitors. Our decision regarding a long-term loan is likely positive, *but* substantially less optimistic than a short-term loan.

Consultant

Cost savings are assumed to derive from paying off current liabilities with money not invested in inventory. Accordingly, cost savings equal (Inventory reduction × 10%). Under the old system, inventory equaled $5 million. This is obtained using the inventory turnover ratio: 20 = $100 million/Average inventory. With the new system, inventory equals $4 million; computed using the new inventory turnover: 25 = $100 million/Average inventory. The cost savings are $100,000–computed from ($5 million − $4 million) × 10%.

Entrepreneur

The main criterion in your analysis is to compare the restaurant's return on assets to the after-tax cost of debt. If your restaurant can continue to earn 9% on assets, then the *after-tax* cost of debt must be less than 9% for you to successfully trade on the equity. Since the tax rate is 40%, you could successfully trade on the equity by adding new debt with an interest rate of 15% or less [9% (1 − 0.40)]. The lower the interest rate is from 15%, the more successful is your trading on the equity. You must recognize that taking on debt increases the riskiness of your business (due to the risk of unsuccessfully trading on the equity). This is because if your restaurant's earnings decline to where return on assets falls below the after-tax cost of debt, then return on equity declines even further. Accordingly, your assessment of earnings stability, or *persistence*, is a crucial part of the decision to add debt.

[4]The model shown here is from Altman, *Corporate Financial Distress* (New York: John Wiley, 1983), pp. 120–124. This model is more generalizable than his earlier 1968 model which can only be applied to publicly traded companies. The earlier model is: $Z = 1.2\,X_1 + 1.4\,X_2 + 3.3\,X_3 + 0.6\,X_4 + 1.0\,X_5$. But X_4 in the earlier model requires the market value of preferred and common equity be available. The new model can be applied to *both* publicly traded and nonpublicly traded companies with no measurable affect on prediction performance. Use of the earlier model is fine provided it is only applied to publicly traded companies.

Analyst

The preferred equity risk is greater for the second company. For the first company, senior securities (to preferred equity) constitute 20% of financing. However, for the second company, senior securities constitute 30% of financing. In a situation of bankruptcy, 30% of residual value must be paid to debtors prior to payments to preferred equity holders. In addition, financial leverage for the second company is potentially greater, although precise assessment of leverage risk depends on the features of preferred stock (features such as fixed return, cumulative, nonparticipating, redeemable, and nonvoting make preferred stock more like debt).

QUESTIONS

11–1 Why is liquidity important in analysis of financial statements? Explain its importance from the viewpoint of more than one type of user.

11–2 Working capital equals current assets less current liabilities. Identify and describe factors impairing the usefulness of working capital as an analysis measure.

11–3 Are fixed assets potentially includable in current assets? Explain. If your answer is yes, describe situations where inclusion is possible.

11–4 Certain installment receivables are not collectible within one year. Why are these receivables sometimes included in current assets?

11–5 Are all inventories included in current assets? Why or why not?

11–6 What is the justification for including prepaid expenses in current assets?

11–7 Assume a company under analysis has few current liabilities but substantial long-term liabilities. Notes to the financial statements report the company has a "revolving loan agreement" with a bank. Is this disclosure relevant to your analysis?

11–8 Certain industries are subject to peculiar financing and operating conditions calling for special consideration in drawing distinctions between *current* and *noncurrent*. How should analysis recognize this in evaluating short-term liquidity?

11–9 Your analysis of two companies reveals identical levels of working capital. Are you confident in concluding their liquidity positions are equivalent?

11–10 What is the current ratio? What does the current ratio measure? What are reasons for using the current ratio for analysis?

11–11 Since cash generally does not yield a return, why does a company hold cash?

11–12 Is there a relation between level of inventories and sales? Are inventories a function of sales? If there is a relation between inventories and sales, is it proportional?

11–13 What are management's objectives in determining a company's investment in inventories and receivables?

11–14 What are the limitations of the current ratio as a measure of liquidity?

11–15 What is the appropriate use of the current ratio as a measure of liquidity?

11–16 What are cash-based ratios of liquidity? What do they measure?

11–17 How can we measure "quality" of current assets?

11–18 What does accounts receivable turnover measure?

11–19 What is the collection period for accounts receivable? What does it measure?

11–20 Assume a company's collection period is 60 days in comparison to 40 days for the prior period. Identify at least three possible reasons for this change.

11–21 What are the repercussions to a company of (*a*) overinvestment and (*b*) underinvestment in inventories?

11–22 What problems are expected in an analysis of a company using the LIFO inventory method when costs are increasing? What effects do price changes have on the (*a*) inventory turnover ratio and (*b*) current ratio?

11–23 Why is the composition of current liabilities relevant to our analysis of the quality of the current ratio?

11–24 A seemingly successful company can have a poor current ratio. Identify possible reasons for this result.

11–25 What is window-dressing of current assets and liabilities? How can we recognize whether financial statements are window-dressed?

11–26 What is the rule of thumb governing the expected level of the current ratio? What risks are there in using this rule of thumb for analysis?

11–27 Describe the importance of sales in assessing a company's current financial condition and the liquidity of its current assets.

11–28 Identify important qualitative considerations in the analysis of a company's liquidity. What SEC disclosures help our analysis in this area?

11–29 What is the importance of what-if analysis on the effects of changes in conditions or policies for a company's cash resources?

11–30 Identify several key elements in the evaluation of solvency.

11–31 Why is analysis of a company's capital structure important?

11–32 What is meant by *financial leverage*? Identify one or more cases where leverage is advantageous.

11–33 Dynamic Electronics, Inc., a successful and high-growth company, consistently experiences a favorable difference between the rate of return on its assets and the interest rate paid on borrowed funds. Explain why this company should not increase its debt to the 90% level of total capitalization and thereby minimize any need for equity financing.

(CFA Adapted)

11–34 How should we treat deferred income taxes in an analysis of capital structure?

11–35 In analysis of capital structure, how should lease obligations not capitalized be treated? Under what conditions should they be considered equivalent to debt?

11–36 What is off-balance-sheet financing? Provide one or more examples.

11–37 What are liabilities for pensions? What factors should our analysis of a company's pension obligations take into consideration?

11–38 When is information on unconsolidated subsidiaries important to solvency analysis?

11–39 Would you classify the items below as equity or liabilities? State your reason(s) and any assumptions.
a. Minority interest in consolidated financial statements.
b. Appropriated retained earnings.
c. Guarantee for product performance on sale.
d. Convertible debt.
e. Preferred stock.

11–40 *a.* Why might an analysis of financial statements need to adjust the book value of assets?
b. Give three examples of the need for possible adjustments to book value.

11–41 In evaluating solvency, why are long-term projections necessary in addition to a short-term analysis? What are some limitations of long-term projections?

11–42 What is the difference between common-size analysis and capital structure ratio analysis? Explain how capital structure ratio analysis is useful to financial statement analysis.

11–43 Equity capital on the balance sheet is reported using historical cost accounting and at times differs considerably from market value. How should our analysis allow for this, if at all, in analyzing capital structure?

11–44 Why is the evaluation of asset composition useful for capital structure analysis?

11–45 What does the earnings to fixed charges ratio measure? What does this ratio add to the other tools of credit analysis?

11–46 In computing the earnings to fixed charges ratio, what broad categories of items are included in fixed charges? What tax adjustments must be considered for these items?

11–47 A company you are analyzing has a purchase commitment of raw materials under a noncancelable contract that is substantial in amount. Under what conditions do you include this purchase commitment in computing fixed charges?

11–48 Is net income a reliable measure of cash available to meet fixed charges?

11–49 Company B is a wholly owned subsidiary of Company A. Company A is also Company B's principal customer. As a potential lender to Company B, what particular facets of this relationship concern you most? What safeguards, if any, do you require in any loan contract?

11–50 Comment on the assertion: *"Debt is a supplement to, not a substitute for, equity financing."*

11–51 A company in need of additional equity financing sells convertible debt. This action postpones equity dilution and the company ultimately sells its shares at an effectively higher price. What are the advantages and disadvantages of this action?

11–52 *a.* What is the reason for restrictive covenants in long-term debt indentures?
b. What is the reason for provisions regarding:
(1) Maintenance of minimum working capital (or current ratio)?
(2) Maintenance of minimum shareholders' equity?
(3) Restrictions on dividend payments?
(4) Power of creditors to elect a majority of the board of directors of the debtor company in the event of default under terms of the loan agreement?

11–53 Why are debt securities regularly rated while equity securities are not?

11–54 What factors do rating agencies emphasize in rating an industrial bond? Describe these factors.

11–55 Can an analysis of financial statements improve on published bond ratings? Explain.

11–56 What is the reason(s) why companies hire bond rating agencies to rate their debt?

EXERCISES

EXERCISE 11–1
Interpreting Effects of Transactions on Liquidity Measures

The Lux Company experiences the following unrelated events and transactions during Year 1. The company's existing current ratio is 2:1 and its quick ratio is 1.2:1.

1. Lux wrote off $5,000 of accounts receivable as uncollectible.
2. A bank notifies Lux that a customer's check for $411 is returned marked insufficient funds. The customer is bankrupt.
3. The owners of Lux Company make an additional cash investment of $7,500.
4. Inventory costing $600 is judged obsolete when a physical inventory is taken.
5. Lux declares a $5,000 cash dividend to be paid during the first week of the next reporting period.
6. Lux purchases long-term investments for $10,000.
7. Accounts payable of $9,000 are paid.
8. Lux borrows $1,200 from a bank and gives a 90-day, 6% promissory note in exchange.
9. Lux sells a vacant lot for $20,000 that had been used in its operations.
10. A three-year insurance policy is purchased for $1,500.

Required:
Separately evaluate the immediate effect of each transaction on the company's:

a. Current ratio *b.* Quick (acid-test) ratio *c.* Working capital

EXERCISE 11–2
Interpreting Effects of Transactions on Liquidity Measures

Interpret the effect of the following six *independent* events and transactions for the:

a. Accounts receivable turnover (currently equals 3.0).
b. Collection period.
c. Inventory turnover (currently equals 3.0).

The three columns to the right of each event and transaction are identified as (*a*), (*b*), and (*c*) corresponding to the three liquidity measures. For each event and transaction indicate the effect as an increase (I); decrease (D); or no effect (NE).

Events and Transactions	(*a*)	(*b*)	(*c*)
1. Beginning inventory understatement of $500 is corrected this period.	______	______	______
2. Sales on account are underreported by $10,000.	______	______	______
3. $10,000 of accounts receivable are written off by a charge to the allowance for doubtful accounts.	______	______	______
4. $10,000 of accounts receivable are written off by a charge to bad debts expense (direct method).	______	______	______
5. Under the lower-of-cost-or-market method, inventory is reduced to market by $1,000.	______	______	______
6. Beginning inventory overstatement of $500 is corrected this period.	______	______	______

EXERCISE 11–3
Interpreting Effects of Transactions on Liquidity Measures

Interpret the effect of the following six *independent* events and transactions for the:

a. Accounts receivable turnover (equals 4.0 prior to the event).

b. Collection period.

c. Inventory turnover (equals 4.0 prior to the event).

The three columns to the right of each event and transaction are identified as (*a*), (*b*), and (*c*) corresponding to the three liquidity measures. For each event and transaction indicate the effect as an increase (I); decrease (D); or no effect (NE).

Events and Transactions	(*a*)	(*b*)	(*c*)
1. $5,000 of accounts receivable are written off by a charge to allowance for doubtful accounts.	______	______	______
2. Beginning inventory understatement of $1,000 is corrected this period.	______	______	______
3. Under the lower-of-cost-or-market method, inventory is reduced to market by $2,000.	______	______	______
4. Obsolete inventory of $3,000 is identified and written off.	______	______	______
5. Beginning inventory overstatement of $2,000 is corrected this period.	______	______	______
6. Sales on account are overstated by $10,000 and corrected this period.	______	______	______

EXERCISE 11–4
Identifying Window-Dressing

The management of a corporation wishes to improve the appearance of its current financial position as reflected in the current and quick ratios.

Required:

a. Describe four ways in which management can window-dress the financial statements to accomplish this objective.

b. For each technique you identify in (*a*), describe the procedures, if any, you can use in your analysis to detect the window-dressing.

(CFA Adapted)

EXERCISE 11–5
Determining the Effect of Transactions on Solvency Ratios

Financial data ($ thousands) for Wisconsin Wilderness, Inc., are reproduced below:

Short-term liabilities	$ 500
Long-term liabilities	800
Equity capital	1,200
Cash from operations	300
Pretax income	200
Interest expense	40

Indicate the effect that each of the Wisconsin Wilderness transactions and events (1 through 10) on the next page has on each of the four ratios below. (Each transaction or event is independent of others–consider only the immediate effect.) Use I for increase, D for decrease, and NE for no effect.

a. Total debt to equity.

b. Long-term debt to equity.

c. Earnings to fixed charges (exceeds 1.0 before transactions and events).

d. Cash flow to fixed charges (exceeds 1.0 before transactions and events).

	a	b	c	d
1. Increase in tax rate.				
2. Retire bonds—paid in cash.				
3. Issue bonds to finance expansion.				
4. Issue preferred stock to finance expansion.				
5. Depreciation expense increases.				
6. Collect accounts receivable.				
7. Refinance debt resulting in higher interest cost.				
8. Capitalize higher proportion of interest expense.				
9. Convert convertible debt into common stock.				
10. Acquire inventory on credit.				

EXERCISE 11–6
What-If Analysis of Capital Structure (multiple choice)

The following information is relevant for Questions 1 and 2:
Austin Corporation's Year 8 financial statement notes include the following information:

a. Austin recently entered into operating leases with total future payments of $40 million that equal a discounted present value of $20 million.

b. Long-term assets include held-to-maturity debt securities carried at their amortized cost of $10 million. Fair market value of these securities is $12 million.

c. Austin guarantees a $5 million bond issue, due in Year 13. The bonds are issued by Healey, a nonconsolidated 30%-owned affiliate.

After analysis, you decide to adjust Austin's balance sheet for each of the above three items.

1. Among the effects of these adjustments for the times interest earned coverage ratio is (choose one of the following):
   a. Lease capitalization increases this ratio.
   b. Lease capitalization decreases this ratio.
   c. Recognizing the debt guarantee decreases this ratio.
   d. Held-to-maturity debt securities adjustment increases this ratio.
2. Among the effects of these adjustments for the long-term debt to equity ratio is (choose one of the following):
   a. Only the held-to-maturity debt securities adjustment decreases this ratio.
   b. Only lease capitalization decreases this ratio.
   c. All three adjustments decrease this ratio.
   d. All three adjustments increase this ratio.
3. What is the effect of a cash dividend payment on the following ratios (all else equal)?

Times Interest Earned	Long-Term Debt to Equity
a. Increase	Increase
b. No effect	Increase
c. No effect	No effect
d. Decrease	Decrease

4. What is the effect of selling inventory for profit on the following ratios (all else equal)?

Times Interest Earned	Long-Term Debt to Equity
a. Increase	Increase
b. Increase	Decrease
c. Decrease	Increase
d. Decrease	Decrease

5. The existence of uncapitalized operating leases is to (choose one of the following):
   a. Overstate the earnings to fixed charges coverage ratio.
   b. Overstate fixed charges.
   c. Overstate working capital.
   d. Understate the long-term debt to equity ratio.

(CFA Adapted)

PROBLEMS

PROBLEM 11–1
Analyzing Measures of Short-Term Liquidity

Campbell Soup Company

Refer to the financial statements of **Campbell Soup Company** in Appendix A.

Required:

a. Compute the following liquidity measures for Year 10:
  (1) Current ratio.
  (2) Acid-test ratio.
  (3) Accounts receivable turnover (accounts receivable balance at end of Year 9 is $564.1).
  (4) Inventory turnover (inventory balance at end of Year 9 is $816.0).
  (5) Days' sales in receivables.
  (6) Days' sales in inventory.
  (7) Conversion period (operating cycle).
  (8) Cash and cash equivalents to current assets.
  (9) Cash and cash equivalents to current liabilities.
  (10) Days' purchases in accounts payable.
  (11) Net trade cycle.
  (12) Cash flow ratio.

b. Assess Campbell's liquidity position using results from (*a*).

c. For Year 10, compute ratios 1, 4, 5, 6, and 7 using inventories valued on a FIFO basis (FIFO inventory at the end of Year 9 is $904).

d. What are the limitations of the current ratio as a measure of liquidity?

e. How can analysis and use of other related measures (other than the current ratio) enhance the evaluation of liquidity?

CHECK
(a) 7. 105.54
10. 46.36
11. 59.18

PROBLEM 11–2
What-If Analysis of Cash Requirements

Selected financial data of Future Technologies, Inc., at December 31, Year 1, are shown below:

Cash	$ 42,000	Accounts payable	$ 78,000
Accounts receivable	90,000	Notes payable	21,000
Inventory	39,000	Accrued taxes	10,800
Fixed assets	120,000	Capital stock	120,000
Accumulated depreciation	25,800	Retained earnings	35,400

The following additional information is available for the year ended December 31, Year 1:

Sales	$450,000	Depreciation	$15,000
Cost of goods sold (excluding depreciation)	312,000	Net income	12,000
Purchases	210,000		

For Year 2, Future Technologies anticipates a 5% sales growth. To counterbalance this lower than expected growth rate, the company implements cost-cutting strategies to reduce cost of goods sold by 2% from the Year 1 level. All other expenses are expected to increase by 5%. Expected net income for Year 2 is $20,000. Ending Year 2 inventory is estimated at $90,000 and there is no expected balance in accrued taxes. The company requires $175,000 to buy new equipment in Year 2. The minimum desired cash balance is $30,000. The company offers a discount of 2% of sales if payment is received in 10 days. It is expected that 10% of sales take advantage of this discount, while the remaining 90% are collected (on average) in 60 days.

Required:

Prepare a what-if analysis of cash needs (cash forecast) for Year 2. Will Future Technologies need to borrow money?

CHECK
Predicted borrowing, $103,232

PROBLEM 11–3
What-If Analysis of Changes in Credit Policy

Shown below are selected financial accounts of RAM Corp. as of December 31, Year 1:

Cash	$ 80,000	Accounts payable	$130,000
Accounts receivable	150,000	Notes payable	35,000
Inventory	65,000	Accrued taxes	20,000
Fixed assets	200,000	Capital stock	200,000
Accumulated depreciation	45,000		

The following additional information is available for Year 1:

Sales	$800,000	Depreciation	$25,000
Cost of sales (excludes depreciation)	520,000	Net income	20,000
Purchases	350,000		

RAM Corp. anticipates growth of 10% in sales for the coming year. All corresponding revenue and expense items are expected to increase by 10%, except for depreciation, which remains the same. All expenses are paid in cash as incurred during the year. Year 2 ending inventory is predicted at $150,000. By the end of Year 2, the company expects a notes payable balance of $50,000 and no accrued taxes. The company maintains a minimum cash balance of $50,000 as a managerial policy.

Required:

Consider each of the following circumstances separately and independently of each other and focus only on changes described. (*Hint:* Prepare an analysis of cash needs (cash forecast) for Year 2, and then calculate the effect of each of these three separate alternative scenarios.)

a. RAM is considering changing its credit policy. This change implies ending accounts receivable would represent 90 days of sales. What is the impact of this policy change on RAM's current cash position? Will the company be required to borrow?

b. RAM is considering a change to a 120-day collection period based on ending accounts receivable. What is the effect(s) of this change on its cash position?

c. Suppliers are considering changing their policy of extending credit to RAM to require payment on purchases within 60 days; there would be no change in RAM's collection period. What is the effect(s) of this change on its cash position?

CHECK
(a) Cash excess, $33,500
(c) Cash needed, $46,000

PROBLEM 11–4
What-If Analysis of Cash Demands

Reproduced below are selected financial data at the end of Year 5 and *forecasts* for the end of Year 6 for Top Corporation:

Account	Year 5	Year 6 (Forecast)	Account	Year 5	Year 6 (Forecast)
Cash	$ 35,000	?	Accounts payable	$ 65,000	$122,000
Accounts receivable	75,000	?	Notes payable	17,500	15,000
Inventory	32,000	$ 75,000	Accrued taxes	9,000	0
Fixed assets	100,000	100,000	Capital stock	100,000	100,000
Accumulated depreciation	21,500	25,000			

Additional forecast estimates for Year 6:

Sales	$412,500	Net income	$10,000
Cost of sales	70% of sales forecast	Days' sales in receivables	90 days

Required:

Assuming all expenses are paid in cash when incurred and that cost of sales is exclusive of depreciation, forecast the ending cash balance for Year 6. If Top Corp. wishes to maintain a minimum cash balance of $50,000, must it borrow?

CHECK
Cash needed, $27,125

PROBLEM 11–5
Qualitative Assessment of Liquidity

You are an investment analyst at Valley Insurance. Robert Jollie, a CFA and your superior, recently asked you to prepare a report on Gant Corporation's liquidity. Gant is a manufacturer of heavy equipment for the agricultural, forestry, and mining industries. Most of its plant capacity is located in the U.S. and a majority of its sales are international. Gant's investment bankers are offering Valley Insurance a participation in a private placement debenture issue. Beyond the traditional ratio analysis, your memo to Jollie stresses the following:

1. Gant's current ratio is 2:1.
2. During the prior fiscal year, Gant's working capital increased substantially.
3. While Gant's earnings are below record levels, rigorous cost controls yield an acceptable level of profitability and provide a basis for continued liquidity.

After reviewing your memo, Jollie dismisses it as "totally inadequate"–not because it did not include a quantitative analysis of financial ratios, but because it did not effectively address liquidity. Jollie writes:

> Liquidity is a cash issue, and liquidity analysis is a process of evaluating the risk of whether a company can pay its debts as they come due. The vagaries and inconsistencies of working capital definitions do not adequately address this issue. Working capital analysis simply accounts for the change in a company's working capital position and adds little to an assessment of liquidity.

Required:

a. Identify five key information items directly reflecting on Gant's liquidity that you should attempt to derive from this company's financial statements and management interviews.

b. Identify five *qualitative* financial and economic assessments specific to Gant and its industry that you should consider in further analyzing Gant's liquidity.

(CFA Adapted)

PROBLEM 11–6
Interpreting Measures of Short-Term Liquidity

As lending officer for Prudent Bank you are analyzing the financial statements of ZETA Corporation (see Case CC–2 in the Comprehensive Case Chapter for data) as part of ZETA's loan application. Your superior requests you evaluate ZETA's liquidity using the two-year financial information available. The following additional information is acquired (in $ thousands): Inventory at January 1, Year 5, $32,000.

Required:

a. Compute the following measures for both Years 5 and 6:
(1) Current ratio.
(2) Days' sales in receivables.
(3) Inventory turnover.
(4) Days' sales in inventory.
(5) Days' purchases in accounts payable (assume all cost of sales items are purchased).
(6) Cash flow ratio.

b. Comment on any significant year-to-year changes identified from the analysis in (*a*).

CHECK
(5) Year 5, 79
Year 6, 76

PROBLEM 11–7
Computing and Interpreting Solvency Ratios

Quaker Oats Company

Refer to the financial statements of **Quaker Oats Company** in Appendix A.

Required:

a. Compute the following ratios for Years 9, 10, and 11. Assume a statutory income tax rate of 34% in all ratios except the fixed-charge coverage ratios (where you are to use the effective tax rate). Consider all deferred taxes as liabilities. Assume fixed charges include the interest portion of operating rental expense, equal to one-third of the operating lease expense.
(1) Long-term debt to equity.
(2) Total debt ratio.

(3) Total debt to equity.
(4) Preferred stock to equity (use stated value of preferred stock for all years).
(5) Earnings to fixed charges.
(6) Cash flow to fixed charges.
(7) Cash from operations to long-term debt.
(8) Earnings coverage of preferred dividends.
(9) Equity capital to net fixed assets.

b. Discuss the importance of both level and trend for each of the above measures.

CHECK
Year 11
(4) 0.53%
(5) 4.45
(6) 6.83
(8) 4.22
(9) 0.73

PROBLEM 11–8
Calculating Solvency Ratios

Campbell Soup Company

Refer to the financial statements of **Campbell Soup Company** in Appendix A.

Required:

a. Compute the following measures for Year 10. (Assume 50% of deferred income taxes will reverse in the foreseeable future—the remainder should be considered equity.)
(1) Total debt to equity.
(2) Total debt ratio.
(3) Long-term liabilities to equity.
(4) Total equity to total liabilities.
(5) Fixed assets to equity.
(6) Short-term liabilities to total debt.
(7) Earnings to fixed charges.
(8) Cash flow to fixed charges.
(9) Working capital to total debt.

b. Under the heading "Balance Sheets" in its Management's Discussion and Analysis section, Campbell refers to the ratio of total debt to capitalization (33.7%). Verify Campbell's computation for Year 10.

CHECK
(1) 1.21
(7) 2.14
(8) 5.27

PROBLEM 11–9
Computing and Analyzing Earnings Coverage Ratios

The income statement of Kimberly Corporation for the year ended December 31, Year 1, is reproduced below:

KIMBERLY CORPORATION
Consolidated Income Statement ($ thousands)
For Year Ended December 31, Year 1

Sales		$14,000
Undistributed income of less than 50%-owned affiliates		300
Total revenue		14,300
Cost of goods sold	$6,000	
Selling and administrative expenses	2,000	
Depreciation	600	
Rental expense	500	
Share of minority interest in consolidated income	200	
Interest expense	400	(9,700)
Income before taxes		4,600
Income taxes:		
Current	900	
Deferred	400	(1,300)
Net income		$ 3,300
Less dividends:		
Common stock	$ 300	
Preferred stock	400	$ (700)
Earnings retained for the year		$ 2,600

Additional Information:

1. The following changes occurred in current assets and current liabilities for Year 1:

Current accounts	Increase (decrease)	Current accounts	Increase (decrease)
Accounts receivable	$900	Notes payable to bank	$(200)
Inventories	(800)	Accounts payable	700
Dividend payable	(100)		

2. The effective tax rate is 40%.
3. Shares of minority interests in consolidated income do not have fixed charges.
4. Interest expense includes:

Interest incurred (except items below)	$600
Amortization of bond premium	(300)
Interest on capitalized leases	140
Interest incurred	440
Less interest capitalized	(40)
Interest expense	$400

5. Amortization of previously capitalized interest (included in depreciation) is $60.
6. Interest implicit in operating lease rental payment (included in rental expense) is $120.

Required:

CHECK
(1) 8.71
(2) 11.11

a. Compute the following earnings coverage ratios:
(1) Earnings to fixed charges.
(2) Cash flow to fixed charges.
(3) Earnings coverage of preferred dividends.

b. Analyze and interpret the earnings coverage ratios in (*a*).

PROBLEM 11–10
Computing and Analyzing Earnings Coverage Ratios

The income statement of Lot Corp. for the year ended December 31, Year 1, follows:

LOT CORPORATION
Income Statement ($ thousands)
For Year Ended December 31, Year 1

Sales		$27,400
Undistributed income of less than 50%-owned affiliates		400
Total revenue		27,800
Less: Cost of goods sold		(14,000)
Gross profit		13,800
Selling and administrative expenses	$3,600	
Depreciation[(a)]	1,200	
Rental expense[(b)]	1,400	
Share of minority interest in consolidated income[(c)]	600	
Interest expense[(d)]	1,200	(8,000)
Income before taxes		5,800
Income taxes:		
Current	2,000	
Deferred	1,000	(3,000)
Net income		$ 2,800

(continued)

Dividends:		
Preferred stock	$ 400	
Common stock	1,000	$ (1,400)
Earnings retained for the year		$ 1,400

[a] Represents depreciation excluded from all other expense categories and includes $100 amortization of previously capitalized interest.
[b] Includes $400 of interest implicit in operating lease rental payments that should be considered as having financing characteristics.
[c] These subsidiaries have fixed charges.
[d] Interest expense includes:

Interest incurred (except items below)	*$ 880*
Amortization of bond discount	*100*
Interest portion of capitalized leases	*340*
Interest capitalized	*(120)*
	$1,200

Additional Information:

1. The following changes occurred in current assets and liabilities for Year 1:

Current accounts	Increase (decrease)	Current accounts	Increase (decrease)
Accounts receivable	$(1,600)	Notes payable	$ (400)
Inventories	2,000	Accounts payable	2,000
Dividend payable	240		

2. Tax rate is 40%.

Required:

a. Compute the following earnings coverage ratios:
   (1) Earnings to fixed charges.
   (2) Cash flow to fixed charges.
   (3) Earnings coverage of preferred dividends.

b. Analyze and interpret the earnings coverage ratios in (*a*).

CHECK
(1) 4.48
(2) 6.04

PROBLEM 11–11
Analyzing Coverage Ratios

Your supervisor is considering purchasing the bonds and preferred shares of ARC Corp. She furnishes you the following ARC income statement and expresses concern about the coverage of fixed charges.

ARC CORPORATION
Consolidated Income Statement
For Year Ended December 31, Year 5

Sales		$27,400
Income of less than 50%-owned affiliates (note 1)		800
Total revenue		28,200
Cost of goods sold		(14,000)
Gross profit		14,200
Selling and administrative expenses	$3,600	
Depreciation (note 2)	1,200	
Rental expenses (note 3)	1,400	
Share of minority interests in consolidated income (note 4)	600	
Interest expense (note 5)	1,200	(8,000)
Income before income taxes		6,200

(continued)

Income taxes:		
Current	$2,000	
Deferred	1,000	$ (3,000)
Net income		$ 3,200
Dividends:		
Preferred stock	$ 400	
Common stock	1,000	$ (1,400)
Increase in retained earnings		$ 1,800

Notes:

1. *For the income from affiliates, $600 is undistributed.*
2. *Includes $80 amortization of previously capitalized interest.*
3. *Includes $400 of interest implicit in operating lease rental payments.*
4. *These subsidiaries do not have fixed charges.*
5. *Interest expense includes:*

Interest incurred (except items below)	*$ 880*
Amortization of bond discount	*100*
Interest portion of capitalized leases	*340*
Interest capitalized	*(120)*
	$1,200

6. *The following changes occurred in current year balance sheet accounts:*

Accounts receivable	*$(600)*
Inventories	*160*
Payables and accrued expenses	*120*
Dividends payable	*(80)*
Current portion of long-term debt	*(100)*

7. *Tax rate is 40 percent.*

CHECK
(1) 4.23
(2) 5.56

Required:

a. Compute the following earnings coverage ratios:
(1) Earnings to fixed charges.
(2) Cash flow to fixed charges.
(3) Earnings coverage of preferred dividends.

b. Analyze and interpret the earnings coverage ratios in (*a*).

PROBLEM 11–12
Calculating Financial Ratios on Debt and Equity Securities

Refer to the following financial data of Fox Industries Ltd.:

FOX INDUSTRIES LIMITED
Condensed Income Statement ($ thousands)

	FISCAL YEAR ENDED				
	Year 7	**Year 6**	**Year 5**	**Year 4**	**Year 3**
Earnings before depreciation, interest on long-term debt, and taxes	$8,750	$8,250	$8,000	$7,750	$7,250
Less: Depreciation	(4,000)	(3,750)	(3,500)	(3,500)	(3,250)
Earnings before interest on long-term debt and taxes	$4,750	$4,500	$4,500	$4,250	$4,000

FOX INDUSTRIES LIMITED

Capitalization at December 31, Year 7 ($ thousands)

Long-term debt:	
First mortgage bonds:	
5.00% serial bonds due Year 8 to Year 10	$ 7,500
6.00% sinking fund bonds due Year 15 (note 1)	17,500
Debentures:	
6.50% sinking fund debentures due Year 16 (note 1)	10,000
Total long-term debt	$35,000
Capital stock:	
$1.10 cumulative redeemable preferred, stated value $5.00 per share (redeemable at $20.00 share)	$ 1,500
400,000 Class A shares, no-par value (note 2)	14,000
1,000,000 common shares, no par value	6,000
Total capital stock	$21,500
Paid-in capital	7,000
Retained earnings	18,500
Total long-term debt and equity	$82,000

Notes:

1. Combined annual sinking fund payments are $500.

2. Subject to the rights of the preferred shares, the Class A shares are entitled to fixed cumulative dividends at the rate of $2.50 per share per annum, and are convertible at the holder's option, at any time, into common shares on the basis of two common shares for one Class A share.

Required:

a. Compute the (1) earnings coverage ratio for Year 7, and (2) average earnings coverage ratio for the five-year period Year 3 through Year 7 (inclusive), separately on the first mortgage bonds and on the sinking fund debentures at the end of Year 7.

b. Compute the long-term debt to equity ratio as of December 31, Year 7, and identify the proportion of equity represented by shares senior to common shares.

c. Assuming a 50% income tax rate, calculate the (1) earnings coverage ratio for Year 7, and (2) average earnings coverage ratio for the five-year period Year 3 through Year 7 (inclusive), on the $1.10 cumulative redeemable preferred shares at the end of Year 7.

d. Assuming a 50% income tax rate and full conversion of the Class A shares, calculate earnings per common share for the end of Year 7.

(CFA Adapted)

CHECK

(c) 1. 1.7
2. 1.6
(d) $0.56

PROBLEM 11–13

Analyzing Alternative Financing Strategies

TOPP Company is planning to invest $20,000,000 in an expansion program expected to increase income before interest and taxes by $4,000,000. TOPP currently is earning $5 per share on 1,000,000 shares of common stock outstanding. TOPP's capital structure prior to the investment is:

Total debt	$20,000,000
Shareholders' equity	50,000,000
Total capitalization	$70,000,000

Expansion can be financed by the sale of 400,000 shares at $50 each or by issuing long-term debt at 6%. TOPP's most recent income statement follows:

Sales		$100,000,000
Variable costs	$60,000,000	
Fixed costs	20,000,000	
Total costs		(80,000,000)
Income before interest and taxes		20,000,000
Interest expense (6% rate)		(1,000,000)
Income before taxes		19,000,000
Income taxes (40% rate)		(7,600,000)
Net income		$ 11,400,000

Required:

CHECK
(a) 1. $6.54

a. Assuming TOPP maintains its current income level and achieves the expected income from expansion, what will be TOPP's earnings per share:
   (1) If expansion is financed by debt? (2) If expansion is financed by equity?

b. At what level of income before interest and taxes will earnings per share be equal under both alternatives?

PROBLEM 11–14
Analytical Adjustment of the Debt to Capitalization Ratio

You are a senior portfolio manager with Reilly Investment Management reviewing the biweekly printout of equity value screens prepared by a brokerage firm. One of the screens used to identify companies is a "low long-term debt/total long-term capital ratio." The printout indicates this ratio for Lubbock Corporation is 23.9%. Your reaction is that Lubbock might be a potential takeover target and you proceed to analyze Lubbock's balance sheet reproduced below:

LUBBOCK CORPORATION
Condensed Balance Sheet, ($ millions)
December 31, Year 7

Assets	
Cash and equivalents	$ 100
Receivables	350
Marketable securities	150
Inventory	800
Other current assets	400
Total current assets	1,800
Plant and equipment, net	1,800
Total assets	$3,600
Liabilities and Equity	
Note payable	$ 125
Accounts payable	175
Taxes payable	150
Other current liabilities	75
Total current liabilities	525
Long-term debt	675
Deferred taxes (noncurrent)	175
Other noncurrent liabilities	75
Minority interest	100
Common stock	400
Retained earnings	1,650
Total liabilities and equity	$3,600

Further analysis of Lubbock's financial statements reveals the following notes:

1. A subsidiary, Lubbock Property Corp., holds, as joint venture partner, a 50% interest in its head office building in Chicago, and 10 regional shopping centers in the United States. The parent company has guaranteed the indebtedness of these properties, which total $250,000,000 at December 31, Year 7.

2. The LIFO cost basis was used in the valuation of inventories at December 31, Year 7. If the FIFO method of inventory was used in place of LIFO, inventories would have exceeded reported amounts by $200,000,000.
3. The company leases most of its facilities under long-term contracts. These leases are categorized as operating leases for accounting purposes. Future minimum rental payments as of December 31, Year 7 are: $90,000,000 per year for Year 8 through Year 27. These leases carry an implicit interest rate factor of 10%, which translates to a present value of approximately $750,000,000.

Required:

a. Explain how the information in each note is used to adjust items on Lubbock's balance sheet.

b. Calculate an adjusted *long-term debt to total long-term capitalization* ratio applying the proposed adjustments from (*a*). Ignore potential income tax effects.

c. As a potential investor, you consider other accounting factors in evaluating Lubbock's balance sheet including:

(1) Valuation of marketable securities. (2) Treatment of deferred taxes.

Discuss how each of these accounting factors can impact Lubbock's *long-term debt to total long-term capitalization* ratio.

(CFA Adapted)

PROBLEM 11–15
Analyzing and Interpreting Financial Ratios

You are analyzing the bonds of ZETA Company (see Case CC–2 in the Comprehensive Case Chapter for data) as a potential long-term investment. As part of your decision-making process, you compute various ratios for Years 5 and 6. Additional data and information to be considered only for purposes of this problem follow ($ thousands):

1. Interest consists of:

	Year 6	Year 5
Interest incurred (except items below)	$ 9,200	$5,000
Amortization of bond discount	2,500	2,000
Interest portion of capitalized leases	80	—
Interest capitalized	(1,780)	(1,000)
	$10,000	$6,000

2. Depreciation includes amortization of previously capitalized interest of $1,200 for Year 6 and $1,000 for Year 5.
3. Interest portion of operating rental expense considered a fixed charge: $20 in Year 6 and $16 in Year 5.
4. The associated company is less than 50% owned.
5. Deferred taxes constitute a long-term liability.
6. Present value of noncapitalized financing leases is $200 for both years.
7. Excess of the projected pension benefit obligation over the accumulated pension benefit obligation is $2,800 for both years.
8. End of Year 4 total assets and equity capital are $94,500 and $42,000, respectively.
9. Average market price per share of ZETA's common stock is $40 and $45 for Year 6 and Year 5, respectively.

Required:

a. Compute the following analytical measures for both Year 6 and Year 5:
(1) Total debt ratio.
(2) Total debt to equity.
(3) Long-term debt to equity.
(4) Earnings to fixed charges.
(5) Cash flow to fixed charges.

b. Analyze and interpret both the level and year-to-year trend in these measures.

CHECK
Year 6
(4) 2.61
(5) 2.17

PROBLEM 11–16
Analysis of Creditworthiness with Merger Activity

As a new employee of Clayton Asset Management, you are assigned to evaluate the credit quality of BRT Corp. bonds. Clayton holds the bonds in its high-yield bond portfolio. The following information is provided to assist in the analysis.

1. BRT Corporation is a rapidly growing company in the broadcast industry. It has grown primarily through a series of aggressive acquisitions.

2. Early in Year 6, BRT announced it was acquiring a competitor in a hostile takeover that would double its assets but also increase debt. The credit rating of BRT debt fell from BBB to BB. The acquisition reduced the financial flexibility of BRT but increased its presence in the broadcasting industry.
3. In the middle of Year 7, BRT announced it is merging with another large entertainment company. The merger will alter BRT's capital structure and also make it the leader in the broadcast industry. The Year 6 acquisition combined with this merger will increase the total assets of BRT by a factor of four. A large portion of the total assets are intangible, representing franchise and distribution rights.
4. While the outlook for the broadcasting industry remains strong, large telecommunication companies attempting to enter the broadcasting industry are keeping competitive pressures high. Laws and regulations also promote the competitiveness of the environment, but initial start-up costs make it difficult for new companies to enter the industry. Large capital expenditures are required to maintain and improve existing systems as well as to expand current business.
5. For your analysis, you are provided with the financial data shown here:

BRT CORPORATION
Balance Sheet Data (in millions)
At December 31

	Year 3	Year 4	Year 5	Year 6	Projected Year 7
Current assets	$ 654	$ 718	$2,686	$ 2,241	$ 5,255
Fixed assets, net	391	379	554	1,567	2,583
Other assets (intangibles)	2,982	3,090	3,176	8,946	20,435
Total assets	$4,027	$4,187	$6,416	$12,754	$28,273
Current liabilities	$ 799	$ 876	$ 966	$ 1,476	$ 3,731
Long-term debt	2,537	2,321	2,378	7,142	15,701
Other liabilities	326	292	354	976	349
Total equity	365	698	2,718	3,160	8,492
Total liabilities and equity	$4,027	$4,187	$6,416	$12,754	$28,273

BRT CORPORATION
Income Statement Data
(In Millions Except per Share Data)
For Year Ended December 31

	Year 3	Year 4	Year 5	Year 6	Projected Year 7
Net sales	$1,600	$1,712	$2,005	$4,103	$9,436
Operating expenses	(1,376)	(1,400)	(1,620)	(3,683)	(8,603)
Operating income	224	312	385	420	833
Interest expense	(296)	(299)	(155)	(270)	(825)
Income taxes	(20)	(42)	(130)	(131)	(4)
Net income	$ (92)	$ (29)	$ 100	$ 19	$ 4
Earnings per share	$ (0.86)	$ (0.24)	$ 0.83	$ 0.09	$ 0.01
Average price per share	$26.30	$34.10	$44.90	$40.10	$40.80
Average shares outstanding	107	120	121	198	359

BRT CORPORATION
Selected Ratios

	Year 3	Year 4	Year 5	Year 6	Projected Year 7
Operating income to sales	14.0%	18.2%	19.2%	10.2%	*
Sales to total assets	0.39	0.41	0.31	0.32	0.33
Earnings before interest and taxes to total assets	5.5%	7.4%	6.0%	3.3%	*
Times interest earned	0.76	1.04	2.48	1.55	*
Long-term debt to total assets	63.0%	55.4%	37.0%	55.9%	*

CLAYTON ASSET MANAGEMENT
Credit Rating Standards

	AVERAGE RATIOS BY RATING CATEGORY						
Financial Ratios	**AA**	**A**	**BBB**	**BB**	**B**	**CCC**	**CC**
Operating income to sales (%)	16.2	13.4	12.1	10.3	8.5	6.4	5.2
Sales to total assets	2.50	2.00	1.50	1.00	0.75	0.50	0.25
Earnings before interest and taxes to total assets	15.0%	10.0%	8.0%	6.0%	4.0%	3.0%	2.0%
Times interest earned	5.54	3.62	2.29	1.56	1.04	0.79	0.75
Long-term debt to total assets	19.5%	30.4%	40.2%	51.8%	71.8%	81.0%	85.4%
Bond Credit Spread Information							
Current yield spread in basis points over 10-year Treasuries	45	55	85	155	225	275	350

Required:

a. Calculate the following ratios using the projected Year 7 financial information:
(1) Operating income to sales.
(2) Earnings before interest and taxes to total assets.
(3) Times interest earned.
(4) Long-term debt to total assets.

b. Discuss the effect of the Year 7 merger on the creditworthiness of BRT through an analysis of each of the ratios in (*a*).

c. BRT Corporation 10-year bonds are currently rated BB and are trading at a yield to maturity of 7.70%. The current 10-year Treasury note is yielding 6.15%. Based on your work in (*a*) and (*b*), the background information, and information on Selected Ratios and Credit Rating Standards, state and justify whether Clayton should hold or sell the BRT Corporation bonds in its portfolio. Include qualitative factors in your discussion.

(CFA adapted)

PROBLEM 11–17
Comparative Credit Analysis of Companies

Assume you are a fixed-income analyst at an investment management firm. You are following the developments at two companies, Sturdy Machines and Patriot Manufacturing, which are both U.S. based industrial companies that sell their products worldwide. Both companies operate in cyclical industries. Sturdy Machines' profits have suffered from a rising dollar and a slump in its business. The company has said that major cuts in its operating expenses are likely to be necessary if it is to make a profit next year. On the other hand, Patriot Manufacturing has been able to maintain its profitability and enhance its balance sheet. Selected data for both companies follow:

Ratio	Year 5	Year 6	Year 7
Sturdy Machines			
Cash flow/total debt (%)	37.3	31.0	33.0
Total debt/capital (%)	38.2	40.1	41.3
Pretax interest coverage (times)	4.2	2.3	1.1
Patriot Manufacturing			
Cash flow/total debt (%)	34.6	38.0	43.1
Total debt/capital (%)	40.0	37.3	34.9
Pretax interest coverage (times)	2.7	4.5	6.1

You are monitoring the bonds of these companies for possible purchase. You notice that a rating agency recently downgraded the senior debt of Sturdy Machines from A to AA and upgraded the senior debt of Patriot Manufacturing from AAA to AA. You received the following yield quotes from a broker:

- Sturdy Machines 7.50% due June 1, 2008, quoted at 7.10%.
- Patriot Manufacturing 7.50% due June 1, 2008, quoted at 7.10%.

Required:

Recommend which of the above bonds you should buy. Justify your choice with reference to at least two ratios and two qualitative factors from the information provided.

(CFA adapted)

CASES

CASE 11–1

Assessing Short-Term Liquidity and Cash Requirements

Refer to the financial statements of **Quaker Oats Company** in Appendix A.

Quaker Oats Company

Part I

a. Construct a table containing the following liquidity ratios for Years 9 through 11.
   (1) Current ratio.
   (2) Acid-test ratio.
   (3) Cash to current assets ratio.
   (4) Accounts receivable turnover.
   (5) Collection period.
   (6) Inventory turnover.
   (7) Days to sell inventory.
   (8) Days' purchases in accounts payable.
   (9) Operating cycle (conversion period).
   (10) Net trade cycle.
   (11) Cash flow ratio.

b. Based on computations in (*a*), prepare a one-page report analyzing Quaker Oats' liquidity.

Part II

Quaker Oats' management projects a 15% growth in sales, purchases, and expenses for Year 12. The inventory turnover for Year 12 is expected to be 6.5. To achieve these operating goals, management set the receivable collection period at 40 days, based on *year-end* accounts receivable. Ending accounts payable for Year 12 is expected to be $380 million and accounts payable turnover is expected to be 8.0. Also, $40 million in notes are to be paid off. Management desires to maintain a minimum cash balance of $70 million. The effective income tax rate for Year 12 is expected to be 45%, and 10% of tax expense is expected to be deferred. Dividends will be $4.3 million on preferred stock and $128 million for common stock.

CHECK
Forecast NI, $250.3
Forecast excess cash, $296.7

Required:

Will Quaker Oats need to borrow money in Year 12? (*Hint:* Prepare a forecasted income statement and a forecasted statement of cash receipts and payments for Year 12.)

CASE 11–2
Preparing and Interpreting Cash Flow Forecasts

Fax Corporation's income statement and balance sheet for the year ended December 31, Year 1, are reproduced below:

FAX CORPORATION
Income Statement
For Year Ended December 31, Year 1

Net sales		$960,000
Cost of goods sold (excluding depreciation)		(550,000)
Gross profit		410,000
Depreciation expense	$ 30,000	
Selling and administrative expenses	160,000	(190,000)
Income before taxes		220,000
Income taxes (state and federal)		(105,600)
Net income		$114,400

FAX CORPORATION
Balance Sheet
December 31, Year 1

Assets		
Current assets:		
Cash	$ 30,000	
Marketable securities	5,500	
Accounts receivable	52,000	
Inventory	112,500	
Total current assets		$200,000
Plant and equipment	630,000	
Less: Accumulated depreciation	(130,000)	500,000
Total assets		$700,000
Liabilities and Equity		
Current liabilities:		
Accounts payable	$ 60,000	
Notes payable	50,000	
Total current liabilities		$110,000
Long-term debt		150,000
Equity:		
Capital stock	250,000	
Retained earnings	190,000	440,000
Total liabilities and equity		$700,000

Additional Information:

1. Purchases in Year 1 are $480,000.
2. In Year 2, management expects 15% sales growth and a 10% increase in all expenses except for depreciation, which increases by 5%.
3. Management expects an inventory turnover ratio of 5.5 for Year 2.
4. A receivable collection period of 90 days, based on *year-end* accounts receivable, is planned for Year 2.
5. Year 2 income taxes, at the same rate of pretax income for Year 1, will be paid in cash.
6. Notes payable at the end of Year 2 will be $30,000.
7. Long-term debt of $25,000 will be paid in Year 2.
8. FAX desires a minimum cash balance of $20,000 in Year 2.

9. The ratio of accounts payable to purchases for Year 2 is the same as in Year 1.
10. All selling and administrative expenses will be paid in cash in Year 2.
11. Marketable securities and equity accounts at the end of Year 2 are the same as in Year 1.

Required:

CHECK
Forecast cash needed, $55,920

a. Prepare a statement of forecasted cash inflows and outflows (what-if analysis) for the year ended December 31, Year 2.

b. Will FAX Corporation have to borrow money in Year 2?

CASE 11–3
Preparing and Interpreting Cash Flow Forecasts

Kopp Corporation's income statement and balance sheet for the year ending December 31, Year 1, are reproduced below:

KOPP CORPORATION
Income Statement
For Year Ended December 31, Year 1

Net sales		$960,000
Cost of goods sold		(550,000)
Gross profit		410,000
Depreciation expense	$ 30,000	
Selling and administrative expenses	160,000	(190,000)
Income before taxes		220,000
Income taxes (48%)		(57,600)
Net income		$162,400

KOPP CORPORATION
Balance Sheet
December 31, Year 1

Assets		
Current assets:		
Cash	$ 30,000	
Marketable securities	5,500	
Accounts receivable	52,500	
Inventory	112,000	
Total current assets		$200,000
Plant and equipment	630,000	
Less: Accumulated depreciation	(130,000)	500,000
Total assets		$700,000
Liabilities and Equity		
Current liabilities:		
Accounts payable	$ 60,000	
Notes payable	50,000	
Total current liabilities		$110,000
Long-term debt		150,000
Equity:		
Capital stock	250,000	
Retained earnings	190,000	440,000
Total liabilities and equity		$700,000

Additional Information:

1. Purchases in Year 1 are $450,000.
2. In Year 2, management expects 15% sales growth and a 10% increase in all expenses except for depreciation, which increases by 5%.

3. Inventory turnover for Year 1 is 5.0, and management expects an inventory turnover ratio of 6.0 for Year 2.
4. A receivable collection period of 90 days, based on *year-end* accounts receivable, is planned for Year 2.
5. Year 2 income taxes, at the same rate on pretax income in Year 1, will be paid in cash.
6. Notes payable of $20,000 will be paid in Year 2.
7. Long-term debt of $25,000 will be repaid in Year 2.
8. Kopp desires a minimum cash balance of $20,000 in Year 2.
9. The ratio of accounts payable to purchases will remain the same in Year 2 as in Year 1.

Required:

a. Prepare a statement of forecasted cash inflows and outflows (what-if analysis) for the year ending December 31, Year 2.

b. Will Kopp Corporation have to borrow money in Year 2?

CHECK
Forecasted cash need, $35,898

CASE 11–4
Making a Lending Decision

Ian Manufacturing Company was organized five years ago and manufactures toys. Its most recent three years' balance sheets and income statements are reproduced below:

IAN MANUFACTURING COMPANY
Balance Sheets
June 30, Year 5, Year 4, and Year 3

	Year 5	Year 4	Year 3
Assets			
Cash	$ 12,000	$ 15,000	$ 16,000
Accounts receivable, net	183,000	80,000	60,000
Inventory	142,000	97,000	52,000
Other current assets	5,000	6,000	4,000
Plant and equipment (net)	160,000	110,000	70,000
Total assets	$502,000	$308,000	$202,000
Liabilities and Equity			
Accounts payable	$147,800	$ 50,400	$ 22,000
Federal income tax payable	30,000	14,400	28,000
Long-term liabilities	120,000	73,000	22,400
Common stock, $5 par value	110,000	110,000	80,000
Retained earnings	94,200	60,200	49,600
Total liabilities and equity	$502,000	$308,000	$202,000

IAN MANUFACTURING COMPANY
Condensed Income Statements
For Years Ended June 30, Year 5, Year 4, Year 3

	Year 5	Year 4	Year 3
Net sales	$1,684,000	$1,250,000	$1,050,000
Cost of goods sold	(927,000)	(810,000)	(512,000)
Gross profit	757,000	440,000	538,000
Marketing and administrative costs	(670,000)	(396,700)	(467,760)
Operating income	87,000	43,300	70,240
Interest cost	(12,000)	(7,300)	(2,240)
Income before income tax	75,000	36,000	68,000
Income tax	(30,000)	(14,400)	(28,000)
Net income	$ 45,000	$ 21,600	$ 40,000

A reconciliation of retained earnings for years ended June 30, Year 4, and Year 5, follows:

IAN MANUFACTURING COMPANY
Statement of Retained Earnings
For Years Ended June 30, Year 5 and Year 4

	Year 5	Year 4
Balance, beginning	$ 60,200	$49,600
Add: Net income	45,000	21,600
Subtotal	105,200	71,200
Deduct: Dividends paid	(11,000)	(11,000)
Balance, ending	$ 94,200	$60,200

Additional Information:

1. All sales are on account.
2. Long-term liabilities are owed to the company's bank.
3. Terms of sale are net 30 days.

Required:

CHECK
(a) 5. Year 5, 28.10
8. Year 5, 1.46

a. Compute the following measures for both Years 4 and 5:
(1) Working capital.
(2) Current ratio.
(3) Acid-test ratio.
(4) Accounts receivable turnover.
(5) Collection period of receivables.
(6) Inventory turnover.
(7) Days to sell inventory.
(8) Debt-to-equity ratio.
(9) Times interest earned.

b. Using Year 3 as the base year, compute an index-number trend series for:
(1) Sales.
(2) Cost of goods sold.
(3) Gross profit.
(4) Marketing and administrative costs.
(5) Net income.

c. Based on your analysis in (*a*) and (*b*), prepare a one-page report yielding a recommendation on whether to grant a loan to Ian Manufacturing. Support your recommendation with relevant analysis.

CASE 11–5
Determining Bond Rating

Philip Morris Companies

Philip Morris Companies is a major manufacturer and distributor of consumer products. It has a history of steady growth in sales, earnings, and cash flows. In recent years Philip Morris has diversified with acquisitions of Miller Brewing and General Foods. In Year 8, Philip Morris acted to further diversify by announcing an unsolicited cash tender offer for all the 124 million outstanding shares of Kraft at $90 per share. After negotiation, Kraft accepts a $106 per share all-cash offer from Philip Morris. Assume you are an analyst with Investment Services, and that soon after the cash tender offer you are requested by your supervisor to review the potential acquisition of Kraft and assess its impact on Philip Morris' credit standing. You assemble various information using the following projected Year 8 and Year 9 financial data:

PHILIP MORRIS COMPANIES, INC.
Projected Financial Data ($ millions)

	Year 8 Estimate	YEAR 9 ESTIMATE			
	Excluding Kraft	Before Kraft	Kraft Only	Adjustments	Consolidated
Selected Income Statement Data					
Sales:					
Domestic tobacco	$ 8,300	$ 8,930			$ 8,930
International tobacco	8,000	8,800			8,800
General Foods	10,750	11,600			11,600
Kraft			$11,610		11,610
Beer	3,400	3,750			3,750
Total sales	30,450	33,080	11,610		44,690

Operating income:					
Domestic tobacco	$ 3,080	$ 3,520		$ 35	$ 3,555
International tobacco	800	940			940
General Foods	810	870			870
Kraft			$ 1,050	50	1,100
Beer	190	205			205
Other	105	125			125
Goodwill amortization	(110)	(110)		(295)	(405)
Total operating income	4,875	5,550	1,050	(210)	6,390
Percent of sales	16.0%	16.8%	9.0%		14.3%
Interest expense	(575)	(500)	(75)	(1,025)	(1,600)
Corporate expense	(200)	(225)	(100)	(40)	(365)
Other expense	(5)	(5)			(5)
Pre-tax income	4,095	4,820	875	(1,275)	4,420
Percent of sales	13.4%	14.6%	7.5%		9.9%
Income taxes	(1,740)	(2,000)	(349)	493	(1,856)
Tax rate	42.5%	41.5%	40.0%		42.0%
Net income	$ 2,355	$ 2,820	$ 526	$ (782)	$ 2,564
Selected Year-End Balance Sheet Data					
Short-term debt	$ 1,125	$ 1,100	$ 683		$ 1,783
Long-term debt	4,757	3,883	895	$11,000	15,778
Stockholders' equity	8,141	9,931	2,150	(2,406)	9,675
Other Selected Financial Data					
Depreciation and amortization	720	750	190	295	1,235
Deferred taxes	100	100	10	280	390
Equity in undistributed earnings of unconsolidated subsidiaries	110	125			125

Required:

a. You arrange a visit with Philip Morris management. Given the information you have assembled above, identify and discuss five major industry considerations you should pursue when questioning management.

b. Additional information is collected showing median ratio values along with their bond rating category for three financial ratios. Using this information reported in the excerpt below along with the projections above:
  (1) Calculate these same three ratios for Philip Morris for Year 9 using:
    (*a*) Amounts *before* accounting for the Kraft acquisition.
    (*b*) Consolidated amounts *after* the Kraft acquisition.
  (2) Discuss and interpret the two sets of ratios from 1 compared to the median values for each bond rating category. Determine and support your recommendation on a rating category for Philip Morris *after* the Kraft acquisition.

(CFA Adapted)

CHECK
(1b) 3 ratios:
3.76, .619, .231

Additional Information:

MEDIAN RATIO VALUES ACCORDING TO BOND RATING CATEGORIES

Ratio	AAA	AA	A	BBB	BB	B	CCC
Pretax interest coverage	14.10	9.67	5.40	3.63	2.25	1.58	(0.42)
Long-term debt as a percent of capitalization	11.5%	18.7%	28.3%	34.3%	48.4%	57.2%	73.2%
Cash flow* as a percent of total debt	111.8%	86.0%	50.9%	34.2%	22.8%	14.1%	6.2%

* *For the purpose of calculating this ratio, Standard & Poor's defines* cash flow *as net income plus depreciation, amortization, and deferred taxes, less equity in undistributed earnings of unconsolidated subsidiaries.*
Source: Standard & Poor's.

CASE 11–6

Comprehensive Analysis of Creditworthiness

Assume you are an analyst at a brokerage firm. One of the companies you follow is ABEX Chemicals, Inc., which is rapidly growing into a major producer of petrochemicals (principally polyethylene). You are uneasy about competitors in the petrochemical business, their aggressive expansion, and the possibility of a recession in the next year or two. In response, you compile a summary of relevant industry statistics. Your analysis suggests prices of petrochemicals produced by ABEX will likely decline over the next 12 to 18 months. Primarily for this reason, you consider ABEX's credit standing as risky. You also note that ABEX common stock recently declined from \$15 to \$9 per share. Because of this price decline and subsequent instability, you further extend your credit analysis of ABEX. You focus on the external environment, company fundamentals, and stock price behavior. A description of your findings follows:

External environment. While uncertainty about the economy persists, you conclude the key issue for the petrochemical industry is not demand but overcapacity. As revealed in Exhibit I, polyethylene production is expected to remain flat in Year 10 and capacity to increase, causing operating rates to fall. The result is increased competition and lower product prices. In the long run you expect use of polyethylene to grow 4% per annum and prices to rise 5% per annum, beginning in Year 12.

Company fundamentals. ABEX's operating income depends primarily on two businesses: pipeline distribution of natural gas (gas transmission) and petrochemical production. The gas transmission business is declining due to lower gas production and price constraints, but your outlook is for modest increases in volume and transmission rates. Your summary of key statistics for pipeline operations is included in Exhibit I. The more unpredictable component of ABEX's operating income is the petrochemical operation. Operating income from petrochemicals are sensitive to selling price, production costs, and volume of polyethylene sales. A key to estimating operating income is estimation of future prices and costs, and ABEX's market share. ABEX's management is confident their lower cost structure makes them price competitive and permits a higher capacity operating rate than their competitors. Exhibit I includes a summary of key statistics for polyethylene operations.

Stock price evaluation. Some investors value companies using discounted cash flows, but you are increasingly emphasizing the quality of cash flow, earning power, yield, book value, and earnings components. You also assemble financial statements and key financial ratios for ABEX (see Exhibits II–IV).

Required:

Your firm's fixed income portfolio manager asks you to further extend your investigation of ABEX. The manager wants your assessment of whether the credit quality (risk) of ABEX's debt has changed during the most recent three years–Year 7 through Year 9. You decide to analyze key financial ratios for ABEX, focusing on areas of (1) asset protection, (2) liquidity, and (3) earning power.

a. Identify *five ratios* from Exhibit IV relevant to at least one of these three areas of analysis. Discuss and interpret both levels and trends in these five key ratios from Year 7 through Year 9.

b. Compare and analyze the pipeline and petrochemical divisions using three *qualitative* measures relevant to ABEX's credit quality for the period Year 7 through Year 9.

c. Using your analysis from (*a*) and (*b*), discuss whether ABEX's credit quality has changed from Year 7 through Year 9.

(CFA Adapted)

Exhibit I

Total U.S. Polyethylene Capacity, Production, and Prices

	Year 5	Year 6	Year 7	Year 8	Year 9	Projected Year 10	Projected Year 11	Compound Annual Growth
Total production (lbs. millions)	15,600	16,100	17,600	18,900	19,700	19,700	19,800	
Growth rate	7.6%	3.2%	9.3%	7.4%	4.2%	0.0%	0.5%	4.5%
Total capacity (lbs. millions)	17,600	17,700	18,600	20,100	21,200	23,400	24,300	
Growth rate	2.9%	0.6%	5.1%	8.1%	5.5%	10.4%	3.8%	5.2%
Capacity operating rate	88.6%	91.0%	94.6%	94.0%	92.9%	84.2%	81.5%	
Average price per pound	$0.41	$0.37	$0.36	$0.51	$0.52	$0.47	$0.57	
Percent change	−9.8%	−10.8%	−2.7%	24.4%	2.0%	−9.6%	21.3%	1.2%

ABEX CHEMICALS, INC.

Selected Key Statistics

	Year 5	Year 6	Year 7	Year 8	Year 9	Projected Year 10
Polyethylene operations:						
Production (lbs. millions)	1,840	1,975	2,870	4,835	5,000	4,950
Approximate capacity (lbs. millions)	1,900	2,100	2,950	5,000	5,500	5,500
Capacity operating rate	97%	94%	97%	97%	91%	90%
Average price received	$0.411	$0.367	$0.356	$0.511	$0.515	$0.470
Average cost/pound produced	$0.338	$0.307	$0.285	$0.350	$0.394	$0.370
Pipeline transportation operations:						
$/1,000 cubic feet (price)	$0.286	$0.253	$0.248	$0.221	$0.192	$0.187
Gas transported (trillion cubic feet)	4.64	4.88	4.67	5.00	5.85	6.29
Operating profit margin	25.6%	27.2%	27.3%	25.9%	26.8%	27.0%

Exhibit II

ABEX CHEMICALS, INC.

Consolidated Income Statements ($ millions)

	Year 5	Year 6	Year 7	Year 8	Year 9
Revenues:					
Petrochemicals	$ 757	$ 725	$ 1,021	$ 2,472	$ 2,575
Pipelines	1,328	1,235	1,156	1,106	1,123
Total revenues	2,085	1,960	2,177	3,578	3,698
Operating costs:*					
Petrochemicals	(622)	(607)	(818)	(1,691)	(1,970)
Pipelines	(988)	(899)	(840)	(820)	(822)
Total operating costs	(1,610)	(1,506)	(1,658)	(2,511)	(2,792)
Operating income:					
Petrochemicals	135	118	203	781	605
Pipelines	340	336	316	286	301
Total operating income	475	454	519	1,067	906
Interest on long-term debt:					
Petrochemicals	(60)	(84)	(78)	(211)	(266)
Pipelines	(169)	(166)	(166)	(172)	(178)
Total interest expense	(229)	(250)	(244)	(383)	(444)
Administrative expenses	(22)	(24)	(23)	(28)	(40)
Rental expenses	(15)	(17)	(17)	(20)	(22)
Income from investments	25	8	4	7	4
Income before taxes	234	171	239	643	405
Income taxes:					
Current	(78)	(30)	(45)	(40)	(44)
Deferred	(23)	(35)	(67)	(201)	(136)
Total taxes	(101)	(65)	(112)	(241)	(180)
Net income	133	106	127	402	225
Preferred dividends	(77)	(74)	(26)	(17)	(17)
Net available for common	$ 56	$ 32	$ 101	$ 385	$ 208
Average shares outstanding† (millions)	128	135	185	231	253
Basic earnings per common share	$0.44	$0.24	$0.54	$1.67	$0.82
Common dividends per share	0.40	0.40	0.40	0.40	0.50
Cash flow per common share	2.52	2.44	2.26	3.85	2.85

* *Operating costs include costs of goods sold and depreciation, where depreciation equals ($ millions):*

	Year 5	Year 6	Year 7	Year 8	Year 9
Petrochemicals	*$ 48*	*$ 60*	*$ 62*	*$135*	*$233*
Pipelines	*96*	*95*	*97*	*98*	*102*
Total depreciation	*$144*	*$155*	*$159*	*$233*	*$335*

† *Year 10 estimate is 305 million shares outstanding.*

Exhibit III

ABEX CHEMICALS, INC.
Consolidated Balance Sheets ($ millions)

	Year 5	Year 6	Year 7	Year 8	Year 9
Assets					
Current assets:					
Cash and short-term investments	$ 45	$ 48	$ 74	$ 102	$ 133
Accounts receivable	279	300	414	868	923
Inventories	125	121	128	501	535
Total current assets	449	469	616	1,471	1,591
Investments and other assets	631	380	167	252	400
Goodwill	35	90	105	330	560
Property, plant, and equipment (net):					
Petrochemicals	1,184	1,245	1,323	2,670	3,275
Pipelines	2,282	2,484	2,547	2,540	2,530
Total assets	$4,581	$4,668	$4,758	$7,263	$8,356
Liabilities					
Current liabilities:					
Bank indebtedness	$ 226	$ 77	$ 72	$ 215	$ 245
Accounts payable and accrued liabilities	333	312	377	768	787
Current portion of long-term debt	99	70	76	86	136
Other current payables	35	33	32	34	54
Total current liabilities	693	492	557	1,103	1,222
Long-term debt:					
Petrochemicals	553	743	721	2,017	2,176
Pipelines	1,686	1,648	1,638	1,702	1,725
Advances—gas contracts	115	135	186	290	210
Deferred income taxes	125	160	227	428	564
Total liabilities	3,172	3,178	3,329	5,540	5,897
Shareholders' Equity					
Preferred stock	861	826	329	216	216
Common stock and retained earnings	548	664	1,100	1,507	2,243
Total shareholders' equity	1,409	1,490	1,429	1,723	2,459
Total liabilities and shareholders' equity	$4,581	$4,668	$4,758	$7,263	$8,356
Average shares outstanding (millions)*	128	135	185	231	253

** Year 10 estimate is 305 million shares outstanding.*

Exhibit IV

ABEX CHEMICALS, INC.
Selected Financial Ratios

	Year 5	Year 6	Year 7	Year 8	Year 9
Petrochemicals operating margin	17.8%	16.3%	19.9%	31.6%	23.5%
Pipeline operating margin	25.6%	27.2%	27.3%	25.9%	26.8%
Return on assets (EBIT/total assets)	10.1%	9.0%	10.2%	14.1%	10.2%
Pretax profit margin	11.2%	8.7%	11.0%	18.0%	10.9%
Tax rate	43.0%	38.0%	46.9%	37.5%	44.4%
Petrochemicals asset turnover (sales/fixed assets)	0.64	0.58	0.77	0.93	0.79
Pipelines asset turnover (sales/fixed assets)	0.58	0.50	0.45	0.44	0.44
Turnover (sales/total assets)	0.46	0.42	0.46	0.49	0.44
Debt to common equity	4.30	3.80	2.31	2.66	1.83
Net tangible assets to long-term debt	58.4%	55.4%	52.0%	34.7%	46.2%
Long-term debt to total capitalization	62.6%	62.9%	64.0%	70.0%	62.6%
Total assets to total shareholders' equity	3.25	3.13	3.33	4.22	3.40
Pretax interest coverage	1.63	1.46	1.80	2.54	1.84
Operating cash flow to long-term debt	20.2%	18.0%	20.4%	26.6%	22.1%
Collection period	48 days	55 days	68 days	87 days	90 days
Inventory turnover	11.0	11.0	12.0	7.2	4.7
Short-term debt to total debt	12.1%	5.5%	5.8%	7.5%	9.3%
Petrochemicals average cost of long-term debt	10.9%	11.3%	10.8%	10.5%	12.2%
Pipeline average cost of long-term debt	10.0%	10.1%	10.1%	10.1%	10.3%
Average cost of preferreds	8.9%	9.0%	7.9%	7.9%	7.9%

CASE 11–7

Analyzing Liquidity, Solvency, and Financial Flexibility

Use the annual report of Kodak in Appendix A to answer the following questions.

a. Calculate the following liquidity measures for 2001 and 2000.
(1) Common-size composition of current assets.
(2) Common-size composition of inventory (see its note 2).
(3) Allowance for doubtful accounts as a percentage of gross accounts receivable.
(4) Working capital.
(5) Current ratio.
(6) Acid-test (quick) ratio.
(7) Cash to current assets ratio.
(8) Cash to current liabilities ratio.
(9) Collection period (accounts receivable at year-end 1999 is $2,537).
(10) Days to sell inventory (inventory at year-end 1999 is $1,519).
(11) Operating cycle.
(12) Cash flow ratio.

b. Using its notes 8 and 9 and the annual report, assess Kodak's financial flexibility.

c. Using your analysis results from (*a*) and (*b*), assess Kodak's liquidity.

d. Perform an analysis of Kodak's 2001 and 2000 capital structure and solvency. Your analysis should (at a minimum) include analysis and interpretation of the following measures:
(1) Financial leverage ratio.
(2) Common-size analysis.
(3) Capital structure ratios.
(4) Asset composition.
(5) Asset coverage.
(6) Both earnings and cash flow to fixed charges ratios.
(7) Relevant qualitative considerations.

e. Use Altman's *Z*-score to evaluate the probability of bankruptcy for Kodak.

WEB ACTIVITIES

The Web Activities are located on the book's website at www.mhhe.com/wild8e.

12

EQUITY ANALYSIS AND VALUATION

A LOOK BACK <

Prior chapters on financial analysis dealt with analysis of company returns, both profitability and return on invested capital, along with prospective and credit analysis.

A LOOK AT THIS CHAPTER •

This chapter emphasizes equity analysis and valuation. Our earnings-based analysis focuses on assessing earnings persistence and earning power. Attention is directed at techniques to aid us in measuring and applying these analysis concepts. Our discussion of equity valuation focuses on issues in estimating company values and forecasting earnings.

A LOOK AHEAD >

The Comprehensive Case applies many of the financial statement analysis tools and insights described in the book. These are illustrated using financial information from Campbell Soup Company. Explanation and interpretation accompany all analyses.

ANALYSIS OBJECTIVES

- Analyze earnings persistence, its determinants, and its relevance for earnings forecasting.
- Explain recasting and adjusting of earnings and earnings components for analysis.
- Describe earnings-based equity valuation and its relevance for financial analysis.
- Analyze earning power and its usefulness for forecasting and valuation.
- Explain earnings forecasting, its mechanics, and its effectiveness in assessing company performance.
- Analyze interim reports and consider their value in monitoring and revising earnings estimates.

Analysis Feature

Earnings Hocus-Pocus

OMAHA, NB–Warren Buffett, chairman of Berkshire Hathaway, recently commented, "Bad terminology is the enemy of good thinking. When companies or investment professionals use terms such as *EBITDA* and *pro forma,* they want you to unthinkingly accept concepts that are dangerously flawed. In golf, my score is frequently below par on a *pro forma* basis: I have firm plans to 'restructure' my putting stroke and therefore only count the swings I take before reaching the green."

Pro forma earnings gained in popularity in the 1990s as companies sought to redefine the benchmark against which they would be evaluated by the market. Any expense that might be deemed unfavorable was quickly excluded while transitory income items, like gains on asset sales and pension income, remained. Pro forma earnings quickly became known as EBUI, or earnings before unpleasant items.

Companies' desire to redefine earnings stems from the mechanics of valuing stock prices. This process involves projecting earnings or cash flows into the future and then discounting them to the present in order to arrive at price. To be meaningful, projections must focus only on the portion of earnings that is likely to persist into the future, that is, core earnings. The higher core earnings are, the higher the resulting stock price. That's why companies offer a myriad of definitions of core earnings, each designed to portray their business in the most favorable light.

Bad terminology is the enemy of good thinking.

In an attempt to rectify this reporting problem, Standard & Poor's redefined core earnings to eliminate three popular financial strategies that companies use to bolster their numbers. Its definition of core earnings expenses stock options as regular compensation (which hits high-tech companies), excludes pension gains (which hits large industrial companies with big pension funds), and includes restructuring charges from ongoing operations while excluding gains and losses from asset sales (which hurts big companies trying to smooth out earnings gains over time).

This is dramatic stuff. Under the Standard & Poor's core earnings measure, expensing of option grants lowers Cisco's EPS by 21 cents and earnings at General Electric Co. drop by 30 cents per share, mainly by eliminating big gains from pension income. Stock price estimates are only as good as the projections of core earnings. Investors need to analyze reported income closely to separate transitory and persistent components, and they should not rely on definitions proposed by companies.

Source: Berkshire Hathaway 2001 annual report and 2003 Website; Business Week, May 2002.

PREVIEW OF CHAPTER 12

Earnings-based equity analysis is the focus of this chapter. Previous chapters examined return and profitability analyses of financial statements. This chapter extends these analyses to consider earnings persistence, valuation, and forecasting.

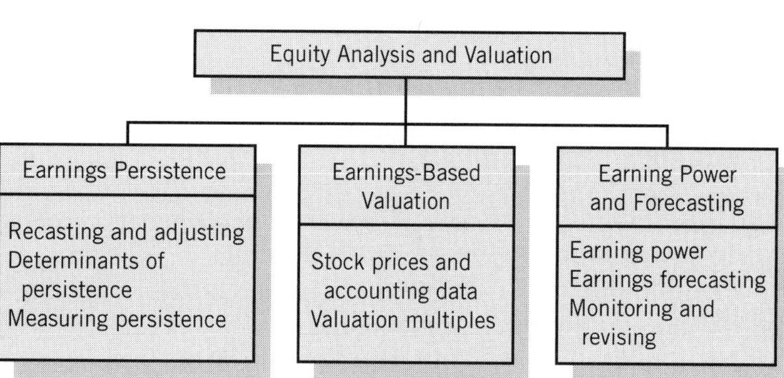

Earnings persistence is broadly defined to include the stability, predictability, variability, and trend in earnings. We consider earnings management as a determinant of persistence. Our *equity valuation* analysis emphasizes earnings and other accounting measures for computing company value. *Earnings forecasting* considers earning power, estimation techniques, and monitoring mechanisms. This chapter also describes several useful tools for earnings-based equity analysis. Specifically, we describe recasting and adjustment of financial statements. We also distinguish between recurring and nonrecurring, operating and nonoperating, and extraordinary and nonextraordinary earnings components. Throughout the chapter we emphasize the application of earnings-based analysis with several illustrations.

EARNINGS PERSISTENCE

A good financial analysis identifies components in earnings that exhibit stability and predictability–that is, *persistent* components. We separate these persistent components from random or nonrecurring components. This analysis aids us in producing reliable forecasts of earning power for valuation. Analysis also must be alert to earnings management and income smoothing. Earnings management and income smoothing can imply more stability and predictability than present in the underlying characteristics. Company management often asserts that such activities remove distortions or peculiarities from operating results. Yet these activities can mask natural and cyclical irregularities that are part of a company's environment and experience. Identifying these influences is important for us in assessing a company's risk. This section considers elements bearing on analysis of earnings persistence, including earnings level, trend, and components.

Target's Operating EPS and Stock Price

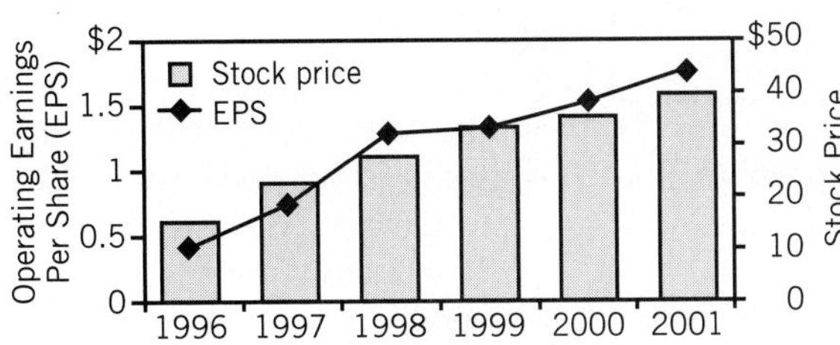

Recasting and Adjusting Earnings

One task in equity analysis is to recast earnings and earnings components so that stable, normal, and continuing elements that constitute earnings are separated and distinguished from random, erratic, unusual, and nonrecurring elements. The latter elements require separate analytical treatment or investigation. Recasting also aims to identify elements included in current earnings that should more properly be included in the operating results of one or more prior periods.

Information on Earnings Persistence

ANALYSIS AID
To help assess earnings persistence we: (1) Recast the income statement, and then (2) Adjust the income statement.

Analysis of operating results for the recasting and adjusting of earnings requires reliable and relevant information. Major sources of this information include the:

- Income statement, including its components:
  - Income from continuing operations.
  - Income from discontinued operations.
  - Extraordinary gains and losses.
  - Cumulative effect of changes in accounting principles.
- Other financial statements and notes.
- Management Discussion and Analysis.

We often find "unusual" items separated within the income statement (typically on a pretax basis), but their disclosure is optional and does not always include sufficient information to assess their significance or persistence. We access all available information sources and management, if possible, to obtain this information. Relevant information includes that affecting earnings comparability and interpretation. Examples are product-mix changes, technological innovations, work stoppages, and raw material constraints.

Recasting Earnings and Earnings Components

Once we secure all available information, we recast and adjust the income statements of several years (typically at least five) to assess earnings persistence. Recasting and adjusting earnings aids in determining the earning power of a company. We explain recasting in this section and adjusting in the next, although both can be performed in one statement.

Recasting aims at rearranging earnings components to provide a meaningful classification and relevant format for analysis. Components can be rearranged, subdivided, or tax effected, but the total must reconcile to net income of each period. Discretionary expenses should be segregated. The same applies to components like equity in income (loss) of unconsolidated subsidiaries or affiliates, often reported net of tax. Components reported pretax must be removed along with their tax effects if reclassified apart from income from continuing operations.

Income tax disclosures enable us to separate factors that either reduce or increase taxes. This separation permits us to analyze the recurring nature of these factors. All permanent tax differences and credits are included. This analytical procedure involves computing taxes at the statutory rate and deducting tax benefits arising from various items such as tax credits, capital gains rates, tax-free income, or lower foreign tax rates. We also must add factors such as additional foreign taxes, nontax-deductible expenses, and state and local taxes (net of federal tax benefit). Immaterial items can be considered in a lump sum labeled *other*.

Analytically recast income statements contain as much detail as necessary for our analysis objectives and are supplemented by notes. Exhibit 12.1 on pages 594 and 595 shows the analytically recast income statements for Campbell Soup Company. These statements are annotated with key numbers referencing Campbell's financial statements in Appendix A. Financial data preceding Year 10 are taken from company reports summarized in the Comprehensive Case chapter, which also contains a discussion and an integration of Exhibit 12.1.

HINT
"Adjusting" aims to assign earnings components to the periods in which they best belong.

Adjusting Earnings and Earnings Components

The adjusting process uses data from recast income statements and other available information to assign earnings components to periods where they most properly belong. We must be especially careful in assigning extraordinary or unusual items (net of tax) to periods. Also, the income tax benefit of a carryforward of operating losses should normally be moved to the year of the loss occurrence. Costs or benefits from settlements of lawsuits can relate to one or more preceding periods. Similarly, gains or losses from disposal of discontinued operations usually relate to operating results of several years. For changes in accounting principles or estimates, all years under analysis should be adjusted to a comparable basis. If the new principle is the desirable one, prior years should be restated to this new method. This restatement redistributes the "cumulative effect of change in accounting principle" to the relevant prior years. Changes in estimates are accounted for prospectively in practice with few exceptions. Our ability to adjust all periods to a comparable basis depends on information availability.

Exhibit 12.1 **Recast Income Statements**

CAMPBELL SOUP COMPANY

Recast Income Statements for Year 6 through Year 11
($ millions)

Reference Item		Year 11	Year 10	Year 9	Year 8	Year 7	Year 6
13	Net sales	$6,204.1	$6,205.8	$5,672.1	$4,868.9	$4,490.4	$4,286.8
19	Interest income	26.0	17.6	38.3	33.2	29.5	27.4
	Total revenues	6,230.1	6,223.4	5,710.4	4,902.1	4,519.9	4,314.2
	Costs and expenses:						
	Cost of products sold (see Note 1 below)	3,727.1	3,893.5	3,651.8	3,077.8	2,897.8	2,820.5
	Marketing and selling expenses (see Note 2 below)	760.8	760.1	605.9	514.2	422.7	363.0
145	Advertising (see Note 2 below)	195.4	220.4	212.9	219.1	203.5	181.4
144	Repairs and maintenance (see Note 1 below)	173.9	180.6	173.9	155.6	148.8	144.0
16	Administrative expenses	306.7	290.7	252.1	232.6	213.9	195.9
17	Research and development expenses	56.3	53.7	47.7	46.9	44.8	42.2
102	Stock price-related incentive programs (see Note 3 below)	15.4	(0.1)	17.4	(2.7)	—	8.5
20	Foreign exchange adjustment	0.8	3.3	19.3	16.6	4.8	0.7
104	Other, net (see Note 3 below)	(3.3)	(2.0)	(1.4)	(4.7)	(0.4)	(9.0)
162A	Depreciation (see Note 1 below)	194.5	184.1	175.9	162.0	139.0	120.8
103	Amortization of intangible and other assets (see Note 3 below)	14.1	16.8	16.4	8.9	5.6	6.0
18	Interest expense	116.2	111.6	94.1	53.9	51.7	56.0
	Total costs and expenses	5,557.9	5,712.7	5,266.0	4,480.2	4,132.2	3,930.0
23	Earnings before equity in earnings of affiliates and minority interests	672.2	510.7	444.4	421.9	387.7	384.2
24	Equity in earnings of affiliates	2.4	13.5	10.4	6.3	15.1	4.3
25	Minority interests	(7.2)	(5.7)	(5.3)	(6.3)	(4.7)	(3.9)
26	Income before taxes	667.4	518.5	449.5	421.9	398.1	384.6
	Income taxes at statutory rate*	(226.9)	(176.3)	(152.8)	(143.5)	(179.1)	(176.9)
	Income from continuing operations	440.5	342.2	296.7	278.4	219.0	207.7
135	State taxes (net of federal tax benefit)	(20.0)	(6.6)	(3.8)	(11.8)	(8.6)	(8.0)
	Investment tax credit	—	—	—	—	4.4	11.6
137	Nondeductible amortization of intangibles	(4.0)	(1.6)	(1.2)	(2.6)	(1.4)	—†
138	Foreign earnings not taxed or taxed at other than statutory rate	2.0	(2.2)	(0.2)	3.2	11.1	15.2
139	Other: Tax effects	(17.0)	(2.2)	(0.1)	(3.7)	7.5	(4.7)

(continued)

Exhibit 12.1 *(concluded)*

Reference Item		Year 11	Year 10	Year 9	Year 8	Year 7	Year 6
	Alaska Native Corporation transaction	—	—	—	—	4.5	—
22	Divestitures, restructuring, and unusual charges	—	(339.1)	(343.0)	(40.6)	—	—
	Tax effect of divestitures, restructuring, and unusual charges (Note 4)	—	13.9	64.7	13.9	—	—
	Gain on sale of businesses in Year 8 and subsidiary in Year 7	—	—	—	3.1	9.7	—
	Loss on sale of exercise equipment subsidiary, net of tax	—	—	—	—	(1.7)	—
	LIFO liquidation gain (see Note 1 below)	—	—	—	1.7	2.8	1.4
	Income before cumulative effect of accounting change	401.5	4.4	13.1	241.6	247.3	223.2
153A	Cumulative effect of accounting change for income taxes	—	—	—	32.5	—	—
28	Net income as reported	$ 401.5	$ 4.4	$ 13.1	$ 274.1	$ 247.3	$ 223.2
14	**Note 1:** Cost of products sold	$4,095.5	$4,258.2	$4,001.6	$3,392.8	$3,180.5	$3,082.8
144	Less: Repair and maintenance expenses	(173.9)	(180.6)	(173.9)	(155.6)	(148.8)	(144.0)
162A	Less: Depreciation[(a)]	(194.5)	(184.1)	(175.9)	(162.0)	(139.0)	(120.8)
153A	Plus: LIFO liquidation gain[(b)]	—	—	—	2.6	5.1	2.5
		$3,727.1	$3,893.5	$3,651.8	$3,077.8	$2,897.8	$2,820.5
15	**Note 2:** Marketing and selling expenses	$ 956.2	$ 980.5	$ 818.8	$ 733.3	$ 626.2	$ 544.4
145	Less: Advertising	(195.4)	(220.4)	(212.9)	(219.1)	(203.5)	(181.4)
		$ 760.8	$ 760.1	$ 605.9	$ 514.2	$ 422.7	$ 363.0
21	**Note 3:** Other expenses (income)	$ 26.2	$ 14.7	$ 32.4	$ (3.2)	$ (9.5)	$ 5.5
102	Less: Stock price-related incentive programs	(15.4)	0.1	(17.4)	2.7	—	(8.5)
103	Less: Amortization of intangible and other assets	(14.1)	(16.8)	(16.4)	(8.9)	(5.6)	(6.0)
	Less: Gain on sale of businesses (Year 8) and subsidiary (Year 7)	—	—	—	4.7	14.7	—
104	Other net	$ (3.3)	$ (2.0)	$ (1.4)	$ (4.7)	$ (0.4)	$ (9.0)
	Note 4: Tax effect of divestitures, restructuring, and unusual charges at statutory rate	—	$ 115.3[(c)]	$ 116.6[(d)]	$ 13.9	—	—
136	Nondeductible divestitures, restructuring, and unusual charges	—	(101.4)[(e)]	(51.9)[(f)]	—	—	—
		—	$ 13.9	$ 64.7	$ 13.9	—	—

* *The statutory, federal tax rate a 34% in Year 8 through Year 11, 45% in Year 7, and 46% in Year 6.*

† *This amount is not reported for Year 6.*

(a) *We assume most depreciation is included in cost of products sold.*

(b) *LIFO liquidation gain before tax—for example, for Year 8 this is $2.5 million, computed as $1.7/(1 − 0.34).*

(c) *$339.1 22 × 0.34 = $115.3.*

(d) *$343.0 22 × 0.34 = $116.6.*

(e) *$179.4 26 × 0.565 136 = $101.4.*

(f) *$106.5 26 × 0.487 136 = $51.9.*

Before we assess earnings persistence it is necessary to obtain the best possible income statement numbers with our adjustments. Exhibit 12.2 shows the adjusted income statements of Campbell Soup Company. All earnings components must be considered. If we decide a component should be excluded from the period it is reported, we can either (1) shift it (net of tax) to the operating results of one or more prior periods or (2) spread (average) it over earnings for the period under analysis. We should only spread it over prior periods' earnings when it cannot be identified with a specific period. While spreading (averaging) helps us in determining earning power, it is not helpful in determining earnings trends. We also must realize that moving gains or losses to other periods does not remedy the misstatements of prior years' results. For example, a damage award for patent infringement in one period implies prior periods suffered from lost sales or other impairments. Further details and analyses of Exhibit 12.2 are identified and discussed in the Comprehensive Case.

Analysis must also recognize that certain management characterizations of revenue or expense items as unusual, nonrecurring, infrequent, or extraordinary are attempts to reduce earnings volatility or minimize selected earnings components. These characterizations also extend to the inclusion in equity of transactions such as gains and losses on available-for-sale securities and foreign currency translation adjustments. We often exclude equity effects from our adjustment process. Yet these items are part of a company's lifetime earnings. These items increase or decrease equity and affect earning power. Accordingly, even if we omit these items from the adjustment process, they belong in the analysis of average earning power.

Exhibit 12.2 ***Adjusted Income Statements***

CAMPBELL SOUP COMPANY

Adjusted Income Statements for Year 6 through Year 11

($ millions)

	Year 11	Year 10	Year 9	Year 8	Year 7	Year 6	Total
Net income as reported	$401.5	$ 4.4	$ 13.1	$274.1	$247.3	$223.2	$1,163.6
Divestitures, restructuring & unusual charges		339.1	343.0	40.6			
Tax effect of divestitures, restructuring, etc.		(13.9)	(64.7)	(13.9)			
Gain on sale of businesses (Year 8) and sale of subsidiary (Year 7), net of tax				(3.1)	(9.7)		
Loss on sale of exercise equipment subsidiary					1.7		
Alaska Native Corporation transaction					(4.5)		
LIFO liquidation gain				(1.7)	(2.8)	(1.4)	
Cumulative effect of change in accounting for income taxes				(32.5)			
Adjusted net income	$401.5	$329.6	$291.4	$263.5	$232.0	$221.8	
Total net income for the period							$1,739.80
Average net income for the period							$ 289.97*

* *One measure of average earning power.*

Determinants of Earnings Persistence

After recasting and adjusting earnings, our analysis next focuses on determining earnings persistence. Earnings management, variability, trends, and incentives are all potential determinants of earnings persistence. We also should assess earnings persistence over both the business cycle and the long run.

Earnings Trend and Persistence

Earnings that reflect a steady growth trend are desirable. We can assess earnings trends by statistical methods or with **trend statements.** Examples of trend statements using selected financial data of Campbell Soup are reported in Exhibits CC.8 and CC.9 in the Comprehensive Case chapter. Trend analysis uses earnings numbers taken from the recasting and adjusting procedures illustrated in Exhibit 12.2. Earnings trends often reveal important clues to a company's current and future performance (cyclical, growth, defensive) and bear on the quality of management. We must be alert to accounting distortions affecting trends. Especially important are changes in accounting principles and the effect of business combinations, particularly purchases. We must make adjustments for these changes. Probably one major motivation of earnings management is to effect earnings trends. Earnings management practices assume earnings trends are important for valuation. They also reflect a belief that retroactive revisions of earnings previously reported have little impact on security prices. For example, once a company incurs and reports a loss, this perspective suggests its existence is often as important as its magnitude for valuation purposes. These assumptions and the propensities of some managers to use accounting as a means of improving earnings trend has led to sophisticated earnings management techniques, including income smoothing.

Earnings Management and Persistence

There are several requirements to meet the definition of *earnings management.* These requirements are important as they distinguish earnings management from misrepresentations and distortions. Earnings management uses acceptable accounting reporting principles for purposes of reporting specific results. It uses the available discretion in selecting and applying accounting principles to achieve its goals, and it is arguably performed within the framework of accepted practice. It is a matter of form rather than of substance. It does not affect actual transactions (such as postponing outlays to later periods) but, instead, does affect a redistribution of credits or charges across periods. A main goal is to moderate earnings variability across periods by shifting earnings between good and bad years, between future and current years, or various combinations. Actual earnings management takes many forms. Some forms of earnings management that we should be especially alert to include:

- *Changes in accounting methods or assumptions.* Examples of companies that changed methods or assumptions include Chrysler, who revised upward the assumed rate of return on its pension portfolio and substantially increased earnings when sales were slumping, and Continental Airlines who lengthened depreciable lives and increased residual values of aircraft, thereby boosting subsequent earnings.
- *Offsetting extraordinary (and unusual) gains and losses.* This practice removes unusual or unexpected earnings effects that can adversely impact earnings trend.
- *Big baths.* This technique recognizes future periods' costs in the current period, when the current period is unavoidably badly performing. This practice relieves future periods' earnings of these costs.
- *Write-downs.* Write-downs of operating assets such as plant and equipment or intangibles such as goodwill when operating results are poor is another earnings

management tool. Companies often justify write-downs by arguing that current economics do not support reported asset values. An example is Cisco Systems that wrote off $2.25 billion of inventories as part of a restructuring program.

- *Timing revenue and expense recognition.* This technique times revenue and expense recognition to manage earnings, including trend. Examples are the timing of revenue recognition, asset sales, research expenditures, advertising, maintenance, and repairs. Unlike most earnings management techniques, these decisions can involve the timing of actual transactions. An example is General Electric which offset gains with restructuring expenses to smooth earnings fluctuations.

Management Incentives and Persistence

We previously described the impact of management incentives on both the accounting and the analysis of financial statements (see Chapters 1–6). This is especially evident in assessing earning persistence and in performing credit analysis. Experience shows that some managers, owners, and employees manipulate and distort reported earnings for personal benefits. Companies in financial distress are particularly vulnerable to these pressures. Such practices are too often justified by these individuals as a battle for survival. Prosperous companies also sometimes try to preserve hard-earned reputations as earnings growth companies through earnings management. Compensation plans and other accounting-based incentives or constraints provide added motivation for managers to manage earnings. The impacts of management incentives reveal themselves in the following cases:

Analysts must recognize the incentives confronting managers with regard to earnings. Earnings management is often initially achieved by understating reported earnings. This creates a "reserve" to call on in any future low earnings periods. For example, Sears boosted its allowance for uncollectible accounts and used the reserve to inflate earnings for many years. While this point is arguable, this is not the purpose of financial reporting. We are better served by full disclosure of earnings components along with management's explanation. We can then average, smooth, or adjust reported earnings in accordance with our analysis objectives. Another probable instance of earnings management is that of General Motors–see Illustration 12.1.

ILLUSTRATION 12.1

GM reported a revision in useful lives of its plant and equipment–reducing depreciation and amortization charges by $1.2 billion. GM's chairperson reported *"GM earned $3.6 billion for the year, up 21% . . . despite a 9% reduction in worldwide unit sales."* Yet without the $1.2 billion decline in depreciation and amortization, earnings would have decreased. This accounting change followed a year earlier provision of $1.3 billion for plant closings and restructurings. However, only $0.5 billion had been charged against this provision four years later, leaving the rest to absorb still future years' costs. After yet another change in leadership at GM, there was an additional $2.1 billion charge to earnings to cover costs of closing several more plants, including closings planned several years into the future. This sequence of events impairs confidence in both financial statements and management. Accordingly, we must work to reliably estimate earning power using techniques like averaging, recasting, and adjusting of earnings.

Given the performance incentives of managers, and the use of accounting numbers to control and monitor their performance, analysis must recognize the potential for earnings management and even misstatements. Analysis must identify companies with strong incentives to manage earnings, and then scrutinize these companies' accounting practices to ensure the integrity of financial statements.

Persistent and Transitory Items in Earnings

Recasting and adjusting earnings for equity valuation rely on separating stable, persistent earnings components from random, transitory components. Assessing persistence is important in determining earning power. Earnings forecasting also relies on persistence. A crucial part of analysis is to assess the persistence of the gain and loss components of earnings. This section describes how we can determine the persistence of nonrecurring, unusual, or extraordinary items. We also discuss how they should be handled in evaluating earnings level, management performance, and earnings forecasting.

Analyzing and Interpreting Transitory Items

The purpose of analyzing and interpreting extraordinary items is twofold:

1. Determine whether an item is transitory (less persistent). This involves assessing whether an item is unusual, nonoperating, or nonrecurring.
2. Determine adjustments that are necessary given assessment of persistence. Special adjustments are sometimes necessary for both evaluating and forecasting earnings.

We describe both of these analyses in this section.

Determining Persistence (Transitory Nature) of Items. Given the incentives confronting managers in reporting transitory items, we must render independent evaluation of whether a gain or loss is transitory. We also must determine how to adjust for them. For this purpose we arrange items into two broad categories: nonrecurring operating and nonrecurring nonoperating.

1. *Nonrecurring operating gains and losses.* These gains and losses relate to operating activities but recur infrequently or unpredictably. Operating items relate to a company's *normal business activities.* The concept of normal operations is far less clear than many realize. A plant's operating revenues and expenses are those associated with the workings of the plant. In contrast, proceeds from selling available-for-sale marketable securities are nonoperating gains or losses. But a gain (or loss) on the sale of equipment, even if disposed of to make room for a more productive one, is a nonoperating item. The other important concept, that of *recurrence,* is one of frequency. There are no predetermined generally accepted boundaries separating a recurring event from a nonrecurring one. For example, a regular event generating a gain or loss is classified as recurring. An unpredictable event, which occurs infrequently, is classified as nonrecurring. Yet an event occurring infrequently but whose occurrence is predictable raises questions as to its classification. An example is the relining of blast furnaces–they endure for many years and their replacement is infrequent, but the need for it is predictable. Some companies provide for these types of replacements with a reserve.

Analysis of nonrecurring operating gains and losses must recognize their inherent infrequencies and lack of recurring patterns. We treat them as belonging to the reporting period. We must also address the question of normal operations. For example, it is a bakery's purpose to bake bread, rolls, and cakes, but it is presumably outside normal activities to buy and sell marketable securities for gains and losses, or even to sell baking machinery that is replaced with more efficient machinery. This limited interpretation of operating activities can be challenged. Some argue the objective is not baking but for management to increase equity or stock values. This is accomplished through strategic classification of financing, investing, and operating activities. It is not limited to a narrow view of normal operations. We can usefully evaluate a much wider range of gains and losses as being derived from operating activities. This view results in many nonrecurring operating gains and losses considered as part of operating activities in the period when they occur.

Analysis of nonrecurring operating items does not readily fit a mechanical rule. We must review the information and will doubtless find some items more likely to be recurring than others and some more operating than others. This review affects our recasting, adjusting, and forecasting of earnings. We should also recognize the magnitude of an item as an important factor. Once we complete the analysis of recurring earnings, we often need to focus on average earnings experience over a few years rather than the result of a single year. A focus on average earnings is especially important for companies with fluctuating amounts of nonrecurring and other extraordinary items. A single year is too short and too arbitrary a period to evaluate the earning power of a company or for forecasting earnings. Illustration 12.2 sheds more light on this point.

ILLUSTRATION 12.2

The past few years have seen several large charges to earnings for reorganization, redeployment, or regrouping. Companies taking substantial write-offs include ($ billions) AT&T $2.6, Occidental Petroleum $2, Continental Airlines $1.8, Digital Equipment $1, Columbia Gas System $.8, General Dynamics $.6, and Bethlehem Steel $.6. Information supplied with these events is often limited, but there is no denying these companies' enormous "revisions" of previously reported results. In one stroke, these write-offs *correct* prior years' overreporting of earnings. Analysis must be alert to aggressive write-offs to relieve future periods of charges properly attributable to them.

2. *Nonrecurring nonoperating gains and losses.* These items are nonrepeating and unpredictable and fall outside normal operations. Events driving these items are typically extraneous, unintended, and unplanned, yet they are rarely entirely unexpected. Business is subject to risks of adverse events and random shocks, be they natural or man-made. Business transactions are subject to the same. An example is damage to plant facilities due to the crash of an aircraft when your plant is not located near an airport. Other examples might include: (1) substantial uninsured casualty losses not within the usual risks of the company, (2) expropriation by a foreign government of assets owned by the company, and (3) seizure or destruction of property from war, insurrection, or civil disorders when not expected. These occurrences are typically nonrecurring but their relation to operating activities varies. All are occurrences in the regular course of business. Even assets destroyed by acts of nature reflect the risks of business. Unique events are rare. What often appears unique is frequently symptomatic of new risks affecting earning power and future operations. Analysis must consider this possibility. But barring evidence to the contrary, these items are regarded as extraordinary and omitted from operating results of a single year. They are, nevertheless, part of the long-term performance of a company.

Adjustments to Extraordinary Items Reflecting Persistence. The second step in analyzing transitory items is to consider their effects on both the resources of the company and the evaluation of management.

- *Effects of transitory items on company resources.* Every transitory gain and loss has a dual effect. For example, when recording a gain, a company also records an increase in resources. Similarly, a loss results in a decrease in resources. Since return on invested capital measures the relations of net income to resources, transitory gains and losses affect this measure. The larger the transitory item, the larger its effect on return. If we use earnings and current events in forecasting, then transitory items convey more than past performance. That is, if a transitory loss decreases capital for expected returns, then future returns are lost. Conversely, a transitory gain increases capital and future expected returns. In forecasting profitability and return on investment, analysis must take account of the effects of recorded transitory items and the likelihood of future events causing transitory items.

- *Effect of transitory items on evaluation of management.* One implication frequently associated with transitory gains and losses is their lack of association with normal or planned business activities. Because of this they are often not used when evaluating management performance. Analysis should question their exclusion from management performance evaluation. What are the normal or planned activities that relate to management's decisions? Whether we consider securities transactions, plant asset transactions, or activities of divisions and subsidiaries, these all reflect on actions taken by management with specific purposes. These actions typically require more consideration or deliberation than ordinary operating decisions because they are often unusual in nature and involve substantial amounts. All of these actions reflect on management's ability as evidenced in the following:

ANALYSIS EXCERPT

Standard Oil Co. reported a transitory charge of $1.15 billion in writing down its ill-fated investment in Kennecott. This loss implies prior years' earnings were overstated *and* it also raises questions about the competence of management in making sound investment decisions.

Management should be aware of the risks of natural or manmade disasters and impediments. Business decisions are managers' responsibility. For example, a decision to pursue international activities is made with the knowledge of the risks involved. A decision to insure or not is a normal operating decision. Essentially, nothing is entirely unexpected or unforeseeable. Management does not engage in, or is at least not expected to engage in, business activities unknowingly. Decision making is within the expected activities of a business. Every company is subject to inherent risks, and management should not blindly pursue activities without weighing these risks.

In an assessment of operating results, distinguishing between normal and transitory items is sometimes meaningless. Management's beliefs about the quality of its decisions are nearly always related to the normalcy, or lack thereof, of business conditions. This is evident in the Management Discussion and Analysis. Yet the best managers anticipate the unexpected. When failures or shortcomings occur, poor managers typically take time to "explain" these in a way to avoid responsibility. While success rarely requires explanation, failure evokes long explanations and blame to unusual or unforeseeable events. In a competitive economy, normal conditions rarely prevail for any length of time. Management is paid to anticipate and expect the unusual. Explanations are not a substitute for performance.

ANALYSIS VIEWPOINT ... YOU ARE THE ANALYST/FORECASTER

You are analyzing a company's earnings persistence in preparing its earnings forecasts for publication in your company's online forecasting service. Its earnings and earnings components ("net income" and "income from continuing operations") are stable and exhibit a steady growth trend. However, you find "unusual gains" relating to litigation comprising 40% of current earnings. You also find "extraordinary losses" from environmental costs. How do these disclosures affect your earnings persistence estimate?

Answer–p. 613

EARNINGS-BASED EQUITY VALUATION

Company valuation is an important objective for many users of financial statements. Reliable estimates of value enable us to make buy/sell/hold decisions regarding securities, assess the value of a company for credit decisions, estimate values for business combinations, determine prices for public offerings of a company's securities, and pursue many other useful applications. This section continues our discussion of accounting-based equity valuation and incorporates it within the analysis of financial statements.

Traditional descriptions of company equity valuation rely on the *discounted cash flow (DCF) method.* Under the DCF method, the value of a company's equity is computed based on forecasts of cash flows available to equity investors. These forecasts are then discounted using the company's cost of equity capital.[1] It is important to emphasize that the accounting-based equity valuation model introduced earlier in this book and discussed in this section is theoretically consistent with the DCF method.

Relation between Stock Prices and Accounting Data

Recall the accounting-based equity valuation model introduced in Chapter 1:

$$V_t = BV_t + \frac{E(RI_{t+1})}{(1+k)^1} + \frac{E(RI_{t+2})}{(1+k)^2} + \frac{E(RI_{t+3})}{(1+k)^3} + \cdots \frac{E(RI_{t+n})}{(1+k)^n} + \cdots$$

where BV_t is book value at the end of period t, RI_{t+n} is residual income in period $t + n$, and k is cost of capital. **Residual income** at time t is defined as comprehensive net income minus a charge on beginning book value, that is, $RI_t = NI_t - (k \times BV_{t-1})$. The model directly shows the importance of future profitability in estimating company value–that is, by using estimates of future net income and book values. Accurate estimates of these measures can be made only after consideration of the quality and persistence of a company's earnings and earning power.

A common criticism of accounting-based valuation methods is that earnings are subject to manipulation and distortion at the hands of management whose personal objectives and interests depend on reported accounting numbers. Indeed, a good portion of the book focuses on the need for our analysis to go "beyond the numbers." A reasonable question, therefore, is: Does the potential manipulation of accounting data influence the accuracy of accounting-based estimates, or forecasts, of company value? The answer is both yes *and* no.

The numerical example in Illustration 12.3 confirms the "no" part of the answer. We demonstrate that while accounting choices necessarily affect both earnings and book value, valuation is unaffected. Although conservative (aggressive) accounting results in lower (higher) book values of stockholders' equity, this is exactly offset by higher (lower) expected residual income.

The "yes" part of the answer is based on the reality that analysis uses reported accounting data (and other information) as a basis for projecting future profitability. To the extent accounting choices mask the true economic performance of the company, a less experienced analyst can be misled regarding the company's current and future performance. Consequently, the analysis techniques described in this book are important for equity analysis even though the accounting-based valuation model is mathematically immune from accounting manipulations.

[1] A common alternative is to discount expected cash flows available to both debt and equity holders using the company's weighted-average cost of debt and equity capital. This yields an estimate of the total value of the company. The value of a company's equity is obtained by subtracting the value of its debt.

ILLUSTRATION 12.3

Consider two identical companies. These companies use the same accounting methods and are expected to report income of $20 million before depreciation in all future years. At the beginning of Year 0, each company has a book value of $40 million; and during the year, each incurs a cash expenditure of $10 million. Company A decides to capitalize the expenditure and depreciate it over the next two years under the straight-line method. Company B chooses to expense the expenditure immediately. Each company has a cost of equity capital of 15% and does not intend to pay dividends in the foreseeable future. Since earnings for both companies are identical after Year 2, the difference in valuation of the two companies will be affected only by differences in earnings through Year 2. Accordingly, we assume that residual income for Year 3 and beyond equals zero. Ignoring income taxes, the companies report the following results:

Company A:	Year 0	Year 1	Year 2
Income before effect of expenditure	$20	$20	$20
Depreciation of $10 expenditure	0	5	5
Net income	$20	$15	$15
Book value at year-end	$60	$75	$90

Company B:	Year 0	Year 1	Year 2
Income before effect of expenditure	$20	$20	$20
Depreciation of $10 expenditure	10	0	0
Net income	$10	$20	$20
Book value at year-end	$50	$70	$90

The valuations of Company A and Company B, computed at the end of Year 0, follow:

$$\text{Company A valuation} = \$60 + [\$15 - (15\% \times \$60)]/1.15 + [\$15 - (15\% \times \$75)]/1.15^2 = \$68.05$$

$$\text{Company B valuation} = \$50 + [\$20 - (15\% \times \$50)]/1.15 + [\$20 - (15\% \times \$70)]/1.15^2 = \$68.05$$

Generally, the phrase *conservative accounting* is applied to methods that result in lower income and lower book values in early years. Accordingly, by immediately expensing the $10 expenditure, Company B is using more conservative accounting. Despite the use of different accounting treatments for the $10 expenditure, the estimated values for Companies A and B are equal. Mathematically, the accounting-based equity valuation model yields the same valuation estimates for any accounting system that follows the clean surplus relation.

Fundamental Valuation Multiples

Two widely cited valuation measures are the price-to-book (PB) and price-to-earnings (PE) ratios. Users often base investment decisions on the observed values of these ratios. We describe how an analysis can arrive at "fundamental" PB and PE ratios without referring to the trading price of a company's shares. By comparing our fundamental ratios to those implicit in current stock prices, we can evaluate the investment merits of a publicly traded company. For those companies whose shares are not traded in active markets, the fundamental ratios serve as a means for estimating equity value.

Price-to-Book (PB) Ratio

The **price-to-book (PB) ratio** is expressed as:

$$\frac{\text{Market value of equity}}{\text{Book value of equity}}$$

Analysis Research

EARNINGS PERSISTENCE

Earnings persistence plays an important role in company valuation. Analysis research indicates nonrecurring earnings increase company value on a dollar-for-dollar basis, while the stock price reaction to persistent sources of earnings is higher and positively associated with the degree of persistence.

An analyst cannot rely solely on income statement classifications in assessing the persistence of a company's earnings. Research indicates that many types of nonrecurring items often are included in income from continuing operations. Examples are gains and losses from asset disposals, changes in accounting estimates, asset writedowns, and provisions for future losses. Analysis must carefully examine the financial statement notes, MD&A, and other disclosures for the existence of these items. Evidence also shows that extraordinary items and discontinued operations (special items) may be partly predictable and can provide information regarding future profitability.

Recent analysis research indicates that companies currently reporting negative income along with special items are more likely to report special items in the following year. These subsequent years' special items are likely to be of the same sign. Profitable companies with discontinued operations are more likely to report higher earnings in subsequent years.

By substituting the accounting-based expression for equity value in the numerator, the PB ratio can be expressed in terms of accounting data as follows:

$$\frac{V_t}{BV_t} = 1 + \left[\frac{(ROCE_{t+1} - k)}{(1+k)}\right] + \left[\frac{(ROCE_{t+2} - k)}{(1+k)^2} \times \frac{BV_{t+1}}{BV_t}\right] + \left[\frac{(ROCE_{t+3} - k)}{(1+k)^3} \times \frac{BV_{t+2}}{BV_t}\right] + \cdots$$

This expression yields several important insights. As future ROCE and/or growth in book value increase, the PB ratio increases. Also, as the cost (risk) of equity capital, k, increases, the PB ratio decreases. Recognize that PB ratios deviate from 1.0 when the market expects abnormal earnings (both positive and negative) in the future. If the present value of future abnormal earnings is positive (negative), the PB ratio is greater (less) than 1.0.

Price-to-Earnings (PE) Ratio

The **price-to-earnings (PE) ratio** is expressed as:

$$\frac{\text{Market value of equity}}{\text{Net income}}$$

Ohlson and Juettner-Nauroth (2000) show that the PE ratio can be written as a function of short-term (STG) and long-term growth (LTG) of earning per share (eps) as follows:

$$\frac{P_0}{eps_1} = \frac{1}{r} \times \frac{STG - LTG}{r - LTG}$$

where r is the cost of equity capital, STG (LTG) is the expected short-term (long-term) percentage change in eps relative to expected "normal" growth, STG > LTG and LTG < r.[2] STG can be thought of as analysts' consensus five-year growth rate in eps and LTG as the long-run rate of inflation beyond the forecast horizon.

This equation yields two important insights: (1) The PE ratio is inversely related to the cost of capital, that is, it will be lower (higher) the higher (lower) than the cost of equity capital, and (2) The PE ratio is positively related to the expected growth in eps relative to normal growth.

The PE ratio does not say anything about the absolute level of earnings (whether eps is high or low), only the rate at which eps is expected to increase relative to normal expected growth.

[2] Expected normal growth is at the rate of the cost of capital, that is, $eps_1 = eps_0 \times (1 + r)$ and eps includes the normal return on any dividends paid during the year (e.g., $r \times$ dividends).

An interesting case is one in which the long-term expected growth in eps relative to normal eps is expected to remain at a constant level (for example, when LTG = 0). In this case, the ratio reduces to

$$\frac{P}{eps} = \frac{STG}{r^2}$$

In this form, the PE ratio is related to the short-term growth in eps relative to expected normal growth. This provides the rationale for the **PEG ratio,** a popular stock-screening device. As an example, assume that a stock's PE ratio is 20 and the cost of capital is 10%. Proponents of this method classify a stock as fairly priced if the expected growth in eps is 20%, underpriced if the expected growth in eps is greater than 20% and overpriced if the expected growth in eps is less than 20%. While the validity of the PEG ratio has yet to be demonstrated empirically, its widespread use highlights investors' appreciation of the relation between PE and eps growth.

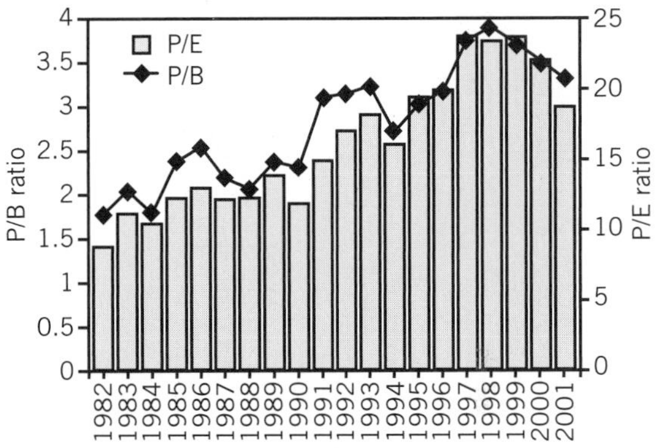

Articulation of PB and PE Ratios

By studying actual PB and PE ratios jointly, our analysis gains insight into the market's expectations of future profitability. As we showed, the PB ratio is a function of future profitability relative to book value and growth in book value, while the PE ratio is a function of future profitability relative to the current level of earnings. The following table summarizes the implications of various combinations of PB and PE ratios:

	High P/B	Low P/B
High P/E	I **(High-performing companies)** Expected positive RI Increasing income	III **(Improving companies)** Expected negative RI Increasing income
Low P/E	II **(Declining companies)** Expected positive RI Decreasing income	IV **(Poor-performing companies)** Expected negative RI Decreasing income

Firms with high P/B and high P/E ratios (cell I) are those with positive expected RI and net income (I) that is expected to increase from current levels. These are the highest-performing (high-growth) companies. Conversely, low P/B with low P/E ratios (cell IV) indicate negative expected residual income and future earnings less than current levels. Clearly, these firms are facing serious difficulties as their existing investments are not expected to earn a return in excess of the cost of capital, and profitability is expected to decline from current levels. Firms with high P/B and low P/E (cell II) are expected to report positive residual profits but falling earnings. These firms are still generating productive (positive net present value) investments, but are in a state of decline. And firms with low P/B and high P/E ratios (cell III) are unable to generate positive net present value investment opportunities, but profitability is expected to increase from current levels. These are firms that are improving their operations, but have not yet resolved their operating difficulties.

Illustration of Earnings-Based Valuation

We illustrate earnings-based valuation using financial information from Christy Company. The book value of equity for Christy Company at January 1, Year 1, is $50,000. The company has a 15% cost of equity capital (*k*). After careful study of the company and its prospects using analysis techniques described in this book, we obtain the following predictions of accounting data:

	Year 1	Year 2	Year 3	Year 4	Year 5*
Sales	$100,000	$113,000	$127,690	$144,290	$144,290
Operating expenses	77,500	90,000	103,500	118,000	119,040
Depreciation	10,000	11,300	12,770	14,430	14,430
Net income	$ 12,500	$ 11,700	$ 11,420	$ 11,860	$ 10,820
Dividends	$ 6,000	$ 4,355	$ 3,120	$ 11,860	$ 10,820

* *Note: For Year 6 and beyond, both accounting data and dividends are expected to approximate Year 5 levels.*

To apply the accounting-based valuation model, we compute expected future book values and ROCEs using the accounting predictions above. For example, expected book value at January 1, Year 2, is computed as $56,500 ($50,000 beginning book value + $12,500 net income − $6,000 dividends). Expected book values at January 1, Years 3 through 5, are $63,845, $72,145, and $72,145, respectively.

Recall that the accounting-based valuation model uses ROCEs computed using *beginning-of-period* book value. Therefore, expected ROCE for Year 1 is 25% ($12,500 ÷ $50,000). Expected ROCEs for Years 2 through 5 are 20.71%, 17.89%, 16.44%, and 15%, respectively.

The value of Christy Company's equity at January 1, Year 1, is computed using the accounting-based valuation model as follows:

$$\$58{,}594 = 50{,}000 + \frac{(0.25 - 0.15) \times 50{,}000}{1.15} + \frac{(0.2071 - 0.15) \times 56{,}500}{1.15^2}$$

$$+ \frac{(0.1789 - 0.15) \times 63{,}845}{1.15^3} + \frac{(0.1644 - 0.15) \times 72{,}145}{1.15^4} + \frac{(0.15 - 0.15) \times 72{,}145}{1.15^5} + 0 + \cdots$$

This accounting-based valuation implies that Christy's stock should sell at a PB ratio of 1.17 ($58,594 ÷ $50,000) at January 1, Year 1. To the extent that expectations of stock market participants differ from those implied by the valuation model, the PB ratio using actual stock price will differ from 1.17. In this case, we must consider two possibilities: (1) estimates of future profitability are too optimistic or pessimistic, and/or (2) the company's stock is mispriced. This determination is a major part of fundamental analysis. Three additional observations regarding this illustration are important.

1. Expected ROCE equals 15% for Year 5 and beyond. This 15% return is equal to Christy Company's cost of capital for those years. Since ROCE equals the cost of capital for Year 5 and beyond, these years' results do not change the value of Christy Company (that is, abnormal earnings equal zero for those years). Our assumption that ROCE gradually nears the cost of capital arises from basic economics. That is, if companies in an industry are able to earn ROCEs in excess of the cost of capital, other companies will enter the industry and drive abnormal earnings to zero.[3] The anticipated effects of competition are implicit in estimates

[3] We must be alert to the possibility that even when abnormal earnings are zero, conservatism in accounting principles can create the *appearance* of abnormal profitability. While this issue is not pursued here, our analysis must consider the effects of conservative accounting principles on future ROCEs. For example, due to mandated expensing of most research and development costs, firms in the pharmaceutical industry are characterized by relatively high ROCEs.

of future profitability. For example, net income as a percentage of sales steadily decreases from 12.5% ($12,500 ÷ $100,000) in Year 1 to 7.5% ($10,820 ÷ $144,290) in Year 5 and beyond.

2. Since PE ratios are based on both *current* and *future* earnings, a PE ratio for Christy Company as of January 1, Year 1, cannot be calculated since prior years' data are unavailable. We can compute the PE ratio at January 1, Year 2. It is calculated as follows (we calculate Christy's abnormal earnings in Problem 12-5):

$$\underline{\underline{4.91}} = \frac{1.15}{0.15} + \frac{\left(\frac{1.15}{0.15}\right)}{12{,}500}\left[\frac{3{,}225-5{,}000}{1.15} + \frac{1{,}844-3{,}226}{1.15^2} + \frac{1{,}039-1{,}845}{1.15^3} + \frac{0-1{,}039}{1.15^4}\right] - \frac{6{,}000}{12{,}500}$$

3. Valuation estimates assume dividend payments occur at the end of each year. A more realistic assumption is that, on average, these cash outflows occur midway through the year. To adjust valuation estimates for midyear discounting, we multiply the present value of future abnormal earnings by $(1 + k/2)$. For Christy Company the adjusted valuation estimate equals $59,239. This is computed as $50,000 plus [1 + (.15/2)] × $8,594.

EARNING POWER AND FORECASTING FOR VALUATION

This section expands on the role of earning power and earnings forecasts for valuation. We also discuss the use of interim reports to monitor and revise these valuation inputs.

Earning Power

Earning power refers to the earnings level for a company that is expected to persist into the foreseeable future. With few exceptions, earning power is recognized as a primary factor in company valuation. Accounting-based valuation models include the capitalization of earning power, where capitalization involves using a factor or multiplier reflecting the cost of capital and its future expected risks and returns. Many analyses of earnings and financial statements are aimed at determining earning power.

Measuring Earning Power

Earning power is a concept derived from financial analysis, not accounting. It focuses on the stability and persistence of earnings and earnings components. Financial statements are used in computing earning power. This computation requires knowledge, judgment, experience, and perspective. Earnings are the most reliable and relevant measure for valuation purposes. While valuation is future oriented, we must recognize the relevance of current and prior company performance for estimating future performance. Recent periods' earnings extending over a business cycle represent actual operating performance and provide us a perspective on operating activities from which we can estimate future performance. Valuation is extremely important for many decisions (such as investing, lending, tax planning, adjudication of valuation disputes). Accordingly, valuation estimates must be credible and defensible, and we must scrutinize departures from the norm.

Time Horizon for Earning Power

A one-year period is often too short a period to reliably measure earnings. This is because of the long-term nature of many investing and financing activities, the effects of business cycles, and the existence of various nonrecurring factors. We can usually best measure a company's earning power by using average (or cumulative) earnings over several years. The preferred time horizon in measuring earning power varies across

PRICE IS RIGHT
Accelerated first-day gains for IPOs suggest that bank clients—not issuers—are raking in the big money (*Business Week*, September 9, 2002):

	Average First-Day Increase: Share Price	Market Value (mil.)
1980–1989	7%	$ 2.6
1990–1998	15	9.3
1999–2000	65	79.0

industries and other factors. A typical horizon is 5 years (and sometimes up to 10 years) in computing average earnings. This extended period is less subject to distortions, irregularities, and other transitory effects impairing the relevance of a single year's results. A five-year earnings computation often retains an emphasis on recent experience while avoiding less relevant performance.

Our discussion of both earnings quality and persistence emphasizes the importance of several earnings attributes including trend. Earnings trend is an important factor in measuring earning power. If earnings exhibit a sustainable trend, we can adjust the averaging process to weigh recent earnings more heavily. As an example, in a five-year earnings computation, the most recent earnings might be given a weight of 5/15, the next most recent earnings a weight of 4/15, and so on until earnings from five years ago receives a weight of 1/15. The more a company's recent experience is representative of future activities, the more relevant it is in the earnings forecast computation. If recent performance is unlike a company's future plans, then less emphasis is placed on prior earnings and more on earnings forecasts.

Adjusting Earnings per Share

Earning power is measured using *all* earnings components. Every item of revenue and expense is part of a company's operating experience. The issue is to what year we assign these items when computing earning power. In certain cases our earnings analysis might be limited to a short time horizon. As described earlier in this chapter, we adjust short time series of earnings for items that better relate to other periods. If this is done on a per share basis, every item must be adjusted for its tax effect using the company's effective tax rate unless the applicable tax rate is specified. All items must also be divided by the number of shares used in computing earnings per share (see Appendix 6A). An example of analytical adjustments for A. H. Robins Company appears in Illustration 12.4.

ILLUSTRATION 12.4 **An Example of per Share Earnings Adjustments**

Item	Year 2	Year 1
Effective tax rate change	+$0.02	
Settlement of litigation	+0.07	+$0.57
Change to straight-line depreciation	+0.02	
Reserves for losses on foreign assets	+0.02	−0.15
Loss on sale of divisions	−0.19	
Change to LIFO	−0.07	
Litigation settlements and expense	−0.09	−0.12
Foreign exchange translation	−0.03	−0.04
R&D expenditures exceeding prior levels	−0.11	
Higher percent allowance for doubtful accounts	−0.02	
± Per share earnings impact	−$0.38	+$0.26
Per share earnings as reported	$1.01	$1.71
Add back negative (−) impact to Year 2	0.38	
Subtract positive (+) impact from Year 1		(0.26)
Adjusted earnings per share	$1.39	$1.45

Earnings Forecasting

A major part of financial statement analysis and valuation is earnings forecasting. From an analytical perspective, evaluating earnings level is closely related to forecasting earnings. This is because a relevant forecast of earnings involves an analysis of earnings components and an assessment of their future levels. Accordingly, much of this chapter's previous discussion is applicable to earnings forecasting. Earnings forecasting follows an analysis of earnings components and involves generating estimates of their future levels. We should consider interactions among components and future business conditions. We should also consider persistence and stability of earnings components. This includes analysis of permanent (recurring) and transitory (nonrecurring) elements.

Mechanics of Earnings Forecasting

Forecasting requires us to effectively use all available information, including prior periods' earnings. Forecasting also benefits from disaggregation. Disaggregation involves using data by product lines or segments and is especially useful when these segments differ by risk, profitability, or growth. Divisional earnings for TechCom, Inc., reveal how strikingly different divisional performance can be masked by aggregate results:

	TECHCOM EARNINGS ($ MILLIONS)			
	1998	1999	2000	2001
Electronic products	$1,800	$1,700	$1,500	$1,200
Customer services	600	800	1,100	1,400
Total net income	$2,400	$2,500	$2,600	$2,600

We must also differentiate forecasting from extrapolation. *Extrapolation* typically assumes the continuation of a trend and mechanically projects that trend into the future.

Analysis research reveals various statistical properties in earnings. Annual earnings growth often behaves in a random fashion. Some users interpret this as implying earnings growth cannot be forecasted. We must remember these studies reflect aggregate behavior and not individual company behavior. Furthermore, reliable earnings forecasting is not done by naive extrapolation of past earnings growth or trends. It is done by analyzing earnings components and considering all available information, both quantitative and qualitative. It involves forecasting these components and speculating about future business conditions.

An often useful source of relevant information for earnings forecasting is the Management Discussion and Analysis. It contains information on management's views and attitudes about the future, along with a discussion of factors influencing company performance. While companies have been slow to respond to the market demand for numerical forecasts of financial position and performance, they are encouraged to report forward-looking information in the MD&A.

Elements in Earnings Forecasting

While earnings forecasting depends on future prospects, the forecasting process must rely on current and past evidence. We forecast expected future conditions in light of this evidence. Analysis must assess continuity and momentum of company performance, including its industry, but it should be put in perspective. We should not confuse a company's past with its future and the uncertainty of forecasting. We must also remember that earnings is total revenues less total expenses, and that earnings forecasts reflect these components. A relatively minor change in a component can cause a large change in earnings.

Another element in earnings forecasting is checking on a forecast's reasonableness. We often use return on invested capital for this purpose. If the earnings forecast yields returns substantially different from returns realized in the past or from industry returns, we should reassess the forecasts and the process. Differences in forecast returns from what is reasonable must be explained. Return on invested capital depends on earnings–where earnings are a product of management quality and asset management.

- *Management quality.* It takes resourceful management to "breathe life" into assets by profitably and efficiently using them. To assume stability of relations and trends implies there is no major change in the skill, depth, and continuity of management. It also implies no major changes in the type of business where management's skills are proven.
- *Asset management.* A second element of profitable operations is asset management and success in financing those assets. Companies require assets to expand operations. Continuity of success and forecasts of growth depend on financing sources and their effects on earnings.

A company's financial condition is another element to earnings forecasting. Lack of liquidity can constrain successful management, and risky capital structure can limit management's actions. These and other economic, industry, and competitive factors are relevant to earnings forecasting. In forecasting earnings we must add expectations about the future to our knowledge of the past. We should also evaluate earnings trends with special emphasis on indicators of future performance like capital expenditures, order backlogs, and demand trends for products and services. It is important for us to realize that earnings forecasting is accompanied by considerable uncertainty. Forecasts may prove quite different from realizations because of unpredictable events or circumstances. We counter uncertainty by continual monitoring of performance relative to forecasts and revising forecasts as appropriate.

Reporting Earnings Forecasts

Recent years have witnessed increased interest in disclosures of earnings forecasts by companies. We should recognize that management (insider) forecasting is different from forecasts made by financial analysts (outsiders). The reliability of forecasts depends on information access and assumptions made. Use of management or analyst forecasts in our analysis depends on an assessment of the assumptions underlying them. The SEC encourages forecasts made in *good faith* that have a reasonable basis. It recommends they be reported in financial statement format and accompanied by information adequate for investors to assess reliability. To encourage forecast disclosures, the SEC has "safe harbor" rules protecting companies from lawsuits in case their predictions do not come true. These rules protect companies provided their forecasts are reasonably based and made in good faith. Because of practical legal considerations, few companies avail themselves of these safe harbor rules and publish forecasts. The following caveat from The Limited is typical of companies' reluctance to report forecasts:

ANALYSIS EXCERPT

The Company cautions that any forward-looking statements . . . involve risks and uncertainties, and are subject to . . . changes in consumer spending patterns, consumer preferences and overall economic conditions, the impact of competition and pricing, changes in weather patterns, political stability, currency and exchange risks and changes in existing or potential duties, tariffs, quotas, postal rate increases and charges; paper and printing costs, availability of suitable store locations at appropriate terms, ability to develop new merchandise and ability to hire and train associates.

Interim Reports for Monitoring and Revising Earnings Estimates

Best Buy Quarterly EPS from Continuing Operations

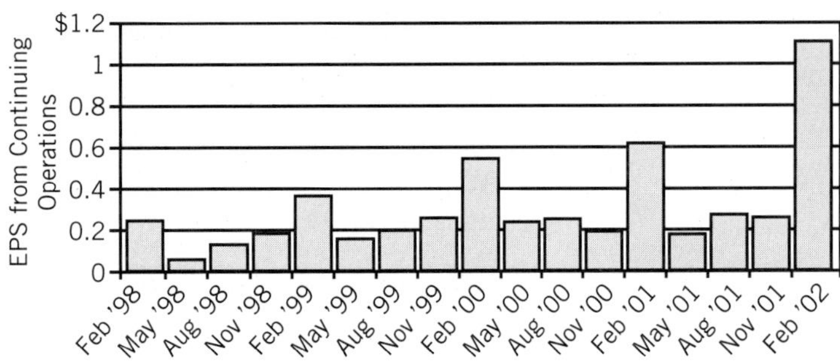

Assessing the earning power or earnings forecasts of a company relies on estimates of future conditions not amenable to verification. Our analysis must continually monitor company performance and compare it with the most recent forecasts and assumptions. We should regularly revise forecasts to incorporate current business conditions. Interim (less than one year) financial statements are a valuable source of information for monitoring performance. Interim statements are usually issued quarterly and are designed to meet users' needs. They are useful in revising estimates of earning power and earnings forecasts. Yet we must recognize certain limitations in interim reporting related to difficulties in assigning earnings components to periods of under one year in length. The remainder of this chapter describes these limitations and their effects on interim reports.

Period-End Accounting Adjustments

Determining operating results for a one-year period requires many accrual adjustments and estimates. These year-end adjustments are often complex, time-consuming, and costly. Examples include revenue recognition, determining inventory costs, allocating overhead, obtaining market values of securities, and estimating bad debts. Adjustments for interim periods are often less complete and use less reliable information than their year-end counterparts. This likely yields a less accurate earnings measure for interim periods.

Seasonality in Business Activities

Many companies experience seasonality in their business activities. Sales, production, and other operating activities are often unevenly distributed across interim periods. This can distort comparisons of interim earnings. It also creates problems in allocating certain discretionary costs like advertising, research, development, repairs, and maintenance. If these expenses vary with sales, they are usually accrued on the basis of expected sales for the entire year. Reporting problems also extend to allocating fixed costs across interim periods. Illustration 12.5 shows an example.

ILLUSTRATION 12.5

Seasonality led to the following adjustments in the interim reports of Toronto Electech: "Because of seasonality in the production cycle, and in accordance with practices followed by the Company in reporting interim financial statements, $435,000 of unabsorbed factory overhead is deferred at June 30, 2000. Due to uncertainties in production and sales for the entire 2000 year, $487,000 of unabsorbed overhead is expensed during the first 6 months of the year."

Integral Reporting Method

Interim reports are generally reported in a manner consistent with annual reporting requirements. Adopting the view that quarterly reports are integral to the entire year rather than a discrete period, practice requires accrual of revenues and expenses across interim periods. This includes accruals for inventory shrinkages, quantity discounts, and uncollectible accounts. Losses are not usually deferred beyond the interim period when they occur, and extraordinary items are reported in the interim period when they occur. But accrual of advertising costs is not acceptable on the basis that their benefits cannot be anticipated. Similarly, LIFO inventory liquidations are not considered for interim periods and only permanent declines in inventory values are recorded for interim reports. In contrast, income taxes are accrued using the effective tax rate expected for the annual period.

SEC Interim Reporting Requirements

The SEC is keenly interested in interim reporting. It requires quarterly reports (Form 10-Q), reports on current developments (Form 8-K), disclosure of separate fourth-quarter results, and details of year-end adjustments. Several reporting requirements exist for interim reports filed with the SEC. Principal requirements include:

- Comparative interim and year-to-date income statement data–can be labeled *unaudited* but must be included in annual reports (small companies are exempt).
- Comparative balance sheets.
- Year-to-date statement of cash flows.
- Pro forma information on business combinations accounted for as purchases.
- Conformity with accepted accounting principles and disclosure of accounting changes, including a letter from the auditor reporting whether the changes are preferable.
- Management's narrative analysis of operating results, with explanations of changes in revenues and expenses across interim periods.
- Disclosure as to whether a Form 8-K is filed during the period–reporting either unusual earnings adjustments or change of auditor.

These disclosures are believed to assist users in better understanding a company's business activities. They also are believed to assist users in estimating the trend in business activities across periods in a timely manner.

Analysis Implications of Interim Reports

Our analysis must be aware of estimation errors and the discretion inherent in interim reports. The limited involvement of auditors with interim reports reduces their reliability relative to annual audited financial statements. Exchange regulations offer some, albeit limited, assurance. Yet not all reporting requirements for interim reports are necessarily best for our analysis. For example, including extraordinary items in the interim period when they occur requires adjustment for use in analysis. Similarly, while accruing expenses across interim periods is reasonable, our analysis must remember there are no precise rules governing these accruals. Shifting expenses across interim periods is often easier than shifting revenues. Therefore, analysis often emphasizes interim revenues as a measure of interim performance. We also should remember that common stock prices influence a company's earnings per share (see Appendix 6A). Our analysis of per share results should separate price effects from operating performance. Certain seasonality problems with interim reports are overcome by computing *year-to-date cumulative numbers,* including the results of the most recent quarter.

GUIDANCE ANSWERS TO ANALYSIS VIEWPOINTS

ANALYST/FORECASTER

More persistent earnings reflect recurring, stable, and predictable operating elements. Your estimate of earnings persistence should consider these elements. More persistent earnings comprise recurring operating elements. Finding 40% of earnings from unusual gains implies less persistence because its source is nonoperating. You can also question classification of litigation gains as unusual–they are sometimes better viewed as extraordinary. The extraordinary loss component also implies less persistence. In this case you need to assess whether environmental costs are truly extraordinary for this company's business. Together, these components suggest less persistence than suggested by the stable and steady growth trend in aggregate earnings. This lower persistence should be reflected in both the level and uncertainty of your earnings forecast.

QUESTIONS

12–1 Why is analysis of research and development expenses important in assessing and forecasting earnings? What are some concerns in analyzing research and development expenses?

12–2 What is the relation between the reported values of assets and reported earnings? What is the relation between the reported values of liabilities, including provisions, and reported earnings?

12–3 What is the purpose in recasting the income statement for analysis?

12–4 Where do we find the data necessary for analysis of operating results and for their recasting and adjustment?

12–5 Describe the recasting process. What is the aim of the recasting process in analysis?

12–6 Describe the adjustment of the income statement for financial statement analysis.

12–7 Explain earnings management. How is earnings management distinguished from fraudulent reporting?

12–8 Identify and explain at least three types of earnings management.

12–9 What factors and incentives motivate companies (management) to engage in earnings management? What are the implications of these incentives for financial statement analysis?

12–10 Why is management interested in the reporting of extraordinary gains and losses?

12–11 What are the analysis objectives in evaluating extraordinary items?

12–12 What three categories can unusual or extraordinary items be usefully subdivided into for purposes of analysis? Provide examples for each category. How should an analysis treat items in each of these categories? Is a certain treatment implied under all circumstances? Explain.

12–13 Describe the effects of extraordinary items on:
a. Company resources. *b.* Management evaluation.

12–14 Comment on the following statement: "Extraordinary gains or losses do not result from 'normal' or 'planned' business activities and, consequently, they should not be used in evaluating managerial performance." Do you agree?

12–15 Can accounting manipulations influence earnings-based estimates of company valuation? Explain.

12–16 *a.* Identify major determinants of PB and PE ratios.
b. How can the analyst use jointly the values of PB and PE ratios in assessing the merits of a particular stock investment?

12–17 What is the difference between forecasting and extrapolation of earnings?

12–18 How do MD&A disclosure requirements aid in earnings forecasting?

12–19 What is earning power? Why is earning power important for financial statement analysis?

12–20 How are interim financial statements used in analysis? What accounting problems with interim statements must we be alert to in an analysis?

12–21 Interim financial reports are subject to limitations and distortions. Identify and discuss at least two reasons for this.

12–22 What are major disclosure requirements for interim reports? What are the objectives of these requirements?

12–23 What are the implications of interim reports for financial analysis?

EXERCISES

EXERCISE 12–1

Analyzing and Interpreting Maintenance and Repairs Expense

CHECK
(4) i. 1.75%
ii. 7.80%

Refer to the financial statements of **Quaker Oats Company** in Appendix A.

Quaker Oats Company

Required:

a. Prepare a schedule where maintenance and repairs expense is shown (i) as a percent of revenues and (ii) as a percent of property, plant, and equipment (net) for:
(1) Year 9 and Year 10, separately.
(2) Total of Years 9 and 10.
(3) Average of Years 9 and 10.
(4) Year 11.

b. Interpret the comparison of the spending level for maintenance and repairs in Year 11 with the average level of spending for Years 9 and 10.

EXERCISE 12–2

Interpreting Extraordinary Items

The president of Vancouver Viacom made the following comments to shareholders:

> Regarding management attitudes, Vancouver Viacom has resisted joining an increasing number of companies who along with earnings announcements make extraordinary or nonrecurring loss announcements. Many of these cases read like regular operating problems. When we close plants, we charge earnings for the costs involved or reserved as we approach the event. These costs, in my judgment, are usually a normal operating expense and something that good management should expect or anticipate. That, of course, raises the question of what earnings figure should be used in assessing a price-earnings ratio and the quality of earnings.

Required:

a. Discuss your reactions to these comments.

b. What factors determine whether a gain or loss is extraordinary?

c. Explain whether you would classify the following items as extraordinary and why.
(1) Loss suffered by foreign subsidiaries due to a change in the foreign exchange rate.
(2) Write-down of inventory from cost to market.
(3) Loss attributable to an improved product developed by a competitor.
(4) Decrease in net income from higher tax rates.
(5) Increase in income from liquidation of low-cost LIFO inventories due to a strike.
(6) Expenses incurred in relocating plant facilities.
(7) Expenses incurred in liquidating unprofitable product lines.
(8) Research and development costs written off from a product failure (non-marketed).
(9) Software costs written off because demand for a product was weaker than expected.
(10) Financial distress of a major customer yielding a bad debts provision.
(11) Loss on sale of rental cars by a car rental company.
(12) Gains on sales of fixed assets.
(13) Rents received from employees who occupy company-owned houses.
(14) Uninsured casualty losses.
(15) Expropriation by a foreign government of an entire division of the company.
(16) Seizure or destruction of property from an act of war.

CHECK
(1) No
(5) No
(10) No

EXERCISE 12–3

Extraordinary Items in Financial Statement Analysis

A financial analyst's comments on income statement classifications follow:

> We should drop the word extraordinary and leave it to users to decide whether items like a strike will recur next year or not, and to decide whether a lease abandonment will recur or not. We need an all-inclusive statement with no extraordinary items. Let users apply the income statement for predictive purposes by eliminating items that will not recur. But let the record show all events that have an impact–there are really no values that "don't count." The current operating performance approach to reporting has no merit. I argue that everything is relevant and needs to be included. By omitting items from current operating performance we are relegating them to a lesser role. I do not believe this is conceptually correct. We include everything to better evaluate

management and forecast earnings. Users can individually decide on the merits of an inventory write-off or the planned sale or abandonment of a plant. Both items deserve to adversely affect income because they reflect management performance. Both items can be excluded by the user in forecasting earnings. The current system yields abuses. Even an earthquake is part of the picture. A lease abandonment recurs in the oil industry. No man is wise enough to cut the Gordian knot on this issue by picking and choosing what is extraordinary, recurring, typical, or customary.

Required:

a. Describe your views on this statement. What is your opinion on how extraordinary items should be reported?

b. Discuss how extraordinary items should be treated in financial analysis.

EXERCISE 12–4
Interpreting Disclosures in Interim Financial Statements

Interim accounting statements comprise a major part of financial reporting. There is ongoing discussion considering the relevance of reporting on business activities for interim periods.

Required:

a. Discuss how revenues are recognized for interim periods. Comment on differences in revenue recognition for companies (1) subject to large seasonal fluctuations in revenue, and (2) having long-term contracts accounted for using percentage of completion for annual periods.

b. Explain how product and period costs are recognized for interim periods.

c. Discuss how inventory and cost of goods sold can be given special accounting treatment for interim periods.

d. Describe how the provision for income taxes is computed and reported in interim reports.

(AICPA Adapted)

EXERCISE 12–5
Identifying Sources of Variability in Financial Data

An analyst needs to understand the sources and implications of variability in financial statement data.

Required:
Identify factors affecting variability in earnings per share, dividends per share, and market price per share that derive from

a. The company

b. The economy

(CFA Adapted)

PROBLEMS

PROBLEM 12–1
Recasting of the Income Statement

CHECK
Recast cont. income Years 11–9, $252.7, $224.5, $126.8

Quaker Oats Company

Refer to the financial statements of **Quaker Oats Company** in Appendix A.

Required:

a. Recast Quaker Oats' income statements for Years 11, 10, and 9 (*Hint:* Use its notes 13, 14, and 15 for discretionary expenses, and estimate federal income tax at the statutory rate of 34%).

b. Interpret trends revealed by the recast income statements.

PROBLEM 12–2
Recasting the Income Statement

CHECK
Recast cont. income Years 11–9, $440.48, $342.21, $296.67

Campbell Soup Company

Refer to the financial statements of **Campbell Soup Company** in Appendix A.

Required:

a. Recast Campbell Soup's income statements for Years 11, 10, and 9. Show computations.

b. Interpret trends revealed by the recast income statements.

PROBLEM 12–3

Analyzing Pre- and Post-acquisition Financial Statements

You are considering the purchase of all outstanding stock of Finex, Inc., for $700,000 on January 2, Year 2. Finex's financial statements for Year 1 are reproduced below:

FINEX, INC.
Balance Sheet
As of December 31, Year 1

Cash	$ 55,000
U.S. government bonds	25,000
Accounts receivable (net)	150,000
Merchandise inventory	230,000
Land	40,000
Buildings (net)[a]	360,000
Equipment (net)[b]	130,000
Total assets	$990,000
Accounts payable	$170,000
Notes payable (current)	50,000
Bonds payable (due Year 12)[c]	200,000
Preferred stock (6%, $100 par)	100,000
Common stock ($100 par)	400,000
Paid-in capital	43,000
Retained earnings[d]	27,000
Liabilities and equity	$990,000

Income Statement
For Year Ended December 31, Year 1

Net sales	$860,000
Cost of good sold	546,000
Gross profit	$314,000
Selling and administrative expenses	240,000
Net operating income	$ 74,000
Income tax expense	34,000
Net income	$ 40,000

[a] *Accumulated depreciation on buildings, $35,000. Depreciation expense in Year 1, $7,900.*
[b] *Accumulated depreciation on equipment, $20,000. Depreciation expense in Year 1, $9,000.*
[c] *Bonds are sold at par.*
[d] *Dividends paid in Year 1: preferred, $6,000; common, $20,000.*

You need to adjust net income to estimate the earnings potential of an acquisition. The company uses the FIFO method of inventory valuation and all inventories can be sold without loss. With the change in ownership you expect an additional 5% of accounts receivable to be uncollectible. You assume sales and all remaining financial relations are constant.

Required:

a. What reported value would be individually assigned to Land, Buildings, and Equipment after the proposed purchase? (*Hint:* Allocate the amount paid for these three assets in proportion to their respective book values on the Year 1 balance sheet.)

b. Prepare a balance sheet for Finex, Inc., immediately after your proposed purchase.

c. Estimate Finex, Inc.'s net operating income for Year 2 under your ownership. (*Hint:* Use the same ratio of depreciation expense to assets; and one-third of depreciation is charged to cost of goods sold.)

d. Assuming your minimum required ratio of net operating income to net sales is 8%, should you purchase Finex, Inc.?

CHECK
(b) Total assets, $1,120,000
(c) Net oper. inc., $64,508

PROBLEM 12–4
Analyzing Credit Constraints for a Bank Loan

Aspero, Inc., has sales of approximately $500,000 per year. Aspero requires a short-term loan of $100,000 to finance its working capital requirements. Two banks are considering Aspero's loan request but each bank requires certain minimum conditions be satisfied. Bank America requires at least a 25% gross margin on sales, and Bank Boston requires a 2:1 current ratio. The following information is available for Aspero for the current year:

- Sales returns and allowances are 10% of sales.
- Purchases returns and allowances are 2% of purchases.
- Sales discounts are 2% of sales.
- Purchase discounts are 1% of purchases.
- Ending inventory is $138,000.
- Cash is 10% of accounts receivable.
- Credit terms to Aspero's customers are 45 days.
- Credit terms Aspero receives from its suppliers are 90 days.
- Purchases for the year are $400,000.
- Ending inventory is 38% greater than beginning inventory.
- Accounts payable are the only current liability.

Required:

Assess whether Aspero, Inc., meets the credit constraint for a loan from either or both banks. Show computations.

CHECK
Bank America rejects loan.

PROBLEM 12–5
Accounting-Based Equity Valuation

Use the data from Christy Company in the chapter to answer the following.

a. Calculate Christy Company's abnormal earnings for each of Year 1 through Year 5.

b. Use the accounting-based equity valuation model to estimate the value of Christy's equity at January 1 of each of Year 2 through Year 5.

c. Adjust the estimates in (*a*) for mid-year discounting.

d. The chapter's discussion of Christy Company assumes that accounting for book value is not conservative. How does the use of conservative accounting principles affect the accounting-based valuation task?

e. Use the PB formula to determine the PB ratio at January 1 of each of Year 2 through Year 5.

f. Use the PE formula to determine the PE ratio at January 1 of each of Year 3 through Year 5.

CHECK
1/1/Year 2
(b) $60,747
(c) $61,066
(e) 1.09

CASES

CASE 12–1
Analyzing and Interpreting Trends in Earnings and Earnings Components

Ferro Corporation

Income statements of **Ferro Corporation,** along with its note 7 on income taxes and selected information from its Form 10-K, are reproduced below:

CONSOLIDATED STATEMENT OF INCOME
Years Ended December 31, Year 6 and Year 5

($ thousands)	Year 6	Year 5
Net sales	$376,485	$328,005
Cost of sales	266,846	237,333
Selling and administrative expenses	58,216	54,140
Research and development	9,972	8,205
Operating expenses	$335,034	$299,678
Operating income	$ 41,451	$ 28,327

	Year 6	Year 5
Other income:		
Equity in net earnings of affiliated companies	$ 1,394	$ 504
Royalties	710	854
Interest earned	1,346	1,086
Miscellaneous	1,490	1,761
Total other income	$ 4,940	$ 4,205
Other charges:		
Interest expense	4,055	4,474
Unrealized foreign currency translation loss	4,037	1,851
Miscellaneous	1,480	1,448
Total other charges	$ 9,572	$ 7,773
Income before taxes	$ 36,819	$ 24,759
U.S. and foreign income taxes (note 7)	16,765	11,133
Net income	$ 20,054	$ 13,626

Notes to Financial Statements:

7. Income tax expense is comprised of the following components ($ thousands):

	U.S. Federal	Foreign	Total		U.S. Federal	Foreign	Total
Year 6:				Year 5:			
Current	$5,147	$11,125	$16,272	Current	$2,974	$ 8,095	$11,069
Deferred	353	140	493	Deferred	180	(116)	64
Total	$5,500	$11,265	$16,765	Total	$3,154	$ 7,979	$11,133

Deferred income taxes were mainly the result of using accelerated depreciation for income tax purposes and straight-line depreciation in the consolidated financial statements. State and local income taxes totaling approximately $750,000 and $698,000 in Year 6 and Year 5, respectively, are included in other expense categories. A reconciliation between the U.S. federal income tax rate and the effective tax rate for Year 6 and Year 5 follows:

	Year 6	Year 5
U.S. federal income tax rate	48.0%	48.0%
Earnings of consolidated subsidiaries taxed at rates less than the U.S. federal income tax rate	(5.3)	(5.3)
Equity in after-tax earnings of affiliated companies	(1.4)	(0.8)
Unrealized foreign exchange translation loss	5.3	3.6
Additional U.S. taxes on dividends from subsidiaries and affiliates	0.8	1.0
Investment tax credit	(1.5)	(0.9)
Miscellaneous	(0.4)	(0.6)
Effective tax rate	45.5%	45.0%

The following information from Ferro Corporation's Form 10-K is available:

	Year 6	Year 5
Cost of sales includes ($ thousands):		
Repairs and maintenance	$15,000	$20,000
Loss on disposal of chemicals division	—	7,000
Selling and administrative expenses include ($ thousands):		
Advertising	$ 6,000	$ 7,000
Employee training program	4,000	5,000

Required:

a. Recast Ferro's income statements for Years 5 and 6. Show computations.

b. Identify factors causing income tax expense to differ from 48% of pretax income. Identify any random or unstable factors.

c. What significant changes can you identify in Ferro's operating policies for Year 6? (*Hint:* Limit your analysis to outlays for repairs and maintenance, advertising, and employee training programs.)

CHECK
Recast oper. income,
Year 6 = $20,520;
Year 5 = $17,215

CASE 12–2
Assessing Earnings Quality and Proposed Accounting Changes

Canada Steel, Ltd., produces steel castings and metal fabrications for sale to manufacturers of heavy construction machinery and agricultural equipment. Early in Year 3 the company's president sent the following memorandum to the financial vice president:

TO: Robert Kinkaid, Financial Vice President

FROM: Richard Johnson, President

SUBJECT: Accounting and Financial Policies

Fiscal Year 2 was a difficult year, and the recession is likely to continue into Year 3. While the entire industry is suffering, we might be hurting our performance unnecessarily with accounting and business policies that are not appropriate. Specifically:

(1) We depreciate most fixed assets over their estimated useful lives on a "tonnage-of-production" method. Accelerated methods and shorter lives are used for tax purposes. A switch to straight-line for financial reporting purposes could: (a) eliminate the deferred tax liability on our balance sheet, and (b) leverage our profits if business picks up.

(2) Several years ago you convinced me to change from the FIFO to LIFO inventory method. Since inflation is now down to a 4% annual rate, and balance sheet strength is important in our current environment, I estimate we can increase shareholders' equity by about $2.0 million, working capital by $4.0 million, and Year 3 earnings by $0.5 million if we return to FIFO in Year 3. This adjustment is real–these profits were earned by us over the past several years and should be recognized.

(3) If we make the inventory change, our stock repurchase program can be continued. The same shareholder who sold us 50,000 shares last year at $100 per share would like to sell another 20,000 shares at the same price. However, to obtain additional bank financing, we must maintain the current ratio at 3:1 or better. It seems prudent to decrease our capitalization if return on assets is unsatisfactory. Also, interest rates are lower (11% prime) and we can save $60,000 after taxes annually once our $3.00 per share dividend is resumed.

These actions would favorably affect our profitability and liquidity ratios as shown in the pro forma income statement and balance sheet data for Year 3 ($ millions):

	Year 1	Year 2	Year 3 Estimate
Net sales	$50.6	$42.3	$29.0
Net income (loss)	$ 2.0	$ (5.7)	$ 0.1
Net profit margin	4.0%	—	0.3%
Dividends	$ 0.7	$ 0.6	$ 0.0
Return on assets	7.2%	—	0.4%
Return on equity	11.3%	—	0.9%
Current assets	$17.6	$14.8	$14.5
Current liabilities	$ 6.6	$ 4.9	$ 4.5
Long-term debt	$ 2.0	$ 6.1	$ 8.1
Shareholders' equity	$17.7	$11.4	$11.5
Shares outstanding (000s)	226.8	170.5	150.5

Per common share:			
Book value	$78.05	$66.70	$76.41
Market price range	$42–34	$65–45	$62–55*

* *Year to date.*

Required:

Assume you are Robert Kinkaid, the financial vice president. Appraise the president's rationale for each of the proposals. You should place special emphasis on how each accounting or business decision affects earnings quality. Support your response with ratio analysis.

(CFA Adapted)

CASE 12–3
Accounting-Based Equity Valuation

After careful financial statement analysis, we obtain these predictions for Colin Technology:

Year	Net Income	Beginning Book Value	Year	Net Income	Beginning Book Value
1	$1,034	$5,308	5	$1,278	$6,728
2	1,130	5,292	6	1,404	7,266
3	1,218	5,834	7	1,546	7,856
4	1,256	6,338			

Colin Technology's cost of equity capital is estimated at 13 percent.

CHECK
(a) $7,205
(d) $8,644

Required:

a. Abnormal earnings are expected to be $0 per year after Year 7. Use the accounting-based equity valuation model to estimate Colin's value at the beginning of Year 1.

b. Determine Colin's PB ratio using the results in (*a*). Colin's actual market-based PB ratio is 1.95. What do you conclude from this PB comparison?

c. Determine Colin's PE ratio using the results in (*a*). Colin's actual market-based PE ratio is 10. What do you conclude from this PE comparison?

d. If we expect Colin's sales and profit margin to remain unchanged after Year 7 with a stable book value of $8,506, use the accounting-based equity valuation model to estimate Colin's value at the beginning of Year 1.

CASE 12–4
IT Professional Service Company Valuations–Revenue Multiples

IT service companies develop Web storefronts that are integrated with back-end implementation systems. Only a small number of companies offer such extensive e-business integration. The industry continues to grow because of customer demand. Unlike traditional valuation, companies in the IT services sector are valued based on revenue multiples. Following are two tables that summarize comparable valuation multiples and operating metrics as of November 22, 1999–a leading Wall Street investment bank, using its own estimates and company data, compiled these tables.

Valuation Multiples:

				REVENUE ESTIMATES					REVENUE MULTIPLE	
Company	Price at 11/22/99	Shares (millions)	Market Value	1999	2000	Growth	Latest Quarter Revenue	Latest Quarter Growth	1999	2000
Breakaway Solutions	$ 62.63	23.9	$1,497	25	43	72%	7	38%	59.9	34.8
Rare Medium	31.25	78.0	2,438	50	100	100	5	100	48.8	24.4
Scient	129.38	38.9	5,033	95	222	134	31	88	53.0	22.7
Viant	87.00	26.0	2,262	59	110	86	19	71	38.3	20.6
Proxicom	73.50	29.2	2,146	79	122	54	24	45	27.2	17.6
US Interactive	41.25	22.1	912	34	55	62	10	29	26.8	16.6

Razorfish	73.50	46.5	3,420	148	230	55	41	20	23.1	14.9
AppNet	48.63	31.3	1,522	109	150	38	30	20	14.0	10.1
iXL Enterprises	37.00	64.5	2,388	200	370	85	64	39	11.9	6.5
Modem Media	54.00	11.7	632	71	102	44	21	32	8.9	6.2
Luminant Worldwide	38.38	23.7	909	94	149	58	25	—	9.6	6.1
USWeb/CKS	42.50	89.1	3,787	506	925	83	138	22	7.5	4.1
Selected averages	—	—	—	—	—	73%	—	46%	27.4	15.4
Selected medians	—	—	—	—	—	67%	—	38%	25.0	15.7

Operating Metrics:

Company	Gross Margin	Revenue/ Headcount	Billable Headcount	Billing Rates	Annual Turnover	Average Utilization
Breakaway Solutions	52.4%	$214,000	140	$138	20%	73%
Rare Medium	51.0	188,000	327	200	—	70
Scient	53.8	303,000	484	—	12	71
Viant	55.0	324,000	254	—	28	67
Proxicom	48.8	214,000	492	149	17	79
US Interactive	44.2	187,000	212	160	24	68
Razorfish	57.8	197,000	868	153	18	62
AppNet	45.1	175,000	715	115	16	73
iXL Enterprises	44.0	217,000	1,260	152	30	73
Modem Media	44.7	209,000	455	132	8	78
Luminant Worldwide	—	180,000	—	—	24	73
USWeb/CKS	40.0	223,000	3,190	155	21	69
Selected averages	48.8%	$219,283	—	$150	20%	71%
Selected medians	48.8%	$211,500	—	$152	20%	72%

Required:

a. Considering that the IT services sector is still in its infancy, explain why analysts employ a revenue multiple model when valuing these companies. How do the "nonfinancial" operating metrics supplement this model?

b. Can you explain why the distribution of revenue multiples appears to have such a wide variance? Notice that billing rates do not appear to be as varied.

c. Most operating metrics are based on headcount. This can be a problem for an industry enjoying such rapid growth. Can you explain how this can be a problem? (*Hint:* Average utilization is the percentage of the 2,080 normal work year that is billed to clients beginning on the day that the employee is hired.)

d. Explain why the revenue multiples for year 2000 are all lower than the comparable revenue multiples for 1999.

e. With such rapid industry expansion comes consolidation through business combinations. Shortly after the above tables were compiled, Razorfish completed a merger with International Integration (I-Cube), another company in the IT services sector. Razorfish offered I-Cube shareholders 0.875 share of Razorfish for each one I-Cube share. The deal was valued at $24.72 per share, nearly 18% above what I-Cube was trading for prior to the announcement. At the time of the acquisition announcement, I-Cube was trading at a price-to-revenue multiple of seven. What is your assessment of the price that Razorfish paid to acquire I-Cube?

WEB ACTIVITIES

The Web Activities are located on the book's website at www.mhhe.com/wild8e.

CC

COMPREHENSIVE CASE

APPLYING FINANCIAL STATEMENT ANALYSIS

A LOOK BACK

Chapters 1 and 2 provided us a broad overview of financial statement analysis using Kodak as a primary example. Chapters 3–6 described the accounting analysis of financing, investing, and operating activities, and offered us insights into company performance and financial condition. Chapters 7–12 emphasized the application and interpretation of key financial analysis tools and techniques.

A LOOK AT THIS CASE

This case is a comprehensive analysis of financial statements and related notes. We use Campbell Soup Company as a focus. We describe the steps in analyzing financial statements, the building blocks of analysis, and essential attributes of an analysis report. We support our analysis using many of the tools and techniques described throughout the book. Explanation and interpretation accompany all of our analyses.

ANALYSIS OBJECTIVES

- Describe the steps in analyzing financial statements.
- Review the building blocks of financial statement analysis.
- Explain important attributes of reporting on financial statement analysis.
- Describe implications for financial statement analysis of evaluating companies in specialized industries or with unique characteristics.
- Analyze in a comprehensive manner the financial statements and notes of Campbell Soup Company.

Mmmm-Mmmm Good, but for How Long?

CAMDEN, NJ–Kurt Warner of the St. Louis Rams has joined a long list of celebrities selling Chunky Soup. Campbell hopes that these rugged salesmen will convince consumers that "soup is great for *eating*." Campbell will need more than slogans, however, to jump-start its sales. The company is the world's largest maker and marketer of soup, and a leading producer of juice beverages, sauces, biscuits, and confectionery products. Its industry, however, remains a competitive, slow-growth environment. And one of its major competitors, General Mills, is poised for attack following its acquisition of Pillsbury.

All of this weighs heavily on Campbell's new CEO, Douglas Conant, who needs to begin the long, hard task of fundamentally remaking the company. Slow-growing for years, Campbell has resisted change and missed opportunities. Its slavish devotion to condensed soup left faster-growing products lacking for research and development funds and marketing support. Without a major makeover, the core product appears destined for irrelevance. Says Prudential Securities analyst John M. McMillin: "You really have to ask yourself: 'Is this the next buggy whip?' "

Is this the next buggy whip?

Campbell's history is one of opportunities found, then squandered. Several years ago, it considered using less heat to improve its soups' taste and texture, but backed off because retooling cost $100 million. Progresso beat it to the punch. Says a former exec: "It's definitely a risk-averse, control-oriented culture. It's all about two things: financial control and how much they can squeeze out of a tomato."

Conant expects to grow Campbell's sales by 3–4% annually and EPS by 8% compounded. To achieve this goal, the company has cut its dividend to help finance an aggressive capital expenditure program to support improved manufacturing technology and increased research and development geared to the development of new products. The transformation, if it comes, will take time. In the interim, Kurt Warner needs to keep the Chunky gravy train rolling. Without the continued growth of that cash cow to finance the transformation, Campbell's prospects aren't looking M'm! M'm! Good!

Sources: Business Week, June 2001; Campbell Soup 2001 Annual Report and 2002 Website.

PREVIEW OF COMPREHENSIVE CASE

A comprehensive case analysis of the financial statements and notes of Campbell Soup Company is our focus. This book has prepared us to tackle all facets of financial statement analysis. This comprehensive case analysis provides us the opportunity to illustrate and apply these analysis tools and techniques. This case also gives us the opportunity to show how we draw conclusions and inferences from detailed analysis. We review the basic steps of analysis, the building blocks, and key attributes of an expert

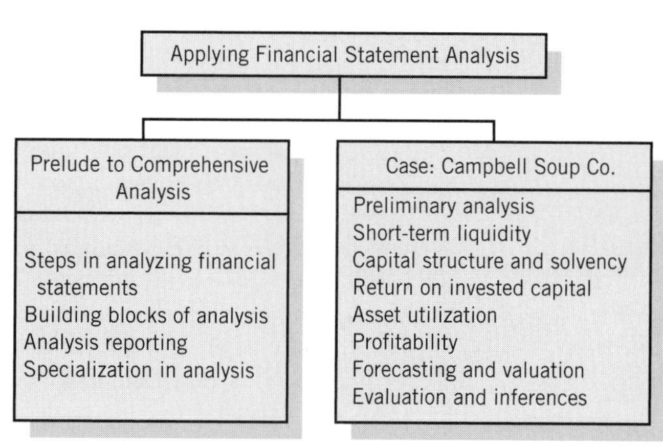

analysis report. Throughout the case we emphasize applications and inferences associated with financial statement analysis.

STEPS IN ANALYZING FINANCIAL STATEMENTS

Our task in analyzing financial statements can be usefully summarized for consistency and organizational efficiency. There are generalizations and guidelines that help us conduct financial statement analysis. Still, we must remember that analysis depends on judgments and thus should be flexible. This flexibility is necessary because of the diversity of situations and circumstances in practice and the need for us to aggressively apply ideas, experience, and knowledge.

Financial statement analysis is oriented toward achieving specific objectives. *The first step is to explicitly define the analysis objectives.* Our evaluation of the issues and concerns leading up to specification of objectives is an important part of analysis. This evaluation helps us develop an understanding of pertinent and relevant objectives. It also helps eliminate extraneous objectives and avoid unnecessary analysis. Identifying objectives is important to an effective and efficient analysis. Effectiveness in analysis implies a focus on the important and relevant elements of financial statements. Efficiency in analysis implies economy of time and effort–see Illustration CC.1a.

ILLUSTRATION CC.1a

Assume you are a bank loan officer handling a request for a short-term loan to finance inventory. A reasonable objective is for you to *assess the intent and ability of the borrower to repay the loan in a timely manner.* Your analysis concentrates on what information is necessary to assess the borrower's intent and ability. You need not focus on extraneous issues like long-term industry conditions affecting the borrower's long-run performance.

The second step in analysis is to formulate specific questions and criteria consistent with the analysis objectives. Answers to these questions should be both relevant to achieving the analysis objectives and reliable for making business decisions. Criteria for answers must be consistent with our risk and return requirements–see Illustration CC.1b.

ILLUSTRATION CC.1b

In your role as bank loan officer you need to specify relevant questions and criteria for making the loan decision in Illustration CC.1a. Criteria for the borrower include:

- Willingness to repay the short-term loan.
- Ability to repay the short-term loan (liquidity).
- Identification of future sources and uses of cash during the loan period.

Addressing analysis questions and defining criteria depend on a variety of information sources, including those bearing on the borrower's character. Financial statement analysis can answer many of these questions, but not all. Tools other than financial statement analysis (such as strategy analysis) must be used to answer some of these questions.

The third step in analysis is identifying the most effective and efficient tools of analysis. These tools must be relevant in answering the questions posed and the criteria established, and must be appropriate for the business decision at hand. These tools include many of the procedures and techniques discussed throughout the book–see Illustration CC.1c.

ILLUSTRATION CC.1c

Your role as loan officer requires decisions regarding what financial statement analysis tools to use for the short-term loan request in Illustration CC.1a. You will probably choose one or more of the following analysis tools:

- Short-term liquidity measures.
- Inventory turnover measures.
- Cash flow and earnings forecasts.
- Pro forma analysis.

Many of these analysis tools include estimates and projections of future conditions. This future orientation is a common thread of all analysis tools.

The fourth step in analysis is interpreting the evidence. Interpretation of financial data and measures is the basis of our decision and subsequent action. This is a crucial and difficult step in analysis, and requires us to apply our skills and knowledge of business and nonbusiness factors. It is a step demanding study and evaluation. It requires us to picture the business reality and environment behind the numbers. There is no mechanical substitute for this step. Yet the quality of our interpretation depends on properly identifying the objectives of analysis, defining the questions and their decision criteria, and selecting efficient and effective analysis tools–see Illustration CC.1d.

ILLUSTRATION CC.1d

Your loan decision requires you to integrate and evaluate the evidence, and then interpret it for purposes of reaching a decision on whether to make the loan or not. It can also include various loan parameters: amount, interest rate, term, payment pattern, and loan restrictions. It also requires an analysis of the client's business strategy and an assessment of the business environment.

This step is similar to the skill requirements of several professions. For example, weather forecasting offers an abundance of analytical data demanding interpretation. Most of us exposed to weather information could not reliably interpret barometric pressure, relative humidity, or wind velocity. We only need to know the weather forecast resulting from the professional interpretation of weather data. Medicine, law, engineering, biology, and genetics provide similar examples.

Our analysis and interpretation of financial statements must remember that the data depict a richer reality. Analysis of financial data result in further levels of abstraction. As an example, no map or picture of the Rocky Mountains conveys their magnificence. One must visit these mountains to fully appreciate them because maps or pictures, like financial statements, are abstractions. This is why it is often advantageous for us to go beyond financial statements and "visit" companies–that is, use their products, buy services, visit stores, talk with customers, and immerse oneself in companies' business activities. The static reality portrayed by abstractions in financial statements is unnatural. Reality is dynamic and evolving. Recognizing the limitations of financial statements is necessary in analysis. This does not detract from their importance. Financial statements are the means by which a company's financial realities are reduced to a common denominator. This common denominator is quantifiable, can be statistically evaluated, and is amenable to prediction.

BUILDING BLOCKS OF FINANCIAL STATEMENT ANALYSIS

Financial statement analysis focuses on one or more elements of a company's financial condition or operating results. Our analysis emphasizes six areas of inquiry–with varying degrees of importance. We described these six areas of inquiry and illustrated them throughout the book. They are considered "building blocks" of financial statement analysis.

1. **Short-term liquidity.** Ability to meet short-term obligations.
2. **Capital structure and solvency.** Ability to generate future revenues and meet long-term obligations.
3. **Return on invested capital.** Ability to provide financial rewards sufficient to attract and retain financing.
4. **Asset turnover.** Asset intensity in generating revenues to reach a sufficient profitability level.
5. **Operating performance and profitability.** Success at maximizing revenues and minimizing expenses from operating activities over the long run.
6. **Forecasting and valuation.** Projection of operating performance, ability to generate sufficient cash flows to fund investment needs, and valuation.

Applying the building blocks to financial statement analysis involves determining:

- Objectives of the analysis.
- Relative emphasis among the building blocks.

To illustrate, an equity investor when evaluating the investment merit of a common stock often emphasizes earnings- and returns-based analyses. This involves assessing operating performance and return on invested capital. A thorough analysis requires an equity investor to assess other building blocks although with perhaps lesser emphasis. Attention to these other areas is necessary to assess risk exposure. This usually involves some analysis of liquidity, solvency, and financing. Further analysis can reveal important risks that outweigh earning power and lead to major changes in the financial statement analysis of a company.

We distinguish among these six building blocks to emphasize important aspects of a company's financial condition and performance. Yet we must remember these areas of analysis are interrelated. For example, a company's operating performance is affected by availability of financing and short-term liquidity conditions. Similarly, a company's credit standing is not limited to satisfactory short-term liquidity, but also depends on its operating performance and asset turnover. Early in the analysis, we must tentatively determine the relative emphasis of each building block and the order of analysis. Order of emphasis and analysis can subsequently change due to evidence collected and/or changes in the business environment.

REPORTING ON FINANCIAL STATEMENT ANALYSIS

The foundation of a reliable analysis is an understanding of its objectives. This understanding leads to efficiency of effort, effectiveness in application, and relevance in focus. Most analyses face constraints on availability of information. Decisions must be made using incomplete or inadequate information. One goal of financial statement analysis is reducing uncertainty through a rigorous and sound evaluation. A **financial statement analysis report** helps on each of these points by addressing all the building blocks of analysis. It helps identify weaknesses in inference by requiring explanation, and it forces us to organize our reasoning and to verify the flow and logic of analysis. The report also serves as a communication device with readers. The writing process reinforces judgments and vice versa, and it helps refine inferences from evidence bearing on key building blocks.

A good report separates interpretations and conclusions of analysis from the information underlying them. This separation enables readers to see the process and rationale of analysis. It also enables the reader to draw personal conclusions and make modifications as appropriate. A good analysis report typically contains at least six sections devoted to:

1. **Executive summary.** Brief summary focused on important analysis results; it launches the analysis report.
2. **Analysis overview.** Background material on the company, its industry, and its economic environment.
3. **Evidential matter.** Financial statements and information used in the analysis. This includes ratios, trends, statistics, and all analytical measures assembled.
4. **Assumptions.** Identification of important assumptions regarding a company's industry and business environment, and other important assumptions for estimates and forecasts, including its business strategy.
5. **Crucial factors.** Listing of important favorable and unfavorable factors, both quantitative and qualitative, for company performance–usually listed by areas of analysis.
6. **Inferences.** Includes forecasts, estimates, interpretations, and conclusions drawing on all prior sections of the report.

We must remember that *importance* is defined by the user. The analysis report should include a brief table of contents to help readers focus on those areas most relevant to their decisions. All irrelevant matter must be eliminated. For example, decades-old details of the beginnings of a company and a detailing of the miscues of analysis are irrelevant. Ambiguities and qualifications to avoid responsibility or hedge inferences should also be eliminated. Finally, writing is important. Mistakes in grammar and errors of fact compromise the credibility of analysis.

SPECIALIZATION IN FINANCIAL STATEMENT ANALYSIS

Analysis of financial statements is usually viewed from the perspective of a "typical" company. Yet we must recognize the existence of several distinct factors (such as unique accounting methods and business environments). These factors arise from several influences including special industry conditions, government regulations, social concerns, and political visibility. Analysis of financial statements for these companies requires we understand their accounting peculiarities. We must prepare for this by learning the specialized areas of accounting relevant to the company under analysis. For example, analysis of an oil and gas company would require knowledge of accounting concepts peculiar to that industry, including determining cost centers, prediscovery costs, discovery costs, and disposing of capitalized costs. In addition, analysis of an oil and gas company would confront special problems in analyzing exploratory, development, and related expenditures, and in amortization and depletion practices. Another example is insurance accounting. This analysis would require knowledge of the industry and its regulations. Challenges arise in understanding recognition of premium revenues, accounting for acquisition costs of new business, and determination of policy reserves. Another example is public utilities. Regulation results in specialized accounting concepts and problems for analysis. There are questions related to the adequacy of provisions for depreciation, and problems concerning the utility's "rate base" and the method used in determining it. Like any profession, specialized areas of inquiry require specialized knowledge. Financial statement analysis is no exception.

COMPREHENSIVE CASE: CAMPBELL SOUP COMPANY

We illustrate many of the major components of financial statement analysis using information and data from Campbell Soup Company.

Preliminary Financial Analysis

Campbell Soup Company is one of the world's largest food companies focusing on convenience foods for human consumption. The company's operations are organized within three divisions: Campbell North America, Campbell Biscuit and Bakery, and Campbell International. Within each division there are groups and business units. Major groups within the Campbell North America division are Soups, Convenience Meals, Grocery, Condiments, and Canadian operations.

The company's products are primarily for home use, but various items are also manufactured for restaurants, vending machines, and institutions. The company distributes its products through direct customer sales. These include chain stores, wholesalers, distributors (with central warehouses), institutional and industrial customers, convenience stores, club stores, and government agencies. In the United States, sales solicitation activities are conducted by subsidiaries, independent brokers, and contract distributors. No major part of Campbell's business depends on a single customer. Shipments are made promptly after receipt and acceptance of orders as reflected in no significant backlog of unfilled orders.

Sales Analysis by Source

Campbell's Sales by Divisions

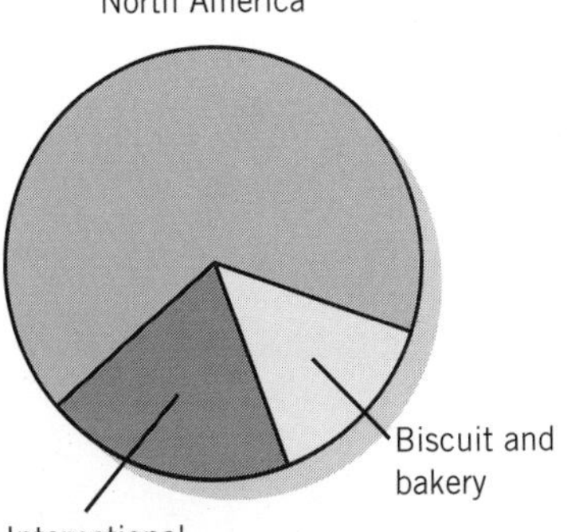

Campbell's sales by division from Year 6 through Year 11 are shown in Exhibit CC.1. Its North American and International divisions are the largest contributors of sales, accounting for 68.7% and 19.7%, respectively, in Year 11.

Soup is the primary business of Campbell U.S., capturing about 60% of the entire soup market. This includes dry, ramen noodle, and microwavable soups. Other Campbell Soup brands include ready-to-serve soups: Home Cooking, Chunky, and Healthy Request. An integral part of its soup business is Swanson's canned chicken broth. Americans purchase more than 2.5 billion cans of Campbell's soups each year, and on average have nine cans in their pantry at any time during the year.

Fiscal Year 11 is a successful transition year for Campbell. It completed major divestitures and accomplished significant restructuring and reorganization projects. Corporate goals concerning earnings, returns, and cash flows are being met. The North American and International divisions

Exhibit CC.1

CAMPBELL SOUP COMPANY
Sales Contribution and Percentage of Sales by Division
($ millions)

	Year 11	Year 10	Year 9	Year 8	Year 7	Year 6
Sales Contribution:						
Campbell North America:						
Campbell USA	$3,911.8	$3,932.7	$3,666.9	$3,094.1	$2,881.4	$2,910.1
Campbell Canada	352.0	384.0	313.4	313.1	312.8	255.1
	4,263.8	4,316.7	3,980.3	3,407.2	3,194.2	3,165.2
Campbell Biscuit and Bakery:						
Pepperidge Farm	569.0	582.0	548.4	495.0	458.5	420.1
International Biscuit	219.4	195.3	178.0	—	—	—
	788.4	777.3	726.4	495.0	458.5	420.1
Campbell International	1,222.9	1,189.8	1,030.3	1,036.5	897.8	766.2
Interdivision	(71.0)	(78.0)	(64.9)	(69.8)	(60.1)	(64.7)
Total sales	$6,204.1	$6,205.8	$5,672.1	$4,868.9	$4,490.4	$4,286.8
Percentage of Sales:						
Campbell North America:						
Campbell U.S.A.	63.0%	63.4%	64.7%	63.6%	64.2%	67.9%
Campbell Canada	5.7	6.2	5.5	6.4	6.9	5.9
	68.7	69.6	70.2	70.0	71.1	73.8
Campbell Biscuit and Bakery:						
Pepperidge Farm	9.2	9.4	9.7	10.2	10.2	9.8
International Biscuit	3.5	3.1	3.1	—	—	—
	12.7	12.5	12.8	10.2	10.2	9.8
Campbell International	19.7	19.2	18.2	21.3	20.0	17.9
Interdivision	(1.1)	(1.3)	(1.2)	(1.4)	(1.3)	(1.5)
Total sales	100.0%	100.0%	100.0%	100.0%	100.0%	100.0%

produced strong earnings results. The company enters Year 12 with a reconfigured product portfolio, positioned to support continued solid financial performance. This performance gives Campbell an opportunity to increase consumer advertising and to further the introduction of new product lines and continue support for flagship products.

Comparative Financial Statements

Complete financial statements and related information for Campbell Soup are in Appendix A. These reports include information from SEC Form 10-K. Comparative financial statements for Campbell for Years 6 through 11 are presented in Exhibits CC.2, CC.3, and CC.4. The auditor's opinions on its financial statements for the past six years are unqualified.

Exhibit CC.2

CAMPBELL SOUP COMPANY
Income Statements (in millions except per share data)
For Year 6 through Year 11

	Year 11	Year 10	Year 9	Year 8	Year 7	Year 6
Net sales	$6,204.1	$6,205.8	$5,672.1	$4,868.9	$4,490.4	$4,286.8
Costs and expenses:						
Cost of products sold	$4,095.5	$4,258.2	$4,001.6	$3,392.8	$3,180.5	$3,082.7
Marketing and selling expenses	956.2	980.5	818.8	733.3	626.2	544.4
Administrative expenses	306.7	290.7	252.1	232.6	213.9	195.9
Research and development expenses	56.3	53.7	47.7	46.9	44.8	42.2
Interest expense	116.2	111.6	94.1	53.9	51.7	56.0
Interest income	(26.0)	(17.6)	(38.3)	(33.2)	(29.5)	(27.4)
Foreign exchange losses, net	0.8	3.3	19.3	16.6	4.8	0.7
Other expense (income)	26.2	14.7	32.4	(3.2)	(9.5)	5.5
Divestitures, restructuring, and unusual charges	0.0	339.1	343.0	40.6	0.0	0.0
Total costs and expenses	5,531.9	6,034.2	5,570.7	4,480.3	4,082.9	3,900.0
Earnings before equity in earnings of affiliates and minority interests	672.2	171.6	101.4	388.6	407.5	386.8
Equity in earnings of affiliates	2.4	13.5	10.4	6.3	15.1	4.3
Minority interests	(7.2)	(5.7)	(5.3)	(6.3)	(4.7)	(3.9)
Earnings before taxes	667.4	179.4	106.5	388.6	417.9	387.2
Taxes on earnings	265.9	175.0	93.4	147.0	170.6	164.0
Earnings before cumulative effect of accounting change	401.5	4.4	13.1	241.6	247.3	223.2
Cumulative effect of change in accounting for income taxes	0	0	0	32.5	0	0
Net earnings	$ 401.5	$ 4.4	$ 13.1	$ 274.1	$ 247.3	$ 223.2
Earnings per share	$3.16	$0.03	$0.10	$2.12*	$1.90	$1.72
Weighted-average shares outstanding	127.00	126.60	129.30	129.30	129.90	129.50

* Including $0.25 per share cumulative effect of change in accounting for income taxes.

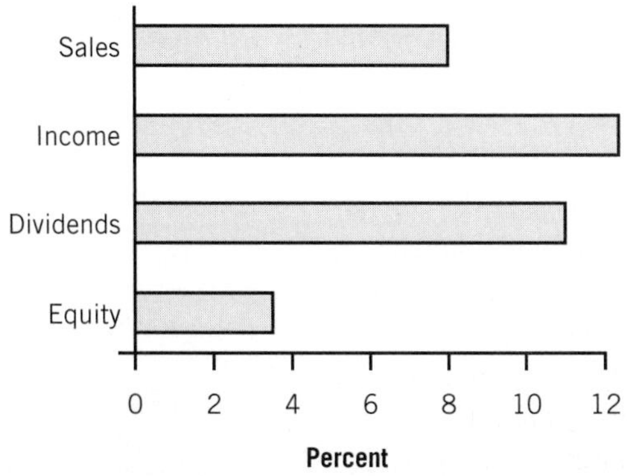

Further Analysis of Financial Statements

Growth rates for important financial measures, annually compounded, are reported in Exhibit CC.5. These rates are computed using four different periods and are based on per share data (see Exhibit CC.9). Most impressive is the growth in net income per share over the past five years (12.93%). Growth in sales per share over the same recent five-year period is at a rate less than that of net income. Equity per share growth in the recent 5-year period declined compared to the 10-year period. This finding, including the two negative growth rates in the exhibit, is due to divestitures and restructurings in Years 9 and 10. We also compute common-size income statements and balance sheets in Exhibits CC.6 and CC.7. Exhibit CC.8 presents the trend indexes of selected accounts for Campbell Soup. Exhibit CC.9 shows Campbell Soup's per share results.

Exhibit CC.3

CAMPBELL SOUP COMPANY
Balance Sheets ($ millions)
At the End of Year 6 through Year 11

	Year 11	Year 10	Year 9	Year 8	Year 7	Year 6
Assets						
Current assets:						
Cash and cash equivalents	$ 178.90	$ 80.70	$ 120.90	$ 85.80	$ 145.00	$ 155.10
Other temporary investments	12.80	22.50	26.20	35.00	280.30	238.70
Accounts receivable	527.40	624.50	538.00	486.90	338.90	299.00
Inventories	706.70	819.80	816.00	664.70	623.60	610.50
Prepaid expenses	92.70	118.00	100.40	90.50	50.10	31.50
Total current assets	1,518.50	1,665.50	1,601.50	1,362.90	1,437.90	1,334.80
Plant assets, net of depreciation	1,790.40	1,717.70	1,540.60	1,508.90	1,349.00	1,168.10
Intangible assets, net of amortization	435.50	383.40	466.90	496.60	—	—
Other assets	404.60	349.00	323.10	241.20	310.50	259.90
Total assets	$4,149.00	$4,115.60	$3,932.10	$3,609.60	$3,097.40	$2,762.80
Liabilities and Shareowners' Equity						
Current liabilities:						
Notes payable	$ 282.20	$ 202.30	$ 271.50	$ 138.00	$ 93.50	$ 88.90
Payable to suppliers and others	482.40	525.20	508.20	446.70	374.80	321.70
Accrued liabilities	408.70	491.90	392.60	236.90	182.10	165.90
Dividend payable	37.00	32.30	29.70	—	—	—
Accrued income taxes	67.70	46.40	30.10	41.70	43.40	49.60
Total current liabilities	1,278.00	1,298.10	1,232.10	863.30	693.80	626.10
Long-term debt	772.60	805.80	629.20	525.80	380.20	362.30
Other liabilities, mainly deferred income tax	305.00	319.90	292.50	325.50	287.30	235.50
Shareowners' equity:						
Preferred stock; authorized 40,000,000 sh.; none issued	—	—	—	—	—	—
Capital stock, $0.15 par value; authorized 140,000,000 sh.; issued 135,622,676 sh.	20.30	20.30	20.30	20.30	20.30	20.30
Capital surplus	107.30	61.90	50.80	42.30	41.10	38.10
Earnings retained in the business	1,912.60	1,653.30	1,775.80	1,879.10	1,709.60	1,554.00
Capital stock in treasury, at cost	(270.40)	(107.20)	(70.70)	(75.20)	(46.80)	(48.40)
Cumulative translation adjustments	23.60	63.50	2.10	28.50	11.90	(25.10)
Total shareowners' equity	1,793.40	1,691.80	1,778.30	1,895.00	1,736.10	1,538.90
Total liabilities and shareowners' equity	$4,149.00	$4,115.60	$3,932.10	$3,609.60	$3,097.40	$2,762.80

Analysis of Exhibit CC.4 reveals operating cash flows are a steady and growing source of cash, with a substantial increase in Year 11 net operating cash flows ($805 million). The slight cash downturn in Year 9 is due primarily to an increase in inventories ($113 million) and a decrease (negative) in deferred taxes ($68 million). The increase in inventories is tied to management's desire to improve customer service, and the decrease in deferred taxes relates to restructuring and unusual charges that are not tax

Exhibit CC.4

CAMPBELL SOUP COMPANY
Statements of Cash Flows ($ millions)
For Year 6 through Year 11

	Year 11	Year 10	Year 9	Year 8	Year 7	Year 6	Total
Cash flows from operating activities:							
Net earnings	$ 401.5	$ 4.4	$ 13.1	$ 274.1	$ 247.3	$ 223.2	$ 1,163.6
To reconcile net earnings to net cash provided by operating activities:							
Depreciation and amortization	208.6	200.9	192.3	170.9	144.6	126.8	1,044.1
Divestitures and restructuring	—	339.1	343.0	17.6	—	—	699.7
Deferred taxes	35.5	3.9	(67.8)	13.4	45.7	29.0	59.7
Other, net	63.2	18.6	37.3	43.0	28.0	16.6	206.7
Cumulative effect of accounting change	—	—	—	(32.5)	—	—	(32.5)
(Increase) decrease in accounts receivable	17.1	(60.4)	(46.8)	(104.3)	(36.3)	(3.6)	(234.3)
(Increase) decrease in inventories	48.7	10.7	(113.2)	54.2	(3.9)	23.1	19.6
Net change in other current assets and liabilities	30.6	(68.8)	(0.6)	30.2	42.9	48.7	83.0
Net cash from operating activities	805.2	448.4	357.3	466.6	468.3	463.8	3,009.6
Cash flows from investing activities:							
Purchases of plant assets	(361.1)	(387.6)	(284.1)	(245.3)	(303.7)	(235.3)	(1,817.1)
Sale of plant assets	43.2	34.9	39.8	22.6	—	29.8	170.3
Businesses acquired	(180.1)	(41.6)	(135.8)	(471.9)	(7.3)	(20.0)	(856.7)
Sale of businesses	67.4	21.7	4.9	23.5	20.8	—	138.3
Increase in other assets	(57.8)	(18.6)	(107.0)	(40.3)	(50.1)	(18.0)	(291.8)
Net change in other temporary investments	9.7	3.7	9.0	249.2	(60.7)	(144.1)	66.8
Net cash used in investing activities	(478.7)	(387.5)	(473.2)	(462.2)	(401.0)	(387.6)	(2,590.2)
Cash flows from financing activities:							
Long-term borrowings	402.8	12.6	126.5	103.0	4.8	203.9	853.6
Repayments of long-term borrowings	(129.9)	(22.5)	(53.6)	(22.9)	(23.9)	(164.7)	(417.5)
Increase (decrease) in short-term borrowings*	(137.9)	(2.7)	108.2	8.4	(20.7)	4.6	(40.1)
Other short-term borrowings	117.3	153.7	227.1	77.0	89.3	72.9	737.3
Repayments of other short-term borrowings	(206.4)	(89.8)	(192.3)	(87.6)	(66.3)	(88.5)	(730.9)
Dividends paid	(137.5)	(124.3)	(86.7)	(104.6)	(91.7)	(104.6)	(649.4)
Treasury stock purchases	(175.6)	(41.1)	(8.1)	(29.3)	—	—	(254.1)
Treasury stock issued	47.7	12.4	18.5	0.9	1.6	4.0†	85.1
Other, net	(0.1)	(0.1)	23.5	2.3	18.6	17.9	62.1
Net cash from (used in) financing activities	(219.6)	(101.8)	163.1	(52.8)	(88.3)	(54.5)	(353.9)
Effect of exchange rate change on cash	(8.7)	0.7	(12.1)	(10.8)	(7.1)	(3.7)	(41.7)
Net increase (decrease) in cash and cash equivalents	$ 98.2	$ (40.2)	$ 35.1	$ (59.2)	$ (28.1)	$ 18.0	$ 23.8
Cash and cash equivalents at the beginning of year	80.7	120.9	85.8	145.0	173.1	155.1	760.6
Cash and cash equivalents at end of year	$ 178.9	$ 80.7	$ 120.9	$ 85.8	$ 145.0	$ 173.1	$ 784.4

* With less than three month maturities.
† Stock of $2.8 issued for a pooling of interest.

Exhibit CC.5

CAMPBELL SOUP COMPANY

Five-Year Growth Rates*

Per share	Years 6 to 11	[Average for Years 6 to 8] to [Average for Years 9 to 11]
Sales	8.09%	5.95%
Net income	12.93	−10.53
Dividends	11.50	6.69
Equity	3.55	0.53

Ten-Year Growth Rates*

Per share	Years 1 to 11	[Average for Years 1 to 3] to [Average for Years 9 to 11]
Sales	8.51%	7.22%
Net income	12.19	−0.44
Dividends	8.18	6.62
Equity	6.22	5.13

* Growth rates (annually compounded) are computed using the compound interest method (where n = compounding period, and r = Rate of growth):

$$\text{Future value (FV)} = \text{Present value (PV)} \times \left(1 + \frac{r}{100}\right)^n$$

For example, net sales per share during Years 6 to 11 grew at a rate of:

$$\text{FV} = \text{PV}\left(1 + \frac{r}{100}\right)^n \Leftrightarrow \$48.85 = \$33.10\left(1 + \frac{r}{100}\right)^5$$

$$r = 8.09\%$$

deductible, resulting in $78 million of credits to tax expense but higher current tax liabilities. We also see that the declines in net income for Years 9 and 10 are not reflected in operating cash flows. This is because these declines are from restructuring and divestiture charges having no immediate cash flow effects.

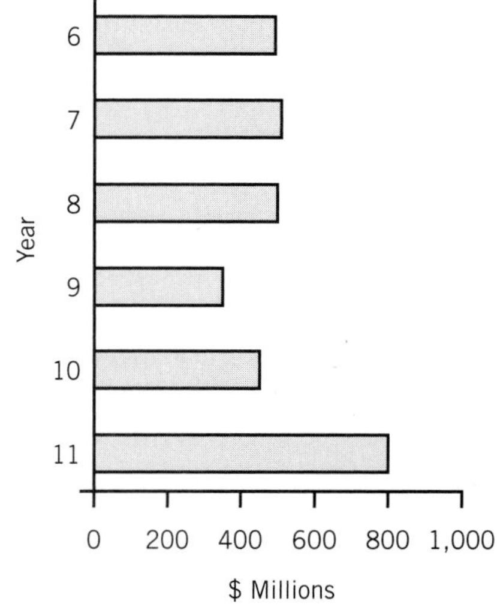

Campbell's common-size statements of cash flows for the six years ending with Year 11 are shown in Exhibit CC.10. This exhibit reveals several patterns in the company's cash flows over these six years. Transitory fluctuations in cash, such as those due to the high usage of cash for investing activities in Year 7 (62%), are put in perspective by including aggregate figures in a total column. Total operating cash flows constitute more than one-half of all cash inflows. This finding along with evidence that financing activities (using 7% of cash inflows) are mostly refinancing is indicative of Campbell's financial strength and financing practices. The total column reveals that cash used for acquiring assets and businesses consumes nearly 50% of cash inflows, and about 12% of cash inflows are used for dividends. Overall, cash inflows from operations (56%) are used for both financing (7%) and investing (48%) activities. Campbell's net cash position over these six years is stable, never deviating more than 7% from the prior year. Its growth for the entire six-year period is less than 1%.

Exhibit CC.6

CAMPBELL SOUP COMPANY
Common-Size Income Statements
For Year 6 through Year 11

	Year 11	Year 10	Year 9	Year 8	Year 7	Year 6
Net sales	100.00%	100.00%	100.00%	100.00%	100.00%	100.00%
Costs and expenses:						
Cost of products sold	66.01%	68.62%	70.55%	69.68%	70.83%	71.91%
Marketing and selling expenses	15.41	15.80	14.44	15.06	13.95	12.70
Administrative expenses	4.94	4.68	4.44	4.78	4.76	4.57
Research and development expenses	0.91	0.87	0.84	0.96	1.00	0.98
Interest expense	1.87	1.80	1.66	1.11	1.15	1.31
Interest income	(0.42)	(0.28)	(0.68)	(0.68)	(0.66)	(0.64)
Foreign exchange losses, net	0.01	0.05	0.34	0.34	0.11	0.02
Other expense (income)	0.42	0.24	0.57	(0.07)	(0.21)	0.13
Divestitures, restructuring, and unusual charges	—	5.46	6.05	0.83	—	—
Total costs and expenses	89.17%	97.23%	98.21%	92.02%	90.93%	90.98%
Earnings before equity in earnings of affiliates and minority interests	10.83%	2.77%	1.79%	7.98%	9.07%	9.02%
Equity in earnings of affiliates	0.04	0.22	0.18	0.13	0.34	0.10
Minority interests	(0.12)	(0.09)	(0.09)	(0.13)	(0.10)	(0.09)
Earnings before taxes	10.76%	2.89%	1.88%	7.98%	9.31%	9.03%
Taxes on earnings	4.29	2.82	1.65	3.02	3.80	3.83
Earnings before cumulative effect of accounting change	6.47%	0.07%	0.23%	4.96%	5.51%	5.21%
Cumulative effect of accounting change for income taxes	—	—	—	0.67	—	—
Net earnings	6.47%	0.07%	0.23%	5.63%	5.51%	5.21%

It is often useful to construct a summary of cash inflows and cash outflows by major categories of activities. Using Exhibit CC.4, we prepare the following chart of summary cash inflows and cash outflows:

($ in millions)	Year 11	Year 10	Year 9	Year 8	Year 7	Year 6	Total
Operating activities	$805.2	$448.4	$357.3	$466.6	$468.3	$463.8	$3,009.6
Investing activities	(478.7)	(387.5)	(473.2)	(462.2)	(401.0)	(387.6)	(2,590.2)
Financing activities	(219.6)	(101.8)	163.1	(52.8)	(88.3)	(54.5)	(353.9)
Increase (decrease) in cash	98.2	(40.2)	35.1	(59.2)	(28.1)	18.0	23.8

The picture emerging from this summary is that Campbell has major outlays for (1) investing–$2,590.2 million–and (2) financing (including dividends)–$353.9 million. Despite these outlays, Campbell experienced a slight cumulative increase of $23.8 million in cash. Notably, these activities are funded by Campbell's net operating cash inflows of $3,009.6 million. Notice that in Years 7, 8, and 10 the cash balances are drawn down to fund investing and financing activities. Still, operating cash flows for this

Exhibit CC.7

CAMPBELL SOUP COMPANY
Common-Size Balance Sheets
At the End of Year 6 through Year 11

	Year 11	Year 10	Year 9	Year 8	Year 7	Year 6	Year 11 Industry Composite*
Current assets:							
Cash and cash equivalents	4.31%	1.96%	3.07%	2.38%	4.69%	5.61%	3.4%
Other temporary investments	0.31	0.55	0.67	0.97	9.05	8.64	
Accounts receivable	12.71	15.17	13.68	13.49	10.94	10.82	16.5
Inventories	17.03	19.92	20.75	18.41	20.13	22.10	38.6
Prepaid expenses	2.23	2.87	2.55	2.51	1.62	1.14	2.2
Total current assets	36.60%	40.47%	40.73%	37.76%	46.43%	48.31%	60.7%
Plant assets, net of depreciation	43.15	41.74	39.18	41.80	43.55	42.28	21.0
Intangible assets, net of amortization	10.50	9.32	11.87	13.76	—	—	
Other assets	9.75	8.48	8.22	6.68	10.02	9.41	18.3
Total assets	100.00%	100.00%	100.00%	100.00%	100.00%	100.00%	100.0%
Current liabilities:							
Notes payable	6.80%	4.92%	6.90%	3.82%	3.02%	3.22%	6.7%
Payable to suppliers and others	11.63	12.76	12.92	12.38	12.10	11.64	10.2
Accrued liabilities	9.85	11.95	9.98	6.56	5.88	6.00	15.8
Dividend payable	0.89	0.78	0.76	—	—	—	
Accrued income taxes	1.63	1.13	0.77	1.16	1.40	1.80	
Total current liabilities	30.80%	31.54%	31.33%	23.92%	22.40%	22.66%	32.7%
Long-term debt	18.62	19.58	16.00	14.57	12.27	13.11	19.7
Other liabilities, mainly deferred taxes	7.35	7.77	7.44	9.02	9.28	8.52	1.5
Shareowners' equity:							
Preferred stock; authorized 40,000,000 sh.; none issued	—	—	—	—	—	—	
Capital stock, $0.15 par value; authorized 140,000,000 sh.; issued 135,622,676 sh.	0.49	0.49	0.52	0.56	0.66	0.73	
Capital surplus	2.59	1.50	1.29	1.17	1.33	1.38	
Earnings retained in the business	46.10	40.17	45.16	52.06	55.19	56.25	
Capital stock in treasury, at cost	(6.52)	(2.60)	(1.80)	(2.08)	(1.51)	(1.75)	
Cumulative translation adjustments	0.57	1.54	0.05	0.79	0.38	(0.91)	
Total shareowners' equity	43.22%	41.11%	45.23%	52.50%	56.05%	55.70%	46.1%
Total liabilities and equity	100.00%	100.00%	100.00%	100.00%	100.00%	100.00%	100.0%

* Reported for accounts where data are available.

six-year period are sufficient to fund *all* of Campbell's investing and financing needs and still leave excess cash of $23.8 million.

Exhibit CC.8

CAMPBELL SOUP COMPANY
Trend Index of Selected Accounts (Year 6 = 100%)

	Year 11	Year 10	Year 9	Year 8	Year 7	Year 6
Cash and cash equivalents	115%	52%	78%	55%	93%	$ 155.1
Accounts receivable	176	209	180	163	113	299.0
Temporary investments	5	9	11	15	117	238.7
Inventory	116	134	134	109	102	610.5
Total current assets	114	125	120	102	108	1,334.8
Total current liabilities	204	207	197	138	111	626.1
Working capital	34	52	52	70	105	708.7
Plant assets, net	153	147	132	129	115	1,168.1
Other assets	156	134	124	93	119	259.9
Long-term debt	213	222	174	145	105	362.3
Total liabilities	192	198	176	140	111	1,223.9
Shareowners' equity	117	110	116	123	113	1,538.9
Net sales	145	145	132	114	105	4,286.8
Cost of products sold	133	138	130	110	103	3,082.7
Administrative expenses	157	148	129	119	109	195.9
Marketing and sales expenses	176	180	150	135	115	544.4
Interest expense	208	199	168	96	92	56.0
Total costs and expenses	142	155	143	115	105	3,900.0
Earnings before taxes	172	46	28	100	108	387.2
Net income	180	2*	6*	123	111	223.2

* Excluding the effect (net of statutory tax) of divestitures, restructuring, and unusual charges would change these amounts to: Year 10—102% and Year 9—104%.

Exhibit CC.9

CAMPBELL SOUP COMPANY
Per Share Results

	Year 11	Year 10	Year 9	Year 8	Year 7	Year 6
Sales	$48.85	$47.88	$43.87	$37.63	$34.57	$33.10
Net income	3.16	0.03	0.10	2.12	1.90	1.72
Dividends	1.12	0.98	0.90	0.81	0.71	0.65
Book value	14.12	13.09	13.76	14.69	13.35	11.86
Average shares outstanding (mil.)	127.0	129.6	129.3	129.4	129.9	129.5

Two additional measures of Campbell's cash flows are reported in Exhibit CC.11. The cash flow adequacy ratio provides insight into whether Campbell generates sufficient cash from operations to cover capital expenditures, investments in inventories, and cash dividends. Campbell's cash flow adequacy ratio for the six-year period is 0.875, implying that funds generated from operations are insufficient to cover these items (see denominator) and that there is a need for external financing. We must remember this is

Exhibit CC.10

CAMPBELL SOUP COMPANY
Common-Size Statements of Cash Flows*
For Year 6 through Year 11

	Year 11	Year 10	Year 9	Year 8	Year 7	Year 6	Total
Cash flows from operating activities:							
Net earnings	26.89%	0.54%	1.15%	25.14%	38.42%	27.88%	21.54%
To reconcile net earnings to net cash provided by operating activities:							
Depreciation and amortization	13.97	24.58	16.82	15.67	22.47	15.84	19.33
Divestitures and restructuring provisions	—	41.49	30.00	1.61	—	—	12.95
Deferred taxes	2.38	0.48	(5.93)	1.23	7.10	3.62	1.11
Other, net	4.23	2.28	3.26	3.94	4.35	2.07	3.83
Cumulative effect of accounting change	—	—	—	(2.98)	—	—	(0.60)
(Increase) decrease in accounts receivable	1.15	(7.39)	(4.09)	(9.57)	(5.64)	(0.45)	(4.34)
(Increase) decrease in inventories	3.26	1.31	(9.90)	4.97	(0.61)	2.89	0.36
Net change in other current assets and liabilities	2.05	(8.42)	(0.05)	2.77	6.67	6.08	1.54
Net cash provided by operating activities	53.92%	54.86%	31.25%	42.80%	72.76%	57.94%	55.72%
Cash flows from investing activities:							
Purchase of plant assets	(24.18)%	(47.42)%	(24.85)%	(22.50)%	(47.19)%	(29.39)%	(33.64)%
Sale of plant assets	2.89	4.27	3.48	2.07	—	3.72	3.15
Businesses acquired	(12.06)	(5.09)	(11.88)	(43.28)	(1.13)	(2.50)	(15.86)
Sale of businesses	4.51	2.66	0.43	2.16	3.23	—	2.56
Increase in other assets	(3.87)	(2.28)	(9.36)	(3.70)	(7.78)	(2.25)	(5.40)
Net change in other temporary investments	0.65	0.45	0.79	22.86	(9.43)	(18.00)	1.24
Net cash used in investing activities	(32.06)%	(47.41)%	(41.39)%	(42.39)%	(62.31)%	(48.42)%	(47.95)%
Cash flows from financing activities:							
Long-term borrowings	26.97%	1.54%	11.07%	9.45%	0.75%	25.47%	15.80%
Repayments of long-term borrowings	(8.70)	(2.75)	(4.69)	(2.10)	(3.71)	(20.57)	(7.73)
Increase (decrease) in short-term borrowings	(9.23)	(0.33)	9.46	0.77	(3.22)	0.57	(0.74)
Other short-term borrowings	7.86	18.81	19.87	7.06	13.88	9.11	13.65
Repayments of other short-term borrowings	(13.82)	(10.99)	(16.82)	(8.03)	(10.30)	(11.06)	(13.53)
Dividends paid	(9.21)	(15.21)	(7.58)	(9.59)	(14.25)	(13.07)	(12.02)
Treasury stock purchases	(11.76)	(5.03)	(0.71)	(2.69)	—	—	(4.70)
Treasury stock issued	3.19	1.52	1.62	0.08	0.25	0.50	1.58
Other, net	(0.01)	(0.01)	2.06	0.21	2.89	2.24	1.15
Net cash from (used in) financing activities	(14.71)%	(12.46)%	14.27%	(4.84)%	(13.72)%	(6.81)%	(6.55)%
Effect of exchange rate change on cash	(0.58)	0.09	(1.06)	(0.99)	(1.10)	(0.46)	(0.77)
Net increase (decrease) in cash and cash equivalents	6.58%	(4.92)%	3.07%	(5.43)%	(4.37)%	2.25%	0.44%

*Common-size percentages are based on total cash inflows = 100%. For Year 11, the 100 percent consists of CFO (26.89 + 13.97 + 2.38 + 4.23 + 1.15 + 3.26 + 2.05) + Sale of plant assets (2.89) + Sale of bus. (4.51) + Decrease in temp. invest. (0.65) + LT borrowings (26.97) + ST borrowings (7.86) + Treas. st. issued (3.19).

an aggregate (six-year sum) ratio. When we look at individual years, including Year 11, the cash flow adequacy ratio suggests sufficient cash resources. The exceptions are

Exhibit CC.11

CAMPBELL SOUP COMPANY
Analysis of Cash Flow Ratios ($ millions)

$$\text{(1) Cash flow adequacy ratio*} = \frac{\text{6-year sum of sources of cash from operations}}{\text{6-year sum of capital expenditures, inventory additions, and cash dividends}}$$

$$= \frac{\$3{,}009.6}{(\$1{,}817.1 + \$856.7) + (\$113.2 + \$3.9) + \$649.4}$$

$$= 0.875$$

$$\text{(2) Cash reinvestment ratio}^{\dagger} = \frac{\text{Cash provided by operations} - \text{Dividends}}{\text{Gross PPE} + \text{Investments} + \text{Other assets} + \text{Working capital}}$$

$$\text{Year 6 to Year 11 average} = \frac{\$3{,}009.6 - \$649.4}{\$15{,}183.7 + \$1{,}888.3 + \$2{,}929.7} = 11.8\%$$

$$\text{Year 11} = \frac{\$805.2 - \$137.5}{\$2{,}921.9 + \$404.6 + \$240.5} = 18.7\%$$

$$\text{Year 10} = \frac{\$448.4 - \$124.3}{\$2{,}734.9 + \$349.0 + \$367.4} = 9.4\%$$

$$\text{Year 9} = \frac{\$357.3 - \$86.7}{\$2{,}543.0 + \$323.1 + \$369.4} = 8.4\%$$

$$\text{Year 8} = \frac{\$466.6 - \$104.6}{\$2{,}539.7 + \$241.2 + \$499.6} = 11.0\%$$

$$\text{Year 7} = \frac{\$468.3 - \$91.7}{\$2{,}355.1 + \$310.5 + \$744.1} = 11.0\%$$

$$\text{Year 6} = \frac{\$463.8 - \$104.6}{\$2{,}089.1 + \$259.9 + \$708.7} = 11.7\%$$

* All amounts are from the statement of cash flows.
† Numerator amounts are from the statement of cash flows and denominator amounts are from the balance sheet.

Years 7 and 9. A second measure, the cash reinvestment ratio, provides insight into the amount of cash retained and reinvested into the company for both asset replacement and growth. Campbell's cash reinvestment ratio is 11.8% for the six-year period. This reinvestment rate is satisfactory for the industry. The Year 11 reinvestment ratio is much higher (18.7%) than normal. Years 9 and 10 show a lower ratio due to decreases in operating cash flows.

Short-Term Liquidity

Various measures of short-term liquidity for the most recent six years are reported in Exhibit CC.12. This exhibit also includes industry composite data for Year 11. Several findings should be noted. The current ratio in Year 11 is at its lowest level for the past six years. Its value of 1.19 is measurably lower than the industry composite of 1.86. This is due in part to growth in current liabilities over recent years. Current liabilities are

Exhibit CC.12

CAMPBELL SOUP COMPANY
Short-Term Liquidity Analysis

	Units	Measure	Year 11	Year 10	Year 9	Year 8	Year 7	Year 6	Year 11 Industry Composite
1.	Ratio	Current ratio	1.19	1.28	1.30	1.58	2.07	2.13	1.86
2.	Ratio	Acid-test ratio	0.56	0.56	0.56	0.70	1.10	1.11	0.61
3.	Times	Accounts receivable turnover	10.77	10.68	11.07	11.79	14.08	15.13	8.37
4.	Times	Inventory turnover	5.37	5.21	5.41	5.27	5.15	5.14	2.53
5.	Days	Days' sales in receivables	30.60	36.23	34.15	36.00	27.17	25.11	43.01
6.	Days	Days' sales in inventory	62.12	69.31	73.41	70.53	70.59	71.29	142.03
7.	Days	Approximate conversion period	92.72	105.54	107.56	106.53	97.76	96.40	185.32
8.	Percent	Cash to current assets	11.78%	4.84%	7.55%	6.30%	10.14%	11.62%	5.60%
9.	Percent	Cash to current liabilities	14.00%	6.22%	9.81%	9.94%	20.90%	24.77%	10.40%
10.	$ mil.	Working capital	240.50	367.40	369.40	499.60	744.10	708.70	54.33
11.	Days	Days' purchases in accounts payable	46.03	46.56	46.20	49.30	44.25	39.33	—
12.	Days	Average net trade cycle	46.69	58.98	61.36	57.23	53.51	57.07	—
13.	Percent	Cash provided by operations to average current liabilities	62.51%	35.44%	34.10%	60.22%	71.36%	77.34%	—

Notes:
For Year 11, the computations are as follows ($ in millions):

(3) $\frac{\text{Net sales [13]}}{\text{Average accounts receivable [33]}} = \frac{\$6,204.1}{(\$527.4 + \$624.5)/2} = 10.77$

(4) $\frac{\text{Cost of products sold [14]}}{\text{Average inventory [34]}} = \frac{\$4,095.5}{(\$706.7 + \$819.8)/2} = 5.37$

(5) $\frac{\text{Ending accounts receivable [33]}}{\text{Sales [13]/360}} = \frac{\$527.4}{\$6,204.1/360} = 30.60$

(6) $\frac{\text{Ending inventory [34]}}{\text{Cost of products sold [14]/360}} = \frac{\$706.7}{\$4,095.5/360} = 62.12$

(7) Approximate conversion period = (5) Days' sales in receivables + (6) Days' sales in inventory

(11) $\frac{\text{Accounts payable [41]}}{\text{Purchases per day}^{\dagger}} = \frac{\$482.4}{10.48} = 46.03$

†From Exhibit CC.14.

(12) Number of days' sales in:

Accounts receivable	30.60
Inventories	62.12
Subtotal	92.72
Less: accounts payable	46.03
Total	46.69

(13) $\frac{\text{Cash from operations [64]}}{(\text{Beginning current liabilities + Ending current liabilities [45]}) \div 2} = \frac{\$805.2}{\$1,288} = 62.51$

double what they were in Year 6, while current assets in Year 11 are but 114% of its Year 6 level. A substantial amount of notes payable are reclassified as long-term debt in Year 10. This helps improve the current ratio. Also, Exhibit CC.13 reveals that cash and cash equivalents in Year 11 represent a larger proportion of current assets (11.78%) compared with the industry (5.60%).

Exhibit CC.13

CAMPBELL SOUP COMPANY
Common-Size Analysis of Current Assets and Current Liabilities

	Year 11	Year 10	Year 9	Year 8	Year 7	Year 6	Year 11 Industry Composite
Current assets:							
Cash and cash equivalents	11.78%	4.85%	7.55%	6.30%	10.09%	11.62%	5.60%
Other temporary investments	0.84	1.35	1.64	2.57	19.49	17.88	—
Accounts receivable	34.73	37.50	33.59	35.72	23.57	22.40	27.18
Inventories	46.54	49.22	50.95	48.77	43.37	45.74	63.60
Prepaid expenses	6.11	7.08	6.27	6.64	3.48	2.36	3.62
Total current assets	100.00%	100.00%	100.00%	100.00%	100.00%	100.00%	100.00%
Current liabilities:							
Notes payable	22.08%	15.58%	22.04%	15.99%	13.48%	14.20%	20.49%
Payable to suppliers and others	37.75	40.46	41.25	51.74	54.02	51.38	31.19
Accrued liabilities	31.98	37.89	31.86	27.44	26.25	26.50 }	
Dividend payable	2.89	2.49	2.41	—	—	— } =	48.32
Accrued income taxes	5.30	3.58	2.44	4.83	6.25	7.92 }	
Total current liabilities	100.00%	100.00%	100.00%	100.00%	100.00%	100.00%	100.00%

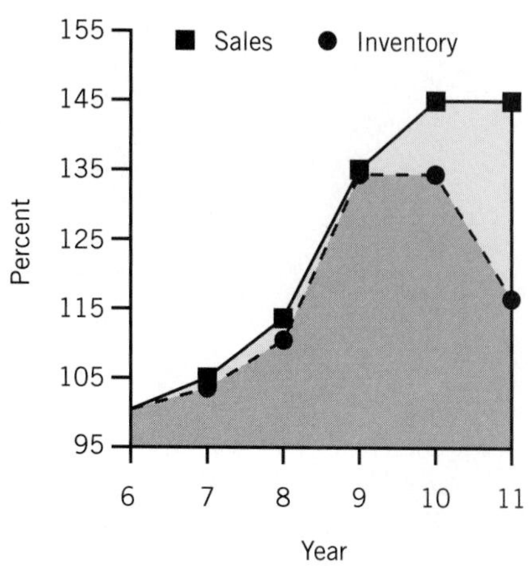

Campbell's acid-test ratio for the past three years (0.56) is slightly below the Year 11 industry composite (0.61)–see Exhibit CC.12. The assets and liabilities composing the acid-test ratio can be compared with the industry composite using Exhibit CC.7. This exhibit along with Exhibit CC.13 reveals that inventories constitute a lower proportion of total assets (17%) and total current assets (47%) than they do for the industry (39% and 64%, respectively). Also, inventory turnover for Campbell in Year 11 is 5.37 versus 2.53 for the industry. These measures indicate Campbell has less funds invested in inventory relative to the industry. This conclusion is supported with evidence from Exhibit CC.8 where inventory growth is less than sales growth (116% versus 145%). These improvements in inventory management are concurrent with Campbell's launching of the just-in-time inventory system. This improvement is especially evident with raw materials. Exhibit CC.14 reports inventory data showing a decline in the proportion of raw materials to total inventories consistent with this inference.

The LIFO inventory method is used in accounting for approximately 70% of its inventories in Year 11 and 64% in Year 10 (see annual report note 14 in Appendix A). Exhibit CC.15 compares income and cost of goods sold using the LIFO and FIFO inventory methods. When prices are rising, LIFO income is typically lower than FIFO. In Campbell's case LIFO yielded income less than FIFO in Years 7, 9, and 11. During other years the reverse occurs. This might be due to declining costs or inventory liquidation.

Exhibit CC.14

CAMPBELL SOUP COMPANY

Inventory Data ($ millions)

	Year 11	Year 10	Year 9	Year 8	Year 7	Year 6
1. Beginning inventory	$ 819.8	$ 816.0	$ 664.7	$ 623.6	$ 610.5	$ 623.1
2. Plus: production inputs	3,982.4	4,262.0	4,152.9	3,433.9	3,193.6	3,070.1
3. Goods available for sale	4,802.2	5,078.0	4,817.6	4,057.5	3,804.1	3,693.2
4. Less: Ending inventory	(706.7)	(819.8)	(816.0)	(664.7)	(623.6)	(610.5)
5. Cost of products sold	4,095.5	4,258.2	4,001.6	3,392.8	3,180.5	3,082.7
6. Depreciation	208.6	200.9	192.3	170.9	144.6	126.8
7. Purchases = (2) − (6)	3,773.8	4,061.1	3,960.6	3,263.0	3,049.0	2,943.3
8. Purchases per day = (7)/360	$ 10.48	$ 11.28	$ 11.00	$ 9.06	$ 8.47	$ 8.18
Ending inventories:						
Raw materials, containers, and supplies	$ 342.3	$ 384.4	$ 385.0	$ 333.4	$ 333.6	$ 340.4
Finished products	454.0	520.0	519.0	412.5	372.4	348.1
Subtotal	796.3	904.4	904.0	745.9	706.0	688.5
Less: Adjustment of inventories to LIFO	89.6	84.6	88.0	81.2	82.4	78.5
Total ending inventories	$ 706.7	$ 819.8	$ 816.0	$ 664.7	$ 623.6	$ 610.5
Raw materials, containers, and supplies	43.0%	42.5%	42.6%	44.7%	47.3%	49.4%
Finished products	57.0	57.5	57.4	55.3	52.7	50.6
	100.0%	100.0%	100.0%	100.0%	100.0%	100.0%

Exhibit CC.15

CAMPBELL SOUP COMPANY

Inventory Data Using FIFO versus LIFO ($ millions)

	Year 11	Year 10	Year 9	Year 8	Year 7	Year 6
Beginning inventory	$ 904.4	$ 904.0	$ 745.9	$ 706.0	$ 688.5	$ 707.0
Production inputs (same as LIFO)	3,982.4	4,262.0	4,152.9	3,433.9	3,193.6	3,070.1
Goods available for sale	4,886.8	5,166.0	4,898.8	4,139.9	3,882.1	3,777.1
Less: Ending inventory	796.3	904.4	904.0	745.9	706.0	688.5
Cost of products sold (FIFO)	$4,090.5	$4,261.6	$3,994.8	$3,394.0	$3,176.1	$3,088.6
Cost of products sold (LIFO)	$4,095.5	$4,258.2	$4,001.6	$3,392.8	$3,180.5	$3,082.7
Effect of restatement to FIFO increases (decreases) cost of products sold by:	$ (5.0)	$ 3.4	$ (6.8)	$ 1.2	$ (4.4)	$ 5.9
Net of tax* effect of restatement to FIFO decreases (increases) net income by:	$ (3.3)	$ 2.2	$ (4.5)	$ 0.8	$ (2.4)	$ 3.2

* Tax rate is 34% for Years 8 through 11, 45% for Year 7, and 46% for Year 6.

Campbell's accounts receivable turnover has been declining over the past six years, but it is still above the industry level in Year 11 (see Exhibit CC.12). We also see from Exhibit CC.8 that accounts receivable are growing faster than sales, reaching a peak in Year 10 (209%) with a decline in Year 11 (176%). This is suggestive of a more aggressive credit policy. The collection period for accounts receivable (see Exhibit CC.12) worsened between Years 6 and 10, but improved slightly in Year 11. Similar behavior is evidenced with the inventory conversion period, with a general worsening from Years 6 through 10. Yet the conversion period in Year 11 returns to 92.7 days versus the 96.4 days for Year 6. This is mainly due to improved inventory turnover, which helps Campbell in comparison to industry norms.

Campbell's success in managing current liabilities is varied. While the days' purchases in accounts payable increased from Year 6 through Year 8, the recent three years' results have leveled off (see Exhibit CC.12). Similarly, its average net trade cycle fluctuates over the past six years. But by Year 11, this period (nearly 47 days) is below the Year 6 level of roughly 57 days. This finding is consistent with the company's improving liquidity.

Capital Structure and Solvency

We next analyze Campbell's capital structure and solvency (the analysis above related to cash forecasting is relevant to solvency). Changes in the company's capital structure

Exhibit CC.16

CAMPBELL SOUP COMPANY
Analysis of Capital Structure ($ millions)

	Year 11	Year 10	Year 9	Year 8	Year 7	Year 6
Long-term liabilities:						
Notes payable	$ 757.8	$ 792.9	$ 610.3	$ 507.1	$ 358.8	$ 346.7
Capital lease obligation	14.8	12.9	18.9	18.7	21.4	15.6
Total long-term debt	772.6	805.8	629.2	525.8	380.2	362.3
Deferred income taxes*	129.3	117.6	109.0	140.3	124.0	99.6
Other long-term liabilities	23.0	28.5	19.6	15.6	15.8	16.3
Total long-term liabilities	924.9	951.9	757.8	681.7	520.0	478.2
Current liabilities†	1,278.0	1,298.1	1,232.1	863.3	693.8	626.1
Total liabilities	$2,202.9	$2,250.0	$1,989.9	$1,545.0	$1,213.8	$1,104.3
Equity capital:						
Common shareholders' equity	$1,793.4	$1,691.8	$1,778.3	$1,895.0	$1,736.1	$1,538.9
Minority interests	23.5	56.3	54.9	29.3	23.5	20.1
Deferred income taxes*	129.2	117.5	109.0	140.3	124.0	99.5
Total equity capital	1,946.1	1,865.6	1,942.2	2,064.6	1,883.6	1,658.5
Total liabilities and equity	$4,149.0	$4,115.6	$3,932.1	$3,609.6	$3,097.4	$2,762.8

* For analytical purposes, 50% of deferred income taxes are considered debt and the remainder equity.
† Including the current portion of notes payable.

are measured using various analyses and comparisons. Campbell's capital structure for the six years ending in Year 11 is depicted in Exhibit CC.16. For analytical purposes, one-half of deferred taxes is considered a long-term liability and the other half as equity. Exhibit CC.17 shows a common-size analysis of capital structure. For Year 11, liabilities constitute 53% and equity 47% of Campbell's financing.

Selected capital structure and long-term solvency ratios are reported in Exhibit CC.18. The total debt to equity ratio increases markedly in the past three years, yet remains at or below the industry norm (1.17). The source of this increase is attributed to long-term debt, see Exhibit CC.8. In particular, Exhibit CC.8 shows the trend index of long-term debt (213) exceeds that for current liabilities (204), total liabilities (192), and shareowners' equity (117). This is also evident in Campbell's long-term debt to equity ratio, where in Year 11 the ratio for Campbell (48%) exceeds the industry composite of 43%. Campbell is moving away from its historically conservative capital structure toward a more aggressive one. This is evidenced by a lower level of fixed charge coverage ratios using both earnings and operating cash flows compared with Years 6 through 8. Consistent with our analysis, Campbell's long-term debt is rated AA by the major rating agencies–down from the AAA rating the company enjoyed previously, but still an excellent rating. The company's creditors enjoy sound asset protection and superior earning power.

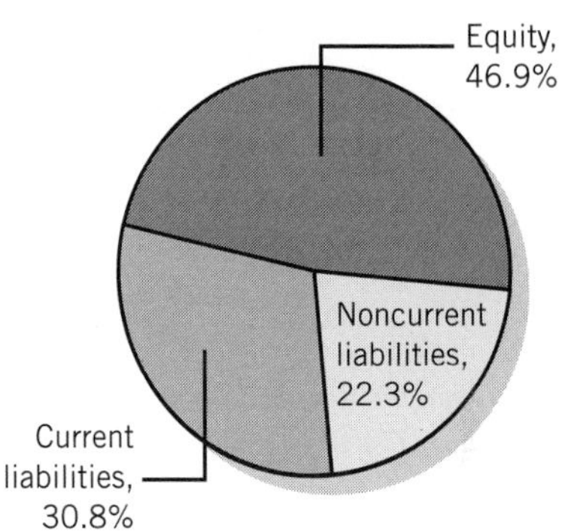

Exhibit CC.17

CAMPBELL SOUP COMPANY
Common-Size Analysis of Capital Structure

	Year 11	Year 10	Year 9	Year 8	Year 7	Year 6
Long-term liabilities:						
Notes payable	18.26%	19.27%	15.52%	14.05%	11.59%	12.55%
Capital lease obligation	0.36	0.31	0.48	0.52	0.69	0.56
Total long-term debt	18.62%	19.58%	16.00%	14.57%	12.28%	13.11%
Deferred income taxes*	3.12	2.86	2.77	3.88	4.00	3.61
Other long-term liabilities	0.55	0.69	0.50	0.43	0.51	0.59
Total long-term liabilities	22.29%	23.13%	19.27%	18.88%	16.79%	17.31%
Current liabilities†	30.80	31.54	31.34	23.92	22.40	22.66
Total liabilities	53.09%	54.67%	50.61%	42.80%	39.19%	39.97%
Equity capital:						
Common shareholders' equity	43.22%	41.11%	45.22%	52.50%	56.05%	55.70%
Minority interests	0.57	1.37	1.40	0.81	0.76	0.73
Deferred income taxes*	3.12	2.85	2.77	3.89	4.00	3.60
Total equity capital	46.91%	45.33%	49.39%	57.20%	60.81%	60.03%
Total liabilities and equity	100.00%	100.00%	100.00%	100.00%	100.00%	100.00%

* For analytical purposes, 50% of deferred income taxes are considered debt and the remainder equity.
† Including the current portion of notes payable.

Exhibit CC.18

CAMPBELL SOUP COMPANY
Capital Structure and Solvency Ratios

	Year 11	Year 10	Year 9	Year 8	Year 7	Year 6	Year 11 Industry Composite
1. Total debt to equity	1.13	1.21	1.02	0.75	0.64	0.67	1.17
2. Total debt ratio	0.53	0.55	0.51	0.43	0.39	0.40	0.54
3. Long-term debt to equity	0.48	0.51	0.39	0.33	0.28	0.29	0.43
4. Equity to total debt	0.88	0.83	0.98	1.34	1.56	1.50	0.86
5. Fixed assets to equity	0.92	0.92	0.79	0.73	0.72	0.70	0.46
6. Current liabilities to total liabilities	0.58	0.58	0.62	0.56	0.58	0.57	0.61
7. Earnings to fixed charges	5.16	2.14	1.84	6.06	6.41	6.28	—
8. Cash flow to fixed charges	7.47	5.27	5.38	8.94	8.69	9.26	—

The computations for Year 11 are shown here:

(1) $\frac{\text{Total debt*}}{\text{Equity capital*}} = \frac{2{,}202.9}{1{,}946.1} = 1.13$

(2) $\frac{\text{Total debt*}}{\text{Total debt and equity [55]}} = \frac{2{,}202.9}{4{,}149.0} = 0.53$

(3) $\frac{\text{Long-term debt*}}{\text{Equity capital*}} = \frac{924.9}{1{,}946.1} = 0.48$

(4) $\frac{\text{Equity capital*}}{\text{Total debt*}} = \frac{1{,}946.1}{2{,}202.9} = 0.88$

(5) $\frac{\text{Plant assets [37]}}{\text{Equity capital*}} = \frac{1{,}790.4}{1{,}946.1} = 0.92$

(6) $\frac{\text{Current liabilities [45]}}{\text{Total liabilities*}} = \frac{1{,}278.0}{2{,}202.9} = 0.58$

(7) $\frac{\text{Pretax income [26]} + \text{Interest expense [18]} + \text{Interest portion of rent expense}^{\dagger} - \text{Undistributed equity in earnings in affiliates [24], [169A]}}{\text{Interest incurred [98]} + \text{Interest portion of rent expense}^{*}\text{ [143]}} = \frac{667.4 + 116.2 + 20 - (2.4 - 8.2)}{136.9 + 20} = 5.16$

(8) $\frac{\text{Cash flows from operations [64]} + \text{Current tax expense [124A]} + \text{Interest expense [18]} + \text{Interest portion of rent expense}^{\dagger}\text{ [143]}}{\text{Interest incurred [98]} + \text{Interest portion of rent expense}^{\dagger}\text{ [143]}} = \frac{805.2 + 230.4 + 116.2 + 20}{136.9 + 20} = 7.47$

* From Exhibit CC.16.

† One-third of rent expense under operating leases. For Year 11: ⅓ of $59.7 [143].

Return on Invested Capital

The return on invested capital ratios for Campbell are reported in Exhibit CC.19. These ratios reveal several insights. The return on assets is stable during Years 6 through 8, declines sharply for Years 9 and 10, and then rebounds strongly to 11.75% in Year 11. Analysis of Years 9 and 10 shows these years' low returns are due to divestitures and restructuring charges. Yet we must keep in mind the marked increase in return for Year 11 is probably due in part to the two prior years' write-offs.

Exhibit CC.19

CAMPBELL SOUP COMPANY

Return on Invested Capital Ratios

	Year 11	Year 10*	Year 9*	Year 8	Year 7	Year 6	Year 11 Industry Composite
1. Return on assets (ROA)	11.75%	2.08%	2.13%	9.42%	9.57%	9.90%	9.20%
2. Return on common equity (ROCE)*	21.52%	0.24%	0.67%	14.07%	14.14%	14.40%	19.80%
3. Return on long-term debt and equity	17.07%	3.04%	2.96%	12.27%	12.35%	12.90%	13.50%
4. Equity growth rate	13.85%	−6.30%	−3.67%	8.59%	8.79%	8.96%	—
5. Disaggregation of return on common equity*							
Adjusted profit margin	6.47%	0.07%	0.23%	5.63%	5.51%	5.10%	6.60%
	×	×	×	×	×	×	×
Asset turnover	1.50	1.54	1.50	1.45	1.53	1.68	1.38
	×	×	×	×	×	×	×
Financial leverage ratio	2.22	2.18	1.92	1.72	1.68	1.68	2.17
	21.52%	0.24%	0.67%	14.07%	14.14%	14.40%	19.80%

The computations for Year 11 are shown here:

$$\text{(1) ROA} = \frac{\text{Net income} + \text{Interest expense (1} - \text{Tax rate)} + \text{Minority interest (MI)}}{\text{Average total assets}} = \frac{401.5 + 116.2\,(1 - 0.34) + 7.2}{(4{,}149.0 + 4{,}115.6)/2} = 11.75\%$$

$$\text{ROA disaggregated} = \frac{\text{Net income} + \text{Interest expense (1} - \text{Tax rate)} + \text{Minority interest}}{\text{Sales}} \times \frac{\text{Sales}}{\text{Average total assets}}$$

$$= \left[\frac{401.5 + 116.2\,(1 - 0.34) + 7.2}{6{,}204.1} = 7.83\%\right] \times \left[\frac{6{,}204.1}{(4{,}149.0 + 4{,}115.6)/2} = 1.5\right] = 11.75\%$$

$$\text{Industry ROA composite} = 6.6\% \times 1.4 = 9.24\%$$

$$\text{(2) ROCE} = \frac{\text{Net income} - \text{Preferred dividend}}{\text{Average common equity}^{\dagger}} = \frac{401.5}{[(1{,}946.1 - 23.5) + (1{,}865.6 - 56.3)]/2} = 21.52\%$$

$$\text{ROCE disaggregated} = \text{Adjusted profit margin} \times \text{Asset turnover} \times \text{Financial leverage ratio} = \frac{401.5}{6{,}204.1} \times \frac{6{,}204.1}{(4{,}149.0 + 4{,}115.6)/2} \times \frac{(4{,}149.0 + 4{,}115.6)/2}{1{,}856.95^{\dagger}}$$

$$= 6.47\% \times 1.50 \times 2.22 = 21.52\%$$

$$\text{(3) Return on LTD and equity} = \frac{\text{Net income} + \text{Interest expense (1} - \text{Tax rate)} + \text{MI}}{\text{Average long-term liabilities}^{\ddagger} + \text{Average equity}^{\dagger}} = \frac{401.5 + 116.2\,(1 - 0.34) + 7.2}{(924.9 + 951.9)/2 + (1{,}946.1 + 1{,}865.6)/2} = 17.07\%$$

$$\text{(4) Equity growth rate} = \frac{\text{Net income} - \text{Dividends paid}}{\text{Average common equity}^{\dagger}} = \frac{401.5 - 137.5}{(1{,}946.1 + 1{,}865.6)/2} = 13.85\%$$

* Excluding the effect of divestitures, restructuring, and unusual charges, net of tax, of $301.6 million in Year 10, and $260.8 million in Year 9, drastically changes these ratios. For example, ROA, for Year 10 and Year 9 becomes 9.57% and 9.03%, respectively.

† Including 50% of deferred taxes assumed as equity, and excluding minority interests (MI). See Exhibit CC.16.

‡ Including 50% of deferred taxes. See Exhibit CC.16.

Further analysis of return on assets for Year 11 shows it is comprised of a 7.83% profit margin (not shown in Exhibit CC.19) and an asset turnover of 1.50. Both these components show improvement over their values from Year 8 (comparisons with Year 10 and Year 9 ratios are less relevant due to accounting charges). They also compare favorably with industry norms. Campbell's management hopes these improvements for Year 11 are reflective of its major restructuring, closings, and business reorganizations during Years 9 and 10. Because of those restructuring programs and cost-cutting efforts, profit margins are higher. Prior years' returns are depressed by several poorly performing or ill-fitting businesses. Those businesses are now divested and Campbell has streamlined and modernized its manufacturing.

Campbell's return on common equity (21.52%) exceeds both the industry norm and its most recent performance. The source of improvement is due to a solid net income margin and leverage ratio. Like the profit component in return on assets, the improved net income margin likely benefits from write-offs in Years 10 and 9. Disaggregation of Campbell's return on equity (item 5 in Exhibit CC.19) shows that changes in the net income margin are primarily responsible for fluctuations in return on equity during recent years. Net income margin is as low as 0.07 percent in Year 10 from the divestitures and restructurings, and it is as high as 6.47 percent in Year 11 partly due to the rebound from prior year changes and potential cost overprovisions. The other two components are reasonably stable. Asset turnover declined slightly in Year 7 from Year 6, but remained relatively level through other years. The leverage ratio increases gradually during the six-year period because of Campbell's increasingly leveraged capital structure.

Comparisons of these disaggregated components with industry norms reveal a favorable asset turnover ratio (1.50 versus 1.38), a normal leverage ratio (2.22 versus 2.17), and a normal or slightly unfavorable net income margin (6.47 versus 6.60). This implies Campbell's higher asset turnover (1.50) and higher leverage ratio (2.22) are primarily responsible for the favorable return on equity (21.52%) compared to the industry norm (19.8%). Recall that Campbell's increased leverage ratio also helped produce some negative consequences such as a lower credit rating.

Campbell's Financial Leverage

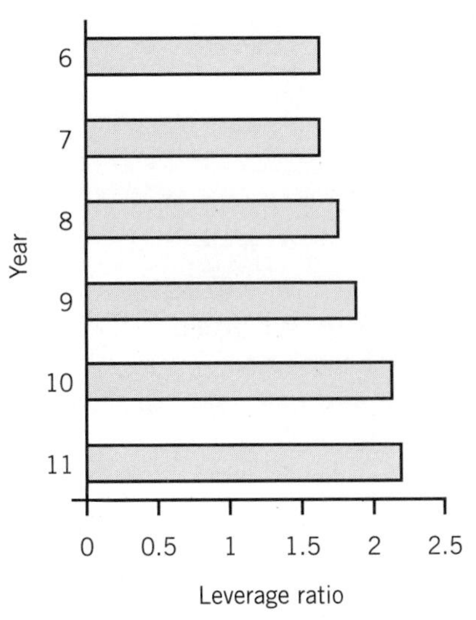

The leverage ratio for Year 11 implies that Campbell is borrowing $1.22 on each dollar of equity. This inference is based on considering 50% of deferred taxes as interest-free debt. The total $2.22 in funds are then able to generate $3.33 in sales because assets are turning over at a rate of 1.50 times. This $3.33 in sales earns 6.47% in net income, yielding a return on equity of 21.52%.

Campbell's return on long-term debt and equity displays a pattern similar to return on equity over the past six years. For Year 11, return on long-term liabilities and equity is 17.07%. This compares favorably with the industry composite of 13.50%.

Notice that Campbell's Year 11 equity growth rate (13.85%) markedly improved relative to prior years. Even if we exclude Years 9 and 10, this rate is nearly double the level for Years 6 through 8. The negative ratios for Years 9 and 10 are because Campbell maintained its dividend payout with its divestitures and restructuring. The strong rebound in this ratio for Year 11 bodes well for future growth in sales and earnings. A higher level of reinvestment frees Campbell from reliance on outside financing sources to fund its growth. The Year 11 net income of $401.5 million and dividends of $142.2 million leave sufficient funds for reinvestment and internally financed growth.

Analysis of Asset Utilization

Campbell's asset utilization measures are reported in Exhibit CC.20. Campbell's asset turnover (1.5 for Year 11) is stable over the past six years. Yet this stability in asset turnover masks significant changes in turnover for individual asset components. Cash and cash equivalents evidence the most variability during this period. Variability in cash

Exhibit CC.20

CAMPBELL SOUP COMPANY
Asset Utilization Ratios

	Year 11	Year 10	Year 9	Year 8	Year 7	Year 6	Year 11 Industry Composite
1. Sales to cash and equivalents	34.7	76.9	46.9	56.8	31.0	27.6	40.6
2. Sales to receivables	11.8	9.9	10.5	10.0	13.2	14.3	8.4
3. Sales to inventories	8.8	7.6	7.0	7.3	7.2	7.0	3.6
4. Sales to working capital	25.8	16.9	15.4	9.8	6.0	6.1	4.9
5. Sales to fixed assets	3.5	3.6	3.7	3.2	3.3	3.7	6.6
6. Sales to other assets*	7.4	8.5	7.2	6.6	14.5	16.5	7.5
7. Sales to total assets	1.5	1.5	1.4	1.4	1.5	1.6	1.4
8. Sales to short-term liabilities	4.9	4.8	4.6	5.6	6.5	6.9	4.2

* Including intangible assets.

and cash equivalents is also evidenced in both the sales to working capital turnover ratio and in the common-size balance sheet in Exhibit CC.7. Exhibit CC.7 reveals a gradual disposal of temporary investments. The sizeable $98.2 million increase in Year 11 cash and cash equivalents is primarily due to improvements in operating performance (see Exhibit CC.4).

Campbell's accounts receivable turnover shows a slight improvement in Years 8 through 11 relative to earlier years. The continued improvement in Year 11 is helped by this year's decrease of $97.1 million in receivables. Regarding inventory turnover, Campbell's expressed desire to decrease inventories at every stage of its manufacturing process is revealing itself through an improved inventory turnover ratio (8.8). It is important to see that Campbell's asset and asset component turnover ratios often compare favorably to industry norms. In several key areas like receivables (11.8 versus 8.4), inventories (8.8 versus 3.6), and working capital (25.8 versus 4.9), its turnover ratio is better than the industry composite.

Analysis of Operating Performance and Profitability

Selected profit margin ratios for Campbell are reported in Exhibit CC.21. We see that Campbell's gross profit margin for Year 11 is better than the industry norm (34.0% versus 29.3%). However its net profit margin is at or slightly below the industry level (6.47% versus 6.60%). After the divestitures and restructuring of Years 9 and 10, Campbell's net profit margin is better than it was in Years 6 through 8. These moves included eliminating administrative personnel and unsuccessful divisions. Results in Year 11 already show indications of tighter control over several areas of operating expenses. Continued cost control should allow Campbell to further improve its profitability and exceed industry norms.

Campbell's Sales and Cost of Sales Growth

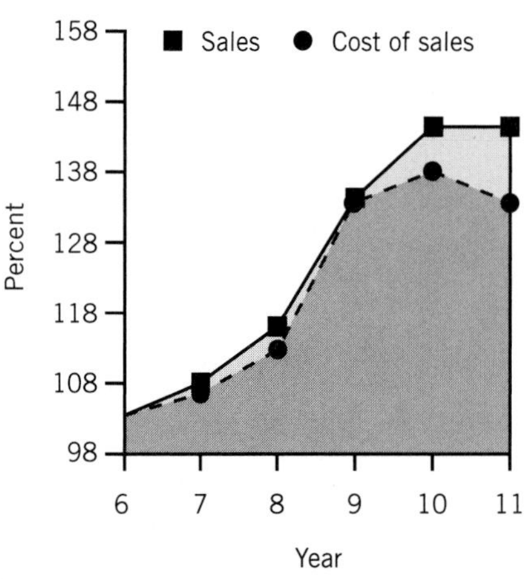

Exhibit CC.21

CAMPBELL SOUP COMPANY
Analysis of Profit Margin Ratios

Profit margins	Year 11	Year 10	Year 9	Year 8	Year 7	Year 6	Year 11 Industry Composite
1. Gross profit margin	34.00%	31.38%	29.45%	30.32%	29.17%	28.09%	29.30%
2. Operating profit margin	12.63%	4.69%	3.54%	9.09%	10.46%	10.34%	—
3. Net profit margin	6.47%	0.07%	0.23%	5.63%	5.51%	5.21%	6.60%

Computations for Year 11 are shown here:

$$\text{(1) Gross profit margin} = \frac{\text{Net sales} - \text{Cost of products sold}}{\text{Net sales}} = \frac{6{,}204.1 - 4{,}095.5}{6{,}204.1} = 34\%$$

$$\text{(2) Operating profit margin} = \frac{\text{Income before taxes and interest expense}}{\text{Net sales}} = \frac{667.4 + 116.2}{6{,}204.1} = 12.63\%$$

We link these profitability measures with evidence in earlier analyses. Improvement evidenced in the gross profit margin confirms earlier results in Exhibit CC.6 showing a gradual decline in cost of products sold (66.01% in Year 11 versus 71.91% in Year 6). While continued improvement in gross profit margin is possible, it will be difficult to achieve. The key for a profit ratio to benefit from improved gross profit margin is continued control over administrative and marketing expenses. This analysis is corroborated by our earlier trend index analysis. Exhibit CC.8 shows sales in Year 11 are 145% higher than for Year 6. Yet cost of products sold is only 133% greater, and the total of costs and expenses is 142% greater. This combination yields a net income that is 180% larger than the Year 6 level. The general inference from these trend indexes is that sales, gross margin, and net income are growing at a relatively faster rate than costs and expenses.

Exhibit CC.8 reveals that interest expense grew throughout the six-year period but at a relatively lower rate than did total liabilities, except for Year 11. This reflects a lower cost of borrowing resulting primarily from lower interest rates. We also note that Campbell is probably a more risky borrower compared to three to five years earlier as reflected in its increasing debt to equity ratio.

The Supplemental Schedule of Sales and Earnings in Campbell's annual report (item [1]) shows the contributions of international operations to Year 11. International earnings total $92.3 million, including $35.3 million from Campbell Canada, $17.6 million from International Biscuit, and $39.4 million from Campbell International. International earnings represents about 11.6% of total operating earnings. In Years 10 and 9, international operations contribute negatively to total earnings. This is due to the restructuring in those years, reducing total operating earnings by $134.1 million in Year 10 and by $82.3 million in Year 9. These negative contributions are in addition to losses from foreign currency translation of $3.3 million and $19.3 million in Years 10 and 9, respectively. Foreign currency translation is not significant in Year 11. Nevertheless, international operations for the past six years comprise nearly 20% of total sales (see Exhibit CC.1). International operations are expected to continue to exert a significant impact on Campbell's profitability.

Campbell's effective tax rate (note 9) is 39.8% in Year 11, 97.5% in Year 10, and 87.7% in Year 9. The extraordinarily high rates for the latter two years are due mainly to the

Exhibit CC.22

CAMPBELL SOUP COMPANY
Analysis of Depreciation

	Year 11	Year 10	Year 9	Year 8	Year 7	Year 6
1. Accumulated depreciation as a percent of gross plant assets*	44.6%	42.3%	43.1%	43.7%	46.6%	48.6%
2. Annual depreciation expenses as a percent of gross plant	7.7%	7.7%	7.6%	6.9%	6.4%	6.4%
3. Annual depreciation expenses as a percent of sales	3.1%	3.0%	3.1%	3.3%	3.1%	2.8%

Computations for Year 11 are shown here:

$$(1)\ \frac{1{,}131.5\ \boxed{162}}{758.7\ \boxed{159} + 1{,}779.3\ \boxed{160}} = 44.6\%$$

$$(2)\ \frac{194.5\ \boxed{162A}}{758.7\ \boxed{159} + 1{,}779.3\ \boxed{160}} = 7.7\%$$

$$(3)\ \frac{194.5\ \boxed{162A}}{6{,}204.1\ \boxed{13}} = 3.1\%$$

*Exclusive of land and projects in progress.

large amounts of nondeductible divestiture, restructuring, and unusual charges, representing 56.5 and 48.7% of earnings before taxes, respectively (note 9). If we exclude these divestitures, the effective tax rate declines to about 40%. Campbell is also taking advantage of tax loss carryforward benefits from international subsidiaries. At the end of Year 11 the company has $77.4 million remaining in unused tax loss carryforward benefits. About one-half of these expire by Year 16 and the remainder are available indefinitely. Most deferred taxes result from pensions, depreciation timing differences, divestiture, restructuring, and unusual charges. Deferred taxes due to depreciation differences are relatively large through Year 10, then decline to a low of $5.9 million in Year 11.

Analysis of depreciation data for Campbell is reported in Exhibit CC.22. This evidence shows that accumulated depreciation as a percentage of gross plant assets remains stable (44.6% in Year 11). Stability in depreciation expense, as a percentage of either plant assets or sales, is also evident in Exhibit CC.22. Accordingly, there is no evidence that earnings quality is affected due to changes in depreciation.

Analysis of discretionary expenditures in Exhibit CC.23 shows spending in all major categories during Year 11 declines compared to most prior years. This potentially results from more controlled spending and enhanced efficiencies. Recall our common-size analysis of factors affecting net earnings in Exhibit CC.6. This analysis is corroborative of some of the factors evidenced in Exhibit CC.23. For example, gross margin is increasing while (on a relative basis) increases in marketing, selling, interest, and "other" expenses outpace increases in sales. Administrative expenses and research and development expenses are not increasing with sales. Statutory tax rates decline over this period, thereby holding down growth in tax expenses. Profitability increases because the growth in gross margin is not offset with increases in expenses.

Recast income statements of Campbell for the most recent six years were reported in Exhibit 12.1. These recast statements support many of the observations recognized in this section. Campbell's adjusted income statements for this same period are shown in Exhibit 12.2. The adjusted statements reveal an increasing trend in net income from

Exhibit CC.23

CAMPBELL SOUP COMPANY

Analysis of Discretionary Expenditures ($ millions)

	Year 11	Year 10	Year 9	Year 8	Year 7	Year 6
Net sales	$6,204.1	$6,205.8	$5,672.1	$4,868.9	$4,490.4	$4,286.8
Plant assets (net)*	1,406.5	1,386.9	1,322.6	1,329.1	1,152.0	974.1
Maintenance and repairs	173.9	180.6	173.9	155.6	148.8	144.0
Advertising	195.4	220.4	212.9	219.1	203.5	181.4
Research & development (R&D)	56.3	53.7	47.7	46.9	44.8	42.2
Maintenance and repairs ÷ sales	2.8%	2.9%	3.1%	3.2%	3.3%	3.4%
Maintenance and repairs ÷ plant	12.4	13.0	13.1	11.7	12.9	14.8
Advertising ÷ sales	3.1	3.6	3.8	4.5	4.5	4.2
R&D ÷ sales	0.9	0.9	0.8	1.0	1.0	1.0

* Exclusive of land and projects in process.

Year 9 to Year 10–this contrasts with reported income. The average earning power calculation for the six-year period includes all charges and is $193.9 million.

Forecasting and Valuation

The final step in the analysis process is forecasting future financial performance. The inferences we expect to draw from this analysis depend on the analyst's perspective. For example, if our perspective is that of the company's creditor we are interested in forecasts of future cash flows, either short term or long term depending on the length of our credit arrangement. These cash flow forecasts are derived from our projection of the company's income statement and balance sheet as illustrated in Chapter 10. If the perspective of the analysis is that of an equity investor, we are interested in the company's ability to realize the benefits of its strategic plan. Specifically, our focus is on whether the company can generate positive residual profits in the future. Again, forecasts of the income statement and balance sheet are required.

Exhibit CC.24 reproduces the historical income statements for Campbell Soup's Years 6–11 together with a forecast for Year 12. Also included are selected historical ratios and our assumptions for the Year 12 forecast. The forecasting process begins with our expectations for the level of sales. Campbell Soup's sales growth had been strong (4.75% to 16.5% per year) until Year 11 when sales declined slightly. As the company discussed in its MD&A section (see Appendix A), the sales decline is primarily attributable to the divestiture (discontinuation) of several businesses (product lines). Absent these effects, the company reveals that sales would have increased by 4% for the year. Our forecast of Year 12 sales is based on an expected increase of 5%.

Campbell Soup's gross profit margin has been steadily increasing from 29% to 31% in Year 10. Year 11's gross profit margin increased significantly to 34%. The MD&A section does not provide an explanation for this increase and 30–31% is more in line with recent history. As a result, we use 31% for the gross profit margin in our forecast. Cost of goods sold, then, is computed as the difference between sales and gross profit.

Selling, general, and administrative (SG&A) expenses have remained fairly constant at 20–21% of sales. We use 21.26%, the most recent percentage, in our forecast. Interest and other expenses have fluctuated widely over the period under review, from 0.16% to 7.14% and, most recently, 1.97% of sales. This category includes interest expense (revenue), foreign exchange gains (losses) and transitory items like restructuring charges

Exhibit CC.24

CAMPBELL SOUP COMPANY

Forecasted Income Statement ($ millions)

	Year 12 Estimate	Year 11	Year 10	Year 9	Year 8	Year 7	Year 6
Net sales	$6,514.3	$6,204.1	$6,205.8	$5,672.1	$4,868.9	$4,490.4	$4,286.8
Cost of products sold	4,494.9	4,095.5	4,258.2	4,001.6	3,392.8	3,180.5	3,082.7
Gross profit	2,019.4	2,108.6	1,947.6	1,670.5	1,476.1	1,309.9	1,204.1
Marketing, selling, administrative, and R&D expenses	1,385.2	1,319.2	1,324.9	1,118.6	1,012.8	884.9	782.5
Interest & other expenses	128.1	122.0	443.3	445.4	74.7	7.1	34.4
Earnings before taxes	506.2	667.4	179.4	106.5	388.6	417.9	387.2
Taxes on earnings	201.7	265.9	175.0	93.4	147.0	170.6	164.0
Cumulative loss (gain) from accounting change	0.0	0.0	0.0	0.0	(32.5)	0	0
Net earnings	$ 304.5	$ 401.5	$ 4.4	$ 13.1	$ 274.1	$ 247.3	$ 223.2
Shares outstanding	127.0	127.0	126.6	129.3	129.3	129.9	129.5
Selected ratios							
Sales growth	5.00%	−0.03%	9.41%	16.50%	8.43%	4.75%	
Gross profit margin	31.00%	33.99%	31.38%	29.45%	30.32%	29.17%	
Selling, general, and administrative expenses/Sales	21.26%	21.26%	21.35%	19.72%	20.80%	19.71%	
Depreciation expense/Prior year plant assets (net)	12.14%	12.14%	13.04%	12.74%	12.67%	12.38%	
Interest and other expenses/Sales	1.97%	1.97%	7.14%	7.85%	1.53%	0.16%	
Taxes on earnings/Earnings before taxes	39.84%	39.84%	97.55%	87.70%	37.83%	40.82%	

and expenses resulting from divestitures. This last category was particularly large in Years 9 and 10, amounting to 6.0% and 5.4% of sales, respectively. Absent these transitory items, interest and other expenses would have been in the 2% range. Since we have no knowledge of planned restructuring expenses or divestitures in Year 12, we use 1.97% in our projection, the most recent percentage of sales.

Projected sales less projected expenses yield our forecast of pretax profits. We then subtract income tax expense to arrive at our projected net profit. Tax expense as a percentage of pretax profit has fluctuated widely for the period under review, from 37.8% to 97.6% in Year 10. The higher percentages of tax expense are typically due to nondeductible expenses in reported earnings. These include restructuring expenses that are accrued for financial reporting purposes, but are not deductible for tax purposes until paid. As a result, the higher percentages are probably not realistic for our projections and we use 39.8%, the most recent experience, to project Year 12 net profit.

Exhibit CC.25 reproduces the historical balance sheets of Campbell Soup for Years 6–11 together with our initial forecast for Year 12. Receivables, inventories, accounts payable, and accruals are all projected using their most recent turnover rates and our projections for sales and cost of goods sold. Receivable turnover rates, for example, have fluctuated between 9.94 and 14.34 times with 11.76 the most recent turnover rate. We use the recent turnover in our forecast and forecast receivables using projected sales as follows:

$$\text{Projected accounts receivable} = \frac{\text{Projected sales}}{\text{Turnover rate}} = \frac{6{,}514.3}{11.76} = 553.8$$

Other working capital accounts are forecasted similarly. Accrued expenses are projected using sales and the accrued expense turnover rate of 15.18 for Year 11. Inventories and accounts payable are likewise projected using cost of goods sold and their respective

Exhibit CC.25

CAMPBELL SOUP COMPANY
Forecasted Balance Sheet ($ millions)

	Year 12 Initial Estimate	Year 11	Year 10	Year 9	Year 8	Year 7	Year 6
Cash and cash equivalents	$ (99.4)	$ 178.9	$ 80.7	$ 120.9	$ 85.8	$ 145.0	$ 155.1
Accounts receivable	553.8	527.4	624.5	538.0	486.9	338.9	299.0
Inventories	775.6	706.7	819.8	816.0	664.7	623.6	610.5
Other current assets	105.5	105.5	140.5	126.6	125.5	330.4	270.2
Total current assets	1,335.5	1,518.5	1,665.5	1,601.5	1,362.9	1,437.9	1,334.8
Plant assets, net of depreciation	1,963.8	1,790.4	1,717.7	1,540.6	1,508.9	1,349.0	1,168.1
Other long-term assets	840.1	840.1	732.4	790.0	737.8	310.5	259.9
Total assets	$4,139.4	$4,149.0	$4,115.6	$3,932.1	$3,609.6	$3,097.4	$2,762.8
Payable to suppliers and others	$ 529.4	$ 482.4	$ 525.2	$ 508.2	$ 446.7	$ 374.8	$ 321.7
Notes payable	173.4	282.2	202.3	271.5	138.0	93.5	88.9
Accrued liabilities	429.1	408.7	491.9	392.6	236.9	182.1	165.9
Accrued income taxes	51.3	67.7	46.4	30.1	41.7	43.4	49.6
Dividend payable	37.0	37.0	32.3	29.7	0	0	0
Total current liabilities	1,220.3	1,278.0	1,298.1	1,232.1	863.3	693.8	626.1
Long-term debt	653.7	772.6	805.8	629.2	525.8	380.2	362.3
Deferred income tax and other liabilities	305.0	305.0	319.9	292.5	325.5	287.3	235.5
Total liabilities	2,179.0	2,355.6	2,423.8	2,153.8	1,714.6	1,361.3	1,223.9
Preferred stock	0.0	0.0	0.0	0.0	0.0	0.0	0.0
Capital stock	20.3	20.3	20.3	20.3	20.3	20.3	20.3
Capital surplus	107.3	107.3	61.9	50.8	42.3	41.1	38.1
Earnings retained and cumulative translation adjustments	2,103.2	1,936.2	1,716.8	1,777.9	1,907.6	1,721.5	1,528.9
Capital stock in treasury	(270.4)	(270.4)	(107.2)	(70.7)	(75.2)	(46.8)	(48.4)
Total shareowners' equity	1,960.4	1,793.4	1,691.8	1,778.3	1,895.0	1,736.1	1,538.9
Total liabilities and shareholders' equity	$4,139.4	$4,149.0	$4,115.6	$3,932.1	$3,609.6	$3,097.4	$2,762.8
Accounts receivable turnover*	11.76	11.76	9.94	10.54	10.00	13.25	14.34
Inventory turnover*	5.80	5.80	5.19	4.90	5.10	5.10	5.05
Accounts payable turnover*	8.49	8.49	8.11	7.87	7.60	8.49	9.58
Accruals turnover	15.18	15.18	12.62	14.45	20.55	24.66	25.84
Taxes payable/Tax expense	25.46%	25.46%	26.51%	32.23%	28.37%	25.44%	30.24%
Financial leverage (Total assets/Stockholders' equity)	2.11	2.31	2.43	2.21	1.90	1.78	1.80
Dividends paid per share	$1.083	$1.083	$0.982	$0.671	$0.81	$0.71	$0.81
Capital expenditures	390.9	361.1	387.6	284.1	245.3	303.7	235.3
Capital expenditures/sales	6.00%	5.82%	6.25%	5.01%	5.04%	6.76%	5.49%
Depreciation expense	217.4	208.6	200.9	192.3	170.9	144.6	126.8

*Computed using ending balances only.

turnover rates. Other current assets and liabilities are assumed equal to the Year 11 balance.

Short-term debt is assumed equal to the Year 11 balance. Current maturities of long-term debt are projected using amounts provided in the long-term debt footnote 19. Campbell Soup reports that scheduled maturities of long-term debt are $227.7 million for Year 12. This amount is included in current liabilities for Year 11. Projected maturities of long-term debt in Year 13 are reported at $118.9 million, a reduction of $108.8

million. As a result, assuming other short-term debt remains constant at Year 12 levels, the short-term and current maturities of long-term debt account is projected to decline by $108.8 million from $282.2 million in Year 11 to a projected level of $173.4 million for Year 12.

Property, plant, and equipment expense is projected at the prior year's balance plus projected capital expenditures and less depreciation. Capital expenditures as a percentage of sales have remained fairly constant at 5–6% of sales. We use 6% in our forecast. Likewise, depreciation expense as a percentage of the prior year's balance of PP&E has ranged from 12.14% (most recently) to 13.04%. We use 12.14% as this reflects the most recent depreciation policies of the company.

Other long-term assets are projected at the Year 11 balance. These consist of intangible assets, such as goodwill, and miscellaneous other long-term assets. Since goodwill is no longer amortized, we use the prior year's balance as we have no knowledge of expected changes in other long-term assets.

Long-term debt is initially projected at the balance of long-term debt in Year 11 less the portion now recognized as current maturities of long-term debt in current liabilities ($118.9 million). Once the initial cash balance is computed, we will adjust this for any new financing required. Other long-term debt is assumed to remain at Year 1 levels.

Common stock, capital surplus, and treasury stock are assumed to remain at Year 11 levels. Projected retained earnings are equal to the Year 11 retained earnings balance plus the projected profit of $304.5 million less projected dividends of $137.5 million (Year 11's payout of $1.083 per share for 127 million outstanding shares).

Setting total assets equal to total liabilities and subtracting forecasted current assets (other than cash) and long-term assets yields an initial negative estimate for cash of $(99.4 million). We, then, add $350 million to long-term debt, representing the financing that Campbell Soup will require based on our projections. This yields a forecasted cash balance of $250.6 million, in line with previous year's levels of cash. In addition, the leverage ratio (total assets / total equity) is projected at 2.29, about the same as the Year 11 level. The revised balance sheet forecast is provided in Exhibit CC.26.

We conclude this section by valuing the Campbell Soup common stock as of Year 11 and using forecasts for Year 12 and beyond. The valuation analysis is provided in Exhibit CC.27. We use a five-year forecast horizon, beginning with Year 12 forecasted above and continuing through Year 16. Year 17 is the assumed terminal year and we project sales growth at the rate of inflation from that period forward. To simplify the analysis, we project only the five parameters we utilized in our valuation example in Chapter 10:

1. Sales growth.
2. Net profit margin (Net income/Sales).
3. Net working capital turnover (Sales/Net working capital).
4. Fixed asset turnover (Sales/Fixed assets).
5. Financial leverage (Operating assets/Equity).

The summary balance sheet and income statement begin with our estimate for Year 12. Years 13–17 are computed using the same sales growth, net profit margin, working capital, and fixed asset turnover rates and leverage used for Year 12. These could, of course, be modified if we had information indicating an expected change in one or more of the forecast parameters. Finally, we assume a cost of equity capital of 7%.[1]

The expected level of profits, based on beginning stockholders' equity of $1,793 million and a 7% yield, is $126 million. The forecasted net income for Year 12 is $305 million. Residual profits are, therefore, projected at $179 million. These are discounted to

[1] Under CAPM, with long-term government bond yields of 5%, a beta for Campbell Soup stock of 0.394, and an equity risk premium of 5%, the cost of equity capital is 5% + (0.394 × 5%) = 6.97, or approximately 7%.

Exhibit CC.26

CAMPBELL SOUP COMPANY
Final Forecasted Balance Sheet ($ millions)

	Year 12 Final Estimate	Year 12 Initial Estimate
Cash and cash equivalents	$ 250.6	$ (99.4)
Accounts receivable	553.8	553.8
Inventories	775.6	775.6
Other current assets	105.5	105.5
Total current assets	1,685.5	1,335.5
Plant assets, net of depreciation	1,963.8	1,963.8
Other long-term assets	840.1	840.1
Total assets	$4,489.4	$4,139.4
Payable to suppliers and others	$ 529.4	$ 529.4
Notes payable	173.4	173.4
Accrued liabilities	429.1	429.1
Accrued income taxes	51.3	51.3
Dividend payable	37.0	37.0
Total current liabilities	1,220.3	1,220.3
Long-term debt	1,003.7	653.7
Deferred income tax and other liabilities	305.0	305.0
Total liabilities	2,529.0	2,179.0
Preferred stock	0.0	0.0
Capital stock	20.3	20.3
Capital surplus	107.3	107.3
Earnings retained and cumulative translation adjustments	2,103.2	2,103.2
Capital stock in treasury	(270.4)	(270.4)
Total shareowners' equity	1,960.4	1,960.4
Total liabilities and shareowners' equity	$4,489.4	$4,139.4

the present with a factor of .89 (1/1.12) as discussed in Chapter 10. We forecast residual income for each additional year and also discount these to the present. The terminal year residual income is treated as a perpetuity beginning in Year 6. The present value of this perpetuity is also discounted. The cumulative present value of the projected residual income is $5,193 million ($787 million + $4,406 million) which, when added to the beginning book value of $1,793 million, yields a value for the common equity of $6,987 million, or $55.01 per share based on 127 million outstanding common shares.

Our estimate of $55.01 is considerably lower than the market price range of $72.38–$84.88 for Campbell Soup in the fourth quarter of Year 11 as reported in note 24. Clearly, the market is expecting stronger performance than we have assumed. One possibility is the company's gross profit margin. We have assumed that the reported gross profit margin of nearly 34% in Year 11 is an aberration and that it will revert to historical levels of 31%. If the market is, in fact, expecting gross profit margins to remain at 34%, the net profit margin will increase by 1.8% after tax to 6.47%. The resulting stock price estimate is $82.76 per share. Similarly, the market may be forecasting higher growth rates in sales or increasing improvement in asset turnover ratios.

Exhibit CC.27

CAMPBELL SOUP COMPANY
Valuation of Common Stock

	HISTORICAL FIGURES		FORECAST HORIZON					TERMINAL YEAR
	Year 10	Year 11	Year 12	Year 13	Year 14	Year 15	Year 16	Year 17
Sales growth	9.43%	−0.03%	5.00%	5.00%	5.00%	5.00%	5.00%	3.50%
Net profit margin (Net income/Sales)	0.07%	6.47%	4.67%	4.67%	4.67%	4.67%	4.67%	4.67%
Net working capital (NWC) turnover								
Sales/Average NWC	16.89	25.80	14.00	14.00	14.00	14.00	14.00	14.00
Fixed assets turnover								
Sales/Average fixed assets	2.53	2.36	2.32	2.32	2.32	2.32	2.32	2.32
Total operating assets/Total equity	1.67	1.60	1.67	1.67	1.67	1.67	1.67	1.67
Cost of equity			7.0%					
(in $ thousands)								
Net sales	$6,206	$6,204	$6,514	$6,840	$7,182	$7,541	$7,918	$8,195
Net earnings ($ millions)	4	402	305	320	336	353	370	383
Net working capital	367	241	465	488	513	539	565	585
Long-term assets	2,450	2,631	2,804	2,944	3,091	3,246	3,408	3,527
Total operating assets	2,818	2,871	3,269	3,433	3,604	3,784	3,974	4,113
Long-term liabilities	1,126	1,078	1,309	1,374	1,443	1,515	1,591	1,646
Total shareowners' equity ($ millions)	1,692	1,793	1,960	2,058	2,161	2,269	2,383	2,466
Residual Income Computation								
Net income			305	320	336	353	370	383
Beginning-year equity			1,793	1,960	2,058	2,161	2,269	2,383
Required equity return			7.0%	7.0%	7.0%	7.0%	7.0%	7.0%
Expected earnings			126	137	144	151	159	167
Residual income			179	183	192	201	211	216
Discount factor			0.93	0.87	0.82	0.76	0.71	
Present value of residual income			167	159	156	154	151	
Cumulative present value of residual income			167	327	483	637	787	
Terminal value of abnormal earnings							4,406	
Beginning book value of equity							1,793	
Value of equity (abnormal earnings)							6,987	
Common shares outstanding (millions)							127	
Value of equity per share							$55.01	

Summary Evaluation and Inferences

This case analysis considered all facets of Campbell Soup Company's operating results and financial position. We also forecasted the company's income statement, balance sheet, and statement of cash flows. This type of analysis, modified for the analysis perspective, is valuable for informed business decisions. While these data and information from our analysis are indispensable, they are not sufficient in arriving at final decisions. This is because other qualitative and quantitative factors from outside of the financial statements should be brought to bear on these decisions.

Since lending, investing, or other business analysis decisions require more information than provided in accounting and financial analysis, we often summarize the analysis and its inferences in a financial analysis report. This report (see the discussion earlier in this chapter) lists the most relevant and salient findings from the analysis, which depend on the analysis perspective. The remainder of this section provides a brief listing of the main findings of our analysis of Campbell Soup Company.

Short-Term Liquidity

The assessment of Campbell's short-term liquidity is a mixed one. Both current and acid-test ratios do not compare favorably with industry norms. Yet Campbell's cash position compares favorably with its industry, and its accounts receivable and inventory turnover ratios are better than industry norms. Moreover, Campbell's conversion period is better (less) than that of the industry, and its cash position is strong, allowing for cash to be used for nonoperating activities like acquisitions and retirement of debt.

Capital Structure and Solvency

Campbell has aggressively transformed its capital structure in recent years to a less conservative one. This inference is drawn from absolute and industry comparative measures. Total liabilities make up about 53% of total financing, and long-term liabilities equal about one-half of equity. On the positive side, both earnings to fixed charges and cash flow to fixed charges ratios are strong, the exception being earnings coverage ratios for Years 9 and 10 (due to restructuring). These strong ratios imply good protection for Campbell's creditors. The company also has the strength to take on additional debt, and the market continues to assign Campbell a superior credit rating (AA).

Return on Invested Capital

Campbell's return on assets varies. In Years 6 through 8 it is stable at around 9.5%, but in Years 9 and 10 it declines to a low of around 2% due primarily to divestiture, restructuring, and unusual charges. In Year 11, return on assets rebounds to a strong 11.75%, composed of a 6.47% profit margin and an asset turnover of 1.50. Campbell's return on assets for Year 11 compares favorably to the industry average of 9.2%. Campbell's return on common equity is 21.52% for Year 11 and exceeds the industry average of 19.8%. This return also evidences setbacks in Years 9 and 10 for the same reasons as the return on assets. An important factor affecting return on common equity (beyond the same components comprising return on assets) is financial leverage. The leverage ratio equals 2.22 in Year 11 and is higher than in prior years mainly due to a more risky capital structure. A favorable finding is Campbell's increased equity growth rate for Year 11, due in large part to strong earnings and a higher rate of earnings retention.

Asset Turnover (Utilization)

Campbell's asset turnover is relatively stable. While its turnover of cash and cash equivalents fluctuates from year to year, Campbell's accounts receivable and inventory turnovers are improving and exceed industry norms. These improvements are due mainly to Campbell's efforts to reduce working capital through, among other activities, less receivables and inventories. Nevertheless, asset turnover compares favorably to the industry despite the relatively low cash turnover and fixed assets turnover.

Operating Performance and Profitability

Campbell's gross profit margin is steadily improving and above the industry average. Yet its net profit margin is not as solid. This is due primarily to increased operating expenses, and the inability of Campbell's management in controlling these expenses. Recent activities suggest that Campbell is attempting to gain greater control over these expenses.

Financial Market Measures

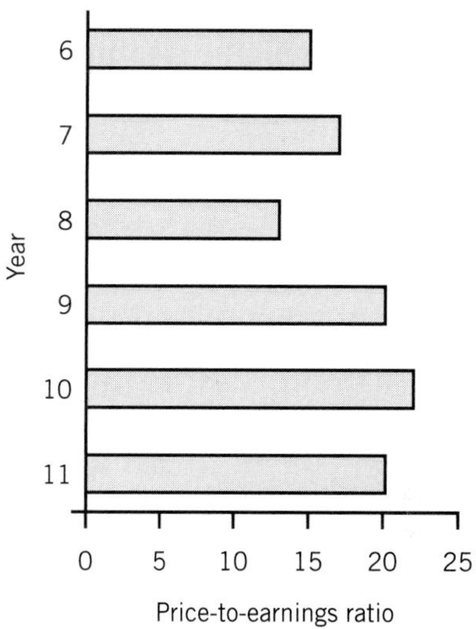

Source: Exhibit CC.28.

Selected financial market measures for Campbell are shown in Exhibit CC.28. The first four measures reflect the market's valuation of Campbell's equity securities, while the fifth (dividend payout) reflects management discretion. Earnings per share figures for Years 9 and 10 are adjusted to exclude the effect of divestitures, restructuring, and unusual charges. While earnings per share increases from $1.72 in Year 6 to $3.16 in Year 11, the earnings yield declines over the same period because of steadily increasing price-to-earnings and price-to-book ratios. This is mainly due to a strong equity market. Similarly, while dividends per share increase from $0.65 in Year 6 to $1.12 in Year 11, the dividend yield declines from 2.5% to 1.74% over the same period. Declines in earnings yield and dividend yield are attributable mainly to steady increases in price-to-earnings and price-to-book ratios. Both ratios reflect the market's appreciation and confidence in Campbell's prior and expected performance. This analysis shows Campbell's operating performance is strong despite temporary declines in Years 9 and 10.

Higher price-to-earnings and price-to-book ratios benefit a company in several ways. These include the ability to raise a given amount of equity capital by issuing fewer shares and the ability to use common stock as a means of payment for acquisitions. Yet, increasing stock valuations expose existing and especially new common shareholders to increasing risks, including the risk of stagnating or reversing stock valuations. This occurs because, unlike in early stages of a bull market, prices can potentially deviate from company fundamentals in reflecting upward price momentum. Consider, for example, the difference between the current market price for Campbell Soup and our estimate in the case analysis. When stock valuations reflect this price momentum, experience shows it is promptly erased once information on the fundamentals fails to support the high stock price. Assessing price momentum, as important and crucial as it is for equity investing, cannot be gauged by

Exhibit CC.28

CAMPBELL SOUP COMPANY
Market Measures

	Year 11	Year 10*	Year 9*	Year 8	Year 7	Year 6
1. Price-to-earning (range)	27–14	26–18	29–12	16–11	19–14	20–10
2. Price-to-book (range)	6.0–3.1	4.7–3.2	4.5–1.8	2.3–1.6	2.7–2.0	2.9–1.5
3. Earnings yield	4.91%	4.53%	4.91%	7.45%	6.20%	6.61%
4. Dividend yield	1.74%	1.88%	2.08%	2.85%	2.32%	2.50%
5. Dividend payout ratio	35.44%	41.53%	42.45%	38.21%	37.37%	37.79%

Computations for Year 11 are shown here:
(1) High and Low for the year: High—84.88/3.16 = 27; Low—43.75/3.16 = 14 [see item 184].
(2) High and Low for the year: High—84.88/14.12 = 6.0; Low—43.75/14.12 = 3.1 [see item 185].
(3) Earnings per share/Average market price = 3.16/[(84.88 + 43.75)/2] = 4.91%.
(4) Dividend per share/Average market price = 1.12/64.32 = 1.74%.
(5) Dividend per share/Earnings per share = 1.12/3.16 = 35.44%.
* Year 10 and Year 9 results are shown for EPS before effects of divestitures, restructuring, and unusual charges of $2.33 and $2.02 per share, respectively.

means of the analysis tools here. They involve the study of market expectations and cycles. The difference between Campbell's return on its invested capital and an equity investor's return on investment is discussed in Chapter 8.

Using Financial Statement Analysis

Our analysis of the financial statements of Campbell Soup Company consisted of two major parts: (1) detailed analysis and (2) summary and inferences. In our *analysis report,* the summary and inferences (executive summary) often precede detailed analysis. The detailed analysis section is usually directed at a specific user. For example, our bank loan officer who must decide on a short-term loan application typically directs attention to short-term liquidity and cash flow analysis and forecasting. A secondary objective of the loan officer is to assess capital structure and operating performance. Regarding the investment committee of our insurance company scenario, it would take a more long-term perspective. This implies more attention needs to be directed at capital structure and long-term solvency. Its secondary focus is on operating performance, return on invested capital, asset utilization, and short-term liquidity (in order of emphasis). Finally, the potential investor in Campbell shares has varying interest in all aspects of our analysis. The emphasis across areas is different for this user, and the likely order of priority is operating performance, return on invested capital, capital structure, long-term solvency, and short-term liquidity. A competent financial statement analysis contains sufficient detailed evaluation along with enough information and inferences to permit its use by different users with varying perspectives.

QUESTIONS

CC–1. Identify and describe the six major building blocks of financial statement analysis. What is the initial step in applying the building blocks to an analysis of financial statements?

CC–2. What type of investigation should precede analysis of financial statements?

CC–3. What are the analytical implications of recognizing that financial statements are an abstraction of a company's underlying business transactions and events?

CC–4. What additional knowledge and analytical skills must an analysis of financial statements bring to bear on companies operating in specialized or regulated industries?

CC–5. What are the attributes of a good financial analysis report? What distinct sections constitute a complete financial analysis report?

EXERCISES

EXERCISE CC-1

Evaluating Financial Ratios in Determining Price-to-Earnings (PE)

The following financial data are available for each of two manufacturers of mountain bikes.

	AXEL	BIKE
Capital structure:		
5%, 20-year notes	$10,000,000	—
Common equity	$20,000,000	$30,000,000
Number of common shares	500,000	750,000
Earnings per share:		
Year 6	$ 4.25	$ 3.00
Year 5	3.50	2.50
Year 4	2.25	1.67
Year 3	2.75	2.00
Year 2	1.70	1.95
Sales (Year 6)	30,000,000	30,000,000
Net income (Year 6)	2,125,000	2,250,000

	AXEL	BIKE
Selected balance sheet data at end of Year 6:		
Cash and cash equivalents	$ 3,000,000	$ 5,850,000
Accounts receivable	5,000,000	3,750,000
Inventories	12,000,000	10,000,000
Total current assets	20,000,000	19,600,000
Accounts payable	4,000,000	3,500,000
Accrued expenses	2,000,000	2,000,000
Taxes payable	1,000,000	1,100,000
Total current liabilities	7,000,000	6,600,000
Plant and equipment, net	13,000,000	15,900,000
Patents, net	4,000,000	100,000

Required:

Compute and analyze each of the following seven factors and ratios. For each factor and ratio, does the evidence imply a higher or lower PE for Axel or Bike?

a. Growth in earnings per share.
b. Financial leverage ratio.
c. Return on common equity.
d. Net income as % of sales.
e. Current ratio, receivables turnover, and sales to plant and equipment.
f. Patent position.
g. Return on long-term assets.

(CFA Adapted)

CHECK
Axel
(a) 21%
(b) 33%
(g) 13.3%

EXERCISE CC-2
Identifying Industry Classification by Company Financial Statements

Reproduced below are condensed common-size financial statements of companies operating in nine different industries. The nine industries represented are:

a. Tobacco manufacturing
b. Pharmaceuticals
c. Health care
d. Utilities
e. Investment advising
f. Breweries
g. Grocery stores
h. Computer equipment
i. Public opinion surveys

Required:

Examine the relations in these balance sheets and income statements and match the (1) through (9) companies with the (*a*) through (*i*) industries. It might be helpful to consult published industry ratios.

Company Balance Sheets*

Account	(1)	(2)	(3)	(4)	(5)	(6)	(7)	(8)	(9)
Current receivables	9.77%	19.20%	3.35%	25.96%	0.55%	8.10%	26.34%	17.38%	15.33%
Inventories	6.22	14.87	5.18	0.00	7.91	20.11	31.69	0.00	0.00
Plant and equipment, net	224.39	28.20	51.20	24.52	6.94	26.25	31.36	88.97	3.19
Other assets	46.56	29.15	5.48	26.65	3.71	18.50	16.91	24.35	219.59
Total assets	286.94%	91.42%	65.21%	77.13%	19.11%	72.96%	106.30%	130.70%	238.11%
Cost of P&E (gross)	279.83%	39.06%	70.33%	35.78%	9.64%	39.31%	45.91%	106.64%	6.29%
Current liabilities	18.78%	22.70%	11.19%	29.92%	7.31%	13.31%	19.30%	19.33%	76.89%
Long-term liabilities	158.69	9.22	26.65	10.19	6.06	16.40	4.11	73.32	72.18
Shareholders' equity	109.47	59.50	27.37	37.02	5.74	43.25	82.89	38.05	89.04
Total liabilities and equity	286.94%	91.42%	65.21%	77.13%	19.11%	72.96%	106.30%	130.70%	238.11%

* All numbers expressed as a percentage of total revenues.

Company Income Statements

Account	(1)	(2)	(3)	(4)	(5)	(6)	(7)	(8)	(9)
Revenues	100.00%	100.00%	100.00%	100.00%	100.00%	100.00%	100.00%	100.00%	100.00%
Cost of sales	49.50	31.11	67.48	63.29*	77.20	68.16	56.24	81.06*	16.55*
Depreciation expense	8.36	2.26	2.47	3.51	1.14	3.50	4.76	4.33	0.81
Interest expense	8.81	1.14	2.03	0.47	0.59	1.26	0.31	4.04	10.75
Advertising expense	0.00	2.39	4.82	0.12	3.89	6.97	3.86	0.00	6.24
R&D expense	0.76	7.95	0.24	0.00	0.00	0.00	11.06	0.00	0.00
Income taxes	11.47	8.11	2.44	6.80	0.77	4.71	2.98	4.44	33.01
All other items (net)	6.63	29.08	15.59	18.54	15.50	8.89	14.15	(0.46)	0.73
Total expenses	85.53%	82.04%	95.07%	92.73%	99.09%	93.49%	93.36%	93.41%	68.09%
Net income	14.47%	17.96%	4.93%	7.27%	0.91%	6.51%	6.64%	6.59%	31.91%

* Companies (4), (8), and (9) carry zero inventory, meaning that cost of sales is primarily operating expenses.

PROBLEMS

PROBLEM CC-1
Analysis of Credit Quality

Selected financial ratios from the (i) S&P 400, (ii) the brewing industry, and (iii) **Anheuser-Busch Companies** (BUD), for Years 2 through 6 are reproduced below.

Anheuser-Busch Companies

Required:

a. Using these financial ratios, analyze the relative credit position of:
(1) Brewing industry compared with the S&P 400.
(2) Anheuser-Busch compared with the brewing industry.
(3) Anheuser-Busch compared with the S&P 400.

b. Using these financial ratios and your analysis from (*a*), describe the current position of Anheuser-Busch and discuss whether you feel there has been a change in the credit quality of Anheuser-Busch during this five-year period.

	YEAR 2			YEAR 3			YEAR 4			YEAR 5			YEAR 6		
	S&P 400	Brewing Industry	BUD	S&P 400	Brewing Industry	BUD	S&P 400	Brewing Industry	BUD	S&P 400	Brewing Industry	BUD	S&P 400	Brewing Industry	BUD
Current ratio	1.5	1.3	1.1	1.5	1.4	1.2	1.5	1.3	1.1	1.4	1.5	1.2	1.4	1.4	1.0
Quick ratio	0.9	0.7	0.4	0.9	0.8	0.7	0.8	0.7	0.05	0.8	1.0	0.6	0.7	0.8	0.4
Long-term debt/total assets (%)	24	21	25	23	18	22	25	15	18	26	15	17	27	17	19
Total debt ratio (%)*	43	37	41	42	36	39	44	31	34	48	32	33	48	34	37
Times interest earned	4.0	7.2	12.2	4.6	7.5	12.7	4.8	7.6	13.3	4.2	10.1	14.9	3.6	11.0	9.8
Cash flow/long-term debt (%)	54	52	43	61	70	55	65	84	71	57	88	79	51	80	73
Cash flow/total debt (%)*	23	29	26	25	35	32	25	39	38	20	40	40	20	38	38
Total asset turnover	1.2	1.2	1.2	1.2	1.4	1.4	1.2	1.5	1.6	1.2	1.3	1.5	1.1	1.3	1.4
Net profit margin (%)	3.95	5.36	6.3	4.42	5.58	5.8	4.77	5.12	6.0	3.84	5.73	6.3	3.75	6.16	6.17
Return on assets (%)	4.64	6.46	7.4	5.10	7.98	8.0	5.80	7.47	8.7	4.41	7.66	8.7	3.97	7.90	8.89

* Total debt is defined as long-term debt plus current liabilities.

PROBLEM CC-2
Forecasting Future Income, and What-If Analysis

CHECK
(a) Oper. inc., $812.58
(c) 1. $0.34/sh. incr.

Refer to the financial statement data of ABEX Chemicals, Inc., reproduced in Case 11–6.

Required:

a. Prepare a forecast of ABEX's total operating income for Year 10. (*Hint:* Refer to forecast data for volume, price, and cost.)

b. Identify additional information necessary to prepare a forecast of earnings per share (EPS) for Year 10, and identify five primary sources where you can obtain this information (you should identify *primary* sources and not necessarily external sources for the information needed).

c. Forecast and explain incremental changes in ABEX's earnings per share based on each of the following two independent scenarios for the petrochemical division only.
   (1) Price of polyethylene in Year 10 is 8% higher than shown in the selected key statistics.
   (2) Volume of production and sales of polyethylene is 8% higher than shown in the selected key statistics.

(CFA Adapted)

PROBLEM CC-3
Analysis of Bond Investment, Ratio Analysis, and Financial Distress

Florida Gypsum Corporation

You are the portfolio manager of a high-yield bond portfolio at Solomon Group. You are concerned about the financial stability of **Florida Gypsum Corporation** (FGC), whose bonds represent one of the holdings in your portfolio at the *middle of Year 6.* The bonds you hold, 13.25% senior subordinated debentures due in Year 16, were issued at par in Year 5, and are currently priced in your portfolio at 53. Your high-yield bond sales staff is not optimistic they can even develop a bid at that level. FGC is a large producer of gypsum products, accounting for approximately one-third of total gypsum sales. The company also manufactures ceiling tile, caulks, sealants, floor and wall adhesives, and other specialty building products.

In Year 5, FGC did a leveraged recapitalization of its balance sheet. This involved paying a large dividend to common shareholders financed with several new subordinated debt financings, including the 13.25% debentures that you hold. The company's primary competitor, American Gypsum, is highly leveraged, following its acquisition by a large Canadian company. Due to a downturn in residential and commercial construction activity beginning in Year 4, demand for gypsum wallboard fell off through the middle of Year 6. However, capacity continues to expand at a rate of nearly 2% per year. As a result, capacity utilization has declined to 85% currently, from 87% in Year 4 and a peak of 95% in Years 1 and 2. The price of wallboard, which peaked in Year 2, has subsequently declined by more than 30%.

To help you in analyzing FGC's prospects, you assemble various financial data that follow. The director of fixed income research at Solomon Group suggests that you look carefully at ratios of short-term liquidity and operating performance, specifically the quick ratio, accounts receivable turnover ratio, inventory turnover ratio, and operating profit margin. You prepare the table below and schedule a meeting with the director to discuss what the firm should do with FGC.

FLORIDA GYPSUM CORPORATION
Selected Liquidity and Operating Performance Ratios

	YEAR ENDED		Six Months Ended
	Year 4	Year 5	Mid-Year 6
Quick (acid-test) ratio	0.73	0.78	0.77
Accounts receivable turnover	8.9	8.1	7.4
Inventory turnover	11.4	12.4	13.3
Operating profit margin*	16.6%	13.3%	14.9%

* Computed before interest and taxes.

Financial statement data for Florida Gypsum Corporation include the following:

FLORIDA GYPSUM CORPORATION
Balance Sheets ($ millions)

	End of Year 4	End of Year 5	At middle of Year 6
Assets			
Current assets:			
Cash & cash equivalents	$ 31.3	$ 250.0	$ 95.6
Accounts receivable	274.1	278.3	320.4
Inventories	144.1	124.6	128.4
Net assets of discontinued operations	415.1	20.4	—
Total current assets	864.6	673.3	544.4
Property, plant, & equipment	909.0	906.4	878.4
Purchased goodwill	148.9	146.5	144.5
Other assets	35.0	95.0	90.0
Total assets	$1,957.5	$1,821.2	$1,657.3
Liabilities and shareholders' equity			
Current liabilities:			
Commercial paper & notes payable	$ 38.3	$ 1.3	$ 1.6
Accounts payable	141.6	125.4	125.2
Accrued expenses	188.2	256.9	244.0
Other current liabilities	14.8	38.7	13.7
Current portion of long-term debt	33.0	259.3	154.5
Total current liabilities	415.9	681.6	539.0
Long-term debt	724.9	2,384.3	2,344.0
Deferred income tax	194.1	206.2	212.6
Minority interest	12.8	20.0	22.0
Shareholders' equity	609.8	(1,470.9)	(1,460.3)
Total liabilities and shareholders' equity	$1,957.5	$1,821.2	$1,657.3

FLORIDA GYPSUM CORPORATION
Income Statements ($ millions)

	YEAR ENDED		Six Months Ended
	Year 4	Year 5	Mid-year 6
Net sales	$2,254.4	$2,248.0	$1,107.7
Cost of goods sold	(1,598.6)	(1,671.9)	(841.4)
Gross profit	655.8	576.1	266.3
Selling and administrative expenses	(268.7)	(253.7)	(122.9)
Interest expense	(69.2)	(178.3)	(148.9)
Interest income	5.3	12.7	4.8
Recapitalization & restructuring expenses	(53.4)	(20.0)	—
Other expenses, net	34.3	(15.9)	17.0
Pre-tax earnings from continuing operations	304.1	120.9	16.3
Income taxes	(130.9)	(48.2)	(5.9)
Earnings from continuing operations	$ 173.2	$ 72.7	$ 10.4

FLORIDA GYPSUM CORPORATION
Selected Cash Flow Data ($ millions)

	YEAR ENDED		Six Months Ended
	Year 4	Year 5	Mid-year 6
Cash Flow from Operations:			
Earnings from continuing operations	$173.2	$ 72.7	$ 10.4
Depreciation, depletion, & amortization	76.6	83.0	42.5
Noncash interest expense	—	19.1	22.3
Minority interest	13.2	9.1	4.0
Deferred income taxes	1.5	12.6	6.4
Other noncash items relating to operations	15.2	(6.1)	(11.7)
(Increase) decrease in noncash working capital	43.8	91.8	(84.1)
Other cash flows from operations	(24.0)	(62.0)	3.9
Total net cash flow from operations	$299.5	$220.2	$ (6.3)
Net Liquid Balance:			
Cash and cash equivalents	$ 31.3	$250.0	$ 95.6
Less current notes payable	(38.3)	(1.3)	(1.6)
Less current portion of long-term debt	(33.0)	(259.3)	(154.5)
Net liquid balance	$ (40.0)	$ (10.6)	$ (60.5)
Net liquid balance as percent of total assets	(2.0)%	(0.6)%	(3.7)%

Required:

a. The director of fixed income research subsequently argues that the four ratios computed do not reveal important changes in the financial condition of FGC. Discuss limitations of these ratios in assessing the liquidity and operating performance of a company like FGC.

b. Identify at least two better measures of short-term liquidity and operating performance for FGC. Calculate their values and discuss their trend over the period Year 4 through middle of Year 6. Explain why these measures better reflect FGC's liquidity and operating performance.

c. Based on the analysis performed in (*b*) and on the background information provided, recommend and justify whether you should attempt to sell the FGC bonds, retain them, or buy more FGC bonds.

(CFA Adapted)

CHECK
(b) Examine CFO, Net liquid bal., Times int. earned, ROA, ROCE

CASES

CASE CC-1
Comprehensive Financial Analysis

Select a company from a nonregulated industry for which you can obtain complete financial statements for at least the most recent six years.

Required:

Based on these financial statements, the company's background, industry statistics, and other market and company information, prepare a financial statement analysis report covering the following points:

a. Executive summary of the company and its industry.

b. Detailed evaluation of:
 (1) Short-term liquidity (current debt-paying ability).
 (2) Cash forecasting and pro forma analysis.
 (3) Capital structure and solvency.
 (4) Return on invested capital.
 (5) Asset turnover (utilization).
 (6) Profitability and equity analysis.

Note: You are expected to use a variety of financial analysis tools in answering (*b*). Your analysis should yield inferences for each of these six areas.

c. Comment on the usefulness of the financial statements of this company for your analysis.

d. How did accounting principles used in the financial statements affect your analytical measures?

e. Prepare a forecast of the income statement, balance sheet, and statement of cash flows for a five-year horizon and a terminal year in Year 6.

f. Estimate the value of your company's common stock per share using the valuation analysis and procedures described in the Comprehensive Case.

CASE CC-2

Comprehensive Financial Analysis

The financial statements and notes of ZETA Corporation are reproduced over the next several pages.

Required:

Answer the following questions and provide supporting calculations. Explain the accounts and amounts used in each analysis.

a. What transactions and events explain the $7,000 increase in stockholders' equity for Year 6?

b. Note 6 discloses "capitalized lease obligations" of $1,000. What accounts are increased in Year 6, and by what amounts, to reflect these leases? Explain. How are these leases reflected in the statement of cash flows?

CHECK
(c) Repaid $2,500

c. Use T-account analysis to determine how much long-term debt is paid in Year 6. Does your answer agree with the amount reported by ZETA?

d. Note 1 describes a change in accounting principle.
(1) What effect did this change in accounting have on the Year 6 balance sheet and income statement?
(2) Describe the necessary adjustments in the Year 5 balance sheet and income statement for an effective comparison of Year 5 with Year 6.
(3) How would the $1,000 "cumulative effect" for Year 6 be reported in a statement of cash flows (direct method). (*Hint:* Reconstruct the accounts and amounts affected to record the $1,000 effect.)

e. Note 3 describes ZETA's acquisition of TRO Company.
(1) Is TRO a separate legal entity at December 31, Year 6, or is it dissolved into ZETA?
(2) What effect did the acquisition of TRO Company have at December 31, Year 6 (date of acquisition), on the:
i. ZETA balance sheet?
ii. Consolidated balance sheet?
(3) What are TRO's revenues for Year 6?

CHECK
(e) 3. $19,000

ZETA CORPORATION
Consolidated Balance Sheets ($ thousands)
As of December 31, Year 6 and Year 5

	Year 6	Year 5
Assets		
Current assets:		
Cash	$ 2,000	$ 2,000
Receivables	25,000	20,000
Inventories (notes 1 and 2)	56,000	38,000
Prepaid expenses	1,000	1,000
Total current assets	$ 84,000	$ 61,000
Investment in associated companies	14,000	11,000
Property, plant, and equipment	61,000	52,000
Less: accumulated depreciation	(23,000)	(19,000)
Net property, plant, and equipment	$ 38,000	$ 33,000
Goodwill	2,000	—
Total assets	$138,000	$105,000
Liabilities and Stockholders' Equity		
Current liabilities:		
Notes payable to banks	$ 16,000	$ 14,000
Accounts payable and accruals	29,000	23,000
Income taxes payable	7,000	2,000
Current portion of long-term debt (note 6)	2,000	1,000
Total current liabilities	$ 54,000	$ 40,000
Long-term debt (note 6)	25,000	15,200
Deferred income taxes (note 5)	3,600	2,000
Minority interest	1,400	800
Stockholders' equity (note 7):		
Common stock, $5 par value	5,500	5,000
Paid-in capital	24,500	15,000
Retained earnings	24,000	27,000
Total stockholders' equity	$ 54,000	$ 47,000
Total liabilities and stockholders' equity	$138,000	$105,000

ZETA CORPORATION
Consolidated Income Statement ($ thousands)
For Years Ended December 31, Year 6 and Year 5

	Year 6	Year 5
Net sales	$186,000	$155,000
Equity in income (loss) of associated companies	2,000	(1,000)
Expenses:		
Cost of sales	120,000	99,000
Selling and administrative expenses	37,000	33,000
Interest expense	10,000	6,000
Total costs and expenses	$167,000	$138,000
Income before taxes and minority interest	$ 21,000	$ 16,000
Income tax expense (note 5)	10,000	7,800
Income before minority interest	$ 11,000	$ 8,200
Minority interest	200	—
Income from continuing operations	$ 10,800	$ 8,200
Discontinued operations (note 4):		
Operations, net of tax	(1,100)	(1,200)
Loss on disposal, net of tax	(700)	—
Total gain (loss) from discontinued operations	$ (1,800)	$ (1,200)
Income before cumulative effect of accounting change	$ 9,000	$ 7,000
Cumulative effect of change in accounting, net of tax (note 1)	1,000	—
Net income	$ 10,000	$ 7,000
Pro forma income (assuming change in accounting is applied retroactively):		
Income from continuing operations	$ 10,800	$ 8,500
Discontinued operations	(1,800)	(1,200)
Total pro forma net income	$ 9,000	$ 7,300

f. For the asset "Investment in associated companies":
(1) Explain all changes during Year 6.
(2) Identify all effects in the statement of cash flows relating to this investment.

g. For the "Minority interest" reported in the balance sheet:
(1) Explain all changes during Year 6.
(2) Show how this account relates to the asset "Investment in associated companies."

CHECK
(h) $750 incr.

h. If the FIFO method of inventory valuation is used (instead of LIFO), how much would Year 6 net income be increased or decreased?

i. Note 4 describes "discontinued operations":
(1) What accounts (and amounts) are effected on October 31, Year 6, to record the loss on disposal?
(2) What effect did the loss on disposal of $700 have on the statement of cash flows? (Identify specific items and amounts.)
(3) How should the discontinued operation and $1,100 operating loss be reported in a statement of cash flows using the direct format, assuming we desire to include these operations among cash inflows and outflows?

j. How is goodwill reflected in the Year 7 (next year) statement of cash flows?

k. Explain all changes during Year 6 in the Net Property, Plant, and Equipment account.

ZETA CORPORATION
Consolidated Statement of Cash Flows ($ thousands)
For Years Ended December 31, Year 6 and Year 5

		Year 6	Year 5
Cash provided from (used for) operations:			
Net income		$ 10,000	$ 7,000
Add (deduct) adjustments to cash basis:			
Depreciation		6,000	4,000
Deferred income taxes		1,600	1,000
Minority interest		200	—
Undistributed income of associated companies		(1,400)	1,300
Loss on discontinued operations		700	—
Increase in accounts receivable (5,000 − 2,000†)		(3,000)	(2,400)
Increase in inventories (18,000 + 100* − 2,200†)		(15,900)	(6,000)
Increase in prepaid expenses		—	(200)
Increase in accounts payable and accruals (6,000 − 300* − 3,200†)		2,500	2,000
Increase in income taxes payable (5,000 + 700)*		5,700	1,000
Net cash provided from (used for) operations		6,400	7,700
Cash provided from (used for) investing activities:			
Additions to property, plant, and equipment		(6,500)	(5,800)
Acquisition of TRO Company (excluding cash of $4,200):			
Property, plant, and equipment	$(6,000)		
Goodwill	(2,000)		
Long-term debt	4,800		
Minority interest	400		
Current assets (receivables and inventories)	(4,200)		
Current liabilities	3,200	(3,800)	—
Investment in associated companies		(1,600)	—
Proceeds from disposal of equipment		500	—
Net cash used for investing activities		(11,400)	(5,800)
Cash provided from (used for) financing:			
Issuance of long-term debt		7,500	5,000
Reduction in long-term debt		(1,500)	(1,000)
Dividends paid		(3,000)	(2,000)
Increase (decrease) in notes payable to bank		2,000	(3,500)
Net cash provided from (used for) financing activities		5,000	(1,500)
Net increase (decrease) in cash‡		$ 0	$ 400

* Adjustments of noncash transactions arising from discontinued operations (see note 4).
† Adjustments relating to acquisition of TRO Co (note 3).
‡ Supplemental disclosures of cash flow information:

	Year 6	Year 5
Cash paid for interest	10,000	6,000
Cash paid for income taxes	2,600	4,800

Schedule of noncash activities:
Capital lease of $1,000 incurred on the lease of equipment

ZETA CORPORATION

Notes to Consolidated Financial Statements
(in thousands)

Note 1: Change in accounting principle

During Year 6, the company broadened its definition of overhead costs to be included in the determination of inventories to more properly match costs with revenues. The effect of the change in Year 6 is to increase income from continuing operations by $400. The adjustment of $1,000 (after reduction for income taxes of $1,000) for the cumulative effect for prior years is shown in the net income for Year 6. The pro forma amounts show the effect of retroactive application of the revised inventory costing assuming that the new method had been in effect for all prior years.

Note 2: Inventories

Inventories are priced at cost (principally last-in, first-out [LIFO] method of determination) not in excess of replacement market. If the first-in, first-out (FIFO) method of inventory accounting had been used, inventories would have been $6,000 and $4,500 higher than reported at December 31, Year 6, and December 31, Year 5, respectively.

Note 3: Acquisition of TRO Company

Effective December 31, Year 6, the company purchased most of the outstanding common stock of TRO Company for $8,000 in cash. The excess of the acquisition cost over fair value of the net assets acquired, $2,000, will be recorded as goodwill and not amortized. The following unaudited supplemental pro forma information shows the condensed results of operations as though TRO Company had been acquired as of January 1, Year 5.

	Year 6	Year 5
Revenues	$205,000	$172,000
Net income	10,700	7,400

Details of acquisition (resources and obligations assumed):

Cash	$4,200
Accounts Receivable	2,000
Inventories	2,200
Property, Plant, & Equipment	6,000
Long-Term Debt	4,800
Accounts Payable & Accruals	3,200

Note 4: Discontinued operations

As of October 31, Year 6, the board of directors adopted a plan authorizing the disposition of the assets and business of its wholly owned subsidiary, Zachary Corporation. The "Loss on Disposal" is $700 (net of income tax credits of $700) and is based upon the estimated realizable value of the assets to be sold plus a provision for costs of $300 for operating the business until its expected disposition in early Year 7. Property, plant, and equipment is reduced by $1,000 and inventories are reduced by $100 to net realizable value. The provision for costs of $300 is included in "Accounts payable and accruals" and is reduced to $200 at year-end. Net sales of the operations to be discontinued are $18,000 in Year 6 and $23,000 in Year 5.

Note 5: Income taxes

The income tax expense consists of the following:

	Year 6	Year 5
Current	$ 8,400	$6,800
Deferred	1,600	1,000
Total	$10,000	$7,800

The effective tax rates of 47.6% and 48.8% for Year 6 and Year 5, respectively, differ from the statutory federal income tax rate of 50% due to research and development tax credits of $500 in Year 6 and $200 in Year 5. Deferred taxes result from the use of accelerated depreciation methods for income tax reporting and the straight-line method for financial reporting.

Note 6: Long-term debt

	Year 6	Year 5
10% promissory notes to institutional investors payable in annual installments of $900 through Year 10	$13,000	$13,900
Unsecured notes to banks—interest 1% over prime	4,000	—
Capitalized lease obligations—payable to Year 9 with an average interest rate of 8%	1,000	—
11% subordinated note payable in annual installments of $500 from Year 7 through Year 16	5,000	—
Other mortgages and notes	4,000	2,300
	$27,000	$16,200
Less current maturities	2,000	1,000
Total long-term debt	$25,000	$15,200

The various loan agreements place certain restrictions on the corporation including the payment of cash dividends on common stock and require the maintenance of working capital, as defined, of not less than $18,000. Approximately $10,000 of retained earnings is available for payment of cash dividends on common stock at December 31, Year 6. The corporation entered into several long-term noncancelable leases of equipment during Year 6 which have been capitalized for financial reporting. There are no other significant lease arrangements.

Note 7: Stockholders' equity

The corporation has 5 million shares of authorized common stock, par value $5. There are 1 million shares outstanding at December 31, Year 5, and this is increased by a 10% dividend payable in common stock during Year 6. The changes in retained earnings are as follows:

	Year 6	Year 5
Beginning balance	$ 27,000	$22,000
Add net income	10,000	7,000
Less cash dividends	(3,000)	(2,000)
Less 10% stock dividend	(10,000)	—
Ending balance	$ 24,000	$27,000

CASE CC-3

Comprehensive Analysis of Equity Investments

Coca-Cola Company
Coca-Cola Enterprises

The Policy Committee of your company decides to change investment strategies. This change entails an increase in exposure to the stocks of large companies producing consumer products dominated by leading brands. The committee decides the soft drink industry, specifically **Coca-Cola Company** (KO) and **Coca-Cola Enterprises** (CCE) qualify as potential purchases for your company's portfolio. As the company's beverage industry expert, you must prepare a financial analysis of these two soft drink producers.

KO owns the brands included in its broad product line. Its marketing efforts center on worldwide advertising promoting these soft drinks. KO manufactures primarily soft drink extract. The production process requires only low-cost raw materials and relatively limited fixed asset investment. Extract is inexpensive to ship and requires limited numbers of production facilities throughout the world. KO's position as a leading soft drink extract producer is protected by the technical nature of its manufacturing process, the restricted formula for its product, and strong brand names established from over a century of operations. Competition is limited essentially to one competitor, PepsiCo. KO plays almost no direct role in domestic manufacturing and distribution beyond the output of soft drink extract.

CCE's business is also dominated by soft drinks. CCE purchases extract from KO and transforms it into completed products sold in a wide variety of retail outlets throughout the United States. This costly, complex production and distribution system requires hundreds of plants and warehouses, and thousands of vehicles. Marketing efforts emphasize local promotion. Competition consists of a large number of highly automated, similarly organized companies also manufacturing soft drinks from extract.

Selected financial statements and notes for these two companies are reproduced below:

Consolidated Balance Sheets ($ millions)
December 31, Year 8

	Coca-Cola Company (KO)	Coca-Cola Enterprises (CCE)
Assets		
Current assets:		
Cash and cash equivalents	$1,231	$ —
Trade accounts receivable	627	294
Inventories	779	125
Other current assets	608	69
Total current assets	3,245	488
Other investments:		
Investments in affiliates	1,912	—
Other	478	66
Total other investments	2,390	66
Fixed assets:		
Land	117	135
Plant and equipment	2,500	1,561
Other	293	42
Total fixed assets	2,910	1,738
Less: accumulated depreciation	(1,150)	(558)
Total fixed assets, net	1,760	1,180
Goodwill	57	2,935
Total assets	$7,451	$4,669

	Coca-Cola Company (KO)	Coca-Cola Enterprises (CCE)
Liabilities & shareholders' equity		
Current liabilities:		
Short-term debt	$1,363	$ 148
Accounts payable	1,081	402
Other current liabilities	425	—
Total current liabilities	2,869	550
Long-term debt	761	2,062
Deferred income taxes	270	222
Other long-term liabilities	206	27
Shareholders' equity:		
Preferred stock	300	250
Common stock	3,045	1,558
Total shareholders' equity	3,345	1,808
Total liabilities & shareholders' equity	$7,451	$4,669

Year 8 Consolidated Statements of Income
($ millions except per share data)

	Coca-Cola Company (KO)	Coca-Cola Enterprises (CCE)
Revenues	$8,338	$3,874
Cost of goods sold	(3,702)	(2,268)
Gross profit	4,636	1,606
Selling & administrative expenses	(3,038)	(1,225)
Provision for restructuring	—	(27)
Operating profit	1,598	354
Interest expense	(231)	(211)
Gain on sale of operations	—	104
Equity in income of affiliates	48	—
Other income	167	21
Pretax income	1,582	268
Income taxes	(538)	(115)
Net income	$1,044	$ 153
Preferred cash dividends	(6)	(10)
Income available for common	$1,038	$ 143
Earnings per share	$ 2.85	$ 1.03

Data Extracted from Financial Statement Footnotes

Coca-Cola Company (KO)

1. Certain soft drink and citrus inventories are valued on the last-in first-out (LIFO) method. The excess of current costs over LIFO stated values amount to approximately $30 million at December 31, Year 8.
2. The market value of the company's investments in publicly traded equity investees exceed the company's carrying value at December 31, Year 8, by approximately $291 million.
3. The company is contingently liable for guarantees of indebtedness owed by some of its licensees and others, totaling approximately $133 million at December 31, Year 8.
4. Pension plan assets total $496 million. The projected benefit obligation for all plans totals $413 million.

Coca-Cola Enterprises (CCE)

1. Inventory cost is computed principally on the last-in first-out (LIFO) method. At December 31, Year 8, the LIFO reserve is $2,077,000.
2. In December Year 8, the company repurchases for cash various outstanding bond issues. These transactions result in a pretax gain of approximately $8.5 million.
3. The company leases office and warehouse space, and machinery and equipment under lease agreements. At December 31, Year 8, future minimum lease payments under noncancellable operating leases are as follows ($ thousand):

Year 9	$11,749
Year 10	8,436
Year 11	6,881
Year 12	4,972
Year 13	3,485
Later years	11,181
Total	$46,704

4. Pension plan assets total $197 million. Total projected benefit obligation for all plans is $151 million.

Selected Financial Ratios*

For Year 8

	Coca-Cola Company (KO)	Coca-Cola Enterprises (CCE)
Return on assets	0.16	0.06
Total debt ratio	0.55	0.61
Net profit margin	0.13	0.04
Receivables turnover	13.30	13.18
Property, plant, & equipment turnover	4.74	3.28
Return on common equity	0.34	0.09
Current ratio	1.13	0.89
Inventory turnover	4.75	18.14
Long-term debt to equity	0.23	1.14
Gross profit margin	0.56	0.41
Acid-test ratio	0.65	0.53
Asset turnover	1.12	0.83
Times interest earned	7.85	2.27

* For simplicity, ratios are computed using year-end data rather than on Year 8 average data when applicable.

Required:

Use *only* the financial information reproduced here in answering requirements (*a*) and (*b*).

a. Your comparative analysis of these two soft drink companies requires using the ratios reported. You identify four key areas of comparison in your analysis:
   (1) Short-term liquidity.
   (2) Capital structure and solvency.
   (3) Asset utilization.
   (4) Profitability.
   Discuss differences between KO and CCE in each of these four areas.

b. Using the financial statement information, identify *five* adjustments to the financial statements you feel would enhance their comparability and usefulness for financial analysis. For each of your five adjustments, discuss the effects of these adjustments on your answer to (*a*).

(CFA Adapted)

WEB ACTIVITIES

The Web Activities are located on the book's website at www.mhhe.com/wild8e.

FINANCIAL STATEMENTS

Appendix A contains selections from both the Annual Report and Form 10-K filings for three companies: Eastman Kodak, Campbell Soup, and Quaker Oats. Numerous chapter illustrations and assignment materials refer to information in this appendix.

Eastman Kodak

To Our Shareholders

No question about it: 2001 was an extraordinary and difficult year for the nation, for the world and for nearly every business, including Kodak. The continuing worldwide economic slump, coupled with the tragic events of September 11, severely impacted industries important to our business, including travel, theme parks, lodging, advertising and entertainment.

Through these challenging times, we focused on strengthening Kodak's value as an investment, maintaining our market share in key segments of our business and laying the groundwork for future growth. In the broad category of infoimaging—our strategic framework going forward—we're driving the convergence of images and information beyond traditional boundaries, and into new image applications and business opportunities for Kodak.

While our revenues and earnings were down for the year, our successful drive to generate cash—including continuing, aggressive cost-reduction programs—produced a strong balance sheet and healthy dividend payouts. We maintained our full-year market share in the U.S. consumer film business and increased it slightly worldwide. We drove Kodak digital imaging to record revenues, with consumer-friendly products and services—including online and retail photo printing and the highly successful Kodak EasyShare camera launch—that are in the forefront of this burgeoning business.

We gained market share in our Health Imaging business, but pricing pressures and some operating issues led to margin declines. We moved quickly to put in place corrective measures that are returning that segment to its promising, profitable path.

Cash Management

Consistent with current economic reality, we have reduced our cost base and increased our focus on cash generation. On the cost front, we took a number of steps to reduce worldwide employment by about 9% and expect to see much of the resulting savings in our full-year 2002 results. We drove inventories down by 34 percent, or $581 million. We reduced receivables and continued our tight restraint on capital expenditures, with the latter decreasing 21% year-over-year.

All these actions contributed to a greatly strengthened cash position compared to a year earlier. Cash flow for 2001 was $373 million after paying dividends. Excluding a December 2001 accelerated dividend payment, cash flow was $504 million.

Investing for the Long Term

At the same time we were managing cash and costs, we continued to invest in our long-term future. We invested in fundamental research and development (R&D), and made strategic acquisitions that will position us well going forward. In a very cash-efficient way, we invested in a business venture for the manufacture of flat-panel displays for consumer devices such as cameras and personal data assistants (PDAs). We acquired a number of wholesale photofinishing laboratories in Europe, which will allow us to offer more pan-European services. We acquired Ofoto, Inc., a leading online photography service that will accelerate our growth in that desirable market. We also acquired the imaging services business of Bell & Howell Company to expand the existing services portfolio in document imaging, and made selective, smaller acquisitions in certain strategic areas.

Sharpening Our Focus

In November, we introduced a new operating model that is centered around strategic product groups—enabling a sharper focus on the customers and markets we serve. Our new alignment will reduce complexity, provide key managers with more decision-making authority and enable business groups and product managers to concentrate on processes and decisions that have the greatest influence on generating profitable growth.

As part of this effort, we integrated strategic product groups from our existing businesses and geographic regions into units that share common technology and product platforms and customer sets.

- The Photography Group, our largest business, includes Consumer Imaging, Digital & Applied Imaging, the photography portion of our Kodak Professional business and Entertainment Imaging.
- Health Imaging, our second-largest business, remains a stand-alone business.
- Commercial Imaging consists of Document Imaging, Commercial & Government Systems, Graphics and Wide-Format Inkjet. Included in the group are two joint venture operations, Kodak Polychrome Graphics and NexPress. The Wide-Format Inkjet business has been consolidated into our recent acquisition of ENCAD, Inc.
- The Components Group includes Kodak's Display Products, Image Sensor Solutions, and the Optics business, which was formerly part of Commercial & Government Systems. These businesses will spearhead our diversification into high-growth product areas consistent with our historical strengths in image and materials science.

2001 Business/Market Highlights

Photography Group U.S. industry film sales declined steadily through the first three quarters, but at a slower rate in the fourth. Our U.S. consumer film share for the full year held steady for the fourth consecutive year and worldwide share increased slightly. We saw good growth in many of our newer online and other digital services and we introduced several exciting new products in traditional photography.

Consumer use of our Kodak picture maker kiosks grew at double-digit rates. Our focus now is on creating new channels and increasing usage to an even higher level to drive output media.

In U.S. wholesale photofinishing, Qualex scanning rates have shown steady growth despite the economic downturn. More consumers are enjoying the advantages of receiving film images in digital form. The principal drivers are Kodak picture CD and our retail online partners. The average penetration rate for the number of rolls of film scanned grew from 4.1% in the first quarter to 6.7% in just the second half of the year. The number of images scanned showed a fourth-quarter, year-over-year increase of 49%. Our acquisition of wholesale photofinishing operations in Europe will allow us to expand this capability outside the U.S. photo market, which is the most digitally advanced. In addition, Ofoto is off and running, with our customer base growing by 12% a month.

In emerging markets, we continued to expand the number of outlets for Kodak consumer products. There are now more than 14,000 Kodak Express photo stores in Greater Asia, including China. In addition, we completed launching a new concept called "Photoshops" in India. More than 4,300 retail "Photoshops" were in place in key cities by year-end 2001, expanding the availability and distribution of Kodak consumer products.

Turning to our consumer digital imaging product offerings, our new line of EasyShare digital cameras has drawn a great response from consumers. The cameras continue to receive rave reviews and our docking station has truly brought "You Press the Button, We Do the Rest" simplicity to the art of digital photography.

In digital output, Kodak inkjet photo papers continue to attract consumers and maintain a high market share. In addition to continued growth in digital printing services through Ofoto, we see the launch of services from our Phogenix joint venture helping to drive even greater popularity for printing digital photo files.

Our professional product offerings returned to basics with the move of graphics and wide-format inkjet to Commercial Imaging. Our professional products include both traditional and digital solutions and services to professional photographers and labs. Products recently introduced include Kodak Portra sepia black-and-white paper, color metallic paper and day/night display materials offering exciting output choices, and the Kodak Professional DCS 760 digital camera and the DCS pro back plus.

Our products and services offered to the entertainment industry turned in a good performance despite a very challenging year. The threat of strikes in the entertainment industry pulled most production schedules into the first half of the year, creating a slower second half. In addition, film sales for television commercials were impacted as advertisers reduced their spend due to the economy and the aftermath of September 11th.

Health Imaging In Health Imaging, sales of traditional products declined, while the corresponding growth in digital products and services slowed somewhat due to the economy. However, Kodak increased its market share in both traditional analog x-ray media and digital output for diagnostic medical imaging. Sales of digital capture and PACS (picture archiving and communications systems) products and DryView media continued to grow at double-digit rates.

Commercial Imaging Growth in document imaging-related products and services sales benefited from the Bell & Howell acquisition and from increased sales of document scanners. Over the past five years, we have become the market leader in document scanning and preservation, building on our heritage in microfilm. Our new iNnovation series scanners are bundled with application software for document management, text recognition and photo management and have earned many industry awards.

Specialized imaging products and solutions for commercial and government customers continue to generate strong sales growth. The operations are exploring new business opportunities across a broad range of image management applications in real estate, government, insurance, telecommunications, transportation, mineral exploration and other industries.

In the graphics product offerings, our Kodak Polychrome Graphics joint venture contributed to positive earnings and expanded its growth opportunities by acquiring the color proofing and software businesses of Imation Corp. A joint venture between Kodak and Heidelberg achieved a key milestone with the successful launch of the NexPress 2100 printer, a digital short-run production color press that sets new industry standards for reliability, image quality and print consistency.

In the commercial inkjet printing market, we introduced the new 5260 wide-format printer. This product has expanded our presence in this rapidly growing market. In January 2002, we completed our acquisition of ENCAD, Inc., a leading supplier of commercial inkjet products, to further leverage our new product distribution efforts in this market.

Components Group Our flat-panel display business is off and running with the creation of SK Display Corporation, a business venture with SANYO Electric Co., Ltd., to manufacture displays for consumer devices such as cameras and PDAs. The business venture will feature the world's first full-scale manufacturing facility dedicated to full-color, organic light emitting diode (OLED) displays.

Additions to Board of Directors

Kodak's Board consists of "outside" Directors and only one company-employed member. In 2001, we welcomed three people to our Board—two new Directors and a returning member. Former U.S. Senator, Olympian and Pro Basketball Hall of Famer William W. Bradley joined the Board in May. Mr. Bradley is a Managing Director of Allen & Company Incorporated, and Chair of the Advisory Board of McKinsey & Company's Institute for Management of Nonprofits. Timothy M. Donahue, elected to the Board in October, is President & Chief Executive Officer of Nextel Communications, Inc. We were honored to welcome back Delano E. Lewis, who was re-elected to the Board in July. Mr. Lewis had served on Kodak's Board from May 1998 until he became U.S. Ambassador to South Africa in December 1999.

Outlook

We expect the balance of 2002 will continue to be challenging. We have very modest earnings expectations for the first half of the year, with some improvement in the second half as the cost-reduction efforts and operational improvements we made in 2001 begin to take hold. We do not expect to see any real upturn in the economy until 2003, with a very gradual return to consumer spending habits and behavior that will positively affect our business growth.

Our actions are consistent with Kodak's fundamental, long-term business strategy, and we expect to build on that foundation as the economy strengthens. We will continue to invest in R&D as a critical path to our future success—delivering innovative, customer-focused imaging products, systems and services. Of course, we will work to maintain or increase share positions in all of our businesses and we will continue to pay close attention to costs, managing the business for maximum cash. As we announced in late January, we are confident Kodak is capable of generating at least $6 billion in cash over the next six years.

Growth Strategy

We will leverage our unparalleled reputation for quality to ALL infoimaging processes and products, a category with a $225 billion total market potential. Kodak's imaging technologies, products and services position us well for success in this growing category. In 2002, we are aligning the entire Kodak organization to focus on four related growth paths for the future. Together, we will:

- *Expand the benefits of film.* The traditional film business is healthy, and developing in new markets around the world. Some digital substitution is happening—as we expected—particularly in the professional markets, and we are at the forefront of products for the digital market, as well. One of our key thrusts is to leverage and extend the benefits of our film-related businesses far into the future. We are doing this through the application of digital technology in such areas as wholesale and retail photofinishing and by expanding our presence in emerging film markets.
- *Drive image output in all forms.* Ofoto's capabilities and Health Imaging's DryView laser imaging system are examples of how the company is extracting value from image output. So is our worldwide population of 35,000 Kodak picture maker kiosks. We will also be introducing the Kodak I.Lab system, with exceptionally high-quality, digitally enhanced output on silver-halide paper.
- *Facilitate ease of use in digital imaging.* Our EasyShare camera line's success demonstrates that for the consumer, we are making digital imaging one-button simple. Look for even better things to come from this product line.
- *Develop new businesses in new markets.* We are exploring and developing new business opportunities that may be higher in risk, but will position Kodak and its technology to capture a broader share of the infoimaging category.

While these have been exceptionally challenging times for our industry and for Kodak, we are working through them and continuing to do what we do best—provide top-quality products and services, leverage a brand that is second to none, maintain a strong balance sheet and cash position, and pursue growth paths that will fulfill our promising future. We have unique strengths: brand and share leadership, a well-deserved reputation for innovation, and unparalleled development and production expertise. We have a strong, diverse management team, talented and dedicated employees and an active, involved Board of Directors.

On behalf of everyone in the extended Kodak family—customers, employees, the Board and the communities in which we operate around the world—I thank you, our investors, for your confidence and support.

Daniel A. Carp
Chairman & Chief Executive Officer,
President & Chief Operating Officer

Management's Discussion and Analysis
of Financial Condition and Results of Operations

Critical Accounting Policies and Estimates

The accompanying consolidated financial statements and notes to consolidated financial statements contain information that is pertinent to management's discussion and analysis of financial condition and results of operations. The preparation of financial statements in conformity with accounting principles generally accepted in the United States of America requires management to make estimates and assumptions that affect the reported amounts of assets, liabilities, revenue and expenses, and the related disclosure of contingent assets and liabilities. Actual results may differ from these estimates and assumptions.

The Company believes that the critical accounting policies discussed below involve additional management judgment due to the sensitivity of the methods, assumptions and estimates necessary in determining the related asset, liability, revenue and expense amounts.

Kodak recognizes revenue when it is realized or realizable and earned. For the sale of multiple-element arrangements whereby equipment is combined with services, including maintenance and training, and other elements, including software and products, the Company allocates to and recognizes revenue from the various elements based on verifiable objective evidence of fair value (if software is incidental to the transaction) or Kodak-specific objective evidence of fair value if software is other than incidental to the sales transaction as a whole. Revisions to these determinants of fair value would affect the timing of revenue allocated to the various elements in the arrangement and would impact the results of operations of the Company. For full-service solutions sales, which consist of the sale of equipment and software which may or may not require significant production, modification or customization, there are two acceptable methods of accounting: percentage of completion accounting and completed contract accounting. For certain of the Company's full-service solutions, the completed contract method of accounting is being followed by the Company. This is due to the Company's lack of historical experience resulting in the inability to provide reasonably dependable estimates of the revenues and costs applicable to the various stages of such contracts as would be necessary under the percentage of completion methodology. Furthermore, the Company records estimated reductions to revenue for customer incentive programs offered including cash discounts, price protection, promotional and advertising allowances and volume discounts. If market conditions were to decline, the Company may take actions to expand these customer offerings which may result in incremental reductions to revenue.

Kodak assesses the carrying value of its identifiable intangible assets, long-lived assets and goodwill whenever events or changes in circumstances indicate that the carrying amount of the underlying asset may not be recoverable. Certain factors which may occur and indicate that an impairment exists include, but are not limited to: significant underperformance relative to expected historical or projected future operating results; significant changes in the manner of the Company's use of the underlying assets; and significant adverse industry or market economic trends. In the event that the carrying value of assets are determined to be unrecoverable, the Company would record an adjustment to the respective carrying value.

Kodak maintains provisions for uncollectible accounts for estimated losses resulting from the inability of its customers to remit payments. If the financial condition of customers were to deteriorate, thereby resulting in an inability to make payments, additional allowances may be required.

Kodak provides estimated inventory allowances for excess, slow-moving and obsolete inventory as well as inventory whose carrying value is in excess of net realizable value. These reserves are based on current assessments about future demands, market conditions and related management initiatives. If market conditions and actual demands are less favorable than those projected by management, additional inventory write-downs may be required.

Kodak holds minority interests in certain publicly traded and privately held companies having operations or technology within its strategic area of focus. The Company's policy is to record an impairment charge on these investments when they experience declines in value which are considered to be other-than-temporary. Poor operating results of the investees or adverse changes in market conditions in the future may cause losses or an inability of the Company to recover its carrying value in these underlying investments.

Kodak evaluates the realizability of its deferred tax assets on an ongoing basis by assessing its valuation allowance and by adjusting the amount of such allowance, if necessary. In the determination of the valuation allowance, the Company has considered future taxable income and the feasibility of tax planning initiatives. Should the Company determine that it is more likely than not that it will realize certain of its deferred tax assets in the future, an adjustment would be required to reduce the existing valuation allowance and increase income. On the contrary, if the Company determined that it would not be able to realize its recorded net deferred tax asset, an adjustment to increase the valuation allowance would be charged to the results of operations in the period such conclusion was made. In addition, the Company operates within multiple taxing jurisdictions and is subject to audit in these jurisdictions. These audits can involve complex issues, which may require an extended period of time for resolution. Although management believes that adequate consideration has been made for such issues, there is the possibility that the ultimate resolution of such issues could have an adverse effect on the results of operations of the Company.

Management estimates expected product failure rates, material usage and service costs in the development of its warranty obligations. In the event that the actual results of these items differ from the estimates, an adjustment to the warranty obligation would be recorded.

Pension assets and liabilities are determined on an actuarial basis and are affected by the estimated market-related value of plan assets, estimates of the expected return on plan assets, discount rates and other assumptions inherent in these valuations. The Company annually reviews the assumptions underlying the actuarial calculations and makes changes to these assumptions, based on current market conditions, as necessary. Actual changes in the fair market value of plan assets and differences between the actual return on plan assets and the expected return on plan assets will affect the amount of pension (income) expense ultimately recognized. The other postretirement benefits liability is also determined on an actuarial basis and is affected by assumptions including the discount rate and expected trends in healthcare costs. Changes in the discount rate and differences between actual and expected healthcare costs will affect the recorded amount of other postretirement benefits expense.

Environmental liabilities are accrued based on estimates of known environmental remediation exposures. The liabilities include accruals for sites owned by Kodak, sites formerly owned by Kodak, and other third-party sites where Kodak was designated as a potentially responsible party (PRP). The amounts accrued for such sites are based on these estimates, which may be affected by changing determinations of what constitutes an environmental liability or an acceptable level of remediation. To the extent that the current work plans are not effective in achieving targeted results, the proposals to regulatory agencies for desired methods and outcomes of remediation are not acceptable, or additional exposures are identified, Kodak's estimate of its environmental liabilities may change.

Summary (in millions, except per share data)	2001	Change	2000	Change	1999
Net sales	$ 13,234	–5%	$ 13,994	–1%	$ 14,089
Earnings from operations	345	–84%	2,214	+11%	1,990
Net earnings	76	–95%	1,407	+1%	1,392
Basic earnings per share	.26	–94%	4.62	+5%	4.38
Diluted earnings per share	.26	–94%	4.59	+6%	4.33

2001

The Company's results for the year included the following:

Charges of $830 million ($583 million after tax) related to the restructuring programs implemented in the second, third and fourth quarters and other asset impairments. See further discussion in Management's Discussion and Analysis of Financial Condition and Results of Operations (MD&A) and Note 14.

A charge of $41 million ($28 million after tax) for environmental exposures. See MD&A and Note 10.

A charge of $20 million ($14 million after tax) for the Kmart bankruptcy. See MD&A and Note 2.

Income tax benefits of $31 million, including a favorable tax settlement of $11 million and a $20 million benefit representing a decline in the year-over-year effective tax rate.

Excluding the above items, net earnings were $670 million, or $2.30 per basic and diluted share.

2000

The Company's results for the year included the following:

Charges of approximately $50 million ($33 million after tax) associated with the sale and exit of one of the Company's equipment manufacturing facilities. The costs for this effort, which began in 1999, related to accelerated depreciation of assets still in use prior to the sale of the facility in the second quarter, and costs for relocation of the operations.

Excluding the above, net earnings were $1,440 million. Basic earnings per share were $4.73 and diluted earnings per share were $4.70.

1999

The Company's results for the year included the following:

A restructuring charge of $350 million ($231 million after tax) related to worldwide manufacturing and photofinishing consolidation and reductions in selling, general and administrative positions worldwide. In addition, the Company incurred charges of $11 million ($7 million after tax) related to accelerated depreciation of assets still in use during 1999 and sold in 2000, in connection with the exit of one of the Company's equipment manufacturing facilities.

Charges totaling approximately $103 million ($68 million after tax) associated with the exits of the Eastman Software business ($51 million) and Entertainment Imaging's sticker print kiosk product line ($32 million) as well as the write-off of the Company's Calcomp investment ($20 million), which was determined to be unrecoverable.

Gains of approximately $120 million ($79 million after tax) related to the sale of The Image Bank ($95 million gain) and the Motion Analysis Systems Division ($25 million gain).

Excluding the above items, net earnings were $1,619 million. Basic earnings per share were $5.09 and diluted earnings per share were $5.03.

Detailed Results of Operations

Net Sales by Reportable Segment and All Other (in millions)	2001	Change	2000	Change	1999
Photography					
Inside the U.S.	$ 4,482	–10%	$ 4,960	+4%	$ 4,756
Outside the U.S.	4,921	–7%	5,271	–4%	5,509
Total Photography	9,403	–8%	10,231	0%	10,265
Health Imaging					
Inside the U.S.	1,089	+2%	1,067	+8%	984
Outside the U.S.	1,173	+2%	1,153	–2%	1,175
Total Health Imaging	2,262	+2%	2,220	+3%	2,159
Commercial Imaging					
Inside the U.S.	820	+15%	715	–4%	741
Outside the U.S.	639	–9%	702	–5%	738
Total Commercial Imaging	1,459	+3%	1,417	–4%	1,479
All Other					
Inside the U.S.	68	0%	68	–40%	113
Outside the U.S.	42	–28%	58	–21%	73
Total All Other	110	–13%	126	–32%	186
Total Net Sales	$ 13,234	–5%	$ 13,994	–1%	$ 14,089
Earnings from Operations by Reportable Segment and All Other (in millions)					
Photography	$ 787	–45%	$ 1,430	–16%	$ 1,709
Health Imaging	323	–38%	518	+7%	483
Commercial Imaging	165	–29%	233	–9%	257
All Other	(60)		(11)		(109)
Total of segments	1,215	–44%	2,170	–7%	2,340
Restructuring costs and credits and asset impairments	(732)		44		(350)
Wolf charge	(77)		–		–
Environmental reserve	(41)		–		–
Kmart charge	(20)		–		–
Consolidated total	$ 345	–84%	$ 2,214	+11%	$ 1,990
Net Earnings by Reportable Segment and All Other (in millions)					
Photography	$ 535	–48%	$ 1,034	–18%	$ 1,261
Health Imaging	221	–38%	356	+10%	324
Commercial Imaging	80	–11%	90	–49%	178
All Other	(38)		(2)		(61)
Total of segments	798	–46%	1,478	–13%	1,702
Restructuring costs and credits and asset impairments	(735)		44		(350)
Wolf charge	(77)		–		–
Environmental reserve	(41)		–		–
Kmart charge	(20)		–		–
Interest expense	(219)		(178)		(142)
Other corporate items	8		26		22
Income tax effects on above items and taxes not allocated to segments	362		37		160
Consolidated total	$ 76	–95%	$ 1,407	+1%	$ 1,392

2001 Compared with 2000

Consolidated Net worldwide sales were $13,234 million for 2001 as compared with $13,994 million for 2000, representing a decrease of $760 million, or 5% as reported, or 3% excluding the negative impact of exchange. Net sales in the U.S. were $6,459 million for 2001 as compared with $6,810 million for 2000, representing a decrease of $351 million, or 5%. Net sales outside the U.S. were $6,775 million for 2001 as compared with $7,184 million for 2000, representing a decrease of $409 million, or 6% as reported, or 2% excluding the negative impact of exchange. The U.S. economic condition throughout the year and the events of September 11th adversely impacted the Company's sales, particularly in the consumer film product groups within the Photography segment. The total decrease in net worldwide sales of $760 million, or 5%, was comprised of declines in Photography sales of $828 million, or 8%, and All Other sales of $16 million, or 13%, partially offset by increases in Health Imaging sales of $42 million, or 2%, and Commercial Imaging of $42 million or 3%. The decrease in Photography sales was driven by declines in consumer, entertainment origination and professional film products, consumer and professional color paper, photofinishing revenues and consumer and professional digital cameras.

Sales in emerging markets decreased 4% from 2000 to 2001. The net decrease in emerging market sales was comprised of decreases in Latin America, Asia, Greater China and the European, African and Middle Eastern Region (EAMER) Emerging Markets of 5%, 4%, 7% and 7%, respectively, partially offset by an increase in sales in the Greater Russia market of 17%.

Gross profit declined 19% with margins declining 5.7 percentage points from 40.2% in 2000 to 34.5% in 2001. Excluding special charges to cost of goods sold in 2001 and 2000 of $156 million and $50 million, respectively, gross profit margins decreased 4.8 percentage points from 40.5% in 2000 to 35.7% in 2001. The decline in margin was driven primarily by lower prices across many of the Company's traditional and digital product groups within the Photography segment, a significant decline in the margin in the Health Imaging segment, which was caused by declining prices and mix, and the negative impact of exchange.

Selling, general and administrative expenses (SG&A) increased $113 million, or 4%, in 2001 as compared to 2000. The increase in SG&A expenses is primarily attributable to charges of $73 million that the Company recorded in 2001 relating to Kmart's bankruptcy, environmental issues and the write-off of certain strategic investments that were impaired.

Research and development (R&D) expenses remained flat, decreasing $5 million from $784 million in 2000 to $779 million in 2001.

Earnings from operations decreased $1,869 million from $2,214 million in 2000 to $345 million in 2001. The decrease in earnings from operations is partially attributable to charges taken in 2001 totaling $891 million primarily relating to restructuring and asset impairments, significant customer bankruptcies and environmental issues. The remaining decrease in earnings from operations is attributable to the decrease in sales and gross profit margin percentage for the reasons described above.

Net earnings decreased $1,331 million from $1,407 million in 2000 to $76 million in 2001. The decrease in net earnings is attributable to lower earnings from operations, as described above, the increase in interest expense due to higher average borrowings during 2001, and the decrease in other income (charges) due to lower gains on the sale of investments.

The actual tax rates for the years ended December 31, 2001 and December 31, 2000 were 30% and 34%, respectively. The decline in the Company's 2001 actual tax rate as compared with the 2000 actual tax rate is primarily attributable to an increase in creditable foreign taxes and an $11 million tax benefit related to favorable tax settlements reached in the third quarter, which were partially offset by restructuring costs recorded in the second, third and fourth quarters, which provided reduced tax benefits to the Company.

Photography Net worldwide sales for the Photography segment were $9,403 million for 2001 as compared with $10,231 million for 2000, representing a decrease of $828 million, or 8% as reported, or 6% excluding the negative impact of exchange. Photography net sales in the U.S. were $4,482 million for 2001 as compared with $4,960 million for 2000, representing a decrease of $478 million, or 10%. Photography net sales outside the U.S. were $4,921 million for 2001 as compared with $5,271 million for 2000, representing a decrease of $350 million, or 7% as reported, or 3% excluding the negative impact of exchange.

Net worldwide sales of consumer film products, which include traditional 35mm film, Advantix film and one-time-use cameras in both the traditional and APS formats, decreased 7% in 2001 relative to 2000, reflecting a 3% decline in volume and a 2% decline in both exchange and price/mix. The composition of consumer film products in 2001 as compared with 2000 reflects a 2% decrease in volumes for Advantix film, a 7% increase in volume of one-time-use cameras and a 4% decline in volume of traditional film product lines. Sales of the Company's consumer film products within the U.S. decreased, reflecting a 5% decline in volume in 2001 as compared with 2000. Sales of consumer film products outside the U.S. decreased 9% in 2001 as compared with 2000, reflecting a 2% decrease in volume, 3% decline in price/mix and 4% decline due to foreign exchange. During 2001, the Company continued the efforts it began in 1998 to shift consumers to the differentiated, higher value Max and Advantix film product lines. For 2001, sales of the Max and Advantix product lines as a percentage of total consumer roll film revenue increased from a level of 62% in the fourth quarter of 2000 to 68% by the fourth quarter of 2001. The U.S.

film industry volume was down slightly in 2001 relative to 2000; however, the Company maintained full-year U.S. consumer film market share for the fourth consecutive year. During 2001, the Company reached its highest worldwide consumer film market share position in the past nine years. The Company's traditional film business is developing in new markets, and management believes the business is strong. However, digital substitution is occurring and the Company continues its development and application of digital technology in such areas as wholesale and retail photofinishing. Digital substitution is occurring more quickly in Japan and more slowly in the U.S., Europe and China.

Net worldwide sales of origination and print film to the entertainment industry decreased 4% in 2001 as compared with 2000. Origination film sales decreased 12%, reflecting a 9% decline in volume and a 3% decline due to the negative impact of exchange. The decrease in origination film sales was partially offset by an increase in print film of 4%, reflecting a 9% increase in volume, offset by declines attributable to exchange and price of 3% and 2%, respectively. After several consecutive years of growth in origination film sales, this decrease reflects a slight downward trend beginning in the second half of 2001 due to continued economic weakness in the U.S., which caused a decrease in television advertising spend and the resulting decline in the production of television commercials. Additionally, the events of September 11th caused a number of motion picture film releases and television show productions to be delayed or postponed.

Net worldwide sales of professional film products, which include color negative, color reversal and black-and-white film, decreased 13% in 2001 as compared with 2000. The downward trend in the sale of professional film products existed throughout 2001 and is the result of ongoing digital capture substitution and continued economic weakness in a number of markets worldwide.

Net worldwide sales of consumer color paper decreased 11% in 2001 as compared with 2000, reflecting a 4% decline in both volume and price/mix and a 3% decline due to exchange. The downward trend in color paper sales existed throughout 2001 and is due to industry declines resulting from digital substitution, market trends toward on-site processing where there is a decreasing trend in double prints, and a reduction in mail-order processing where Kodak has a strong share position. Effective January 1, 2001, the Company and Mitsubishi Paper Mills Ltd. formed the business venture, Diamic Ltd., a consolidated sales subsidiary, which is expected to improve the Company's color paper market share in Japan. Net worldwide sales of sensitized professional paper decreased 2% in 2001 as compared with 2000, reflecting a 4% increase in volume, offset by a 4% decrease in price and a 2% decline attributable to exchange.

Net worldwide revenues from on-site and overnight photofinishing equipment, products and services decreased 16% in 2001 as compared with 2000. This downward trend, which existed throughout 2001, is the result of a significant reduction in the placement of on-site photofinishing equipment due to the saturation of the U.S. market and the market's anticipation of the availability of new digital minilabs. During the fourth quarter of 2001, the Company purchased two wholesale, overnight photofinishing businesses in Europe. The Company acquired Spector Photo Group's wholesale photofinishing and distribution activities in France, Germany and Austria, and ColourCare Limited's wholesale processing and printing operations in the U.K. The Company believes that these acquisitions will facilitate its strategy to enhance retail photofinishing activities, provide access to a broader base of customers, create new service efficiencies and provide consumers with technologically advanced digital imaging services.

Net worldwide sales of the Company's consumer digital cameras decreased 3% in 2001 as compared with 2000, reflecting volume growth of 35% offset by declining prices and a 2% decrease due to negative exchange impact. The significant volume growth over the 2000 levels was driven by strong market acceptance of the new consumer EasyShare digital camera system, competitive pricing initiatives, and a shift in the go-to-market strategy to mass-market distribution channels. These factors have moved the Company into the number two consumer market share position in the U.S., up from the number three position as of the end of 2000. Net worldwide sales of professional digital cameras decreased 12% in 2001 as compared with 2000, primarily attributable to a 20% decline in volume.

Net worldwide sales of the Company's inkjet photo paper increased 55% in 2001 as compared with 2000, reflecting volume growth of 42% and increased prices. The inkjet photo paper demonstrated double-digit growth year-over-year throughout 2001, reflecting the Company's increased promotional activity at key retail accounts, improved merchandising and broader channel distribution of the entire line of inkjet paper within the product group. Net worldwide sales of professional thermal paper remained flat, reflecting an 8% increase in volume offset by declines attributable to price and negative exchange impact of 7% and 1%, respectively.

The Company continued its strong focus on the consumer imaging digital products and services, which include the picture maker kiosks and related media and consumer digital services revenue from picture CD, "You've Got Pictures" and Retailer.com. Combined revenues from the placement of picture maker kiosks and the related media decreased 2% in 2001 as compared with 2000, reflecting a decline in the volume of new kiosk placements partially offset by a 15% increase in kiosk media volume. This trend in increased media usage reflects the Company's focus on creating new sales channels and increasing the media burn per kiosk. Revenue from consumer digital services increased 15% in 2001 as compared with 2000. In addition, the Company experienced an increase in digital penetration in its Qualex wholesale labs. The principal products which contributed to this increase were picture CD and Retail.com. The average digital penetration rate for the number of rolls processed increased each quarter during 2001 up to a rate of 6.7% in the fourth quarter, reflecting a 49% increase over the fourth quarter of 2000. In certain major retail accounts, the digital penetration reached levels of up to 15%.

During the second quarter of 2001, the Company purchased Ofoto, Inc. The Company believes that Ofoto will solidify the Company's leading position in online imaging products and services. Since the acquisition, Ofoto has demonstrated strong order growth, with the average order size increasing by 31% over the 2000 level. In addition, the Ofoto customer base reflected growth of approximately 12% per month throughout 2001.

The gross profit margin for the Photography segment was 36.2% in 2001 as compared with 40.1% in 2000. The 3.9 percentage point decrease in gross margin for the Photography segment was primarily attributable to continued lower effective selling prices across virtually all product groups, including the Company's core products of traditional film, paper, and digital cameras, unfavorable exchange and flat distribution costs on a lower sales base.

SG&A expenses remained flat, decreasing 1% in 2001 as compared with 2000. As a percentage of sales, SG&A increased from 19.3% in 2000 to 20.9% in 2001. SG&A, excluding advertising, increased 4%, representing 14.6% of sales in 2001 and 12.9% of sales in 2000. R&D expenses decreased 6% in 2001 as compared with 2000. As a percentage of sales, R&D increased slightly from 5.6% in 2000 to 5.8% in 2001.

Earnings from operations decreased $643 million, or 45%, from $1,430 million in 2000 to $787 million in 2001, reflecting the lower sales and gross profit levels described above. Net earnings decreased $499 million, or 48%, from $1,034 million in 2000 to $535 million in 2001 due primarily to lower earnings from operations.

Health Imaging Net worldwide sales for the Health Imaging segment were $2,262 million for 2001 as compared with $2,220 million for 2000, representing an increase of $42 million, or 2% as reported, or a 4% increase excluding the negative impact of exchange. Net sales in the U.S. were $1,089 million for 2001 as compared with $1,067 million for 2000, representing an increase of $22 million or 2%, while net sales outside the U.S. were $1,173 million for 2001 as compared with $1,153 million for 2000, representing an increase of $20 million, or 2% as reported, or 6% excluding the negative impact of exchange. Sales in emerging markets increased slightly, up 4% from 2000 to 2001.

Net sales of digital products, which include laser imagers (DryView imagers and wet laser printers), digital media (DryView and wet laser media), digital capture equipment (computed radiography capture equipment and direct radiography equipment) and picture archiving and communications systems (PACS), increased 11% in 2001 as compared with 2000. The increase in digital sales was principally the result of a 184% increase in digital capture revenues resulting from a 201% increase in volume, partially offset by declines attributable to price and foreign exchange. Laser imaging equipment, services and film also contributed to the increase in digital sales, as sales in these combined categories increased 3% in 2001 as compared with 2000. The 3% increase in these product groups was the result of increases in DryView laser imagers and media of 8% and 33%, respectively, which were partially offset by the expected decreases in wet laser printers and media of 8% and 29%, respectively, in 2001 as compared with 2000. Sales of PACS increased 9% in 2001 as compared with 2000, reflecting a 16% increase in volume, partially offset by declines attributable to price and foreign exchange of 4% and 3%, respectively.

Sales of traditional medical products, which include analog film, equipment, chemistry and services, decreased 7% in 2001 as compared with 2000. This decline was primarily attributable to a 12% decrease in non-specialty medical sales. The decrease in these sales was partially offset by an increase in specialty Mammography and Oncology sales, which increased 4%, reflecting a 12% increase in volume, offset by declines attributable to price/mix and foreign exchange of 6% and 2%, respectively. Additionally, Dental sales increased 3% in 2001 as compared with 2000, reflecting a 5% increase in volume, which was partially offset by declines of 1% attributable to both price/mix and foreign exchange.

The gross profit margin for the Health Imaging segment was 38.4% in 2001 as compared with 46.6% in 2000. The 8.2 percentage point decrease in gross margin is primarily attributable to selling price declines in 2001, driven by the continued conversion of customers to lower pricing levels under the Company's Novation Group Purchasing Organization contracts and a larger product mix shift from higher margin traditional analog film toward lower margin digital capture and printing equipment. Additionally, in 2001 as compared with 2000, the Company incurred higher service costs due to an increase in volume of new digital capture equipment and systems placements, compounded by short-term start-up reliability issues with the new equipment.

SG&A expenses increased 4% in 2001 as compared with 2000. As a percentage of sales, SG&A increased from 15.8% in 2000 to 16.2% in 2001. R&D expenses increased 10% in 2001 as compared with 2000. As a percentage of sales, R&D increased from 6.2% in 2000 to 6.7% in 2001.

Earnings from operations decreased $195 million, or 38%, from $518 million in 2000 to $323 million in 2001, which is attributable to the decrease in the gross profit percentage in 2001 as compared with 2000, as described above. Net earnings decreased $135 million, or 38%, from $356 million in 2000 to $221 million in 2001 due to lower earnings from operations as described above.

Commercial Imaging Net worldwide sales for the Commercial Imaging segment were $1,459 million for 2001 as compared with $1,417 million for 2000, representing an increase of $42 million, or 3% as reported, or 5% excluding the negative impact of exchange. Net sales in the U.S.

were $820 million for 2001 as compared with $715 million for 2000, representing an increase of $105 million, or 15%. Net sales outside the U.S. were $639 million for 2001 as compared with $702 million for 2000, representing a decrease of $63 million, or 9% as reported, or 4% excluding the negative impact of exchange.

Net worldwide sales of document imaging equipment, products and services increased 8% in 2001 as compared with 2000. The increase in sales was primarily attributable to an increase in service revenue due to the acquisition of the Bell & Howell Imaging business in the first quarter of 2001. With the acquisition of the Bell & Howell Imaging business, the Company continues to secure new exclusive third-party maintenance agreements. The increase in revenue was also due to strong demand for the Company's iNnovation series scanners, specifically the new i800 series high-volume document scanner.

Net worldwide sales of the Company's commercial and government products and services increased 16% in 2001 as compared with 2000. The increase in sales was principally due to an increase in revenues from government products and services under its government contracts.

Net worldwide sales for wide-format inkjet products were a contributor to the net increase in Commercial Imaging sales as these revenues increased 9% in 2001 as compared with 2000, reflecting year-over-year sales increases throughout 2001. The Company continues to focus on initiatives to grow this business as reflected in the worldwide launch of the 5260 wide-format inkjet printer in the fourth quarter of 2001 and the acquisition of ENCAD, Inc. in January of 2002. Given ENCAD's strong distribution position in this industry, the acquisition of ENCAD is expected to provide the Company with a strong channel to the wide-format inkjet printer market, which Kodak had not previously served.

Net worldwide sales of graphic arts products to Kodak Polychrome Graphics (KPG), an unconsolidated joint venture affiliate in which the Company has a 50% ownership interest, decreased 15% in 2001 as compared with 2000. The largest contributor to this decline in sales was graphics film, which experienced a 20% decrease, reflecting a 19% decrease in volume and small declines attributable to price/mix and foreign exchange. The decrease in sales to KPG is attributable to continued technology substitution and economic weakness. During 2001, KPG continued to implement the operational improvements it began in 2000, which returned the joint venture to profitability in the first quarter and throughout 2001. In the fourth quarter of 2001, KPG completed its acquisition of Imation's color proofing and software business. The Company believes that Imation's portfolio of products will complement and expand KPG's offerings in the marketplace, which should drive sell-through of Kodak's graphics products. The Company is the exclusive provider of graphic arts products to KPG.

Net worldwide sales of products to NexPress, an unconsolidated joint venture affiliate in which the Company has a 50% ownership interest, decreased in 2001 as compared with 2000, reflecting a 15% decrease in volume and declines in price/mix. In September 2001, the joint venture achieved its key milestone in launching the NexPress 2100 printer product at the Print '01 trade show. There is strong customer demand for the new printer, which the Company believes should drive increased sell-through of Kodak's products through the joint venture.

The gross profit margin for the Commercial Imaging segment was 30.7% in 2001 as compared with 33.4% in 2000. The 2.7 percentage point decrease in gross margin is primarily attributable to lower selling prices in a number of product groups within the segment.

SG&A expenses increased 19% in 2001 as compared with 2000. As a percentage of sales, SG&A increased from 12.4% in 2000 to 14.4% in 2001. R&D expenses decreased 5%. As a percentage of sales, R&D decreased from 4.3% in 2000 to 4.0% in 2001.

Earnings from operations decreased $68 million, or 29%, from $233 million in 2000 to $165 million in 2001, which is attributable to the decrease in the gross profit percentage and an increase in SG&A expenses in 2001 as compared with 2000, as described above. Net earnings decreased $10 million, or 11%, from $90 million in 2000 to $80 million in 2001. Net earnings include positive earnings from the Company's equity in the income of KPG.

All Other Net worldwide sales of businesses comprising All Other were $110 million for 2001 as compared with $126 million for 2000, representing a decrease of $16 million, or 13% as reported, with no impact from exchange. Net sales in the U.S. were flat at $68 million for both 2001 and 2000, while net sales outside the U.S. were $42 million for 2001 as compared with $58 million for 2000, representing a decrease of $16 million, or 28% as reported, or 30% excluding the impact of exchange.

The decrease in worldwide net sales was primarily attributable to a decrease in optics revenues of 39% and a decrease in revenues due to the divestment of the Eastman Software business in 2000. These decreases were partially offset by a 10% increase in the sale of sensors.

In December 2001, the Company and SANYO announced the formation of a business venture, SK Display Corporation, to manufacture and sell active matrix organic light emitting diode (OLED) displays for consumer devices. Kodak will have a 34% ownership interest in this venture. For 2001, there were no sales relating to this business. In the future, the Company will derive revenue through royalty income and sales of raw materials and finished displays.

Earnings from operations decreased $49 million from a loss of $11 million in 2000 to a loss of $60 million in 2001. The increase in the loss is attributable to increased costs incurred for the continued development of the OLED technology, the establishment of the SK Display business venture and costs incurred to grow the existing optics and sensor businesses.

Restructuring Costs and Other

The following table summarizes the activity with respect to the restructuring charges and reversals recorded in 2001, 2000 and 1999 and the remaining balance in the related restructuring and asset impairment reserves at December 31, 2001:

(in millions)

	Number of Employees	Severance Reserve	Inventory Reserve	Long-term Assets Reserve	Exit Costs Reserve	Total
1999 charges	3,400	$ 250	$ –	$ 90	$ 10	$ 350
1999 utilization	(400)	(21)	–	(90)	–	(111)
Ending balance at December 31, 1999	3,000	229	–	–	10	239
2000 reversal	(500)	(44)	–	–	–	(44)
2000 utilization	(2,500)	(185)	–	–	(10)	(195)
Ending balance at December 31, 2000	–	–	–	–	–	–
2001 charges	7,200	351	84	215	48	698
2001 reversal	(275)	(20)	–	–	–	(20)
2001 utilization	(2,700)	(56)	(84)	(215)	(5)	(360)
Ending balance at December 31, 2001	4,225	$ 275	$ –	$ –	$ 43	$ 318

2001 Restructuring Programs and Other

During 2001, the Company recorded a total charge for its two separate restructuring programs, the first of which was implemented in the second and third quarters of 2001 and the second of which was implemented in the fourth quarter of 2001, of $698 million, primarily for the rationalization of the U.S. photofinishing operations, the elimination of excess manufacturing capacity, the exit of certain operations and reductions in research and development positions and selling, general and administrative positions worldwide. The total restructuring amount of $698 million was comprised of charges for severance, long-term assets, inventory, and exit costs of $351 million, $215 million, $84 million, and $48 million, respectively. Additionally, during 2001, the Company recorded asset impairments relating to the Wolf Camera bankruptcy, its photofinishing operations, relocation costs in connection with a closed manufacturing site and investments in strategic and non-strategic ventures (See Note 6) of $77 million, $42 million, $18 million and $15 million, respectively.

Approximately $351 million of the charges of $698 million was for employee severance covering 7,200 worldwide positions. The geographic breakdown includes approximately 4,300 employees in the U.S. and Canada and 2,900 throughout the rest of the world. The 7,200 personnel were associated with the realignment of manufacturing (2,450), service and photofinishing operations (1,950), R&D (425) and administrative (2,375) functions in various locations of the Company's worldwide operations. Approximately 2,700 positions were eliminated by the end of 2001, with the majority of the remaining positions to be eliminated during the early part of 2002. In the fourth quarter of 2001, the Company reversed $20 million of the second quarter severance charge as certain severance actions, primarily in the European, African and Middle Eastern Region (EAMER) and Japan, will be completed at a total cost less than originally estimated. This is the result of a lower actual severance cost per employee as compared with the original amounts estimated.
In addition, approximately 275 (150 service and photofinishing, 100 administrative and 25 R&D) fewer employees will be separated. The original severance accrual of $351 million and the $20 million reversal were included in restructuring costs and other.

The Company included $119 million of the $698 million provision in cost of goods sold, representing an $84 million inventory write-down associated with product line discontinuances and $35 million related to accelerated depreciation on assets presently used in operations which were disposed of during the latter part of 2001 or will be disposed of through abandonment within the first three months of 2002.

Also included in restructuring costs and other were write-offs and costs associated with the Company's exit from non-strategic operations and investments, consisting of $180 million for the write-off of capital assets, goodwill and investments, and $48 million for exit costs. The exit costs consist principally of lease termination expenses, shutdown costs and vendor penalty payments, which have been accrued on an undiscounted basis.

Restructuring actions related to the Photography, Health and Commercial segments amounted to $360 million, $43 million and

$21 million, respectively. The remaining $254 million were for actions associated with the manufacturing, research and development, and selling and administrative functions shared across all the segments.

The Company realized savings of approximately $50 million from these programs in 2001. Total savings in 2002 are estimated to be $450 million from these programs. The net cash cost of these programs will be recovered by the end of 2002. All actions under these programs will be completed by the end of 2002.

In 2001, the Company recorded a $77 million charge associated with the bankruptcy of the Wolf Camera Inc. consumer retail business. This amount is reflected in restructuring costs and other.

During 2001, the Company recorded a $42 million charge representing the write-off of certain lease residuals, receivables and capital assets resulting primarily from technology changes in the transition from optical to digital photofinishing equipment within the Company's onsite photofinishing operations. The charges for the lease residuals and capital assets totaling $19 million have been included in cost of goods sold. The remaining $23 million has been included in restructuring costs and other.

Outlook

The Company expects 2002 to be another difficult economic year, with full year revenues level with 2001 and some earnings improvement in the second half of 2002. We do not expect to see any real upturn in the economy until 2003, with a very gradual return to consumer spending habits and behavior that will positively affect our business growth. The Company will continue to take actions to minimize the financial impact of this slowdown. These actions include efforts to better manage production and inventory levels and reduce capital spending, while at the same time reducing discretionary spending to further hold down costs. The Company will also complete the implementation of the restructuring programs announced in 2001 to make its operations more cost competitive and improve margins, particularly in its health imaging and consumer digital camera businesses.

During 2000, the Company completed an ongoing program of real estate divestitures and portfolio rationalization that contributed to other income (charges) reaching an annual average of $100 million over the past three years. Now that this program is largely complete, the other income (charges) category is expected to run in the negative $50 million to negative $100 million range annually.

The Company expects its effective tax rate to approximate 29% in 2002. The lower rate is attributable to favorable tax benefits from the elimination of goodwill amortization and expected increased earnings from operations in certain lower-taxed jurisdictions outside the U.S.

From a liquidity and capital resource perspective, the Company expects to generate $6 billion in cash flow after dividends during the next six years, with approximately $400 million of this being achieved in 2002. This will enable the Company to maintain its dividend, pay down debt and make acquisitions that promote profitable growth. Cash flow is defined as net cash flows (after dividends), excluding the impacts from debt and transactions in the Company's own equity, such as stock repurchases and proceeds from the exercise of stock options.

The Euro

The Treaty on European Union provided that an economic and monetary union (EMU) be established in Europe whereby a single European currency, the Euro, replaces the currencies of participating member states. The Euro was introduced on January 1, 1999, at which time the value of participating member state currencies was irrevocably fixed against the Euro and the European Currency Unit (ECU) was replaced at the rate of one Euro to one ECU. For the three-year transitional period ending December 31, 2001, the national currencies of member states continued to circulate, but as sub-units of the Euro. New public debt was issued in Euros and existing debt was redenominated into Euros. At the end of the transitional period, Euro banknotes and coins were issued, and the national currencies of the member states will cease to be legal tender no later than June 30, 2002. The countries that adopted the Euro on January 1, 1999 were Austria, Belgium, Finland, France, Germany, Ireland, Italy, Luxembourg, The Netherlands, Portugal, and Spain. Greece was part of the transition. The Company has operations in all of these countries.

As a result of the Euro conversion, it is possible that selling prices of the Company's products and services will experience downward pressure, as current price variations among countries are reduced due to easy comparability of Euro prices across countries. Prices will tend to harmonize, although value-added taxes and transportation costs will still justify price differentials. Adoption of the Euro will probably accelerate existing market and pricing trends including pan-European buying and general price erosion.

On the other hand, currency exchange and hedging costs will be reduced; lower prices and pan-European buying will benefit the Company in its purchasing endeavors; the number of banks and suppliers needed will be reduced; there will be less variation in payment terms; and it will be easier for the Company to expand into new marketing channels such as mail-order and Internet marketing.

The Company made changes in areas such as marketing and pricing, purchasing, contracts, payroll, taxes, cash management and treasury operations. Under the "no compulsion no prohibition" rules, billing systems were modified so that the Company is able to show total gross, value-added tax, and net in Euros on national currency invoices. This enables customers to pay in the new Euro currency if they wish to do so. Countries that have installed ERP/SAP software in connection with the Company's enterprise resource planning project are able to invoice and receive payments in Euros as well as in other currencies. Systems for pricing, payroll and expense reimbursements continued to use national currencies until year-end 2001. The functional currencies in the affected countries were the national currencies until May 2001 (except Germany and Austria (October 2001)), when they changed to the Euro. Systems changes for countries not on SAP (Finland and Greece) were implemented in 2001.

Liquidity and Capital Resources

2001 Net cash provided by operating activities in 2001 was $2,065 million, as net earnings of $76 million, adjusted for depreciation and amortization, and restructuring costs, asset impairments and other charges provided $1,825 million of operating cash. Also contributing to operating cash was a decrease in receivables of $252 million and a decrease in inventories of $461 million. This was partially offset by decreases in liabilities, excluding borrowings, of $529 million related primarily to severance payments for restructuring programs and reductions in accounts payable and accrued benefit costs. Net cash used in investing activities of $1,047 million in 2001 was utilized primarily for capital expenditures of $743 million and business acquisitions of $306 million. Net cash used in financing activities of $808 million in 2001 was primarily the result of stock repurchases and dividend payments as discussed below.

The Company declared cash dividends per share of $.44 in each of the first three quarters and $.89 in the fourth quarter of 2001. Total cash dividends of $643 million were paid in 2001. In October 2001, the Company's Board of Directors approved a change in dividend policy from quarterly dividend payments to semi-annual dividend payments. Dividends, when declared, will be paid on the 10th business day of July and December to shareholders of record on the first business day of the preceding month. These payment dates serve to better align the dividend disbursements with the seasonal cash flow pattern of the business, which is more concentrated in the second half of the year. This action resulted in the Company making five dividend payments in 2001.

Net working capital, excluding short-term borrowings and the current portion of long-term debt, decreased to $863 million from $1,482 million at year-end 2000. This decrease is mainly attributable to lower receivable and inventory balances, as discussed above.

Capital additions, excluding equipment purchased for lease, were $680 million in 2001, with the majority of the spending supporting new products, manufacturing productivity and quality improvements, infrastructure improvements, ongoing environmental and safety initiatives, and renovations due to relocations associated with restructuring actions taken in 1999. In 2002, the Company expects to reduce its capital spending, excluding acquisitions and equipment purchased for lease, to a range of $550 million to $600 million. Capital additions by segment are included in Note 21.

Under the $4 billion stock repurchase program announced on April 15, 1999 and December 7, 2000, the Company repurchased $44 million of its shares in 2001. As of March 2, 2001, the Company suspended the stock repurchase program in a move designed to accelerate debt reduction and increase financial flexibility. At the time of the suspension of the program, the Company had repurchased approximately $1.8 billion of its shares under this program.

The Company anticipates the net cash cost of the restructuring charge recorded in 2001 to be approximately $182 million after tax, which will be recovered through cost savings in less than two years. A majority of the severance-related actions associated with this charge are expected to be completed in the early part of 2002.

The Company currently expects to fund expenditures for capital requirements, dividend payments and liquidity needs from cash generated from operations. Cash balances and financing arrangements will be used to bridge timing differences between expenditures and cash generated from operations. The Company has $2.45 billion in revolving credit facilities established in 2001, which are available to support the Company's commercial paper program and for general corporate purposes. The credit agreements are comprised of a 364-day commitment at $1.225 billion expiring in July 2002 and a 5-year commitment at $1.225 billion expiring in July 2006. If unused, they have a commitment fee of $3 million per year, at the Company's current credit rating. Interest on amounts borrowed under these facilities is calculated at rates based on spreads above certain reference rates and the Company's credit rating.

At December 31, 2001, the Company had $1.1 billion in commercial paper outstanding, with a weighted average interest rate of 3.6%. In addition, the Company had short-term borrowings, excluding the current portion of long-term debt, of $238 million at December 31, 2001, with a weighted average interest rate of 6.2%.

During the second quarter of 2001, the Company increased its medium-term note program from $1.0 billion to $2.2 billion for issuance of debt securities due nine months or more from date of issue. At December 31, 2001, the Company had debt securities outstanding of $850 million under this medium-term note program, with $150 million of this balance due within one year. The Company has $1.35 billion available under its medium-term note program for the issuance of new notes. Total long-term debt at December 31, 2001, including these amounts, was as follows:

Description and Interest Rates of 2001 Borrowings	Maturity Dates of 2001 Borrowings	2001	2000
Notes:			
3.74%	2003	$ 10	$ -
6.38% - 8.25%	2002 - 2006	959	473
9.20% - 9.95%	2003 - 2021	191	191
Debentures:			
1.11% - 3.16%	2003 - 2004	42	61
Other:			
2.42%	2004	190	-
5.94% - 6.66%	2002 - 2010	430	591
		$ 1,822	$ 1,316

During the fourth quarter of 2001, the Company's credit ratings were lowered by Standard & Poor's and Moody's to A- and A3 for long-term debt and A2 and P2 for short-term debt, respectively. These actions were due to lower earnings as a result of the economic slowdown, industry factors and other world events. The lower credit ratings caused the Company to experience slightly higher interest rates, although the relative cost of borrowing was very low on a comparative basis.

The Company is in compliance with all covenants or other requirements set forth in its credit agreements or indentures. Further, the Company does not have any rating downgrade triggers that would accelerate the maturity dates of its debt, with the exception of a $110 million note due in 2003 that can be accelerated if the Company's rating falls below BBB. However, further downgrades in the Company's credit rating or disruptions in the capital markets could adversely impact borrowing costs and the nature of its funding alternatives. The Company has access to $2.45 billion in bank revolving credit facilities to meet unanticipated funding needs should it be necessary.

The Company guarantees debt and other obligations under agreements with certain affiliated companies and customers. At December 31, 2001, these guarantees totaled approximately $277 million. Within the total amount of $277 million, the Company is guaranteeing debt in the amount of $175 million for Kodak Polychrome Graphics, an unconsolidated affiliate in which the Company has a 50% ownership interest. The balance of the amount is principally comprised of other loan guarantees and guarantees of customer amounts due to banks in connection with various banks' financing of customers' purchase of equipment and products from Kodak. These guarantees would require payment from Kodak only in the event of default on payment by the respective debtor. Management believes the likelihood is remote that material payments will be required under these guarantees.

In connection with the formation of the SK Display Corporation with SANYO Electric Co., Ltd., the Company will contribute approximately $119 million, comprised of $19 million in cash and $100 million in loan guarantees during 2002 and 2003.

Qualex, a wholly-owned subsidiary of Kodak, has a 50% ownership interest in Express Stop Financing (ESF), which is a joint venture partnership between Qualex and Dana Credit Corporation (DCC), a wholly-owned subsidiary of Dana Corporation. Qualex accounts for its investment in ESF under the equity method of accounting. ESF provides a long-term financing solution to Qualex's photofinishing customers in connection with Qualex's leasing of photofinishing equipment to third parties, as opposed to Qualex extending long-term credit. As part of the operations of its photofinishing business, Qualex sells equipment under a sales-type lease arrangement and records a long-term receivable. These long-term receivables are subsequently sold to ESF without recourse to Qualex. ESF incurs long-term debt to finance a portion of the purchase of the receivables from Qualex. This debt is collateralized solely by the long-term receivables purchased from Qualex and, in part, by a $60 million guarantee from DCC. Qualex provides no guarantee or collateral to ESF's creditors in connection with the debt, and ESF's debt is non-recourse to Qualex. Qualex's only continued involvement in connection with the sale of the long-term receivables is the servicing of the related equipment under the leases. Qualex has continued revenue streams in connection with this equipment through future sales of photofinishing consumables, including paper and chemicals, and maintenance.

Qualex has risk with respect to the ESF arrangement as it relates to its continued ability to procure spare parts from the primary photofinishing equipment vendor to fulfill its servicing obligations under the leases. The primary photofinishing equipment vendor is currently experiencing financial difficulty, which raises concern about Qualex's ability to procure the required service parts. Although the lessees' requirement to pay ESF under the lease agreements is not contingent upon Qualex's fulfillment of its servicing obligations under the leases, under the agreement with ESF, Qualex would be responsible for any deficiency in the amount of rent not paid to ESF as a result of any lessee's claim regarding maintenance or supply services not provided by Qualex. Such lease payments would be made in accordance with the original lease terms, which generally extend over 5 to 7 years. ESF's outstanding lease receivable amount was approximately $570 million at December 31, 2001. To mitigate the risk of not being able to fulfill its service obligations, Qualex has built up its inventory of these spare parts and has begun refurbishing used parts. Additionally, Qualex has entered into spare parts escrow agreements under which bills of materials, parts drawings, intellectual property and other information necessary to manufacture the parts were put into escrow arrangements. In the event that the primary photofinishing equipment vendor were unable to supply the necessary parts to Qualex, Qualex would gain access to the information in the escrow arrangements to either manufacture or have manufactured the parts necessary to fulfill its servicing obligations. Management is currently negotiating alternatives with the photofinishing equipment vendor to further mitigate the above risks.

In December 2001, Standard & Poor's downgraded the credit ratings of Dana Corporation to BB for long-term debt and B for short-term debt, which are below investment grade. This action created a Guarantor Termination Event under the Receivables Purchase Agreement (RPA) that ESF has with its banks under the RPA. To cure the Guarantor Termination Event, in January 2002, ESF posted $60 million of additional collateral in the form of cash and long-term lease receivables. At that time, if Dana Corporation were downgraded to below BB by Standard & Poor's or below Ba2 by Moody's, that action would constitute a Termination Event under the RPA and ESF would be forced to renegotiate its debt arrangements with the banks. On February 22, 2002, Moody's downgraded Dana Corporation to a Ba3 credit rating, thus creating a Termination Event.

Under the Termination Event, the banks can require ESF to put up an additional 6% collateral against the debt (on a debt balance of approximately $405 million at the time of filing the annual report, the additional collateral would be approximately $24 million), the interest rate on the debt could be increased 2 percentage points and Qualex could be precluded from selling any new receivables to ESF until the Termination Event has been waived by the banks. ESF does not currently have the ability to put up the additional collateral and, therefore, ESF would require additional capital infusions by DCC and Qualex. If DCC and/or Qualex do not provide the additional capital funding to ESF, the banks could accelerate the debt and force ESF to liquidate its long-term lease receivables to service the debt. Management believes that it is unlikely that the banks would accelerate the debt, and force ESF to sell the receivables to a third party to generate cash to satisfy the debt, due to the high-quality nature of the underlying long-term receivable portfolio. Furthermore, under this scenario, the banks would not have any recourse against Qualex; rather, the impact on Qualex would be limited to the need to find an alternative source of financing for future photofinishing equipment placements. Additionally, under this scenario, it is not expected that the operations of the customers who are leasing the equipment under these long-term lease arrangements would be affected such that Qualex's revenue stream for future sales of photofinishing consumables would be jeopardized. ESF is beginning negotiations with the banks to resolve the Termination Event.

The current RPA arrangement expires on July 23, 2002, at which time the RPA can be extended or terminated. If the RPA is terminated, Qualex will no longer be able to sell its lease receivables to ESF and will need to find an alternative financing solution for future sales of its photofinishing equipment. Under the partnership agreement between Qualex and DCC, subject to certain conditions, ESF has exclusivity rights to purchase Qualex's long-term lease receivables. The term of the partnership agreement continues through October 6, 2003. In light of the Termination Event referred to above and the timing of the partnership termination, Qualex is currently considering alternative financing solutions for prospective leasing activity with its customers.

At December 31, 2001, the Company had outstanding letters of credit totaling $42 million and surety bonds in the amount of $94 million to ensure the completion of environmental remediations and payment of possible casualty and workers' compensation claims. See Note 10 for other commitments of the Company.

New Accounting Pronouncements

In June 2001, the Financial Accounting Standards Board (FASB or the Board) issued Statement of Financial Accounting Standards (SFAS) No. 141, "Business Combinations," and SFAS No. 142, "Goodwill and Other Intangible Assets," collectively referred to as the "Standards," which are effective for the Company as of January 1, 2002, except as noted below. SFAS No. 141 supercedes Accounting Principles Board Opinion (APB) No. 16, "Business Combinations." The provisions of SFAS No. 141 (1) require that the purchase method of accounting be used for all business combinations initiated after June 30, 2001, (2) provide specific criteria for the initial recognition and measurement of intangible assets apart from goodwill, and (3) require that unamortized negative goodwill be written off immediately as an extraordinary gain instead of being deferred and amortized. SFAS No. 141 also requires that, upon adoption of SFAS No. 142, the Company reclassify the carrying amounts of certain intangible assets into or out of goodwill, based on certain criteria. SFAS No. 142 supercedes APB No. 17, "Intangible Assets," and is effective for fiscal years beginning after December 15, 2001. SFAS No. 142 primarily addresses the accounting for goodwill and intangible assets subsequent to their initial recognition. The provisions of SFAS No. 142 (1) prohibit the amortization of goodwill and indefinite-lived intangible assets, (2) require that goodwill and indefinite-lived intangible assets be tested annually for impairment (and in interim periods if certain events occur indicating that the carrying value of goodwill and/or indefinite-lived intangible assets may be impaired), (3) require that reporting units be identified for the purpose of assessing potential future impairments of goodwill, and (4) remove the forty-year limitation on the amortization period of intangible assets that have finite lives.

The Company will adopt the provisions of SFAS No. 142 in its first quarter ended March 31, 2002. The Company is in the process of preparing for its adoption of SFAS No. 142 and is making the determinations as to its reporting units and the amounts of goodwill, intangible assets, other assets, and liabilities allocated to those reporting units. The Company will no longer record annual amortization relating to its existing goodwill ($154 million for 2002, $131 million after tax). The Company is evaluating the useful lives assigned to its intangible assets and does not anticipate any material changes to such useful lives.

SFAS No. 142 requires that goodwill be tested annually for impairment using a two-step process. The first step of the goodwill impairment test is to test for a potential impairment. The second step of the goodwill impairment test is to measure the amount of the impairment loss. The Company expects to complete steps one and two of the goodwill impairment test during the first quarter of 2002. The Company does not believe that the results of these impairment test steps will have a material impact on the Company's consolidated financial statements.

In August 2001, the FASB issued SFAS No. 144, "Accounting for the Impairment or Disposal of Long-Lived Assets." SFAS No. 144 addresses financial accounting and reporting for the impairment or disposal of long-lived assets to be held and used, to be disposed of other than by sale and to be disposed of by sale. Although the Statement retains certain of the provisions of SFAS No. 121, "Accounting for the Impairment of Long-Lived Assets and for Long-Lived Assets to Be Disposed Of," it supercedes SFAS No. 121 and APB Opinion No. 30, "Reporting the Results of Operations–Reporting the Effects of Disposal of a Segment of a Business, and Extraordinary, Unusual and Infrequently Occurring Events and Transactions," for the disposal of a segment of a business. SFAS No. 144 also amends Accounting Research Bulletin (ARB) No. 51, "Consolidated Financial Statements," to eliminate the exception to consolidation for a subsidiary for which control is likely to be temporary. The Statement is effective for financial statements issued for fiscal years beginning after December 15, 2001 and interim periods within those fiscal years, and will thus be adopted by the Company, as required, on January 1, 2002. The adoption of SFAS No. 144 is not expected to have a material impact on the Company's consolidated financial statements.

The Emerging Issues Task Force (EITF) has issued EITF Issue No. 01-09, "Accounting for Consideration Given by a Vendor to a Customer (Including a Reseller of the Vendor's Products)." The EITF provides guidance with respect to the statement of earnings classification of and the accounting for recognition and measurement of consideration given by a vendor to a customer, which includes sales incentive offers labeled as discounts, coupons, rebates and free product or services as well as arrangements labeled as slotting fees, cooperative advertising and buydowns. The guidance with respect to the appropriate statement of earnings classification of the consideration given by a vendor to a customer is effective for annual and interim periods beginning after December 15, 2001. Upon adoption, financial statements for prior periods presented for comparative purposes should be reclassified to comply with the requirements under the EITF.

The guidance with respect to the accounting for recognition and measurement of consideration given by a vendor to a customer is effective for annual and interim periods beginning after December 15, 2001. The impact on the statement of earnings resulting from the adoption of the EITF should be reported as a cumulative effect of a change in accounting principle or applied prospectively to new sales incentives offered on or after the effective date. The impact of the guidance under EITF 01-09 on the Company's financial statements has not yet been determined.

Other

Cash expenditures for pollution prevention and waste treatment for the Company's current manufacturing facilities were as follows:

(in millions)	2001	2000	1999
Recurring costs for pollution prevention and waste treatment	$ 68	$ 72	$ 69
Capital expenditures for pollution prevention and waste treatment	27	36	20
Site remediation costs	2	3	5
Total	$ 97	$ 111	$ 94

At December 31, 2001 and 2000, the Company's undiscounted accrued liabilities for environmental remediation costs amounted to $162 million and $113 million, respectively. These amounts are reported in other long-term liabilities.

The Company is currently implementing a Corrective Action Program required by the Resource Conservation and Recovery Act (RCRA) at the Kodak Park site in Rochester, NY. As part of this Program, the Company has completed the RCRA Facility Assessment (RFA), a broad-based environmental investigation of the site. The Company is currently in the process of completing, and in some cases has completed, RCRA Facility Investigations (RFIs) and Corrective Measures Studies (CMS) for areas at the site. At December 31, 2001, estimated future remediation costs of $70 million are accrued on an undiscounted basis by the Company and are included in the environmental accruals reported in other long-term liabilities.

Additionally, the Company has retained certain obligations for environmental remediation and Superfund matters related to certain sites associated with the non-imaging health businesses sold in 1994. In addition, the Company has been identified as a potentially responsible party (PRP) in connection with the non-imaging health businesses in five active Superfund sites. At December 31, 2001, estimated future remediation costs of $51 million are accrued on an undiscounted basis by the Company and are included in the environmental accruals reported in other long-term liabilities.

The Company recorded a $41 million charge in the fourth quarter of 2001 for additional environmental reserves. This amount has been included in selling, general and administrative expenses. Approximately $34 million has been provided for two former manufacturing sites located outside the United States. Investigations were completed by an external environmental consultant in the fourth quarter of 2001, which facilitated the completion of cost estimates for the future remediation and monitoring of these sites. In addition, the accrual incorporates the Company's estimate of its cost to repurchase one of the sites and demolish the buildings in preparation for its possible conversion to a public park. The establishment of these accruals is consistent with Kodak's policy to record accruals for environmental remediation obligations generally no later than the completion of feasibility studies. The additional $7 million recorded during the fourth quarter 2001 represents the estimated increased costs associated with the site remediation of the non-imaging health businesses sold in 1994 discussed above ($4 million) and increases in estimated costs ($3 million) associated with the remediation of other facilities which are not material to the Company's financial position, results of operation, cash flows or competitive position. These aforementioned environmental accruals have been established on an undiscounted basis.

Cash expenditures for the aforementioned remediation and monitoring activities are expected to be incurred over the next thirty years for each site. The accrual reflects the Company's cost estimate of the amount it will incur under the agreed-upon or proposed work plans. The Company's cost estimate is based upon existing technology and has not been reduced by possible recoveries from third parties. The Company's estimate includes equipment and operating costs for remediation and long-term monitoring of the sites.

A Consent Decree was signed in 1994 in settlement of a civil complaint brought by the U.S. Environmental Protection Agency and the

U.S. Department of Justice under which the Company is subject to a Compliance Schedule by which the Company improved its waste characterization procedures, upgraded one of its incinerators, and is evaluating and upgrading its industrial sewer system. The total expenditures required to complete this program are currently estimated to be approximately $24 million over the next nine years. These expenditures are primarily capital in nature and, therefore, are not included in the environmental accrual at December 31, 2001.

The Company is presently designated as a PRP under the Comprehensive Environmental Response, Compensation, and Liability Act of 1980, as amended (the Superfund law), or under similar state laws, for environmental assessment and cleanup costs as the result of the Company's alleged arrangements for disposal of hazardous substances at six active Superfund sites. With respect to each of these sites, the Company's actual or potential allocated share of responsibility is small. Furthermore, numerous other PRPs have also been designated at these sites, and although the law imposes joint and several liability on PRPs, the Company's historical experience demonstrates that these costs are shared with other PRPs. Settlements and costs paid by the Company in Superfund matters to date have not been material. Future costs are also not expected to be material to the Company's financial position or results of operations.

The Clean Air Act Amendments were enacted in 1990. Expenditures to comply with the Clean Air Act implementing regulations issued to date have not been material and have been primarily capital in nature. In addition, future expenditures for existing regulations, which are primarily capital in nature, are not expected to be material. Many of the regulations to be promulgated pursuant to this Act have not been issued.

Uncertainties associated with environmental remediation contingencies are pervasive and often result in wide ranges of reasonably possible outcomes. Estimates developed in the early stages of remediation can vary significantly. A finite estimate of cost does not normally become fixed and determinable at a specific point in time. Rather, the costs associated with environmental remediation become estimable over a continuum of events and activities that help to frame and define a liability and the Company continually updates its cost estimates. It is reasonably possible that the Company's recorded estimates of its liabilities may change and there is no assurance that additional costs greater than the amounts accrued will not be incurred or that changes in environmental laws or their interpretation will not require that additional amounts be spent.

Factors which cause uncertainties for the Company include, but are not limited to, the effectiveness of the current work plans in achieving targeted results and proposals of regulatory agencies for desired methods and outcomes. It is possible that financial position, results of operations, cash flows or competitive positions could be affected by the impact of the ultimate resolution of these matters.

Market Price Data

	2001		2000	
Price per share:	High	Low	High	Low
1st Qtr.	$ 46.65	$ 38.19	$ 67.50	$ 53.31
2nd Qtr.	49.95	37.76	63.63	53.19
3rd Qtr.	47.38	30.75	65.69	39.75
4th Qtr.	36.10	24.40	48.50	35.31

Quantitative and Qualitative Disclosures About Market Risk

The Company, as a result of its global operating and financing activities, is exposed to changes in foreign currency exchange rates, commodity prices, and interest rates, which may adversely affect its results of operations and financial position. In seeking to minimize the risks and/or costs associated with such activities, the Company may enter into derivative contracts. See also Note 11.

Foreign currency forward contracts are used to hedge existing foreign currency denominated assets and liabilities, especially those of the Company's International Treasury Center, as well as forecasted foreign currency denominated intercompany sales. Silver forward contracts are used to mitigate the Company's risk to fluctuating silver prices. The Company's exposure to changes in interest rates results from its investing and borrowing activities used to meet its liquidity needs. Long-term debt is generally used to finance long-term investments, while short-term debt is used to meet working capital requirements. An interest rate swap agreement was used to convert some floating-rate debt to fixed-rate debt. The Company does not utilize financial instruments for trading or other speculative purposes.

A sensitivity analysis indicates that if foreign currency exchange rates at December 31, 2001 and 2000 increased 10%, the Company would incur losses of $25 million and $88 million on foreign currency forward contracts outstanding at December 31, 2001 and 2000, respectively. Such losses would be substantially offset by gains from the revaluation or settlement of the underlying positions hedged.

A sensitivity analysis indicates that, based on broker-quoted termination values, if the price of silver decreased 10% from spot rates at December 31, 2001 and 2000, the fair value of silver forward contracts would be reduced by $11 million and $27 million, respectively. Such losses in fair value, if realized, would be offset by lower costs of manufacturing silver-containing products.

The Company is exposed to interest rate risk primarily through its borrowing activities, and to a lesser extent, through investments in marketable securities. The Company utilizes U.S. dollar denominated and foreign currency denominated borrowings to fund its working capital and investment needs. The majority of short-term and long-term borrowings are in fixed-rate instruments. There is inherent roll-over risk for debt and marketable securities as they mature and are renewed at current market rates. The extent of this risk is not predictable because of the variability of future interest rates and business financing requirements.

Using a yield-to-maturity analysis, if December 31, 2001 interest rates increased 10% (about 43 basis points) with the current period's level of debt, there would be decreases in fair value of short-term and long-term borrowings of $1 million and $28 million, respectively. If December 31, 2000 interest rates increased 10% (about 62 basis points) with the December 31, 2000 level of debt, there would be decreases in fair value of short-term and long-term borrowings of $2 million and $20 million, respectively.

The Company's financial instrument counterparties are high-quality investment or commercial banks with significant experience with such instruments. The Company manages exposure to counterparty credit risk by requiring specific minimum credit standards and diversification of counterparties. The Company has procedures to monitor the credit exposure amounts. The maximum credit exposure at December 31, 2001 was not significant to the Company.

Management's Responsibility for Financial Statements

Management is responsible for the preparation and integrity of the consolidated financial statements and related notes which appear on pages 50 through 77. These financial statements have been prepared in accordance with accounting principles generally accepted in the United States of America, and include certain amounts that are based on management's best estimates and judgments.

The Company's accounting systems include extensive internal controls designed to provide reasonable assurance of the reliability of its financial records and the proper safeguarding and use of its assets. Such controls are based on established policies and procedures, are implemented by trained, skilled personnel with an appropriate segregation of duties, and are monitored through a comprehensive internal audit program. The Company's policies and procedures prescribe that the Company and all employees are to maintain the highest ethical standards and that its business practices throughout the world are to be conducted in a manner which is above reproach.

The consolidated financial statements have been audited by PricewaterhouseCoopers LLP, independent accountants, who were responsible for conducting their audits in accordance with auditing standards generally accepted in the United States of America. Their resulting report follows.

The Board of Directors exercises its responsibility for these financial statements through its Audit Committee, which consists entirely of non-management Board members. The independent accountants and internal auditors have full and free access to the Audit Committee. The Audit Committee meets periodically with the independent accountants and the Director of Corporate Auditing, both privately and with management present, to discuss accounting, auditing and financial reporting matters.

Robert H. Brust

Chief Financial Officer, and
Executive Vice President
January 23, 2002

Dan Carp

Chairman & Chief Executive Officer,
President & Chief Operating Officer
January 23, 2002

Report of Independent Accountants

To the Board of Directors and Shareholders of Eastman Kodak Company

In our opinion, the accompanying consolidated financial statements appearing on pages 50 through 77 of this Annual Report present fairly, in all material respects, the financial position of Eastman Kodak Company and its subsidiaries at December 31, 2001 and 2000, and the results of their operations and their cash flows for each of the three years in the period ended December 31, 2001, in conformity with accounting principles generally accepted in the United States of America. These financial statements are the responsibility of the Company's management; our responsibility is to express an opinion on these financial statements based on our audits. We conducted our audits of these statements in accordance with auditing standards generally accepted in the United States of America, which require that we plan and perform the audit to obtain reasonable assurance about whether the financial statements are free of material misstatement. An audit includes examining, on a test basis, evidence supporting the amounts and disclosures in the financial statements, assessing the accounting principles used and significant estimates made by management, and evaluating the overall financial statement presentation. We believe that our audits provide a reasonable basis for our opinion.

PricewaterhouseCoopers LLP

Rochester, New York
January 23, 2002

Eastman Kodak Company and Subsidiary Companies

Consolidated Statement of Earnings

(in millions, except per share data)	For the Year Ended December 31 2001	2000	1999
Net sales	$ 13,234	$ 13,994	$ 14,089
Cost of goods sold	8,670	8,375	8,086
Gross profit	4,564	5,619	6,003
Selling, general and administrative expenses	2,627	2,514	2,701
Research and development costs	779	784	817
Goodwill amortization	154	151	145
Restructuring costs (credits) and other	659	(44)	350
Earnings from operations	345	2,214	1,990
Interest expense	219	178	142
Other income (charges)	(18)	96	261
Earnings before income taxes	108	2,132	2,109
Provision for income taxes	32	725	717
Net Earnings	$ 76	$ 1,407	$ 1,392
Basic earnings per share	$ .26	$ 4.62	$ 4.38
Diluted earnings per share	$ .26	$ 4.59	$ 4.33
Earnings used in basic and diluted earnings per share	$ 76	$ 1,407	$ 1,392
Number of common shares used in basic earnings per share	290.6	304.9	318.0
Incremental shares from assumed conversion of options	0.4	1.7	3.5
Number of common shares used in diluted earnings per share	291.0	306.6	321.5
Cash dividends per share	$ 2.21	$ 1.76	$ 1.76

The accompanying notes are an integral part of these consolidated financial statements.

Eastman Kodak Company and Subsidiary Companies

Consolidated Statement of Financial Position

(in millions, except share and per share data)	At December 31 2001	2000
Assets		
Current Assets		
Cash and cash equivalents	$ 448	$ 246
Receivables, net	2,337	2,653
Inventories, net	1,137	1,718
Deferred income taxes	521	575
Other current assets	240	299
Total current assets	4,683	5,491
Property, plant and equipment, net	5,659	5,919
Goodwill, net	948	947
Other long-term assets	2,072	1,855
Total Assets	$ 13,362	$ 14,212
Liabilities and Shareholders' Equity		
Current Liabilities		
Accounts payable and other current liabilities	$ 3,276	$ 3,403
Short-term borrowings	1,378	2,058
Current portion of long-term debt	156	148
Accrued income taxes	544	606
Total current liabilities	5,354	6,215
Long-term debt, net of current portion	1,666	1,166
Postemployment liabilities	2,728	2,722
Other long-term liabilities	720	681
Total Liabilities	10,468	10,784
Commitments and Contingencies (Note 10)		
Shareholders' Equity		
Common stock, $2.50 par value		
950,000,000 shares authorized; issued 391,292,760 shares in 2001 and 2000; 290,929,701 and 290,484,266 shares outstanding in 2001 and 2000	978	978
Additional paid in capital	849	871
Retained earnings	7,431	7,869
Accumulated other comprehensive loss	(597)	(482)
	8,661	9,236
Treasury stock, at cost		
100,363,059 shares in 2001 and 100,808,494 shares in 2000	5,767	5,808
Total Shareholders' Equity	2,894	3,428
Total Liabilities and Shareholders' Equity	$ 13,362	$ 14,212

The accompanying notes are an integral part of these consolidated financial statements.

Eastman Kodak Company and Subsidiary Companies

Consolidated Statement of Shareholders' Equity

(in millions, except share and per share data)	Common Stock*	Additional Paid In Capital	Retained Earnings	Accumulated Other Comprehensive Income (Loss)	Treasury Stock	Total
Shareholders' Equity December 31, 1998	$ 978	$ 902	$ 6,163	$ (111)	$ (3,944)	$ 3,988
Net earnings	–	–	1,392	–	–	1,392
Other comprehensive income (loss):						
Unrealized gains on available-for-sale securities ($115 million pre-tax)	–	–	–	83	–	83
Reclassification adjustment for gains on available-for-sale securities included in net earnings ($20 million pre-tax)	–	–	–	(13)	–	(13)
Currency translation adjustments	–	–	–	(118)	–	(118)
Minimum pension liability adjustment ($26 million pre-tax)	–	–	–	14	–	14
Other comprehensive loss	–	–	–	(34)	–	(34)
Comprehensive income	–	–	–	–	–	1,358
Cash dividends declared ($1.76 per common share)	–	–	(560)	–	–	(560)
Treasury stock repurchased (13,482,648 shares)	–	–	–	–	(925)	(925)
Treasury stock issued under employee plans (1,105,220 shares)	–	(24)	–	–	64	40
Tax reductions - employee plans	–	11	–	–	–	11
Shareholders' Equity December 31, 1999	978	889	6,995	(145)	(4,805)	3,912
Net earnings	–	–	1,407	–	–	1,407
Other comprehensive income (loss):						
Unrealized losses on available-for-sale securities ($77 million pre-tax)	–	–	–	(48)	–	(48)
Reclassification adjustment for gains on available-for-sale securities included in net earnings ($94 million pre-tax)	–	–	–	(58)	–	(58)
Unrealized loss arising from hedging activity ($55 million pre-tax)	–	–	–	(34)	–	(34)
Reclassification adjustment for hedging related gains included in net earnings ($6 million pre-tax)	–	–	–	(4)	–	(4)
Currency translation adjustments	–	–	–	(194)	–	(194)
Minimum pension liability adjustment ($2 million pre-tax)	–	–	–	1	–	1
Other comprehensive loss	–	–	–	(337)	–	(337)
Comprehensive income	–	–	–	–	–	1,070
Cash dividends declared ($1.76 per common share)	–	–	(533)	–	–	(533)
Treasury stock repurchased (21,575,536 shares)	–	–	–	–	(1,099)	(1,099)
Treasury stock issued under employee plans (1,638,872 shares)	–	(33)	–	–	96	63
Tax reductions - employee plans	–	15	–	–	–	15
Shareholders' Equity December 31, 2000	978	871	7,869	(482)	(5,808)	3,428
Net earnings	–	–	76	–	–	76
Other comprehensive income (loss):						
Unrealized losses on available-for-sale securities ($34 million pre-tax)	–	–	–	(21)	–	(21)
Reclassification adjustment for gains on available-for-sale securities included in net earnings ($13 million pre-tax)	–	–	–	8	–	8
Unrealized gain arising from hedging activity ($6 million pre-tax)	–	–	–	4	–	4
Reclassification adjustment for hedging related losses included in net earnings ($48 million pre-tax)	–	–	–	29	–	29
Currency translation adjustments	–	–	–	(98)	–	(98)
Minimum pension liability adjustment ($60 million pre-tax)	–	–	–	(37)	–	(37)
Other comprehensive loss	–	–	–	(115)	–	(115)
Comprehensive loss	–	–	–	–	–	(39)
Cash dividends declared ($2.21 per common share)	–	–	(514)	–	–	(514)
Treasury stock repurchased (947,670 shares)	–	–	–	–	(41)	(41)
Treasury stock issued under employee plans (1,393,105 shares)	–	(25)	–	–	82	57
Tax reductions - employee plans	–	3	–	–	–	3
Shareholders' Equity December 31, 2001	$ 978	$ 849	$ 7,431	$ (597)	$ (5,767)	$ 2,894

* There are 100 million shares of $10 par value preferred stock authorized, none of which have been issued.

The accompanying notes are an integral part of these consolidated financial statements.

Eastman Kodak Company and Subsidiary Companies

Consolidated Statement of Cash Flows

(in millions)	2001	2000	1999
	For the Year Ended December 31		
Cash flows from operating activities:			
Net earnings	$ 76	$ 1,407	$ 1,392
Adjustments to reconcile to net cash provided by operating activities:			
Depreciation and amortization	919	889	918
Gain on sales of businesses/assets	–	(117)	(162)
Restructuring costs, asset impairments and other charges	830	–	453
(Benefit) provision for deferred income taxes	(44)	235	247
Decrease (increase) in receivables	252	(247)	(121)
Decrease (increase) in inventories	461	(282)	(201)
Decrease in liabilities excluding borrowings	(529)	(755)	(478)
Other items, net	100	(148)	(115)
Total adjustments	1,989	(425)	541
Net cash provided by operating activities	2,065	982	1,933
Cash flows from investing activities:			
Additions to properties	(743)	(945)	(1,127)
Net proceeds from sales of businesses/assets	–	277	422
Acquisitions, net of cash acquired	(306)	(130)	(3)
Marketable securities - sales	54	84	127
Marketable securities - purchases	(52)	(69)	(104)
Net cash used in investing activities	(1,047)	(783)	(685)
Cash flows from financing activities:			
Net (decrease) increase in borrowings with original maturities of 90 days or less	(695)	939	(136)
Proceeds from other borrowings	1,907	1,310	1,343
Repayment of other borrowings	(1,355)	(936)	(1,118)
Dividends to shareholders	(643)	(545)	(563)
Exercise of employee stock options	22	43	44
Stock repurchase programs	(44)	(1,125)	(897)
Net cash used in financing activities	(808)	(314)	(1,327)
Effect of exchange rate changes on cash	(8)	(12)	(5)
Net increase (decrease) in cash and cash equivalents	202	(127)	(84)
Cash and cash equivalents, beginning of year	246	373	457
Cash and cash equivalents, end of year	$ 448	$ 246	$ 373

Supplemental Cash Flow Information	2001	2000	1999
Cash paid for interest and income taxes was:			
Interest, net of portion capitalized of $12, $40 and $36	$ 214	$ 166	$ 120
Income taxes	120	486	445
The following transactions are not reflected in the Consolidated Statement of Cash Flows:			
Contribution of assets to Kodak Polychrome Graphics joint venture	$ –	$ –	$ 13
Minimum pension liability adjustment	37	(1)	(14)
Liabilities assumed in acquisitions	142	31	–

The accompanying notes are an integral part of these consolidated financial statements.

Eastman Kodak Company and Subsidiary Companies

Notes to Financial Statements

Note 1: Significant Accounting Policies

Company Operations Eastman Kodak Company (the Company or Kodak) is engaged primarily in developing, manufacturing, and marketing traditional and digital imaging products, services and solutions to consumers, the entertainment industry, professionals, healthcare providers and other customers. The Company's products are manufactured in a number of countries in North and South America, Europe, Australia and Asia. The Company's products are marketed and sold in many countries throughout the world.

Basis of Consolidation The consolidated financial statements include the accounts of Kodak and its majority owned subsidiary companies. Intercompany transactions are eliminated and net earnings are reduced by the portion of the earnings of subsidiaries applicable to minority interests. The equity method of accounting is used for joint ventures and investments in associated companies over which Kodak has significant influence, but does not have effective control. Significant influence is generally deemed to exist when the Company has an ownership interest in the voting stock of the investee of between 20% and 50%, although other factors, such as representation on the investee's Board of Directors, voting rights and the impact of commercial arrangements, are considered in determining whether the equity method of accounting is appropriate. The cost method of accounting is used for investments in which Kodak has less than a 20% ownership interest, and the Company does not have the ability to exercise significant influence. These investments are carried at cost and are adjusted only for other-than-temporary declines in fair value. The carrying value of these investments is reported in other long-term assets. The Company's equity in the net income and losses of these investments is reported in other income (charges). See Note 6 and Note 12.

Use of Estimates The preparation of financial statements in conformity with generally accepted accounting principles requires management to make estimates and assumptions that affect the reported amounts of assets and liabilities and disclosure of contingent assets and liabilities at year end and the reported amounts of revenues and expenses during the reporting period. Actual results could differ from those estimates.

Foreign Currency For most subsidiaries and branches outside the U.S., the local currency is the functional currency. In accordance with the Statement of Financial Accounting Standards (SFAS) No. 52, "Foreign Currency Translation," the financial statements of these subsidiaries and branches are translated into U.S. dollars as follows: assets and liabilities at year-end exchange rates; income, expenses and cash flows at average exchange rates; and shareholders' equity at historical exchange rates. For those subsidiaries for which the local currency is the functional currency, the resulting translation adjustment is recorded as a component of accumulated other comprehensive income in the accompanying balance sheet. Translation adjustments are not tax-effected since they relate to investments which are permanent in nature.

For certain other subsidiaries and branches, operations are conducted primarily in U.S. dollars, which is therefore the functional currency. Monetary assets and liabilities, and the related revenue, expense, gain and loss accounts, of these foreign subsidiaries and branches are remeasured at year-end exchange rates. Non-monetary assets and liabilities, and the related revenue, expense, gain and loss accounts, are remeasured at historical rates.

The Company has operations in Argentina. Prior to December 31, 2001, the Argentine peso had been pegged to the U.S. dollar at an exchange rate of 1 to 1. In late December 2001, although the official exchange rate between the peso and the dollar remained at 1 to 1, exchange houses started exchanging at a rate of 1.4 pesos to the dollar in anticipation that the government would announce a devaluation of the peso. The exchange houses were then closed, and at year-end 2001 there was no exchangeability between the peso and the dollar. The exchangeability between the peso and the dollar was first re-established on January 11, 2002, and the day's closing rate for buying U.S. dollars was approximately 1.7 Argentine pesos to the dollar. The situation relating to the devaluation in Argentina did not have a material impact on the Company's Consolidated Statement of Financial Position or Consolidated Statement of Earnings as of and for the year ended December 31, 2001.

Foreign exchange gains and losses arising from transactions denominated in a currency other than the functional currency of the entity involved are included in income. The effects of foreign currency transactions, including related hedging activities, were losses of $9 million, $13 million, and $2 million in the years 2001, 2000, and 1999, respectively, and are included in other income (charges).

Concentration of Credit Risk Financial instruments that potentially subject the Company to significant concentrations of credit risk consist principally of cash and cash equivalents, receivables, foreign currency forward contracts, commodity forward contracts and interest rate swap arrangements. The Company places its cash and cash equivalents with high-quality financial institutions and limits the amount of credit exposure to any one institution. With respect to receivables, such receivables arise from sales to numerous customers in a variety of industries, markets, and geographies around the world. Receivables arising from these sales are generally not collateralized. The Company performs ongoing credit evaluations of its customers' financial conditions and no single customer accounts for greater than 10% of the sales of the Company. The Company maintains reserves for potential credit losses and such losses, in the aggregate, have not exceeded management's expectations. With respect to the foreign currency forward contracts, commodity forward contracts and interest rate swap arrangements, the counterparties to these contracts are major financial institutions. The

Company has never experienced non-performance by any of its counterparties.

Cash Equivalents All highly liquid investments with a remaining maturity of three months or less at date of purchase are considered to be cash equivalents.

Marketable Securities and Noncurrent Investments The Company has evaluated its investment policies consistent with SFAS No. 115, "Accounting for Certain Investments in Debt and Equity Securities" which requires that investment securities be classified as either held-to-maturity, available-for-sale or trading. The Company's debt and equity investment securities are classified as held-to-maturity and available-for-sale, respectively. Held-to-maturity investments are carried at amortized cost and available-for-sale securities are carried at fair value, with the unrealized gains and losses reported in Shareholders' Equity under the caption Accumulated Other Comprehensive Income (Loss).

At December 31, 2001, the Company had short-term investments classified as held-to-maturity of $3 million. These investments were included in other current assets. In addition, the Company had long-term marketable securities and other investments classified as held-to-maturity and available-for-sale equity securities of $1 million and $33 million, respectively, which were included in other long-term assets at December 31, 2001.

At December 31, 2000, the Company had short-term investments classified as held-to-maturity of $5 million, which were included in other current assets. In addition, the Company had long-term marketable securities and other investments classified as held-to-maturity and available-for-sale equity securities of $5 million and $49 million, respectively, which were included in other long-term assets at December 31, 2000.

Inventories Inventories are stated at the lower of cost or market. The cost of most inventories in the U.S. is determined by the "last-in, first-out" (LIFO) method. The cost of all of the Company's remaining inventories in and outside the U.S. is determined by the "first-in, first-out" (FIFO) or average cost method, which approximates current cost. The Company provides inventory reserves for excess, obsolete or slow-moving inventory based on changes in customer demand, technology developments or other economic factors.

Properties Properties are recorded at cost, net of accumulated depreciation. The Company principally calculates depreciation expense using the straight-line method over the assets' estimated useful lives, which are as follows:

	Years
Buildings and building improvements	10–40
Machinery and equipment	3–20

Maintenance and repairs are charged to expense as incurred. Upon sale or other disposition, the applicable amounts of asset cost and accumulated depreciation are removed from the accounts and the net amount, less proceeds from disposal, is charged or credited to income.

Goodwill Goodwill represents the excess of purchase price over the fair value of the net assets acquired, and for the three-year period ended December 31, 2001, goodwill was charged to earnings on a straight-line basis over the period estimated to be benefited, generally ten years. See Note 5.

Effective January 1, 2002, the Company will be accounting for goodwill under SFAS No. 142, "Goodwill and Other Intangible Assets." Under SFAS No. 142 the Company will no longer amortize its goodwill which, as of December 31, 2001, had a net balance of $948 million. Under SFAS No. 142, the Company's goodwill will be subject to an impairment test, at least annually, and therefore, will only be charged to operations to the extent it has been determined to be impaired. See the Recently Issued Accounting Standards within Note 1.

Revenue The Company's revenue transactions include sales of the following: products; equipment; services; equipment bundled with products and/or services; and integrated solutions. The Company recognizes revenue when realized or realizable and earned, which is when the following criteria are met: persuasive evidence of an arrangement exists; delivery has occurred; the sales price is fixed and determinable; and collectibility is reasonably assured. At the time revenue is recognized, the Company provides for the estimated costs of warranties and reduces revenue for estimated returns.

For product sales, the recognition criteria are generally met when title and risk of loss have transferred from the Company to the buyer, which may be upon shipment or upon delivery to the customer sites, based on contract terms or legal requirements in foreign jurisdictions. Service revenues are recognized as such services are rendered.

For equipment sales, the recognition criteria are generally met when the equipment is delivered and installed at the customer site. In instances in which the agreement with the customer contains a customer acceptance clause, revenue is deferred until customer acceptance is obtained, provided the customer acceptance clause is considered to be substantive. For certain agreements, the Company does not consider these customer acceptance clauses to be substantive because the Company can and does replicate the customer acceptance test environment and performs the agreed upon product testing prior to shipment. In these instances, revenue is recognized upon installation of the equipment.

The sale of equipment combined with services, including maintenance, and/or other elements, including products and software, represent multiple element arrangements. The Company allocates revenue to the various elements based on verifiable objective evidence of fair value (if software is not included or is incidental to the transaction) or Kodak-specific objective evidence of fair value if software is other than incidental to the sales transaction as a whole. Revenue allocated to an individual element is recognized when all other revenue recognition criteria are met for that element.

Revenue from the sale of integrated solutions, which includes transactions which require significant production, modification or customization of software, is recognized in accordance with contract accounting. Under contract accounting, revenue should be recognized utilizing either the percentage-of-completion or completed-contract method. The Company currently utilizes the completed-contract method for all solution sales as sufficient history does not currently exist to allow the Company to accurately estimate total costs to complete these transactions. Revenue from other long-term contracts, government contracts, is generally recognized using the percentage-of-completion method.

The Company may offer customer financing to assist customers in their acquisition of Kodak's products, primarily in the area of on-site photofinishing equipment. At the time a financing transaction is consummated, which qualifies as a sales-type lease, the Company records the total lease receivable net of unearned income and the estimated residual value of the equipment. Unearned income is recognized as finance income using the interest method over the term of the lease. Leases not qualifying as sales-type leases are accounted for as operating leases. The underlying equipment is depreciated on a straight-line basis over the assets' estimated useful life.

Net sales reflects reductions in gross revenues attributable to cash discounts, promotional and advertising allowances and volume discounts the Company offers in connection with certain of its sales transactions.

In December 1999, the Securities and Exchange Commission (SEC) issued Staff Accounting Bulletin (SAB) No. 101, "Revenue Recognition in Financial Statements." This guidance summarizes the SEC staff's views in applying generally accepted accounting principles to revenue recognition in financial statements. Upon its adoption effective January 1, 2000, SAB No. 101 did not have a material impact on the Company's results of operations.

The Company's sales of tangible products is the only class of revenues that exceeds 10% of total consolidated net sales. All other sales classes are individually less than 10%, and therefore, have been combined with sales of tangible products on the same line in accordance with Regulation S-X.

Research and Development Costs Research and development costs, which include costs in connection with new product development, fundamental and exploratory research, process improvement, product use technology and product accreditation are charged to operations in the period in which they are incurred.

Advertising Advertising costs are expensed as incurred and included in selling, general and administrative expenses. Advertising expenses amounted to $634 million, $701 million and $717 million in 2001, 2000 and 1999, respectively.

Shipping and Handling Costs Amounts charged to customers and costs incurred by the Company related to shipping and handling are included in net sales and cost of goods sold, respectively, in accordance with Emerging Issues Task Force (EITF) Issue No. 00-10, "Accounting for Shipping and Handling Fees and Costs." Prior to January 1, 2001, costs incurred for shipping and handling and other distribution costs were reported in selling, general and administrative expenses. The shipping and handling and other distribution costs for 2000 and 1999 of $482 million and $480 million, respectively, have been reclassified from selling, general and administrative expenses to cost of goods sold to conform with the 2001 presentation of these amounts.

Impairment of Long-Lived Assets The Company reviews the carrying value of its long-lived assets, including goodwill and other intangible assets, whenever events or changes in circumstances indicate that the carrying amount of the asset may not be recoverable. The Company assesses recoverability of the carrying value of the asset by grouping assets at the lowest level for which there are identifiable cash flows that are largely independent of the cash flows of other groups of assets. The Company then estimates the undiscounted future cash flows expected to result from the asset grouping, including the proceeds from its eventual disposal. An impairment loss would be recognized when the estimated undiscounted future cash flows expected to result from the use of the asset and its eventual disposal are less than its carrying amount. In such instances, the carrying value of long-lived assets is reduced to the estimated fair value, as determined using an appraisal or discounted cash flow, as appropriate.

Effective January 1, 2002, the Company will assess recoverability of its long-lived assets, other than goodwill, under the guidance of SFAS No. 144, "Accounting for the Impairment or Disposal of Long-Lived Assets." See the Recently Issued Accounting Standards within Note 1.

Derivative Financial Instruments The Company adopted SFAS No. 133, "Accounting for Derivative Instruments and Hedging Activities," on January 1, 2000. All derivative instruments are recognized as either assets or liabilities and are measured at fair value. Certain derivatives are designated and accounted for as hedges. The Company does not use derivatives for trading or other speculative purposes.

The Company has cash flow hedges to manage foreign currency exchange risk, commodity price risk, and interest rate risk related to forecasted transactions. The Company also uses foreign currency forward contracts to offset currency-related changes in foreign currency denominated assets and liabilities; these are marked to market through earnings.

The fair value of foreign currency forward contracts designated as hedges of forecasted foreign currency denominated intercompany sales is reported in other current assets and/or current liabilities, and is recorded in other comprehensive income. When the related inventory is sold to third parties, the hedge gains or losses as of the date of the intercompany sale are transferred from other comprehensive income to cost of goods sold.

The fair value of silver forward contracts designated as hedges of forecasted worldwide silver purchases is reported in other current assets and/or current liabilities, and is recorded in other comprehensive income. When the silver-containing products are sold to third parties, the hedge gains or losses as of the date of the purchase of raw silver are transferred from other comprehensive income to cost of goods sold.

The fair value of the interest rate swap designated as a hedge of forecasted floating-rate interest payments is reported in current liabilities, and is recorded in other comprehensive income. As interest expense is accrued, an amount equal to the difference between the fixed and floating-rate interest payments is transferred from other comprehensive income to interest expense.

Environmental Expenditures Environmental expenditures that relate to current operations are expensed or capitalized, as appropriate. Expenditures that relate to an existing condition caused by past operations and that do not provide future benefits, are expensed as incurred. Liabilities are recorded when environmental assessments are made or the requirement for remedial efforts is probable, and the costs can be reasonably estimated. The timing of these accruals is generally no later than the completion of feasibility studies.

Income Taxes The Company accounts for income taxes in accordance with SFAS No. 109, "Accounting for Income Taxes." The asset and liability approach underlying SFAS No. 109 requires the recognition of deferred tax liabilities and assets for the expected future tax consequences of temporary differences between the carrying amounts and tax basis of the Company's assets and liabilities. Management provides valuation allowances against the net deferred tax asset for amounts which are not considered more likely than not to be realized.

Earnings Per Share Basic earnings-per-share computations are based on the weighted-average number of shares of common stock outstanding during the year. Diluted earnings-per-share calculations reflect the assumed exercise and conversion of employee stock options that have an exercise price that is below the average market price of the common shares for the respective periods.

Options to purchase 43.7 million and 32.3 million shares of common stock at weighted-average per share prices of $61.30 and $61.98 for the years ended December 31, 2001 and 2000, respectively, were outstanding during the years presented but were not included in the computation of diluted earnings per share because the options' exercise price was greater than the average market price of the common shares for the respective periods.

Comprehensive Income SFAS No. 130, "Reporting Comprehensive Income," establishes standards for the reporting and display of comprehensive income and its components in financial statements. SFAS No. 130 requires that all items that are required to be recognized under accounting standards as components of comprehensive income be reported in a financial statement with the same prominence as other financial statements. Comprehensive income consists of net earnings, the net unrealized gains or losses on available-for-sale marketable securities, foreign currency translation adjustments, minimum pension liability adjustments and unrealized gains and losses on financial instruments qualifying for hedge accounting and is presented in the Consolidated Statement of Shareholders' Equity in accordance with SFAS No. 130.

Stock-Based Compensation The Company accounts for its employee stock incentive plans under Accounting Principles Board (APB) Opinion No. 25, "Accounting for Stock Issued to Employees" and the related interpretations under Financial Accounting Standards Board (FASB) Interpretation No. 44, "Accounting for Certain Transactions Involving Stock Compensation." Accordingly, no compensation cost is recognized for stock-based compensation unless the quoted market price of the stock at the grant date is in excess of the price the employee must pay to acquire the stock.

SFAS No. 123, "Accounting for Stock-Based Compensation," allows, but does not require, companies to record compensation cost for stock-based employee compensation plans at fair value. The Company has chosen to continue using the intrinsic method prescribed in APB No. 25 as described above. The Company has adopted the disclosure-only provisions of SFAS No. 123. See Note 18.

Segment Reporting The Company reports net sales, operating income, net income, certain expense, asset and geographical information about its operating segments in accordance with SFAS No. 131, "Disclosures about Segments of an Enterprise and Related Information." SFAS No. 131 requires public companies to report information about their business activities, which meet the criteria of a reportable segment. Reportable segments are components of an enterprise for which separate financial information is available that is evaluated regularly by the chief operating decision maker in deciding how to allocate resources and in assessing performance. The Company has three reportable segments. See Note 21 for a discussion of the change in the Company's operating structure in 2001.

Recently Issued Accounting Standards In June 2001, the FASB issued SFAS No. 141, "Business Combinations," and SFAS No. 142, "Goodwill and Other Intangible Assets," collectively referred to as the "Standards," which are effective for the Company as of January 1, 2002, except as noted below. SFAS No. 141 supercedes APB No. 16, "Business Combinations." The provisions of SFAS No. 141 (1) require that the purchase method of accounting be used for all business combinations initiated after June 30, 2001, (2) provide specific criteria for the initial recognition and measurement of intangible assets apart from goodwill, and (3) require that unamortized negative goodwill be written off immediately as an extraordinary gain instead of being deferred and amortized. SFAS No. 141 also requires that, upon adoption of SFAS No. 142, the Company reclassify the carrying amounts of certain intangible assets into or out of goodwill, based on certain criteria. SFAS No. 142 supercedes APB No. 17, "Intangible Assets," and is effective for fiscal years beginning after December 15, 2001. SFAS No. 142 primarily addresses the accounting for goodwill and intangible assets subsequent to their initial recognition. The provisions of SFAS No. 142 (1) prohibit the amortization of goodwill and indefinite-lived intangible assets, (2) require that goodwill and indefinite-lived intangible assets be tested annually for impairment (and in interim periods if certain events occur indicating that the carrying value of goodwill and/or indefinite-lived intangible assets may be impaired), (3) require that reporting units be identified for the purpose of assessing potential future impairments of goodwill, and (4) remove the forty-year limitation on the amortization period of intangible assets that have finite lives.

The Company will adopt the provisions of SFAS No. 142 in its first quarter ended March 31, 2002. The Company is in the process of preparing for its adoption of SFAS No. 142 and is making the determinations as to its reporting units and the amounts of goodwill, intangible assets, other assets, and liabilities allocated to those reporting units. The Company is evaluating the useful lives assigned to its intangible assets and does not anticipate any material changes to such useful lives.

SFAS No. 142 requires that goodwill be tested annually for impairment using a two-step process. The first step of the goodwill impairment test is to test for a potential impairment. The second step of the goodwill impairment test is to measure the amount of the impairment loss. The Company expects to complete steps one and two of the goodwill impairment test during the first quarter of 2002. The Company does not believe that the results of these impairment test steps will have a material impact on the Company's consolidated financial statements.

In August 2001, the FASB issued SFAS No. 144, "Accounting for the Impairment or Disposal of Long-Lived Assets." SFAS No. 144 addresses financial accounting and reporting for the impairment or disposal of long-lived assets to be held and used, to be disposed of other than by sale and to be disposed of by sale. Although the Statement retains certain of the provisions of SFAS No. 121, "Accounting for the Impairment of Long-Lived Assets and for Long-Lived Assets to Be Disposed Of," it supercedes SFAS No. 121 and APB Opinion No. 30, "Reporting the Results of Operations—Reporting the Effects of Disposal of a Segment of a Business, and Extraordinary, Unusual and Infrequently Occurring Events and Transactions," for the disposal of a segment of a business. SFAS No. 144 also amends Accounting Research Bulletin (ARB) No. 51, "Consolidated Financial Statements," to eliminate the exception to consolidation for a subsidiary for which control is likely to be temporary. The Statement is effective for financial statements issued for fiscal years beginning after December 15, 2001 and interim periods within those fiscal years, and will thus be adopted by the Company, as required, on January 1, 2002. The adoption of SFAS No. 144 is not expected to have a material impact on the Company's consolidated financial statements.

The EITF has issued EITF Issue No. 01-09, "Accounting for Consideration Given by a Vendor to a Customer (Including a Reseller of the Vendor's Products)." The EITF provides guidance with respect to the statement of earnings classification of and the accounting for recognition and measurement of consideration given by a vendor to a customer, which includes sales incentive offers labeled as discounts, coupons, rebates and free products or services as well as arrangements labeled as slotting fees, cooperative advertising and buydowns. The guidance with respect to the appropriate statement of earnings classification of the consideration given by a vendor to a customer is effective for annual and interim periods beginning after December 15, 2001. Upon adoption, financial statements for prior periods presented for comparative purposes should be reclassified to comply with the requirements under the EITF.

The guidance with respect to the accounting for recognition and measurement of consideration given by a vendor to a customer is effective for annual and interim periods beginning after December 15, 2001. The impact on the statement of earnings resulting from the adoption of the EITF should be reported as a cumulative effect of a change in accounting principle or applied prospectively to new sales incentives offered on or after the effective date. The impact of the guidance under EITF 01-09 on the Company's consolidated financial statements has not yet been determined.

Reclassifications Certain reclassifications of prior financial information and related footnote amounts have been made to conform with the 2001 presentation.

Note 2: Receivables, net

(in millions)	2001	2000
Trade receivables	$ 1,966	$ 2,245
Miscellaneous receivables	371	408
Total (net of allowances of $109 and $89)	$ 2,337	$ 2,653

In the fourth quarter of 2001, the Company recorded a charge of $20 million to provide for the potential uncollectible amounts due from Kmart, who filed a petition for reorganization under Chapter 11 of the United States Bankruptcy Code in January 2002. The amount of $20 million is included in selling, general and administrative expenses and in the total allowance of $109 million at December 31, 2001.

Note 3: Inventories, net

(in millions)	2001	2000
At FIFO or average cost (approximates current cost)		
Finished goods	$ 851	$ 1,155
Work in process	318	423
Raw materials and supplies	412	589
	1,581	2,167
LIFO reserve	(444)	(449)
Total	$ 1,137	$ 1,718

Inventories valued on the LIFO method are approximately 48% and 47% of total inventories in 2001 and 2000, respectively. During 2001, inventory usage resulted in liquidations of LIFO inventory quantities. In the aggregate, these inventories were carried at the lower costs prevailing in prior years as compared with the cost of current purchases. The effect of these LIFO liquidations was to reduce cost of goods sold by $14 million in 2001. No LIFO layer liquidations occurred in 2000 or 1999.

The Company provides for potentially excess, obsolete or slow-moving inventory based on management's analysis of inventory levels and future sales forecasts. The Company also provides for inventories whose cost is in excess of market. At December 31, 2001 and 2000, aggregate excess, obsolete, slow-moving and lower of cost or market reserves were $99 million and $96 million, respectively.

Note 4: Property, Plant and Equipment, net

(in millions)	2001	2000
Land	$ 127	$ 141
Buildings and building improvements	2,602	2,285
Machinery and equipment	9,884	9,585
Construction in progress	369	952
	12,982	12,963
Accumulated depreciation	(7,323)	(7,044)
Net properties	$ 5,659	$ 5,919

Depreciation expense was $765 million, $738 million and $773 million for the years 2001, 2000, and 1999, respectively.

Note 5: Goodwill, net

(in millions)	2001	2000
Goodwill	$ 1,868	$ 1,724
Accumulated amortization	920	777
Goodwill, net	$ 948	$ 947

During 2001, the Company purchased Ofoto, Inc. and substantially all of the imaging service operations of the Bell & Howell Company. The Company recorded goodwill in connection with these two acquisitions of $37 million and $70 million, respectively. The additional net increase in goodwill results from additional acquisitions, which are all individually immaterial. See Note 19.

Note 6: Investments

At December 31, 2001, the Company's significant equity method investees and the Company's approximate ownership interest in each investee were as follows:

Kodak Polychrome Graphics (KPG)	50%
NexPress Solutions LLC	50%
Phogenix Imaging LLC	50%
Matsushita-Ultra Technologies Battery Corporation	30%
Express Stop Financing (ESF)	50%
SK Display Corporation	34%

At December 31, 2001 and 2000, the Company's equity investment in these unconsolidated affiliates was $360 million and $317 million, respectively, and is reported within other long-term assets. The Company records its equity in the income or losses of these investees and reports such amounts in other income (charges). See Note 12. These investments do not meet the Regulation S-X significance test requiring the inclusion of separate investee financial statements.

The Company also has certain investments with less than a 20% ownership interest in various private companies whereby the Company does not have the ability to exercise significant influence. Such investments are accounted for under the cost method. At December 31, 2001 and 2000, the carrying value of these investments aggregated $51 million and $55 million, respectively, and is reported in other long-term assets. During 2001, the Company recorded an asset impairment charge of $15 million on certain strategic and non-strategic investments which exhibited other-than-temporary declines in their fair value. See Note 14.

Kodak sells certain of its long-term lease receivables relating to the sale of photofinishing equipment to ESF without recourse to the Company. Sales of long-term lease receivables to ESF were approximately $83 million, $153 million and $397 million in 2001, 2000 and 1999, respectively. See Note 10.

The Company sells graphics film and other products to its equity affiliate, KPG. Sales to KPG for the years ended December 31, 2001, 2000 and 1999 amounted to $350 million, $419 million and $540 million, respectively, and cost of goods sold on these sales amounted to $258 million, $290 million and $359 million for the years ended December 31, 2001, 2000 and 1999, respectively. These sales and cost of goods sold amounts are reported in the Consolidated Statement of Earnings. The Company eliminates profits on these sales, to the extent the inventory has not been sold through to third parties on the basis of its 50% interest. At December 31, 2001 and 2000, amounts due from KPG on such sales were $40 million and $52 million, respectively, and are reported in receivables, net. Additionally, the Company has guaranteed certain debt obligations of KPG up to $175 million which is included in the total guarantees amount of $277 million at December 31, 2001, as discussed in Note 10.

The Company also sells toner products to its 50% owned equity affiliate, NexPress. However, these sales transactions are not material to the Company's results of operations or financial position.

Kodak has no other material activities with its investees.

Note 7: Accounts Payable and Other Current Liabilities

(in millions)	2001	2000
Accounts payable, trade	$ 674	$ 817
Accrued advertising and promotional expenses	568	578
Accrued employment-related liabilities	749	780
Accrued restructuring liabilities	318	–
Dividends payable	–	128
Other	967	1,100
Total payables	$ 3,276	$ 3,403

The Other component above consists of other miscellaneous current liabilities which, individually, are less than 5% of the Total current liabilities component within the Consolidated Statement of Financial Position, and therefore, have been aggregated in accordance with Regulation S-X.

Note 8: Short-Term Borrowings and Long-Term Debt

Short-Term Borrowings

The Company's short-term borrowings at December 31, 2001 and 2000 were as follows:

(in millions)	2001	2000
Commercial paper	$ 1,140	$ 1,809
Current portion of long-term debt	156	148
Short-term bank borrowings	238	249
Total short-term borrowings	$ 1,534	$ 2,206

The weighted-average interest rates for commercial paper outstanding during 2001 and 2000 were 3.6% and 6.6%, respectively. The weighted-average interest rates for short-term borrowings outstanding during 2001 and 2000 were 6.2% and 5.4%, respectively.

The Company has $2.45 billion in revolving credit facilities established in 2001, which are available to support the Company's commercial paper program and for general corporate purposes. The credit agreements are comprised of a 364-day commitment at $1.225 billion expiring in July 2002 and a 5-year commitment at $1.225 billion expiring in July 2006. If unused, they have a commitment fee of $3 million per year, at the Company's current credit rating. Interest on amounts borrowed under these facilities is calculated at rates based on the Company's credit rating and spreads above certain reference rates. There were no amounts outstanding under these arrangements or the prior year arrangement at December 31, 2001 and 2000, respectively. The facility includes a covenant which requires the Company to maintain a certain EBITDA (earnings before interest, income taxes, depreciation and amortization) to interest ratio. In the event of violation of the covenant, the facility would not be available for borrowing until the covenant provisions were waived, amended or satisfied. The Company does not anticipate that a violation is likely to occur.

Long-Term Debt

Description and Interest Rates of 2001 Borrowings	Maturity Dates of 2001 Borrowings		
(in millions)		2001	2000
Notes:			
3.74%	2003	$ 10	$ –
6.38%–8.25%	2002–2006	959	473
9.20%–9.95%	2003–2021	191	191
Debentures:			
1.11%–3.16%	2003–2004	42	61
Other:			
2.42%	2004	190	–
5.94%–6.66%	2002–2010	430	591
		1,822	1,316
Current portion of long-term debt		(156)	(150)
Long-term debt, net of current portion		$ 1,666	$ 1,166

Annual maturities (in millions) of long-term debt outstanding at December 31, 2001 are as follows: 2002: $13; 2003: $394; 2004: $379; 2005: $333; 2006: $500; 2007 and beyond: $47.

During the second quarter of 2001, the Company issued Medium-Term Notes consisting of floating-rate notes in the amount of $150 million maturing on September 16, 2002 and 6.375% fixed notes in the amount of $500 million maturing on June 15, 2006. The proceeds from this offering were used to pay down a portion of the Company's outstanding commercial paper.

The Company has a shelf registration statement for medium-term notes of which $1.35 billion remains available for issuance.

Note 9: Other Long-Term Liabilities

(in millions)	2001	2000
Deferred compensation	$ 164	$ 166
Minority interest in Kodak companies	84	93
Environmental liabilities	162	113
Deferred income taxes	81	61
Other	229	248
Total	$ 720	$ 681

The Other component above consists of other miscellaneous long-term liabilities which, individually, are less than 5% of the Total liabilities component in the Consolidated Statement of Financial Position, and therefore, have been aggregated in accordance with Regulation S-X.

Note 10: Commitments and Contingencies

Environmental Cash expenditures for pollution prevention and waste treatment for the Company's current manufacturing facilities were as follows:

(in millions)	2001	2000	1999
Recurring costs for pollution prevention and waste treatment	$ 68	$ 72	$ 69
Capital expenditures for pollution prevention and waste treatment	27	36	20
Site remediation costs	2	3	5
Total	$ 97	$ 111	$ 94

At December 31, 2001 and 2000, the Company's undiscounted accrued liabilities for environmental remediation costs amounted to $162 million and $113 million, respectively. These amounts are reported in other long-term liabilities.

The Company is currently implementing a Corrective Action Program required by the Resource Conservation and Recovery Act (RCRA) at the Kodak Park site in Rochester, NY. As part of this Program, the Company has completed the RCRA Facility Assessment (RFA), a broad-based environmental investigation of the site. The Company is currently in the process of completing, and in some cases has completed, RCRA Facility Investigations (RFIs) and Corrective Measures Studies (CMS) for areas at the site. At December 31, 2001, estimated future remediation costs of $70 million are accrued on an undiscounted basis by the Company and are included in remediation accruals reported in other long-term liabilities.

Additionally, the Company has retained certain obligations for environmental remediation and Superfund matters related to certain sites associated with the non-imaging health businesses sold in 1994. In addition, the Company has been identified as a potentially responsible party (PRP) in connection with the non-imaging health businesses in five active Superfund sites. At December 31, 2001, estimated future remediation costs of $51 million are accrued on an undiscounted basis by the Company and are included in the environmental accruals reported in other long-term liabilities.

The Company recorded a $41 million charge in the fourth quarter of 2001 for additional environmental reserves. This amount has been included in selling, general and administrative expenses. Approximately $34 million has been provided for two former manufacturing sites located outside the United States. Investigations were completed by an external environmental consultant in the fourth quarter of 2001, which facilitated the completion of cost estimates for the future remediation and monitoring of these sites. In addition, the accrual incorporates the Company's estimate of its cost to repurchase one of the sites and demolish the buildings in preparation for its possible conversion to a public park. The establishment of these accruals is consistent with Kodak's policy to record accruals for environmental remediation obligations generally no later than the completion of feasibility studies. The additional $7 million recorded during the fourth quarter of 2001 represents the estimated increased costs associated with the site remediation of the non-imaging health businesses sold in 1994 discussed above ($4 million) and increases in estimated costs ($3 million) associated with the remediation of other facilities which are not material to the Company's financial position, results of operations, cash flows or competitive position. These aforementioned environmental accruals have been established on an undiscounted basis.

Cash expenditures for the aforementioned remediation and monitoring activities are expected to be incurred over the next thirty years for each site. The accrual reflects the Company's cost estimate of the amount it will incur under the agreed-upon or proposed work plans. The Company's cost estimate is based upon existing technology and has not been reduced by possible recoveries from third parties. The Company's estimate includes equipment and operating costs for remediation and long-term monitoring of the sites.

A Consent Decree was signed in 1994 in settlement of a civil complaint brought by the U.S. Environmental Protection Agency and the U.S. Department of Justice under which the Company is subject to a Compliance Schedule by which the Company improved its waste characterization procedures, upgraded one of its incinerators, and is evaluating and upgrading its industrial sewer system. The total expenditures required to complete this program are currently estimated to be approximately $24 million over the next nine years. These expenditures are primarily capital in nature and, therefore, are not included in the environmental accrual at December 31, 2001.

The Company is presently designated as a PRP under the Comprehensive Environmental Response, Compensation, and Liability Act of 1980, as amended (the Superfund law), or under similar state laws, for environmental assessment and cleanup costs as the result of the Company's alleged arrangements for disposal of hazardous substances at six active Superfund sites. With respect to each of these sites, the Company's actual or potential allocated share of responsibility is small. Furthermore, numerous other PRPs have also been designated at these sites, and although the law imposes joint and several liability on PRPs, the Company's historical experience demonstrates that these costs are shared with other PRPs. Settlements and costs paid by the Company in Superfund matters to date have not been material. Future costs are also not expected to be material to the Company's financial position or results of operations.

The Clean Air Act Amendments were enacted in 1990. Expenditures to comply with the Clean Air Act implementing regulations issued to date have not been material and have been primarily capital in nature. In addition, future expenditures for existing regulations, which are primarily capital in nature, are not expected to be material. Many of the regulations to be promulgated pursuant to this Act have not been issued.

Uncertainties associated with environmental remediation contingencies are pervasive and often result in wide ranges of reasonably possible outcomes. Estimates developed in the early stages of remediation can vary significantly. A finite estimate of cost does not normally become fixed and determinable at a specific point in time. Rather, the costs associated with environmental remediation become estimable over a continuum of events and activities that help to frame and define a liability and the Company continually updates its cost estimates. It is reasonably possible that the Company's recorded estimates of its liabilities may change and there is no assurance that additional costs greater than the amounts accrued will not be incurred or that changes in environmental laws or their interpretation will not require that additional amounts be spent.

Factors which cause uncertainties for the Company include, but are not limited to, the effectiveness of the current work plans in achieving targeted results and proposals of regulatory agencies for desired methods and outcomes. It is possible that financial position, results of operations, cash flows or competitive positions could be affected by the impact of the ultimate resolution of these matters.

Other Commitments and Contingencies The Company has entered into agreements with several companies which provide Kodak with products and services to be used in its normal operations. The minimum payments for these agreements are approximately $221 million in 2002, $191 million in 2003, $165 million in 2004, $137 million in 2005, $82 million in 2006 and $246 million in 2007 and thereafter.

The Company guarantees debt and other obligations under agreements with certain affiliated companies and customers. At December 31, 2001, these guarantees totaled approximately $277 million. Within the total amount of $277 million, the Company is guaranteeing debt in the amount of $175 million for Kodak Polychrome Graphics, an unconsolidated affiliate in which the Company has a 50% ownership interest. The balance of the amount is principally comprised of other loan guarantees and guarantees of customer amounts due to banks in connection with various banks' financing of customers' purchase of equipment and products from Kodak. These guarantees would require payment from Kodak only in the event of default on payment by the respective debtor. Management believes the likelihood is remote that material payments will be required under these guarantees.

Qualex, a wholly-owned subsidiary of Kodak, has a 50% ownership interest in ESF, which is a joint venture partnership between Qualex and Dana Credit Corporation (DCC), a wholly-owned subsidiary of Dana Corporation. Qualex accounts for its investment in ESF under the equity method of accounting. ESF provides a long-term financing solution to Qualex's photofinishing customers in connection with Qualex's leasing of photofinishing equipment to third parties, as opposed to Qualex extending long-term credit. As part of the operations of its photofinishing services, Qualex sells equipment under a sales-type lease arrangement and records a long-term receivable. These long-term receivables are subsequently sold to ESF without recourse to Qualex. ESF incurs long-term debt to finance a portion of the purchase of the receivables from Qualex. This debt is collateralized solely by the long-term receivables purchased from Qualex, and in part, by a $60 million guarantee from DCC. Qualex provides no guarantee or collateral to ESF's creditors in connection with the debt, and ESF's debt is non-recourse to Qualex. Qualex's only continued involvement in connection with the sale of the long-term receivables is the servicing of the related equipment under the leases. Qualex has continued revenue streams in connection with this equipment through future sales of photofinishing consumables, including paper and chemicals, and maintenance.

Qualex has risk with respect to the ESF arrangement as it relates to its continued ability to procure spare parts from the primary photofinishing equipment vendor to fulfill its servicing obligations under the leases. The primary photofinishing equipment vendor is currently experiencing financial difficulty, which raises concern about Qualex's ability to procure the required service parts. Although the lessees' requirement to pay ESF under the lease agreements is not contingent upon Qualex's fulfillment of its servicing obligations under the leases, under the agreement with ESF, Qualex would be responsible for any deficiency in the amount of rent not paid to ESF as a result of any lessee's claim regarding maintenance or supply services not provided by Qualex. Such lease payments would be made in accordance with the original lease terms, which generally extend over 5 to 7 years. ESF's outstanding lease receivable amount was approximately $570 million at December 31, 2001. To mitigate the risk of not being able to fulfill its service obligations, Qualex has built up its inventory of these spare parts and has begun refurbishing used parts. Additionally, Qualex has entered into spare parts escrow agreements under which bills of materials, parts drawings, intellectual property and other information necessary to manufacture the parts were put into escrow arrangements. In the event that the primary photofinishing equipment vendor were unable to supply the necessary parts to Qualex, Qualex would gain access to the information in the escrow arrangements to either manufacture or have manufactured the parts necessary to fulfill its servicing obligations. Management is currently negotiating alternatives with the photofinishing equipment vendor to further mitigate the above risks.

In December 2001, Standard & Poor's downgraded the credit ratings of Dana Corporation to BB for long-term debt and B for short-term debt, which are below investment grade. This action created a Guarantor Termination Event under the Receivables Purchase Agreement (RPA) that ESF has with its banks under the RPA. To cure the Guarantor Termination Event, in January 2002, ESF posted $60 million of additional collateral in the form of cash and long-term lease receivables. At that time, if Dana Corporation were downgraded below BB by Standard & Poor's or below Ba2 by Moody's, that action would constitute a Termination Event under the RPA and ESF would be forced to renegotiate its debt arrangements with the banks. On February 22, 2002, Moody's downgraded Dana Corporation to a Ba3 credit rating, thus creating a Termination Event.

Under the Termination Event, the banks can require ESF to put up an additional 6% collateral against the debt (on a debt balance of approximately $405 million at the time of filing the annual report, the additional collateral would be approximately $24 million), the interest rate on the debt could be increased 2 percentage points and Qualex could be precluded from selling any new receivables to ESF until the Termination Event has been waived by the banks. ESF does not currently have the ability to put up the additional collateral, and therefore, ESF would require additional capital infusions by DCC and Qualex. If DCC and/or Qualex do not provide the additional capital funding to ESF, the banks could accelerate the debt and force ESF to liquidate its long-term lease receivables to service the debt. Management believes that it is unlikely that the banks would accelerate the debt, and force ESF to sell the receivables to a third party to generate cash to satisfy the debt, due to the high-quality nature of the underlying long-term receivable portfolio. Furthermore, under this scenario, the banks would not have any recourse against Qualex; rather, the impact on Qualex would be limited to the need to find an alternative source of financing for future photofinishing equipment placements. Additionally, under this scenario, it is not expected that the operations of the customers who are leasing the equipment under these long-term lease arrangements would be affected such that Qualex's revenue stream for future sales of photofinishing consumables would be jeopardized. ESF is beginning negotiations with the banks to resolve the Termination Event.

The current RPA arrangement expires on July 23, 2002, at which time the RPA can be extended or terminated. If the RPA is terminated, Qualex will no longer be able to sell its lease receivables to ESF and will need to find an alternative financing solution for future sales of its photofinishing equipment. Under the partnership agreement between Qualex and DCC, subject to certain conditions, ESF has exclusivity rights to purchase Qualex's long-term lease receivables. The term of the partnership agreement continues through October 6, 2003. In light of the Termination Event referred to above and the timing of the partnership termination, Qualex is currently considering alternative financing solutions for prospective leasing activity with its customers.

At December 31, 2001, the Company had outstanding letters of credit totaling $42 million and surety bonds in the amount of $94 million to ensure the completion of environmental remediations and payment of possible casualty and workers' compensation claims.

Rental expense, net of minor sublease income, amounted to $126 million in 2001, $155 million in 2000 and $142 million in 1999. The approximate amounts of noncancelable lease commitments with terms of more than one year, principally for the rental of real property, reduced by minor sublease income, are $106 million in 2002, $85 million in 2003, $70 million in 2004, $36 million in 2005, $25 million in 2006 and $45 million in 2007 and thereafter.

The Company and its subsidiary companies are involved in lawsuits, claims, investigations and proceedings, including product liability, commercial, environmental, and health and safety matters, which are being handled and defended in the ordinary course of business. There are no such matters pending that the Company and its General Counsel expect to be material in relation to the Company's business, financial position or results of operations.

Note 11: Financial Instruments

The following table presents the carrying amounts of the assets (liabilities) and the estimated fair values of financial instruments at December 31, 2001 and 2000:

	2001		2000	
(in millions)	Carrying Amount	Fair Value	Carrying Amount	Fair Value
Marketable securities:				
Current	$ 3	$ 3	$ 5	$ 5
Long-term	34	34	54	53
Other investments	–	–	2	2
Long-term debt	(1,666)	(1,664)	(1,166)	(1,184)
Foreign currency forwards	1	1	(44)	(44)
Silver forwards	1	1	(17)	(17)
Interest rate swap	(2)	(2)	–	–

Marketable securities and other investments are valued at quoted market prices. The fair values of long-term borrowings are determined by reference to quoted market prices or by obtaining quotes from dealers. The fair values for the remaining financial instruments in the above table are based on dealer quotes and reflect the estimated amounts the Company would pay or receive to terminate the contracts. The carrying values of cash and cash equivalents, receivables, short-term borrowings and payables approximate their fair values.

The Company, as a result of its global operating and financing activities, is exposed to changes in foreign currency exchange rates, commodity prices, and interest rates which may adversely affect its results of operations and financial position. The Company manages such exposures, in part, with derivative financial instruments. The fair value of these derivative contracts is reported in other current assets or accounts payable and other current liabilities.

Foreign currency forward contracts are used to hedge existing foreign currency denominated assets and liabilities, especially those of the Company's International Treasury Center, as well as forecasted foreign currency denominated intercompany sales. Silver forward contracts are used to mitigate the Company's risk to fluctuating silver prices. The Company's exposure to changes in interest rates results from its investing and borrowing activities used to meet its liquidity needs. Long-term debt is generally used to finance long-term investments, while short-term debt is used to meet working capital requirements. An interest rate swap agreement was used to convert some floating-rate debt to fixed-rate debt. The Company does not utilize financial instruments for trading or other speculative purposes.

On January 1, 2000, the Company adopted SFAS No. 133, "Accounting for Derivative Instruments and Hedging Activities." This statement requires that an entity recognize all derivatives as either assets or liabilities and measure those instruments at fair value. If certain conditions are met, a derivative may be designated as a hedge. The accounting for changes in the fair value of a derivative depends on the intended use of the derivative and the resulting designation.

The transition adjustment was a loss of $1 million recorded in other income (charges) for marking foreign exchange forward contracts to fair value, and an unrealized gain of $3 million recorded in other comprehensive income for marking silver forward contracts to fair value. These items were not displayed in separate captions as cumulative effects of a change in accounting principle, due to their immateriality. The fair value of the contracts is reported in other current assets or in current liabilities.

The Company has entered into foreign currency forward contracts that are designated as cash flow hedges of exchange rate risk related to forecasted foreign currency denominated intercompany sales. At December 31, 2001, the Company had cash flow hedges for the Euro, the Canadian dollar, the Australian dollar, and the Korean won, with maturity dates ranging from January 2002 to July 2002.

At December 31, 2001, the fair value of all open foreign currency forward contracts was an unrealized gain of $1 million, recorded in other comprehensive income. Additionally, realized losses of less than $1 million, related to closed foreign currency contracts, have been deferred in other comprehensive income. If all amounts deferred to other comprehensive income related to these contracts were to be realized, less than $1 million of gains would be reclassified into cost of goods sold over the next twelve months as the inventory transferred in connection with the intercompany sales is sold to third parties. During 2001, a loss of $13 million was reclassified from other comprehensive income to cost of goods sold. Hedge ineffectiveness was insignificant.

The Company does not apply hedge accounting to the foreign currency forward contracts used to offset currency-related changes in the fair value of foreign currency denominated assets and liabilities. These contracts are marked to market through earnings at the same time that the exposed assets and liabilities are remeasured through earnings (both in other income). The majority of the contracts held by the Company are denominated in Euros, Australian dollars, British pounds, Canadian dollars, and Chinese renminbi.

The Company has entered into silver forward contracts that are designated as cash flow hedges of price risk related to forecasted worldwide silver purchases. The Company used silver forward contracts to minimize its exposure to increases in silver prices in 2000 and 2001. At December 31, 2001, the Company had open forward contracts with maturity dates ranging from January 2002 to June 2002.

At December 31, 2001, the fair value of open silver forward contracts was an unrealized gain of $1 million, recorded in other comprehensive income. If this amount were to be realized, all of it would be reclassified into cost of goods sold during the next twelve months. During 2001, a realized loss of $35 million was recorded in cost of goods sold. At December 31, 2001, realized losses of $7 million, related to closed silver contracts, were recorded in other comprehensive income. These losses will be reclassified into cost of goods sold as silver-containing products are sold, all within the next twelve months. Hedge ineffectiveness was insignificant.

In July 2001, the Company entered into an interest rate swap agreement designated as a cash flow hedge of the LIBOR-based floating-rate interest payments on $150 million of debt issued June 26, 2001 and maturing September 16, 2002. The swap effectively converts interest expense on that debt to a fixed annual rate of 4.06%.

At December 31, 2001, the fair value of the swap was a loss of $2 million, recorded in other comprehensive income. If this amount were to be realized, all of this loss would be reclassified into interest expense within the next twelve months. During 2001, less than $1 million was charged to interest expense related to the swap. There was no hedge ineffectiveness.

The Company's financial instrument counterparties are high-quality investment or commercial banks with significant experience with such instruments. The Company manages exposure to counterparty credit risk by requiring specific minimum credit standards and diversification of counterparties. The Company has procedures to monitor the credit exposure amounts. The maximum credit exposure at December 31, 2000 was not significant to the Company.

Note 12: Other Income (Charges)

(in millions)	2001	2000	1999
Investment income	$ 15	$ 36	$ 37
Loss on foreign exchange transactions	(9)	(13)	(2)
Equity in income (losses) of unconsolidated affiliates	(79)	(110)	(11)
Gain on sales of investments	18	127	41
Gain on sales of capital assets	3	51	28
(Loss) gain on sales of subsidiaries	—	(9)	120
Interest on past-due receivables	10	14	15
Minority interest	11	(11)	30
Other	13	11	3
Total	$ (18)	$ 96	$ 261

Note 13: Income Taxes

The components of earnings before income taxes and the related provision for U.S. and other income taxes were as follows:

(in millions)	2001	2000	1999
Earnings (loss) before income taxes			
U.S.	$ (266)	$ 1,294	$ 1,398
Outside the U.S.	374	838	711
Total	$ 108	$ 2,132	$ 2,109
U.S. income taxes			
Current (benefit) provision	$ (65)	$ 145	$ 185
Deferred (benefit) provision	(69)	225	215
Income taxes outside the U.S.			
Current provision	177	268	225
Deferred (benefit) provision	(5)	37	23
State and other income taxes			
Current provision	3	35	60
Deferred (benefit) provision	(9)	15	9
Total	$ 32	$ 725	$ 717

The differences between the provision for income taxes and income taxes computed using the U.S. federal income tax rate were as follows:

(in millions)	2001	2000	1999
Amount computed using the statutory rate	$ 38	$ 746	$ 738
Increase (reduction) in taxes resulting from:			
State and other income taxes, net of federal	(4)	33	45
Goodwill amortization	45	40	36
Export sales and manufacturing credits	(19)	(48)	(45)
Operations outside the U.S.	(10)	(70)	(41)
Valuation allowance	(18)	(9)	5
Tax settlement	(11)	–	–
Other, net	11	33	(21)
Provision for income taxes	$ 32	$ 725	$ 717

During the third quarter of 2001, the Company reached a favorable tax settlement, which resulted in a tax benefit of $11 million. In addition, during the fourth quarter the Company recorded a $20 million tax benefit due to a reduction in the estimated effective tax rate for the full year. The reduction in the estimated effective tax rate was primarily attributable to a shift in actual earnings versus estimates toward lower tax rate jurisdictions, and an increase in creditable foreign tax credits as compared to estimates.

The significant components of deferred tax assets and liabilities were as follows:

(in millions)	2001	2000
Deferred tax assets		
Postemployment obligations	$ 867	$ 916
Restructuring programs	122	–
Employee deferred compensation	120	116
Inventories	99	139
Tax loss carryforwards	56	103
Other	739	768
Total deferred tax assets	2,003	2,042
Deferred tax liabilities		
Depreciation	612	555
Leasing	188	225
Other	535	591
Total deferred tax liabilities	1,335	1,371
Valuation allowance	56	103
Net deferred tax assets	$ 612	$ 568

Deferred income tax assets (liabilities) are reported in the following components within the Consolidated Statement of Financial Position:

(in millions)	2001	2000
Deferred income tax charges (current)	$ 521	$ 575
Other long-term assets	201	88
Accrued income taxes	(29)	(34)
Other long-term liabilities	(81)	(61)
Net deferred income tax assets	$ 612	$ 568

The valuation allowance is primarily attributable to certain net operating loss carryforwards outside the U.S. The primary reason for the decline in the valuation allowance from 2000 to 2001 was attributable to utilization of tax loss carryforwards by certain units outside the U.S. A majority of the net operating loss carryforwards are subject to a five-year expiration period. Management believes that it is more likely than not that it will generate taxable income in certain jurisdictions sufficient to realize the remaining tax benefit associated with the future deductible temporary differences identified above. This belief is based upon a review of all available evidence, including historical operating results and projections of future taxable income.

Retained earnings of subsidiary companies outside the U.S. were approximately $1,491 million and $1,574 million at December 31, 2001 and 2000, respectively. Retained earnings at December 31, 2001 are considered to be reinvested indefinitely. It is not practicable to determine the deferred tax liability for temporary differences related to these retained earnings if they were to be remitted.

Note 14: Restructuring Costs and Other

The following table summarizes the activity with respect to the restructuring charges and reversals recorded in 2001, 2000 and 1999 and the remaining balance in the related restructuring and asset impairment reserves at December 31, 2001:

(in millions)

	Number of Employees	Severance Reserve	Inventory Reserve	Long-term Assets Reserve	Exit Costs Reserve	Total
1999 charges	3,400	$ 250	$ –	$ 90	$ 10	$ 350
1999 utilization	(400)	(21)	–	(90)	–	(111)
Ending balance at December 31, 1999	3,000	229	–	–	10	239
2000 reversal	(500)	(44)	–	–	–	(44)
2000 utilization	(2,500)	(185)	–	–	(10)	(195)
Ending balance at December 31, 2000	–	–	–	–	–	–
2001 charges	7,200	351	84	215	48	698
2001 reversal	(275)	(20)	–	–	–	(20)
2001 utilization	(2,700)	(56)	(84)	(215)	(5)	(360)
Ending balance at December 31, 2001	4,225	$ 275	$ –	$ –	$ 43	$ 318

2001 Restructuring Programs and Other

During 2001, the Company recorded a total charge for its two separate restructuring programs, the first of which was implemented in the second and third quarters of 2001 and the second of which was implemented in the fourth quarter of 2001, of $698 million, primarily for the rationalization of the U.S. photofinishing operations, the elimination of excess manufacturing capacity, the exit of certain operations and reductions in research and development positions and selling, general and administrative positions worldwide. The total restructuring amount of $698 million was comprised of charges for severance, long-term assets, inventory, and exit costs of $351 million, $215 million, $84 million, and $48 million, respectively. Additionally, during 2001, the Company recorded asset impairments relating to the Wolf Camera bankruptcy, its photofinishing operations, relocation costs in connection with a closed manufacturing site and investments in strategic and non-strategic ventures (See Note 6) of $77 million, $42 million, $18 million and $15 million, respectively.

Approximately $351 million of the charges of $698 million was for employee severance covering 7,200 worldwide positions. The geographic breakdown includes approximately 4,300 employees in the U.S. and Canada and 2,900 throughout the rest of the world. The 7,200 personnel were associated with the realignment of manufacturing (2,450), service and photofinishing operations (1,950), R&D (425) and administrative (2,375) functions in various locations of the Company's worldwide operations. Approximately 2,700 positions were eliminated by the end of 2001, with the majority of the remaining positions to be eliminated during the early part of 2002. In the fourth quarter of 2001, the Company reversed $20 million of the second quarter severance charge as certain severance actions, primarily in the European, African and Middle Eastern Region (EAMER) and Japan, will be completed at a total cost less than originally estimated. This is the result of a lower actual severance cost per employee as compared with the original amounts estimated. In addition, approximately 275 (150 service and photofinishing, 100 administrative and 25 R&D) fewer employees will be separated. The original severance accrual of $351 million and the $20 million reversal were included in restructuring costs and other.

The Company included $119 million of the $698 million provision in cost of goods sold, representing an $84 million inventory write-down associated with product line discontinuances and $35 million related to accelerated depreciation on assets presently used in operations which were disposed of during the latter part of 2001 or will be disposed of through abandonment within the first three months of 2002.

Also included in restructuring costs and other were write-offs and costs associated with the Company's exit from non-strategic operations and investments, consisting of $180 million for the write-off of capital assets, goodwill and investments, and $48 million for exit costs. The exit costs consist principally of lease termination expenses, shutdown costs and vendor penalty payments, which have been accrued on an undiscounted basis.

In 2001, the Company recorded a $77 million charge associated with the bankruptcy of the Wolf Camera Inc. consumer retail business. This amount is reflected in restructuring costs and other.

During 2001, the Company recorded a $42 million charge representing the write-off of certain lease residuals, receivables and capital assets resulting primarily from technology changes in the transition from optical to digital photofinishing equipment within the Company's onsite photofinishing operations. The charges for the lease residuals and capital assets totaling $19 million have been included in cost of goods sold. The remaining $23 million has been included in restructuring costs and other.

Note 15: Retirement Plans

Substantially all U.S. employees are covered by a noncontributory plan, the Kodak Retirement Income Plan (KRIP), which is funded by Company contributions to an irrevocable trust fund. The funding policy for KRIP is to contribute amounts sufficient to meet minimum funding requirements as determined by employee benefit and tax laws plus additional amounts the Company determines to be appropriate. Generally, benefits are based on a formula recognizing length of service and final average earnings. Assets in the fund are held for the sole benefit of participating employees and retirees. The assets of the trust fund are comprised of corporate equity and debt securities, U.S. government securities, partnership and joint venture investments, interests in pooled funds, and various types of interest rate, foreign currency and equity market financial instruments. Kodak common stock represents approximately 3.4% of trust assets.

On March 25, 1999, the Company amended this plan to include a separate cash balance formula for all U.S. employees hired after February 1999. All U.S. employees hired prior to that date were granted the option to choose the KRIP plan or the Cash Balance Plus plan. Written elections were made by employees in 1999, and were effective January 1, 2000. The Cash Balance Plus plan credits employees' accounts with an amount equal to 4% of their pay, plus interest based on the 30-year treasury bond rate. In addition, for employees participating in this plan and the Company's defined contribution plan, the Savings and Investment Plan (SIP), the Company will match SIP contributions for an amount up to 3% of pay, for employee contributions of up to 5% of pay. Company contributions to SIP were $15 million and $11 million for 2001 and 2000, respectively. As a result of employee elections to the Cash Balance Plus plan, the reductions in future pension expense will be almost entirely offset by the cost of matching employee contributions to SIP. The impact of the Cash Balance Plus plan is shown as a plan amendment.

Most subsidiaries and branches operating outside the U.S. have retirement plans covering substantially all employees. Contributions by the Company for these plans are typically deposited under government or other fiduciary-type arrangements. Retirement benefits are generally based on contractual agreements that provide for benefit formulas using years of service and/or compensation prior to retirement. The actuarial assumptions used for these plans reflect the diverse economic environments within the various countries in which the Company operates.

Changes in the Company's benefit obligation, plan assets and funded status for major plans are as follows:

	2001		2000	
(in millions)	U.S.	Non-U.S.	U.S.	Non-U.S.
Change in Benefit Obligation				
Projected benefit obligation at January 1	$ 5,530	$ 1,805	$ 5,798	$ 1,905
Service cost	94	33	89	35
Interest cost	406	101	408	114
Participant contributions	–	6	–	12
Plan amendment	–	–	(67)	(3)
Benefit payments	(555)	(106)	(578)	(111)
Actuarial loss (gain)	182	21	(115)	12
Settlements	–	(3)	–	(13)
Curtailments	–	–	(5)	–
Currency adjustments	–	(75)	–	(120)
Projected benefit obligation at December 31	$ 5,657	$ 1,782	$ 5,530	$ 1,831
Change in Plan Assets				
Fair value of plan assets at January 1	$ 7,290	$ 1,880	$ 7,340	$ 1,917
Actual return on plan assets	(418)	(115)	528	187
Employer contributions	–	33	–	38
Participant contributions	–	6	–	12
Benefit payments	(555)	(106)	(578)	(111)
Settlements	–	(3)	–	(13)
Currency adjustments	–	(75)	–	(126)
Other	–	5	–	1
Fair value of plan assets at December 31	$ 6,317	$ 1,625	$ 7,290	$ 1,905
Funded Status at December 31	$ 660	$ (157)	$ 1,760	$ 74
Unamortized:				
Transition asset	(56)	(22)	(115)	(33)
Net (gain) loss	(125)	338	(1,323)	65
Prior service cost	3	5	3	12
Net amount recognized at December 31	$ 482	$ 164	$ 325	$ 118

Amounts recognized in the Statement of Financial Position for major plans are as follows:

Prepaid pension cost	$ 482	$ 180	$ 325	$ 139
Accrued benefit liability	–	(16)	–	(21)
Net amount recognized at December 31	$ 482	$ 164	$ 325	$ 118

The prepaid pension cost asset amounts for the U.S. and Non-U.S. for 2001 of $482 million and $180 million, respectively, and $325 million and $139 million, respectively, for 2000 are included in other long-term assets.

Pension expense (income) for all plans included:

(in millions)	2001 U.S.	2001 Non-U.S.	2000 U.S.	2000 Non-U.S.	1999 U.S.	1999 Non-U.S.
Service cost	$ 94	$ 33	$ 89	$ 36	$ 107	$ 34
Interest cost	406	101	408	114	426	111
Expected return on plan assets	(599)	(149)	(572)	(157)	(537)	(137)
Amortization of:						
Transition asset	(59)	(9)	(59)	(10)	(59)	(10)
Prior service cost	1	7	1	8	10	8
Actuarial loss	–	1	–	3	2	10
	(157)	(16)	(133)	(6)	(51)	16
Curtailments	–	–	(3)	–	(1)	–
Settlements	–	1	–	1	–	–
Net pension (income) expense	(157)	(15)	(136)	(5)	(52)	16
Other plans including unfunded plans	48	82	41	69	33	51
Total net pension (income) expense	$ (109)	$ 67	$ (95)	$ 64	$ (19)	$ 67

There was no curtailment gain or loss recognized as a result of the 2001 restructuring programs. The Company recorded a $3 million curtailment gain in 2000 and a $9 million curtailment loss in 1999 as a result of the reduction in employees from the 1997 restructuring program. Additionally, the Company recorded a $10 million curtailment gain in 1999 as a result of the sale of the Office Imaging operations.

The weighted assumptions used to compute pension amounts for major plans were as follows:

	2001 U.S.	2001 Non-U.S.	2000 U.S.	2000 Non-U.S.
Discount rate	7.25%	5.90%	7.50%	6.00%
Salary increase rate	4.30%	3.10%	4.30%	3.10%
Long-term rate of return on plan assets	9.50%	8.50%	9.50%	8.70%

The Company also sponsors an unfunded plan for certain U.S. employees, primarily executives. The benefits of this plan are obtained by applying KRIP provisions to all compensation, including amounts being deferred, and without regard to the legislated qualified plan maximums, reduced by benefits under KRIP. At December 31, 2001 and 2000, the projected benefit obligations of this plan amounted to $200 million and $187 million, respectively. The Company has accrued in postemployment liabilities its unfunded accumulated benefit obligation (ABO) of $183 million and $171 million as of December 31, 2001 and 2000, respectively. Pension expense recorded in 2001, 2000 and 1999 related to this plan was $18 million, $34 million and $21 million, respectively.

Note 16: Other Postretirement Benefits

The Company provides healthcare, dental and life insurance benefits to U.S. eligible retirees and eligible survivors of retirees. In general, these benefits are provided to U.S. retirees that are covered by the Company's KRIP plan. These benefits are funded from the general assets of the Company as they are incurred. Certain non-U.S. subsidiaries offer healthcare benefits; however, the cost of such benefits is not material to the Company.

Changes in the Company's benefit obligation and funded status are as follows:

(in millions)	2001	2000
Net benefit obligation at		
beginning of year	$ 2,602	$ 2,307
Service cost	14	12
Interest cost	195	169
Plan participants' contributions	2	3
Plan amendments	–	62
Actuarial loss	446	229
Curtailments	–	1
Benefit payments	(213)	(181)
Net benefit obligation at end of year	$ 3,046	$ 2,602

	2001	2000
Funded status at end of year	$ (3,046)	$ (2,602)
Unamortized net loss	1,106	700
Unamortized plan amendments	(450)	(510)
Net amount recognized and recorded at end of year	$ (2,390)	$ (2,412)

The weighted-average assumptions used to compute other postretirement benefit amounts were as follows:

	2001	2000
Discount rate	7.25%	7.50%
Salary increase rate	4.30%	4.30%
Healthcare cost trend[(a)]	10.00%	8.00%

(a) decreasing to 5.00% by 2007

(in millions)	2001	2000	1999
Components of net postretirement benefit cost			
Service cost	$ 14	$ 12	$ 13
Interest cost	195	169	152
Amortization of:			
Prior service cost	(60)	(67)	(68)
Actuarial loss	40	18	8
	189	132	105
Curtailments	–	(6)	(90)
Total net postretirement benefit cost	$ 189	$ 126	$ 15

There were no curtailment gains or losses recognized as a result of the 2001 restructuring programs.

The Company recorded curtailment gains of $6 million and $71 million in 2000 and 1999, respectively, as a result of the reduction in employees from the 1997 restructuring program. Additionally, the Company recorded curtailment gains in 1999 of $15 million as a result of the sale of the Office Imaging operations, and $4 million related to the establishment of the NexPress joint venture.

The Company will no longer fund healthcare and dental benefits for employees who elected to participate in the Company's Cash Balance Plus plan, effective January 1, 2000. This change is not expected to have a material impact on the Company's future postretirement benefit cost.

Assumed healthcare cost trend rates have a significant effect on the amounts reported for the healthcare plans. A one percentage point change in assumed healthcare cost trend rates would have the following effects:

	1% increase	1% decrease
Effect on total service and interest cost components	$ 7	$ (3)
Effect on postretirement benefit obligation	102	(58)

Note 17: Accumulated Other Comprehensive (Loss) Income

The components of accumulated other comprehensive (loss) income at December 31, 2001, 2000 and 1999 were as follows:

(in millions)	2001	2000	1999
Accumulated unrealized holding (losses) gains related to available-for-sale securities	$ (6)	$ 7	$ 113
Accumulated unrealized losses related to hedging activity	(5)	(38)	–
Accumulated translation adjustments	(524)	(425)	(231)
Accumulated minimum pension liability adjustments	(62)	(26)	(27)
Total	$ (597)	$ (482)	$ (145)

Note 18: Stock Option and Compensation Plans

The Company's stock incentive plans consist of the 2000 Omnibus Long-Term Compensation Plan (the 2000 Plan), the 1995 Omnibus Long-Term Compensation Plan (the 1995 Plan), and the 1990 Omnibus Long-Term Compensation Plan (the 1990 Plan). The Plans are administered by the Executive Compensation and Development Committee of the Board of Directors.

Under the 2000 Plan, 22 million shares of the Company's common stock may be granted to a variety of employees between January 1, 2000 and December 31, 2004. The 2000 Plan is substantially similar to, and is intended to replace, the 1995 Plan, which expired on December 31, 1999.

Under the 1995 Plan, 22 million shares of the Company's common stock were eligible for grant to a variety of employees between February 1, 1995 and December 31, 1999. Option prices are not less than 100% of the per share fair market value on the date of grant, and the options generally expire ten years from the date of grant, but may expire sooner if the optionee's employment terminates. The 1995 Plan also provides for Stock Appreciation Rights (SARs) to be granted, either in tandem with options or freestanding. SARs allow optionees to receive payment equal to the difference between the Company's stock market price on grant date and exercise date. At December 31, 2001, 226,515 freestanding SARs were outstanding at option prices ranging from $56.31 to $71.81.

Under the 1990 Plan, 22 million shares of the Company's common stock were eligible for grant to key employees between February 1, 1990 and January 31, 1995. Option prices could not be less than 50% of the per share fair market value on the date of grant; however, no options below fair market value were granted. The options generally expire ten years from the date of grant, but may expire sooner if the optionee's employment terminates. The 1990 Plan also provided that options with dividend equivalents, tandem SARs and freestanding SARs could be granted. At December 31, 2001, 98,046 freestanding SARs were outstanding at option prices ranging from $32.50 to $44.50.

In January 2002, the Company's shareholders voted in favor of a proposed stock option exchange program for its employees. The voluntary program offers employees a one-time opportunity to exchange stock options they currently hold for new options. The new options are expected to be granted on or about August 26, 2002. The new options will have a grant price equal to the fair market value of Kodak common stock on the new grant date. The number of new options employees will ultimately receive has been determined, prior to the inception of the exchange program, based on the fair value of the existing options, as determined using the Black-Scholes option pricing model. In most cases, employees will receive fewer options in exchange for their current options. The exchange generally applies to all outstanding options held by employees, including two all-employee grants made in 1998 and 2000. The exchange program is not expected to result in the recording of any compensation expense.

Further information relating to options is as follows:

(Amounts in thousands, except per share amounts)	Shares Under Option	Range of Price Per Share	Weighted Average Exercise Price Per Share
Outstanding on			
December 31, 1998	34,331	$30.25–$92.31	$61.04
Granted	4,276	$60.13–$79.63	$65.17
Exercised	1,101	$30.25–$74.31	$39.73
Terminated, Canceled or Surrendered	473	$31.45–$92.31	$63.80
Outstanding on			
December 31, 1999	37,033	$30.25–$92.31	$62.12
Granted	12,533	$37.25–$69.53	$54.38
Exercised	1,326	$30.25–$58.63	$32.64
Terminated, Canceled or Surrendered	3,394	$31.45–$90.50	$62.22
Outstanding on			
December 31, 2000	44,846	$32.50–$92.31	$60.87
Granted	8,575	$26.90–$74.31	$36.49
Exercised	615	$32.50–$43.18	$35.91
Terminated, Canceled or Surrendered	2,351	$32.50–$90.75	$50.33
Outstanding on			
December 31, 2001	50,455	$25.92–$92.31	$57.53
Exercisable on			
December 31, 1999	19,913	$30.25–$92.31	$57.08
Exercisable on			
December 31, 2000	28,783	$32.50–$92.31	$62.13
Exercisable on			
December 31, 2001	31,571	$26.90–$92.31	$63.54

The table above excludes approximately 68,000 options granted by the Company at an exercise price of $.05–$21.91 as part of an acquisition.

As allowed by SFAS No. 123, "Accounting for Stock-Based Compensation," the Company has elected to continue to follow APB Opinion No. 25, "Accounting for Stock Issued to Employees," in accounting for its stock option plans. Under APB No. 25, the Company does not recognize compensation expense upon the issuance of its stock options because the option terms are fixed and the exercise price equals the market price of the underlying stock on the grant date. The Company has determined the pro forma information as if the Company had accounted for stock options granted under the fair value method of SFAS No. 123. The Black-Scholes option pricing model was used with the following weighted-average assumptions for options issued in each year:

	2001	2000	1999
Risk-free interest rates	4.2%	6.2%	5.1%
Expected option lives	6 years	7 years	7 years
Expected volatilities	34%	29%	28%
Expected dividend yields	4.43%	3.19%	2.76%

The weighted-average fair value of options granted was $8.37, $16.79 and $18.77 for 2001, 2000 and 1999, respectively.

For purposes of pro forma disclosures, the estimated fair value of the options is amortized to expense over the options' vesting period (2–3 years). The Company's pro forma information follows:

	Year Ended December 31		
(in millions, except per share data)	2001	2000	1999
Net earnings			
As reported	$ 76	$1,407	$1,392
Pro forma	(3)	1,346	1,263
Basic earnings per share			
As reported	$ .26	$ 4.62	$ 4.38
Pro forma	(.01)	4.41	3.97
Diluted earnings per share			
As reported	$ .26	$ 4.59	$ 4.33
Pro forma	(.01)	4.41	3.96

The following table summarizes information about stock options at December 31, 2001:

(Number of options in thousands)		Options Outstanding			Options Exercisable	
Range of Exercise Prices						
At Least	Less Than	Options	Weighted-Average Remaining Contractual Life	Weighted-Average Exercise Price	Options	Weighted-Average Exercise Price
$25 –	$40	6,175	7.98	$ 32.08	1,351	$ 33.81
$40 –	$55	14,356	6.26	$ 47.87	4,999	$ 45.31
$55 –	$70	20,060	6.55	$ 62.52	15,711	$ 63.44
$70 –	$85	7,512	5.16	$ 73.42	7,158	$ 73.40
Over $85		2,352	5.17	$ 90.01	2,352	$ 90.01
		50,455			31,571	

Note 19: Acquisitions, Joint Ventures and Business Ventures

2001 On December 4, 2001, the Company and SANYO Electric Co., Ltd. announced the formation of a global business venture, the SK Display Corporation, to manufacture organic light emitting diode (OLED) displays for consumer devices such as cameras, personal data assistants (PDAs), and portable entertainment machines. Kodak will hold a 34% stake in the business venture and will contribute approximately $19 million in cash and $100 million in loan guarantees during 2002 and 2003. SANYO will hold a 66% stake in the business venture and will contribute approximately $36 million in cash and $195 million in loan guarantees during the same periods.

On June 4, 2001, the Company completed its acquisition of Ofoto, Inc. The purchase price of this stock acquisition was approximately $58 million in cash. The acquisition was accounted for as a purchase with $10 million allocated to tangible net assets, $37 million allocated to goodwill and $11 million allocated to other intangible assets. The acquisition of Ofoto will accelerate Kodak's growth in the online photography market and help drive more rapid adoption of digital and online services. Ofoto offers digital processing of digital images and traditional film, top-quality prints, private online image storage, sharing, editing and creative tools, frames, cards and other merchandise.

On February 7, 2001, the Company completed its acquisition of substantially all of the imaging services operations of Bell & Howell Company. The purchase price of this stock and asset acquisition was $141 million in cash. The acquisition was accounted for as a purchase with $15 million allocated to tangible net assets, $70 million allocated to goodwill, and $56 million allocated to other intangible assets, primarily customer contracts. The acquired units provide customers worldwide with maintenance for document imaging components, micrographic-related equipment, supplies, parts and service.

During 2001, the Company also completed additional acquisitions, none of which are individually material to the Company's financial position, results of operations or cash flows, which had an aggregate purchase price of approximately $122 million in cash and stock.

Note 20: Sales of Assets and Divestitures

1999 In April 1999, the Company sold its digital printer, copier-duplicator, and roller assembly operations primarily associated with its Office Imaging operations, which included its operations in Rochester, NY, Muehlhausen, Germany and Tijuana, Mexico to Heidelberg for approximately $80 million. The transaction did not have a material effect on the Company's results of operations or financial position.

In November 1999, the Company sold The Image Bank, a wholly-owned subsidiary which markets and licenses image reproduction rights, to Getty Images, Inc. for $183 million in cash. As a result of this transaction, the Company recorded a gain of $95 million in other income (charges).

In November 1999, the Company sold its Motion Analysis Systems Division, which manufactures digital cameras and digital video cameras for the automotive and industrial markets, to Roper Industries, Inc. for approximately $50 million in cash. As a result of this transaction, the Company recorded a gain of $25 million in other income (charges).

Note 21: Segment Information

Beginning in the fourth quarter of 2001, the Company changed its operating structure, which was previously comprised of seven business units, to be centered around strategic product groups. The strategic product groups from existing businesses and geographies have been integrated into segments that share common technology, manufacturing and product platforms and customer sets. In accordance with the change in the operating structure, certain of the Company's product groups were realigned to reflect how senior management now reviews the business, makes investing and resource allocation decisions and assesses operating performance. The realignment of certain of the Company's strategic product groups resulted in changes to the composition of the reportable segments.

As a result of the change in composition of the reportable segments, the accompanying 1999 and 2000 segment information has been presented in accordance with the new structure and to conform to the 2001 presentation. The Company has three reportable segments: Photography; Health Imaging; and Commercial Imaging.

The Photography segment derives revenues from consumer film products, sales of origination and print film to the entertainment industry, sales of professional film products, traditional and inkjet photo paper, chemicals, traditional and digital cameras, photoprocessing equipment and services, and digitization services, including online services. The Health Imaging segment derives revenues from the sale of digital products, including laser imagers, media, computed and direct radiography equipment and picture archiving and communications systems, as well as traditional medical products, including analog film, equipment, chemistry, services and specialty products for the mammography, oncology and dental fields. The Commercial Imaging segment derives revenues from microfilm equipment and media, printers, scanners, other business equipment, media sold to commercial and government customers, and from graphics film products sold to the Kodak Polychrome Graphics joint venture. The All Other group derives revenues from the sale of organic light emitting diode (OLED) displays, imaging sensor solutions and optical products to other manufacturers.

Transactions between segments, which are immaterial, are made on a basis intended to reflect the market value of the products, recognizing prevailing market prices and distributor discounts. Differences between the reportable segments' operating results and net assets, and the Company's consolidated financial statements relate primarily to items held at the corporate level, and to other items excluded from segment operating measurements.

Segment financial information is shown below.

(in millions)	2001	2000	1999
Net sales:			
Photography	$ 9,403	$ 10,231	$ 10,265
Health Imaging	2,262	2,220	2,159
Commercial Imaging	1,459	1,417	1,479
All Other	110	126	186
Consolidated total	$ 13,234	$ 13,994	$ 14,089
Earnings from operations:			
Photography	$ 787	$ 1,430	$ 1,709
Health Imaging	323	518	483
Commercial Imaging	165	233	257
All Other	(60)	(11)	(109)
Total of segments	1,215	2,170	2,340
Restructuring costs and credits and asset impairments	(732)	44	(350)
Wolf charge	(77)	–	–
Environmental reserve	(41)	–	–
Kmart charge	(20)	–	–
Consolidated total	$ 345	$ 2,214	$ 1,990
Net earnings:			
Photography	$ 535	$ 1,034	$ 1,261
Health Imaging	221	356	324
Commercial Imaging	80	90	178
All Other	(38)	(2)	(61)
Total of segments	798	1,478	1,702
Restructuring costs and credits and asset impairments	(735)	44	(350)
Wolf charge	(77)	–	–
Environmental reserve	(41)	–	–
Kmart charge	(20)	–	–
Interest expense	(219)	(178)	(142)
Other corporate items	8	26	22
Income tax effects on above items and taxes not allocated to segments	362	37	160
Consolidated total	$ 76	$ 1,407	$ 1,392

(in millions)	2001	2000	1999
Operating net assets:			
Photography	$ 6,288	$ 7,100	$ 6,875
Health Imaging	1,426	1,491	1,229
Commercial Imaging	1,085	1,045	963
All Other	(219)	(92)	(123)
Total of segments	8,580	9,544	8,944
LIFO inventory reserve	(444)	(449)	(465)
Cash and marketable securities	451	251	393
Dividends payable	–	(128)	(139)
Net deferred income tax (liabilities) and assets	97	(4)	191
Noncurrent other postemployment liabilities	(2,180)	(2,209)	(2,289)
Other corporate net assets	(410)	(205)	(624)
Consolidated net assets (1)	$ 6,094	$ 6,800	$ 6,011

(1) Consolidated net assets are derived from the Consolidated Statement of Financial Position, as follows:

(in millions)	2001	2000	1999
Total assets	$ 13,362	$ 14,212	$ 14,370
Total liabilities	10,468	10,784	10,458
Less: Short-term borrowings and current portion of long-term debt	(1,534)	(2,206)	(1,163)
Less: Long-term debt, net of current portion	(1,666)	(1,166)	(936)
Non-interest-bearing liabilities	7,268	7,412	8,359
Consolidated net assets	$ 6,094	$ 6,800	$ 6,011

(in millions)	2001	2000	1999
Depreciation expense:			
Photography	$ 599	$ 557	$ 592
Health Imaging	96	92	82
Commercial Imaging	69	80	76
All Other	1	9	23
Consolidated total	$ 765	$ 738	$ 773
Goodwill amortization expense:			
Photography	$ 110	$ 120	$ 113
Health Imaging	28	27	24
Commercial Imaging	16	3	4
All Other	0	1	4
Consolidated total	$ 154	$ 151	$ 145
Capital additions:			
Photography	$ 555	$ 721	$ 938
Health Imaging	128	120	92
Commercial Imaging	56	98	84
All Other	4	6	13
Consolidated total	$ 743	$ 945	$ 1,127
Net sales to external customers attributed to(2):			
The United States	$ 6,419	$ 6,800	$ 6,714
Europe, Middle East and Africa	3,275	3,464	3,734
Asia Pacific	2,215	2,349	2,267
Canada and Latin America	1,325	1,381	1,374
Consolidated total	$ 13,234	$ 13,994	$ 14,089

(2) Sales are reported in the geographic area in which they originate.

	2001	2000	1999
Long-lived assets located in:			
The United States	$ 3,738	$ 3,913	$ 3,904
Europe, Middle East and Africa	672	647	715
Asia Pacific	977	1,056	1,024
Canada and Latin America	272	303	304
Consolidated total	$ 5,659	$ 5,919	$ 5,947

Note 22: Quarterly Sales and Earnings Data—Unaudited

(in millions, except per share data)	4th Qtr.	3rd Qtr.	2nd Qtr.	1st Qtr.
2001				
Net sales	$ 3,359	$ 3,308	$ 3,592	$ 2,975
Gross profit	1,027	1,132	1,338	1,067
Net (loss) earnings	(206)(4)	96(3)	36(1,2)	150(1)
Basic (loss) earnings per share(6)	(.71)	.33	.12	.52
Diluted (loss) earnings per share(6)	(.71)	.33	.12	.52
2000				
Net sales	$ 3,560	$ 3,590	$ 3,749	$ 3,095
Gross profit	1,244	1,516	1,626	1,261
Net earnings	194(5)	418(5)	506(5)	289(5)
Basic earnings per share(6)	.66	1.37	1.63	.93
Diluted earnings per share(6)	.66	1.36	1.62	.93

(1) Includes relocation charges (included in cost of goods sold) related to the sale and exit of a manufacturing facility of $10 million and $8 million, which reduced net earnings by $7 million and $5 million in the first and second quarters, respectively.

(2) Includes $316 million ($57 million included in cost of goods sold and $259 million included in restructuring costs and other) of restructuring costs, which reduced net earnings by $232 million; and $77 million (included in restructuring costs and other) for the Wolf bankruptcy charge, which reduced net earnings by $52 million.

(3) Includes $53 million ($41 million included in cost of goods sold and $12 million included in restructuring costs and other) of restructuring costs, which reduced net earnings by $41 million; $42 million ($23 million included in restructuring costs and other and $19 million included in cost of goods sold) for a charge related to asset impairments associated with certain of the Company's photofinishing operations, which reduced net earnings by $26 million; and an $11 million (included in provision for income taxes) tax benefit related to favorable tax settlements reached during the quarter.

(4) Includes $309 million ($21 million included in cost of goods sold and $288 million included in restructuring costs and other) of restructuring costs, which reduced net earnings by $210 million; $15 million ($12 million included in selling, general and administrative expenses and $3 million included in other income (charges)) for asset impairments related to venture investments, which reduced net earnings by $10 million; a $41 million (included in selling, general and administrative expenses) charge for environmental reserves, which reduced net earnings by $28 million; a $20 million (included in selling, general and administrative expenses) Kmart bankruptcy charge, which reduced net earnings by $14 million, and a $20 million (included in provision for income taxes) tax benefit related to a decline in the year-over-year effective tax rate.

(5) Includes accelerated depreciation and relocation charges (included in cost of goods sold) related to the sale and exit of a manufacturing facility of $11 million, $12 million, $18 million, and $9 million, which reduced net earnings by $7 million, $8 million, $12 million, and $6 million in the first, second, third and fourth quarters, respectively.

(6) Each quarter is calculated as a discrete period and the sum of the four quarters may not equal the full year amount.

EASTMAN KODAK

Eastman Kodak Company and Subsidiary Companies

Summary of Operating Data

(Dollar amounts and shares in millions, except per share data)	2001	2000	1999	1998	1997
Net sales	$ 13,234	$ 13,994	$ 14,089	$ 13,406	$ 14,538
Earnings from operations	345	2,214	1,990	1,888	130
Net earnings	76(1)	1,407(2)	1,392(3)	1,390(4)	5(6)
Earnings and Dividends					
Net earnings					
— % of sales	0.6%	10.1%	9.9%	10.4%	0.0%
— % return on average shareholders' equity	2.4%	38.3%	35.2%	38.9%	0.1%
Basic earnings per share	.26	4.62	4.38	4.30	.01
Diluted earnings per share	.26	4.59	4.33	4.24	.01
Cash dividends paid					
— on common shares	643	545	563	569	567
— per common share	2.21	1.76	1.76	1.76	1.76
Common shares outstanding at year end	290.9	290.5	310.4	322.8	323.1
Shareholders at year end	91,893	113,308	131,719	129,495	135,132
Statement of Financial Position Data					
Operational working capital(8)	$ 863	$ 1,482	$ 838	$ 939	$ 909
Working capital	(671)	(724)	(325)	(579)	298
Property, plant and equipment, net	5,659	5,919	5,947	5,914	5,509
Total assets	13,362	14,212	14,370	14,733	13,145
Short-term borrowings and current portion of long-term debt	1,534	2,206	1,163	1,518	611
Long-term debt, net of current portion	1,666	1,166	936	504	585
Total shareholders' equity	2,894	3,428	3,912	3,988	3,161
Supplemental Information					
Sales — Photography	$ 9,403	$ 10,231	$ 10,265	$ 10,063	$ 10,620
— Health Imaging	2,262	2,220	2,159	1,526	1,532
— Commercial Imaging	1,459	1,417	1,479	1,296	1,740
— All Other	110	126	187	521	646
Research and development costs	779	784	817	922(5)	1,230(7)
Depreciation	765	738	773	737	748
Taxes (excludes payroll, sales and excise taxes)	154	933	806	809	164
Wages, salaries and employee benefits	3,824	3,726	3,962	4,306	4,985
Employees at year end					
— in the U.S.	42,000	43,200	43,300	46,300	54,800
— worldwide	75,100	78,400	80,650	86,200	97,500

(1) Includes $678 million of restructuring charges; $42 million for a charge related to asset impairments associated with certain of the Company's photofinishing operations; $15 million for asset impairments related to venture investments; $41 million for a charge for environmental reserves; $77 million for the Wolf bankruptcy; a $20 million charge for the Kmart bankruptcy; $18 million of relocation charges related to the sale and exit of a manufacturing facility; an $11 million tax benefit related to a favorable tax settlement; and a $20 million tax benefit representing a decline in the year-over-year effective tax rate. These items reduced net earnings by $594 million.

(2) Includes accelerated depreciation and relocation charges related to the sale and exit of a manufacturing facility of $50 million, which reduced net earnings by $33 million.

(3) Includes $350 million of restructuring charges, and an additional $11 million of charges related to this restructuring program; $103 million of charges associated with business exits; a gain of $95 million on the sale of The Image Bank; and a gain of $25 million on the sale of the Motion Analysis Systems Division. These items reduced net earnings by $227 million.

(4) Includes $35 million of litigation charges; $132 million of Office Imaging charges; $45 million primarily for a write-off of in-process R&D associated with the Imation acquisition; a gain of $87 million on the sale of NanoSystems; and a gain of $66 million on the sale of part of the Company's investment in Gretag. These items reduced net earnings by $39 million.

(5) Includes a $42 million charge for the write-off of in-process R&D associated with the Imation acquisition.

(6) Includes $1,455 million of restructuring costs, asset impairments and other charges; $186 million for a write-off of in-process R&D associated with the Wang acquisition; and a $46 million litigation charge. These items reduced net earnings by $1,143 million.

(7) Includes a $186 million charge for the write-off of in-process R&D associated with the Wang acquisition.

(8) Excludes short-term borrowings and current portion of long-term debt.

Campbell Soup

(million dollars)

	Year 11		Year 10		Year 9	
	Sales	***Earnings***	Sales	Earnings	Sales	Earnings
1 **CONTRIBUTIONS BY DIVISION:**						
Campbell North America						
Campbell U.S.A.	***$3,911.8***	***$632.7***	$3,932.7	$370.8	$3,666.9	$242.3
Campbell Canada	***352.0***	***35.3***	384.0	25.6	313.4	23.8
	4,263.8	***668.0***	4,316.7	396.4	3,980.3	266.1
Campbell Biscuit and Bakery						
Pepperidge Farm	***569.0***	***73.6***	582.0	57.0	548.4	53.6
International Biscuit	***219.4***	***17.6***	195.3	8.9	178.0	11.7
	788.4	***91.2***	777.3	65.9	726.4	65.3
Campbell International	***1,222.9***	***39.4***	1,189.8	(168.6)	1,030.3	(117.8)
Interdivision	***(71.0)***		(78.0)		(64.9)	
TOTAL SALES	***$6,204.1***		$6,205.8		$5,672.1	
TOTAL OPERATING EARNINGS		***798.6***		293.7		213.6
Unallocated corporate expenses		***(41.1)***		(16.5)		(31.3)
Interest, net		***(90.2)***		(94.0)		(55.8)
Foreign currency translation adjustments		***.1***		(3.8)		(20.0)
Taxes on earnings		***(265.9)***		(175.0)		(93.4)
NET EARNINGS		***$401.5***		$4.4		$13.1
NET EARNINGS PER SHARE		***$3.16***		$.03		$.10

Contributions by division in Year 10 include the effects of divestitures, restructuring and unusual charges of $339.1 million as follows: Campbell U.S.A. $121.8 million, Campbell Canada $6.6 million, Pepperidge Farm $11.0 million, International Biscuit $14.3 million, and Campbell International $185.4 million. Contributions by division in Year 9 include the effects of restructuring and unusual charges of $343.0 million as follows: Campbell U.S.A. $183.1 million, Campbell Canada $6.0 million, Pepperidge Farm $7.1 million, International Biscuit $9.5 million, and Campbell International $137.3 million.

2 RESULTS OF OPERATIONS

Overview

Campbell had record net earnings in Year 11 of $401.5 million, or $3.16 per share, compared to net earnings of $4.4 million, or 3 cents per share, in Year 10. Excluding Year 10's divestiture and restructuring charges, earnings per share increased 34% in Year 11. In Year 11, the Company sold five non-strategic businesses, sold or closed several manufacturing plants, and discontinued certain unprofitable product lines. Net sales of $6.2 billion in Year 11 were even with Year 10. Sales were up 4% excluding businesses that were divested and product lines that were discontinued in Year 11.

In Year 10 the Company incurred charges for divestitures and restructuring of $2.33 per share, reducing net earnings to 3 cents per share. In Year 9 restructuring charges of $2.02 per share reduced earnings to 10 cents per share. Excluding these charges from both years, earnings per share rose 11% in Year 10. Sales increased 9%. In Year 10 the company's domestic divisions had strong earnings performances, excluding the divestiture and restructuring charges, but the International Division's performance was disappointing principally due to the poor performance of United Kingdom frozen food and Italian biscuit operations. The Italian biscuit operations were divested in Year 11.

The divestiture and restructuring programs were designed to strengthen the Company's core businesses and improve long-term profitability. The Year 10 divestiture program involved the sale of several low-return or non-strategic businesses. The Year 10 restructuring charges provided for the elimination of underperforming assets and unnecessary facilities and included a write-off of goodwill. The restructuring charges in Year 9 involved plant consolidations, work force reductions, and goodwill write-offs.

Year 11 Compared to Year 10

3 RESULTS BY DIVISION

Campbell North America—Operating earnings of Campbell North America, the Company's largest division, were $668.0 million in Year 11 compared to $396.4 million in Year 10 after restructuring charges of $128.4 million. Operating earnings increased 27% in Year 11 over Year 10, excluding the restructuring charges from Year 10. All of the division's core businesses had very strong earnings growth. Continued benefits of restructuring drove significant improvements in operating margins.

Sales were $4.26 billion in Year 11. Excluding divested businesses and discontinued product lines, sales increased 2% with overall volume down 2%. Soup volume was off 1.5% as a result of reduced year-end trade promotional activities. Significant volume increases were achieved in the cooking soup, ramen noodle and family-size soup categories and "Healthy Request" soup. Exceptionally strong volume performances were turned in by "Swanson" frozen dinners, "Franco-American" gravies and "Prego" spaghetti sauces with positive volume results for "LeMenu Healthy" entrees, Food Service frozen soups and entrees, and Casera Foods in Puerto Rico.

Campbell Biscuit and Bakery—Operating earnings of the Biscuit and Bakery division, which includes Pepperidge Farm in the United States, Delacre in Europe and an equity interest in Arnotts Limited in Australia, were $91.2 million in Year 11 compared with $65.9 million in Year 10 after restructuring charges of $25.3 million. Operating earnings were flat in Year 11 excluding the restructuring charges from Year 10. Sales increased 1%, however, volume declined 3%.

Pepperidge Farm operating earnings in Year 11 increased despite a drop in sales, which reflects the adverse effect of the recession on premium cookies. Several new varieties of "Hearty Slices" bread performed well. Delacre, benefiting from new management and integration into the worldwide biscuit and bakery organization, turned in significant improvement in Year 11 sales and operating earnings. Arnotts' performance in Year 11 was disappointing and included restructuring charges. Its restructuring program should have a positive impact on fiscal Year 12 results. The Year 11 comparison with Year 10 was also adversely impacted by gains of $4.0 million realized in Year 10 on the sales of businesses by Arnotts.

Campbell International—Operating earnings of the International division were $39.4 million in Year 11 compared to an operating loss of $168.6 million in Year 10 after restructuring charges of $185.4 million.

In Year 11, Campbell International achieved a significant turnaround. Operating earnings for the year more than doubled above the pre-restructuring results of the prior year. There were margin improvements throughout the system. Europe led the division's positive results. A key component was the United Kingdom's move from a loss position to profitability, driven by the benefits of restructuring and product line reconfiguration.

European Food and Confectionery units turned in another year of solid earnings growth. Mexican operations, strengthened by a new management team, also turned around from a loss to a profit position. Sales were $1.22 billion in Year 11, an increase of 6%, excluding divested businesses and discontinued product lines, and the effects of foreign currency rates. Volume was approximately the same as in Year 10.

4 STATEMENTS OF EARNINGS

Sales in Year 11 were even with Year 10. Excluding divested businesses and unprofitable product lines discontinued during Year 11, sales increased 4% while volume declined approximately 2%. The decline in volume was caused by reduced year-end trade promotional activities and the adverse effect of the recession on certain premium products.

Gross margins improved 2.6 percentage points to 34.0% in Year 11 from 31.4% in Year 10. All divisions improved due to the significant benefits from restructuring and the divestitures and product-pruning activities. Productivity improvements worldwide and declining commodity prices also contributed to the higher margins.

Marketing and selling expenses, as a percentage of net sales, were 15.4% in Year 11 compared to 15.8% in Year 10. The decrease in Year 11 is due to more focused marketing efforts and controlled new product introductions. For each of the prior 10 fiscal years, these expenses had increased significantly. Advertising was down 11% in Year 11. Management expects advertising expenditures to increase in Year 12 in order to drive volume growth of core products and to support the introduction of new products.

Administrative expenses, as a percentage of net sales, were 4.9% in Year 11 compared to 4.7% in Year 10. The increase in Year 11 results principally from annual executive incentive plan accruals due to outstanding financial performance and foreign currency rates.

Interest expense increased in Year 11 due to timing of fourth quarter borrowings in order to obtain favorable long-term interest rates. Interest income was also higher in Year 11 as the proceeds from these borrowings were invested temporarily until needed. Interest expense, net of interest income, decreased from $94.0 million in Year 10 to $90.2 million in Year 11 as the increased cash flow from operations exceeded cash used for share repurchases and acquisitions.

Foreign exchange losses declined principally due to reduced effects of currency devaluations in Argentina.

Other expense was $26.2 million in Year 11 compared to $14.7 million in Year 10. The increase results principally from accruals for long-term incentive compensation plans reflecting changes in Campbell's stock price.

As discussed in the "Overview" section above, Year 10 results include divestiture, restructuring, and unusual charges of $339.1 million ($301.6 million or $2.33 per share after taxes).

Equity in earnings of affiliates declined in Year 11 principally due to the disappointing performance at Arnotts and to a $4.0 million gain on sales of businesses realized by Arnotts in Year 10.

Year 10 Compared to Year 9

5 RESULTS BY DIVISION

CAMPBELL NORTH AMERICA—In Year 10, Campbell North America had operating earnings of $396.4 million after restructuring charges of $128.4 million. In Year 9 the division had operating earnings of $266.1 million, after restructuring charges of $189.1 million. Excluding restructuring charges from both Year 10 and Year 9 operating earnings increased 15% in Year 10, led by strong performances by the soup, grocery, "Mrs. Paul's" frozen seafood, and Canadian sectors. The olives business performed poorly in Year 10.

Sales increased 8% in Year 10 to $4.32 billion on a 3% increase in volume. There were solid volume increases in ready-to-serve soups, "Great Starts" frozen breakfasts, and "Prego" spaghetti sauces. Overall soup volume was up 1%. "Mrs. Paul's" regained the number one share position in frozen prepared seafood.

CAMPBELL BISCUIT AND BAKERY—In Year 10, Campbell Biscuit and Bakery had operating earnings of $65.9 million after restructuring charges of $25.3 million. In Year 9, the division's operating earnings were $65.3 million after restructuring charges of $16.6 million. Excluding restructuring charges from both Year 10 and Year 9, operating earnings of the division increased 11% in Year 10. The increase in operating earnings was driven by Pepperidge Farm's biscuit and bakery units along with Arnott's gain on sales of businesses. Pepperidge Farm's frozen unit and Delacre performed poorly. Sales increased 7% to $777.3 million. Volume increased 1%, with Pepperidge Farm's biscuit, bakery and food service units and Delacre the main contributors to the growth.

CAMPBELL INTERNATIONAL—In Year 10, Campbell International had an operating loss of $168.6 million after restructuring charges of $185.4 million. In Year 9, the division sustained an operating loss of $117.8 million after restructuring charges of $137.3 million. Excluding restructuring charges from both Year 10 and Year 9, operating earnings declined 14% in Year 10, as strong performances in the European Food and Confectionery and Argentine operations were more than offset by poor performances in the United Kingdom frozen food and Italian biscuit operations. Sales in Year 10 were $1.19 billion, an increase of 15%. Volume was up 14% of which 11% came from acquisitions.

6 STATEMENTS OF EARNINGS

In Year 10 sales increased 9% on a 5% increase in volume, about half of which came from established businesses.

Gross margins improved by 1.9 percentage points to 31.4% in Year 10 from 29.5% in Year 9. All divisions had improved margins in Year 10, with Campbell North America operations posting substantial improvements.

Marketing and selling expenses, as a percentage of net sales, were 15.8% in Year 10 compared to 14.4% in Year 9. The Year 10 increase was due to heavy marketing expenditures by Campbell U.S.A. at both the national and regional levels.

Administrative expenses, as a percentage of net sales, were 4.7% in Year 10 compared to 4.4% in Year 9. The increase in Year 10 was driven by some unusual one-time expenditures, employee benefits, the weakening dollar and acquisitions.

Interest expense increased in Year 10 due to higher debt levels resulting from funding of acquisitions, higher inventory levels during the year, purchases of Campbell's stock for the treasury and restructuring program expenditures. Interest income declined in Year 10 because of a shift from local currency to lower-yielding dollar denominated temporary investments in Latin America to minimize foreign exchange losses.

Foreign exchange losses resulted principally from currency devaluations in Argentina. There was a large devaluation in Argentina in Year 9. Also, Year 10 losses were lower due to the shift in temporary investments described in the previous paragraph.

Other expense was $14.7 million in Year 10 compared to $32.4 million in Year 9. This decline results principally from reduced accruals for long-term incentive compensation plans reflecting changes in Campbell's stock price.

As discussed in the "Overview" section above, results include divestiture, restructuring and unusual charges of $339.1 million ($301.6 million or $2.33 per share after taxes) in Year 10 and $343.0 million ($260.8 million or $2.02 per share after taxes) in Year 9.

Equity in earnings of affiliates increased in Year 10 principally due to a $4.0 million gain on sales of businesses realized by Arnotts in Year 10.

7 **Income Taxes**

The effective income tax rate was 39.8% in Year 11, 97.5% in Year 10 an 87.7% in Year 9. The principal reason for the high tax rates in Year 10 and Year 9 is that certain of the divestiture, restructuring and unusual charges are not tax deductible. Excluding the effect of these charges, the rate would be 41.0% in Year 10 and 38.9% in Year 9. The variances in all years are principally due to the level of certain foreign losses for which no tax benefit is currently available.

8 **Inflation**

The Company attempts to mitigate the effects of inflation on sales and earnings by appropriately increasing selling prices and aggressively pursuing an ongoing cost improvement effort which includes capital investments in more efficient plants and equipment. Also, the divestiture and restructuring programs enacted in Year 9 and Year 10 have made the Company a more cost-effective producer, as previously discussed with reference to cost of products sold.

9 **Recent Developments**

The Financial Accounting Standards Board Statement of Financial Accounting Standards No. 106, "Employer's Accounting for Post-retirement Benefits Other Than Pensions," requires employers to account for retiree health obligations on an accrual basis beginning with the Company's Year 14 fiscal year. For a discussion of its impact on the Company, see Note 8 to the Consolidated Financial Statements.

10 **LIQUIDITY AND CAPITAL RESOURCES**

The Consolidated Statements of Cash Flows and Balance Sheets demonstrate the Company's continued superior financial strength.

11 **Statements of Cash Flows**

Operating Activities—Cash provided by operations was $805.2 million in Year 11, an 80% increase from $448.4 million in Year 10. This increased cash flow was driven by the Company's record earnings level and reduced working capital resulting from improved asset management and the restructuring program.

Investing Activities—The majority of the Company's investing activities involve the purchase of new plant assets to maintain modern manufacturing processes and increase productivity. Capital expenditures for plant assets amounted to $371.1 million in Year 11, including $10.0 million of capital lease activity, down slightly from Year 10. The Company expects capital expenditures in Year 12 to be about $400 million.

Another key investing activity of the Company is acquisitions. The total cost of acquisitions in Year 11 was $180.1 million, most of which was spent to acquire the publicly held shares of the Company's 71% owned subsidiary, Campbell Soup Company Ltd. in Canada. This will allow Campbell North America to more efficiently integrate its U.S. and Canadian operations to provide Campbell with competitive advantage in North America.

One of the Company's strategies has been to prune low-return assets and businesses from its portfolio. In Year 11 the Company realized over $100 million in cash from these activities, with $67.4 million coming from sales of businesses and $43.2 million realized from asset sales.

Also, during Year 11 the Company made contributions to its pension plans substantially in excess of the amounts expensed. This was the principal reason for the increase in other assets.

Financing Activities—During Year 11, the Company issued debt in the public markets for a total of $400 million: $100 million of 9% Notes due Year 18. $100 million of Medium-Term Notes due Year 21 at interest rates from 8.58% to 8.75%, and $200 million of 8.875%. Debentures due Year 41. The proceeds were used to reduce short-term debt by $227 million, pay off long-term debt maturing in Year 11 of $129.9 million, and to fund the purchase of the minority interest of Campbell Canada.

During Year 11, the Company repurchased approximately 3.4 million shares of its capital stock at a cost of $175.6 million. Cash received from the issuance of approximately 1.1 million treasury shares pursuant to the stock option and long-term incentive plans amounted to $47.7 million in Year 11.

Dividends of $137.5 million represent the dividends paid in Year 11. Dividends declared in Year 11 were $142.2 million or $1.12 per share, an increase of 14% over Year 10.

12 **Balance Sheets**

Total borrowings at the end of fiscal Year 11 were $1.055 billion compared to $1.008 billion at the end of Year 10. Even after the effects of the borrowing and treasury stock activity previously discussed, total debt as a percentage of total capitalization was 33.7%—the same as a year ago. The Company has ample sources of funds. It has access to the commercial paper markets with the highest rating. The Company's long-term debt is rated double A by the major rating agencies. It has filed a shelf registration with the Securities and Exchange Commission for the issuance from time to time of up to $100 million of debt securities. Also, the Company has unused lines of credit of approximately $635 million.

Debt-related activity is discussed in the Statements of Cash Flows section above. In addition to that, the debt balances on the Balance Sheets were affected by current maturities of long-term debt and by the classification of commercial paper to be refinanced as long-term debt in Year 10.

Aggressive management of working capital and the effect of divested businesses are evidenced by a $235.5 million decrease in current assets exclusive of changes in cash and temporary investments. Receivables are down $97.1 million and inventories declined $113.1 million from Year 10. Accounts payable are down $42.8 million because of the reduced inventory levels and divestitures. Accrued liabilities and accrued income taxes declined $61.9 million as increases due to higher earnings levels and the timing of certain payments were offset by payments and charges resulting from the divestitures and restructuring programs.

Plant assets increased $72.7 million due to capital expenditures of $371.1 million offset by the annual provision for depreciation of $194.5 million, asset sales and divestitures. Intangible assets increased $52.1 million as the acquisitions resulted in $132.3 million of additional goodwill. Amortization and divestitures accounted for the remainder of the change. Other assets increased principally as the result of the pension contribution.

Other liabilities decreased $14.9 million as the reduction of minority interest resulting from the purchase of the publicly-held shares of Campbell Canada and changes in foreign currency rates of other liabilities offset the annual deferred tax provision.

CAMPBELL SOUP

(millions)

		Year 11	Year 10	Year 9
13	**NET SALES**	**$6,204.1**	$6,205.8	$5,672.1
	Costs and expenses			
14	Cost of products sold	**4,095.5**	4,258.2	4,001.6
15	Marketing and selling expenses	**956.2**	980.5	818.8
16	Administrative expenses	**306.7**	290.7	252.1
17	Research and development expenses	**56.3**	53.7	47.7
18	Interest expense (Note 3)	**116.2**	111.6	94.1
19	Interest income	**(26.0)**	(17.6)	(38.3)
20	Foreign exchange losses, net (Note 4)	**.8**	3.3	19.3
21	Other expense (Note 5)	**26.2**	14.7	32.4
22	Divestitures, restructuring and unusual charges (Note 6)	—	339.1	343.0
22A	Total costs and expenses	**5,531.9**	6,034.2	5,570.7
23	Earnings before equity in earnings of affiliates and minority interests	**672.2**	171.6	101.4
24	Equity in earnings of affiliates	**2.4**	13.5	10.4
25	Minority interests	**(7.2)**	(5.7)	(5.3)
26	Earnings before taxes	**667.4**	179.4	106.5
27	Taxes on earnings (Note 9)	**265.9**	175.0	93.4
28	**NET EARNINGS**	**$401.5**	$4.4	$13.1
29	**NET EARNINGS PER SHARE (NOTE 22)**	**$3.16**	$.03	$.10
30	Weighted average shares outstanding	**127.0**	129.6	129.3

The accompanying Summary of Significant Accounting Policies and Notes are an integral part of the financial statements.

(million dollars)

		July 28, Year 11	July 29, Year 10
	CURRENT ASSETS		
31	Cash and cash equivalents (Note 12)	***$178.9***	$80.7
32	Other temporary investments, at cost which approximates market	***12.8***	22.5
33	Accounts receivable (Note 13)	***527.4***	624.5
34	Inventories (Note 14)	***706.7***	819.8
35	Prepaid expenses (Note 15)	***92.7***	118.0
36	Total current assets	***1,518.5***	1,665.5
37	**PLANT ASSETS, NET OF DEPRECIATION (NOTE 16)**	***1,790.4***	1,717.7
38	**INTANGIBLE ASSETS, NET OF AMORTIZATION (NOTE 17)**	***435.5***	383.4
39	**OTHER ASSETS (NOTE 18)**	***404.6***	349.0
	Total Assets	***$4,149.0***	$4,115.6
	CURRENT LIABILITIES		
40	Notes payable (Note 19)	***$282.2***	$202.3
41	Payable to suppliers and others	***482.4***	525.2
42	Accrued liabilities (Note 20)	***408.7***	491.9
43	Dividend payable	***37.0***	32.3
44	Accrued income taxes	***67.7***	46.4
45	Total current liabilities	***1,278.0***	1,298.1
46	**LONG-TERM DEBT (NOTE 19)**	***772.6***	805.8
47	**OTHER LIABILITIES, PRINCIPALLY DEFERRED INCOME TAXES (NOTE 21)**	***305.0***	319.9
	SHAREOWNERS' EQUITY (NOTE 22)		
48	Preferred stock; authorized 40,000,000 shares; none issued	—	—
49	Capital stock, $.15 par value; authorized 140,000,000 shares; issued 135,622,676 shares	***20.3***	20.3
50	Capital surplus	***107.3***	61.9
51	Earnings retained in the business	***1,912.6***	1,653.3
52	Capital stock in treasury, 8,618,911 shares in Year 11 and 6,353,697 shares in Year 10, at cost	***(270.4)***	(107.2)
53	Cumulative translation adjustments (Note 4)	***23.6***	63.5
54	Total shareowners' equity	***1,793.4***	1,691.8
55	Total liabilities and shareowners' equity	***$4,149.0***	$4,115.6

The accompanying Summary of Significant Accounting Policies and Notes are an integral part of the financial statements.

(million dollars)

		Year 11	Year 10	Year 9
	CASH FLOWS FROM OPERATING ACTIVITIES:			
56	Net earnings	***$401.5***	$4.4	$13.1
	To reconcile net earnings to net cash provided by operating activities:			
57	Depreciation and amortization	***208.6***	200.9	192.3
58	Divestitures and restructuring provisions		339.1	343.0
59	Deferred taxes	***35.5***	3.9	(67.8)
60	Other, net	***63.2***	18.6	37.3
61	(Increase) decrease in accounts receivable	***17.1***	(60.4)	(46.8)
62	(Increase) decrease in inventories	***48.7***	10.7	(113.2)
63	Net change in other current assets and liabilities	***30.6***	(68.8)	(.6)
64	Net cash provided by operating activities	***805.2***	448.4	357.3
	CASH FLOWS FROM INVESTING ACTIVITIES:			
65	Purchases of plant assets	***(361.1)***	(387.6)	(284.1)
66	Sales of plant assets	***43.2***	34.9	39.8
67	Businesses acquired	***(180.1)***	(41.6)	(135.8)
68	Sales of businesses	***67.4***	21.7	4.9
69	Increase in other assets	***(57.8)***	(18.6)	(107.0)
70	Net change in other temporary investments	***9.7***	3.7	9.0
71	Net cash used in investing activities	***(478.7)***	(387.5)	(473.2)
	CASH FLOWS FROM FINANCING ACTIVITIES:			
72	Long-term borrowings	***402.8***	12.6	126.5
73	Repayments of long-term borrowings	***(129.9)***	(22.5)	(53.6)
74	Increase (decrease) in borrowings with less than three month maturities	***(137.9)***	(2.7)	108.2
75	Other short-term borrowings	***117.3***	153.7	227.1
76	Repayments of other short-term borrowings	***(206.4)***	(89.8)	(192.3)
77	Dividends paid	***(137.5)***	(124.3)	(86.7)
78	Treasury stock purchases	***(175.6)***	(41.1)	(8.1)
79	Treasury stock issued	***47.7***	12.4	18.5
80	Other, net	***(.1)***	(.1)	23.5
81	Net cash provided by (used in) financing activities	***(219.6)***	(101.8)	163.1
82	Effect of exchange rate changes on cash	***(8.7)***	.7	(12.1)
83	**NET INCREASE (DECREASE) IN CASH AND CASH EQUIVALENTS**	***98.2***	(40.2)	35.1
84	Cash and cash equivalents at beginning of year	***80.7***	120.9	85.8
85	**CASH AND CASH EQUIVALENTS AT END OF YEAR**	***$178.9***	$80.7	$120.9

The accompanying Summary of Significant Accounting Policies and Notes are an integral part of the financial statements.
Prior years have been reclassified to conform to the Year 11 presentation.

(million dollars)

		Preferred stock	Capital stock	Capital surplus	Earnings retained in the business	Capital stock in treasury	Cumulative translation adjustments	Total Shareowners' Equity
86	Balance at July 31, Year 8	—	$20.3	$42.3	$1,879.1	$(75.2)	$28.5	$1,895.0
	Net earnings				13.1			13.1
	Cash dividends ($.90 per share)				(116.4)			(116.4)
	Treasury stock purchased					(8.1)		(8.1)
	Treasury stock issued under Management incentive and Stock option plans			8.5		12.6		21.1
	Translation adjustments						(26.4)	(26.4)
87	Balance at July 30, Year 9	—	20.3	50.8	1,775.8	(70.7)	2.1	1,778.3
	Net earnings				4.4			4.4
	Cash dividends ($.98 per share)				(126.9)			(126.9)
	Treasury stock purchased					(41.1)		(41.1)
	Treasury stock issued under Management incentive and Stock option plans			11.1		4.6		15.7
	Translation adjustments						61.4	61.4
	Balance at July 29, Year 10	—	20.3	61.9	1,653.3	(107.2)	63.5	1,691.8
88	**Net earnings**				***401.5***			***401.5***
89	**Cash dividends ($1.12 per share)**				***(142.2)***			***(142.2)***
90	**Treasury stock purchased**					***(175.6)***		***(175.6)***
91	**Treasury stock issued under Management incentive and Stock option plans**			***45.4***		***12.4***		***57.8***
92	**Translation adjustments**						***(29.9)***	***(29.9)***
93	**Sale of foreign operations**						***(10.0)***	***(10.0)***
94	**Balance at July 28, Year 11**	—	***$20.3***	***$107.3***	***$1,912.6***	***$(270.4)***	***$23.6***	***$1,793.4***

95 CHANGES IN NUMBER OF SHARES

(thousands of shares)

	Issued	Out-standing	In Treasury
Balance at July 31, Year 8	135,622.7	129,038.6	6,584.1
Treasury stock purchased		(250.6)	250.6
Treasury stock issued under Management incentive and Stock option plans		790.6	(790.6)
Balance at July 30, Year 9	135,622.7	129,578.6	6,044.1
Treasury stock purchased		(833.0)	833.0
Treasury stock issued under Management incentive and Stock option plans		523.4	(523.4)
Balance at July 29, Year 10	135,622.7	129,269.0	6,353.7
Treasury stock purchased		***(3,395.4)***	***3,395.4***
Treasury stock issued under Management incentive and Stock option plans		***1,130.2***	***(1,130.2)***
Balance at July 28, Year 11	***135,622.7***	***127,003.8***	***8,618.9***

(million dollars)

96 **1 SUMMARY OF SIGNIFICANT ACCOUNTING POLICIES**

CONSOLIDATION—The consolidated financial statements include the accounts of the Company and its majority-owned subsidiaries. Significant intercompany transactions are eliminated in consolidation. Investments in affiliated owned 20% or more are accounted for by the equity method.

INVENTORIES—Substantially all domestic inventories are priced at the lower of cost or market, with cost determined by the last-in, first-out (LIFO) method. Other inventories are priced at the lower of average cost or market.

INTANGIBLES—The excess of cost of investments over net assets of purchased companies is amortized on a straight-line basis over periods not exceeding forty years.

PLANT ASSETS—Alterations and major overhauls which substantially extend the lives of properties or materially increase their capacity are capitalized. The amounts for property disposals are removed from plant asset and accumulated depreciation accounts and any resultant gain or loss is included in earnings. Ordinary repairs and maintenance are charged to operating costs.

DEPRECIATION—Depreciation provided in costs and expenses is on the straight-line method. The United States, Canadian and certain other foreign companies use accelerated methods of depreciation for income tax purposes.

PENSION PLANS—Pension costs are accrued over employees' careers based on plan benefit formulas.

CASH AND CASH EQUIVALENTS—All highly liquid debt instruments purchased with a maturity of three months or less are classified as Cash Equivalents.

FINANCIAL INSTRUMENTS—In managing interest rate exposure, the Company at times enters into interest rate swap agreements. When interest rates change, the difference to be paid or received is accrued and recognized as interest expense over the life of the agreement. In order to hedge foreign currency exposures on firm commitments, the Company at times enters into forward foreign exchange contracts. Gains and losses resulting from these instruments are recognized in the same period as the underlying hedged transaction. The Company also at times enters into foreign currency swap agreements which are effective as hedges of net investments in foreign subsidiaries. Realized and unrealized gains and losses on these currency swaps are recognized in the Cumulative Translation Adjustments account in Shareowners' Equity.

97 **2 GEOGRAPHIC AREA INFORMATION**

The Company is predominantly engaged in the prepared convenience foods industry. The following presents information about operations in different geographic areas:

	Year 11	Year 10	Year 9
Net sales			
United States	***$4,495.6***	$4,527.2	$4,233.4
Europe	***1,149.1***	1,101.4	983.7
Other foreign countries	***656.0***	673.6	542.9
Adjustment and elimination	***(96.6)***	(96.4)	(87.9)
Consolidated	***$6,204.1***	$6,205.8	$5,672.1
Earnings (loss) before taxes			
United States	***$694.8***	$427.8	$294.5
Europe	***48.8***	(178.7)	(21.3)
Other foreign countries	***55.0***	44.6	(59.6)
	798.6	293.7	213.6
Unallocated corporate expenses	***(41.1)***	(16.5)	(31.3)
Interest, net	***(90.2)***	(94.0)	(55.8)
Foreign currency translation adjustment	***.1***	(3.8)	(20.0)
Consolidated	***$667.4***	$179.4	$106.5
Identifiable assets			
United States	***$2,693.4***	$2,535.0	$2,460.5
Europe	***711.3***	942.2	886.9
Other foreign countries	***744.3***	638.4	584.7
Consolidated	***$4,149.0***	$4,115.6	$3,932.1

Transfers between geographic areas are recorded at cost plus markup or at market. Identifiable assets are all assets identified with operations in each geographic area.

3 INTEREST EXPENSE

	Year 11	Year 10	Year 9
98 Interest expense	***$136.9***	$121.9	$97.6
99 Less interest expense capitalized	***20.7***	10.3	3.5
100	***$116.2***	$111.6	$94.1

(million dollars)

101 **4 FOREIGN CURRENCY TRANSLATION**

Fluctuations in foreign exchange rates resulted in decreases in net earnings of $.3 in Year 11, $3.2 in Year 10 and $19.1 in Year 9.

The balances in the Cumulative translation adjustments account are the following:

	Year 11	Year 10	Year 9
Europe	***$ 5.6***	$43.2	$(3.5)
Canada	***3.8***	3.6	(2.5)
Australia	***13.4***	16.1	7.3
Other	***.8***	.6	.8
	$23.6	$63.5	$ 2.1

5 OTHER EXPENSE

Included in other expense are the following:

	Year 11	Year 10	Year 9
102 Stock price related incentive programs	***$15.4***	$ (.1)	$17.4
103 Amortization of intangible and other assets	***14.1***	16.8	16.4
104 Other, net	***(3.3)***	(2.0)	(1.4)
	$26.2	$14.7	$32.4

105 **6 DIVESTITURES, RESTRUCTURING AND UNUSUAL CHARGES**

In Year 10, charges for divestiture and restructuring programs, designed to strengthen the Company's core businesses and improve long-term profitability, reduced operating earnings by $339.1; $301.6 after taxes, or $2.33 per share. The divestiture program involves the sale of several low-return or non-strategic businesses. The restructuring charges provide for the elimination of underperforming assets and unnecessary facilities and include a charge of $113 to write off goodwill in the United Kingdom.

In Year 9, charges for a worldwide restructuring program reduced operating earnings by $343.0; $260.8 after taxes, or $2.02 per share. The restructuring program involved plant consolidations, work force reductions, and goodwill write-offs.

106 **7 ACQUISITIONS**

Prior to July Year 11, the Company owned approximately 71% of the capital stock of Campbell Soup Company Ltd. ("Campbell Canada"), which processes, packages and distributes a wide range of prepared foods exclusively in Canada under many of the Company's brand names. The financial position and results of operations of Campbell Canada are consolidated with those of the Company. In July Year 11, the Company acquired the remaining shares (29%) of Campbell Canada which it did not already own at a cost of $159.7. In addition, the Company made one other acquisition at a cost of $20.4. The total cost of Year 11 acquisitions of $180.1 was allocated as follows:

107

Working capital	$ 5.1
Fixed assets	4.7
Intangibles, principally goodwill	132.3
Other assets	1.5
Elimination of minority interest	36.5
	$180.1

During Year 10 the Company made several small acquisitions at a cost of $43.1 which was allocated as follows:

108

Working capital	$ 7.8
Fixed assets	24.7
Intangibles, principally goodwill	18.5
Long-term liabilities and other	(7.9)
	$43.1

During Year 9, the Company made several acquisitions at a cost of $137.9, including a soup and pickle manufacturing business in Canada. The cost of the acquisitions was allocated as follows:

109

Working capital	$ 39.9
Fixed assets	34.6
Intangibles, principally goodwill	65.5
Long-term liabilities and other	(2.1)
	$137.9

These acquisition were accounted for as purchase transactions, and operations of the acquired companies are included in the financial statements from the dates the acquisitions were recorded. Proforma results

(million dollars)

of operations have not been presented as they would not vary materially from the reported amounts and would not be indicative of results anticipated following acquisition due to significant changes made to acquired companies' operations.

110 **8 PENSION PLANS AND RETIREMENT BENEFITS**

Pension Plans—Substantially all of the employees of the Company and its domestic and Canadian subsidiaries are covered by noncontributory defined benefit pension plans. Plan benefits are generally based on years of service and employees' compensation during the last years of employment. Benefits are paid from funds previously provided to trustees and insurance companies or are paid directly by the Company or its subsidiaries. Actuarial assumptions and plan provisions are reviewed regularly by the Company and its independent actuaries to ensure that plan assets will be adequate to provide pension and survivor benefits. Plan assets consist primarily of shares of or units in common stock, fixed income, real estate and money market funds.

Pension expense included the following:

		Year 11	Year 10	Year 9
	For Domestic and Canadian trusteed plans:			
111	Service cost-benefits earned during the year	***$ 22.1***	$ 19.3	$ 17.2
112	Interest cost on projected benefit obligation	***69.0***	63.3	58.8
113	Actual return on plan assets	***(73.4)***	(27.1)	(113.8)
114	Net amortization and deferral	***6.3***	(38.2)	57.8
		24.0	17.3	20.0
115	Other pension expense	***7.4***	6.4	6.8
116	Consolidated pension expense	***$ 31.4***	$ 23.7	$ 26.8

Principal actuarial assumptions used in the United States were:

	Measurements of projected benefit obligation—			
117	Discount rate	***8.75%***	9.00%	9.00%
118	Long-term rate of compensation increase	***5.75%***	5.50%	5.00%
119	Long-term rate of return on plan assets	***9.00%***	9.00%	9.00%

The funded status of the plans was as follows:

120	***July 28, Year 11***	July 29, Year 10
Actuarial present value of benefit obligations:		
Vested	***$(679.6)***	$(624.4)
Non-vested	***(34.8)***	(35.0)
Accumulated benefit obligation	***(714.4)***	(659.4)
Effect of projected future salary increases	***(113.3)***	(101.0)
Projected benefit obligation	***(827.7)***	(760.4)
Plan assets at market value	***857.7***	773.9
Plan assets in excess of projected benefit obligation	***30.0***	13.5
Unrecognized net loss	***122.9***	86.3
Unrecognized prior service cost	***54.9***	55.9
Unrecognized net assets at transition	***(35.3)***	(39.5)
Prepaid pension expense	***$ 172.5***	$ 116.2

Pension coverage for employees of the Company's foreign subsidiaries, other than Canada, and other supplemental pension benefits of the Company are provided to the extent determined appropriate through their respective plans. Obligations under such plans are systematically provided for by depositing funds with trusts or under insurance contracts. The assets and obligations of these plans are not material.

Savings Plans—The Company sponsors employee savings plans which cover substantially all domestic employees. After one year of continuous service the Company matches 50% of employee contributions up to five percent of compensation within certain limits. In fiscal Year 12, the Company will increase its contribution by up to 20% if certain earnings' goals are achieved. Amounts charged to costs and expenses were $10.0 in Year 11, $10.6 in Year 10, and $10.7 in Year 9.

(million dollars)

Retiree Benefits—The Company and its domestic subsidiaries provide certain health care and life insurance benefits to substantially all retired employees and their dependents. The cost of these retiree health and life insurance benefits are expensed as claims are paid and amounted to $15.3 in Year 11, $12.6 in Year 10, and $11.0 in Year 9. Substantially all retirees of foreign subsidiaries are provided health care benefits by government sponsored plans. The cost of life insurance provided to retirees of certain foreign subsidiaries is not significant.

121 **9 TAXES ON EARNINGS**

The provision for income taxes consists of the following:

		Year 11	Year 10	Year 9
	Currently payable			
122	Federal	***$185.8***	$132.4	$118.8
123	State	***23.4***	20.8	20.9
124	Foreign	***21.2***	17.9	21.5
124A		***230.4***	171.1	161.2
	Deferred			
125	Federal	***21.9***	1.2	(49.3)
126	State	***7.5***	2.6	(8.0)
127	Foreign	***6.1***	.1	(10.5)
127A		***35.5***	3.9	(67.8)
127B		***$265.9***	$175.0	$ 93.4

The deferred income taxes result from temporary differences between financial statement earnings and taxable earnings as follows:

		Year 11	Year 10	Year 9
128	Depreciation	***$ 5.9***	$ 18.6	$ 11.9
129	Pensions	***13.6***	11.7	8.3
130	Prefunded employee benefits	***(3.3)***	(4.8)	(3.4)
131	Accruals not currently deductible for tax purposes	***(11.4)***	(5.8)	(5.3)
132	Divestitures, restructuring and unusual charges	***29.3***	(11.1)	(78.2)
133	Other	***1.4***	(4.7)	(1.1)
		$35.5	$ 3.9	$(67.8)

The following is a reconciliation of effective income tax rates with the statutory Federal income tax rate:

		Year 11	Year 10	Year 9
134	Statutory Federal income tax rate	***34.0%***	34.0%	34.0%
135	State income taxes (net of Federal tax benefit)	***3.0***	3.7	3.6
136	Nondeductible divestitures, restructuring and unusual charges		56.5	48.7
137	Nondeductible amortization of intangibles	***.6***	.9	1.1
138	Foreign earnings not taxed or taxed at other than statutory Federal rate	***(.3)***	1.2	.2
139	Other	***2.5***	1.2	.1
140	Effective income tax rate	***39.8%***	97.5%	87.7%

The provision for income taxes was reduced by $3.2 in Year 11, $5.2 in Year 10 and $3.5 in Year 9 due to the utilization of loss carryforwards by certain foreign subsidiaries.

Certain foreign subsidiaries of the Company have tax loss carryforwards of approximately $103.4 ($77.4 for financial purposes), of which $10.5 relate to periods prior to acquisition of the subsidiaries by the Company. Of these carryforwards, $54.8 expire through Year 16 and $48.6 may be carried forward indefinitely. The current statutory tax rates in these foreign countries range from 20% to 51%.

(million dollars)

Income taxes have not been accrued on undistributed earnings of foreign subsidiaries of $219.7 which are invested in operating assets and are not expected to be remitted. If remitted, tax credits are available to substantially reduce any resultant additional taxes.

The following are earnings before taxes of United States and foreign companies.

		Year 11	Year 10	Year 9
141	United States	***$570.9***	$277.0	$201.5
142	Foreign	***96.5***	(97.6)	(95.0)
		$667.4	$179.4	$106.5

143 **10 LEASES**

Rent expense was $59.7 in Year 11, $62.4 in Year 10 and $60.2 in Year 9 and generally relates to leases of machinery and equipment. Future minimum lease payments under operating leases are $71.9.

11 SUPPLEMENTARY STATEMENTS OF EARNINGS INFORMATION

		Year 11	Year 10	Year 9
144	Maintenance and repairs	***$173.9***	$180.6	$173.9
145	Advertising	***$195.4***	$220.4	$212.9

146 **12 CASH AND CASH EQUIVALENTS**

Cash and Cash Equivalents includes cash equivalents of $140.7 at July 28, Year 11, and $44.1 at July 29, Year 10.

13 ACCOUNTS RECEIVABLE

		Year 11	Year 10
147	Customers	***$478.0***	$554.0
148	Allowances for cash discounts and bad debts	***(16.3)***	(19.9)
		461.7	534.1
149	Other	***65.7***	90.4
150		***$527.4***	$624.5

14 INVENTORIES

		Year 11	Year 10
151	Raw materials, containers and supplies	***$342.3***	$384.4
152	Finished products	***454.0***	520.0
		796.3	904.4
153	Less—adjustments of inventories to LIFO basis	***89.6***	84.6
		$706.7	$819.8

Liquidation of LIFO inventory quantities had no significant effect on net earnings in Year 11, Year 10, or Year 9. Inventories for which the LIFO method of determining cost is used represented approximately 70% of consolidated inventories in Year 11 and 64% in Year 10.

15 PREPAID EXPENSES

		Year 11	Year 10
154	Pensions	***$19.8***	$ 22.3
155	Deferred taxes	***36.6***	37.7
156	Prefunded employee benefits	***1.2***	13.9
157	Other	***35.1***	44.1
		$92.7	$118.0

16 PLANT ASSETS

		Year 11	Year 10
158	Land	***$ 56.3***	$ 63.8
159	Buildings	***758.7***	746.5
160	Machinery and equipment	***1,779.3***	1,657.6
161	Projects in progress	***327.6***	267.0
161A		***2,921.9***	2,734.9
162	Accumulated depreciation	***(1,131.5)***	(1,017.2)
		$1,790.4	$1,717.7

Depreciation provided in costs and expenses was $194.5 in Year 11, $184.1 in Year 10 and $175.9 in Year 9. Approximately $158.2 of capital expenditures is required to complete projects in progress at July 28, Year 11.

(million dollars)

17 INTANGIBLE ASSETS

		Year 11	Year 10
163	Cost of investments in excess of net assets of purchased companies (goodwill)	**$347.8**	$281.1
164	Other intangibles	**129.8**	134.0
		477.6	415.1
165	Accumulated amortization	**(42.1)**	(31.7)
		$435.5	$383.4

18 OTHER ASSETS

		Year 11	Year 10
166	Investment in affiliates	**$155.8**	$169.4
167	Noncurrent prepaid pension expense	**152.7**	93.9
168	Other noncurrent investments	**44.2**	52.0
169	Other	**51.9**	33.7
169A		**$404.6**	$349.0

Investment in affiliates consists principally of the Company's ownership of 33% of the outstanding capital stock of Arnotts Limited, an Australian biscuit manufacturer. This investment is being accounted for by the equity method. Included in this investment is goodwill of $28.3 which is being amortized over 40 years. At July 28, Year 11, the market value of the investment based on quoted market prices was $213.8. The Company's equity in the earnings of Arnotts Limited was $1.5 in Year 11, $13.0 in Year 10 and $8.7 in Year 9. The Year 10 amount includes a $4.0 gain realized by Arnotts on the sales of businesses. Dividends received were $8.2 in Year 11, $7.4 in Year 10 and $6.6 in Year 9. The Company's equity in the undistributed earnings of Arnotts was $15.4 at July 28, Year 11 and $22.1 at July 29, Year 10.

170 19 NOTES PAYABLE AND LONG-TERM DEBT

Notes payable consists of the following:

	Year 11	Year 10
Commercial paper	**$ 24.7**	$191.8
8.25% Notes due Year 11		100.3
13.99% Notes due Year 12	**182.0***	
Banks	**23.6**	91.1
Other	**51.9**	69.4
Amounts reclassified to long-term debt		(250.3)
	$282.2	$202.3

**Present value of $200.0 zero coupon notes, net of unamortized discount of $18.0.*

At July 29, Year 10, $150 of outstanding commercial paper and $100.3 of currently maturing notes were reclassified to long-term debt and were refinanced in Year 11.

Information on notes payable follows:

171	Year 11	Year 10	Year 9
Maximum amount payable at end of any monthly accounting period during the year	**$603.3**	$518.7	$347.1
Approximate average amount outstanding during the year	**$332.5**	$429.7	$273.5
Weighted average interest rate at year-end	**10.1%**	10.7%	12.1%
Approximate weighted average interest rate during the year	**9.8%**	10.8%	10.6%

The amount of unused lines of credit at July 28, Year 11 approximates $635. The lines of credit are unconditional and generally cover loans for a period of a year at prime commercial interest rates.

CAMPBELL SOUP

(million dollars)

Long-term debt consists of the following:

	Fiscal year maturities	***Year 11***	Year 10
172	13.99% Notes due Year 12	**$**	$159.7***
	9.125% Notes due Year 14	***100.6***	100.9
	10.5% Notes due Year 16*	***100.0***	100.0
	7.5% Notes due Year 18*	***99.6***	99.5
	9.0% Notes due Year 18	***99.8***	
	8.58%–8.75% Medium-Term Notes due Year 21**	***100.0***	
	8.875% Debentures due Year 41	***199.6***	
	Other Notes due Year 12–24 (interest 4.7%–14.4%)	***58.2***	82.5
	Notes payable, reclassified		250.3
	Capital lease obligations	***14.8***	12.9
		$772.6	$805.8

**Redeemable in Year 13.*
***$50 redeemable in Year 18.*
****Present value of $200.0 zero coupon notes, net of unamortized discount of $40.3.*

173 Future minimum lease payments under capital leases are $28.0 and the present value of such payments, after deducting implicit interest of $6.5, is $21.5 of which $6.7 is included in current liabilities.

Principle amounts of long-term debt mature as follows: Year 12-$227.7 (in current liabilities); Year 13-$118.9; Year 14-$17.8; Year 15-$15.9; Year 16-$108.3 and beyond-$511.7.

The Company has filed a shelf registration statement with the Securities and Exchange Commission for the issuance from time to time of up to $300 of debt securities, of which $100 remains unissued.

Information on financial instruments follows:

At July 28, Year 11, the Company had an interest rate swap agreement with financial institutions having a notional principal amount of $100, which is intended to reduce the impact of changes in interest rates on floating rate commercial paper. In addition, at July 28, Year 11, the Company had two swap agreements with financial institutions which covered both interest rates and foreign currencies. These agreements have a total notional principal amount of $103, and are intended to reduce exposure to higher foreign interest rates and to hedge the Company's net investments in the United Kingdom and Australia. The Company is exposed to credit loss in the event of nonperformance by the other parties to the interest rate swap agreements; however, the Company does not anticipate nonperformance by the counterparties.

At July 28, Year 11, the Company had contracts to purchase approximately $109 in foreign currency. The contracts are mostly for European currencies and have maturities through Year 12.

20 ACCRUED LIABILITIES

		Year 11	Year 10
174	Divestiture and restructuring charges	***$ 88.4***	$238.8
175	Other	***320.3***	253.1
		$408.7	$491.9

21 OTHER LIABILITIES

		Year 11	Year 10
176	Deferred income taxes	***$258.5***	$235.1
177	Other liabilities	***23.0***	28.5
178	Minority interests	***23.5***	56.3
		$305.0	$319.9

(million dollars)

179 ## 22 SHAREOWNERS' EQUITY

The Company has authorized 140 million shares of Capital Stock of $.15 par value and 40 million shares of Preferred Stock issuable in one or more classes, with or without par as may be authorized by the Board of Directors. No Preferred Stock has been issued.

The following summarizes the activity in option shares under the Company's employee stock option plans:

(thousands of shares)	*Year 11*	Year 10	Year 9
Beginning of year	***4,301.1***	3,767.9	3,257.0
Granted under the Year 4 long-term incentive plan at average price of $63.64 in Year 11; $47.27 in Year 10; $30.37 in Year 9	***2,136.3***	1,196.0	1,495.5
Exercised at average price of $29.82 in Year 11; $24.78 in Year 10; $20.65 in Year 9 in form of:			
Stock appreciation rights	***(14.9)***	(110.2)	(137.3)
Shares	***(1,063.7)***	(367.2)	(615.1)
Terminated	***(216.9)***	(185.4)	(232.2)
End of year	***5,141.9***	4,301.1	3,767.9
Exercisable at end of year	***2,897.0***	2,654.4	2,104.1
Shares under option-price per share:			
Range of prices: Low	***$14.68***	$ 6.98	$ 6.98
High	***$83.31***	$57.61	$34.31
Average	***$46.73***	$33.63	$28.21

In addition to options granted under the Year 4 long-term incentive plan, 233,200 restricted shares of capital stock were granted to certain key management employees in Year 11; 168,850 in Year 10; and 162,000 in Year 9.

There are 4,229,111 shares available for grant under the long-term incentive plan.

Net earnings per share are based on the weighted average shares outstanding during the applicable periods. The potential dilution from the exercise of stock options is not material.

23 STATEMENTS OF CASH FLOWS

		Year 11	Year 10	Year 9
180	Interest paid, net of amounts capitalized	***$101.3***	$116.3	$ 88.9
181	Interest received	***$ 27.9***	$ 17.1	$ 35.5
182	Income taxes paid	***$199.3***	$152.8	$168.6
183	Capital lease obligations incurred	***$ 10.0***	$ 9.7	$ 18.0

184 ## 24 QUARTERLY DATA (unaudited)

	Year 11			
	First	*Second*	*Third*	*Fourth*
Net sales	***$1,594.3***	***$1,770.9***	***$1,490.8***	***$1,348.1***
Cost of products sold	***1,082.7***	***1,152.6***	***981.6***	***878.6***
Net earnings	***105.1***	***135.3***	***76.4***	***84.7***
Per share				
Net earnings	***.82***	***1.07***	***.60***	***.67***
Dividends	***.25***	***.29***	***.29***	***.29***
Market price				
High	***54.00***	***60.38***	***87.13***	***84.88***
Low	***43.75***	***48.50***	***58.75***	***72.38***

	Year 10			
	First	*Second*	*Third*	*Fourth*
Net sales	$1,523.5	$1,722.5	$1,519.6	$1,440.2
Cost of products sold	1,057.2	1,173.0	1,049.3	978.7
Net earnings (loss)	83.0	105.2	54.6	(238.4)
Per share				
Net earnings (loss)	.64	.81	.42	(1.84)
Dividends	.23	.25	.25	.25
Market price				
High	58.50	59.63	54.13	62.00
Low	42.13	42.50	45.00	50.13

The fourth quarter of Year 10 includes divestitures, restructuring and unusual charges of $301.6 after taxes, or $2.33 per share.

CAMPBELL SOUP

ELEVEN YEAR REVIEW–CONSOLIDATED

(millions except per share amounts)

Fiscal Year	***Year 11***	Year 10	Year 9
185 **SUMMARY OF OPERATIONS**		(a)	(b)
Net sales	***$6,204.1***	$6,205.8	$5,672.1
Earnings before taxes	***667.4***	179.4	106.5
Earnings before cumulative effect of accounting change	***401.5***	4.4	13.1
Net earnings	***401.5***	4.4	13.1
Percent of sales	***6.5%***	.1%	.2%
Return on average shareowners' equity	***23.0%***	.3%	.7%
FINANCIAL POSITION			
Working capital	***$ 240.5***	$ 367.4	$ 369.4
Plant assets–net	***1,790.4***	1,717.7	1,540.6
Total assets	***4,149.0***	4,115.6	3,932.1
Long-term debt	***772.6***	805.8	629.2
Shareowners' equity	***1,793.4***	1,691.8	1,778.3
PER SHARE DATA			
Earnings before cumulative effect of accounting change	**$ 3.16**	$ .03	$ .10
Net earnings	**3.16**	.03	.10
Dividends declared	**1.12**	.98	.90
Shareowners' equity	**14.12**	13.09	13.76
OTHER STATISTICS			
Salaries, wages, pensions, etc.	**$1,401.0**	$1,422.5	$1,333.9
Capital expenditures	**371.1**	397.3	302.0
Number of shareowners (in thousands)	**37.7**	43.0	43.7
Weighted average shares outstanding	**127.0**	129.6	129.3

(a) Year 10 includes pre-tax divestiture and restructuring charges of $339.1 million; 301.6 million or $2.33 per share after taxes.

(b) Year 9 includes pre-tax restructuring charges of $343.0 million; $260.8 million or $2.02 per share after taxes.

(c) Year 8 includes pre-tax restructuring charges of $49.3 million; $29.4 million or 23 cents per share after taxes. Year 8 also includes cumulative effect of change in accounting for income taxes of $32.5 million or 25 cents per share.

(d) Includes employees under the Employee Stock Ownership Plan terminated in Year 7.

Year 8	Year 7	Year 6	Year 5	Year 4	Year 3	Year 2	Year 1
(c)							
$4,868.9	*$4,490.4*	*$4,286.8*	*$3,916.6*	*$3,636.9*	*$3,292.4*	*$2,955.6*	*$2,797.7*
388.6	*417.9*	*387.2*	*333.7*	*332.4*	*306.0*	*276.9*	*244.4*
241.6	*247.3*	*223.2*	*197.8*	*191.2*	*165.0*	*149.6*	*129.7*
274.1	*247.3*	*223.2*	*197.8*	*191.2*	*165.0*	*149.6*	*129.7*
5.6%	*5.5%*	*5.2%*	*5.1%*	*5.3%*	*5.0%*	*5.1%*	*4.6%*
15.1%	*15.1%*	*15.3%*	*15.0%*	*15.9%*	*15.0%*	*14.6%*	*13.2%*
$ 499.6	$ 744.1	$ 708.7	$ 579.4	$ 541.5	$ 478.9	$ 434.6	$ 368.2
1,508.9	1,349.0	1,168.1	1,027.5	970.9	889.1	815.4	755.1
3,609.6	3,097.4	2,762.8	2,437.5	2,210.1	1,991.5	1,865.5	1,722.9
525.8	380.2	362.3	297.1	283.0	267.5	236.2	150.6
1,895.0	1,736.1	1,538.9	1,382.5	1,259.9	1,149.4	1,055.8	1,000.5
$ 1.87	$ 1.90	$ 1.72	$ 1.53	$ 1.48	$ 1.28	$ 1.16	$ 1.00
2.12	1.90	1.72	1.53	1.48	1.28	1.16	1.00
.81	.71	.65	.61	.57	.54	.53	.51
14.69	13.35	11.86	10.69	9.76	8.92	8.19	7.72
$1,222.9	$1,137.3	$1,061.0	$ 950.1	$ 889.5	$ 755.1	$ 700.9	$ 680.9
261.9	328.0	251.3	212.9	183.1	154.1	147.6	135.4
43.0	41.0	50.9*(d)*	49.5*(d)*	49.4*(d)*	40.1	39.7	41.6
129.4	129.9	129.5	129.1	129.0	129.0	129.0	129.6

CAMPBELL SOUP

CAMPBELL SOUP

CAMPBELL SOUP COMPANY AND CONSOLIDATED SUBSIDIARIES
Property, Plant, and Equipment at Cost
(million dollars)

	Land	*Buildings*	*Machinery and equipment*	*Projects in progress*	*Total*
Balance at July 31, Year 8	$53.2	$735.5	$1,624.4	$126.6	$2,539.7
Additions	2.8	47.6	216.4	35.2	302.0
Acquired assets*	4.8	13.6	22.6	—	41.0
Retirements and sales	(4.5)	(88.4)	(238.3)	—	(331.2)
Translation adjustments	(.5)	(2.5)	(5.9)	.4	(8.5)
Balance at July 30, Year 9	55.8	705.8	1,619.2	162.2	2,543.0
Additions	3.2	69.2	219.6	105.3	397.3
Acquired assets*	3.8	14.1	6.8	—	24.7
Retirements and sales	(2.8)	(64.0)	(222.9)	(1.1)	(290.8)
Translation adjustments	3.8	21.4	34.9	.6	60.7
Balance at July 29, Year 10	63.8	746.5	1,657.6	267.0	2,734.9
Additions	1.5	70.2	239.5	59.9	371.1
Acquired assets*	.5	3.3	.9	—	4.7
Retirements and sales	(7.5)	(49.3)	(99.9)	—	(156.7)
Rate variance	(2.0)	(12.0)	(18.8)	.7	(32.1)
Balance at July 28, Year 11	$56.3	$758.7	$1,779.3	$327.6	$2,921.9

*See "Acquisitions" in Notes to Consolidated Financial Statements.

CAMPBELL SOUP COMPANY AND CONSOLIDATED SUBSIDIARIES
Accumulated Depreciation and Amortization of Property, Plant and Equipment
(million dollars)

	Buildings	*Machinery and Equipment*	*Total*
Balance at July 31, Year 8	$285.4	$745.4	$1,030.8
Additions charged to income	31.5	144.4	175.9
Retirements and sales	(57.8)	(143.5)	(201.3)
Translations adjustments	(.8)	(2.2)	(3.0)
Balance at July 30, Year 9	258.3	744.1	1,002.4
Additions charged to income	34.2	149.9	184.1
Retirements and sales	(32.5)	(154.7)	(187.2)
Translations adjustments	5.2	12.7	17.9
Balance at July 29, Year 10	265.2	752.0	1,017.2
Additions charged to income	35.3	159.2	194.5
Retirements and sales	(17.4)	(52.1)	(69.5)
Translations adjustments	(2.8)	(7.9)	(10.7)
Balance at July 28, Year 11	$280.3	$851.2	$1,131.5

Quaker Oats

The Quaker Oats Company and Subsidiaries

Consolidated Statements of Income

Dollars in Millions (Except Per Share Data)

	Year Ended June 30	Year 11	Year 10	Year 9
1	**Net Sales**	**$5,491.2**	$5,030.6	$4,879.4
2	Cost of goods sold	**2,839.7**	2,685.9	2,655.3
3	Gross profit	**2,651.5**	2,344.7	2,224.1
4	Selling, general and administrative expenses	**2,121.2**	1,844.1	1,779.0
5	Interest expense—net of $9.0, $11.0 and $12.4 interest income	**86.2**	101.8	56.4
6	Other expense—net	**32.6**	16.4	149.6
7	**Income from Continuing Operations Before Income Taxes**	**411.5**	382.4	239.1
8	Provision for income taxes	**175.7**	153.5	90.2
9	**Income from Continuing Operations**	**235.8**	228.9	148.9
10	Income (loss) from discontinued operations—net of tax	**(30.0)**	(59.9)	54.1
11	**Net Income**	**205.8**	169.0	203.0
12	Preferred dividends—net of tax	**4.3**	4.5	—
13	**Net Income Available for Common**	**$ 201.5**	$ 164.5	$ 203.0
	Per Common Share:			
14	**Income from Continuing Operations**	**$ 3.05**	$ 2.93	$ 1.88
15	Income (loss) from discontinued operations	**(.40)**	(.78)	.68
16	**Net Income**	**$ 2.65**	$ 2.15	$ 2.56
17	Dividends declared	**$ 1.56**	$ 1.40	$ 1.20
18	**Average Number of Common Shares Outstanding** (in 000's)	**75,904**	76,537	79,307

See accompanying notes to the consolidated financial statements.

Consolidated Statements of Cash Flows

Dollars in Millions

	Year Ended June 30	Year 11	Year 10	Year 9
	Cash Flows from Operating Activities:			
19	Net income	**$ 205.8**	$ 169.0	$ 203.0
	Adjustments to reconcile net income to net cash (used in) provided by operating activities:			
20	Depreciation and amortization	**177.7**	162.5	135.5
21	Deferred income taxes and other items	**45.3**	15.2	79.9
22	Provision for restructuring charges	**10.0**	(17.5)	124.3
	Changes in operating assets and liabilities—continuing operations:			
23	Change in receivables	**(97.8)**	(55.9)	(77.1)
24	Change in inventories	**30.7**	(2.2)	(90.3)
25	Change in other current assets	**(13.7)**	(14.1)	(48.9)
26	Change in trade accounts payable	**26.1**	31.4	102.2
27	Change in other current liabilities	**43.2**	83.4	(53.1)
28	Other—net	**9.5**	0.4	(8.4)
29	Change in payable to Fisher-Price	**29.6**	—	—
30	Change in net current assets of discontinued operations	**66.0**	74.9	14.5
31	Net Cash Provided by Operating Activities	**532.4**	447.1	381.6
	Cash Flows from Investing Activities:			
32	Additions to property, plant and equipment	**(240.6)**	(275.6)	(223.2)
33	Cost of acquisitions, excluding working capital	**—**	—	(112.9)
34	Change in other receivables and investments	**(10.7)**	(22.6)	(5.7)
35	Disposals of property, plant and equipment	**17.9**	11.9	26.7
36	Other—discontinued operations	**(19.8)**	(58.4)	(46.7)
37	Net Cash Used in Investing Activities	**(253.2)**	(344.7)	(361.8)
	Cash Flows from Financing Activities:			
38	Cash dividends	**(123.0)**	(110.5)	(95.2)
39	Proceeds from issuance of debt for spin-off	**141.1**	—	—
40	Change in deferred compensation	**(0.2)**	3.5	(248.4)
41	Change in short-term debt	**(265.6)**	(7.2)	42.1
42	Proceeds from long-term debt	**1.8**	252.1	251.2
43	Reduction of long-term debt	**(39.7)**	(34.8)	(30.1)
44	Issuance of common treasury stock	**25.6**	12.8	10.1
45	Purchase of common stock	**—**	(223.2)	(68.5)
46	Issuance of preferred stock	**—**	—	100.0
47	Purchase of preferred stock	**(0.7)**	—	—
48	Net Cash Used in Financing Activities	**(260.7)**	(107.3)	(38.8)
49	**Effect of Exchange Rate Changes on Cash and Cash Equivalents**	**(6.0)**	1.6	(7.4)
50	**Net Increase (Decrease) in Cash and Cash Equivalents**	**$ 12.5**	$ (3.3)	$ (26.4)
51	**Cash and Cash Equivalents—Beginning of Year**	**$ 17.7**	$ 21.0	$ 47.4
52	**Cash and Cash Equivalents—End of Year**	**$ 30.2**	$ 17.7	$ 21.0

See accompanying notes to the consolidated financial statements.

The Quaker Oats Company and Subsidiaries

Consolidated Balance Sheets

Assets

	June 30	**Year 11**	Year 10	Year 9
	Current Assets:			
53	Cash and cash equivalents	**$ 30.2**	$ 17.7	$ 21.0
54	Short-term investments, at cost which approximates market	**—**	.6	2.7
55	Receivables—net of allowances	**691.1**	629.9	594.4
	Inventories:			
56	Finished goods	**309.1**	324.1	326.0
57	Grain and raw materials	**86.7**	110.7	114.1
58	Packaging materials and supplies	**26.5**	39.1	39.0
59	Total inventories	**422.3**	473.9	479.1
60	Other current assets	**114.5**	107.0	94.2
61	Net current assets of discontinued operations	**—**	252.2	328.5
62	Total current assets	**1,258.1**	1,481.3	1,519.9
63	**Other Receivables and Investments**	**79.1**	63.5	26.4
64	Property, plant and equipment	**1,914.6**	1,745.6	1,456.9
65	Less accumulated depreciation	**681.9**	591.5	497.3
66	**Properties—Net**	**1,232.7**	1,154.1	959.6
67	**Intangible Assets, Net of Amortization**	**446.2**	466.7	484.7
68	**Net Non-current Assets of Discontinued Operations**	**—**	160.5	135.3
69	**Total Assets**	**$3,016.1**	$3,326.1	$3,125.9

See accompanying notes to the consolidated financial statements.

Dollars in Millions

Liabilities and Common Shareholders' Equity

	June 30	**Year 11**	Year 10	Year 9
	Current Liabilities:			
70	Short-term debt	**$ 80.6**	$ 343.2	$ 102.2
71	Current portion of long-term debt	**32.9**	32.3	30.0
72	Trade accounts payable	**350.9**	354.0	333.8
73	Accrued payrolls, pensions and bonuses	**116.3**	106.3	118.1
74	Accrued advertising and merchandising	**105.7**	92.6	67.1
75	Income taxes payable	**45.1**	36.3	8.0
76	Payable to Fisher-Price	**29.6**	—	—
77	Other accrued liabilities	**165.8**	173.8	164.9
78	Total current liabilities	**926.9**	1,138.5	824.1
79	**Long-term Debt**	**701.2**	740.3	766.8
80	**Other Liabilities**	**115.5**	100.3	89.5
81	**Deferred Income Taxes**	**366.7**	327.7	308.4
82	**Preferred Stock,** no pay value, authorized 1,750,000 shares; issued 1,282,051 of $5.46 cumulative convertible shares in Year 9 (liquidating preference $78 per share)	**100.0**	100.0	100.0
83	**Deferred Compensation**	**(94.5)**	(98.2)	(100.0)
84	**Treasury Preferred Stock,** at cost, 10,089 shares at June 30, Year 11	**(.7)**	—	—
	Common Shareholders' Equity:			
85	Common stock, $5 par value, authorized 200,000,000 shares; issued 83,989,396 shares	**420.0**	420.0	420.0
86	Additional paid-in capital	**7.2**	12.9	18.1
87	Reinvested earnings	**1,047.5**	1,164.7	1,106.2
88	Cumulative exchange adjustment	**(52.9)**	(29.3)	(56.6)
89	Deferred compensation	**(168.0)**	(164.1)	(165.8)
90	Treasury common stock, at cost, 7,660,675 shares; 8,402,871 shares; and 5,221,981 shares, respectively	**(352.8)**	(386.7)	(184.8)
91	Total common shareholders' equity	**901.0**	1,017.5	1,137.1
92	**Total Liabilities and Common Shareholders' Equity**	**$3,016.1**	$3,326.1	$3,125.9

Consolidated Statements of Common Shareholders' Equity

Dollars in Millions

		Common Stock Issued		Additional Paid-in Capital	Reinvested Earnings	Common Stock in Treasury		Cumulative Exchange Adjustment	Deferred Compensation	Total
		Shares	Amount			Shares	Amount			
93	Balance at June 30, Year 8	83,989,396	$420.0	$19.5	$ 998.4	4,593,664	$(132.9)	$(36.5)	$ (17.4)	$1,251.1
94	Net income				203.0					203.0
95	Cash dividends declared on common stock				(95.2)					(95.2)
96	Common stock issued for stock option, stock purchase and profit-sharing plans			(1.4)		(601,383)	16.7			15.3
97	Repurchases of common stock					1,229,700	(68.6)			(68.6)
98	Current year foreign currency adjustments (net of allocated income taxes of $1.2)							(20.1)		(20.1)
99	Deferred compensation								(148.4)	(148.4)
100	Balance at June 30, Year 9	83,989,396	$420.0	$18.1	$1,106.2	5,221,981	$(184.8)	$(56.6)	$(165.8)	$1,137.1
101	Net income				169.0					169.0
102	Cash dividends declared on common stock				(106.9)					(106.9)
103	Cash dividends declared on preferred stock				(3.6)					(3.6)
104	Common stock issued for stock purchase and incentive plans			(5.2)		(522,110)	21.3			16.1
105	Repurchases of common stock					3,703,000	(223.2)			(223.2)
106	Current year foreign currency adjustments (net of allocated income taxes of $6.4)							27.3		27.3
107	Deferred compensation								1.7	1.7
108	Balance at June 30, Year 10	83,989,396	$420.0	$12.9	$1,164.7	8,402,871	$(386.7)	$(29.3)	$(164.1)	$1,017.5
109	Net income				205.8					205.8
110	Cash dividends declared on common stock				(118.7)					(118.7)
111	Cash dividends declared on preferred stock				(4.3)					(4.3)
112	Distribution of equity to shareholders from spin-off of Fisher-Price				(200.0)					(200.0)
113	Common stock issued for stock purchase and incentive plans			(5.7)		(742,196)	33.9			28.2
114	Current year foreign currency adjustments (net of allocated income taxes of $3.0)							(23.6)		(23.6)
115	Deferred compensation								(3.9)	(3.9)
116	Balance at June 30, Year 11	83,989,396	$420.0	$ 7.2	$1,047.5	7,660,675	$(352.8)	$(52.9)	$(168.0)	$ 901.0

See accompanying notes to the consolidated financial statements.

QUAKER OATS

The Quaker Oats Company and Subsidiaries

Eleven-Year Selected Financial Data

Dollars in Millions (Except Per Share Data)

Year Ended June 30	5-Year Compound Growth Rate	10-Year Compound Growth Rate	**Year 11**	Year 10	Year 9	Year 8	Year 7	Year 6	Year 5	Year 4	Year 3	Year 2	Year 1
118 **Operating Results** *(a)(b)(c)(d)*													
Net sales	13.1%	10.7%	**$5,491.2**	$5,030.6	$4,879.4	$4,508.0	$3,823.9	$2,968.6	$2,925.6	$2,830.9	$2,172.4	$2,114.7	$1,989.8
Gross profit	15.3%	14.5%	**2,651.5**	2,344.7	2,224.1	2,111.0	1,751.9	1,299.1	1,174.7	1,085.7	879.1	790.6	683.7
Income from continuing operations before income taxes	10.0%	11.1%	**411.5**	382.4	239.1	314.6	295.9	255.8	238.8	211.3	180.1	158.9	144.1
Provision for income taxes	9.2%	10.7%	**175.7**	153.5	90.2	118.1	141.3	113.4	110.3	99.0	81.9	68.4	63.7
Income from continuing operations	10.6%	11.4%	**235.8**	228.9	148.9	196.5	154.6	142.4	128.5	112.3	98.2	90.5	80.4
Income (loss) from discontinued operations—net of tax			**(30.0)**	(59.9)	54.1	59.2	33.5	37.2	28.1	26.4	14.1	26.8	24.8
Income (loss) from the disposal of discontinued operations—net of tax			—	—	—	—	55.8	—	—	—	(55.5)	(20.4)	—
119 Net income	2.8%	6.9%	**$ 205.8**	$ 169.0	$ 203.0	$ 255.7	$ 243.9	$ 179.6	$ 156.6	$ 138.7	$ 56.8	$ 96.9	$ 105.2
Per common share:													
Income from continuing operations	11.5%	12.5%	**$ 3.05**	$ 2.93	$ 1.88	$ 2.46	$ 1.96	$ 1.77	$ 1.53	$ 1.35	$ 1.19	$ 1.11	$ .94
Income (loss) from discontinued operations			**(.40)**	(.78)	.68	.74	.43	.47	.35	.32	.17	.34	.31
Income (loss) from the disposal of discontinued operations			—	—	—	—	.71	—	—	—	(.70)	(.26)	—
120 Net income	3.4%	7.8%	**$ 2.65**	$ 2.15	$ 2.56	$ 3.20	$ 3.10	$ 2.24	$ 1.88	$ 1.67	$ .66	$ 1.19	$ 1.25
121 Dividends declared:													
Common stock	16.5%	14.0%	**$ 118.7**	$ 106.9	$ 95.2	$ 79.9	$ 63.2	$ 55.3	$ 50.5	$ 44.4	$ 39.5	$ 35.3	$ 31.9
Per common share	17.4%	14.6%	**$ 1.56**	$ 1.40	$ 1.20	$ 1.00	$ .80	$ .70	$ .62	$ .55	$ .50	$ .45	$ .40
Redeemable preference and preferred stock			**$ 4.3**	$ 3.6	—	—	—	$ 2.3	$ 3.6	$ 3.9	$ 4.1	$ 4.3	$ 4.6
122 Average number of common shares outstanding (000's)			**75,904**	76,537	79,307	79,835	78,812	79,060	81,492	80,412	79,008	77,820	80,322

(a) Excludes the operating results of businesses reported as discontinued operations (see Note 2).
(b) See Management's Discussion and Analysis for discussion of fiscal Year 9 through Year 11 restructuring charges and credits.
(c) Fiscal Year 9 net income was decreased by $16 million (after tax) or $.20 per share due to the adoption of the last-in, first-out ("LIFO") method of valuing inventories.
(d) Per share data reflect the November Year 6 and Year 4 two-for-one stock split-ups.

The Quaker Oats Company and Subsidiaries

QUAKER OATS

Eleven-Year Selected Financial Data

Dollars in Millions (Except Per Share Data)

Year Ended June 30	5-Year Compound Growth Rate	10-Year Compound Growth Rate	Year 11	Year 10	Year 9	Year 8	Year 7	Year 6	Year 5	Year 4	Year 3	Year 2	Year 1
Financial Statistics *(a)(b)(c)*													
123 Current ratio			**1.4**	1.3	1.8	1.4	1.4	1.4	1.7	1.6	1.6	1.6	1.6
Working capital	2.2%	2.8%	**$ 331.2**	$ 342.8	$ 695.8	$ 417.5	$ 507.9	$ 296.8	$ 400.7	$ 316.8	$ 261.9	$ 266.6	$ 252.4
Working capital turnover *(d)*			**16.3**	9.7	8.8	9.7	9.5	8.5	8.2	9.8	8.2	8.1	7.7
124 Property, plant and equipment—net	12.3%	8.4%	**$1,232.7**	$1,154.1	$ 959.6	$ 922.5	$ 898.6	$ 691.0	$ 616.5	$ 650.1	$ 533.0	$ 533.8	$ 552.2
125 Depreciation expense	16.2%	14.3%	**$ 125.2**	$ 103.5	$ 94.2	$ 88.3	$ 81.6	$ 59.1	$ 56.3	$ 57.4	$ 40.1	$ 35.2	$ 32.9
126 Total assets	9.2%	8.3%	**$3,016.1**	$3,326.1	$3,125.9	$2,886.1	$3,136.5	$1,944.5	$1,760.3	$1,726.5	$1,391.9	$1,383.3	$1,360.3
127 Long-term debt			**$ 701.2**	$ 740.3	$ 766.8	$ 299.1	$ 527.7	$ 160.9	$ 168.2	$ 200.1	$ 152.8	$ 162.1	$ 164.5
128 Preferred stock net of deferred compensation, and preference stock			**$ 4.8**	$ 1.8	—	—	—	—	$ 37.9	$ 38.5	$ 41.3	$ 45.4	$ 46.7
129 Common shareholders' equity			**$ 901.0**	$1,017.5	$1,137.1	$1,251.1	$1,087.5	$ 831.7	$ 786.9	$ 720.1	$ 639.4	$ 630.5	$ 612.6
130 Book value per common share			**$ 11.80**	$ 13.46	$ 14.44	$ 15.76	$ 13.68	$ 10.64	$ 9.76	$ 8.89	$ 8.02	$ 8.04	$ 7.99
131 Return on average common shareholders' equity			**24.1%**	20.8%	12.5%	16.8%	16.1%	17.3%	16.6%	15.9%	14.8%	13.9%	12.7%
132 Gross profit as a percentage of sales			**48.3%**	46.6%	45.6%	46.8%	45.8%	43.8%	40.2%	38.4%	40.5%	37.4%	34.4%
133 Advertising and merchandising as a percentage of sales			**25.6%**	23.8%	23.4%	24.9%	22.9%	21.7%	19.4%	18.4%	18.6%	16.6%	15.3%
134 Research and development as a percentage of sales			**.8%**	.9%	.8%	.8%	.8%	.8%	.7%	.8%	.8%	1.0%	1.0%
135 Income from continuing operations as a percentage of sales			**4.3%**	4.6%	3.1%	4.4%	4.0%	4.8%	4.4%	4.0%	4.5%	4.3%	4.0%
136 Long-term debt ratio *(e)*			**43.6%**	42.1%	40.3%	19.3%	32.7%	16.2%	16.9%	20.9%	18.3%	19.4%	20.0%
Total debt ratio *(f)*			**47.4%**	52.3%	44.2%	33.8%	50.2%	35.7%	28.9%	35.4%	32.9%	32.4%	35.2%
Common dividends as a percentage of income available for common shares			**58.9%**	65.1%	46.9%	31.3%	25.9%	31.2%	33.0%	32.9%	75.8%	37.8%	32.0%
Number of common shareholders			**33,603**	33,859	34,347	34,231	32,358	27,068	26,670	26,785	27,943	29,552	30,418
Number of employees worldwide			**20,900**	28,200	31,700	31,300	30,800	29,500	28,700	28,400	25,200	26,000	30,900
137 Market price range of common stock—High			**$ 64⅞**	$ 68⅞	$ 66¼	$ 57⅜	$ 57⅝	$ 39¾	$ 26⅛	$ 16⅛	$ 12⅞	$ 10⅞	$ 9⅜
Low			**$ 41¾**	$ 45⅛	$ 42⅝	$ 31	$ 32⅝	$ 23½	$ 14¾	$ 10⅝	$ 8¾	$ 7¾	$ 6⅜

(a) Income-related statistics exclude the results of business which have been reported as discontinued operations. Balance sheets and related statistics have not been restated for discontinued operations other than Fisher-Price due to immateriality.
(b) Per share data reflect the November Year 6 and Year 4 two-for-one stock split-ups.
(c) During fiscal Year 11 common shareholders equity and book value per common share, as well as number of employees worldwide, were reduced by the split-off of Fisher-Price (see Note 2).

(d) Net sales divided by average working capital.
(e) Long-term debt divided by long-term debt plus total equity including preferred stock net of related deferred compensation and preference stock.
(f) Total debt divided by total debt plus total equity including preferred stock net of related deferred compensation and preference stock.

Management's Discussion and Analysis

138 **Financial Review**

On June 28, Year 11, the Company completed the distribution of Fisher-Price to its shareholders and Fisher-Price, Inc., an independent, free-standing company, was created (see Note 2). Fisher-Price has been presented as a discontinued operation within these financial statements for all periods shown. Also in fiscal Year 11, the Company recorded a $10 million pretax restructuring charge, or 8 cents per share, to close a Golden grain pasta manufacturing plant.

In fiscal Year 10, the Company reassessed a previously announced plan to close two European pet food facilities and invest in a new pet food plant. This reassessment resulted in management's decision to upgrade existing facilities and forego building a new plant. As a result, reserves of $17.5 million, 18 cents per share, charged to fiscal Year 9 earnings were reversed in fiscal Year 10.

In fiscal Year 9, the Company recorded a variety of restructuring charges aimed at improving productivity and lowering costs. The most significant of these related to the closure of its Marion, Ohio Pet Foods Division plant, which resulted in a $70 million pretax charge to income. Also in fiscal Year 9, the Company recorded a charge of $20.7 million for the planned consolidation of European pet food facilities (referenced above). In total, these restructuring charges reduced pretax income by approximately $125 million, or $1.00 per share.

139 **Fiscal Year 11 Compared with Fiscal Year 10**

Operations

Fiscal Year 11 consolidated sales reached a record $5.5 billion, up 9 percent over fiscal Year 10, aided by a solid unit volume increase of 5 percent. U.S. and Canadian Grocery Products sales of $3.9 billion were up 7 percent on a 5 percent volume increase. Most businesses had volume increases, led by *Gatorade* thirst quencher, up over 15 percent. International Grocery Products sales of $1.6 billion were up 15 percent on a 5 percent volume increase. The sales gain was driven by the European and Mexican businesses, due to favorable currency trends and strong volume gains in *Gatorade* and pet foods.

Gross profit margin rose to 48 percent of net sales versus 47 percent in fiscal Year 10 due largely to lower commodity and packaging costs in the domestic grocery business.

Selling, general and administrative expenses of $2.1 billion rose 15 percent over fiscal Year 10, and were also higher as a percentage of sales versus last year. The increases in both dollar and percentage terms were due to higher planned advertising and merchandising (A&M) expenditures in the domestic cereals and *Gatorade* business as well as the expansion of *Gatorade* thirst quencher in Europe.

140

Net interest expense declined 15 percent to $86.2 million due primarily to lower financing costs in Brazil due to the hyper-inflationary environment in that country in fiscal Year 10.

Fiscal Year 11 other expense included foreign exchange gains of $5.1 million compared to losses of $25.7 million in fiscal Year 10, due largely to improvement in Brazil. Restructuring items included in other expense were a $10 million Golden Grain plant closing charge in fiscal Year 11 and a $17.5 million credit in fiscal Year 10.

Consolidated operating income was $533 million compared to $544.2 million last year. Excluding restructuring charges and credits in both years, operating income would have been $543 million in fiscal Year 11, or 3 percent higher than the $526.7 million of a year ago. Operating income for U.S. and Canadian Grocery Products for fiscal Year 11 was $429 million, up 15 percent from last year's $372.5 million. Excluding the fiscal Year 11 restructuring charge of $10 million, operating income rose 18 percent for the year. InternationalGrocery Products operating income in fiscal Year 11 was $104 million, versus last year's $171.7 million. The year-to-year comparisons largely reflect the impact of a hyper-inflationary economic environment in Brazil in fiscal Year 10, and a downturn in the business in fiscal Year 11 because of deteriorating economic conditions in that country, as well as the fiscal Year 10 restructuring credit of $17.5 million. The operating income shortfall in Brazil was largely offset by lower financing costs in that country. In addition, significant A&M expenditures were incurred to launch *Gatorade* thirst quencher into Germany, France, Spain and Mexico. A more detailed discussion of operating performance by segment is provided in the Operations Review section of this report.

Income from continuing operations of $235.8 million increased 3 percent over fiscal Year 10. See Note 2 for a discussion of discontinued operations, which include the Company' Fisher-Price business.

141 **Fiscal Year 10 Compared with Fiscal Year 9**

Operations

Fiscal Year 10 sales of $5 billion rose 3 percent above fiscal Year 9, driven by solid gains in International Grocery Products. U.S. and Canadian Grocery Products sales of $3.6 billion were essentially even with the prior year, although volumes declined 6 percent.

The gross profit margin increased to 47 percent of net sales versus 46 percent in fiscal Year 9 due primarily to sharply higher margins from the Company's Brazilian business. This resulted from aggressive pricing during a period of dramatic inflation in that country and from lower commodity costs, especially oats, in the domestic grocery business. Partially offsetting the benefit of lower commodity costs were charges of approximately $15 million, recorded in fiscal Year 10 for oat bran inventory write-downs.

Selling, general and administrative expenses increased 4 percent over fiscal Year 9 to $1.8 billion but remained steady with fiscal Year 9 as a percent of net sales. The dollar increase was driven by higher advertising and merchandising spending, especially for the expansion of *Gatorade* thirst quencher in Europe.

Net interest expense increased 80 percent to $101.8 million due primarily to higher financing costs in Brazil and, to a lesser extent, domestic interest expense incurred on debt used for the repurchase of the Company's common stock.

Fiscal Year 9 other expense included approximately $125 million in restructuring charges.

Operating income increased 56 percent from fiscal Year 9. The increase is attributable to the above-mentioned restructuring charges in fiscal Year 9 and credits in fiscal Year 10 as well as significantly higher operating income from the Brazilian business. The higher Brazilian operating income was achieved in that country's hyper-inflationary environment and was largely offset by accompanying higher financing costs.

Income from continuing operations increased 54 percent over fiscal Year 9 due primarily to the restructuring charges in fiscal Year 9 and credits in Year 10.

142

Liquidity and Capital Resources

The ability to generate funds internally remains one of the Company's most significant financial strengths. Net cash flow from operations of $532.4, $447.1 and $381.6 million during fiscal Year 11, Year 10 and Year 9 respectively, was well in excess of the Company's dividend and capital expenditure requirements. Capital expenditures for fiscal Year 11, Year 10, and Year 9 were $240.6, $275.6 and $223.2 million, respectively, with no material individual commitments outstanding.

Short-term and long-term debt (total debt) decreased $301.1 million from last year, due primarily to proceeds from debt spun off with the Fisher-Price business. Total debt increased $216.8 million from June 30, Year 9 to June 30, Year 10, driven primarily by the common share repurchase program (see Note 7). During fiscal Year 10, the company repurchased 3.7 million shares of outstanding common stock as part of a 7 million share repurchase program announced in May Year 9. No shares were repurchased in fiscal Year 11, because of the impending spin-off of Fisher-Price, leaving 3.3 million shares available to repurchase under this program. The Company's debt to total capitalization ratio was 47.4 percent at June 30, Year 11 compared to 52.3 percent and 44.2 percent at June 30, Year 10 and June 30, Year 9 respectively.

On January 31, Year 10, the Company filed a shelf registration with the Securities and Exchange Commission covering $600 million of debt securities. As of June 30, Year 11, no securities have been issued under this registration statement.

Commercial paper has been the Company's primary source of short-term financing. Quaker's ratings of "A1" (Standard & Poor's) and "PI" (Moody's) have been maintained throughout the year. The available levels of borrowings are adequate to meet the Company's seasonal working capital needs. The Company maintains domestic and non-U.S. bank lines of credit for future corporate general requirements. For a discussion of these lines of credit, see Note 5.

Notes to the Consolidated Financial Statements

143 **Note 1**
Summary of Significant Accounting Policies

Consolidation. The consolidated financial statements include The Quaker Oats Company and all of its subsidiaries ("the Company"). All significant intercompany transactions have been eliminated. Businesses acquired are included in the results of operations since their acquisition date. The Company's toy and juvenile products segment ("Fisher-Price") is reflected in the accompanying financial statements as a discontinued operation (see Note 2). Accordingly, unless otherwise indicated, the following notes relate to continuing operations only.

Foreign Currency Translation. Assets and liabilities of the Company's foreign affiliates, other than those located in highly inflationary countries, are translated at current exchange rates, while income and expenses are translated at average rates for the period. For entities in highly inflationary countries, a combination of current and historical rates is used to determine currency gains and losses resulting from financial statement translation and those resulting from transactions. Translation gains and losses are reported as a component of shareholders' equity, except for those associated with highly inflationary countries, which are reported directly in the Consolidated Statements of Income.

Cash and Cash Equivalents. Cash equivalents are composed of all highly liquid investments with an original maturity of three months or less. All other temporary investments are classified as short-term investments.

Inventories. Inventories are valued at the lower of cost or market, using various cost methods, and include the cost of raw materials, labor and overhead. The percentage of year-end inventories valued using each of the methods is as follows:

June 30	Year 11	Year 10	Year 9
Last-in, first-out (LIFO)	**61%**	62%	63%
Average quarterly cost	**27%**	27%	22%
First-in, first-out (FIFO)	**12%**	11%	15%

If the LIFO method of valuing certain inventories were not used, total inventories would have been $18.9 million, $27.9 million, and $31 million higher than reported at June 30, Year 11, Year 10 and Year 9, respectively.

The Company takes positions in the commodity futures and options markets as part of its overall raw materials purchasing strategy in order to reduce the risk associated with price fluctuations of commodities used in manufacturing The gains and losses on futures contracts and options are included as a part of product cost.

Properties and Depreciation. Property, plant and equipment are carried at cost and depreciated on a straight-line basis over their estimated useful lives. Useful lives range from 5 to 50 years for buildings and improvements and from 3 to 20 years for machinery and equipment.

Intangibles. Intangible assets consist principally of excess purchase price over net tangible assets of businesses acquired (goodwill).

Goodwill is amortized on a straight-line basis over periods not exceeding 40 years. Accumulated goodwill amortization as of June 30, Year 11, Year 10 and Year 9 is $86.5 million, $71.2 million and $55.6 million, respectively.

Income Taxes. Deferred income taxes are provided when tax laws and financial accounting standards differ in respect to the recording of depreciation, capitalized leases and other items. Federal income taxes have been provided on $96.1 million of the $311.5 million of unremitted earnings from foreign subsidiaries. Taxes are not provided on earnings expected to be indefinitely reinvested.

Interest Rate Futures, Currency Swaps, Options and Forward Contracts. The Company enters into a variety of interest rate futures, currency swaps, options and forward contracts in its management of interest rate and foreign currency exposures. Realized and unrealized gains and losses on interest rate futures and options are deferred and recognized as interest expense over the borrowing period. Realized and unrealized gains and losses on foreign currency options and forward contracts which hedge operating income are recognized currently in other income and expense. Realized and unrealized gains and losses on foreign currency options that hedge exchange rate exposure on future raw material purchases are deferred and recognized in cost of sales in the period in which purchases occur. Realized and unrealized gains and losses on foreign currency options, currency swaps, and forward contracts which are effective as net investment hedges are recognized in shareholders' equity.

Income Per Common Share. Income per common share is based on the weighted average number of common shares outstanding during the period.

Software Costs. As of July 1, Year 9, the Company began deferring significant software development project costs, which had previously been expensed as incurred. Software costs of $12.2 million and $6.8 million were deferred during fiscal Year 11 and Year 10, respectively, pending capitalization at the projects' completion. In fiscal Year 11, $3 million of the deferred costs were capitalized and are being amortized over a three-year period.

144 **Note 2**
Discontinued Operations

In April Year 10, the Company's Board of Directors approved in principle the distribution of Fisher-Price to the Company's shareholders. Accordingly, Fisher-Price has been reflected as a discontinued operation in the accompanying financial statements for all periods presented. The tax-free distribution was completed on June 28, Year 11 and Fisher-Price, Inc., an independent free-standing company, was created. The distribution reduced reinvested earnings by $200 million. The $29.6 million payable to Fisher-Price at June 30, Year 11 represents an estimate of the final cash settlement pursuant to the Distribution Agreement. Each holder of Quaker common stock on July 8, Year 11 received one share of Fisher-Price, Inc., common stock for every five shares of Quaker common stock held as of such date. Fisher-Price, Inc., common stock is publicly traded.

The loss from discontinued operations for fiscal Year 10 was $59.9 million, or 78 cents per share, including $25.5 million, or 33 cents per share, for the loss from the first nine months of fiscal Year 10 and an after-tax provision of $34.4 million, or 45 cents per share, recorded in the fourth quarter. The third-quarter results included charges of $10.7 million, or 8 cents per share, for the East Aurora, New York manufacturing facility closing and $17 million, or 23 cents per share, for anticipated transaction expenses of the planned spin-off and projected operating losses (including allocated interest expense) through the expected completion date of the spin-off. The fourth-quarter provision included charges of $8.6 million, or 7 cents per share, for the pending closing of Fisher-Price's Holland, New York manufacturing facility and $4.8 million, or 4 cents per share, for costs relating to staff reductions. The fourth-quarter provision also included $25.4 million, or 21 cents per share, for inventory write-downs and the cost of maintaining related trade programs and $18.1 million, or 13 cents per share, for higher projected operating losses through the spin-off date due to lower than previously anticipated sales volumes.

During fiscal Year 11, the Company recorded an additional $50 million pretax charge ($30 million after tax), or 40 cents per share to discontinued operations. The charge related primarily to receivables credit risk exposure, product recall reserves and severance costs.

The following summarizes the results of operations for discontinued operations:

Dollars in Millions	Year 11	Year 10	Year 9
Sales	**$601.0**	$702.6	$844.8
Pretax earnings (loss)	**$(50.0)**	$(96.2)	$89.6
Income taxes (benefit)	**(20.0)**	(36.3)	35.5
Income (loss) from discontinued operations	**$(30.0)**	$(59.9)	$54.1

Fisher-Price operating loss for fiscal Year 11 was approximately $35 million.

Fisher-Price operating losses for the fourth quarter of fiscal Year 10, including the Holland, New York plant closing and severance charges, were $40 million, including allocated interest expense of $1.2 million. Interest expense of $6.7 million, $7.4 million and $7.1 million was allocated to discontinued operations in fiscal Year 11, Year 10 and Year 9, respectively.

145 **Note 3**
Accounts Receivable Allowances

Dollars in Millions	Year 11	Year 10	Year 9
Balance at beginning of year	**$16.5**	$16.5	$18.1
Provision for doubtful accounts	**5.8**	3.8	2.8
Provision for discounts and allowances	**15.8**	6.7	7.2
Write-offs of doubtful accounts, net of recoveries	**(4.6)**	(2.0)	(5.3)
Discounts and allowances taken	**(14.8)**	(8.5)	(6.3)
Balance at end of year	**$18.7**	$16.5	$16.5

146 **Note 4**
Property, Plant and Equipment

Dollars in Millions Year 11	Balance at Beginning of Year	Additions	Retirements and Sales	Other Changes	Balance at End of Year
Gross property:					
Land	$ 31.0	$ .8	$ (.2)	$ (.6)	$ 31.0
Buildings and improvements	395.2	41.5	(4.4)	(5.1)	427.2
Machinery and equipment	1,319.4	198.3	(38.1)	(23.2)	1,456.4
Total	$1,745.6	$240.6	$ (42.7)	$(28.9)	$1,914.6
Accumulated depreciation:					
Buildings and improvements	$ 94.1	$ 13.6	$ (1.8)	$ (1.8)	$ 104.1
Machinery and equipment	497.4	115.0	(23.0)	(11.6)	577.8
Total	$ 591.5	$128.6	$ (24.8)	$(13.4)	$ 681.9
Year 10					
Gross property:					
Land	$ 30.6	$ .5	$ (1.1)	$ 1.0	$ 31.0
Buildings and improvements	348.2	36.4	(1.5)	12.1	395.2
Machinery and equipment	1,078.1	238.7	(36.1)	38.7	1,319.4
Total	$1,456.9	$275.6	$ (38.7)	$ 51.8	$1,745.6
Accumulated depreciation:					
Buildings and improvements	$ 80.9	$ 11.3	$ (.7)	$ 2.6	$ 94.1
Machinery and equipment	416.4	95.2	(26.2)	12.0	497.4
Total	$ 497.3	$106.5	$ (26.9)	$ 14.6	$ 591.5
Year 9					
Gross property:					
Land	$ 30.1	$ 3.9	$ (3.7)	$ .3	$ 30.6
Buildings and improvements	341.7	36.4	(24.3)	(5.6)	348.2
Machinery and equipment	1,031.3	208.4	(142.5)	(19.1)	1,078.1
Total	$1,403.1	$248.7	$(170.5)	$(24.4)	$1,456.9
Accumulated depreciation:					
Buildings and improvements	$ 75.0	$ 11.1	$ (3.7)	$ (1.5)	$ 80.9
Machinery and equipment	405.6	85.9	(66.2)	(8.9)	416.4
Total	$ 480.6	$ 97.0	$ (69.9)	$(10.4)	$ 497.3

The "Additions" column for fiscal Year 9 includes acquisitions made by the Company during that year. Included in the "Other Changes" column for fiscal Year 11, Year 10 and Year 9 are net increases (decreases) of $(18.1), $22.7 and $(13.2) million, respectively, reflecting the effect of translating non-U.S. property at current exchange rates as required by SFAS #52.

147
Note 5
Short-Term Debt and Lines of Credit

Dollars in Millions	Year 11	Year 10	Year 9
Notes payable—			
Non-U.S. subsidiaries	**$ 67.6**	$127.1	$ 49.6
Commercial paper—U.S.			
Dealer-placed on the open market	**13.0**	216.1	302.6
Commercial paper to be refinanced	—	—	(250.0)
	$ 80.6	$343.2	$ 102.2
Weighted average interest rates on debt outstanding at end of year—			
Notes payable to banks—non U.S.	**12.1%**	17.4%	14.5%
Commercial paper—U.S.	**5.9%**	8.2%	9.4%
Weighted average interest rates on debt outstanding during the year—			
Notes payable to banks—non US (computed on month-end balances)	**50.7%(a)**	76%(a)	50.5%(a)
Commercial paper—U.S. (computed on daily balances)	**7.2%**	8.5%	8.9%
Average amount of debt outstanding during the year	**$263.5**	$264.6	$ 357.7
Maximum month-end balance during the year	**$391.4**	$355.7	$ 486.5

(a) The interest rate on debt outstanding was driven principally by periods of high real interest rates in Latin America combined with proportionately lower devaluation of local currencies resulting in high interest rates in dollar terms.

The consolidated balance sheet at June 30, Year 9 reflects the reclassification of $250 million of short-term debt, reflecting the Company's intent to refinance this debt on a long-term basis. During fiscal Year 10, the Company issued $250 million of medium term notes. (See Note 6).

The Company has a Revolving Credit Agreement with various banks, which supports its commercial paper borrowings and is also available for direct borrowings. The amount of available borrowings under the agreement was $500 million. The Agreement, which expires no sooner than June 30, Year 16, requires a commitment fee of one-eight percent per annum, payable on any available and unused portion. There were no borrowings under the Agreement during fiscal Year 11, Year 10 or Year 9. As of July 2, Year 11, the amount available borrowings under the Agreement was reduced to $300 million.

The Company's non-U.S. subsidiaries have additional unused short-term lines of credit of approximately $195 million at June 30, Year 11.

Under the most restrictive terms of the various loan agreements in effect at June 30, Year 11, minimum working capital of $250 million must be maintained.

148 **Note 6**
Long-Term Debt

Dollars in Millions	Year 11	Year 10	Year 9
Sinking Fund Debentures:			
7.7% due through Year 21	**$ 16.1**	$ 18.5	$ 21.5
8% due through Year 19	**8.4**	9.5	10.6
Industrial Revenue Bonds:			
6%-11.5% due through Year 30, tax exempt	**39.0**	46.0	46.0
4.5%-8.375% due through Year 23, taxable	**7.1**	8.2	7.4
Non-interesting bearing installment note due Year 34	**3.1**	2.7	2.4
7.83% Senior ESOP Notes due through Year 22	**94.5**	98.2	100.0
8.07% Senior ESOP Notes due through Year 22	**148.2**	150.0	150.0
8.75% ESOP installment loan due through Year 16	**12.2**	14.1	15.8
7.2%-7.9% Series A Medium-term Notes due through Year 20	**119.6**	134.6	157.1
5.415% and 6.63% deutsche mark swaps due Year 13 and Year 18	**25.6**	27.9	23.8
8.15%-9.34% Series B Medium-term Notes due Year 13 through Year 40	**250.0**	250.0	—
Commercial paper to be refinanced	—	—	250.0
Other	**10.3**	12.9	12.2
	$734.1	$772.6	$ 796.8
Less: Current portion	**32.9**	32.3	30.0
Net Long-term Debt	**$701.2**	$740.3	$ 766.8

All maturity dates presented refer to fiscal years.

Aggregate required payments of maturities on long-term debt for the next five fiscal years are as follows:

Dollars in Millions Year ended June 30	Year 12	Year 13	Year 14	Year 15	Year 16
Required Payments	$32.9	$45.3	$48.5	$46.1	$38.9

During fiscal Year 10, the Company issued $250 million of Series B Medium-term Notes bearing interest rates ranging from 8.15 percent to 9.34 percent per annum with maturities from 3 to 30 years. The debt issuance was covered under a $250 million shelf registration filed with the Securities and Exchange Commission during March Year 7. Although none of these securities were issued as of June 30, Year 9, the consolidated balance sheet as of that date reflects a reclassification of $250 million of commercial paper to long-term debt due to the Company's intent to issue the medium-term notes in fiscal Year 10.

During January Year 10, the Company filed a shelf registration with the Securities and Exchange Commission covering $600 million worth of debt securities. No securities have been issued under the registration statement as of June 30, Year 11.

The Quaker Employee Stock Ownership Plan (ESOP) was expanded during fiscal Year 9 through two separate transactions:

—In January Year 9, the ESOP through a trust issued $150 million. Senior ESOP Notes bearing interest at a rate of 8.07 percent per annum. The proceeds from these notes were used to purchase the Company's common stock on the open market.

—In June Year 9, the ESOP incurred an additional $100 million of indebtedness through the issuance via a trust of 7.83 percent Senior ESOP Notes. The proceeds from these notes were used to acquire shares of the Company's Series B ESOP Convertible Preferred Stock.

Both issues of Senior ESOP Notes are due through fiscal Year 22 and are unconditionally guaranteed by the Company. See Note 8 for a further description of these transactions.

In July Year 7, $25 million of 8.55 and 9.2 percent medium-term notes were issued, completing the $200 million Series A Medium-term Note offering begun in January Year 7. The notes mature during fiscal years Year 13 and Year 18. This note offering was concurrently swapped into deutsche marks at interest rates of 5.415 percent and 6.63 percent. The swap is effective as a net investment hedge.

The non-interest bearing note for $55.5 million (due fiscal Year 34) has an unamortized discount of $52.4 million, $52.8 million and $53.1 million as of June 30, Year 11, Year 10 and Year 9, respectively, based on an imputed interest rate of 13 percent.

The 7.7 percent sinking fund debenture requires annual payments of $1.8 million through fiscal Year 20 and a final payment of $6.8 million due in June Year 21. The 8 percent sinking fund debenture, which is an obligation of Stokely-Van Camp, Inc., a subsidiary of the Company, requires annual payments of $1.3 million through October Year 17 with a final payment of $5.3 million due in October Year 18. Amounts held in treasury for these sinking fund requirements were as follows:

Dollars in Millions

June 30	**Year 11**	Year 10	Year 9
7.7% Sinking Fund Debenture	**$6.9**	$6.3	$5.1
8% Sinking Fund Debenture	**$5.2**	$5.2	$5.2

149 **Note 7**

Capital Stock

In May Year 9, the Company announced its intent to repurchase, from time to time, up to seven million shares of its outstanding common stock through open market purchases and privately negotiated transactions. As of June 30, Year 11, 3,703,000 shares have been repurchased. In June Year 9, the ESOP through a trust issued $100 million of Senior ESOP Notes due through fiscal Year 22, and bearing interest at a rate of 7.83 percent per annum. Concurrently, the company sold 1,282,051 shares of the newly authorized issue of Series B ESOP Convertible Preferred Stock to the ESOP. Each share of the preferred stock, of which 1,750,000 shares are authorized, is convertible into one share of the Company's common stock and pays a dividend of $5.46. The preferred stock will be issued only for the ESOP and will not trade on the open market.

In June Year 9, the Company completed the repurchase of two million shares under a program announced in fiscal Year 8, and in January Year 8 completed a two million share repurchase program (adjusted for the November Year 6 stock split-up), announced in fiscal Year 6. Repurchased shares are used for general corporate purposes including stock option and incentive plans.

The Company is authorized to issue one million shares of redeemable preference stock and an additional ten million shares of a new class of preferred stock to be issued in series, whose term will be fixed by resolution of the Board of Directors. As of June 30, Year 11, none of the preference stock and 1,282,051 shares of the preferred stock have been issued.

The Dividend Reinvestment and Stock Purchase Plan exists for eligible employees and shareholders. The Plan allows for the use of open market, unissued or treasury shares. The shares used in fiscal Year 11, Year 10 and Year 9 were open market shares.

150 **Note 8**

Deferred Compensation

The Quaker Employee Stock Ownership Plan (ESOP) was expanded during fiscal Year 9 through two separate transactions. In January Year 9, the ESOP through a trust issued $150 million Senior ESOP Notes due through fiscal Year 22 and bearing interest at a rate of 8.07 percent per annum. The proceeds from the notes, which were received by the trust, were used to purchase 2,813,152 shares of the Company's common stock on the open market. The Senior ESOP Notes are unconditionally guaranteed by the Company.

During May Year 9, the Company announced that its Board of Directors authorized the ESOP to incur up to an additional $125 million of indebtedness, which would also be guaranteed by the Company. The Company announced that a new issue of up to $125 million of convertible preferred stock for the ESOP would be purchased with the proceeds of the ESOP debt. In June Year 9, the ESOP through a trust issued $100 million of Senior ESOP Notes due through fiscal Year 22 and bearing interest at a rate of 7.83 percent per annum. The proceeds from these notes were used to acquire 1,282,051 shares of Series B ESOP Convertible Preferred Stock.

These transactions represent an expansion of the original ESOP, which was adopted during fiscal Year 6. The loans from the original and expanded ESOP programs are included as long-term debt on the Company's consolidated balance sheets. Deferred compensation of $262.5 million represents primarily the Company's payment of future compensation expense related to the original and expanded ESOP programs.

QUAKER OATS

As the Company makes annual contributions to the ESOP, these contributions, along with the dividends accumulated on the Company's common and preferred stock held by the ESOP, will be used to repay the outstanding loans. As the loans are repaid, common and preferred stock is allocated to ESOP participants, and deferred compensation is reduced by the amount of the principal payment on the loans.

The following table presents the ESOP loan repayments:

Dollars in Millions

	Year 11	Year 10	Year 9
Principal payments	**$ 7.4**	$ 3.5	$1.6
Interest payments	**20.9**	17.4	1.5
Total ESOP payments	**$28.3**	$20.9	$3.1

As of June 30, Year 11, 883,395 shares of common stock and 166,470 shares of preferred stock have been allocated to the accounts of ESOP participants.

151 **Note 9**

Employee Stock Option and Award Plans

During fiscal Year 10, Quaker shareholders approved the adoption of The Quaker Long-Term Incentive Plan of Year 10 ("the Plan"). The purpose of the Plan is to promote the interests of the Company and its shareholders by providing the officers and other key employees with additional incentive and the opportunity through stock ownership to increase their proprietary interest in the Company and their personal interest in its continued success. The Plan provides for benefits to be awarded in the form of options, stock appreciation rights, restricted stock (with corresponding cash awards), performance shares, performance units, and other stock based awards. Six million shares of common stock have been authorized for grant under the Plan. Previously, stock options were issued under the Year 4 Long-Term Incentive Plan, which expired by its terms on December 31, Year 10. Restricted stock awards were previously issued under the Year 4 Restricted Stock Plan, which was terminated during fiscal Year 10. Officers and other managerial employees may be granted options for the purchase of common stock at a price not less than the fair market value at date of grant. Options are generally exercisable after one or more years and expire no later than ten years from date of grant. As of June 30, Year 11, 534 persons held such options. Changes in stock options outstanding are summarized as follows:

	Shares	Options Price (Per Share)
Balance at June 30, Year 8	3,226,408	$ 5.64-44.25
Granted	796,820	53.88
Exercised	(651,108)	5.64-44.25
Expired or terminated	(87,633)	10.67-53.88
Balance at June 30, Year 9	3,284,487	$ 6.74-53.88
Granted	809,300	57.00
Exercised	(535,194)	6.74-53.88
Expired or terminated	(103,356)	6.74-57.00
Balance at June 30, Year 10	3,455,237	$ 7.08-57.00
Granted	781,100	49.50
Exercised	(600,065)	7.08-57.00
Expired or terminated	(210,554)	28.69-57.00
Balance at June 30, Year 11	3,425,718	$ 8.30-57.00

During July Year 11, the number and exercise price of all options outstanding at the time of the Fisher-Price spin-off (see Note 2) were adjusted to compensate for decreases in the economic value of the options as a result of the distribution to shareholders. This adjustment increased the number of options outstanding by 293,241 and decreased the exercise price of the options outstanding by approximately 8 percent.

At June 30, Year 11, options for 2,664,490 shares were exercisable. As of June 30, Year 11, the average per share option price of unexercised options expiring during the period January 13, Year 12 to January 9, Year 21 was $43.46.

Since fiscal Year 3, the stock option plans have provided for the granting of stock appreciation rights in tandem with the granting of stock options. At June 30, Year 11, 42,156 stock appreciation rights were attached to outstanding options.

Restricted stock awards grant shares of the Company's common stock to key officers and employees. These shares are subject to a restriction period from the date of grant, during which they may not be sold, assigned, pledged or otherwise encumbered. The number of shares of the Company's common stock awarded were 172,700, 3,700 and 10,200 in fiscal years Year 11, Year 10, and Year 9, respectively. Restrictions on these awards lapse after a period of time designated by the Plan committee. In addition, participants may receive a cash award at the end of the restricted period not to exceed 200 percent of the current market value of the shares received as designated by the committee.

152 **Note 10**
Shareholder Rights Plan

The Company's Shareholder Rights Plan, adopted July 9, Year 6, and amended July 12, Year 9, is designed to deter coercive or unfair takeover tactics and to prevent a person or group from gaining control of the Company without offering a fair price to all shareholders.

Under the terms of the plan, all common shareholders of record on July 30, Year 6 received for each share owned one "Right" entitling them to purchase from the Company one one-hundredth of a newly issued share of Series A Junior Participating Preferred stock at an exercise price of $300.

The Rights become exercisable (1) ten days after a public announcement that a person or group has acquired shares representing 20 percent or more of the voting power of the Company's capital stock, (2) ten business days following commencement of a tender offer for more than 20 percent of such voting power, or (3) ten business days after a holder of at least 15 percent of such voting power is determined to be an adverse person by the Board of Directors. The time periods can be extended by the Company. Unless the Board of Directors has made a determination that any person is an adverse person, the Company can redeem the Rights for $.05 per Right at any time prior to their becoming exercisable. The Rights will expire on July 30, Year 6 unless redeemed earlier by the Company.

If after the Rights become exercisable the Company is involved in a merger or other business combination at any time when there is a holder of 20 percent or more of Quaker's stock, the Rights will then entitle a holder, upon exercise of the Rights, to receive shares of common stock of the acquiring company with a market value equal to twice the exercise price of each Right. Alternatively, if a 20 percent holder acquires the Company by means of a reverse merger in which the Company and its stock survive, or if any person acquires 20 percent or more of the Company's voting power or acquires 15 percent of Company's voting power and is determined by the Board to be an adverse person, each Right not owned by such 20 percent shareholder or adverse person would, upon exercise of the Right, entitle the holder to common stock of the Company (or in certain circumstances other consideration) having a market value equal to twice the exercise price of the Right. The rights described in this paragraph shall not apply to an acquisition, merger or consolidation which is determined by a majority of the Company's independent directors, after consulting one or more investment banking firms, to be fair and otherwise in the best interest of the Company and its shareholders.

153
Note 11
Pension Plans and Other Post-Employment Benefits

The Company has various pension plans covering substantially all of its domestic and certain foreign employees. Plan benefits are based on years of service and earnings. Company policy is to make contributions to its U.S. plans within the maximum amount deductible for federal income tax purposes. Plan assets consist primarily of equity securities as well as government, corporate and other fixed-income obligations.

The components of net pension cost for defined benefit plans are detailed below:

Dollars in Millions	**Year 11**	Year 10	Year 9
Service cost (benefits earned during the year)	**$ 28.5**	$ 26.7	$ 22.7
Interest cost on projected benefit obligation	**39.7**	36.5	34.1
Actual return on plan assets	**(70.5)**	(66.7)	(51.6)
Net amortization and deferral	**9.8**	10.6	(3.3)
U.S. and Canadian pension cost	**7.5**	7.1	1.9
Multi-employer plans	**.7**	.8	.7
Foreign plans	**3.2**	.6	3.7
Net pension cost	**$ 11.4**	$ 8.5	$ 6.3

Reconciliations of the funded status of the Company's defined benefit plans to the accrued pension asset (liability) included in the consolidated balance sheets are as follows:

	Overfunded			Underfunded		
Dollars in Millions	**Year 11**	Year 10	Year 9	**Year 11**	Year 10	Year 9
Vested benefits	**$363.6**	$336.8	$307.7	**$ 43.6**	$ 42.8	$ 37.8
Non-vested benefits	**8.1**	12.9	10.5	**.2**	.6	.3
Accumulated benefit obligation	**371.7**	349.7	318.2	**43.8**	43.4	38.1
Effect of projected future salary increases	**54.2**	61.7	56.7	**5.4**	11.8	7.1
Projected benefit obligation	**425.9**	411.4	374.9	**49.2**	55.2	45.2
Plan assets at market value	**588.2**	543.7	499.3	**28.0**	26.7	25.5
Projected benefit obligations less (greater) than plan assets	**162.3**	132.3	124.4	**(21.2)**	(28.5)	(19.7)
Unrecognized net (gain)	**(81.3)**	(39.5)	(12.4)	**(14.1)**	(5.7)	(6.3)
Unrecognized prior service cost	**10.4**	9.1	9.5	**5.6**	6.3	1.6
Unrecognized net (asset) liability at transition	**(83.8)**	(90.8)	(109.0)	**5.6**	6.3	7.1
Prepaid (accrued) pension costs (in the Balance Sheet)	**$ 7.6**	$ 11.1	$ 12.5	**$(24.1)**	$(21.6)	$(17.3)

Assumptions:
Weighted average discount rate: 9%
Rate of future compensation increases: 6%
Long-term rate of return on plan assets: 9%

Foreign pension plan assets and accumulated benefit obligations are not significant in the aggregate. Therefore, SFAS #87 disclosures have not been presented for these plans.

In addition, the Company provides certain health care and life insurance benefits to its retired employees. A substantial number of the Company's domestic employees and certain employees in foreign countries become eligible for these benefits if they meet retirement age and service requirements while still working for the Company. These costs are expensed as incurred and amounted to $7.4 million, $6.9 million and $6.4 million in fiscal Year 11, Year 10 and Year 9, respectively.

154 **Note 12**
Leases and Other Commitments

Certain equipment and operating properties are rented under non-cancelable operating leases that expire at various dates through Year 22. Total rental expense under operating leases was $44.5 million, $44.3 million and $42.4 million in fiscal Year 11, Year 10 and Year 9, respectively. Contingent rentals and subleases are not significant. Capital leases, which are included in fixed assets, and minimum lease payments under such leases are not significant.

The following is a schedule of future minimum annual rentals on non-cancelable operating leases, primarily for sales offices, warehouses and corporate headquarters in effect at June 30 Year 11.

Dollars in Millions	*Year 12*	*Year 13*	*Year 14*	*Year 15*	*Year 16*	*Later*	*Total*
Total payments	$16.5	$16.5	$15.7	$15.2	$15.0	$66.8	$145.7

155
Note 13
Supplementary Expense Data

Dollars in Millions	**Year 11**	Year 10	Year 9
Advertising, media and production	**$ 277.5**	$ 282.8	$ 256.5
Merchandising	**1,129.9**	912.5	886.2
Total advertising and merchandising	**$1,407.4**	$1,195.3	$1,142.7
Maintenance and repairs	**$ 96.1**	$ 96.6	$ 93.8
Depreciation expense	**$ 125.2**	$ 103.5	$ 94.5
Research and development	**$ 44.3**	$ 43.3	$ 39.3

156
Note 14
Interest (Income) Expense

Dollars in Millions	**Year 11**	Year 10	Year 9
Interest expense on long-term debt	**$ 43.3**	$ 38.3	$ 25.7
Interest expense on short-term debt and other	**60.5**	84.7	52.4
Interest expense capitalized net	**(1.9)**	(2.8)	(2.2)
Total interest expense	**101.9**	120.2	75.9
Interest income on securities	**(5.5)**	(7.2)	(7.3)
Interest income, other	**(3.5)**	(3.8)	(5.1)
Total interest income	**(9.0)**	(11.0)	(12.4)
Net interest allocated to discontinued operations	**(6.7)**	(7.4)	(7.1)
Total net interest expense	**$ 86.2**	$101.8	$ 56.4

157 **Note 15**

Other (Income) Expense

Dollars in Millions	**Year 11**	Year 10	Year 9
Foreign exchange (gains) losses—net	**$(5.1)**	$ 25.7	$ 14.8
Amortization of intangibles	**22.4**	22.2	18.2
Losses (gains) from plant closings and operations sold or to be sold—net	**8.8**	(23.1)	119.4
Miscellaneous—net	**6.5**	(8.4)	(2.8)
Net other expense	**$32.6**	$ 16.4	$149.6

158 **Note 16**

Provision for Income Taxes

Provisions for income taxes applicable to continuing operations were as follows:

Dollars in Millions	**Year 11**	Year 10	Year 9
Currently payable—			
Federal	**$103.0**	$ 72.7	$12.7
Non-U.S.	**36.6**	44.3	26.9
State	**21.8**	17.9	10.0
Total currently payable	**161.4**	134.9	49.6
Deferred—net			
Federal	**6.7**	13.4	30.8
Non-U.S.	**4.1**	5.4	8.2
State	**3.5**	(.2)	1.6
Total deferred—net	**14.3**	18.6	40.6
Total income tax provision	**$175.7**	$153.5	$90.2

158A

The components of the deferred income tax provision were as follows:

Dollars in Millions	**Year 11**	Year 10	Year 9
Accelerated tax depreciation	**$ 8.4**	$14.5	$15.0
Receipt of tax benefits	**(1.3)**	(2.8)	(2.1)
Long-term tax liability	—	—	18.2
Tax benefits—ANC(a)	—	—	(1.7)
Other—net	**7.2**	6.9	11.2
Total deferred income tax provision	**$14.3**	$18.6	$40.6

158B

The sources of pretax income from continuing operations were as follows:

Dollars in Millions	**Year 11**	Year 10	Year 9
U.S. sources	**$328.7**	$265.2	$162.2
Non-U.S. sources	**82.8**	117.2	76.9
Total income before taxes	**$411.5**	$382.4	$239.1

A reconciliation of the statutory federal income tax rate to the effective income tax rate follows:

158C

	Year 11		Year 10		Year 9	
Dollars in Millions	**Amount**	**% of Pretax Income**	Amount	% of Pretax Income	Amount	% of Pretax Income
Tax provision based on the federal statutory rate	**$139.9**	**34.0%**	$130.0	34.0%	$81.3	34.0%
State and local income taxes, net of federal income tax benefit	**16.7**	**4.1**	11.9	3.1	7.7	3.2
ANC benefit(a)	—	—	—	—	(1.7)	(.7)
Repatriation of foreign earnings	**4.3**	**1.0**	4.8	1.3	(2.1)	(.9)
Non-U.S. tax rate differential	**8.2**	**2.0**	9.8	2.5	8.8	3.7
U.S. tax credits	**(.2)**	—	(.1)	—	(.7)	(.3)
Miscellaneous items—net	**6.8**	**1.6**	(2.9)	(.8)	(3.1)	(1.3)
Actual tax provision	**$175.7**	**42.7%**	$153.5	40.1%	$90.2	37.7%

(a) In fiscal Year 9, the Company recognized $1.7 million of tax benefits in its provision for income taxes related to Alaskan Native Corporation (ANC) agreements. The ANC agreements granted the Company the right to utilize net operating losses of the ANC's for tax purposes during fiscal Year 7 and Year 8. At June 30, Year 11, $67.8 million relating to these agreements are included in deferred taxes.

159 **Note 17**

Supplemental Cash Flow Information

Dollars in Millions	**Year 11**	Year 10	Year 9
Interest paid	**$101.7**	$96.8	$ 73.8
Income taxes paid	**$ 88.7**	$90.7	$140.0

Interest paid and income taxes paid include amounts related to Fisher-Price. The Company assumed liabilities in conjunction with acquisitions in fiscal Year 9 of $13.6 million.

160 **Note 18**

Financial Instruments

Foreign Currency Forward Contracts. At June 30, Year 11, the Company had forward contracts for the purchase and sale of European and Canadian currencies to hedge foreign exchange operating income and balance sheet exposure, purchases totaling $47.2 million and sales totaling $148.9 million. While the contracts generally mature in less than 12 months, the total sales include obligations to sell $8.2 million in British pounds in fiscal Year 18 and $7.6 million in Canadian dollars in fiscal Year 14.

Deutsche Mark Swap. During fiscal Year 8, the Company swapped $25 million for deutsche marks in two separate transactions. The Company is committed to re-exchange 18.5 million deutsche marks for $10 million in August Year 12, and 27.9 million deutsche marks for $15 million in August Year 17. The Company is also committed to make semi-annual interest payments of 1.4 million deutsche marks through August Year 12 and, thereafter, 0.9 million deutsche marks through August Year 17.

161 **Note 19**

Litigation

On December 18, Year 10, Judge Prentice H. Marshall of the United States District Court for the Northern District of Illinois issued a memorandum opinion stating that the Court would enter judgment against the Company in favor of Sands, Taylor & Wood Co. The Court found that the use of the words "thirst aid" in advertising *Gatorade* thirst quencher infringed the Plaintiff's rights in the trademark THIRST-AID. On July 9, Year 11, Judge Marshall entered a judgment of $42.6 million, composed of $31.4 million in principal, plus prejudgment interest of $10.6 million, and fees, expenses and costs of $0.6 million. The order enjoins use of the phrase "THIRST-AID" in connection with the advertising or sale of *Gatorade* thirst quencher in the United States. The Company and its subsidiary, Stokely-Van Camp, Inc., ceased use of the words "thirst aid" in December Year 10. The Company on the advice of inside and outside counsel, strongly believes that it will prevail in an appeal of the judgment. Therefore, no provision for loss has been made in the accompanying financial statements.

The Company is not a party to any other pending legal proceedings which it believes will have a material adverse effect on its financial position or results of operations.

162 **Note 20**

Quarterly Financial Data (Unaudited)

Year Ended June 30	*Dollars in Million (Except Per Share Data)*			
Year 11	First Quarter	Second Quarter(a)	Third Quarter	Fourth Quarter(b)
Net sales	$1,326.5	$1,293.8	$1,334.6	$1,536.3
Cost of goods sold	685.2	689.0	682.3	783.2
Gross profit	$ 641.3	$ 604.8	$ 652.3	$ 753.1
Income from continuing operations	$ 33.2	$ 33.1	$ 63.1	$ 106.4
(Loss) from discontinued operations, net of tax	—	(30.0)	—	—
Net income	$ 33.2	$ 3.1	$ 63.1	$ 106.4
Per common share:				
Income from continuing operations	$ 0.42	$ 0.43	$ 0.82	$ 1.38
(Loss) from discontinued operations	—	(0.40)	—	—
Net income	$ 0.42	$ 0.03	$ 0.82	$ 1.38
Cash dividends declared	$ 0.39	$ 0.39	$ 0.39	$ 0.39
Market price range:				
High	$ 50⅜	$ 53	$ 60¾	$ 64⅞
Low	$ 41¼	$ 42⅞	$ 47¾	$ 55⅛

(a) Includes a provision for discontinued operations of $30 million after-tax ($.40 per share) for Fisher-Price receivables credit risk exposure, product recall reserves, and severance costs.
(b) Includes a charge of $6.6 million after-tax ($.08 per share) for the closing of a Golden Grain pasta manufacturing facility. Also includes a $4.2 million after tax ($.05) per share) credits for favorable LIFO price variances that were not projected in the prior fiscal Year 11 quarters.

INTEREST TABLES

Table 1: Future Value of 1, $f = (1 + i)^n$

Periods	2%	2½%	3%	4%	5%	6%	7%	8%	9%	10%
1	1.02000	1.02500	1.03000	1.04000	1.05000	1.06000	1.07000	1.08000	1.09000	1.10000
2	1.04040	1.05063	1.06090	1.08160	1.10250	1.12360	1.14490	1.16640	1.18810	1.21000
3	1.06121	1.07689	1.09273	1.12486	1.15763	1.19102	1.22504	1.25971	1.29503	1.33100
4	1.08243	1.10381	1.12551	1.16986	1.21551	1.26248	1.31080	1.36049	1.41158	1.46410
5	1.10408	1.13141	1.15927	1.21665	1.27628	1.33823	1.40255	1.46933	1.53862	1.61051
6	1.12616	1.15969	1.19405	1.26532	1.34010	1.41852	1.50073	1.58687	1.67710	1.77156
7	1.14869	1.18869	1.22987	1.31593	1.40710	1.50363	1.60578	1.71382	1.82804	1.94872
8	1.17166	1.21840	1.26677	1.36857	1.47746	1.59385	1.71819	1.85093	1.99256	2.14359
9	1.19509	1.24886	1.30477	1.42331	1.55133	1.68948	1.83846	1.99900	2.17189	2.35795
10	1.21899	1.28008	1.34392	1.48024	1.62889	1.79085	1.96715	2.15892	2.36736	2.59374
11	1.24337	1.31209	1.38423	1.53945	1.71034	1.89830	2.10485	2.33164	2.58043	2.85312
12	1.26824	1.34489	1.42576	1.60103	1.79586	2.01220	2.25219	2.51817	2.81266	3.13843
13	1.29361	1.37851	1.46853	1.66507	1.88565	2.13293	2.40985	2.71962	3.06580	3.45227
14	1.31948	1.41297	1.51259	1.73168	1.97993	2.26090	2.57853	2.93719	3.34173	3.79750
15	1.34587	1.44830	1.55797	1.80094	2.07893	2.39656	2.75903	3.17217	3.64248	4.17725
16	1.37279	1.48451	1.60471	1.87298	2.18287	2.54035	2.95216	3.42594	3.97031	4.59497
17	1.40024	1.52162	1.65285	1.94790	2.29202	2.69277	3.15882	3.70002	4.32763	5.05447
18	1.42825	1.55966	1.70243	2.02582	2.40662	2.85434	3.37993	3.99602	4.71712	5.55992
19	1.45681	1.59865	1.75351	2.10685	2.52695	3.02560	3.61653	4.31570	5.14166	6.11591
20	1.48595	1.63862	1.80611	2.19112	2.65330	3.20714	3.86968	4.66096	5.60441	6.72750
21	1.51567	1.67958	1.86029	2.27877	2.78596	3.39956	4.14056	5.03383	6.10881	7.40025
22	1.54598	1.72157	1.91610	2.36992	2.92526	3.60354	4.43040	5.43654	6.65860	8.14027
23	1.57690	1.76461	1.97359	2.46472	3.07152	3.81975	4.74053	5.87146	7.25787	8.95430
24	1.60844	1.80873	2.03279	2.56330	3.22510	4.04893	5.07237	6.34118	7.91108	9.84973
25	1.64061	1.85394	2.09378	2.66584	3.38635	4.29187	5.42743	6.84848	8.62308	10.83471

Periods	11%	12%	14%	15%	16%	18%	20%	22%	24%	25%
1	1.11000	1.12000	1.14000	1.15000	1.16000	1.18000	1.20000	1.22000	1.24000	1.25000
2	1.23210	1.25440	1.29960	1.32250	1.34560	1.39240	1.44000	1.48840	1.53760	1.56250
3	1.36763	1.40493	1.48154	1.52088	1.56090	1.64303	1.72800	1.81585	1.90662	1.95313
4	1.51807	1.57352	1.68896	1.74901	1.81064	1.93878	2.07360	2.21533	2.36421	2.44141
5	1.68506	1.76234	1.92541	2.01136	2.10034	2.28776	2.48832	2.70271	2.93163	3.05176
6	1.87041	1.97382	2.19497	2.31306	2.43640	2.69955	2.98598	3.29730	3.63522	3.81470
7	2.07616	2.21068	2.50227	2.66002	2.82622	3.18547	3.58318	4.02271	4.50767	4.76837
8	2.30454	2.47596	2.85259	3.05902	3.27841	3.75886	4.29982	4.90771	5.58951	5.96046
9	2.55804	2.77308	3.25195	3.51788	3.80296	4.43545	5.15978	5.98740	6.93099	7.45058
10	2.83942	3.10585	3.70722	4.04556	4.41144	5.23384	6.19174	7.30463	8.59443	9.31323
11	3.15176	3.47855	4.22623	4.65239	5.11726	6.17593	7.43008	8.91165	10.65709	11.64153
12	3.49845	3.89598	4.81790	5.35025	5.93603	7.28759	8.91610	10.87221	13.21479	14.55192
13	3.88328	4.36349	5.49241	6.15279	6.88579	8.59936	10.69932	13.26410	16.38634	18.18989
14	4.31044	4.88711	6.26135	7.07571	7.98752	10.14724	12.83918	16.18220	20.31906	22.73737
15	4.78459	5.47357	7.13794	8.13706	9.26552	11.97375	15.40702	19.74229	25.19563	28.42171
16	5.31089	6.13039	8.13725	9.35762	10.74800	14.12902	18.48843	24.08559	31.24259	35.52714
17	5.89509	6.86604	9.27646	10.76126	12.46768	16.67225	22.18611	29.38442	38.74081	44.40892
18	6.54355	7.68997	10.57517	12.37545	14.46251	19.67325	26.62333	35.84899	48.03860	55.51115
19	7.26334	8.61276	12.05569	14.23177	16.77652	23.21444	31.94800	43.73577	59.56786	69.38894
20	8.06231	9.64629	13.74349	16.36654	19.46076	27.39303	38.33760	53.35764	73.86415	86.73617
21	8.94917	10.80385	15.66758	18.82152	22.57448	32.32378	46.00512	65.09632	91.59155	108.42022
22	9.93357	12.10031	17.86104	21.64475	26.18640	38.14206	55.20614	79.41751	113.57352	135.52527
23	11.02627	13.55235	20.36158	24.89146	30.37622	45.00763	66.24737	96.88936	140.83116	169.40659
24	12.23916	15.17863	23.21221	28.62518	35.23642	53.10901	79.49685	118.20502	174.63064	211.75824
25	13.58546	17.00006	26.46192	32.91895	40.87424	62.66863	95.39622	144.21013	216.54199	264.69780

Table 2: Present Value of 1, $p = \frac{1}{(1 + i)^n}$

Periods	2%	2½%	3%	4%	5%	6%	7%	8%	9%	10%
1	.98039	.97561	.97087	.96154	.95238	.94340	.93458	.92593	.91743	.90909
2	.96177	.95181	.94260	.92456	.90703	.89000	.87344	.85734	.84168	.82645
3	.94232	.92860	.91514	.88900	.86384	.83962	.81630	.79383	.77218	.75131
4	.92385	.90595	.88849	.85480	.82270	.79209	.76290	.73503	.70843	.68301
5	.90573	.88385	.86261	.82193	.78353	.74726	.71299	.68058	.64993	.62092
6	.88797	.86230	.83748	.79031	.74622	.70496	.66634	.63017	.59627	.56447
7	.87056	.84127	.81309	.75992	.71068	.66506	.62275	.58349	.54703	.51316
8	.85349	.82075	.78941	.73069	.67684	.62741	.58201	.54027	.50187	.46651
9	.83676	.80073	.76642	.70259	.64461	.59190	.54393	.50025	.46043	.42410
10	.82035	.78120	.74409	.67556	.61391	.55839	.50835	.46319	.42241	.38554
11	.80426	.76214	.72242	.64958	.58468	.52679	.47509	.42888	.38753	.35049
12	.78849	.74356	.70138	.62460	.55684	.49697	.44401	.39711	.35553	.31863
13	.77303	.72542	.68095	.60057	.53032	.46884	.41496	.36770	.32618	.28966
14	.75788	.70773	.66112	.57748	.50507	.44230	.38782	.34046	.29925	.26333
15	.74301	.69047	.64186	.55526	.48102	.41727	.36245	.31524	.27454	.23939
16	.72845	.67362	.62317	.53391	.45811	.39365	.33873	.29189	.25187	.21763
17	.71416	.65720	.60502	.51337	.43630	.37136	.31657	.27027	.23107	.19784
18	.70016	.64117	.58739	.49363	.41552	.35034	.29586	.25025	.21199	.17986
19	.68643	.62553	.57029	.47464	.39573	.33051	.27651	.23171	.19449	.16351
20	.67297	.61027	.55368	.45639	.37689	.31180	.25842	.21455	.17843	.14864
21	.65978	.59539	.53755	.43883	.35894	.29416	.24151	.19866	.16370	.13513
22	.64684	.58086	.52189	.42196	.34185	.27751	.22571	.18394	.15018	.12285
23	.63416	.56670	.50669	.40573	.32557	.26180	.21095	.17032	.13778	.11168
24	.62172	.55288	.49193	.39012	.31007	.24698	.19715	.15770	.12640	.10153
25	.60953	.53939	.47761	.37512	.29530	.23300	.18425	.14602	.11597	.09230

Periods	11%	12%	14%	15%	16%	18%	20%	22%	24%	25%
1	.90090	.89286	.87719	.86957	.86207	.84746	.83333	.81967	.80645	.80000
2	.81162	.79719	.76947	.75614	.74316	.71818	.69444	.67186	.65036	.64000
3	.73119	.71178	.67497	.65752	.64066	.60863	.57870	.55071	.52449	.51200
4	.65873	.63552	.59208	.57175	.55229	.51579	.48225	.45140	.42297	.40960
5	.59345	.56743	.51937	.49718	.47611	.43711	.40188	.37000	.34111	.32768
6	.53464	.50663	.45559	.43233	.41044	.37043	.33490	.30328	.27509	.26214
7	.48166	.45235	.39964	.37594	.35383	.31393	.27908	.24859	.22184	.20972
8	.43393	.40388	.35056	.32690	.30503	.26604	.23257	.20376	.17891	.16777
9	.39092	.36061	.30751	.28426	.26295	.22546	.19381	.16702	.14428	.13422
10	.35218	.32197	.26974	.24718	.22668	.19106	.16151	.13690	.11635	.10737
11	.31728	.28748	.23662	.21494	.19542	.16192	.13459	.11221	.09383	.08590
12	.28584	.25668	.20756	.18691	.16846	.13722	.11216	.09198	.07567	.06872
13	.25751	.22917	.18207	.16253	.14523	.11629	.09346	.07539	.06103	.05498
14	.23199	.20462	.15971	.14133	.12520	.09855	.07789	.06180	.04921	.04398
15	.20900	.18270	.14010	.12289	.10793	.08352	.06491	.05065	.03969	.03518
16	.18829	.16312	.12289	.10686	.09304	.07078	.05409	.04152	.03201	.02815
17	.16963	.14564	.10780	.09293	.08021	.05998	.04507	.03403	.02581	.02252
18	.15282	.13004	.09456	.08081	.06914	.05083	.03756	.02789	.02082	.01801
19	.13768	.11611	.08295	.07027	.05961	.04308	.03130	.02286	.01679	.01441
20	.12403	.10367	.07276	.06110	.05139	.03651	.02608	.01874	.01354	.01153
21	.11174	.09256	.06383	.05313	.04430	.03094	.02174	.01536	.01092	.00922
22	.10067	.08264	.05599	.04620	.03819	.02622	.01811	.01259	.00880	.00738
23	.09069	.07379	.04911	.04017	.03292	.02222	.01509	.01032	.00710	.00590
24	.08170	.06588	.04308	.03493	.02838	.01883	.01258	.00846	.00573	.00472
25	.07361	.05882	.03779	.03038	.02447	.01596	.01048	.00693	.00462	.00378

Table 3: Future Value of an Ordinary Annuity of n Payments of 1 Each,

$$F_0 = \frac{(1+i)^n - 1}{i}$$

Periods (n)	2%	2½%	3%	4%	5%	6%	7%	8%	9%	10%
1	1.00000	1.00000	1.00000	1.00000	1.00000	1.00000	1.00000	1.00000	1.00000	1.00000
2	2.02000	2.02500	2.03000	2.04000	2.05000	2.06000	2.07000	2.08000	2.09000	2.10000
3	3.06040	3.07563	3.09090	3.12160	3.15250	3.18360	3.21490	3.24640	3.27810	3.31000
4	4.12161	4.15252	4.18363	4.24646	4.31013	4.37462	4.43994	4.50611	4.57313	4.64100
5	5.20404	5.25633	5.30914	5.41632	5.52563	5.63709	5.75074	5.86660	5.98471	6.10510
6	6.30812	6.38774	6.46841	6.63298	6.80191	6.97532	7.15329	7.33593	7.52333	7.71561
7	7.43428	7.54753	7.66246	7.89829	8.14201	8.39384	8.65402	8.92280	9.20043	9.48717
8	8.58297	8.73612	8.89234	9.21423	9.54911	9.89747	10.25980	10.63663	11.02847	11.43589
9	9.75463	9.95452	10.15911	10.58280	11.02656	11.49132	11.97799	12.48756	13.02104	13.57948
10	10.94972	11.20338	11.46388	12.00611	12.57789	13.18079	13.81645	14.48656	15.19293	15.93742
11	12.16872	12.48347	12.80780	13.48635	14.20679	14.97164	15.78360	16.64549	17.56029	18.53117
12	13.41209	13.79555	14.19203	15.02581	15.91713	16.86994	17.88845	18.97713	20.14072	21.38428
13	14.68033	15.14044	15.61779	16.62684	17.71298	18.88214	20.14064	21.49530	22.95338	24.52271
14	15.97394	16.51895	17.08632	18.29191	19.59863	21.01507	22.55049	24.21492	26.01919	27.97498
15	17.29342	17.93193	18.59891	20.02359	21.57856	23.27597	25.12902	27.15211	29.36092	31.77248
16	18.63929	19.38022	20.15688	21.82453	23.65749	25.67253	27.88805	30.32428	33.00340	35.94973
17	20.01207	20.86473	21.76159	23.69751	25.84037	28.21288	30.84022	33.75023	36.97370	40.54470
18	21.41231	22.38635	23.41444	25.64541	28.13238	30.90565	33.99903	37.45024	41.30134	45.59917
19	22.84056	23.94601	25.11687	27.67123	30.53900	33.75999	37.37896	41.44626	46.01846	51.15909
20	24.29737	25.54466	26.87037	29.77808	33.06595	36.78559	40.99549	45.76196	51.16012	57.27500
21	25.78332	27.18327	28.67649	31.96920	35.71925	39.99273	44.86518	50.42292	56.76453	64.00250
22	27.29898	28.86286	30.53678	34.24797	38.50521	43.39229	49.00574	55.45676	62.87334	71.40275
23	28.84496	30.58443	32.45288	36.61789	41.43048	46.99583	53.43614	60.89330	69.53194	79.54302
24	30.42186	32.34904	34.42647	39.08260	44.50200	50.81558	58.17667	66.76476	76.78981	88.49733
25	32.03030	34.15776	36.45926	41.64591	47.72710	54.86451	63.24904	73.10594	84.70090	98.34706

Periods (n)	11%	12%	14%	15%	16%	18%	20%	22%	24%	25%
1	1.00000	1.00000	1.00000	1.00000	1.00000	1.00000	1.00000	1.00000	1.00000	1.00000
2	2.11000	2.12000	2.14000	2.15000	2.16000	2.18000	2.20000	2.22000	2.24000	2.25000
3	3.34210	3.37440	3.43960	3.47250	3.50560	3.57240	3.64000	3.70840	3.77760	3.81250
4	4.70973	4.77933	4.92114	4.99338	5.06650	5.21543	5.36800	5.52425	5.68422	5.76563
5	6.22780	6.35285	6.61010	6.74238	6.87714	7.15421	7.44160	7.73958	8.04844	8.20703
6	7.91286	8.11519	8.53552	8.75374	8.97748	9.44197	9.92992	10.44229	10.98006	11.25879
7	9.78327	10.08901	10.73049	11.06680	11.41387	12.14152	12.91590	13.73959	14.61528	15.07349
8	11.85943	12.29969	13.23276	13.72682	14.24009	15.32700	16.49908	17.76231	19.12294	19.84186
9	14.16397	14.77566	16.08535	16.78584	17.51851	19.08585	20.79890	22.67001	24.71245	25.80232
10	16.72201	17.54874	19.33730	20.30372	21.32147	23.52131	25.95868	28.65742	31.64344	33.25290
11	19.56143	20.65458	23.04452	24.34928	25.73290	28.75514	32.15042	35.96205	40.23787	42.56613
12	22.71319	24.13313	27.27075	29.00167	30.85017	34.93107	39.58050	44.87370	50.89495	54.20766
13	26.21164	28.02911	32.08865	34.35192	36.78620	42.21866	48.49660	55.74591	64.10974	68.75958
14	30.09492	32.39260	37.58107	40.50471	43.67199	50.81802	59.19592	69.01001	80.49608	86.94947
15	34.40536	37.27971	43.84241	47.58041	51.65951	60.96527	72.03511	85.19221	100.81514	109.68684
16	39.18995	42.75328	50.98035	55.71747	60.92503	72.93901	87.44213	104.93450	126.01077	138.10855
17	44.50084	48.88367	59.11760	65.07509	71.67303	87.06804	105.93056	129.02009	157.25336	173.63568
18	50.39594	55.74971	68.39407	75.83636	84.14072	103.74028	128.11667	158.40451	195.99416	218.04460
19	56.93949	63.43968	78.96923	88.21181	98.60323	123.41353	154.74000	194.25350	244.03276	273.55576
20	64.20283	72.05244	91.02493	102.44358	115.37975	146.62797	186.68800	237.98927	303.60062	342.94470
21	72.26514	81.69874	104.76842	118.81012	134.84051	174.02100	225.02560	291.34691	377.46477	429.68087
22	81.21431	92.50258	120.43600	137.63164	157.41499	206.34479	271.03072	356.44323	469.05632	538.10109
23	91.14788	104.60289	138.29704	159.27638	183.60138	244.48685	326.23686	435.86075	582.62984	673.62636
24	102.17415	118.15524	158.65862	184.16784	213.97761	289.49448	392.48424	532.75011	723.46100	843.03295
25	114.41331	133.33387	181.87083	212.79302	249.21402	342.60349	471.98108	650.95513	898.09164	1054.79118

Table 4: Present Value of an Ordinary Annuity of n Payments of 1 Each,

$$P_0 = \frac{1 - \dfrac{1}{(1+i)^n}}{i}$$

Periods (n)	2%	2½%	3%	4%	5%	6%	7%	8%	9%	10%
1	.98039	.97561	.97087	.96154	.95238	.94340	.93458	.92593	.91743	.90909
2	1.94156	1.92742	1.91347	1.88609	1.85941	1.83339	1.80802	1.78326	1.75911	1.73554
3	2.88388	2.85602	2.82861	2.77509	2.72325	2.67301	2.62432	2.57710	2.53129	2.48685
4	3.80773	3.76197	3.71710	3.62990	3.54595	3.46511	3.38721	3.31213	3.23972	3.16987
5	4.71346	4.64583	4.57971	4.45182	4.32948	4.21236	4.10020	3.99271	3.88965	3.79079
6	5.60143	5.50813	5.41719	5.24214	5.07569	4.91732	4.76654	4.62288	4.48592	4.35526
7	6.47199	6.34939	6.23028	6.00205	5.78637	5.58238	5.38929	5.20637	5.03295	4.86842
8	7.32548	7.17014	7.01969	6.73274	6.46321	6.20979	5.97130	5.74664	5.53482	5.33493
9	8.16224	7.97087	7.78611	7.43533	7.10782	6.80169	6.51523	6.24689	5.99525	5.75902
10	8.98259	8.75206	8.53020	8.11090	7.72173	7.36009	7.02358	6.71008	6.41766	6.14457
11	9.78685	9.51421	9.25262	8.76048	8.30641	7.88687	7.49867	7.13896	6.80519	6.49506
12	10.57534	10.25776	9.95400	9.38507	8.86325	8.38384	7.94269	7.53608	7.16073	6.81369
13	11.34837	10.98318	10.63496	9.98565	9.39357	8.85268	8.35765	7.90378	7.48690	7.10336
14	12.10625	11.69091	11.29607	10.56312	9.89864	9.29498	8.74547	8.24424	7.78615	7.36669
15	12.84926	12.38138	11.93794	11.11839	10.37966	9.71225	9.10791	8.55948	8.06069	7.60608
16	13.57771	13.05500	12.56110	11.65230	10.83777	10.10590	9.44665	8.85137	8.31256	7.82371
17	14.29187	13.71220	13.16612	12.16567	11.27407	10.47726	9.76322	9.12164	8.54363	8.01255
18	14.99203	14.35336	13.75351	12.65930	11.68959	10.82760	10.05909	9.37189	8.75563	8.20141
19	15.67846	14.97889	14.32380	13.13394	12.08532	11.15812	10.33560	9.60360	8.95011	8.36492
20	16.35143	15.58916	14.87747	13.59033	12.46221	11.46992	10.59401	9.81815	9.12855	8.51356
21	17.01121	16.18455	15.41502	14.02916	12.82115	11.76408	10.83553	10.01680	9.29224	8.64869
22	17.65805	16.76541	15.93692	14.45112	13.16300	12.04158	11.06124	10.20074	9.44243	8.77154
23	18.29220	17.33211	16.44361	14.85684	13.48857	12.30338	11.27219	10.37106	9.58021	8.88322
24	18.91393	17.88499	16.93554	15.24696	13.79864	12.55036	11.46933	10.52876	9.70661	8.98474
25	19.52346	18.42438	17.41315	15.62208	14.09394	12.78336	11.65358	10.67478	9.82258	9.07704

Periods (n)	11%	12%	14%	15%	16%	18%	20%	22%	24%	25%
1	.90090	.89286	.87719	.86957	.86207	.84746	.83333	.81967	.80645	.80000
2	1.71252	1.69005	1.64666	1.62571	1.60523	1.56564	1.52778	1.49153	1.45682	1.44000
3	2.44371	2.40183	2.32163	2.28323	2.24589	2.17427	2.10648	2.04224	1.98130	1.95200
4	3.10245	3.03735	2.91371	2.85498	2.79818	2.69006	2.58873	2.49364	2.40428	2.36160
5	3.69590	3.60478	3.43308	3.35216	3.27429	3.12717	2.99061	2.86364	2.74538	2.68928
6	4.23054	4.11141	3.88867	3.78448	3.68474	3.49760	3.32551	3.16692	3.02047	2.95142
7	4.71220	4.56376	4.28830	4.16042	4.03857	3.81153	3.60459	3.41551	3.24232	3.16114
8	5.14612	4.96764	4.63886	4.48732	4.34359	4.07757	3.83716	3.61927	3.42122	3.32891
9	5.53705	5.32825	4.94647	4.77158	4.60654	4.30302	4.03097	3.78628	3.56550	3.46313
10	5.88923	5.65022	5.21612	5.01877	4.83323	4.49409	4.19247	3.92318	3.68186	3.57050
11	6.20652	5.93770	5.45273	5.23371	5.02864	4.65601	4.32706	4.03540	3.77569	3.65640
12	6.49236	6.19437	5.66029	5.42062	5.19711	4.79322	4.43922	4.12737	3.85136	3.72512
13	6.74987	6.42355	5.84236	5.58315	5.34233	4.90951	4.53268	4.20277	3.91239	3.78010
14	6.98187	6.62817	6.00207	5.72448	5.46753	5.00806	4.61057	4.26456	3.96160	3.82408
15	7.19087	6.81086	6.14217	5.84737	5.57546	5.09158	4.67547	4.31522	4.00129	3.85926
16	7.37916	6.97399	6.26506	5.95423	5.66850	5.16235	4.72956	4.35673	4.03330	3.88741
17	7.54879	7.11963	6.37286	6.04716	5.74870	5.22233	4.77463	4.39077	4.05911	3.90993
18	7.70162	7.24967	6.46742	6.12797	5.81785	5.27316	4.81219	4.41866	4.07993	3.92794
19	7.83929	7.36578	6.55037	6.19823	5.87746	5.31624	4.84350	4.44152	4.09672	3.94235
20	7.96333	7.46944	6.62313	6.25933	5.92884	5.35275	4.86958	4.46027	4.11026	3.95388
21	8.07507	7.56200	6.68696	6.31246	5.97314	5.38368	4.89132	4.47563	4.12117	3.96311
22	8.17574	7.64465	6.74294	6.35866	6.01133	5.40990	4.90943	4.48822	4.12998	3.97049
23	8.26643	7.71843	6.79206	6.39884	6.04425	5.43212	4.92453	4.49854	4.13708	3.97639
24	8.34814	7.78432	6.83514	6.43377	6.07263	5.45095	4.93710	4.50700	4.14281	3.98111
25	8.42174	7.84314	6.87293	6.46415	6.09709	5.46691	4.94759	4.51393	4.14742	3.98489

REFERENCES

Abarbanell, J. S. "Do Analysts' Earnings Forecasts Incorporate Information in Prior Stock Price Changes?" *Journal of Accounting and Economics,* June 1991, pp. 147–166.

Abarbanell, J.; and B. Bushee. "Fundamental Analysis, Future Earnings, and Stock Prices." *Journal of Accounting Research* 35, 1997, pp. 1–24.

Abdel-khalik, R. A. *Economic Effects on Leases of FASB Statement No. 13, Accounting for Leases.* Stamford, CT: Financial Accounting Standards Board, 1981.

Aboody, D.. "Market Valuation of Employee Stock Options." *Journal of Accounting and Economics* 22, 1996, pp. 357–91.

Aboody, D.; and B. Lev. "The Value Relevance of Intangibles: The Case of Software Capitalization." *Journal of Accounting Research* 36, 1998, pp. 161–91.

"Accounting by Creditors for Impairment of a Loan." *Statement of Financial Accounting Standards No. 114.* Norwalk, CT: 1993.

"Accounting by Creditors for Impairment of a Loan–Income Recognition and Disclosures." *Statement of Financial Accounting Standards No. 118.* Norwalk, CT: Financial Accounting Standards Board, 1994.

"Accounting for Leases: A New Approach." *FASB Special Report.* Norwalk, CT: Financial Accounting Standards Board, 1996.

"Accounting for the Costs of Computer Software Developed or Obtained for Internal Use." *AICPA Proposed Statement of Position.* New York: American Institute of Certified Public Accountants, 1997.

"Accounting for the Impairment of Long-Lived Assets to Be Disposed Of." *Statement of Financial Accounting Standards No. 121.* Norwalk, CT: Financial Accounting Standards Board, 1995.

"Accounting for Transfers and Servicing of Financial Assets and Extinguishments of Liabilities. *Statement of Financial Accounting Standards No. 125.* Norwalk, CT: Financial Accounting Standards Board, 1996.

Ahmed, A. "Accounting Earnings and Future Economic Rents: An Empirical Analysis." *Journal of Accounting and Economics* 17, 1994, pp. 377–400.

Ajinkya, B.; and M. Gift. "Corporate Managers' Earnings Forecasts and Symmetrical Adjustments of Market Expectations." *Journal of Accounting Research* 22, Autumn 1984, pp. 425–44.

Albrecht, W.; L. Lookabill; and J. McKeown. "The Time Series Properties of Annual Earnings." *Journal of Accounting Research* 15, 1977, pp. 226–44.

Ali, A.; A. Klein; and J. Rosenfeld. "Analysts' Use of Information About Permanent and Transitory Earnings Components in Forecasting Annual EPS." *Accounting Review* 67, 1992, pp. 183–98.

Ali, A.; L. Hwang; and M. Trombley. "Accruals and Future Returns: Tests of the Naive Investor Hypothesis." working paper, 1999, University of Arizona.

Altman, Edward I. "Financial Ratios, Discriminant Analysis and the Prediction of Corporate Bankruptcy." *Journal of Finance,* September 1968, pp. 589–609.

Amir, E. "The Effect of Accounting Aggregation on the Value-Relevance of Financial Disclosures: The Case of SFAS No. 106." *Accounting Review* 71, 1996, pp. 573–90.

Amir, E. "The Market Valuation of Accounting Information: The Case of Postretirement Benefits Other than Pensions." *Accounting Review* 68, 1993, pp. 703–24.

Amir, E.; T. S. Harris; and E. K. Venuti. "A Comparison of Value-Relevance of U.S. versus Non-U.S. GAAP Accounting Measures Using Form 20-F Reconciliations." *Journal of Accounting Research Supplement* 31, 1993, pp. 230–64.

Amir, E.; M. Kirschenheiler; and K. Willard. "The Valuation of Deferred Taxes." *Contemporary Accounting Research* 14, 1997, pp. 597–622.

Anthony, J.; and K. Ramesh. "Association between Accounting Performance Measures and Stock Prices: A Test of the Life Cycle Hypothesis." *Journal of Accounting and Economics* 15, 1992, pp. 203–27.

Atiase, R. K. "Predisclosure Information, Firm Capitalization and Security Price Behavior Around Earnings Announcements." *Journal of Accounting Research,* Spring 1985, pp. 21–36.

Atiase, R. K.; L. S. Bamber; and R. N. Freeman. "Accounting Disclosures Based on Company Size: Regulations and Capital Markets Evidence." *Accounting Horizons* 2, no. 1, March 1988, pp. 18–26.

Ayers, B. C. "Deferred Tax Accounting under SFAS No. 109: An Empirical Investigation of Its Incremental Value-Relevance Relative to APB No. 11." *Accounting Review* 73, 1998, pp. 195–212.

Backer, M.; and M. L. Gosman. *Financial Reporting and Business Liquidity.* New York: National Association of Accountants, 1978.

Bahnson, P.; P. Miller; and B. Budge. "Nonarticulation in Cash Flow Statements and Implications for Education, Research, and Practice." *Accounting Horizons* 10, 1996, pp. 1–15.

Baldwin, B. A. "Segment Earnings Disclosure and the Ability of Security Analysts to Forecast Earnings per Share." *The Accounting Review,* July 1984, pp. 376–89.

Ball, B. "The Mysterious Disappearance of Retained Earnings." *Harvard Business Review,* July–August 1987.

Ball, R.; and P. Brown. "An Empirical Evaluation of Accounting Income Numbers." *Journal of Accounting Research,* Autumn 1968, pp. 159–78.

Ball, R.; and R. Watts. "Some Time Series Properties of Accounting Income." *Journal of Finance* 27, 1972, pp. 663–82.

Balsam, S.; and R. Lipka. "Share Prices and Alternative Measures of Earnings per Share." *Accounting Review* 12, 1998, pp. 234–49.

Banz, R. W. "The Relation between Return and Market Value of Common Stocks." *Journal of Financial Economics* 9, 1981, pp. 3–18.

Barclay, M.; D. Gode; and S. Kothari. "Measuring Delivered Performance." working paper, 1999, Massachusetts Institute of Technology.

Barth, M. E. "Fair Value Accounting: Evidence from Investment Securities and the Market Valuation of Banks." *Accounting Review* 69, 1994, pp. 1–25.

Barth, M. E. "Relative Measurement Errors among Alternative Pension Asset and Liability Measures." *The Accounting Review* 66, 1991, pp. 433–63.

Barth, M. E.; W. H. Beaver; and W. Landsman. "The Market Valuation Implications of Net Periodic Pension Cost Components." *Journal of Accounting and Economics* 15, 1992, pp. 27–62.

Barth, M. E.; W. H. Beaver; and W. Landsman. "Value-Relevance of Banks' Fair Value Disclosures under SFAS No. 107." *The Accounting Review* 71, 1996, pp. 513–37.

Barth, M.; W. Beaver; and W. Landsman. "Relative Valuation Roles of Equity Book Value and Net Income as a Function of Financial Health." *Journal of Accounting and Economics* 25, 1998, pp. 1–34.

Barth, M. E.; and G. Clinch. "Revalued Financial Tangible, and Intangible Assets: Associations with Share Prices and Non Market-Based Value Estimates." *Journal of Accounting Research* 36, 1998, pp. 199–233.

Barth, M. E.; D. P. Cram; and K. K. Nelson. "Accruals and the Prediction of Future Cash Flows." working paper, 1999, Stanford University.

Barth, M. E.; M. Clement; G. Foster; and R. Kasznik; "Brand Values and Capital Market Valuation." *Review of Accounting Studies* 3, 1998, pp. 41–68.

Barth M. E.; and M. F. McNichols. "Estimation and Valuation of Environmental Liabilities." *Journal of Accounting Research,* Supplement 1994, pp. 177–209.

Bartov, E. "Foreign Currency Exposure of Multinational Firms: Accounting Measures and Market Valuation." *Contemporary Accounting Research* 14, 1997, pp. 623–52.

Bartov, Eli. "The Timing of Asset Sales and Earnings Manipulation." *The Accounting Review,* October 1993, pp. 840–55.

Basu, S. "The Conservatism Principle and the Asymmetric Timeliness of Earnings." *Journal of Accounting and Economics* 24, 1997, pp. 3–37.

Basu, S. "The Relationship between Earnings Yield, Market Value and Return for NYSE Common Stocks: Further Evidence." *Journal of Financial Economics* 12, 1983, pp. 129–56.

Bauman, C. C., M P. Bauman, R. F. Halsey. "Do Firms Use the Deferred Tax Asset Valuation Allowance to Manage Earnings?" University of Wisconsin–Milwaukee, August 2000.

Bauman, M. P. "A Review of Fundamental Analysis Research in Accounting." *Journal of Accounting Literature,* 1996, pp. 1–33.

Bauman, M. P. "A Summary of Fundamental Analysis Research in Accounting." *Journal of Accounting Literature,* 1996.

Beaver, W. H. *Financial Reporting: An Accounting Revolution.* 2nd edition. Prentice-Hall, Englewood Cliffs, NJ, 1998.

Beaver, W.; and D. Morse. "What Determines Price-Earnings Ratios?" *Financial Analysts' Journal* 34, 1978, pp. 65–76.

Beaver, William H.; Paul Kettler; and Myron Scholes. "The Association between Market-Determined and Accounting Determined Risk Measures." *The Accounting Review,* October 1970, pp. 654–82.

Beneish, M.; and E. Press. "The Resolution of Technical Default." *The Accounting Review,* April 1995, pp. 337–53.

Bernard, V. "The Feltham-Ohlson Framework: Implications for Empiricists." *Contemporary Accounting Research,* Spring 1995, pp. 733–47.

Bernard, V. L. "Accounting-Based Valuation Methods, Determinants of Market-to-Book Ratios and Implications for Financial Statements Analysis." University of Michigan (December 1994).

Bernard, V.; and J. Noel. "Do Inventory Disclosures Predict Sales and Earnings?" *Journal of Accounting, Auditing and Finance,* Spring 1991, pp. 145–181.

Bernard, V.; and J. Thomas. "Post Earnings Announcement Drift: Delayed Price Response or Risk Premium?" *Journal of Accounting Research* (Supplement) 1989, pp. 1–48.

Bernard, V.; and T. Stober. "The Nature and Amount of Information in Cash Flows and Accruals." *The Accounting Review* 64, October 1989, pp. 624–52.

Biddle, G. C.; R. M. Bowen; and J. S. Wallace. "Does EVA Beat Earnings? Evidence on Associations with Stock Returns and Firm Values." *Journal of Accounting and Economics* 24, 1997, pp. 301–36.

Biddle, G. C.; and W. E. Ricks. "Analyst Forecast Errors and Stock Price Behavior Near the Earnings Announcement Dates of LIFO Adopters." *Journal of Accounting Research,* Autumn 1988, pp. 169–194.

Biddle, Gary C.; and Frederick W. Lindahl. "Stock Price Reactions to LIFO Adoptions: The Association Between Excess Returns and LIFO Tax Savings." *Journal of Accounting Research,* Autumn 1982, Part II, pp. 551–88.

Biggs, Stanley F.; and John J. Wild. "An Investigation of Auditor Judgment in Analytical Review." *The Accounting Review* LX, no. 4, October 1985, pp. 607–33.

Black, E. "Which Is More Value Relevant: Earnings or Cash Flows?" working paper, 1999, University of Arkansas.

Blankley, Alan I.; and Edward P. Swanson. "A Longitudinal Study of SFAS 87 Pension Rate Assumptions." *Accounting Horizons,* December 1995, pp. 1–21.

Boblitz, B.; and M. Ettredge. "The Information in Discretionary Outlays: Advertising, Research and Development." *The Accounting Review,* January 1989, pp. 108–124.

Botosan, C. "Disclosure Level and the Cost of Equity Capital." *The Accounting Review* 72, 1997, pp. 323–50.

Bowen, R. M.; D. Burgstahler; and L. A. Daley. "Evidence of the Relationships between Earnings and Various Measures of Cash Flow." *The Accounting Review* 61, 1986, pp. 713–25.

Bowen, R. M.; D. Burgstahler; and L. A. Daley. "The Incremental Information Content of Accruals versus Cash Flows." *The Accounting Review* 62, October 1987, pp. 723–47.

Bowen, R.; L. DuCharme; and D. Shores. "Stakeholders' Implicit Claims and Accounting Method Choice. *Journal of Accounting and Economics* 20, no. 3, 1995.

Bowman, R. G. "The Theoretical Relationship between Systematic Risk and Financial Variables." *Journal of Finance,* June 1979, pp. 617–630.

Brealey, R.; and S. Myers. *Principles of Corporate Finance,* 5th edition, McGraw-Hill, NY, 1996.

Brown, L.; and J. Han. "Do Stock Prices Reflect the Implications of Current Earnings for Future Earnings for ARI Firms?" *Journal of Accounting Research.*

Bulow, Jeremy. "What Are Corporate Pension Liabilities?" *Quarterly Journal of Economics,* August 1982, pp. 435–42.

Burgstahler, D.; and I. Dichev. "Earnings Management to Avoid Earnings Decreases and Losses." *Journal of Accounting and Economics* 24, 1997, pp. 99–126.

Burgstahler; D.; and I. Dichev. "Earnings, Adaptation, and Equity Value." *The Accounting Review* 72, 1997, pp. 187–215.

Burgstahler, D.; J. Jiambalvo; and Y. Pyo. "The Informativeness of Cash Flows for Future Cash Flows." working paper, 1998, University of Washington.

"Business Combinations Prior to an Initial Public Offering and Determination of the Acquiring Corporation," *SEC Staff Accounting Bulletin 97.* Washington DC: SEC, 1996.

Callen, J. L.; J. Livnat; and S. Ryan. "Capital Expenditures: Value Relevance and Fourth Quarter Effects." *The Journal of Financial Statement Analysis,* Spring 1996, pp. 13–24.

Carhart, M. "On the Persistence of Mutual Fund Performance." *Journal of Finance* 52, 1997, pp. 57–73.

Chaney, P. K.; and D. C. Jeter. "The Effect of Deferred Taxes on Security Prices." *Journal of Accounting, Auditing and Finance* 9, 1994, pp. 91–116.

Chaney, P.; C. Hogan; and D. Jeter. "The Effect of Reporting Restructuring Charges on Analysts' Forecast Revisions and Errors." *Journal of Accounting and Economics* 27, 1999, pp. 261–84.

Chen, K.; and J. Wei. "Creditors' Decisions to Waive Violations of Accounting-Based Debt Covenants." *The Accounting Review,* April 1993, pp. 218–32.

Chen, Kung H.; and Thomas A. Shimerda. "An Empirical Analysis of Useful Financial Ratios." *Financial Management,* Spring 1981, pp. 51–60.

Cheng, C. S. A.; C. Lui; and T. F. Schaefer. "The Value-Relevance of SFAS No. 95 Cash Flows from Operations as Assessed by Security Market Effects." *Accounting Horizons* 11, 1997, pp. 1–15.

Choi, B.; D. W. Collins; and W. B. Johnson. "Valuation Implications of Reliability Differences: The Case of Nonpension Postretirement Obligations." *Accounting Review* 72, 1997, pp. 351–83.

Coller, M.; and J. L. Higgs. "Firm Valuation and Accounting for Employee Stock Options." *Financial Analyst Journal* 53, 1997, pp. 26–34.

Collins, D. W. "Predicting Earnings with Subentity Data: Some Further Evidence." *Journal of Accounting Research,* Spring 1976, pp. 163–177.

Collins, D. W.; and S. P. Kothari. "An Analysis of Intertemporal and Cross-Sectional Determinants of Earnings Response Coefficients." *Journal of Accounting and Economics* 11, 1989, pp. 143–81.

Collins, D. W.; E. L. Maydew ; and I. S. Weiss. "Changes in the Value-Relevance of Earnings and Book Values over the Past Forty Years." *Journal of Accounting and Economics* 24, 1997, pp. 39–67.

Collins, D. W.; S. P. Kothari; and J. Rayburn. "Firm Size and the Information Content of Prices with Respect to Earnings." *Journal of Accounting and Economics,* March 1987.

Collis, David J.; and Cynthia Montgomery. *Corporate Strategy: Resources and the Scope of the Firm.* Burr Ridge, IL: Irwin/McGraw-Hill, 1997.

"Consolidated Financial Statements: Policy and Procedures," *FASB Exposure Draft.* Norwalk, CT: Financial Accounting Standards Board, 1996.

"Consolidation of Special-Purpose Entities under FAS 125." *EITF Report 96-20.* Norwalk, CT: Financial Accounting Standards Board, 1996.

Copeland, R. M.; and M. L. Moore. "The Financial Bath: Is It Common?" *MSU Business Topics,* Autumn 1972, pp. 63–69.

Copeland, T.; T. Koller; and J. Murrin. *Valuation: Measuring and Managing the Value of Companies,* 2nd ed. New York: John Wiley and Sons, 1996.

Cushing, B. E.; and M. J. LeClere. "Evidence on the Determinants of Inventory Accounting Policy Choice." *The Accounting Review,* April 1992, pp. 355–66.

Davis, H. Z.; and Y. C. Peles. "Measuring Equilibrating Forces of Financial Ratios." *The Accounting Review,* October 1993, pp. 725–47.

Davis, Harry Z.; Nathan Kahn; and Etzmun Rosen. "LIFO Inventory Liquidations: An Empirical Study." *Journal of Accounting Research,* Autumn 1984, pp. 480–96.

Davis, M. L. "Differential Market Reaction to Pooling and Purchase Methods." *The Accounting Review,* July 1990, pp. 696–709.

DeBondt, W.; and R. Thaler. "Further Evidence of Investor Overreaction and Stock Market Seasonality." *Journal of Finance* 42, 1987, pp. 557–81.

Dechow, P. M. "Accounting Earnings and Cash Flows as Measures of Firm Performance: The Role of Accounting Accruals." *Journal of Accounting and Economics* 18, 1994, pp. 3–42.

Dechow, P. M.; S. P. Kothari; and R. L. Watts. "The Relation between Earnings and Cash Flows." *Journal of Accounting and Economics* 25, 1998, pp. 133–68.

"Derivatives and Hedging: Questions, Answers, and Illustrative Examples." *FASB Staff Paper.* Norwalk, CT: Financial Accounting Standards Board, 1996.

Dhaliwal, D.; D. Guenther; and M. Trombley. "Inventory Accounting Method and Earnings-Price Ratios." *Contemporary Accounting Research.*

Dhaliwal, D.; K. R. Subramanyam; and R. Trezevant. "Is Comprehensive Income Superior to Net Income as a Measure of Firm Performance?" *Journal of Accounting and Economics* 26, 2000, pp. 43–67.

Dhaliwal, Dan S. "Measurement of Financial Leverage in the Presence of Unfunded Pension Liabilities." *The Accounting Review,* October 1986, pp. 651–61.

Dharan, B.; and B. Lev. "The Valuation Consequences of Accounting Changes: A Multiyear Examination." *Journal of Accounting, Auditing, and Finance* 8, 1993, pp. 475–94.

"Disclosure of Accounting Policies for Derivative Financial Instruments and Derivative Commodity Instruments and Disclosure of Quantitative and Qualitative Information about Market Risk Inherent in Derivative Financial Instruments." *SEC Release 33-7386.* Washington, DC: SEC, 1997.

"Disclosure of Information about Capital Structure." *Statement of Financial Accounting Standards No. 129.* Norwalk, CT: 1997.

Dopuch, N.; and M. Pincus. "Evidence of the Choice of Inventory Accounting Methods: LIFO versus FIFO." *Journal of Accounting Research,* Spring 1988, pp. 28–59.

Duke, J. C., and H. G. Hunt. "An Empirical Examination of Debt Covenant Restrictions and Accounting-Related Debt Proxies." *Journal of Accounting and Economics,* January 1990, pp. 45–63.

Dukes, R. E. "An Investigation of the Effects of Expensing Research and Development Costs on Security Prices." In *Proceedings of the Conference on Topical Research in Accounting,* ed. M. Schiff and G. Sorter, New York: Ross Institute of Accounting Research, New York University, 1976.

Dunne, K. M. "An Empirical Analysis of Management's Choice of Accounting Treatment for Business Combinations." *Journal of Accounting and Public Policy,* July 1990, pp. 111–133.

Durkee, D. A.; J. E. Groff; and J. R. Boatsman. "The Effect of Costly vs. Costless Pension Disclosure on Common Share Prices: The Case of SFAS 36." *Journal of Accounting Literature* 7, 1988, pp. 180–96.

"Earnings per Share." *Statement of Financial Accounting Standards No. 128.* Norwalk, CT: 1997.

Easton, P. D.; and T. S. Harris. "Earnings as an Explanatory Variable for Returns." *Journal of Accounting Research,* Spring 1991, pp. 19–36.

Easton, P. D.; T. S. Harris; and J. A. Ohlson. "Accounting Earnings Can Explain Most of Security Returns: The Case of Long Event Windows." *Journal of Accounting and Economics,* June/September 1992, pp. 119–42.

Easton, Peter D.; Trevor Harris; and James Ohlson. "Aggregate Accounting Earnings Can Explain Most of Security Returns: The Case of Long Run Intervals." *Journal of Accounting and Economics,* June/September 1992, pp. 119–42.

Eccher, E. A.; K. Ramesh; and S. R. Thiagarajan. "Fair Value Disclosures by Bank Holding Companies." *Journal of Accounting and Economics* 22, 1996, pp. 79–117.

Elam, Rick. "The Effect of Lease Data on the Predictive Ability of Financial Ratios." *The Accounting Review,* January 1975, pp. 25–53.

El-Gazzar, S. M.; S. Lilien; and V. Pastena. "Accounting for Leases by Lessees." *Journal of Accounting and Economics,* October 1986, pp. 217–37.

Elliott, J.; and D. Hanna. "Repeated Accounting Write-Offs and the Information Content of Earnings." *Journal of Accounting Research Supplement* 34, 1996, pp. 135–55.

Elliott, J. A; and W. H. Shaw. "Write-Offs as Accounting Procedures to Manage Perceptions." *Journal of Accounting Research,* Supplement 1988, pp. 91–119.

Elliott, John A.; and Donna R. Philbrick. "Accounting Changes and Earnings Predictability." *The Accounting Review,* January 1990, pp. 157–74.

Ely, K.; and G. Waymire. "Accounting Standard-Setting Organizations and Earnings Relevance: Longitudinal Evidence from NYSE Common Stocks 1927–93." *Journal of Accounting Research* 37, 1999, pp. 293–317.

Emery, G. W.; and K. O. Cogger. "The Measurement of Liquidity." *Journal of Accounting Research,* Autumn 1982, pp. 290–303.

"Employers' Accounting for Postemployment Benefits." *Statement of Financial Accounting Standards No. 112.* Norwalk, CT: Financial Accounting Standards Board, 1992.

Fairfield, P. "P/E, P/B and the Present Value of Future Dividends." *Financial Analysts Journal,* July/August 1994, pp. 23–31.

Fairfield, P. M.; R. J. Sweeney; and T. L. Yohn. "Accounting Classification and the Predictive Content of Earnings." *The Accounting Review,* July 1996, pp. 337–56.

Fairfield, P. M.; R. J. Sweeney; and T. L. Yohn. "Non-Recurring Items and Earnings Predictions." *The Journal of Financial Statement Analysis,* Summer 1996, pp. 30–40.

Fama, E. "Efficient Capital Markets: A Review of Theory and Empirical Work." *Journal of Finance,* 1970.

Fama, E. "Efficient Markets: II." *Journal of Finance* 46, 1991, pp. 1575–617.

Fama, E.; and K. French. "Forecasting Profitability and Earnings." *Journal of Business,* 2000.

Fama, E.; and K. French. "The Cross-Section of Expected Stock Returns." *Journal of Finance* 47, 1992, pp. 427–65.

Fama, E.; and K. French. "Size and Book-to-Market Factors in Earnings and Returns." *Journal of Finance* 50, 1995, pp. 131–56.

Fama, E.; and K. French. "Common Risk Factors in the Returns on Stocks and Bonds." *Journal of Financial Economics* 33, 1993, pp. 3–56.

Feltham, J.; and J. A. Ohlson. "Valuation and Clean Surplus Accounting for Operating and Financial Activities." *Contemporary Accounting Research,* Spring 1995, pp. 689–731.

Fesler, R. D. "Disclosure of Litigation Contingencies." *Journal of Accountancy,* July 1990, p. 15.

Finger, C. "The Ability of Earnings to Predict Future Earnings and Cash Flow." *Journal of Accounting Research* 32, 1994, pp. 210–23.

Francis, J.; P. Olsson; and D. Oswald. "Comparing the Accuracy and Explainability of Dividends, Cash Flows, and Abnormal Earnings Equity Valuation Models." working paper, 1997, University of Chicago.

Francis, J.; D. Hanna; and L. Vincent, "Causes and Consequences of Discretionary Asset Write-Offs." *Journal of Accounting Research,* Supplement, 1996, pp. 117–34.

Francis, J.; and K. Schipper. "Have Financial Statements Lost Their Relevance?" *Journal of Accounting Research* 37, 1999, pp. 319–52.

Freeman, R. N. "The Association between Accounting Earnings and Security Returns for Large and Small Firms." *Journal of Accounting and Economics,* July 1987, pp. 195–228.

Freeman, R.; J. Ohlson; and S. Penman. "Book Rate-of-Return and Prediction of Earnings Changes: An Empirical Investigation." *Journal of Accounting Research* 20, 1982, pp. 639–53.

Fried, D.; and D. Givoly. "Financial Analysts' Forecasts of Earnings: A Better Surrogate for Market Expectations." *Journal of Accounting and Economics,* October 1982, pp. 85–108.

Fried, D.; M. Schiff; and A. C. Sondhi. *Impairments and Writeoffs of Long-Lived Assets.* Montvale, NJ: National Association of Accountants, 1989.

Gaver, J. J.; K. M. Gaver; and J. R. Austin. "Additional Evidence on the Association between Income Management and Earnings-Based Bonus Plans." *Journal of Accounting and Economics,* February 1995, pp. 3–28.

Gentry, J. A.; P. Newbold; and D. Whitford. "Classifying Bankrupt Firms with Funds Flow Components." *Journal of Accounting Research,* Spring 1985, pp. 146–60.

Gibbons. M. R.; and P. Hess. "Day of the Week Effects and Asset Returns." *Journal of Business* 54, 1981, pp. 579–96.

Gill, S.; R. Gore; and L. Rees. "An Investigation of Asset Writedowns and Concurrent Abnormal Accruals." *Journal of Accounting Research,* Supplement 1997.

Ginay, W. "The Impact of Derivatives on Form Risk: An Examination of New Derivative Users." *Journal of Accounting and Economics* 26, 1999.

Givoly, D.; and C. Hayn. "The Valuation of the Deferred Tax Liability: Evidence from the Stock Market." *The Accounting Review,* April 1992, pp. 394–410.

Givoly, D.; and C. Hayn. "Transitory Accounting Items: Information Content and Earnings Management." Tel Aviv University and Northwestern University, 1993.

Gombola, M. F.; M. E. Haskins; J. E. Katz; and D. D. Williams. "Cash Flow in Bankrupt Prediction." *Financial Management,* Winter 1987.

Gopalakrishnan, V. "The Effect of Cognition vs. Disclosure on Investor Valuation: The Case of Pension Accounting." *Review of Quantitative Finance and Accounting* 4, 1994, pp. 383–96.

Gopalakrishnan, V.; and T. F. Sugrue. "An Empirical Investigation of Stock Market Valuation of Corporate Projected Pension Liabilities." *Journal of Business Finance and Accounting* 20, September 1993, pp. 711–24.

Greenstein, M. M.; and H. Sami. "The Impact of the SEC's Segment Disclosure Requirement on Bid-Ask Spreads." *The Accounting Review,* January 1994, pp. 179–99.

Guenther, D. A.; and M. A. Trombley. "The 'LIFO Reserve' and the Value of the Firm: Theory and Empirical Evidence." *Contemporary Accounting Research,* Spring 1994, pp. 433–52.

Guenther, D. A.; E. L. Maydew; and S. E. Nutter. "Financial Reporting, Tax Costs, and Book-Tax Conformity." *Journal of Accounting and Economics* 23, 1997, pp. 225–48.

Hackel, K. S.; and J. Livnat. *Cash Flow and Security Analysis,* 2nd ed. Homewood, IL: Business One-Irwin, 1995.

Hagerman, R. L.; M. E. Zmijewski; and P. Shah. "The Association Between the Magnitude of Quarterly Earnings Forecast Errors and Risk-Adjusted Stock Returns." *Journal of Accounting Research,* Autumn 1984, pp. 526–40.

Han, Jerry C. Y.; and John J. Wild. "Stock Price Behavior Associated with Managers' Earnings and Revenue Forecasts." *Journal of Accounting Research* 29, no. 1, Spring 1991, pp. 79–95.

Han, Jerry C. Y.; and John J. Wild. "Timeliness of Reporting and Earnings Information Transfers." *Journal of Business Finance and Accounting* 24, nos. 3–4, April 1997, pp. 527–40.

Han, Jerry C. Y.; John J. Wild; and K. Ramesh. "Managers' Earnings Forecasts and Intra-Industry Information Transfers." *Journal of Accounting and Economics* 11, no. 1, February 1989, pp. 3–33.

Han, Jerry C. Y.; and John J. Wild. "Unexpected Earnings and Intra-Industry Information Transfers: Further Evidence." *Journal of Accounting Research* 28, no. 1, Spring 1990, pp. 211–19.

Hand, J. "Resolving LIFO Uncertainty–A Theoretical and Empirical Reexamination of 1974–1975 LIFO Adoptions and Non-adoptions." *Journal of Accounting Research,* Spring 1993, pp. 21–49.

Harris, T. S.; and J. A. Ohlson. "Accounting Disclosures and the Market's Valuation of Oil and Gas Properties." *Accounting Review* 62, 1987, pp. 651–70.

Hawkins, D. F.; and W. J. Campbell. *Equity Valuation: Models, Analysis and Implications.* New York: Financial Executives Research Foundation, 1978.

Hayn, C. "The Information Content of Losses." *Journal of Accounting and Economics* 20, 1995, pp. 125–53.

Healy, P. "The Effect of Bonus Schemes on Accounting Decisions." *Journal of Accounting and Economics* 7, 1985, pp. 85–107.

Healy, P.; S. Myers; and C. Howe. "R&D Accounting and the Tradeoff between Relevance and Objectivity." working paper, 1999, Massachusetts Institute of Technology.

Heian, J. B.; and B. Thies. "Consolidation of Finance Subsidiaries: $230 Billion in Off-Balance-Sheet Financing Comes Home to Roost." *Accounting Horizons,* March 1989, pp. 1–9.

Henning, S. L.; and T. Stock. "The Value-Relevance of Goodwill Write-Offs." Unpublished working paper, 1997, Southern Methodist University.

Hickman, W. B. *Corporate Bond Quality and Investor Experience.* Princeton, NJ: Princeton University Press, 1958.

Hicks, J. R. *Value and Capital,* 2nd ed. Oxford: Chaundon Press, 1946.

Holthausen, R. W. "Evidence on the Effect of Bond Covenants and Management Compensation Contracts on the Choice of Accounting Techniques: The Case of the Depreciation Switch-Back." *Journal of Accounting and Economics* 3, 1981, pp. 73–79.

Holthausen, R. W.; and K. Palepu. "Research Investigating the Economic Consequences of Accounting Standards." Unpublished working paper, 1995, University of Pennsylvania.

Holthausen, R. W.; D. F. Larcker; and R. G. Sloan. "Annual Bonus Schemes and the Manipulation of Earnings." *Journal of Accounting and Economics* 19, 1995, pp. 29–74.

Hong, H.; R. S. Kaplan; and G. Mandelker. "Pooling vs. Purchase: The Effects of Accounting for Mergers on Stock Prices." *The Accounting Review,* January 1978, pp. 31–47.

Hopwood, W.; P. Newbold; and P. A. Silhan. "The Potential for Gains in Predictive Ability Through Disaggregation: Segmented Annual Earnings." *Journal of Accounting Research,* Autumn 1982, pp. 724–32.

Imhoff, E. A., Jr.; and J. K. Thomas. "Economic Consequences of Accounting Changes: The Lease Disclosure Rule Change." *Journal of Accounting and Economics,* December 1988, pp. 277–310.

"Impact of FASB Statement No. 125, 'Accounting for Transfers and Servicing of Financial Assets and Extinguishments of Liabilities,' on EITF Issues." *FASB Staff Paper.* Norwalk, CT: Financial Accounting Standards Board, 1996.

Jennings, R.; D. Mest; and R. B. Thompson. "Investor Reaction to Disclosures of 1974–75 LIFO Adoption Decisions." *The Accounting Review,* April 1992, pp. 337–54.

Jennings, R.; J. Robinson; R. B. Thompson II; and L. Duvall. "The Relation between Accounting Goodwill Numbers and Equity Values." *Journal of Business, Finance and Accounting,* June 1996, pp. 513–34.

Jennings, R.; P. Simko; and R. Thompson. "Does LIFO Inventory Accounting Improve the Income Statement at the Expense of the Balance Sheet?" *Journal of Accounting Research* 34, no. 1, 1996.

Johnson, W. B.; and D. S. Dhaliwal. "LIFO Abandonment." *Journal of Accounting Research,* Autumn 1988, pp. 236–72.

Kang, S. "A Conceptual Framework for the Stock Price Effect of LIFO Tax Benefits." *Journal of Accounting Research,* Spring 1993, pp. 50–61.

Kang, S.; and K. Sivaramakrishnan. "Issues in Testing Earnings Management and an Instrumental Variable Approach." *Journal of Accounting Research* 33, 1995, pp. 353–67.

Kim, M.; and G. Moore. "Economic vs. Accounting Depreciation." *Journal Accounting and Economics,* April 1988, pp. 111–25.

Kimmel, P.; and T. D. Warfield. "The Usefulness of Hybrid Security Classifications–Evidence from Redeemable Preferred Stock." *The Accounting Review,* January 1995, pp. 151–67.

Kimmel, P.; and T. D. Warfield. "Variation in Attributes of Redeemable Preferred Stock: Implications for Accounting Standards." *Accounting Horizons,* June 1993, pp. 30–40.

Kinney, M.; and R. H. Trezevant. "Taxes and the Timing of Corporate Capital Expenditures." *The Journal of the American Taxation Association,* 1993, pp. 40–62.

Klammer, T. P.; and S. A. Reed. "Operating Cash Flow Formats: Does Format Influence Decisions?" *Journal of Accounting and Public Policy,* 1990, pp. 217–35.

Kleim, D. B. "Size Related Anomalies and Return Seasonality: Further Empirical Evidence." *Journal of Financial Economics* 12, 1983, pp. 13–32.

Kormendi, R.; and R. Lipe. "Earnings Innovations, Earnings Persistence, and Stock Returns." *Journal of Business* 60, July 1987, pp. 323–45.

Kothari, S. P. "Capital Markets Research in Accounting." Unpublished working paper. Massachusetts Institute of Technology.

Kothari, S.; and J. Zimmerman. "Price and Return Models." *Journal of Accounting and Economics* 20, 1995, pp. 155–92.

Kross, W.; and D. Schroeder. "Firm Prominence and the Differential Information Content of Quarterly Earnings Announcements." *Journal of Business, Finance and Accounting,* Spring 1989, pp. 55–74.

Kwon, Sung S.; and John J. Wild. "The Informativeness of Annual Reports for Firms in Financial Distress." *Contemporary Accounting Research* 11, no. 1–II, Fall 1994, pp. 331–51.

Lakonishok, J.; A. Shleifer; and R. W. Vishny. "Contrarian Investment, Extrapolation and Risk." *Journal of Finance* 49, pp. 1541–578.

Lakonishok, J.; and S. Smidt. "Are Seasonal Anomalies Real? A Ninety Year Perspective." *Review of Financial Studies* 1, 1988, pp. 435–55.

Landsman, W. "An Empirical Investigation of Pension and Property Rights." *The Accounting Review,* October 1986, pp. 662–91.

Lasman, D. A.; and R. L. Weil. "Adjusting the Debt-Equity Ratio." *Financial Analysts Journal,* September/October 1978, pp. 49–58.

Lee, C. "Accounting-Based Valuation: A Commentary." *Accounting Horizons* 13, 1999, pp. 413–25.

Lee, C. "Inventory Accounting and Earnings/Price Ratios: A Puzzle." *Contemporary Accounting Research* 26, 1988, pp. 371–88.

Lee, C.; J. Myers; and B. Swaminathan. "What Is the Intrinsic Value of the Dow?" *Journal of Finance* 54, 1999, pp. 1693–742.

Lee, C.; A. Shleifer; and R. Thaler. "Investor Sentiment and the Closed-End Fund Puzzle." *Journal of Finance* 14, 1991, pp. 75–109.

Leftwich, R. W. "Accounting Information in Private Markets: Evidence from Private Lending Agreements." *The Accounting Review* 63, January 1983, pp. 23–42.

Lev, B. "On the Association between Operating Leverage and Risk." *Journal of Financial and Quantitative Analysis,* 1974, pp. 627–41.

Lev, B.; and S. R. Thiagarajan. "Fundamental Information Analysis." *Journal of Accounting Research* 31, Autumn 1993, pp. 190–215.

Lev, B.; and T. Sougiannis. "The Capitalization, Amortization, and Value-Relevance of R&D." *Journal of Accounting and Economics,* February 1996, pp. 107–38.

Lev, B.; and P. Zarowin. "The Boundaries of Financial Reporting and How to Extend Them." *Journal of Accounting Research* 37, 1999, pp. 353–86.

"Liability Recognition for Certain Employee Termination Benefits and Other Costs to Exit an Activity (Including Certain Costs Incurred in a Restructuring)." *EITF 94-3.* Norwalk, CT: Financial Accounting Standards Board, 1994.

Lin, H.; and M. McNichols. "Underwriting Relationships and Analysts' Earnings Forecasts and Investment Recommendations." *Journal of Accounting and Economics* 25, 1998, pp. 101–27.

Lipe, R. C. "The Information Contained in the Components of Earnings." *Journal of Accounting Research,* Supplement 1986, pp. 37–64.

Liu, C.; J. Livnat; and S. G. Ryan. "Forward-Looking Financial Information: The Order Backlog as a Predictor of Future Sales." *The Journal of Financial Statement Analysis,* Fall 1996, pp. 89–99.

Livnat, J.; and P. Zarowin. "The Incremental Information Content of Cash-Flow Components." *Journal of Accounting and Economics* 25, 1990, pp. 133–68.

Lys, T.; and L. Vincent. "An Analysis of Value Destruction at AT&T's Acquisition of NCR." *Journal of Financial Economics* 39, 1995, pp. 353–78.

Lys, T. Z. "Abandoning the Transactions-Based Accounting Model: Weighing the Evidence." *Journal of Accounting and Economics* 22, 1996, pp. 155–75.

Malkiel, B. *A Random Walk Down Wall Street.* J. B. Norton and Co., 1999.

Mandelker, G. M.; and S. G. Rhee. "The Impact of the Degrees of Operating and Financial Leverage on Systematic Risk of Common Stock." *Journal of Financial and Quantitative Analysis,* March 1984, pp. 45–57.

Martin, L. G.; and G. V. Henderson. "On Bond Ratings and Pension Obligations: A Note." *Journal of Financial and Quantitative Analysis,* December 1983, pp. 463–70.

McConnell, J. J.; and C. J. Muscarella. "Corporate Capital Expenditure Decisions and the Market Value of the Firm." *Journal of Financial Economics,* 1985, pp. 399–422.

McNichols, L.; and P. Wilson. "Evidence of Earnings Management from the Provision of Bad Debts." *Journal of Accounting Research Supplement* 26, 1988, pp. 1–31.

Mellman, M.; and L. A. Bernstein. "Lease Capitalization under APB Opinion No. 5." *The New York Certified Public Accountant,* February 1966, pp. 115–122.

Mendenhall, R. "Evidence on the Possible Underweighting of Earnings Related Information." *Journal of Accounting Research,* Spring 1991, pp. 170–79.

Mikhail, M.; B. Walther; and R. Willis. "Does Forecast Accuracy Matter to Security Analysts?" *The Accounting Review* 74, 1999, pp. 185–200.

Mittelstaedt, H. F.; W. D. Nichols; and P. R. Regier. "SFAS No. 106 and Benefit Reduction in Employer-Sponsored Retiree Health Care Plans." *The Accounting Review,* October 1995, pp. 535–56.

Mittelstaedt, H. F.; and M. J. Warshawski. "The Impact of Liabilities for Retiree Health Benefits on Share Prices." *Journal of Risk and Insurance* 60, 1993, pp. 13–35.

Mohrman, M. B. "The Use of Fixed GAAP Provisions in Debt Contracts." *Accounting Horizons,* September 1996, pp. 78–91.

Morck, R.; A. Shleifer; and R. W. Vishny. "Do Managerial Objectives Drive Bad Acquisitions?" *Journal of Finance,* March 1990, pp. 31–48.

Moses, D. "Income Smoothing and Incentives: Empirical Tests Using Accounting Changes." *The Accounting Review,* April 1987, pp. 358–77.

Mulford, C. W. "The Importance of a Market Value Measurement of Debt in Leverage Ratios: Replications and Extensions." *Journal of Accounting Research,* Autumn 1985, pp. 897–906.

Murdoch, B. "The Information Content of FAS 33 Returns on Equity." *The Accounting Review,* April 1986, pp. 273–87.

Nakayama, M.; S. Lilien; and M. Benis. "Due Process and FAS No. 13." *Management Accounting,* April 1981, pp. 49–53.

Nathan, K. "Do Firms Pay to Pool? Some Empirical Evidence." *Journal of Accounting and Public Policy* 7, 1988, pp. 185–200.

Nissim, D.; and S. Penman, unpublished manuscript, March 1999.

Noe, C. "Voluntary Disclosures and Insider Transactions." *Journal of Accounting and Economics* 27, 1999, pp. 305–26.

Ohlson, J. A. "Earnings, Book Values, and Dividends in Equity Valuation." *Contemporary Accounting Research,* Spring 1995, pp. 661–87.

Ohlson, J. A.; and B. E. Juettuer-Nauroth. "Expected EPS and EPS Growth as Determinants of Value." Working paper, September 2000.

Ou, J. A.; and S. H. Penman. "Accounting Measurement, Price-Earnings Ratio, and the Information Content of Security Prices." *Journal of Accounting Research,* Supplement 1989, pp. 111–44.

Ou, J. A.; and S. H. Penman. "Financial Statement Analysis and the Prediction of Stock Returns." *Journal of Accounting and Economics,* November 1989, pp. 295–329.

Penman, S. "The Articulation of Price-Earnings Ratios and Market-to-Book Ratios and the Evaluation of Growth." *Journal of Accounting Research,* Autumn 1996, pp. 235–59.

Penman, S. H. "Return to Fundamentals." *Journal of Accounting, Auditing and Finance,* Fall 1992, pp. 465–83.

Penman, S. H. "An Evaluation of Accounting Rate-of-Return." *Journal of Accounting, Auditing and Finance,* Spring 1991, pp. 233–255.

Penman, S.; and T. Sougiannis. "A Comparison of Dividend, Cash Flow, and Earnings Approaches to Equity Valuation." working paper, 1995, University of California at Berkeley.

Pfeiffer, R. J.; P. T. Elgers; M. H. Lo; and L. L. Rees. "Additional Evidence on the Incremental Information Content of Cash Flows and Accruals: The Impact of Errors in Measuring Market Expectations." *The Accounting Review* 73, July 1998, pp. 373–86.

Philbrick, D.; and W. Ricks. "Using Value Line and IBES Analyst Forecasts in Accounting Research." *Journal of Accounting Research* 29, 1991, pp. 397–417.

Porter, Michael E. *Competitive Advantage: Creating and Sustaining Superior Performance.* New York: The Free Press, 1985.

Porter, Michael E. *Competitive Strategy.* New York: The Free Press, 1980.

Pourciau, S. "Earnings Management and Nonroutine Executive Changes." *Journal of Accounting and Economics* 16, 1993, pp. 317–36.

Pownall, G.; C. Wasley; and G. Waymire. "The Stock Price Effects of Alternative Types of Management Earnings Forecasts." *The Accounting Review* 68, 1993, pp. 896–912.

Press, E. G.; and J. B. Weintrop. "Accounting-Based Constraints in Public and Private Debt Agreements." *Journal of Accounting and Economics,* January 1990, pp. 65–95.

Ramakrishnan, R.; and R. Thomas. "Valuation of Permanent, Transitory, and Price-Irrelevant Components of Reported Earnings." *Journal of Accounting and Finance* 13, 1998.

Ramakrishnan, R.; and R. Thomas. "What Matters from the Past: Market Value, Book Value, or Earnings? Earnings Valuation and Sufficient Statistics for Prior Information." *Journal of Accounting and Finance* 7, 1992, pp. 423–64.

Rayburn, J. "The Association of Operating Cash Flow and Accruals with Security Returns." *Journal of Accounting Research* 24, Supplement 1986, pp. 112–133.

"Recognition of Liabilities in Connection with a Purchase Business Combination." *EITF 95-3.* Norwalk, CT: Financial Accounting Standards Board, 1994.

Rees, L.; and P. Elgers. "The Market's Valuation of Nonreported Accounting Measures: Retrospective Reconciliations of non-U.S. and U.S. GAAP." *Journal of Accounting Research* 35, 1997, pp. 115–27.

Reeve, J. H.; and K. G. Stanga. "The LIFO Pooling Decision: Some Empirical Results from Accounting Practices." *Accounting Horizons,* March 1987, pp. 25–34.

Reilly, F. K. "Using Cash Flows and Financial Ratios to Predict Bankruptcies." *Analyzing Investment Opportunities in Distressed and Bankrupt Companies.* Charlottesville, VA: The Institute of Chartered Financial Analysts, 1991.

Reinganum, M. R. "Misspecification of Capital Asset Pricing: Empirical Anomalies Based on Earnings Yields and Market Values." *Journal of Financial Economics* 9, 1981, pp. 19–46.

Robinson, J. R., and P. B. Shane. "Acquisition Accounting Method and Bid Premia for Target Firms." *The Accounting Review,* January 1990, pp. 25–48.

Schipper, K. "Commentary on Earnings Management." *Accounting Horizons* 3, 1989, pp. 91–102.

Schrand, C. M. "The Association between Stock-Price Interest Rate Sensitivity and Disclosures about Derivative Instruments." *Accounting Review* 72, 1997, pp. 87–109.

Selling, T. I.; and C. P. Stickney. "Disaggregating the Rate of Return on Common Shareholders' Equity: A New Approach." *Accounting Horizons,* December 1990, pp. 9–17.

Shevlin, T. "The Valuation of R&D Firms with R&D Limited Partnerships." *The Accounting Review* 66, January 1991, pp. 1–21.

Shevlin, T. J. "Taxes and Off-Balance-Sheet Financing: Research and Development Limited Partnerships." *The Accounting Review,* July 1987, pp. 480–509.

Shiller, R. J. *Market Volatility.* Cambridge, Massachusetts: The MIT Press, 1989.

Skinner, D. J. "Are Disclosures about Bank Derivatives and Employee Stock Options 'Value-Relevant'?" *Journal of Accounting and Economics* 22, 1996, pp. 393–405.

Skinner, D. J. "How Well Does Net Income Measure Firm Performance? A Discussion of Two Studies." *Journal of Accounting and Economics* 26, 1999, pp. 105–11.

Skinner, R. C. "Fixed Asset Lives and Replacement Cost Accounting." *Journal of Accounting Research,* Spring 1982; pp. 210–26.

Sloan, R. "Do Stock Prices Fully Reflect Information in Accruals and Cash Flows about Future Earnings?" *The Accounting Review* 71, July 1996, pp. 289–315.

Smith, C., and J. B. Warner. "On Financial Contracting: An Analysis of Bond Covenants." *Journal of Financial Economics,* June 1979, 117–161.

Smith, C.; and L. M. Wakeman. "Determinants of Corporate Leasing Policy." *Journal of Finance,* July 1985, pp. 895–908.

Soffer, L.; and T. Lys. "Post-Earnings Announcement Drift and the Dissemination of Predictable Information." *Contemporary Accounting Research* 16, 1999, pp. 305–31.

Sougiannis, T. "The Accounting Based Valuation of Corporate R&D." *The Accounting Review* (January 1994): pp. 44–68.

Stewart, G., III. *The Quest for Value.* New York: Harper Business, 1991.

Stickel, S. E. "The Effect of Value Line Investment Survey Rank Changes on Common Stock Prices." *Journal of Financial Economics* 14, 1985, pp. 121–44.

Stober, T. L. "The Incremental Information Content of Financial Statement Disclosures: The Case of LIFO Liquidations." *Journal of Accounting Research,* Supplement 1986, pp. 138–60.

"Streamlining Disclosure Requirements Relating to Significant Business Acquisitions," *SEC Release 33-7355.* Washington, DC: SEC, 1996.

Subramanyam, K. "The Pricing of Discretionary Accruals." *Journal of Accounting and Economics* 22, 1996, pp. 249–81.

Subramanyam, K. "Uncertain Precision and Price Reaction to Information." *The Accounting Review* 71, 1996, pp. 207–20.

Subramanyam, K. R.; and J. J. Wild. "Going Concern Status, Earnings Persistence, and Informativeness of Earnings." *Contemporary Accounting Research* 13, no. 1 (Spring 1996), pp. 251–273.

Swaminathan, S. "The Impact of SEC Mandated Segment Data on Price Variability and Divergence of Beliefs." *The Accounting Review,* January 1991, pp. 23–41.

Sweeney, A. P. "Debt-Covenant Violations and Managers' Accounting Responses." *Journal of Accounting and Economics* 17, 1994, pp. 281–308.

Teoh, S. H.; I. Welch; and T. J. Wong. "Earnings Management and the Long-Run Performance of IPOs." *Journal of Finance* 53, 1998, pp. 1935–974.

Teoh, S.; I. Welch; and T. Wong. "Earnings Management and the Long-Run Underperformance of Seasoned Equity Offerings." *Journal of Financial Economics* 50, 1998, pp. 63–100.

"The Valuation of R&D Firms with R&D Limited Partnerships." *The Accounting Review,* January 1991, pp. 1–22.

Thomas, J. K. "Why Do Firms Terminate Their Overfunded Pension Plans?" *Journal of Accounting and Economics,* November 1989, pp. 361–98.

Trombley, M. A.; and D. A. Guenther. "Should Earnings and Book Values Be Adjusted for LIFO?" *The Journal of Financial Statement Analysis,* Fall 1995, pp. 26–32.

Tse, S. "LIFO Liquidations." *Journal of Accounting Research,* Spring 1990, pp. 229–38.

Venkatachalam, M. "Value-Relevance of Banks' Derivatives Disclosures." *Journal of Accounting and Economics* 22, 1996, pp. 327–55.

Vigeland, R. L. "The Market Reaction to Statement of Financial Accounting Standards No. 2." *The Accounting Review,* April 1981, pp. 309–25.

Vincent, L. "Equity Valuation Implications of Purchase versus Pooling Accounting." *Journal of Financial Statement Analysis* 2, 1997, pp. 5–20.

Warfield, T. D. and J. J. Wild. "Accounting Recognition and the Relevance of Earnings as an Explanatory Variable for Returns." *The Accounting Review* 67, October 1992, pp. 821–42.

Warfield, T.; J. J. Wild; and K. L. Wild. "Managerial Ownership, Accounting Choices, and Informativeness of Earnings." *Journal of Accounting and Economics* 20, July 1995, pp. 61–91.

Whisenant, J. S. "Does Fundamental Analysis Produce More Value-Relevant Summary Measures?" Unpublished working paper, 1998, Georgetown University.

Wild, John J. "The Audit Committee and Earnings Quality." *Journal of Accounting, Auditing and Finance* 11, no. 2, Winter 1996.

Wild, John J. "Stock Price Informativeness of Accounting Numbers: Evidence on Earnings, Book Values, and Their Components." *Journal of Accounting and Public Policy* 11, no. 2, Summer 1992, pp. 119–54.

Wild, J. J. "The Prediction Performance of a Structural Model of Accounting Numbers." *Journal of Accounting Research* 25, no. 1, Spring 1987, pp. 139–60.

Wild, J. J.; and S. S. Kwon. "Earnings Expectations, Firm Size, and the Informativeness of Stock Prices." *Journal of Business Finance and Accounting* 21, no. 7 (October 1994), pp. 975–96.

Williamson, R. W. "Evidence on the Selective Reporting of Financial Ratios." *The Accounting Review,* April 1984, pp. 296–99.

Wilson, P. G. "The Relative Information Content of Accruals and Cash Flows: Combined Evidence at the Earnings Announcement and Annual Report Release Date." *Journal of Accounting Research,* Supplement 1986, pp. 165–200.

Xie, H. "Are Discretionary Accruals Mispriced? A Reexamination." working paper, 1997, University of Iowa.

Zarowin, P. "What Determines Earnings-Price Ratios: Revisited." *Journal of Accounting Auditing and Finance,* Summer 1990, pp. 439–54.

Ziebart, D. A.; and D. H. Kim. "An Examination of the Market Reactions Associated with SFAS No. 8 and SFAS No. 52." *The Accounting Review,* April 1987, pp. 343–57.

INDEX

Summary of Key Financial Statement An

Return on invested capital	Profitability	Asset utilization and efficiency
Return on assets (ROA) Return on common equity (ROCE) Equity growth rate Sustainable equity growth Dividend payout rate Effective tax rate	Gross profit margin Operating profit margin Net profit margin Pretax profit margin Earnings per share Book value per share Effective interest rate Operating cash flow to income	Total assets turnover Cash turnover Accounts receivable turnover Days' sales in receivables Days' sales in inventory Sales to inventory Working capital turnover Fixed asset turnover Current liabilities turnover

† *Certain measures can be cla*

Definitions

Return on invested capital
Return on assets (ROA) = [net income + interest expense (1 − tax rate) + minority interest in income]/average total assets
Return on common equity (ROCE) = (net income − preferred dividend)/average common shareholders' equity
Equity growth rate = (net income − preferred dividend − dividend payout)/average common equity
Sustainable equity growth = ROCE × (1 − dividend payout rate)
Dividend payout rate = cash dividends paid/net income
Effective tax rate = tax expense/income before income tax

Profitability
Gross profit margin = (sales − cost of sales)/sales
Operating profit margin = operating income/sales
Net profit margin = net income/sales
Pretax profit margin = income before income tax/sales
Earnings per share (basic) = (net income − preferred dividend)/weighted average of shares outstanding
Book value per share = (shareholders' equity − preferred equity)/number of shares outstanding
Effective interest rate = total interest incurred/average interest-bearing indebtedness
Operating cash flow to income = operating cash flow/net income

Asset utilization and efficiency
Total assets turnover = sales/average total assets
Cash turnover = sales/average cash and cash equivalents
Accounts receivable turnover = sales/average accounts receivable
Days' sales in receivables = (accounts receivable × 360)/sales
Days' sales in inventory = (inventory × 360)/cost of sales
Sales to inventory = sales/average inventory
Working capital turnover = sales/average working capital
Fixed asset turnover = sales/average fixed assets
Current liabilities turnover = sales/average current liabilities

Liquidity
Current ratio = current assets/current liabilities
Working capital = current assets − current liabilities
Acid-test (quick) ratio = (cash + cash equivalents + marketable securities + accounts receivable)/current liabilities
Cash ratio = (cash + cash equivalents + marketable securities)/current assets
Collection period = (average accounts receivable × 360)/sales
Inventory turnover = cost of sales/average inventory
Days to sell inventory = (average inventory × 360)/cost of sales

‡ *Number of days in a year is 360 for ratio*